HOW TO PROGRAM

SEVENTH EDITION

STUDENT ACCESS CARD

Thank you for purchasing a new copy of C++ *How to Program, Seventh Edition*, by Deitel and Deitel. The information below provides instruction on how to access the Deitel Companion Website. This Website provides access to premium Web content. Including:

- Video Notes
- Bonus Chapters
- Appendices
- Source Code

To access the Companion Website for Deitel's 7th Edition, please follow these steps:

1. Go to www.pearsonhighered.com/deitel
2. Click Companion Website.
3. There you can register as a First-Time User and Returning User.
4. Use a coin to scratch off the coating below and reveal your student access code.

**Do not use a knife or other sharp object as it may damage the code.*

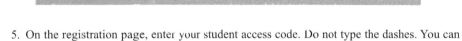

5. On the registration page, enter your student access code. Do not type the dashes. You can use lower or uppercase letters.
6. Follow the on-screen instructions. If you need help during the online registration process, simply click Need Help?
7. Once your personal Login Name and Password are confirmed, you can begin viewing the Website.

To login to the Companion Website for the first time after you've registered:
Follow steps 1 and 2 to return to the Website. Then, follow the prompts for "Returning User" to enter your Login Name and Password.

Note to Instructors: For access to the Instructor Resource Center, contact your Pearson representative.

IMPORTANT The access code on this page can only be used once to establish a subscription to the Deitel, C++ *How to Program, Seventh Edition* premium Web content. If this access code has already been scratched off, it may no longer be valid. You may purchase a subscription by going to the www.pearsonhighered.com/deitel website, selecting Companion Website and then selecting "Get Access".

www.pearsonhighered.c

C++

HOW TO PROGRAM

SEVENTH EDITION

Deitel® Ser

How To Program Series

Java How to Program, 8/E

Java How to Program, Late Objects Version, 8/E

C++ How to Program, 7/E

C How to Program, 6/E

Internet & World Wide Web How to Program, 4/E

Visual Basic® 2008 How to Program

Visual C#® 2008 How to Program, 3/E

Visual C++® 2008 How to Program, 2/E

Small Java™ How to Program, 6/E

Small C++ How to Program, 5/E

Simply Series

Simply C++: An Application-Driven Tutorial Approach

Simply Java™ Programming: An Application-Driven Tutorial Approach

Simply C#: An Application-Driven Tutorial Approach

Simply Visual Basic® 2008, 3/E: An Application-Driven Tutorial Approach

CourseSmart Web Books

www.deitel.com/books/CourseSmart/

C++ How to Program, 5/E & 6/E

Java How to Program, 6/E, 7/E & 8/E

Simply C++: An Application-Driven Tutorial Approach

Simply Visual Basic 2008: An Application-Driven Tutorial Approach, 3/E

Small C++ How to Program, 5/E

Small Java How to Program, 6/E

Visual Basic 2008 How to Program

Visual C# 2008 How to Program, 3/E

ies Page

Deitel® Developer Series

AJAX, Rich Internet Applications and Web Development for Programmers

C++ for Programmers

C# 2008 for Programmers, 3/E

iPhone for Programmers

Java for Programmers

Javascript for Programmers

LiveLessons Video Learning Products

www.deitel.com/books/LiveLessons/

Java Fundamentals Parts 1 and 2

C# Fundamentals Parts 1 and 2

C++ Fundamentals Parts 1 and 2

JavaScript Fundamentals Parts 1 and 2

To receive updates on Deitel publications, Resource Centers, training courses, partner offers and more, please register for the free *Deitel® Buzz Online* e-mail newsletter at:

www.deitel.com/newsletter/subscribe.html

follow us on Twitter®

@deitel

and become a Deitel & Associates fan on Facebook®

www.deitel.com/deitelfan/

To communicate with the authors, send e-mail to:

deitel@deitel.com

For information on government and corporate *Dive-Into®* *Series* on-site seminars offered by Deitel & Associates, Inc. worldwide, visit:

www.deitel.com/training/

or write to

deitel@deitel.com

For continuing updates on Prentice Hall/Deitel publications visit:

www.deitel.com
www.pearsonhighered.com/deitel

Check out our Resource Centers for valuable web resources that will help you master Java, other important programming languages, software and Internet- and web-related topics:

www.deitel.com/ResourceCenters.html

Library of Congress Cataloging-in-Publication Data
On file

Vice President and Editorial Director, ECS: *Marcia J. Horton*
Editor-in-Chief, Computer Science: *Michael Hirsch*
Associate Editor: *Carole Snyder*
Supervisor/Editorial Assistant: *Dolores Mars*
Director of Team-Based Project Management: *Vince O'Brien*
Senior Managing Editor: *Scott Disanno*
Managing Editor: *Robert Engelhardt*
A/V Production Editor: *Greg Dulles*
Art Director: *Kristine Carney*
Cover Design: *Abbey S. Deitel, Harvey M. Deitel, Francesco Santalucia, Kristine Carney*
Interior Design: *Harvey M. Deitel, Kristine Carney*
Manufacturing Manager: *Alexis Heydt-Long*
Manufacturing Buyer: *Lisa McDowell*
Director of Marketing: *Margaret Waples*
Marketing Manager: *Erin Davis*

 © 2010 by Pearson Education, Inc.
Upper Saddle River, New Jersey 07458

10 9 8 7 6 5 4 3 2

ISBN-10: 0-13-611726-0

ISBN-13: 978-0-13-611726-1

Pearson Education Ltd., *London*
Pearson Education Australia Pty. Ltd., *Sydney*
Pearson Education Singapore, Pte. Ltd.
Pearson Education North Asia Ltd., *Hong Kong*
Pearson Education Canada, Inc., *Toronto*
Pearson Educación de Mexico, S.A. de C.V.
Pearson Education–Japan, *Tokyo*
Pearson Education Malaysia, Pte. Ltd.
Pearson Education, Inc., *Upper Saddle River, New Jersey*

C++

HOW TO PROGRAM

SEVENTH EDITION

P. J. Deitel
Deitel & Associates, Inc.

H. M. Deitel
Deitel & Associates, Inc.

Upper Saddle River, New Jersey 07458

Trademarks

DEITEL, the double-thumbs-up bug and DIVE INTO are registered trademarks of Deitel and Associates, Inc.

Java and all Java-based marks are trademarks or registered trademarks of Sun Microsystems, Inc. in the United States and other countries. Pearson Education is independent of Sun Microsystems, Inc.

Microsoft, Internet Explorer and the Windows logo are either registered trademarks or trademarks of Microsoft Corporation in the United States and/or other countries.

Pong® classic video game courtesy of Atari Interactive, Inc. ©2009 Atari Interactive, Inc. All rights reserved. Used with permission.

UNIX is a registered trademark of The Open Group.

In memory of Joseph Weizenbaum
MIT Professor Emeritus of Computer Science:
For making us think.

Paul and Harvey Deitel

Deitel Resource Centers

Our Resource Centers focus on the vast amounts of free content available online. Find resources, downloads, tutorials, documentation, books, e-books, journals, articles, blogs, RSS feeds and more on many of today's hottest programming and technology topics. For the most up-to-date list of our Resource Centers, visit:

www.deitel.com/ResourceCenters.html

Let us know what other Resource Centers you'd like to see! Also, please register for the free *Deitel®* *Buzz Online* e-mail newsletter at:

www.deitel.com/newsletter/subscribe.html

Computer Science
Functional Programming
Regular Expressions

Programming
Apple iPhone
ASP.NET 3.5
Adobe Flex
Ajax
Apex
ASP.NET Ajax
ASP.NET
C
C++
C++ Boost Libraries
C++ Game Programming
C#
Code Search Engines and Code Sites
Computer Game Programming
CSS 2.1
Dojo
Facebook Developer Platform
Flash 9
Functional Programming
Java
Java Certification and Assessment Testing
Java Design Patterns
Java EE 5
Java SE 6
Java SE 7 (Dolphin) Resource Center
JavaFX
JavaScript
JSON
Microsoft LINQ
Microsoft Popfly
.NET
.NET 3.0
.NET 3.5
OpenGL
Perl
PHP
Programming Projects
Python
Regular Expressions
Ruby

Ruby on Rails
Silverlight
UML
Visual Basic
Visual C++
Visual Studio Team System
Web 3D Technologies
Web Services
Windows Presentation Foundation
XHTML
XML

Games and Game Programming
Computer Game Programming
Computer Games
Mobile Gaming
Sudoku

Internet Business
Affiliate Programs
Competitive Analysis
Facebook Social Ads
Google AdSense
Google Analytics
Google Services
Internet Advertising
Internet Business Initiative
Internet Public Relations
Link Building
Location-Based Services
Online Lead Generation
Podcasting
Search Engine Optimization
Selling Digital Content
Sitemaps
Web Analytics
Website Monetization
YouTube and AdSense

Java
Java
Java Certification and Assessment Testing
Java Design Patterns
Java EE 5

Java SE 6
Java SE 7 (Dolphin) Resource Center
JavaFX

Microsoft
ASP.NET
ASP.NET 3.5
ASP.NET Ajax
C#
DotNetNuke (DNN)
Internet Explorer 7 (IE7)
Microsoft LINQ
.NET
.NET 3.0
.NET 3.5
SharePoint
Silverlight
Visual Basic
Visual C++
Visual Studio Team System
Windows Presentation Foundation
Windows Vista
Microsoft Popfly

Open Source and LAMP Stack
Apache
DotNetNuke (DNN)
Eclipse
Firefox
Linux
MySQL
Open Source
Perl
PHP
Python
Ruby

Software
Apache
DotNetNuke (DNN)
Eclipse
Firefox
Internet Explorer 7 (IE7)
Linux
MySQL
Open Source

Search Engines
SharePoint
Skype
Web Servers
Wikis
Windows Vista

Web 2.0
Alert Services
Attention Economy
Blogging
Building Web Communities
Community Generated Content
Facebook Developer Platform
Facebook Social Ads
Google Base
Google Video
Google Web Toolkit (GWT)
Internet Video
Joost
Location-Based Services
Mashups
Microformats
Recommender Systems
RSS
Social Graph
Social Media
Social Networking
Software as a Service (SaaS)
Virtual Worlds
Web 2.0
Web 3.0
Widgets

Dive Into® **Web 2.0 eBook**
Web 2 eBook

Other Topics
Computer Games
Computing Jobs
Gadgets and Gizmos
Ring Tones
Sudoku

Contents

Chapters 23–27 and Appendices F–I are PDF documents posted online at the book's Companion Website (located at www.pearsonhighered.com/deitel).

6   Functions and an Introduction to Recursion   207

7   Arrays and Vectors   282

12   Object-Oriented Programming: Inheritance   521

13   Object-Oriented Programming: Polymorphism   572

14 Templates 626

15 Stream Input/Output 645

16 Exception Handling   683

17 File Processing   713

18 Class `string` and String Stream Processing   **755**

19 Searching and Sorting   **784**

20 Data Structures   **806**

21 Bits, Characters, C Strings and `structs`   **852**

22 Standard Template Library (STL)   916

Chapters on the Web   1005

Chapters 23–27 are PDF documents posted online at the book's Companion Website (located at **www.pearsonhighered.com/deitel**).

23   Boost Libraries, Technical Report 1 and C++0x   I

24   Other Topics   XL

25   ATM Case Study, Part 1: Object-Oriented Design with the UML   LXVII

26 ATM Case Study, Part 2: Implementing an Object-Oriented Design   CIX

27 Game Programming with Ogre   CLVIII

Appendices on the Web 1036

Appendices F–I are PDF documents posted online at the book's Companion Website (located at www.pearsonhighered.com/deitel).

Preface

"The chief merit of language is clearness ..."
—Galen

Welcome to the world of C++ programming and *C++ How to Program, Seventh Edition*! This book presents leading-edge computing technologies for students, instructors and software development professionals.

At the heart of the book is the Deitel signature "live-code approach." Concepts are presented in the context of complete working C++ programs, rather than in code snippets. Each code example is immediately followed by one or more sample executions. All the source code is available at www.deitel.com/books/cpphtp7/.

New and Updated Features

Here are the updates we've made for *C++ How to Program, 7/e*:

- *"Making a Difference" Exercise Sets.* We encourage you to use computers and the Internet to research and solve problems that really matter. These new exercises are meant to increase awareness of important issues the world is facing. We hope you'll approach them with your own values, politics and beliefs.

- *Prefer string Objects to C Strings.* C++ offers two types of strings—string class objects (which we use starting in Chapter 3) and C-style, pointer-based strings. We continue to include some early discussions of C strings to give you practice with pointer manipulations, to illustrate dynamic memory allocation with new and delete and to prepare you for working with C strings in the "legacy code" that you'll encounter in industry. In new development, you should favor string class objects. We've replaced most occurrences of C strings with instances of C++ class string to make programs more robust and eliminate many of the security problems that can be caused by manipulating C strings.

- *Prefer vectors to C Arrays.* Similarly, C++ offers two types of arrays—vector class objects (which we use starting in Chapter 7) and C-style, pointer-based arrays. As appropriate, we use class template vector instead of C arrays throughout the book. However, we begin by discussing C arrays in Chapter 7 to prepare you for working with legacy code and to use as a basis for building your own customized Array class in Chapter 11, Operator Overloading.

- *New Companion Website (www.pearsonhighered.com/deitel/).* This edition's Companion Website includes a wealth of material to help you with your study of C++ programming. We provide an extensive number of VideoNotes that walk you through the code examples in 14 of the key chapters, solutions to many of the book's exercises, bonus chapters, and more (see the Companion Website section later in this Preface).

- *Dynamic Memory Allocation.* We moved dynamic memory allocation later in the book to Chapter 11, where it's first needed. The "proxy class" discussion (which uses dynamic memory) has also been moved to Chapter 11.

- *Titled Programming Exercises.* We've titled all the programming exercises. This and the previous two features help instructors tune assignments for their classes.

- *Eliminated "Magic" Numbers.* We eliminated all uses of truly "magic" numbers and replaced them with named constants or enums as appropriate. In a few cases in which the context is absolutely clear, we don't consider numbers to be "magic."

- *Enhanced Use of `const`.* We increased our use of `const` bookwide to encourage better software engineering.

- *Eliminated "`return 0;`".* According to the C++ standard, any `main` function that does not contain "`return 0;`" as its last statement is assumed to return 0. For this reason, we've eliminated "`return 0;`" from all but the first program in the book.

- *Use "`using namespace std;`".* Previously, we specified a `using` declaration for every individual item that we referenced from a C++ Standard Library header file. Since these items are well known and unlikely to have name collisions with other C++ libraries, we now use "`using namespace std;`" for all C++ Standard Library components from Chapter 3 forward. This simplifies the programs and saves many lines of code.

- *New Design.* The book has a new interior design that graphically serves to organize, clarify and highlight the information, and enhances the book's pedagogy.

- *Reorganized Optional OOD Case Study.* We tuned the Object-Oriented Design/ UML automated teller machine (ATM) case study and reorganized it into two optional chapters (25 and 26) that present the ATM's design and complete code implementation. This is a nice business example that most students can relate to. Working through these two chapters as a unit will help you tie together many of the object-oriented programming (OOP) concepts you learn in Chapters 1–13. A key concept in OOP is the interactions among objects. In most textbooks, the code examples create and use only one or two objects. The ATM case study gives you the opportunity to examine the interactions among *many* objects that provide the functionality of a substantial system. For instructors who wish to cover the case study in a distributed manner, we've indicated where each section in Chapters 25 and 26 can be covered inline with earlier chapters in the book.

- *Function Pointer Exercises.* We added several real-world function-pointers exercises. These are available at the Companion Website and at www.deitel.com/ books/cpphtp7/.

- *Improved Terminology Sections.* We've added page numbers for the defining occurrences of all terms in the terminology lists for easy reference.

New Features in the Next C++ Standard

We discuss four new language features that will be part of the next C++ standard and are already implemented by some of today's C++ compilers. These include:

- *Initializer Lists for User-Defined Types.* These enable objects of your own types to be initialized using the same syntax as built-in arrays.

- *Range-Based **for** Statement.* A version of the `for` statement that iterates over all the elements of an array or container (such as an object of the `vector` class).

- *Lambda Expressions.* These enable you to create anonymous functions that can be passed to other functions as arguments.

- *Concepts.* These enable template programmers to specify the requirements for data types that will be used with a particular template. Compilers can then provide more meaningful error messages when data types do not meet a template's requirements.

Other Features

Other features of *C++ How to Program, 7/e,* include:

- *Game Programming.* The computer-game industry's revenues are already greater than those of the first-run movie business, creating lots of career opportunities. Chapter 27, Game Programming with Ogre, introduces game programming and graphics with the open source Ogre 3D graphics engine. We discuss basic issues involved in game programming. Then we show how to use Ogre to create a simple game featuring a play mechanic similar to the classic video game Pong®, originally developed by Atari. We demonstrate how to create a scene with 3D color graphics, smoothly animate moving objects, use timers to control animation speed, detect collisions between objects, add sound, accept keyboard input and display text output.

- *Future of C++.* Chapter 23 considers the future of C++—we introduce the Boost C++ Libraries, Technical Report 1 (TR1) and C++0x. The free Boost open source libraries are created by members of the C++ community. Technical Report 1 describes the proposed changes to the C++ Standard Library, many of which are based on current Boost libraries. The C++ Standards Committee is revising the C++ Standard. The main goals for the new standard are to make C++ easier to learn, improve library building capabilities, and increase compatibility with the C programming language. The last standard was published in 1998. The new standard is likely to be released in 2010 or 2011. It will include changes to the core language and many of the libraries in TR1. We overview the Boost libraries and provide code examples for the "regular expression" and "smart pointer" libraries. Regular expressions are used to match specific character patterns in text. They can be used, for example, to validate data to ensure that it's in a particular format, to replace parts of one string with another, or to split a string. Many common bugs in C and C++ code are related to pointers, a powerful programming capability you'll study in Chapter 8, Pointers. Smart pointers help you avoid errors by providing additional functionality to standard pointers.

- *Integrated Case Studies.* We provide several case studies spanning multiple sections and chapters. These include the development of the `GradeBook` class in Chapters 3–7, the `Time` class in Chapters 9–10, the `Employee` class in Chapters 12–13, and the optional OOD/UML ATM case study in Chapters 25–26.

- *Integrated GradeBook Case Study.* The `GradeBook` case study uses classes and objects in Chapters 3–7 to incrementally build a `GradeBook` class that represents an instructor's grade book and performs various calculations based on a set of student grades, such as calculating the average grade, finding the maximum and minimum, and printing a bar chart.

- *Unified Modeling Language™ 2 (UML 2).* The Unified Modeling Language (UML) has become the preferred graphical modeling language for designers of object-oriented systems. We use UML class diagrams to visually represent classes and their inheritance relationships, and we use UML activity diagrams to demonstrate the flow of control in each of C++'s control statements. We use six types of UML diagrams in the optional OOD/UML ATM case study

- *Compilation and Linking Process for Multiple-Source-File Programs.* Chapter 3 includes a detailed diagram and discussion of the compilation and linking process that produces an executable program.

- *Function Call Stack Explanation.* In Chapter 6, we provide a detailed discussion (with illustrations) of the function call stack and activation records to explain how C++ is able to keep track of which function is currently executing, how automatic variables of functions are maintained in memory and how a function knows where to return after it completes execution.

- *Tuned Treatment of Inheritance and Polymorphism.* Chapters 12–13 have been carefully tuned using an `Employee` class hierarchy to make the treatment of inheritance and polymorphism clear and accessible for students who are new to OOP.

- *Discussion and Illustration of How Polymorphism Works "Under the Hood."* Chapter 13 contains a detailed diagram and explanation of how C++ can implement polymorphism, `virtual` functions and dynamic binding internally. This gives students a solid understanding of how these capabilities really work.

- *Standard Template Library (STL).* This might be one of the most important topics in the book in terms of your appreciation of software reuse. The STL defines powerful, template-based, reusable components that implement many common data structures and algorithms used to process those data structures. Chapter 22 introduces the STL and discusses its three key components—containers, iterators and algorithms. We show that using STL components provides tremendous expressive power, often reducing many lines of code to a single statement.

- *ISO/IEC C++ Standard Compliance.* We've audited our presentation against the most recent ISO/IEC C++ standard document.

- *Debugger Appendices.* We provide two Using the Debugger appendices on the book's Companion Website—Appendix H, Using the Visual Studio Debugger, and Appendix I, Using the GNU C++ Debugger.

- *Code Testing on Multiple Platforms.* We tested the code examples on various popular C++ platforms including GNU C++ on Linux and Microsoft and Visual C++ on Windows. For the most part, the book's examples port to popular standard-compliant compilers.

We believe that this book and its support materials will give you an informative, interesting, challenging and entertaining C++ educational experience.

As you read the book, if you have questions, send an e-mail to deitel@deitel.com; we'll respond promptly. For updates on this book and the status of all supporting C++ software, and for the latest news on all Deitel publications and services, visit www.deitel.com.

Optional Case Study: Using the UML 2 to Develop an Object-Oriented ATM Design

The optional Software Engineering Case Study in Chapters 25 and 26 presents a carefully paced introduction to object-oriented design using the UML. It will help you prepare for the kinds of substantial projects you'll encounter in industry. We design and fully implement the software for a simple automated teller machine (ATM). The case study has been reviewed through many editions by a distinguished team of OOD/UML academics and industry professionals, including leaders in the field from Rational (the creators of the UML) and the Object Management Group (responsible for evolving the UML).

We introduce a simple, concise subset of the UML, then guide you through a first design experience intended for the novice. The case study is not an exercise—it's an end-to-end learning experience that concludes with a detailed walkthrough of the complete C++ code (850 lines).

At the end of Chapter 1, we introduce basic concepts and terminology of OOD. In Chapter 25, we analyze a typical requirements document that specifies a system to be built, determine the objects needed to implement that system, determine the attributes these objects need to have, determine the behaviors these objects need to exhibit, and specify how the objects must interact with one another to meet the system requirements. In Chapter 26, we include a complete C++ code implementation of the ATM, using key object-oriented programming notions, including classes, objects, encapsulation, visibility, composition, inheritance and polymorphism.

Companion Website

We include a set of free, web-based student supplements to the book—the Companion Website—available with new books purchased from Pearson (see the scratch card at the front of the book for your access code). To access the Companion Website, visit www.pearsonhighered.com/deitel/ and select the Companion Website link in the section for this book. *If the access code in front of your book is already redeemed, you can purchase access to this material directly from the Companion Website.*

The Companion Website contains the following chapters and appendices in searchable PDF format:

- Chapter 23, Boost Libraries, Technical Report 1 and C++0x
- Chapter 24, Other Topics
- Chapter 25, ATM Case Study, Part 1: Object-Oriented Design with the UML
- Chapter 26, ATM Case Study, Part 2: Implementing an Object-Oriented Design
- Chapter 27, Game Programming with Ogre
- Appendix F, C Legacy Code Topics
- Appendix G, UML 2: Additional Diagram Types
- Appendix H, Using the Visual Studio Debugger
- Appendix I, Using the GNU C++ Debugger

The Companion Website also includes:

- VideoNotes in which you can watch and listen as Paul Deitel shows you the important features of the code examples in Chapters 2–13 and portions of Chapters 16 and 17.

- Two true/false questions per section with answers for self-review.
- Solutions to approximately half of the solved exercises in the book.

The following additional materials are posted at both the Companion Website and at www.deitel.com/books/cpphtp7/:

- An arrays of pointers to functions example and additional function pointer exercises (from Chapter 8).
- String Class Operator Overloading Case Study (from Chapter 11).
- Building Your Own Compiler exercise descriptions (from Chapter 20).

Dependency Chart

The chart on the next page shows the dependencies among the chapters to help instructors plan their syllabi. *C++ How to Program, 7/e* is appropriate for CS1 and CS2 courses.

Teaching Approach

C++ How to Program, 7/e, contains a rich collection of examples. The book concentrates on the principles of good software engineering and stresses program clarity. We teach by example. We are educators who teach leading-edge programming languages and software-related topics in academic, government, military and industry classrooms worldwide.

Live-Code Approach. *C++ How to Program, 7/e,* is loaded with "live-code" examples. Most new concepts are presented in the context of complete working C++ applications, followed by one or more executions showing program inputs and outputs.

Syntax Coloring. For readability, we syntax color all the C++ code, similar to the way most C++ integrated-development environments and code editors syntax color code. Our syntax-coloring conventions are as follows:

```
comments appear in green
keywords appear in dark blue
errors appear in red
constants and literal values appear in light blue
all other code appears in black
```

Code Highlighting. We place yellow rectangles around key code segments.

Using Fonts for Emphasis. We place the key terms and the index's page reference for each defining occurrence in **bold maroon** text for easy reference. We emphasize on-screen components in the **bold Helvetica** font (e.g., the **File** menu) and C++ program text in the Lucida font (for example, int x = 5;).

Web Access. All of the source-code examples are available for download from:

```
www.deitel.com/books/cpphtp7/
www.pearsonhighered.com/deitel/
```

Quotations. Each chapter begins with quotations. We hope that you enjoy relating these to the chapter material.

Objectives. The quotes are followed by a list of chapter objectives.

Illustrations/Figures. Abundant charts, tables, line drawings, UML diagrams, programs and program output are included.

Chapter Dependency Chart

[*Note:* Arrows pointing into a chapter indicate that chapter's dependencies.]

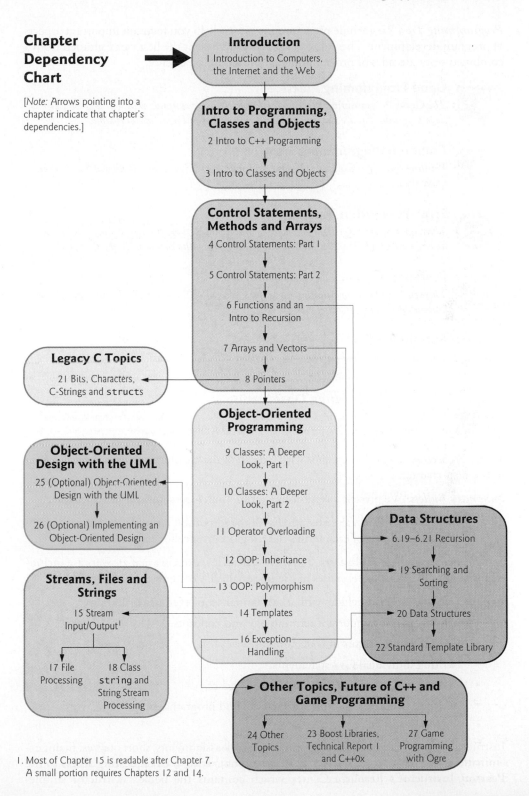

Introduction

1 Introduction to Computers, the Internet and the Web

Intro to Programming, Classes and Objects

2 Intro to C++ Programming

3 Intro to Classes and Objects

Control Statements, Methods and Arrays

4 Control Statements: Part 1

5 Control Statements: Part 2

6 Functions and an Intro to Recursion

7 Arrays and Vectors

8 Pointers

Legacy C Topics

21 Bits, Characters, C-Strings and structs

Object-Oriented Programming

9 Classes: A Deeper Look, Part 1

10 Classes: A Deeper Look, Part 2

11 Operator Overloading

12 OOP: Inheritance

13 OOP: Polymorphism

14 Templates

16 Exception Handling

Object-Oriented Design with the UML

25 (Optional) Object-Oriented Design with the UML

26 (Optional) Implementing an Object-Oriented Design

Streams, Files and Strings

15 Stream Input/Output[1]

17 File Processing

18 Class string and String Stream Processing

Data Structures

6.19–6.21 Recursion

19 Searching and Sorting

20 Data Structures

22 Standard Template Library

Other Topics, Future of C++ and Game Programming

24 Other Topics

23 Boost Libraries, Technical Report 1 and C++0x

27 Game Programming with Ogre

1. Most of Chapter 15 is readable after Chapter 7. A small portion requires Chapters 12 and 14.

Programming Tips. We include programming tips to help you focus on important aspects of program development. These tips and practices represent the best we've gleaned from a combined seven decades of programming and teaching experience.

Good Programming Practice

The Good Programming Practices *call attention to techniques that will help you produce programs that are clearer, more understandable and more maintainable.*

Common Programming Error

Pointing out these Common Programming Errors *reduces the likelihood that you'll make them.*

Error-Prevention Tip

These tips contain suggestions for exposing and removing bugs from your programs; many describe aspects of C++ that prevent bugs from getting into programs in the first place.

Performance Tip

These tips highlight opportunities for making your programs run faster or minimizing the amount of memory that they occupy.

Portability Tip

The Portability Tips *help you write code that will run on a variety of platforms.*

Software Engineering Observation

The Software Engineering Observations *highlight architectural and design issues that affect the construction of software systems, especially large-scale systems.*

Wrap-Up Section. Each chapter ends with a recap of the chapter content, then transitions to the next chapter.

Summary Bullets. We present a section-by-section bullet-list summary of the chapter.

Terminology. We include an alphabetized list of the important terms defined in each chapter with the page number of each term's defining occurrence for easy reference.

Self-Review Exercises and Answers. Extensive self-review exercises *and* answers are included for self study. All of the exercises in the optional ATM case study are fully solved.

Exercises. Each chapter concludes with a substantial set of exercises including:

- simple recall of important terminology and concepts,
- identifying the errors in code samples,
- writing individual C++ statements,
- writing small portions of functions and classes,
- writing complete C++ functions, classes and programs, and
- major projects.

Instructors can use these exercises to form homework assignments, short quizzes, major examinations and term projects. [*NOTE:* **Please do not write to us requesting access to the Pearson Instructor's Resource Center which contains the book's instructor supple-**

ments, including the exercise solutions. Access is limited strictly to college instructors teaching from the book. Instructors may obtain access only through their Pearson representatives. Solutions are *not* provided for "project" exercises.] Check out our Programming Projects Resource Center (www.deitel.com/ProgrammingProjects/) for lots of additional exercise and project possibilities.

Index. We've included an extensive index, which is especially useful when you use the book as a reference. Defining occurrences of key terms are highlighted with a **bold maroon** page number.

Student Resources

Many C++ development tools are available. We wrote *C++ How to Program, 7/e* primarily using Microsoft's free Visual C++ Express Edition (which is available free for download at www.microsoft.com/express/vc/) and the free GNU C++ (gcc.gnu.org/install/binaries.html), which is already installed on most Linux systems and can be installed on Mac OS X and Windows systems as well. You can learn more about Visual C++ Express at msdn.microsoft.com/vstudio/express/visualc. You can learn more about GNU C++ at gcc.gnu.org. Apple includes GNU C++ in their Xcode development tools, which Mac OS X users can download from developer.apple.com/tools/xcode.

For additional resources and software downloads see our C++ Resource Center:

```
www.deitel.com/cplusplus/
```

For other C++ compilers that are available free for download:

```
www.thefreecountry.com/developercity/ccompilers.shtml
www.compilers.net/Dir/Compilers/CCpp.htm
```

CourseSmart Web Books

Today's students and instructors have increasing demands on their time and money. Pearson has responded to that need by offering digital texts and course materials online through CourseSmart. CourseSmart allows faculty to review course materials online saving time and costs. It is also environmentally sound and offers students a high-quality digital version of the text for as much as 50% off the cost of a print copy of the text. Students receive the same content offered in the print textbook enhanced by search, note-taking, and printing tools. For more information, visit www.coursesmart.com.

Instructor Supplements

The following supplements are available to qualified instructors only through Pearson Education's Instructor Resource Center (www.pearsonhighered.com/irc):

- *Solutions Manual* with solutions to most of the end-of-chapter exercises and Lab Manual exercises. We've also graded the difficulty of each programming exercise in the book, and have posted a file that assigns a grade level to each programming exercise (in increasingly challenging order: 1, 2, 3 and Project).

- *Test Item File* of multiple-choice questions (approximately two per book section)

- Customizable PowerPoint® slides containing all the code and figures in the text, plus bulleted items that summarize the key points in the text

If you are not already a registered faculty member, contact your Pearson representative or visit www.pearsonhighered.com/educator/replocator/.

Deitel® Buzz Online Free E-mail Newsletter

The *Deitel® Buzz Online* e-mail newsletter will keep you posted about issues related to *C++ How to Program, 7/e*. It also includes commentary on industry trends and developments, links to free articles and resources from our published books and upcoming publications, product-release schedules, errata, challenges, anecdotes, information on our corporate instructor-led training courses and more. To subscribe, visit

    www.deitel.com/newsletter/subscribe.html

The Deitel Online Resource Centers

Our website www.deitel.com provides more than 100 Resource Centers on various topics including programming languages, software development, Web 2.0, Internet business and open-source projects—see the list of Resource Centers in the first few pages of this book and visit www.deitel.com/ResourceCenters.html. We've found many exceptional resources online, including tutorials, documentation, software downloads, articles, blogs, podcasts, videos, code samples, books, e-books and more—most of them are free. Each week we announce our latest Resource Centers in our newsletter, the *Deitel® Buzz Online*. Some of the Resource Centers you might find helpful while studying this book are C++, C++ Boost Libraries, C++ Game Programming, Visual C++, UML, Code Search Engines and Code Sites, Game Programming and Programming Projects.

Follow Deitel on Twitter and Facebook

To receive updates on Deitel publications, Resource Centers, training courses, partner offers and more, follow us on Twitter®

    @deitel

and join the Deitel & Associates group on Facebook®

    http://www.deitel.com/deitelfan/

Acknowledgments

It's a pleasure to acknowledge the efforts of people whose names do not appear on the cover, but whose hard work, cooperation, friendship and understanding were crucial to the book's production. Many people at Deitel & Associates, Inc., devoted long hours to this project—thanks especially to Abbey Deitel and Barbara Deitel.

We would also like to thank the participants of our Honors Internship program who contributed to this publication—Matthew Pearson, a Computer Science graduate of Cornell University; and Christine Chen, an Operations Research and Information Engineering major at Cornell University.

We are fortunate to have worked on this project with the dedicated team of publishing professionals at Pearson. We appreciate the efforts of Marcia Horton, Editorial Director of Pearson's Engineering and Computer Science Division, and Michael Hirsch, Editor-in-Chief of Computer Science. Carole Snyder recruited the book's review team and managed the review process. Francesco Santalucia (an independent artist) and Kristine Carney of

Pearson designed the book's cover—we provided the concept, and they made it happen. Scott Disanno and Bob Engelhardt managed the book's production. Erin Davis and Margaret Waples marketed the book through academic and professional channels.

C++ How to Program, 7/e *Reviewers*

We wish to acknowledge the efforts of our reviewers. Adhering to a tight time schedule, they scrutinized the text and the programs and provided countless suggestions for improving the accuracy and completeness of the presentation:

Academic Reviewers:

- Thomas J. Borrelli (Rochester Institute of Technology)
- Peter J. DePasquale (The College of New Jersey)
- Jack Hagemeister (Washington State University)
- Williams M. Higdon (University of Indiana)
- Dean Mathias (Utah State University)
- Robert A. McLain (Tidewater Community College)
- Dave Topham (Ohlone College)

Industry Reviewers:

- Chris Cox (Adobe Systems)
- Gregory Dai (Kernel Development)
- Doug Gregor (Apple, Inc.)
- April Reagan (Microsoft)
- José Antonio González Seco (Parliament of Andalusia, Spain)

Well, there you have it! Welcome to the exciting world of C++ and object-oriented programming. We hope you enjoy this look at contemporary computer programming. As you read the book, we would sincerely appreciate your comments, criticisms, corrections and suggestions for improving the text. Please address all correspondence to:

```
deitel@deitel.com
```

We'll respond promptly, and post corrections and clarifications on:

```
www.deitel.com/books/cpphtp7/
```

We hope you enjoy reading *C++ How to Program, Seventh Edition* as much as we enjoyed writing it!

Paul Deitel
Harvey Deitel
Maynard, Massachusetts
July 2009

About the Authors

Paul J. Deitel, CEO and Chief Technical Officer of Deitel & Associates, Inc., is a graduate of MIT's Sloan School of Management, where he studied Information Technology.

Through Deitel & Associates, Inc., he has delivered C++, C, Java, C#, Visual Basic and Internet programming courses to industry clients, including Cisco, IBM, Sun Microsystems, Dell, Lucent Technologies, Fidelity, NASA at the Kennedy Space Center, the National Severe Storm Laboratory, White Sands Missile Range, Rogue Wave Software, Boeing, SunGard Higher Education, Stratus, Cambridge Technology Partners, Open Environment Corporation, One Wave, Hyperion Software, Adra Systems, Entergy, CableData Systems, Nortel Networks, Puma, iRobot, Invensys and many more. He holds the Java Certified Programmer and Java Certified Developer certifications and has been designated by Sun Microsystems as a Java Champion. He has also lectured on Java and C++ for the Boston Chapter of the Association for Computing Machinery. He and his co-author, Dr. Harvey M. Deitel, are the world's best-selling programming-language textbook authors.

Dr. Harvey M. Deitel, Chairman and Chief Strategy Officer of Deitel & Associates, Inc., has 48 years of academic and industry experience in the computer field. Dr. Deitel earned B.S. and M.S. degrees from MIT and a Ph.D. from Boston University. He has extensive college teaching experience, including earning tenure and serving as the Chairman of the Computer Science Department at Boston College before founding Deitel & Associates, Inc., with his son, Paul J. Deitel. He and Paul are the co-authors of dozens of books and multimedia packages and they are writing many more. With translations published in Japanese, German, Russian, Traditional Chinese, Simplified Chinese, Spanish, Korean, French, Polish, Italian, Portuguese, Greek, Urdu and Turkish, the Deitels' texts have earned international recognition. Dr. Deitel has delivered hundreds of professional seminars to major corporations, academic institutions, government organizations and the military.

About Deitel & Associates, Inc.

Deitel & Associates, Inc., is an internationally recognized authoring and corporate training organization specializing in computer programming languages, Internet and web software technology, object-technology education and Internet business development. The company provides instructor-led courses delivered at client sites worldwide on major programming languages and platforms, such as C++, Visual C++®, C, Java™, Visual C#®, Visual Basic®, XML®, Python®, object technology, Internet and web programming, and a growing list of additional programming and software-development-related courses. The founders of Deitel & Associates, Inc., are Paul J. Deitel and Dr. Harvey M. Deitel. The company's clients include many of the world's largest companies, government agencies, branches of the military, and academic institutions. Through its 33-year publishing partnership with Prentice Hall/Pearson, Deitel & Associates, Inc., publishes leading-edge programming textbooks, professional books, interactive multimedia *Cyber Classrooms*, *LiveLessons* DVD-based and web-based video courses, and e-content for popular course-management systems. Deitel & Associates, Inc., and the authors can be reached via e-mail at:

```
deitel@deitel.com
```

To learn more about Deitel & Associates, Inc., its publications and its *Dive Into*® Series Corporate Training curriculum delivered at client locations worldwide, visit:

```
www.deitel.com/training/
```

and subscribe to the free *Deitel® Buzz Online* e-mail newsletter at:

```
www.deitel.com/newsletter/subscribe.html
```

Individuals wishing to purchase Deitel books, and *LiveLessons* DVD and web-based training courses can do so through www.deitel.com. Bulk orders by corporations, the government, the military and academic institutions should be placed directly with Pearson. For more information, visit www.prenhall.com/mischtm/support.html#order.

Introduction to Computers, the Internet and the World Wide Web

1

The chief merit of language is clearness.
—Galen

Our life is frittered away by detail. ... Simplify, simplify.
—Henry David Thoreau

Man is still the most extraordinary computer of all.
—John F. Kennedy

Objectives

In this chapter you'll learn:

- Basic hardware and software concepts.

- Object-technology concepts, such as classes, objects, attributes, behaviors, encapsulation and inheritance.

- The different types of programming languages.

- A typical C++ program development environment.

- The history of the industry-standard object-oriented system modeling language, the UML.

- The history of the Internet and the World Wide Web, and the Web 2.0 phenomenon.

- To test-drive C++ applications in GNU C++ on Linux and Microsoft's Visual C++® on Windows®.

1.1 Introduction

Welcome to C++! We've worked hard to create what we hope you'll find to be an informative, entertaining and challenging learning experience. C++ is a powerful computer programming language that is appropriate for technically oriented people with little or no programming experience and for experienced programmers to use in building substantial information systems. *C++ How to Program, Seventh Edition*, is an effective learning tool for each of these audiences.

The core of the book emphasizes achieving program clarity through the proven techniques of object-oriented programming. We teach C++ features in the context of complete working C++ programs and show the outputs produced when those programs are run on a computer—we call this the **live-code approach**. You may download the example programs from www.deitel.com/books/cpphtp7/.

The early chapters introduce the fundamentals of computers, computer programming and the C++ computer programming language, providing a solid foundation for the deeper treatment of C++ in the later chapters.

Most people are at least somewhat familiar with the exciting things computers do. Using this textbook, you'll learn how to command computers to do those things. Computers (often referred to as **hardware**) are controlled by **software** (i.e., the instructions you write to command the computer to perform **actions** and make **decisions**). C++ is one of today's most popular software development languages. This text provides an introduction to programming in the version of C++ standardized in the United States through the **American National Standards Institute (ANSI)** and worldwide through the efforts of the **International Organization for Standardization (ISO)**.

Computer use is increasing in most fields of endeavor. Computing costs have decreased dramatically due to rapid developments in both hardware and software technologies. Computers that might have filled large rooms and cost millions of dollars a few decades ago can now be inscribed on silicon chips smaller than a fingernail, costing a few dollars each. Those large computers were called **mainframes** and current versions are widely used today in business, government and industry. Fortunately, silicon is one of the most abundant materials on earth—it's an ingredient in common sand. Silicon chip technology has made computing so economical that more than a billion general-purpose computers are in use worldwide, helping people in business, industry and government, and in their personal lives.

Over the years, many programmers learned the programming methodology called structured programming. You'll learn structured programming and an exciting newer methodology, object-oriented programming. Why do we teach both? Object orientation is the key programming methodology used by programmers today. You'll create and work with many software objects in this text. You'll discover, however, that their internal structure is often built using structured-programming techniques. Also, the logic of manipulating objects is occasionally expressed with structured programming.

To keep up to date with C++ developments at Deitel & Associates, please register for our free e-mail newsletter, the *Deitel® Buzz Online,* at

```
www.deitel.com/newsletter/subscribe.html
```

Please check out our growing list of C++ and related Resource Centers at

```
www.deitel.com/ResourceCenters.html
```

Some Resource Centers that will be valuable to you as you read this book are C++, Visual C++, C++ Game Programming, C++ Boost Libraries, Code Search Engines and Code Sites, Computer Game Programming, Programming Projects, Eclipse, Linux and Open Source. Each week we announce our latest Resource Centers in the newsletter. Errata and updates for this book are posted at

```
www.deitel.com/books/cpphtp7/
```

You are embarking on a challenging and rewarding path. As you proceed, if you have any questions, please send e-mail to

```
deitel@deitel.com
```

We'll respond promptly. We hope that you'll enjoy learning with *C++ How to Program, Seventh Edition.*

1.2 Computers: Hardware and Software

A **computer** is a device that can perform computations and make logical decisions billions of times faster than human beings can. For example, many of today's personal computers can perform several billion additions per second. A person operating a desk calculator could spend an entire lifetime performing calculations and still not complete as many calculations as a powerful personal computer can perform in one second! (Points to ponder: How would you know whether the person added the numbers correctly? How would you know whether the computer added the numbers correctly?) Today's fastest **supercomput-**

ers can perform *thousands of trillions (quadrillions)* of instructions per second! To put that in perspective, a quadrillion-instruction-per-second computer can perform more than 100,000 calculations per second for every person on the planet!

Computers process **data** under the control of sets of instructions called **computer programs**. These programs guide the computer through orderly sets of actions specified by people called **computer programmers**.

A computer consists of various devices referred to as hardware (e.g., the keyboard, screen, mouse, hard disk, memory, DVDs and processing units). The programs that run on a computer are referred to as software. Hardware costs have been declining dramatically in recent years, to the point that personal computers have become a commodity. In this book, you'll learn proven methods that are reducing software development costs—object-oriented programming and (in our optional Software Engineering Case Study on building an automated teller machine in Chapters 25–26) object-oriented design.

1.3 Computer Organization

Regardless of differences in physical appearance, virtually every computer may be envisioned as divided into six **logical units** or sections:

1. **Input unit**. This "receiving" section obtains information (data and computer programs) from **input devices** and places it at the disposal of the other units so that it can be processed. Most information is entered into computers through keyboards and mouse devices. Information also can be entered in many other ways, including by speaking to your computer, scanning images and barcodes, reading from secondary storage devices (like hard drives, CD drives, DVD drives and USB drives—also called "thumb drives") and having your computer receive information from the Internet (such as when you download videos from You-Tube™, e-books from Amazon and the like).

2. **Output unit**. This "shipping" section takes information that the computer has processed and places it on various **output devices** to make it available for use outside the computer. Most information that is output from computers today is displayed on screens, printed on paper, played on audio players (such as Apple's popular iPods), or used to control other devices. Computers also can output their information to networks, such as the Internet.

3. **Memory unit**. This rapid-access, relatively low-capacity "warehouse" section retains information that has been entered through the input unit, making it immediately available for processing when needed. The memory unit also retains processed information until it can be placed on output devices by the output unit. Information in the memory unit is **volatile**—it's typically lost when the computer's power is turned off. The memory unit is often called either **memory** or **primary memory**.

4. **Arithmetic and logic unit (ALU)**. This "manufacturing" section performs calculations, such as addition, subtraction, multiplication and division. It also contains the decision mechanisms that allow the computer, for example, to compare two items from the memory unit to determine whether they're equal. In today's systems, the ALU is usually implemented as part of the next logical unit, the CPU.

5. **Central processing unit (CPU).** This "administrative" section coordinates and supervises the operation of the other sections. The CPU tells the input unit when information should be read into the memory unit, tells the ALU when information from the memory unit should be used in calculations and tells the output unit when to send information from the memory unit to certain output devices. Many of today's computers have multiple CPUs and, hence, can perform many operations simultaneously—such computers are called **multiprocessors**. A **multi-core processor** implements multiprocessing on a single integrated circuit chip—for example a dual-core processor has two CPUs and a quad-core processor has four CPUs.

6. **Secondary storage unit.** This is the long-term, high-capacity "warehousing" section. Programs or data not actively being used by the other units normally are placed on secondary storage devices (e.g., your hard drive) until they're again needed, possibly hours, days, months or even years later. Therefore, information on secondary storage devices is said to be **persistent**—it is preserved even when the computer's power is turned off. Secondary storage information takes much longer to access than information in primary memory, but the cost per unit of secondary storage is much less than that of primary memory. Examples of secondary storage devices include CDs, DVDs and flash drives (sometimes called memory sticks), which can hold hundreds of millions to billions of characters.

1.4 Personal, Distributed and Client/Server Computing

In 1977, Apple Computer popularized **personal computing**. Computers became so economical that people could buy them for their own personal or business use. In 1981, IBM, the world's largest computer vendor, introduced the IBM Personal Computer (PC). This quickly legitimized personal computing in business, industry and government organizations, where IBM mainframes were heavily used.

These computers were "stand-alone" units—people transported disks back and forth between them to share information (this was often called "sneakernet"). These machines could be linked together in computer networks, sometimes over telephone lines and sometimes in **local area networks (LANs)** within an organization. This led to the phenomenon of **distributed computing**, in which an organization's computing, instead of being performed only at some central computer installation, is distributed over networks to the sites where the organization's work is performed. Personal computers were powerful enough to handle the computing requirements of individual users as well as the basic communications tasks of passing information between computers electronically.

Today's personal computers are as powerful as the million-dollar machines of just a few decades ago. Information is shared easily across computer networks, where computers called **servers** (file servers, database servers, web servers, etc.) offer a common data store that may be used by **client** computers distributed throughout the network, hence the term **client/server computing**. C++ has become widely used for writing software for operating systems, for computer networking and for distributed client/server applications. Today's popular operating systems such as UNIX, Linux, Mac OS X and Microsoft's Windows-based systems provide the kinds of capabilities discussed in this section.

1.5 The Internet and the World Wide Web

The **Internet**—a global network of computers—was initiated in the late 1960s with funding supplied by the U.S. Department of Defense. Originally designed to connect the main computer systems of about a dozen universities and research organizations, the Internet today is accessible by computers worldwide.

With the introduction of the **World Wide Web**—which allows computer users to locate and view multimedia-based documents on almost any subject over the Internet—the Internet has exploded into the world's premier communication mechanism.

The Internet and the World Wide Web are surely among humankind's most important and profound creations. In the past, most computer applications ran on computers that were not connected to one another. Today's applications can be written to communicate among the world's computers. The Internet mixes computing and communications technologies. It makes our work easier. It makes information instantly and conveniently accessible worldwide. It enables individuals and local small businesses to get worldwide exposure. It's changing the way business is done. People can search for the best prices on virtually any product or service. Special-interest communities can stay in touch with one another. Researchers can be made instantly aware of the latest breakthroughs.

1.6 Web 2.0[1]

In 2006, *TIME Magazine*'s "Person of the Year"[2] was "you." In this article, Web 2.0 and the associated social phenomena were recognized as a shift away from a powerful few to an empowered many. **Web 2.0** has no single definition but can be explained through a series of Internet trends, one being the empowerment of the user. Companies such as eBay, Facebook and Twitter are built almost entirely on **community-generated content**. Web 2.0 takes advantage of **collective intelligence**, the idea that collaboration will result in intelligent ideas. For example, **wikis**, such as the encyclopedia Wikipedia, allow users access to edit content. **Tagging**, or labeling content, is another key part of the collaborative theme of Web 2.0, which can be seen in sites such as Flickr, a photo-sharing site, and del.icio.us, a social bookmarking site.

Social networking sites, which keep track of users' interpersonal relationships, have experienced extraordinary growth as part of Web 2.0. Sites such as MySpace, Facebook and LinkedIn rely heavily on **network effects**, attracting users only if their friends or colleagues are also members. Similarly, social media sites, such as YouTube (an online video site) and Last.fm (a social music platform), have gained immense popularity, partly due to the increased availability of **broadband Internet**, often referred to as high-speed Internet.

Blogs—websites characterized by short postings in reverse chronological order—have become a major social phenomenon within Web 2.0. Many bloggers are recognized as part

---

1. O'Reilly, T. "What is Web 2.0: Design Patterns and Business Models for the Next Generation of Software." September 2005 <http://www.oreillynet.com/pub/a/oreilly/tim/news/2005/09/30/what-is-web-20.html?page=1>.
2. Grossman, L. "Time's Person of the Year: You." *Time*, December 2006 <http://www.time.com/time/magazine/article/0,9171,1569514,00.html>.

of the media, and companies are reaching out to the **blogosphere**, or blogging community, to track consumer opinions.

The increased popularity of **open source** software—a style of developing software in which individuals and companies develop, maintain and evolve software in exchange for the right to use that software for their own purposes—has made it cheaper and easier to start Web 2.0 companies. **Web services**—software components accessible by applications (or other software components) over the Internet—are on the rise, favoring the "**webtop**" over the desktop in much new development. **Mashups** combine two or more existing web applications to serve a new purpose and are dependent on open access to web services. For example, housingmaps.com is a mashup of Google Maps and real-estate listings on Craigslist. In our book *Internet & World Wide Web How to Program, 4/e* we describe key Web 2.0 technologies, including XML, RSS, Ajax, RIA, Podcasting, Internet video and others.

Many Web 2.0 companies use advertising as their main source of monetization. Internet advertising programs such as **Google AdSense** match advertisers with website publishers. Another website monetization model is **premium content**, providing additional services or information for a fee.

Web 3.0 refers to the next movement in web development—one that realizes the full potential of the web. The Internet in its current state is a giant conglomeration of single websites with loose connections. Web 3.0 will resolve this by moving toward the **Semantic Web**—or the "web of meaning"—in which the web becomes a giant database meaning-fully searchable by computers. See our Web 3.0 Resource Center at www.deitel.com/web3.0/ for more information.

1.7 Machine Languages, Assembly Languages and High-Level Languages

Programmers write instructions in various programming languages, some directly understandable by computers and others requiring intermediate **translation** steps. Hundreds of computer languages are in use today. These may be divided into three general types:

1. Machine languages
2. Assembly languages
3. High-level languages

Any computer can directly understand only its own **machine language**. Machine language is the "natural language" of a computer and as such is defined by its hardware design. [*Note:* Machine language is often referred to as **object code**. This term predates "object-oriented programming." These two uses of "object" are unrelated.] Machine languages generally consist of strings of numbers (ultimately reduced to 1s and 0s) that instruct computers to perform their most elementary operations one at a time. Machine languages are **machine dependent** (i.e., a particular machine language can be used on only one type of computer). Such languages are cumbersome for humans, as illustrated by the following section of an early machine-language program that adds overtime pay to base pay and stores the result in gross pay:

```
+1300042774
+1400593419
+1200274027
```

Machine-language programming was simply too slow, tedious and error prone for most programmers. Instead of using the strings of numbers that computers could directly understand, programmers began using English-like abbreviations to represent elementary operations. These abbreviations formed the basis of **assembly languages**. **Translator programs** called **assemblers** were developed to convert early assembly-language programs to machine language at computer speeds. The following section of an assembly-language program also adds overtime pay to base pay and stores the result in gross pay:

```
load    basepay
add     overpay
store   grosspay
```

Although such code is clearer to humans, it's incomprehensible to computers until translated to machine language.

Computer usage increased rapidly with the advent of assembly languages, but programmers still had to use many instructions to accomplish even the simplest tasks. To speed the programming process, **high-level languages** were developed in which single statements could be written to accomplish substantial tasks. Translator programs called **compilers** convert high-level language programs into machine language. High-level languages allow programmers to write instructions that look almost like everyday English and contain commonly used mathematical notations. A payroll program written in a high-level language might contain a statement such as

```
grossPay = basePay + overTimePay;
```

From your standpoint, obviously, high-level languages are preferable to machine and assembly language. C, C++, Microsoft's .NET languages (e.g., Visual Basic, Visual C++ and Visual C#) and Java are among the most widely used high-level programming languages.

The process of compiling a high-level language program into machine language can take a considerable amount of computer time. **Interpreter** programs were developed to execute high-level language programs directly (without the delay of compilation), although slower than compiled programs run.

1.8 History of C and C++

C++ evolved from C, which evolved from two previous programming languages, BCPL and B. BCPL was developed in 1967 by Martin Richards as a language for writing operating systems software and compilers for operating systems. Ken Thompson modeled many features in his language B after their counterparts in BCPL and used B to create early versions of the UNIX operating system at Bell Laboratories in 1970.

The C language was evolved from B by Dennis Ritchie at Bell Laboratories. C uses many important concepts of BCPL and B. C initially became widely known as the development language of the UNIX operating system. Today, most operating systems are written in C and/or C++. C is available for most computers and is hardware independent. With careful design, it's possible to write C programs that are **portable** to most computers.

The widespread use of C with various kinds of computers (sometimes called **hardware platforms**) unfortunately led to many variations. This was a serious problem for program developers, who needed to write portable programs that would run on several platforms.

A standard version of C was needed. The American National Standards Institute (ANSI) cooperated with the International Organization for Standardization (ISO) to standardize C worldwide; the joint standard document was published in 1990 and is referred to as *ANSI/ISO 9899: 1990.*

C99 is the latest ANSI standard for the C programming language. It was developed to evolve the C language to keep pace with increasingly powerful hardware and ever more demanding user requirements. C99 also makes C more consistent with C++. For more information on C and C99, see our book *C How to Program, 6/e* and our C Resource Center (located at www.deitel.com/C).

Portability Tip 1.1
Because C is a standardized, hardware-independent, widely available language, applications written in C can be run with little or no modification on a wide range of computers.

C++, an extension of C, was developed by Bjarne Stroustrup in the early 1980s at Bell Laboratories. C++ provides a number of features that "spruce up" the C language, but more importantly, it provides capabilities for **object-oriented programming.**

A revolution is brewing in the software community. Building software quickly, correctly and economically remains an elusive goal, and this at a time when the demand for new and more powerful software is soaring. **Objects** are essentially reusable software **components** that model items in the real world. Software developers are discovering that a modular, object oriented design and implementation approach can make them much more productive than can previous popular programming techniques. Object-oriented programs are easier to understand, correct and modify.

You'll be introduced to the basic concepts and terminology of object technology in Section 1.19 and will begin developing customized, reusable classes and objects in Chapter 3, Introduction to Classes and Objects. The book is object oriented, where appropriate, from the start and throughout the text. Object-oriented programming is not trivial by any means, but it's fun to write object-oriented programs, and you'll see immediate results.

We also provide an optional automated teller machine (ATM) case study in Chapters 25–26, which contains a complete C++ implementation. The case study presents a carefully paced introduction to object-oriented design using the UML—an industry standard graphical modeling language for developing object-oriented systems. We guide you through a friendly design experience intended for the novice.

1.9 C++ Standard Library

C++ programs consist of pieces called **classes** and **functions.** You can program each piece yourself, but most C++ programmers take advantage of the rich collections of classes and functions in the **C++ Standard Library**. Thus, there are really two parts to learning the C++ "world." The first is learning the C++ language itself; the second is learning how to use the classes and functions in the C++ Standard Library. We discuss many of these classes and functions. P. J. Plauger's book, *The Standard C Library* (Upper Saddle River, NJ: Prentice Hall PTR, 1992), is a must read for programmers who need a deep understanding of the ANSI C library functions included in C++. Many special-purpose class libraries are supplied by independent software vendors.

Software Engineering Observation 1.1

*Use a "building-block" approach to create programs. Avoid reinventing the wheel. Use existing pieces wherever possible. Called **software reuse**, this practice is central to object-oriented programming.*

Software Engineering Observation 1.2

When programming in C++, you typically will use the following building blocks: classes and functions from the C++ Standard Library, classes and functions you and your colleagues create and classes and functions from various popular third-party libraries.

We include many **Software Engineering Observations** throughout the book to explain concepts that affect and improve the overall architecture and quality of software systems. We also highlight other kinds of tips, including **Good Programming Practices** (to help you write programs that are clearer, more understandable, more maintainable and easier to test and **debug**—or remove programming errors), **Common Programming Errors** (problems to watch out for and avoid), **Performance Tips** (techniques for writing programs that run faster and use less memory), **Portability Tips** (techniques to help you write programs that can run, with little or no modification, on a variety of computers) and **Error-Prevention Tips** (techniques for removing programming errors—also known as bugs—from your programs and, more important, techniques for writing bug-free programs in the first place).

The advantage of creating your own functions and classes is that you'll know exactly how they work. You'll be able to examine the C++ code. The disadvantage is the time-consuming and complex effort that goes into designing, developing and maintaining new functions and classes that are correct and that operate efficiently.

Performance Tip 1.1

Using C++ Standard Library functions and classes instead of writing your own versions can improve program performance, because they're written carefully to perform efficiently. This technique also shortens program development time.

Portability Tip 1.2

Using C++ Standard Library functions and classes instead of writing your own improves program portability, because they're included in every C++ implementation.

1.10 History of Java

Microprocessors are having a profound impact in intelligent consumer electronic devices. Recognizing this, Sun Microsystems in 1991 funded an internal corporate research project code-named Green. The project resulted in the development of a C++-based language that its creator, James Gosling, called Oak after an oak tree outside his window at Sun. It was later discovered that there already was a computer language called Oak. When a group of Sun people visited a local coffee shop, the name **Java** was suggested and it stuck.

The Green project ran into some difficulties. The marketplace for intelligent consumer electronic devices did not develop in the early 1990s as quickly as Sun had anticipated. The project was in danger of being canceled. By sheer good fortune, the World Wide Web exploded in popularity in 1993, and Sun saw the immediate potential of using

Java to add **dynamic content** (e.g., interactivity, animations and the like) to web pages. This breathed new life into the project.

Sun formally announced Java at an industry conference in May 1995. Java garnered the attention of the business community because of the phenomenal interest in the World Wide Web. Java is now used to develop large-scale enterprise applications, to enhance the functionality of web servers (the computers that provide the content we see in our web browsers), to provide applications for consumer devices (e.g., cell phones, pagers and personal digital assistants) and for many other purposes.

1.11 Fortran, COBOL, Pascal and Ada

Hundreds of high-level languages have been developed, but few have achieved broad acceptance. **FORTRAN** (FORmula TRANslator) was developed by IBM Corporation in the mid-1950s to be used for scientific and engineering applications that require complex mathematical computations. Fortran is still widely used in engineering applications.

COBOL (COmmon Business Oriented Language) was developed in the late 1950s by computer manufacturers, the U.S. government and industrial computer users. COBOL is used for commercial applications that require precise and efficient manipulation of large amounts of data. Much business software is still programmed in COBOL.

During the 1960s, many large software development efforts encountered severe difficulties. Software deliveries were often late, costs greatly exceeded budgets and the finished products were unreliable. People realized that software development was a more complex activity than they had imagined. Research in the 1960s resulted in the evolution of **structured programming**—a disciplined approach to writing programs that are clearer and easier to test, debug and modify than large programs produced with previous techniques.

One of the more tangible results of this research was the development of the **Pascal** programming language by Professor Niklaus Wirth in 1971. Named after the seventeenth-century mathematician and philosopher Blaise Pascal, it was designed for teaching structured programming and rapidly became the preferred programming language in most colleges. Pascal lacks many features needed in commercial, industrial and government applications, so it was not widely accepted outside academia.

The **Ada** language was developed under the sponsorship of the U.S. Department of Defense (DoD) during the 1970s and early 1980s. Hundreds of separate languages were being used to produce the DoD's massive command-and-control software systems. The DoD wanted one language that would fill most of its needs. The Ada language was named after Lady Ada Lovelace, daughter of the poet Lord Byron. Lady Lovelace is credited with writing the world's first computer program in the early 1800s (for the Analytical Engine mechanical computing device designed by Charles Babbage). One important capability of Ada, called **multitasking**, allows programmers to specify that many activities are to occur in parallel. Java, through a technique called *multithreading*, also enables programmers to write programs with parallel activities. Although multithreading is not part of standard C++, it's available through various add-on class libraries such as Boost (www.boost.org).

1.12 BASIC, Visual Basic, Visual C++, C# and .NET

The **BASIC** (Beginner's All-purpose Symbolic Instruction Code) programming language was developed in the mid-1960s at Dartmouth College as a means of writing simple programs. BASIC's primary purpose was to familiarize novices with programming techniques. Microsoft's Visual Basic language, introduced in the early 1990s to simplify the development of Microsoft Windows applications, has become one of the most popular programming languages in the world.

Microsoft's latest development tools are part of its corporate-wide strategy for integrating the Internet and the web into computer applications. This strategy is implemented in Microsoft's **.NET platform**, which provides the capabilities developers need to create and run computer applications that can execute on computers distributed across the Internet. Microsoft's three primary programming languages are **Visual Basic** (based on the original BASIC), **Visual C++** (based on C++) and **Visual C#** (a new language based on C++ and Java that was developed expressly for the .NET platform).

1.13 Key Software Trend: Object Technology

One of the authors, Harvey Deitel, remembers the great frustration felt in the 1960s by software development organizations, especially those working on large-scale projects. During his undergraduate years, he had the privilege of working summers at a leading computer vendor on the teams developing timesharing, virtual memory operating systems. This was a great experience for a college student. But, in the summer of 1967, reality set in when the company "decommitted" from producing as a commercial product the particular system on which hundreds of people had been working for many years. It was difficult to get this software right—software is "complex stuff."

Improvements to software technology did emerge, with the benefits of structured programming (and the related disciplines of **structured systems analysis and design**) being realized in the 1970s. Not until the technology of object-oriented programming became widely used in the 1990s, though, did software developers feel they had the necessary tools for making major strides in the software development process.

Actually, object technology dates back to the mid 1960s. The C++ programming language, developed at AT&T by Bjarne Stroustrup in the early 1980s, is based on two languages—C and Simula 67, a simulation programming language developed in Europe and released in 1967. C++ absorbed the features of C and added Simula's capabilities for creating and manipulating objects. Neither C nor C++ was originally intended for wide use beyond the AT&T research laboratories. But grass roots support rapidly developed for each.

Object technology is a packaging scheme that helps us create meaningful software units. There are date objects, time objects, paycheck objects, invoice objects, audio objects, video objects, file objects, record objects and so on. In fact, almost any *noun* can be reasonably represented as an object.

We live in a world of objects. There are cars, planes, people, animals, buildings, traffic lights, elevators and the like. Before object-oriented languages appeared, procedural programming languages (such as Fortran, COBOL, Pascal, BASIC and C) were focused on actions (verbs) rather than on things or objects (nouns). Programmers living in a world of objects programmed primarily using verbs. This made it awkward to write programs. Now, with the availability of popular object-oriented languages such as C++, Java and C#, programmers continue to live in an object-oriented world and can program in an object-oriented manner. This is a more natural process than procedural programming and has resulted in significant productivity gains.

A key problem with procedural programming is that the program units do not effectively mirror real-world entities, so these units are not particularly reusable. It isn't unusual for programmers to "start fresh" on each new project and have to write similar software "from scratch." This wastes time and money, as people repeatedly "reinvent the wheel." With object technology, the software entities created (called **classes**), if properly designed, tend to be reusable on future projects. Using libraries of reusable componentry can greatly reduce effort required to implement certain kinds of systems (compared to the effort that would be required to reinvent these capabilities on new projects).

Software Engineering Observation 1.3

Extensive class libraries of reusable software components are available on the Internet. Many of these libraries are free.

Some organizations report that the key benefit of object-oriented programming is not software reuse but, rather, that the software they produce is more understandable, better organized and easier to maintain, modify and debug. This can be significant, because perhaps as much as 80 percent of software costs are associated not with the original efforts to develop the software, but with the continued evolution and maintenance of that software throughout its lifetime. Whatever the perceived benefits, it's clear that object-oriented programming will be the key programming methodology for the next several decades.

1.14 Typical C++ Development Environment

Let's consider the steps in creating and executing a C++ application using a C++ development environment (illustrated in Fig. 1.1). C++ systems generally consist of three parts: a program development environment, the language and the C++ Standard Library. C++ programs typically go through six phases: **edit, preprocess, compile, link, load** and **execute.** The following discussion explains a typical C++ program development environment.

Phase 1: Creating a Program
Phase 1 consists of editing a file with an **editor program** (normally known simply as an **editor**). You type a C++ program (typically referred to as **source code**) using the editor, make corrections and save the program on a secondary storage device, such as your hard drive. C++ source code filenames often end with the .cpp, .cxx, .cc or .C extensions (note that C is in uppercase) which indicate that a file contains C++ source code. See the documentation for your C++ compiler for more information on file-name extensions.

Two editors widely used on UNIX systems are vi and emacs. C++ software packages for Microsoft Windows such as Microsoft Visual C++ (msdn.microsoft.com/vstudio/express/visualc/default.aspx) have editors integrated into the programming environment. You can also use a simple text editor, such as Notepad in Windows, to write your C++ code.

Phases 2 and 3: Preprocessing and Compiling a C++ Program
In phase 2, you give the command to **compile** the program. In a C++ system, a **preprocessor** program executes automatically before the compiler's translation phase begins (so we call preprocessing phase 2 and compiling phase 3). The C++ preprocessor obeys commands called **preprocessor directives,** which indicate that certain manipulations are to be performed on the program before compilation. These manipulations usually include

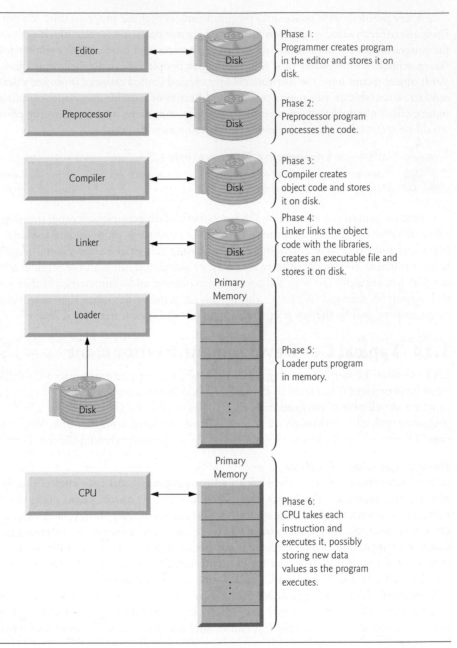

Fig. 1.1 | Typical C++ environment.

other text files to be compiled, and perform various text replacements. The most common preprocessor directives are discussed in the early chapters; a detailed discussion of preprocessor features appears in Appendix E, Preprocessor. In phase 3, the compiler translates the C++ program into machine-language code (also referred to as object code).

Phase 4: Linking

Phase 4 is called **linking.** C++ programs typically contain references to functions and data defined elsewhere, such as in the standard libraries or in the private libraries of groups of programmers working on a particular project. The object code produced by the C++ compiler typically contains "holes" due to these missing parts. A **linker** links the object code with the code for the missing functions to produce an **executable program** (with no missing pieces). If the program compiles and links correctly, an executable image is produced.

Phase 5: Loading

Phase 5 is called **loading.** Before a program can be executed, it must first be placed in memory. This is done by the **loader,** which takes the executable image from disk and transfers it to memory. Additional components from shared libraries that support the program are also loaded.

Phase 6: Execution

Finally, the computer, under the control of its CPU, **executes** the program one instruction at a time.

Problems That May Occur at Execution Time

Programs do not always work on the first try. Each of the preceding phases can fail because of various errors that we discuss throughout the book. For example, an executing program might attempt to divide by zero (an illegal operation for whole number arithmetic in C++). This would cause the C++ program to display an error message. If this occurs, you'd have to return to the edit phase, make the necessary corrections and proceed through the remaining phases again to determine that the corrections fix the problem(s).

Most programs in C++ input and/or output data. Certain C++ functions take their input from cin (the **standard input stream**; pronounced "see-in"), which is normally the keyboard, but cin can be redirected to another device. Data is often output to cout (the **standard output stream**; pronounced "see out"), which is normally the computer screen, but cout can be redirected to another device. When we say that a program prints a result, we normally mean that the result is displayed on a screen. Data may be output to other devices, such as disks and hardcopy printers. There is also a **standard error stream** referred to as **cerr.** The cerr stream (normally connected to the screen) is used for displaying error messages. It's common for users to assign cout to a device other than the screen while keeping cerr assigned to the screen, so that normal outputs are separated from errors.

Common Programming Error 1.1

*Errors such as division by zero occur as a program runs, so they're called **runtime errors** or **execution-time errors**. **Fatal runtime errors** cause programs to terminate immediately without having successfully performed their jobs. **Nonfatal runtime errors** allow programs to run to completion, often producing incorrect results. [Note: On some systems, divide-by-zero is not a fatal error. Please see your system documentation.]*

1.15 Notes About C++ and C++ *How to Program, 7/e*

Experienced C++ programmers sometimes take pride in being able to create weird, convoluted uses of the language. This is a poor programming practice. It makes programs more difficult to read, more likely to behave strangely, more difficult to test and debug, and more difficult to adapt to changing requirements. This book is geared for novice programmers, so we stress program *clarity*. Here's our first "good programming practice."

Good Programming Practice 1.1

Write your C++ programs in a simple and straightforward manner. This is sometimes referred to as KIS ("keep it simple"). Do not "stretch" the language by trying bizarre usages.

You've heard that C and C++ are portable languages, and that programs written in C and C++ can run on many different computers. *Portability is an elusive goal.* The ANSI C standard document contains a lengthy list of portability issues, and complete books have been written that discuss portability.

Portability Tip 1.3

Although it's possible to write portable programs, there are many problems among different C and C++ compilers and different computers that can make portability difficult to achieve. Writing programs in C and C++ does not guarantee portability. You often will need to deal directly with compiler and computer variations. As a group, these are sometimes called **platform** *variations.*

If you need additional technical details on C++, you may want to read the C++ standard document, which can be ordered from ANSI at

```
webstore.ansi.org
```

The title of the document is "Information Technology – Programming Languages – C++" and its document number is INCITS/ISO/IEC 14882-2003.

We list many websites relating to C++ and object-oriented programming in our C++ Resource Center at www.deitel.com/cplusplus/, which provides links to free C++ compilers, resource sites, some fun C++ games, game programming tutorials and much more.

Good Programming Practice 1.2

Read the documentation for the version of C++ you are using. Refer to this documentation frequently to be sure you are aware of the rich collection of C++ features and that you are using them correctly.

Good Programming Practice 1.3

If, after reading your C++ language documentation, you still are not sure how a feature of C++ works, experiment using a small test program and see what happens. Set your compiler options for "maximum warnings." Study each message that the compiler generates and correct the program to eliminate the messages.

1.16 Test-Driving a C++ Application

In this section, you'll run and interact with your first C++ application. You'll begin by running an entertaining guess-the-number game, which picks a number from 1 to 1000 and prompts you to guess it. If your guess is correct, the game ends. If your guess is not correct, the application indicates whether your guess is higher or lower than the correct number. There is no limit on the number of guesses you can make. [*Note:* For this test drive only, we've modified this application from the exercise you'll be asked to create in Chapter 6, Functions and an Introduction to Recursion. Normally this application randomly selects the correct answer as you execute the program. The modified application uses the same correct answer every time the program executes (though this may vary by compiler), so you can use the same guesses we use in this section and see the same results as we walk you through interacting with your first C++ application.

We'll demonstrate running a C++ application using the Windows **Command Prompt** and a shell on Linux. The application runs similarly on both platforms. Many development environments are available in which you can compile, build and run C++ applications, such as Code Gear's C++Builder, GNU C++, Microsoft Visual C++, etc. Consult your instructor for information on your specific development environment.

In the following steps, you'll run the application and enter various numbers to guess the correct number. The elements and functionality that you see in this application are typical of those you'll learn to program in this book. We use fonts to distinguish between features you see on the screen (e.g., the **Command Prompt**) and elements that are not directly related to the screen. We emphasize screen features like titles and menus (e.g., the **File** menu) in a semibold **sans-serif Helvetica** font and to emphasize filenames, text displayed by an application and values you should enter into an application (e.g., `Guess-Number` or `500`) in a `sans-serif Lucida` font. As you've noticed, the **defining occurrence** of each term is set in maroon, bold type. For the figures in this section, we point out significant parts of the application. To make these features more visible, we've modified the background color of the **Command Prompt** window (for the Windows test drive only). To modify the **Command Prompt** colors on your system, open a **Command Prompt** by selecting **Start > All Programs > Accessories > Command Prompt**, then right click the title bar and select **Properties**. In the **"Command Prompt" Properties** dialog box that appears, click the **Colors** tab, and select your preferred text and background colors.

Running a C++ Application from the Windows Command Prompt

1. *Checking your setup.* It's important to read the Before You Begin section at `www.deitel.com/books/cpphtp7/` to make sure that you've copied the book's examples to your hard drive correctly.

2. *Locating the completed application.* Open a **Command Prompt** window. To change to the directory for the completed **GuessNumber** application, type **cd C:\examples\ch01\GuessNumber\Windows**, then press *Enter* (Fig. 1.2). The command `cd` is used to change directories.

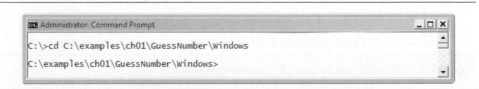

Fig. 1.2 | Opening a **Command Prompt** window and changing the directory.

3. *Running the GuessNumber application.* Now that you are in the directory that contains the **GuessNumber** application, type the command **GuessNumber** (Fig. 1.3) and press *Enter*. [*Note:* `GuessNumber.exe` is the actual name of the application; however, Windows assumes the `.exe` extension by default.]

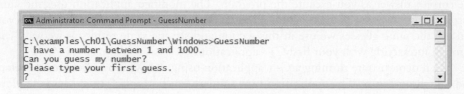

```
[■] Administrator: Command Prompt - GuessNumber                        _ □ ×
C:\examples\ch01\GuessNumber\Windows>GuessNumber
I have a number between 1 and 1000.
Can you guess my number?
Please type your first guess.
?
```

Fig. 1.3 | Running the **GuessNumber** application.

4. *Entering your first guess.* The application displays "Please type your first guess.", then displays a question mark (?) as a prompt on the next line (Fig. 1.3). At the prompt, enter **500** (Fig. 1.4).

```
[■] Administrator: Command Prompt - GuessNumber                        _ □ ×
C:\examples\ch01\GuessNumber\Windows>GuessNumber
I have a number between 1 and 1000.
Can you guess my number?
Please type your first guess.
? 500
Too high. Try again.
?
```

Fig. 1.4 | Entering your first guess.

5. *Entering another guess.* The application displays "Too high. Try again.", meaning that the value you entered is greater than the number the application chose as the correct guess. So, you should enter a lower number for your next guess. At the prompt, enter **250** (Fig. 1.5). The application again displays "Too high. Try again.", because the value you entered is still greater than the number that the application chose as the correct guess.

```
[■] Administrator: Command Prompt - GuessNumber                        _ □ ×
C:\examples\ch01\GuessNumber\Windows>GuessNumber
I have a number between 1 and 1000.
Can you guess my number?
Please type your first guess.
? 500
Too high. Try again.
? 250
Too high. Try again.
?
```

Fig. 1.5 | Entering a second guess and receiving feedback.

6. *Entering additional guesses.* Continue to play the game by entering values until you guess the correct number. The application will display "Excellent! You guessed the number!" (Fig. 1.6).

7. *Playing the game again or exiting the application.* After you guess correctly, the application asks if you'd like to play another game (Fig. 1.6). At the "Would you like to play again (y or n)?" prompt, entering the one character **y** causes the

```
Administrator: Command Prompt - GuessNumber                    _ □ X
Too high. Try again.
? 125
Too low. Try again.
? 187
Too high. Try again.
? 156
Too high. Try again.
? 140
Too high. Try again.
? 132
Too high. Try again.
? 128
Too low. Try again.
? 130
Too low. Try again.
? 131

Excellent! You guessed the number!
Would you like to play again (y or n)?
```

Fig. 1.6 | Entering additional guesses and guessing the correct number.

application to choose a new number and displays the message "Please type your first guess." followed by a question mark prompt (Fig. 1.7) so you can make your first guess in the new game. Entering the character **n** ends the application and returns you to the application's directory at the **Command Prompt** (Fig. 1.8). Each time you execute this application from the beginning (i.e., *Step 3*), it will choose the same numbers for you to guess.

8. *Close the* **Command Prompt** *window.*

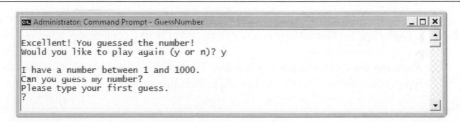

Fig. 1.7 | Playing the game again.

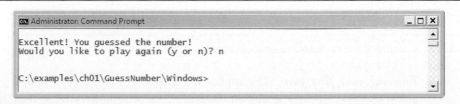

Fig. 1.8 | Exiting the game.

Running a C++ Application Using GNU C++ with Linux
For this test drive, we assume that you know how to copy the examples into your home directory. Please see your instructor if you have any questions regarding copying the files

to your Linux system. Also, for the figures in this section, we use a bold highlight to point out the user input required by each step. The prompt in the shell on our system uses the tilde (~) character to represent the home directory, and each prompt ends with the dollar sign ($) character. The prompt will vary among Linux systems.

1. ***Locating the completed application.*** From a Linux shell, change to the completed **GuessNumber** application directory (Fig. 1.9) by typing

   ```
   cd Examples/ch01/GuessNumber/GNU_Linux
   ```

   then pressing *Enter*. The command cd is used to change directories.

```
~$ cd examples/ch01/GuessNumber/GNU_Linux
~/examples/ch01/GuessNumber/GNU_Linux$
```

Fig. 1.9 | Changing to the **GuessNumber** application's directory.

2. ***Compiling the GuessNumber application.*** To run an application on the GNU C++ compiler, you must first compile it by typing

   ```
   g++ GuessNumber.cpp -o GuessNumber
   ```

   as in Fig. 1.10. This command compiles the application and produces an executable file called GuessNumber.

```
~/examples/ch01/GuessNumber/GNU_Linux$ g++ GuessNumber.cpp -o GuessNumber
~/examples/ch01/GuessNumber/GNU_Linux$
```

Fig. 1.10 | Compiling the **GuessNumber** application using the g++ command.

3. ***Running the GuessNumber application.*** To run the executable file GuessNumber, type ./GuessNumber at the next prompt, then press *Enter* (Fig. 1.11).

```
~/examples/ch01/GuessNumber/GNU_Linux$ ./GuessNumber
I have a number between 1 and 1000.
Can you guess my number?
Please type your first guess.
?
```

Fig. 1.11 | Running the **GuessNumber** application.

4. ***Entering your first guess.*** The application displays "Please type your first guess.", then displays a question mark (?) as a prompt on the next line (Fig. 1.11). At the prompt, enter **500** (Fig. 1.12). [*Note:* This is the same application that we modified and test-drove for Windows, but the outputs could vary based on the compiler being used.]

5. ***Entering another guess.*** The application displays "Too high. Try again.", meaning that the value you entered is greater than the number the application chose as

```
~/examples/ch01/GuessNumber/GNU_Linux$ ./GuessNumber
I have a number between 1 and 1000.
Can you guess my number?
Please type your first guess.
? 500
Too high. Try again.
?
```

Fig. 1.12 | Entering an initial guess.

the correct guess (Fig. 1.12). At the next prompt, enter **250** (Fig. 1.13). This time the application displays "Too low. Try again.", because the value you entered is less than the correct guess.

```
~/examples/ch01/GuessNumber/GNU_Linux$ ./GuessNumber
I have a number between 1 and 1000.
Can you guess my number?
Please type your first guess.
? 500
Too high. Try again.
? 250
Too low. Try again.
?
```

Fig. 1.13 | Entering a second guess and receiving feedback.

6. *Entering additional guesses.* Continue to play the game (Fig. 1.14) by entering values until you guess the correct number. When you guess correctly, the application displays "Excellent! You guessed the number." (Fig. 1.14).

```
Too low. Try again.
? 375
Too low. Try again.
? 437
Too high. Try again.
? 406
Too high. Try again.
? 391
Too high. Try again.
? 383
Too low. Try again.
? 387
Too high. Try again.
? 385
Too high. Try again.
? 384
Excellent! You guessed the number.
Would you like to play again (y or n)?
```

Fig. 1.14 | Entering additional guesses and guessing the correct number.

7. *Playing the game again or exiting the application.* After you guess the correct number, the application asks if you'd like to play another game. At the "Would you like to play again (y or n)?" prompt, entering the one character **y** causes the application to choose a new number and displays the message "Please type your first guess." followed by a question mark prompt (Fig. 1.15) so you can make your first guess in the new game. Entering the character **n** ends the application and returns you to the application's directory in the shell (Fig. 1.16). Each time you execute this application from the beginning (i.e., *Step 3*), it will choose the same numbers for you to guess.

```
Excellent! You guessed the number.
Would you like to play again (y or n)? y

I have a number between 1 and 1000.
Can you guess my number?
Please type your first guess.
?
```

Fig. 1.15 | Playing the game again.

```
Excellent! You guessed the number.
Would you like to play again (y or n)? n

~/examples/ch01/GuessNumber/GNU_Linux$
```

Fig. 1.16 | Exiting the game.

1.17 Software Technologies

In this section, we discuss a number of software engineering buzzwords that you'll hear in the software development community. We've created Resource Centers on most of them.

Agile Software Development is a set of methodologies that try to get software implemented quickly with fewer resources than previous methodologies. Check out the Agile Alliance (www.agilealliance.org) and the Agile Manifesto (www.agilemanifesto.org).

Refactoring involves reworking code to make it clearer and easier to maintain while preserving its functionality. It's widely employed with agile development methodologies. Many refactoring tools are available to do major portions of the reworking automatically.

Design patterns are proven architectures for constructing flexible and maintainable object-oriented software. The field of design patterns tries to enumerate those recurring patterns, encouraging software designers to reuse them to develop better quality software with less time, money and effort.

Game programming. The computer game business is larger than the first-run movie business. College courses and even majors are now devoted to the sophisticated software techniques used in game programming. Check out our Resource Centers on Game Programming, C++ Game Programming and Programming Projects.

Open source software is a style of developing software in contrast to proprietary development that dominated software's early years. With open source development, individuals and companies contribute their efforts in developing, maintaining and evolving software in exchange for the right to use that software for their own purposes, typically at no charge. Open source code generally gets scrutinized by a much larger audience than proprietary software, so bugs get removed faster. Open source also encourages more innovation. Sun recently announced that it's open sourcing Java. Some organizations you'll hear a lot about in the open source community are the Eclipse Foundation (the Eclipse IDE is popular for C++ and Java software development), the Mozilla Foundation (creators of the Firefox browser), the Apache Software Foundation (creators of the Apache web server) and SourceForge (which provides the tools for managing open source projects and currently has hundreds of thousands of open source projects under development).

Linux is an open source operating system and one of the greatest successes of the open source movement. **MySQL** is an open source database management system. **PHP** is the most popular open source server-side "scripting" language for developing Internet-based applications. **LAMP** is an acronym for the set of open source technologies that many developers used to build web applications—it stands for Linux, Apache, MySQL and PHP (or Perl or Python—two other languages used for similar purposes).

Ruby on Rails combines the scripting language Ruby with the Rails web application framework developed by the company 37Signals. Their book, *Getting Real*, is a must read for today's web application developers; read it free at `gettingreal.37signals.com/toc.php`. Many Ruby on Rails developers have reported significant productivity gains over using other languages when developing database-intensive web applications.

Software has generally been viewed as a product; most software still is offered this way. If you want to run an application, you buy a software package from a software vendor. You then install that software on your computer and run it as needed. As new versions of the software appear, you upgrade your software, often at significant expense. This process can become cumbersome for organizations with tens of thousands of systems that must be maintained on a diverse array of computer equipment. With **Software as a Service (SaaS)** the software runs on servers elsewhere on the Internet. When those servers are updated, all clients worldwide see the new capabilities; no local installation is needed. You typically access the service through a browser—these are quite portable, so you can run the same applications on different kinds of computers from anywhere in the world. Salesforce.com, Google, and Microsoft's Office Live and Windows Live all offer SaaS.

1.18 Future of C++: Open Source Boost Libraries, TR1 and C++0x

Bjarne Stroustrup, the creator of C++, has expressed his vision for the future of C++. The main goals for the new standard are to make C++ easier to learn, improve library building capabilities, and increase compatibility with the C programming language.

Chapter 23 considers the future of C++—we introduce the Boost C++ Libraries, Technical Report 1 (TR1) and C++0x. The **Boost C++ Libraries** are free, open source libraries created by members of the C++ community. Boost has grown to over 80 libraries, with more being added regularly. Today there are thousands of programmers in the Boost open source community. Boost provides C++ programmers with useful, well-designed libraries that work well with the existing C++ Standard Library. The Boost libraries can be used by C++ programmers working on a wide variety of platforms with many different compilers. We overview the libraries included in TR1 and provide code examples for the "regular expression" and "smart pointer" libraries.

Regular expressions are used to match specific character patterns in text. They can be used to validate data to ensure that it's in a particular format, to replace parts of one string with another, or to split a string.

Many common bugs in C and C++ code are related to pointers, a powerful programming capability C++ absorbed from C. **Smart pointers** help you avoid errors by providing additional functionality beyond standard pointers. This functionality typically strengthens the process of memory allocation and deallocation.

Technical Report 1 describes the proposed changes to the C++ Standard Library, many of which are based on current Boost libraries. These libraries add useful functionality to C++. The C++ Standards Committee is currently revising the C++ Standard. The last standard was published in 1998. Work on the new standard, currently referred to as **C++0x**, began in 2003. The new standard is likely to be released soon. It will include changes to the core language and most of the libraries in TR1.

1.19 Software Engineering Case Study: Introduction to Object Technology and the UML

Now we begin our early introduction to object orientation, a natural way of thinking about the world and writing computer programs. Optional Chapters 25–26 present a carefully paced introduction to object orientation. Our goal here is to help you develop an object-oriented way of thinking and to introduce you to the **Unified Modeling Language™ (UML™)**—a graphical language that allows people who design object-oriented software systems to use an industry-standard notation to represent them.

In this required section, we introduce basic object-oriented concepts and terminology. The optional chapters present an object-oriented design and implementation of the software for a simple automated teller machine (ATM) system. In Chapter 25, we

- analyze a typical requirements specification that describes a software system (the ATM) to be built
- determine the objects required to implement that system
- determine the attributes the objects will have
- determine the behaviors these objects will exhibit
- specify how the objects interact with one another to meet the system requirements

In Chapter 26 we modify and enhance the design presented in Chapter 25 and present a complete, working C++ implementation of the object-oriented ATM system.

Although our case study is a scaled-down version of an industry-level problem, we cover many common industry practices. You'll experience a solid introduction to object-oriented design with the UML. Also, you'll sharpen your code-reading skills by touring the complete, carefully written and well-documented C++ implementation of the ATM.

Basic Object Technology Concepts

We begin our introduction to object orientation with some key terminology. Everywhere you look in the real world you see **objects**—people, animals, plants, cars, planes, buildings, computers, monitors and so on. Humans think in terms of objects. Telephones, houses, traffic lights, microwave ovens and water coolers are just a few more objects we see around us every day.

We sometimes divide objects into two categories: animate and inanimate. Animate objects are "alive" in some sense—they move around and do things. Inanimate objects do not move on their own. Objects of both types, however, have some things in common. They all have **attributes** (e.g., size, shape, color and weight), and they all exhibit **behaviors** (e.g., a ball rolls, bounces, inflates and deflates; a baby cries, sleeps, crawls, walks and blinks; a car accelerates, brakes and turns; a towel absorbs water). We'll study the kinds of attributes and behaviors that software objects have.

Humans learn about existing objects by studying their attributes and observing their behaviors. Different objects can have similar attributes and can exhibit similar behaviors. Comparisons can be made, for example, between babies and adults, and between humans and chimpanzees.

Object-oriented design (OOD) models software in terms similar to those that people use to describe real-world objects. It takes advantage of class relationships, where objects of a certain class, such as a class of vehicles, have the same characteristics—cars, trucks, little red wagons and roller skates have much in common. OOD takes advantage of **inheritance** relationships, where new classes of objects are derived by absorbing characteristics of existing classes and adding unique characteristics of their own. An object of class "convertible" certainly has the characteristics of the more general class "automobile," but more specifically, the roof goes up and down.

Object-oriented design provides a natural and intuitive way to view the software design process—namely, modeling objects by their attributes, behaviors and interrelationships just as we describe real-world objects. OOD also models communication between objects. Just as people send messages to one another (e.g., a sergeant commands a soldier to stand at attention), objects also communicate via messages. A bank account object may receive a message to decrease its balance by a certain amount because the customer has withdrawn that amount of money.

OOD **encapsulates** (i.e., wraps) attributes and **operations** (behaviors) into objects—an object's attributes and operations are intimately tied together. Objects have the property of **information hiding**. This means that objects may know how to communicate with one another across well-defined **interfaces**, but normally they're not allowed to know how other objects are implemented—implementation details are hidden within the objects themselves. We can drive a car effectively, for instance, without knowing the details of how engines, transmissions, brakes and exhaust systems work internally—as long as we know how to use the accelerator pedal, the brake pedal, the steering wheel and so on. Information hiding, as we'll see, is crucial to good software engineering.

Languages like C++ are **object oriented**. Programming in such a language is called **object-oriented programming (OOP)**, and it allows computer programmers to implement object-oriented designs as working software systems. Languages like C, on the other hand, are **procedural**, so programming tends to be **action oriented**. In C, the unit of programming is the **function.** In C++, the unit of programming is the **class** from which objects are eventually **instantiated** (an OOP term for "created"). C++ classes contain functions that implement operations and data that implements attributes.

C programmers concentrate on writing functions. Programmers group actions that perform some common task into functions, and group functions to form programs. Data is certainly important in C, but the view is that data exists primarily in support of the actions that functions perform. The **verbs** in a system specification help the C programmer determine the set of functions that will work together to implement the system.

Classes, Data Members and Member Functions

C++ programmers concentrate on creating their own **user-defined types** called **classes**. Each class contains data as well as the set of functions that manipulate that data and provide services to **clients** (i.e., other classes or functions that use the class). The data components of a class are called **data members**. For example, a bank account class might include an account number and a balance. The function components of a class are called **member functions** (typically called **methods** in other object-oriented programming languages such as Java). For example, a bank account class might include member functions to make a deposit (increasing the balance), make a withdrawal (decreasing the balance) and inquire what the current balance is. You use built-in types (and other user-defined types) as the "building blocks" for constructing new user-defined types (classes). The **nouns** in a system specification help the C++ programmer determine the set of classes from which objects are created that work together to implement the system.

Classes are to objects as blueprints are to houses—a class is a "plan" for building an object of the class. Just as we can build many houses from one blueprint, we can instantiate (create) many objects from one class. You cannot cook meals in the kitchen of a blueprint; you can cook meals in the kitchen of a house. You cannot sleep in the bedroom of a blueprint; you can sleep in the bedroom of a house.

Classes can have relationships—called **associations**—with other classes. For example, in an object-oriented design of a bank, the "bank teller" class needs to relate to other classes, such as the "customer" class, the "cash drawer" class, the "safe" class, and so on.

Packaging software as classes makes it possible for future software systems to **reuse** the classes. Groups of related classes are often packaged as reusable **components**. Many people say that the most important factor affecting the future of software development is reuse.

 Software Engineering Observation 1.4

Reuse of existing classes when building new classes and programs saves time and money. Reuse also helps you build more reliable and effective systems, because existing classes and components often have gone through extensive testing, debugging and performance tuning.

Indeed, with object technology, you can build much of the new software you'll need by combining existing classes, just as automobile manufacturers combine interchangeable parts. Each new class you create will have the potential to become a valuable *software asset* that you and other programmers can reuse to speed and enhance the quality of future software development efforts.

Introduction to Object-Oriented Analysis and Design (OOAD)

Soon you'll be writing programs in C++. How will you create the code for your programs? Perhaps, like many beginning programmers, you'll simply turn on your computer and start typing. This approach may work for small programs, but what if you were asked to create a software system to control thousands of automated teller machines for a major bank? Or suppose you were asked to work on a team of 1000 software developers building the next U.S. air traffic control system. For projects so large and complex, you could not simply sit down and start writing programs.

To create the best solutions, you should follow a process for **analyzing** your project's **requirements** (i.e., determining *what* the system should do) and developing a **design** that satisfies them (i.e., deciding *how* the system should do it). Ideally, you'd go through this process and carefully review the design (or have your design reviewed by other software professionals) before writing any code. If this process involves analyzing and designing your system from an object-oriented point of view, it's called an **object-oriented analysis and design (OOAD) process**. Analysis and design can save many hours by helping you to avoid an ill-planned system-development approach that has to be abandoned part of the way through its implementation, possibly wasting considerable time, money and effort.

OOAD is the generic term for the process of analyzing a problem and developing an approach for solving it. Small problems do not require an exhaustive OOAD process. It may be sufficient to write **pseudocode** before we begin writing C++ code. Pseudocode is an informal means of expressing program logic. It isn't actually a programming language, but we can use it as a kind of outline to guide us as we write our code. We introduce pseudocode in Chapter 4, Control Statements: Part 1.

As problems and the groups of people solving them increase in size, the methods of OOAD become more appropriate than pseudocode. Ideally, members of a group should agree on a strictly defined process for solving their problem and a uniform way of communicating the results of that process to one another. Although many different OOAD processes exist, a single graphical language for communicating the results of *any* OOAD process has come into wide use. This language, known as the Unified Modeling Language (UML), was developed in the mid-1990s under the initial direction of three software methodologists—Grady Booch, James Rumbaugh and Ivar Jacobson.

History of the UML

In the 1980s, increasing numbers of organizations began using OOP to build their applications, and a need developed for a standard OOAD process. Many methodologists—including Booch, Rumbaugh and Jacobson—individually produced and promoted separate processes to satisfy this need. Each process had its own notation, or "language" (in the form of graphical diagrams), to convey the results of analysis and design.

By the early 1990s, different organizations, and even divisions within the same organization, were using their own unique processes and notations. At the same time, these organizations also wanted to use software tools that would support their particular processes. Software vendors found it difficult to provide tools for so many processes. A standard notation and standard processes were needed.

In 1994, James Rumbaugh joined Grady Booch at Rational Software Corporation (now a division of IBM), and they began working to unify their popular processes. They soon were joined by Ivar Jacobson. In 1996, the group released early versions of the UML to the software engineering community and requested feedback. Around the same time, an organization known as the **Object Management Group™ (OMG™)** invited submissions for a common modeling language. The OMG (www.omg.org) is a nonprofit organization that promotes the standardization of object-oriented technologies by issuing guidelines and specifications, such as the UML. Several corporations—among them HP, IBM, Microsoft, Oracle and Rational Software—had already recognized the need for a common modeling language. In response to the OMG's request for proposals, these companies formed **UML Partners**—the consortium that developed the UML version 1.1 and submitted it to the OMG. The OMG accepted the proposal and, in 1997, assumed responsibility for the continuing maintenance and revision of the UML. We present UML 2 terminology and notation throughout this book.

What Is the UML?

The UML is now the most widely used graphical representation scheme for modeling object-oriented systems. It has unified the various popular notational schemes. Those who design systems use the language (in the form of diagrams) to model their systems. UML modelers are free to use various processes in designing systems, but all developers can now express their designs with one standard set of graphical notations. In the Software Engineering Case Study in optional Chapters 25–26, we present a simple, concise subset of the UML. For more information, visit our UML Resource Center at www.deitel.com/UML/.

Section 1.19 Self-Review Exercises

1.1   List three examples of real-world objects that we did not mention. For each object, list several attributes and behaviors.

1.2   Pseudocode is _____.
   a)   another term for OOAD
   b)   a programming language used to display UML diagrams
   c)   an informal means of expressing program logic
   d)   a graphical representation scheme for modeling object-oriented systems

1.3   The UML is used primarily to _____.
   a)   test object-oriented systems
   b)   design object-oriented systems
   c)   implement object-oriented systems
   d)   Both a and b

Answers to Section 1.19 Self-Review Exercises

1.1   [*Note:* Answers may vary.] a) A television's attributes include the size of the screen, the number of colors it can display, its current channel and its current volume. A television turns on and off, changes channels, displays video and plays sounds. b) A coffee maker's attributes include the maximum volume of water it can hold, the time required to brew a pot of coffee and the temperature of the heating plate under the coffee pot. A coffee maker turns on and off, brews coffee and heats coffee. c) A turtle's attributes include its age, the size of its shell and its weight. A turtle walks, retreats into its shell, emerges from its shell and eats vegetation.

1.2   c.

1.3   b.

1.20 Wrap-Up

This chapter introduced basic hardware and software concepts. You studied the history of the Internet and the World Wide Web and learned about the Web 2.0 phenomenon. We discussed the different types of programming languages, their history and which programming languages are most widely used. We also discussed the C++ Standard Library which contains reusable classes and functions that help C++ programmers create portable C++ programs.

   We presented basic object technology concepts, including classes, objects, attributes, behaviors, encapsulation and inheritance. You also learned about the history and purpose of the UML—the industry-standard graphical language for modeling object-oriented software systems.

You learned the typical steps for creating and executing a C++ application, and you "test-drove" a sample C++ application. We discussed several key software technologies and concepts, and looked to the future of C++. In a later chapter, you'll study the Boost open source library for broadly enhancing the C++ Standard Library's capabilities.

In the next chapter, you'll create your first C++ applications. You'll see several examples that demonstrate how programs display messages on the screen and obtain information from the user at the keyboard for processing.

1.21 Web Resources

This section provides links to our C++ and related Resource Centers that will be useful to you as you learn C++. These Resource Centers include various C++ resources, C++ development tools for students and professionals and links to games built with C++.

Deitel & Associates Websites

www.deitel.com/books/cpphtp7/
The Deitel & Associates *C++ How to Program, 7/e* site. Here you'll find links to the book's examples and other resources.

www.deitel.com/cplusplus/
www.deitel.com/visualcplusplus/
www.deitel.com/cplusplusgameprogramming/
www.deitel.com/cplusplusboostlibraries/
www.deitel.com/codesearchengines
www.deitel.com/programmingprojects
Check these Resource Centers for compilers, code downloads, tutorials, documentation, books, e-books, articles, blogs, RSS feeds and more that will help you develop C++ applications.

www.deitel.com
Check this site for updates, corrections and additional resources for all Deitel publications.

www.deitel.com/newsletter/subscribe.html
Visit this site to subscribe for the *Deitel® Buzz Online* e-mail newsletter to follow the Deitel & Associates publishing program, including updates and errata to *C++ How to Program, 7/e.*

Summary

Section 1.1 Introduction
- Computers (often referred to as hardware) are controlled by software (i.e., the instructions you write to command the computer to perform actions and make decisions).
- Computing costs have been decreasing dramatically due to rapid developments in both hardware and software technologies.
- Object orientation is the key programming methodology used by programmers today.

Section 1.2 Computers: Hardware and Software
- A computer is capable of performing computations and making logical decisions at speeds billions of times faster than human beings can.
- Computers process data under the control of sets of instructions called computer programs, which guide the computer through orderly sets of actions specified by computer programmers.

- The various devices that comprise a computer system are referred to as hardware.
- The computer programs that run on a computer are referred to as software.

Section 1.3 Computer Organization

- The input unit is the "receiving" section of the computer. It obtains information from input devices and places it at the disposal of the other units for processing.
- The output unit is the "shipping" section of the computer. It takes information processed by the computer and places it on output devices to make it available for use outside the computer.
- The memory unit is the rapid-access, relatively low-capacity "warehouse" section of the computer. It retains information that has been entered through the input unit, making it immediately available for processing when needed, and retains information that has already been processed until it can be placed on output devices by the output unit.
- The arithmetic and logic unit (ALU) is the "manufacturing" section of the computer. It's responsible for performing calculations and making decisions.
- The central processing unit (CPU) is the "administrative" section of the computer. It coordinates and supervises the operation of the other sections.
- The secondary storage unit is the long-term, high-capacity "warehousing" section of the computer. Programs or data not being used by the other units are normally placed on secondary storage devices (e.g., disks) until they're needed, possibly hours, days, months or even years later.

Section 1.4 Personal, Distributed and Client/Server Computing

- Apple Computer popularized personal computing.
- IBM's Personal Computer quickly legitimized personal computing in business, industry and government organizations, where IBM mainframes are heavily used.
- Early personal computers could be linked together in computer networks. This led to the phenomenon of distributed computing.
- Information is shared easily across networks, where computers called servers (file servers, database servers, web servers, etc.) offer a common data store and other capabilities that may be used by client computers distributed throughout the network, hence the term client/server computing.
- C++ has become widely used for writing software for operating systems, for computer networking and for distributed client/server applications.

Section 1.5 The Internet and the World Wide Web

- The Internet—a global network of computers—was initiated almost four decades ago with funding supplied by the U.S. Department of Defense.
- With the introduction of the World Wide Web—which allows computer users to locate and view multimedia-based documents on almost any subject over the Internet—the Internet has exploded into the world's premier communication mechanism.

Section 1.6 Web 2.0

- Web 2.0 can be explained through a series of Internet trends, one being the empowerment of the user. Companies such as eBay are built almost entirely on community-generated content.
- Web 2.0 takes advantage of collective intelligence—collaboration will result in intelligent ideas.
- Tagging, or labeling content, is another key part of the collaborative theme of Web 2.0.
- Social networking sites help users manage their interpersonal relationships.

- Blogs, websites characterized by short postings in reverse chronological order, have become a major social phenomenon within Web 2.0. Many bloggers are recognized as part of the media, and companies are reaching out to the blogosphere to track consumer opinions.
- Open source software makes it cheaper and easier to start Web 2.0 companies.
- Mashups combine two or more existing web applications to serve a new purpose and are dependent on small modular pieces and open access to web services APIs, which allow developers to integrate other web services into their applications.

Section 1.7 Machine Languages, Assembly Languages and High-Level Languages
- Any computer can directly understand only its own machine language, which generally consist of strings of numbers that instruct computers to perform their most elementary operations.
- English-like abbreviations form the basis of assembly languages. Translator programs called assemblers convert assembly-language programs to machine language.
- Compilers translate high-level language programs into machine-language programs. High-level languages (like C++) contain English words and conventional mathematical notations.
- Interpreter programs directly execute high-level language programs, eliminating the need to compile them into machine language.

Section 1.8 History of C and C++
- C++ enhances the C language and provides capabilities for object-oriented programming.
- Objects are reusable software components that model items in the real world. Using a modular, object-oriented design and implementation approach can make software development groups more productive than with previous programming techniques.

Section 1.9 C++ Standard Library
- You can program each class and function you need, but most C++ programmers take advantage of the rich collections of existing classes and functions in the C++ Standard Library.

Section 1.10 History of Java
- Java is used to create dynamic and interactive content for web pages, develop enterprise applications, enhance web server functionality, provide applications for consumer devices and more.

Section 1.11 Fortran, COBOL, Pascal and Ada
- FORTRAN was developed by IBM Corporation in the 1950s for scientific and engineering applications that require complex mathematical computations.
- COBOL was developed in the 1950s for commercial applications that require precise and efficient data manipulation.
- Ada was developed under the sponsorship of the United States Department of Defense (DoD) during the 1970s and early 1980s. Ada provides multitasking, which allows programmers to specify that many activities are to occur in parallel.

Section 1.12 BASIC, Visual Basic, Visual C++, C# and .NET
- BASIC was developed in the 1960s at Dartmouth College for programming novices.
- Visual Basic was introduced in the 1990s to simplify developing Windows applications.
- Microsoft has a corporate-wide strategy for integrating the Internet and the web into computer applications. This strategy is implemented in Microsoft's .NET platform.

- The .NET platform's three primary programming languages are Visual Basic (based on the original BASIC), Visual C++ (based on C++) and Visual C# (a new language based on C++ and Java that was developed expressly for the .NET platform).

Section 1.13 Key Software Trend: Object Technology

- Not until object-oriented programming became widely used in the 1990s did software developers feel they had the tools to make major strides in the software development process.
- C++ absorbed the features of C and added Simula's object capabilities.
- Object technology is a packaging scheme that helps us create meaningful software units.
- With object technology, the software entities created (called classes), if properly designed, tend to be reusable on future projects.
- Some organizations report the key benefit of object-oriented programming is the production of software which is more understandable, better organized and easier to maintain and debug.

Section 1.14 Typical C++ Development Environment

- C++ systems generally consist of three parts: a program development environment, the language and the C++ Standard Library.
- C++ programs typically go through six phases: *edit, preprocess, compile, link, load* and *execute*.
- C++ source code filenames often end with the .cpp, .cxx, .cc or .C extensions.
- A preprocessor program executes automatically before the compiler's translation phase begins. The C++ preprocessor obeys commands called preprocessor directives, which indicate that certain manipulations are to be performed on the program before compilation.
- The object code produced by the C++ compiler typically contains "holes" due to references to functions and data defined elsewhere. A linker links the object code with the code for the missing functions to produce an executable program (with no missing pieces).
- The loader takes the executable program from disk and transfers it to memory for execution.
- Data is often input from cin (the standard input stream) which is normally the keyboard. Data is often output to cout (the standard output stream), which is normally the computer screen. The cerr stream is used to display error messages.

Section 1.17 Software Technologies

- Agile Software Development is a set of methodologies that try to get software implemented quickly with fewer resources then previous methodologies.
- Refactoring involves reworking code to make it clearer and easier to maintain.
- Design patterns are proven architectures for constructing object-oriented software.
- With open source software development, individuals and companies develop, maintain and evolve software in exchange for the right to use that software for their own purposes. Bugs get removed faster and open source encourages innovation.
- Linux is an open source operating system.
- MySQL is an open source database management system.
- PHP is an open source server-side "scripting" language for developing Internet applications.
- LAMP is an acronym for a set of open source technologies used to build web applications—it stands for Linux, Apache, MySQL and PHP (or Perl or Python).
- Ruby on Rails combines the scripting language Ruby with the Rails web application framework.
- With Software as a Service (SaaS) the software runs on servers. When those are updated, all clients are updated; no local installation is needed. You typically access the service through a browser.

Section 1.18 Future of C++: Open Source Boost Libraries, TR1 and C++0x
- The free, open source Boost C++ Libraries work well with the C++ Standard Library.
- Technical Report 1 describes the proposed changes to the C++ Standard Library, many of which are based on current Boost libraries.
- C++0x is the working name for the next version of the C++ Standard. It includes some changes to the core language and many of the library additions described in TR1.

Section 1.19 Software Engineering Case Study: Introduction to Object Technology and the UML
- The Unified Modeling Language (UML) is a graphical language that allows people who build systems to represent their object-oriented designs in a common notation.
- Object-oriented design (OOD) models software components in terms of real-world objects. It takes advantage of class relationships, where objects of a certain class have the same characteristics. It also takes advantage of inheritance relationships, where newly created classes of objects are derived by absorbing characteristics of existing classes and adding unique characteristics of their own. OOD encapsulates data (attributes) and functions (behavior) into objects—the data and functions of an object are intimately tied together.
- Objects have the property of information hiding—objects normally are not allowed to know how other objects are implemented.
- C++ programmers create their own user-defined types called classes. Each class contains data (known as data members) and the set of functions (known as member functions) that manipulate that data and provide services to clients.
- Classes can have relationships with other classes. These relationships are called associations.
- Packaging software as classes makes it possible for future software systems to reuse the classes.
- An instance of a class is called an object.
- The process of analyzing and designing a system from an object-oriented point of view is called object-oriented analysis and design (OOAD).

Terminology

Self-Review Exercises

1.1 Fill in the blanks in each of the following:
  a) The company that popularized personal computing was _____.
  b) The computer that made personal computing legitimate in business and industry was the _____.
  c) Computers process data under the control of sets of instructions called computer _____.
  d) The six key logical units of the computer are the _____, _____, _____, _____, _____ and the _____.
  e) The three types of languages discussed in the chapter are _____, _____, and _____.
  f) The programs that translate high-level language programs into machine language are called _____.
  g) C is widely known as the development language of the _____ operating system.
  h) The _____ language was developed by Wirth for teaching structured programming.
  i) The Department of Defense developed the Ada language with a capability called _____, which allows programmers to specify activities that can proceed in parallel.
  j) _____, or labeling content, is another key part of the collaborative theme of Web 2.0.
  k) With Internet applications, the desktop evolves to the _____.
  l) _____ involves reworking code to make it clearer and easier to maintain while preserving its functionality.
  m) With _____ development, individuals and companies contribute their efforts in developing, maintaining and evolving software in exchange for the right to use that software for their own purposes, typically at no charge.
  n) _____ are used to match specific character patterns in text. They can be used to validate data to ensure that it's in a particular format, to replace parts of one string with another, or to split a string.

1.2 Fill in the blanks in each of the following sentences about the C++ environment.
  a) C++ programs are normally typed into a computer using a(n) _____ program.
  b) In a C++ system, a(n) _____ program executes before the compiler's translation phase begins.

    c) The _____ program combines the output of the compiler with various library functions to produce an executable program.

    d) The _____ program transfers the executable program from disk to memory.

1.3   Fill in the blanks in each of the following statements (based on Section 1.19):

    a) Objects have the property of _____—although objects may know how to communicate with one another across well-defined interfaces, they normally are not allowed to know how other objects are implemented.

    b) C++ programmers concentrate on creating _____, which contain data members and the member functions that manipulate those data members and provide services to clients.

    c) Classes can have relationships with other classes. These relationships are called _____.

    d) The process of analyzing and designing a system from an object-oriented point of view is called _____.

    e) OOD also takes advantage of _____ relationships, where new classes of objects are derived by absorbing characteristics of existing classes, then adding unique characteristics of their own.

    f) _____ is a graphical language that allows people who design software systems to use an industry-standard notation to represent them.

    g) The size, shape, color and weight of an object are considered _____ of the object.

Answers to Self-Review Exercises

1.1   a) Apple. b) IBM Personal Computer. c) programs. d) input unit, output unit, memory unit, arithmetic and logic unit, central processing unit, secondary storage unit. e) machine languages, assembly languages and high-level languages. f) compilers. g) UNIX. h) Pascal. i) multitasking. j) Tagging. k) webtop. l) Refactoring. m) open source. n) Regular expressions.

1.2   a) editor. b) preprocessor. c) linker. d) loader.

1.3   a) information hiding. b) classes. c) associations. d) object-oriented analysis and design (OOAD). e) inheritance. f) The Unified Modeling Language (UML). g) attributes.

Exercises

1.4   Categorize each of the following items as either hardware or software:

    a) CPU

    b) C++ compiler

    c) ALU

    d) C++ preprocessor

    e) input unit

    f) an editor program

1.5   Why might you want to write a program in a machine-independent language instead of a machine-dependent language? Why might a machine-dependent language be more appropriate for writing certain types of programs?

1.6   Fill in the blanks in each of the following statements:

    a) Which logical unit of the computer receives information from outside the computer for use by the computer? _____.

    b) The process of instructing the computer to solve specific problems is called _____.

    c) What type of computer language uses English-like abbreviations for machine-language instructions? _____.

d) Which logical unit of the computer sends information that has already been processed by the computer to various devices so that the information may be used outside the computer? _____.

e) Which logical units of the computer retain information? _____.

f) Which logical unit of the computer performs calculations? _____.

g) Which logical unit of the computer makes logical decisions? _____.

h) The level of computer language most convenient for you to write programs quickly and easily is _____.

i) The only language that a computer directly understands is called that computer's _____.

j) Which logical unit of the computer coordinates the activities of all the other logical units? _____.

1.7 Why is so much attention today focused on object-oriented programming?

1.8 Distinguish between the terms fatal error and nonfatal error. Why might you prefer to experience a fatal error rather than a nonfatal error?

1.9 Give a brief answer to each of the following questions:

a) Why does this text discuss structured programming in addition to object-oriented programming?

b) What kinds of messages do people send to one another?

c) Objects send messages to one another across well-defined interfaces. What interfaces does a car radio (object) present to its user (a person object)?

1.10 *(The Watch as an Object)* You are probably wearing on your wrist one of the world's most common types of objects—a watch. Discuss how each of the following terms and concepts applies to the notion of a watch: object, attributes, behaviors, class, inheritance (consider, for example, an alarm clock), encapsulation, interface, information hiding, data members and member functions.

1.11 Fill in the blanks in each of the following statements (based on Section 1.17):

a) The open source database management system used in LAMP development is _____.

b) A key advantage of Software as a Service (SaaS) is _____.

c) _____ are proven architectures for constructing flexible and maintainable object-oriented software.

d) _____ is the most popular open source server-side "scripting" language for developing Internet-based applications.

Making a Difference

1.12 *(Test Drive: Carbon Footprint Calculator)* Some scientists believe that carbon emissions, especially from the burning of fossil fuels, contribute significantly to global warming and that this can be combatted if individuals take steps to limit their use of carbon-based fuels. Organizations and individuals are increasingly concerned about their "carbon footprints." Websites such as TerraPass

```
www.terrapass.com/carbon-footprint-calculator/
```

and Carbon Footprint

```
www.carbonfootprint.com/calculator.aspx
```

provide carbon footprint calculators. Test drive these calculators to determine your carbon footprint. Exercises in later chapters will ask you to program your own carbon footprint calculator. To prepare for this, use the web to research the formulas for calculating carbon footprints.

1.13 *(Test Drive: Body Mass Index Calculator)* By recent estimates, two-thirds of the people in the United States are overweight and about half of those are obese. This causes significant increases in illnesses such as diabetes and heart disease. To determine whether a person is overweight or obese, you can use a measure called the body mass index (BMI). The United States Department of Health and Human Services provides a BMI calculator at www.nhlbisupport.com/bmi/. Use it to calculate your own BMI. An exercise in Chapter 2 will ask you to program your own BMI calculator. To prepare for this, use the web to research the formulas for calculating BMI.

1.14 *(Attributes of Hybrid Vehicles)* In this chapter you learned the basics of classes. Now you'll "flesh out" aspects of a class called "Hybrid Vehicle." Hybrid vehicles are becoming increasingly popular, because they often get much better mileage than purely gasoline-powered vehicles. Browse the web and study the features of four or five of today's popular hybrid cars, then list as many of their hybrid-related attributes as you can. Some common attributes include city-miles-per-gallon and highway-miles-per-gallon. Also list the attributes of the batteries (type, weight, etc.).

1.15 *(Gender Neutrality)* Many people want to eliminate sexism in all forms of communication. You've been asked to create a program that can process a paragraph of text and replace gender-specific words with gender-neutral ones. Assuming that you've been given a list of gender-specific words and their gender-neutral replacements (e.g., replace "wife" with "spouse," "man" with "person," "daughter" with "child" and so on), explain the procedure you'd use to read through a paragraph of text and manually perform these replacements. How might your procedure generate a strange term like "woperchild," which is actually listed in the Urban Dictionary (www.urbandictionary.com)? In Chapter 4, you'll learn that a more formal term for "procedure" is "algorithm," and that an algorithm specifies the steps to be performed and the order in which to perform them.

Introduction to C++ Programming

What's in a name? that which we call a rose By any other name would smell as sweet.
—William Shakespeare

When faced with a decision, I always ask, "What would be the most fun?"
—Peggy Walker

"Take some more tea," the March Hare said to Alice, very earnestly. "I've had nothing yet," Alice replied in an offended tone: "so I can't take more." "You mean you can't take less," said the Hatter: "it's very easy to take more than nothing."
—Lewis Carroll

High thoughts must have high language.
—Aristophanes

Objectives

In this chapter you'll learn:

- To write simple computer programs in C++.
- To write simple input and output statements.
- To use fundamental types.
- Basic computer memory concepts.
- To use arithmetic operators.
- The precedence of arithmetic operators.
- To write simple decision-making statements.

2.1 Introduction

We now introduce C++ programming, which facilitates a disciplined approach to program design. Most of the C++ programs you'll study in this book process information and display results. In this chapter, we present five examples that demonstrate how your programs can display messages and obtain information from the user for processing. The first three examples simply display messages on the screen. The next obtains two numbers from a user, calculates their sum and displays the result. The accompanying discussion shows you how to perform various arithmetic calculations and save their results for later use. The fifth example demonstrates decision-making fundamentals by showing you how to compare two numbers, then display messages based on the comparison results. We analyze each program one line at a time to help you ease your way into C++ programming. To help you apply the skills you learn here, we provide many programming problems in the chapter's exercises.

2.2 First Program in C++: Printing a Line of Text

C++ uses notations that may appear strange to nonprogrammers. We now consider a simple program that prints a line of text (Fig. 2.1). This program illustrates several important features of the C++ language. We consider each line in detail.

```
1   // Fig. 2.1: fig02_01.cpp
2   // Text-printing program.
3   #include <iostream> // allows program to output data to the screen
4
5   // function main begins program execution
6   int main()
7   {
8      std::cout << "Welcome to C++!\n"; // display message
9
10     return 0; // indicate that program ended successfully
11  } // end function main
```

```
Welcome to C++!
```

Fig. 2.1 | Text-printing program.

Lines 1 and 2

```
// Fig. 2.1: fig02_01.cpp
// Text-printing program.
```

each begin with **//**, indicating that the remainder of each line is a **comment**. You insert comments to document your programs and to help other people read and understand them. Comments do not cause the computer to perform any action when the program is run—they're ignored by the C++ compiler and do not cause any machine-language object code to be generated. The comment Text-printing program describes the purpose of the program. A comment beginning with // is called a **single-line comment** because it terminates at the end of the current line. [*Note:* You also may use C's style in which a comment—possibly containing many lines—begins with /* and ends with */.]

Good Programming Practice 2.1
Every program should begin with a comment that describes the purpose of the program.

Line 3

```
#include <iostream> // allows program to output data to the screen
```

is a **preprocessor directive**, which is a message to the C++ preprocessor (introduced in Section 1.14). Lines that begin with **#** are processed by the preprocessor before the program is compiled. This line notifies the preprocessor to include in the program the contents of the **input/output stream header file <iostream>**. This file must be included for any program that outputs data to the screen or inputs data from the keyboard using C++-style stream input/output. The program in Fig. 2.1 outputs data to the screen, as we'll soon see. We discuss header files in more detail in Chapter 6 and explain the contents of <iostream> in Chapter 15.

Common Programming Error 2.1
Forgetting to include the <iostream> header file in a program that inputs data from the keyboard or outputs data to the screen causes the compiler to issue an error message, because the compiler cannot recognize references to the stream components (e.g., cout).

Line 4 is simply a blank line. You use blank lines, space characters and tab characters (i.e., "tabs") to make programs easier to read. Together, these characters are known as **white space**. White-space characters are normally ignored by the compiler. In this chapter and several that follow, we discuss conventions for using white-space characters to enhance program readability.

Good Programming Practice 2.2
Use blank lines, space characters and tabs to enhance program readability.

Line 5

```
// function main begins program execution
```

is another single-line comment indicating that program execution begins at the next line.

Line 6

```
int main()
```

is a part of every C++ program. The parentheses after main indicate that **main** is a program building block called a **function**. C++ programs typically consist of one or more functions and classes (as you'll learn in Chapter 3). Exactly one function in every program must be named main. Figure 2.1 contains only one function. C++ programs begin executing at function main, even if main is not the first function in the program. The keyword int to the left of main indicates that main "returns" an integer (whole number) value. A **keyword** is a word in code that is reserved by C++ for a specific use. The complete list of C++ keywords can be found in Fig. 4.3. We'll explain what it means for a function to "return a value" when we demonstrate how to create your own functions in Section 3.4 and when we study functions in greater depth in Chapter 6. For now, simply include the keyword int to the left of main in each of your programs.

The **left brace**, **{**, (line 7) must begin the **body** of every function. A corresponding **right brace**, **}**, (line 11) must end each function's body. Line 8

```
std::cout << "Welcome to C++!\n"; // display message
```

instructs the computer to **perform an action**—namely, to print the **string** of characters contained between the double quotation marks. A string is sometimes called a **character string** or a **string literal**. We refer to characters between double quotation marks simply as **strings**. White-space characters in strings are not ignored by the compiler.

The entire line 8, including std::cout, the **<< operator**, the string "Welcome to C++!\n" and the **semicolon** (**;**), is called a **statement**. Every C++ statement must end with a semicolon (also known as the **statement terminator**). Preprocessor directives (like #include) do not end with a semicolon. Output and input in C++ are accomplished with **streams** of characters. Thus, when the preceding statement is executed, it sends the stream of characters Welcome to C++!\n to the **standard output stream object—std::cout**—which is normally "connected" to the screen. We discuss std::cout's many features in detail in Chapter 15, Stream Input/Output.

The std:: before cout is required when we use names that we've brought into the program by the preprocessor directive #include <iostream>. The notation std::cout specifies that we are using a name, in this case cout, that belongs to "namespace" std. The names cin (the standard input stream) and cerr (the standard error stream)—introduced in Chapter 1—also belong to namespace std. Namespaces are an advanced C++ feature that we discuss in depth in Chapter 24, Other Topics. For now, you should simply remember to include std:: before each mention of cout, cin and cerr in a program. This can be cumbersome—in Fig. 2.13, we introduce the using declaration, which will enable us to omit std:: before each use of a name in the std namespace.

The << operator is referred to as the **stream insertion operator**. When this program executes, the value to the operator's right, the right **operand**, is inserted in the output stream. Notice that the operator points in the direction of where the data goes. The right operand's characters normally print exactly as they appear between the double quotes. However, the characters \n are not printed on the screen (Fig. 2.1). The backslash (\) is called an **escape character**. It indicates that a "special" character is to be output. When a backslash is encountered in a string of characters, the next character is combined with the backslash to form an **escape sequence**. The escape sequence \n means **newline**. It causes the **cursor** (i.e., the current screen-position indicator) to move to the beginning of the next line on the screen. Some common escape sequences are listed in Fig. 2.2.

Escape sequence	Description
\n	Newline. Position the screen cursor to the beginning of the next line.
\t	Horizontal tab. Move the screen cursor to the next tab stop.
\r	Carriage return. Position the screen cursor to the beginning of the current line; do not advance to the next line.
\a	Alert. Sound the system bell.
\\	Backslash. Used to print a backslash character.
\'	Single quote. Use to print a single quote character.
\"	Double quote. Used to print a double quote character.

Fig. 2.2 | Escape sequences.

Common Programming Error 2.2

*Omitting the semicolon at the end of a C++ statement is a syntax error. (Again, prepro-cessor directives do not end in a semicolon.) The **syntax** of a programming language spec-ifies the rules for creating proper programs in that language. A **syntax error** occurs when the compiler encounters code that violates C++'s language rules (i.e., its syntax). The com-piler normally issues an error message to help you locate and fix the incorrect code. Syntax errors are also called **compiler errors**, **compile-time errors** or **compilation errors**, because the compiler detects them during the compilation phase. You cannot execute your program until you correct all the syntax errors in it. As you'll see, some compilation errors are not syntax errors.*

Line 10

```
return 0; // indicate that program ended successfully
```

is one of several means we'll use to **exit a function**. When the **return statement** is used at the end of main, as shown here, the value 0 indicates that the program has terminated suc-cessfully. In Chapter 6 we discuss functions in detail, and the reasons for including this statement will become clear. The right brace, }, (line 11) indicates the end of function main. According to the C++ standard, if program execution reaches the end of main with-out encountering a return statement, it's assumed that the program terminated success-fully—exactly as when the last statement in main is a return statement with the value 0. For that reason, we omit the return statement at the end of main in subsequent programs.

Good Programming Practice 2.3

Indent the entire body of each function one level within the braces that delimit the body of the function. This makes a program's functional structure stand out and makes the pro-gram easier to read.

Good Programming Practice 2.4

Set a convention for the size of indent you prefer, then apply it uniformly. The tab key may be used to create indents, but tab stops may vary. We recommend using either 1/4-inch tab stops or (preferably) three spaces to form a level of indent.

2.3 Modifying Our First C++ Program

This section continues our introduction to C++ programming with two examples, showing how to modify the program in Fig. 2.1 to print text on one line by using multiple statements, and to print text on several lines by using a single statement.

Printing a Single Line of Text with Multiple Statements
Welcome to C++! can be printed several ways. For example, Fig. 2.3 performs stream insertion in multiple statements (lines 8–9), yet produces the same output as the program of Fig. 2.1. [*Note:* From this point forward, we use a yellow background to highlight the key features each program introduces.] Each stream insertion resumes printing where the previous one stopped. The first stream insertion (line 8) prints Welcome followed by a space, and because this string did not end with \n, the second stream insertion (line 9) begins printing on the same line immediately following the space. In general, C++ allows you to express statements in a variety of ways.

```
1   // Fig. 2.3: fig02_03.cpp
2   // Printing a line of text with multiple statements.
3   #include <iostream> // allows program to output data to the screen
4
5   // function main begins program execution
6   int main()
7   {
8      std::cout << "Welcome ";
9      std::cout << "to C++!\n";
10  } // end function main
```

```
Welcome to C++!
```

Fig. 2.3 | Printing a line of text with multiple statements.

Printing Multiple Lines of Text with a Single Statement
A single statement can print multiple lines by using newline characters, as in line 8 of Fig. 2.4. Each time the \n (newline) escape sequence is encountered in the output stream, the screen cursor is positioned to the beginning of the next line. To get a blank line in your output, place two newline characters back to back, as in line 8.

```
1   // Fig. 2.4: fig02_04.cpp
2   // Printing multiple lines of text with a single statement.
3   #include <iostream> // allows program to output data to the screen
```

Fig. 2.4 | Printing multiple lines of text with a single statement. (Part 1 of 2.)

```
4
5   // function main begins program execution
6   int main()
7   {
8      std::cout << "Welcome\nto\n\nC++!\n";
9   } // end function main
```

```
Welcome
to

C++!
```

Fig. 2.4 | Printing multiple lines of text with a single statement. (Part 2 of 2.)

2.4 **Another C++ Program: Adding Integers**

Our next program uses the input stream object **std::cin** and the **stream extraction operator**, **>>**, to obtain two integers typed by a user at the keyboard, computes the sum of these values and outputs the result using std::cout. Figure 2.5 shows the program and sample inputs and outputs. In the output window, we highlight the user's input in bold.

```
 1   // Fig. 2.5: fig02_05.cpp
 2   // Addition program that displays the sum of two integers.
 3   #include <iostream> // allows program to perform input and output
 4
 5   // function main begins program execution
 6   int main()
 7   {
 8      // variable declarations
 9      int number1; // first integer to add
10      int number2; // second integer to add
11      int sum; // sum of number1 and number2
12
13      std::cout << "Enter first integer: "; // prompt user for data
14      std::cin >> number1; // read first integer from user into number1
15
16      std::cout << "Enter second integer: "; // prompt user for data
17      std::cin >> number2; // read second integer from user into number2
18
19      sum = number1 + number2; // add the numbers; store result in sum
20
21      std::cout << "Sum is " << sum << std::endl; // display sum; end line
22   } // end function main
```

```
Enter first integer: 45
Enter second integer: 72
Sum is 117
```

Fig. 2.5 | Addition program that displays the sum of two integers entered at the keyboard.

The comments in lines 1 and 2

```
// Fig. 2.5: fig02_05.cpp
// Addition program that displays the sum of two numbers.
```

state the name of the file and the purpose of the program. The C++ preprocessor directive

```
#include <iostream> // allows program to perform input and output
```

in line 3 includes the contents of the <iostream> header file in the program.

The program begins execution with function main (line 6). The left brace (line 7) begins main's body and the corresponding right brace (line 22) ends it.

Lines 9–11

```
int number1; // first integer to add
int number2; // second integer to add
int sum; // sum of number1 and number2
```

are **declarations**. The identifiers number1, number2 and sum are the names of **variables**. A variable is a location in the computer's memory where a value can be stored for use by a program. These declarations specify that the variables number1, number2 and sum are data of type **int**, meaning that these variables will hold **integer** values, i.e., whole numbers such as 7, –11, 0 and 31914. All variables must be declared with a name and a data type before they can be used in a program. Several variables of the same type may be declared in one declaration or in multiple declarations. We could have declared all three variables in one declaration as follows:

```
int number1, number2, sum;
```

This makes the program less readable and prevents us from providing comments that describe each variable's purpose. If more than one name is declared in a declaration (as shown here), the names are separated by commas (,); this is referred to as a **comma-separated list**.

Good Programming Practice 2.5

Place a space after each comma (,) to make programs more readable.

We'll soon discuss the data type double for specifying real numbers, and the data type char for specifying character data. Real numbers are numbers with decimal points, such as 3.4, 0.0 and –11.19. A char variable may hold only a single lowercase letter, a single uppercase letter, a single digit or a single special character (e.g., $ or *). Types such as int, double and char are called **fundamental types**. Fundamental-type names are keywords and therefore must appear in all lowercase letters. Appendix C contains the complete list of fundamental types.

A variable name (such as number1) is any valid **identifier** that is not a keyword. An identifier is a series of characters consisting of letters, digits and underscores (_) that does not begin with a digit. C++ is **case sensitive**—uppercase and lowercase letters are different, so a1 and A1 are different identifiers.

Portability Tip 2.1

C++ allows identifiers of any length, but your C++ implementation may restrict identifier lengths. Use identifiers of 31 characters or fewer to ensure portability.

Good Programming Practice 2.6

*Choosing meaningful identifiers makes a program **self-documenting**—a person can understand the program simply by reading it rather than having to refer to manuals or comments.*

Good Programming Practice 2.7

Avoid using abbreviations in identifiers. This promotes program readability.

Good Programming Practice 2.8

Avoid identifiers that begin with underscores and double underscores, because C++ compilers may use names like that for their own purposes internally. This will prevent names you choose from being confused with names the compilers choose.

Error-Prevention Tip 2.1

Languages like C++ are "moving targets." As they evolve, more keywords could be added to the language. Avoid using "loaded" words like "object" as identifiers. Even though "object" is not currently a keyword in C++, it could become one; therefore, future compiling with new compilers could break existing code.

Declarations of variables can be placed almost anywhere in a program, but they must appear before their corresponding variables are used in the program. For example, in the program of Fig. 2.5, the declaration in line 9

```
int number1; // first integer to add
```

could have been placed immediately before line 14

```
std::cin >> number1; // read first integer from user into number1
```

the declaration in line 10

```
int number2; // second integer to add
```

could have been placed immediately before line 17

```
std::cin >> number2; // read second integer from user into number2
```

and the declaration in line 11

```
int sum; // sum of number1 and number2
```

could have been placed immediately before line 19

```
sum = number1 + number2; // add the numbers; store result in sum
```

Good Programming Practice 2.9

Always place a blank line between a declaration and adjacent executable statements. This makes the declarations stand out in the program and contributes to program clarity.

Line 13

```
std::cout << "Enter first integer: "; // prompt user for data
```

displays Enter first integer: followed by a space. This message is called a **prompt** because it directs the user to take a specific action. We like to pronounce the preceding statement as "std::cout *gets* the character string "Enter first integer: "." Line 14

```
std::cin >> number1; // read first integer from user into number1
```

uses the **input stream object cin** (of namespace std) and the **stream extraction operator**, >>, to obtain a value from the keyboard. Using the stream extraction operator with std::cin takes character input from the standard input stream, which is usually the keyboard. We like to pronounce the preceding statement as, "std::cin *gives* a value to number1" or simply "std::cin *gives* number1."

Error-Prevention Tip 2.2

Programs should validate the correctness of all input values to prevent erroneous information from affecting a program's calculations.

When the computer executes the preceding statement, it waits for the user to enter a value for variable number1. The user responds by typing an integer (as characters), then pressing the *Enter* key (sometimes called the *Return* key) to send the characters to the computer. The computer converts the character representation of the number to an integer and assigns (i.e., copies) this number (or **value**) to the variable number1. Any subsequent references to number1 in this program will use this same value.

The std::cout and std::cin stream objects facilitate interaction between the user and the computer. Because this interaction resembles a dialog, it's often called **conversational computing** or **interactive computing.**

Line 16

```
std::cout << "Enter second integer: "; // prompt user for data
```

prints Enter second integer: on the screen, prompting the user to take action. Line 17

```
std::cin >> number2; // read second integer from user into number2
```

obtains a value for variable number2 from the user.

The assignment statement in line 19

```
sum = number1 + number2; // add the numbers; store result in sum
```

adds the values of variables number1 and number2 and assigns the result to variable sum using the **assignment operator =**. The statement is read as, "sum *gets* the value of number1 + number2." Most calculations are performed in assignment statements. The = operator and the + operator are called **binary operators** because each has two operands. In the case of the + operator, the two operands are number1 and number2. In the case of the preceding = operator, the two operands are sum and the value of the expression number1 + number2.

Good Programming Practice 2.10

Place spaces on either side of a binary operator. This makes the operator stand out and makes the program more readable.

Line 21

```
std::cout << "Sum is " << sum << std::endl; // display sum; end line
```

displays the character string Sum is followed by the numerical value of variable sum followed by std::endl—a so-called **stream manipulator**. The name endl is an abbreviation for "end line" and belongs to namespace std. The std::endl stream manipulator outputs a newline, then "flushes the output buffer." This simply means that, on some systems where outputs accumulate in the machine until there are enough to "make it worthwhile" to display them on the screen, std::endl forces any accumulated outputs to be displayed at that moment. This can be important when the outputs are prompting the user for an action, such as entering data.

The preceding statement outputs multiple values of different types. The stream insertion operator "knows" how to output each type of data. Using multiple stream insertion operators (<<) in a single statement is referred to as **concatenating**, **chaining** or **cascading stream insertion operations**. It's unnecessary to have multiple statements to output multiple pieces of data.

Calculations can also be performed in output statements. We could have combined the statements in lines 19 and 21 into the statement

```
std::cout << "Sum is " << number1 + number2 << std::endl;
```

thus eliminating the need for the variable sum.

A powerful feature of C++ is that users can create their own data types called classes (we introduce this capability in Chapter 3 and explore it in depth in Chapters 9 and 10). Users can then "teach" C++ how to input and output values of these new data types using the >> and << operators (this is called **operator overloading**—a topic we explore in Chapter 11).

2.5 Memory Concepts

Variable names such as number1, number2 and sum actually correspond to **locations** in the computer's memory. Every variable has a name, a type, a size and a value.

In the addition program of Fig. 2.5, when the statement

```
std::cin >> number1; // read first integer from user into number1
```

in line 14 is executed, the characters typed by the user are converted to an integer that is placed into a memory location to which the name number1 has been assigned by the C++ compiler. Suppose the user enters the number 45 as the value for number1. The computer will place 45 into location number1, as shown in Fig. 2.6.

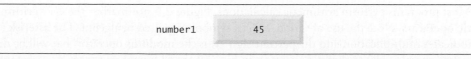

number1   45

Fig. 2.6 | Memory location showing the name and value of variable number1.

When a value is placed in a memory location, the value overwrites the previous value in that location; thus, placing a new value into a memory location is said to be **destructive**.

Returning to our addition program, when the statement

```
std::cin >> number2; // read second integer from user into number2
```

in line 17 is executed, suppose the user enters the value 72. This value is placed into location `number2`, and memory appears as in Fig. 2.7. These locations are not necessarily adjacent in memory.

number1	45
number2	72

Fig. 2.7 | Memory locations after storing values for `number1` and `number2`.

Once the program has obtained values for `number1` and `number2`, it adds these values and places the sum into variable `sum`. The statement

```
sum = number1 + number2; // add the numbers; store result in sum
```

that performs the addition also replaces whatever value was stored in `sum`. This occurs when the calculated sum of `number1` and `number2` is placed into location `sum` (without regard to what value may already be in `sum`; that value is lost). After `sum` is calculated, memory appears as in Fig. 2.8. The values of `number1` and `number2` appear exactly as they did before they were used in the calculation of `sum`. These values were used, but not destroyed, as the computer performed the calculation. Thus, when a value is read out of a memory location, the process is **nondestructive**.

number1	45
number2	72
sum	117

Fig. 2.8 | Memory locations after calculating and storing the `sum` of `number1` and `number2`.

2.6 Arithmetic

Most programs perform arithmetic calculations. Figure 2.9 summarizes the C++ **arithmetic operators**. Note the use of various special symbols not used in algebra. The **asterisk** (*) indicates multiplication and the **percent sign** (%) is the **modulus** operator that will be discussed shortly. The arithmetic operators in Fig. 2.9 are all binary operators, i.e., operators that take two operands. For example, the expression `number1 + number2` contains the binary operator + and the two operands `number1` and `number2`.

Integer division (i.e., where both the numerator and the denominator are integers) yields an integer quotient; for example, the expression 7 / 4 evaluates to 1 and the expression 17 / 5 evaluates to 3. Any fractional part in integer division is discarded (i.e., **truncated**)—no rounding occurs.

C++ operation	C++ arithmetic operator	Algebraic expression	C++ expression
Addition	+	$f + 7$	f + 7
Subtraction	-	$p - c$	p - c
Multiplication	*	bm or $b\,m$	b * m
Division	/	x / y or $\frac{x}{y}$ or $x \div y$	x / y
Modulus	%	$r \bmod s$	r % s

Fig. 2.9 | Arithmetic operators.

C++ provides the **modulus operator**, %, that yields the remainder after integer division. The modulus operator can be used only with integer operands. The expression x % y yields the remainder after x is divided by y. Thus, 7 % 4 yields 3 and 17 % 5 yields 2. In later chapters, we discuss many interesting applications of the modulus operator, such as determining whether one number is a multiple of another (a special case of this is determining whether a number is odd or even).

Common Programming Error 2.3
Attempting to use the modulus operator (%) with noninteger operands is a compilation error.

Arithmetic Expressions in Straight-Line Form

Arithmetic expressions in C++ must be entered into the computer in **straight-line form**. Thus, expressions such as "a divided by b" must be written as a / b, so that all constants, variables and operators appear in a straight line. The algebraic notation

$$\frac{a}{b}$$

is generally not acceptable to compilers, although some special-purpose software packages do support more natural notation for complex mathematical expressions.

Parentheses for Grouping Subexpressions

Parentheses are used in C++ expressions in the same manner as in algebraic expressions. For example, to multiply a times the quantity b + c we write a * (b + c).

Rules of Operator Precedence

C++ applies the operators in arithmetic expressions in a precise sequence determined by the following **rules of operator precedence**, which are generally the same as those followed in algebra:

1. Operators in expressions contained within pairs of parentheses are evaluated first. Parentheses are said to be at the "highest level of precedence." In cases of **nested**, or **embedded**, **parentheses**, such as

   ```
   ( a * ( b + c ) )
   ```

   the operators in the innermost pair of parentheses are applied first.

2. Multiplication, division and modulus operations are applied next. If an expression contains several multiplication, division and modulus operations, oper-

ators are applied from left to right. Multiplication, division and modulus are said to be on the same level of precedence.

3. Addition and subtraction operations are applied last. If an expression contains several addition and subtraction operations, operators are applied from left to right. Addition and subtraction also have the same level of precedence.

The set of rules of operator precedence defines the order in which C++ applies operators. When we say that certain operators are applied from left to right, we are referring to the **associativity** of the operators. For example, in the expression

```
a + b + c
```

the addition operators (+) associate from left to right, so a + b is calculated first, then c is added to that sum to determine the value of the whole expression. We'll see that some operators associate from right to left. Figure 2.10 summarizes these rules of operator precedence. This table will be expanded as additional C++ operators are introduced. A complete precedence chart is included in Appendix A.

Operator(s)	Operation(s)	Order of evaluation (precedence)
( )	Parentheses	Evaluated first. If the parentheses are nested, the expression in the innermost pair is evaluated first. If there are several pairs of parentheses "on the same level" (i.e., not nested), they're evaluated left to right.
*, /, %	Multiplication, Division, Modulus	Evaluated second. If there are several, they're evaluated left to right.
+ −	Addition Subtraction	Evaluated last. If there are several, they're evaluated left to right.

Fig. 2.10 | Precedence of arithmetic operators.

Sample Algebraic and C++ Expressions

Now consider several expressions in light of the rules of operator precedence. Each example lists an algebraic expression and its C++ equivalent. The following is an example of an arithmetic mean (average) of five terms:

Algebra: $m = \dfrac{a + b + c + d + e}{5}$

The parentheses are required because division has higher precedence than addition. The entire quantity (a + b + c + d + e) is to be divided by 5. If the parentheses are erroneously omitted, we obtain a + b + c + d + e / 5, which evaluates incorrectly as

$a + b + c + d + \dfrac{e}{5}$

The following is an example of the equation of a straight line:

Algebra: $y = mx + b$

C++:   y = m * x + b;

No parentheses are required. The multiplication is applied first because multiplication has a higher precedence than addition.

The following example contains modulus (%), multiplication, division, addition, subtraction and assignment operations:

> *Algebra:* $\quad z = pr\%q + w/x - y$
>
> *C++:* $\quad$ z = p * r % q + w / x - y;
> $\qquad\qquad$ 6 $\quad$ 1 $\quad$ 2 $\quad$ 4 $\quad$ 3 $\quad$ 5

The circled numbers under the statement indicate the order in which C++ applies the operators. The multiplication, modulus and division are evaluated first in left-to-right order (i.e., they associate from left to right) because they have higher precedence than addition and subtraction. The addition and subtraction are applied next. These are also applied left to right. Then the assignment operator is applied because its precedence is lower than that of any of the arithmetic operators.

Evaluation of a Second-Degree Polynomial

To develop a better understanding of the rules of operator precedence, consider the evaluation of a second-degree polynomial ($y = ax^2 + bx + c$):

> y = a * x * x + b * x + c;
> $\quad$ 6 $\quad$ 1 $\quad$ 2 $\quad$ 4 $\quad$ 3 $\quad$ 5

The circled numbers under the statement indicate the order in which C++ applies the operators. There is no arithmetic operator for exponentiation in C++, so we've represented x^2 as x * x. We'll soon discuss the standard library function pow ("power") that performs exponentiation. Because of some subtle issues related to the data types required by pow, we defer a detailed explanation of pow until Chapter 6.

Common Programming Error 2.4

*Some programming languages use operators ** or ^ to represent exponentiation. C++ does not support these exponentiation operators; using them for exponentiation results in errors.*

Suppose variables a, b, c and x in the preceding second-degree polynomial are initialized as follows: a = 2, b = 3, c = 7 and x = 5. Figure 2.11 illustrates the order in which the operators are applied.

As in algebra, it's acceptable to place unnecessary parentheses in an expression to make the expression clearer. These are called **redundant parentheses**. For example, the preceding assignment statement could be parenthesized as follows:

> y = (a * x * x) + (b * x) + c;

Good Programming Practice 2.11

Using redundant parentheses in complex arithmetic expressions can make the expressions clearer.

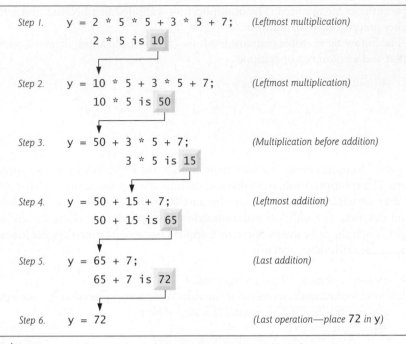

Step 1.	y = 2 * 5 * 5 + 3 * 5 + 7;	*(Leftmost multiplication)*
	2 * 5 is 10	
Step 2.	y = 10 * 5 + 3 * 5 + 7;	*(Leftmost multiplication)*
	10 * 5 is 50	
Step 3.	y = 50 + 3 * 5 + 7;	*(Multiplication before addition)*
	3 * 5 is 15	
Step 4.	y = 50 + 15 + 7;	*(Leftmost addition)*
	50 + 15 is 65	
Step 5.	y = 65 + 7;	*(Last addition)*
	65 + 7 is 72	
Step 6.	y = 72	*(Last operation—place 72 in y)*

Fig. 2.11 | Order in which a second-degree polynomial is evaluated.

2.7 Decision Making: Equality and Relational Operators

We now introduce a simple version of C++'s **if statement** that allows a program to take alternative action based on whether a **condition** is true or false. If the condition is true, the statement in the body of the if statement is executed. If the condition is false, the body statement is not executed. We'll see an example shortly.

Conditions in if statements can be formed by using the **equality operators** and **relational operators** summarized in Fig. 2.12. The relational operators all have the same level of precedence and associate left to right. The equality operators both have the same level of precedence, which is lower than that of the relational operators, and associate left to right.

Common Programming Error 2.5

A syntax error will occur if any of the operators ==, !=, >= and <= appears with spaces between its pair of symbols.

Common Programming Error 2.6

*Reversing the order of the pair of symbols in any of the operators !=, >= and <= (by writing them as =!, => and =<, respectively) is normally a syntax error. In some cases, writing != as =! will not be a syntax error, but almost certainly will be a **logic error** that has an effect at execution time. You'll understand why when you learn about logical operators in Chapter 5. A **fatal logic error** causes a program to fail and terminate prematurely. A **nonfatal logic error** allows a program to continue executing, but usually produces incorrect results.*

Standard algebraic equality or relational operator	C++ equality or relational operator	Sample C++ condition	Meaning of C++ condition
Relational operators			
>	>	x > y	x is greater than y
<	<	x < y	x is less than y
$\geq$	>=	x >= y	x is greater than or equal to y
$\leq$	<=	x <= y	x is less than or equal to y
Equality operators			
=	==	x == y	x is equal to y
$\neq$	!=	x != y	x is not equal to y

Fig. 2.12 | Equality and relational operators.

Common Programming Error 2.7

Confusing the equality operator == with the assignment operator = results in logic errors. The equality operator should be read "is equal to," and the assignment operator should be read "gets" or "gets the value of" or "is assigned the value of." Some people prefer to read the equality operator as "double equals." As we discuss in Section 5.9, confusing these operators may not necessarily cause an easy-to-recognize syntax error, but may cause extremely subtle logic errors.

The following example uses six if statements to compare two numbers input by the user. If the condition in any of these if statements is satisfied, the output statement associated with that if statement is executed. Figure 2.13 shows the program and the input/output dialogs of three sample executions.

```
1   // Fig. 2.13: fig02_13.cpp
2   // Comparing integers using if statements, relational operators
3   // and equality operators.
4   #include <iostream> // allows program to perform input and output
5
6   using std::cout; // program uses cout
7   using std::cin; // program uses cin
8   using std::endl; // program uses endl
9
10  // function main begins program execution
11  int main()
12  {
13     int number1; // first integer to compare
14     int number2; // second integer to compare
15
16     cout << "Enter two integers to compare: "; // prompt user for data
17     cin >> number1 >> number2; // read two integers from user
```

Fig. 2.13 | Comparing integers using if statements, relational operators and equality operators. (Part 1 of 2.)

```
18
19      if ( number1 == number2 )
20         cout << number1 << " == " << number2 << endl;
21
22      if ( number1 != number2 )
23         cout << number1 << " != " << number2 << endl;
24
25      if ( number1 < number2 )
26         cout << number1 << " < " << number2 << endl;
27
28      if ( number1 > number2 )
29         cout << number1 << " > " << number2 << endl;
30
31      if ( number1 <= number2 )
32         cout << number1 << " <= " << number2 << endl;
33
34      if ( number1 >= number2 )
35         cout << number1 << " >= " << number2 << endl;
36   } // end function main
```

```
Enter two integers to compare: 3 7
3 != 7
3 < 7
3 <= 7
```

```
Enter two integers to compare: 22 12
22 != 12
22 > 12
22 >= 12
```

```
Enter two integers to compare: 7 7
7 == 7
7 <= 7
7 >= 7
```

Fig. 2.13 | Comparing integers using if statements, relational operators and equality operators. (Part 2 of 2.)

Lines 6–8

```
using std::cout; // program uses cout
using std::cin; // program uses cin
using std::endl; // program uses endl
```

are **using declarations** that eliminate the need to repeat the std:: prefix as we did in earlier programs. Once we insert these using declarations, we can write cout instead of std::cout, cin instead of std::cin and endl instead of std::endl, respectively, in the remainder of the program.

In place of lines 6–8, many programmers prefer to use the declaration

```
using namespace std;
```

which enables a program to use all the names in any standard C++ header file (such as
<iostream>) that a program might include. From this point forward in the book, we'll use
the preceding declaration in our programs.

Lines 13–14

```
int number1; // first integer to compare
int number2; // second integer to compare
```

declare the variables used in the program. Remember that variables may be declared in one
declaration or in separate declarations.

The program uses cascaded stream extraction operations (line 17) to input two integers. Remember that we are allowed to write cin (instead of std::cin) because of line 7.
First a value is read into variable number1, then a value is read into variable number2.

The if statement in lines 19–20

```
if ( number1 == number2 )
    cout << number1 << " == " << number2 << endl;
```

compares the values of variables number1 and number2 to test for equality. If the values are
equal, the statement in line 20 displays a line of text indicating that the numbers are equal.
If the conditions are true in one or more of the if statements starting in lines 22, 25, 28,
31 and 34, the corresponding body statement displays an appropriate line of text.

Each if statement in Fig. 2.13 has a single statement in its body and each body statement is indented. In Chapter 4 we show how to specify if statements with multiple-state-
ment bodies (by enclosing the body statements in a pair of braces, { }, creating what is
called a **compound statement** or a **block**).

Good Programming Practice 2.12

Indent the statement(s) in the body of an if statement to enhance readability.

Good Programming Practice 2.13

For readability, there should be no more than one statement per line in a program.

Common Programming Error 2.8

*Placing a semicolon immediately after the right parenthesis after the condition in an if
statement is often a logic error (although not a syntax error). The semicolon causes the body
of the if statement to be empty, so the if statement performs no action, regardless of
whether or not its condition is true. Worse yet, the original body statement of the if statement now becomes a statement in sequence with the if statement and always executes,
often causing the program to produce incorrect results.*

Note the use of white space in Fig. 2.13. Recall that white-space characters, such as
tabs, newlines and spaces, are normally ignored by the compiler. So, statements may be
split over several lines and may be spaced according to your preferences. It's a syntax error
to split identifiers, strings (such as "hello") and constants (such as the number 1000) over
several lines.

Common Programming Error 2.9

It's a syntax error to split an identifier by inserting white-space characters (e.g., writing main as ma in).

Good Programming Practice 2.14

A lengthy statement may be spread over several lines. If a single statement must be split across lines, choose meaningful breaking points, such as after a comma in a comma-separated list, or after an operator in a lengthy expression. If a statement is split across two or more lines, indent all subsequent lines and left-align the group of indented lines.

Figure 2.14 shows the precedence and associativity of the operators introduced in this chapter. The operators are shown top to bottom in decreasing order of precedence. All these operators, with the exception of the assignment operator =, associate from left to right. Addition is left-associative, so an expression like x + y + z is evaluated as if it had been written (x + y) + z. The assignment operator = associates from right to left, so an expression such as x = y = 0 is evaluated as if it had been written x = (y = 0), which, as we'll soon see, first assigns 0 to y, then assigns the result of that assignment—0—to x.

Operators				Associativity	Type
()				left to right	parentheses
*	/	%		left to right	multiplicative
+	-			left to right	additive
<<	>>			left to right	stream insertion/extraction
<	<=	>	>=	left to right	relational
==	!=			left to right	equality
=				right to left	assignment

Fig. 2.14 | Precedence and associativity of the operators discussed so far.

Good Programming Practice 2.15

Refer to the operator precedence and associativity chart when writing expressions containing many operators. Confirm that the operators in the expression are performed in the order you expect. If you are uncertain about the order of evaluation in a complex expression, break the expression into smaller statements or use parentheses to force the order of evaluation, exactly as you'd do in an algebraic expression. Be sure to observe that some operators such as assignment (=) associate right to left rather than left to right.

2.8 Wrap-Up

You learned many important basic features of C++ in this chapter, including displaying data on the screen, inputting data from the keyboard and declaring variables of fundamental types. In particular, you learned to use the output stream object cout and the input stream object cin to build simple interactive programs. We explained how variables are stored in and retrieved from memory. You also learned how to use arithmetic operators to perform calculations. We discussed the order in which C++ applies operators (i.e., the rules of operator precedence), as well as the associativity of the operators. You also learned how C++'s if statement allows a program to make decisions. Finally, we introduced the equality and relational operators, which you use to form conditions in if statements.

The non-object-oriented applications presented here introduced you to basic programming concepts. As you'll see in Chapter 3, C++ applications typically contain just a few lines of code in function main—these statements normally create the objects that perform the work of the application, then the objects "take over from there." In Chapter 3, you'll learn how to implement your own classes and use objects of those classes in applications.

Summary

Section 2.2 First Program in C++: Printing a Line of Text

- Single-line comments begin with //. You insert comments to document your programs and improve their readability.

- Comments do not cause the computer to perform any action when the program is run—they're ignored by the compiler and do not cause any machine-language object code to be generated.

- A preprocessor directive begins with # and is a message to the C++ preprocessor. Preprocessor directives are processed before the program is compiled and don't end with a semicolon.

- The line #include <iostream> tells the C++ preprocessor to include the contents of the input/output stream header file in the program. This file contains information necessary to compile programs that use std::cin and std::cout and the stream insertion (<<) and stream extraction (>>) operators.

- White space (i.e., blank lines, space characters and tab characters) makes programs easier to read. White-space characters outside of literals are ignored by the compiler.

- C++ programs begin executing at main, even if main does not appear first in the program.

- The keyword int to the left of main indicates that main "returns" an integer value.

- A left brace, {, must begin the body of every function. A corresponding right brace, }, must end each function's body.

- A string in double quotes is sometimes referred to as a character string, message or string literal. White-space characters in strings are *not* ignored by the compiler.

- Every statement must end with a semicolon (also known as the statement terminator).

- Output and input in C++ are accomplished with streams of characters.

- The output stream object std::cout—normally connected to the screen—is used to output data. Multiple data items can be output by concatenating stream insertion (<<) operators.

- The input stream object std::cin—normally connected to the keyboard—is used to input data. Multiple data items can be input by concatenating stream extraction (>>) operators.

- The std::cout and std::cin stream objects facilitate interaction between the user and the computer. Because this interaction resembles a dialog, it's often called conversational computing or interactive computing.

- The notation std::cout specifies that we are using cout from "namespace" std.

- When a backslash (i.e., an escape character) is encountered in a string of characters, the next character is combined with the backslash to form an escape sequence.

- The escape sequence \n means newline. It causes the cursor (i.e., the current screen-position indicator) to move to the beginning of the next line on the screen.

- A message that directs the user to take a specific action is known as a prompt.
- C++ keyword return is one of several means to exit a function.

Section 2.4 Another C++ Program: Adding Integers
- All variables in a C++ program must be declared before they can be used.
- A variable name in C++ is any valid identifier that is not a keyword. An identifier is a series of characters consisting of letters, digits and underscores (_). Identifiers cannot start with a digit. C++ identifiers can be any length; however, some systems and/or C++ implementations may impose some restrictions on the length of identifiers.
- C++ is case sensitive.
- Most calculations are performed in assignment statements.
- A variable is a location in memory where a value can be stored for use by a program.
- Variables of type int hold integer values, i.e., whole numbers such as 7, –11, 0, 31914.

Section 2.5 Memory Concepts
- Every variable stored in the computer's memory has a name, a value, a type and a size.
- Whenever a new value is placed in a memory location, the process is destructive; i.e., the new value replaces the previous value in that location. The previous value is lost.
- When a value is read from memory, the process is nondestructive; i.e., a copy of the value is read, leaving the original value undisturbed in the memory location.
- The std::endl stream manipulator outputs a newline, then "flushes the output buffer."

Section 2.6 Arithmetic
- C++ evaluates arithmetic expressions in a precise sequence determined by the rules of operator precedence and associativity.
- Parentheses may be used to group expressions.
- Integer division (i.e., both the numerator and the denominator are integers) yields an integer quotient. Any fractional part in integer division is truncated—no rounding occurs.
- The modulus operator, %, yields the remainder after integer division. The modulus operator can be used only with integer operands.

Section 2.7 Decision Making: Equality and Relational Operators
- The if statement allows a program to take alternative action based on whether a condition is met. The format for an if statement is

      if (*condition*)
         statement;

  If the condition is true, the statement in the body of the if is executed. If the condition is not met, i.e., the condition is false, the body statement is skipped.
- Conditions in if statements are commonly formed by using equality operators and relational operators. The result of using these operators is always the value true or false.
- The declaration

      using std::cout;

  is a using declaration that informs the compiler where to find cout (namespace std) and eliminates the need to repeat the std:: prefix. The declaration

      using namespace std;

  enables the program to use all the names in any included standard library header file.

Terminology

Self-Review Exercises

2.1 Fill in the blanks in each of the following.

    a) Every C++ program begins execution at the function _____.

b) A _____ begins the body of every function and a _____ ends the body.

c) Every C++ statement ends with a(n) _____.

d) The escape sequence \n represents the _____ character, which causes the cursor to position to the beginning of the next line on the screen.

e) The _____ statement is used to make decisions.

2.2   State whether each of the following is *true* or *false*. If *false*, explain why. Assume the statement using std::cout; is used.

a) Comments cause the computer to print the text after the // on the screen when the program is executed.

b) The escape sequence \n, when output with cout and the stream insertion operator, causes the cursor to position to the beginning of the next line on the screen.

c) All variables must be declared before they're used.

d) All variables must be given a type when they're declared.

e) C++ considers the variables number and NuMbEr to be identical.

f) Declarations can appear almost anywhere in the body of a C++ function.

g) The modulus operator (%) can be used only with integer operands.

h) The arithmetic operators *, /, %, + and – all have the same level of precedence.

i) A C++ program that prints three lines of output must contain three statements using cout and the stream insertion operator.

2.3   Write a single C++ statement to accomplish each of the following (assume that using declarations have not been used):

a) Declare the variables c, thisIsAVariable, q76354 and number to be of type int.

b) Prompt the user to enter an integer. End your prompting message with a colon (:) followed by a space and leave the cursor positioned after the space.

c) Read an integer from the user at the keyboard and store it in integer variable age.

d) If the variable number is not equal to 7, print "The variable number is not equal to 7".

e) Print the message "This is a C++ program" on one line.

f) Print the message "This is a C++ program" on two lines. End the first line with C++.

g) Print the message "This is a C++ program" with each word on a separate line.

h) Print the message "This is a C++ program". Separate each word from the next by a tab.

2.4   Write a statement (or comment) to accomplish each of the following (assume that using declarations have been used for cin, cout and endl):

a) State that a program calculates the product of three integers.

b) Declare the variables x, y, z and result to be of type int (in separate statements).

c) Prompt the user to enter three integers.

d) Read three integers from the keyboard and store them in the variables x, y and z.

e) Compute the product of the three integers contained in variables x, y and z, and assign the result to the variable result.

f) Print "The product is " followed by the value of the variable result.

g) Return a value from main indicating that the program terminated successfully.

2.5   Using the statements you wrote in Exercise 2.4, write a complete program that calculates and displays the product of three integers. Add comments to the code where appropriate. [*Note:* You'll need to write the necessary using declarations.]

2.6   Identify and correct the errors in each of the following statements (assume that the statement using std::cout; is used):

a) if (c < 7);
        cout << "c is less than 7\n";

b) if (c => 7)
        cout << "c is equal to or greater than 7\n";

Answers to Self-Review Exercises

2.1 a) main. b) left brace ({), right brace (}). c) semicolon. d) newline. e) if.

2.2 a) False. Comments do not cause any action to be performed when the program is executed. They're used to document programs and improve their readability.
b) True.
c) True.
d) True.
e) False. C++ is case sensitive, so these variables are unique.
f) True.
g) True.
h) False. The operators *, / and % have the same precedence, and the operators + and - have a lower precedence.
i) False. One statement with cout and multiple \n escape sequences can print several lines.

2.3 a) `int c, thisIsAVariable, q76354, number;`
b) `std::cout << "Enter an integer: ";`
c) `std::cin >> age;`
d) `if ( number != 7 )`
    `std::cout << "The variable number is not equal to 7\n";`
e) `std::cout << "This is a C++ program\n";`
f) `std::cout << "This is a C++\nprogram\n";`
g) `std::cout << "This\nis\na\nC++\nprogram\n";`
h) `std::cout << "This\tis\ta\tC++\tprogram\n";`

2.4 a) `// Calculate the product of three integers`
b) `int x;`
   `int y;`
   `int z;`
   `int result;`
c) `cout << "Enter three integers: ";`
d) `cin >> x >> y >> z;`
e) `result - x * y * z;`
f) `cout << "The product is " << result << endl;`
g) `return 0;`

2.5 (See program below.)

```
 1   // Calculate the product of three integers
 2   #include <iostream> // allows program to perform input and output
 3   using namespace std; // program uses names from the std namespace
 4
 5   // function main begins program execution
 6   int main()
 7   {
 8      int x; // first integer to multiply
 9      int y; // second integer to multiply
10      int z; // third integer to multiply
11      int result; // the product of the three integers
12
13      cout << "Enter three integers: "; // prompt user for data
14      cin >> x >> y >> z; // read three integers from user
15      result = x * y * z; // multiply the three integers; store result
16      cout << "The product is " << result << endl; // print result; end line
17   } // end function main
```

2.6   a) *Error:* Semicolon after the right parenthesis of the condition in the if statement.
Correction: Remove the semicolon after the right parenthesis. [*Note:* The result of this error is that the output statement executes whether or not the condition in the if statement is true.] The semicolon after the right parenthesis is a null (or empty) statement that does nothing. We'll learn more about the null statement in Chapter 4.

b) *Error:* The relational operator =>.
Correction: Change => to >=, and you may want to change "equal to or greater than" to "greater than or equal to" as well.

Exercises

2.7   Discuss the meaning of each of the following objects:
a) std::cin
b) std::cout

2.8   Fill in the blanks in each of the following:
a) _____ are used to document a program and improve its readability.
b) The object used to print information on the screen is _____.
c) A C++ statement that makes a decision is _____.
d) Most calculations are normally performed by _____ statements.
e) The _____ object inputs values from the keyboard.

2.9   Write a single C++ statement or line that accomplishes each of the following:
a) Print the message "Enter two numbers".
b) Assign the product of variables b and c to variable a.
c) State that a program performs a payroll calculation (i.e., use text that helps to document a program).
d) Input three integer values from the keyboard into integer variables a, b and c.

2.10   State which of the following are *true* and which are *false*. If *false*, explain your answers.
a) C++ operators are evaluated from left to right.
b) The following are all valid variable names: _under_bar_, m928134, t5, j7, her_sales, his_account_total, a, b, c, z, z2.
c) The statement cout << "a = 5;"; is a typical example of an assignment statement.
d) A valid C++ arithmetic expression with no parentheses is evaluated from left to right.
e) The following are all invalid variable names: 3g, 87, 67h2, h22, 2h.

2.11   Fill in the blanks in each of the following:
a) What arithmetic operations are on the same level of precedence as multiplication? _____.
b) When parentheses are nested, which set of parentheses is evaluated first in an arithmetic expression? _____.
c) A location in the computer's memory that may contain different values at various times throughout the execution of a program is called a _____.

2.12   What, if anything, prints when each of the following C++ statements is performed? If nothing prints, then answer "nothing." Assume x = 2 and y = 3.
a) cout << x;
b) cout << x + x;
c) cout << "x=";
d) cout << "x = " << x;
e) cout << x + y << " = " << y + x;
f) z = x + y;
g) cin >> x >> y;

h) `// cout << "x + y = " << x + y;`

i) `cout << "\n";`

2.13 Which of the following C++ statements contain variables whose values are replaced?

a) `cin >> b >> c >> d >> e >> f;`

b) `p = i + j + k + 7;`

c) `cout << "variables whose values are replaced";`

d) `cout << "a = 5";`

2.14 Given the algebraic equation $y = ax^3 + 7$, which of the following, if any, are correct C++ statements for this equation?

a) `y = a * x * x * x + 7;`

b) `y = a * x * x * ( x + 7 );`

c) `y = ( a * x ) * x * ( x + 7 );`

d) `y = (a * x) * x * x + 7;`

e) `y = a * ( x * x * x ) + 7;`

f) `y = a * x * ( x * x + 7 );`

2.15 *(Order of Evaluation)* State the order of evaluation of the operators in each of the following C++ statements and show the value of x after each statement is performed.

a) `x = 7 + 3 * 6 / 2 - 1;`

b) `x = 2 % 2 + 2 * 2 - 2 / 2;`

c) `x = ( 3 * 9 * ( 3 + ( 9 * 3 / ( 3 ) ) ) );`

2.16 *(Arithmetic)* Write a program that asks the user to enter two numbers, obtains the two numbers from the user and prints the sum, product, difference, and quotient of the two numbers.

2.17 *(Printing)* Write a program that prints the numbers 1 to 4 on the same line with each pair of adjacent numbers separated by one space. Do this several ways:

a) Using one statement with one stream insertion operator.

b) Using one statement with four stream insertion operators.

c) Using four statements.

2.18 *(Comparing Integers)* Write a program that asks the user to enter two integers, obtains the numbers from the user, then prints the larger number followed by the words `"is larger."` If the numbers are equal, print the message `"These numbers are equal."`

2.19 *(Arithmetic, Smallest and Largest)* Write a program that inputs three integers from the keyboard and prints the sum, average, product, smallest and largest of these numbers. The screen dialog should appear as follows:

```
Input three different integers: 13 27 14
Sum is 54
Average is 18
Product is 4914
Smallest is 13
Largest is 27
```

2.20 *(Diameter, Circumference and Area of a Circle)* Write a program that reads in the radius of a circle as an integer and prints the circle's diameter, circumference and area. Use the constant value 3.14159 for π. Do all calculations in output statements. [*Note:* In this chapter, we've discussed only integer constants and variables. In Chapter 4 we discuss floating-point numbers, i.e., values that can have decimal points.]

2.21 *(Displaying Shapes with Asterisks)* Write a program that prints a box, an oval, an arrow and a diamond as follows:

```
********            ***            *               *
*       *         *     *         ***             * *
*       *         *     *        *****           *   *
*       *         *     *          *            *     *
*       *         *     *          *           *       *
*       *         *     *          *          *         *
*       *         *     *          *         *    *
*       *           *     *        *          * *
********            ***            *             *
```

2.22 What does the following code print?

```
cout << "*\n**\n***\n****\n*****" << endl;
```

2.23 *(Largest and Smallest Integers)* Write a program that reads in five integers and determines and prints the largest and the smallest integers in the group. Use only the programming techniques you learned in this chapter.

2.24 *(Odd or Even)* Write a program that reads an integer and determines and prints whether it's odd or even. [*Hint:* Use the modulus operator. An even number is a multiple of two. Any multiple of two leaves a remainder of zero when divided by 2.]

2.25 *(Multiples)* Write a program that reads in two integers and determines and prints if the first is a multiple of the second. [*Hint:* Use the modulus operator.]

2.26 *(Checkerboard Pattern)* Display the following checkerboard pattern with eight output statements, then display the same pattern using as few statements as possible.

```
* * * * * * * *
 * * * * * * * *
* * * * * * * *
 * * * * * * * *
* * * * * * * *
 * * * * * * * *
* * * * * * * *
 * * * * * * * *
```

2.27 *(Integer Equivalent of a Character)* Here is a peek ahead. In this chapter you learned about integers and the type int. C++ can also represent uppercase letters, lowercase letters and a considerable variety of special symbols. C++ uses small integers internally to represent each different character. The set of characters a computer uses and the corresponding integer representations for those characters are called that computer's **character set**. You can print a character by enclosing that character in single quotes, as with

```
cout << 'A'; // print an uppercase A
```

You can print the integer equivalent of a character using static_cast as follows:

```
cout << static_cast< int >( 'A' ); // print 'A' as an integer
```

This is called a **cast** operation (we formally introduce casts in Chapter 4). When the preceding statement executes, it prints the value 65 (on systems that use the **ASCII character set**). Write a program that prints the integer equivalent of a character typed at the keyboard. Store the input in a variable of type char. Test your program several times using uppercase letters, lowercase letters, digits and special characters (like $).

2.28 *(Digits of an Integer)* Write a program that inputs a five-digit integer, separates the integer into its digits and prints them separated by three spaces each. [*Hint:* Use the integer division and modulus operators.] For example, if the user types in 42339, the program should print:

```
4   2   3   3   9
```

2.29   *(Table)* Using the techniques of this chapter, write a program that calculates the squares and cubes of the integers from 0 to 10. Use tabs to print the following neatly formatted table of values:

```
integer square  cube
0       0       0
1       1       1
2       4       8
3       9       27
4       16      64
5       25      125
6       36      216
7       49      343
8       64      512
9       81      729
10      100     1000
```

Making a Difference

2.30   *(Body Mass Index Calculator)* We introduced the body mass index (BMI) calculator in Exercise 1.12. The formulas for calculating BMI are

$$BMI = \frac{weightInPounds \times 703}{heightInInches \times heightInInches}$$

or

$$BMI = \frac{weightInKilograms}{heightInMeters \times heightInMeters}$$

Create a BMI calculator application that reads the user's weight in pounds and height in inches (or, if you prefer, the user's weight in kilograms and height in meters), then calculates and displays the user's body mass index. Also, the application should display the following information from the Department of Health and Human Services/National Institutes of Health so the user can evaluate his/her BMI:

```
BMI VALUES
Underweight: less than 18.5
Normal:      between 18.5 and 24.9
Overweight:  between 25 and 29.9
Obese:       30 or greater
```

[*Note:* In this chapter, you learned to use the int type to represent whole numbers. The BMI calculations when done with int values will both produce whole-number results. In Chapter 4 you'll learn to use the double type to represent numbers with decimal points. When the BMI calculations are performed with doubles, they'll both produce numbers with decimal points—these are called "floating-point" numbers.]

2.31   *(Car-Pool Savings Calculator)* Research several car-pooling websites. Create an application that calculates your daily driving cost, so that you can estimate how much money could be saved by car pooling, which also has other advantages such as reducing carbon emissions and reducing traffic congestion. The application should input the following information and display the user's cost per day of driving to work:

a) Total miles driven per day.
b) Cost per gallon of gasoline.
c) Average miles per gallon.
d) Parking fees per day.
e) Tolls per day.

3

Introduction to Classes and Objects

Nothing can have value without being an object of utility.
—Karl Marx

Your public servants serve you right.
—Adlai E. Stevenson

*Knowing how to answer one who speaks,
To reply to one who sends a message.*
—Amenemopel

Objectives

In this chapter you'll learn:

- How to define a class and use it to create an object.
- How to define member functions in a class to implement the class's behaviors.
- How to declare data members in a class to implement the class's attributes.
- How to call a member function of an object to perform a task.
- The differences between data members of a class and local variables of a function.
- How to use a constructor to initialize an object's data when the object is created.
- How to engineer a class to separate its interface from its implementation and encourage reuse.

3.1 **Introduction**

In Chapter 2, you created simple programs that displayed messages to the user, obtained information from the user, performed calculations and made decisions. In this chapter, you'll begin writing programs that employ the basic concepts of object-oriented programming that we introduced in Section 1.19. One common feature of every program in Chapter 2 was that all the statements that performed tasks were located in function main. Typically, the programs you develop in this book will consist of function main and one or more classes, each containing data members and member functions. If you become part of a development team in industry, you might work on software systems that contain hundreds, or even thousands, of classes. In this chapter, we develop a simple, well-engineered framework for organizing object-oriented programs in C++.

First, we motivate the notion of classes with a real-world example. Then we present a carefully paced sequence of seven complete working programs to demonstrate creating and using your own classes. These examples begin our integrated case study on developing a grade-book class that instructors can use to maintain student test scores. This case study is enhanced over the next several chapters, culminating with the version presented in Chapter 7, Arrays and Vectors. We also introduce the C++ standard library class string in this chapter.

3.2 **Classes, Objects, Member Functions and Data Members**

Let's begin with a simple analogy to help you reinforce your understanding from Section 1.19 of classes and their contents. Suppose you want to drive a car and make it go faster by pressing down on its accelerator pedal. What must happen before you can do this? Well, before you can drive a car, someone has to *design* it and *build* it. A car typically begins as engineering drawings, similar to the blueprints used to design a house. These drawings include the design for an accelerator pedal that the driver will use to make the car go faster. In a sense, the pedal "hides" the complex mechanisms that actually make the car go faster, just as the brake pedal "hides" the mechanisms that slow the car, the steering wheel "hides" the mechanisms that turn the car and so on. This enables people with little or no knowledge of how cars are engineered to drive a car easily, simply by using the accelerator pedal, the brake pedal, the steering wheel, the transmission shifting mechanism and other such simple and user-friendly "interfaces" to the car's complex internal mechanisms.

Unfortunately, you cannot drive the engineering drawings of a car—before you can drive a car, it must be built from the engineering drawings that describe it. A completed car will have an actual accelerator pedal to make the car go faster. But even that's not enough—the car will not accelerate on its own, so the driver must press the accelerator pedal to tell the car to go faster.

Now let's use our car example to introduce the key object-oriented programming concepts of this section. Performing a task in a program requires a function (such as main, as described in Chapter 2). The function describes the mechanisms that actually perform its tasks. The function hides from its user the complex tasks that it performs, just as the accelerator pedal of a car hides from the driver the complex mechanisms of making the car go faster. In C++, we begin by creating a program unit called a class to house a function, just as a car's engineering drawings house the design of an accelerator pedal. Recall from Section 1.19 that a function belonging to a class is called a member function. In a class, you provide one or more member functions that are designed to perform the class's tasks. For example, a class that represents a bank account might contain one member function to deposit money into the account, another to withdraw money from the account and a third to inquire what the current account balance is.

Just as you cannot drive an engineering drawing of a car, you cannot "drive" a class. Just as someone has to build a car from its engineering drawings before you can actually drive the car, *you must create an object of a class before you can get a program to perform the tasks the class describes*. That is one reason C++ is known as an object-oriented programming language. Note also that just as *many* cars can be built from the same engineering drawing, *many* objects can be built from the same class.

When you drive a car, pressing its gas pedal sends a message to the car to perform a task—that is, make the car go faster. Similarly, you send **messages** to an object—each message is known as a **member-function call** and tells a member function of the object to perform its task. This is often called **requesting a service from an object**.

Thus far, we've used the car analogy to introduce classes, objects and member functions. In addition to the capabilities a car provides, it also has many attributes, such as its color, the number of doors, the amount of gas in its tank, its current speed and its total miles driven (i.e., its odometer reading). Like the car's capabilities, these attributes are represented as part of a car's design in its engineering diagrams. As you drive a car, these attributes are always associated with the car. Every car maintains its own attributes. For example, each car knows how much gas is in its own gas tank, but not how much is in the tanks of other cars. Similarly, an object has attributes that are carried with the object as it's used in a program. These attributes are specified as part of the object's class. For example, a bank account object has a balance attribute that represents the amount of money in the account. Each bank account object knows the balance in the account it represents, but not the balances of the other accounts in the bank. Attributes are specified by the class's data members.

The remainder of this chapter presents seven simple examples that demonstrate the concepts we introduced in the context of the car analogy.

3.3 Defining a Class with a Member Function

We begin with an example (Fig. 3.1) that consists of class GradeBook (lines 8–16), which, when it is fully developed in Chapter 7, will represent a grade book that an instructor can use to maintain student test scores, and a main function (lines 19–23) that creates a Grade-Book object. Function main uses this object and its member function to display a message on the screen welcoming the instructor to the grade-book program.

```cpp
1   // Fig. 3.1: fig03_01.cpp
2   // Define class GradeBook with a member function displayMessage,
3   // create a GradeBook object, and call its displayMessage function.
4   #include <iostream>
5   using namespace std;
6
7   // GradeBook class definition
8   class GradeBook
9   {
10  public:
11     // function that displays a welcome message to the GradeBook user
12     void displayMessage()
13     {
14        cout << "Welcome to the Grade Book!" << endl;
15     } // end function displayMessage
16  }; // end class GradeBook
17
18  // function main begins program execution
19  int main()
20  {
21     GradeBook myGradeBook; // create a GradeBook object named myGradeBook
22     myGradeBook.displayMessage(); // call object's displayMessage function
23  } // end main
```

```
Welcome to the Grade Book!
```

Fig. 3.1 | Define class GradeBook with a member function displayMessage, create a GradeBook object and call its displayMessage function.

First we describe how to define a class and a member function, then how an object is created and how to call an object's member function. The first few examples contain in the same file function main and the GradeBook class it uses. Later in the chapter, we introduce more sophisticated ways to structure programs for better software engineering.

Class GradeBook

Before function main (lines 19–23) can create a GradeBook object, we must tell the compiler what member functions and data members belong to the class—known as **defining a class**. The GradeBook **class definition** (lines 8–16) begins with keyword **class** and contains a member function called displayMessage (lines 12–15) that displays a message on the screen (line 14). Recall that a class is like a blueprint—so we need to make an object of class GradeBook (line 21) and call its displayMessage member function (line 22) to get line 14 to execute and display the welcome message. We'll soon explain lines 21–22 in detail.

The class definition begins in line 8 with the keyword class followed by the class name GradeBook. By convention, the name of a user-defined class begins with a capital letter, and for readability, each subsequent word in the class name begins with a capital letter. This capitalization style is often referred to as **camel case**, because the pattern of uppercase and lowercase letters resembles the silhouette of a camel.

Every class's **body** is enclosed in a pair of left and right braces ({ and }), as in lines 9 and 16. The class definition terminates with a semicolon (line 16).

Common Programming Error 3.1

Forgetting the semicolon at the end of a class definition is a syntax error.

Recall that the function main is always called automatically when you execute a program. Most functions do not get called automatically. As you'll soon see, you must call member function displayMessage explicitly to tell it to perform its task.

Line 10 contains the **access-specifier label public:**. The keyword **public** is an **access specifier**. Lines 12–15 define member function displayMessage. This member function appears after access specifier public: to indicate that the function is "available to the public"—that is, it can be called by other functions in the program (such as main), and by member functions of other classes (if there are any). Access specifiers are always followed by a colon (:). For the remainder of the text, when we refer to the access specifier public, we'll omit the colon as we did in this sentence. Section 3.5 introduces a second access specifier, private. Later in the book we'll study the access specifier protected.

Each function in a program performs a task and may return a value when it completes its task—for example, a function might perform a calculation, then return the result of that calculation. When you define a function, you must specify a **return type** to indicate the type of the value returned by the function when it completes its task. In line 12, keyword **void** to the left of the function name displayMessage is the function's return type. Return type void indicates that displayMessage will *not* return (i.e., give back) any data to its **calling function** (in this example, main, as we'll see in a moment) when it completes its task. In Fig. 3.5, you'll see an example of a function that returns a value.

The name of the member function, displayMessage, follows the return type. By convention, function names begin with a lowercase first letter and all subsequent words in the name begin with a capital letter. The parentheses after the member function name indicate that this is a function. An empty set of parentheses, as shown in line 12, indicates that this member function does not require additional data to perform its task. You'll see an example of a member function that does require additional data in Section 3.4. Line 12 is commonly referred to as the **function header**. Every function's body is delimited by left and right braces ({ and }), as in lines 13 and 15.

The body of a function contains statements that perform the function's task. In this case, member function displayMessage contains one statement (line 14) that displays the message "Welcome to the Grade Book!". After this statement executes, the function has completed its task.

Common Programming Error 3.2

Returning a value from a function whose return type has been declared void is a compilation error.

Common Programming Error 3.3

Defining a function inside another function (i.e., "nesting" functions) is a syntax error.

Testing Class *GradeBook*

Next, we'd like to use class GradeBook in a program. As you learned in Chapter 2, function main (lines 19–23) begins the execution of every program.

In this program, we'd like to call class GradeBook's displayMessage member function to display the welcome message. Typically, you cannot call a member function of a class until you create an object of that class. (As you'll learn in Section 10.6, static member functions are an exception.) Line 21 creates an object of class GradeBook called myGrade-Book. The variable's type is GradeBook—the class we defined in lines 8–16. When we declare variables of type int, as we did in Chapter 2, the compiler knows what int is—it's a fundamental type. In line 21, however, the compiler does not automatically know what type GradeBook is—it's a **user-defined type**. We tell the compiler what GradeBook is by including the class definition (lines 8–16). If we omitted these lines, the compiler would issue an error message (such as "'GradeBook': undeclared identifier" in Microsoft Visual C++ or "'GradeBook': undeclared" in GNU C++). Each class you create becomes a new type that can be used to create objects. You can define new class types as needed; this is one reason why C++ is known as an **extensible language**.

Line 22 calls the member function displayMessage (defined in lines 12–15) using variable myGradeBook followed by the **dot operator** (.), the function name display-Message and an empty set of parentheses. This call causes the displayMessage function to perform its task. At the beginning of line 22, "myGradeBook." indicates that main should use the GradeBook object that was created in line 21. The empty parentheses in line 12 indicate that member function displayMessage does not require additional data to perform its task, which is why we called this function with empty parentheses in line 22. (In Section 3.4, you'll see how to pass data to a function.) When displayMessage completes its task, the program reaches the end of main and terminates.

UML Class Diagram for Class *GradeBook*

Recall from Section 1.19 that the UML is a standardized graphical language used by software developers to represent their object-oriented systems. In the UML, each class is modeled in a **UML class diagram** as a rectangle with three compartments. Figure 3.2 presents a class diagram for class GradeBook (Fig. 3.1). The top compartment contains the class's name centered horizontally and in boldface type. The middle compartment contains the class's attributes, which correspond to data members in C++. This compartment is currently empty, because class GradeBook does not have any attributes. (Section 3.5 presents a version of class GradeBook with an attribute.) The bottom compartment contains the class's operations, which correspond to member functions in C++. The UML models operations by listing the operation name followed by a set of parentheses. Class GradeBook has only one member function, displayMessage, so the bottom compartment of Fig. 3.2 lists one operation with this name. Member function displayMessage does not require additional information to perform its tasks, so the parentheses following displayMessage in the class diagram are empty, just as they are in the member function's header in line 12 of Fig. 3.1. The plus sign (+) in front of the operation name indicates that display-Message is a public operation in the UML (i.e., a public member function in C++).

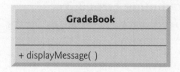

Fig. 3.2 | UML class diagram indicating that class GradeBook has a public displayMessage operation.

3.4 Defining a Member Function with a Parameter

In our car analogy from Section 3.2, we mentioned that pressing a car's gas pedal sends a message to the car to perform a task—make the car go faster. But how fast should the car accelerate? As you know, the farther down you press the pedal, the faster the car accelerates. So the message to the car includes both the task to perform and additional information that helps the car perform the task. This additional information is known as a **parameter**—the value of the parameter helps the car determine how fast to accelerate. Similarly, a member function can require one or more parameters that represent additional data it needs to perform its task. A function call supplies values—called **arguments**—for each of the function's parameters. For example, to make a deposit into a bank account, suppose a deposit member function of an Account class specifies a parameter that represents the deposit amount. When the deposit member function is called, an argument value representing the deposit amount is copied to the member function's parameter. The member function then adds that amount to the account balance.

Defining and Testing Class GradeBook

Our next example (Fig. 3.3) redefines class GradeBook (lines 9–18) with a display-Message member function (lines 13–17) that displays the course name as part of the welcome message. The new version of displayMessage requires a parameter (courseName in line 13) that represents the course name to output.

Before discussing the new features of class GradeBook, let's see how the new class is used in main (lines 21–34). Line 23 creates a variable of type **string** called nameOfCourse that will be used to store the course name entered by the user. A variable of type string represents a string of characters such as "CS101 Introduction to C++ Programming". A string is actually an object of the C++ Standard Library class string. This class is defined in **header file <string>**, and the name string, like cout, belongs to namespace std. To enable line 23 to compile, line 5 includes the <string> header file. The using declaration in line 6 allows us to simply write string in line 23 rather than std::string. For now, you can think of string variables like variables of other types such as int. You'll learn additional string capabilities in Section 3.9.

Line 24 creates an object of class GradeBook named myGradeBook. Line 27 prompts the user to enter a course name. Line 28 reads the name from the user and assigns it to the nameOfCourse variable, using the library function **getline** to perform the input. Before we explain this line of code, let's explain why we cannot simply write

```
cin >> nameOfCourse;
```

```cpp
1   // Fig. 3.3: fig03_03.cpp
2   // Define class GradeBook with a member function that takes a parameter;
3   // Create a GradeBook object and call its displayMessage function.
4   #include <iostream>
5   #include <string> // program uses C++ standard string class
6   using namespace std;
7
8   // GradeBook class definition
9   class GradeBook
10  {
11  public:
12     // function that displays a welcome message to the GradeBook user
13     void displayMessage( string courseName )
14     {
15        cout << "Welcome to the grade book for\n" << courseName << "!"
16           << endl;
17     } // end function displayMessage
18  }; // end class GradeBook
19
20  // function main begins program execution
21  int main()
22  {
23     string nameOfCourse; // string of characters to store the course name
24     GradeBook myGradeBook; // create a GradeBook object named myGradeBook
25
26     // prompt for and input course name
27     cout << "Please enter the course name:" << endl;
28     getline( cin, nameOfCourse ); // read a course name with blanks
29     cout << endl; // output a blank line
30
31     // call myGradeBook's displayMessage function
32     // and pass nameOfCourse as an argument
33     myGradeBook.displayMessage( nameOfCourse );
34  } // end main
```

```
Please enter the course name:
CS101 Introduction to C++ Programming

Welcome to the grade book for
CS101 Introduction to C++ Programming!
```

Fig. 3.3 | Define class GradeBook with a member function that takes a parameter, create a GradeBook object and call its displayMessage function.

to obtain the course name. In our sample program execution, we use the course name "CS101 Introduction to C++ Programming," which contains multiple words. (Recall that we highlight user-supplied input in bold.) When cin is used with the stream extraction operator, it reads characters until the first white-space character is reached. Thus, only "CS101" would be read by the preceding statement. The rest of the course name would have to be read by subsequent input operations.

In this example, we'd like the user to type the complete course name and press *Enter* to submit it to the program, and we'd like to store the entire course name in the string variable nameOfCourse. The function call getline(cin, nameOfCourse) in line 28 reads characters (including the space characters that separate the words in the input) from the standard input stream object cin (i.e., the keyboard) until the newline character is encountered, places the characters in the string variable nameOfCourse and discards the newline character. When you press *Enter* while typing program input, a newline is inserted in the input stream. Also, the <string> header file must be included in the program to use function getline and that the name getline belongs to namespace std.

Line 33 calls myGradeBook's displayMessage member function. The nameOfCourse variable in parentheses is the argument that is passed to member function displayMessage so that it can perform its task. The value of variable nameOfCourse in main becomes the value of member function displayMessage's parameter courseName in line 13. When you execute this program, member function displayMessage outputs as part of the welcome message the course name you type (in our sample execution, CS101 Introduction to C++ Programming).

More on Arguments and Parameters
To specify that a function requires data to perform its task, you place additional information in the function's **parameter list**, which is located in the parentheses following the function name. The parameter list may contain any number of parameters, including none at all (represented by empty parentheses as in Fig. 3.1, line 12) to indicate that a function does not require any parameters. Member function displayMessage's parameter list (Fig. 3.3, line 13) declares that the function requires one parameter. Each parameter must specify a type and an identifier. In this case, the type string and the identifier courseName indicate that member function displayMessage requires a string to perform its task. The member function body uses the parameter courseName to access the value that is passed to the function in the function call (line 33 in main). Lines 15–16 display parameter courseName's value as part of the welcome message. The parameter variable's name (line 13) can be the same as or different from the argument variable's name (line 33)—you'll learn why in Chapter 6, Functions and an Introduction to Recursion.

A function can specify multiple parameters by separating each parameter from the next with a comma (we'll see an example in Figs. 6.4–6.5). The number and order of arguments in a function call must match the number and order of parameters in the parameter list of the called member function's header. Also, the argument types in the function call must be consistent with the types of the corresponding parameters in the function header. (As you'll learn in subsequent chapters, an argument's type and its corresponding parameter's type need not always be identical, but they must be "consistent.") In our example, the one string argument in the function call (i.e., nameOfCourse) exactly matches the one string parameter in the member-function definition (i.e., courseName).

Common Programming Error 3.4
Placing a semicolon after the right parenthesis enclosing the parameter list of a function definition is a syntax error.

Common Programming Error 3.5
Defining a function parameter again as a variable in the function's body is a compilation error.

Good Programming Practice 3.1
To avoid ambiguity, do not use the same names for the arguments passed to a function and the corresponding parameters in the function definition.

Good Programming Practice 3.2
Choosing meaningful function names and meaningful parameter names makes programs more readable and helps avoid excessive use of comments.

Updated UML Class Diagram for Class GradeBook

The UML class diagram of Fig. 3.4 models class GradeBook of Fig. 3.3. Like the class GradeBook defined in Fig. 3.1, this GradeBook class contains public member function displayMessage. However, this version of displayMessage has a parameter. The UML models a parameter by listing the parameter name, followed by a colon and the parameter type in the parentheses following the operation name. The UML has its own data types similar to those of C++. The UML is language independent—it's used with many different programming languages—so its terminology does not exactly match that of C++. For example, the UML type String corresponds to the C++ type string. Member function displayMessage of class GradeBook (Fig. 3.3, lines 13–17) has a string parameter named courseName, so Fig. 3.4 lists courseName : String between the parentheses following the operation name displayMessage. This version of the GradeBook class still does not have any data members.

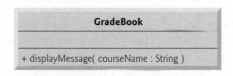

Fig. 3.4 | UML class diagram indicating that class GradeBook has a public displayMessage operation with a courseName parameter of UML type String.

3.5 Data Members, *set* Functions and *get* Functions

In Chapter 2, we declared all of a program's variables in its main function. Variables declared in a function definition's body are known as **local variables** and can be used only from the line of their declaration in the function to closing right brace (}) of the block in which they're declared. A local variable must be declared before it can be used in a function. A local variable cannot be accessed outside the function in which it's declared. When a function terminates, the values of its local variables are lost. (You'll see an exception to this in Chapter 6 when we discuss static local variables.) Recall from Section 3.2 that an object has attributes that are carried with it as it's used in a program. Such attributes exist throughout the life of the object.

A class normally consists of one or more member functions that manipulate the attributes that belong to a particular object of the class. Attributes are represented as variables in a class definition. Such variables are called **data members** and are declared inside a class definition but outside the bodies of the class's member-function definitions. Each object of a class maintains its own copy of its attributes in memory. The example in this section demonstrates a GradeBook class that contains a courseName data member to represent a particular GradeBook object's course name.

GradeBook *Class with a Data Member, a* set *Function and a* get *Function*

In our next example, class GradeBook (Fig. 3.5) maintains the course name as a data member so that it can be used or modified at any time during a program's execution. The class contains member functions setCourseName, getCourseName and displayMessage. Member function setCourseName stores a course name in a GradeBook data member. Member function getCourseName obtains the course name from that data member. Member function displayMessage—which now specifies no parameters—still displays a welcome message that includes the course name. However, as you'll see, the function now obtains the course name by calling another function in the same class—getCourseName.

Good Programming Practice 3.3

Place a blank line between member-function definitions to enhance program readability.

A typical instructor teaches multiple courses, each with its own course name. Line 34 declares that courseName is a variable of type string. Because the variable is declared in the class definition (lines 10–35) but outside the bodies of the class's member-function definitions (lines 14–17, 20–23 and 26–32), the variable is a data member. Every instance (i.e., object) of class GradeBook contains one copy of each of the class's data members—if there are two GradeBook objects, each has its own copy of courseName (one per object), as you'll see in the example of Fig. 3.7. A benefit of making courseName a data member is that all the member functions of the class (in this case, class GradeBook) can manipulate any data members that appear in the class definition (in this case, courseName).

```
1   // Fig. 3.5: fig03_05.cpp
2   // Define class GradeBook that contains a courseName data member
3   // and member functions to set and get its value;
4   // Create and manipulate a GradeBook object with these functions.
5   #include <iostream>
6   #include <string> // program uses C++ standard string class
7   using namespace std;
8
9   // GradeBook class definition
10  class GradeBook
11  {
12  public:
13     // function that sets the course name
14     void setCourseName( string name )
15     {
16        courseName = name; // store the course name in the object
17     } // end function setCourseName
18
```

Fig. 3.5 | Defining and testing class GradeBook with a data member and *set* and *get* functions. (Part 1 of 2.)

```
19      // function that gets the course name
20      string getCourseName()
21      {
22         return courseName; // return the object's courseName
23      } // end function getCourseName
24
25      // function that displays a welcome message
26      void displayMessage()
27      {
28         // this statement calls getCourseName to get the
29         // name of the course this GradeBook represents
30         cout << "Welcome to the grade book for\n" << getCourseName() << "!"
31            << endl;
32      } // end function displayMessage
33   private:
34      string courseName; // course name for this GradeBook
35   }; // end class GradeBook
36
37   // function main begins program execution
38   int main()
39   {
40      string nameOfCourse; // string of characters to store the course name
41      GradeBook myGradeBook; // create a GradeBook object named myGradeBook
42
43      // display initial value of courseName
44      cout << "Initial course name is: " << myGradeBook.getCourseName()
45         << endl;
46
47      // prompt for, input and set course name
48      cout << "\nPlease enter the course name:" << endl;
49      getline( cin, nameOfCourse ); // read a course name with blanks
50      myGradeBook.setCourseName( nameOfCourse ); // set the course name
51
52      cout << endl; // outputs a blank line
53      myGradeBook.displayMessage(); // display message with new course name
54   } // end main
```

```
Initial course name is:

Please enter the course name:
CS101 Introduction to C++ Programming

Welcome to the grade book for
CS101 Introduction to C++ Programming!
```

Fig. 3.5 | Defining and testing class GradeBook with a data member and *set* and *get* functions. (Part 2 of 2.)

Access Specifiers **public** *and* **private**

Most data-member declarations appear after the access-specifier label **private:** (line 33). Like public, keyword private is an access specifier. Variables or functions declared after access specifier private (and before the next access specifier) are accessible only to member functions of the class for which they're declared. Thus, data member courseName can be used only in member functions setCourseName, getCourseName and displayMessage of (every object of) class GradeBook. Data member courseName, because it's private, cannot be accessed by functions outside the class (such as main) or by member functions of other classes in the program. Attempting to access data member courseName in one of these program locations with an expression such as myGradeBook.courseName would result in a compilation error containing a message similar to

```
cannot access private member declared in class 'GradeBook'
```

Software Engineering Observation 3.1

Generally, data members should be declared private and member functions should be declared public. (We'll see that it's appropriate to declare certain member functions private, if they're to be accessed only by other member functions of the class.)

Common Programming Error 3.6

An attempt by a function, which is not a member of a particular class (or a friend of that class, as we'll see in Chapter 10, Classes: A Deeper Look, Part 2), to access a private member of that class is a compilation error.

The default access for class members is private so all members after the class header and before the first access specifier are private. The access specifiers public and private may be repeated, but this is unnecessary and can be confusing.

Good Programming Practice 3.4

Despite the fact that the public and private access specifiers may be repeated and intermixed, list all the public members of a class first in one group then list all the private members in another group. This focuses the programmer's attention on the class's public interface, rather than on the class's implementation.

Good Programming Practice 3.5

If you choose to list the private members first in a class definition, explicitly use the private access specifier despite the fact that private is assumed by default. This improves program clarity.

Declaring data members with access specifier private is known as **data hiding**. When a program creates (instantiates) a GradeBook object, data member courseName is encapsulated (hidden) in the object and can be accessed only by member functions of the object's class. In class GradeBook, member functions setCourseName and getCourseName manipulate the data member courseName directly (and displayMessage could do so if necessary).

Software Engineering Observation 3.2

You'll learn in Chapter 10 that functions and classes declared by a class to be "friends" can access the private members of the class.

Error-Prevention Tip 3.1

Making the data members of a class private and the member functions of the class public facilitates debugging because problems with data manipulations are localized to either the class's member functions or the friends of the class.

Member Functions *setCourseName and getCourseName*

Member function setCourseName (defined in lines 14–17) does not return any data when it completes its task, so its return type is void. The member function receives one parameter—name—which represents the course name that will be passed to it as an argument (as we'll see in line 50 of main). Line 16 assigns name to data member courseName. In this example, setCourseName does not attempt to validate the course name—i.e., the function does not check that the course name adheres to any particular format or follows any other rules regarding what a "valid" course name looks like. Suppose, for instance, that a university can print student transcripts containing course names of only 25 characters or fewer. In this case, we might want class GradeBook to ensure that its data member courseName never contains more than 25 characters. We discuss basic validation techniques in Section 3.9.

Member function getCourseName (defined in lines 20–23) returns a particular GradeBook object's courseName. The member function has an empty parameter list, so it does not require additional data to perform its task. The function specifies that it returns a string. When a function that specifies a return type other than void is called and completes its task, the function uses a **return statement** (as in line 22) to return a result to its calling function. For example, when you go to an automated teller machine (ATM) and request your account balance, you expect the ATM to give you back a value that represents your balance. Similarly, when a statement calls member function getCourseName on a GradeBook object, the statement expects to receive the GradeBook's course name (in this case, a string, as specified by the function's return type). If you have a function square that returns the square of its argument, the statement

```
result = square( 2 );
```

returns 4 from function square and assigns to variable result the value 4. If you have a function maximum that returns the largest of three integer arguments, the statement

```
biggest = maximum( 27, 114, 51 );
```

returns 114 from function maximum and assigns to variable biggest the value 114.

Common Programming Error 3.7
Forgetting to return a value from a function that is supposed to return a value is a compilation error.

The statements in lines 16 and 22 each use variable courseName (line 34) even though it was not declared in any of the member functions. We can use courseName in the member functions of class GradeBook because courseName is a data member of the class. So member function getCourseName could be defined before member function setCourseName.

Member Function *displayMessage*

Member function displayMessage (lines 26–32) does not return any data when it completes its task, so its return type is void. The function does not receive parameters, so its parameter list is empty. Lines 30–31 output a welcome message that includes the value of data member courseName. Line 30 calls member function getCourseName to obtain the value of courseName. Member function displayMessage could also access data member courseName directly, just as member functions setCourseName and getCourseName do.

We explain shortly why we choose to call member function getCourseName to obtain the value of courseName.

Testing Class GradeBook

The main function (lines 38–54) creates one object of class GradeBook and uses each of its member functions. Line 41 creates a GradeBook object named myGradeBook. Lines 44–45 display the initial course name by calling the object's getCourseName member function. The first line of the output does not show a course name, because the object's courseName data member (i.e., a string) is initially empty—by default, the initial value of a string is the so-called **empty string**, i.e., a string that does not contain any characters. Nothing appears on the screen when an empty string is displayed.

Line 48 prompts the user to enter a course name. Local string variable nameOfCourse (declared in line 40) is set to the course name entered by the user, which is obtained by the call to the getline function (line 49). Line 50 calls object myGradeBook's setCourseName member function and supplies nameOfCourse as the function's argument. When the function is called, the argument's value is copied to parameter name (line 14) of member function setCourseName. Then the parameter's value is assigned to data member courseName (line 16). Line 52 skips a line; then line 53 calls object myGradeBook's displayMessage member function to display the welcome message containing the course name.

Software Engineering with Set *and* Get *Functions*

A class's private data members can be manipulated only by member functions of that class (and by "friends" of the class, as we'll see in Chapter 10). So a **client of an object**—that is, any class or function that calls the object's member functions from outside the object—calls the class's public member functions to request the class's services for particular objects of the class. This is why the statements in function main call member functions setCourseName, getCourseName and displayMessage on a GradeBook object. Classes often provide public member functions to allow clients of the class to *set* (i.e., assign values to) or *get* (i.e., obtain the values of) private data members. These member function names need not begin with set or get, but this naming convention is common. In this example, the member function that *sets* the courseName data member is called setCourseName, and the member function that *gets* the value of the courseName data member is called getCourseName. *Set* functions are also sometimes called **mutators** (because they mutate, or change, values), and *get* functions are also sometimes called **accessors** (because they access values).

Recall that declaring data members with access specifier private enforces data hiding. Providing public *set* and *get* functions allows clients of a class to access the hidden data, but only *indirectly*. The client knows that it's attempting to modify or obtain an object's data, but the client does not know how the object performs these operations. In some cases, a class may internally represent a piece of data one way, but expose that data to clients in a different way. For example, suppose a Clock class represents the time of day as a private int data member time that stores the number of seconds since midnight. However, when a client calls a Clock object's getTime member function, the object could return the time with hours, minutes and seconds in a string in the format "HH:MM:SS". Similarly, suppose the Clock class provides a *set* function named setTime that takes a string parameter in the "HH:MM:SS" format. Using string capabilities presented in Chapter 18, the setTime function could convert this string to a number of seconds, which the function stores in its `private` data member. The *set* function could also check that the value it receives represents a valid time (e.g., `"12:30:45"` is valid but `"42:85:70"` is not). The *set* and *get* functions allow a client to interact with an object, but the object's `private` data remains safely encapsulated (i.e., hidden) in the object itself.

The *set* and *get* functions of a class also should be used by other member functions within the class to manipulate the class's `private` data, although these member functions *can* access the `private` data directly. In Fig. 3.5, member functions `setCourseName` and `getCourseName` are `public` member functions, so they're accessible to clients of the class, as well as to the class itself. Member function `displayMessage` calls member function `getCourseName` to obtain the value of data member `courseName` for display purposes, even though `displayMessage` can access `courseName` directly—accessing a data member via its *get* function creates a better, more robust class (i.e., a class that is easier to maintain and less likely to stop working). If we decide to change the data member `courseName` in some way, the `displayMessage` definition will not require modification—only the bodies of the *get* and *set* functions that directly manipulate the data member will need to change. For example, suppose we want to represent the course name as two separate data members— `courseNumber` (e.g., `"CS101"`) and `courseTitle` (e.g., `"Introduction to C++ Programming"`). Member function `displayMessage` can still issue a single call to member function `getCourseName` to obtain the full course name to display as part of the welcome message. In this case, `getCourseName` would need to build and return a `string` containing the `courseNumber` followed by the `courseTitle`. Member function `displayMessage` would continue to display the complete course title "CS101 Introduction to C++ Programming," because it's unaffected by the change to the class's data members. The benefits of calling a *set* function from another member function of a class will become clear when we discuss validation in Section 3.9.

Good Programming Practice 3.6
Always try to localize the effects of changes to a class's data members by accessing and manipulating the data members through their get and set functions. Changes to the name of a data member or the data type used to store a data member then affect only the corresponding get and set functions, but not the callers of those functions.

Software Engineering Observation 3.3
Write programs that are understandable and easy to maintain. Change is the rule rather than the exception. You should anticipate that your code will be modified.

Software Engineering Observation 3.4
Provide set or get functions for each `private` data item only when appropriate. Services useful to the client should typically be provided in the class's `public` interface.

GradeBook's UML Class Diagram with a Data Member and set and get Functions
Figure 3.6 contains an updated UML class diagram for the version of class `GradeBook` in Fig. 3.5. This diagram models `GradeBook`'s data member `courseName` as an attribute in the middle compartment. The UML represents data members as attributes by listing the attribute name, followed by a colon and the attribute type. The UML type of attribute `courseName` is `String`, which corresponds to `string` in C++. Data member `courseName` is `private` in C++, so the class diagram lists a minus sign (–) in front of the corresponding

attribute's name. The minus sign in the UML is equivalent to the `private` access specifier in C++. Class `GradeBook` contains three `public` member functions, so the class diagram lists three operations in the third compartment. Operation `setCourseName` has a `String` parameter called `name`. The UML indicates the return type of an operation by placing a colon and the return type after the parentheses following the operation name. Member function `getCourseName` of class `GradeBook` has a `string` return type in C++, so the class diagram shows a `String` return type in the UML. Operations `setCourseName` and `displayMessage` do not return values (i.e., they return `void`), so the UML class diagram does not specify a return type after the parentheses of these operations.

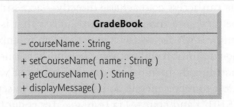

Fig. 3.6 | UML class diagram for class `GradeBook` with a private `courseName` attribute and public operations `setCourseName`, `getCourseName` and `displayMessage`.

3.6 Initializing Objects with Constructors

As mentioned in Section 3.5, when an object of class `GradeBook` (Fig. 3.5) is created, its data member `courseName` is initialized to the empty string by default. What if you want to provide a course name when you create a `GradeBook` object? Each class you declare can provide a **constructor** that can be used to initialize an object of the class when the object is created. A constructor is a special member function that must be defined with the same name as the class, so that the compiler can distinguish it from the class's other member functions. An important difference between constructors and other functions is that constructors cannot return values, so they cannot specify a return type (not even `void`). Normally, constructors are declared `public`.

C++ requires a constructor call for each object that is created, which helps ensure that each object is initialized before it's used in a program. The constructor call occurs implicitly when the object is created. If a class does not explicitly include a constructor, the compiler provides a **default constructor**—that is, a constructor with no parameters. For example, when line 41 of Fig. 3.5 creates a `GradeBook` object, the default constructor is called. The default constructor provided by the compiler creates a `GradeBook` object without giving any initial values to the object's fundamental type data members. [*Note:* For data members that are objects of other classes, the default constructor implicitly calls each data member's default constructor to ensure that the data member is initialized properly. This is why the `string` data member `courseName` (in Fig. 3.5) was initialized to the empty string—the default constructor for class `string` sets the `string`'s value to the empty string. You'll learn more about initializing data members that are objects of other classes in Section 10.3.]

In the example of Fig. 3.7, we specify a course name for a `GradeBook` object when the object is created (e.g., line 46). In this case, the argument `"CS101 Introduction to C++`

Programming" is passed to the GradeBook object's constructor (lines 14–17) and used to initialize the courseName. Figure 3.7 defines a modified GradeBook class containing a constructor with a string parameter that receives the initial course name.

```cpp
1   // Fig. 3.7: fig03_07.cpp
2   // Instantiating multiple objects of the GradeBook class and using
3   // the GradeBook constructor to specify the course name
4   // when each GradeBook object is created.
5   #include <iostream>
6   #include <string> // program uses C++ standard string class
7   using namespace std;
8
9   // GradeBook class definition
10  class GradeBook
11  {
12  public:
13     // constructor initializes courseName with string supplied as argument
14     GradeBook( string name )
15     {
16        setCourseName( name ); // call set function to initialize courseName
17     } // end GradeBook constructor
18
19     // function to set the course name
20     void setCourseName( string name )
21     {
22        courseName = name; // store the course name in the object
23     } // end function setCourseName
24
25     // function to get the course name
26     string getCourseName()
27     {
28        return courseName; // return object's courseName
29     } // end function getCourseName
30
31     // display a welcome message to the GradeBook user
32     void displayMessage()
33     {
34        // call getCourseName to get the courseName
35        cout << "Welcome to the grade book for\n" << getCourseName()
36           << "!" << endl;
37     } // end function displayMessage
38  private:
39     string courseName; // course name for this GradeBook
40  }; // end class GradeBook
41
42  // function main begins program execution
43  int main()
44  {
45     // create two GradeBook objects
46     GradeBook gradeBook1( "CS101 Introduction to C++ Programming" );
47     GradeBook gradeBook2( "CS102 Data Structures in C++" );
```

Fig. 3.7 | Instantiating multiple objects of the GradeBook class and using the GradeBook constructor to specify the course name when each GradeBook object is created. (Part 1 of 2.)

```
48
49        // display initial value of courseName for each GradeBook
50        cout << "gradeBook1 created for course: " << gradeBook1.getCourseName()
51           << "\ngradeBook2 created for course: " << gradeBook2.getCourseName()
52           << endl;
53     } // end main
```

```
gradeBook1 created for course: CS101 Introduction to C++ Programming
gradeBook2 created for course: CS102 Data Structures in C++
```

Fig. 3.7 | Instantiating multiple objects of the GradeBook class and using the GradeBook constructor to specify the course name when each GradeBook object is created. (Part 2 of 2.)

Defining a Constructor

Lines 14–17 of Fig. 3.7 define a constructor for class GradeBook. Notice that the constructor has the same name as its class, GradeBook. A constructor specifies in its parameter list the data it requires to perform its task. When you create a new object, you place this data in the parentheses that follow the object name (as we did in lines 46–47). Line 14 indicates that class GradeBook's constructor has a string parameter called name. Line 14 does not specify a return type, because constructors cannot return values (or even void).

Line 16 in the constructor's body passes the constructor's parameter name to member function setCourseName (lines 20–23), which simply assigns the value of its parameter to data member courseName. You might be wondering why we bother making the call to setCourseName in line 16—the constructor certainly could perform the assignment courseName = name. In Section 3.9, we modify setCourseName to perform validation (ensuring that, in this case, the courseName is 25 or fewer characters in length). At that point the benefits of calling setCourseName from the constructor will become clear. Both the constructor (line 14) and the setCourseName function (line 20) use a parameter called name. You can use the same parameter names in different functions because the parameters are local to each function; they do not interfere with one another.

Testing Class GradeBook

Lines 43–53 of Fig. 3.7 define the main function that tests class GradeBook and demonstrates initializing GradeBook objects using a constructor. Line 46 creates and initializes a GradeBook object called gradeBook1. When this line executes, the GradeBook constructor (lines 14–17) is called (implicitly by C++) with the argument "CS101 Introduction to C++ Programming" to initialize gradeBook1's course name. Line 47 repeats this process for the GradeBook object called gradeBook2, this time passing the argument "CS102 Data Structures in C++" to initialize gradeBook2's course name. Lines 50–51 use each object's getCourseName member function to obtain the course names and show that they were indeed initialized when the objects were created. The output confirms that each GradeBook object maintains its own copy of data member courseName.

Two Ways to Provide a Default Constructor for a Class

Any constructor that takes no arguments is called a default constructor. A class gets a default constructor in one of two ways:

1. The compiler implicitly creates a default constructor in a class that does not define a constructor. Such a constructor does not initialize the class's data members, but does call the default constructor for each data member that is an object of another class. An uninitialized variable typically contains a "garbage" value.

2. You explicitly define a constructor that takes no arguments. Such a default constructor will call the default constructor for each data member that is an object of another class and will perform additional initialization specified by you.

If you define a constructor *with* arguments, C++ will not implicitly create a default constructor for that class. For each version of class GradeBook in Fig. 3.1, Fig. 3.3 and Fig. 3.5 the compiler implicitly defined a default constructor.

Error-Prevention Tip 3.2

Unless no initialization of your class's data members is necessary (almost never), provide a constructor to ensure that your class's data members are initialized with meaningful values when each new object of your class is created.

Software Engineering Observation 3.5

Data members can be initialized in a constructor, or their values may be set later after the object is created. However, it's a good software engineering practice to ensure that an object is fully initialized before the client code invokes the object's member functions. You should not rely on the client code to ensure that an object gets initialized properly.

Adding the Constructor to Class *GradeBook's* UML Class Diagram

The UML class diagram of Fig. 3.8 models class GradeBook of Fig. 3.7, which has a constructor with a name parameter of type string (represented by type String in the UML). Like operations, the UML models constructors in the third compartment of a class in a class diagram. To distinguish a constructor from a class's operations, the UML places the word "constructor" between guillemets (« and ») before the constructor's name. It's customary to list the class's constructor before other operations in the third compartment.

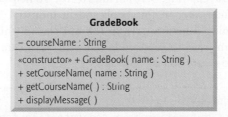

Fig. 3.8 | UML class diagram indicating that class GradeBook has a constructor with a name parameter of UML type String.

3.7 Placing a Class in a Separate File for Reusability

One of the benefits of creating class definitions is that, when packaged properly, our classes can be reused by programmers—potentially worldwide. For example, we can reuse C++

Standard Library type string in any C++ program by including the header file <string> (and, as we'll see, by being able to link to the library's object code).

Programmers who wish to use our GradeBook class cannot simply include the file from Fig. 3.7 in another program. As you learned in Chapter 2, function main begins the execution of every program, and every program must have exactly one main function. If other programmers include the code from Fig. 3.7, they get extra baggage—our main function—and their programs will then have two main functions. Attempting to compile a program with two main functions in Microsoft Visual C++ produces an error such as

```
error C2084: function 'int main(void)' already has a body
```

when the compiler tries to compile the second main function it encounters. Similarly, the GNU C++ compiler produces the error

```
redefinition of 'int main()'
```

These errors indicate that a program already has a main function. So, placing main in the same file with a class definition prevents that class from being reused by other programs. In this section, we demonstrate how to make class GradeBook reusable by separating it into another file from the main function.

Header Files
Each of the previous examples in the chapter consists of a single .cpp file, also known as a **source-code file**, that contains a GradeBook class definition and a main function. When building an object-oriented C++ program, it's customary to define reusable source code (such as a class) in a file that by convention has a .h filename extension—known as a **header file**. Programs use #include preprocessor directives to include header files and take advantage of reusable software components, such as type string provided in the C++ Standard Library and user-defined types like class GradeBook.

Our next example separates the code from Fig. 3.7 into two files—GradeBook.h (Fig. 3.9) and fig03_10.cpp (Fig. 3.10). As you look at the header file in Fig. 3.9, notice that it contains only the GradeBook class definition (lines 8–38), the appropriate header files and a using declaration. The main function that uses class GradeBook is defined in the source-code file fig03_10.cpp (Fig. 3.10) in lines 8–18. To help you prepare for the larger programs you'll encounter later in this book and in industry, we often use a separate source-code file containing function main to test our classes (this is called a **driver program**). You'll soon learn how a source-code file with main can use the class definition found in a header file to create objects of a class.

```
1   // Fig. 3.9: GradeBook.h
2   // GradeBook class definition in a separate file from main.
3   #include <iostream>
4   #include <string> // class GradeBook uses C++ standard string class
5   using namespace std;
6
7   // GradeBook class definition
8   class GradeBook
9   {
```

Fig. 3.9 | GradeBook class definition in a separate file from main. (Part 1 of 2.)

```
10   public:
11      // constructor initializes courseName with string supplied as argument
12      GradeBook( string name )
13      {
14         setCourseName( name ); // call set function to initialize courseName
15      } // end GradeBook constructor
16
17      // function to set the course name
18      void setCourseName( string name )
19      {
20         courseName = name; // store the course name in the object
21      } // end function setCourseName
22
23      // function to get the course name
24      string getCourseName()
25      {
26         return courseName; // return object's courseName
27      } // end function getCourseName
28
29      // display a welcome message to the GradeBook user
30      void displayMessage()
31      {
32         // call getCourseName to get the courseName
33         cout << "Welcome to the grade book for\n" << getCourseName()
34            << "!" << endl;
35      } // end function displayMessage
36   private:
37      string courseName; // course name for this GradeBook
38   }; // end class GradeBook
```

Fig. 3.9 | GradeBook class definition in a separate file from `main`. (Part 2 of 2.)

```
1    // Fig. 3.10: fig03_10.cpp
2    // Including class GradeBook from file GradeBook.h for use in main.
3    #include <iostream>
4    #include "GradeBook.h" // include definition of class GradeBook
5    using namespace std;
6
7    // function main begins program execution
8    int main()
9    {
10      // create two GradeBook objects
11      GradeBook gradeBook1( "CS101 Introduction to C++ Programming" );
12      GradeBook gradeBook2( "CS102 Data Structures in C++" );
13
14      // display initial value of courseName for each GradeBook
15      cout << "gradeBook1 created for course: " << gradeBook1.getCourseName()
16         << "\ngradeBook2 created for course: " << gradeBook2.getCourseName()
17         << endl;
18   } // end main
```

Fig. 3.10 | Including class GradeBook from file GradeBook.h for use in `main`. (Part 1 of 2.)

```
gradeBook1 created for course: CS101 Introduction to C++ Programming
gradeBook2 created for course: CS102 Data Structures in C++
```

Fig. 3.10 | Including class `GradeBook` from file `GradeBook.h` for use in `main`. (Part 2 of 2.)

Including a Header File That Contains a User-Defined Class
A header file such as `GradeBook.h` (Fig. 3.9) cannot be used to begin program execution, because it does not contain a `main` function. If you try to compile and link `GradeBook.h` by itself to create an executable application, Microsoft Visual C++ 2008 produces the linker error message:

```
error LNK2001: unresolved external symbol _mainCRTStartup
```

To compile and link with GNU C++ on Linux, you must first include the header file in a `.cpp` source-code file, then GNU C++ produces a linker error message containing:

```
undefined reference to 'main'
```

This error indicates that the linker could not locate the program's `main` function. To test class `GradeBook` (defined in Fig. 3.9), you must write a separate source-code file containing a `main` function (such as Fig. 3.10) that instantiates and uses objects of the class.

The compiler does not know what a `GradeBook` is because it's a user-defined type. In fact, the compiler doesn't even know the classes in the C++ Standard Library. To help it understand how to use a class, we must explicitly provide the compiler with the class's definition—that's why, for example, to use type `string`, a program must include the `<string>` header file. This enables the compiler to determine the amount of memory that it must reserve for each object of the class and ensure that a program calls the class's member functions correctly.

To create `GradeBook` objects `gradeBook1` and `gradeBook2` in lines 11–12 of Fig. 3.10, the compiler must know the size of a `GradeBook` object. While objects conceptually contain data members and member functions, C++ objects contain only data. The compiler creates only *one* copy of the class's member functions and *shares* that copy among all the class's objects. Each object, of course, needs its own copy of the class's data members, because their contents can vary among objects (such as two different `BankAccount` objects having two different `balance` data members). The member-function code, however, is not modifiable, so it can be shared among all objects of the class. Therefore, the size of an object depends on the amount of memory required to store the class's data members. By including `GradeBook.h` in line 4, we give the compiler access to the information it needs (Fig. 3.9, line 37) to determine the size of a `GradeBook` object and to determine whether objects of the class are used correctly (in lines 11–12 and 15–16 of Fig. 3.10).

Line 4 instructs the C++ preprocessor to replace the directive with a copy of the contents of `GradeBook.h` (i.e., the `GradeBook` class definition) *before* the program is compiled. When the source-code file `fig03_10.cpp` is compiled, it now contains the `GradeBook` class definition (because of the `#include`), and the compiler is able to determine how to create `GradeBook` objects and see that their member functions are called correctly. Now that the class definition is in a header file (without a `main` function), we can include that header in *any* program that needs to reuse our `GradeBook` class.

How Header Files Are Located

Notice that the name of the GradeBook.h header file in line 4 of Fig. 3.10 is enclosed in quotes (" ") rather than angle brackets (< >). Normally, a program's source-code files and user-defined header files are placed in the same directory. When the preprocessor encounters a header file name in quotes, it attempts to locate the header file in the same directory as the file in which the #include directive appears. If the preprocessor cannot find the header file in that directory, it searches for it in the same location(s) as the C++ Standard Library header files. When the preprocessor encounters a header file name in angle brackets (e.g., <iostream>), it assumes that the header is part of the C++ Standard Library and does not look in the directory of the program that is being preprocessed.

Error-Prevention Tip 3.3

To ensure that the preprocessor can locate header files correctly, #include preprocessor directives should place the names of user-defined header files in quotes (e.g., "Grade-Book.h") and place the names of C++ Standard Library header files in angle brackets (e.g., <iostream>).

Additional Software Engineering Issues

Now that class GradeBook is defined in a header file, the class is reusable. Unfortunately, placing a class definition in a header file as in Fig. 3.9 still reveals the entire implementation of the class to the class's clients—GradeBook.h is simply a text file that anyone can open and read. Conventional software engineering wisdom says that to use an object of a class, the client code needs to know only what member functions to call, what arguments to provide to each member function and what return type to expect from each member function. The client code does not need to know how those functions are implemented.

If client code *does* know how a class is implemented, the client-code programmer might write client code based on the class's implementation details. Ideally, if that implementation changes, the class's clients should not have to change. Hiding the class's implementation details makes it easier to change the class's implementation while minimizing, and hopefully eliminating, changes to client code.

In Section 3.8, we show how to break up the GradeBook class into two files so that

1. the class is reusable,

2. the clients of the class know what member functions the class provides, how to call them and what return types to expect, and

3. the clients do *not* know how the class's member functions are implemented.

3.8 Separating Interface from Implementation

In the preceding section, we showed how to promote software reusability by separating a class definition from the client code (e.g., function main) that uses the class. We now introduce another fundamental principle of good software engineering—**separating interface from implementation**.

Interface of a Class

Interfaces define and standardize the ways in which things such as people and systems interact with one another. For example, a radio's controls serve as an interface between the radio's users and its internal components. The controls allow users to perform a limited set of operations (such as changing the station, adjusting the volume, and choosing between AM and FM stations). Various radios may implement these operations differently—some provide push buttons, some provide dials and some support voice commands. The interface specifies *what* operations a radio permits users to perform but does not specify *how* the operations are implemented inside the radio.

Similarly, the **interface of a class** describes *what* services a class's clients can use and how to *request* those services, but not *how* the class carries out the services. A class's public interface consists of the class's public member functions (also known as the class's **public services**). For example, class GradeBook's interface (Fig. 3.9) contains a constructor and member functions setCourseName, getCourseName and displayMessage. GradeBook's clients (e.g., main in Fig. 3.10) use these functions to request the class's services. As you'll soon see, you can specify a class's interface by writing a class definition that lists only the member-function names, return types and parameter types.

Separating the Interface from the Implementation
In our prior examples, each class definition contained the complete definitions of the class's public member functions and the declarations of its private data members. However, it's better software engineering to define member functions *outside* the class definition, so that their implementation details can be hidden from the client code. This practice *ensures* that you do not write client code that depends on the class's implementation details. If you were to do so, the client code would be more likely to "break" if the class's implementation changed.

The program of Figs. 3.11–3.13 separates class GradeBook's interface from its implementation by splitting the class definition of Fig. 3.9 into two files—the header file GradeBook.h (Fig. 3.11) in which class GradeBook is defined, and the source-code file GradeBook.cpp (Fig. 3.12) in which GradeBook's member functions are defined. By convention, member-function definitions are placed in a source-code file of the same base name (e.g., GradeBook) as the class's header file but with a .cpp filename extension. The source-code file fig03_13.cpp (Fig. 3.13) defines function main (the client code). The code and output of Fig. 3.13 are identical to that of Fig. 3.10. Figure 3.14 shows how this three-file program is compiled from the perspectives of the GradeBook class programmer and the client-code programmer—we'll explain this figure in detail.

GradeBook.h: Defining a Class's Interface with Function Prototypes
Header file GradeBook.h (Fig. 3.11) contains another version of GradeBook's class definition (lines 9–18). This version is similar to the one in Fig. 3.9, but the function definitions in Fig. 3.9 are replaced here with **function prototypes** (lines 12–15) that describe the class's public interface without revealing the class's member-function implementations. A function prototype is a declaration of a function that tells the compiler the function's name, its return type and the types of its parameters. Also, the header file still specifies the class's private data member (line 17) as well. Again, the compiler must know the data members of the class to determine how much memory to reserve for each object of the class. Including the header file GradeBook.h in the client code (line 5 of Fig. 3.13) provides the compiler with the information it needs to ensure that the client code calls the member functions of class GradeBook correctly.

```
 1   // Fig. 3.11: GradeBook.h
 2   // GradeBook class definition. This file presents GradeBook's public
 3   // interface without revealing the implementations of GradeBook's member
 4   // functions, which are defined in GradeBook.cpp.
 5   #include <string> // class GradeBook uses C++ standard string class
 6   using namespace std;
 7
 8   // GradeBook class definition
 9   class GradeBook
10   {
11   public:
12      GradeBook( string ); // constructor that initializes courseName
13      void setCourseName( string ); // function that sets the course name
14      string getCourseName(); // function that gets the course name
15      void displayMessage(); // function that displays a welcome message
16   private:
17      string courseName; // course name for this GradeBook
18   }; // end class GradeBook
```

Fig. 3.11 | GradeBook class definition containing function prototypes that specify the interface of the class.

The function prototype in line 12 (Fig. 3.11) indicates that the constructor requires one string parameter. Recall that constructors do not have return types, so no return type appears in the function prototype. Member function setCourseName's function prototype indicates that setCourseName requires a string parameter and does not return a value (i.e., its return type is void). Member function getCourseName's function prototype indicates that the function does not require parameters and returns a string. Finally, member function displayMessage's function prototype (line 15) specifies that displayMessage does not require parameters and does not return a value. These function prototypes are the same as the corresponding function headers in Fig. 3.9, except that the parameter names (which are optional in prototypes) are not included and each function prototype must end with a semicolon.

Common Programming Error 3.8

Forgetting the semicolon at the end of a function prototype is a syntax error.

Good Programming Practice 3.7

Although parameter names in function prototypes are optional (they're ignored by the compiler), many programmers use these names for documentation purposes.

Error-Prevention Tip 3.4

Parameter names in a function prototype (which, again, are ignored by the compiler) can be misleading if the names used do not match those used in the function definition. For this reason, many programmers create function prototypes by copying the first line of the corresponding function definitions (when the source code for the functions is available), then appending a semicolon to the end of each prototype.

GradeBook.cpp: *Defining Member Functions in a Separate Source-Code File*
Source-code file `GradeBook.cpp` (Fig. 3.12) *defines* class `GradeBook`'s member functions, which were *declared* in lines 12–15 of Fig. 3.11. The definitions appear in lines 9–32 and are nearly identical to the member-function definitions in lines 12–35 of Fig. 3.9.

```cpp
1   // Fig. 3.12: GradeBook.cpp
2   // GradeBook member-function definitions. This file contains
3   // implementations of the member functions prototyped in GradeBook.h.
4   #include <iostream>
5   #include "GradeBook.h" // include definition of class GradeBook
6   using namespace std;
7
8   // constructor initializes courseName with string supplied as argument
9   GradeBook::GradeBook( string name )
10  {
11     setCourseName( name ); // call set function to initialize courseName
12  } // end GradeBook constructor
13
14  // function to set the course name
15  void GradeBook::setCourseName( string name )
16  {
17     courseName = name; // store the course name in the object
18  } // end function setCourseName
19
20  // function to get the course name
21  string GradeBook::getCourseName()
22  {
23     return courseName; // return object's courseName
24  } // end function getCourseName
25
26  // display a welcome message to the GradeBook user
27  void GradeBook::displayMessage()
28  {
29     // call getCourseName to get the courseName
30     cout << "Welcome to the grade book for\n" << getCourseName()
31        << "!" << endl;
32  } // end function displayMessage
```

Fig. 3.12 | `GradeBook` member-function definitions represent the implementation of class `GradeBook`.

Notice that each member-function name in the function headers (lines 9, 15, 21 and 27) is preceded by the class name and `::`, which is known as the **binary scope resolution operator**. This "ties" each member function to the (now separate) `GradeBook` class definition (Fig. 3.11), which declares the class's member functions and data members. Without "`GradeBook::`" preceding each function name, these functions would not be recognized by the compiler as member functions of class `GradeBook`—the compiler would consider them "free" or "loose" functions, like `main`. These are also called global functions. Such functions cannot access `GradeBook`'s `private` data or call the class's member functions, without specifying an object. So, the compiler would not be able to compile these functions. For example, lines 17 and 23 that access variable `courseName` would cause compilation errors because courseName is not declared as a local variable in each function—the compiler would not know that courseName is already declared as a data member of class GradeBook.

Common Programming Error 3.9
When defining a class's member functions outside that class, omitting the class name and binary scope resolution operator (::) preceding the function names causes compilation errors.

To indicate that the member functions in GradeBook.cpp are part of class GradeBook, we must first include the GradeBook.h header file (line 5 of Fig. 3.12). This allows us to access the class name GradeBook in the GradeBook.cpp file. When compiling Grade-Book.cpp, the compiler uses the information in GradeBook.h to ensure that

1. the first line of each member function (lines 9, 15, 21 and 27) matches its prototype in the GradeBook.h file—for example, the compiler ensures that getCourse-Name accepts no parameters and returns a string, and that

2. each member function knows about the class's data members and other member functions—for example, lines 17 and 23 can access variable courseName because it's declared in GradeBook.h as a data member of class GradeBook, and lines 11 and 30 can call functions setCourseName and getCourseName, respectively, because each is declared as a member function of the class in GradeBook.h (and because these calls conform with the corresponding prototypes).

*Testing Class **GradeBook***
Figure 3.13 performs the same GradeBook object manipulations as Fig. 3.10. Separating GradeBook's interface from the implementation of its member functions does not affect the way that this client code uses the class. It affects only how the program is compiled and linked, which we discuss in detail shortly.

```cpp
 1   // Fig. 3.13: fig03_13.cpp
 2   // GradeBook class demonstration after separating
 3   // its interface from its implementation.
 4   #include <iostream>
 5   #include "GradeBook.h" // include definition of class GradeBook
 6   using namespace std;
 7
 8   // function main begins program execution
 9   int main()
10   {
11      // create two GradeBook objects
12      GradeBook gradeBook1( "CS101 Introduction to C++ Programming" );
13      GradeBook gradeBook2( "CS102 Data Structures in C++" );
14
15      // display initial value of courseName for each GradeBook
16      cout << "gradeBook1 created for course: " << gradeBook1.getCourseName()
17         << "\ngradeBook2 created for course: " << gradeBook2.getCourseName()
18         << endl;
19   } // end main
```

Fig. 3.13 | GradeBook class demonstration after separating its interface from its implementation. (Part 1 of 2.)

```
gradeBook1 created for course: CS101 Introduction to C++ Programming
gradeBook2 created for course: CS102 Data Structures in C++
```

Fig. 3.13 | GradeBook class demonstration after separating its interface from its implementation. (Part 2 of 2.)

As in Fig. 3.10, line 5 of Fig. 3.13 includes the GradeBook.h header file so that the compiler can ensure that GradeBook objects are created and manipulated correctly in the client code. Before executing this program, the source-code files in Fig. 3.12 and Fig. 3.13 must both be compiled, then linked together—that is, the member-function calls in the client code need to be tied to the implementations of the class's member functions—a job performed by the linker.

The Compilation and Linking Process
The diagram in Fig. 3.14 shows the compilation and linking process that results in an executable GradeBook application that can be used by instructors. Often a class's interface and implementation will be created and compiled by one programmer and used by a separate programmer who implements the client code that uses the class. So, the diagram shows what is required by both the class-implementation programmer and the client-code programmer. The dashed lines in the diagram show the pieces required by the class-implementation programmer, the client-code programmer and the GradeBook application user, respectively. [*Note:* Figure 3.14 is *not* a UML diagram.]

A class-implementation programmer responsible for creating a reusable GradeBook class creates the header file GradeBook.h and the source-code file GradeBook.cpp that #includes the header file, then compiles the source-code file to create GradeBook's object code. To hide the class's member-function implementation details, the class-implementation programmer would provide the client-code programmer with the header file Grade-Book.h (which specifies the class's interface and data members) and the GradeBook object code (i.e., the machine-language instructions that represent GradeBook's member functions). The client-code programmer is not given GradeBook.cpp, so the client remains unaware of how GradeBook's member functions are implemented.

The client code needs to know only GradeBook's interface to use the class and must be able to link its object code. Since the interface of the class is part of the class definition in the GradeBook.h header file, the client-code programmer must have access to this file and must #include it in the client's source-code file. When the client code is compiled, the compiler uses the class definition in GradeBook.h to ensure that the main function creates and manipulates objects of class GradeBook correctly.

To create the executable GradeBook application, the last step is to link

1. the object code for the main function (i.e., the client code),
2. the object code for class GradeBook's member-function implementations and
3. the C++ Standard Library object code for the C++ classes (e.g., string) used by the class-implementation programmer and the client-code programmer.

The linker's output is the executable GradeBook application that instructors can use to manage their students' grades. Compilers and IDEs typically invoke the linker for you after compiling your code.

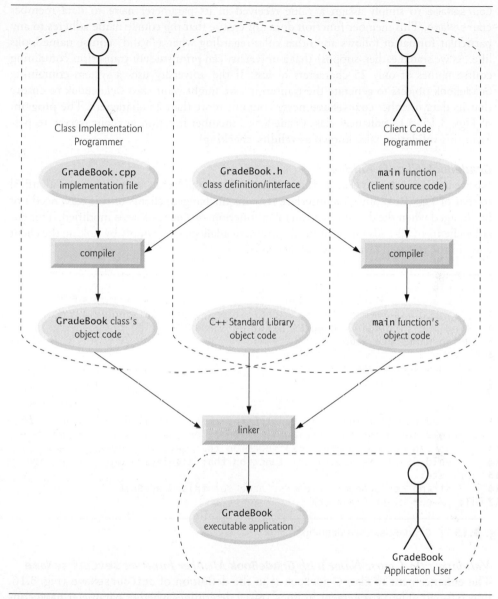

Fig. 3.14 | Compilation and linking process that produces an executable application.

For further information on compiling multiple-source-file programs, see your compiler's documentation. We provide links to various C++ compilers in our C++ Resource Center at www.deitel.com/cplusplus/.

3.9 Validating Data with *set* Functions

In Section 3.5, we introduced *set* functions for allowing clients of a class to modify the value of a private data member. In Fig. 3.5, class GradeBook defines member function set-

CourseName to simply assign a value received in its parameter name to data member courseName. This member function does not ensure that the course name adheres to any particular format or follows any other rules regarding what a "valid" course name looks like. As we stated earlier, suppose that a university can print student transcripts containing course names of only 25 characters or less. If the university uses a system containing GradeBook objects to generate the transcripts, we might want class GradeBook to ensure that its data member courseName never contains more than 25 characters. The program of Figs. 3.15–3.17 enhances class GradeBook's member function setCourseName to perform this **validation** (also known as **validity checking**).

GradeBook Class Definition
Notice that GradeBook's class definition (Fig. 3.15)—and hence, its interface—is identical to that of Fig. 3.11. Since the interface remains unchanged, clients of this class need not be changed when the definition of member function setCourseName is modified. This enables clients to take advantage of the improved GradeBook class simply by linking the client code to the updated GradeBook's object code.

```
1   // Fig. 3.15: GradeBook.h
2   // GradeBook class definition presents the public interface of
3   // the class. Member-function definitions appear in GradeBook.cpp.
4   #include <string> // program uses C++ standard string class
5   using namespace std;
6
7   // GradeBook class definition
8   class GradeBook
9   {
10  public:
11     GradeBook( string ); // constructor that initializes a GradeBook object
12     void setCourseName( string ); // function that sets the course name
13     string getCourseName(); // function that gets the course name
14     void displayMessage(); // function that displays a welcome message
15  private:
16     string courseName; // course name for this GradeBook
17  }; // end class GradeBook
```

Fig. 3.15 | GradeBook class definition.

Validating the Course Name with GradeBook Member Function setCourseName
The enhancement to class GradeBook is in the definition of setCourseName (Fig. 3.16, lines 16–29). The if statement in lines 18–19 determines whether parameter name contains a valid course name (i.e., a string of 25 or fewer characters). If the course name is valid, line 19 stores it in data member courseName. Note the expression name.length() in line 18. This is a member-function call just like myGradeBook.displayMessage(). The C++ Standard Library's string class defines a member function **length** that returns the number of characters in a string object. Parameter name is a string object, so the call name.length() returns the number of characters in name. If this value is less than or equal to 25, name is valid and line 19 executes.

The if statement in lines 21–28 handles the case in which setCourseName receives an invalid course name (i.e., a name that is more than 25 characters long). Even if parameter

```
 1    // Fig. 3.16: GradeBook.cpp
 2    // Implementations of the GradeBook member-function definitions.
 3    // The setCourseName function performs validation.
 4    #include <iostream>
 5    #include "GradeBook.h" // include definition of class GradeBook
 6    using namespace std;
 7
 8    // constructor initializes courseName with string supplied as argument
 9    GradeBook::GradeBook( string name )
10    {
11       setCourseName( name ); // validate and store courseName
12    } // end GradeBook constructor
13
14    // function that sets the course name;
15    // ensures that the course name has at most 25 characters
16    void GradeBook::setCourseName( string name )
17    {
18       if ( name.length() <= 25 ) // if name has 25 or fewer characters
19          courseName = name; // store the course name in the object
20
21       if ( name.length() > 25 ) // if name has more than 25 characters
22       {
23          // set courseName to first 25 characters of parameter name
24          courseName = name.substr( 0, 25 ); // start at 0, length of 25
25
26          cout << "Name \"" << name << "\" exceeds maximum length (25).\n"
27             << "Limiting courseName to first 25 characters.\n" << endl;
28       } // end if
29    } // end function setCourseName
30
31    // function to get the course name
32    string GradeBook::getCourseName()
33    {
34       return courseName; // return object's courseName
35    } // end function getCourseName
36
37    // display a welcome message to the GradeBook user
38    void GradeBook::displayMessage()
39    {
40       // call getCourseName to get the courseName
41       cout << "Welcome to the grade book for\n" << getCourseName()
42          << "!" << endl;
43    } // end function displayMessage
```

Fig. 3.16 | Member-function definitions for class GradeBook with a *set* function that validates
the length of data member courseName.

name is too long, we still want to leave the GradeBook object in a **consistent state**—that is,
a state in which the object's data member courseName contains a valid value (i.e., a string
of 25 characters or less). Thus, we truncate the specified course name and assign the first
25 characters of name to the courseName data member (unfortunately, this could truncate
the course name awkwardly). Standard class string provides member function **substr**
(short for "substring") that returns a new string object created by copying part of an

existing string object. The call in line 24 (i.e., name.substr(0, 25)) passes two integers (0 and 25) to name's member function substr. These arguments indicate the portion of the string name that substr should return. The first argument specifies the starting position in the original string from which characters are copied—the first character in every string is considered to be at position 0. The second argument specifies the number of characters to copy. Therefore, the call in line 24 returns a 25-character substring of name starting at position 0 (i.e., the first 25 characters in name). For example, if name holds the value "CS101 Introduction to Programming in C++", substr returns "CS101 Introduction to Pro". After the call to substr, line 24 assigns the substring returned by substr to data member courseName. In this way, setCourseName ensures that courseName is always assigned a string containing 25 or fewer characters. If the member function has to truncate the course name to make it valid, lines 26–27 display a warning message.

The if statement in lines 21–28 contains two body statements—one to set the courseName to the first 25 characters of parameter name and one to print an accompanying message to the user. Both statements should execute when name is too long, so we place them in a pair of braces, { }. Recall from Chapter 2 that this creates a block. You'll learn more about placing multiple statements in a control statement's body in Chapter 4.

The statement in lines 26–27 could also appear without a stream insertion operator at the start of the second line of the statement, as in:

```
cout << "Name \"" << name << "\" exceeds maximum length (25).\n"
   "Limiting courseName to first 25 characters.\n" << endl;
```

The C++ compiler combines adjacent string literals, even if they appear on separate lines of a program. Thus, in the statement above, the C++ compiler would combine the string literals "\" exceeds maximum length (25).\n" and "Limiting courseName to first 25 characters.\n" into a single string literal that produces output identical to that of lines 26–27 in Fig. 3.16. This behavior allows you to print lengthy strings by breaking them across lines in your program without including additional stream insertion operations.

Testing Class GradeBook

Figure 3.17 demonstrates the modified version of class GradeBook (Figs. 3.15–3.16) featuring validation. Line 12 creates a GradeBook object named gradeBook1. Recall that the GradeBook constructor calls setCourseName to initialize data member courseName. In previous versions of the class, the benefit of calling setCourseName in the constructor was not evident. Now, however, the constructor takes advantage of the validation provided by setCourseName. The constructor simply calls setCourseName, rather than duplicating its validation code. When line 12 of Fig. 3.17 passes an initial course name of "CS101 Introduction to Programming in C++" to the GradeBook constructor, the constructor passes this value to setCourseName, where the actual initialization occurs. Because this course name contains more than 25 characters, the body of the second if statement executes, causing courseName to be initialized to the truncated 25-character course name "CS101 Introduction to Pro" (the truncated part is highlighted in red in line 12). The output in Fig. 3.17 contains the warning message output by lines 26–27 of Fig. 3.16 in member function setCourseName. Line 13 creates another GradeBook object called gradeBook2—the valid course name passed to the constructor is exactly 25 characters.

Lines 16–19 of Fig. 3.17 display the truncated course name for gradeBook1 (we highlight this in red in the program output) and the course name for gradeBook2. Line 22 calls

```cpp
1   // Fig. 3.17: fig03_17.cpp
2   // Create and manipulate a GradeBook object; illustrate validation.
3   #include <iostream>
4   #include "GradeBook.h" // include definition of class GradeBook
5   using namespace std;
6
7   // function main begins program execution
8   int main()
9   {
10     // create two GradeBook objects;
11     // initial course name of gradeBook1 is too long
12     GradeBook gradeBook1( "CS101 Introduction to Programming in C++" );
13     GradeBook gradeBook2( "CS102 C++ Data Structures" );
14
15     // display each GradeBook's courseName
16     cout << "gradeBook1's initial course name is: "
17        << gradeBook1.getCourseName()
18        << "\ngradeBook2's initial course name is: "
19        << gradeBook2.getCourseName() << endl;
20
21     // modify myGradeBook's courseName (with a valid-length string)
22     gradeBook1.setCourseName( "CS101 C++ Programming" );
23
24     // display each GradeBook's courseName
25     cout << "\ngradeBook1's course name is: "
26        << gradeBook1.getCourseName()
27        << "\ngradeBook2's course name is: "
28        << gradeBook2.getCourseName() << endl;
29  } // end main
```

```
Name "CS101 Introduction to Programming in C++" exceeds maximum length (25).
Limiting courseName to first 25 characters.

gradeBook1's initial course name is: CS101 Introduction to Pro
gradeBook2's initial course name is: CS102 C++ Data Structures

gradeBook1's course name is: CS101 C++ Programming
gradeBook2's course name is: CS102 C++ Data Structures
```

Fig. 3.17 | Creating and manipulating a GradeBook object in which the course name is limited to 25 characters in length.

gradeBook1's setCourseName member function directly, to change the course name in the GradeBook object to a shorter name that does not need to be truncated. Then, lines 25–28 output the course names for the GradeBook objects again.

Additional Notes on Set Functions

A public *set* function such as setCourseName should carefully scrutinize any attempt to modify the value of a data member (e.g., courseName) to ensure that the new value is appropriate for that data item. For example, an attempt to *set* the day of the month to 37 should be rejected, an attempt to *set* a person's weight to zero or a negative value should be rejected, an attempt to *set* a grade on an exam to 185 (when the proper range is zero to 100) should be rejected, and so on

Software Engineering Observation 3.6

Making data members private *and controlling access, especially write access, to those data members through* public *member functions helps ensure data integrity.*

Error-Prevention Tip 3.5

The benefits of data integrity are not automatic simply because data members are made private*—you must provide appropriate validity checking and report the errors.*

A class's *set* functions can return values to the class's clients indicating that attempts were made to assign invalid data to objects of the class. A client can test the return value of a *set* function to determine whether the attempt to modify the object was successful and to take appropriate action. In Chapter 16, we demonstrate how clients of a class can be notified via the exception-handling mechanism when an attempt is made to modify an object with an inappropriate value. To keep the program of Figs. 3.15–3.17 simple at this early point in the book, setCourseName in Fig. 3.16 just prints an appropriate message.

3.10 Wrap-Up

In this chapter, you created user-defined classes, and created and used objects of those classes. We declared data members of a class to maintain data for each object of the class. We also defined member functions that operate on that data. You learned how to call an object's member functions to request the services the object provides and how to pass data to those member functions as arguments. We discussed the difference between a local variable of a member function and a data member of a class. We also showed how to use a constructor to specify initial values for an object's data members. You learned how to separate the interface of a class from its implementation to promote good software engineering. We presented a diagram that shows the files that class-implementation programmers and client-code programmers need to compile the code they write. We demonstrated how *set* functions can be used to validate an object's data and ensure that objects are maintained in a consistent state. UML class diagrams were used to model classes and their constructors, member functions and data members. In the next chapter, we begin our introduction to control statements, which specify the order in which a function's actions are performed.

Summary

Section 3.2 Classes, Objects, Member Functions and Data Members

- Performing a task in a program requires a function. The function hides from its user the complex tasks that it performs.

- A function in a class is known as a member function and performs one of the class's tasks.

- You must create an object of a class before a program can perform the tasks the class describes.

- Each message sent to an object is a member-function call that tells the object to perform a task.

- An object has attributes that are carried with the object as it's used in a program. These attributes are specified as data members in the object's class.

Section 3.3 Defining a Class with a Member Function

- A class definition contains the data members and member functions that define the class's attributes and behaviors, respectively.

- A class definition begins with the keyword class followed immediately by the class name.
- By convention, the name of a user-defined class begins with a capital letter and, for readability, each subsequent word in the class name begins with a capital letter.
- Every class's body is enclosed in a pair of braces ({ and }) and ends with a semicolon.
- Member functions that appear after access specifier public can be called by other functions in a program and by member functions of other classes.
- Access specifiers are always followed by a colon (:).
- Keyword void is a special return type which indicates that a function will perform a task but will not return any data to its calling function when it completes its task.
- By convention, function names begin with a lowercase first letter and all subsequent words in the name begin with a capital letter.
- An empty set of parentheses after a function name indicates that the function does not require additional data to perform its task.
- Every function's body is delimited by left and right braces ({ and }).
- Typically, you cannot call a member function until you create an object of its class.
- Each new class you create becomes a new type in C++.
- In the UML, each class is modeled in a class diagram as a rectangle with three compartments. The top compartment contains the class name. The middle compartment contains the class's attributes. The bottom compartment contains the class's operations.
- The UML models operations as the operation name followed by parentheses. A plus sign (+) preceding the name indicates a public operation (i.e., a public member function in C++).

Section 3.4 Defining a Member Function with a Parameter
- A member function can require one or more parameters that represent additional data it needs to perform its task. A function call supplies arguments for each of the function's parameters.
- A member function is called by following the object name with a dot operator (.), the function name and a set of parentheses containing the function's arguments.
- A variable of C++ Standard Library class string represents a string of characters. This class is defined in header file <string>, and the name string belongs to namespace std.
- Function getline (from header <string>) reads characters from its first argument until a newline character is encountered, then places the characters (not including the newline) in the string variable specified as its second argument. The newline character is discarded.
- A parameter list may contain any number of parameters, including none at all (represented by empty parentheses) to indicate that a function does not require any parameters.
- The number of arguments in a function call must match the number of parameters in the parameter list of the called member function's header. Also, the argument types in the function call must be consistent with the types of the corresponding parameters in the function header.
- The UML models a parameter of an operation by listing the parameter name, followed by a colon and the parameter type between the parentheses following the operation name.
- The UML has its own data types. Not all the UML data types have the same names as the corresponding C++ types. The UML type String corresponds to the C++ type string.

Section 3.5 Data Members, set Functions and get Functions
- Variables declared in a function's body are local variables and can be used only from the point of their declaration in the function to the immediately following closing right brace (}). When a function terminates, the values of its local variables are lost.

- A local variable must be declared before it can be used in a function. A local variable cannot be accessed outside the function in which it's declared.

- Data members normally are `private`. Variables or functions declared `private` are accessible only to member functions of the class in which they're declared, or to friends of the class.

- When a program creates (instantiates) an object of a class, its `private` data members are encapsulated (hidden) in the object and can be accessed only by member functions of the object's class.

- When a function that specifies a return type other than `void` is called and completes its task, the function returns a result to its calling function.

- By default, the initial value of a `string` is the empty string—i.e., a string that does not contain any characters. Nothing appears on the screen when an empty string is displayed.

- Classes often provide `public` member functions to allow clients of the class to *set* or *get* `private` data members. The names of these member functions normally begin with *set* or *get*.

- *Set* and *get* functions allow clients of a class to indirectly access the hidden data. The client does not know how the object performs these operations.

- A class's *set* and *get* functions should be used by other member functions of the class to manipulate the class's `private` data. If the class's data representation is changed, member functions that access the data only via the *set* and *get* functions will not require modification.

- A `public` *set* function should carefully scrutinize any attempt to modify the value of a data member to ensure that the new value is appropriate for that data item.

- The UML represents data members as attributes by listing the attribute name, followed by a colon and the attribute type. Private attributes are preceded by a minus sign (–) in the UML.

- The UML indicates the return type of an operation by placing a colon and the return type after the parentheses following the operation name.

- UML class diagrams do not specify return types for operations that do not return values.

Section 3.6 Initializing Objects with Constructors
- Each class should provide a constructor to initialize an object of the class when the object is created. A constructor must be defined with the same name as the class.

- A difference between constructors and functions is that constructors cannot return values, so they cannot specify a return type (not even `void`). Normally, constructors are declared `public`.

- C++ requires a constructor call at the time each object is created, which helps ensure that every object is initialized before it's used in a program.

- A constructor with no parameters is a default constructor. If you do not provide a constructor, the compiler provides a default constructor. You can also define a default constructor explicitly. If you define a constructor for a class, C++ will not create a default constructor.

- The UML models constructors as operations in a class diagram's third compartment with the word "constructor" between guillemets (« and ») before the constructor's name.

Section 3.7 Placing a Class in a Separate File for Reusability
- Class definitions, when packaged properly, can be reused by programmers worldwide.

- It's customary to define a class in a header file that has a `.h` filename extension.

- If the class's implementation changes, the class's clients should not be required to change.

- Interfaces define and standardize the ways in which things such as people and systems interact.

- A class's `public` interface describes the `public` member functions that are made available to the class's clients. The interface describes *what* services clients can use and how to *request* those services, but does not specify *how* the class carries out the services.

Section 3.8 Separating Interface from Implementation

- Separating interface from implementation makes programs easier to modify. Changes in the class's implementation do not affect the client as long as the class's interface remains unchanged.

- A function prototype contains a function's name, its return type and the number, types and order of the parameters the function expects to receive.

- Once a class is defined and its member functions are declared (via function prototypes), the member functions should be defined in a separate source-code file

- For each member function defined outside of its corresponding class definition, the function name must be preceded by the class name and the binary scope resolution operator (::).

Section 3.9 Validating Data with set Functions

- Class string's length member function returns the number of characters in a string object.

- Class string's member function substr returns a new string object containing a copy of part of an existing string object. The first argument specifies the starting position in the original string. The second argument specifies the number of characters to copy.

Terminology

access specifier 72
access-specifier label public: 72
accessor 82
argument 74
binary scope resolution operator (::) 94
body of a class definition 72
calling function 72
camel case 72
class definition 71
class keyword 71
client of an object 82
consistent state 99
constructor 84
data hiding 80
data member 77
default constructor 84
defining a class 71
dot operator (.) 73
driver program 88
empty string 82
extensible language 73
function header 72
function prototype 92
get function 82
getline function of <string> library 74
header file 88

interface of a class 92
interface 91
length member function of class string 98
local variable 77
member-function call 70
message (send to an object) 70
mutator 82
parameter 74
parameter list 76
private: access specifier 79
public access specifier 72
public services of a class 92
request a service from an object 70
return statement 81
return type 72
separate interface from implementation 91
set function 82
source-code file 88
string class 74
<string> header file 74
substr member function of class string 99
UML class diagram 73
user-defined type 73
validation 98
validity checking 98
void return type 72

Self-Review Exercises

3.1 Fill in the blanks in each of the following:
   a) A house is to a blueprint as a(n) _____ is to a class.
   b) Every class definition contains the keyword _____ followed immediately by the class's name.

    c) A class definition is typically stored in a file with the _____ filename extension.

    d) Each parameter in a function header must specify both a(n) _____ and a(n) _____.

    e) When each object of a class maintains its own copy of an attribute, the variable that represents the attribute is also known as a(n) _____.

    f) Keyword public is a(n) _____.

    g) Return type _____ indicates that a function will perform a task but will not return any information when it completes its task.

    h) Function _____ from the <string> library reads characters until a newline character is encountered, then copies those characters into the specified string.

    i) When a member function is defined outside the class definition, the function header must include the class name and the _____, followed by the function name to "tie" the member function to the class definition.

    j) The source-code file and any other files that use a class can include the class's header file via a(n) _____ preprocessor directive.

3.2 State whether each of the following is *true* or *false*. If *false*, explain why.

    a) By convention, function names begin with a capital letter and all subsequent words in the name begin with a capital letter.

    b) Empty parentheses following a function name in a function prototype indicate that the function does not require any parameters to perform its task.

    c) Data members or member functions declared with access specifier private are accessible to member functions of the class in which they're declared.

    d) Variables declared in the body of a particular member function are known as data members and can be used in all member functions of the class.

    e) Every function's body is delimited by left and right braces ({ and }).

    f) Any source-code file that contains int main() can be used to execute a program.

    g) The types of arguments in a function call must be consistent with the types of the corresponding parameters in the function prototype's parameter list.

3.3 What is the difference between a local variable and a data member?

3.4 Explain the purpose of a function parameter. What is the difference between a parameter and an argument?

Answers to Self-Review Exercises

3.1 a) object. b) class. c) .h. d) type, name. e) data member. f) access specifier. g) void. h) getline. i) binary scope resolution operator (::). j) #include.

3.2 a) False. Function names begin with a lowercase letter and all subsequent words in the name begin with a capital letter. b) True. c) True. d) False. Such variables are local variables and can be used only in the member function in which they're declared. e) True. f) True. g) True.

3.3 A local variable is declared in the body of a function and can be used only from the point at which it's declared to the closing brace of the block in which it's declared. A data member is declared in a class, but not in the body of any of the class's member functions. Every object of a class has a separate copy of the class's data members. Data members are accessible to all member functions of the class.

3.4 A parameter represents additional information that a function requires to perform its task. Each parameter required by a function is specified in the function header. An argument is the value supplied in the function call. When the function is called, the argument value is passed into the function parameter so that the function can perform its task.

Exercises

3.5 Explain the difference between a function prototype and a function definition.

3.6 What is a default constructor? How are an object's data members initialized if a class has only an implicitly defined default constructor?

3.7 Explain the purpose of a data member.

3.8 What is a header file? What is a source-code file? Discuss the purpose of each.

3.9 Explain how a program could use class string without inserting a using declaration.

3.10 Explain why a class might provide a *set* function and a *get* function for a data member.

3.11 *(Modifying Class GradeBook)* Modify class GradeBook (Figs. 3.11–3.12) as follows:
    a) Include a second string data member that represents the course instructor's name.
    b) Provide a *set* function to change the instructor's name and a *get* function to retrieve it.
    c) Modify the constructor to specify course name and instructor name parameters.
    d) Modify function displayMessage to output the welcome message and course name, then the string "This course is presented by: " followed by the instructor's name.

Use your modified class in a test program that demonstrates the class's new capabilities.

3.12 *(Account Class)* Create an Account class that a bank might use to represent customers' bank accounts. Include a data member of type int to represent the account balance. [*Note:* In subsequent chapters, we'll use numbers that contain decimal points (e.g., 2.75)—called floating-point values—to represent dollar amounts.] Provide a constructor that receives an initial balance and uses it to initialize the data member. The constructor should validate the initial balance to ensure that it's greater than or equal to 0. If not, set the balance to 0 and display an error message indicating that the initial balance was invalid. Provide three member functions. Member function credit should add an amount to the current balance. Member function debit should withdraw money from the Account and ensure that the debit amount does not exceed the Account's balance. If it does, the balance should be left unchanged and the function should print a message indicating "Debit amount exceeded account balance." Member function getBalance should return the current balance. Create a program that creates two Account objects and tests the member functions of class Account.

3.13 *(Invoice Class)* Create a class called Invoice that a hardware store might use to represent an invoice for an item sold at the store. An Invoice should include four data members—a part number (type string), a part description (type string), a quantity of the item being purchased (type int) and a price per item (type int). [*Note:* In subsequent chapters, we'll use numbers that contain decimal points (e.g., 2.75)—called floating-point values—to represent dollar amounts.] Your class should have a constructor that initializes the four data members. Provide a *set* and a *get* function for each data member. In addition, provide a member function named getInvoiceAmount that calculates the invoice amount (i.e., multiplies the quantity by the price per item), then returns the amount as an int value. If the quantity is not positive, it should be set to 0. If the price per item is not positive, it should be set to 0. Write a test program that demonstrates class Invoice's capabilities.

3.14 *(Employee Class)* Create a class called Employee that includes three pieces of information as data members—a first name (type string), a last name (type string) and a monthly salary (type int). [*Note:* In subsequent chapters, we'll use numbers that contain decimal points (e.g., 2.75)—called floating-point values—to represent dollar amounts.] Your class should have a constructor that initializes the three data members. Provide a *set* and a *get* function for each data member. If the monthly salary is not positive, set it to 0. Write a test program that demonstrates class Employee's capabilities. Create two Employee objects and display each object's *yearly* salary. Then give each Employee a 10 percent raise and display each Employee's yearly salary again.

3.15   *(Date Class)* Create a class called Date that includes three pieces of information as data members—a month (type int), a day (type int) and a year (type int). Your class should have a constructor with three parameters that uses the parameters to initialize the three data members. For the purpose of this exercise, assume that the values provided for the year and day are correct, but ensure that the month value is in the range 1–12; if it isn't, set the month to 1. Provide a *set* and a *get* function for each data member. Provide a member function displayDate that displays the month, day and year separated by forward slashes (/). Write a test program that demonstrates class Date's capabilities.

Making a Difference

3.16   *(Target-Heart-Rate Calculator)* While exercising, you can use a heart-rate monitor to see that your heart rate stays within a safe range suggested by your trainers and doctors. According to the American Heart Association (AHA) (www.americanheart.org/presenter.jhtml?identifier=4736), the formula for calculating your *maximum heart rate* in beats per minute is 220 minus your age in years. Your *target heart rate* is a range that is 50–85% of your maximum heart rate. *[Note: These formulas are estimates provided by the AHA. Maximum and target heart rates may vary based on the health, fitness and gender of the individual. Always consult a physician or qualified health care professional before beginning or modifying an exercise program.]* Create a class called HeartRates. The class attributes should include the person's first name, last name and date of birth (consisting of separate attributes for the month, day and year of birth). Your class should have a constructor that receives this data as parameters. For each attribute provide *set* and *get* functions. The class also should include a function getAge that calculates and returns the person's age (in years), a function getMaxiumumHeartRate that calculates and returns the person's maximum heart rate and a function getTargetHeartRate that calculates and returns the person's target heart rate. Since you do not yet know how to obtain the current date from the computer, function getAge should prompt the user to enter the current month, day and year before calculating the person's age. Write an application that prompts for the person's information, instantiates an object of class HeartRates and prints the information from that object—including the person's first name, last name and date of birth—then calculates and prints the person's age in (years), maximum heart rate and target-heart-rate range.

3.17   *(Computerization of Health Records)* A health care issue that has been in the news lately is the computerization of health records. This possibility is being approached cautiously because of sensitive privacy and security concerns, among others. [We address such concerns in later exercises.] Computerizing health records could make it easier for patients to share their health profiles and histories among their various health care professionals. This could improve the quality of health care, help avoid drug conflicts and erroneous drug prescriptions, reduce costs and in emergencies, could save lives. In this exercise, you'll design a "starter" HealthProfile class for a person. The class attributes should include the person's first name, last name, gender, date of birth (consisting of separate attributes for the month, day and year of birth), height (in inches) and weight (in pounds). Your class should have a constructor that receives this data. For each attribute, provide *set* and *get* functions. The class also should include functions that calculate and return the user's age in years, maximum heart rate and target-heart-rate range (see Exercise 3.16), and body mass index (BMI; see Exercise 2.30). Write an application that prompts for the person's information, instantiates an object of class HealthProfile for that person and prints the information from that object—including the person's first name, last name, gender, date of birth, height and weight—then calculates and prints the person's age in years, BMI, maximum heart rate and target-heart-rate range. It should also display the "BMI values" chart from Exercise 2.30. Use the same technique as Exercise 3.16 to calculate the person's age.

Control Statements: Part 1

4

Let's all move one place on.
—Lewis Carroll

The wheel is come full circle.
—William Shakespeare

How many apples fell on Newton's head before he took the hint!
—Robert Frost

All the evolution we know of proceeds from the vague to the definite.
—Charles Sanders Peirce

Objectives

In this chapter you'll learn:

- Basic problem-solving techniques.

- To develop algorithms through the process of top-down, stepwise refinement.

- To use the if and if...else selection statements to choose among alternative actions.

- To use the while repetition statement to execute statements in a program repeatedly.

- Counter-controlled repetition and sentinel-controlled repetition.

- To use the increment, decrement and assignment operators.

4.1 Introduction

Before writing a program to solve a problem, we must have a thorough understanding of the problem and a carefully planned approach to solving it. When writing a program, we must also understand the types of building blocks that are available and employ proven program construction techniques. In this chapter and in Chapter 5, Control Statements: Part 2, we discuss these issues as we present the theory and principles of structured programming. The concepts presented here are crucial to building effective classes and manipulating objects.

In this chapter, we introduce C++'s if, if...else and while statements, three of the building blocks that allow you to specify the logic required for member functions to perform their tasks. We devote a portion of this chapter (and Chapters 5 and 7) to further developing the GradeBook class introduced in Chapter 3. In particular, we add a member function to the GradeBook class that uses control statements to calculate the average of a set of student grades. Another example demonstrates additional ways to combine control statements. We introduce C++'s assignment operators and explore C++'s increment and decrement operators. These additional operators abbreviate and simplify many program statements.

4.2 Algorithms

Any solvable computing problem can be solved by the execution of a series of actions in a specific order. A **procedure** for solving a problem in terms of

1. the **actions** to execute and
2. the **order** in which the actions execute

is called an **algorithm**. The following example demonstrates that correctly specifying the order in which the actions execute is important.

Consider the "rise-and-shine algorithm" followed by one junior executive for getting out of bed and going to work: (1) Get out of bed, (2) take off pajamas, (3) take a shower, (4) get dressed, (5) eat breakfast, (6) carpool to work. This routine gets the executive to work well prepared to make critical decisions. Suppose that the same steps are performed in a slightly different order: (1) Get out of bed, (2) take off pajamas, (3) get dressed, (4) take a shower, (5) eat breakfast, (6) carpool to work. In this case, our junior executive shows up for work soaking wet. Specifying the order in which statements (actions) execute in a computer program is called **program control**. This chapter investigates program control using C++'s **control statements**.

4.3 Pseudocode

Pseudocode (or "fake" code) is an artificial and informal language that helps you develop algorithms without having to worry about the strict details of C++ language syntax. The pseudocode we present here is particularly useful for developing algorithms that will be converted to structured portions of C++ programs. Pseudocode is similar to everyday English; it's convenient and user friendly, although it isn't an actual computer programming language.

Pseudocode does not execute on computers. Rather, it helps you "think out" a program before attempting to write it in a programming language, such as C++. This chapter provides several examples of how to use pseudocode to develop C++ programs.

The style of pseudocode we present consists purely of characters, so you can type pseudocode conveniently, using any editor program. The computer can produce a freshly printed copy of a pseudocode program on demand. A carefully prepared pseudocode program can easily be converted to a corresponding C++ program. In many cases, this simply requires replacing pseudocode statements with C++ equivalents.

Pseudocode normally describes only **executable statements**, which cause specific actions to occur after a programmer converts a program from pseudocode to C++ and the program is run on a computer. Declarations (that do not have initializers or do not involve constructor calls) are not executable statements. For example, the declaration

```
int counter;
```

tells the compiler variable `counter`'s type and instructs the compiler to reserve space in memory for the variable. This declaration does not cause any action—such as input, output or a calculation—to occur when the program executes. We typically do not include variable declarations in our pseudocode. However, some programmers choose to list variables and mention their purposes at the beginning of pseudocode programs.

Let's look at an example of pseudocode that may be written to help a programmer create the addition program of Fig. 2.5. This pseudocode (Fig. 4.1) corresponds to the algorithm that inputs two integers from the user, adds these integers and displays their sum. Although we show the complete pseudocode listing here, we'll show how to *create* pseudocode from a problem statement later in the chapter.

Lines 1–2 correspond to the statements in lines 13–14 of Fig. 2.5. Notice that the pseudocode statements are simply English statements that convey what task is to be performed in C++. Likewise, lines 4–5 correspond to the statements in lines 16–17 of Fig. 2.5 and lines 7–8 correspond to the statements in lines 19 and 21 of Fig. 2.5.

Notice that the pseudocode in Fig. 4.1 corresponds to code only in function `main`. This occurs because pseudocode is normally used for algorithms, not complete programs. In this case, the pseudocode represents the algorithm. The function in which this code is placed is not important to the algorithm itself.

1	*Prompt the user to enter the first integer*
2	*Input the first integer*
3	
4	*Prompt the user to enter the second integer*
5	*Input the second integer*
6	
7	*Add first integer and second integer, store result*
8	*Display result*

Fig. 4.1 | Pseudocode for the addition program of Fig. 2.5.

4.4 **Control Structures**

Normally, statements in a program execute one after the other in the order in which they're written. This is called **sequential execution**. Various C++ statements we'll soon discuss enable you to specify that the next statement to execute may be other than the next one in sequence. This is called **transfer of control**.

During the 1960s, it became clear that the indiscriminate use of transfers of control was the root of much difficulty experienced by software development groups. The finger of blame was pointed at the **goto statement**, which allows you to specify a transfer of control to one of a wide range of possible destinations in a program (creating what's often called "spaghetti code"). The notion of so-called **structured programming** became almost synonymous with "**goto elimination**."

The research of Böhm and Jacopini[1] demonstrated that programs could be written without any goto statements. It became the challenge of the era for programmers to shift their styles to "goto-less programming." It was not until the 1970s that programmers started taking structured programming seriously. The results have been impressive, as software development groups have reported reduced development times, more frequent on-time delivery of systems and more frequent within-budget completion of software projects. The key to these successes is that structured programs are clearer, are easier to debug, test and modify and are more likely to be bug-free in the first place.

Böhm and Jacopini's work demonstrated that all programs could be written in terms of only three **control structures**, namely, the **sequence structure**, the **selection structure** and the **repetition structure**. The term "control structures" comes from the field of computer science. When we introduce C++'s implementations of control structures, we'll refer to them in the terminology of the C++ standard document as "control statements."

Sequence Structure in C++

The sequence structure is built into C++. Unless directed otherwise, the computer executes C++ statements one after the other in the order in which they're written—that is, in sequence. The Unified Modeling Language (UML) **activity diagram** of Fig. 4.2 illustrates a typical sequence structure in which two calculations are performed in order. C++ allows us to have as many actions as we want in a sequence structure. As we'll soon see, anywhere a single action may be placed, we may place several actions in sequence.

---

1. Böhm, C., and G. Jacopini, "Flow Diagrams, Turing Machines, and Languages with Only Two Formation Rules," *Communications of the ACM*, Vol. 9, No. 5, May 1966, pp. 366–371.

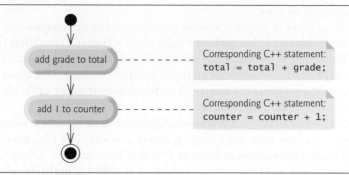

Fig. 4.2 | Sequence-structure activity diagram.

In this figure, the two statements add a grade to a `total` variable and add the value 1 to a `counter` variable. Such statements might appear in a program that averages several student grades. To calculate an average, the total of the grades being averaged is divided by the number of grades. A counter variable would be used to keep track of the number of values being averaged. You'll see similar statements in the program of Section 4.8.

Activity diagrams are part of the UML. An activity diagram models the **workflow** (also called the **activity**) of a portion of a software system. Such workflows may include a portion of an algorithm, such as the sequence structure in Fig. 4.2. Activity diagrams are composed of special-purpose symbols, such as **action state symbols** (a rectangle with its left and right sides replaced with arcs curving outward), **diamonds** and **small circles**; these symbols are connected by **transition arrows**, which represent the flow of the activity.

Activity diagrams help you develop and represent algorithms, but many programmers prefer pseudocode. Activity diagrams clearly show how control structures operate.

Consider the sequence-structure activity diagram of Fig. 4.2. It contains two **action states** that represent actions to perform. Each action state contains an **action expression**—e.g., "add grade to total" or "add 1 to counter"—that specifies a particular action to perform. Other actions might include calculations or input/output operations. The arrows in the activity diagram are called transition arrows. These arrows represent **transitions**, which indicate the order in which the actions represented by the action states occur—the program that implements the activities illustrated by the activity diagram in Fig. 4.2 first adds `grade` to `total`, then adds 1 to `counter`.

The **solid circle** at the top of the diagram represents the activity's **initial state**—the beginning of the workflow before the program performs the modeled activities. The solid circle surrounded by a hollow circle that appears at the bottom of the activity diagram represents the **final state**—the end of the workflow after the program performs its activities.

Figure 4.2 also includes rectangles with the upper-right corners folded over. These are called **notes** in the UML. Notes are explanatory remarks that describe the purpose of symbols in the diagram. Notes can be used in any UML diagram—not just activity diagrams. Figure 4.2 uses UML notes to show the C++ code associated with each action state in the activity diagram. A **dotted line** connects each note with the element that the note describes. Activity diagrams normally do not show the C++ code that implements the activity. We use notes for this purpose here to illustrate how the diagram relates to C++ code. For more information on the UML, see our optional case study, which appears in Chapters 25–26, or visit our UML Resource Center at www.deitel.com/UML/.

Selection Statements in C++

C++ provides three types of selection statements (discussed in this chapter and Chapter 5). The if selection statement either performs (selects) an action if a condition (predicate) is true or skips the action if the condition is false. The if...else selection statement performs an action if a condition is true or performs a different action if the condition is false. The switch selection statement (Chapter 5) performs one of many different actions, depending on the value of an integer expression.

The if selection statement is a **single-selection statement** because it selects or ignores a single action (or, as we'll soon see, a single group of actions). The if...else statement is called a **double-selection statement** because it selects between two different actions (or groups of actions). The switch selection statement is called a **multiple-selection statement** because it selects among many different actions (or groups of actions).

Repetition Statements in C++

C++ provides three types of repetition statements (also called **looping statements** or **loops**) for performing statements repeatedly while a condition (called the **loop-continuation condition**) remains true. These are the **while**, **do...while** and **for** statements. (Chapter 5 presents the do...while and for statements.) The while and for statements perform the action (or group of actions) in their bodies zero or more times—if the loop-continuation condition is initially false, the action (or group of actions) will not execute. The do...while statement performs the action (or group of actions) in its body at least once.

Each of the words if, else, switch, while, do and for is a C++ keyword. These words are reserved by the C++ programming language to implement various features, such as C++'s control statements. Keywords must not be used as identifiers, such as variable names. Figure 4.3 provides a complete list of C++ keywords.

C++ Keywords				
Keywords common to the C and C++ programming languages				
auto	break	case	char	const
continue	default	do	double	else
enum	extern	float	for	goto
if	int	long	register	return
short	signed	sizeof	static	struct
switch	typedef	union	unsigned	void
volatile	while			
C++-only keywords				
and	and_eq	asm	bitand	bitor
bool	catch	class	compl	const_cast
delete	dynamic_cast	explicit	export	false
friend	inline	mutable	namespace	new
not	not_eq	operator	or	or_eq
private	protected	public	reinterpret_cast	static_cast
template	this	throw	true	try
typeid	typename	using	virtual	wchar_t
xor	xor_eq			

Fig. 4.3 | C++ keywords.

Common Programming Error 4.1

Using a keyword as an identifier is a syntax error.

Common Programming Error 4.2

Spelling a keyword with any uppercase letters is a syntax error. All of C++'s keywords contain only lowercase letters.

Summary of Control Statements in C++

C++ has only three kinds of control structures, which from this point forward we refer to as control statements: the sequence statement, selection statements (three types—if, if...else and switch) and repetition statements (three types—while, for and do...while). Each program combines as many of these control statements as is appropriate for the algorithm the program implements. We can model each control statement as an activity diagram with an initial state and a final state that represent a control statement's entry point and exit point, respectively. These **single-entry/single-exit control statements** make it easy to build programs—control statements are attached to one another by connecting the exit point of one to the entry point of the next. This is similar to the way a child stacks building blocks, so we call this **control-statement stacking**. We'll learn shortly that there is only one other way to connect control statements—called **control-statement nesting**, in which one control statement is contained inside another. Thus, algorithms in C++ programs are constructed from only three kinds of control statements, combined in only two ways.

Software Engineering Observation 4.1

Any C++ program we'll ever build can be constructed from only seven different types of control statements (sequence, if, if...else, switch, while, do...while and for) combined in only two ways (control-statement stacking and control-statement nesting).

4.5 if Selection Statement

Programs use selection statements to choose among alternative courses of action. For example, suppose the passing grade on an exam is 60. The pseudocode statement

> *If student's grade is greater than or equal to 60*
> > *Print "Passed"*

determines whether the condition "student's grade is greater than or equal to 60" is true or false. If the condition is true, "Passed" is printed and the next pseudocode statement in order is "performed" (remember that pseudocode is not a real programming language). If the condition is false, the print statement is ignored and the next pseudocode statement in order is performed. The indentation of the second line is optional, but it's recommended because it emphasizes the inherent structure of structured programs.

Good Programming Practice 4.1

Consistently applying reasonable indentation conventions throughout your programs greatly improves program readability. We suggest three blanks per indent. Some people prefer using tabs, but these can vary across editors, causing a program written on one editor to align differently when used with another.

The preceding pseudocode *If* statement can be written in C++ as

```cpp
if ( grade >= 60 )
   cout << "Passed";
```

The C++ code corresponds closely to the pseudocode. This is one of the properties of pseudocode that make it such a useful program development tool.

Figure 4.4 illustrates the single-selection `if` statement. It contains what is perhaps the most important symbol in an activity diagram—the diamond or **decision symbol**, which indicates that a decision is to be made. A decision symbol indicates that the workflow will continue along a path determined by the symbol's associated **guard conditions**, which can be true or false. Each transition arrow emerging from a decision symbol has a guard condition (specified in square brackets above or next to the transition arrow). If a particular guard condition is true, the workflow enters the action state to which that transition arrow points. In Fig. 4.4, if the grade is greater than or equal to 60, the program prints "Passed" to the screen, then transitions to the final state of this activity. If the grade is less than 60, the program immediately transitions to the final state without displaying a message.

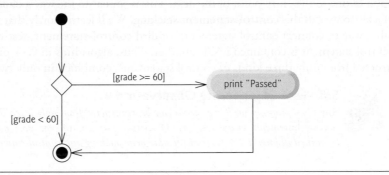

Fig. 4.4 | `if` single-selection statement activity diagram.

We learned in Chapter 2 that decisions can be based on conditions containing relational or equality operators. Actually, in C++, a decision can be based on any expression—if the expression evaluates to zero, it's treated as false; if the expression evaluates to nonzero, it's treated as true. C++ provides the data type **bool** for variables that can hold only the values **true** and **false**—each of these is a C++ keyword.

Portability Tip 4.1

For compatibility with earlier versions of C, which used integers for Boolean values, the bool *value* true *also can be represented by any nonzero value (compilers typically use 1) and the* bool *value* false *also can be represented as the value zero.*

The `if` statement is a single-entry/single-exit statement. We'll see that the activity diagrams for the remaining control statements also contain initial states, transition arrows, action states that indicate actions to perform, decision symbols (with associated guard conditions) that indicate decisions to be made and final states. This is consistent with the **action/decision model of programming** we've been emphasizing.

Envision seven bins, each containing only empty UML activity diagrams of one of the seven types of control statements. Your task, then, is assembling a program from the activity diagrams of as many of each type of control statement as the algorithm demands, combining the activity diagrams in only two possible ways (stacking or nesting), then filling in the action states and decisions with action expressions and guard conditions in a manner appropriate to form a structured implementation for the algorithm. We'll discuss the variety of ways in which actions and decisions may be written.

4.6 if...else Double-Selection Statement

The if single-selection statement performs an indicated action only when the condition is true; otherwise the action is skipped. The if...else double-selection statement allows you to specify an action to perform when the condition is true and a different action to perform when the condition is false. For example, the pseudocode statement

> *If student's grade is greater than or equal to 60*
> *Print "Passed"*
> *Else*
> *Print "Failed"*

prints "Passed" if the student's grade is greater than or equal to 60, but prints "Failed" if the student's grade is less than 60. In either case, after printing occurs, the next pseudocode statement in sequence is "performed."

The preceding pseudocode *If...Else* statement can be written in C++ as

```
if ( grade >= 60 )
    cout << "Passed";
else
    cout << "Failed";
```

The body of the else is also indented.

Good Programming Practice 4.2

Whatever indentation convention you choose should be applied consistently throughout your programs. It's difficult to read programs that do not obey uniform spacing conventions.

Good Programming Practice 4.3

Indent both body statements of an if...else statement.

Good Programming Practice 4.4

If there are several levels of indentation, each level should be indented the same additional amount of space to promote readability and maintainability.

Figure 4.5 illustrates the the if...else statement's flow of control. Once again, the symbols in the UML activity diagram (besides the initial state, transition arrows and final state) represent action states and decisions.

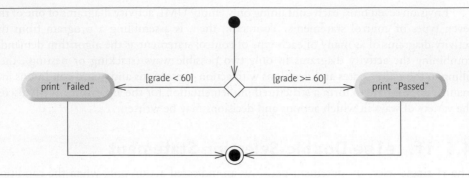

Fig. 4.5 | if...else double-selection statement activity diagram.

Conditional Operator (?:)

C++ provides the **conditional operator** (**?:**), which is closely related to the if...else statement. The conditional operator is C++'s only **ternary operator**—it takes three operands. The operands, together with the conditional operator, form a **conditional expression**. The first operand is a condition, the second operand is the value for the entire conditional expression if the condition is true and the third operand is the value for the entire conditional expression if the condition is false. For example, the output statement

```
cout << ( grade >= 60 ? "Passed" : "Failed" );
```

contains a conditional expression, grade >= 60 ? "Passed" : "Failed", that evaluates to the string "Passed" if the condition grade >= 60 is true, but evaluates to "Failed" if the condition is false. Thus, the statement with the conditional operator performs essentially the same as the preceding if...else statement. As we'll see, the precedence of the conditional operator is low, so the parentheses in the preceding expression are required.

Error-Prevention Tip 4.1
To avoid precedence problems (and for clarity), place conditional expressions (that appear in larger expressions) in parentheses.

The values in a conditional expression also can be actions to execute. For example, the following conditional expression also prints "Passed" or "Failed":

```
grade >= 60 ? cout << "Passed" : cout << "Failed";
```

The preceding conditional expression is read, "If grade is greater than or equal to 60, then cout << "Passed"; otherwise, cout << "Failed"." This, too, is comparable to the preceding if...else statement. Conditional expressions can appear in some program locations where if...else statements cannot.

Nested if...else Statements

Nested if...else statements test for multiple cases by placing if...else selection statements inside other if...else selection statements. For example, the following pseudocode if...else statement prints A for exam grades greater than or equal to 90, B for grades in the range 80 to 89, C for grades in the range 70 to 79, D for grades in the range 60 to 69 and F for all other grades:

> *If student's grade is greater than or equal to 90*
>> *Print "A"*
> *Else*
>> *If student's grade is greater than or equal to 80*
>>> *Print "B"*
>> *Else*
>>> *If student's grade is greater than or equal to 70*
>>>> *Print "C"*
>>> *Else*
>>>> *If student's grade is greater than or equal to 60*
>>>>> *Print "D"*
>>>> *Else*
>>>>> *Print "F"*

This pseudocode can be written in C++ as

```cpp
if ( studentGrade >= 90 ) // 90 and above gets "A"
   cout << "A";
else
   if ( studentGrade >= 80 ) // 80-89 gets "B"
      cout << "B";
   else
      if ( studentGrade >= 70 ) // 70-79 gets "C"
         cout << "C";
      else
         if ( studentGrade >= 60 ) // 60-69 gets "D"
            cout << "D";
         else // less than 60 gets "F"
            cout << "F";
```

If studentGrade is greater than or equal to 90, the first four conditions are true, but only the output statement after the first test executes. Then, the program skips the else-part of the "outermost" if...else statement. Most write the preceding if...else statement as

```cpp
if ( studentGrade >= 90 ) // 90 and above gets "A"
   cout << "A";
else if ( studentGrade >= 80 ) // 80-89 gets "B"
   cout << "B";
else if ( studentGrade >= 70 ) // 70-79 gets "C"
   cout << "C";
else if ( studentGrade >= 60 ) // 60-69 gets "D"
   cout << "D";
else // less than 60 gets "F"
   cout << "F";
```

The two forms are identical except for the spacing and indentation, which the compiler ignores. The latter form is popular because it avoids deep indentation of the code to the right, which can force lines to wrap.

Performance Tip 4.1

A nested if...else statement can perform much faster than a series of single-selection if statements because of the possibility of early exit after one of the conditions is satisfied.

Performance Tip 4.2

In a nested if...else statement, test the conditions that are more likely to be true *at the beginning of the nested statement. This will enable the nested if...else statement to run faster by exiting earlier than they would if infrequently occurring cases were tested first.*

Dangling-else Problem

The C++ compiler always associates an else with the immediately preceding if unless told to do otherwise by the placement of braces ({ and }). This behavior can lead to what's referred to as the **dangling-else problem**. For example,

```
if ( x > 5 )
    if ( y > 5 )
        cout << "x and y are > 5";
else
    cout << "x is <= 5";
```

appears to indicate that if x is greater than 5, the nested if statement determines whether y is also greater than 5. If so, "x and y are > 5" is output. Otherwise, it appears that if x is not greater than 5, the else part of the if...else outputs "x is <= 5".

Beware! This nested if...else statement does not execute as it appears. The compiler actually interprets the statement as

```
if ( x > 5 )
    if ( y > 5 )
        cout << "x and y are > 5";
    else
        cout << "x is <= 5";
```

in which the body of the first if is a nested if...else. The outer if statement tests whether x is greater than 5. If so, execution continues by testing whether y is also greater than 5. If the second condition is true, the proper string—"x and y are > 5"—is displayed. However, if the second condition is false, the string "x is <= 5" is displayed, even though we know that x is greater than 5.

To force the nested if...else statement to execute as originally intended, we can write it as follows:

```
if ( x > 5 )
{
    if ( y > 5 )
        cout << "x and y are > 5";
}
else
    cout << "x is <= 5";
```

The braces ({}) indicate to the compiler that the second if statement is in the body of the first if and that the else is associated with the first if. Exercises 4.23–4.24 further investigate the dangling-else problem.

Blocks

The if selection statement expects only one statement in its body. Similarly, the if and else parts of an if...else statement each expect only one body statement. To include several statements in the body of an `if` or in either part of an `if...else`, enclose the statements in braces ({ and }). A set of statements contained within a pair of braces is called a **compound statement** or a **block**. We use the term "block" from this point forward.

Software Engineering Observation 4.2

A block can be placed anywhere in a program that a single statement can be placed.

The following example includes a block in the `else` part of an `if...else` statement.

```
if ( studentGrade >= 60 )
    cout << "Passed.\n";
else
{
    cout << "Failed.\n";
    cout << "You must take this course again.\n";
}
```

In this case, if `studentGrade` is less than 60, the program executes both statements in the body of the `else` and prints

```
Failed.
You must take this course again.
```

Notice the braces surrounding the two statements in the `else` clause. These braces are important. Without the braces, the statement

```
cout << "You must take this course again.\n";
```

would be outside the body of the `else` part of the `if` and would execute regardless of whether the grade was less than 60. This is a logic error.

Common Programming Error 4.3

Forgetting one or both of the braces that delimit a block can lead to syntax errors or logic errors in a program.

Good Programming Practice 4.5

Always putting the braces in an `if...else` statement (or any control statement) helps prevent their accidental omission, especially when adding statements to an `if` or `else` clause at a later time. To avoid omitting one or both of the braces, some programmers prefer to type the beginning and ending braces of blocks even before typing the individual statements within the braces.

Just as a block can be placed anywhere a single statement can be placed, it's also possible to have no statement at all—called a **null statement** (or an **empty statement**). The null statement is represented by placing a semicolon (;) where a statement would normally be.

Common Programming Error 4.4

Placing a semicolon after the condition in an `if` statement leads to a logic error in single-selection `if` statements and a syntax error in double-selection `if...else` statements (when the `if` part contains an actual body statement).

4.7 `while` Repetition Statement

A **repetition statement** (also called a **looping statement** or a **loop**) allows you to specify that a program should repeat an action while some condition remains true. The pseudocode statement

> *While there are more items on my shopping list*
> *Purchase next item and cross it off my list*

describes the repetition that occurs during a shopping trip. The condition, "there are more items on my shopping list" is either true or false. If it's true, then the action, "Purchase next item and cross it off my list" is performed. This action will be performed repeatedly while the condition remains true. The statement contained in the *While* repetition statement constitutes the body of the *While*, which can be a single statement or a block. Eventually, the condition will become false (when the last item on the shopping list has been purchased and crossed off the list). At this point, the repetition terminates, and the first pseudocode statement after the repetition statement executes.

As an example of C++'s `while` repetition statement, consider a program segment designed to find the first power of 3 larger than 100. Suppose the integer variable `product` has been initialized to 3. When the following `while` repetition statement finishes executing, `product` contains the result:

```
int product = 3;

while ( product <= 100 )
    product = 3 * product;
```

When the `while` statement begins execution, `product`'s value is 3. Each repetition multiplies `product` by 3, so `product` takes on the values 9, 27, 81 and 243 successively. When `product` becomes 243, the `while` statement condition—`product <= 100`—becomes `false`. This terminates the repetition, so the final value of `product` is 243. At this point, program execution continues with the next statement after the `while` statement.

Common Programming Error 4.5

Not providing, in the body of a `while` statement, an action that eventually causes the condition in the `while` to become false normally results in a logic error called an infinite loop, *in which the repetition statement never terminates. This can make a program appear to "hang" or "freeze" if the loop body does not contain statements that interact with the user.*

The UML activity diagram of Fig. 4.6 illustrates the flow of control that corresponds to the preceding `while` statement. Once again, the symbols in the diagram (besides the initial state, transition arrows, a final state and three notes) represent an action state and a decision. This diagram also introduces the UML's **merge symbol**, which joins two flows of activity into one flow of activity. The UML represents both the merge symbol and the decision symbol as diamonds. In this diagram, the merge symbol joins the transitions from the initial state and from the action state, so they both flow into the decision that determines whether the loop should begin (or continue) executing. The decision and merge symbols can be distinguished by the number of "incoming" and "outgoing" transition arrows. A decision symbol has one transition arrow pointing to the diamond and two or more transition arrows pointing out from the diamond to indicate possible transitions from that point. In addition, each transition arrow pointing out of a decision symbol has a guard condition next to it. A merge symbol has two or more transition arrows pointing to the diamond and only one transition arrow pointing from the diamond, to indicate multiple activity flows merging to continue the activity. Unlike the decision symbol, the merge symbol does not have a counterpart in C++ code.

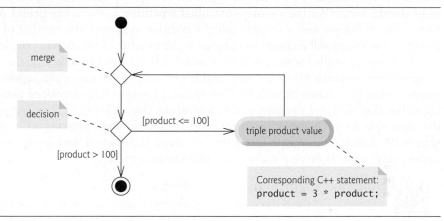

Fig. 4.6 | `while` repetition statement UML activity diagram.

The diagram of Fig. 4.6 clearly shows the repetition of the `while` statement discussed earlier in this section. The transition arrow emerging from the action state points to the merge, which transitions back to the decision that is tested each time through the loop until the guard condition `product > 100` becomes true. Then the `while` statement exits (reaches its final state) and control passes to the next statement in sequence in the program.

Imagine a deep bin of empty UML `while` repetition statement activity diagrams—as many as you might need to stack and nest with the activity diagrams of other control statements to form a structured implementation of an algorithm. You fill in the action states and decision symbols with action expressions and guard conditions appropriate to the algorithm.

Performance Tip 4.3

Many of the Performance Tips we mention in this text result in only small improvements, so you might be tempted to ignore them. However, a small performance improvement for code that executes many times in a loop can result in substantial overall performance improvement.

4.8 Formulating Algorithms: Counter-Controlled Repetition

To illustrate how programmers develop algorithms, this section and Section 4.9 solve two variations of a class average problem. Consider the following problem statement:

A class of ten students took a quiz. The grades (integers in the range 0 to 100) for this quiz are available to you. Calculate and display the total of all student grades and the class average on the quiz.

The class average is equal to the sum of the grades divided by the number of students. The algorithm for solving this problem on a computer must input each of the grades, calculate the average and print the result.

Pseudocode Algorithm with Counter-Controlled Repetition

Let's use pseudocode to list the actions to execute and specify the order in which these actions should occur. We use **counter-controlled repetition** to input the grades one at a time. This technique uses a variable called a **counter** to control the number of times a group of statements will execute (also known as the number of **iterations** of the loop).

Counter-controlled repetition is often called **definite repetition** because the number of repetitions is known before the loop begins executing. In this example, repetition terminates when the counter exceeds 10. This section presents a fully developed pseudocode algorithm (Fig. 4.7) and a version of class GradeBook (Fig. 4.8–Fig. 4.9) that implements the algorithm in a C++ member function. The section then presents an application (Fig. 4.10) that demonstrates the algorithm in action. In Section 4.9 we demonstrate how to use pseudocode to develop such an algorithm from scratch.

Software Engineering Observation 4.3

Experience has shown that the most difficult part of solving a problem on a computer is developing the algorithm for the solution. The process of producing a working C++ program from the algorithm is typically straightforward.

---

1 *Set total to zero*
2 *Set grade counter to one*
3
4 *While grade counter is less than or equal to ten*
5   *Prompt the user to enter the next grade*
6   *Input the next grade*
7   *Add the grade into the total*
8   *Add one to the grade counter*
9
10 *Set the class average to the total divided by ten*
11 *Print the total of the grades for all students in the class*
12 *Print the class average*

Fig. 4.7 | Pseudocode for solving the class average problem with counter-controlled repetition.

Note the references in the pseudocode algorithm of Fig. 4.7 to a total and a counter. A **total** is a variable used to accumulate the sum of several values. A **counter** is a variable used to count—in this case, the grade counter indicates which of the 10 grades is about to be entered by the user. Variables used to store totals are normally initialized to zero before being used in a program; otherwise, the sum would include the previous value stored in the total's memory location.

Enhancing GradeBook Validation

Let's consider an enhancement we made to class GradeBook. In Fig. 3.16, our setCourse-Name member function validated the course name by testing whether the course name's length was less than or equal to 25 characters, using an if statement. If this was true, the course name would be set. This code was followed by an if statement that tested whether the course name's length was larger than 25 characters (in which case the course name would be shortened). The second if statement's condition is the exact opposite of the first if statement's condition. If one condition evaluates to true, the other must evaluate to false. Such a situation is ideal for an if...else statement, so we've modified our code, replacing the two if statements with one if...else statement (lines 18–25 of Fig. 4.9).

Implementing Counter-Controlled Repetition in Class *GradeBook*

Class GradeBook (Fig. 4.8–Fig. 4.9) contains a constructor (declared in line 11 of Fig. 4.8 and defined in lines 9–12 of Fig. 4.9) that assigns a value to the class's data member courseName (declared in line 17 of Fig. 4.8). Lines 16–26, 29–32 and 35–29 of Fig. 4.9 define member functions setCourseName, getCourseName and displayMessage, respectively. Lines 42–68 define member function determineClassAverage, which implements the class average algorithm described by the pseudocode in Fig. 4.7.

```cpp
1   // Fig. 4.8: GradeBook.h
2   // Definition of class GradeBook that determines a class average.
3   // Member functions are defined in GradeBook.cpp
4   #include <string> // program uses C++ standard string class
5   using namespace std;
6
7   // GradeBook class definition
8   class GradeBook
9   {
10  public:
11     GradeBook( string ); // constructor initializes course name
12     void setCourseName( string ); // function to set the course name
13     string getCourseName(); // function to retrieve the course name
14     void displayMessage(); // display a welcome message
15     void determineClassAverage(); // averages grades entered by the user
16  private:
17     string courseName; // course name for this GradeBook
18  }; // end class GradeBook
```

Fig. 4.8 | Class average problem using counter-controlled repetition: GradeBook header file.

```cpp
1   // Fig. 4.9: GradeBook.cpp
2   // Member-function definitions for class GradeBook that solves the
3   // class average program with counter-controlled repetition.
4   #include <iostream>
5   #include "GradeBook.h" // include definition of class GradeBook
6   using namespace std;
7
8   // constructor initializes courseName with string supplied as argument
9   GradeBook::GradeBook( string name )
10  {
```

Fig. 4.9 | Class average problem using counter-controlled repetition: GradeBook source code file. (Part 1 of 3.)

```
11      setCourseName( name ); // validate and store courseName
12  } // end GradeBook constructor
13
14  // function to set the course name;
15  // ensures that the course name has at most 25 characters
16  void GradeBook::setCourseName( string name )
17  {
18      if ( name.length() <= 25 ) // if name has 25 or fewer characters
19          courseName = name; // store the course name in the object
20      else // if name is longer than 25 characters
21      { // set courseName to first 25 characters of parameter name
22          courseName = name.substr( 0, 25 ); // select first 25 characters
23          cout << "Name \"" << name << "\" exceeds maximum length (25).\n"
24              << "Limiting courseName to first 25 characters.\n" << endl;
25      } // end if...else
26  } // end function setCourseName
27
28  // function to retrieve the course name
29  string GradeBook::getCourseName()
30  {
31      return courseName;
32  } // end function getCourseName
33
34  // display a welcome message to the GradeBook user
35  void GradeBook::displayMessage()
36  {
37      cout << "Welcome to the grade book for\n" << getCourseName() << "!\n"
38          << endl;
39  } // end function displayMessage
40
41  // determine class average based on 10 grades entered by user
42  void GradeBook::determineClassAverage()
43  {
44      int total; // sum of grades entered by user
45      int gradeCounter; // number of the grade to be entered next
46      int grade; // grade value entered by user
47      int average; // average of grades
48
49      // initialization phase
50      total = 0; // initialize total
51      gradeCounter = 1; // initialize loop counter
52
53      // processing phase
54      while ( gradeCounter <= 10 ) // loop 10 times
55      {
56          cout << "Enter grade: "; // prompt for input
57          cin >> grade; // input next grade
58          total = total + grade; // add grade to total
59          gradeCounter = gradeCounter + 1; // increment counter by 1
60      } // end while
61
```

Fig. 4.9 | Class average problem using counter-controlled repetition: GradeBook source code file. (Part 2 of 3.)

```
62      // termination phase
63      average = total / 10; // integer division yields integer result
64
65      // display total and average of grades
66      cout << "\nTotal of all 10 grades is " << total << endl;
67      cout << "Class average is " << average << endl;
68   } // end function determineClassAverage
```

Fig. 4.9 | Class average problem using counter-controlled repetition: GradeBook source code file. (Part 3 of 3.)

Lines 44–47 (Fig. 4.9) declare local variables total, gradeCounter, grade and average to be of type int. Variable grade stores the user input. Notice that the preceding declarations appear in the body of member function determineClassAverage.

In this chapter's versions of class GradeBook, we simply read and process a set of grades. The averaging calculation is performed in member function determineClass-Average using local variables—we do not preserve any information about student grades in the class's data members. In Chapter 7, Arrays and Vectors, we modify class GradeBook to maintain the grades in memory using a data member that refers to a data structure known as an array. This allows a GradeBook object to perform various calculations on a set of grades without requiring the user to enter the grades multiple times.

Good Programming Practice 4.6
Separate declarations from other statements in functions with a blank line for readability.

Lines 50–51 initialize total to 0 and gradeCounter to 1 they're used in calculations. Counter variables are normally initialized to zero or one, depending on their use. An uninitialized variable contains a **"garbage" value** (also called an **undefined value**)—the value last stored in the memory location reserved for that variable. The variables grade and average (for the user input and calculated average, respectively) need not be initialized before they're used—their values will be assigned as they're input or calculated later in the function.

Common Programming Error 4.6
Not initializing counters and totals can lead to logic errors.

Error-Prevention Tip 4.2
Initialize each counter and total, either in its declaration or in an assignment statement. Totals are normally initialized to 0. Counters are normally initialized to 0 or 1, depending on how they're used.

Good Programming Practice 4.7
Declare each variable on a separate line with its own comment for readability.

Line 54 indicates that the while statement should continue looping (also called **iterating**) as long as gradeCounter's value is less than or equal to 10. While this condition remains true, the while statement repeatedly executes the statements between the braces that delimit its body (lines 55–60).

Line 56 displays the prompt "Enter grade: ". This line corresponds to the pseudocode statement *"Prompt the user to enter the next grade."* Line 57 reads the grade entered by the user and assigns it to variable grade. This line corresponds to the pseudocode statement *"Input the next grade."* Recall that variable grade was not initialized earlier in the program, because the program obtains the value for grade from the user during each iteration of the loop. Line 58 adds the new grade entered by the user to the total and assigns the result to total, which replaces its previous value.

Line 59 adds 1 to gradeCounter to indicate that the program has processed a grade and is ready to input the next grade from the user. Incrementing gradeCounter eventually causes gradeCounter to exceed 10. At that point the while loop terminates because its condition (line 54) becomes false.

When the loop terminates, line 63 performs the averaging calculation and assigns its result to the variable average. Line 66 displays the text "Total of all 10 grades is " followed by variable total's value. Line 67 then displays the text "Class average is " followed by variable average's value. Member function determineClassAverage then returns control to the calling function (i.e., main in Fig. 4.10).

Demonstrating Class *GradeBook*

Figure 4.10 contains this application's main function, which creates an object of class GradeBook and demonstrates its capabilities. Line 9 of Fig. 4.10 creates a new GradeBook object called myGradeBook. The string in line 9 is passed to the GradeBook constructor (lines 9–12 of Fig. 4.9). Line 11 of Fig. 4.10 calls myGradeBook's displayMessage member function to display a welcome message to the user. Line 12 then calls myGradeBook's determineClassAverage member function to allow the user to enter 10 grades, for which the member function then calculates and prints the average—the member function performs the algorithm shown in the pseudocode of Fig. 4.7.

```
1  // Fig. 4.10: fig04_10.cpp
2  // Create GradeBook object and invoke its determineClassAverage function.
3  #include "GradeBook.h" // include definition of class GradeBook
4
5  int main()
6  {
7     // create GradeBook object myGradeBook and
8     // pass course name to constructor
9     GradeBook myGradeBook( "CS101 C++ Programming" );
10
11    myGradeBook.displayMessage(); // display welcome message
12    myGradeBook.determineClassAverage(); // find average of 10 grades
13  } // end main
```

Fig. 4.10 | Class average problem using counter-controlled repetition: Creating an object of class GradeBook (Fig. 4.8–Fig. 4.9) and invoking its determineClassAverage member function. (Part 1 of 2.)

```
Welcome to the grade book for
CS101 C++ Programming

Enter grade: 67
Enter grade: 78
Enter grade: 89
Enter grade: 67
Enter grade: 87
Enter grade: 98
Enter grade: 93
Enter grade: 85
Enter grade: 82
Enter grade: 100

Total of all 10 grades is 846
Class average is 84
```

Fig. 4.10 | Class average problem using counter-controlled repetition: Creating an object of class GradeBook (Fig. 4.8–Fig. 4.9) and invoking its determineClassAverage member function. (Part 2 of 2.)

Notes on Integer Division and Truncation

The averaging calculation performed in response to the function call in line 12 of Fig. 4.10 produces an integer result. The sample execution indicates that the sum of the grade values is 846, which, when divided by 10, should yield 84.6—a number with a decimal point. However, the result of the calculation total / 10 (line 63 of Fig. 4.9) is the integer 84, because total and 10 are both integers. Dividing two integers results in integer division— any fractional part of the calculation is lost (i.e., **truncated**). We'll see how to obtain a result that includes a decimal point from the averaging calculation in the next section.

Common Programming Error 4.7

Assuming that integer division rounds (rather than truncates) can lead to incorrect results. For example, 7 ÷ 4, which yields 1.75 in conventional arithmetic, truncates to 1 in integer arithmetic, rather than rounding to 2.

In Fig. 4.9, if line 63 used gradeCounter rather than 10, the output for this program would display an incorrect value, 76. This would occur because in the final iteration of the while statement, gradeCounter was incremented to the value 11 in line 59.

Common Programming Error 4.8

*Using a loop's counter-control variable in a calculation after the loop often causes a common logic error called an **off-by-one error**. In a counter-controlled loop that counts up by one each time through the loop, the loop terminates when the counter's value is one higher than its last legitimate value (i.e., 11 in the case of counting from 1 to 10).*

4.9 Formulating Algorithms: Sentinel-Controlled Repetition

Let's generalize the class average problem. Consider the following problem:

Develop a class average program that processes grades for an arbitrary number of students each time it's run.

In the previous example, the problem statement specified the number of students, so the number of grades (10) was known in advance. In this example, no indication is given of how many grades the user will enter during the program's execution. The program must process an arbitrary number of grades. How can the program determine when to stop the input of grades? How will it know when to calculate and print the class average?

To solve this problem, we can use a special value called a **sentinel value** (also called a **signal value**, a **dummy value** or a **flag value**) to indicate "end of data entry." After typing the legitimate grades, the user types the sentinel value to indicate that the last grade has been entered. Sentinel-controlled repetition is often called **indefinite repetition** because the number of repetitions is not known before the loop begins executing.

The sentinel value must be chosen so that it is not confused with an acceptable input value. Grades are normally nonnegative integers, so –1 is an acceptable sentinel value. Thus, a run of the program might process inputs such as 95, 96, 75, 74, 89 and –1. The program would then compute and print the class average for the grades 95, 96, 75, 74 and 89. Since –1 is the sentinel value, it should not enter into the averaging calculation.

Common Programming Error 4.9

Choosing a sentinel value that is also a legitimate data value is a logic error.

Developing the Pseudocode Algorithm with Top-Down, Stepwise Refinement: The Top and First Refinement

We approach the class average program with a technique called **top-down, stepwise refinement**, a technique that is essential to the development of well-structured programs. We begin with a pseudocode representation of the **top**—a single statement that conveys the overall function of the program:

Determine the class average for the quiz for an arbitrary number of students

The top is, in effect, a *complete* representation of a program. Unfortunately, the top (as in this case) rarely conveys sufficient detail from which to write a program. So we now begin the refinement process. We divide the top into a series of smaller tasks and list these in the order in which they need to be performed. This results in the following **first refinement**.

Initialize variables
Input, sum and count the quiz grades
Calculate and print the total of all student grades and the class average

This refinement uses only the sequence structure—these steps execute in order.

Software Engineering Observation 4.4

Each refinement, as well as the top itself, is a complete specification of the algorithm; only the level of detail varies.

Software Engineering Observation 4.5

Many programs can be divided logically into three phases: an initialization phase that initializes the program variables; a processing phase that inputs data values and adjusts program variables (such as counters and totals) accordingly; and a termination phase that calculates and outputs the final results.

Proceeding to the Second Refinement

The preceding *Software Engineering Observation* is often all you need for the first refinement in the top-down process. In the **second refinement**, we commit to specific variables. In this example, we need a running total of the numbers, a count of how many numbers have been processed, a variable to receive the value of each grade as it's input by the user and a variable to hold the calculated average. The pseudocode statement

> *Initialize variables*

can be refined as follows:

> *Initialize total to zero*
> *Initialize counter to zero*

Only the variables *total* and *counter* need to be initialized before they're used. The variables *average* and *grade* (for the calculated average and the user input, respectively) need not be initialized, because their values will be replaced as they're calculated or input.

The pseudocode statement

> *Input, sum and count the quiz grades*

requires a repetition statement (i.e., a loop) that successively inputs each grade. We don't know in advance how many grades are to be processed, so we'll use **sentinel-controlled repetition**. The user enters legitimate grades one at a time. After entering the last legitimate grade, the user enters the sentinel value. The program tests for the sentinel value after each grade is input and terminates the loop when the user enters the sentinel value. The second refinement of the preceding pseudocode statement is then

> *Prompt the user to enter the first grade*
> *Input the first grade (possibly the sentinel)*
>
> *While the user has not yet entered the sentinel*
>   *Add this grade into the running total*
>   *Add one to the grade counter*
>   *Prompt the user to enter the next grade*
>   *Input the next grade (possibly the sentinel)*

In pseudocode, we do not use braces around the statements that form the body of the *While* structure. We simply indent the statements under the *While* to show that they belong to the *While*. Again, pseudocode is only an informal program development aid.

The pseudocode statement

> *Calculate and print the total of all student grades and the class average*

can be refined as follows:

> *If the counter is not equal to zero*
>   *Set the average to the total divided by the counter*
>   *Print the total of the grades for all students in the class*
>   *Print the class average*
> *else*
>   *Print "No grades were entered"*

We're careful here to test for the possibility of division by zero—normally a **fatal logic error** that, if undetected, would cause the program to fail (often called "**crashing**"). The complete second refinement of the pseudocode for the class average problem is shown in Fig. 4.11.

Common Programming Error 4.10
An attempt to divide by zero normally causes a fatal runtime error.

Error-Prevention Tip 4.3
When performing division by an expression whose value could be zero, explicitly test for this possibility and handle it appropriately in your program (such as by printing an error message) rather than allowing the fatal error to occur.

1	*Initialize total to zero*
2	*Initialize counter to zero*
3	
4	*Prompt the user to enter the first grade*
5	*Input the first grade (possibly the sentinel)*
6	
7	*While the user has not yet entered the sentinel*
8	*Add this grade into the running total*
9	*Add one to the grade counter*
10	*Prompt the user to enter the next grade*
11	*Input the next grade (possibly the sentinel)*
12	
13	*If the counter is not equal to zero*
14	*Set the average to the total divided by the counter*
15	*Print the total of the grades for all students in the class*
16	*Print the class average*
17	*else*
18	*Print "No grades were entered"*

Fig. 4.11 | Class average problem pseudocode algorithm with sentinel-controlled repetition.

In Fig. 4.7 and Fig. 4.11, we include some blank lines and indentation in the pseudocode to make it more readable. The blank lines separate the pseudocode algorithms into their various phases, and the indentation emphasizes the control statement bodies.

The pseudocode algorithm in Fig. 4.11 solves the more general class average problem. This algorithm was developed after only two levels of refinement. Sometimes more levels are necessary.

Software Engineering Observation 4.6
Terminate the top-down, stepwise refinement process when the pseudocode algorithm is specified in sufficient detail for you to be able to convert the pseudocode to C++. Typically, implementing the C++ program is then straightforward.

Software Engineering Observation 4.7

Many experienced programmers write programs without ever using program development tools like pseudocode. These programmers feel that their ultimate goal is to solve the problem on a computer and that writing pseudocode merely delays the production of final outputs. Although this method might work for simple and familiar problems, it can lead to serious difficulties in large, complex projects.

Implementing Sentinel-Controlled Repetition in Class *GradeBook*

Figures 4.12–4.13 show class GradeBook containing member function determineClassAverage that implements the pseudocode algorithm of Fig. 4.11 (this class is demonstrated in Fig. 4.14). Although each grade entered is an integer, the averaging calculation is likely to produce a number with a decimal point—in other words, a real number or **floating-point number** (e.g., 7.33, 0.0975 or 1000.12345). The type int cannot represent such a number, so this class must use another type to do so. C++ provides several data types for storing floating-point numbers in memory, including **float** and **double**. The primary difference between these types is that, compared to float variables, double variables can typically store numbers with larger magnitude and finer detail (i.e., more digits to the right of the decimal point—also known as the number's **precision**). This program introduces a special operator called a **cast operator** to force the averaging calculation to produce a floating-point numeric result. These features are explained in detail as we discuss the program.

In this example, we see that control statements can be stacked on top of one another (in sequence) just as a child stacks building blocks. The while statement (lines 60–68 of Fig. 4.13) is immediately followed by an if...else statement (lines 71–83) in sequence. Much of the code in this program is identical to the code in Fig. 4.9, so we concentrate on the new features and issues.

Line 48 declares the double variable average. Recall that we used an int variable in the preceding example to store the class average. Using type double in the current example allows us to store the class average calculation's result as a floating-point number. Line 52

```
1   // Fig. 4.12: GradeBook.h
2   // Definition of class GradeBook that determines a class average.
3   // Member functions are defined in GradeBook.cpp
4   #include <string> // program uses C++ standard string class
5   using namespace std;
6
7   // GradeBook class definition
8   class GradeBook
9   {
10  public:
11     GradeBook( string ); // constructor initializes course name
12     void setCourseName( string ); // function to set the course name
13     string getCourseName(); // function to retrieve the course name
14     void displayMessage(); // display a welcome message
15     void determineClassAverage(); // averages grades entered by the user
16  private:
17     string courseName; // course name for this GradeBook
18  }; // end class GradeBook
```

Fig. 4.12 | Class average problem using sentinel-controlled repetition: GradeBook header file.

```cpp
1   // Fig. 4.13: GradeBook.cpp
2   // Member-function definitions for class GradeBook that solves the
3   // class average program with sentinel-controlled repetition.
4   #include <iostream>
5   #include <iomanip> // parameterized stream manipulators
6   #include "GradeBook.h" // include definition of class GradeBook
7   using namespace std;
8
9   // constructor initializes courseName with string supplied as argument
10  GradeBook::GradeBook( string name )
11  {
12     setCourseName( name ); // validate and store courseName
13  } // end GradeBook constructor
14
15  // function to set the course name;
16  // ensures that the course name has at most 25 characters
17  void GradeBook::setCourseName( string name )
18  {
19     if ( name.length() <= 25 ) // if name has 25 or fewer characters
20        courseName = name; // store the course name in the object
21     else // if name is longer than 25 characters
22     { // set courseName to first 25 characters of parameter name
23        courseName = name.substr( 0, 25 ); // select first 25 characters
24        cout << "Name \"" << name << "\" exceeds maximum length (25).\n"
25           << "Limiting courseName to first 25 characters.\n" << endl;
26     } // end if...else
27  } // end function setCourseName
28
29  // function to retrieve the course name
30  string GradeBook::getCourseName()
31  {
32     return courseName;
33  } // end function getCourseName
34
35  // display a welcome message to the GradeBook user
36  void GradeBook::displayMessage()
37  {
38     cout << "Welcome to the grade book for\n" << getCourseName() << "!\n"
39        << endl;
40  } // end function displayMessage
41
42  // determine class average based on 10 grades entered by user
43  void GradeBook::determineClassAverage()
44  {
45     int total; // sum of grades entered by user
46     int gradeCounter; // number of grades entered
47     int grade; // grade value
48     double average; // number with decimal point for average
49
50     // initialization phase
51     total = 0; // initialize total
```

Fig. 4.13 | Class average problem using sentinel-controlled repetition: GradeBook source code file. (Part 1 of 2.)

```
52      gradeCounter = 0; // initialize loop counter
53
54      // processing phase
55      // prompt for input and read grade from user
56      cout << "Enter grade or -1 to quit: ";
57      cin >> grade; // input grade or sentinel value
58
59      // loop until sentinel value read from user
60      while ( grade != -1 ) // while grade is not -1
61      {
62          total = total + grade; // add grade to total
63          gradeCounter = gradeCounter + 1; // increment counter
64
65          // prompt for input and read next grade from user
66          cout << "Enter grade or -1 to quit: ";
67          cin >> grade; // input grade or sentinel value
68      } // end while
69
70      // termination phase
71      if ( gradeCounter != 0 ) // if user entered at least one grade...
72      {
73          // calculate average of all grades entered
74          average = static_cast< double >( total ) / gradeCounter;
75
76          // display total and average (with two digits of precision)
77          cout << "\nTotal of all " << gradeCounter << " grades entered is "
78              << total << endl;
79          cout << "Class average is " << setprecision( 2 ) << fixed << average
80              << endl;
81      } // end if
82      else // no grades were entered, so output appropriate message
83          cout << "No grades were entered" << endl;
84  } // end function determineClassAverage
```

Fig. 4.13 | Class average problem using sentinel-controlled repetition: GradeBook source code file. (Part 2 of 2.)

initializes the variable gradeCounter to 0, because no grades have been entered yet. Remember that this program uses sentinel-controlled repetition. To keep an accurate record of the number of grades entered, the program increments variable gradeCounter only when the user enters a valid grade value (i.e., not the sentinel value) and the program completes the processing of the grade. Finally, notice that both input statements (lines 57 and 67) are preceded by an output statement that prompts the user for input.

Good Programming Practice 4.8

Prompt the user for each keyboard input. The prompt should indicate the form of the input and any special input values. For example, in a sentinel-controlled loop, the prompts requesting data entry should explicitly remind the user what the sentinel value is.

Program Logic for Sentinel-Controlled Repetition vs. Counter-Controlled Repetition
Compare the program logic for sentinel-controlled repetition in this application with that for counter-controlled repetition in Fig. 4.9. In counter-controlled repetition, each itera-

```
 1  // Fig. 4.14: fig04_14.cpp
 2  // Create GradeBook object and invoke its determineClassAverage function.
 3  #include "GradeBook.h" // include definition of class GradeBook
 4
 5  int main()
 6  {
 7     // create GradeBook object myGradeBook and
 8     // pass course name to constructor
 9     GradeBook myGradeBook( "CS101 C++ Programming" );
10
11     myGradeBook.displayMessage(); // display welcome message
12     myGradeBook.determineClassAverage(); // find average of 10 grades
13  } // end main
```

```
Welcome to the grade book for
CS101 C++ Programming

Enter grade or -1 to quit: 97
Enter grade or -1 to quit: 88
Enter grade or -1 to quit: 72
Enter grade or -1 to quit: -1

Total of all 3 grades entered is 257
Class average is 85.67
```

Fig. 4.14 | Class average problem using sentinel-controlled repetition: Creating a `GradeBook` object and invoking its `determineClassAverage` member function.

tion of the `while` statement (lines 54–60 of Fig. 4.9) reads a value from the user, for the specified number of iterations. In sentinel-controlled repetition, the program reads the first value (lines 56–57 of Fig. 4.13) before reaching the `while`. This value determines whether the program's flow of control should enter the body of the `while`. If the condition of the `while` is false, the user entered the sentinel value, so the body of the `while` does not execute (i.e., no grades were entered). If, on the other hand, the condition is true, the body begins execution, and the loop adds the `grade` value to the `total` (line 62) and increments `gradeCounter` (line 63). Then lines 66–67 in the loop's body prompt for and input the next value from the user. Next, program control reaches the closing right brace (}) of the body in line 68, so execution continues with the test of the `while`'s condition (line 60). The condition uses the most recent `grade` input by the user to determine whether the loop's body should execute again. The value of variable `grade` is always input from the user immediately before the program tests the `while` condition. This allows the program to determine whether the value just input is the sentinel value *before* the program processes that value (i.e., adds it to the `total` and increments `gradeCounter`). If the sentinel value is input, the loop terminates, and the program does not add –1 to the `total`.

After the loop terminates, the `if...else` statement in lines 71–83 executes. The condition in line 71 determines whether any grades were entered. If none were, the `else` part (lines 82–83) of the `if...else` statement executes and displays the message `"No grades were entered"` and the member function returns control to the calling function.

Notice the block in the `while` loop in Fig. 4.13. Without the braces, the last three statements in the body of the loop would fall outside the loop, causing the computer to interpret this code incorrectly, as follows:

```
   // loop until sentinel value read from user
   while ( grade != -1 )
      total = total + grade; // add grade to total
   gradeCounter = gradeCounter + 1; // increment counter

   // prompt for input and read next grade from user
   cout << "Enter grade or -1 to quit: ";
   cin >> grade;
```

This would cause an infinite loop in the program if the user did not input –1 for the first grade (in line 57).

Common Programming Error 4.11
Omitting the braces that delimit a block can lead to logic errors, such as infinite loops. To prevent this problem, some programmers enclose the body of every control statement in braces, even if the body contains only a single statement.

Floating-Point Number Precision and Memory Requirements

Variables of type `float` represent **single-precision floating-point numbers** and have seven significant digits on most 32-bit systems. Variables of type `double` represent **double-precision floating-point numbers**. These require twice as much memory as `float` variables and provide 15 significant digits on most 32-bit systems—approximately double the precision of `float` variables. For the range of values required by most programs, variables of type `float` should suffice, but you can use `double` to "play it safe." In some programs, even variables of type `double` will be inadequate—such programs are beyond the scope of this book. Most programmers represent floating-point numbers with type `double`. In fact, C++ treats all floating-point numbers you type in a program's source code (such as 7.33 and 0.0975) as `double` values by default. Such values in the source code are known as **floating-point constants**. See Appendix C, Fundamental Types, for the ranges of values for `float`s and `double`s.

Floating-point numbers often arise as a result of division. In conventional arithmetic, when we divide 10 by 3, the result is 3.3333333…, with the sequence of 3s repeating infinitely. The computer allocates only a fixed amount of space to hold such a value, so clearly the stored floating-point value can be only an approximation.

Common Programming Error 4.12
Using floating-point numbers in a manner that assumes they're represented exactly (e.g., using them in comparisons for equality) can lead to incorrect results. Floating-point numbers are represented only approximately.

Although floating-point numbers are not always 100 percent precise, they have numerous applications. For example, when we speak of a "normal" body temperature of 98.6, we do not need to be precise to a large number of digits. When we read the temperature on a thermometer as 98.6, it may actually be 98.5999473210643. Calling this number simply 98.6 is fine for most applications involving body temperatures. Due to the imprecise nature of floating-point numbers, type `double` is preferred over type `float`, because `double` variables can represent floating-point numbers more accurately. For this reason, we use type `double` throughout the book.

Converting Between Fundamental Types Explicitly and Implicitly

The variable average is declared to be of type double (line 48 of Fig. 4.13) to capture the fractional result of our calculation. However, total and gradeCounter are both integer variables. Recall that dividing two integers results in integer division, in which any fractional part of the calculation is lost (i.e., **truncated**). In the following statement:

```
average = total / gradeCounter;
```

the division occurs first—the result's fractional part is lost before it's assigned to average. To perform a floating-point calculation with integers, we must create temporary floating-point values. C++ provides the **unary cast operator** to accomplish this task. Line 74 uses the cast operator **static_cast**<double>(total) to create a *temporary* floating-point copy of its operand in parentheses—total. Using a cast operator in this manner is called **explicit conversion**. The value stored in total is still an integer.

The calculation now consists of a floating-point value (the temporary double version of total) divided by the integer gradeCounter. The compiler knows how to evaluate only expressions in which the operand types of are identical. To ensure that the operands are of the same type, the compiler performs an operation called **promotion** (also called **implicit conversion**) on selected operands. For example, in an expression containing values of data types int and double, C++ **promotes** int operands to double values. In our example, we are treating total as a double (by using the unary cast operator), so the compiler promotes gradeCounter to double, allowing the calculation to be performed—the result of the floating-point division is assigned to average. In Chapter 6, Functions and an Introduction to Recursion, we discuss all the fundamental data types and their order of promotion.

Common Programming Error 4.13

The cast operator can be used to convert between fundamental numeric types, such as int and double, and between related class types (as we discuss in Chapter 13, Object-Oriented Programming: Polymorphism). Casting to the wrong type may cause errors.

Cast operators are available for use with every data type and with class types as well. The static_cast operator is formed by following keyword static_cast with angle brackets (< and >) around a data-type name. The cast operator is a **unary operator**—an operator that takes only one operand. In Chapter 2, we studied the binary arithmetic operators. C++ also supports unary versions of the plus (+) and minus (-) operators, so that you can write such expressions as -7 or +5. Cast operators have higher precedence than other unary operators, such as unary + and unary -. This precedence is higher than that of the **multiplicative operators** *, / and %, and lower than that of parentheses. We indicate the cast operator with the notation static_cast<*type*>() in our precedence charts.

Formatting for Floating-Point Numbers

The formatting capabilities in Fig. 4.13 are discussed here briefly and explained in depth in Chapter 15, Stream Input/Output. The call to **setprecision** in line 79 (with an argument of 2) indicates that double variable average should be printed with two digits of **precision** to the right of the decimal point (e.g., 92.37). This call is referred to as a **parameterized stream manipulator** (because of the 2 in parentheses). Programs that use these calls must contain the preprocessor directive (line 5)

```
#include <iomanip>
```

The manipulator `endl` is a **nonparameterized stream manipulator** (because it isn't followed by a value or expression in parentheses) and does not require the `<iomanip>` header file. If the precision is not specified, floating-point values are normally output with six digits of precision (i.e., the **default precision** on most 32-bit systems today), although we'll see an exception to this in a moment.

The stream manipulator **`fixed`** (line 79) indicates that floating-point values should be output in so-called **fixed-point format**, as opposed to **scientific notation**. Scientific notation is a way of displaying a number as a floating-point number between the values of 1.0 and 10.0, multiplied by a power of 10. For instance, the value 3,100.0 would be displayed in scientific notation as 3.1×10^3. Scientific notation is useful when displaying values that are very large or very small. Formatting using scientific notation is discussed further in Chapter 15. Fixed-point formatting, on the other hand, is used to force a floating-point number to display a specific number of digits. Specifying fixed-point formatting also forces the decimal point and trailing zeros to print, even if the value is a whole number amount, such as 88.00. Without the fixed-point formatting option, such a value prints in C++ as 88 without the trailing zeros and without the decimal point. When the stream manipulators `fixed` and `setprecision` are used in a program, the printed value is **rounded** to the number of decimal positions indicated by the value passed to `setprecision` (e.g., the value 2 in line 79), although the value in memory remains unaltered. For example, the values 87.946 and 67.543 are output as 87.95 and 67.54, respectively. It's also possible to force a decimal point to appear by using stream manipulator **`showpoint`**. If `showpoint` is specified without `fixed`, then trailing zeros will not print. Like `endl`, stream manipulators `fixed` and `showpoint` do not use parameters, nor do they require the `<iomanip>` header file. Both can be found in header `<iostream>`.

Lines 79 and 80 of Fig. 4.13 output the class average. In this example, we display the class average rounded to the nearest hundredth and output it with exactly two digits to the right of the decimal point. The parameterized stream manipulator (line 79) indicates that variable `average`'s value should be displayed with two digits of precision to the right of the decimal point—indicated by `setprecision( 2 )`. The three grades entered during the sample execution of the program in Fig. 4.14 total 257, which yields the average 85.666666.... The parameterized stream manipulator `setprecision` causes the value to be rounded to the specified number of digits. In this program, the average is rounded to the hundredths position and displayed as `85.67`.

4.10 Formulating Algorithms: Nested Control Statements

For the next example, we once again formulate an algorithm by using pseudocode and top-down, stepwise refinement, and write a corresponding C++ program. We've seen that control statements can be stacked on top of one another (in sequence) just as a child stacks building blocks. In this case study, we examine the only other structured way control statements can be connected, namely, by **nesting** one control statement within another.

Consider the following problem statement:

A college offers a course that prepares students for the state licensing exam for real estate brokers. Last year, ten of the students who completed this course took the exam. The college wants to know how well its students did on the exam. You've been asked to write a program to summarize the results. You've been given a list of these 10 students. Next to each name is written a 1 if the student passed the exam or a 2 if the student failed.

Your program should analyze the results of the exam as follows:

1. *Input each test result (i.e., a 1 or a 2). Display the prompting message "Enter result" each time the program requests another test result.*

2. *Count the number of test results of each type.*

3. *Display a summary of the test results indicating the number of students who passed and the number who failed.*

4. *If more than eight students passed the exam, print the message "Bonus to instructor!"*

After reading the problem statement carefully, we make the following observations:

1. The program must process test results for 10 students. A counter-controlled loop can be used because the number of test results is known in advance.

2. Each test result is a number—either a 1 or a 2. Each time the program reads a test result, the program must determine whether the number is a 1 or a 2. We test for a 1 in our algorithm. If the number is not a 1, we assume that it's a 2. (Exercise 4.20 considers the consequences of this assumption.)

3. Two counters are used to keep track of the exam results—one to count the number of students who passed the exam and one to count the number of students who failed the exam.

4. After the program has processed all the results, it must decide whether more than eight students passed the exam.

Let's proceed with top-down, stepwise refinement. We begin with a pseudocode representation of the top:

Analyze exam results and decide whether tuition should be raised

Once again, it's important to emphasize that the top is a *complete* representation of the program, but several refinements are likely to be needed before the pseudocode evolves naturally into a C++ program.

Our first refinement is

Initialize variables
Input the 10 exam results, and count passes and failures
Print a summary of the exam results and decide if tuition should be raised

Here, too, even though we have a complete representation of the entire program, further refinement is necessary. We now commit to specific variables. Counters are needed to record the passes and failures, a counter will be used to control the looping process and a variable is needed to store the user input. The last variable is not initialized, because its value is read from the user during each iteration of the loop.

The pseudocode statement

Initialize variables

can be refined as follows:

> *Initialize passes to zero*
> *Initialize failures to zero*
> *Initialize student counter to one*

Notice that only the counters are initialized at the start of the algorithm.
The pseudocode statement

> *Input the 10 exam results, and count passes and failures*

requires a loop that successively inputs the result of each exam. Here it's known in advance that there are precisely 10 exam results, so counter-controlled looping is appropriate. Inside the loop (i.e., **nested** within the loop), an `if...else` statement will determine whether each exam result is a pass or a failure and will increment the appropriate counter. The refinement of the preceding pseudocode statement is then

> *While student counter is less than or equal to 10*
>   *Prompt the user to enter the next exam result*
>   *Input the next exam result*
>
>   *If the student passed*
>   *Add one to passes*
>   *Else*
>   *Add one to failures*
>
>   *Add one to student counter*

We use blank lines to isolate the *If...Else* control structure, which improves readability.
The pseudocode statement

> *Print a summary of the exam results and decide whether tuition should be raised*

can be refined as follows:

> *Print the number of passes*
> *Print the number of failures*
>
> *If more than eight students passed*
>   *Print "Bonus to instructor!"*

The complete second refinement appears in Fig. 4.15. Blank lines are used to set off the *While* structure for readability. This pseudocode is now sufficiently refined for conversion to C++.

---

1   *Initialize passes to zero*
2   *Initialize failures to zero*
3   *Initialize student counter to one*
4

Fig. 4.15 | Pseudocode for examination-results problem. (Part 1 of 2.)

5	*While student counter is less than or equal to 10*
6	*Prompt the user to enter the next exam result*
7	*Input the next exam result*
8	
9	*If the student passed*
10	*Add one to passes*
11	*Else*
12	*Add one to failures*
13	
14	*Add one to student counter*
15	
16	*Print the number of passes*
17	*Print the number of failures*
18	
19	*If more than eight students passed*
20	*Print "Bonus to instructor!"*

Fig. 4.15 | Pseudocode for examination-results problem. (Part 2 of 2.)

Conversion to Class Analysis

The program that implements the pseudocode algorithm and two sample executions are shown in Fig. 4.16.

```cpp
1   // Fig. 4.16: fig04_16.cpp
2   // Examination-results problem: Nested control statements.
3   #include <iostream>
4   using namespace std;
5
6   int main()
7   {
8      // initializing variables in declarations
9      int passes = 0; // number of passes
10     int failures = 0; // number of failures
11     int studentCounter = 1; // student counter
12     int result; // one exam result (1 = pass, 2 = fail)
13
14     // process 10 students using counter-controlled loop
15     while ( studentCounter <= 10 )
16     {
17        // prompt user for input and obtain value from user
18        cout << "Enter result (1 = pass, 2 = fail): ";
19        cin >> result; // input result
20
21        // if...else nested in while
22        if ( result == 1 )          // if result is 1,
23           passes = passes + 1;     // increment passes;
24        else                        // else result is not 1, so
25           failures = failures + 1; // increment failures
26
```

Fig. 4.16 | Examination-results problem: Nested control statements. (Part 1 of 2.)

```
27          // increment studentCounter so loop eventually terminates
28          studentCounter = studentCounter + 1;
29       } // end while
30
31       // termination phase; display number of passes and failures
32       cout << "Passed " << passes << "\nFailed " << failures << endl;
33
34       // determine whether more than eight students passed
35       if ( passes > 8 )
36          cout << "Bonus to instructor!" << endl;
37    } // end main
```

```
Enter result (1 = pass, 2 = fail): 1
Enter result (1 = pass, 2 = fail): 1
Enter result (1 = pass, 2 = fail): 1
Enter result (1 = pass, 2 = fail): 1
Enter result (1 = pass, 2 = fail): 2
Enter result (1 = pass, 2 = fail): 1
Enter result (1 = pass, 2 = fail): 1
Enter result (1 = pass, 2 = fail): 1
Enter result (1 = pass, 2 = fail): 1
Enter result (1 = pass, 2 = fail): 1
Passed 9
Failed 1
Bonus to instructor!
```

```
Enter result (1 = pass, 2 = fail): 1
Enter result (1 = pass, 2 = fail): 2
Enter result (1 = pass, 2 = fail): 2
Enter result (1 = pass, 2 = fail): 1
Enter result (1 = pass, 2 = fail): 1
Enter result (1 = pass, 2 = fail): 1
Enter result (1 = pass, 2 = fail): 2
Enter result (1 = pass, 2 = fail): 1
Enter result (1 = pass, 2 = fail): 1
Enter result (1 = pass, 2 = fail): 2
Passed 6
Failed 4
```

Fig. 4.16 | Examination-results problem: Nested control statements. (Part 2 of 2.)

Lines 9–12 declare the variables used to process the examination results. We've taken advantage of a feature of C++ that allows variable initialization to be incorporated into declarations (passes is initialized to 0, failures is initialized to 0 and studentCounter is initialized to 1). Looping programs may require initialization at the beginning of each repetition; such reinitialization normally would be performed by assignment statements rather than in declarations or by moving the declarations inside the loop bodies.

The while statement (lines 15–29) loops 10 times. Each iteration inputs and processes one exam result. The if...else statement (lines 22–25) for processing each result is nested in the while statement. If the result is 1, the if...else statement increments passes; otherwise, it assumes the result is 2 and increments failures. Line 28 increments studentCounter before the loop condition is tested again in line 15. After 10 values have been input, the loop terminates and line 32 displays the number of passes and the number of `failures`. The `if` statement in lines 35–36 determines whether more than eight students passed the exam and, if so, outputs the message `"Bonus to instructor!"`.

Figure 4.16 shows the input and output from two sample executions of the program. At the end of the first sample execution, the condition in line 35 is true—more than eight students passed the exam, so the program outputs a message indicating that the instructor should receive a bonus.

4.11 Assignment Operators

C++ provides several **assignment operators** for abbreviating assignment expressions. For example, the statement

```
c = c + 3;
```

can be abbreviated with the **addition assignment operator +=** as

```
c += 3;
```

The += operator adds the value of the expression on the right of the operator to the value of the variable on the left of the operator and stores the result in the variable on the left of the operator. Any statement of the form

variable = *variable operator expression*;

in which the same *variable* appears on both sides of the assignment operator and *operator* is one of the binary operators +, -, *, /, or % (or others we'll discuss later in the text), can be written in the form

variable operator= expression;

Thus the assignment c += 3 adds 3 to c. Figure 4.17 shows the arithmetic assignment operators, sample expressions using these operators and explanations.

Assignment operator	Sample expression	Explanation	Assigns
Assume: int c = 3, d = 5, e = 4, f = 6, g = 12;			
+=	c += 7	c = c + 7	10 to c
-=	d -= 4	d = d - 4	1 to d
*=	e *= 5	e = e * 5	20 to e
/=	f /= 3	f = f / 3	2 to f
%=	g %= 9	g = g % 9	3 to g

Fig. 4.17 | Arithmetic assignment operators.

4.12 Increment and Decrement Operators

In addition to the arithmetic assignment operators, C++ also provides two unary operators for adding 1 to or subtracting 1 from the value of a numeric variable. These are the unary increment operator, ++, and the unary **decrement operator**, --, which are summarized in Fig. 4.18. A program can increment by 1 the value of a variable called c using the increment operator, ++, rather than the expression c = c + 1 or c += 1. An increment or decrement operator that is prefixed to (placed before) a variable is referred to as the **prefix increment** or **prefix decrement operator**, respectively. An increment or decrement operator that is postfixed to (placed after) a variable is referred to as the **postfix increment** or **postfix decrement operator**, respectively.

Operator	Called	Sample expression	Explanation
++	preincrement	++a	Increment a by 1, then use the new value of a in the expression in which a resides.
++	postincrement	a++	Use the current value of a in the expression in which a resides, then increment a by 1.
--	predecrement	--b	Decrement b by 1, then use the new value of b in the expression in which b resides.
--	postdecrement	b--	Use the current value of b in the expression in which b resides, then decrement b by 1.

Fig. 4.18 | Increment and decrement operators.

Using the prefix increment (or decrement) operator to add (or subtract) 1 from a variable is known as **preincrementing** (or **predecrementing**) the variable. Preincrementing (or predecrementing) causes the variable to be incremented (decremented) by 1, then the new value of the variable is used in the expression in which it appears. Using the postfix increment (or decrement) operator to add (or subtract) 1 from a variable is known as **postincrementing** (or **postdecrementing**) the variable. Postincrementing (or postdecrementing) causes the current value of the variable to be used in the expression in which it appears, then the variable's value is incremented (decremented) by 1.

Good Programming Practice 4.9
Unlike binary operators, the unary increment and decrement operators should be placed next to their operands, with no intervening spaces.

Figure 4.19 demonstrates the difference between the prefix increment and postfix increment versions of the ++ increment operator. The decrement operator (--) works similarly. This example does not contain a class—it contains just a source code file with function main performing all the application's work. In this chapter and in Chapter 3, you've seen examples consisting of one class (including the header and source code files for this class), as well as another source code file testing the class. This source code file contained function main, which created an object of the class and called its member functions. In this example, we simply want to show the mechanics of the ++ operator, so we use only one source code file with function main. Occasionally, when it does not make sense to try to create a reusable class to demonstrate a simple concept, we'll use a mechanical example contained entirely within the main function of a single source code file.

```cpp
 1   // Fig. 4.19: fig04_19.cpp
 2   // Preincrementing and postincrementing.
 3   #include <iostream>
 4   using namespace std;
 5
 6   int main()
 7   {
 8      int c;
 9
10      // demonstrate postincrement
11      c = 5; // assign 5 to c
12      cout << c << endl; // print 5
13      cout << c++ << endl; // print 5 then postincrement
14      cout << c << endl; // print 6
15
16      cout << endl; // skip a line
17
18      // demonstrate preincrement
19      c = 5; // assign 5 to c
20      cout << c << endl; // print 5
21      cout << ++c << endl; // preincrement then print 6
22      cout << c << endl; // print 6
23   } // end main
```

```
5
5
6

5
6
6
```

Fig. 4.19 | Preincrementing and postincrementing.

Line 11 initializes c to 5, and line 12 outputs c's initial value. Line 13 outputs the value of the expression c++. This postincrements the variable c, so c's original value (5) is output, then c's value is incremented. Thus, line 13 outputs c's initial value (5) again. Line 14 outputs c's new value (6) to prove that the variable's value was incremented in line 13.

Line 19 resets c's value to 5, and line 20 outputs that value. Line 21 outputs the value of the expression ++c. This expression preincrements c, so its value is incremented, then the new value (6) is output. Line 22 outputs c's value again to show that the value of c is still 6 after line 21 executes.

The arithmetic assignment operators and the increment and decrement operators can be used to simplify program statements. The three assignment statements in Fig. 4.16:

```cpp
passes = passes + 1;
failures = failures + 1;
studentCounter = studentCounter + 1;
```

can be written more concisely with assignment operators as

```cpp
passes += 1;
failures += 1;
studentCounter += 1;
```

with prefix increment operators as

```
++passes;
++failures;
++studentCounter;
```

or with postfix increment operators as

```
passes++;
failures++;
studentCounter++;
```

When you increment (++) or decrement (--) a variable in a statement by itself, the preincrement and postincrement forms have the same effect, and the predecrement and postdecrement forms have the same effect. It's only when a variable appears in the context of a larger expression that preincrementing the variable and postincrementing the variable have different effects (and similarly for predecrementing and postdecrementing).

Common Programming Error 4.14

Attempting to use the increment or decrement operator on an expression other than a modifiable variable name or reference, e.g., writing ++(x + 1), is a syntax error.

Figure 4.20 shows the precedence and associativity of the operators introduced to this point. The operators are shown top-to-bottom in decreasing order of precedence. The second column indicates the associativity of the operators at each level of precedence. Notice that the conditional operator (?:), the unary operators preincrement (++), predecrement (--), plus (+) and minus (-), and the assignment operators =, +=, -=, *=, /= and %= associate from right to left. All other operators in the operator precedence chart of Fig. 4.20 associate from left to right. The third column names the various groups of operators.

Operators			Associativity	Type
::			left to right	scope resolution
()			left to right	parentheses
++	--	static_cast<*type*>()	left to right	unary (postfix)
++	--	+ -	right to left	unary (prefix)
*	/	%	left to right	multiplicative
+	-		left to right	additive
<<	>>		left to right	insertion/extraction
<	<=	> >=	left to right	relational
==	!=		left to right	equality
?:			right to left	conditional
=	+=	-= *= /= %=	right to left	assignment

Fig. 4.20 | Operator precedence for the operators encountered so far in the text.

4.13 Wrap-Up

This chapter presented basic problem-solving techniques that you use in building classes and developing member functions for these classes. We demonstrated how to construct an algorithm (i.e., an approach to solving a problem) in pseudocode, then how to refine the algorithm through pseudocode development, resulting in C++ code that can be executed as part of a function. You learned how to use top-down, stepwise refinement to plan out the actions that a function must perform and the order in which it must perform them.

You learned that only three types of control structures—sequence, selection and repetition—are needed to develop any algorithm. We demonstrated two of C++'s selection statements—the if single-selection statement and the if...else double-selection statement. The if statement is used to execute a set of statements based on a condition—if the condition is true, the statements execute; if it isn't, the statements are skipped. The if...else double-selection statement is used to execute one set of statements if a condition is true, and another set of statements if the condition is false. We then discussed the while repetition statement, where a set of statements are executed repeatedly as long as a condition is true. We used control-statement stacking to total and compute the average of a set of student grades with counter- and sentinel-controlled repetition, and we used control-statement nesting to analyze and make decisions based on a set of exam results. We introduced assignment operators, which can be used for abbreviating statements. We presented the increment and decrement operators, which can be used to add or subtract the value 1 from a variable. In Chapter 5, Control Statements: Part 2, we continue our discussion of control statements, introducing the for, do...while and switch statements.

Summary

Section 4.2 Algorithms
- An algorithm is a procedure for solving a problem in terms of the actions to execute and the order in which to execute them.
- Specifying the order in which statements execute in a program is called program control.

Section 4.3 Pseudocode
- Pseudocode helps you think out a program before writing it in a programming language.
- Activity diagrams are part of the UML—an industry standard for modeling software systems.

Section 4.4 Control Structures
- An activity diagram models the workflow (also called the activity) of a software system.
- Activity diagrams are composed of symbols, such as action state symbols, diamonds and small circles, that are connected by transition arrows representing the flow of the activity.
- Like pseudocode, activity diagrams help you develop and represent algorithms.
- An action state is represented as a rectangle with its left and right sides replaced with arcs curving outward. The action expression appears inside the action state.
- The arrows in an activity diagram represent transitions, which indicate the order in which the actions represented by action states occur.
- The solid circle in an activity diagram represents the initial state—the beginning of the workflow before the program performs the modeled actions.

- The solid circle surrounded by a hollow circle that appears at the bottom of the activity diagram represents the final state—the end of the workflow after the program performs its actions.
- Rectangles with the upper-right corners folded over are called notes in the UML. A dotted line connects each note with the element that the note describes.
- A decision symbol in an activity diagram indicates that a decision is to be made. The workflow follows a path determined by the associated guard conditions. Each transition arrow emerging from a decision symbol has a guard condition. If a guard condition is true, the workflow enters the action state to which the transition arrow points.
- A merge symbol has two or more transition arrows pointing to the diamond and only one transition arrow pointing from it, to indicate multiple activity flows merging to continue the activity.
- Top-down, stepwise refinement is a process for refining pseudocode by maintaining a complete representation of the program during each refinement.
- There are three types of control structures—sequence, selection and repetition.
- The sequence structure is built in—by default, statements execute in the order they appear.
- A selection structure chooses among alternative courses of action.

Section 4.5 `if` Selection Statement
- The `if` single-selection statement either performs (selects) an action if a condition is true, or skips the action if the condition is false.

Section 4.6 `if...else` Double-Selection Statement
- The `if...else` double-selection statement performs (selects) an action if a condition is true and performs a different action if the condition is false.
- To include several statements in an `if`'s body (or the body of an `else` for an `if...else` statement), enclose the statements in braces ({ and }). A set of statements contained in braces is called a block. A block can be placed anywhere in a program that a single statement can be placed.
- A null statement, indicating that no action is to be taken, is indicated by a semicolon (;).

Section 4.7 `while` Repetition Statement
- A repetition statement repeats an action while some condition remains true.
- A value that contains a fractional part is referred to as a floating-point number and is represented approximately by data types such as `float` and `double`.

Section 4.8 Formulating Algorithms: Counter-Controlled Repetition
- Counter-controlled repetition is used when the number of repetitions is known before a loop begins executing, i.e., when there is definite repetition.
- The unary cast operator `static_cast<double>` can be used to create a temporary floating-point copy of its operand.
- Unary operators take only one operand; binary operators take two.
- The parameterized stream manipulator `setprecision` indicates the number of digits of precision that should be displayed to the right of the decimal point.
- The stream manipulator `fixed` indicates that floating-point values should be output in so-called fixed-point format, as opposed to scientific notation.

Section 4.9 Formulating Algorithms: Sentinel-Controlled Repetition
- Sentinel-controlled repetition is used when the number of repetitions is not known before a loop begins executing, i.e., when there is indefinite repetition.

Section 4.10 Formulating Algorithms: Nested Control Statements
- A nested control statement appears in the body of another control statement.

Section 4.11 Assignment Operators
- The arithmetic operators +=, -=, *=, /= and %= abbreviate assignment expressions.

Section 4.12 Increment and Decrement Operators
- The increment operator, ++, and the decrement operator, --, increment or decrement a variable by 1, respectively. If the operator is prefixed to the variable, the variable is incremented or decremented by 1 first, then its new value is used in the expression in which it appears. If the operator is postfixed to the variable, the variable is first used in the expression in which it appears, then the variable's value is incremented or decremented by 1.

Terminology

action/decision model of programming 116
action 110
action expression 113
action state symbol 113
activity 113
activity diagram 112
addition assignment operator (+=) 144
algorithm 110
assignment operators 144
block 121
bool fundamental type 116
cast operator 133
compound statement 121
conditional expression 118
conditional operator (?:) 118
control-statement nesting 115
control-statement stacking 115
control statements 111
control structures 112
counter 124
counter-controlled repetition 124
"crashing" 132
dangling-else problem 120
decision symbol 116
decrement operator (--) 145
default precision 139
definite repetition 124
diamond 113
divide by zero 132
do...while repetition statement 114
double fundamental type 133
double-precision floating-point number 137
double-selection statement 114
dummy value 130
empty statement 121

executable statement 111
explicit conversion 138
false 116
fatal logic error 132
final state symbol 113
first refinement 130
fixed 139
fixed-point format 139
fixed stream manipulator 139
flag value 130
float fundamental type 133
floating-point constants 137
floating-point number 133
for repetition statement 114
"garbage" value 127
goto elimination 112
goto statement 112
guard condition 116
implicit conversion 138
increment operator (++) 145
indefinite repetition 130
initial state 113
iteration of a loop 124
loop-continuation condition 114
looping statement 114
loops 114
merge symbol 122
multiple-selection statement 114
multiplicative operator 138
nested control statement 139
nested if...else statement 118
nonparameterized stream manipulator 139
note in the UML 113
null statement 121
off-by-one error 129
order 110

Self-Review Exercises

4.1 Answer each of the following questions.
   a) All programs can be written in terms of three types of control structures: _____,
      _____ and _____.
   b) The _____ selection statement is used to execute one action when a condition is true
      or a different action when that condition is false.
   c) Repeating a set of instructions a specific number of times is called _____ repeti-
      tion.
   d) When it isn't known in advance how many times a set of statements will be repeated,
      a(n) _____ value can be used to terminate the repetition.

4.2 Write four different C++ statements that each add 1 to integer variable x.

4.3 Write C++ statements to accomplish each of the following:
   a) In one statement, assign the sum of the current value of x and y to z and postincrement
      the value of x.
   b) Determine whether the value of the variable count is greater than 10. If it is, print
      "Count is greater than 10."
   c) Predecrement the variable x by 1, then subtract it from the variable total.
   d) Calculate the remainder after q is divided by divisor and assign the result to q. Write
      this statement two different ways.

4.4 Write C++ statements to accomplish each of the following tasks.
   a) Declare variables sum and x to be of type int.
   b) Set variable x to 1.
   c) Set variable sum to 0.

     d) Add variable x to variable sum and assign the result to variable sum.

     e) Print "The sum is: " followed by the value of variable sum.

4.5   Combine the statements that you wrote in Exercise 4.4 into a program that calculates and prints the sum of the integers from 1 to 10. Use the while statement to loop through the calculation and increment statements. The loop should terminate when the value of x becomes 11.

4.6   State the values of *each* variable after the calculation is performed. Assume that, when each statement begins executing, all variables have the integer value 5.

     a) `product *= x++;`

     b) `quotient /= ++x;`

4.7   Write single C++ statements or portions of statements that do the following:

     a) Input integer variable x with cin and >>.

     b) Input integer variable y with cin and >>.

     c) Set integer variable i to 1.

     d) Set integer variable power to 1.

     e) Multiply variable power by x and assign the result to power.

     f) Preincrement variable i by 1.

     g) Determine whether i is less than or equal to y.

     h) Output integer variable power with cout and <<.

4.8   Write a C++ program that uses the statements in Exercise 4.7 to calculate x raised to the y power. The program should have a while repetition statement.

4.9   Identify and correct the errors in each of the following:

     a)
```
while ( c <= 5 )
   {
       product *= c;
       ++c;
```

     b) `cin << value;`

     c)
```
if ( gender == 1 )
       cout << "Woman" << endl;
   else;
       cout << "Man" << endl;
```

4.10   What's wrong with the following while repetition statement?

```
while ( z >= 0 )
   sum += z;
```

Answers to Self-Review Exercises

4.1   a) Sequence, selection and repetition. b) if...else. c) Counter-controlled or definite. d) Sentinel, signal, flag or dummy.

4.2
```
x = x + 1;
x += 1;
++x;
x++;
```

4.3   a) `z = x++ + y;`

     b)
```
if ( count > 10 )
       cout << "Count is greater than 10" << endl;
```

     c) `total -= --x;`

     d)
```
q %= divisor;
   q = q % divisor;
```

4.4 a) `int sum;`
       `int x;`
    b) `x = 1;`
    c) `sum = 0;`
    d) `sum += x;`
      or
      `sum = sum + x;`
    e) `cout << "The sum is: " << sum << endl;`

4.5 See the following code:

```
1   // Exercise 4.5 Solution: ex04_05.cpp
2   // Calculate the sum of the integers from 1 to 10.
3   #include <iostream>
4   using namespace std;
5
6   int main()
7   {
8      int sum; // stores sum of integers 1 to 10
9      int x; // counter
10
11     x = 1; // count from 1
12     sum = 0; // initialize sum
13
14     while ( x <= 10 ) // loop 10 times
15     {
16        sum += x; // add x to sum
17        ++x; // increment x
18     } // end while
19
20     cout << "The sum is: " << sum << endl;
21  } // end main
```

```
The sum is: 55
```

4.6 a) `product = 25, x = 6;`
    b) `quotient = 0, x = 6;`

```
1   // Exercise 4.6 Solution: ex04_06.cpp
2   // Calculate the value of product and quotient.
3   #include <iostream>
4   using namespace std;
5
6   int main()
7   {
8      int x = 5;
9      int product = 5;
10     int quotient = 5;
11
12     // part a
13     product *= x++; // part a statement
14     cout << "Value of product after calculation: " << product << endl;
15     cout << "Value of x after calculation: " << x << endl << endl;
16
```

```
17      // part b
18      x = 5; // reset value of x
19      quotient /= ++x; // part b statement
20      cout << "Value of quotient after calculation: " << quotient << endl;
21      cout << "Value of x after calculation: " << x << endl << endl;
22    } // end main
```

```
Value of product after calculation: 25
Value of x after calculation: 6

Value of quotient after calculation: 0
Value of x after calculation: 6
```

4.7   a) cin >> x;
       b) cin >> y;
       c) i = 1;
       d) power = 1;
       e) power *= x;
           or
           power = power * x;
       f) ++i;
       g) if (i <= y)
       h) cout << power << endl;

4.8   See the following code:

```
 1    // Exercise 4.8 Solution: ex04_08.cpp
 2    // Raise x to the y power.
 3    #include <iostream>
 4    using namespace std;
 5
 6    int main()
 7    {
 8       int x; // base
 9       int y; // exponent
10       int i; // counts from 1 to y
11       int power; // used to calculate x raised to power y
12
13       i = 1; // initialize i to begin counting from 1
14       power = 1; // initialize power
15
16       cout << "Enter base as an integer: ";  // prompt for base
17       cin >> x; // input base
18
19       cout << "Enter exponent as an integer: "; // prompt for exponent
20       cin >> y; // input exponent
21
22       // count from 1 to y and multiply power by x each time
23       while ( i <= y )
24       {
25          power *= x;
26          ++i;
27       } // end while
28
29       cout << power << endl; // display result
30    } // end main
```

```
Enter base as an integer: 2
Enter exponent as an integer: 3
8
```

4.9 a) *Error:* Missing the closing right brace of the `while` body.
Correction: Add closing right brace after the statement `c++;`.
b) *Error:* Used stream insertion instead of stream extraction.
Correction: Change `<<` to `>>`.
c) *Error:* Semicolon after `else` results in a logic error. The second output statement will always be executed.
Correction: Remove the semicolon after `else`.

4.10 The value of the variable `z` is never changed in the `while` statement. Therefore, if the loop-continuation condition (`z >= 0`) is initially `true`, an infinite loop is created. To prevent the infinite loop, `z` must be decremented so that it eventually becomes less than 0.

Exercises

4.11 Identify and correct the error(s) in each of the following:
a)
```
if ( age >= 65 );
    cout << "Age is greater than or equal to 65" << endl;
else
    cout << "Age is less than 65 << endl";
```
b)
```
if ( age >= 65 )
    cout << "Age is greater than or equal to 65" << endl;
else;
    cout << "Age is less than 65 << endl";
```
c)
```
int x = 1, total;

while ( x <= 10 )
{
    total += x;
    ++x;
}
```
d)
```
While ( x <= 100 )
    total += x;
    ++x;
```
e)
```
while ( y > 0 )
{
    cout << y << endl;
    ++y;
}
```

4.12 What does the following program print?

```
1    // Exercise 4.12: ex04_12.cpp
2    // What does this program print?
3    #include <iostream>
4    using namespace std;
5
6    int main()
7    {
```

```
8    int y; // declare y
9    int x = 1; // initialize x
10   int total = 0; // initialize total
11
12   while ( x <= 10 ) // loop 10 times
13   {
14      y = x * x; // perform calculation
15      cout << y << endl; // output result
16      total += y; // add y to total
17      x++; // increment counter x
18   } // end while
19
20   cout << "Total is " << total << endl; // display result
21 } // end main
```

For Exercises 4.13–4.16, perform each of these steps:

    a) Read the problem statement.
    b) Formulate the algorithm using pseudocode and top-down, stepwise refinement.
    c) Write a C++ program.
    d) Test, debug and execute the C++ program.

4.13 *(Gas Mileage)* Drivers are concerned with the mileage obtained by their automobiles. One driver has kept track of several tankfuls of gasoline by recording miles driven and gallons used for each tankful. Develop a C++ program that uses a while statement to input the miles driven and gallons used for each tankful. The program should calculate and display the miles per gallon obtained for each tankful and print the combined miles per gallon obtained for all tankfuls up to this point.

```
Enter miles driven (-1 to quit): 287
Enter gallons used: 13
MPG this tankful: 22.076923
Total MPG: 22.076923

Enter miles driven (-1 to quit): 200
Enter gallons used: 10
MPG this tankful: 20.000000
Total MPG: 21.173913

Enter the miles driven (-1 to quit): 120
Enter gallons used: 5
MPG this tankful: 24.000000
Total MPG: 21.678571

Enter the miles used (-1 to quit): -1
```

4.14 *(Credit Limit Calculator)* Develop a C++ program that will determine whether a department-store customer has exceeded the credit limit on a charge account. For each customer, the following facts are available:

    a) Account number (an integer)
    b) Balance at the beginning of the month
    c) Total of all items charged by this customer this month
    d) Total of all credits applied to this customer's account this month
    e) Allowed credit limit

The program should use a while statement to input each of these facts, calculate the new balance (= beginning balance + charges − credits) and determine whether the new balance exceeds the customer's credit limit. For those customers whose credit limit is exceeded, the program should display the customer's account number, credit limit, new balance and the message "Credit Limit Exceeded."

```
Enter account number (or -1 to quit): 100
Enter beginning balance: 5394.78
Enter total charges: 1000.00
Enter total credits: 500.00
Enter credit limit: 5500.00
New balance is 5894.78
Account:        100
Credit limit: 5500.00
Balance:       5894.78
Credit Limit Exceeded.

Enter Account Number (or -1 to quit): 200
Enter beginning balance: 1000.00
Enter total charges: 123.45
Enter total credits: 321.00
Enter credit limit: 1500.00
New balance is 802.45

Enter Account Number (or -1 to quit): -1
```

4.15 *(Sales Commission Calculator)* A large company pays its salespeople on a commission basis. The salespeople each receive $200 per week plus 9% of their gross sales for that week. For example, a salesperson who sells $5000 worth of chemicals in a week receives $200 plus 9% of $5000, or a total of $650. Develop a C++ program that uses a while statement to input each salesperson's gross sales for last week and calculates and displays that salesperson's earnings. Process one salesperson's figures at a time.

```
Enter sales in dollars (-1 to end): 5000.00
Salary is: $650.00

Enter sales in dollars (-1 to end): 6000.00
Salary is: $740.00

Enter sales in dollars (-1 to end): 7000.00
Salary is: $830.00

Enter sales in dollars (-1 to end): -1
```

4.16 *(Salary Calculator)* Develop a C++ program that uses a while statement to determine the gross pay for each of several employees. The company pays "straight time" for the first 40 hours worked by each employee and pays "time-and-a-half" for all hours worked in excess of 40 hours. You are given a list of the employees of the company, the number of hours each employee worked last week and the hourly rate of each employee. Your program should input this information for each employee and should determine and display the employee's gross pay.

```
Enter hours worked (-1 to end): 39
Enter hourly rate of the employee ($00.00): 10.00
Salary is $390.00

Enter hours worked (-1 to end): 40
Enter hourly rate of the employee ($00.00): 10.00
Salary is $400.00

Enter hours worked (-1 to end): 41
Enter hourly rate of the employee ($00.00): 10.00
Salary is $415.00

Enter hours worked (-1 to end): -1
```

4.17 *(Find the Largest)* The process of finding the largest number (i.e., the maximum of a group of numbers) is used frequently in computer applications. For example, a program that determines the winner of a sales contest inputs the number of units sold by each salesperson. The salesperson who sells the most units wins the contest. Write a C++ program that uses a while statement to determine and print the largest number of 10 numbers input by the user. Your program should use three variables, as follows:

counter:	A counter to count to 10 (i.e., to keep track of how many numbers have been input and to determine when all 10 numbers have been processed).
number:	The current number input to the program.
largest:	The largest number found so far.

4.18 *(Tabular Output)* Write a C++ program that uses a while statement and the tab escape sequence \t to print the following table of values:

N	10*N	100*N	1000*N
1	10	100	1000
2	20	200	2000
3	30	300	3000
4	40	400	4000
5	50	500	5000

4.19 *(Find the Two Largest Numbers)* Using an approach similar to that in Exercise 4.17, find the *two* largest values among the 10 numbers. [*Note:* You must input each number only once.]

4.20 *(Validating User Input)* The examination-results program of Fig. 4.16 assumes that any value input by the user that is not a 1 must be a 2. Modify the application to validate its inputs. On any input, if the value entered is other than 1 or 2, keep looping until the user enters a correct value.

4.21 What does the following program print?

```cpp
1   // Exercise 4.21: ex04_21.cpp
2   // What does this program print?
3   #include <iostream>
4   using namespace std;
5
6   int main()
7   {
8      int count = 1; // initialize count
9
10     while ( count <= 10 ) // loop 10 times
11     {
12        // output line of text
13        cout << ( count % 2 ? "****" : "++++++++" ) << endl;
14        ++count; // increment count
15     } // end while
16  } // end main
```

4.22 What does the following program print?

```cpp
1   // Exercise 4.22: ex04_22.cpp
2   // What does this program print?
3   #include <iostream>
4   using namespace std;
5
```

```
6   int main()
7   {
8      int row = 10; // initialize row
9      int column; // declare column
10
11     while ( row >= 1 ) // loop until row < 1
12     {
13        column = 1; // set column to 1 as iteration begins
14
15        while ( column <= 10 ) // loop 10 times
16        {
17           cout << ( row % 2 ? "<" : ">" ); // output
18           ++column; // increment column
19        } // end inner while
20
21        --row; // decrement row
22        cout << endl; // begin new output line
23     } // end outer while
24  } // end main
```

4.23   *(Dangling-else Problem)* State the output for each of the following when x is 9 and y is 11 and when x is 11 and y is 9. The compiler ignores the indentation in a C++ program. The C++ compiler always associates an else with the previous if unless told to do otherwise by the placement of braces {}. On first glance, you may not be sure which if and else match, so this is referred to as the "dangling-else" problem. We eliminated the indentation from the following code to make the problem more challenging. [*Hint:* Apply indentation conventions you've learned.]

a)
```
if ( x < 10 )
if ( y > 10 )
cout << "*****" << endl;
else
cout << "#####" << endl;
cout << "$$$$$" << endl;
```

b)
```
if ( x < 10 )
{
if ( y > 10 )
cout << "*****" << endl;
}
else
{
cout << "#####" << endl;
cout << "$$$$$" << endl;
}
```

4.24   *(Another Dangling-else Problem)* Modify the following code to produce the output shown. Use proper indentation techniques. You must not make any changes other than inserting braces. The compiler ignores indentation in a C++ program. We eliminated the indentation from the following code to make the problem more challenging. [*Note:* It's possible that no modification is necessary.]

```
if ( y == 8 )
if ( x == 5 )
cout << "@@@@@" << endl;
else
cout << "#####" << endl;
cout << "$$$$$" << endl;
cout << "&&&&&" << endl;
```

a) Assuming x = 5 and y = 8, the following output is produced.

```
@@@@@
$$$$$
&&&&&
```

b) Assuming x = 5 and y = 8, the following output is produced.

```
@@@@@
```

c) Assuming x = 5 and y = 8, the following output is produced.

```
@@@@@
&&&&&
```

d) Assuming x = 5 and y = 7, the following output is produced. [*Note:* The last three output statements after the else are all part of a block.]

```
#####
$$$$$
&&&&&
```

4.25 *(Square of Asterisks)* Write a program that reads in the size of the side of a square then prints a hollow square of that size out of asterisks and blanks. Your program should work for squares of all side sizes between 1 and 20. For example, if your program reads a size of 5, it should print

```
*****
*   *
*   *
*   *
*****
```

4.26 *(Palindromes)* A palindrome is a number or a text phrase that reads the same backward as forward. For example, each of the following five-digit integers is a palindrome: 12321, 55555, 45554 and 11611. Write a program that reads in a five-digit integer and determines whether it's a palindrome. [*Hint:* Use the division and modulus operators to separate the number into its individual digits.]

4.27 *(Printing the Decimmal Equivalent of a Binary Number)* Input an integer containing only 0s and 1s (i.e., a "binary" integer) and print its decimal equivalent. Use the modulus and division operators to pick off the "binary" number's digits one at a time from right to left. Much as in the decimal number system, where the rightmost digit has a positional value of 1, the next digit left has a positional value of 10, then 100, then 1000, and so on, in the binary number system the rightmost digit has a positional value of 1, the next digit left has a positional value of 2, then 4, then 8, and so on. Thus the decimal number 234 can be interpreted as 2 * 100 + 3 * 10 + 4 * 1. The decimal equivalent of binary 1101 is 1 * 1 + 0 * 2 + 1 * 4 + 1 * 8 or 1 + 0 + 4 + 8, or 13. [*Note:* To learn more about binary numbers, refer to Appendix D.]

4.28 *(Checkerboard Pattern of Asterisks)* Write a program that displays the checkerboard pattern shown below. Your program must use only three output statements, one of each of the following forms:

```
cout << "* ";
cout << ' ';
cout << endl;
```

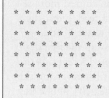

4.29 *(Multiples of 2 with an Infinite Loop)* Write a program that prints the powers of the integer 2, namely 2, 4, 8, 16, 32, 64, etc. Your while loop should not terminate (i.e., you should create an infinite loop). To do this, simply use the keyword true as the expression for the while statement. What happens when you run this program?

4.30 Write a program that reads the radius of a circle (as a double value) and computes and prints the diameter, the circumference and the area. Use the value 3.14159 for π.

4.31 What's wrong with the following statement? Provide the correct statement to accomplish what the programmer was probably trying to do.

```
cout << ++( x + y );
```

4.32 *(Sides of a Triangle)* Write a program that reads three nonzero double values and determines and prints whether they could represent the sides of a triangle.

4.33 *(Sides of a Right Triangle)* Write a program that reads three nonzero integers and determines and prints whether they could be the sides of a right triangle.

4.34 *(Factorial)* The factorial of a nonnegative integer n is written $n!$ (pronounced "n factorial") and is defined as follows:

$n! = n \cdot (n-1) \cdot (n-2) \cdot \ldots \cdot 1$ (for values of n greater than 1)

and

$n! = 1$ (for $n = 0$ or $n = 1$).

For example, $5! = 5 \cdot 4 \cdot 3 \cdot 2 \cdot 1$, which is 120. Use while statements in each of the following:

a) Write a program that reads a nonnegative integer and computes and prints its factorial.

b) Write a program that estimates the value of the mathematical constant e by using the formula:

$$e = 1 + \frac{1}{1!} + \frac{1}{2!} + \frac{1}{3!} + \ldots$$

Prompt the user for the desired accuracy of e (i.e., the number of terms in the summation).

c) Write a program that computes the value of e^x by using the formula

$$e^x = 1 + \frac{x}{1!} + \frac{x^2}{2!} + \frac{x^3}{3!} + \ldots$$

Prompt the user for the desired accuracy of e (i.e., the number of terms in the summation).

Making a Difference

4.35 *(Enforcing Privacy with Cryptography)* The explosive growth of Internet communications and data storage on Internet-connected computers has greatly increased privacy concerns. The field of cryptography is concerned with coding data to make it difficult (and hopefully—with the most advanced schemes—impossible) for unauthorized users to read. In this exercise you'll investigate a simple scheme for encrypting and decrypting data. A company that wants to send data over the Internet has asked you to write a program that will encrypt it so that it may be transmitted more securely. All the data is transmitted as four-digit integers. Your application should read a four-digit integer entered by the user and encrypt it as follows: Replace each digit with the result of adding 7 to the digit and getting the remainder after dividing the new value by 10. Then swap the first digit with the third, and swap the second digit with the fourth. Then print the encrypted integer. Write a separate application that inputs an encrypted four-digit integer and decrypts it (by reversing the encryption scheme) to form the original number. [*Optional reading project:* Research "public key cryptography" in general and the PGP (Pretty Good Privacy) specific public key scheme. You may also want to investigate the RSA scheme, which is widely used in industrial-strength applications.]

4.36 *(World Population Growth)* World population has grown considerably over the centuries. Continued growth could eventually challenge the limits of breathable air, drinkable water, arable cropland and other limited resources. There is evidence that growth has been slowing in recent years and that world population could peak some time this century, then start to decline.

For this exercise, research world population growth issues online. *Be sure to investigate various viewpoints.* Get estimates for the current world population and its growth rate (the percentage by which it is likely to increase this year). Write a program that calculates world population growth each year for the next 75 years, *using the simplifying assumption that the current growth rate will stay constant.* Print the results in a table. The first column should display the year from year 1 to year 75. The second column should display the anticipated world population at the end of that year. The third column should display the numerical increase in the world population that would occur that year. Using your results, determine the year in which the population would be double what it is today, if this year's growth rate were to persist.

Control Statements: Part 2

5

Not everything that can be counted counts, and not every thing that counts can be counted.
—Albert Einstein

Who can control his fate?
—William Shakespeare

The used key is always bright.
—Benjamin Franklin

Intelligence ... is the faculty of making artificial objects, especially tools to make tools.
—Henri Bergson

Objectives

In this chapter you'll learn:

- The essentials of counter-controlled repetition.

- To use **for** and **do...while** to execute statements in a program repeatedly.

- To implement multiple selection using the **switch** selection statement.

- How **break** and **continue** alter the flow of control.

- To use the logical operators to form complex conditional expressions in control statements.

- To avoid the consequences of confusing the equality and assignment operators.

5.1 Introduction

Chapter 4 began our introduction to the types of building blocks that are available for problem solving. We used those building blocks to employ proven program construction techniques. In this chapter, we continue our presentation of structured programming by introducing C++'s remaining control statements. The control statements we study here and in Chapter 4 will help us in building and manipulating objects. We continue our early emphasis on object-oriented programming that began with a discussion of basic concepts in Chapter 1 and extensive object-oriented code examples and exercises in Chapters 3–4.

In this chapter, we demonstrate the `for`, `do...while` and `switch` statements. Through short examples using `while` and `for`, we explore counter-controlled repetition. We expand the `GradeBook` class presented in Chapters 3–4. In particular, we create a version of class `GradeBook` that uses a `switch` statement to count the number of A, B, C, D and F grades in a set of letter grades entered by the user. We introduce the `break` and `continue` program control statements. We discuss the logical operators, which enable you to use more powerful conditional expressions. We also examine the common error of confusing the equality (==) and assignment (=) operators, and how to avoid it. Finally, we summarize C++'s control statements and the proven problem-solving techniques presented in this chapter and Chapter 4.

5.2 Essentials of Counter-Controlled Repetition

This section uses the `while` repetition statement to formalize the elements required to perform counter-controlled repetition. Counter-controlled repetition requires

1. the **name of a control variable** (or loop counter)

2. the **initial value** of the control variable

3. the **loop-continuation condition** that tests for the **final value** of the control variable (i.e., whether looping should continue)

4. the **increment** (or **decrement**) by which the control variable is modified each time through the loop.

The program in Fig. 5.1 prints the numbers from 1 to 10. The declaration in line 8 *names* the control variable (`counter`), declares it to be an integer, reserves space for it in memory and sets it to an *initial value* of 1. Declarations that require initialization are, in effect, executable statements. In C++, it's more precise to call a declaration that also reserves memory a **definition**. Because definitions are declarations, too, we'll use the term "declaration" except when the distinction is important.

```
1   // Fig. 5.1: fig05_01.cpp
2   // Counter-controlled repetition.
3   #include <iostream>
4   using namespace std;
5
6   int main()
7   {
8      int counter = 1; // declare and initialize control variable
9
10     while ( counter <= 10 ) // loop-continuation condition
11     {
12        cout << counter << " ";
13        counter++; // increment control variable by 1
14     } // end while
15
16     cout << endl; // output a newline
17  } // end main
```

```
1 2 3 4 5 6 7 8 9 10
```

Fig. 5.1 | Counter-controlled repetition.

The declaration and initialization of counter (line 8) also could have been accomplished with the statements

```
int counter; // declare control variable
counter = 1; // initialize control variable to 1
```

We use both methods of initializing variables.

Line 13 *increments* the loop counter by 1 each time the loop's body is performed. The loop-continuation condition (line 10) in the while statement determines whether the value of the control variable is less than or equal to 10 (the final value for which the condition is true). The body of this while executes even when the control variable is 10. The loop terminates when the control variable is greater than 10 (i.e., when counter is 11).

Figure 5.1 can be made more concise by initializing counter to 0 and by replacing the while statement with

```
while ( ++counter <= 10 ) // loop-continuation condition
   cout << counter << " ";
```

This code saves a statement, because the incrementing is done in the while condition before the condition is tested. Also, the code eliminates the braces around the body of the while, because the while now contains only one statement. Coding in such a condensed fashion can lead to programs that are more difficult to read, debug, modify and maintain.

Common Programming Error 5.1

Floating-point values are approximate, so controlling counting loops with floating-point variables can result in imprecise counter values and inaccurate tests for termination.

Error-Prevention Tip 5.1

Control counting loops with integer values.

Good Programming Practice 5.1

Put a blank line before and after each control statement to make it stand out in the program.

Good Programming Practice 5.2

Too many levels of nesting can make a program difficult to understand. As a rule, try to avoid using more than three levels of indentation.

Good Programming Practice 5.3

Vertical spacing above and below control statements and indentation of the bodies of control statements give programs a two-dimensional appearance that improves readability.

5.3 for Repetition Statement

In addition to while, C++ provides the **for repetition statement**, which specifies the counter-controlled repetition details in a single line of code. To illustrate the power of for, let's rewrite the program of Fig. 5.1. The result is shown in Fig. 5.2.

```cpp
1   // Fig. 5.2: fig05_02.cpp
2   // Counter-controlled repetition with the for statement.
3   #include <iostream>
4   using namespace std;
5
6   int main()
7   {
8      // for statement header includes initialization,
9      // loop-continuation condition and increment.
10     for ( int counter = 1; counter <= 10; counter++ )
11        cout << counter << " ";
12
13     cout << endl; // output a newline
14  } // end main
```

```
1 2 3 4 5 6 7 8 9 10
```

Fig. 5.2 | Counter-controlled repetition with the for statement.

When the for statement (lines 10–11) begins executing, the control variable counter is declared and initialized to 1. Then, the loop-continuation condition (line 10 between the semicolons) counter <= 10 is checked. The initial value of counter is 1, so the condition is satisfied and the body statement (line 11) prints the value of counter, namely 1. Then, the expression counter++ increments control variable counter and the loop begins again with the loop-continuation test. The control variable is now equal to 2, so the final value is not exceeded and the program performs the body statement again. This process continues until the loop body has executed 10 times and the control variable counter is incremented to 11—this causes the loop-continuation test to fail and repetition to terminate. The program continues by performing the first statement after the for statement (in this case, the output statement in line 13).

for *Statement Header Components*
Figure 5.3 takes a closer look at the for statement header (line 10) of Fig. 5.2. Notice that the for statement header "does it all"—it specifies each of the items needed for counter-controlled repetition with a control variable. If there is more than one statement in the body of the for, braces are required to enclose the body of the loop.

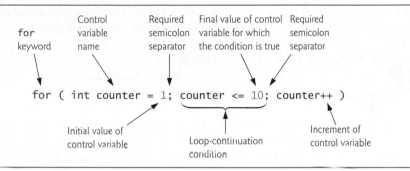

Fig. 5.3 | for statement header components.

If you incorrectly wrote counter < 10 as the loop-continuation condition in Fig. 5.2, then the loop would execute only 9 times. This is a common **off-by-one error**.

Common Programming Error 5.2
Using an incorrect relational operator or using an incorrect final value of a loop counter in the condition of a while *or* for *statement can cause off-by-one errors.*

Good Programming Practice 5.4
Using the final value in the condition of a while *or* for *statement and using the* <= *relational operator will help avoid off-by-one errors. For a loop used to print the values 1 to 10, for example, the loop-continuation condition should be* counter <= 10 *rather than* counter < 10 *(which is an off-by-one error) or* counter < 11 *(which is nevertheless correct). Many programmers prefer so-called* **zero-based counting***, in which, to count 10 times through the loop,* counter *would be initialized to zero and the loop-continuation test would be* counter < 10.

The general form of the for statement is

```
for ( initialization; loopContinuationCondition; increment )
    statement
```

where the *initialization* expression initializes the loop's control variable, *loopContinuationCondition* determines whether the loop should continue executing and *increment* increments the control variable. In most cases, the for statement can be represented by an equivalent while statement, as follows:

```
    initialization;

    while ( loopContinuationCondition )
    {
        statement
        increment;
    }
```

There is an exception to this rule, which we'll discuss in Section 5.7.

If the *initialization* expression declares the control variable (i.e., its type is specified before its name), the control variable can be used only in the body of the `for` statement—the control variable will be unknown outside the `for` statement. This restricted use of the control variable name is known as the variable's **scope**. The scope of a variable specifies where it can be used in a program. Scope is discussed in detail in Chapter 6.

Common Programming Error 5.3

When the control variable is declared in the initialization section of the `for` statement, using the control variable after the body is a compilation error.

As we'll see, the *initialization* and *increment* expressions can be comma-separated lists of expressions. The commas, as used in these expressions, are **comma operators**, which guarantee that lists of expressions evaluate from left to right. The comma operator has the lowest precedence of all C++ operators. The value and type of a comma-separated list of expressions is the value and type of the rightmost expression. The comma operator is often used in `for` statements. Its primary application is to enable you to use multiple initialization expressions and/or multiple increment expressions. For example, there may be several control variables in a single `for` statement that must be initialized and incremented.

Good Programming Practice 5.5

Place only expressions involving the control variables in the initialization and increment sections of a `for` statement. Manipulations of other variables should appear either before the loop (if they should execute only once, like initialization statements) or in the loop body (if they should execute once per repetition, like incrementing or decrementing statements).

The three expressions in the `for` statement header are optional (but the two semicolon separators are required). If the *loopContinuationCondition* is omitted, C++ assumes that the condition is true, thus creating an infinite loop. One might omit the *initialization* expression if the control variable is initialized earlier in the program. One might omit the *increment* expression if the increment is calculated by statements in the body of the `for` or if no increment is needed. The increment expression in the `for` statement acts as a stand-alone statement at the end of the body of the `for`. Therefore, the expressions

```
    counter = counter + 1
    counter += 1
    ++counter
    counter++
```

are all equivalent in the incrementing portion of the `for` statement's header (when no other code appears there). Many programmers prefer the form counter++, because for loops evaluate the increment expression after the loop body executes. The postincrementing form therefore seems more natural. The variable being incremented here does not appear in a larger expression, so both preincrementing and postincrementing actually have the same effect.

Common Programming Error 5.4
Using commas instead of the two required semicolons in a for *header is a syntax error.*

Common Programming Error 5.5
Placing a semicolon immediately to the right of the right parenthesis of a for *header makes the body of that* for *statement an empty statement. This is usually a logic error.*

The initialization, loop-continuation condition and increment expressions of a for statement can contain arithmetic expressions. For example, if x = 2 and y = 10, and x and y are not modified in the loop body, the for header

```
for ( int j = x; j <= 4 * x * y; j += y / x )
```

is equivalent to

```
for ( int j = 2; j <= 80; j += 5 )
```

The "increment" of a for statement can be negative, in which case it's really a decrement and the loop actually counts downward (as shown in Section 5.4).

If the loop-continuation condition is initially false, the body of the for statement is not performed. Instead, execution proceeds with the statement following the for.

Frequently, the control variable is printed or used in calculations in the body of a for statement, but this is not required. It's common to use the control variable for controlling repetition while never mentioning it in the body of the for statement.

Error-Prevention Tip 5.2
Although the value of the control variable can be changed in the body of a for *statement, avoid doing so, because this practice can lead to subtle logic errors.*

for *Statement UML Activity Diagram*

The for repetition statement's UML activity diagram is similar to that of the while statement (Fig. 4.6). Figure 5.4 shows the activity diagram of the for statement in Fig. 5.2. The diagram makes it clear that initialization occurs once before the loop-continuation test is evaluated the first time, and that incrementing occurs each time through the loop *after* the body statement executes. Note that (besides an initial state, transition arrows, a merge, a final state and several notes) the diagram contains only action states and a decision. Imagine, again, that you have a bin of empty for statement UML activity diagrams—as many as you might need to stack and nest with the activity diagrams of other control statements to form a structured implementation of an algorithm. You fill in the action states and decision symbols with action expressions and guard conditions appropriate to the algorithm.

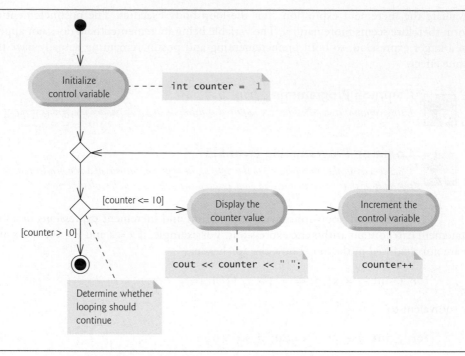

Fig. 5.4 | UML activity diagram for the for statement in Fig. 5.2.

5.4 Examples Using the for Statement

The following examples show methods of varying the control variable in a for statement. In each case, we write the appropriate for statement header. Note the change in the relational operator for loops that decrement the control variable.

a) Vary the control variable from 1 to 100 in increments of 1.

```
for ( int i = 1; i <= 100; i++ )
```

b) Vary the control variable from 100 down to 1 in decrements of 1.

```
for ( int i = 100; i >= 1; i-- )
```

c) Vary the control variable from 7 to 77 in steps of 7.

```
for ( int i = 7; i <= 77; i += 7 )
```

d) Vary the control variable from 20 down to 2 in steps of -2.

```
for ( int i = 20; i >= 2; i -= 2 )
```

e) Vary the control variable over the following sequence of values: 2, 5, 8, 11, 14, 17.

```
for ( int i = 2; i <= 17; i += 3 )
```

f) Vary the control variable over the following sequence of values: 99, 88, 77, 66, 55.

```
for ( int i = 99; i >= 55; i -= 11 )
```

Common Programming Error 5.6

Not using the proper relational operator in the loop-continuation condition of a loop that counts downward (such as incorrectly using i <= 1 instead of i >= 1 in a loop counting down to 1) is a logic error that yields incorrect results when the program runs.

Application: Summing the Even Integers from 2 to 20

The program of Fig. 5.5 uses a for statement to sum the even integers from 2 to 20. Each iteration of the loop (lines 11–12) adds control variable number's value to variable total.

```cpp
1   // Fig. 5.5: fig05_05.cpp
2   // Summing integers with the for statement.
3   #include <iostream>
4   using namespace std;
5
6   int main()
7   {
8      int total = 0; // initialize total
9
10     // total even integers from 2 through 20
11     for ( int number = 2; number <= 20; number += 2 )
12        total += number;
13
14     cout << "Sum is " << total << endl; // display results
15  } // end main
```

```
Sum is 110
```

Fig. 5.5 | Summing integers with the for statement.

The body of the for statement in Fig. 5.5 actually could be merged into the increment portion of the for header by using the comma operator as follows:

```cpp
for ( int number = 2; // initialization
      number <= 20; // loop continuation condition
      total += number, number += 2 ) // total and increment
   ; // empty body
```

Good Programming Practice 5.6

Although statements preceding a for and statements in the body of a for often can be merged into the for header, doing so can make the program more difficult to read, maintain, modify and debug.

Good Programming Practice 5.7

Limit the size of control statement headers to a single line, if possible.

Application: Compound Interest Calculations

Consider the following problem statement:

A person invests $1000.00 in a savings account yielding 5 percent interest. Assuming that all interest is left on deposit in the account, calculate and print the amount of *money in the account at the end of each year for 10 years. Use the following formula for determining these amounts:*

$$a = p\,(1 + r)^n$$

where

p *is the original amount invested (i.e., the principal),*
r *is the annual interest rate,*
n *is the number of years and*
a *is the amount on deposit at the end of the nth year.*

This problem involves a loop that performs the indicated calculation for each of the 10 years the money remains on deposit. The solution is shown in Fig. 5.6.

```cpp
1   // Fig. 5.6: fig05_06.cpp
2   // Compound interest calculations with for.
3   #include <iostream>
4   #include <iomanip>
5   #include <cmath> // standard C++ math library
6   using namespace std;
7
8   int main()
9   {
10     double amount; // amount on deposit at end of each year
11     double principal = 1000.0; // initial amount before interest
12     double rate = .05; // interest rate
13
14     // display headers
15     cout << "Year" << setw( 21 ) << "Amount on deposit" << endl;
16
17     // set floating-point number format
18     cout << fixed << setprecision( 2 );
19
20     // calculate amount on deposit for each of ten years
21     for ( int year = 1; year <= 10; year++ )
22     {
23        // calculate new amount for specified year
24        amount = principal * pow( 1.0 + rate, year );
25
26        // display the year and the amount
27        cout << setw( 4 ) << year << setw( 21 ) << amount << endl;
28     } // end for
29  } // end main
```

```
Year     Amount on deposit
  1            1050.00
  2            1102.50
  3            1157.63
  4            1215.51
  5            1276.28
  6            1340.10
  7            1407.10
  8            1477.46
  9            1551.33
 10            1628.89
```

Fig. 5.6 | Compound interest calculations with for.

The for statement (lines 21–28) executes its body 10 times, varying a control variable from 1 to 10 in increments of 1. C++ does not include an exponentiation operator, so we use the **standard library function pow** (line 24). The function pow(x, y) calculates the value of x raised to the yth power. In this example, the algebraic expression $(1 + r)^n$ is written as pow(1.0 + rate, year), where variable rate represents r and variable year represents n. Function pow takes two arguments of type double and returns a double value.

This program will not compile without including header file <cmath> (line 5). Function pow requires two double arguments. Variable year is an integer. Header <cmath> includes information that tells the compiler to convert the value of year to a temporary double representation before calling the function. This information is contained in pow's function prototype. Chapter 6 summarizes other math library functions.

Common Programming Error 5.7

Forgetting to include the appropriate header file when using standard library functions (e.g., <cmath> in a program that uses math library functions) is a compilation error.

A Caution about Using Type *float* or *double* for Monetary Amounts

Notice that lines 10–12 declare the double variables amount, principal and rate. We did this for simplicity because we're dealing with fractional parts of dollars, and we need a type that allows decimal points in its values. Unfortunately, this can cause trouble. Here is a simple explanation of what can go wrong when using float or double to represent dollar amounts (assuming setprecision(2) is used to specify two digits of precision when printing): Two dollar amounts stored in the machine could be 14.234 (which prints as 14.23) and 18.673 (which prints as 18.67). When these amounts are added, they produce the internal sum 32.907, which prints as 32.91. Thus your printout could appear as

```
   14.23
 + 18.67
 -------
   32.91
```

but a person adding the individual numbers as printed would expect the sum 32.90! You've been warned!

Good Programming Practice 5.8

Do not use variables of type float or double to perform monetary calculations. The imprecision of floating-point numbers can cause incorrect monetary values. In the exercises, we explore the use of integers to perform monetary calculations. [Note: Some third-party vendors sell C++ class libraries that perform precise monetary calculations.]

Using Stream Manipulators to Format Numeric Output

The output statement in line 18 before the for loop and the output statement in line 27 in the for loop combine to print the values of the variables year and amount with the formatting specified by the parameterized stream manipulators setprecision and **setw** and the nonparameterized stream manipulator fixed. The stream manipulator setw(4) specifies that the next value output should appear in a **field width** of 4—i.e., cout prints the value with at least 4 character positions. If the value to be output is less than 4 character positions wide, the value is **right justified** in the field by default. If the value to be output is more than 4 character positions wide, the field width is extended to accommodate the entire value. To indicate that values should be output **left justified**, simply output nonparameterized stream manipulator **left** (found in header <iostream>). Right justification can be restored by outputting nonparameterized stream manipulator **right**.

The other formatting in the output statements indicates that variable amount is printed as a fixed-point value with a decimal point (specified in line 18 with the stream manipulator fixed) right justified in a field of 21 character positions (specified in line 27 with setw(21)) and two digits of precision to the right of the decimal point (specified in line 18 with manipulator setprecision(2)). We applied the stream manipulators fixed and setprecision to the output stream (i.e., cout) before the for loop because these format settings remain in effect until they're changed—such settings are called **sticky settings** and they do not need to be applied during each iteration of the loop. However, the field width specified with setw applies only to the next value output. We discuss C++'s powerful input/output formatting capabilities in Chapter 15, Stream Input/Output.

The calculation 1.0 + rate, which appears as an argument to the pow function, is contained in the body of the for statement. In fact, this calculation produces the same result during each iteration of the loop, so repeating it's wasteful—it should be performed once before the loop.

Performance Tip 5.1
Avoid placing expressions whose values do not change inside loops—but, even if you do, many of today's sophisticated optimizing compilers will automatically place such expressions outside the loops in the generated machine-language code.

Performance Tip 5.2
Many compilers contain optimization features that improve the performance of the code you write, but it's still better to write good code from the start.

Be sure to try our Peter Minuit problem in Exercise 5.29. This problem demonstrates the wonders of compound interest.

5.5 do...while Repetition Statement

The do...while repetition statement is similar to the while statement. In the while statement, the loop-continuation condition test occurs at the beginning of the loop before the body of the loop executes. The do...while statement tests the loop-continuation condition *after* the loop body executes; therefore, *the loop body always executes at least once*. When a do...while terminates, execution continues with the statement after the while clause. It's not necessary to use braces in the do...while statement if there is only one statement in the body; however, most programmers include the braces to avoid confusion between the while and do...while statements. For example,

```
while ( condition )
```

normally is regarded as the header of a while statement. A do...while with no braces around the single statement body appears as

```
do
    statement
while ( condition );
```

which can be confusing. You might misinterpret the last line—while(*condition*);—as a while statement containing as its body an empty statement. Thus, the do...while with one statement often is written as follows to avoid confusion:

```
do
{
    statement
} while ( condition );
```

Good Programming Practice 5.9

Always including braces in a do...while statement helps eliminate ambiguity between the while statement and the do...while statement containing one statement.

Figure 5.7 uses a do...while statement to print the numbers 1–10. Upon entering the do...while statement, line 12 outputs counter's value and line 13 increments counter. Then the program evaluates the loop-continuation test at the bottom of the loop (line 14). If the condition is true, the loop continues from the first body statement in the do...while (line 12). If the condition is false, the loop terminates and the program continues with the next statement after the loop (line 16).

```cpp
1   // Fig. 5.7: fig05_07.cpp
2   // do...while repetition statement.
3   #include <iostream>
4   using namespace std;
5
6   int main()
7   {
8      int counter = 1; // initialize counter
9
10     do
11     {
12        cout << counter << " "; // display counter
13        counter++; // increment counter
14     } while ( counter <= 10 ); // end do...while
15
16     cout << endl; // output a newline
17   } // end main
```

```
1 2 3 4 5 6 7 8 9 10
```

Fig. 5.7 | do...while repetition statement.

do...while Statement UML Activity Diagram

Figure 5.8 contains the do...while statement's UML activity diagram, which makes it clear that the loop-continuation condition is not evaluated until after the loop performs its body at least once. Compare this activity diagram with that of the while statement (Fig. 4.6). Again, note that (besides an initial state, transition arrows, a merge, a final state and several notes) the diagram contains only action states and a decision.

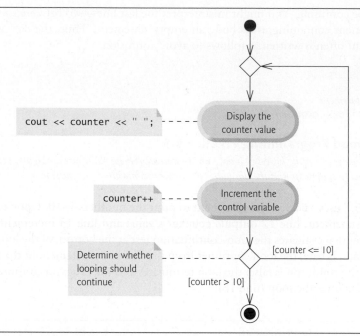

Fig. 5.8 | UML activity diagram for the do...while repetition statement of Fig. 5.7.

5.6 switch Multiple-Selection Statement

C++ provides the **switch multiple-selection** statement to perform many different actions based on the possible values of a variable or expression. Each action is associated with the value of a **constant integral expression** (i.e., any combination of character and integer constants that evaluates to a constant integer value).

GradeBook *Class with* switch *Statement to Count A, B, C, D and F Grades*

We now present an enhanced version of the GradeBook class introduced in Chapter 3 and further developed in Chapter 4. The new version of the class asks the user to enter a set of letter grades, then displays a summary of the number of students who received each grade. The class uses a switch to determine whether each grade entered is an A, B, C, D or F and to increment the appropriate grade counter. Class GradeBook is defined in Fig. 5.9, and its member-function definitions appear in Fig. 5.10. Figure 5.11 shows sample inputs and outputs of the main program that uses class GradeBook to process a set of grades.

Like earlier versions of the class definition, the GradeBook class definition (Fig. 5.9) contains function prototypes for member functions setCourseName (line 12), getCourse-Name (line 13) and displayMessage (line 14), as well as the class's constructor (line 11). The class definition also declares private data member courseName (line 18).

Class GradeBook (Fig. 5.9) now contains five additional private data members (lines 19–23)—counter variables for each grade category (i.e., A, B, C, D and F). The class also contains two additional public member functions—inputGrades and displayGradeReport. Member function inputGrades (declared in line 15) reads an arbitrary number of letter grades from the user using sentinel-controlled repetition and updates the appropriate

```
1    // Fig. 5.9: GradeBook.h
2    // Definition of class GradeBook that counts A, B, C, D and F grades.
3    // Member functions are defined in GradeBook.cpp
4    #include <string> // program uses C++ standard string class
5    using namespace std;
6
7    // GradeBook class definition
8    class GradeBook
9    {
10   public:
11      GradeBook( string ); // constructor initializes course name
12      void setCourseName( string ); // function to set the course name
13      string getCourseName(); // function to retrieve the course name
14      void displayMessage(); // display a welcome message
15      void inputGrades(); // input arbitrary number of grades from user
16      void displayGradeReport(); // display a report based on the grades
17   private:
18      string courseName; // course name for this GradeBook
19      int aCount; // count of A grades
20      int bCount; // count of B grades
21      int cCount; // count of C grades
22      int dCount; // count of D grades
23      int fCount; // count of F grades
24   }; // end class GradeBook
```

Fig. 5.9 | GradeBook class definition.

grade counter for each grade entered. Member function displayGradeReport (declared in line 16) outputs a report containing the number of students who received each letter grade.

Source-code file GradeBook.cpp (Fig. 5.10) contains the member-function definitions for class GradeBook. Notice that lines 13–17 in the constructor initialize the five grade counters to 0—when a GradeBook object is first created, no grades have been entered yet. As you'll soon see, these counters are incremented in member function inputGrades as the user enters grades. The definitions of member functions setCourseName, getCourseName and displayMessage are identical to those found in the earlier versions of class GradeBook. Let's consider the new GradeBook member functions in detail.

```
1    // Fig. 5.10: GradeBook.cpp
2    // Member-function definitions for class GradeBook that
3    // uses a switch statement to count A, B, C, D and F grades.
4    #include <iostream>
5    #include "GradeBook.h" // include definition of class GradeBook
6    using namespace std;
7
8    // constructor initializes courseName with string supplied as argument;
9    // initializes counter data members to 0
10   GradeBook::GradeBook( string name )
11   {
12      setCourseName( name ); // validate and store courseName
13      aCount = 0; // initialize count of A grades to 0
```

Fig. 5.10 | GradeBook class uses switch statement to count letter grades. (Part 1 of 3.)

```
14        bCount = 0; // initialize count of B grades to 0
15        cCount = 0; // initialize count of C grades to 0
16        dCount = 0; // initialize count of D grades to 0
17        fCount = 0; // initialize count of F grades to 0
18   } // end GradeBook constructor
19
20   // function to set the course name; limits name to 25 or fewer characters
21   void GradeBook::setCourseName( string name )
22   {
23        if ( name.length() <= 25 ) // if name has 25 or fewer characters
24           courseName = name; // store the course name in the object
25        else // if name is longer than 25 characters
26        { // set courseName to first 25 characters of parameter name
27           courseName = name.substr( 0, 25 ); // select first 25 characters
28           cout << "Name \"" << name << "\" exceeds maximum length (25).\n"
29              << "Limiting courseName to first 25 characters.\n" << endl;
30        } // end if...else
31   } // end function setCourseName
32
33   // function to retrieve the course name
34   string GradeBook::getCourseName()
35   {
36        return courseName;
37   } // end function getCourseName
38
39   // display a welcome message to the GradeBook user
40   void GradeBook::displayMessage()
41   {
42        // this statement calls getCourseName to get the
43        // name of the course this GradeBook represents
44        cout << "Welcome to the grade book for\n" << getCourseName() << "!\n"
45           << endl;
46   } // end function displayMessage
47
48   // input arbitrary number of grades from user; update grade counter
49   void GradeBook::inputGrades()
50   {
51        int grade; // grade entered by user
52
53        cout << "Enter the letter grades." << endl
54           << "Enter the EOF character to end input." << endl;
55
56        // loop until user types end-of-file key sequence
57        while ( ( grade = cin.get() ) != EOF )
58        {
59           // determine which grade was entered
60           switch ( grade ) // switch statement nested in while
61           {
62              case 'A': // grade was uppercase A
63              case 'a': // or lowercase a
64                 aCount++; // increment aCount
65                 break; // necessary to exit switch
66
```

Fig. 5.10 | GradeBook class uses switch statement to count letter grades. (Part 2 of 3.)

```
67        case 'B': // grade was uppercase B
68        case 'b': // or lowercase b
69           bCount++; // increment bCount
70           break; // exit switch
71
72        case 'C': // grade was uppercase C
73        case 'c': // or lowercase c
74           cCount++; // increment cCount
75           break; // exit switch
76
77        case 'D': // grade was uppercase D
78        case 'd': // or lowercase d
79           dCount++; // increment dCount
80           break; // exit switch
81
82        case 'F': // grade was uppercase F
83        case 'f': // or lowercase f
84           fCount++; // increment fCount
85           break; // exit switch
86
87        case '\n': // ignore newlines,
88        case '\t': // tabs,
89        case ' ': // and spaces in input
90           break; // exit switch
91
92        default: // catch all other characters
93           cout << "Incorrect letter grade entered."
94              << " Enter a new grade." << endl;
95           break; // optional; will exit switch anyway
96     } // end switch
97   } // end while
98 } // end function inputGrades
99
100 // display a report based on the grades entered by user
101 void GradeBook::displayGradeReport()
102 {
103    // output summary of results
104    cout << "\n\nNumber of students who received each letter grade:"
105       << "\nA: " << aCount // display number of A grades
106       << "\nB: " << bCount // display number of B grades
107       << "\nC: " << cCount // display number of C grades
108       << "\nD: " << dCount // display number of D grades
109       << "\nF: " << fCount // display number of F grades
110       << endl;
111 } // end function displayGradeReport
```

Fig. 5.10 | GradeBook class uses switch statement to count letter grades. (Part 3 of 3.)

Reading Character Input

The user enters letter grades for a course in member function inputGrades (lines 49–98). Inside the while header, in line 57, the parenthesized assignment (grade = cin.get()) executes first. The cin.get() function reads one character from the keyboard and stores that character in integer variable grade (declared in line 51). Normally, characters are stored in variables of type **char**; however, characters can be stored in any integer data type, because types short, int and long are guaranteed to be at least as big as type char. Thus, we can treat a character either as an integer or as a character, depending on its use. For example, the statement

```
cout << "The character (" << 'a' << ") has the value "
    << static_cast< int > ( 'a' ) << endl;
```

prints the character a and its integer value as follows:

```
The character (a) has the value 97
```

The integer 97 is the character's numerical representation in the computer. Most computers today use the Unicode character set in which 97 represents the lowercase letter 'a'. Appendix B shows the characters and decimal equivalents from the **ASCII** (**American Standard Code for Information Interchange**) **character set**, which is a subset of Unicode.

Generally, assignment statements have the value that is assigned to the variable on the left side of the =. Thus, the value of the assignment expression grade = cin.get() is the same as the value returned by cin.get() and assigned to the variable grade.

The fact that assignment expressions have values can be useful for assigning the same value to several variables. For example,

```
a = b = c = 0;
```

first evaluates c = 0 (because the = operator associates from right to left). The variable b is then assigned the value of c = 0 (which is 0). Then, a is assigned the value of b = (c = 0) (which is also 0). In the program, the value of grade = cin.get() is compared with the value of EOF (a symbol whose acronym stands for "end-of-file"). We use EOF (which normally has the value −1) as the sentinel value. *However, you do not type the value −1, nor do you type the letters EOF as the sentinel value.* Rather, you type a system-dependent keystroke combination that means "end-of-file" to indicate that you have no more data to enter. EOF is a symbolic integer constant defined in the <iostream> header file. If the value assigned to grade is equal to EOF, the while loop (lines 57–97) terminates. We've chosen to represent the characters entered into this program as ints, because EOF has type int.

On UNIX/Linux systems and many others, end-of-file is entered by typing

    <Ctrl> d

on a line by itself. This notation means to press and hold down the *Ctrl* key, then press the *d* key. On other systems such as Microsoft Windows, end-of-file can be entered by typing

    <Ctrl> z

[*Note:* In some cases, you must press *Enter* after the preceding key sequence. Also, the characters ^Z sometimes appear on the screen to represent end-of-file, as shown in Fig. 5.11.]

Portability Tip 5.1

The keystroke combinations for entering end-of-file are system dependent.

Portability Tip 5.2

Testing for the symbolic constant EOF rather than −1 makes programs more portable. The ANSI/ISO C standard, from which C++ adopts the definition of EOF, states that EOF is a negative integral value, so EOF could have different values on different systems.

In this program, the user enters grades at the keyboard. When the user presses the *Enter* (or *Return*) key, the characters are read by the cin.get() function, one character at a time. If the character entered is not end-of-file, the flow of control enters the switch statement (lines 60–96), which increments the appropriate letter-grade counter.

switch *Statement Details*

The switch statement consists of a series of **case labels** and an optional **default** case. These are used in this example to determine which counter to increment, based on a grade. When the flow of control reaches the switch, the program evaluates the expression in the parentheses (i.e., grade) following keyword switch (line 60). This is called the **controlling expression**. The switch statement compares the value of the controlling expression with each case label. Assume the user enters the letter C as a grade. The program compares C to each case in the switch. If a match occurs (case 'C': in line 72), the program executes the statements for that case. For the letter C, line 74 increments cCount by 1. The break statement (line 75) causes program control to proceed with the first statement after the switch—in this program, control transfers to line 97. This line marks the end of the body of the while loop that inputs grades (lines 57–97), so control flows to the while's condition (line 57) to determine whether the loop should continue executing.

The cases in our switch explicitly test for the lowercase and uppercase versions of the letters A, B, C, D and F. Note the cases in lines 62–63 that test for the values 'A' and 'a' (both of which represent the grade A). Listing cases consecutively with no statements between them enables the cases to perform the same set of statements—when the controlling expression evaluates to either 'A' or 'a', the statements in lines 64–65 will execute. Each case can have multiple statements. The switch selection statement does not require braces around multiple statements in each case.

Without break statements, each time a match occurs in the switch, the statements for that case and subsequent cases execute until a break statement or the end of the switch is encountered. This is often referred to as "falling through" to the statements in subsequent cases. (This feature is perfect for writing a concise program that displays the iterative song "The Twelve Days of Christmas" in Exercise 5.28.)

Common Programming Error 5.8

Forgetting a break statement when one is needed in a switch statement is a logic error.

Common Programming Error 5.9

Omitting the space between the word case and the integral value being tested in a switch statement—e.g., writing case3: instead of case 3:—is a logic error. The switch statement will not perform the appropriate actions when the controlling expression has a value of 3.

Providing a **default** *Case*

If no match occurs between the controlling expression's value and a case label, the default case (lines 92–95) executes. We use the default case in this example to process all controlling-expression values that are neither valid grades nor newline, tab or space characters. If no match occurs, the default case executes, and lines 93–94 print an error message indicating that an incorrect letter grade was entered. If no match occurs in a switch statement that does not contain a `default` case, program control continues with the first statement after the `switch`.

Good Programming Practice 5.10

Provide a `default` case in `switch` statements. Cases not explicitly tested in a `switch` statement without a `default` case are ignored. Including a `default` case focuses you on the need to process exceptional conditions. There are situations in which no `default` processing is needed. Although the `case` clauses and the `default` case clause in a `switch` statement can occur in any order, it's common practice to place the `default` clause last.

Good Programming Practice 5.11

The last `case` in a `switch` statement does not require a `break` statement. Some programmers include this `break` for clarity and for symmetry with other cases.

Ignoring Newline, Tab and Blank Characters in Input

Lines 87–90 in the `switch` statement of Fig. 5.10 cause the program to skip newline, tab and blank characters. Reading characters one at a time can cause some problems. To have the program read the characters, we must send them to the computer by pressing the *Enter* key. This places a newline character in the input after the character we wish to process. Often, this newline character must be specially processed. By including the preceding `cases` in our `switch` statement, we prevent the error message in the `default` case from being printed each time a newline, tab or space is encountered in the input.

Common Programming Error 5.10

Not processing newline and other white-space characters in the input when reading characters one at a time can cause logic errors.

Testing Class GradeBook

Figure 5.11 creates a `GradeBook` object (line 8). Line 10 invokes the its `displayMessage` member function to output a welcome message to the user. Line 11 invokes member function object's `inputGrades` to read a set of grades from the user and keep track of how many students received each grade. The output window in Fig. 5.11 shows an error message displayed in response to entering an invalid grade (i.e., E). Line 12 invokes `GradeBook` member function `displayGradeReport` (defined in lines 101–111 of Fig. 5.10), which outputs a report based on the grades entered (as in the output in Fig. 5.11).

```
1   // Fig. 5.11: fig05_11.cpp
2   // Create GradeBook object, input grades and display grade report.
3   #include "GradeBook.h" // include definition of class GradeBook
4
5   int main()
6   {
7      // create GradeBook object
8      GradeBook myGradeBook( "CS101 C++ Programming" );
9
10     myGradeBook.displayMessage(); // display welcome message
```

Fig. 5.11 | Creating a `GradeBook` object and calling its member functions. (Part 1 of 2.)

```
11      myGradeBook.inputGrades(); // read grades from user
12      myGradeBook.displayGradeReport(); // display report based on grades
13   } // end main
```

```
Welcome to the grade book for
CS101 C++ Programming!

Enter the letter grades.
Enter the EOF character to end input.
a
B
c
C
A
d
f
C
E
Incorrect letter grade entered. Enter a new grade.
D
A
b
^Z


Number of students who received each letter grade:
A: 3
B: 2
C: 3
D: 2
F: 1
```

Fig. 5.11 | Creating a GradeBook object and calling its member functions. (Part 2 of 2.)

switch Statement UML Activity Diagram

Figure 5.12 shows the UML activity diagram for the general switch multiple-selection statement. Most switch statements use a break in each case to terminate the switch statement after processing the case. Figure 5.12 emphasizes this by including break statements in the activity diagram. Without the break statement, control would not transfer to the first statement after the switch statement after a case is processed. Instead, control would transfer to the next case's actions.

The diagram makes it clear that the break statement at the end of a case causes control to exit the switch statement immediately. Again, note that (besides an initial state, transition arrows, a final state and several notes) the diagram contains action states and decisions. Also, the diagram uses merge symbols to merge the transitions from the break statements to the final state.

When using the switch statement, remember that each case can be used to test only a *constant* integral expression—any combination of character constants and integer constants that evaluates to a constant integer value. A character constant is represented as the specific character in single quotes, such as 'A'. An integer constant is simply an integer value. Also, each case label can specify only one constant integral expression.

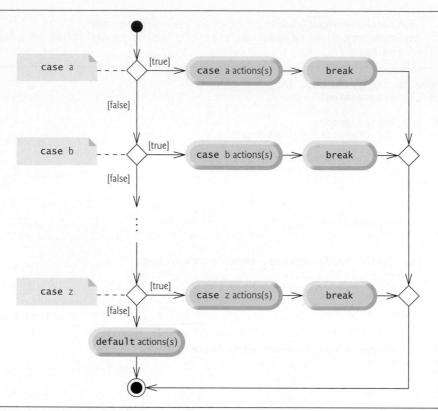

Fig. 5.12 | switch multiple-selection statement UML activity diagram with **break** statements.

Common Programming Error 5.11
Specifying a nonconstant integral expression in a switch's case *label is a syntax error.*

Common Programming Error 5.12
Providing identical case labels in a switch *statement is a compilation error. Providing case labels containing different expressions that evaluate to the same value also is a compilation error. For example, placing* case 4 + 1: *and* case 3 + 2: *in the same* switch *statement is a compilation error, because these are both equivalent to* case 5:.

In Chapter 13, we present a more elegant way to implement switch logic. We'll use a technique called polymorphism to create programs that are often clearer, more concise, easier to maintain and easier to extend than programs that use switch logic.

Notes on Data Types
C++ has flexible data type sizes (see Appendix C, Fundamental Types). Different applications, for example, might need integers of different sizes. C++ provides several integer types. The range of integer values for each type depends on the particular computer's hardware. In addition to the types int and char, C++ provides the types short (an abbreviation of short int) and long (an abbreviation of long int). The minimum range of values

for short integers is –32,768 to 32,767. For the vast majority of integer calculations, long integers are sufficient. The minimum range of values for long integers is –2,147,483,648 to 2,147,483,647. On most computers, ints are equivalent either to short or to long. The range of values for an int is at least the same as that for short integers and no larger than that for long integers. The data type char can be used to represent any of the characters in the computer's character set. It also can be used to represent small integers.

Portability Tip 5.3

Because ints can vary in size between systems, use long integers if you expect to process integers outside the range –32,768 to 32,767 and you'd like to run the program on several different computer systems.

Performance Tip 5.3

If memory is at a premium, it might be desirable to use smaller integer sizes.

5.7 break and continue Statements

C++ also provides statements break and continue to alter the flow of control. The preceding section showed how break can be used to terminate a switch statement's execution. This section discusses how to use break in a repetition statement.

break *Statement*

The **break statement**, when executed in a while, for, do...while or switch statement, causes immediate exit from that statement. Program execution continues with the next statement. Common uses of the break statement are to escape early from a loop or to skip the remainder of a switch statement. Figure 5.13 demonstrates the break statement (line 13) exiting a for repetition statement.

```cpp
1   // Fig. 5.13: fig05_13.cpp
2   // break statement exiting a for statement.
3   #include <iostream>
4   using namespace std;
5
6   int main()
7   {
8      int count; // control variable also used after loop terminates
9
10     for ( count = 1; count <= 10; count++ ) // loop 10 times
11     {
12        if ( count == 5 )
13           break; // break loop only if x is 5
14
15        cout << count << " ";
16     } // end for
17
18     cout << "\nBroke out of loop at count = " << count << endl;
19  } // end main
```

Fig. 5.13 | break statement exiting a for statement. (Part 1 of 2.)

```
1 2 3 4
Broke out of loop at count = 5
```

Fig. 5.13 | break statement exiting a for statement. (Part 2 of 2.)

When the if statement detects that count is 5, the break statement executes. This terminates the for statement, and the program proceeds to line 18 (immediately after the for statement), which displays a message indicating the control variable value that terminated the loop. The for statement fully executes its body only four times instead of 10. The control variable count is defined outside the for statement header, so that we can use the control variable both in the loop's body and after the loop completes its execution.

continue Statement

The **continue statement**, when executed in a while, for or do...while statement, skips the remaining statements in the body of that statement and proceeds with the next iteration of the loop. In while and do...while statements, the loop-continuation test evaluates immediately after the continue statement executes. In the for statement, the increment expression executes, then the loop-continuation test evaluates.

Figure 5.14 uses the continue statement (line 11) in a for statement to skip the output statement (line 13) when the nested if (lines 10–11) determines that the value of count is 5. When the continue statement executes, program control continues with the increment of the control variable in the for header (line 8) and loops five more times.

```
 1   // Fig. 5.14: fig05_14.cpp
 2   // continue statement terminating an iteration of a for statement.
 3   #include <iostream>
 4   using namespace std;
 5
 6   int main()
 7   {
 8      for ( int count = 1; count <= 10; count++ ) // loop 10 times
 9      {
10         if ( count == 5 ) // if count is 5,
11            continue;       // skip remaining code in loop
12
13         cout << count << " ";
14      } // end for
15
16      cout << "\nUsed continue to skip printing 5" << endl;
17   } // end main
```

```
1 2 3 4 6 7 8 9 10
Used continue to skip printing 5
```

Fig. 5.14 | continue statement terminating a single iteration of a for statement.

In Section 5.3, we stated that the while statement could be used in most cases to represent the for statement. The one exception occurs when the increment expression in the while statement follows the continue statement. In this case, the increment does not execute before the program tests the loop-continuation condition, and the while does not execute in the same manner as the for.

Good Programming Practice 5.12

Some programmers feel that break and continue violate structured programming. The effects of these statements can be achieved by structured programming techniques we soon will learn, so these programmers do not use break and continue. Most programmers consider the use of break in switch statements acceptable.

Performance Tip 5.4

The break and continue statements, when used properly, perform faster than do the corresponding structured techniques.

Software Engineering Observation 5.1

There is a tension between achieving quality software engineering and achieving the best-performing software. Often, one of these goals is achieved at the expense of the other. For all but the most performance-intensive situations, apply the following guidelines: First, make your code simple and correct; then make it fast and small, but only if necessary.

5.8 Logical Operators

So far we've studied only **simple conditions**, such as counter <= 10, total > 1000 and number != sentinelValue. We expressed these conditions in terms of the relational operators >, <, >= and <=, and the equality operators == and !=. Each decision tested precisely one condition. To test multiple conditions while making a decision, we performed these tests in separate statements or in nested if or if…else statements.

C++ provides **logical operators** that are used to form more complex conditions by combining simple conditions. The logical operators are && (logical AND), || (logical OR) and ! (logical NOT, also called logical negation).

Logical AND (&&) Operator

Suppose that we wish to ensure that two conditions are *both* true before we choose a certain path of execution. In this case, we can use the && (**logical AND**) operator, as follows:

```
if ( gender == 1 && age >= 65 )
    seniorFemales++;
```

This if statement contains two simple conditions. The condition gender == 1 is used here to determine whether a person is a female. The condition age >= 65 determines whether a person is a senior citizen. The simple condition to the left of the && operator evaluates first. If necessary, the simple condition to the right of the && operator evaluates next. As we'll discuss shortly, the right side of a logical AND expression is evaluated only if the left side is true. The if statement then considers the combined condition

```
gender == 1 && age >= 65
```

This condition is true if and only if both of the simple conditions are true. Finally, if this combined condition is indeed true, the statement in the if statement's body increments the count of seniorFemales. If either (or both) of the simple conditions are false, then the program skips the incrementing and proceeds to the statement following the `if`. The preceding combined condition can be made more readable by adding redundant parentheses:

```
( gender == 1 ) && ( age >= 65 )
```

Common Programming Error 5.13

Although 3 < x < 7 is a mathematically correct condition, it does not evaluate as you might expect in C++. Use (3 < x && x < 7) to get the proper evaluation in C++.

Figure 5.15 summarizes the `&&` operator. The table shows all four possible combinations of `false` and `true` values for *expression1* and *expression2*. Such tables are often called **truth tables**. C++ evaluates to `false` or `true` all expressions that include relational operators, equality operators and/or logical operators.

expression1	expression2	expression1 && expression2
false	false	false
false	true	false
true	false	false
true	true	true

Fig. 5.15 | && (logical AND) operator truth table.

Logical OR (| |) Operator

Now let's consider the `||` (**logical OR**) operator. Suppose we wish to ensure that either *or* both of two conditions are `true` before we choose a certain path of execution. In this case, we use the `||` operator, as in the following program segment:

```
if ( ( semesterAverage >= 90 ) || ( finalExam >= 90 ) )
    cout << "Student grade is A" << endl;
```

This preceding condition contains two simple conditions. The simple condition `semesterAverage >= 90` evaluates to determine whether the student deserves an "A" in the course because of a solid performance throughout the semester. The simple condition `finalExam >= 90` evaluates to determine whether the student deserves an "A" in the course because of an outstanding performance on the final exam. The `if` statement then considers the combined condition

```
( semesterAverage >= 90 ) || ( finalExam >= 90 )
```

and awards the student an "A" if either or both of the simple conditions are `true`. The message "`Student grade is A`" prints unless both of the simple conditions are `false`. Figure 5.16 is a truth table for the logical OR operator (`||`).

The `&&` operator has a higher precedence than the `||` operator. Both operators associate from left to right. An expression containing `&&` or `||` operators evaluates only until the truth or falsehood of the expression is known. Thus, evaluation of the expression

```
( gender == 1 ) && ( age >= 65 )
```

expression1	expression2	expression1 || expression2
false	false	false
false	true	true
true	false	true
true	true	true

Fig. 5.16 | \|\| (logical OR) operator truth table.

stops immediately if gender is not equal to 1 (i.e., the entire expression is false) and continues if gender is equal to 1 (i.e., the entire expression could still be true if the condition age >= 65 is true). This performance feature for the evaluation of logical AND and logical OR expressions is called **short-circuit evaluation**.

Performance Tip 5.5

In expressions using operator &&, if the separate conditions are independent of one another, make the condition most likely to be false the leftmost condition. In expressions using operator \|\|, make the condition most likely to be true the leftmost condition. This use of short-circuit evaluation can reduce a program's execution time.

Logical Negation (!) Operator

C++ provides the ! (**logical NOT**, also called **logical negation**) operator to "reverse" a condition's meaning. The unary logical negation operator has only a single condition as an operand. The unary logical negation operator is placed before a condition when we are interested in choosing a path of execution if the original condition (without the logical negation operator) is false, such as in the following program segment:

```
if ( !( grade == sentinelValue ) )
    cout << "The next grade is " << grade << endl;
```

The parentheses around the condition grade == sentinelValue are needed because the logical negation operator has a higher precedence than the equality operator.

You can often avoid the ! operator by using an appropriate relational or equality operator. For example, the preceding if statement also can be written as follows:

```
if ( grade != sentinelValue )
    cout << "The next grade is " << grade << endl;
```

This flexibility often can help a programmer express a condition in a more "natural" or convenient manner. Figure 5.17 is a truth table for the logical negation operator (!).

expression	!expression
false	true
true	false

Fig. 5.17 | ! (logical negation) operator truth table.

Logical Operators Example

Figure 5.18 demonstrates the logical operators by producing their truth tables. The output shows each expression that is evaluated and its bool result. By default, bool values true and false are displayed by cout and the stream insertion operator as 1 and 0, respectively. We use **stream manipulator boolalpha** (a sticky manipulator) in line 9 to specify that the value of each bool expression should be displayed as either the word "true" or the word "false." For example, the result of the expression false && false in line 10 is false, so the second line of output includes the word "false." Lines 9–13 produce the truth table for &&. Lines 16–20 produce the truth table for ||. Lines 23–25 produce the truth table for !.

```cpp
1   // Fig. 5.18: fig05_18.cpp
2   // Logical operators.
3   #include <iostream>
4   using namespace std;
5
6   int main()
7   {
8      // create truth table for && (logical AND) operator
9      cout << boolalpha << "Logical AND (&&)"
10        << "\nfalse && false: " << ( false && false )
11        << "\nfalse && true: " << ( false && true )
12        << "\ntrue && false: " << ( true && false )
13        << "\ntrue && true: " << ( true && true ) << "\n\n";
14
15      // create truth table for || (logical OR) operator
16      cout << "Logical OR (||)"
17        << "\nfalse || false: " << ( false || false )
18        << "\nfalse || true: " << ( false || true )
19        << "\ntrue || false: " << ( true || false )
20        << "\ntrue || true: " << ( true || true ) << "\n\n";
21
22      // create truth table for ! (logical negation) operator
23      cout << "Logical NOT (!)"
24        << "\n!false: " << ( !false )
25        << "\n!true: " << ( !true ) << endl;
26   } // end main
```

```
Logical AND (&&)
false && false: false
false && true: false
true && false: false
true && true: true

Logical OR (||)
false || false: false
false || true: true
true || false: true
true || true: true

Logical NOT (!)
!false: true
!true: false
```

Fig. 5.18 | Logical operators.

Summary of Operator Precedence and Associativity
Figure 5.19 adds the logical and comma operators to the operator precedence and associativity chart. The operators are shown from top to bottom, in decreasing order of precedence.

Operators						Associativity	Type
::						left to right	scope resolution
()						left to right	parentheses
++	--	static_cast< *type* >()				left to right	unary (postfix)
++	--	+	-	!		right to left	unary (prefix)
*	/	%				left to right	multiplicative
+	-					left to right	additive
<<	>>					left to right	insertion/extraction
<	<=	>	>=			left to right	relational
==	!=					left to right	equality
&&						left to right	logical AND
||						left to right	logical OR
?:						right to left	conditional
=	+=	-=	*=	/=	%=	right to left	assignment
,						left to right	comma

Fig. 5.19 | Operator precedence and associativity

5.9 **Confusing the Equality (==) and Assignment (=) Operators**

There is one type of error that C++ programmers, no matter how experienced, tend to make so frequently that we feel it requires a separate section. That error is accidentally swapping the operators == (equality) and = (assignment). What makes these swaps so damaging is the fact that they ordinarily do not cause syntax errors. Rather, statements with these errors tend to compile correctly and the programs run to completion, often generating incorrect results through runtime logic errors. [*Note:* Some compilers issue a warning when = is used in a context where == typically is expected.]

Two aspects of C++ contribute to these problems. One is that *any expression that produces a value can be used in the decision portion of any control statement.* If the value of the expression is zero, it's treated as false, and if the value is nonzero, it's treated as true. The second is that assignments produce a value—namely, the value assigned to the variable on the left side of the assignment operator. For example, suppose we intend to write

```
if ( payCode == 4 )
    cout << "You get a bonus!" << endl;
```

but we accidentally write

```
if ( payCode = 4 )
    cout << "You get a bonus!" << endl;
```

The first if statement properly awards a bonus to the person whose payCode is equal to 4. The second one—with the error—evaluates the assignment expression in the if condition to the constant 4. *Any nonzero value is interpreted as* true, so this condition is always true and the person always receives a bonus regardless of what the actual paycode is! Even worse, the paycode has been modified when it was only supposed to be examined!

Common Programming Error 5.14

Using operator == for assignment and using operator = for equality are logic errors.

Error-Prevention Tip 5.3

Programmers normally write conditions such as x == 7 with the variable name on the left and the constant on the right. By placing the constant on the left, as in 7 == x, you'll be protected by the compiler if you accidentally replace the == operator with =. The compiler treats this as a compilation error, because you can't change the value of a constant. This will prevent the potential devastation of a runtime logic error.

Variable names are said to be **lvalues** (for "left values") because they can be used on the *left* side of an assignment operator. Constants are said to be **rvalues** (for "right values") because they can be used on only the *right* side of an assignment operator. *Lvalues* can also be used as *rvalues*, but not vice versa.

There is another equally unpleasant situation. Suppose you want to assign a value to a variable with a simple statement like

```
x = 1;
```

but instead write

```
x == 1;
```

Here, too, this is not a syntax error. Rather, the compiler simply evaluates the conditional expression. If x is equal to 1, the condition is true and the expression evaluates to the value true. If x is not equal to 1, the condition is false and the expression evaluates to the value false. Regardless of the expression's value, there is no assignment operator, so the value simply is lost. The value of x remains unaltered, probably causing an execution-time logic error. Unfortunately, we do not have a handy trick available to help you with this problem!

Error-Prevention Tip 5.4

Use your text editor to search for all occurrences of = in your program and check that you have the correct assignment operator or logical operator in each place.

5.10 Structured Programming Summary

Just as architects design buildings by employing the collective wisdom of their profession, so should programmers design programs. Our field is younger than architecture is, and our collective wisdom is sparser. We've learned that structured programming produces programs that are easier than unstructured programs to understand, test, debug, modify, and even prove correct in a mathematical sense.

Figure 5.20 uses activity diagrams to summarize C++'s control statements. The initial and final states indicate the single entry point and the single exit point of each control

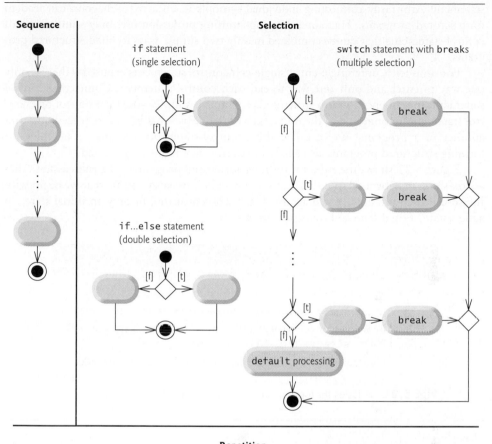

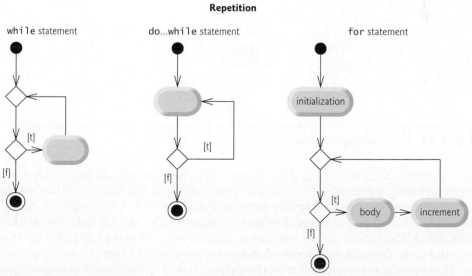

Fig. 5.20 | C++'s single-entry/single-exit sequence, selection and repetition statements.

statement. Arbitrarily connecting individual symbols in an activity diagram can lead to unstructured programs. Therefore, the programming profession uses only a limited set of control statements that can be combined in only two simple ways to build structured programs.

For simplicity, only single-entry/single-exit control statements are used—there is only one way to enter and only one way to exit each control statement. Connecting control statements in sequence to form structured programs is simple—the final state of one control statement is connected to the initial state of the next—that is, they're placed one after another in a program. We've called this "control-statement stacking." The rules for forming structured programs also allow for control statements to be nested.

Figure 5.21 shows the rules for forming structured programs. The rules assume that action states may be used to indicate any action. The rules also assume that we begin with the so-called simplest activity diagram (Fig. 5.22), consisting of only an initial state, an action state, a final state and transition arrows.

Rules for forming structured programs
1) Begin with the "simplest activity diagram" (Fig. 5.22).
2) Any action state can be replaced by two action states in sequence.
3) Any action state can be replaced by any control statement (sequence, if, if...else, switch, while, do...while or for).
4) Rules 2 and 3 can be applied as often as you like and in any order.

Fig. 5.21 | Rules for forming structured programs.

Fig. 5.22 | Simplest activity diagram.

Applying the rules of Fig. 5.21 always results in an activity diagram with a neat, building-block appearance. For example, repeatedly applying Rule 2 to the simplest activity diagram results in an activity diagram containing many action states in sequence (Fig. 5.23). Rule 2 generates a stack of control statements, so let's call Rule 2 the **stacking rule**. [*Note:* The vertical dashed lines in Fig. 5.23 are not part of the UML. We use them to separate the four activity diagrams that demonstrate Rule 2 of Fig. 5.21 being applied.]

Rule 3 is the **nesting rule**. Repeatedly applying Rule 3 to the simplest activity diagram results in one with neatly nested control statements. For example, in Fig. 5.24, the action state in the simplest activity diagram is replaced with a double-selection (if...else) state-

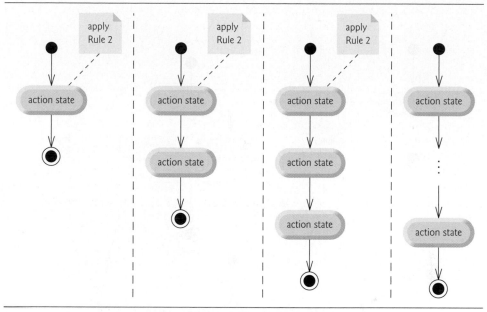

Fig. 5.23 | Repeatedly applying Rule 2 of Fig. 5.21 to the simplest activity diagram.

ment. Then Rule 3 is applied again to the action states in the double-selection statement, replacing each with a double-selection statement. The dashed action-state symbols around each of the double-selection statements represent an action state that was replaced in the preceding activity diagram. [*Note:* The dashed arrows and dashed action state symbols shown in Fig. 5.24 are not part of the UML. They're used here as pedagogic devices to illustrate that any action state may be replaced with a control statement.]

Rule 4 generates larger, more involved and more deeply nested statements. The diagrams that emerge from applying the rules in Fig. 5.21 constitute the set of all possible activity diagrams and hence the set of all possible structured programs. The beauty of the structured approach is that we use only seven simple single-entry/single-exit control statements and assemble them in only two simple ways.

If the rules in Fig. 5.21 are followed, an activity diagram with illegal syntax (such as that in Fig. 5.25) cannot be created. If you are uncertain about whether a particular diagram is legal, apply the rules of Fig. 5.21 in reverse to reduce the diagram to the simplest activity diagram. If it's reducible to the simplest activity diagram, the original diagram is structured; otherwise, it isn't.

Structured programming promotes simplicity. Böhm and Jacopini have given us the result that only three forms of control are needed:

- Sequence
- Selection
- Repetition

The sequence structure is trivial. Simply list the statements to execute in the order in which they should execute.

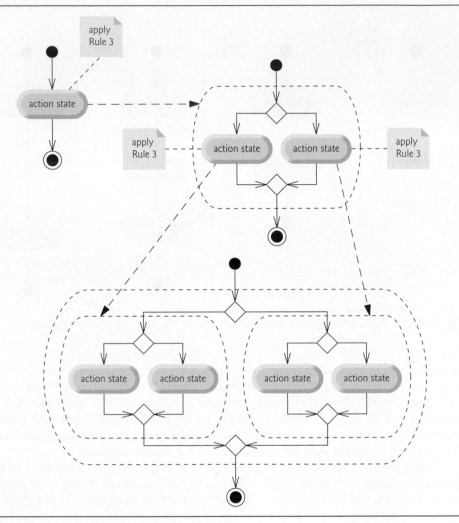

Fig. 5.24 | Applying Rule 3 of Fig. 5.21 to the simplest activity diagram several times.

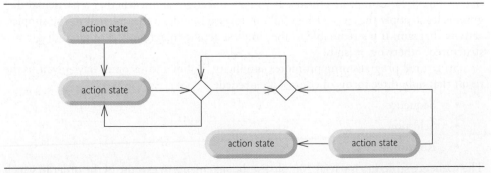

Fig. 5.25 | Activity diagram with illegal syntax.

Selection is implemented in one of three ways:

- `if` statement (single selection)
- `if...else` statement (double selection)
- `switch` statement (multiple selection)

It's straightforward to prove that the simple `if` statement is sufficient to provide any form of selection—everything that can be done with the `if...else` statement and the `switch` statement can be implemented (although perhaps not as clearly and efficiently) by combining `if` statements.

Repetition is implemented in one of three ways:

- `while` statement
- `do...while` statement
- `for` statement

It's straightforward to prove that the `while` statement is sufficient to provide any form of repetition. Everything that can be done with the `do...while` statement and the `for` statement can be done (although perhaps not as smoothly) with the `while` statement.

Combining these results illustrates that any form of control ever needed in a C++ program can be expressed in terms of the following:

- sequence
- `if` statement (selection)
- `while` statement (repetition)

and that these control statements can be combined in only two ways—stacking and nesting. Indeed, structured programming promotes simplicity.

5.11 Wrap-Up

We've now completed our introduction to control statements, which enable you to control the flow of execution in functions. Chapter 4 discussed the `if`, `if...else` and `while` statements. This chapter demonstrated the `for`, `do...while` and `switch` statements. We showed that any algorithm can be developed using combinations of the sequence structure, the three types of selection statements—`if`, `if...else` and `switch`—and the three types of repetition statements—`while`, `do...while` and `for`. We discussed how you can combine these building blocks to utilize proven program construction and problem-solving techniques. You used the `break` and `continue` statements to alter a repetition statement's flow of control. This chapter also introduced logical operators, which enable you to use more complex conditional expressions in control statements. Finally, we examined the common errors of confusing the equality and assignment operators and provided suggestions for avoiding these errors. In Chapter 6, we examine functions in greater depth.

Summary

Section 5.2 Essentials of Counter-Controlled Repetition
- In C++, it's more precise to call a declaration that also reserves memory a definition.

Section 5.3 **for** *Repetition Statement*

- The for repetition statement handles all the details of counter-controlled repetition.

- The general format of the for statement is

```
for ( initialization; loopContinuationCondition; increment )
    statement
```

where *initialization* initializes the control variable, *loopContinuationCondition* determines whether the loop should continue executing and *increment* increments or decrements the control variable.

- Typically, for statements are used for counter-controlled repetition and while statements are used for sentinel-controlled repetition.

- The scope of a variable specifies where it can be used in a program.

- The comma operator has the lowest precedence of all C++ operators. The value and type of a comma-separated list of expressions is the value and type of the rightmost expression in the list.

- The initialization, loop-continuation condition and increment expressions of a for statement can contain arithmetic expressions. Also, the increment of a for statement can be negative.

- If the loop-continuation condition in a for header is initially false, the body of the for statement is not performed. Instead, execution proceeds with the statement following the for.

Section 5.4 Examples Using the **for** *Statement*

- Standard library function pow(x, y) calculates the value of x raised to the yth power. Function pow takes two arguments of type double and returns a double value.

- Parameterized stream manipulator setw specifies the field width in which the next value output should appear. The value is right justified in the field by default. If the value to be output is larger than the field width, the field width is extended to accommodate the entire value. Nonparameterized stream manipulator left (found in header <iostream>) can be used to cause a value to be left justified in a field and right can be used to restore right justification.

- Sticky settings are those output-formatting settings that remain in effect until they're changed.

Section 5.5 **do...while** *Repetition Statement*

- The do...while repetition statement tests the loop-continuation condition at the end of the loop, so the body of the loop will be executed at least once. The format for the do...while statement is

```
do
{
   statement
} while ( condition );
```

Section 5.6 **switch** *Multiple-Selection Statement*

- The switch multiple-selection statement performs different actions based on the possible values of a variable or expression. Each action is associated with the value of a constant integral expression that the variable or expression on which the switch is based may assume.

- The switch statement consists of a series of case labels and an optional default case.

- Function cin.get() reads one character from the keyboard. Characters normally are stored in variables of type char. A character can be treated either as an integer or as a character.

- The end-of-file indicator is a system-dependent keystroke combination that specifies that there is no more data to input. EOF is a constant defined in the <iostream> header file that indicates "end-of-file."

- The expression in the parentheses following keyword switch is called the controlling expression. The switch statement compares the value of the controlling expression with each case label.

- Listing cases consecutively with no statements between them enables the cases to perform the same set of statements.

- Each case can have multiple statements. The switch selection statement differs from other control statements in that it does not require braces around multiple statements in each case.

- Each case can be used only to test only a constant integral expression. A character constant is represented as the specific character in single quotes, such as 'A'. An integer constant is simply an integer value. Also, each case label can specify only one constant integral expression.

- C++ provides several data types to represent integers—int, char, short and long. The range of integer values for each type depends on the particular computer's hardware.

Section 5.7 **break** and **continue** Statements

- The break statement, when executed in one of the repetition statements (for, while and do...while), causes immediate exit from the statement.

- The continue statement, when executed in one of the repetition statements (for, while and do...while), skips any remaining statements in the body of the repetition statement and proceeds with the next iteration of the loop. In a while or do...while statement, execution continues with the next evaluation of the condition. In a for statement, execution continues with the increment expression in the for statement header.

Section 5.8 Logical Operators

- Logical operators enable you to form complex conditions by combining simple conditions. The logical operators are && (logical AND), || (logical OR) and ! (logical negation).

- The && (logical AND) operator ensures that two conditions are *both* true.

- The || (logical OR) operator ensures that either *or* both of two conditions are true.

- An expression containing && or || operators evaluates only until the truth or falsehood of the expression is known. This performance feature for the evaluation of logical AND and logical OR expressions is called short-circuit evaluation.

- The ! (logical NOT, also called logical negation) operator enables a programmer to "reverse" the meaning of a condition. The unary logical negation operator is placed before a condition to choose a path of execution if the original condition (without the logical negation operator) is false. In most cases, you can avoid using logical negation by expressing the condition with an appropriate relational or equality operator.

- When used as a condition, any nonzero value implicitly converts to true; 0 (zero) implicitly converts to false.

- By default, bool values true and false are displayed by cout as 1 and 0, respectively. Stream manipulator boolalpha (a sticky manipulator) specifies that the value of each bool expression should be displayed as either the word "true" or the word "false."

Section 5.9 Confusing the Equality (==) and Assignment (=) Operators

- Any expression that produces a value can be used in the decision portion of any control statement. If the value of the expression is zero, it's treated as false, and if the value is nonzero, it's treated as true.

- An assignment produces a value—namely, the value assigned to the variable on the left side of the assignment operator.

Section 5.10 Structured Programming Summary

- Any form of control can be expressed in terms of sequence, selection and repetition statements, and these can be combined in only two ways—stacking and nesting.

Terminology

!, logical NOT operator 189
&&, logical AND operator 187
||, logical OR operator 188
ASCII (American Standard Code for
    Information Interchange) character set 180
boolalpha stream manipulator 190
break statement 185
case label 181
char fundamental type 179
comma operator 168
constant integral expression 176
continue statement 186
controlling expression of a switch 181
decrement a control variable 164
default case in switch 181
definition 165
field width 173
final value of a control variable 164
for repetition statement 166
increment a control variable 164
initial value of a control variable 164
left justified 174
left stream manipulator 174

logical AND (&&) 187
logical negation (!) 189
logical NOT (!) 189
logical operator 187
logical OR (||) 188
loop-continuation condition 164
lvalue ("left value") 192
name of a control variable 164
nesting rule 194
off-by-one error 167
pow standard library function 173
right justified 173
right stream manipulator 174
rvalue ("right value") 192
scope of a variable 168
setw stream manipulator 173
short-circuit evaluation 189
simple condition 187
stacking rule 194
sticky setting 174
switch multiple-selection statement 176
truth table 188
zero-based counting 167

Self-Review Exercises

5.1 State whether the following are *true* or *false*. If the answer is *false*, explain why.
    a) The default case is required in the switch selection statement.
    b) The break statement is required in the default case of a switch selection statement to exit the switch properly.
    c) The expression (x > y && a < b) is true if either the expression x > y is true or the expression a < b is true.
    d) An expression containing the || operator is true if either or both of its operands are true.

5.2 Write a C++ statement or a set of C++ statements to accomplish each of the following:
    a) Sum the odd integers between 1 and 99 using a for statement. Assume the integer variables sum and count have been declared.
    b) Print the value 333.546372 in a 15-character field with precisions of 1, 2 and 3. Print each number on the same line. Left-justify each number in its field. What three values print?
    c) Calculate the value of 2.5 raised to the power 3 using function pow. Print the result with a precision of 2 in a field width of 10 positions. What prints?
    d) Print the integers from 1 to 20 using a while loop and the counter variable x. Assume that the variable x has been declared, but not initialized. Print only 5 integers per line. [*Hint:* When x % 5 is 0, print a newline character; otherwise, print a tab character.]
    e) Repeat Exercise 5.2(d) using a for statement.

5.3 Find the errors in each of the following code segments and explain how to correct them.
    a)
```
x = 1;
while ( x <= 10 );
    x++;
}
```

b)
```
for ( y = .1; y != 1.0; y += .1 )
    cout << y << endl;
```
c)
```
switch ( n )
{
    case 1:
        cout << "The number is 1" << endl;
    case 2:
        cout << "The number is 2" << endl;
        break;
    default:
        cout << "The number is not 1 or 2" << endl;
        break;
}
```
d) The following code should print the values 1 to 10.
```
n = 1;
while ( n < 10 )
    cout << n++ << endl;
```

Answers to Self-Review Exercises

5.1 a) False. The default case is optional. Nevertheless, it's considered good software engineering to always provide a default case.

b) False. The break statement is used to exit the switch statement. The break statement is not required when the default case is the last case. Nor will the break statement be required if having control proceed with the next case makes sense.

c) False. When using the && operator, both of the relational expressions must be true for the entire expression to be true.

d) True.

5.2 a)
```
sum = 0;
for ( count = 1; count <= 99; count += 2 )
    sum += count;
```
b)
```
cout << fixed << left
    << setprecision( 1 ) << setw( 15 ) << 333.546372
    << setprecision( 2 ) << setw( 15 ) << 333.546372
    << setprecision( 3 ) << setw( 15 ) << 333.546372
    << endl;
```
Output is:
```
333.5          333.55         333.546
```
c)
```
cout << fixed << setprecision( 2 )
    << setw( 10 ) << pow( 2.5, 3 )
    << endl;
```
Output is:
```
     15.63
```
d)
```
x = 1;
while ( x <= 20 )
{
    if ( x % 5 == 0 )
        cout << x << endl;
    else
        cout << x << '\t';
    x++;
}
```

e)
```
for ( x = 1; x <= 20; x++ )
{
    if ( x % 5 == 0 )
        cout << x << endl;
    else
        cout << x << '\t';
}
```

5.3 a) *Error:* The semicolon after the `while` header causes an infinite loop.
   Correction: Replace the semicolon by a {, or remove both the ; and the }.
   b) *Error:* Using a floating-point number to control a `for` repetition statement.
   Correction: Use an `int` and perform the proper calculation to get the values you desire.
   ```
   for ( y = 1; y != 10; y++ )
       cout << ( static_cast< double >( y ) / 10 ) << endl;
   ```
   c) *Error:* Missing `break` statement in the first case.
   Correction: Add a `break` statement at the end of the first case. This is not an error if you want the statement of `case 2:` to execute every time the `case 1:` statement executes.
   d) *Error:* Improper relational operator used in the loop-continuation condition.
   Correction: Use <= rather than <, or change 10 to 11.

Exercises

5.4 Find the error(s), if any, in each of the following:
a)
```
For ( x = 100, x >= 1, x++ )
    cout << x << endl;
```
b) The following code should print whether integer `value` is odd or even:
```
switch ( value % 2 )
{
    case 0:
        cout << "Even integer" << endl;
    case 1:
        cout << "Odd integer" << endl;
}
```
c) The following code should output the odd integers from 19 to 1:
```
for ( x = 19; x >= 1; x += 2 )
    cout << x << endl;
```
d) The following code should output the even integers from 2 to 100:
```
counter = 2;
do
{
    cout << counter << endl;
    counter += 2;
} While ( counter < 100 );
```

5.5 *(Summing Integers)* Write a program that uses a `for` statement to sum a sequence of integers. Assume that the first integer read specifies the number of values remaining to be entered. Your program should read only one value per input statement. A typical input sequence might be

   5 100 200 300 400 500

where the 5 indicates that the subsequent 5 values are to be summed.

5.6 *(Averaging Integers)* Write a program that uses a `for` statement to calculate the average of several integers. Assume the last value read is the sentinel 9999. A typical input sequence might be

   10 8 11 7 9 9999

indicating that the program should calculate the average of all the values preceding 9999.

5.7   What does the following program do?

```
1   // Exercise 5.7: ex05_07.cpp
2   // What does this program print?
3   #include <iostream>
4   using namespace std;
5
6   int main()
7   {
8      int x; // declare x
9      int y; // declare y
10
11     // prompt user for input
12     cout << "Enter two integers in the range 1-20: ";
13     cin >> x >> y;  // read values for x and y
14
15     for ( int i = 1; i <= y; i++ ) // count from 1 to y
16     {
17        for ( int j = 1; j <= x; j++ ) // count from 1 to x
18           cout << '@'; // output @
19
20        cout << endl; // begin new line
21     } // end outer for
22  } // end main
```

5.8   *(Find the Smallest Integer)* Write a program that uses a for statement to find the smallest of several integers. Assume that the first value read specifies the number of values remaining.

5.9   *(Product of Odd Integers)* Write a program that uses a for statement to calculate and print the product of the odd integers from 1 to 15.

5.10   *(Factorials)* The factorial function is used frequently in probability problems. Using the definition of factorial in Exercise 4.34, write a program that uses a for statement to evaluate the factorials of the integers from 1 to 5. Print the results in tabular format. What difficulty might prevent you from calculating the factorial of 20?

5.11   *(Compound Interest)* Modify the compound interest program of Section 5.4 to repeat its steps for the interest rates 5%, 6%, 7%, 8%, 9% and 10%. Use a for statement to vary the interest rate.

5.12   *(Drawing Patterns with Nested for Loops)* Write a program that uses for statements to print the following patterns separately, one below the other. Use for loops to generate the patterns. All asterisks (*) should be printed by a single statement of the form cout << '*'; (this causes the asterisks to print side by side). [*Hint:* The last two patterns require that each line begin with an appropriate number of blanks. *Extra credit:* Combine your code from the four separate problems into a single program that prints all four patterns side by side by making clever use of nested for loops.]

(a)	(b)	(c)	(d)
*	**********	**********	*
**	*********	*********	**
***	********	********	***
****	*******	*******	****
*****	******	******	*****
******	*****	*****	******
*******	****	****	*******
********	***	***	********
*********	**	**	*********
**********	*	*	**********

5.13   *(Bar Chart)* One interesting application of computers is drawing graphs and bar charts. Write a program that reads five numbers (each between 1 and 30). Assume that the user enters only valid values. For each number that is read, your program should print a line containing that number of adjacent asterisks. For example, if your program reads the number 7, it should print *******.

5.14   *(Calculating Total Sales)* A mail order house sells five different products whose retail prices are: product 1 — $2.98, product 2—$4.50, product 3—$9.98, product 4—$4.49 and product 5—$6.87. Write a program that reads a series of pairs of numbers as follows:
  a) product number
  b) quantity sold

Your program should use a switch statement to determine the retail price for each product. Your program should calculate and display the total retail value of all products sold. Use a sentinel-controlled loop to determine when the program should stop looping and display the final results.

5.15   *(GradeBook Modification)* Modify the GradeBook program of Fig. 5.9–Fig. 5.11 to calculate the grade-point average. A grade of A is worth 4 points, B is worth 3 points, and so on.

5.16   *(Compound Interest Calculation)* Modify Fig. 5.6 so it uses only integers to calculate the compound interest. [*Hint:* Treat all monetary amounts as numbers of pennies. Then "break" the result into its dollar and cents portions by using the division and modulus operations. Insert a period.]

5.17   *(What Prints?)* Assume i = 1, j = 2, k = 3 and m = 2. What does each statement print?
  a) `cout << ( i == 1 ) << endl;`
  b) `cout << ( j == 3 ) << endl;`
  c) `cout << ( i >= 1 && j < 4 ) << endl;`
  d) `cout << ( m <= 99 && k < m ) << endl;`
  e) `cout << ( j >= i || k == m ) << endl;`
  f) `cout << ( k + m < j || 3 - j >= k ) << endl;`
  g) `cout << ( !m ) << endl;`
  h) `cout << ( !( j - m ) ) << endl;`
  i) `cout << ( !( k > m ) ) << endl;`

5.18   *(Number Systems Table)* Write a program that prints a table of the binary, octal and hexadecimal equivalents of the decimal numbers in the range 1–256. If you are not familiar with these number systems, read Appendix D, Number Systems, first. [*Hint:* You can use the stream manipulators dec, oct and hex to display integers in decimal, octal and hexadecimal formats, respectively.]

5.19   *(Calculating π)* Calculate the value of π from the infinite series

$$\pi = 4 - \frac{4}{3} + \frac{4}{5} - \frac{4}{7} + \frac{4}{9} - \frac{4}{11} + \cdots$$

Print a table that shows the approximate value of π after each of the first 1000 terms of this series.

5.20   *(Pythagorean Triples)* A right triangle can have sides that are all integers. A set of three integer values for the sides of a right triangle is called a Pythagorean triple. These three sides must satisfy the relationship that the sum of the squares of two of the sides is equal to the square of the hypotenuse. Find all Pythagorean triples for side1, side2 and hypotenuse all no larger than 500. Use a triple-nested for loop that tries all possibilities. This is an example of **brute force** computing. You'll learn in more advanced computer science courses that there are many interesting problems for which there is no known algorithmic approach other than sheer brute force.

5.21   *(Calculating Salaries)* A company pays its employees as managers (who receive a fixed weekly salary), hourly workers (who receive a fixed hourly wage for up to the first 40 hours they work and "time-and-a-half"—1.5 times their hourly wage—for overtime hours worked), commission workers (who receive $250 plus 5.7 percent of their gross weekly sales), or pieceworkers (who receive a fixed amount of money per item for each of the items they produce—each pieceworker in this company works on only one type of item). Write a program to compute the weekly pay for each employee. You do not know the number of employees in advance. Each type of employee has its own pay code:

Managers have code 1, hourly workers have code 2, commission workers have code 3 and pieceworkers have code 4. Use a switch to compute each employee's pay according to that employee's paycode. Within the switch, prompt the user (i.e., the payroll clerk) to enter the appropriate facts your program needs to calculate each employee's pay according to that employee's paycode.

5.22 *(De Morgan's Laws)* In this chapter, we discussed the logical operators &&, || and !. De Morgan's laws can sometimes make it more convenient for us to express a logical expression. These laws state that the expression !(*condition1* && *condition2*) is logically equivalent to the expression (!*condition1* || !*condition2*). Also, the expression !(*condition1* || *condition2*) is logically equivalent to the expression (!*condition1* && !*condition2*). Use De Morgan's laws to write equivalent expressions for each of the following, then write a program to show that the original expression and the new expression in each case are equivalent:

a) !(x < 5) && !(y >= 7)
b) !(a == b) || !(g != 5)
c) !((x <= 8) && (y > 4))
d) !((i > 4) || (j <= 6))

5.23 *(Diamond of Asterisks)* Write a program that prints the following diamond shape. You may use output statements that print a single asterisk (*), a single blank or a single newline. Maximize your use of repetition (with nested for statements) and minimize the number of output statements.

```
       *
      ***
     *****
    *******
   *********
    *******
     *****
      ***
       *
```

5.24 *(Diamond of Asterisks)* Modify Exercise 5.23 to read an odd number in the range 1 to 19 to specify the number of rows in the diamond, then display a diamond of the appropriate size.

5.25 *(Removing **break** and **continue**)* A criticism of the break and continue statements is that each is unstructured. These statements can always be replaced by structured statements. Describe in general how you'd remove any break statement from a loop in a program and replace it with some structured equivalent. [*Hint:* The break statement leaves a loop from within the body of the loop. Another way to leave is by failing the loop-continuation test. Consider using in the loop-continuation test a second test that indicates "early exit because of a 'break' condition."] Use the technique you developed here to remove the break statement from the program of Fig. 5.13.

5.26 What does the following program segment do?

```
1   for ( int i = 1; i <= 5; i++ )
2   {
3      for ( int j = 1; j <= 3; j++ )
4      {
5         for ( int k = 1; k <= 4; k++ )
6            cout << '*';
7
8         cout << endl;
9      } // end inner for
10
11      cout << endl;
12   } // end outer for
```

5.27 *(Removing the* `continue` *Statement)* Describe in general how you'd remove any `continue` statement from a loop in a program and replace it with some structured equivalent. Use the technique you developed here to remove the `continue` statement from the program of Fig. 5.14.

5.28 *("The Twelve Days of Christmas" Song)* Write a program that uses repetition and `switch` statements to print the song "The Twelve Days of Christmas." One `switch` statement should be used to print the day (i.e., "first," "second," etc.). A separate `switch` statement should be used to print the remainder of each verse. Visit the website www.12days.com/library/carols/12daysofxmas.htm for the complete lyrics to the song.

5.29 *(Peter Minuit Problem)* Legend has it that, in 1626, Peter Minuit purchased Manhattan Island for $24.00 in barter. Did he make a good investment? To answer this question, modify the compound interest program of Fig. 5.6 to begin with a principal of $24.00 and to calculate the amount of interest on deposit if that money had been kept on deposit until this year (e.g., 384 years through 2010). Place the `for` loop that performs the compound interest calculation in an outer `for` loop that varies the interest rate from 5% to 10% to observe the wonders of compound interest.

Making a Difference

5.30 *(Global Warming Facts Quiz)* The controversial issue of global warming has been widely publicized by the film "An Inconvenient Truth," featuring former Vice President Al Gore. Mr. Gore and a U.N. network of scientists, the Intergovernmental Panel on Climate Change, shared the 2007 Nobel Peace Prize in recognition of "their efforts to build up and disseminate greater knowledge about man-made climate change." Research *both* sides of the global warming issue online (you might want to search for phrases like "global warming skeptics"). Create a five-question multiple-choice quiz on global warming, each question having four possible answers (numbered 1–4). Be objective and try to fairly represent both sides of the issue. Next, write an application that administers the quiz, calculates the number of correct answers (zero through five) and returns a message to the user. If the user correctly answers five questions, print "Excellent"; if four, print "Very good"; if three or fewer, print "Time to brush up on your knowledge of global warming," and include a list of the websites where you found your facts.

5.31 *(Tax Plan Alternatives; The "FairTax")* There are many proposals to make taxation fairer. Check out the FairTax initiative in the United States at

www.fairtax.org/site/PageServer?pagename=calculator

Research how the proposed FairTax works. One suggestion is to eliminate income taxes and most other taxes in favor of a 23% consumption tax on all products and services that you buy. Some FairTax opponents question the 23% figure and say that because of the way the tax is calculated, it would be more accurate to say the rate is 30%—check this carefully. Write a program that prompts the user to enter expenses in various expense categories they have (e.g., housing, food, clothing, transportation, education, health care, vacations), then prints the estimated FairTax that person would pay.

Functions and an Introduction to Recursion

Form ever follows function.
—Louis Henri Sullivan

E pluribus unum.
(One composed of many.)
—Virgil

O! call back yesterday, bid time
return.
—William Shakespeare

Answer me in one word.
—William Shakespeare

There is a point at which
methods devour themselves.
—Frantz Fanon

Objectives
In this chapter you'll learn:

- To construct programs modularly from functions.
- To use common math library functions.
- The mechanisms for passing data to functions and returning results.
- How the function call/return mechanism is supported by the function call stack and activation records.
- To use random number generation to implement game-playing applications.
- How the visibility of identifiers is limited to specific regions of programs.
- To write and use recursive functions.

6.1 Introduction

Most computer programs that solve real-world problems are much larger than the programs presented in the first few chapters of this book. Experience has shown that the best way to develop and maintain a large program is to construct it from small, simple pieces, or components. This technique is called **divide and conquer**. We emphasize how to declare and use functions to facilitate the design, implementation, operation and maintenance of large programs.

We'll overview a portion of the C++ Standard Library's math functions. Next, you'll learn how to declare a function with more than one parameter. We'll also present additional information about function prototypes and how the compiler uses them to convert the type of an argument in a function call to the type specified in a function's parameter list, if necessary.

Next, we'll take a brief diversion into simulation techniques with random number generation and develop a version of the casino dice game called craps that uses most of the programming techniques you've learned.

We then present C++'s storage classes and scope rules. These determine the period during which an object exists in memory and where its identifier can be referenced in a program. You'll learn how C++ keeps track of which function is currently executing, how parameters and other local variables of functions are maintained in memory and how a function knows where to return after it completes execution. We discuss topics that help improve program performance—inline functions that can eliminate the overhead of a function call and reference parameters that can be used to pass large data items to functions efficiently.

Many of the applications you develop will have more than one function of the same name. This technique, called function overloading, is used to implement functions that perform similar tasks for arguments of different types or possibly for different numbers of arguments. We consider function templates—a mechanism for defining a family of overloaded functions. The chapter concludes with a discussion of functions that call themselves, either directly, or indirectly (through another function)—a topic called recursion.

6.2 Program Components in C++

C++ programs are typically written by combining new functions and classes you write with "prepackaged" functions and classes available in the C++ Standard Library. In this chapter, we concentrate on functions.

The C++ Standard Library provides a rich collection of functions for common mathematical calculations, string manipulations, character manipulations, input/output, error checking and many other useful operations.

Functions (called **methods** or **procedures** in other programming languages) allow you to modularize a program by separating its tasks into self-contained units. You've used a combination of library functions and your own functions in every program you've written. Functions you write are referred to as **user-defined functions** or **programmer-defined functions.** The statements in function bodies are written only once, are reused from perhaps several locations in a program and are hidden from other functions.

There are several motivations for modularizing a program with functions. One is the divide-and-conquer approach. Another is software reuse. For example, in earlier programs, we did not have to define how to read a line of text from the keyboard—C++ provides this capability via the `getline` function of the `<string>` header file. A third motivation is to avoid repeating code. Also, dividing a program into meaningful functions makes the program easier to debug and maintain.

Software Engineering Observation 6.1

To promote software reusability, every function should be limited to performing a single, well-defined task, and the name of the function should express that task effectively.

Software Engineering Observation 6.2

If you cannot choose a concise name that expresses a function's task, your function might be attempting to perform too many diverse tasks. It's usually best to break such a function into several smaller functions.

As you know, a function is invoked by a function call, and when the called function completes its task, it either returns a result or simply returns control to the caller. An analogy to this program structure is the hierarchical form of management (Figure 6.1). A boss (similar to the calling function) asks a worker (similar to the called function) to perform a task and report back (i.e., return) the results after completing the task. The boss function does not know how the worker function performs its designated tasks. The worker may also call other worker functions, unbeknownst to the boss. This hiding of implementation details promotes good software engineering. Figure 6.1 shows the `boss` function communicating with several worker functions in a hierarchical manner. The `boss` function divides the responsibilities among the various `worker` functions, and `worker1` acts as a "boss function" to `worker4` and `worker5`.

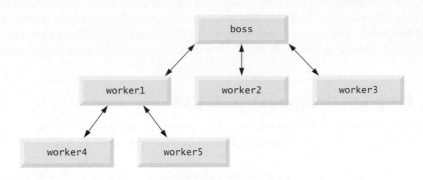

Fig. 6.1 | Hierarchical boss function/worker function relationship.

6.3 **Math Library Functions**

As you know, a class can provide member functions that perform the services of the class. For example, in Chapters 3–5, you've called the member functions of various versions of a GradeBook object to display the GradeBook's welcome message, to set its course name, to obtain a set of grades and to calculate the average of those grades.

Sometimes functions are *not* members of a class. Such functions are called **global functions**. Like a class's member functions, the function prototypes for global functions are placed in header files, so that the global functions can be reused in any program that includes the header file and that can link to the function's object code. For example, recall that we used function pow of the <cmath> header file to raise a value to a power in Figure 5.6. We introduce various functions from the <cmath> header file here to present the concept of global functions that do not belong to a particular class. In this chapter and in subsequent chapters, we use a combination of global functions (such as main) and classes with member functions to implement our example programs.

The <cmath> header file provides a collection of functions that enable you to perform common mathematical calculations. For example, you can calculate the square root of 900.0 with the function call

```
sqrt( 900.0 )
```

The preceding expression evaluates to 30.0. Function sqrt takes an argument of type double and returns a double result. There's no need to create any objects before calling function sqrt. Also, *all* functions in the <cmath> header file are global functions—therefore, each is called simply by specifying the name of the function followed by parentheses containing the function's arguments.

Function arguments may be constants, variables or more complex expressions. If c = 13.0, d = 3.0 and f = 4.0, then the statement

```
cout << sqrt( c + d * f ) << endl;
```

displays the square root of 13.0 + 3.0 * 4.0 = 25.0—namely, 5.0. Some math library functions are summarized in Fig. 6.2. In the figure, the variables x and y are of type double.

Function	Description	Example
ceil(x)	rounds x to the smallest integer not less than x	ceil(9.2) is 10.0 ceil(-9.8) is -9.0
cos(x)	trigonometric cosine of x (x in radians)	cos(0.0) is 1.0
exp(x)	exponential function e^x	exp(1.0) is 2.718282 exp(2.0) is 7.389056
fabs(x)	absolute value of x	fabs(5.1) is 5.1 fabs(0.0) is 0.0 fabs(-8.76) is 8.76
floor(x)	rounds x to the largest integer not greater than x	floor(9.2) is 9.0 floor(-9.8) is -10.0
fmod(x, y)	remainder of x/y as a floating-point number	fmod(2.6, 1.2) is 0.2
log(x)	natural logarithm of x (base e)	log(2.718282) is 1.0 log(7.389056) is 2.0
log10(x)	logarithm of x (base 10)	log10(10.0) is 1.0 log10(100.0) is 2.0
pow(x, y)	x raised to power y (x^y)	pow(2, 7) is 128 pow(9, .5) is 3
sin(x)	trigonometric sine of x (x in radians)	sin(0.0) is 0
sqrt(x)	square root of x (where x is a nonnegative value)	sqrt(9.0) is 3.0
tan(x)	trigonometric tangent of x (x in radians)	tan(0.0) is 0

Fig. 6.2 | Math library functions.

6.4 Function Definitions with Multiple Parameters

Chapters 3–5 presented classes containing simple functions that had at most one parameter. Functions often require more than one piece of information to perform their tasks. We now consider functions with multiple parameters.

The program in Figs. 6.3–6.5 modifies our GradeBook class by including a user-defined function called maximum that determines and returns the largest of three int values. When the application begins execution, the main function (lines 5–13 of Fig. 6.5) creates one object of class GradeBook (line 8) and calls the object's inputGrades member function (line 11) to read three integer grades from the user. In class GradeBook's implementation file (Fig. 6.4), lines 52–53 of member function inputGrades prompt the user to enter three integer values and read them from the user. Line 56 calls member function maximum (defined in lines 60–73). Function maximum determines the largest value, then the return statement (line 72) returns that value to the point at which function inputGrades invoked maximum (line 56). Member function inputGrades then stores maximum's return value in data member maximumGrade. This value is then output by calling function displayGradeReport (line 12 of Fig. 6.5). [*Note:* We named this function displayGradeReport because subsequent versions of class GradeBook will use this function to display a complete grade report, including the maximum and minimum grades.] In Chapter 7, Arrays and Vectors, we'll enhance class GradeBook to process an arbitrary number of grades.

```cpp
 1   // Fig. 6.3: GradeBook.h
 2   // Definition of class GradeBook that finds the maximum of three grades.
 3   // Member functions are defined in GradeBook.cpp
 4   #include <string> // program uses C++ standard string class
 5   using namespace std;
 6
 7   // GradeBook class definition
 8   class GradeBook
 9   {
10   public:
11      GradeBook( string ); // constructor initializes course name
12      void setCourseName( string ); // function to set the course name
13      string getCourseName(); // function to retrieve the course name
14      void displayMessage(); // display a welcome message
15      void inputGrades(); // input three grades from user
16      void displayGradeReport(); // display a report based on the grades
17      int maximum( int, int, int ); // determine max of 3 values
18   private:
19      string courseName; // course name for this GradeBook
20      int maximumGrade; // maximum of three grades
21   }; // end class GradeBook
```

Fig. 6.3 | GradeBook header file.

```cpp
 1   // Fig. 6.4: GradeBook.cpp
 2   // Member-function definitions for class GradeBook that
 3   // determines the maximum of three grades.
 4   #include <iostream>
 5   using namespace std;
 6
 7   #include "GradeBook.h" // include definition of class GradeBook
 8
 9   // constructor initializes courseName with string supplied as argument;
10   // initializes maximumGrade to 0
11   GradeBook::GradeBook( string name )
12   {
13      setCourseName( name ); // validate and store courseName
14      maximumGrade = 0; // this value will be replaced by the maximum grade
15   } // end GradeBook constructor
16
17   // function to set the course name; limits name to 25 or fewer characters
18   void GradeBook::setCourseName( string name )
19   {
20      if ( name.length() <= 25 ) // if name has 25 or fewer characters
21         courseName = name; // store the course name in the object
```

Fig. 6.4 | GradeBook class defines function maximum. (Part 1 of 3.)

```
22      else // if name is longer than 25 characters
23      { // set courseName to first 25 characters of parameter name
24         courseName = name.substr( 0, 25 ); // select first 25 characters
25         cout << "Name \"" << name << "\" exceeds maximum length (25).\n"
26            << "Limiting courseName to first 25 characters.\n" << endl;
27      } // end if...else
28   } // end function setCourseName
29
30   // function to retrieve the course name
31   string GradeBook::getCourseName()
32   {
33      return courseName;
34   } // end function getCourseName
35
36   // display a welcome message to the GradeBook user
37   void GradeBook::displayMessage()
38   {
39      // this statement calls getCourseName to get the
40      // name of the course this GradeBook represents
41      cout << "Welcome to the grade book for\n" << getCourseName() << "!\n"
42         << endl;
43   } // end function displayMessage
44
45   // input three grades from user; determine maximum
46   void GradeBook::inputGrades()
47   {
48      int grade1; // first grade entered by user
49      int grade2; // second grade entered by user
50      int grade3; // third grade entered by user
51
52      cout << "Enter three integer grades: ";
53      cin >> grade1 >> grade2 >> grade3;
54
55      // store maximum in member maximumGrade
56      maximumGrade = maximum( grade1, grade2, grade3 );
57   } // end function inputGrades
58
59   // returns the maximum of its three integer parameters
60   int GradeBook::maximum( int x, int y, int z )
61   {
62      int maximumValue = x; // assume x is the largest to start
63
64      // determine whether y is greater than maximumValue
65      if ( y > maximumValue )
66         maximumValue = y; // make y the new maximumValue
67
68      // determine whether z is greater than maximumValue
69      if ( z > maximumValue )
70         maximumValue = z; // make z the new maximumValue
71
72      return maximumValue;
73   } // end function maximum
74
```

Fig. 6.4 | GradeBook class defines function maximum. (Part 2 of 3.)

```
75   // display a report based on the grades entered by user
76   void GradeBook::displayGradeReport()
77   {
78      // output maximum of grades entered
79      cout << "Maximum of grades entered: " << maximumGrade << endl;
80   } // end function displayGradeReport
```

Fig. 6.4 | GradeBook class defines function maximum. (Part 3 of 3.)

```
1    // Fig. 6.5: fig06_05.cpp
2    // Create GradeBook object, input grades and display grade report.
3    #include "GradeBook.h" // include definition of class GradeBook
4
5    int main()
6    {
7       // create GradeBook object
8       GradeBook myGradeBook( "CS101 C++ Programming" );
9
10      myGradeBook.displayMessage(); // display welcome message
11      myGradeBook.inputGrades(); // read grades from user
12      myGradeBook.displayGradeReport(); // display report based on grades
13   } // end main
```

```
Welcome to the grade book for
CS101 C++ Programming!

Enter three integer grades: 86 67 75
Maximum of grades entered: 86
```

```
Welcome to the grade book for
CS101 C++ Programming!

Enter three integer grades: 67 86 75
Maximum of grades entered: 86
```

```
Welcome to the grade book for
CS101 C++ Programming!

Enter three integer grades: 67 75 86
Maximum of grades entered: 86
```

Fig. 6.5 | Demonstrating function maximum.

Software Engineering Observation 6.3

The commas used in line 56 of Fig. 6.4 to separate the arguments to function maximum are not comma operators as discussed in Section 5.3. The comma operator guarantees that its operands are evaluated left to right. The order of evaluation of a function's arguments, however, is not specified by the C++ standard. Thus, different compilers can evaluate function arguments in different orders. The C++ standard does guarantee that all arguments in a function call are evaluated before the called function executes.

Portability Tip 6.1

Sometimes when a function's arguments are expressions, such as those with calls to other functions, the order in which the compiler evaluates the arguments could affect the values of one or more of the arguments. If the evaluation order changes between compilers, the argument values passed to the function could vary, causing subtle logic errors.

Error-Prevention Tip 6.1

If you have doubts about the order of evaluation of a function's arguments and whether the order would affect the values passed to the function, evaluate the arguments in separate assignment statements before the function call, assign the result of each expression to a local variable, then pass those variables as arguments to the function.

Member function `maximum`'s prototype (Fig. 6.3, line 17) indicates that the function returns an integer value, has the name `maximum` and requires three integer parameters to perform its task. The function header (Fig. 6.4, line 60) matches the function prototype and indicates that the parameter names are x, y and z. When `maximum` is called (Fig. 6.4, line 56), the parameter x is initialized with the value of the argument `grade1`, the parameter y is initialized with the value of the argument `grade2` and the parameter z is initialized with the value of the argument `grade3`. There must be one argument in the function call for each parameter (also called a **formal parameter**) in the function definition.

Notice that multiple parameters are specified in both the function prototype and the function header as a comma-separated list. The compiler refers to the function prototype to check that calls to `maximum` contain the correct number and types of arguments and that the types of the arguments are in the correct order. In addition, the compiler uses the prototype to ensure that the value returned by the function can be used correctly in the expression that called the function (e.g., a function call that returns void cannot be used as the right side of an assignment statement). Each argument must be consistent with the type of the corresponding parameter. For example, a parameter of type double can receive values like 7.35, 22 or –0.03456, but not a string like "hello". If the arguments passed to a function do not match the types specified in the function's prototype, the compiler attempts to convert the arguments to those types. Section 6.5 discusses this conversion.

Common Programming Error 6.1

Declaring function parameters of the same type as `double x, y` *instead of* `double x, double y` *is a syntax error—a type is required for each parameter in the parameter list.*

Common Programming Error 6.2

Compilation errors occur if the function prototype, header and calls do not all agree in the number, type and order of arguments and parameters, and in the return type.

Software Engineering Observation 6.4

A function that has many parameters may be performing too many tasks. Consider dividing the function into smaller functions that perform the separate tasks. Limit the function header to one line if possible.

To determine the maximum value (lines 60–73 of Fig. 6.4), we begin with the assumption that parameter x contains the largest value, so line 62 of function `maximum` declares local variable maximumValue and initializes it with the value of parameter x. Of course, it's possible that parameter y or z contains the actual largest value, so we must compare each of these values with maximumValue. The if statement in lines 65–66 determines whether y is greater than maximumValue and, if so, assigns y to maximumValue. The if statement in lines 69–70 determines whether z is greater than maximumValue and, if so, assigns z to maximumValue. At this point the largest of the three values is in maximumValue, so line 72 returns that value to the call in line 56. When program control returns to the point in the program where maximum was called, maximum's parameters x, y and z are no longer accessible to the program.

There are three ways to return control to the point at which a function was invoked. If the function does not return a result (i.e., it has a void return type), control returns when the program reaches the function-ending right brace, or by execution of the statement

```
return;
```

If the function does return a result, the statement

```
return expression;
```

evaluates *expression* and returns the value of *expression* to the caller.

6.5 Function Prototypes and Argument Coercion

A function prototype (also called a **function declaration**) tells the compiler the name of a function, the type of data returned by the function, the number of parameters the function expects to receive, the types of those parameters and the order in which the parameters of those types are expected.

Software Engineering Observation 6.5

Function prototypes are required. Use #include preprocessor directives to obtain function prototypes for the C++ Standard Library functions from the header files of the appropriate libraries (e.g., the prototype for sqrt is in header file <cmath>; a partial list of C++ Standard Library header files appears in Section 6.6). Also use #include to obtain header files containing function prototypes written by you or other programmers.

Common Programming Error 6.3

If a function is defined before it's invoked, then its definition also serves as the function's prototype, so a separate prototype is unnecessary. If a function is invoked before it's defined, and that function does not have a function prototype, a compilation error occurs.

Software Engineering Observation 6.6

Always provide function prototypes, even though it's possible to omit them when functions are defined before they're used (in which case the function header acts as the function prototype as well). Providing the prototypes avoids tying the code to the order in which functions are defined (which can easily change as a program evolves).

Function Signatures
The portion of a function prototype that includes the name of the function and the types of its arguments is called the **function signature** or simply the **signature**. The function signature does not specify the function's return type. Functions in the same scope must have

unique signatures. The scope of a function is the region of a program in which the function is known and accessible. We'll say more about scope in Section 6.10.

 Common Programming Error 6.4
It's a compilation error if two functions in the same scope have the same signature but different return types.

In Fig. 6.3, if the function prototype in line 17 had been written

```
void maximum( int, int, int );
```

the compiler would report an error, because the `void` return type in the function prototype would differ from the `int` return type in the function header. Similarly, such a prototype would cause the statement

```
cout << maximum( 6, 7, 0 );
```

to generate a compilation error, because that statement depends on `maximum` to return a value to be displayed.

Argument Coercion

An important feature of function prototypes is **argument coercion**—i.e., forcing arguments to the appropriate types specified by the parameter declarations. For example, a program can call a function with an integer argument, even though the function prototype specifies a `double` argument—the function will still work correctly.

Argument Promotion Rules

Sometimes, argument values that do not correspond precisely to the parameter types in the function prototype can be converted by the compiler to the proper type before the function is called. These conversions occur as specified by C++'s **promotion rules**. The promotion rules indicate how to convert between types without losing data. An `int` can be converted to a `double` without changing its value. However, a `double` converted to an `int` truncates the fractional part of the `double` value. Keep in mind that `double` variables can hold numbers of much greater magnitude than `int` variables, so the loss of data may be considerable. Values may also be modified when converting large integer types to small integer types (e.g., `long` to `short`), signed to unsigned or unsigned to signed. Unsigned integers range from 0 to approximately twice the positive range of the corresponding signed type.

The promotion rules apply to expressions containing values of two or more data types; such expressions are also referred to as **mixed-type expressions**. The type of each value in a mixed-type expression is promoted to the "highest" type in the expression (actually a temporary version of each value is created and used for the expression—the original values remain unchanged). Promotion also occurs when the type of a function argument does not match the parameter type specified in the function definition or prototype. Figure 6.6 lists the fundamental data types in order from "highest type" to "lowest type."

Converting values to lower fundamental types can result in incorrect values. Therefore, a value can be converted to a lower fundamental type only by explicitly assigning the value to a variable of lower type (some compilers will issue a warning in this case) or by using a cast operator (see Section 4.9). Function argument values are converted to the parameter types in a function prototype as if they were being assigned directly to variables of those types. If a `square` function that uses an integer parameter is called with a floating-point argument, the argument is converted to `int` (a lower type), and `square` could return an incorrect value. For example, `square(4.5)` returns 16, not 20.25.

Data types	
`long double`	
`double`	
`float`	
`unsigned long int`	(synonymous with unsigned `long`)
`long int`	(synonymous with `long`)
`unsigned int`	(synonymous with `unsigned`)
`int`	
`unsigned short int`	(synonymous with unsigned `short`)
`short int`	(synonymous with `short`)
`unsigned char`	
`char`	
`bool`	

Fig. 6.6 | Promotion hierarchy for fundamental data types.

Common Programming Error 6.5

Converting from a higher data type in the promotion hierarchy to a lower type, or between signed and unsigned, can corrupt the data value, causing a loss of information.

Common Programming Error 6.6

It's a compilation error if the arguments in a function call do not match the number and types of the parameters declared in the corresponding function prototype. It's also an error if the number of arguments in the call matches, but the arguments cannot be implicitly converted to the expected types.

6.6 C++ Standard Library Header Files

The C++ Standard Library is divided into many portions, each with its own header file. The header files contain the function prototypes for the related functions that form each portion of the library. The header files also contain definitions of various class types and functions, as well as constants needed by those functions. A header file "instructs" the compiler on how to interface with library and user-written components.

Figure 6.7 lists some common C++ Standard Library header files, most of which are discussed later in the book. The term "macro" that is used several times in Fig. 6.7 is discussed in detail in Appendix E, Preprocessor. Header file names ending in .h are "old-style" header files that have been superseded by the C++ Standard Library header files. We use only the C++ Standard Library versions of each header file in this book to ensure that our examples will work on most standard C++ compilers.

Standard Library header file	Explanation
`<iostream>`	Contains function prototypes for the C++ standard input and standard output functions, introduced in Chapter 2, and is covered in more detail in Chapter 15, Stream Input/Output. This header file replaces header file `<iostream.h>`.
`<iomanip>`	Contains function prototypes for stream manipulators that format streams of data. This header file is first used in Section 4.9 and is discussed in more detail in Chapter 15, Stream Input/Output. This header file replaces header file `<iomanip.h>`.
`<cmath>`	Contains function prototypes for math library functions (discussed in Section 6.3). This header file replaces header file `<math.h>`.
`<cstdlib>`	Contains function prototypes for conversions of numbers to text, text to numbers, memory allocation, random numbers and various other utility functions. Portions of the header file are covered in Section 6.7; Chapter 11, Operator Overloading; Chapter 16, Exception Handling; Chapter 21, Bits, Characters, C Strings and `structs`; and Appendix F, C Legacy Code Topics. This header file replaces header file `<stdlib.h>`.
`<ctime>`	Contains function prototypes and types for manipulating the time and date. This header file replaces header file `<time.h>`. This header file is used in Section 6.7.
`<vector>`, `<list>`, `<deque>`, `<queue>`, `<stack>`, `<map>`, `<set>`, `<bitset>`	These header files contain classes that implement the C++ Standard Library containers. Containers store data during a program's execution. The `<vector>` header is first introduced in Chapter 7, Arrays and Vectors. We discuss all these header files in Chapter 22, Standard Template Library (STL).
`<cctype>`	Contains function prototypes for functions that test characters for certain properties (such as whether the character is a digit or a punctuation), and function prototypes for functions that can be used to convert lowercase letters to uppercase letters and vice versa. This header file replaces header file `<ctype.h>`. These topics are discussed in Chapter 21, Bits, Characters, C Strings and `structs`.
`<cstring>`	Contains function prototypes for C-style string-processing functions. This header file replaces header file `<string.h>`. This header file is used in Chapter 11, Operator Overloading.
`<typeinfo>`	Contains classes for runtime type identification (determining data types at execution time). This header file is discussed in Section 13.8.
`<exception>`, `<stdexcept>`	These header files contain classes that are used for exception handling (discussed in Chapter 16, Exception Handling).
`<memory>`	Contains classes and functions used by the C++ Standard Library to allocate memory to the C++ Standard Library containers. This header is used in Chapter 16, Exception Handling.

Fig. 6.7 | C++ Standard Library header files. (Part 1 of 2.)

Standard Library header file	Explanation
`<fstream>`	Contains function prototypes for functions that perform input from files on disk and output to files on disk (discussed in Chapter 17, File Processing). This header file replaces header file `<fstream.h>`.
`<string>`	Contains the definition of class `string` from the C++ Standard Library (discussed in Chapter 18, Class `string` and String Stream Processing).
`<sstream>`	Contains function prototypes for functions that perform input from strings in memory and output to strings in memory (discussed in Chapter 18, Class `string` and String Stream Processing).
`<functional>`	Contains classes and functions used by C++ Standard Library algorithms. This header file is used in Chapter 22.
`<iterator>`	Contains classes for accessing data in the C++ Standard Library containers. This header file is used in Chapter 22.
`<algorithm>`	Contains functions for manipulating data in C++ Standard Library containers. This header file is used in Chapter 22.
`<cassert>`	Contains macros for adding diagnostics that aid program debugging. This replaces header file `<assert.h>` from pre-standard C++. This header file is used in Appendix E, Preprocessor.
`<cfloat>`	Contains the floating-point size limits of the system. This header file replaces header file `<float.h>`.
`<climits>`	Contains the integral size limits of the system. This header file replaces header file `<limits.h>`.
`<cstdio>`	Contains function prototypes for the C-style standard input/output library functions. This header file replaces header file `<stdio.h>`.
`<locale>`	Contains classes and functions normally used by stream processing to process data in the natural form for different languages (e.g., monetary formats, sorting strings, character presentation, etc.).
`<limits>`	Contains classes for defining the numerical data type limits on each computer platform.
`<utility>`	Contains classes and functions that are used by many C++ Standard Library header files.

Fig. 6.7 | C++ Standard Library header files. (Part 2 of 2.)

6.7 Case Study: Random Number Generation

We now take a brief and hopefully entertaining diversion into a popular programming application, namely simulation and game playing. In this and the next section, we develop a game-playing program that includes multiple functions. The program uses many of the control statements and concepts discussed to this point.

The element of chance can be introduced into computer applications by using the C++ Standard Library function **rand**. Consider the following statement:

```
i = rand();
```

The function `rand` generates an unsigned integer between 0 and `RAND_MAX` (a symbolic constant defined in the `<cstdlib>` header file). The value of `RAND_MAX` must be at least 32767—the maximum positive value for a two-byte (16-bit) integer. For GNU C++, the value of `RAND_MAX` is 2147483647; for Visual Studio, the value of `RAND_MAX` is 32767. If `rand` truly produces integers at random, every number between 0 and `RAND_MAX` has an equal *chance* (or probability) of being chosen each time `rand` is called.

The range of values produced directly by the function `rand` often is different than what a specific application requires. For example, a program that simulates coin tossing might require only 0 for "heads" and 1 for "tails." A program that simulates rolling a six-sided die would require random integers in the range 1 to 6. A program that randomly predicts the next type of spaceship (out of four possibilities) that will fly across the horizon in a video game might require random integers in the range 1 through 4.

Rolling a Six-Sided Die

To demonstrate `rand`, Fig. 6.8 simulates 20 rolls of a six-sided die and displays the value of each roll. The function prototype for the `rand` function is in `<cstdlib>`. To produce integers in the range 0 to 5, we use the modulus operator (%) with `rand` as follows:

```
rand() % 6
```

This is called **scaling**. The number 6 is called the **scaling factor**. We then **shift** the range of numbers produced by adding 1 to our previous result. Figure 6.8 confirms that the results are in the range 1 to 6.

```cpp
// Fig. 6.8. fig06_08.cpp
// Shifted and scaled random integers.
#include <iostream>
#include <iomanip>
#include <cstdlib> // contains function prototype for rand
using namespace std;

int main()
{
    // loop 20 times
    for ( int counter = 1; counter <= 20; counter++ )
    {
        // pick random number from 1 to 6 and output it
        cout << setw( 10 ) << ( 1 + rand() % 6 );

        // if counter is divisible by 5, start a new line of output
        if ( counter % 5 == 0 )
            cout << endl;
    } // end for
} // end main
```

6	6	5	5	6
5	1	1	5	3
6	6	2	4	2
6	2	3	4	1

Fig. 6.8 | Shifted, scaled integers produced by `1 + rand() % 6`.

Rolling a Six-Sided Die 6,000,000 Times

To show that the numbers produced by rand occur with approximately equal likelihood, Fig. 6.9 simulates 6,000,000 rolls of a die. Each integer in the range 1 to 6 should appear approximately 1,000,000 times. This is confirmed by the program's output.

As the output shows, we can simulate the rolling of a six-sided die by scaling and shifting the values produced by rand. The program should never get to the default case (lines 45–46) in the switch structure, because the switch's controlling expression (face) always has values in the range 1–6; however, we provide the default case as a matter of good practice. After we study arrays in Chapter 7, we show how to replace the entire switch structure in Fig. 6.9 elegantly with a single-line statement.

Error-Prevention Tip 6.2

Provide a default case in a switch to catch errors even if you are absolutely, positively certain that you have no bugs!

```cpp
1   // Fig. 6.9: fig06_09.cpp
2   // Roll a six-sided die 6,000,000 times.
3   #include <iostream>
4   #include <iomanip>
5   #include <cstdlib> // contains function prototype for rand
6   using namespace std;
7
8   int main()
9   {
10      int frequency1 = 0; // count of 1s rolled
11      int frequency2 = 0; // count of 2s rolled
12      int frequency3 = 0; // count of 3s rolled
13      int frequency4 = 0; // count of 4s rolled
14      int frequency5 = 0; // count of 5s rolled
15      int frequency6 = 0; // count of 6s rolled
16
17      int face; // stores most recently rolled value
18
19      // summarize results of 6,000,000 rolls of a die
20      for ( int roll = 1; roll <= 6000000; roll++ )
21      {
22         face = 1 + rand() % 6; // random number from 1 to 6
23
24         // determine roll value 1-6 and increment appropriate counter
25         switch ( face )
26         {
27            case 1:
28               ++frequency1; // increment the 1s counter
29               break;
30            case 2:
31               ++frequency2; // increment the 2s counter
32               break;
33            case 3:
34               ++frequency3; // increment the 3s counter
35               break;
```

Fig. 6.9 | Rolling a six-sided die 6,000,000 times. (Part 1 of 2.)

```
36              case 4:
37                  ++frequency4; // increment the 4s counter
38                  break;
39              case 5:
40                  ++frequency5; // increment the 5s counter
41                  break;
42              case 6:
43                  ++frequency6; // increment the 6s counter
44                  break;
45              default: // invalid value
46                  cout << "Program should never get here!";
47          } // end switch
48      } // end for
49
50      cout << "Face" << setw( 13 ) << "Frequency" << endl; // output headers
51      cout << "  1" << setw( 13 ) << frequency1
52          << "\n   2" << setw( 13 ) << frequency2
53          << "\n   3" << setw( 13 ) << frequency3
54          << "\n   4" << setw( 13 ) << frequency4
55          << "\n   5" << setw( 13 ) << frequency5
56          << "\n   6" << setw( 13 ) << frequency6 << endl;
57  } // end main
```

Face	Frequency
1	999702
2	1000823
3	999378
4	998898
5	1000777
6	1000422

Fig. 6.9 | Rolling a six-sided die 6,000,000 times. (Part 2 of 2.)

Randomizing the Random Number Generator
Executing the program of Fig. 6.8 again produces

6	6	5	5	6
5	1	1	5	3
6	6	2	4	2
6	2	3	4	1

Notice that the program prints exactly the same sequence of values shown in Fig. 6.8. How can these be random numbers? Ironically, this repeatability is an important characteristic of function rand. When debugging a simulation program, this repeatability is essential for proving that corrections to the program work properly.

Function rand actually generates **pseudorandom numbers**. Repeatedly calling rand produces a sequence of numbers that appears to be random. However, the sequence repeats itself each time the program executes. Once a program has been thoroughly debugged, it can be conditioned to produce a different sequence of random numbers for each execution. This is called **randomizing** and is accomplished with the C++ Standard

Library function **srand**. Function srand takes an unsigned integer argument and **seeds** the rand function to produce a different sequence of random numbers for each execution.

Using Function srand

Figure 6.10 demonstrates function srand. The program uses the data type unsigned, which is short for unsigned int. An int is stored in at least two bytes of memory (typically four bytes on 32-bit systems and as much as eight bytes on 64-bit systems) and can have positive and negative values. A variable of type unsigned int is also stored in at least two bytes of memory. A two-byte unsigned int can have only nonnegative values in the range 0–65535. A four-byte unsigned int can have only nonnegative values in the range 0–4294967295. Function srand takes an unsigned int value as an argument. The function prototype for the srand function is in header file <cstdlib>.

```cpp
1    // Fig. 6.10: fig06_10.cpp
2    // Randomizing die-rolling program.
3    #include <iostream>
4    #include <iomanip>
5    #include <cstdlib> // contains prototypes for functions srand and rand
6    using namespace std;
7
8    int main()
9    {
10       unsigned seed; // stores the seed entered by the user
11
12       cout << "Enter seed: ";
13       cin >> seed;
14       srand( seed ); // seed random number generator
15
16       // loop 10 times
17       for ( int counter = 1; counter <= 10; counter++ )
18       {
19          // pick random number from 1 to 6 and output it
20          cout << setw( 10 ) << ( 1 + rand() % 6 );
21
22          // if counter is divisible by 5, start a new line of output
23          if ( counter % 5 == 0 )
24             cout << endl;
25       } // end for
26    } // end main
```

```
Enter seed: 67
         6         1         4         6         2
         1         6         1         6         4
```

```
Enter seed: 432
         4         6         3         1         6
         3         1         5         4         2
```

Fig. 6.10 | Randomizing the die-rolling program. (Part 1 of 2.)

```
Enter seed: 67
        6          1          4          6          2
        1          6          1          6          4
```

Fig. 6.10 | Randomizing the die-rolling program. (Part 2 of 2.)

Let's run the program several times and observe the results. Notice that the program produces a *different* sequence of random numbers each time it executes, provided that the user enters a different seed. We used the same seed in the first and third sample outputs, so the same series of 10 numbers is displayed in each of those outputs.

To randomize without having to enter a seed each time, we may use a statement like

```
srand( time( 0 ) );
```

This causes the computer to read its clock to obtain the value for the seed. Function **time** (with the argument 0 as written in the preceding statement) typically returns the current time as the number of seconds since January 1, 1970, at midnight Greenwich Mean Time (GMT). This value is converted to an unsigned integer and used as the seed to the random number generator. The function prototype for time is in <ctime>.

Generalized Scaling and Shifting of Random Numbers
Previously, we demonstrated how to write a single statement to simulate the rolling of a six-sided die with the statement

```
face = 1 + rand() % 6;
```

which always assigns an integer (at random) to variable face in the range $1 \leq face \leq 6$. The width of this range (i.e., the number of consecutive integers in the range) is 6 and the starting number in the range is 1. Referring to the preceding statement, we see that the width of the range is determined by the number used to scale rand with the modulus operator (i.e., 6), and the starting number of the range is equal to the number (i.e., 1) that is added to the expression rand % 6. We can generalize this result as

$$number = shiftingValue + \text{rand() } \% \; scalingFactor;$$

where *shiftingValue* is equal to the first number in the desired range of consecutive integers and *scalingFactor* is equal to the width of the desired range of consecutive integers.

6.8 Case Study: Game of Chance; Introducing enum

One of the most popular games of chance is a dice game known as "craps," which is played in casinos and back alleys worldwide. The rules of the game are straightforward:

> *A player rolls two dice. Each die has six faces. These faces contain 1, 2, 3, 4, 5 and 6 spots. After the dice have come to rest, the sum of the spots on the two upward faces is calculated. If the sum is 7 or 11 on the first roll, the player wins. If the sum is 2, 3 or 12 on the first roll (called "craps"), the player loses (i.e., the "house" wins). If the sum is 4, 5, 6, 8, 9 or 10 on the first roll, then that sum becomes the player's "point." To win, you must continue rolling the dice until you "make your point." The player loses by rolling a 7 before making the point.*

The program in Fig. 6.11 simulates the game. In the rules, notice that the player must roll two dice on the first roll and on all subsequent rolls. We define function rollDice (lines 63–75) to roll the dice and compute and print their sum. The function is defined once, but called from lines 21 and 45. The function takes no arguments and returns the sum of the two dice, so empty parentheses and the return type int are indicated in the function prototype (line 8) and function header (line 63).

```cpp
1   // Fig. 6.11: fig06_11.cpp
2   // Craps simulation.
3   #include <iostream>
4   #include <cstdlib> // contains prototypes for functions srand and rand
5   #include <ctime> // contains prototype for function time
6   using namespace std;
7
8   int rollDice(); // rolls dice, calculates and displays sum
9
10  int main()
11  {
12     // enumeration with constants that represent the game status
13     enum Status { CONTINUE, WON, LOST }; // all caps in constants
14
15     int myPoint; // point if no win or loss on first roll
16     Status gameStatus; // can contain CONTINUE, WON or LOST
17
18     // randomize random number generator using current time
19     srand( time( 0 ) );
20
21     int sumOfDice = rollDice(); // first roll of the dice
22
23     // determine game status and point (if needed) based on first roll
24     switch ( sumOfDice )
25     {
26        case 7: // win with 7 on first roll
27        case 11: // win with 11 on first roll
28           gameStatus = WON;
29           break;
30        case 2: // lose with 2 on first roll
31        case 3: // lose with 3 on first roll
32        case 12: // lose with 12 on first roll
33           gameStatus = LOST;
34           break;
35        default: // did not win or lose, so remember point
36           gameStatus = CONTINUE; // game is not over
37           myPoint = sumOfDice; // remember the point
38           cout << "Point is " << myPoint << endl;
39           break; // optional at end of switch
40     } // end switch
41
42     // while game is not complete
43     while ( gameStatus == CONTINUE ) // not WON or LOST
44     {
```

Fig. 6.11 | Craps simulation. (Part 1 of 3.)

```
45          sumOfDice = rollDice(); // roll dice again
46
47          // determine game status
48          if ( sumOfDice == myPoint ) // win by making point
49             gameStatus = WON;
50          else
51             if ( sumOfDice == 7 ) // lose by rolling 7 before point
52                gameStatus = LOST;
53       } // end while
54
55       // display won or lost message
56       if ( gameStatus == WON )
57          cout << "Player wins" << endl;
58       else
59          cout << "Player loses" << endl;
60    } // end main
61
62    // roll dice, calculate sum and display results
63    int rollDice()
64    {
65       // pick random die values
66       int die1 = 1 + rand() % 6; // first die roll
67       int die2 = 1 + rand() % 6; // second die roll
68
69       int sum = die1 + die2; // compute sum of die values
70
71       // display results of this roll
72       cout << "Player rolled " << die1 << " + " << die2
73          << " = " << sum << endl;
74       return sum; // end function rollDice
75    } // end function rollDice
```

```
Player rolled 2 + 5 = 7
Player wins
```

```
Player rolled 6 + 6 = 12
Player loses
```

```
Player rolled 1 + 3 = 4
Point is 4
Player rolled 4 + 6 = 10
Player rolled 2 + 4 = 6
Player rolled 6 + 4 = 10
Player rolled 2 + 3 = 5
Player rolled 2 + 4 = 6
Player rolled 1 + 1 = 2
Player rolled 4 + 4 = 8
Player rolled 4 + 3 = 7
Player loses
```

Fig. 6.11 | Craps simulation. (Part 2 of 3.)

```
Player rolled 3 + 3 = 6
Point is 6
Player rolled 5 + 3 = 8
Player rolled 4 + 5 = 9
Player rolled 2 + 1 = 3
Player rolled 1 + 5 = 6
Player wins
```

Fig. 6.11 | Craps simulation. (Part 3 of 3.)

The game is reasonably involved. The player may win or lose on the first roll or on any subsequent roll. The program uses variable gameStatus to keep track of this. Variable gameStatus is declared to be of new type Status. Line 13 declares a user-defined type called an **enumeration**. An enumeration, introduced by the keyword **enum** and followed by a **type name** (in this case, Status), is a set of integer constants represented by identifiers. The values of these **enumeration constants** start at 0, unless specified otherwise, and increment by 1. In the preceding enumeration, the constant CONTINUE has the value 0, WON has the value 1 and LOST has the value 2. The identifiers in an enum must be unique, but separate enumeration constants can have the same integer value.

> **Good Programming Practice 6.1**
> *Capitalize the first letter of an identifier used as a user-defined type name.*

> **Good Programming Practice 6.2**
> *Use only uppercase letters in enumeration constant names. This makes these constants stand out in a program and reminds you that enumeration constants are not variables.*

Variables of user-defined type Status can be assigned only one of the three values declared in the enumeration. When the game is won, the program sets variable gameStatus to WON (lines 28 and 49). When the game is lost, the program sets variable gameStatus to LOST (lines 33 and 52). Otherwise, the program sets variable gameStatus to CONTINUE (line 36) to indicate that the dice must be rolled again.

Another popular enumeration is

```
enum Months { JAN = 1, FEB, MAR, APR, MAY, JUN, JUL, AUG,
   SEP, OCT, NOV, DEC };
```

which creates user-defined type Months with enumeration constants representing the months of the year. The first value in the preceding enumeration is explicitly set to 1, so the remaining values increment from 1, resulting in the values 1 through 12. Any enumeration constant can be assigned an integer value in the enumeration definition, and subsequent enumeration constants each have a value 1 higher than the preceding constant in the list until the next explicit setting.

After the first roll, if the game is won or lost, the program skips the body of the while statement (lines 43–53) because gameStatus is not equal to CONTINUE. The program proceeds to the if...else statement in lines 56–59, which prints "Player wins" if gameStatus is equal to WON and "Player loses" if gameStatus is equal to LOST.

After the first roll, if the game is not over, the program saves the sum in myPoint (line 37). Execution proceeds with the while statement, because gameStatus is equal to CON-

TINUE. During each iteration of the `while`, the program calls `rollDice` to produce a new sum. If sum matches `myPoint`, the program sets `gameStatus` to `WON` (line 49), the `while`-test fails, the `if...else` statement prints `"Player wins"` and execution terminates. If sum is equal to 7, the program sets `gameStatus` to `LOST` (line 52), the `while`-test fails, the `if...else` statement prints `"Player loses"` and execution terminates.

Note the interesting use of the various program control mechanisms we've discussed. The craps program uses two functions—`main` and `rollDice`—and the `switch`, `while`, `if...else`, nested `if...else` and nested `if` statements. In the exercises, we further investigate of the game of craps.

Good Programming Practice 6.3

Using enumerations rather than integer constants can make programs clearer. You can set the value of an enumeration constant once in the enumeration declaration.

Common Programming Error 6.7

Assigning the integer equivalent of an enumeration constant (rather than the enumeration constant, itself) to a variable of the enumeration type is a compilation error.

Common Programming Error 6.8

After an enumeration constant has been defined, attempting to assign another value to the enumeration constant is a compilation error.

6.9 Storage Classes

The programs you've seen so far use identifiers for variable names. The attributes of variables include name, type, size and value. This chapter also uses identifiers as names for user-defined functions. Actually, each identifier in a program has other attributes, including **storage class**, scope and **linkage**.

C++ provides five **storage-class specifiers**: **auto**, **register**, **extern**, **mutable** and **static**. This section discusses storage-class specifiers `auto`, `register`, `extern` and `static`; `mutable` (discussed in Chapter 24, Other Topics) is used exclusively with classes.

Storage Class, Scope and Linkage

An identifier's storage class determines the period during which that identifier exists in memory. Some exist briefly, some are repeatedly created and destroyed and others exist for the entire execution of a program. First we discuss the storage classes **static** and **automatic**.

An identifier's scope is where the identifier can be referenced in a program. Some identifiers can be referenced throughout a program; others can be referenced from only limited portions of a program. Section 6.10 discusses the scope of identifiers.

An identifier's linkage determines whether it's known only in the source file where it's declared or across multiple files that are compiled, then linked together. An identifier's storage-class specifier helps determine its storage class and linkage.

Storage Class Categories

The storage-class specifiers can be split into two storage classes: automatic storage class and static storage class. Keywords `auto` and `register` are used to declare variables of the automatic storage class. Such variables are created when program execution enters the block in which they're defined, they exist while the block is active and they're destroyed when the program exits the block.

Local Variables

Only local variables of a function can be of automatic storage class. A function's local variables and parameters normally are of automatic storage class. The storage class specifier `auto` explicitly declares variables of automatic storage class. For example, the following declaration indicates that `double` variable `x` is a local variable of automatic storage class—it exists only in the nearest enclosing pair of curly braces within the body of the function in which the definition appears:

```
auto double x;
```

Local variables are of automatic storage class by default, so keyword `auto` rarely is used. For the remainder of the text, we refer to variables of automatic storage class simply as automatic variables.

Performance Tip 6.1

Automatic storage is a means of conserving memory, because automatic storage class variables exist in memory only when the block in which they're defined is executing.

Software Engineering Observation 6.7

*Automatic storage is an example of the **principle of least privilege**. In the context of an application, the principle states that code should be granted only the amount of privilege and access that it needs to accomplish its designated task, but no more. Why should we have variables stored in memory and accessible when they're not needed?*

Register Variables

Data in the machine-language version of a program is normally loaded into registers for calculations and other processing.

Performance Tip 6.2

The storage-class specifier `register` can be placed before an automatic variable declaration to suggest that the compiler maintain the variable in one of the computer's high-speed hardware registers rather than in memory. If intensely used variables such as counters or totals are kept in hardware registers, the overhead of repeatedly loading the variables from memory into the registers and storing the results back into memory is eliminated.

The compiler might ignore `register` declarations. For example, there might not be a sufficient number of registers available for the compiler to use. The following definition *suggests* that the integer variable `counter` be placed in one of the computer's registers; regardless of whether the compiler does this, `counter` is initialized to 1:

```
register int counter = 1;
```

The `register` keyword can be used only with local variables and function parameters.

Performance Tip 6.3

Often, `register` is unnecessary. Optimizing compilers can recognize frequently used variables and may place them in registers without needing a `register` declaration.

Static Storage Class

Keywords `extern` and `static` declare identifiers for variables of the static storage class and for functions. Static-storage-class variables exist from the point at which the program begins execution and last for the duration of the program. A static-storage-class variable's storage is allocated when the program begins execution. Such a variable is initialized once when its declaration is encountered. For functions, the name of the function exists when the program begins execution, just as for all other functions. However, even though the variables and the function names exist from the start of program execution, this does not mean that these identifiers can be used throughout the program. Storage class and scope (where a name can be used) are separate issues, as we'll see in Section 6.10.

Identifiers with Static Storage Class

There are two types of identifiers with static storage class—external identifiers (such as **global variables** and global function names) and local variables declared with the storage-class specifier `static`. Global variables are created by placing variable declarations outside any class or function definition. Global variables retain their values throughout the execution of the program. Global variables and global functions can be referenced by any function that follows their declarations or definitions in the source file.

Software Engineering Observation 6.8
Declaring a variable as global rather than local allows unintended side effects to occur when a function that does not need access to the variable accidentally or maliciously modifies it. This is another example of the principle of least privilege. In general, except for truly global resources such as `cin` *and* `cout`, *the use of global variables should be avoided except in certain situations with unique performance requirements.*

Software Engineering Observation 6.9
Variables used only in a particular function should be declared as local variables in that function rather than as global variables.

Local variables declared `static` are still known only in the function in which they're declared, but, unlike automatic variables, `static` local variables retain their values when the function returns to its caller. The next time the function is called, the `static` local variables contain the values they had when the function last completed execution. The following statement declares local variable `count` to be `static` and to be initialized to 1:

```
static int count = 1;
```

All numeric variables of the static storage class are initialized to zero if they're not explicitly initialized by you, but it's nevertheless a good practice to explicitly initialize all variables.

Storage-class specifiers `extern` and `static` have special meaning when they're applied explicitly to external identifiers such as global variables and global function names. In Appendix F, C Legacy Code Topics, we discuss using `extern` and `static` with external identifiers and multiple-source-file programs.

6.10 Scope Rules

The portion of the program where an identifier can be used is known as its scope. For example, when we declare a local variable in a block, it can be referenced only in that block and in blocks nested within that block. This section discusses four scopes for an identifier—**function scope**, **global namespace scope**, **local scope** and **function-prototype scope**. Later we'll see two other scopes—**class scope** (Chapter 9) and **namespace scope** (Chapter 24).

An identifier declared outside any function or class has global namespace scope. Such an identifier is "known" in all functions from the point at which it's declared until the end of the file. Global variables, function definitions and function prototypes placed outside a function all have global namespace scope.

Labels (identifiers followed by a colon such as start:) are the only identifiers with function scope. Labels can be used anywhere in the function in which they appear, but cannot be referenced outside the function body. Labels are used in goto statements (Appendix F). Labels are implementation details that functions hide from one another.

Identifiers declared inside a block have local scope. Local scope begins at the identifier's declaration and ends at the terminating right brace (}) of the block in which the identifier is declared. Local variables have local scope, as do function parameters, which are also local variables of the function. Any block can contain variable declarations. When blocks are nested and an identifier in an outer block has the same name as an identifier in an inner block, the identifier in the outer block is "hidden" until the inner block terminates. The inner block sees the value of its own local identifier and not the value of the identically named identifier in the enclosing block. Local variables declared static still have local scope, even though they exist from the time the program begins execution. Storage duration does not affect the scope of an identifier.

The only identifiers with function prototype scope are those used in the parameter list of a function prototype. As mentioned previously, function prototypes do not require names in the parameter list—only types are required. Names appearing in the parameter list of a function prototype are ignored by the compiler. Identifiers used in a function prototype can be reused elsewhere in the program without ambiguity. In a single prototype, a particular identifier can be used only once.

Common Programming Error 6.9
Accidentally using the same name for an identifier in an inner block that is used for an identifier in an outer block, when in fact you want the identifier in the outer block to be active for the duration of the inner block, is typically a logic error.

Good Programming Practice 6.4
Avoid variable names that hide names in outer scopes. This can be accomplished by avoiding the use of duplicate identifiers in a program.

The program of Fig. 6.12 demonstrates scoping issues with global variables, automatic local variables and static local variables.

Line 10 declares and initializes global variable x to 1. This global variable is hidden in any block (or function) that declares a variable named x. In main, line 14 displays the value of global variable x. Line 16 declares a local variable x and initializes it to 5. Line 19 outputs this variable to show that the global x is hidden in main. Next, lines 20–24 define a new block in main in which another local variable x is initialized to 7 (line 21). Line 23 outputs this variable to show that it hides x in the outer block of main. When the block exits, the variable x with value 7 is destroyed automatically. Next, line 26 outputs the local variable x in the outer block of main to show that it's no longer hidden.

```cpp
1   // Fig. 6.12: fig06_12.cpp
2   // A scoping example.
3   #include <iostream>
4   using namespace std;
5
6   void useLocal(); // function prototype
7   void useStaticLocal(); // function prototype
8   void useGlobal(); // function prototype
9
10  int x = 1; // global variable
11
12  int main()
13  {
14     cout << "global x in main is " << x << endl;
15
16     int x = 5; // local variable to main
17
18     cout << "local x in main's outer scope is " << x << endl;
19
20     { // start new scope
21        int x = 7; // hides both x in outer scope and global x
22
23        cout << "local x in main's inner scope is " << x << endl;
24     } // end new scope
25
26     cout << "local x in main's outer scope is " << x << endl;
27
28     useLocal(); // useLocal has local x
29     useStaticLocal(); // useStaticLocal has static local x
30     useGlobal(); // useGlobal uses global x
31     useLocal(); // useLocal reinitializes its local x
32     useStaticLocal(); // static local x retains its prior value
33     useGlobal(); // global x also retains its prior value
34
35     cout << "\nlocal x in main is " << x << endl;
36  } // end main
37
38  // useLocal reinitializes local variable x during each call
39  void useLocal()
40  {
41     int x = 25; // initialized each time useLocal is called
42
43     cout << "\nlocal x is " << x << " on entering useLocal" << endl;
44     x++;
45     cout << "local x is " << x << " on exiting useLocal" << endl;
46  } // end function useLocal
47
48  // useStaticLocal initializes static local variable x only the
49  // first time the function is called; value of x is saved
50  // between calls to this function
51  void useStaticLocal()
52  {
53     static int x = 50; // initialized first time useStaticLocal is called
```

Fig. 6.12 | Scoping example. (Part 1 of 2.)

```
54
55     cout << "\nlocal static x is " << x << " on entering useStaticLocal"
56        << endl;
57     x++;
58     cout << "local static x is " << x << " on exiting useStaticLocal"
59        << endl;
60  } // end function useStaticLocal
61
62  // useGlobal modifies global variable x during each call
63  void useGlobal()
64  {
65     cout << "\nglobal x is " << x << " on entering useGlobal" << endl;
66     x *= 10;
67     cout << "global x is " << x << " on exiting useGlobal" << endl;
68  } // end function useGlobal
```

```
global x in main is 1
local x in main's outer scope is 5
local x in main's inner scope is 7
local x in main's outer scope is 5

local x is 25 on entering useLocal
local x is 26 on exiting useLocal

local static x is 50 on entering useStaticLocal
local static x is 51 on exiting useStaticLocal

global x is 1 on entering useGlobal
global x is 10 on exiting useGlobal

local x is 25 on entering useLocal
local x is 26 on exiting useLocal

local static x is 51 on entering useStaticLocal
local static x is 52 on exiting useStaticLocal

global x is 10 on entering useGlobal
global x is 100 on exiting useGlobal

local x in main is 5
```

Fig. 6.12 | Scoping example. (Part 2 of 2.)

To demonstrate other scopes, the program defines three functions, each of which takes no arguments and returns nothing. Function useLocal (lines 39–46) declares automatic variable x (line 41) and initializes it to 25. When the program calls useLocal, the function prints the variable, increments it and prints it again before the function returns program control to its caller. Each time the program calls this function, the function recreates automatic variable x and reinitializes it to 25.

Function useStaticLocal (lines 51–60) declares static variable x and initializes it to 50. Local variables declared as static retain their values even when they're out of scope (i.e., the function in which they're declared is not executing). When the program calls useStaticLocal, the function prints x, increments it and prints it again before the function returns program control to its caller. In the next call to this function, static local variable x contains the value 51. The initialization in line 53 occurs only once—the first time useStaticLocal is called.

Function useGlobal (lines 63–68) does not declare any variables. Therefore, when it refers to variable x, the global x (line 10, preceding main) is used. When the program calls useGlobal, the function prints the global variable x, multiplies it by 10 and prints it again before the function returns program control to its caller. The next time the program calls useGlobal, the global variable has its modified value, 10. After executing functions use-Local, useStaticLocal and useGlobal twice each, the program prints the local variable x in main again to show that none of the function calls modified the value of x in main, because the functions all referred to variables in other scopes.

6.11 Function Call Stack and Activation Records

To understand how C++ performs function calls, we first need to consider a data structure (i.e., collection of related data items) known as a **stack**. Think of a stack as analogous to a pile of dishes. When a dish is placed on the pile, it's normally placed at the top (referred to as **pushing** the dish onto the stack). Similarly, when a dish is removed from the pile, it's normally removed from the top (referred to as **popping** the dish off the stack). Stacks are known as **last-in, first-out (LIFO) data structures**—the last item pushed (inserted) on the stack is the first item popped (removed) from the stack.

One of the most important mechanisms for computer science students to understand is the **function call stack** (sometimes referred to as the **program execution stack**). This data structure—working "behind the scenes"—supports the function call/return mechanism. It also supports the creation, maintenance and destruction of each called function's automatic variables. We explained the last-in, first-out (LIFO) behavior of stacks with our dish-stacking example. As we'll see in Figs. 6.14–6.16, this LIFO behavior is exactly what a function does when returning to the function that called it.

As each function is called, it may, in turn, call other functions, which may, in turn, call other functions—all before any of the functions returns. Each function eventually must return control to the function that called it. So, somehow, we must keep track of the return addresses that each function needs to return control to the function that called it. The function call stack is the perfect data structure for handling this information. Each time a function calls another function, an entry is pushed onto the stack. This entry, called a **stack frame** or an **activation record**, contains the return address that the called function needs in order to return to the calling function. It also contains some additional information we'll soon discuss. If the called function returns, instead of calling another function before returning, the stack frame for the function call is popped, and control transfers to the return address in the popped stack frame.

The beauty of the call stack is that each called function always finds the information it needs to return to its caller at the top of the call stack. And, if a function makes a call to another function, a stack frame for the new function call is simply pushed onto the call stack. Thus, the return address required by the newly called function to return to its caller is now located at the top of the stack.

The stack frames have another important responsibility. Most functions have automatic variables—parameters and any local variables the function declares. Automatic variables need to exist while a function is executing. They need to remain active if the function makes calls to other functions. But when a called function returns to its caller, the called function's automatic variables need to "go away." The called function's stack frame is a perfect place to reserve the memory for the called function's automatic variables. That stack frame exists as long as the called function is active. When that function returns—and no longer needs its local automatic variables—its stack frame is popped from the stack, and those local automatic variables are no longer known to the program.

Of course, the amount of memory in a computer is finite, so only a certain amount of memory can be used to store activation records on the function call stack. If more function calls occur than can have their activation records stored on the function call stack, an error known as **stack overflow** occurs.

Function Call Stack in Action

So, as we've seen, the call stack and activation records support the function call/return mechanism and the creation and destruction of automatic variables. Now let's consider how the call stack supports the operation of a square function called by main (lines 9–14 of Fig. 6.13). First the operating system calls main—this pushes an activation record onto the stack (shown in Fig. 6.14). The activation record tells main how to return to the operating system (i.e., transfer to return address R1) and contains the space for main's automatic variable (i.e., a, which is initialized to 10).

Function main—before returning to the operating system—now calls function square in line 13 of Fig. 6.13. This causes a stack frame for square (lines 17–20) to be pushed onto the function call stack (Fig. 6.15). This stack frame contains the return address that square needs to return to main (i.e., R2) and the memory for square's automatic variable (i.e., x).

```cpp
 1   // Fig. 6.13: fig06_13.cpp
 2   // square function used to demonstrate the function
 3   // call stack and activation records.
 4   #include <iostream>
 5   using namespace std;
 6
 7   int square( int ); // prototype for function square
 8
 9   int main()
10   {
11      int a = 10; // value to square (local automatic variable in main)
12
13      cout << a << " squared: " << square( a ) << endl; // display a squared
14   } // end main
15
16   // returns the square of an integer
17   int square( int x ) // x is a local variable
18   {
19      return x * x; // calculate square and return result
20   } // end function square
```

```
10 squared: 100
```

Fig. 6.13 | square function used to demonstrate the function call stack and activation records.

Step 1: Operating system invokes `main` to execute application.

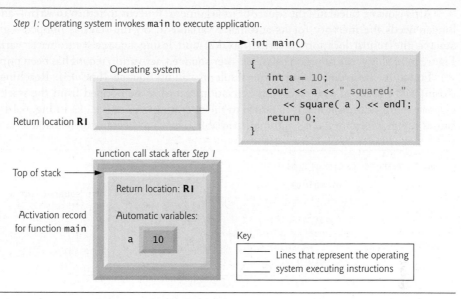

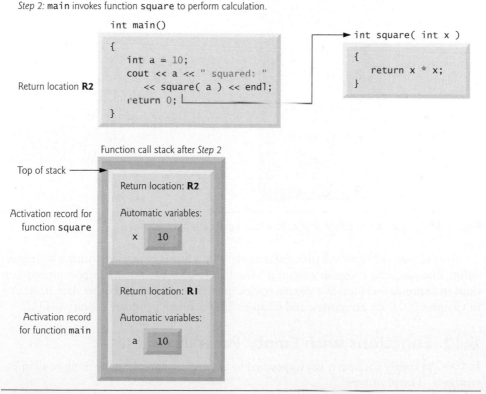

Fig. 6.14 | Function call stack after the operating system invokes `main` to execute the program.

Step 2: `main` invokes function `square` to perform calculation.

Fig. 6.15 | Function call stack after `main` invokes `square` to perform the calculation.

After `square` calculates the square of its argument, it needs to return to `main`—and no longer needs the memory for its automatic variable x. So the stack is popped—giving `square` the return location in `main` (i.e., R2) and losing `square`'s automatic variable. Figure 6.16 shows the function call stack after `square`'s activation record has been popped.

Function `main` now displays the result of calling `square` (line 13). Reaching the closing right brace of `main` causes its activation record to be popped from the stack and gives `main` the address it needs to return to the operating system (i.e., R1 in Fig. 6.14) and causes the memory for `main`'s automatic variable (i.e., a) to become unavailable.

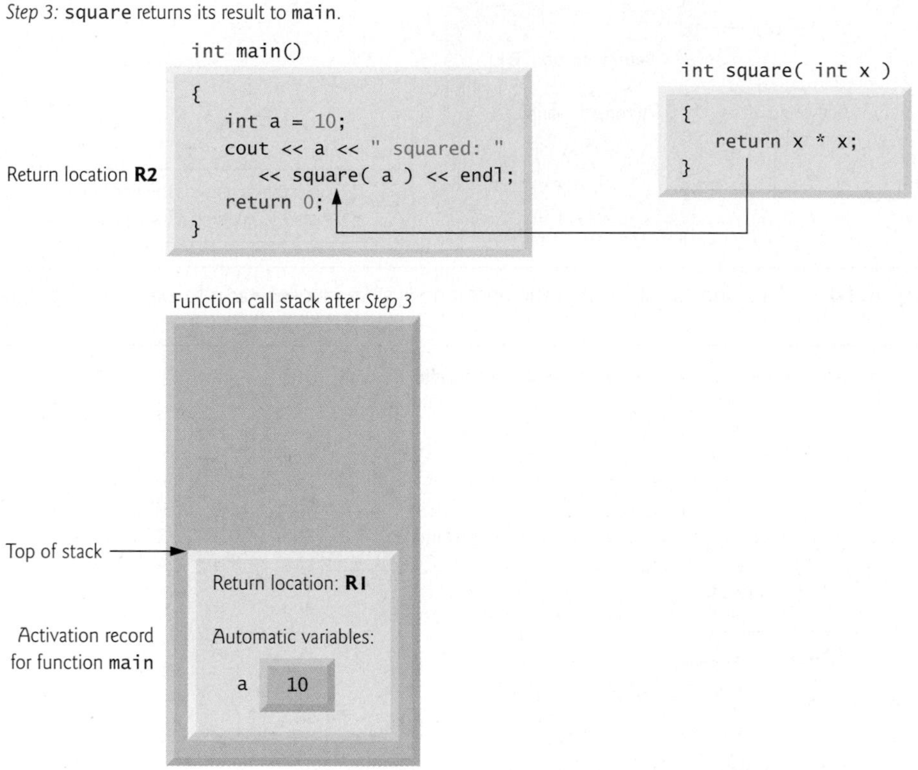

Step 3: `square` returns its result to `main`.

Fig. 6.16 | Function call stack after function `square` returns to `main`.

You've now seen how valuable the stack data structure is in implementing a key mechanism that supports program execution. Data structures have many important applications in computer science. We discuss stacks, queues, lists, trees and other data structures in Chapter 20, Data Structures, and Chapter 22, Standard Template Library (STL).

6.12 Functions with Empty Parameter Lists

In C++, an empty parameter list is specified by writing either `void` or nothing at all in parentheses. The prototype

```
void print();
```

specifies that function print does not take arguments and does not return a value. Figure 6.17 shows both ways to declare and use functions with empty parameter lists.

```cpp
1   // Fig. 6.17: fig06_17.cpp
2   // Functions that take no arguments.
3   #include <iostream>
4   using namespace std;
5
6   void function1(); // function that takes no arguments
7   void function2( void ); // function that takes no arguments
8
9   int main()
10  {
11     function1(); // call function1 with no arguments
12     function2(); // call function2 with no arguments
13  } // end main
14
15  // function1 uses an empty parameter list to specify that
16  // the function receives no arguments
17  void function1()
18  {
19     cout << "function1 takes no arguments" << endl;
20  } // end function1
21
22  // function2 uses a void parameter list to specify that
23  // the function receives no arguments
24  void function2( void )
25  {
26     cout << "function2 also takes no arguments" << endl;
27  } // end function2
```

```
function1 takes no arguments
function2 also takes no arguments
```

Fig. 6.17 | Functions that take no arguments.

 Common Programming Error 6.10

C++ programs do not compile unless function prototypes are provided for every function or each function is defined before it's called.

6.13 Inline Functions

Implementing a program as a set of functions is good from a software engineering standpoint, but function calls involve execution-time overhead. C++ provides **inline functions** to help reduce function call overhead—especially for small functions. Placing the qualifier **inline** before a function's return type in the function definition "advises" the compiler to generate a copy of the function's code in place (when appropriate) to avoid a function call. The trade-off is that multiple copies of the function code are inserted in the program (often making the program larger) rather than there being a single copy of the function to which control is passed each time the function is called. The compiler can ignore the inline qualifier and typically does so for all but the smallest functions.

Software Engineering Observation 6.10

Any change to an `inline` *function requires all clients of the function to be recompiled. This can be significant in some program development and maintenance situations.*

Good Programming Practice 6.5

The `inline` *qualifier should be used only with small, frequently used functions.*

Performance Tip 6.4

Using `inline` *functions can reduce execution time but may increase program size.*

Figure 6.18 uses `inline` function cube (lines 9–12) to calculate the volume of a cube. Keyword **const** in function cube's parameter list (line 9) tells the compiler that the function does not modify variable `side`. This ensures that `side`'s value is not changed by the function during the calculation. (Keyword `const` is discussed in detail in Chapters 7, 8 and 10.) Notice that the complete definition of function cube appears before it's used in the program. This is required so that the compiler knows how to expand a cube function call into its inlined code. For this reason, reusable inline functions are typically placed in header files, so that their definitions can be included in each source file that uses them.

Software Engineering Observation 6.11

The `const` *qualifier should be used to enforce the principle of least privilege. Using the principle of least privilege to properly design software can greatly reduce debugging time and improper side effects and can make a program easier to modify and maintain.*

```cpp
1   // Fig. 6.18: fig06_18.cpp
2   // Using an inline function to calculate the volume of a cube.
3   #include <iostream>
4   using namespace std;
5
6   // Definition of inline function cube. Definition of function appears
7   // before function is called, so a function prototype is not required.
8   // First line of function definition acts as the prototype.
9   inline double cube( const double side )
10  {
11      return side * side * side; // calculate cube
12  } // end function cube
13
14  int main()
15  {
16      double sideValue; // stores value entered by user
17      cout << "Enter the side length of your cube: ";
18      cin >> sideValue; // read value from user
19
20      // calculate cube of sideValue and display result
21      cout << "Volume of cube with side "
22          << sideValue << " is " << cube( sideValue ) << endl;
23  } // end main
```

Fig. 6.18 | `inline` function that calculates the volume of a cube. (Part 1 of 2.)

```
Enter the side length of your cube: 3.5
Volume of cube with side 3.5 is 42.875
```

Fig. 6.18 | `inline` function that calculates the volume of a cube. (Part 2 of 2.)

6.14 **References and Reference Parameters**

Two ways to pass arguments to functions in many programming languages are **pass-by-value** and **pass-by-reference**. When an argument is passed by value, a *copy* of the argument's value is made and passed (on the function call stack) to the called function. Changes to the copy do not affect the original variable's value in the caller. This prevents the accidental side effects that so greatly hinder the development of correct and reliable software systems. Each argument in this chapter has been passed by value.

Performance Tip 6.5

One disadvantage of pass-by-value is that, if a large data item is being passed, copying that data can take a considerable amount of execution time and memory space.

Reference Parameters

This section introduces **reference parameters**—the first of the two means C++ provides for performing pass-by-reference. With pass-by-reference, the caller gives the called function the ability to access the caller's data directly, and to modify that data.

Performance Tip 6.6

Pass-by-reference is good for performance reasons, because it can eliminate the pass-by-value overhead of copying large amounts of data.

Software Engineering Observation 6.12

Pass-by-reference can weaken security; the called function can corrupt the caller's data.

Later, we'll show how to achieve the performance advantage of pass-by-reference while simultaneously achieving the software engineering advantage of protecting the caller's data from corruption.

A reference parameter is an alias for its corresponding argument in a function call. To indicate that a function parameter is passed by reference, simply follow the parameter's type in the function prototype by an ampersand (&); use the same convention when listing the parameter's type in the function header. For example, the following declaration in a function header

```
    int &count
```

when read from right to left is pronounced "count is a reference to an `int`." In the function call, simply mention the variable by name to pass it by reference. Then, mentioning the variable by its parameter name in the body of the called function actually refers to the original variable in the calling function, and the original variable can be modified directly by the called function. As always, the function prototype and header must agree.

Passing Arguments by Value and by Reference

Figure 6.19 compares pass-by-value and pass-by-reference with reference parameters. The "styles" of the arguments in the calls to function `squareByValue` and function `squareByReference` are identical—both variables are simply mentioned by name in the function calls. Without checking the function prototypes or function definitions, it isn't possible to tell from the calls alone whether either function can modify its arguments. Because function prototypes are mandatory, the compiler has no trouble resolving the ambiguity.

Common Programming Error 6.11

Because reference parameters are mentioned only by name in the body of the called function, you might inadvertently treat reference parameters as pass-by-value parameters. This can cause unexpected side effects if the original variables are changed by the function.

```
1   // Fig. 6.19: fig06_19.cpp
2   // Comparing pass-by-value and pass-by-reference with references.
3   #include <iostream>
4   using namespace std;
5
6   int squareByValue( int ); // function prototype (value pass)
7   void squareByReference( int & ); // function prototype (reference pass)
8
9   int main()
10  {
11     int x = 2; // value to square using squareByValue
12     int z = 4; // value to square using squareByReference
13
14     // demonstrate squareByValue
15     cout << "x = " << x << " before squareByValue\n";
16     cout << "Value returned by squareByValue: "
17        << squareByValue( x ) << endl;
18     cout << "x = " << x << " after squareByValue\n" << endl;
19
20     // demonstrate squareByReference
21     cout << "z = " << z << " before squareByReference" << endl;
22     squareByReference( z );
23     cout << "z = " << z << " after squareByReference" << endl;
24  } // end main
25
26  // squareByValue multiplies number by itself, stores the
27  // result in number and returns the new value of number
28  int squareByValue( int number )
29  {
30     return number *= number; // caller's argument not modified
31  } // end function squareByValue
32
33  // squareByReference multiplies numberRef by itself and stores the result
34  // in the variable to which numberRef refers in function main
35  void squareByReference( int &numberRef )
36  {
37     numberRef *= numberRef; // caller's argument modified
38  } // end function squareByReference
```

Fig. 6.19 | Passing arguments by value and by reference. (Part 1 of 2.)

```
x = 2 before squareByValue
Value returned by squareByValue: 4
x = 2 after squareByValue

z = 4 before squareByReference
z = 16 after squareByReference
```

Fig. 6.19 | Passing arguments by value and by reference. (Part 2 of 2.)

Chapter 8 discusses pointers; pointers enable an alternate form of pass-by-reference in which the style of the call clearly indicates pass-by-reference (and the potential for modifying the caller's arguments).

Performance Tip 6.7

For passing large objects, use a constant reference parameter to simulate the appearance and security of pass-by-value and avoid the overhead of passing a copy of the large object.

To specify a reference to a constant, place the `const` qualifier before the type specifier in the parameter declaration. Note the placement of `&` in function `squareByReference`'s parameter list (line 35, Fig. 6.19). Some C++ programmers prefer to write the equivalent form `int& numberRef`.

References as Aliases within a Function

References can also be used as aliases for other variables within a function (although they typically are used with functions as shown in Fig. 6.19). For example, the code

```
int count = 1; // declare integer variable count
int &cRef = count; // create cRef as an alias for count
cRef++; // increment count (using its alias cRef)
```

increments variable `count` by using its alias `cRef`. Reference variables must be initialized in their declarations (see Fig. 6.20 and Fig. 6.21) and cannot be reassigned as aliases to other variables. Once a reference is declared as an alias for another variable, all operations supposedly performed on the alias (i.e., the reference) are actually performed on the original variable. The alias is simply another name for the original variable. Unless it's a reference to a constant, a reference argument must be an *lvalue* (e.g., a variable name), not a constant or expression that returns an *rvalue* (e.g., the result of a calculation). See Section 5.9 for definitions of the terms *lvalue* and *rvalue*.

```
1   // Fig. 6.20: fig06_20.cpp
2   // Initializing and using a reference.
3   #include <iostream>
4   using namespace std;
5
6   int main()
7   {
```

Fig. 6.20 | Initializing and using a reference. (Part 1 of 2.)

```
8      int x = 3;
9      int &y = x; // y refers to (is an alias for) x
10
11     cout << "x = " << x << endl << "y = " << y << endl;
12     y = 7; // actually modifies x
13     cout << "x = " << x << endl << "y = " << y << endl;
14  } // end main
```

```
x = 3
y = 3
x = 7
y = 7
```

Fig. 6.20 | Initializing and using a reference. (Part 2 of 2.)

```
1   // Fig. 6.21: fig06_21.cpp
2   // References must be initialized.
3   #include <iostream>
4   using namespace std;
5
6   int main()
7   {
8      int x = 3;
9      int &y; // Error: y must be initialized
10
11     cout << "x = " << x << endl << "y = " << y << endl;
12     y = 7;
13     cout << "x = " << x << endl << "y = " << y << endl;
14  } // end main
```

Microsoft Visual C++ compiler error message:

```
C:\cpphtp7_examples\ch06\Fig06_21\fig06_21.cpp(9) : error C2530: 'y' :
   references must be initialized
```

GNU C++ compiler error message:

```
fig06_21.cpp:9: error: 'y' declared as a reference but not initialized
```

Fig. 6.21 | Uninitialized reference causes a syntax error.

Returning a Reference from a Function

Functions can return references, but this can be dangerous. When returning a reference to a variable declared in the called function, the variable should be declared static in that function. Otherwise, the reference refers to an automatic variable that is discarded when the function terminates; such a variable is said to be "undefined," and the program's behavior is unpredictable. References to undefined variables are called **dangling references**.

Common Programming Error 6.12

Returning a reference to an automatic variable in a called function is a logic error. Some compilers issue a warning when this occurs.

Error Messages for Uninitialized References
The C++ standard does not specify the error messages that compilers use to indicate particular errors. For this reason, Fig. 6.21 shows the error messages produced by the Microsoft Visual C++ 2008 compiler and GNU C++ compiler when a reference is not initialized.

6.15 Default Arguments

It isn't uncommon for a program to invoke a function repeatedly with the same argument value for a particular parameter. In such cases, you can specify that such a parameter has a **default argument**, i.e., a default value to be passed to that parameter. When a program omits an argument for a parameter with a default argument in a function call, the compiler rewrites the function call and inserts the default value of that argument.

Default arguments must be the rightmost (trailing) arguments in a function's parameter list. When calling a function with two or more default arguments, if an omitted argument is not the rightmost argument in the argument list, then all arguments to the right of that argument also must be omitted. Default arguments must be specified with the first occurrence of the function name—typically, in the function prototype. If the function prototype is omitted because the function definition also serves as the prototype, then the default arguments should be specified in the function header. Default values can be any expression, including constants, global variables or function calls. Default arguments also can be used with `inline` functions.

Figure 6.22 demonstrates using default arguments to calculate a box's volume. The function prototype for `boxVolume` (line 7) specifies that all three parameters have been given default values of 1. We provided variable names in the function prototype for readability. As always, variable names are not required in function prototypes.

```
1   // Fig. 6.22: fig06_22.cpp
2   // Using default arguments.
3   #include <iostream>
4   using namespace std;
5
6   // function prototype that specifies default arguments
7   int boxVolume( int length = 1, int width = 1, int height = 1 );
8
9   int main()
10  {
11     // no arguments--use default values for all dimensions
12     cout << "The default box volume is: " << boxVolume();
13
14     // specify length; default width and height
15     cout << "\n\nThe volume of a box with length 10,\n"
16        << "width 1 and height 1 is: " << boxVolume( 10 );
17
18     // specify length and width; default height
19     cout << "\n\nThe volume of a box with length 10,\n"
20        << "width 5 and height 1 is: " << boxVolume( 10, 5 );
21
```

Fig. 6.22 | Default arguments to a function. (Part 1 of 2.)

```
22     // specify all arguments
23     cout << "\n\nThe volume of a box with length 10,\n"
24        << "width 5 and height 2 is: " << boxVolume( 10, 5, 2 )
25        << endl;
26  } // end main
27
28  // function boxVolume calculates the volume of a box
29  int boxVolume( int length, int width, int height )
30  {
31     return length * width * height;
32  } // end function boxVolume
```

```
The default box volume is: 1

The volume of a box with length 10,
width 1 and height 1 is: 10

The volume of a box with length 10,
width 5 and height 1 is: 50

The volume of a box with length 10,
width 5 and height 2 is: 100
```

Fig. 6.22 | Default arguments to a function. (Part 2 of 2.)

The first call to boxVolume (line 12) specifies no arguments, thus using all three default values of 1. The second call (line 16) passes only a length argument, thus using default values of 1 for the width and height arguments. The third call (line 20) passes arguments for only length and width, thus using a default value of 1 for the height argument. The last call (line 24) passes arguments for length, width and height, thus using no default values. Any arguments passed to the function explicitly are assigned to the function's parameters from left to right. Therefore, when boxVolume receives one argument, the function assigns the value of that argument to its length parameter (i.e., the leftmost parameter in the parameter list). When boxVolume receives two arguments, the function assigns the values of those arguments to its length and width parameters in that order. Finally, when boxVolume receives all three arguments, the function assigns the values of those arguments to its length, width and height parameters, respectively.

Good Programming Practice 6.6

Using default arguments can simplify writing function calls. However, some programmers feel that explicitly specifying all arguments is clearer.

Software Engineering Observation 6.13

If the default values for a function change, all client code using the function must be recompiled.

Common Programming Error 6.13

Specifying and attempting to use a default argument that is not a rightmost argument (while not simultaneously defaulting all the rightmost arguments) is a syntax error.

6.16 **Unary Scope Resolution Operator**

It's possible to declare local and global variables of the same name. C++ provides the **unary scope resolution operator (::)** to access a global variable when a local variable of the same name is in scope. The unary scope resolution operator cannot be used to access a local variable of the same name in an outer block. A global variable can be accessed directly without the unary scope resolution operator if the name of the global variable is not the same as that of a local variable in scope.

Figure 6.23 shows the unary scope resolution operator with local and global variables of the same name (lines 6 and 10). To emphasize that the local and global versions of variable number are distinct, the program declares one variable int and the other double.

```cpp
1   // Fig. 6.23: fig06_23.cpp
2   // Using the unary scope resolution operator.
3   #include <iostream>
4   using namespace std;
5
6   int number = 7; // global variable named number
7
8   int main()
9   {
10      double number = 10.5; // local variable named number
11
12      // display values of local and global variables
13      cout << "Local double value of number = " << number
14          << "\nGlobal int value of number = " << ::number << endl;
15  } // end main
```

```
Local double value of number - 10.5
Global int value of number = 7
```

Fig. 6.23 | Unary scope resolution operator.

Using the unary scope resolution operator (::) with a given variable name is optional when the only variable with that name is a global variable.

Good Programming Practice 6.7
Always using the unary scope resolution operator (::) to refer to global variables makes programs easier to read and understand, because it makes it clear that you are intending to access a global variable rather than a nonglobal variable.

Software Engineering Observation 6.14
Always using the unary scope resolution operator (::) to refer to global variables makes programs easier to modify by reducing the risk of name collisions with nonglobal variables.

Error-Prevention Tip 6.3
Always using the unary scope resolution operator (::) to refer to a global variable eliminates logic errors that might occur if a nonglobal variable hides the global variable.

Error-Prevention Tip 6.4

Avoid using variables of the same name for different purposes in a program. Although this is allowed in various circumstances, it can lead to errors.

6.17 Function Overloading

C++ enables several functions of the same name to be defined, as long as they have different signatures. This is called **function overloading**. The C++ compiler selects the proper function to call by examining the number, types and order of the arguments in the call. Function overloading is used to create several functions of the same name that perform similar tasks, but on different data types. For example, many functions in the math library are overloaded for different numeric types—the C++ standard requires float, double and long double overloaded versions of the math library functions discussed in Section 6.3.

Good Programming Practice 6.8

Overloading functions that perform closely related tasks can make programs more readable and understandable.

Overloaded **square** *Functions*

Figure 6.24 uses overloaded square functions to calculate the square of an int (lines 7–11) and the square of a double (lines 14–18). Line 22 invokes the int version of function square by passing the literal value 7. C++ treats whole number literal values as type int. Similarly, line 24 invokes the double version of function square by passing the literal value 7.5, which C++ treats as a double value. In each case the compiler chooses the proper function to call, based on the type of the argument. The last two lines of the output window confirm that the proper function was called in each case.

```cpp
1   // Fig. 6.24: fig06_24.cpp
2   // Overloaded functions.
3   #include <iostream>
4   using namespace std;
5
6   // function square for int values
7   int square( int x )
8   {
9      cout << "square of integer " << x << " is ";
10     return x * x;
11  } // end function square with int argument
12
13  // function square for double values
14  double square( double y )
15  {
16     cout << "square of double " << y << " is ";
17     return y * y;
18  } // end function square with double argument
19
20  int main()
21  {
```

Fig. 6.24 | Overloaded square functions. (Part 1 of 2.)

```
22        cout << square( 7 ); // calls int version
23        cout << endl;
24        cout << square( 7.5 ); // calls double version
25        cout << endl;
26   } // end main
```

```
square of integer 7 is 49
square of double 7.5 is 56.25
```

Fig. 6.24 | Overloaded `square` functions. (Part 2 of 2.)

How the Compiler Differentiates Overloaded Functions

Overloaded functions are distinguished by their signatures. A signature is a combination of a function's name and its parameter types (in order). The compiler encodes each function identifier with the number and types of its parameters (sometimes referred to as **name mangling** or **name decoration**) to enable **type-safe linkage**. Type-safe linkage ensures that the proper overloaded function is called and that the types of the arguments conform to the types of the parameters.

Figure 6.25 was compiled with GNU C++. Rather than showing the execution output of the program (as we normally would), we show the mangled function names produced in assembly language by GNU C++. Each mangled name (other than `main`) begins with two underscores (__) followed by the letter Z, a number and the function name. The number that follows Z specifies how many characters are in the function's name. For example, function square has 6 characters in its name, so its mangled name is prefixed with __Z6. The function name is then followed by an encoding of its parameter list. In the parameter list for function nothing2 (line 25; see the fourth output line), c represents a char, i represents an int, Rf represents a float & (i.e., a reference to a float) and Rd represents a double & (i.e., a reference to a double). In the parameter list for function nothing1, i represents an int, f represents a float, c represents a char and Ri represents an int &. The two square functions are distinguished by their parameter lists; one specifies d for double and the other specifies i for int. The return types of the functions are not specified in the mangled names. Overloaded functions can have different return types, but if they do, they must also have different parameter lists. Again, you cannot have two functions with the same signature and different return types. Function-name mangling is compiler specific. Also, function main is not mangled, because it cannot be overloaded.

```
1   // Fig. 6.25: fig06_25.cpp
2   // Name mangling.
3
4   // function square for int values
5   int square( int x )
6   {
7      return x * x;
8   } // end function square
9
```

Fig. 6.25 | Name mangling to enable type-safe linkage. (Part 1 of 2.)

```
10    // function square for double values
11    double square( double y )
12    {
13       return y * y;
14    } // end function square
15
16    // function that receives arguments of types
17    // int, float, char and int &
18    void nothing1( int a, float b, char c, int &d )
19    {
20       // empty function body
21    } // end function nothing1
22
23    // function that receives arguments of types
24    // char, int, float & and double &
25    int nothing2( char a, int b, float &c, double &d )
26    {
27       return 0;
28    } // end function nothing2
29
30    int main()
31    {
32    } // end main
```

```
__Z6squarei
__Z6squared
__Z8nothing1ifcRi
__Z8nothing2ciRfRd
_main
```

Fig. 6.25 | Name mangling to enable type-safe linkage. (Part 2 of 2.)

Common Programming Error 6.14

Creating overloaded functions with identical parameter lists and different return types is a compilation error.

The compiler uses only the parameter lists to distinguish between overloaded functions. Such functions need not have the same number of parameters. Use caution when overloading functions with default parameters, because this may cause ambiguity.

Common Programming Error 6.15

A function with default arguments omitted might be called identically to another overloaded function; this is a compilation error. For example, having a program that contains both a function that explicitly takes no arguments and a function of the same name that contains all default arguments results in a compilation error when an attempt is made to use that function name in a call passing no arguments. The compiler does not know which version of the function to choose.

Overloaded Operators

In Chapter 11, we discuss how to overload operators to define how they should operate on objects of user-defined data types. (In fact, we've been using many overloaded operators to this point, including the stream insertion operator << and the stream extraction operator >>, each of which is overloaded to be able to display data of all the fundamental types. We say more about overloading << and >> to be able to handle objects of user-defined types in Chapter 11.) Section 6.18 introduces function templates for automatically generating overloaded functions that perform identical tasks on different data types.

6.18 Function Templates

Overloaded functions are normally used to perform similar operations that involve different program logic on different data types. If the program logic and operations are identical for each data type, overloading may be performed more compactly and conveniently by using **function templates**. You write a single function template definition. Given the argument types provided in calls to this function, C++ automatically generates separate **function template specializations** to handle each type of call appropriately. Thus, defining a single function template essentially defines a whole family of overloaded functions.

Figure 6.26 contains the definition of a function template (lines 3–17) for a maximum function that determines the largest of three values. All function template definitions begin with the **template keyword** (line 3) followed by a **template parameter list** to the function template enclosed in angle brackets (< and >). Every parameter in the template parameter list (often referred to as a **formal type parameter**) is preceded by keyword typename or keyword class (which are synonyms). The formal type parameters are placeholders for fundamental types or user-defined types. These placeholders are used to specify the types of the function's parameters (line 4), to specify the function's return type (line 4) and to declare variables within the body of the function definition (line 6). A function template is defined like any other function, but uses the formal type parameters as placeholders for actual data types.

```
1   // Fig. 6.26: maximum.h
2   // Definition of function template maximum.
3   template < class T >  // or template< typename T >
4   T maximum( T value1, T value2, T value3 )
5   {
6      T maximumValue = value1; // assume value1 is maximum
7
8      // determine whether value2 is greater than maximumValue
9      if ( value2 > maximumValue )
10        maximumValue = value2;
11
12     // determine whether value3 is greater than maximumValue
13     if ( value3 > maximumValue )
14        maximumValue = value3;
15
16     return maximumValue;
17  } // end function template maximum
```

Fig. 6.26 | Function template maximum header file.

The function template in Fig. 6.26 declares a single formal type parameter T (line 3) as a placeholder for the type of the data to be tested by function maximum. The name of a type parameter must be unique in the template parameter list for a particular template definition. When the compiler detects a maximum invocation in the program source code, the type of the data passed to maximum is substituted for T throughout the template definition, and C++ creates a complete function for determining the maximum of three values of the specified data type—all three must have the same type, since we use only one type parameter in this example. Then the newly created function is compiled. Thus, templates are a means of code generation.

Figure 6.27 uses the maximum function template (lines 17, 27 and 37) to determine the largest of three int values, three double values and three char values, respectively. Three functions are created as a result of the calls in lines 17, 27 and 37—expecting three int values, three double values and three char values, respectively. The function template specialization created for type int replaces each occurrence of T with int as follows:

```
int maximum( int value1, int value2, int value3 )
{
   int maximumValue = value1; // assume value1 is maximum

   // determine whether value2 is greater than maximumValue
   if ( value2 > maximumValue )
      maximumValue = value2;

   // determine whether value3 is greater than maximumValue
   if ( value3 > maximumValue )
      maximumValue = value3;

   return maximumValue;
} // end function template maximum
```

```
1   // Fig. 6.27: fig06_27.cpp
2   // Function template maximum test program.
3   #include <iostream>
4   #include "maximum.h" // include definition of function template maximum
5   using namespace std;
6
7   int main()
8   {
9      // demonstrate maximum with int values
10     int int1, int2, int3;
11
12     cout << "Input three integer values: ";
13     cin >> int1 >> int2 >> int3;
14
15     // invoke int version of maximum
16     cout << "The maximum integer value is: "
17        << maximum( int1, int2, int3 );
18
19     // demonstrate maximum with double values
20     double double1, double2, double3;
21
22     cout << "\n\nInput three double values: ";
23     cin >> double1 >> double2 >> double3;
24
```

Fig. 6.27 | Demonstrating function template maximum. (Part 1 of 2.)

```
25      // invoke double version of maximum
26      cout << "The maximum double value is: "
27          << maximum( double1, double2, double3 );
28
29      // demonstrate maximum with char values
30      char char1, char2, char3;
31
32      cout << "\n\nInput three characters: ";
33      cin >> char1 >> char2 >> char3;
34
35      // invoke char version of maximum
36      cout << "The maximum character value is: "
37          << maximum( char1, char2, char3 ) << endl;
38  } // end main
```

```
Input three integer values: 1 2 3
The maximum integer value is: 3

Input three double values: 3.3 2.2 1.1
The maximum double value is: 3.3

Input three characters: A C B
The maximum character value is: C
```

Fig. 6.27 | Demonstrating function template `maximum`. (Part 2 of 2.)

6.19 Recursion

The programs we've discussed are generally structured as functions that call one another in a disciplined, hierarchical manner. For some problems, it's useful to have functions call themselves. A **recursive function** is a function that calls itself, either directly, or indirectly (through another function). [*Note:* Although many compilers allow function main to call itself, Section 3.6.1, paragraph 3, and Section 5.2.2, paragraph 9, of the C++ standard document indicate that main should not be called within a program or recursively. Its sole purpose is to be the starting point for program execution.] Recursion is an important topic discussed at length in upper-level computer science courses. This section and the next present simple examples of recursion. This book contains an extensive treatment of recursion. Figure 6.33 (at the end of Section 6.21) summarizes the recursion examples and exercises in the book.

We first consider recursion conceptually, then examine two programs containing recursive functions. Recursive problem-solving approaches have a number of elements in common. A recursive function is called to solve a problem. The function actually knows how to solve only the simplest case(s), or so-called **base case(s)**. If the function is called with a base case, the function simply returns a result. If the function is called with a more complex problem, it typically divides the problem into two conceptual pieces—a piece that the function knows how to do and a piece that it does not know how to do. To make recursion feasible, the latter piece must resemble the original problem, but be a slightly simpler or smaller version. This new problem looks like the original, so the function calls a copy of itself to work on the smaller problem—this is referred to as a **recursive call** and is also called the **recursion step**. The recursion step often includes the keyword `return`, because its result will be combined with the portion of the problem the function knew how to solve to form the result passed back to the original caller, possibly `main`.

The recursion step executes while the original call to the function is still "open," i.e., it has not yet finished executing. The recursion step can result in many more such recursive calls, as the function keeps dividing each new subproblem with which the function is called into two conceptual pieces. In order for the recursion to eventually terminate, each time the function calls itself with a slightly simpler version of the original problem, this sequence of smaller and smaller problems must eventually converge on the base case. At that point, the function recognizes the base case and returns a result to the previous copy of the function, and a sequence of returns ensues up the line until the original call eventually returns the final result to `main`. This sounds quite exotic compared to the kind of problem solving we've been using to this point. As an example of these concepts at work, let's write a recursive program to perform a popular mathematical calculation.

The factorial of a nonnegative integer n, written $n!$ (and pronounced "n factorial"), is the product

$$n \cdot (n-1) \cdot (n-2) \cdot \ldots \cdot 1$$

with $1!$ equal to 1, and $0!$ defined to be 1. For example, $5!$ is the product $5 \cdot 4 \cdot 3 \cdot 2 \cdot 1$, which is equal to 120.

The factorial of an integer, `number`, greater than or equal to 0, can be calculated **iteratively** (nonrecursively) by using a `for` statement as follows:

```
factorial = 1;

for ( int counter = number; counter >= 1; counter-- )
   factorial *= counter;
```

A recursive definition of the factorial function is arrived at by observing the following algebraic relationship:

$$n! = n \cdot (n-1)!$$

For example, $5!$ is clearly equal to $5 * 4!$ as is shown by the following:

$$5! = 5 \cdot 4 \cdot 3 \cdot 2 \cdot 1$$
$$5! = 5 \cdot (4 \cdot 3 \cdot 2 \cdot 1)$$
$$5! = 5 \cdot (4!)$$

The evaluation of $5!$ would proceed as shown in Fig. 6.28. Figure 6.28(a) shows how the succession of recursive calls proceeds until $1!$ is evaluated to be 1, which terminates the recursion. Figure 6.28(b) shows the values returned from each recursive call to its caller until the final value is calculated and returned.

Figure 6.29 uses recursion to calculate and print the factorials of the integers 0–10. (The choice of the data type `unsigned long` is explained momentarily.) The recursive function `factorial` (lines 18–24) first determines whether the terminating condition `number <= 1` (line 20) is true. If `number` is less than or equal to 1, the `factorial` function returns 1 (line 21), no further recursion is necessary and the function terminates. If `number` is greater than 1, line 23 expresses the problem as the product of `number` and a recursive call to `factorial` evaluating the factorial of `number - 1`, which is a slightly simpler problem than the original calculation `factorial(number)`.

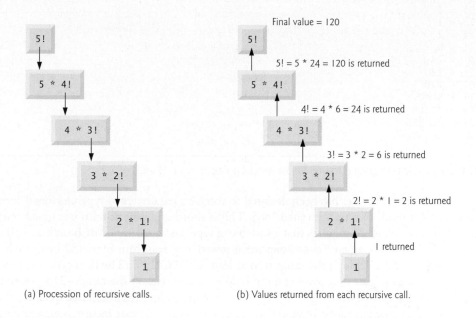

(a) Procession of recursive calls.

(b) Values returned from each recursive call.

Fig. 6.28 | Recursive evaluation of 5!.

```
1   // Fig. 6.29: fig06_29.cpp
2   // Demonstrating the recursive function factorial.
3   #include <iostream>
4   #include <iomanip>
5   using namespace std;
6
7   unsigned long factorial( unsigned long ); // function prototype
8
9   int main()
10  {
11     // calculate the factorials of 0 through 10
12     for ( int counter = 0; counter <= 10; counter++ )
13        cout << setw( 2 ) << counter << "! = " << factorial( counter )
14           << endl;
15  } // end main
16
17  // recursive definition of function factorial
18  unsigned long factorial( unsigned long number )
19  {
20     if ( number <= 1 ) // test for base case
21        return 1; // base cases: 0! = 1 and 1! = 1
22     else // recursion step
23        return number * factorial( number - 1 );
24  } // end function factorial
```

Fig. 6.29 | Demonstrating the recursive function `factorial`. (Part 1 of 2.)

```
 0! = 1
 1! = 1
 2! = 2
 3! = 6
 4! = 24
 5! = 120
 6! = 720
 7! = 5040
 8! = 40320
 9! = 362880
10! = 3628800
```

Fig. 6.29 | Demonstrating the recursive function `factorial`. (Part 2 of 2.)

Function `factorial` has been declared to receive a parameter of type `unsigned long` and return a result of type `unsigned long`. This is shorthand notation for `unsigned long int`. The C++ standard requires that a variable of type `unsigned long int` be at least as big as an `int`. Typically, an `unsigned long int` is stored in at least four bytes (32 bits); such a variable can hold a value in the range 0 to at least 4294967295. (The data type `long int` is also stored in at least four bytes and can hold a value at least in the range –2147483648 to 2147483647.) As can be seen in Fig. 6.29, factorial values become large quickly. We chose the data type `unsigned long` so that the program can calculate factorials greater than 7! on computers with small (such as two-byte) integers. Unfortunately, the function `factorial` produces large values so quickly that even `unsigned long` does not help us compute many factorial values before even the size of an `unsigned long` variable is exceeded.

Variables of type `double` could be used to calculate factorials of larger numbers. This points to a weakness in many programming languages, namely, that the languages are not easily extended to handle the unique requirements of various applications. As we'll see when we discuss object-oriented programming in more depth, C++ is an extensible language that allows us to create classes that can represent arbitrarily large integers if we wish. Such classes already are available in popular class libraries,[1] and we work on similar classes of our own in Exercise 9.14 and Exercise 11.9.

Common Programming Error 6.16

Either omitting the base case, or writing the recursion step incorrectly so that it does not converge on the base case, causes "infinite" recursion, eventually exhausting memory. This is analogous to the problem of an infinite loop in an iterative (nonrecursive) solution.

6.20 Example Using Recursion: Fibonacci Series

The Fibonacci series

$$0, 1, 1, 2, 3, 5, 8, 13, 21, \ldots$$

begins with 0 and 1 and has the property that each subsequent Fibonacci number is the sum of the previous two Fibonacci numbers.

---

1. Such classes can be found at shoup.net/ntl, cliodhna.cop.uop.edu/~hetrick/c-sources.html and www.trumphurst.com/cpplibs/datapage.phtml?category='intro'.

The series occurs in nature and, in particular, describes a form of spiral. The ratio of successive Fibonacci numbers converges on a constant value of 1.618.... This number, too, frequently occurs in nature and has been called the **golden ratio** or the **golden mean.** Humans tend to find the golden mean aesthetically pleasing. Architects often design windows, rooms and buildings whose length and width are in the ratio of the golden mean. Postcards are often designed with a golden mean length/width ratio.

The Fibonacci series can be defined recursively as follows:

fibonacci(0) = 0
fibonacci(1) = 1
fibonacci(n) = fibonacci($n - 1$) + fibonacci($n - 2$)

The program of Fig. 6.30 calculates the nth Fibonacci number recursively by using function `fibonacci`. Fibonacci numbers tend to become large quickly, although slower than factorials do. Therefore, we chose the data type `unsigned long` for the parameter type and the return type in function `fibonacci`. Figure 6.30 shows the execution of the program, which displays the Fibonacci values for several numbers.

The application begins with a `for` statement that calculates and displays the Fibonacci values for the integers 0–10 and is followed by three calls to calculate the Fibonacci values of the integers 20, 30 and 35 (lines 16–18). The calls to `fibonacci` (lines 13 and 16–18) from `main` are not recursive calls, but the calls from line 27 of `fibonacci` are recursive. Each

```
1   // Fig. 6.30: fig06_30.cpp
2   // Testing the recursive fibonacci function.
3   #include <iostream>
4   using namespace std;
5
6   unsigned long fibonacci( unsigned long ); // function prototype
7
8   int main()
9   {
10     // calculate the fibonacci values of 0 through 10
11     for ( int counter = 0; counter <= 10; counter++ )
12        cout << "fibonacci( " << counter << " ) = "
13           << fibonacci( counter ) << endl;
14
15     // display higher fibonacci values
16     cout << "fibonacci( 20 ) = " << fibonacci( 20 ) << endl;
17     cout << "fibonacci( 30 ) = " << fibonacci( 30 ) << endl;
18     cout << "fibonacci( 35 ) = " << fibonacci( 35 ) << endl;
19   } // end main
20
21   // recursive function fibonacci
22   unsigned long fibonacci( unsigned long number )
23   {
24     if ( ( number == 0 ) || ( number == 1 ) ) // base cases
25        return number;
26     else // recursion step
27        return fibonacci( number - 1 ) + fibonacci( number - 2 );
28   } // end function fibonacci
```

Fig. 6.30 | Demonstrating function `fibonacci`. (Part 1 of 2.)

```
fibonacci( 0 ) = 0
fibonacci( 1 ) = 1
fibonacci( 2 ) = 1
fibonacci( 3 ) = 2
fibonacci( 4 ) = 3
fibonacci( 5 ) = 5
fibonacci( 6 ) = 8
fibonacci( 7 ) = 13
fibonacci( 8 ) = 21
fibonacci( 9 ) = 34
fibonacci( 10 ) = 55
fibonacci( 20 ) = 6765
fibonacci( 30 ) = 832040
fibonacci( 35 ) = 9227465
```

Fig. 6.30 | Demonstrating function `fibonacci`. (Part 2 of 2.)

time the program invokes `fibonacci` (lines 22–28), the function immediately tests the base case to determine whether `number` is equal to 0 or 1 (line 24). If this is true, line 25 returns `number`. Interestingly, if `number` is greater than 1, the recursion step (line 27) generates *two* recursive calls, each for a slightly smaller problem than the original call to `fibonacci`.

Figure 6.31 shows how function `fibonacci` would evaluate `fibonacci(3)`. This figure raises some interesting issues about the order in which C++ compilers evaluate the operands of operators. This is a separate issue from the order in which operators are applied to their operands, namely, the order dictated by the rules of operator precedence and associativity. Figure 6.31 shows that evaluating `fibonacci(3)` causes two recursive calls, namely, `fibonacci(2)` and `fibonacci(1)`. In what order are these calls made?

Most programmers simply assume that the operands are evaluated left to right. C++ does not specify the order in which the operands of most operators (including +) are to be evaluated. Therefore, you must make no assumption about the order in which these calls execute. The calls could in fact execute `fibonacci(2)` first, then `fibonacci(1)`, or they

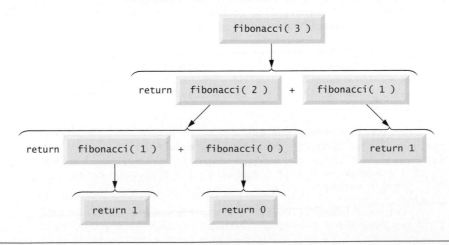

Fig. 6.31 | Set of recursive calls to function `fibonacci`.

could execute in the reverse order: `fibonacci(1)`, then `fibonacci(2)`. In this program and in most others, it turns out that the final result would be the same. However, in some programs the evaluation of an operand can have **side effects** (changes to data values) that could affect the final result of the expression.

C++ specifies the order of evaluation of the operands of only four operators—&&, ||, comma (,) and ?:. The first three are binary operators whose two operands are guaranteed to be evaluated left to right. The last operator is C++'s only ternary operator. Its leftmost operand is always evaluated first; if it evaluates to nonzero (true), the middle operand evaluates next and the last operand is ignored; if the leftmost operand evaluates to zero (false), the third operand evaluates next and the middle operand is ignored.

Common Programming Error 6.17

Writing programs that depend on the order of evaluation of the operands of operators other than &&, ||, ?: and the comma (,) operator can lead to logic errors.

Portability Tip 6.2

Programs that depend on the order of evaluation of the operands of operators other than &&, ||, ?: and the comma (,) operator can function differently with different compilers.

A word of caution is in order about recursive programs like the one we use here to generate Fibonacci numbers. Each level of recursion in function `fibonacci` has a doubling effect on the number of function calls; i.e., the number of recursive calls that are required to calculate the nth Fibonacci number is on the order of 2^n. This rapidly gets out of hand. Calculating only the 20th Fibonacci number would require on the order of 2^{20} or about a million calls, calculating the 30th Fibonacci number would require on the order of 2^{30} or about a billion calls, and so on. Computer scientists refer to this as **exponential complexity**. Problems of this nature humble even the world's most powerful computers! Complexity issues in general, and exponential complexity in particular, are discussed in detail in the upper-level computer science course generally called "Algorithms."

Performance Tip 6.8

Avoid Fibonacci-style recursive programs that result in an exponential "explosion" of calls.

6.21 Recursion vs. Iteration

In the two previous sections, we studied two functions that easily can be implemented recursively or iteratively. This section compares the two approaches and discusses why you might choose one approach over the other in a particular situation.

Both iteration and recursion are based on a control statement: Iteration uses a repetition structure; recursion uses a selection structure. Both iteration and recursion involve repetition: Iteration explicitly uses a repetition structure; recursion achieves repetition through repeated function calls. Iteration and recursion both involve a termination test: Iteration terminates when the loop-continuation condition fails; recursion terminates when a base case is recognized. Iteration with counter-controlled repetition and recursion both gradually approach termination: Iteration modifies a counter until the counter assumes a value that makes the loop-continuation condition fail; recursion produces simpler versions of the original problem until the base case is reached. Both iteration and recursion can occur infinitely: An infinite loop occurs with iteration if the loop-continuation test never becomes false; infinite recursion occurs if the recursion step does not reduce the problem during each recursive call in a manner that converges on the base case.

To illustrate the differences between iteration and recursion, let's examine an iterative solution to the factorial problem (Fig. 6.32). A repetition statement is used (lines 23–24 of Fig. 6.32) rather than the selection statement of the recursive solution (lines 20–23 of Fig. 6.29). Both solutions use a termination test. In the recursive solution, line 20 tests for the base case. In the iterative solution, line 23 tests the loop-continuation condition—if the test fails, the loop terminates. Finally, instead of producing simpler versions of the original problem, the iterative solution uses a counter that is modified until the loop-continuation condition becomes false.

```cpp
1   // Fig. 6.32: fig06_32.cpp
2   // Testing the iterative factorial function.
3   #include <iostream>
4   #include <iomanip>
5   using namespace std;
6
7   unsigned long factorial( unsigned long ); // function prototype
8
9   int main()
10  {
11     // calculate the factorials of 0 through 10
12     for ( int counter = 0; counter <= 10; counter++ )
13        cout << setw( 2 ) << counter << "! = " << factorial( counter )
14           << endl;
15  } // end main
16
17  // iterative function factorial
18  unsigned long factorial( unsigned long number )
19  {
20     unsigned long result = 1;
21
22     // iterative factorial calculation
23     for ( unsigned long i = number; i >= 1; i-- )
24        result *= i;
25
26     return result;
27  } // end function factorial
```

```
 0! = 1
 1! = 1
 2! = 2
 3! = 6
 4! = 24
 5! = 120
 6! = 720
 7! = 5040
 8! = 40320
 9! = 362880
10! = 3628800
```

Fig. 6.32 | Iterative factorial solution.

Recursion has many negatives. It repeatedly invokes the mechanism, and consequently the overhead, of function calls. This can be expensive in both processor time and memory space. Each recursive call causes another copy of the function (actually only the function's variables) to be created; this can consume considerable memory. Iteration normally occurs within a function, so the overhead of repeated function calls and extra memory assignment is omitted. So why choose recursion?

Software Engineering Observation 6.15

Any problem that can be solved recursively can also be solved iteratively (nonrecursively). A recursive approach is normally chosen when the recursive approach more naturally mirrors the problem and results in a program that is easier to understand and debug. Another reason to choose a recursive solution is that an iterative solution is not apparent.

Performance Tip 6.9

Avoid using recursion in performance situations. Recursive calls take time and consume additional memory.

Common Programming Error 6.18

Accidentally having a nonrecursive function call itself, either directly or indirectly (through another function), is a logic error.

Figure 6.33 summarizes the recursion examples and exercises in the text.

Location in text	Recursion examples and exercises
Chapter 6	
Section 6.19, Fig. 6.29	Factorial function
Section 6.20, Fig. 6.30	Fibonacci function
Exercise 6.36	Raising an integer to an integer power
Exercise 6.38	Towers of Hanoi
Exercise 6.40	Visualizing recursion
Exercise 6.41	Greatest common divisor
Exercise 6.45, Exercise 6.46	Mystery "What does this program do?" exercise
Chapter 7	
Exercise 7.18	Mystery "What does this program do?" exercise
Exercise 7.21	Mystery "What does this program do?" exercise
Exercise 7.31	Selection sort
Exercise 7.32	Determine whether a string is a palindrome
Exercise 7.33	Linear search
Exercise 7.34	Eight Queens
Exercise 7.35	Print an array
Exercise 7.36	Print a string backward
Exercise 7.37	Minimum value in an array

Fig. 6.33 | Summary of recursion examples and exercises in the text. (Part 1 of 2.)

Location in text	Recursion examples and exercises
Chapter 8	
Exercise 8.15	Quicksort
Exercise 8.16	Maze traversal
Exercise 8.17	Generating mazes randomly
Chapter 19	
Section 19.3.3, Figs. 19.5–19.7	Mergesort
Exercise 19.8	Linear search
Exercise 19.9	Binary search
Exercise 19.10	Quicksort
Chapter 20	
Section 20.7, Figs. 20.20–20.22	Binary tree insert
Section 20.7, Figs. 20.20–20.22	Preorder traversal of a binary tree
Section 20.7, Figs. 20.20–20.22	Inorder traversal of a binary tree
Section 20.7, Figs. 20.20–20.22	Postorder traversal of a binary tree
Exercise 20.20	Print a linked list backward
Exercise 20.21	Search a linked list
Exercise 20.22	Binary tree delete
Exercise 20.23	Binary tree search
Exercise 20.24	Level order traversal of a binary tree
Exercise 20.25	Printing tree

Fig. 6.33 | Summary of recursion examples and exercises in the text. (Part 2 of 2.)

6.22 Wrap-Up

In this chapter, you learned more about function declarations, including function prototypes, function signatures, function headers and function bodies. We overviewed the math library functions. You learned about argument coercion, or the forcing of arguments to the appropriate types specified by the parameter declarations of a function. We demonstrated how to use functions rand and srand to generate sets of random numbers that can be used for simulations. We showed how to define sets of constants with enums. You also learned about the scope of variables and storage classes. Two different ways to pass arguments to functions were covered—pass-by-value and pass-by-reference. For pass-by-reference, references are used as an alias to a variable. We showed how to implement inline functions and functions that receive default arguments. You learned that multiple functions in one class can be overloaded by providing functions with the same name and different signatures. Such functions can be used to perform the same or similar tasks, using different types or different numbers of parameters. We demonstrated a simpler way of overloading functions using function templates, where a function is defined once but can be used for several different types. You were then introduced to the concept of recursion, where a function calls itself to solve a problem.

In Chapter 7, you'll learn how to maintain lists and tables of data in arrays and object-oriented vectors. You'll see a more elegant array-based implementation of the dice-rolling application and two enhanced versions of the GradeBook case study we presented in Chapters 3–6 that will use arrays to store the actual grades entered.

Summary

Section 6.1 Introduction
- Experience has shown that the best way to develop and maintain a large program is to construct it from small, simple pieces, or components. This technique is called divide and conquer.

Section 6.2 Program Components in C++
- C++ programs are typically written by combining new functions and classes you write with "pre-packaged" functions and classes available in the C++ Standard Library.
- Functions allow you to modularize a program by separating its tasks into self-contained units.
- The statements in the function bodies are written only once, are reused from perhaps several locations in a program and are hidden from other functions.

Section 6.3 Math Library Functions
- Sometimes functions are not members of a class. Such functions are called global functions.
- The prototypes for global functions are placed in header files, so that they can be reused in any program that includes the header file and that can link to the function's object code.

Section 6.4 Function Definitions with Multiple Parameters
- The compiler refers to the function prototype to check that calls to a function contain the correct number and types of arguments, that the types of the arguments are in the correct order and that the value returned by the function can be used correctly in the expression that called the function.
- If a function does not return a result, control returns when the program reaches the function-ending right brace, or by execution of the statement

        return;

    If a function does return a result, the statement

        return *expression*;

    evaluates *expression* and returns the value of *expression* to the caller.

Section 6.5 Function Prototypes and Argument Coercion
- The portion of a function prototype that includes the name of the function and the types of its arguments is called the function signature or simply the signature.
- An important feature of function prototypes is argument coercion—i.e., forcing arguments to the appropriate types specified by the parameter declarations.
- Arguments can be promoted by the compiler to the parameter types as specified by C++'s promotion rules. The promotion rules indicate how to convert between types without losing data.

Section 6.6 C++ Standard Library Header Files
- The C++ Standard Library is divided into many portions, each with its own header file. The header files also contain definitions of various class types, functions and constants.
- A header file "instructs" the compiler on how to interface with library components.

Section 6.7 Case Study: Random Number Generation
- Calling rand repeatedly produces a sequence of pseudorandom numbers. The sequence repeats itself each time the program executes.
- Randomizing the numbers produced by rand is accomplished with function srand, which takes an unsigned integer argument (typically from function time) and seeds the rand function.
- Random numbers in a range can be generated with

  number = *shiftingValue* + rand() % *scalingFactor*;

  where *shiftingValue* is equal to the first number in the desired range of consecutive integers and *scalingFactor* is equal to the width of the desired range of consecutive integers.

Section 6.8 Case Study: Game of Chance; Introducing **enum**
- An enumeration, introduced by the keyword enum and followed by a type name, is a set of named integer constants. Their values start at 0, unless specified otherwise, and increment by 1.

Section 6.9 Storage Classes
- An identifier's storage class determines the period during which that identifier exists in memory.
- An identifier's scope is where the identifier can be referenced in a program.
- An identifier's linkage determines whether an identifier is known only in the source file where it's declared or across multiple files that are compiled, then linked together.
- Keywords auto and register declare variables of the automatic storage class. Such variables are created when program execution enters the block in which they're defined, they exist while the block is active and they're destroyed when the program exits the block.
- Only local variables of a function can be of automatic storage class.
- The storage-class specifier auto explicitly declares variables of automatic storage class. Local variables are of automatic storage class by default, so keyword auto is rarely used.
- Keywords extern and static declare identifiers for variables of the static storage class and for functions. Static-storage-class variables exist from the point at which the program begins execution and last for the duration of the program.
- A static-storage-class variable's storage is allocated when the program begins execution. Such a variable is initialized once when its declaration is encountered. For functions, the name of the function exists when the program begins execution as for all other functions.
- External identifiers (such as global variables and global function names) and local variables declared with the storage class-specifier static have static storage class.
- Global variables are created by placing variable declarations outside any class or function definition. Global variables retain their values throughout the program's execution. Global variables and functions can be referenced by any function that follows their declarations or definitions.

Section 6.10 Scope Rules
- Unlike automatic variables, static local variables retain their values when the function in which they're declared returns to its caller.
- An identifier declared outside any function or class has global namespace scope.
- Labels are the only identifiers with function scope. Labels can be used anywhere in the function in which they appear, but cannot be referenced outside the function body.
- Identifiers declared inside a block have local scope. Local scope begins at the identifier's declaration and ends at the terminating right brace (}) of the block in which the identifier is declared.
- Identifiers in the parameter list of a function prototype have function-prototype scope.

Section 6.11 Function Call Stack and Activation Records
- Stacks are known as last-in, first-out (LIFO) data structures—the last item pushed (inserted) on the stack is the first item popped (removed) from the stack.
- The function call stack supports the function call/return mechanism and the creation, maintenance and destruction of each called function's automatic variables.
- Each time a function calls another function, a stack frame or an activation record is pushed onto the stack containing the return address that the called function needs to return to the calling function, and the function call's automatic variables and parameters.
- The stack frame exists as long as the called function is active. When the called function returns, its stack frame is popped from the stack, and its local automatic variables no longer exist.

Section 6.12 Functions with Empty Parameter Lists
- In C++, an empty parameter list is specified by writing either void or nothing in parentheses.

Section 6.13 Inline Functions
- C++ provides inline functions to help reduce function call overhead—especially for small functions. Placing the qualifier inline before a function's return type in the function definition "advises" the compiler to generate a copy of the function's code in place to avoid a function call.

Section 6.14 References and Reference Parameters
- When an argument is passed by value, a *copy* of the argument's value is made and passed to the called function. Changes to the copy do not affect the original variable's value in the caller.
- With pass-by-reference, the caller gives the called function the ability to access the caller's data directly and to modify it if the called function chooses to do so.
- A reference parameter is an alias for its corresponding argument in a function call.
- To indicate that a function parameter is passed by reference, follow the parameter's type in the function prototype and header by an ampersand (&).
- All operations performed on a reference are actually performed on the original variable.

Section 6.15 Default Arguments
- When a function is called repeatedly with the same argument for a particular parameter, you can specify that such a parameter has a default argument.
- When a program omits an argument for a parameter with a default argument, the compiler inserts the default value of that argument to be passed to the function call.
- Default arguments must be the rightmost (trailing) arguments in a function's parameter list.
- Default arguments are typically specified in the function prototype.

Section 6.16 Unary Scope Resolution Operator
- C++ provides the unary scope resolution operator (::) to access a global variable when a local variable of the same name is in scope.

Section 6.17 Function Overloading
- C++ enables several functions of the same name to be defined, as long as these functions have different sets of parameters. This capability is called function overloading.
- When an overloaded function is called, the C++ compiler selects the proper function by examining the number, types and order of the arguments in the call.
- Overloaded functions are distinguished by their signatures.

- The compiler encodes each function identifier with the number and types of its parameters to enable type-safe linkage. Type-safe linkage ensures that the proper overloaded function is called and that the types of the arguments conform to the types of the parameters.

Section 6.18 Function Templates

- Overloaded functions typically perform similar operations that involve different program logic on different data types. If the program logic and operations are identical for each data type, overloading may be performed more compactly and conveniently using function templates.

- Given the argument types provided in calls to a function template, C++ automatically generates separate function template specializations to handle each type of call appropriately.

- All function template definitions begin with the `template` keyword followed by a template parameter list to the function template enclosed in angle brackets (< and >).

- The formal type parameters are placeholders for fundamental types or user-defined types. These placeholders are used to specify the types of the function's parameters, to specify the function's return type and to declare variables within the body of the function definition.

Section 6.19 Recursion

- A recursive function calls itself, either directly or indirectly.

- A recursive function knows how to solve only the simplest case(s), or so-called base case(s). If the function is called with a base case, the function simply returns a result.

- If the function is called with a more complex problem, the function typically divides the problem into two conceptual pieces—a piece that the function knows how to do and a piece that it does not know how to do. To make recursion feasible, the latter piece must resemble the original problem, but be a slightly simpler or slightly smaller version of it.

- For recursion to terminate, the sequence of recursive calls must converge on the base case.

Section 6.20 Example Using Recursion: Fibonacci Series

- The ratio of successive Fibonacci numbers converges on a constant value of 1.618…. This number frequently occurs in nature and has been called the golden ratio or the golden mean.

Section 6.21 Recursion vs. Iteration

- Iteration and recursion have many similarities: both are based on a control statement, involve repetition, involve a termination test, gradually approach termination and can occur infinitely.

- Recursion repeatedly invokes the mechanism, and consequently the overhead, of function calls. This can be expensive in both processor time and memory space. Each recursive call causes another copy of the function's variables to be created; this can consume considerable memory.

Terminology

Self-Review Exercises

6.1 Answer each of the following:

a) Program components in C++ are called _____ and_____.

b) A function is invoked with a(n) _____.

c) A variable that is known only within the function in which it's defined is called a(n) _____.

d) The _____ statement in a called function passes the value of an expression back to the calling function.

e) The keyword _____ is used in a function header to indicate that a function does not return a value or to indicate that a function contains no parameters.

f) An identifier's _____ is the portion of the program in which the identifier can be used.

g) The three ways to return control from a called function to a caller are _____, _____ and _____.

h) A(n) _____ allows the compiler to check the number, types and order of the arguments passed to a function.

i) Function _____ is used to produce random numbers.

j) Function _____ is used to set the random number seed to randomize a program.

k) The storage-class specifiers are mutable, _____, _____, _____ and _____.

l) Variables declared in a block or in the parameter list of a function are assumed to be of storage class _____ unless specified otherwise.

m) Storage-class specifier _____ is a recommendation to the compiler to store a variable in one of the computer's registers.

n) A variable declared outside any block or function is a(n) _____ variable.

o) For a local variable in a function to retain its value between calls to the function, it must be declared with the _____ storage-class specifier.

p) The six possible scopes of an identifier are _____, _____, _____, _____, _____ and _____.

q) A function that calls itself either directly or indirectly (i.e., through another function) is a(n) _____ function.

r) A recursive function typically has two components—one that provides a means for the recursion to terminate by testing for a(n) _____ case and one that expresses the problem as a recursive call for a slightly simpler problem than the original call.

s) It's possible to have various functions with the same name that operate on different types or numbers of arguments. This is called function _____.

t) The _____ enables access to a global variable with the same name as a variable in the current scope.

u) The _____ qualifier is used to declare read-only variables.

v) A function _____ enables a single function to be defined to perform a task on many different data types.

6.2 For the program in Fig. 6.34, state the scope (either function scope, global namespace scope, local scope or function-prototype scope) of each of the following elements:

a) The variable x in main.

b) The variable y in cube.

c) The function cube.

d) The function main.

e) The function prototype for cube.

f) The identifier y in the function prototype for cube.

```cpp
1   // Exercise 6.2: Ex06_02.cpp
2   #include <iostream>
3   using namespace std;
4
5   int cube( int y ); // function prototype
6
7   int main()
8   {
9      int x;
10
11     for ( x = 1; x <= 10; x++ ) // loop 10 times
12        cout << cube( x ) << endl; // calculate cube of x and output results
13  } // end main
14
15  // definition of function cube
16  int cube( int y )
17  {
18     return y * y * y;
19  } // end function cube
```

Fig. 6.34 | Program for Exercise 6.2.

6.3   Write a program that tests whether the examples of the math library function calls shown in Fig. 6.2 actually produce the indicated results.

6.4   Give the function header for each of the following functions:
   a) Function `hypotenuse` that takes two double-precision, floating-point arguments, `side1` and `side2`, and returns a double-precision, floating-point result.
   b) Function `smallest` that takes three integers, `x`, `y` and `z`, and returns an integer.
   c) Function `instructions` that does not receive any arguments and does not return a value. [*Note:* Such functions are commonly used to display instructions to a user.]
   d) Function `intToDouble` that takes an integer argument, `number`, and returns a double-precision, floating-point result.

6.5   Give the function prototype (without parameter names) for each of the following:
   a) The function described in Exercise 6.4(a).
   b) The function described in Exercise 6.4(b).
   c) The function described in Exercise 6.4(c).
   d) The function described in Exercise 6.4(d).

6.6   Write a declaration for each of the following:
   a) Integer `count` that should be maintained in a register. Initialize `count` to 0.
   b) Double-precision, floating-point variable `lastVal` that is to retain its value between calls to the function in which it's defined.

6.7   Find the error(s) in each of the following program segments, and explain how the error(s) can be corrected (see also Exercise 6.48):

a)
```cpp
int g()
{
    cout << "Inside function g" << endl;

    int h()
    {
        cout << "Inside function h" << endl;
    }
}
```

b)
```cpp
int sum( int x, int y )
{
    int result;

    result = x + y;
}
```

c)
```cpp
int sum( int n )
{
    if ( n == 0 )
        return 0;
    else
        n + sum( n - 1 );
}
```

d)
```cpp
void f( double a );
{
    float a;
    cout << a << endl;
}
```

e)
```cpp
void product()
{
```

```
            int a;
            int b;
            int c;
            int result;
            cout << "Enter three integers: ";
            cin >> a >> b >> c;
            result = a * b * c;
            cout << "Result is " << result;
            return result;
        }
```

6.8 Why would a function prototype contain a parameter type declaration such as double &?

6.9 (True/False) All arguments to function calls in C++ are passed by value.

6.10 Write a complete program that prompts the user for the radius of a sphere, and calculates and prints the volume of that sphere. Use an inline function sphereVolume that returns the result of the following expression: (4.0 / 3.0 * 3.14159 * pow(radius, 3)).

Answers to Self-Review Exercises

6.1 a) functions, classes. b) function call. c) local variable. d) return. e) void. f) scope. g) return;, return *expression*; or encounter the closing right brace of a function. h) function prototype. i) rand. j) srand. k) auto, register, extern, static. l) auto. m) register. n) global. o) static. p) function scope, global namespace scope, local scope, function-prototype scope, class scope, namespace scope. q) recursive. r) base. s) overloading. t) unary scope resolution operator (::). u) const. v) template.

6.2 a) local scope. b) local scope. c) global namespace scope. d) global namespace scope. e) global namespace scope. f) function-prototype scope.

6.3 See the following program:

```
 1    // Exercise 6.3: Ex06_03.cpp
 2    // Testing the math library functions.
 3    #include <iostream>
 4    #include <iomanip>
 5    #include <cmath>
 6    using namespace std;
 7
 8    int main()
 9    {
10       cout << fixed << setprecision( 1 );
11
12       cout << "sqrt(" << 900.0 << ") = " << sqrt( 900.0 )
13          << "\nsqrt(" << 9.0 << ") = " << sqrt( 9.0 );
14       cout << "\nexp(" << 1.0 << ") = " << setprecision( 6 )
15          << exp( 1.0 ) << "\nexp(" << setprecision( 1 ) << 2.0
16          << ") = " << setprecision( 6 ) << exp( 2.0 );
17       cout << "\nlog(" << 2.718282 << ") = " << setprecision( 1 )
18          << log( 2.718282 )
19          << "\nlog(" << setprecision( 6 ) << 7.389056 << ") = "
20          << setprecision( 1 ) << log( 7.389056 );
21       cout << "\nlog10(" << 1.0 << ") = " << log10( 1.0 )
22          << "\nlog10(" << 10.0 << ") = " << log10( 10.0 )
23          << "\nlog10(" << 100.0 << ") = " << log10( 100.0 ) ;
```

```
24        cout << "\nfabs(" << 5.1 << ") = " << fabs( 5.1 )
25            << "\nfabs(" << 0.0 << ") = " << fabs( 0.0 )
26            << "\nfabs(" << -8.76 << ") = " << fabs( -8.76 );
27        cout << "\nceil(" << 9.2 << ") = " << ceil( 9.2 )
28            << "\nceil(" << -9.8 << ") = " << ceil( -9.8 );
29        cout << "\nfloor(" << 9.2 << ") = " << floor( 9.2 )
30            << "\nfloor(" << -9.8 << ") = " << floor( -9.8 );
31        cout << "\npow(" << 2.0 << ", " << 7.0 << ") = "
32            << pow( 2.0, 7.0 ) << "\npow(" << 9.0 << ", "
33            << 0.5 << ") = " << pow( 9.0, 0.5 );
34        cout << setprecision(3) << "\nfmod("
35            << 2.6 << ", " << 1.2 << ") = "
36            << fmod( 2.6, 1.2 ) << setprecision( 1 );
37        cout << "\nsin(" << 0.0 << ") = " << sin( 0.0 );
38        cout << "\ncos(" << 0.0 << ") = " << cos( 0.0 );
39        cout << "\ntan(" << 0.0 << ") = " << tan( 0.0 ) << endl;
40    } // end main
```

```
sqrt(900.0) = 30.0
sqrt(9.0) = 3.0
exp(1.0) = 2.718282
exp(2.0) = 7.389056
log(2.718282) = 1.0
log(7.389056) = 2.0
log10(1.0) = 0.0
log10(10.0) = 1.0
log10(100.0) = 2.0
fabs(5.1) = 5.1
fabs(0.0) = 0.0
fabs(-8.8) = 8.8
ceil(9.2) = 10.0
ceil(-9.8) = -9.0
floor(9.2) = 9.0
floor(-9.8) = -10.0
pow(2.0, 7.0) = 128.0
pow(9.0, 0.5) = 3.0
fmod(2.600, 1.200) = 0.200
sin(0.0) = 0.0
cos(0.0) = 1.0
tan(0.0) = 0.0
```

6.4 a) `double hypotenuse( double side1, double side2 )`
       b) `int smallest( int x, int y, int z )`
       c) `void instructions()`
       d) `double intToDouble( int number )`

6.5 a) `double hypotenuse( double, double );`
       b) `int smallest( int, int, int );`
       c) `void instructions();`
       d) `double intToDouble( int );`

6.6 a) `register int count = 0;`
       b) `static double lastVal;`

6.7 a) *Error:* Function h is defined in function g.
          Correction: Move the definition of h out of the definition of g.
       b) *Error:* The function is supposed to return an integer, but does not.
          Correction: Delete variable result and place the following statement in the function:

          ```
          return x + y;
          ```

c) *Error:* The result of n + sum(n - 1) is not returned; sum returns an improper result.
Correction: Rewrite the statement in the else clause as

```
return n + sum( n - 1 );
```

d) *Errors:* Semicolon after the right parenthesis that encloses the parameter list, and re-defining the parameter a in the function definition.
Corrections: Delete the semicolon after the right parenthesis of the parameter list, and delete the declaration float a;.

e) *Error:* The function returns a value when it isn't supposed to.
Correction: Eliminate the return statement or change the return type.

6.8   This creates a reference parameter of type "reference to double" that enables the function to modify the original variable in the calling function.

6.9   False. C++ enables pass-by-reference using reference parameters (and pointers, as we discuss in Chapter 8).

6.10   See the following program:

```cpp
1   // Exercise 6.10 Solution: Ex06_10.cpp
2   // Inline function that calculates the volume of a sphere.
3   #include <iostream>
4   #include <cmath>
5   using namespace std;
6
7   const double PI = 3.14159; // define global constant PI
8
9   // calculates volume of a sphere
10  inline double sphereVolume( const double radius )
11  {
12     return 4.0 / 3.0 * PI * pow( radius, 3 );
13  } // end inline function sphereVolume
14
15  int main()
16  {
17     double radiusValue;
18
19     // prompt user for radius
20     cout << "Enter the length of the radius of your sphere: ";
21     cin >> radiusValue; // input radius
22
23     // use radiusValue to calculate volume of sphere and display result
24     cout << "Volume of sphere with radius " << radiusValue
25        << " is " << sphereVolume( radiusValue ) << endl;
26  } // end main
```

Exercises

6.11   Show the value of x after each of the following statements is performed:

a) x = fabs(7.5)
b) x = floor(7.5)
c) x = fabs(0.0)
d) x = ceil(0.0)
e) x = fabs(-6.4)
f) x = ceil(-6.4)
g) x = ceil(-fabs(-8 + floor(-5.5)))

6.12 *(Parking Charges)* A parking garage charges a $2.00 minimum fee to park for up to three hours. The garage charges an additional $0.50 per hour for each hour *or part thereof* in excess of three hours. The maximum charge for any given 24-hour period is $10.00. Assume that no car parks for longer than 24 hours at a time. Write a program that calculates and prints the parking charges for each of three customers who parked their cars in this garage yesterday. You should enter the hours parked for each customer. Your program should print the results in a neat tabular format and should calculate and print the total of yesterday's receipts. The program should use the function `calculateCharges` to determine the charge for each customer. Your outputs should appear in the following format:

```
Car      Hours      Charge
1          1.5        2.00
2          4.0        2.50
3         24.0       10.00
TOTAL     29.5       14.50
```

6.13 *(Rounding Numbers)* An application of function `floor` is rounding a value to the nearest integer. The statement

```
y = floor( x + .5 );
```

rounds the number x to the nearest integer and assigns the result to y. Write a program that reads several numbers and uses the preceding statement to round each of these numbers to the nearest integer. For each number processed, print both the original number and the rounded number.

6.14 *(Rounding Numbers)* Function `floor` can be used to round a number to a specific decimal place. The statement

```
y = floor( x * 10 + .5 ) / 10;
```

rounds x to the tenths position (the first position to the right of the decimal point). The statement

```
y = floor( x * 100 + .5 ) / 100;
```

rounds x to the hundredths position (the second position to the right of the decimal point). Write a program that defines four functions to round a number x in various ways:

   a) `roundToInteger( number )`
   b) `roundToTenths( number )`
   c) `roundToHundredths( number )`
   d) `roundToThousandths( number )`

    For each value read, your program should print the original value, the number rounded to the nearest integer, the number rounded to the nearest tenth, the number rounded to the nearest hundredth and the number rounded to the nearest thousandth.

6.15 Answer each of the following questions:
   a) What does it mean to choose numbers "at random?"
   b) Why is the `rand` function useful for simulating games of chance?
   c) Why would you randomize a program by using `srand`? Under what circumstances is it desirable not to randomize?
   d) Why is it often necessary to scale or shift the values produced by `rand`?
   e) Why is computerized simulation of real-world situations a useful technique?

6.16 Write statements that assign random integers to the variable *n* in the following ranges:
   a) $1 \le n \le 2$
   b) $1 \le n \le 100$
   c) $0 \le n \le 9$
   d) $1000 \le n \le 1112$

e) $-1 \le n \le 1$

f) $-3 \le n \le 11$

6.17 Write a single statement that prints a number at random from each of the following sets:

a) 2, 4, 6, 8, 10.

b) 3, 5, 7, 9, 11.

c) 6, 10, 14, 18, 22.

6.18 *(Exponentiation)* Write a function `integerPower(base, exponent)` that returns the value of

$$base^{\,exponent}$$

For example, `integerPower(3, 4) = 3 * 3 * 3 * 3`. Assume that *exponent* is a positive, nonzero integer and that *base* is an integer. Do not use any math library functions.

6.19 *(Hypotenuse Calculations)* Define a function `hypotenuse` that calculates the hypotenuse of a right triangle when the other two sides are given. The function should take two `double` arguments and return the hypotenuse as a `double`. Use this function in a program to determine the hypotenuse for each of the triangles shown below.

Triangle	Side 1	Side 2
1	3.0	4.0
2	5.0	12.0
3	8.0	15.0

6.20 *(Multiples)* Write a function `multiple` that determines for a pair of integers whether the second is a multiple of the first. The function should take two integer arguments and return `true` if the second is a multiple of the first, `false` otherwise. Use this function in a program that inputs a series of pairs of integers.

6.21 *(Even Numbers)* Write a program that inputs a series of integers and passes them one at a time to function `isEven`, which uses the modulus operator to determine whether an integer is even. The function should take an integer argument and return `true` if the integer is even and `false` otherwise.

6.22 *(Square of Asterisks)* Write a function that displays at the left margin of the screen a solid square of asterisks whose side is specified in integer parameter `side`. For example, if `side` is 4, the function displays the following:

```
****
****
****
****
```

6.23 *(Square of Any Character)* Modify the function created in Exercise 6.22 to form the square out of whatever character is contained in character parameter `fillCharacter`. Thus, if `side` is 5 and `fillCharacter` is #, then this function should print the following:

```
#####
#####
#####
#####
#####
```

6.24 *(Separating Digits)* Write program segments that accomplish each of the following:
  a) Calculate the integer part of the quotient when integer a is divided by integer b.
  b) Calculate the integer remainder when integer a is divided by integer b.
  c) Use the program pieces developed in (a) and (b) to write a function that inputs an integer between 1 and 32767 and prints it as a series of digits, each pair of which is separated by two spaces. For example, the integer 4562 should print as follows:

```
4   5   6   2
```

6.25 *(Calculating Number of Seconds)* Write a function that takes the time as three integer arguments (hours, minutes and seconds) and returns the number of seconds since the last time the clock "struck 12." Use this function to calculate the amount of time in seconds between two times, both of which are within one 12-hour cycle of the clock.

6.26 *(Celsius and Fahrenheit Temperatures)* Implement the following integer functions:
  a) Function celsius returns the Celsius equivalent of a Fahrenheit temperature.
  b) Function fahrenheit returns the Fahrenheit equivalent of a Celsius temperature.
  c) Use these functions to write a program that prints charts showing the Fahrenheit equivalents of all Celsius temperatures from 0 to 100 degrees, and the Celsius equivalents of all Fahrenheit temperatures from 32 to 212 degrees. Print the outputs in a neat tabular format that minimizes the number of lines of output while remaining readable.

6.27 *(Find the Minimum)* Write a program that inputs three double-precision, floating-point numbers and passes them to a function that returns the smallest number.

6.28 *(Perfect Numbers)* An integer is said to be a *perfect number* if the sum of its divisors, including 1 (but not the number itself), is equal to the number. For example, 6 is a perfect number, because 6 = 1 + 2 + 3. Write a function isPerfect that determines whether parameter number is a perfect number. Use this function in a program that determines and prints all the perfect numbers between 1 and 1000. Print the divisors of each perfect number to confirm that the number is indeed perfect. Challenge the power of your computer by testing numbers much larger than 1000.

6.29 *(Prime Numbers)* An integer is said to be *prime* if it's divisible by only 1 and itself. For example, 2, 3, 5 and 7 are prime, but 4, 6, 8 and 9 are not.
  a) Write a function that determines whether a number is prime.
  b) Use this function in a program that determines and prints all the prime numbers between 2 and 10,000. How many of these numbers do you really have to test before being sure that you've found all the primes?
  c) Initially, you might think that $n/2$ is the upper limit for which you must test to see whether a number is prime, but you need only go as high as the square root of n. Why? Rewrite the program, and run it both ways. Estimate the performance improvement.

6.30 *(Reverse Digits)* Write a function that takes an integer value and returns the number with its digits reversed. For example, given the number 7631, the function should return 1367.

6.31 *(Greatest Common Divisor)* The *greatest common divisor (GCD)* of two integers is the largest integer that evenly divides each of the numbers. Write a function gcd that returns the greatest common divisor of two integers.

6.32 *(Quality Points for Numeric Grades)* Write a function qualityPoints that inputs a student's average and returns 4 if a student's average is 90–100, 3 if the average is 80–89, 2 if the average is 70–79, 1 if the average is 60–69 and 0 if the average is lower than 60.

6.33 *(Coin Tossing)* Write a program that simulates coin tossing. For each toss of the coin, the program should print Heads or Tails. Let the program toss the coin 100 times and count the number of times each side of the coin appears. Print the results. The program should call a separate function flip that takes no arguments and returns 0 for tails and 1 for heads. [*Note:* If the program realistically simulates the coin tossing, then each side of the coin should appear approximately half the time.]

6.34   *(Guess-the-Number Game)* Write a program that plays the game of "guess the number" as follows: Your program chooses the number to be guessed by selecting an integer at random in the range 1 to 1000. The program then displays the following:

```
I have a number between 1 and 1000.
Can you guess my number?
Please type your first guess.
```

The player then types a first guess. The program responds with one of the following:

```
1. Excellent! You guessed the number!
   Would you like to play again (y or n)?
2. Too low. Try again.
3. Too high. Try again.
```

If the player's guess is incorrect, your program should loop until the player finally gets the number right. Your program should keep telling the player Too high or Too low to help the player "zero in" on the correct answer.

6.35   *(Guess-the-Number Game Modification)* Modify the program of Exercise 6.34 to count the number of guesses the player makes. If the number is 10 or fewer, print "Either you know the secret or you got lucky!" If the player guesses the number in 10 tries, then print "Ahah! You know the secret!" If the player makes more than 10 guesses, then print "You should be able to do better!" Why should it take no more than 10 guesses? Well, with each "good guess" the player should be able to eliminate half of the numbers. Now show why any number from 1 to 1000 can be guessed in 10 or fewer tries.

6.36   *(Recursive Exponentiation)* Write a recursive function power(base, exponent) that, when invoked, returns

$$base^{\ exponent}$$

For example, power(3, 4) = 3 * 3 * 3 * 3. Assume that exponent is an integer greater than or equal to 1. *Hint:* The recursion step would use the relationship

$$base^{\ exponent} = base \cdot base^{\ exponent\ -\ 1}$$

and the terminating condition occurs when exponent is equal to 1, because

$$base^1 = base$$

6.37   *(Fibonacci Series)* The Fibonacci series

$$0, 1, 1, 2, 3, 5, 8, 13, 21, \ldots$$

begins with the terms 0 and 1 and has the property that each succeeding term is the sum of the two preceding terms. (a) Write a *nonrecursive* function fibonacci(n) that uses type int to calculate the *n*th Fibonacci number. (b) Determine the largest int Fibonacci number that can be printed on your system. Modify the program of part (a) to use double instead of int to calculate and return Fibonacci numbers, and use this modified program to repeat part (b).

6.38   *(Towers of Hanoi)* In this chapter, you studied functions that can be easily implemented both recursively and iteratively. In this exercise, we present a problem whose recursive solution demonstrates the elegance of recursion, and whose iterative solution may not be as apparent.

The **Towers of Hanoi** is one of the most famous classic problems every budding computer scientist must grapple with. Legend has it that in a temple in the Far East, priests are attempting to move a stack of golden disks from one diamond peg to another (Fig. 6.35). The initial stack has 64 disks threaded onto one peg and arranged from bottom to top by decreasing size. The priests are attempting to move the stack from one peg to another under the constraints that exactly one disk is moved at a time and at no time may a larger disk be placed above a smaller disk. Three pegs are provided, one being used for temporarily holding disks. Supposedly, the world will end when the priests complete their task, so there is little incentive for us to facilitate their efforts.

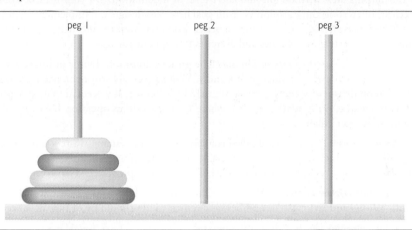

Fig. 6.35 | Towers of Hanoi for the case with four disks.

Let's assume that the priests are attempting to move the disks from peg 1 to peg 3. We wish to develop an algorithm that prints the precise sequence of peg-to-peg disk transfers.

If we were to approach this problem with conventional methods, we would rapidly find ourselves hopelessly knotted up in managing the disks. Instead, attacking this problem with recursion in mind allows the steps to be simple. Moving n disks can be viewed in terms of moving only $n - 1$ disks (hence, the recursion), as follows:

a) Move $n - 1$ disks from peg 1 to peg 2, using peg 3 as a temporary holding area.
b) Move the last disk (the largest) from peg 1 to peg 3.
c) Move the $n - 1$ disks from peg 2 to peg 3, using peg 1 as a temporary holding area.

The process ends when the last task involves moving $n = 1$ disk (i.e., the base case). This task is accomplished by simply moving the disk, without the need for a temporary holding area. Write a program to solve the Towers of Hanoi problem. Use a recursive function with four parameters:

a) The number of disks to be moved
b) The peg on which these disks are initially threaded
c) The peg to which this stack of disks is to be moved
d) The peg to be used as a temporary holding area

Display the precise instructions for moving the disks from the starting peg to the destination peg. To move a stack of three disks from peg 1 to peg 3, the program displays the following moves:

$\quad$ 1 $\rightarrow$ 3 (This means move one disk from peg 1 to peg 3.)
$\quad$ 1 $\rightarrow$ 2
$\quad$ 3 $\rightarrow$ 2
$\quad$ 1 $\rightarrow$ 3
$\quad$ 2 $\rightarrow$ 1
$\quad$ 2 $\rightarrow$ 3
$\quad$ 1 $\rightarrow$ 3

6.39   *(Towers of Hanoi: Iterative Version)* Any program that can be implemented recursively can be implemented iteratively, although sometimes with more difficulty and less clarity. Try writing an iterative version of the Towers of Hanoi. If you succeed, compare your iterative version with the recursive version developed in Exercise 6.38. Investigate issues of performance, clarity and your ability to demonstrate the correctness of the programs.

6.40   *(Visualizing Recursion)* It's interesting to watch recursion "in action." Modify the factorial function of Fig. 6.29 to print its local variable and recursive call parameter. For each recursive call, display the outputs on a separate line and add a level of indentation. Do your utmost to make the outputs clear, interesting and meaningful. Your goal here is to design and implement an output format that helps a person understand recursion better. You may want to add such display capabilities to the many other recursion examples and exercises throughout the text.

6.41   *(Recursive Greatest Common Divisor)* The greatest common divisor of integers x and y is the largest integer that evenly divides both x and y. Write a recursive function gcd that returns the greatest common divisor of x and y, defined recursively as follows: If y is equal to 0, then gcd(x, y) is x; otherwise, gcd(x, y) is gcd(y, x % y), where % is the modulus operator. [*Note:* For this algorithm, x must be larger than y.]

6.42   *(Recursive **main**)* Can main be called recursively on your system? Write a program containing a function main. Include static local variable count and initialize it to 1. Postincrement and print the value of count each time main is called. Compile your program. What happens?

6.43   *(Distance Between Points)* Write function distance that calculates the distance between two points *(x1, y1)* and *(x2, y2)*. All numbers and return values should be of type double.

6.44   What's wrong with the following program?

```
1   // Exercise 6.44: ex06_44.cpp
2   // What is wrong with this program?
3   #include <iostream>
4   using namespace std;
5
6   int main()
7   {
8      int c;
9
10     if ( ( c = cin.get() ) != EOF )
11     {
12        main();
13        cout << c;
14     } // end if
15  } // end main
```

6.45   What does the following program do?

```
1   // Exercise 6.45: ex06_45.cpp
2   // What does this program do?
3   #include <iostream>
4   using namespace std;
5
6   int mystery( int, int ); // function prototype
7
8   int main()
9   {
10     int x, y;
11
12     cout << "Enter two integers: ";
```

```
13      cin >> x >> y;
14      cout << "The result is " << mystery( x, y ) << endl;
15    } // end main
16
17    // Parameter b must be a positive integer to prevent infinite recursion
18    int mystery( int a, int b )
19    {
20      if ( b == 1 ) // base case
21        return a;
22      else // recursion step
23        return a + mystery( a, b - 1 );
24    } // end function mystery
```

6.46   After you determine what the program of Exercise 6.45 does, modify the program to function properly after removing the restriction that the second argument be nonnegative.

6.47   *(Math Library Functions)* Write a program that tests as many of the math library functions in Fig. 6.2 as you can. Exercise each of these functions by having your program print out tables of return values for a diversity of argument values.

6.48   *(Find the Error)* Find the error in each of the following program segments and explain how to correct it:

a) `float cube( float ); // function prototype`

```
cube( float number ) // function definition
{
    return number * number * number;
}
```

b) `register auto int x = 7;`

c) `int randomNumber = srand();`

d) ```
float y = 123.45678;
int x;

x = y;
cout << static_cast< float >(x) << endl;
```

e) ```
double square( double number )
{
    double number;
    return number * number;
}
```

f) ```
int sum(int n)
{
    if (n == 0)
        return 0;
    else
        return n + sum(n);
}
```

**6.49**    *(Craps Game Modification)* Modify the craps program of Fig. 6.11 to allow wagering. Package as a function the portion of the program that runs one game of craps. Initialize variable bankBalance to 1000 dollars. Prompt the player to enter a wager. Use a while loop to check that wager is less than or equal to bankBalance and, if not, prompt the user to reenter wager until a valid wager is entered. After a correct wager is entered, run one game of craps. If the player wins, increase bankBalance by wager and print the new bankBalance. If the player loses, decrease bankBalance by
```

wager, print the new `bankBalance`, check on whether `bankBalance` has become zero and, if so, print the message `"Sorry. You busted!"` As the game progresses, print various messages to create some "chatter" such as `"Oh, you're going for broke, huh?"`, `"Aw cmon, take a chance!"` or `"You're up big. Now's the time to cash in your chips!"`.

6.50 *(Circle Area)* Write a C++ program that prompts the user for the radius of a circle, then calls `inline` function `circleArea` to calculate the area of that circle.

6.51 *(Pass-by-Value vs. Pass-by-Reference)* Write a complete C++ program with the two alternate functions specified below, each of which simply triples the variable `count` defined in `main`. Then compare and contrast the two approaches. These two functions are

  a) function `tripleByValue` that passes a copy of `count` by value, triples the copy and returns the new value and
  a) function `tripleByReference` that passes `count` by reference via a reference parameter and triples the original value of `count` through its alias (i.e., the reference parameter).

6.52 What's the purpose of the unary scope resolution operator?

6.53 *(Function Template `minimum`)* Write a program that uses a function template called `minimum` to determine the smaller of two arguments. Test the program using integer, character and floating-point number arguments.

6.54 *(Function Template `maximum`)* Write a program that uses a function template called `maximum` to determine the larger of two arguments. Test the program using integer, character and floating-point number arguments.

6.55 *(Find the Error)* Determine whether the following program segments contain errors. For each error, explain how it can be corrected. [*Note:* For a particular program segment, it's possible that no errors are present in the segment.]

  a)
```cpp
template < class A >
int sum( int num1, int num2, int num3 )
{
   return num1 + num2 + num3;
}
```
  b)
```cpp
void printResults( int x, int y )
{
   cout << "The sum is " << x + y << '\n';
   return x + y;
}
```
  c)
```cpp
template < A >
A product( A num1, A num2, A num3 )
{
   return num1 * num2 * num3;
}
```
  d)
```cpp
double cube( int );
int cube( int );
```

Making a Difference

As computer costs decline, it becomes feasible for every student, regardless of economic circumstance, to have a computer and use it in school. This creates exciting possibilities for improving the educational experience of all students worldwide as suggested by the next five exercises. [*Note:* Check out initiatives such as the One Laptop Per Child Project (www.laptop.org). Also, research "green" laptops—and note the key "going green" characteristics of these devices? Look into the

Electronic Product Environmental Assessment Tool (www.epeat.net) which can help you assess the "greenness" of desktops, notebooks and monitors to help you decide which products to purchase.]

6.56 *(Computer-Assisted Instruction)* The use of computers in education is referred to as *computer-assisted instruction (CAI)*. Write a program that will help an elementary school student learn multiplication. Use the rand function to produce two positive one-digit integers. The program should then prompt the user with a question, such as

```
How much is 6 times 7?
```

The student then inputs the answer. Next, the program checks the student's answer. If it's correct, display the message "Very good!" and ask another multiplication question. If the answer is wrong, display the message "No. Please try again." and let the student try the same question repeatedly until the student finally gets it right. A separate function should be used to generate each new question. This function should be called once when the application begins execution and each time the user answers the question correctly.

6.57 *(Computer-Assisted Instruction: Reducing Student Fatigue)* One problem in CAI environments is student fatigue. This can be reduced by varying the computer's responses to hold the student's attention. Modify the program of Exercise 6.56 so that various comments are displayed for each answer as follows:

Possible responses to a correct answer:

```
Very good!
Excellent!
Nice work!
Keep up the good work!
```

Possible responses to an incorrect answer:

```
No. Please try again.
Wrong. Try once more.
Don't give up!
No. Keep trying.
```

Use random-number generation to choose a number from 1 to 4 that will be used to select one of the four appropriate responses to each correct or incorrect answer. Use a switch statement to issue the responses.

6.58 *(Computer-Assisted Instruction: Monitoring Student Performance)* More sophisticated computer-assisted instruction systems monitor the student's performance over a period of time. The decision to begin a new topic is often based on the student's success with previous topics. Modify the program of Exercise 6.57 to count the number of correct and incorrect responses typed by the student. After the student types 10 answers, your program should calculate the percentage that are correct. If the percentage is lower than 75%, display "Please ask your teacher for extra help.", then reset the program so another student can try it. If the percentage is 75% or higher, display "Congratulations, you are ready to go to the next level!", then reset the program so another student can try it.

6.59 *(Computer-Assisted Instruction: Difficulty Levels)* Exercise 6.56 through Exercise 6.58 developed a computer-assisted instruction program to help teach an elementary school student multiplication. Modify the program to allow the user to enter a difficulty level. At a difficulty level of 1, the program should use only single-digit numbers in the problems; at a difficulty level of 2, numbers as large as two digits, and so on.

6.60 *(Computer-Assisted Instruction: Varying the Types of Problems)* Modify the program of Exercise 6.59 to allow the user to pick a type of arithmetic problem to study. An option of 1 means addition problems only, 2 means subtraction problems only, 3 means multiplication problems only, 4 means division problems only and 5 means a random mixture of all these types.

7

Arrays and Vectors

*Now go, write it
before them in a table,
and note it in a book.*
—Isaiah 30:8

*Begin at the beginning, … and
go on till you come to the end:
then stop.*
—Lewis Carroll

*To go beyond is as
wrong as to fall short.*
—Confucius

Objectives

In this chapter you'll learn:

- To use the array data structure to represent a set of related data items.

- To use arrays to store, sort and search lists and tables of values.

- To declare arrays, initialize arrays and refer to the individual elements of arrays.

- To pass arrays to functions.

- Basic searching and sorting techniques.

- To declare and manipulate multidimensional arrays.

- To use C++ Standard Library class template **vector**.

7.1 Introduction

This chapter introduces the important topic of **data structures**—collections of related data items. **Arrays** are data structures consisting of related data items of the same type. You learned about classes in Chapter 3. In Chapter 21 we discuss the notion of **structures**. Structures and classes can each hold related data items of possibly different types. Arrays, structures and classes are "static" entities in that they remain the same size throughout program execution. (They may, of course, be of automatic storage class and hence be created and destroyed each time the blocks in which they're defined are entered and exited.)

After discussing how arrays are declared, created and initialized, we present a series of practical examples that demonstrate several common array manipulations. We present an example of searching arrays to find particular elements. The chapter also introduces one of the most important computing applications—sorting data (i.e., putting the data in some particular order). Two sections of the chapter enhance the case study of class Grade-Book in Chapters 3–6. In particular, we use arrays to enable the class to maintain a set of grades in memory and analyze student grades from multiple exams in a semester—two capabilities that were absent from previous versions of the GradeBook class. These and other chapter examples demonstrate the ways in which arrays allow you to organize and manipulate data.

The style of arrays we use throughout most of this chapter are C-style pointer-based arrays. (We'll study pointers in Chapter 8.) In the final section of this chapter, and in Chapter 22, Standard Template Library (STL), we'll cover arrays as full-fledged objects called vectors. We'll discover that these object-based arrays are safer and more versatile than the C-style, pointer-based arrays we discuss in the early part of this chapter.

7.2 Arrays

An array is a consecutive group of memory locations that all have the same type. To refer to a particular location or element in the array, we specify the name of the array and the **position number** of the particular element in the array.

Figure 7.1 shows an integer array called c. This array contains 12 **elements**. A program refers to any one of these elements by giving the name of the array followed by the position number of the particular element in square brackets ([]). The position number is more formally called a **subscript** or **index** (this number specifies the number of elements from the beginning of the array). The first element in every array has **subscript 0** (**zero**) and is sometimes called the **zeroth element**. Thus, the elements of array c are c[0] (pronounced "c sub zero"), c[1], c[2] and so on. The highest subscript in array c is 11, which is 1 less than the number of elements in the array (12). Array names follow the same conventions as other variable names, i.e., they must be identifiers.

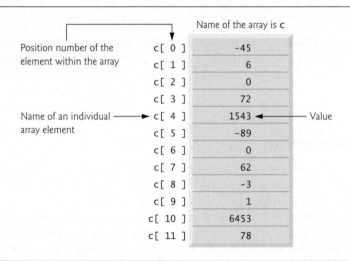

Fig. 7.1 | Array of 12 elements.

A subscript must be an integer or integer expression (using any integral type). If a program uses an expression as a subscript, then the program evaluates the expression to determine the subscript. For example, if we assume that variable a is equal to 5 and that variable b is equal to 6, then the statement

```
c[ a + b ] += 2;
```

adds 2 to array element c[11]. A subscripted array name is an *lvalue*—it can be used on the left side of an assignment, just as nonarray variable names can.

Let's examine array c in Fig. 7.1 more closely. The **name** of the entire array is c. Its 12 elements are referred to as c[0] to c[11]. The **value** of c[0] is -45, the value of c[1] is 6, the value of c[2] is 0, the value of c[7] is 62, and the value of c[11] is 78. To print the sum of the values contained in the first three elements of array c, we'd write

```
cout << c[ 0 ] + c[ 1 ] + c[ 2 ] << endl;
```

To divide the value of c[6] by 2 and assign the result to the variable x, we would write

```
x = c[ 6 ] / 2;
```

Common Programming Error 7.1

*Note the difference between the "seventh element of the array" and "array element 7." Array subscripts begin at 0, so the "seventh element of the array" has a subscript of 6, while "array element 7" has a subscript of 7 and is actually the eighth element of the array. Unfortunately, this distinction frequently is a source of **off-by-one errors**. To avoid such errors, we refer to specific array elements explicitly by their array name and subscript number (e.g., c[6] or c[7]).*

The brackets used to enclose the subscript of an array are actually an operator. Brackets have the same level of precedence as parentheses. Figure 7.2 shows the precedence and associativity of the operators introduced so far. Brackets ([]) have been added to the second row of Fig. 7.2. The operators are shown top to bottom in decreasing order of precedence with their associativity and type.

Operators	Associativity	Type
::	left to right	scope resolution
() []	left to right	highest
++ -- static_cast< *type* >(*operand*)	left to right	unary (postfix)
++ -- + - !	right to left	unary (prefix)
* / %	left to right	multiplicative
+ -	left to right	additive
<< >>	left to right	insertion/extraction
< <= > >=	left to right	relational
== !=	left to right	equality
&&	left to right	logical AND
||	left to right	logical OR
?:	right to left	conditional
= += -= *= /= %=	right to left	assignment
,	left to right	comma

Fig. 7.2 | Operator precedence and associativity.

7.3 **Declaring Arrays**

Arrays occupy space in memory. To specify the type of the elements and the number of elements required by an array use a declaration of the form:

> *type arrayName*[*arraySize*];

The compiler reserves the appropriate amount of memory. (Recall that a declaration which reserves memory is more properly known as a definition in C++.) The *arraySize* must be an integer constant greater than zero. For example, to tell the compiler to reserve 12 elements for integer array c, use the declaration

```
int c[ 12 ]; // c is an array of 12 integers
```

Memory can be reserved for several arrays with a single declaration.

Good Programming Practice 7.1

We declare one array per declaration for readability, modifiability and ease of commenting.

Arrays can be declared to contain values of any nonreference data type. For example, an array of type string can be used to store character strings.

7.4 Examples Using Arrays

This section presents many examples that demonstrate how to declare arrays, how to initialize arrays and how to perform common array manipulations.

7.4.1 Declaring an Array and Using a Loop to Initialize the Array's Elements

The program in Fig. 7.3 declares 10-element integer array n (line 9). Lines 12–13 use a for statement to initialize the array elements to zeros. Like other automatic variables, automatic arrays are not implicitly initialized to zero although static arrays are. The first output statement (line 15) displays the column headings for the columns printed in the subsequent for statement (lines 18–19), which prints the array in tabular format. Remember that setw specifies the field width in which only the *next* value is to be output.

```
1   // Fig. 7.3: fig07_03.cpp
2   // Initializing an array.
3   #include <iostream>
4   #include <iomanip>
5   using namespace std;
6
7   int main()
8   {
9      int n[ 10 ]; // n is an array of 10 integers
10
11     // initialize elements of array n to 0
12     for ( int i = 0; i < 10; i++ )
13        n[ i ] = 0; // set element at location i to 0
14
15     cout << "Element" << setw( 13 ) << "Value" << endl;
16
17     // output each array element's value
18     for ( int j = 0; j < 10; j++ )
19        cout << setw( 7 ) << j << setw( 13 ) << n[ j ] << endl;
20  } // end main
```

Fig. 7.3 | Initializing an array's elements to zeros and printing the array. (Part 1 of 2.)

Element	Value
0	0
1	0
2	0
3	0
4	0
5	0
6	0
7	0
8	0
9	0

Fig. 7.3 | Initializing an array's elements to zeros and printing the array. (Part 2 of 2.)

7.4.2 Initializing an Array in a Declaration with an Initializer List

The elements of an array also can be initialized in the array declaration by following the array name with an equals sign and a brace-delimited comma-separated list of **initializers**. The program in Fig. 7.4 uses an **initializer list** to initialize an integer array with 10 values (line 10) and prints the array in tabular format (lines 12–16).

```
1   // Fig. 7.4: fig07_04.cpp
2   // Initializing an array in a declaration.
3   #include <iostream>
4   #include <iomanip>
5   using namespace std;
6
7   int main()
8   {
9      // use initializer list to initialize array n
10     int n[ 10 ] = { 32, 27, 64, 18, 95, 14, 90, 70, 60, 37 };
11
12     cout << "Element" << setw( 13 ) << "Value" << endl;
13
14     // output each array element's value
15     for ( int i = 0; i < 10; i++ )
16        cout << setw( 7 ) << i << setw( 13 ) << n[ i ] << endl;
17  } // end main
```

Element	Value
0	32
1	27
2	64
3	18
4	95
5	14
6	90
7	70
8	60
9	37

Fig. 7.4 | Initializing the elements of an array in its declaration.

If there are fewer initializers than elements in the array, the remaining array elements are initialized to zero. For example, the elements of array n in Fig. 7.3 could have been initialized to zero with the declaration

```
int n[ 10 ] = {}; // initialize elements of array n to 0
```

The declaration implicitly initializes the elements to zero, because there are fewer initializers (none in this case) than elements in the array. This technique can be used only in the array's declaration, whereas the initialization technique shown in Fig. 7.3 can be used repeatedly during program execution to "reinitialize" an array's elements.

If the array size is omitted from a declaration with an initializer list, the compiler determines the number of elements in the array by counting the number of elements in the initializer list. For example,

```
int n[] = { 1, 2, 3, 4, 5 };
```

creates a five-element array.

If the array size and an initializer list are specified in an array declaration, the number of initializers must be less than or equal to the array size. The array declaration

```
int n[ 5 ] = { 32, 27, 64, 18, 95, 14 };
```

causes a compilation error, because there are six initializers and only five array elements.

Common Programming Error 7.2
Providing more initializers in an array initializer list than there are elements in the array is a compilation error.

7.4.3 Specifying an Array's Size with a Constant Variable and Setting Array Elements with Calculations

Figure 7.5 sets the elements of a 10-element array s to the even integers 2, 4, 6, ..., 20 (lines 14–15) and prints the array in tabular format (lines 17–21). These numbers are generated (line 15) by multiplying each successive value of the loop counter by 2 and adding 2.

```
1   // Fig. 7.5: fig07_05.cpp
2   // Set array s to the even integers from 2 to 20.
3   #include <iostream>
4   #include <iomanip>
5   using namespace std;
6
7   int main()
8   {
9      // constant variable can be used to specify array size
10     const int arraySize = 10;
11
12     int s[ arraySize ]; // array s has 10 elements
13
14     for ( int i = 0; i < arraySize; i++ ) // set the values
15        s[ i ] = 2 + 2 * i;
```

Fig. 7.5 | Generating values to be placed into elements of an array. (Part 1 of 2.)

```
16
17       cout << "Element" << setw( 13 ) << "Value" << endl;
18
19       // output contents of array s in tabular format
20       for ( int j = 0; j < arraySize; j++ )
21          cout << setw( 7 ) << j << setw( 13 ) << s[ j ] << endl;
22    } // end main
```

Element	Value
0	2
1	4
2	6
3	8
4	10
5	12
6	14
7	16
8	18
9	20

Fig. 7.5 | Generating values to be placed into elements of an array. (Part 2 of 2.)

Line 10 uses the **const qualifier** to declare a so-called **constant variable** arraySize with the value 10. Constant variables must be initialized with a constant expression when they're declared and cannot be modified thereafter (as shown in Fig. 7.6 and Fig. 7.7). Constant variables are also called **named constants** or **read-only variables**.

Common Programming Error 7.3

Not assigning a value to a constant variable when it's declared is a compilation error.

```
1    // Fig. 7.6: fig07_06.cpp
2    // Using a properly initialized constant variable.
3    #include <iostream>
4    using namespace std;
5
6    int main()
7    {
8       const int x = 7; // initialized constant variable
9
10      cout << "The value of constant variable x is: " << x << endl;
11   } // end main
```

```
The value of constant variable x is: 7
```

Fig. 7.6 | Initializing and using a constant variable.

```
1    // Fig. 7.7: fig07_07.cpp
2    // A const variable must be initialized.
3
```

Fig. 7.7 | const variables must be initialized. (Part 1 of 2.)

```
4   int main()
5   {
6      const int x; // Error: x must be initialized
7
8      x = 7; // Error: cannot modify a const variable
9   } // end main
```

Microsoft Visual C++ compiler error message:

```
C:\cpphtp7_examples\ch07\fig07_07.cpp(6) : error C2734: 'x' : const object
   must be initialized if not extern
C:\cpphtp7_examples\ch07\fig07_07.cpp(8) : error C3892: 'x' : you cannot
   assign to a variable that is const
```

GNU C++ compiler error message:

```
fig07_07.cpp:6: error: uninitialized const 'x'
fig07_07.cpp:8: error: assignment of read-only variable 'x'
```

Fig. 7.7 | const variables must be initialized. (Part 2 of 2.)

Common Programming Error 7.4
Assigning a value to a constant variable in an executable statement is a compilation error.

In Fig. 7.7, the compilation error produced by Microsoft Visual C++ refers to the int variable x as a "const object." The ISO/IEC C++ standard defines an "object" as any "region of storage." Like objects of classes, fundamental-type variables also occupy space in memory, so they're often referred to as "objects."

Constant variables can be placed anywhere a constant expression is expected. In Fig. 7.5, constant variable arraySize specifies the size of array s in line 12.

Common Programming Error 7.5
Only constants can be used to declare the size of automatic and static arrays. Not using a constant for this purpose is a compilation error.

Using constant variables to specify array sizes makes programs more **scalable**. In Fig. 7.5, the first for statement could fill a 1000-element array by simply changing the value of arraySize in its declaration from 10 to 1000. If the constant variable arraySize had not been used, we would have to change lines 12, 14 and 20 of the program to scale the program to handle 1000 array elements. As programs get larger, this technique becomes more useful for writing clearer, easier-to-modify programs.

Software Engineering Observation 7.1
Defining the size of each array as a constant variable instead of a literal constant can make programs more scalable.

Good Programming Practice 7.2

*Defining the size of an array as a constant variable instead of a literal constant makes programs clearer. This technique eliminates so-called **magic numbers**. For example, repeatedly mentioning the size 10 in array-processing code for a 10-element array gives the number 10 an artificial significance and can be confusing when the program includes other 10s that have nothing to do with the array size.*

7.4.4 Summing the Elements of an Array

Often, the elements of an array represent a series of values to be used in a calculation. For example, if the elements of an array represent exam grades, a professor may wish to total the elements of the array and use that sum to calculate the class average for the exam. The examples using class GradeBook later in the chapter, namely Figs. 7.15–7.16 and Figs. 7.22–7.23, use this technique.

The program in Fig. 7.8 sums the values contained in the 10-element integer array a. The program declares, creates and initializes the array in line 9. The for statement (lines 13–14) performs the calculations. The values being supplied as initializers for array a also could be read into the program from the user at the keyboard, or from a file on disk (see Chapter 17, File Processing). For example, the for statement

```
for ( int j = 0; j < arraySize; j++ )
    cin >> a[ j ];
```

reads one value at a time from the keyboard and stores the value in element a[j].

```
1   // Fig. 7.8: fig07_08.cpp
2   // Compute the sum of the elements of the array.
3   #include <iostream>
4   using namespace std;
5
6   int main()
7   {
8      const int arraySize = 10; // constant variable indicating size of array
9      int a[ arraySize ] = { 87, 68, 94, 100, 83, 78, 85, 91, 76, 87 };
10     int total = 0;
11
12     // sum contents of array a
13     for ( int i = 0; i < arraySize; i++ )
14        total += a[ i ];
15
16     cout << "Total of array elements: " << total << endl;
17  } // end main
```

```
Total of array elements: 849
```

Fig. 7.8 | Computing the sum of the elements of an array.

7.4.5 Using Bar Charts to Display Array Data Graphically

Many programs present data to users in a graphical manner. For example, numeric values are often displayed as bars in a bar chart. In such a chart, longer bars represent proportionally larger numeric values. One simple way to display numeric data graphically is with a bar chart that shows each numeric value as a bar of asterisks (*).

Professors often like to examine the distribution of grades on an exam. A professor might graph the number of grades in each of several categories to visualize the grade distribution. Suppose the grades were 87, 68, 94, 100, 83, 78, 85, 91, 76 and 87. There was one grade of 100, two grades in the 90s, four grades in the 80s, two grades in the 70s, one grade in the 60s and no grades below 60. Our next program (Fig. 7.9) stores this grade distribution data in an array of 11 elements, each corresponding to a category of grades. For example, n[0] indicates the number of grades in the range 0–9, n[7] indicates the number of grades in the range 70–79 and n[10] indicates the number of grades of 100. The two versions of class GradeBook later in the chapter (Figs. 7.15–7.16 and Figs. 7.22–7.23) contain code that calculates these grade frequencies based on a set of grades. For now, we manually create the array by looking at the set of grades.

The program reads the numbers from the array and graphs the information as a bar chart, displaying each grade range followed by a bar of asterisks indicating the number of grades in that range. To label each bar, lines 18–23 output a grade range (e.g., "70-79: ") based on the current value of counter variable i. The nested for statement (lines 26–27)

```cpp
 1   // Fig. 7.9: fig07_09.cpp
 2   // Bar chart printing program.
 3   #include <iostream>
 4   #include <iomanip>
 5   using namespace std;
 6
 7   int main()
 8   {
 9      const int arraySize = 11;
10      int n[ arraySize ] = { 0, 0, 0, 0, 0, 0, 1, 2, 4, 2, 1 };
11
12      cout << "Grade distribution:" << endl;
13
14      // for each element of array n, output a bar of the chart
15      for ( int i = 0; i < arraySize; i++ )
16      {
17         // output bar labels ("0-9:", ..., "90-99:", "100:" )
18         if ( i == 0 )
19            cout << "  0-9: ";
20         else if ( i == 10 )
21            cout << "  100: ";
22         else
23            cout << i * 10 << "-" << ( i * 10 ) + 9 << ": ";
24
25         // print bar of asterisks
26         for ( int stars = 0; stars < n[ i ]; stars++ )
27            cout << '*';
28
29         cout << endl; // start a new line of output
30      } // end outer for
31   } // end main
```

Fig. 7.9 | Bar chart printing program. (Part 1 of 2.)

```
Grade distribution:
   0-9:
  10-19:
  20-29:
  30-39:
  40-49:
  50-59:
  60-69: *
  70-79: **
  80-89: ****
  90-99: **
    100: *
```

Fig. 7.9 | Bar chart printing program. (Part 2 of 2.)

outputs the bars. Note the loop-continuation condition in line 26 (stars < n[i]). Each time the program reaches the inner for, the loop counts from 0 up to n[i], thus using a value in array n to determine the number of asterisks to display. In this example, n[0]–n[5] contain zeros because no students received a grade below 60. Thus, the program displays no asterisks next to the first six grade ranges.

Common Programming Error 7.6

Although it's possible to use the same control variable in a for statement and in a second for statement nested inside, this is confusing and can lead to logic errors.

7.4.6 Using the Elements of an Array as Counters

Sometimes, programs use counter variables to summarize data, such as the results of a survey. In Fig. 6.9, we used separate counters in our die-rolling program to track the number of occurrences of each side of a die as the program rolled the die 6,000,000 times. An array version of this program is shown in Fig. 7.10.

```
 1   // Fig. 7.10: fig07_10.cpp
 2   // Roll a six-sided die 6,000,000 times.
 3   #include <iostream>
 4   #include <iomanip>
 5   #include <cstdlib>
 6   #include <ctime>
 7   using namespace std;
 8
 9   int main()
10   {
11      const int arraySize = 7; // ignore element zero
12      int frequency[ arraySize ] = {}; // initialize elements to 0
13
14      srand( time( 0 ) ); // seed random number generator
15
16      // roll die 6,000,000 times; use die value as frequency index
17      for ( int roll = 1; roll <= 6000000; roll++ )
18         frequency[ 1 + rand() % 6 ]++;
```

Fig. 7.10 | Die-rolling program using an array instead of switch. (Part 1 of 2.)

```
19
20      cout << "Face" << setw( 13 ) << "Frequency" << endl;
21
22      // output each array element's value
23      for ( int face = 1; face < arraySize; face++ )
24         cout << setw( 4 ) << face << setw( 13 ) << frequency[ face ]
25            << endl;
26   } // end main
```

```
Face     Frequency
  1        1000167
  2        1000149
  3        1000152
  4         998748
  5         999626
  6        1001158
```

Fig. 7.10 | Die-rolling program using an array instead of `switch`. (Part 2 of 2.)

Figure 7.10 uses the array `frequency` (line 12) to count the occurrences of each side of the die. *The single statement in line 18 of this program replaces the `switch` statement in lines 25–47 of Fig. 6.9.* Line 18 uses a random value to determine which `frequency` element to increment during each iteration of the loop. The calculation in line 18 produces a random subscript from 1 to 6, so array `frequency` must be large enough to store six counters. However, we use a seven-element array in which we ignore `frequency[0]`—it's more logical to have the die face value 1 increment `frequency[1]` than `frequency[0]`. Thus, each face value is used as a subscript for array `frequency`. We also replace lines 51–56 of Fig. 6.9 by looping through array `frequency` to output the results (lines 23–25).

7.4.7 Using Arrays to Summarize Survey Results

Our next example (Fig. 7.11) uses arrays to summarize the results of data collected in a survey. Consider the following problem statement:

> *Forty students were asked to rate the quality of the food in the student cafeteria on a scale of 1 to 10 (1 meaning awful and 10 meaning excellent). Place the 40 responses in an integer array and summarize the results of the poll.*

This is a typical array-processing application. We wish to summarize the number of responses of each type (i.e., 1 through 10). The array `responses` (lines 14–16) is a 40-element integer array of the students' responses to the survey. The array `responses` is declared `const`, as its values do not (and should not) change. We use an 11-element array `frequency` (line 19) to count the number of occurrences of each response. Each element of the array is used as a counter for one of the survey responses and is initialized to zero. As in Fig. 7.10, we ignore `frequency[0]`.

Software Engineering Observation 7.2

The `const` qualifier should be used to enforce the principle of least privilege. Using the principle of least privilege to properly design software can greatly reduce debugging time and improper side effects and can make a program easier to modify and maintain.

```
 1    // Fig. 7.11: fig07_11.cpp
 2    // Poll analysis program.
 3    #include <iostream>
 4    #include <iomanip>
 5    using namespace std;
 6
 7    int main()
 8    {
 9       // define array sizes
10       const int responseSize = 40; // size of array responses
11       const int frequencySize = 11; // size of array frequency
12
13       // place survey responses in array responses
14       const int responses[ responseSize ] = { 1, 2, 6, 4, 8, 5, 9, 7, 8,
15          10, 1, 6, 3, 8, 6, 10, 3, 8, 2, 7, 6, 5, 7, 6, 8, 6, 7,
16          5, 6, 6, 5, 6, 7, 5, 6, 4, 8, 6, 8, 10 };
17
18       // initialize frequency counters to 0
19       int frequency[ frequencySize ] = {};
20
21       // for each answer, select responses element and use that value
22       // as frequency subscript to determine element to increment
23       for ( int answer = 0; answer < responseSize; answer++ )
24          frequency[ responses[ answer ] ]++;
25
26       cout << "Rating" << setw( 17 ) << "Frequency" << endl;
27
28       // output each array element's value
29       for ( int rating = 1; rating < frequencySize; rating++ )
30          cout << setw( 6 ) << rating << setw( 17 ) << frequency[ rating ]
31             << endl;
32    } // end main
```

Rating	Frequency
1	2
2	2
3	2
4	2
5	5
6	11
7	5
8	7
9	1
10	3

Fig. 7.11 | Poll analysis program.

The first for statement (lines 23–24) takes the responses one at a time from the array responses and increments one of the 10 counters in the frequency array (frequency[1] to frequency[10]). The key statement in the loop is line 24, which increments the appropriate frequency counter, depending on the value of responses[answer].

Let's consider several iterations of the for loop. When control variable answer is 0, the value of responses[answer] is the value of responses[0] (i.e., 1 in line 14), so the program interprets frequency[responses[answer]]++ as

```
frequency[ 1 ]++
```

which increments the value in array element 1. To evaluate the expression, start with the value in the innermost set of square brackets (answer). Once you know answer's value (which is the value of the loop control variable in line 23), plug it into the expression and evaluate the next outer set of square brackets (i.e., responses[answer], which is a value selected from the responses array in lines 14–17). Then use the resulting value as the subscript for the frequency array to specify which counter to increment.

When answer is 1, responses[answer] is the value of responses[1], which is 2, so the program interprets frequency[responses[answer]]++ as

```
frequency[ 2 ]++
```

which increments array element 2.

When answer is 2, responses[answer] is the value of responses[2], which is 6, so the program interprets frequency[responses[answer]]++ as

```
frequency[ 6 ]++
```

which increments array element 6, and so on. Regardless of the number of responses processed in the survey, the program requires only an 11-element array (ignoring element zero) to summarize the results, because all the response values are between 1 and 10 and the subscript values for an 11-element array are 0 through 10.

If the data in responses contained an invalid value, such as 13, the program would have attempted to add 1 to frequency[13], which is outside the bounds of the array. *C++ has no array **bounds checking** to prevent the computer from referring to an element that does not exist.* Thus, an executing program can "walk off" either end of an array without warning. You should ensure that all array references remain within the bounds of the array.

Common Programming Error 7.7

Referring to an element outside the array bounds is an execution-time logic error. It isn't a syntax error.

Error-Prevention Tip 7.1

When looping through an array, the index should never go below 0 and should always be less than the total number of array elements (one less than the size of the array). Make sure that the loop-termination condition prevents accessing elements outside this range.

Portability Tip 7.1

The (normally serious) effects of referencing elements outside the array bounds are system dependent. Often this results in changes to the value of an unrelated variable or a fatal error that terminates program execution.

C++ is an extensible language. Section 7.11 presents C++ Standard Library class template vector, which enables you to perform many operations that are not available for C++'s built-in arrays. For example, we'll be able to compare vectors directly and assign one vector to another. In Chapter 11, we extend C++ further by implementing an array as a user-defined class of our own. This new array definition will enable us to input and output entire arrays with cin and cout, initialize arrays when they're created and prevent access to out-of-range array elements. We'll even be able to use noninteger subscripts.

Error-Prevention Tip 7.2

In Chapter 11, we'll see how to develop a class representing a "smart array," which checks that all subscript references are in bounds at runtime. Using such smart data types helps eliminate bugs.

7.4.8 Static Local Arrays and Automatic Local Arrays

Chapter 6 discussed the storage-class specifier static. A static local variable in a function definition exists for the program's duration but is visible only in the function's body.

Performance Tip 7.1

We can apply static to a local array declaration so that it is not created and initialized each time the program calls the function and is not destroyed each time the function terminates. This can improve performance, especially when using large arrays.

A program initializes static local arrays when their declarations are first encountered. If a static array is not initialized explicitly by you, each element of that array is initialized to zero by the compiler when the array is created. Recall that C++ does not perform such default initialization for automatic variables.

Figure 7.12 demonstrates function staticArrayInit (lines 23–39) with a static local array (line 26) and function automaticArrayInit (lines 42–58) with an automatic local array (line 45).

```
 1   // Fig. 7.12: fig07_12.cpp
 2   // Static arrays are initialized to zero.
 3   #include <iostream>
 4   using namespace std;
 5
 6   void staticArrayInit( void ); // function prototype
 7   void automaticArrayInit( void ); // function prototype
 8   const int arraySize = 3;
 9
10   int main()
11   {
12      cout << "First call to each function:\n";
13      staticArrayInit();
14      automaticArrayInit();
15
16      cout << "\n\nSecond call to each function:\n";
17      staticArrayInit();
18      automaticArrayInit();
19      cout << endl;
20   } // end main
21
22   // function to demonstrate a static local array
23   void staticArrayInit( void )
24   {
```

Fig. 7.12 | static array initialization and automatic array initialization. (Part 1 of 3.)

```
25      // initializes elements to 0 first time function is called
26      static int array1[ arraySize ]; // static local array
27
28      cout << "\nValues on entering staticArrayInit:\n";
29
30      // output contents of array1
31      for ( int i = 0; i < arraySize; i++ )
32         cout << "array1[" << i << "] = " << array1[ i ] << "   ";
33
34      cout << "\nValues on exiting staticArrayInit:\n";
35
36      // modify and output contents of array1
37      for ( int j = 0; j < arraySize; j++ )
38         cout << "array1[" << j << "] = " << ( array1[ j ] += 5 ) << "   ";
39   } // end function staticArrayInit
40
41   // function to demonstrate an automatic local array
42   void automaticArrayInit( void )
43   {
44      // initializes elements each time function is called
45      int array2[ arraySize ] = { 1, 2, 3 }; // automatic local array
46
47      cout << "\n\nValues on entering automaticArrayInit:\n";
48
49      // output contents of array2
50      for ( int i = 0; i < arraySize; i++ )
51         cout << "array2[" << i << "] = " << array2[ i ] << "   ";
52
53      cout << "\nValues on exiting automaticArrayInit:\n";
54
55      // modify and output contents of array2
56      for ( int j = 0; j < arraySize; j++ )
57         cout << "array2[" << j << "] = " << ( array2[ j ] += 5 ) << "   ";
58   } // end function automaticArrayInit
```

```
First call to each function:

Values on entering staticArrayInit:
array1[0] = 0   array1[1] = 0   array1[2] = 0
Values on exiting staticArrayInit:
array1[0] = 5   array1[1] = 5   array1[2] = 5

Values on entering automaticArrayInit:
array2[0] = 1   array2[1] = 2   array2[2] = 3
Values on exiting automaticArrayInit:
array2[0] = 6   array2[1] = 7   array2[2] = 8

Second call to each function:

Values on entering staticArrayInit:
array1[0] = 5   array1[1] = 5   array1[2] = 5
Values on exiting staticArrayInit:
array1[0] = 10   array1[1] = 10   array1[2] = 10
```

Fig. 7.12 | `static` array initialization and automatic array initialization. (Part 2 of 3.)

```
Values on entering automaticArrayInit:
array2[0] = 1  array2[1] = 2  array2[2] = 3
Values on exiting automaticArrayInit:
array2[0] = 6  array2[1] = 7  array2[2] = 8
```

Fig. 7.12 | `static` array initialization and automatic array initialization. (Part 3 of 3.)

Function `staticArrayInit` is called twice (lines 13 and 17). The `static` local array is initialized to zero by the compiler the first time the function is called. The function prints the array, adds 5 to each element and prints the array again. The second time the function is called, the `static` array contains the modified values stored during the first function call. Function `automaticArrayInit` also is called twice (lines 14 and 18). The elements of the automatic local array are initialized (line 45) with the values 1, 2 and 3. The function prints the array, adds 5 to each element and prints the array again. The second time the function is called, the array elements are reinitialized to 1, 2 and 3. The array has automatic storage class, so the array is recreated and reinitialized during each call to `automaticArrayInit`.

Common Programming Error 7.8

Assuming that elements of a function's local static *array are initialized every time the function is called can lead to logic errors in a program.*

7.5 Passing Arrays to Functions

To pass an array argument to a function, specify the name of the array without any brackets. For example, if array `hourlyTemperatures` has been declared as

```
int hourlyTemperatures[ 24 ];
```

the function call

```
modifyArray( hourlyTemperatures, 24 );
```

passes array `hourlyTemperatures` and its size to function `modifyArray`. When passing an array to a function, the array size is normally passed as well, so the function can process the specific number of elements in the array. Otherwise, we would need to build this knowledge into the called function itself or, worse yet, place the array size in a global variable. In Section 7.11, when we present C++ Standard Library class template `vector` to represent a more robust type of array, you'll see that the size of a `vector` is built in—every `vector` object "knows" its own size, which can be obtained by invoking the `vector` object's `size` member function. Thus, when we pass a `vector` *object* into a function, we won't have to pass the size of the `vector` as an argument.

C++ passes arrays to functions by reference—the called functions can modify the element values in the callers' original arrays. The value of the name of the array is the address in the computer's memory of the first element of the array. Because the starting address of the array is passed, the called function knows precisely where the array is stored in memory. Therefore, when the called function modifies array elements in its function body, it's modifying the actual elements of the array in their original memory locations.

Performance Tip 7.2

Passing arrays by reference makes sense for performance reasons. Passing by value would require copying each element. For large, frequently passed arrays, this would be time consuming and would require considerable storage for the copies of the array elements.

Software Engineering Observation 7.3

It's possible to pass an array by value (by using a simple trick we explain in Chapter 21)—however, this is rarely done.

Although entire arrays are passed by reference, individual array elements are passed by value exactly as simple variables are. Such simple single pieces of data are called **scalars** or **scalar quantities**. To pass an element of an array to a function, use the subscripted name of the array element as an argument in the function call. In Chapter 6, we showed how to pass scalars (i.e., individual variables and array elements) by reference with references. In Chapter 8, we show how to pass scalars by reference with pointers.

For a function to receive an array through a function call, the function's parameter list must specify that the function expects to receive an array. For example, the function header for function `modifyArray` might be written as

```
void modifyArray( int b[], int arraySize )
```

indicating that `modifyArray` expects to receive the address of an array of integers in parameter b and the number of array elements in parameter `arraySize`. The array's size is not required in the array brackets. If it's included, the compiler ignores it; thus, arrays of any size can be passed to the function. C++ passes arrays to functions by reference—when the called function uses the array name b, it refers to the actual array in the caller (i.e., array `hourlyTemperatures` discussed at the beginning of this section).

Note the strange appearance of the function prototype for `modifyArray`

```
void modifyArray( int [], int );
```

This prototype could have been written

```
void modifyArray( int anyArrayName[], int anyVariableName );
```

but, as we learned in Chapter 3, C++ compilers ignore variable names in prototypes. Remember, the prototype tells the compiler the number of arguments and the type of each argument (in the order in which the arguments are expected to appear).

The program in Fig. 7.13 demonstrates the difference between passing an entire array and passing an array element. Lines 19–20 print the five original elements of integer array a. Line 25 passes a and its size to function `modifyArray` (lines 40–45), which multiplies each of a's elements by 2 (through parameter b). Then, lines 29–30 print array a again in `main`. As the output shows, the elements of a are indeed modified by `modifyArray`. Next, line 33 prints the value of scalar a[3], then line 35 passes element a[3] to function `modifyElement` (lines 49–53), which multiplies its parameter by 2 and prints the new value. When line 36 prints a[3] again in `main`, the value has not been modified, because individual array elements are passed by value.

There may be situations in your programs in which a function should not be allowed to modify array elements. C++ provides the type qualifier `const` that can be used to prevent modification of array values in the caller by code in a called function. When a

```
1   // Fig. 7.13: fig07_13.cpp
2   // Passing arrays and individual array elements to functions.
3   #include <iostream>
4   #include <iomanip>
5   using namespace std;
6
7   void modifyArray( int [], int ); // appears strange; array and size
8   void modifyElement( int ); // receive array element value
9
10  int main()
11  {
12     const int arraySize = 5; // size of array a
13     int a[ arraySize ] = { 0, 1, 2, 3, 4 }; // initialize array a
14
15     cout << "Effects of passing entire array by reference:"
16        << "\n\nThe values of the original array are:\n";
17
18     // output original array elements
19     for ( int i = 0; i < arraySize; i++ )
20        cout << setw( 3 ) << a[ i ];
21
22     cout << endl;
23
24     // pass array a to modifyArray by reference
25     modifyArray( a, arraySize );
26     cout << "The values of the modified array are:\n";
27
28     // output modified array elements
29     for ( int j = 0; j < arraySize; j++ )
30        cout << setw( 3 ) << a[ j ];
31
32     cout << "\n\n\nEffects of passing array element by value:"
33        << "\n\na[3] before modifyElement: " << a[ 3 ] << endl;
34
35     modifyElement( a[ 3 ] ); // pass array element a[ 3 ] by value
36     cout << "a[3] after modifyElement: " << a[ 3 ] << endl;
37  } // end main
38
39  // in function modifyArray, "b" points to the original array "a" in memory
40  void modifyArray( int b[], int sizeOfArray )
41  {
42     // multiply each array element by 2
43     for ( int k = 0; k < sizeOfArray; k++ )
44        b[ k ] *= 2;
45  } // end function modifyArray
46
47  // in function modifyElement, "e" is a local copy of
48  // array element a[ 3 ] passed from main
49  void modifyElement( int e )
50  {
51     // multiply parameter by 2
52     cout << "Value of element in modifyElement: " << ( e *= 2 ) << endl;
53  } // end function modifyElement
```

Fig. 7.13 | Passing arrays and individual array elements to functions. (Part 1 of 2.)

```
Effects of passing entire array by reference:

The values of the original array are:
   0   1   2   3   4
The values of the modified array are:
   0   2   4   6   8


Effects of passing array element by value:

a[3] before modifyElement: 6
Value of element in modifyElement: 12
a[3] after modifyElement: 6
```

Fig. 7.13 | Passing arrays and individual array elements to functions. (Part 2 of 2.)

function specifies an array parameter that is preceded by the const qualifier, the elements of the array become constant in the function body, and any attempt to modify an element of the array in the function body results in a compilation error. This enables you to prevent accidental modification of array elements in the function's body.

Figure 7.14 demonstrates the const qualifier. Function tryToModifyArray (lines 18–23) is defined with parameter const int b[], which specifies that array b is constant and cannot be modified. Each of the three attempts by the function to modify array b's elements (lines 20–22) results in a compilation error. Some compilers, for example, produce an error like "Cannot modify a const object." This message indicates that using a const object (e.g., b[0]) as an *lvalue* is an error—you cannot assign a new value to a const object by placing it on the left of an assignment operator. Compiler error messages vary between compilers (as shown in Fig. 7.14). The const qualifier will be discussed again in Chapter 10.

 Software Engineering Observation 7.4

Applying the const type qualifier to an array parameter in a function definition to prevent the original array from being modified in the function body is another example of the principle of least privilege. Functions should not be given the capability to modify an array unless it's absolutely necessary.

```
1   // Fig. 7.14: fig07_14.cpp
2   // Demonstrating the const type qualifier.
3   #include <iostream>
4   using namespace std;
5
6   void tryToModifyArray( const int [] ); // function prototype
7
8   int main()
9   {
10      int a[] = { 10, 20, 30 };
```

Fig. 7.14 | const type qualifier applied to an array parameter. (Part 1 of 2.)

```
11
12        tryToModifyArray( a );
13        cout << a[ 0 ] << ' ' << a[ 1 ] << ' ' << a[ 2 ] << '\n';
14    } // end main
15
16    // In function tryToModifyArray, "b" cannot be used
17    // to modify the original array "a" in main.
18    void tryToModifyArray( const int b[] )
19    {
20       b[ 0 ] /= 2; // compilation error
21       b[ 1 ] /= 2; // compilation error
22       b[ 2 ] /= 2; // compilation error
23    } // end function tryToModifyArray
```

Microsoft Visual C++ compiler error message:

```
c:\cpphtp7_examples\ch07\fig07_14\fig07_14.cpp(20) : error C3892: 'b' : you
   cannot assign to a variable that is const
c:\cpphtp7_examples\ch07\fig07_14\fig07_14.cpp(21) : error C3892: 'b' : you
   cannot assign to a variable that is const
c:\cpphtp7_examples\ch07\fig07_14\fig07_14.cpp(22) : error C3892: 'b' : you
   cannot assign to a variable that is const
```

GNU C++ compiler error message:

```
fig07_14.cpp:20: error: assignment of read-only location
fig07_14.cpp:21: error: assignment of read-only location
fig07_14.cpp:22: error: assignment of read-only location
```

Fig. 7.14 | const type qualifier applied to an array parameter. (Part 2 of 2.)

7.6 Case Study: Class GradeBook Using an Array to Store Grades

This section further evolves class GradeBook, introduced in Chapter 3 and expanded in Chapters 4–6. Recall that this class represents a grade book used by a professor to store and analyze student grades. Previous versions of the class process grades entered by the user, but do not maintain the individual grade values in the class's data members. Thus, repeat calculations require the user to reenter the grades. One way to solve this problem would be to store each grade entered in an individual data member of the class. For example, we could create data members grade1, grade2, …, grade10 in class GradeBook to store 10 student grades. However, the code to total the grades and determine the class average would be cumbersome. In this section, we solve this problem by storing grades in an array.

Storing Student Grades in an Array in Class GradeBook
The version of class GradeBook (Figs. 7.15–7.16) presented here uses an array of integers to store the grades of several students on a single exam. This eliminates the need to repeatedly input the same set of grades. Array grades is declared as a data member in line 28 of Fig. 7.15—therefore, each GradeBook object maintains its own set of grades.

```
1   // Fig. 7.15: GradeBook.h
2   // Definition of class GradeBook that uses an array to store test grades.
3   // Member functions are defined in GradeBook.cpp
4   #include <string> // program uses C++ Standard Library string class
5   using namespace std;
6
7   // GradeBook class definition
8   class GradeBook
9   {
10  public:
11     // constant -- number of students who took the test
12     static const int students = 10; // note public data
13
14     // constructor initializes course name and array of grades
15     GradeBook( string, const int [] );
16
17     void setCourseName( string ); // function to set the course name
18     string getCourseName(); // function to retrieve the course name
19     void displayMessage(); // display a welcome message
20     void processGrades(); // perform various operations on the grade data
21     int getMinimum(); // find the minimum grade for the test
22     int getMaximum(); // find the maximum grade for the test
23     double getAverage(); // determine the average grade for the test
24     void outputBarChart(); // output bar chart of grade distribution
25     void outputGrades(); // output the contents of the grades array
26  private:
27     string courseName; // course name for this grade book
28     int grades[ students ]; // array of student grades
29  }; // end class GradeBook
```

Fig. 7.15 | Definition of class **GradeBook** using an array to store test grades.

```
1   // Fig. 7.16: GradeBook.cpp
2   // Member-function definitions for class GradeBook that
3   // uses an array to store test grades.
4   #include <iostream>
5   #include <iomanip>
6   #include "GradeBook.h" // GradeBook class definition
7   using namespace std;
8
9   // constructor initializes courseName and grades array
10  GradeBook::GradeBook( string name, const int gradesArray[] )
11  {
12     setCourseName( name ); // initialize courseName
13
14     // copy grades from gradesArray to grades data member
15     for ( int grade = 0; grade < students; grade++ )
16        grades[ grade ] = gradesArray[ grade ];
17  } // end GradeBook constructor
18
```

Fig. 7.16 | GradeBook class member functions manipulating an array of grades. (Part 1 of 4.)

```cpp
19  // function to set the course name
20  void GradeBook::setCourseName( string name )
21  {
22     courseName = name; // store the course name
23  } // end function setCourseName
24
25  // function to retrieve the course name
26  string GradeBook::getCourseName()
27  {
28     return courseName;
29  } // end function getCourseName
30
31  // display a welcome message to the GradeBook user
32  void GradeBook::displayMessage()
33  {
34     // this statement calls getCourseName to get the
35     // name of the course this GradeBook represents
36     cout << "Welcome to the grade book for\n" << getCourseName() << "!"
37        << endl;
38  } // end function displayMessage
39
40  // perform various operations on the data
41  void GradeBook::processGrades()
42  {
43     outputGrades(); // output grades array
44
45     // display average of all grades and minimum and maximum grades
46     cout << "\nClass average is " << setprecision( 2 ) << fixed <<
47        getAverage() << "\nLowest grade is " << getMinimum() <<
48        "\nHighest grade is " << getMaximum() << endl;
49
50     outputBarChart(); // print grade distribution chart
51  } // end function processGrades
52
53  // find minimum grade
54  int GradeBook::getMinimum()
55  {
56     int lowGrade = 100; // assume lowest grade is 100
57
58     // loop through grades array
59     for ( int grade = 0; grade < students; grade++ )
60     {
61        // if current grade lower than lowGrade, assign it to lowGrade
62        if ( grades[ grade ] < lowGrade )
63           lowGrade = grades[ grade ]; // new lowest grade
64     } // end for
65
66     return lowGrade; // return lowest grade
67  } // end function getMinimum
68
69  // find maximum grade
70  int GradeBook::getMaximum()
71  {
```

Fig. 7.16 | GradeBook class member functions manipulating an array of grades. (Part 2 of 4.)

```
72       int highGrade = 0; // assume highest grade is 0
73
74       // loop through grades array
75       for ( int grade = 0; grade < students; grade++ )
76       {
77          // if current grade higher than highGrade, assign it to highGrade
78          if ( grades[ grade ] > highGrade )
79             highGrade = grades[ grade ]; // new highest grade
80       } // end for
81
82       return highGrade; // return highest grade
83    } // end function getMaximum
84
85    // determine average grade for test
86    double GradeBook::getAverage()
87    {
88       int total = 0; // initialize total
89
90       // sum grades in array
91       for ( int grade = 0; grade < students; grade++ )
92          total += grades[ grade ];
93
94       // return average of grades
95       return static_cast< double >( total ) / students;
96    } // end function getAverage
97
98    // output bar chart displaying grade distribution
99    void GradeBook::outputBarChart()
100   {
101      cout << "\nGrade distribution:" << endl;
102
103      // stores frequency of grades in each range of 10 grades
104      const int frequencySize = 11;
105      int frequency[ frequencySize ] = {}; // initialize elements to 0
106
107      // for each grade, increment the appropriate frequency
108      for ( int grade = 0; grade < students; grade++ )
109         frequency[ grades[ grade ] / students ]++;
110
111      // for each grade frequency, print bar in chart
112      for ( int count = 0; count < frequencySize; count++ )
113      {
114         // output bar labels ("0-9:", ..., "90-99:", "100:" )
115         if ( count == 0 )
116            cout << "  0-9: ";
117         else if ( count == 10 )
118            cout << "  100: ";
119         else
120            cout << count * 10 << "-" << ( count * 10 ) + 9 << ": ";
121
122         // print bar of asterisks
123         for ( int stars = 0; stars < frequency[ count ]; stars++ )
124            cout << '*';
```

Fig. 7.16 | GradeBook class member functions manipulating an array of grades. (Part 3 of 4.)

```
125
126          cout << endl; // start a new line of output
127    } // end outer for
128 } // end function outputBarChart
129
130 // output the contents of the grades array
131 void GradeBook::outputGrades()
132 {
133    cout << "\nThe grades are:\n\n";
134
135    // output each student's grade
136    for ( int student = 0; student < students; student++ )
137       cout << "Student " << setw( 2 ) << student + 1 << ": " << setw( 3 )
138          << grades[ student ] << endl;
139 } // end function outputGrades
```

Fig. 7.16 | GradeBook class member functions manipulating an array of grades. (Part 4 of 4.)

Note that the size of the array in line 28 of Fig. 7.15 is specified by public static const data member students (declared in line 12). This data member is public so that it's accessible to the clients of the class. We'll soon see an example of a client program using this constant. Declaring students with the const qualifier indicates that this data member is constant—its value cannot be changed after being initialized. Keyword static in this variable declaration indicates that the data member is shared by all objects of the class—all GradeBook objects store grades for the same number of students. Recall from Section 3.5 that when each object of a class maintains its own copy of an attribute, the variable that represents the attribute is known as a data member—each object (instance) of the class has a separate copy of the variable in memory. There are variables for which each object of a class does not have a separate copy. That is the case with **static data members**, which are also known as **class variables**. When objects of a class containing static data members are created, all the objects share one copy of the class's static data members. A static data member can be accessed within the class definition and the member-function definitions like any other data member. As you'll soon see, a public static data member can also be accessed outside of the class, even when no objects of the class exist, using the class name followed by the binary scope resolution operator (::) and the name of the data member. You'll learn more about static data members in Chapter 10.

The class's constructor (declared in line 15 of Fig. 7.15 and defined in lines 10–17 of Fig. 7.16) has two parameters—the course name and an array of grades. When a program creates a GradeBook object (e.g., lines 12–13 of fig07_17.cpp), the program passes an existing int array to the constructor, which copies the array's values into the data member grades (lines 15–16 of Fig. 7.16). The grade values in the passed array could have been input from a user or read from a file on disk (as we discuss in Chapter 17, File Processing). In our test program, we simply initialize an array with a set of grade values (Fig. 7.17, lines 9–10). Once the grades are stored in data member grades of class GradeBook, all the class's member functions can access the grades array as needed to perform various calculations.

Member function processGrades (declared in line 20 of Fig. 7.15 and defined in lines 41–51 of Fig. 7.16) contains a series of member function calls that output a report summarizing the grades. Line 43 calls member function outputGrades to print the contents of the array grades. Lines 136–138 in member function outputGrades use a for statement to output each student's grade. Although array indices start at 0, a professor would typically number students starting at 1. Thus, lines 137–138 output student + 1 as the student number to produce grade labels "Student 1: ", "Student 2: ", and so on.

Member function processGrades next calls member function getAverage (line 47) to obtain the average of the grades in the array. Member function getAverage (declared in line 23 of Fig. 7.15 and defined in lines 86–96 of Fig. 7.16) uses a for statement to total the values in array grades before calculating the average. The averaging calculation in line 95 uses static const data member students to determine the number of grades being averaged.

Lines 47–48 in member function processGrades call member functions getMinimum and getMaximum to determine the lowest and highest grades of any student on the exam, respectively. Let's examine how member function getMinimum finds the *lowest* grade. Because the highest grade allowed is 100, we begin by assuming that 100 is the lowest grade (line 56). Then, we compare each of the elements in the array to the lowest grade, looking for smaller values. Lines 59–64 in member function getMinimum loop through the array, and line 62 compares each grade to lowGrade. If a grade is less than lowGrade, lowGrade is set to that grade. When line 66 executes, lowGrade contains the lowest grade in the array. Member function getMaximum (lines 70–83) works similarly to member function getMinimum.

Finally, line 50 in member function processGrades calls member function outputBarChart to print a distribution chart of the grade data using a technique similar to that in Fig. 7.9. In that example, we manually calculated the number of grades in each category (i.e., 0–9, 10–19, …, 90–99 and 100) by simply looking at a set of grades. In this example, lines 108–109 use a technique similar to that in Fig. 7.10 and Fig. 7.11 to calculate the frequency of grades in each category. Line 105 declares and creates array frequency of 11 ints to store the frequency of grades in each grade category. For each grade in array grades, lines 108–109 increment the appropriate element of the frequency array. To determine which element to increment, line 109 divides the current grade by 10 using integer division. For example, if grade is 85, line 109 increments frequency[8] to update the count of grades in the range 80–89. Lines 112–127 next print the bar chart (see Fig. 7.17) based on the values in array frequency. Like lines 26–27 of Fig. 7.9, lines 123–124 of Fig. 7.16 use a value in array frequency to determine the number of asterisks to display in each bar.

Testing Class *GradeBook*

The program of Fig. 7.17 creates an object of class GradeBook (Figs. 7.15–7.16) using the int array gradesArray (declared and initialized in lines 9–10). The binary scope resolution operator (::) is used in the expression "GradeBook::students" (line 9) to access class GradeBook's static constant students. We use this constant here to create an array that is the same size as array grades stored as a data member in class GradeBook. Lines 12–13 pass a course name and gradesArray to the GradeBook constructor. Line 14 displays a welcome message, and line 15 invokes the GradeBook object's processGrades member function. The output reveals the summary of the 10 grades in myGradeBook.

```
1   // Fig. 7.17: fig07_17.cpp
2   // Creates GradeBook object using an array of grades.
3   #include "GradeBook.h" // GradeBook class definition
4
5   // function main begins program execution
6   int main()
7   {
8      // array of student grades
9      int gradesArray[ GradeBook::students ] =
10        { 87, 68, 94, 100, 83, 78, 85, 91, 76, 87 };
11
12     GradeBook myGradeBook(
13        "CS101 Introduction to C++ Programming", gradesArray );
14     myGradeBook.displayMessage();
15     myGradeBook.processGrades();
16  } // end main
```

```
Welcome to the grade book for
CS101 Introduction to C++ Programming!

The grades are:

Student  1:  87
Student  2:  68
Student  3:  94
Student  4: 100
Student  5:  83
Student  6:  78
Student  7:  85
Student  8:  91
Student  9:  76
Student 10:  87

Class average is 84.90
Lowest grade is 68
Highest grade is 100

Grade distribution:
  0-9:
 10-19:
 20-29:
 30-39:
 40-49:
 50-59:
 60-69: *
 70-79: **
 80-89: ****
 90-99: **
  100: *
```

Fig. 7.17 | Creates a GradeBook object using an array of grades, then invokes member function processGrades to analyze them.

7.7 Searching Arrays with Linear Search

Often it may be necessary to determine whether an array contains a value that matches a certain **key value**. The process of finding a particular element of an array is called **search-**

ing. In this section we discuss the simple linear search. Exercise 7.33 at the end of this chapter asks you to implement a recursive version of the linear search. In Chapter 19, Searching and Sorting, we present the more complex, yet more efficient, binary search.

Linear Search

The **linear search** (Fig. 7.18, lines 33–40) compares each element of an array with a **search key** (line 36). Because the array is not in any particular order, it's just as likely that the value will be found in the first element as the last. On average, therefore, the program must compare the search key with half the elements of the array. To determine that a value is not in the array, the program must compare the search key to every element of the array.

```cpp
1   // Fig. 7.18: fig07_18.cpp
2   // Linear search of an array.
3   #include <iostream>
4   using namespace std;
5
6   int linearSearch( const int [], int, int ); // prototype
7
8   int main()
9   {
10     const int arraySize = 100; // size of array a
11     int a[ arraySize ]; // create array a
12     int searchKey; // value to locate in array a
13
14     for ( int i = 0; i < arraySize; i++ )
15        a[ i ] = 2 * i; // create some data
16
17     cout << "Enter integer search key: ";
18     cin >> searchKey;
19
20     // attempt to locate searchKey in array a
21     int element = linearSearch( a, searchKey, arraySize );
22
23     // display results
24     if ( element != -1 )
25        cout << "Found value in element " << element << endl;
26     else
27        cout << "Value not found" << endl;
28   } // end main
29
30   // compare key to every element of array until location is
31   // found or until end of array is reached; return subscript of
32   // element if key is found or -1 if key not found
33   int linearSearch( const int array[], int key, int sizeOfArray )
34   {
35     for ( int j = 0; j < sizeOfArray; j++ )
36        if ( array[ j ] == key ) // if found,
37           return j; // return location of key
38
39     return -1; // key not found
40   } // end function linearSearch
```

Fig. 7.18 | Linear search of an array. (Part 1 of 2.)

```
Enter integer search key: 36
Found value in element 18
```

```
Enter integer search key: 37
Value not found
```

Fig. 7.18 | Linear search of an array. (Part 2 of 2.)

The linear searching method works well for small arrays or for unsorted arrays (i.e., arrays whose elements are in no particular order). However, for large arrays, linear searching is inefficient. If the array is sorted (e.g., its elements are in ascending order), you can use the high-speed binary search technique that you'll learn about in Chapter 19, Searching and Sorting.

7.8 Sorting Arrays with Insertion Sort

Sorting data (i.e., placing the data into some particular order such as ascending or descending) is one of the most important computing applications. A bank sorts all checks by account number so that it can prepare individual bank statements at the end of each month. Telephone companies sort their phone directories by last name and, within that, by first name to make it easy to find phone numbers. Virtually every organization must sort some data and, in many cases, massive amounts of it. Sorting data is an intriguing problem that has attracted some of the most intense research efforts in the field of computer science. In this chapter, we discuss a simple sorting scheme. In Chapter 19, we investigate more complex schemes that yield superior performance, and we introduce Big O (pronounced "Big Oh") notation for characterizing how hard each scheme must work to accomplish its task.

Performance Tip 7.3
Simple algorithms can perform poorly. Their virtue is that they're easy to write, test and debug. More complex algorithms are sometimes needed to realize optimal performance.

Insertion Sort
The program in Fig. 7.19 sorts the values of the 10-element array `data` into ascending order. The technique we use is called **insertion sort**—a simple, but inefficient, sorting algorithm. The first iteration of this algorithm takes the second element and, if it's less than the first element, swaps it with the first element (i.e., the program *inserts* the second element in front of the first element). The second iteration looks at the third element and inserts it into the correct position with respect to the first two elements, so all three elements are in order. At the ith iteration of this algorithm, the first i elements in the original array will be sorted.

Line 10 of Fig. 7.19 declares and initializes array `data` with the following values:

| 34 | 56 | 4 | 10 | 77 | 51 | 93 | 30 | 5 | 52 |

The program first looks at `data[0]` and `data[1]`, whose values are 34 and 56, respectively. These two elements are already in order, so the program continues—if they were out of order, the program would swap them.

```
 1   // Fig. 7.19: fig07_19.cpp
 2   // This program sorts an array's values into ascending order.
 3   #include <iostream>
 4   #include <iomanip>
 5   using namespace std;
 6
 7   int main()
 8   {
 9      const int arraySize = 10; // size of array a
10      int data[ arraySize ] = { 34, 56, 4, 10, 77, 51, 93, 30, 5, 52 };
11      int insert; // temporary variable to hold element to insert
12
13      cout << "Unsorted array:\n";
14
15      // output original array
16      for ( int i = 0; i < arraySize; i++ )
17         cout << setw( 4 ) << data[ i ];
18
19      // insertion sort
20      // loop over the elements of the array
21      for ( int next = 1; next < arraySize; next++ )
22      {
23         insert = data[ next ]; // store the value in the current element
24
25         int moveItem = next; // initialize location to place element
26
27         // search for the location in which to put the current element
28         while ( ( moveItem > 0 ) && ( data[ moveItem - 1 ] > insert ) )
29         {
30            // shift element one slot to the right
31            data[ moveItem ] = data[ moveItem - 1 ];
32            moveItem--;
33         } // end while
34
35         data[ moveItem ] = insert; // place inserted element into the array
36      } // end for
37
38      cout << "\nSorted array:\n";
39
40      // output sorted array
41      for ( int i = 0; i < arraySize; i++ )
42         cout << setw( 4 ) << data[ i ];
43
44      cout << endl;
45   } // end main
```

```
Unsorted array:
  34  56   4  10  77  51  93  30   5  52
Sorted array:
   4   5  10  30  34  51  52  56  77  93
```

Fig. 7.19 | Sorting an array with insertion sort.

In the second iteration, the program looks at the value of data[2], 4. This value is less than 56, so the program stores 4 in a temporary variable and moves 56 one element to the right. The program then checks and determines that 4 is less than 34, so it moves 34 one element to the right. The program has now reached the beginning of the array, so it places 4 in data[0]. The array now is

| 4 | 34 | 56 | 10 | 77 | 51 | 93 | 30 | 5 | 52 |

In the third iteration, the program stores the value of data[3], 10, in a temporary variable. Then the program compares 10 to 56 and moves 56 one element to the right because it's larger than 10. The program then compares 10 to 34, moving 34 right one element. When the program compares 10 to 4, it observes that 10 is larger than 4 and places 10 in data[1]. The array now is

| 4 | 10 | 34 | 56 | 77 | 51 | 93 | 30 | 5 | 52 |

Using this algorithm, at the ith iteration, the first i elements of the original array are sorted. They may not be in their final locations, however, because smaller values may be located later in the array.

The sorting is performed by the for statement in lines 21–36 that loops over the elements of the array. In each iteration, line 23 temporarily stores in variable insert (declared in line 11) the value of the element that will be inserted into the sorted portion of the array. Line 25 declares and initializes the variable moveItem, which keeps track of where to insert the element. Lines 28–33 loop to locate the correct position where the element should be inserted. The loop terminates either when the program reaches the front of the array or when it reaches an element that is less than the value to be inserted. Line 31 moves an element to the right, and line 32 decrements the position at which to insert the next element. After the while loop ends, line 35 inserts the element into place. When the for statement in lines 21–36 terminates, the elements of the array are sorted.

The chief virtue of the insertion sort is that it's easy to program; however, it runs slowly. This becomes apparent when sorting large arrays. In the exercises, we'll investigate some alternate algorithms for sorting an array. We investigate sorting and searching in greater depth in Chapter 19.

7.9 **Multidimensional Arrays**

Arrays with two dimensions (i.e., subscripts) often represent **tables of values** consisting of information arranged in **rows** and **columns**. To identify a particular table element, we must specify two subscripts. By convention, the first identifies the element's row and the second identifies the element's column. Arrays that require two subscripts to identify a particular element are called **two-dimensional arrays** or **2-D arrays**. Arrays with two or more dimensions are known as **multidimensional arrays** and can have more than two dimensions. Figure 7.20 illustrates a two-dimensional array, a. The array contains three rows and four columns, so it's said to be a 3-by-4 array. In general, an array with m rows and n columns is called an m-**by-**n **array**.

Every element in array a is identified in Fig. 7.20 by an element name of the form a[i][j], where a is the name of the array, and i and j are the subscripts that uniquely identify each element in a. Notice that the names of the elements in row 0 all have a first subscript of 0; the names of the elements in column 3 all have a second subscript of 3.

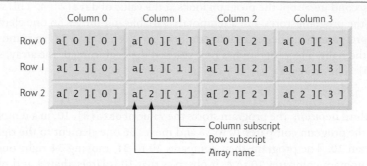

Fig. 7.20 | Two-dimensional array with three rows and four columns.

 Common Programming Error 7.9

Referencing a two-dimensional array element a[x][y] incorrectly as a[x, y] is an error. Actually, a[x, y] is treated as a[y], because C++ evaluates the expression x, y (containing a comma operator) simply as y (the last of the comma-separated expressions).

A multidimensional array can be initialized in its declaration much like a one-dimensional array. For example, a two-dimensional array b with values 1 and 2 in its row 0 elements and values 3 and 4 in its row 1 elements could be declared and initialized with

```
int b[ 2 ][ 2 ] = { { 1, 2 }, { 3, 4 } };
```

The values are grouped by row in braces. So, 1 and 2 initialize b[0][0] and b[0][1], respectively, and 3 and 4 initialize b[1][0] and b[1][1], respectively. If there are not enough initializers for a given row, the remaining elements of that row are initialized to 0. Thus, the declaration

```
int b[ 2 ][ 2 ] = { { 1 }, { 3, 4 } };
```

initializes b[0][0] to 1, b[0][1] to 0, b[1][0] to 3 and b[1][1] to 4.

Figure 7.21 demonstrates initializing two-dimensional arrays in declarations. Lines 12–14 declare three arrays, each with two rows and three columns.

```
1   // Fig. 7.21: fig07_21.cpp
2   // Initializing multidimensional arrays.
3   #include <iostream>
4   using namespace std;
5
6   void printArray( const int [][ 3 ] ); // prototype
7   const int rows = 2;
8   const int columns = 3;
9
10  int main()
11  {
12     int array1[ rows ][ columns ] = { { 1, 2, 3 }, { 4, 5, 6 } };
13     int array2[ rows ][ columns ] = { 1, 2, 3, 4, 5 };
14     int array3[ rows ][ columns ] = { { 1, 2 }, { 4 } };
```

Fig. 7.21 | Initializing multidimensional arrays. (Part 1 of 2.)

```
15
16      cout << "Values in array1 by row are:" << endl;
17      printArray( array1 );
18
19      cout << "\nValues in array2 by row are:" << endl;
20      printArray( array2 );
21
22      cout << "\nValues in array3 by row are:" << endl;
23      printArray( array3 );
24   } // end main
25
26   // output array with two rows and three columns
27   void printArray( const int a[][ columns ] )
28   {
29      // loop through array's rows
30      for ( int i = 0; i < rows; i++ )
31      {
32         // loop through columns of current row
33         for ( int j = 0; j < columns; j++ )
34            cout << a[ i ][ j ] << ' ';
35
36         cout << endl; // start new line of output
37      } // end outer for
38   } // end function printArray
```

```
Values in array1 by row are:
1 2 3
4 5 6

Values in array2 by row are:
1 2 3
4 5 0

Values in array3 by row are:
1 2 0
4 0 0
```

Fig. 7.21 | Initializing multidimensional arrays. (Part 2 of 2.)

The declaration of array1 (line 12) provides six initializers in two sublists. The first sublist initializes row 0 of the array to the values 1, 2 and 3; and the second sublist initializes row 1 of the array to the values 4, 5 and 6. If the braces around each sublist are removed from the array1 initializer list, the compiler initializes the elements of row 0 followed by the elements of row 1, yielding the same result.

The declaration of array2 (line 13) provides only five initializers. The initializers are assigned to row 0, then row 1. Any elements that do not have an explicit initializer are initialized to zero, so array2[1][2] is initialized to zero.

The declaration of array3 (line 14) provides three initializers in two sublists. The sublist for row 0 explicitly initializes the first two elements of row 0 to 1 and 2; the third element is implicitly initialized to zero. The sublist for row 1 explicitly initializes the first element to 4 and implicitly initializes the last two elements to zero.

The program calls function printArray to output each array's elements. Notice that the function prototype (line 6) and definition (lines 27–38) specify the parameter const int a[][columns]. When a function receives a one-dimensional array as an argument, the array brackets are empty in the function's parameter list. The size of a two-dimensional array's first dimension (i.e., the number of rows) is not required either, but all subsequent dimension sizes are required. The compiler uses these sizes to determine the locations in memory of elements in multidimensional arrays. All array elements are stored consecutively in memory, regardless of the number of dimensions. In a two-dimensional array, row 0 is stored in memory followed by row 1. Each row is a one-dimensional array. To locate an element in a particular row, the function must know exactly how many elements are in each row so it can skip the proper number of memory locations when accessing the array. Thus, when accessing a[1][2], the function knows to skip row 0's three elements in memory to get to row 1. Then, the function accesses element 2 of that row.

Many common array manipulations use for repetition statements. For example, the following for statement sets all the elements in row 2 of array a in Fig. 7.20 to zero:

```
for ( column = 0; column < 4; column++ )
   a[ 2 ][ column ] = 0;
```

The for statement varies only the second subscript (i.e., the column subscript). The preceding for statement is equivalent to the following assignment statements:

```
a[ 2 ][ 0 ] = 0;
a[ 2 ][ 1 ] = 0;
a[ 2 ][ 2 ] = 0;
a[ 2 ][ 3 ] = 0;
```

The following nested for statement determines the total of all the elements in array a:

```
total = 0;
for ( row = 0; row < 3; row++ )
   for ( column = 0; column < 4; column++ )
      total += a[ row ][ column ];
```

The for statement totals the elements of the array one row at a time. The outer for statement begins by setting row (i.e., the row subscript) to 0, so the elements of row 0 may be totaled by the inner for statement. The outer for statement then increments row to 1, so the elements of row 1 can be totaled. Then, the outer for statement increments row to 2, so the elements of row 2 can be totaled. When the nested for statement terminates, total contains the sum of all the array elements.

7.10 Case Study: Class GradeBook Using a Two-Dimensional Array

In Section 7.6, we presented class GradeBook (Figs. 7.15–7.16), which used a one-dimensional array to store student grades on a single exam. In most semesters, students take several exams. Professors are likely to want to analyze grades across the entire semester, both for a single student and for the class as a whole.

Storing Student Grades in a Two-Dimensional Array in Class GradeBook
Figures 7.22–7.23 contain a version of class GradeBook that uses a two-dimensional array grades to store the grades of a number of students on multiple exams. Each row of the

array represents a single student's grades for the entire course, and each column represents all the grades the students earned for one particular exam. A client program, such as Fig. 7.24, passes the array as an argument to the GradeBook constructor. In this example, we use a ten-by-three array containing ten students' grades on three exams.

```cpp
1   // Fig. 7.22: GradeBook.h
2   // Definition of class GradeBook that uses a
3   // two-dimensional array to store test grades.
4   // Member functions are defined in GradeBook.cpp
5   #include <string> // program uses C++ Standard Library string class
6   using namespace std;
7
8   // GradeBook class definition
9   class GradeBook
10  {
11  public:
12     // constants
13     static const int students = 10; // number of students
14     static const int tests = 3; // number of tests
15
16     // constructor initializes course name and array of grades
17     GradeBook( string, const int [][ tests ] );
18
19     void setCourseName( string ); // function to set the course name
20     string getCourseName(); // function to retrieve the course name
21     void displayMessage(); // display a welcome message
22     void processGrades(); // perform various operations on the grade data
23     int getMinimum(); // find the minimum grade in the grade book
24     int getMaximum(); // find the maximum grade in the grade book
25     double getAverage( const int [], const int ); // get student's average
26     void outputBarChart(); // output bar chart of grade distribution
27     void outputGrades(); // output the contents of the grades array
28  private:
29     string courseName; // course name for this grade book
30     int grades[ students ][ tests ]; // two-dimensional array of grades
31  }; // end class GradeBook
```

Fig. 7.22 | Definition of class GradeBook with a two-dimensional array to store grades.

```cpp
1   // Fig. 7.23: GradeBook.cpp
2   // Member-function definitions for class GradeBook that
3   // uses a two-dimensional array to store grades.
4   #include <iostream>
5   #include <iomanip> // parameterized stream manipulators
6   using namespace std;
7
8   // include definition of class GradeBook from GradeBook.h
9   #include "GradeBook.h"
10
```

Fig. 7.23 | GradeBook class member-function definitions manipulating a two-dimensional array of grades. (Part 1 of 5.)

```
11    // two-argument constructor initializes courseName and grades array
12    GradeBook::GradeBook( string name, const int gradesArray[][ tests ] )
13    {
14       setCourseName( name ); // initialize courseName
15
16       // copy grades from gradeArray to grades
17       for ( int student = 0; student < students; student++ )
18
19          for ( int test = 0; test < tests; test++ )
20             grades[ student ][ test ] = gradesArray[ student ][ test ];
21    } // end two-argument GradeBook constructor
22
23    // function to set the course name
24    void GradeBook::setCourseName( string name )
25    {
26       courseName = name; // store the course name
27    } // end function setCourseName
28
29    // function to retrieve the course name
30    string GradeBook::getCourseName()
31    {
32       return courseName;
33    } // end function getCourseName
34
35    // display a welcome message to the GradeBook user
36    void GradeBook::displayMessage()
37    {
38       // this statement calls getCourseName to get the
39       // name of the course this GradeBook represents
40       cout << "Welcome to the grade book for\n" << getCourseName() << "!"
41          << endl;
42    } // end function displayMessage
43
44    // perform various operations on the data
45    void GradeBook::processGrades()
46    {
47       outputGrades(); // output grades array
48
49       // call functions getMinimum and getMaximum
50       cout << "\nLowest grade in the grade book is " << getMinimum()
51          << "\nHighest grade in the grade book is " << getMaximum() << endl;
52
53       outputBarChart(); // display distribution chart of grades on all tests
54    } // end function processGrades
55
56    // find minimum grade in the entire gradebook
57    int GradeBook::getMinimum()
58    {
59       int lowGrade = 100; // assume lowest grade is 100
60
```

Fig. 7.23 | GradeBook class member-function definitions manipulating a two-dimensional array of grades. (Part 2 of 5.)

```
61        // loop through rows of grades array
62        for ( int student = 0; student < students; student++ )
63        {
64           // loop through columns of current row
65           for ( int test = 0; test < tests; test++ )
66           {
67              // if current grade less than lowGrade, assign it to lowGrade
68              if ( grades[ student ][ test ] < lowGrade )
69                 lowGrade = grades[ student ][ test ]; // new lowest grade
70           } // end inner for
71        } // end outer for
72
73        return lowGrade; // return lowest grade
74     } // end function getMinimum
75
76     // find maximum grade in the entire gradebook
77     int GradeBook::getMaximum()
78     {
79        int highGrade = 0; // assume highest grade is 0
80
81        // loop through rows of grades array
82        for ( int student = 0; student < students; student++ )
83        {
84           // loop through columns of current row
85           for ( int test = 0; test < tests; test++ )
86           {
87              // if current grade greater than highGrade, assign to highGrade
88              if ( grades[ student ][ test ] > highGrade )
89                 highGrade = grades[ student ][ test ]; // new highest grade
90           } // end inner for
91        } // end outer for
92
93        return highGrade; // return highest grade
94     } // end function getMaximum
95
96     // determine average grade for particular set of grades
97     double GradeBook::getAverage( const int setOfGrades[], const int grades )
98     {
99        int total = 0; // initialize total
100
101       // sum grades in array
102       for ( int grade = 0; grade < grades; grade++ )
103          total += setOfGrades[ grade ];
104
105       // return average of grades
106       return static_cast< double >( total ) / grades;
107    } // end function getAverage
108
109    // output bar chart displaying grade distribution
110    void GradeBook::outputBarChart()
111    {
```

Fig. 7.23 | GradeBook class member-function definitions manipulating a two dimensional array of grades. (Part 3 of 5.)

```
112        cout << "\nOverall grade distribution:" << endl;
113
114        // stores frequency of grades in each range of 10 grades
115        const int frequencySize = 11;
116        int frequency[ frequencySize ] = {}; // initialize elements to 0
117
118        // for each grade, increment the appropriate frequency
119        for ( int student = 0; student < students; student++ )
120
121           for ( int test = 0; test < tests; test++ )
122              ++frequency[ grades[ student ][ test ] / 10 ];
123
124        // for each grade frequency, print bar in chart
125        for ( int count = 0; count < frequencySize; count++ )
126        {
127           // output bar label ("0-9:", ..., "90-99:", "100:" )
128           if ( count == 0 )
129              cout << "  0-9: ";
130           else if ( count == 10 )
131              cout << "  100: ";
132           else
133              cout << count * 10 << "-" << ( count * 10 ) + 9 << ": ";
134
135           // print bar of asterisks
136           for ( int stars = 0; stars < frequency[ count ]; stars++ )
137              cout << '*';
138
139           cout << endl; // start a new line of output
140        } // end outer for
141     } // end function outputBarChart
142
143     // output the contents of the grades array
144     void GradeBook::outputGrades()
145     {
146        cout << "\nThe grades are:\n\n";
147        cout << "            "; // align column heads
148
149        // create a column heading for each of the tests
150        for ( int test = 0; test < tests; test++ )
151           cout << "Test " << test + 1 << "   ";
152
153        cout << "Average" << endl; // student average column heading
154
155        // create rows/columns of text representing array grades
156        for ( int student = 0; student < students; student++ )
157        {
158           cout << "Student " << setw( 2 ) << student + 1;
159
160           // output student's grades
161           for ( int test = 0; test < tests; test++ )
162              cout << setw( 8 ) << grades[ student ][ test ];
```

Fig. 7.23 | GradeBook class member-function definitions manipulating a two-dimensional array of grades. (Part 4 of 5.)

```
163
164        // call member function getAverage to calculate student's average;
165        // pass row of grades and the value of tests as the arguments
166        double average = getAverage( grades[ student ], tests );
167        cout << setw( 9 ) << setprecision( 2 ) << fixed << average << endl;
168     } // end outer for
169  } // end function outputGrades
```

Fig. 7.23 | GradeBook class member-function definitions manipulating a two-dimensional array of grades. (Part 5 of 5.)

Five member functions (declared in lines 23–27 of Fig. 7.22) perform array manipulations to process the grades. Each of these member functions is similar to its counterpart in the earlier one-dimensional array version of class GradeBook (Figs. 7.15–7.16). Member function getMinimum (defined in lines 57–74 of Fig. 7.23) determines the lowest grade of all students for the semester. Member function getMaximum (defined in lines 77–94 of Fig. 7.23) determines the highest grade of all students for the semester. Member function getAverage (lines 97–107 of Fig. 7.23) determines a particular student's semester average. Member function outputBarChart (lines 110–141 of Fig. 7.23) outputs a bar chart of the distribution of all student grades for the semester. Member function outputGrades (lines 144–169 of Fig. 7.23) outputs the two-dimensional array in a tabular format, along with each student's semester average.

Member functions getMinimum, getMaximum, outputBarChart and outputGrades each loop through array grades by using nested for statements. For example, consider the nested for statement in member function getMinimum (lines 62–71). The outer for statement begins by setting student (i.e., the row subscript) to 0, so the elements of row 0 can be compared with variable lowGrade in the body of the inner for statement. The inner for statement loops through the grades of a particular row and compares each grade with lowGrade. If a grade is less than lowGrade, lowGrade is set to that grade. The outer for statement then increments the row subscript to 1. The elements of row 1 are compared with variable lowGrade. The outer for statement then increments the row subscript to 2, and the elements of row 2 are compared with variable lowGrade. This repeats until all rows of grades have been traversed. When execution of the nested statement is complete, lowGrade contains the smallest grade in the two-dimensional array. Member function getMaximum works similarly to member function getMinimum.

Member function outputBarChart in Fig. 7.23 is nearly identical to the one in Fig. 7.16. However, to output the overall grade distribution for a whole semester, the function uses a nested for statement (lines 119–122) to create the one-dimensional array frequency based on all the grades in the two-dimensional array. The rest of the code in each of the two outputBarChart member functions that displays the chart is identical.

Member function outputGrades (lines 144–169) also uses nested for statements to output values of the array grades, in addition to each student's semester average. The output in Fig. 7.24 shows the result, which resembles the tabular format of a professor's physical grade book. Lines 150–151 print the column headings for each test. We use a counter-controlled for statement so that we can identify each test with a number. Similarly, the for statement in lines 156–168 first outputs a row label using a counter variable to identify each student (line 158). Although array indices start at 0, lines 151 and 158 output `test + 1` and `student + 1`, respectively, to produce test and student numbers starting at 1 (see Fig. 7.24). The inner `for` statement in lines 161–162 uses the outer `for` statement's counter variable `student` to loop through a specific row of array `grades` and output each student's test grade. Finally, line 166 obtains each student's semester average by passing the current row of `grades` (i.e., `grades[student]`) to member function `getAverage`.

Member function `getAverage` (lines 97–107) takes two arguments—a one-dimensional array of test results for a particular student and the number of test results in the array. When line 166 calls `getAverage`, the first argument is `grades[student]`, which specifies that a particular row of the two-dimensional array `grades` should be passed to `getAverage`. For example, based on the array created in Fig. 7.24, the argument `grades[1]` represents the three values (a one-dimensional array of grades) stored in row 1 of the two-dimensional array `grades`. A two-dimensional array can be considered an array whose elements are one-dimensional arrays. Member function `getAverage` calculates the sum of the array elements, divides the total by the number of test results and returns the floating-point result as a `double` value (line 106).

*Testing Class **GradeBook***

The program in Fig. 7.24 creates an object of class `GradeBook` (Figs. 7.22–7.23) using the two-dimensional array of `int`s named `gradesArray` (declared and initialized in lines 10–20). Line 10 accesses class `GradeBook`'s `static` constants `students` and `tests` to indicate the size of each dimension of array `gradesArray`. Lines 22–23 pass a course name and `gradesArray` to the `GradeBook` constructor. Lines 24–25 then invoke `myGradeBook`'s `displayMessage` and `processGrades` member functions to display a welcome message and obtain a report summarizing the students' grades for the semester, respectively.

```
1   // Fig. 7.24: fig07_24.cpp
2   // Creates GradeBook object using a two-dimensional array of grades.
3
4   #include "GradeBook.h" // GradeBook class definition
5
6   // function main begins program execution
7   int main()
8   {
9      // two-dimensional array of student grades
10     int gradesArray[ GradeBook::students ][ GradeBook::tests ] =
11        { { 87, 96, 70 },
12          { 68, 87, 90 },
13          { 94, 100, 90 },
14          { 100, 81, 82 },
15          { 83, 65, 85 },
16          { 78, 87, 65 },
17          { 85, 75, 83 },
18          { 91, 94, 100 },
19          { 76, 72, 84 },
20          { 87, 93, 73 } };
```

Fig. 7.24 | Creates a `GradeBook` object using a two-dimensional array of grades, then invokes member function `processGrades` to analyze them. (Part 1 of 2.)

```
21
22      GradeBook myGradeBook(
23         "CS101 Introduction to C++ Programming", gradesArray );
24      myGradeBook.displayMessage();
25      myGradeBook.processGrades();
26   } // end main
```

```
Welcome to the grade book for
CS101 Introduction to C++ Programming!

The grades are:

            Test 1  Test 2  Test 3  Average
Student  1      87      96      70    84.33
Student  2      68      87      90    81.67
Student  3      94     100      90    94.67
Student  4     100      81      82    87.67
Student  5      83      65      85    77.67
Student  6      78      87      65    76.67
Student  7      85      75      83    81.00
Student  8      91      94     100    95.00
Student  9      76      72      84    77.33
Student 10      87      93      73    84.33

Lowest grade in the grade book is 65
Highest grade in the grade book is 100

Overall grade distribution:
  0-9:
 10-19:
 20-29:
 30-39:
 40-49:
 50-59:
 60-69: ***
 70-79: ******
 80-89: ***********
 90-99: *******
   100: ***
```

Fig. 7.24 | Creates a GradeBook object using a two-dimensional array of grades, then invokes member function processGrades to analyze them. (Part 2 of 2.)

7.11 Introduction to C++ Standard Library Class Template vector

We now introduce C++ Standard Library class template **vector**, which represents a more robust type of array featuring many additional capabilities. As you'll see in later chapters, C-style pointer-based arrays (i.e., the type of arrays presented thus far) have great potential for errors. For example, as mentioned earlier, a program can easily "walk off" either end of an array, because C++ does not check whether subscripts fall outside the range of an array. Two arrays cannot be meaningfully compared with equality operators or relational operators. As you'll learn in Chapter 8, pointer variables (known more commonly as pointers) contain memory addresses as their values. Array names are simply pointers to where the arrays begin in memory, and, of course, two arrays will always be at different memory locations. When an array is passed to a general-purpose function designed to handle arrays of any size, the size of the array must be passed as an additional argument. Furthermore, one array cannot be assigned to another with the assignment operator(s)—array names are const pointers, and, as you'll learn in Chapter 8, a constant pointer cannot be used on the left side of an assignment operator. These and other capabilities certainly seem like "naturals" for dealing with arrays, but C++ does not provide such capabilities. However, the C++ Standard Library provides class template vector to allow you to create a more powerful and less error-prone alternative to arrays. In Chapter 11, we present the means to implement such array capabilities as those provided by vector. You'll learn how to customize operators for use with your own classes (a technique known as operator overloading).

The vector class template is available to anyone building applications with C++. The notations that the vector example uses might be unfamiliar to you, because vectors use template notation. Recall that Section 6.18 discussed function templates. In Chapter 14, we discuss class templates. For now, you should feel comfortable using class template vector by mimicking the syntax in the example we show in this section. You'll deepen your understanding as we study class templates in Chapter 14. Chapter 22 presents class template vector (and several other standard C++ container classes) in detail.

The program of Fig. 7.25 demonstrates capabilities provided by C++ Standard Library class template vector that are not available for C-style pointer-based arrays. Standard class template vector provides many of the same features as the Array class that we construct in Chapter 11. Standard class template vector is defined in header <vector> (line 5) and belongs to namespace std. Chapter 22 discusses the full functionality of standard class template vector.

```cpp
 1   // Fig. 7.25: fig07_25.cpp
 2   // Demonstrating C++ Standard Library class template vector.
 3   #include <iostream>
 4   #include <iomanip>
 5   #include <vector>
 6   using namespace std;
 7
 8   void outputVector( const vector< int > & ); // display the vector
 9   void inputVector( vector< int > & ); // input values into the vector
10
11   int main()
12   {
13      vector< int > integers1( 7 ); // 7-element vector< int >
14      vector< int > integers2( 10 ); // 10-element vector< int >
15
16      // print integers1 size and contents
17      cout << "Size of vector integers1 is " << integers1.size()
18         << "\nvector after initialization:" << endl;
19      outputVector( integers1 );
20
```

Fig. 7.25 | C++ Standard Library class template vector. (Part 1 of 4.)

```
21    // print integers2 size and contents
22    cout << "\nSize of vector integers2 is " << integers2.size()
23       << "\nvector after initialization:" << endl;
24    outputVector( integers2 );
25
26    // input and print integers1 and integers2
27    cout << "\nEnter 17 integers:" << endl;
28    inputVector( integers1 );
29    inputVector( integers2 );
30
31    cout << "\nAfter input, the vectors contain:\n"
32       << "integers1:" << endl;
33    outputVector( integers1 );
34    cout << "integers2:" << endl;
35    outputVector( integers2 );
36
37    // use inequality (!=) operator with vector objects
38    cout << "\nEvaluating: integers1 != integers2" << endl;
39
40    if ( integers1 != integers2 )
41       cout << "integers1 and integers2 are not equal" << endl;
42
43    // create vector integers3 using integers1 as an
44    // initializer; print size and contents
45    vector< int > integers3( integers1 ); // copy constructor
46
47    cout << "\nSize of vector integers3 is " << integers3.size()
48       << "\nvector after initialization:" << endl;
49    outputVector( integers3 );
50
51    // use overloaded assignment (=) operator
52    cout << "\nAssigning integers2 to integers1:" << endl;
53    integers1 = integers2; // assign integers2 to integers1
54
55    cout << "integers1:" << endl;
56    outputVector( integers1 );
57    cout << "integers2:" << endl;
58    outputVector( integers2 );
59
60    // use equality (==) operator with vector objects
61    cout << "\nEvaluating: integers1 == integers2" << endl;
62
63    if ( integers1 == integers2 )
64       cout << "integers1 and integers2 are equal" << endl;
65
66    // use square brackets to create rvalue
67    cout << "\nintegers1[5] is " << integers1[ 5 ];
68
69    // use square brackets to create lvalue
70    cout << "\n\nAssigning 1000 to integers1[5]" << endl;
71    integers1[ 5 ] = 1000;
72    cout << "integers1:" << endl;
73    outputVector( integers1 );
```

Fig. 7.25 | C++ Standard Library class template vector. (Part 2 of 4.)

```
74
75      // attempt to use out-of-range subscript
76      cout << "\nAttempt to assign 1000 to integers1.at( 15 )" << endl;
77      integers1.at( 15 ) = 1000; // ERROR: out of range
78   } // end main
79
80   // output vector contents
81   void outputVector( const vector< int > &array )
82   {
83      size_t i; // declare control variable
84
85      for ( i = 0; i < array.size(); i++ )
86      {
87         cout << setw( 12 ) << array[ i ];
88
89         if ( ( i + 1 ) % 4 == 0 ) // 4 numbers per row of output
90            cout << endl;
91      } // end for
92
93      if ( i % 4 != 0 )
94         cout << endl;
95   } // end function outputVector
96
97   // input vector contents
98   void inputVector( vector< int > &array )
99   {
100     for ( size_t i = 0; i < array.size(); i++ )
101        cin >> array[ i ];
102  } // end function inputVector
```

```
Size of vector integers1 is 7
vector after initialization:
          0              0              0              0
          0              0              0

Size of vector integers2 is 10
vector after initialization:
          0              0              0              0
          0              0              0              0
          0              0

Enter 17 integers:
1 2 3 4 5 6 7 8 9 10 11 12 13 14 15 16 17

After input, the vectors contain:
integers1:
          1              2              3              4
          5              6              7
integers2:
          8              9             10             11
         12             13             14             15
         16             17
```

Fig. 7.25 | C++ Standard Library class template `vector`. (Part 3 of 4.)

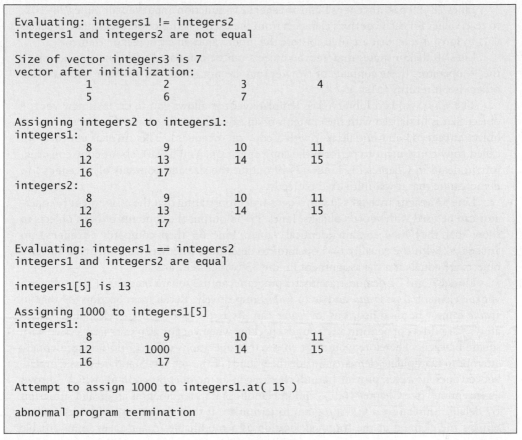

```
Evaluating: integers1 != integers2
integers1 and integers2 are not equal

Size of vector integers3 is 7
vector after initialization:
           1            2            3            4
           5            6            7

Assigning integers2 to integers1:
integers1:
           8            9           10           11
          12           13           14           15
          16           17
integers2:
           8            9           10           11
          12           13           14           15
          16           17

Evaluating: integers1 == integers2
integers1 and integers2 are equal

integers1[5] is 13

Assigning 1000 to integers1[5]
integers1:
           8            9           10           11
          12         1000           14           15
          16           17

Attempt to assign 1000 to integers1.at( 15 )

abnormal program termination
```

Fig. 7.25 | C++ Standard Library class template vector. (Part 4 of 4.)

Lines 13–14 create two vector objects that store values of type int—integers1 contains seven elements, and integers2 contains 10 elements. By default, all the elements of each vector object are set to 0. Note that vectors can be defined to store any data type, by replacing int in vector<int> with the appropriate data type. This notation, which specifies the type stored in the vector, is similar to the template notation that Section 6.18 introduced with function templates.

Line 17 uses vector member function **size** to obtain the size (i.e., the number of elements) of integers1. Line 19 passes integers1 to function outputVector (lines 81–95), which uses square brackets, [] (line 87), to obtain the value in each element of the vector for output. Note the resemblance of this notation to that used to access the value of an array element. Lines 22 and 24 perform the same tasks for integers2.

Member function size of class template vector returns the number of elements in a vector as a value of type size_t (which represents the type unsigned int on many systems). As a result, line 83 declares the control variable i to be of type size_t, too. On some compilers, declaring i as an int causes the compiler to issue a warning message, since the loop-continuation condition (line 85) would compare a signed value (i.e., int i) and an unsigned value (i.e., a value of type size_t returned by function size).

Lines 28–29 pass `integers1` and `integers2` to function `inputVector` (lines 98–102) to read values for each `vector`'s elements from the user. The function uses square brackets (`[]`) to form *lvalues* that are used to store the input values in each `vector` element.

Line 40 demonstrates that `vector` objects can be compared with one another using the `!=` operator. If the contents of two `vectors` are not equal, the operator returns `true`; otherwise, it returns `false`.

The C++ Standard Library class template `vector` allows you to create a new `vector` object that is initialized with the contents of an existing `vector`. Line 45 creates a `vector` object `integers3` and initializes it with a copy of `integers1`. This invokes `vector`'s so-called copy constructor to perform the copy operation. You'll learn about copy constructors in detail in Chapter 11. Lines 47–49 output the size and contents of `integers3` to demonstrate that it was initialized correctly.

Line 53 assigns `integers2` to `integers1`, demonstrating that the assignment (`=`) operator can be used with `vector` objects. Lines 55–58 output the contents of both objects to show that they now contain identical values. Line 63 then compares `integers1` to `integers2` with the equality (`==`) operator to determine whether the contents of the two objects are equal after the assignment in line 53 (which they are).

Lines 67 and 71 demonstrate that a program can use square brackets (`[]`) to obtain a `vector` element as an *rvalue* and as an *lvalue*, respectively. Recall from Section 5.9 that an *rvalue* cannot be modified, but an *lvalue* can. As is the case with C-style pointer-based arrays, C++ does not perform any bounds checking when `vector` elements are accessed with square brackets. Therefore, you must ensure that operations using `[]` do not accidentally attempt to manipulate elements outside the bounds of the `vector`. Standard class template `vector` does, however, provide bounds checking in its member function **at**, which "throws an exception" (see Chapter 16, Exception Handling) if its argument is an invalid subscript. By default, this causes a C++ program to terminate. If the subscript is valid, function `at` returns the element at the specified location as a modifiable *lvalue* or an unmodifiable *lvalue*, depending on the context in which the call appears. An unmodifiable *lvalue* is an expression that identifies an object in memory (such as an element in a `vector`), but cannot be used to modify that object. Line 77 demonstrates a call to function `at` with an invalid subscript. The resulting output varies by compiler.

In this section, we demonstrated the C++ Standard Library class template `vector`, a robust, reusable class that can replace C-style pointer-based arrays. In Chapter 11, you'll see that `vector` achieves many of its capabilities by "overloading" C++'s built-in operators, and you'll learn how to customize operators for use with your own classes in similar ways. For example, we create an `Array` class that, like class template `vector`, improves upon basic array capabilities. Our `Array` class also provides additional features, such as the ability to input and output entire arrays with operators `>>` and `<<`, respectively.

7.12 Wrap-Up

This chapter began our introduction to data structures, exploring the use of arrays and vectors to store data in and retrieve data from lists and tables of values. The chapter examples demonstrated how to declare an array, initialize an array and refer to individual elements of an array. We also illustrated how to pass arrays to functions and how to use the `const` qualifier to enforce the principle of least privilege. Chapter examples also presented basic searching and sorting techniques. You learned how to declare and manipulate multidimensional arrays. Finally, we demonstrated the capabilities of C++ Standard Library class template vector, which provides a more robust alternative to arrays.

We continue our coverage of data structures in Chapter 14, Templates, where we build a stack class template and in Chapter 20, Data Structures, which introduces other dynamic data structures, such as lists, queues, stacks and trees, that can grow and shrink as programs execute. Chapter 22, introduces several of the C++ Standard Library's predefined data structures, which you can use instead of building their own. Chapter 22 presents the full functionality of class template vector and discusses many additional data structure classes, including list and deque, which are array-like data structures that can grow and shrink in response to a program's changing storage requirements.

We've now introduced the basic concepts of classes, objects, control statements, functions and arrays. In Chapter 8, we present one of C++'s most powerful features—the pointer. Pointers keep track of where data and functions are stored in memory, which allows us to manipulate those items in interesting ways. After introducing basic pointer concepts, we examine in detail the close relationship among arrays, pointers and strings.

Summary

Section 7.1 Introduction
- Data structures are collections of related data items. Arrays are data structures consisting of related data items of the same type. Arrays are "static" entities in that they remain the same size throughout program execution. (They may, of course, be of automatic storage class and hence be created and destroyed each time the blocks in which they're defined are entered and exited.)

Section 7.2 Arrays
- An array is a consecutive group of memory locations that share the same type.
- To refer to a particular location or element in an array, we specify the name of the array and the position number of the particular element in the array.
- A program refers to any one of an array's elements by giving the name of the array followed by the index of the particular element in square brackets ([]).
- The first element in every array has index zero and is sometimes called the zeroth element.
- A index must be an integer or integer expression (using any integral type).
- The brackets used to enclose the index are an operator with the same precedence as parentheses.

Section 7.3 Declaring Arrays
- Arrays occupy space in memory. You specify the type of each element and the number of elements required by an array as follows:

    type arrayName[*arraySize*];

  and the compiler reserves the appropriate amount of memory.
- Arrays can be declared to contain any data type. For example, an array of type char can be used to store a character string.

Section 7.4 Examples Using Arrays
- The elements of an array can be initialized in the array declaration by following the array name with an equals sign and an initializer list—a comma-separated list (enclosed in braces) of constant

initializers. When initializing an array with an initializer list, if there are fewer initializers than elements in the array, the remaining elements are initialized to zero.

- If the array size is omitted from a declaration with an initializer list, the compiler determines the number of elements in the array by counting the number of elements in the initializer list.

- If the array size and an initializer list are specified in an array declaration, the number of initializers must be less than or equal to the array size.

- Constants must be initialized with a constant expression when they're declared and cannot be modified thereafter. Constants can be placed anywhere a constant expression is expected.

- C++ has no array bounds checking. You should ensure that all array references remain within the bounds of the array.

- A static local variable in a function definition exists for the duration of the program but is visible only in the function body.

- A program initializes static local arrays when their declarations are first encountered. If a static array is not initialized explicitly by you, each element of that array is initialized to zero by the compiler when the array is created.

Section 7.5 Passing Arrays to Functions

- To pass an array argument to a function, specify the name of the array without any brackets. To pass an element of an array to a function, use the subscripted name of the array element as an argument in the function call.

- Arrays are passed to functions by reference—the called functions can modify the element values in the callers' original arrays. The value of the name of the array is the address in the computer's memory of the first element of the array. Because the starting address of the array is passed, the called function knows precisely where the array is stored in memory.

- Individual array elements are passed by value exactly as simple variables are. Such simple single pieces of data are called scalars or scalar quantities.

- To receive an array argument, a function's parameter list must specify that the function expects to receive an array. The size of the array is not required between the array brackets.

- C++ provides the type qualifier const that can be used to prevent modification of array values in the caller by code in a called function. When an array parameter is preceded by the const qualifier, the elements of the array become constant in the function body, and any attempt to modify an element of the array in the function body results in a compilation error.

Section 7.6 Case Study: Class **GradeBook** Using an Array to Store Grades

- Class variables (static data members) are shared by all objects of the class in which the variables are declared.

- A static data member can be accessed within the class definition and the member-function definitions like any other data member.

- A public static data member can also be accessed outside of the class, even when no objects of the class exist, using the class name followed by the binary scope resolution operator (::) and the name of the data member.

Section 7.7 Searching Arrays with Linear Search

- The linear search compares each array element with a search key. Because the array is not in any particular order, it's just as likely that the value will be found in the first element as the last. On average, a program must compare the search key with half the array elements. To determine that a value is not in the array, the program must compare the search key to every element in the array.

Section 7.8 Sorting Arrays with Insertion Sort

- An array can be sorted using insertion sort. The first iteration of this algorithm takes the second element and, if it's less than the first element, swaps it with the first element (i.e., the program *inserts* the second element in front of the first element). The second iteration looks at the third element and inserts it into the correct position with respect to the first two elements, so all three elements are in order. At the ith iteration of this algorithm, the first i elements in the original array will be sorted. For small arrays, the insertion sort is acceptable, but for larger arrays it's inefficient compared to other more sophisticated sorting algorithms.

Section 7.9 Multidimensional Arrays

- Multidimensional arrays with two dimensions are often used to represent tables of values consisting of information arranged in rows and columns.

- Arrays that require two subscripts to identify a particular element are called two-dimensional arrays. An array with m rows and n columns is called an *m-by-n* array.

Section 7.11 Introduction to C++ Standard Library Class Template **vector**

- C++ Standard Library class template vector represents a more robust alternative to arrays featuring many capabilities that are not provided for C-style pointer-based arrays.

- By default, all the elements of an integer vector object are set to 0.

- A vector can be defined to store any data type using a declaration of the form

      vector< *type* > *name*(*size*);

- Member function size of class template vector returns the number of elements in the vector on which it's invoked.

- The value of an element of a vector can be accessed or modified using square brackets ([]).

- Objects of standard class template vector can be compared directly with the equality (==) and inequality (!=) operators. The assignment (=) operator can also be used with vector objects.

- An unmodifiable *lvalue* is an expression that identifies an object in memory (such as an element in a vector), but cannot be used to modify that object. A modifiable *lvalue* also identifies an object in memory, but can be used to modify the object.

- Standard class template vector provides bounds checking in its member function at, which "throws an exception" if its argument is an invalid subscript. By default, this causes a C++ program to terminate.

Terminology

2-D array 313
array 283
array initializer list 288
at member function of vector 328
bounds checking 296
class variable 307
column of a two-dimensional array 313
const qualifier 289
const type qualifier 302
constant variable 289
data structure 283
element of an array 284
index 284
index zero 284

initializer list 287
initializers 287
insertion sort 311
key value 309
linear search 310
magic number 291
m-by-n array 313
multidimensional array 313
name of an array 284
named constant 289
off-by-one error 285
position number 284
read-only variables 289
row of a two-dimensional array 313

Self-Review Exercises

7.1   Answer each of the following:
a) Lists and tables of values can be stored in _____ or _____.
b) The elements of an array are related by the fact that they have the same _____ and
_____.
c) The number used to refer to a particular element of an array is called its _____.
d) A(n) _____ should be used to declare the size of an array, because it makes the program more scalable.
e) The process of placing the elements of an array in order is called _____ the array.
f) The process of determining if an array contains a particular key value is called
_____ the array.
g) An array that uses two subscripts is referred to as a(n) _____ array.

7.2   State whether the following are *true* or *false*. If the answer is *false*, explain why.
a) An array can store many different types of values.
b) An array subscript should normally be of data type float.
c) If there are fewer initializers in an initializer list than the number of elements in the array, the remaining elements are initialized to the last value in the initializer list.
d) It's an error if an initializer list has more initializers than there are elements in the array.
e) An individual array element that is passed to a function and modified in that function
will contain the modified value when the called function completes execution.

7.3   Write one or more statements that perform the following tasks for and array called fractions:
a) Define a constant integer variable arraySize initialized to 10.
b) Declare an array with arraySize elements of type double, and initialize the elements to
0.
c) Name the fourth element of the array.
d) Refer to array element 4.
e) Assign the value 1.667 to array element 9.
f) Assign the value 3.333 to the seventh element of the array.
g) Print array elements 6 and 9 with two digits of precision to the right of the decimal
point, and show the output that is actually displayed on the screen.
h) Print all the array elements using a for statement. Define the integer variable i as a control variable for the loop. Show the output.

7.4   Answer the following questions regarding an array called table:
a) Declare the array to be an integer array and to have 3 rows and 3 columns. Assume that
the constant variable arraySize has been defined to be 3.
b) How many elements does the array contain?
c) Use a for statement to initialize each element of the array to the sum of its subscripts.
Assume that the integer variables i and j are declared as control variables.

d) Write a program segment to print the values of each element of array `table` in tabular format with 3 rows and 3 columns. Assume that the array was initialized with the declaration

```
int table[ arraySize ][ arraySize ] = { { 1, 8 }, { 2, 4, 6 }, { 5 } };
```

and the integer variables i and j are declared as control variables. Show the output.

7.5   Find the error in each of the following program segments and correct the error:
a) `#include <iostream>;`
b) `arraySize = 10; // arraySize was declared const`
c) Assume that `int b[ 10 ] = {};`
```
for ( int i = 0; i <= 10; i++ )
    b[ i ] = 1;
```
d) Assume that `int a[ 2 ][ 2 ] = { { 1, 2 }, { 3, 4 } };`
```
a[ 1, 1 ] = 5;
```

Answers to Self-Review Exercises

7.1   a) arrays, vectors. b) array name, type. c) subscript or index.   d) constant variable.
e) sorting. f) searching. g) two-dimensional.

7.2   a) False. An array can store only values of the same type.
b) False. An array subscript should be an integer or an integer expression.
c) False. The remaining elements are initialized to zero.
d) True.
e) False. Individual elements of an array are passed by value. If the entire array is passed to a function, then any modifications to the elements will be reflected in the original.

7.3   a) `const int arraySize = 10;`
b) `double fractions[ arraySize ] = { 0.0 };`
c) `fractions[ 3 ]`
d) `fractions[ 4 ]`
e) `fractions[ 9 ] = 1.667;`
f) `fractions[ 6 ] = 3.333;`
g) `cout << fixed << setprecision( 2 );`
   `cout << fractions[ 6 ] << ' ' << fractions[ 9 ] << endl;`
   Output: 3.33 1.67.
h) `for ( int i = 0; i < arraySize; i++ )`
   `    cout << "fractions[" << i << "] = " << fractions[ i ] << endl;`
   Output:
   ```
   fractions[ 0 ] = 0.0
   fractions[ 1 ] = 0.0
   fractions[ 2 ] = 0.0
   fractions[ 3 ] = 0.0
   fractions[ 4 ] = 0.0
   fractions[ 5 ] = 0.0
   fractions[ 6 ] = 3.333
   fractions[ 7 ] = 0.0
   fractions[ 8 ] = 0.0
   fractions[ 9 ] = 1.667
   ```

7.4   a) `int table[ arraySize ][ arraySize ];`
b) Nine.

```
  c)  for ( i = 0; i < arraySize; i++ )
          for ( j = 0; j < arraySize; j++ )
              table[ i ][ j ] = i + j;
  d)  cout << "      [0]   [1]   [2]" << endl;

      for ( int i = 0; i < arraySize; i++ ) {
          cout << '[' << i << "] ";

          for ( int j = 0; j < arraySize; j++ )
              cout << setw( 3 ) << table[ i ][ j ] << "   ";
          cout << endl;
      }
```
Output:
```
        [0]  [1]  [2]
  [0]    1    8    0
  [1]    2    4    6
  [2]    5    0    0
```

7.5   a) *Error:* Semicolon at end of #include preprocessor directive.
           Correction: Eliminate semicolon.
       b) *Error:* Assigning a value to a constant variable using an assignment statement.
           Correction: Initialize the constant variable in a const int arraySize declaration.
       c) *Error:* Referencing an array element outside the bounds of the array (b[10]).
           Correction: Change the final value of the control variable to 9 or change <= to <.
       d) *Error:* Array subscripting done incorrectly.
           Correction: Change the statement to a[1][1] = 5;

Exercises

7.6   Fill in the blanks in each of the following:
       a) The names of the four elements of array p (int p[4];) are _____, _____,
           _____ and _____.
       b) Naming an array, stating its type and specifying the number of elements in the array is
           called _____ the array.
       c) By convention, the first subscript in a two-dimensional array identifies an element's
           _____ and the second subscript identifies an element's _____.
       d) An *m*-by-*n* array contains _____ rows, _____ columns and _____ elements.
       e) The name of the element in row 3 and column 5 of array d is _____.

7.7   Determine whether each of the following is *true* or *false*. If *false*, explain why.
       a) To refer to a particular location or element within an array, we specify the name of the
           array and the value of the particular element.
       b) An array definition reserves space for an array.
       c) To indicate that 100 locations should be reserved for integer array p, you write the dec-
           laration

               p[100];

       d) A for statement must be used to initialize the elements of a 15-element array to zero.
       e) Nested for statements must be used to total the elements of a two-dimensional array.

7.8   Write C++ statements to accomplish each of the following:
       a) Display the value of element 6 of character array f.
       b) Input a value into element 4 of one-dimensional floating-point array b.

c) Initialize each of the 5 elements of one-dimensional integer array g to 8.
d) Total and print the elements of floating-point array c of 100 elements.
e) Copy array a into the first portion of array b. Assume double a[11], b[34];
f) Determine and print the smallest and largest values contained in 99-element floating-point array w.

7.9   Consider a 2-by-3 integer array t.
a) Write a declaration for t.
b) How many rows does t have?
c) How many columns does t have?
d) How many elements does t have?
e) Write the names of all the elements in row 1 of t.
f) Write the names of all the elements in column 2 of t.
g) Write a single statement that sets the element of t in the first row and second column to zero.
h) Write a series of statements that initialize each element of t to zero. Do not use a loop.
i) Write a nested for statement that initializes each element of t to zero.
j) Write a statement that inputs the values for the elements of t from the keyboard.
k) Write a series of statements that determine and print the smallest value in array t.
l) Write a statement that displays the elements in row 0 of t.
m) Write a statement that totals the elements in column 3 of t.
n) Write a series of statements that prints the array t in neat, tabular format. List the column subscripts as headings across the top and list the row subscripts at the left of each row.

7.10   *(Salesperson Salary Ranges)* Use a one-dimensional array to solve the following problem. A company pays its salespeople on a commission basis. The salespeople each receive $200 per week plus 9 percent of their gross sales for that week. For example, a salesperson who grosses $5000 in sales in a week receives $200 plus 9 percent of $5000, or a total of $650. Write a program (using an array of counters) that determines how many of the salespeople earned salaries in each of the following ranges (assume that each salesperson's salary is truncated to an integer amount):
a) $200–299
b) $300–399
c) $400–499
d) $500–599
e) $600–699
f) $700–799
g) $800–899
h) $900–999
i) $1000 and over

7.11   *(Bubble Sort)* In the **bubble sort algorithm**, smaller values gradually "bubble" their way upward to the top of the array like air bubbles rising in water, while the larger values sink to the bottom. The bubble sort makes several passes through the array. On each pass, successive pairs of elements are compared. If a pair is in increasing order (or the values are identical), we leave the values as they are. If a pair is in decreasing order, their values are swapped in the array. Write a program that sorts an array of 10 integers using bubble sort.

7.12   *(Bubble Sort Enhancements)* The bubble sort described in Exercise 7.11 is inefficient for large arrays. Make the following simple modifications to improve the performance of the bubble sort:
a) After the first pass, the largest number is guaranteed to be in the highest-numbered element of the array; after the second pass, the two highest numbers are "in place," and so on. Instead of making nine comparisons on every pass, modify the bubble sort to make eight comparisons on the second pass, seven on the third pass, and so on.

b) The data in the array may already be in the proper order or near-proper order, so why make nine passes if fewer will suffice? Modify the sort to check at the end of each pass if any swaps have been made. If none have been made, then the data must already be in the proper order, so the program should terminate. If swaps have been made, then at least one more pass is needed.

7.13 Write single statements that perform the following one-dimensional array operations:
a) Initialize the 10 elements of integer array counts to zero.
b) Add 1 to each of the 15 elements of integer array bonus.
c) Read 12 values for double array monthlyTemperatures from the keyboard.
d) Print the 5 values of integer array bestScores in column format.

7.14 Find the error(s) in each of the following statements:
a) Assume that: int a[3];

```
cout << a[ 1 ] << " " << a[ 2 ] << " " << a[ 3 ] << endl;
```

b) double f[3] = { 1.1, 10.01, 100.001, 1000.0001 };
c) Assume that: double d[2][10];

```
d[ 1, 9 ] = 2.345;
```

7.15 *(Duplicate Elimination)* Use a one-dimensional array to solve the following problem. Read in 20 numbers, each of which is between 10 and 100, inclusive. As each number is read, validate it and store it in the array only if it isn't a duplicate of a number already read. After reading all the values, display only the unique values that the user entered. Provide for the "worst case" in which all 20 numbers are different. Use the smallest possible array to solve this problem.

7.16 Label the elements of a 3-by-5 two-dimensional array sales to indicate the order in which they're set to zero by the following program segment:

```
for ( row = 0; row < 3; row++ )
    for ( column = 0; column < 5; column++ )
        sales[ row ][ column ] = 0;
```

7.17 *(Dice Rolling)* Write a program that simulates the rolling of two dice. The program should use rand to roll the first die and should use rand again to roll the second die. The sum of the two values should then be calculated. [*Note:* Each die can show an integer value from 1 to 6, so the sum of the two values will vary from 2 to 12, with 7 being the most frequent sum and 2 and 12 being the least frequent sums.] Figure 7.26 shows the 36 possible combinations of the two dice. Your program should roll the two dice 36,000 times. Use a one-dimensional array to tally the numbers of times each possible sum appears. Print the results in a tabular format. Also, determine if the totals are reasonable (i.e., there are six ways to roll a 7, so approximately one-sixth of all the rolls should be 7).

	1	2	3	4	5	6
1	2	3	4	5	6	7
2	3	4	5	6	7	8
3	4	5	6	7	8	9
4	5	6	7	8	9	10
5	6	7	8	9	10	11
6	7	8	9	10	11	12

Fig. 7.26 | The 36 possible outcomes of rolling two dice.

7.18   What does the following program do?

```cpp
// Ex. 7.18: Ex07_18.cpp
// What does this program do?
#include <iostream>
using namespace std;

int whatIsThis( int [], int ); // function prototype

int main()
{
   const int arraySize = 10;
   int a[ arraySize ] = { 1, 2, 3, 4, 5, 6, 7, 8, 9, 10 };

   int result = whatIsThis( a, arraySize );

   cout << "Result is " << result << endl;
} // end main

// What does this function do?
int whatIsThis( int b[], int size )
{
   if ( size == 1 ) // base case
      return b[ 0 ];
   else // recursive step
      return b[ size - 1 ] + whatIsThis( b, size - 1 );
} // end function whatIsThis
```

7.19   *(Craps Game Modification)* Modify the program of Fig. 6.11 to play 1000 games of craps. The program should keep track of the statistics and answer the following questions:

   a)   How many games are won on the 1st roll, 2nd roll, …, 20th roll, and after the 20th roll?
   b)   How many games are lost on the 1st roll, 2nd roll, …, 20th roll, and after the 20th roll?
   c)   What are the chances of winning at craps? [*Note:* You should discover that craps is one of the fairest casino games. What do you suppose this means?]
   d)   What's the average length of a game of craps?
   e)   Do the chances of winning improve with the length of the game?

7.20   *(Airline Reservations System)* A small airline has just purchased a computer for its new automated reservations system. You've been asked to program the new system. You are to write a program to assign seats on each flight of the airline's only plane (capacity: 10 seats).

Your program should display the following menu of alternatives—Please type 1 for "First Class" and Please type 2 for "Economy". If the person types 1, your program should assign a seat in the first class section (seats 1–5). If the person types 2, your program should assign a seat in the economy section (seats 6–10). Your program should print a boarding pass indicating the person's seat number and whether it's in the first class or economy section of the plane.

Use a one-dimensional array to represent the seating chart of the plane. Initialize all the elements of the array to false to indicate that all seats are empty. As each seat is assigned, set the corresponding elements of the array to true to indicate that the seat is no longer available.

Your program should, of course, never assign a seat that has already been assigned. When the first class section is full, your program should ask the person if it's acceptable to be placed in the economy section (and vice versa). If yes, then make the appropriate seat assignment. If no, then print the message "Next flight leaves in 3 hours."

7.21 What does the following program do?

```cpp
// Ex. 7.21: Ex07_21.cpp
// What does this program do?
#include <iostream>
using namespace std;

void someFunction( int [], int, int ); // function prototype

int main()
{
   const int arraySize = 10;
   int a[ arraySize ] = { 1, 2, 3, 4, 5, 6, 7, 8, 9, 10 };

   cout << "The values in the array are:" << endl;
   someFunction( a, 0, arraySize );
   cout << endl;
} // end main

// What does this function do?
void someFunction( int b[], int current, int size )
{
   if ( current < size )
   {
      someFunction( b, current + 1, size );
      cout << b[ current ] << "  ";
   } // end if
} // end function someFunction
```

7.22 *(Sales Summary)* Use a two-dimensional array to solve the following problem. A company has four salespeople (1 to 4) who sell five different products (1 to 5). Once a day, each salesperson passes in a slip for each different type of product sold. Each slip contains the following:

a) The salesperson number

b) The product number

c) The total dollar value of that product sold that day

Thus, each salesperson passes in between 0 and 5 sales slips per day. Assume that the information from all of the slips for last month is available. Write a program that will read all this information for last month's sales and summarize the total sales by salesperson by product. All totals should be stored in the two-dimensional array `sales`. After processing all the information for last month, print the results in tabular format with each of the columns representing a particular salesperson and each of the rows representing a particular product. Cross total each row to get the total sales of each product for last month; cross total each column to get the total sales by salesperson for last month. Your tabular printout should include these cross totals to the right of the totaled rows and to the bottom of the totaled columns.

7.23 *(Turtle Graphics)* The Logo language, which is popular among elementary school children, made the concept of *turtle graphics* famous. Imagine a mechanical turtle that walks around the room under the control of a C++ program. The turtle holds a pen in one of two positions, up or down. While the pen is down, the turtle traces out shapes as it moves; while the pen is up, the turtle moves about freely without writing anything. In this problem, you'll simulate the operation of the turtle and create a computerized sketchpad as well.

Use a 20-by-20 array `floor` that is initialized to `false`. Read commands from an array that contains them. Keep track of the current position of the turtle at all times and whether the pen is currently up or down. Assume that the turtle always starts at position (0, 0) of the floor with its pen up. The set of turtle commands your program must process are shown in Fig. 7.27.

Command	Meaning
1	Pen up
2	Pen down
3	Turn right
4	Turn left
5,10	Move forward 10 spaces (or a number other than 10)
6	Print the 20-by-20 array
9	End of data (sentinel)

Fig. 7.27 | Turtle graphics commands.

Suppose that the turtle is somewhere near the center of the floor. The following "program" would draw and print a 12-by-12 square and end with the pen in the up position:

```
2
5,12
3
5,12
3
5,12
3
5,12
1
6
9
```

As the turtle moves with the pen down, set the appropriate elements of array floor to true. When the 6 command (print) is given, wherever there is a true in the array, display an asterisk or some other character you choose. Wherever there is a zero, display a blank. Write a program to implement the turtle graphics capabilities discussed here. Write several turtle graphics programs to draw interesting shapes. Add other commands to increase the power of your turtle graphics language.

7.24 (*Knight's Tour*) One of the more interesting puzzlers for chess buffs is the Knight's Tour problem. The question is this: Can the chess piece called the knight move around an empty chessboard and touch each of the 64 squares once and only once? We study this intriguing problem in depth in this exercise.

The knight makes L-shaped moves (over two in one direction then over one in a perpendicular direction). Thus, from a square in the middle of an empty chessboard, the knight can make eight different moves (numbered 0 through 7) as shown in Fig. 7.28.

a) Draw an 8-by-8 chessboard on a sheet of paper and attempt a Knight's Tour by hand. Put a 1 in the first square you move to, a 2 in the second square, a 3 in the third, etc. Before starting the tour, estimate how far you think you'll get, remembering that a full tour consists of 64 moves. How far did you get? Was this close to your estimate?

b) Now let's develop a program that will move the knight around a chessboard. The board is represented by an 8-by-8 two-dimensional array board. Each of the squares is initialized to zero. We describe each of the eight possible moves in terms of both their horizontal and vertical components. For example, a move of type 0, as shown in Fig. 7.28, consists of moving two squares horizontally to the right and one square vertically upward. Move 2 consists of moving one square horizontally to the left and two squares vertically upward. Horizontal moves to the left and vertical moves upward are indicated

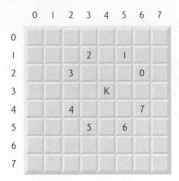

Fig. 7.28 | The eight possible moves of the knight.

with negative numbers. The eight moves may be described by two one-dimensional arrays, horizontal and vertical, as follows:

```
horizontal[ 0 ] = 2      vertical[ 0 ] = -1
horizontal[ 1 ] = 1      vertical[ 1 ] = -2
horizontal[ 2 ] = -1     vertical[ 2 ] = -2
horizontal[ 3 ] = -2     vertical[ 3 ] = -1
horizontal[ 4 ] = -2     vertical[ 4 ] = 1
horizontal[ 5 ] = -1     vertical[ 5 ] = 2
horizontal[ 6 ] = 1      vertical[ 6 ] = 2
horizontal[ 7 ] = 2      vertical[ 7 ] = 1
```

Let the variables currentRow and currentColumn indicate the row and column of the knight's current position. To make a move of type moveNumber, where moveNumber is between 0 and 7, your program uses the statements

```
currentRow += vertical[ moveNumber ];
currentColumn += horizontal[ moveNumber ];
```

Keep a counter that varies from 1 to 64. Record the latest count in each square the knight moves to. Remember to test each potential move to see if the knight has already visited that square, and, of course, test every potential move to make sure that the knight does not land off the chessboard. Now write a program to move the knight around the chessboard. Run the program. How many moves did the knight make?

c) After attempting to write and run a Knight's Tour program, you've probably developed some valuable insights. We'll use these to develop a **heuristic** (or strategy) for moving the knight. Heuristics do not guarantee success, but a carefully developed heuristic greatly improves the chance of success. You may have observed that the outer squares are more troublesome than the squares nearer the center of the board. In fact, the most troublesome, or inaccessible, squares are the four corners.

Intuition may suggest that you should attempt to move the knight to the most troublesome squares first and leave open those that are easiest to get to, so when the board gets congested near the end of the tour, there will be a greater chance of success.

We may develop an "accessibility heuristic" by classifying each square according to how accessible it's then always moving the knight to the square (within the knight's L-shaped moves, of course) that is most inaccessible. We label a two-dimensional array accessibility with numbers indicating from how many squares each particular square is accessible. On a blank chessboard, each center square is rated as 8, each corner square is rated as 2 and the other squares have accessibility numbers of 3, 4 or 6 as follows:

```
2  3  4  4  4  4  3  2
3  4  6  6  6  6  4  3
4  6  8  8  8  8  6  4
4  6  8  8  8  8  6  4
4  6  8  8  8  8  6  4
4  6  8  8  8  8  6  4
3  4  6  6  6  6  4  3
2  3  4  4  4  4  3  2
```

Now write a version of the Knight's Tour program using the accessibility heuristic. At any time, the knight should move to the square with the lowest accessibility number. In case of a tie, the knight may move to any of the tied squares. Therefore, the tour may begin in any of the four corners. [*Note:* As the knight moves around the chessboard, your program should reduce the accessibility numbers as more and more squares become occupied. In this way, at any given time during the tour, each available square's accessibility number will remain equal to precisely the number of squares from which that square may be reached.] Run this version of your program. Did you get a full tour? Now modify the program to run 64 tours, one starting from each square of the chessboard. How many full tours did you get?

d) Write a version of the Knight's Tour program which, when encountering a tie between two or more squares, decides what square to choose by looking ahead to those squares reachable from the "tied" squares. Your program should move to the square for which the next move would arrive at a square with the lowest accessibility number.

7.25 (*Knight's Tour: Brute Force Approaches*) In Exercise 7.24, we developed a solution to the Knight's Tour problem. The approach used, called the "accessibility heuristic," generates many solutions and executes efficiently.

As computers continue increasing in power, we'll be able to solve more problems with sheer computer power and relatively unsophisticated algorithms. This is the "brute force" approach to problem solving.

a) Use random number generation to enable the knight to walk around the chessboard (in its legitimate L-shaped moves, of course) at random. Your program should run one tour and print the final chessboard. How far did the knight get?

b) Most likely, the preceding program produced a relatively short tour. Now modify your program to attempt 1000 tours. Use a one-dimensional array to keep track of the number of tours of each length. When your program finishes attempting the 1000 tours, it should print this information in neat tabular format. What was the best result?

c) Most likely, the preceding program gave you some "respectable" tours, but no full tours. Now "pull all the stops out" and simply let your program run until it produces a full tour. [*Caution:* This version of the program could run for hours on a powerful computer.] Once again, keep a table of the number of tours of each length, and print this table when the first full tour is found. How many tours did your program attempt before producing a full tour? How much time did it take?

d) Compare the brute force version of the Knight's Tour with the accessibility heuristic version. Which required a more careful study of the problem? Which algorithm was more difficult to develop? Which required more computer power? Could we be certain (in advance) of obtaining a full tour with the accessibility heuristic approach? Could we be certain (in advance) of obtaining a full tour with the brute force approach? Argue the pros and cons of brute force problem solving in general.

7.26 (*Eight Queens*) Another puzzler for chess buffs is the Eight Queens problem. Simply stated: Is it possible to place eight queens on an empty chessboard so that no queen is "attacking" any other, i.e., no two queens are in the same row, the same column, or along the same diagonal? Use the thinking developed in Exercise 7.24 to formulate a heuristic for solving the Eight Queens problem. Run your program. [*Hint:* It's possible to assign a value to each square of the chessboard indicating how many squares of an empty chessboard are "eliminated" if a queen is placed in that square. Each of the corners would be assigned the value 22, as in Fig. 7.29. Once these "elimination numbers" are placed in all 64 squares, an appropriate heuristic might be: Place the next queen in the square with the smallest elimination number. Why is this strategy intuitively appealing?]

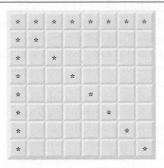

Fig. 7.29 | The 22 squares eliminated by placing a queen in the upper-left corner.

7.27 (*Eight Queens: Brute Force Approaches*) In this exercise, you'll develop several brute-force approaches to solving the Eight Queens problem introduced in Exercise 7.26.
  a) Solve the Eight Queens exercise, using the random brute force technique developed in Exercise 7.25.
  b) Use an exhaustive technique, i.e., try all possible combinations of eight queens on the chessboard.
  c) Why do you suppose the exhaustive brute force approach may not be appropriate for solving the Knight's Tour problem?
  d) Compare and contrast the random brute force and exhaustive brute force approaches in general.

7.28 (*Knight's Tour: Closed-Tour Test*) In the Knight's Tour, a full tour occurs when the knight makes 64 moves touching each square of the chess board once and only once. A closed tour occurs when the 64th move is one move away from the location in which the knight started the tour. Modify the Knight's Tour program you wrote in Exercise 7.24 to test for a closed tour if a full tour has occurred.

7.29 (*The Sieve of Eratosthenes*) A prime integer is any integer that is evenly divisible only by itself and 1. The Sieve of Eratosthenes is a method of finding prime numbers. It operates as follows:
  a) Create an array with all elements initialized to 1 (true). Array elements with prime subscripts will remain 1. All other array elements will eventually be set to zero. You'll ignore elements 0 and 1 in this exercise.
  b) Starting with array subscript 2, every time an array element is found whose value is 1, loop through the remainder of the array and set to zero every element whose subscript is a multiple of the subscript for the element with value 1. For array subscript 2, all elements beyond 2 in the array that are multiples of 2 will be set to zero (subscripts 4, 6, 8, 10, etc.); for array subscript 3, all elements beyond 3 in the array that are multiples of 3 will be set to zero (subscripts 6, 9, 12, 15, etc.); and so on.

When this process is complete, the array elements that are still set to one indicate that the subscript is a prime number. These subscripts can then be printed. Write a program that uses an array of 1000 elements to determine and print the prime numbers between 2 and 999. Ignore element 0 of the array.

7.30 (*Bucket Sort*) A **bucket sort** begins with a one-dimensional array of positive integers to be sorted and a two-dimensional array of integers with rows subscripted from 0 to 9 and columns subscripted from 0 to $n - 1$, where n is the number of values in the array to be sorted. Each row of the two-dimensional array is referred to as a bucket. Write a function bucketSort that takes an integer array and the array size as arguments and performs as follows:

a) Place each value of the one-dimensional array into a row of the bucket array based on the value's ones digit. For example, 97 is placed in row 7, 3 is placed in row 3 and 100 is placed in row 0. This is called a "distribution pass."

b) Loop through the bucket array row by row, and copy the values back to the original array. This is called a "gathering pass." The new order of the preceding values in the one-dimensional array is 100, 3 and 97.

c) Repeat this process for each subsequent digit position (tens, hundreds, thousands, etc.).

On the second pass, 100 is placed in row 0, 3 is placed in row 0 (because 3 has no tens digit) and 97 is placed in row 9. After the gathering pass, the order of the values in the one-dimensional array is 100, 3 and 97. On the third pass, 100 is placed in row 1, 3 is placed in row zero and 97 is placed in row zero (after the 3). After the last gathering pass, the original array is now in sorted order.

Note that the two-dimensional array of buckets is 10 times the size of the integer array being sorted. This sorting technique provides better performance than an insertion sort, but requires much more memory. The insertion sort requires space for only one additional element of data. This is an example of the space-time trade-off: The bucket sort uses more memory than the insertion sort, but performs better. This version of the bucket sort requires copying all the data back to the original array on each pass. Another possibility is to create a second two-dimensional bucket array and repeatedly swap the data between the two bucket arrays.

Recursion Exercises

7.31 (*Selection Sort*) A **selection sort** searches an array looking for the smallest element. Then, the smallest element is swapped with the first element of the array. The process is repeated for the subarray beginning with the second element of the array. Each pass of the array results in one element being placed in its proper location. This sort performs comparably to the insertion sort—for an array of n elements, $n - 1$ passes must be made, and for each subarray, $n - 1$ comparisons must be made to find the smallest value. When the subarray being processed contains one element, the array is sorted. Write recursive function selectionSort to perform this algorithm.

7.32 (*Palindromes*) A palindrome is a string that is spelled the same way forward and backward. Examples of palindromes include "radar" and "able was i ere i saw elba." Write a recursive function testPalindrome that returns true if a string is a palindrome, and false otherwise. Note that like an array, the square brackets ([]) operator can be used to iterate through the characters in a string.

7.33 (*Linear Search*) Modify the program in Fig. 7.18 to use recursive function linearSearch to perform a linear search of the array. The function should receive an integer array and the size of the array as arguments. If the search key is found, return the array subscript; otherwise, return –1.

7.34 (*Eight Queens*) Modify the Eight Queens program you created in Exercise 7.26 to solve the problem recursively.

7.35 (*Print an Array*) Write a recursive function printArray that takes an array, a starting subscript and an ending subscript as arguments, returns nothing and prints the array. The function should stop processing and return when the starting subscript equals the ending subscript.

7.36 (*Print a String Backward*) Write a recursive function stringReverse that takes a string and a starting subscript as arguments, prints the string backward and returns nothing. The function should stop processing and return when the end of the string is encountered. Note that like an array the square brackets ([]) operator can be used to iterate through the characters in a string.

7.37 (*Find the Minimum Value in an Array*) Write a recursive function `recursiveMinimum` that takes an integer array, a starting subscript and an ending subscript as arguments, and returns the smallest element of the array. The function should stop processing and return when the starting subscript equals the ending subscript.

vector Exercises

7.38 (*Salesperson Salary Ranges with* **vector**) Use a vector of integers to solve the problem described in Exercise 7.10.

7.39 (*Dice Rolling with* **vector**) Modify the dice-rolling program you created in Exercise 7.17 to use a vector to store the numbers of times each possible sum of the two dice appears.

7.40 (*Find the Minimum Value in a* **vector**) Modify your solution to Exercise 7.37 to find the minimum value in a vector instead of an array.

Making a Difference

7.41 (*Polling*) The Internet and the web are enabling more people to network, join a cause, voice opinions, and so on. The presidential candidates in 2008 used the Internet intensively to get out their messages and raise money for their campaigns. In this exercise, you'll write a simple polling program that allows users to rate five social-consciousness issues from 1 (least important) to 10 (most important). Pick five causes that are important to you (e.g., political issues, global environmental issues). Use a one-dimensional array topics (of type string) to store the five causes. To summarize the survey responses, use a 5-row, 10-column two-dimensional array responses (of type int), each row corresponding to an element in the topics array. When the program runs, it should ask the user to rate each issue. Have your friends and family respond to the survey. Then have the program display a summary of the results, including:
   a) A tabular report with the five topics down the left side and the 10 ratings across the top, listing in each column the number of ratings received for each topic.
   b) To the right of each row, show the average of the ratings for that issue.
   c) Which issue received the highest point total? Display both the issue and the point total.
   d) Which issue received the lowest point total? Display both the issue and the point total.

Pointers

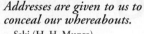

Addresses are given to us to conceal our whereabouts.
—Saki (H. H. Munro)

By indirection find direction out.
—William Shakespeare

*Many things, having full reference
To one consent, may work contrariously.*
—William Shakespeare

You will find it a very good practice always to verify your references, sir!
—Dr. Routh

Objectives

In this chapter you'll learn:

- What pointers are.
- The similarities and differences between pointers and references, and when to use each.
- To use pointers to pass arguments to functions by reference.
- The close relationships between pointers and arrays.
- To use arrays of pointers.
- Basic pointer-based string processing.
- To use pointers to functions.

8.1 Introduction

This chapter discusses one of the most powerful features of the C++ programming language, the pointer. In Chapter 6, we saw that references can be used to perform pass-by-reference. Pointers also enable pass-by-reference and can be used to create and manipulate dynamic data structures that can grow and shrink, such as linked lists, queues, stacks and trees. This chapter explains basic pointer concepts and reinforces the intimate relationship among arrays and pointers. The view of arrays as pointers derives from the C programming language. As we saw in Chapter 7, the C++ Standard Library class vector provides an implementation of arrays as full-fledged objects.

Similarly, C++ actually offers two types of strings—string class objects (which we've been using since Chapter 3) and C-style, pointer-based strings. This chapter on pointers briefly introduces C strings to deepen your knowledge of pointers. C strings are widely used in legacy C and C++ systems. We discuss C strings in depth in Chapter 21. In new software development projects, you should favor string class objects.

We'll examine the use of pointers with classes in Chapter 13, Object-Oriented Programming: Polymorphism, where we'll see that the so-called "polymorphic processing" associated with object-oriented programming is performed with pointers and references. Chapter 20, Data Structures, presents examples of creating and using dynamic data structures that are implemented with pointers.

8.2 Pointer Variable Declarations and Initialization

Pointer variables contain memory addresses as their values. Normally, a variable directly contains a specific value. A pointer contains the memory address of a variable that, in turn, contains a specific value. In this sense, a variable name **directly references a value**, and a pointer **indirectly references a value** (Fig. 8.1). Referencing a value through a pointer is called **indirection**. Diagrams typically represent a pointer as an arrow from the variable that contains an address to the variable located at that address in memory.

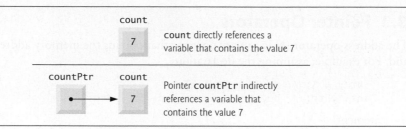

Fig. 8.1 | Directly and indirectly referencing a variable.

Pointers, like any other variables, must be declared before they can be used. For example, for the pointer in Fig. 8.1, the declaration

```
int *countPtr, count;
```

declares the variable countPtr to be of type int * (i.e., a pointer to an int value) and is read (right to left), "countPtr is a pointer to int."Also, variable count in the preceding declaration is declared to be an int, not a pointer to an int. The * in the declaration applies only to countPtr. Each variable being declared as a pointer must be preceded by an asterisk (*). For example, the declaration

```
double *xPtr, *yPtr;
```

indicates that both xPtr and yPtr are pointers to double values. When * appears in a declaration, it isn't an operator; rather, it indicates that the variable being declared is a pointer. Pointers can be declared to point to objects of any data type.

Common Programming Error 8.1

*Assuming that the * used to declare a pointer distributes to all variable names in a declaration's comma-separated list of variables can lead to errors. Each pointer must be declared with the * prefixed to the name (either with or without spaces in between—the compiler ignores the space). Declaring only one variable per declaration helps avoid these types of errors and improves program readability.*

Good Programming Practice 8.1

Although it isn't a requirement, including the letters Ptr in a pointer variable name makes it clear that the variable is a pointer and that it must be handled accordingly.

Pointers should be initialized either when they're declared or in an assignment. A pointer may be initialized to 0, NULL or an address of the corresponding type. A pointer with the value 0 or NULL points to nothing and is known as a **null pointer**. Symbolic constant NULL is defined in header file <iostream> (and in several other standard library header files) to represent the value 0. Initializing a pointer to NULL is equivalent to initializing a pointer to 0, but in C++, 0 is used by convention. When 0 is assigned, it's converted to a pointer of the appropriate type. The value 0 is the only integer value that can be assigned directly to a pointer variable without first casting the integer to a pointer type.

Error-Prevention Tip 8.1

Initialize pointers to prevent pointing to unknown or uninitialized areas of memory.

8.3 Pointer Operators

The **address operator (&)** is a unary operator that obtains the memory address of its operand. For example, assuming the declarations

```
int y = 5; // declare variable y
int *yPtr; // declare pointer variable yPtr
```

the statement

```
yPtr = &y; // assign address of y to yPtr
```

assigns the address of the variable y to pointer variable yPtr. Then variable yPtr is said to "point to" y. Now, yPtr indirectly references variable y's value. The use of the & in the preceding statement is not the same as the use of the & in a reference variable declaration, which is always preceded by a data-type name. When declaring a reference, the & is part of the type. In an expression like &y, the & is an operator.

Figure 8.2 shows a schematic representation of memory after the preceding assignment. The "pointing relationship" is indicated by drawing an arrow from the box that represents the pointer yPtr in memory to the box that represents the variable y in memory.

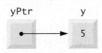

Fig. 8.2 | Graphical representation of a pointer pointing to a variable in memory.

Figure 8.3 shows another pointer representation in memory with integer variable y stored at memory location 600000 and pointer variable yPtr stored at memory location 500000. The operand of the address operator must be an *lvalue*; the address operator cannot be applied to constants or to expressions that do not result in references.

	yPtr		y
location 500000	600000	location 600000	5

Fig. 8.3 | Representation of y and yPtr in memory.

The *** operator**, commonly referred to as the **indirection operator** or **dereferencing operator**, returns a synonym (i.e., an alias or a nickname) for the object to which its pointer operand points. For example (referring again to Fig. 8.2), the statement

```
cout << *yPtr << endl;
```

prints the value of variable y, namely, 5, just as the statement

```
cout << y << endl;
```

would. Using * in this manner is called **dereferencing a pointer**. A dereferenced pointer may also be used on the left side of an assignment statement, as in

```
*yPtr = 9;
```

which would assign 9 to y in Fig. 8.3. The dereferenced pointer may also be used to receive an input value as in

```
cin >> *yPtr;
```

which places the input value in y. The dereferenced pointer is an *lvalue*.

Common Programming Error 8.2

Dereferencing an uninitialized pointer could cause a fatal execution-time error, or it could accidentally modify important data and allow the program to run to completion, possibly with incorrect results.

Common Programming Error 8.3

An attempt to dereference a variable that is not a pointer is a compilation error.

Common Programming Error 8.4

Dereferencing a null pointer is often a fatal execution-time error.

The program in Fig. 8.4 demonstrates the & and * pointer operators. Memory locations are output by << in this example as hexadecimal (i.e., base-16) integers. (See Appendix D, Number Systems, for more information on hexadecimal integers.) The hexadecimal memory addresses output by this program are compiler and operating-system dependent, so you may get different results when you run the program.

Portability Tip 8.1

The format in which a pointer is output is compiler dependent—some use hexadecimal integers, some use decimal integers and some use other formats.

```cpp
1   // Fig. 8.4: fig08_04.cpp
2   // Pointer operators & and *.
3   #include <iostream>
4   using namespace std;
5
6   int main()
7   {
8      int a; // a is an integer
9      int *aPtr; // aPtr is an int * which is a pointer to an integer
10
11     a = 7; // assigned 7 to a
12     aPtr = &a; // assign the address of a to aPtr
13
14     cout << "The address of a is " << &a
15        << "\nThe value of aPtr is " << aPtr;
16     cout << "\n\nThe value of a is " << a
17        << "\nThe value of *aPtr is " << *aPtr;
18     cout << "\n\nShowing that * and & are inverses of "
19        << "each other.\n&*aPtr = " << &*aPtr
20        << "\n*&aPtr = " << *&aPtr << endl;
21  } // end main
```

Fig. 8.4 | Pointer operators & and *. (Part 1 of 2.)

```
The address of a is 0012F580
The value of aPtr is 0012F580

The value of a is 7
The value of *aPtr is 7

Showing that * and & are inverses of each other.
&*aPtr = 0012F580
*&aPtr = 0012F580
```

Fig. 8.4 | Pointer operators & and *. (Part 2 of 2.)

The address of a (line 14) and the value of aPtr (line 15) are identical in the output, confirming that the address of a is indeed assigned to the pointer variable aPtr. The & and * operators are inverses of one another—when they're applied consecutively to aPtr in either order, they "cancel one another out" yielding the same result (the value in aPtr).

Figure 8.5 lists the precedence and associativity of the operators introduced to this point. The address (&) and dereferencing operator (*) are unary operators on the third level.

Operators							Associativity	Type
()	[]						left to right	highest
++	--	static_cast< *type* >(*operand*)					left to right	unary (postfix)
++	--	+	-	!	&	*	right to left	unary (prefix)
*	/	%					left to right	multiplicative
+	-						left to right	additive
<<	>>						left to right	insertion/extraction
<	<=	>	>=				left to right	relational
==	!=						left to right	equality
&&							left to right	logical AND
||							left to right	logical OR
?:							right to left	conditional
=	+=	-=	*=	/=	%=		right to left	assignment
,							left to right	comma

Fig. 8.5 | Operator precedence and associativity.

8.4 Pass-by-Reference with Pointers

There are three ways in C++ to pass arguments to a function—pass-by-value, **pass-by-reference with reference arguments** and **pass-by-reference with pointer arguments**. Chapter 6 compared and contrasted pass-by-value and pass-by-reference with reference arguments. In this section, we explain pass-by-reference with pointer arguments.

As we saw in Chapter 6, return can be used to return one value from a called function to a caller (or to simply return control). We also saw that arguments can be passed to a function using reference arguments. Such arguments enable the called function to modify the original values of the arguments in the caller. Reference arguments also enable programs to pass large data objects to a function and avoid the overhead of passing the objects by value (which, of course, requires making a copy of the object). Pointers, like references, also can be used to modify one or more variables in the caller or to pass pointers to large data objects to avoid the overhead of passing the objects by value.

In C++, you can use pointers and the indirection operator (*) to accomplish pass-by-reference (exactly as pass-by-reference is done in C programs—C does not have references). When calling a function with an argument that should be modified, the address of the argument is passed. This is normally accomplished by applying the address operator (&) to the name of the variable whose value will be modified.

As we saw in Chapter 7, arrays are not passed using operator &, because the name of the array is the starting location in memory of the array (i.e., an array name is already a pointer). The name of an array, arrayName, is equivalent to &arrayName[0]. When the address of a variable is passed to a function, the indirection operator (*) can be used in the function to form a synonym for the name of the variable (i.e., an *lvalue*)—this in turn can be used to modify the variable's value at that location in the caller's memory.

Figure 8.6 and Fig. 8.7 present two versions of a function that cubes an integer—cubeByValue and cubeByReference. Figure 8.6 passes variable number by value to function cubeByValue (line 14). Function cubeByValue (lines 19–22) cubes its argument and passes the new value back to main using a return statement (line 21). The new value is assigned to number (line 14) in main. The calling function has the opportunity to examine the function call's result before modifying variable number's value. For example, we could have stored the result of cubeByValue in another variable, examined its value and assigned the result to number only after determining that the returned value was reasonable.

```cpp
1   // Fig. 8.6: fig08_06.cpp
2   // Pass-by-value used to cube a variable's value.
3   #include <iostream>
4   using namespace std;
5
6   int cubeByValue( int ); // prototype
7
8   int main()
9   {
10      int number = 5;
11
12      cout << "The original value of number is " << number;
13
14      number = cubeByValue( number ); // pass number by value to cubeByValue
15      cout << "\nThe new value of number is " << number << endl;
16   } // end main
17
18   // calculate and return cube of integer argument
19   int cubeByValue( int n )
20   {
21      return n * n * n; // cube local variable n and return result
22   } // end function cubeByValue
```

```
The original value of number is 5
The new value of number is 125
```

Fig. 8.6 | Pass-by-value used to cube a variable's value.

Figure 8.7 passes the variable number to function cubeByReference using pass-by-reference with a pointer argument (line 15)—the address of number is passed to the function. Function cubeByReference (lines 21–24) specifies parameter nPtr (a pointer to int) to receive its argument. The function dereferences the pointer and cubes the value to which nPtr points (line 23). This directly changes the value of number in main.

Common Programming Error 8.5

Not dereferencing a pointer when it's necessary to do so to obtain the value to which the pointer points is an error.

```cpp
1   // Fig. 8.7: fig08_07.cpp
2   // Pass-by-reference with a pointer argument used to cube a
3   // variable's value.
4   #include <iostream>
5   using namespace std;
6
7   void cubeByReference( int * ); // prototype
8
9   int main()
10  {
11     int number = 5;
12
13     cout << "The original value of number is " << number;
14
15     cubeByReference( &number ); // pass number address to cubeByReference
16
17     cout << "\nThe new value of number is " << number << endl;
18  } // end main
19
20  // calculate cube of *nPtr; modifies variable number in main
21  void cubeByReference( int *nPtr )
22  {
23     *nPtr = *nPtr * *nPtr * *nPtr; // cube *nPtr
24  } // end function cubeByReference
```

```
The original value of number is 5
The new value of number is 125
```

Fig. 8.7 | Pass-by-reference with a pointer argument used to cube a variable's value.

A function receiving an address as an argument must define a pointer parameter to receive the address. For example, the header for function cubeByReference (line 21) specifies that cubeByReference receives the address of an int variable (i.e., a pointer to an int) as an argument, stores the address locally in nPtr and does not return a value.

The function prototype for cubeByReference (line 7) contains int * in parentheses. As with other variable types, it isn't necessary to include names of pointer parameters in function prototypes. Parameter names included for documentation purposes are ignored by the compiler.

Figures 8.8–8.9 analyze graphically the execution of the programs in Fig. 8.6 and Fig. 8.7, respectively.

Step 1: Before `main` calls `cubeByValue`:

```
int main()                          number        int cubeByValue( int n )
{                                                  {
    int number = 5;                    5               return n * n * n;
                                                   }
    number = cubeByValue( number );                                        n
}                                                                  undefined
```

Step 2: After `cubeByValue` receives the call:

```
int main()                          number        int cubeByValue( int n )
{                                                  {
    int number = 5;                    5               return n * n * n;
                                                   }
    number = cubeByValue( number );                                        n
}                                                                          5
```

Step 3: After `cubeByValue` cubes parameter `n` and before `cubeByValue` returns to `main`:

```
int main()                          number        int cubeByValue( int n )
{                                                  {               125
    int number = 5;                    5               return n * n * n;
                                                   }                        n
    number = cubeByValue( number );                                        5
}
```

Step 4: After `cubeByValue` returns to `main` and before assigning the result to `number`:

```
int main()                          number        int cubeByValue( int n )
{                                                  {
    int number = 5;                    5               return n * n * n;
                125                                }
    number = cubeByValue( number );                                        n
}                                                                  undefined
```

Step 5: After `main` completes the assignment to `number`:

```
int main()                          number        int cubeByValue( int n )
{                                                  {
    int number = 5;                   125              return n * n * n;
        125             125                        }
    number = cubeByValue( number );                                        n
}                                                                  undefined
```

Fig. 8.8 | Pass-by-value analysis of the program of Fig. 8.6.

Step 1: Before `main` calls `cubeByReference`:

```
int main()                          number
{
    int number = 5;                   5

    cubeByReference( &number );
}
```

```
void cubeByReference( int *nPtr )
{
    *nPtr = *nPtr * *nPtr * *nPtr;
}
                                    nPtr

                                  undefined
```

Step 2: After `cubeByReference` receives the call and before `*nPtr` is cubed:

```
int main()                          number
{
    int number = 5;                   5

    cubeByReference( &number );
}
```

```
void cubeByReference( int *nPtr )
{
    *nPtr = *nPtr * *nPtr * *nPtr;
}
                                    nPtr
```

call establishes this pointer

Step 3: After `*nPtr` is cubed and before program control returns to `main`:

```
int main()                          number
{
    int number = 5;                  125

    cubeByReference( &number );
}
```
called function modifies caller's variable

```
void cubeByReference( int *nPtr )
{                                   125
    *nPtr = *nPtr * *nPtr * *nPtr;
}
                                    nPtr
```

Fig. 8.9 | Pass-by-reference analysis (with a pointer argument) of the program of Fig. 8.7.

Software Engineering Observation 8.1

Use pass-by-value to pass arguments to a function unless the caller explicitly requires that the called function directly modify the value of the argument variable in the caller. This is another example of the principle of least privilege.

In the function header and in the prototype for a function that expects a one-dimensional array as an argument, the pointer notation in the parameter list of `cubeByReference` may be used. The compiler does not differentiate between a function that receives a pointer and a function that receives a one-dimensional array. This, of course, means that the function must "know" when it's receiving an array or simply a single variable which is being passed by reference. When the compiler encounters a function parameter for a one-dimensional array of the form `int b[]`, the compiler converts the parameter to the pointer notation `int *b` (pronounced "b is a pointer to an integer"). Both forms of declaring a function parameter as a one-dimensional array are interchangeable.

8.5 Using const with Pointers

Recall that `const` enables you to inform the compiler that the value of a particular variable should not be modified. Many possibilities exist for using (or not using) `const` with function parameters. How do you choose the most appropriate of these possibilities? Let the principle of least privilege be your guide. Always give a function enough access to the data in its parameters to accomplish its specified task, but no more. This section discusses how to combine const with pointer declarations to enforce the principle of least privilege.

Chapter 6 explained that when an argument is passed by value, a copy of the argument in the function call is made and passed to the function. If the copy is modified in the function, the original value in the caller does not change. In many cases, a value passed to a function is modified in that function. However, in some instances, the value should not be altered in the called function, even though the called function manipulates only a copy of the original value.

Consider a function that takes a one-dimensional array and its size as arguments and subsequently prints the array. Such a function should loop through the array and output each element individually. The size of the array is used in the function body to determine the array's highest subscript so the loop can terminate when the printing completes. The array's size does not change in the function body, so it should be declared const. Because the array is only being printed, it, too, should be declared const. This is especially important because arrays are *always* passed by reference and could easily be changed in the called function. If an attempt is made to modify a const value, an error occurs.

Software Engineering Observation 8.2

If a value does not (or should not) change in the body of a function to which it's passed, the parameter should be declared const.

Error-Prevention Tip 8.2

Before using a function, check its function prototype to determine the parameters that it can modify.

There are four ways to pass a pointer to a function: a nonconstant pointer to nonconstant data, a nonconstant pointer to constant data (Fig. 8.10), a constant pointer to nonconstant data (Fig. 8.11) and a constant pointer to constant data (Fig. 8.12). Each combination provides a different level of access privilege.

Nonconstant Pointer to Nonconstant Data
The highest access is granted by a **nonconstant pointer to nonconstant data**—the data can be modified through the dereferenced pointer, and the pointer can be modified to point to other data. Such a pointer's declaration (e.g., int *countPtr) does not include const.

Nonconstant Pointer to Constant Data
A **nonconstant pointer to constant data** is a pointer that can be modified to point to any data item of the appropriate type, but the data to which it points cannot be modified through that pointer. Such a pointer might be used to receive an array argument to a function that will process each array element, but should not be allowed to modify the data. Any attempt to modify the data in the function results in a compilation error. The declaration for such a pointer places const to the left of the pointer's type, as in

```
const int *countPtr;
```

The declaration is read from right to left as "countPtr is a pointer to an integer constant."

Figure 8.10 demonstrates the compilation error messages produced when attempting to compile a function that receives a nonconstant pointer to constant data, then tries to use that pointer to modify the data.

```
1   // Fig. 8.10: fig08_10.cpp
2   // Attempting to modify data through a
3   // nonconstant pointer to constant data.
4
5   void f( const int * ); // prototype
6
7   int main()
8   {
9      int y;
10
11      f( &y ); // f attempts illegal modification
12   } // end main
13
14   // xPtr cannot modify the value of constant variable to which it points
15   void f( const int *xPtr )
16   {
17      *xPtr = 100; // error: cannot modify a const object
18   } // end function f
```

Microsoft Visual C++ compiler error message:

```
c:\cpphtp7_examples\ch08\Fig08_10\fig08_10.cpp(17) :
   error C3892: 'xPtr' : you cannot assign to a variable that is const
```

GNU C++ compiler error message:

```
fig08_10.cpp: In function `void f(const int*)':
fig08_10.cpp:17: error: assignment of read-only location
```

Fig. 8.10 | Attempting to modify data through a nonconstant pointer to constant data.

As we know, arrays are aggregate data types that store related data items of the same type under one name. When a function is called with an array as an argument, the array is passed to the function by reference. However, by default, objects are passed by value—a copy of the entire object is passed. This requires the execution-time overhead of making a copy of each data item in the object and storing it on the function call stack. When a pointer to an object is passed, only a copy of the address of the object must be made—the object itself is not copied.

Performance Tip 8.1

If they do not need to be modified by the called function, pass large objects using pointers to constant data or references to constant data, to obtain the performance benefits of pass-by-reference.

Software Engineering Observation 8.3

Pass large objects using pointers to constant data, or references to constant data, to obtain the security of pass-by-value.

Constant Pointer to Nonconstant Data

A **constant pointer to nonconstant data** is a pointer that always points to the same memory location; the data at that location *can* be modified through the pointer. An example of such a pointer is an array name, which is a constant pointer to the beginning of the array. All data in the array can be accessed and changed by using the array name and array subscripting. A constant pointer to nonconstant data can be used to receive an array as an argument to a function that accesses array elements using array subscript notation. Pointers that are declared `const` must be initialized when they're declared. If the pointer is a function parameter, it's initialized with a pointer that's passed to the function.

Common Programming Error 8.6

Not initializing a pointer that is declared `const` is a compilation error.

The program of Fig. 8.11 attempts to modify a constant pointer. Line 11 declares pointer `ptr` to be of type `int * const`. The declaration is read from right to left as "ptr is a constant pointer to a nonconstant integer." The pointer is initialized with the address of integer variable `x`. Line 14 attempts to assign the address of `y` to `ptr`, but the compiler generates an error message. No error occurs when line 13 assigns the value 7 to `*ptr`—the nonconstant value to which `ptr` points can be modified using the dereferenced `ptr`, even though `ptr` itself has been declared `const`.

```
 1   // Fig. 8.11: fig08_11.cpp
 2   // Attempting to modify a constant pointer to nonconstant data.
 3
 4   int main()
 5   {
 6      int x, y;
 7
 8      // ptr is a constant pointer to an integer that can
 9      // be modified through ptr, but ptr always points to the
10      // same memory location.
11      int * const ptr = &x; // const pointer must be initialized
12
13      *ptr = 7; // allowed: *ptr is not const
14      ptr = &y; // error: ptr is const; cannot assign to it a new address
15   } // end main
```

Microsoft Visual C++ compiler error message:

```
c:\cpphtp7_examples\ch08\Fig08_11\fig08_11.cpp(14) : error C3892: 'ptr' :
   you cannot assign to a variable that is const
```

GNU C++ compiler error message:

```
fig08_11.cpp: In function `int main()':
fig08_11.cpp:14: error: assignment of read-only variable `ptr'
```

Fig. 8.11 | Attempting to modify a constant pointer to nonconstant data.

Constant Pointer to Constant Data

The minimum access privilege is granted by a **constant pointer to constant data**. Such a pointer always points to the same memory location, and the data at that location cannot be modified via the pointer. This is how an array should be passed to a function that *only reads* the array, using array subscript notation, and *does not modify* the array. The program of Fig. 8.12 declares pointer variable ptr to be of type const int * const (line 13). This declaration is read from right to left as "ptr is a constant pointer to an integer constant." The figure shows the error messages generated when an attempt is made to modify the data to which ptr points (line 17) and when an attempt is made to modify the address stored in the pointer variable (line 18). No errors occur when the program attempts to dereference ptr (line 15), or when the program attempts to output the value to which ptr points, because neither the pointer nor the data it points to is being modified in this statement.

```
1   // Fig. 8.12: fig08_12.cpp
2   // Attempting to modify a constant pointer to constant data.
3   #include <iostream>
4   using namespace std;
5
6   int main()
7   {
8      int x = 5, y;
9
10     // ptr is a constant pointer to a constant integer.
11     // ptr always points to the same location; the integer
12     // at that location cannot be modified.
13     const int *const ptr = &x;
14
15     cout << *ptr << endl;
16
17     *ptr = 7; // error: *ptr is const; cannot assign new value
18     ptr = &y; // error: ptr is const; cannot assign new address
19  } // end main
```

Microsoft Visual C++ compiler error message:

```
c:\cpphtp7_examples\ch08\Fig08_12\fig08_12.cpp(17) : error C3892: 'ptr' :
   you cannot assign to a variable that is const
c:\cpphtp7_examples\ch08\Fig08_12\fig08_12.cpp(18) : error C3892: 'ptr' :
   you cannot assign to a variable that is const
```

GNU C++ compiler error message:

```
fig08_12.cpp: In function `int main()':
fig08_12.cpp:17: error: assignment of read-only location
fig08_12.cpp:18: error: assignment of read-only variable `ptr'
```

Fig. 8.12 | Attempting to modify a constant pointer to constant data.

8.6 Selection Sort Using Pass-by-Reference

In this section, we define a sorting program to demonstrate passing arrays and individual array elements by reference. We use the **selection sort** algorithm, which is an easy-to-program, but unfortunately inefficient, sorting algorithm. The first iteration of the algorithm selects the smallest element in the array and swaps it with the first element. The second iteration selects the second-smallest element (which is the smallest element of the remaining elements) and swaps it with the second element. The algorithm continues until the last iteration selects the second-largest element and swaps it with the second-to-last index, leaving the largest element in the last index. After the ith iteration, the smallest i items of the array will be sorted into increasing order in the first i elements of the array.

As an example, consider the array

| 34 | 56 | 4 | 10 | 77 | 51 | 93 | 30 | 5 | 52 |

A program that implements the selection sort first determines the smallest value (4) in the array, which is contained in element 2. The program swaps the 4 with the value in element 0 (34), resulting in

| **4** | 56 | **34** | 10 | 77 | 51 | 93 | 30 | 5 | 52 |

[*Note:* We use bold to highlight the values that were swapped.] The program then determines the smallest value of the remaining elements (all elements except 4), which is 5, contained in element 8. The program swaps the 5 with the 56 in element 1, resulting in

| 4 | **5** | 34 | 10 | 77 | 51 | 93 | 30 | **56** | 52 |

On the third iteration, the program determines the next smallest value, 10, and swaps it with the value in element 2 (34).

| 4 | 5 | **10** | **34** | 77 | 51 | 93 | 30 | 56 | 52 |

The process continues until the array is fully sorted.

| 4 | 5 | 10 | 30 | 34 | 51 | 52 | 56 | 77 | 93 |

After the first iteration, the smallest element is in the first position. After the second iteration, the two smallest elements are in order in the first two positions. After the third iteration, the three smallest elements are in order in the first three positions.

Figure 8.13 implements selection sort using functions `selectionSort` and `swap`. Function `selectionSort` (lines 32–49) sorts the array. Line 34 declares the variable `smallest`, which will store the index of the smallest element in the remaining array. Lines 37–48 loop `size - 1` times. Line 39 sets the smallest element's index to the current index. Lines 42–45 loop over the remaining array elements. For each element, line 44 compares its value to the value of the smallest element. If the current element is smaller than the smallest element, line 45 assigns the current element's index to `smallest`. When this loop finishes, `smallest` will contain the index of the smallest element in the remaining array. Line 47 calls function `swap` (lines 53–58) to place the smallest remaining element in the next spot in the array (i.e., exchange the array elements `array[i]` and `array[smallest]`).

```
1   // Fig. 8.13: fig08_13.cpp
2   // Selection sort with pass-by-reference. This program puts values into an
3   // array, sorts them into ascending order and prints the resulting array.
4   #include <iostream>
5   #include <iomanip>
```

Fig. 8.13 | Selection sort with pass-by-reference. (Part 1 of 3.)

```
 6   using namespace std;
 7
 8   void selectionSort( int * const, const int ); // prototype
 9   void swap( int * const, int * const ); // prototype
10
11   int main()
12   {
13      const int arraySize = 10;
14      int a[ arraySize ] = { 2, 6, 4, 8, 10, 12, 89, 68, 45, 37 };
15
16      cout << "Data items in original order\n";
17
18      for ( int i = 0; i < arraySize; i++ )
19         cout << setw( 4 ) << a[ i ];
20
21      selectionSort( a, arraySize ); // sort the array
22
23      cout << "\nData items in ascending order\n";
24
25      for ( int j = 0; j < arraySize; j++ )
26         cout << setw( 4 ) << a[ j ];
27
28      cout << endl;
29   } // end main
30
31   // function to sort an array
32   void selectionSort( int * const array, const int size )
33   {
34      int smallest; // index of smallest element
35
36      // loop over size - 1 elements
37      for ( int i = 0; i < size - 1; i++ )
38      {
39         smallest = i; // first index of remaining array
40
41         // loop to find index of smallest element
42         for ( int index = i + 1; index < size; index++ )
43
44            if ( array[ index ] < array[ smallest ] )
45               smallest = index;
46
47         swap( &array[ i ], &array[ smallest ] );
48      } // end if
49   } // end function selectionSort
50
51   // swap values at memory locations to which
52   // element1Ptr and element2Ptr point
53   void swap( int * const element1Ptr, int * const element2Ptr )
54   {
55      int hold = *element1Ptr;
56      *element1Ptr = *element2Ptr;
57      *element2Ptr = hold;
58   } // end function swap
```

Fig. 8.13 | Selection sort with pass-by-reference. (Part 2 of 3.)

```
Data items in original order
   2   6   4   8  10  12  89  68  45  37
Data items in ascending order
   2   4   6   8  10  12  37  45  68  89
```

Fig. 8.13 | Selection sort with pass-by-reference. (Part 3 of 3.)

Let's now look more closely at function swap. Remember that C++ enforces information hiding between functions, so swap does not have access to individual array elements in selectionSort. Because selectionSort *wants* swap to have access to the array elements to be swapped, selectionSort passes each of these elements to swap by reference—the address of each array element is passed explicitly. Although entire arrays are passed by reference, individual array elements are scalars and are ordinarily passed by value. Therefore, selectionSort uses the address operator (&) on each array element in the swap call (line 47) to effect pass-by-reference. Function swap (lines 53–58) receives &array[i] in pointer variable element1Ptr. Information hiding prevents swap from "knowing" the name array[i], but swap can use *element1Ptr as a synonym for array[i]. Thus, when swap references *element1Ptr, it's actually referencing array[i] in selection-Sort. Similarly, when swap references *element2Ptr, it's actually referencing array[smallest] in selectionSort.

Even though swap is not allowed to use the statements

```
hold = array[ i ];
array[ i ] = array[ smallest ];
array[ smallest ] = hold;
```

precisely the same effect is achieved by

```
int hold = *element1Ptr;
*element1Ptr = *element2Ptr;
*element2Ptr = hold;
```

in the swap function of Fig. 8.13.

Several features of function selectionSort should be noted. The function header (line 32) declares array as int * const array, rather than int array[], to indicate that the function receives a one-dimensional array as an argument. Both parameter array's pointer and parameter size are declared const to enforce the principle of least privilege. Although parameter size receives a copy of a value in main and modifying the copy cannot change the value in main, selectionSort does not need to alter size to accomplish its task—the array size remains fixed during the execution of selectionSort. Therefore, size is declared const to ensure that it isn't modified. If the size of the array were to be modified during the sorting process, the sorting algorithm would not run correctly.

Function selectionSort receives the size of the array as a parameter, because the function must have that information to sort the array. When an array is passed to a function, only the memory address of the first element of the array is received by the function; the array size must be passed separately to the function.

By defining function selectionSort to receive the array size as a parameter, we enable the function to be used by any program that sorts one-dimensional int arrays of arbitrary size. The size of the array could have been programmed directly into the function, but this would restrict the function to processing an array of a specific size and reduce the function's reusability—only programs processing one-dimensional int arrays of the specific size "hard coded" into the function could use the function.

Software Engineering Observation 8.4

When passing an array to a function, also pass the size of the array (rather than building into the function knowledge of the array size)—this makes the function more reusable.

8.7 sizeof Operator

The unary operator **sizeof** determines the size of an array (or of any other data type, variable or constant) in bytes during program compilation. When applied to the name of an array, as in Fig. 8.14 (line 13), the sizeof operator returns the total number of bytes in the array as a value of type size_t (an unsigned integer type that is at least as big as unsigned int). This is different from the size of a vector<int>, for example, which is the number of integer elements in the vector. The computer we used to compile this program stores variables of type double in 8 bytes of memory, and array is declared to have 20 elements (line 11), so array uses 160 bytes in memory. When applied to a pointer parameter (line 22) in a function that receives an array as an argument, the sizeof operator returns the size of the pointer in bytes (4 on the system we used)—not the size of the array.

Common Programming Error 8.7

Using the sizeof operator in a function to find the size in bytes of an array parameter results in the size in bytes of a pointer, not the size in bytes of the array.

```
1   // Fig. 8.14: fig08_14.cpp
2   // Sizeof operator when used on an array name
3   // returns the number of bytes in the array.
4   #include <iostream>
5   using namespace std;
6
7   size_t getSize( double * ); // prototype
8
9   int main()
10  {
11     double array[ 20 ]; // 20 doubles; occupies 160 bytes on our system
12
13     cout << "The number of bytes in the array is " << sizeof( array );
14
15     cout << "\nThe number of bytes returned by getSize is "
16        << getSize( array ) << endl;
17  } // end main
18
19  // return size of ptr
20  size_t getSize( double *ptr )
21  {
22     return sizeof( ptr );
23  } // end function getSize
```

Fig. 8.14 | sizeof operator when applied to an array name returns the number of bytes in the array. (Part 1 of 2.)

```
The number of bytes in the array is 160
The number of bytes returned by getSize is 4
```

Fig. 8.14 | `sizeof` operator when applied to an array name returns the number of bytes in the array. (Part 2 of 2.)

The number of elements in an array also can be determined using the results of two `sizeof` operations. For example, consider the following array declaration:

```
double realArray[ 22 ];
```

If variables of data type `double` are stored in eight bytes of memory, array `realArray` contains a total of 176 bytes. To determine the number of elements in the array, the following expression (which is evaluated at compile time) can be used:

```
sizeof realArray / sizeof( realArray[ 0 ] )
```

The expression determines the number of bytes in array `realArray` (176) and divides that value by the number of bytes used in memory to store the array's first element (typically 8 for a `double` value)—the result is the number of elements in `realArray` (22).

Determining the Sizes of the Fundamental Types, an Array and a Pointer
Figure 8.15 uses `sizeof` to calculate the number of bytes used to store most of the standard data types. The output shows that the types `double` and `long double` have the same size. Types may have different sizes based on the platform running the program. On another system, for example, `double` and `long double` may be of different sizes.

```
 1   // Fig. 8.15: fig08_15.cpp
 2   // Demonstrating the sizeof operator.
 3   #include <iostream>
 4   using namespace std;
 5
 6   int main()
 7   {
 8      char c; // variable of type char
 9      short s; // variable of type short
10      int i; // variable of type int
11      long l; // variable of type long
12      float f; // variable of type float
13      double d; // variable of type double
14      long double ld; // variable of type long double
15      int array[ 20 ]; // array of int
16      int *ptr = array; // variable of type int *
17
18      cout << "sizeof c = " << sizeof c
19         << "\tsizeof(char) = " << sizeof( char )
20         << "\nsizeof s = " << sizeof s
21         << "\tsizeof(short) = " << sizeof( short )
22         << "\nsizeof i = " << sizeof i
```

Fig. 8.15 | `sizeof` operator used to determine standard data type sizes. (Part 1 of 2.)

```
23          << "\tsizeof(int) = " << sizeof( int )
24          << "\nsizeof l = " << sizeof l
25          << "\tsizeof(long) = " << sizeof( long )
26          << "\nsizeof f = " << sizeof f
27          << "\tsizeof(float) = " << sizeof( float )
28          << "\nsizeof d = " << sizeof d
29          << "\tsizeof(double) = " << sizeof( double )
30          << "\nsizeof ld = " << sizeof ld
31          << "\tsizeof(long double) = " << sizeof( long double )
32          << "\nsizeof array = " << sizeof array
33          << "\nsizeof ptr = " << sizeof ptr << endl;
34   } // end main
```

```
sizeof c = 1      sizeof(char) = 1
sizeof s = 2      sizeof(short) = 2
sizeof i = 4      sizeof(int) = 4
sizeof l = 4      sizeof(long) = 4
sizeof f = 4      sizeof(float) = 4
sizeof d = 8      sizeof(double) = 8
sizeof ld = 8     sizeof(long double) = 8
sizeof array = 80
sizeof ptr = 4
```

Fig. 8.15 | `sizeof` operator used to determine standard data type sizes. (Part 2 of 2.)

Portability Tip 8.2

The number of bytes used to store a particular data type may vary among systems. When writing programs that depend on data type sizes, and that will run on several computer systems, use `sizeof` to determine the number of bytes used to store the data types.

Operator `sizeof` can be applied to any expression or type name. When `sizeof` is applied to a variable name (which is not an array name) or other expression, the number of bytes used to store the specific type of the expression's value is returned. The parentheses used with `sizeof` are required only if a type name (e.g., `int`) is supplied as its operand. The parentheses used with `sizeof` are not required when `sizeof`'s operand is an expression. Remember that `sizeof` is an operator, not a function, and that it has its effect at compile time, not execution time.

Common Programming Error 8.8

Omitting the parentheses in a `sizeof` operation when the operand is a type name is a compilation error.

Performance Tip 8.2

Because `sizeof` is a compile-time unary operator, not an execution-time operator, using `sizeof` does not negatively impact execution performance.

Error-Prevention Tip 8.3

To avoid errors associated with omitting the parentheses around the operand of operator `sizeof`, include parentheses around every `sizeof` operand.

8.8 **Pointer Expressions and Pointer Arithmetic**

Pointers are valid operands in arithmetic expressions, assignment expressions and comparison expressions. However, not all the operators normally used in these expressions are valid with pointer variables. This section describes the operators that can have pointers as operands and how these operators are used with pointers.

C++ enables **pointer arithmetic**—certain arithmetic operations may be performed on pointers. A pointer may be incremented (++) or decremented (--), an integer may be added to a pointer (+ or +=), an integer may be subtracted from a pointer (- or -=) or one pointer may be subtracted from another of the same type.

Assume that array int v[5] has been declared and that its first element is at memory location 3000. Assume that pointer vPtr has been initialized to point to v[0] (i.e., the value of vPtr is 3000). Figure 8.16 diagrams this situation for a machine with four-byte integers. Variable vPtr can be initialized to point to array v with either of the following statements (because the name of an array is equivalent to the address of its first element):

```
int *vPtr = v;
int *vPtr = &v[ 0 ];
```

> **Portability Tip 8.3**
>
> *Most computers today have two-byte or four-byte integers. Some of the newer machines use eight-byte integers. Because the results of pointer arithmetic depend on the size of the objects a pointer points to, pointer arithmetic is machine dependent.*

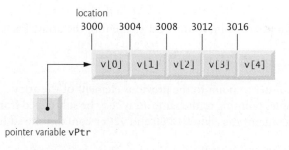

Fig. 8.16 | Array v and a pointer variable int *vPtr that points to v.

In conventional arithmetic, the addition 3000 + 2 yields the value 3002. This is normally not the case with pointer arithmetic. When an integer is added to, or subtracted from, a pointer, the pointer is not simply incremented or decremented by that integer, but by that integer times the size of the object to which the pointer refers. The number of bytes depends on the object's data type. For example, the statement

```
vPtr += 2;
```

would produce 3008 (3000 + 2 * 4), assuming that an int is stored in four bytes of memory. In the array v, vPtr would now point to v[2] (Fig. 8.17). If an integer is stored in two bytes of memory, then the preceding calculation would result in memory location 3004 (3000 + 2 * 2). If the array elements were of a different data type, the preceding statement would increment the pointer by twice the number of bytes it takes to store an object of that data type. When performing pointer arithmetic on a character array, the results will be consistent with regular arithmetic, because each character is one byte long.

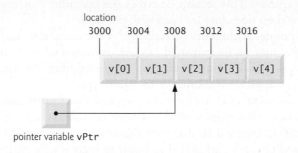

Fig. 8.17 | Pointer `vPtr` after pointer arithmetic.

If `vPtr` had been incremented to 3016, which points to `v[4]`, the statement

```
vPtr -= 4;
```

would set `vPtr` back to 3000—the beginning of the array. If a pointer is being incremented or decremented by one, the increment (`++`) and decrement (`--`) operators can be used. Each of the statements

```
++vPtr;
vPtr++;
```

increments the pointer to point to the next element of the array. Each of the statements

```
--vPtr;
vPtr--;
```

decrements the pointer to point to the previous element of the array.

Pointer variables pointing to the same array may be subtracted from one another. For example, if `vPtr` contains the address 3000 and `v2Ptr` contains the address 3008, the statement

```
x = v2Ptr - vPtr;
```

would assign to `x` the number of array elements from `vPtr` to `v2Ptr`—in this case, 2. Pointer arithmetic is meaningless unless performed on a pointer that points to an array. We cannot assume that two variables of the same type are stored contiguously in memory unless they're adjacent elements of an array.

Common Programming Error 8.9
Using pointer arithmetic on a pointer that does not refer to an array is a logic error.

Common Programming Error 8.10
Subtracting or comparing two pointers that do not refer to elements of the same array is a logic error.

Common Programming Error 8.11

Using pointer arithmetic to move a pointer outside the bounds of an array is a logic error.

A pointer can be assigned to another pointer if both pointers are of the same type. Otherwise, a cast operator (normally a `reinterpret_cast`; discussed in Section 17.8) must be used to convert the value of the pointer on the right of the assignment to the pointer type on the left of the assignment. The exception to this rule is the pointer to `void` (i.e., `void *`), which is a generic pointer capable of representing any pointer type. All pointer types can be assigned to a pointer of type `void *` without casting. However, a pointer of type `void *` cannot be assigned directly to a pointer of another type—the pointer of type `void *` must first be cast to the proper pointer type.

Software Engineering Observation 8.5

Nonconstant pointer arguments can be passed to constant pointer parameters. This is helpful when the body of a program uses a nonconstant pointer to access data, but does not want that data to be modified by a function called in the body of the program.

A `void *` pointer cannot be dereferenced. For example, the compiler "knows" that a pointer to `int` refers to four bytes of memory on a machine with four-byte integers, but a pointer to `void` simply contains a memory address for an unknown data type—the precise number of bytes to which the pointer refers and the type of the data are not known by the compiler. The compiler must know the data type to determine the number of bytes to be dereferenced for a particular pointer—for a pointer to `void`, this number of bytes cannot be determined from the type.

Common Programming Error 8.12

Assigning a pointer of one type to a pointer of another (other than `void *`) without using a cast (normally a `reinterpret_cast`) is a compilation error.

Common Programming Error 8.13

All operations on a `void *` pointer are compilation errors, except comparing `void *` pointers with other pointers, casting `void *` pointers to valid pointer types and assigning addresses to `void *` pointers.

Pointers can be compared using equality and relational operators. Comparisons using relational operators are meaningless unless the pointers point to members of the same array. Pointer comparisons compare the addresses stored in the pointers. A comparison of two pointers pointing to the same array could show, for example, that one pointer points to a higher numbered element of the array than the other pointer does. A common use of pointer comparison is determining whether a pointer is 0 (i.e., the pointer is a null pointer—it does not point to anything).

8.9 Relationship Between Pointers and Arrays

Arrays and pointers are intimately related in C++ and may be used *almost* interchangeably. An array name can be thought of as a constant pointer. Pointers can be used to do any operation involving array subscripting.

Assume the following declarations:

```
int b[ 5 ]; // create 5-element int array b
int *bPtr; // create int pointer bPtr
```

Because the array name (without a subscript) is a (constant) pointer to the first element of the array, we can set bPtr to the address of the first element in array b with the statement

```
bPtr = b; // assign address of array b to bPtr
```

This is equivalent to assigning the address of the first element of the array as follows:

```
bPtr = &b[ 0 ]; // also assigns address of array b to bPtr
```

Array element b[3] can alternatively be referenced with the pointer expression

```
*( bPtr + 3 )
```

The 3 in the preceding expression is the **offset** to the pointer. When the pointer points to the beginning of an array, the offset indicates which array element should be referenced, and the offset value is identical to the subscript. This notation is referred to as **pointer/offset notation**. The parentheses are necessary, because the precedence of * is higher than that of +. Without the parentheses, the preceding expression would add 3 to a copy *bPtr's value (i.e., 3 would be added to b[0], assuming that bPtr points to the beginning of the array). Just as the array element can be referenced with a pointer expression, the address

```
&b[ 3 ]
```

can be written with the pointer expression

```
bPtr + 3
```

The array name (which is implicitly const) can be treated as a pointer and used in pointer arithmetic. For example, the expression

```
*( b + 3 )
```

also refers to the array element b[3]. In general, all subscripted array expressions can be written with a pointer and an offset. In this case, pointer/offset notation was used with the name of the array as a pointer. The preceding expression does not modify the array name in any way; b still points to the first element in the array.

Pointers can be subscripted exactly as arrays can. For example, the expression

```
bPtr[ 1 ]
```

refers to the array element b[1]; this expression uses **pointer/subscript notation**.

Remember that an array name is a constant pointer; it always points to the beginning of the array. Thus, the expression

```
b += 3
```

causes a compilation error, because it attempts to modify the value of the array name (a constant) with pointer arithmetic.

Common Programming Error 8.14

Although array names are pointers to the beginning of the array, array names cannot be modified in arithmetic expressions, because array names are constant pointers.

Good Programming Practice 8.2

For clarity, use array notation instead of pointer notation when manipulating arrays.

Figure 8.18 uses the four notations discussed in this section for referring to array elements—array subscript notation, pointer/offset notation with the array name as a pointer, pointer subscript notation and pointer/offset notation with a pointer—to accomplish the same task, namely printing the four elements of the integer array b.

```cpp
1   // Fig. 8.18: fig08_18.cpp
2   // Using subscripting and pointer notations with arrays.
3   #include <iostream>
4   using namespace std;
5
6   int main()
7   {
8      int b[] = { 10, 20, 30, 40 }; // create 4-element array b
9      int *bPtr = b; // set bPtr to point to array b
10
11     // output array b using array subscript notation
12     cout << "Array b printed with:\n\nArray subscript notation\n";
13
14     for ( int i = 0; i < 4; i++ )
15        cout << "b[" << i << "] = " << b[ i ] << '\n';
16
17     // output array b using the array name and pointer/offset notation
18     cout << "\nPointer/offset notation where "
19        << "the pointer is the array name\n";
20
21     for ( int offset1 = 0; offset1 < 4; offset1++ )
22        cout << "*(b + " << offset1 << ") = " << *( b + offset1 ) << '\n';
23
24     // output array b using bPtr and array subscript notation
25     cout << "\nPointer subscript notation\n";
26
27     for ( int j = 0; j < 4; j++ )
28        cout << "bPtr[" << j << "] = " << bPtr[ j ] << '\n';
29
30     cout << "\nPointer/offset notation\n";
31
32     // output array b using bPtr and pointer/offset notation
33     for ( int offset2 = 0; offset2 < 4; offset2++ )
34        cout << "*(bPtr + " << offset2 << ") = "
35           << *( bPtr + offset2 ) << '\n';
36   } // end main
```

```
Array b printed with:

Array subscript notation
b[0] = 10
b[1] = 20
b[2] = 30
b[3] = 40
```

Fig. 8.18 | Referencing array elements with the array name and with pointers. (Part 1 of 2.)

```
Pointer/offset notation where the pointer is the array name
*(b + 0) = 10
*(b + 1) = 20
*(b + 2) = 30
*(b + 3) = 40

Pointer subscript notation
bPtr[0] = 10
bPtr[1] = 20
bPtr[2] = 30
bPtr[3] = 40

Pointer/offset notation
*(bPtr + 0) = 10
*(bPtr + 1) = 20
*(bPtr + 2) = 30
*(bPtr + 3) = 40
```

Fig. 8.18 | Referencing array elements with the array name and with pointers. (Part 2 of 2.)

8.10 Pointer-Based String Processing

We've already used the C++ Standard Library `string` class to represent strings as full-fledged objects. For example, the `GradeBook` class case study in Chapters 3–7 represents a course name using a `string` object. Chapter 18 presents class `string` in detail. This section introduces C-style, pointer-based strings. *C++'s `string` class is preferred for use in new programs, because it eliminates many of the security problems that can be caused by manipulating C strings.* We cover C strings here for a deeper understanding of arrays. Also, if you work with legacy C++ programs, you may be required to manipulate these pointer-based strings. We cover C-style, pointer-based strings in detail in Chapter 21.

Characters are the fundamental building blocks of C++ source programs. Every program is composed of a sequence of characters that—when grouped together meaningfully—is interpreted by the compiler as a series of instructions used to accomplish a task. A program may contain **character constants**. A character constant is an integer value represented as a character in single quotes. The value of a character constant is the integer value of the character in the machine's character set. For example, `'z'` represents the integer value of z (122 in the ASCII character set; see Appendix B), and `'\n'` represents the integer value of newline (10 in the ASCII character set).

A string is a series of characters treated as a single unit. A string may include letters, digits and various **special characters** such as +, -, *, /and $. **String literals**, or **string constants**, in C++ are written in double quotation marks as follows:

```
"John Q. Doe"              (a name)
"9999 Main Street"         (a street address)
"Maynard, Massachusetts"   (a city and state)
"(201) 555-1212"           (a telephone number)
```

A pointer-based string is an array of characters ending with a **null character (`'\0'`)**, which marks where the string terminates in memory. A string is accessed via a pointer to its first character. The value of a string literal is the address of its first character, but the sizeof a string literal is the length of the string *including* the terminating null character. Pointer-based strings are like arrays, because an array name is also a pointer to its first element.

A string literal may be used as an initializer in the declaration of either a character array or a variable of type char *. The declarations

```
char color[] = "blue";
const char *colorPtr = "blue";
```

each initialize a variable to the string "blue". The first declaration creates a five-element array color containing the characters 'b', 'l', 'u', 'e' and '\0'. The second declaration creates pointer variable colorPtr that points to the letter b in the string "blue" (which ends in '\0') somewhere in memory. String literals have static storage class (they exist for the duration of the program) and may or may not be shared if the same string literal is referenced from multiple locations in a program. The effect modifying a string literal is *undefined*; thus, you should always declare a pointer to a string literal as const char *.

The declaration char color[] = "blue"; could also be written

```
char color[] = { 'b', 'l', 'u', 'e', '\0' };
```

which uses character constants in single quotes (') as initializers for each element of the character array. When declaring a character array to contain a string, the array must be large enough to store the string and its terminating null character. The preceding declaration determines the size of the array, based on the number of initializers provided in the initializer list.

Common Programming Error 8.15
Not allocating sufficient space in a character array to store the null character that terminates a string is an error.

Common Programming Error 8.16
Creating or using a C-style string that does not contain a terminating null character can lead to logic errors.

Error-Prevention Tip 8.4
When storing a string of characters in a character array, be sure that the array is large enough to hold the largest string that will be stored. C++ allows strings of any length to be stored. If a string is longer than the character array in which it's to be stored, characters beyond the end of the array will overwrite data in memory following the array, leading to logic errors.

Because a string is an array of characters, we can access individual characters in a string directly with array subscript notation. For example, color[0] is the character 'b', color[2] is the character 'u' and string1[4] is the null character.

A string can be read into a character array using stream extraction with cin. For example, the following statement reads a string into character array word[20]:

```
cin >> word;
```

The string entered by the user is stored in word. The preceding statement reads characters until a white-space character or end-of-file indicator is encountered. The string should be no longer than 19 characters to leave room for the terminating null character. The `setw` stream manipulator can be used to ensure that the string read into word does not exceed the size of the array. For example, the statement

```
cin >> setw( 20 ) >> word;
```

specifies that `cin` should read a maximum of 19 characters into array word and save the 20th location in the array to store the terminating null character for the string. The `setw` stream manipulator applies only to the next value being input. If more than 19 characters are entered, the remaining characters are not saved in word, but will be read in and can be stored in another variable.

Common Programming Error 8.17
Not providing cin >> *with a character array large enough to store a string typed at the keyboard can result in loss of data in a program and other serious runtime errors.*

In some cases, it's desirable to input an entire line of text into a character array. For this purpose, the `cin` object provides the member function **getline**. The `getline` member function takes three arguments—a character array in which the line of text will be stored, a length and a delimiter character. For example, the statements

```
char sentence[ 80 ];
cin.getline( sentence, 80, '\n' );
```

declare array sentence of 80 characters and read a line of text from the keyboard into the array. The function stops reading characters when the delimiter character '\n' is encountered, when the end-of-file indicator is entered or when the number of characters read so far is one less than the length specified in the second argument. (The last character in the array is reserved for the terminating null character.) If the delimiter character is encountered, it's read and discarded. The third argument to `cin.getline` has '\n' as a default value, so the preceding function call could have been written as follows:

```
cin.getline( sentence, 80 );
```

Chapter 15, Stream Input/Output, provides a detailed discussion of `cin.getline` and other input/output functions.

Common Programming Error 8.18
Processing a single character as a char * *string can lead to a fatal runtime error. A* char * *string is a pointer—probably a respectably large integer. However, a character is a small integer (ASCII values range from 0 to 255). On many systems, dereferencing a* char *value causes an error, because low memory addresses are reserved for special purposes such as operating system interrupt handlers—so "memory access violations" occur.*

Common Programming Error 8.19
Passing a string as an argument to a function when a character is expected is a compilation error.

A character array representing a null-terminated string can be output with `cout` and `<<`. The statement

```
cout << sentence;
```

prints the array sentence. Note that cout <<, like cin >>, does not care how large the character array is. The characters of the string are output until a terminating null character is encountered; the null character is not printed. [*Note:* cin and cout assume that character arrays should be processed as strings terminated by null characters; cin and cout do not provide similar input and output processing capabilities for other array types.]

8.11 Arrays of Pointers

Arrays may contain pointers. A common use of such a data structure is to form an array of pointer-based strings, referred to simply as a **string array**. Each entry in the array is a string, but in C++ a string is essentially a pointer to its first character, so each entry in an array of strings is simply a pointer to the first character of a string. Consider the declaration of string array suit that might be useful in representing a deck of cards:

```
const char * const suit[ 4 ] =
    { "Hearts", "Diamonds", "Clubs", "Spades" };
```

The suit[4] portion of the declaration indicates an array of four elements. The const char * portion of the declaration indicates that each element of array suit is of type "pointer to char constant data." The four values to be placed in the array are "Hearts", "Diamonds", "Clubs" and "Spades". Each is stored in memory as a null-terminated character string that is one character longer than the number of characters between quotes. The four strings are seven, nine, six and seven characters long (including their terminating null characters), respectively. Although it appears as though these strings are being placed in the suit array, only pointers are actually stored in the array, as shown in Fig. 8.19. Each pointer points to the first character of its corresponding string. Thus, even though the suit array is fixed in size, it provides access to character strings of any length. This flexibility is one example of C++'s powerful data-structuring capabilities.

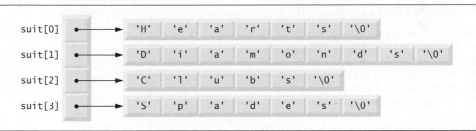

Fig. 8.19 | Graphical representation of the suit array.

The suit strings could be placed into a two-dimensional array, in which each row represents one suit and each column represents one of the letters of a suit name. Such a data structure must have a fixed number of columns per row, and that number must be as large as the largest string. Therefore, considerable memory is wasted when we store a large number of strings, of which most are shorter than the longest string. We use arrays of strings to help represent a deck of cards in the next section.

String arrays are commonly used with **command-line arguments** that are passed to function main when a program begins execution. Such arguments follow the program name when a program is executed from the command line. A typical use of command-line arguments is to pass options to a program. For example, from the command line on a Windows computer, the user can type

```
dir /p
```

to list the contents of the current directory and pause after each screen of information. When the dir command executes, the option /p is passed to dir as a command-line argument. Such arguments are placed in a string array that main receives as an argument. We discuss command-line arguments in Appendix F, C Legacy Code Topics.

8.12 Function Pointers

A **pointer to a function** contains the function's address in memory. We know that an array's name is actually the address in memory of the first element. Similarly, a function's name is actually the starting address in memory of the code that performs the function's task. Pointers to functions can be passed to functions, returned from functions, stored in arrays, assigned to other function pointers and used to call the underlying function.

Multipurpose Selection Sort Using Function Pointers
To illustrate the use of pointers to functions, Fig. 8.20 modifies the selection sort program of Fig. 8.13. Figure 8.20 consists of main (lines 13–50) and the functions selectionSort (lines 54–71), swap (lines 75–80), ascending (lines 84–87) and descending (lines 91–94). Function selectionSort receives a pointer to a function—either function ascending or function descending—as an argument in addition to the integer array to sort and the size of the array. Functions ascending and descending determine the sorting order. The program prompts the user to choose whether the array should be sorted in ascending order or in descending order (lines 20–22). If the user enters 1, a pointer to function ascending is passed to function selectionSort (line 33), causing the array to be sorted into increasing order. If the user enters 2, a pointer to function descending is passed to function selectionSort (line 41), causing the array to be sorted into decreasing order.

```cpp
1   // Fig. 8.20: fig08_20.cpp
2   // Multipurpose sorting program using function pointers.
3   #include <iostream>
4   #include <iomanip>
5   using namespace std;
6
7   // prototypes
8   void selectionSort( int [], const int, bool (*)( int, int ) );
9   void swap( int * const, int * const );
10  bool ascending( int, int ); // implements ascending order
11  bool descending( int, int ); // implements descending order
12
13  int main()
14  {
15     const int arraySize = 10;
16     int order; // 1 = ascending, 2 = descending
17     int counter; // array index
18     int a[ arraySize ] = { 2, 6, 4, 8, 10, 12, 89, 68, 45, 37 };
```

Fig. 8.20 | Multipurpose sorting program using function pointers. (Part 1 of 3.)

```
19
20     cout << "Enter 1 to sort in ascending order,\n"
21        << "Enter 2 to sort in descending order: ";
22     cin >> order;
23     cout << "\nData items in original order\n";
24
25     // output original array
26     for ( counter = 0; counter < arraySize; counter++ )
27        cout << setw( 4 ) << a[ counter ];
28
29     // sort array in ascending order; pass function ascending
30     // as an argument to specify ascending sorting order
31     if ( order == 1 )
32     {
33        selectionSort( a, arraySize, ascending );
34        cout << "\nData items in ascending order\n";
35     } // end if
36
37     // sort array in descending order; pass function descending
38     // as an argument to specify descending sorting order
39     else
40     {
41        selectionSort( a, arraySize, descending );
42        cout << "\nData items in descending order\n";
43     } // end else part of if...else
44
45     // output sorted array
46     for ( counter = 0; counter < arraySize; counter++ )
47        cout << setw( 4 ) << a[ counter ];
48
49     cout << endl;
50  } // end main
51
52  // multipurpose selection sort; the parameter compare is a pointer to
53  // the comparison function that determines the sorting order
54  void selectionSort( int work[], const int size,
55                      bool (*compare)( int, int ) )
56  {
57     int smallestOrLargest; // index of smallest (or largest) element
58
59     // loop over size - 1 elements
60     for ( int i = 0; i < size - 1; i++ )
61     {
62        smallestOrLargest = i; // first index of remaining vector
63
64        // loop to find index of smallest (or largest) element
65        for ( int index = i + 1; index < size; index++ )
66           if ( !(*compare)( work[ smallestOrLargest ], work[ index ] ) )
67              smallestOrLargest = index;
68
69        swap( &work[ smallestOrLargest ], &work[ i ] );
70     } // end if
71  } // end function selectionSort
```

Fig. 8.20 | Multipurpose sorting program using function pointers. (Part 2 of 3.)

```
72
73   // swap values at memory locations to which
74   // element1Ptr and element2Ptr point
75   void swap( int * const element1Ptr, int * const element2Ptr )
76   {
77      int hold = *element1Ptr;
78      *element1Ptr = *element2Ptr;
79      *element2Ptr = hold;
80   } // end function swap
81
82   // determine whether element a is less than
83   // element b for an ascending order sort
84   bool ascending( int a, int b )
85   {
86      return a < b; // returns true if a is less than b
87   } // end function ascending
88
89   // determine whether element a is greater than
90   // element b for a descending order sort
91   bool descending( int a, int b )
92   {
93      return a > b; // returns true if a is greater than b
94   } // end function descending
```

```
Enter 1 to sort in ascending order,
Enter 2 to sort in descending order: 1

Data items in original order
   2   6   4   8  10  12  89  68  45  37
Data items in ascending order
   2   4   6   8  10  12  37  45  68  89
```

```
Enter 1 to sort in ascending order,
Enter 2 to sort in descending order: 2

Data items in original order
   2   6   4   8  10  12  89  68  45  37
Data items in descending order
  89  68  45  37  12  10   8   6   4   2
```

Fig. 8.20 | Multipurpose sorting program using function pointers. (Part 3 of 3.)

The following parameter appears in line 55 of selectionSort's function header:

```
bool ( *compare )( int, int )
```

This parameter specifies a pointer to a function. The keyword bool indicates that the function being pointed to returns a bool value. The text (*compare) indicates the name of the pointer to the function (the * indicates that parameter compare is a pointer). The text (int, int) indicates that the function pointed to by compare takes two integer arguments. Parentheses are needed around *compare to indicate that compare is a pointer to a function. If we had not included the parentheses, the declaration would have been

```
bool *compare( int, int )
```

which declares a function that receives two integers as parameters and returns a pointer to a bool value.

The corresponding parameter in the function prototype of selectionSort (line 8) is

```
bool (*)( int, int )
```

Only types have been included. As always, for documentation purposes, you can include names that the compiler will ignore.

The function passed to selectionSort is called in line 66 as follows:

```
( *compare )( work[ smallestOrLargest ], work[ index ] )
```

Just as a pointer to a variable is dereferenced to access the value of the variable, a pointer to a function is dereferenced to execute the function. The parentheses around *compare are necessary—if they were left out, the * operator would attempt to dereference the value returned from the function call. The call to the function could have been made without dereferencing the pointer, as in

```
compare( work[ smallestOrLargest ], work[ index ] )
```

which uses the pointer directly as the function name. We prefer the first method of calling a function through a pointer, because it explicitly illustrates that compare is a pointer to a function that is dereferenced to call the function. The second method of calling a function through a pointer makes it appear as though compare is the name of an actual function in the program. This may be confusing to a user of the program who would like to see the definition of function compare and finds that it isn't defined in the file. Chapter 22, Standard Template Library (STL), presents many common uses of function pointers.

8.13 Wrap-Up

In this chapter we provided a detailed introduction to pointers—variables that contain memory addresses as their values. We began by demonstrating how to declare and initialize pointers. You saw how to use the address operator (&) to assign the address of a variable to a pointer and the indirection operator (*) to access the data stored in the variable indirectly referenced by a pointer. We discussed passing arguments by reference using both pointer arguments and reference arguments.

You learned how to use const with pointers to enforce the principle of least privilege. We demonstrated using nonconstant pointers to nonconstant data, nonconstant pointers to constant data, constant pointers to nonconstant data, and constant pointers to constant data. We then used selection sort to demonstrate passing arrays and individual array elements by reference. We discussed the sizeof operator, which can be used to determine the sizes of data types and variables in bytes during program compilation.

We demonstrated how to use pointers in arithmetic and comparison expressions. You saw that pointer arithmetic can be used to jump from one element of an array to another. You learned how to use arrays of pointers, and more specifically string arrays (arrays of strings). We discussed function pointers, which enable you to pass functions as parameters. We briefly introduced pointer-based strings.

In the next chapter, we begin our deeper treatment of classes. You'll learn about the scope of a class's members, and how to keep objects in a consistent state. You'll also learn about using special member functions called constructors and destructors, which execute when an object is created and destroyed, respectively, and we'll discuss when constructors and destructors are called. In addition, we'll demonstrate using default arguments with constructors and using default memberwise assignment to assign one object of a class to another object of the same class. We'll also discuss the danger of returning a reference to a `private` data member of a class.

Summary

Section 8.2 Pointer Variable Declarations and Initialization

- Pointers are variables that contain as their values memory addresses of other variables.
- The declaration

      int *ptr;

  declares `ptr` to be a pointer to a variable of type `int` and is read, "`ptr` is a pointer to `int`." The `*` as used here in a declaration indicates that the variable is a pointer.
- There are three values that can be used to initialize a pointer: `0`, `NULL` or an address of an object of the same type.
- The only integer that can be assigned to a pointer without casting is zero.

Section 8.3 Pointer Operators

- The `&` (address) operator obtains the memory address of its operand.
- The operand of the address operator must be a variable name (or another *lvalue*); the address operator cannot be applied to constants or to expressions that do not return a reference.
- The `*` indirection (or dereferencing) operator returns a synonym for the name of the object that its operand points to in memory. This is called dereferencing the pointer.

Section 8.4 Pass-by-Reference with Pointers

- When calling a function with an argument that the caller wants the called function to modify, the address of the argument may be passed. The called function then uses the indirection operator (`*`) to dereference the pointer and modify the value of the argument in the calling function.
- A function receiving an address as an argument must have a pointer as its corresponding parameter.

Section 8.5 Using **const** with Pointers

- The `const` qualifier enables you to inform the compiler that the value of a particular variable cannot be modified through the specified identifier.
- There are four ways to pass a pointer to a function—a nonconstant pointer to nonconstant data, a nonconstant pointer to constant data, a constant pointer to nonconstant data, and a constant pointer to constant data.
- The value of the array name is the address of the array's first element.
- To pass a single array element by reference using pointers, pass the address of the array element.

Section 8.6 Selection Sort Using Pass-by-Reference

- The selection sort algorithm is an easy-to-program, but inefficient, sorting algorithm. The first iteration of the algorithm selects the smallest element in the array and swaps it with the first element. The second iteration selects the second-smallest element (which is the smallest element of the remaining elements) and swaps it with the second element. The algorithm continues until the last iteration selects the second-largest element and swaps it with the second-to-last index, leaving the largest element in the last index. After the ith iteration, the smallest i items of the array will be sorted into increasing order in the first i elements of the array.

Section 8.7 sizeof Operator

• Operator sizeof determines the size in bytes of a data type, variable or constant at compile time.

• When applied to an array name, sizeof returns the total number of bytes in the array.

Section 8.8 Pointer Expressions and Pointer Arithmetic

• The arithmetic operations that may be performed on pointers are incrementing (++) a pointer, decrementing (--) a pointer, adding (+ or +=) an integer to a pointer, subtracting (- or -=) an integer from a pointer and subtracting one pointer from another.

• When an integer is added or subtracted from a pointer, the pointer is incremented or decremented by that integer times the size of the object to which the pointer refers.

• Pointers can be assigned to one another if they are of the same type. Otherwise, a cast must be used. The exception to this is a void * pointer, which is a generic pointer type that can hold pointer values of any type.

• The only valid operations on a void * pointer are comparing void * pointers with other pointers, assigning addresses to void * pointers and casting void * pointers to valid pointer types.

• Pointers can be compared using the equality and relational operators. Comparisons using relational operators are meaningful only if the pointers point to members of the same array.

Section 8.9 Relationship Between Pointers and Arrays

• Pointers that point to arrays can be subscripted exactly as array names can.

• In pointer/offset notation, if the pointer points to the first element of the array, the offset is the same as an array subscript.

• All subscripted array expressions can be written with a pointer and an offset, using either the name of the array as a pointer or using a separate pointer that points to the array.

Section 8.10 Pointer-Based String Processing

• A character constant is an integer value represented as a character in single quotes. The value of a character constant is the integer value of the character in the machine's character set.

• A string is a series of characters treated as a single unit. A string may include letters, digits and various special characters such as +, -, *, /and $.

• String literals, or string constants, in C++ are written in double quotation marks.

• A pointer-based string is an array of characters ending with a null character ('\0'), which marks where the string terminates in memory. A string is accessed via a pointer to its first character.

• The value of a string literal is the address of its first character, but the sizeof a string literal is the length of the string including the terminating null character.

• A string literal may be used as an initializer for a character array or a variable of type char *.

• String literals have static storage class and may or may not be shared if the same string literal is referenced from multiple locations in a program.

• The effect modifying a string literal is undefined; thus, you should always declare a pointer to a string literal as const char *.

• When declaring a character array to contain a string, the array must be large enough to store the string and its terminating null character.

• If a string is longer than the character array in which it's to be stored, characters beyond the end of the array will overwrite data in memory following the array, leading to logic errors.

- You can access individual characters in a string directly with array subscript notation.

- A string can be read into a character array using stream extraction with `cin`.

- The `setw` stream manipulator can be used to ensure that the string read into a character array does not exceed the size of the array.

- The `cin` object provides the member function `getline` to input an entire line of text into a character array. The function takes three arguments—a character array in which the line of text will be stored, a length and a delimiter character. The third argument has `'\n'` as a default value.

- A character array representing a null-terminated string can be output with `cout` and `<<`. The characters of the string are output until a terminating null character is encountered.

Section 8.11 Arrays of Pointers

- Arrays may contain pointers.

- Such a data structure can be used to form an array of pointer-based strings, referred to as a string array. Each entry in the array is a string, but in C++ a string is essentially a pointer to its first character, so each entry in an array of strings is simply a pointer to the first character of a string.

- String arrays are commonly used with command-line arguments that are passed to `main` when a program begins execution.

Section 8.12 Function Pointers

- A pointer to a function is the address where the code for the function resides.

- Pointers to functions can be used to call the functions they point to, passed to functions, returned from functions, stored in arrays, assigned to other pointers.

Terminology

* (pointer dereference or indirection operator) 348
address operator (&) 348
character constant 370
command-line arguments 373
constant pointer to constant data 358
constant pointer to nonconstant data 357
dereferencing a pointer 348
dereferencing operator (*) 348
directly references a value 346
function pointer 374
`getline` function of `cin` 372
indirection 346
indirection (*) operator 348
indirectly references a value 346
nonconstant pointer to constant data 355

nonconstant pointer to nonconstant data 355
null character ('\0') 370
null pointer 347
offset to a pointer 368
pass-by-reference with pointer arguments 350
pass-by-reference with reference arguments 350
pointer arithmetic 365
pointer/offset notation 368
pointer/subscript notation 368
pointer to a function 374
selection sort algorithm 358
`sizeof` operator 362
special characters 370
string array 373
string constant 370
string literals 370

Self-Review Exercises

8.1 Answer each of the following:
  a) A pointer is a variable that contains as its value the _____ of another variable.
  b) The three values that can be used to initialize a pointer are _____, _____ and _____.
  c) The only integer that can be assigned directly to a pointer is _____.

8.2 State whether the following are *true* or *false*. If the answer is *false*, explain why.
   a) The address operator & can be applied only to constants and to expressions.
   b) A pointer that is declared to be of type void * can be dereferenced.
   c) Pointers of different types can't be assigned to one another without a cast operation.

8.3 For each of the following, write C++ statements that perform the specified task. Assume that double-precision, floating-point numbers are stored in eight bytes and that the starting address of the array is at location 1002500 in memory. Each part of the exercise should use the results of previous parts where appropriate.
   a) Declare an array of type double called numbers with 10 elements, and initialize the elements to the values 0.0, 1.1, 2.2, ..., 9.9. Assume that the symbolic constant SIZE has been defined as 10.
   b) Declare a pointer nPtr that points to a variable of type double.
   c) Use a for statement to print the elements of array numbers using array subscript notation. Print each number with one position of precision to the right of the decimal point.
   d) Write two separate statements that each assign the starting address of array numbers to the pointer variable nPtr.
   e) Use a for statement to print the elements of array numbers using pointer/offset notation with pointer nPtr.
   f) Use a for statement to print the elements of array numbers using pointer/offset notation with the array name as the pointer.
   g) Use a for statement to print the elements of array numbers using pointer/subscript notation with pointer nPtr.
   h) Refer to the fourth element of array numbers using array subscript notation, pointer/offset notation with the array name as the pointer, pointer subscript notation with nPtr and pointer/offset notation with nPtr.
   i) Assuming that nPtr points to the beginning of array numbers, what address is referenced by nPtr + 8? What value is stored at that location?
   j) Assuming that nPtr points to numbers[5], what address is referenced by nPtr after nPtr -= 4 is executed? What's the value stored at that location?

8.4 For each of the following, write a single statement that performs the specified task. Assume that floating-point variables number1 and number2 have been declared and that number1 has been initialized to 7.3. Assume that variable ptr is of type char *. Assume that arrays s1 and s2 are each 100-element char arrays that are initialized with string literals.
   a) Declare the variable fPtr to be a pointer to an object of type double.
   b) Assign the address of variable number1 to pointer variable fPtr.
   c) Print the value of the object pointed to by fPtr.
   d) Assign the value of the object pointed to by fPtr to variable number2.
   e) Print the value of number2.
   f) Print the address of number1.
   g) Print the address stored in fPtr. Is the value printed the same as the address of number1?

8.5 Perform the task specified by each of the following statements:
   a) Write the function header for a function called exchange that takes two pointers to double-precision, floating-point numbers x and y as parameters and does not return a value.
   b) Write the function prototype for the function in part (a).
   c) Write the function header for a function called evaluate that returns an integer and that takes as parameters integer x and a pointer to function poly. Function poly takes an integer parameter and returns an integer.
   d) Write the function prototype for the function in part (c).
   e) Write two statements that each initialize character array vowel with the string of vowels, "AEIOU".

8.6   Find the error in each of the following program segments. Assume the following declarations and statements:

```
int *zPtr; // zPtr will reference array z
void *sPtr = 0;
int number;
int z[ 5 ] = { 1, 2, 3, 4, 5 };
```

a) ++zPtr;
b) // use pointer to get first value of array
   number = zPtr;
c) // assign array element 2 (the value 3) to number
   number = *zPtr[2];
d) // print entire array z
   for (int i = 0; i <= 5; i++)
      cout << zPtr[i] << endl;
e) // assign the value pointed to by sPtr to number
   number = *sPtr;
f) ++z;

Answers to Self-Review Exercises

8.1   a) address. b) 0, NULL, an address. c) 0.

8.2   a) False. The operand of the address operator must be an *lvalue*; the address operator cannot be applied to constants or to expressions that do not result in references.
   b) False. A pointer to void cannot be dereferenced. Such a pointer does not have a type that enables the compiler to determine the number of bytes of memory to dereference and the type of the data to which the pointer points.
   c) False. Pointers of any type can be assigned to void pointers. Pointers of type void can be assigned to pointers of other types only with an explicit type cast.

8.3   a) double numbers[SIZE] = { 0.0, 1.1, 2.2, 3.3, 4.4, 5.5, 6.6, 7.7, 8.8, 9.9 };
   b) double *nPtr;
   c) cout << fixed << showpoint << setprecision(1);
       for (int i = 0; i < SIZE; i++)
          cout << numbers[i] << ' ';
   d) nPtr = numbers;
       nPtr = &numbers[0];
   e) cout << fixed << showpoint << setprecision(1);
       for (int j = 0; j < SIZE; j++)
          cout << *(nPtr + j) << ' ';
   f) cout << fixed << showpoint << setprecision(1);
       for (int k = 0; k < SIZE; k++)
          cout << *(numbers + k) << ' ';
   g) cout << fixed << showpoint << setprecision(1);
       for (int m = 0; m < SIZE; m++)
          cout << nPtr[m] << ' ';
   h) numbers[3]
       *(numbers + 3)
       nPtr[3]
       *(nPtr + 3)
   i) The address is 1002500 + 8 * 8 = 1002564. The value is 8.8.

j) The address of numbers[5] is 1002500 + 5 * 8 = 1002540.
The address of nPtr -= 4 is 1002540 - 4 * 8 = 1002508.
The value at that location is 1.1.

8.4   a) `double *fPtr;`
b) `fPtr = &number1;`
c) `cout << "The value of *fPtr is " << *fPtr << endl;`
d) `number2 = *fPtr;`
e) `cout << "The value of number2 is " << number2 << endl;`
f) `cout << "The address of number1 is " << &number1 << endl;`
g) `cout << "The address stored in fPtr is " << fPtr << endl;`
Yes, the value is the same.

8.5   a) `void exchange( double *x, double *y )`
b) `void exchange( double *, double * );`
c) `int evaluate( int x, int (*poly)( int ) )`
d) `int evaluate( int, int (*)( int ) );`
e) `char vowel[] = "AEIOU";`
`char vowel[] = { 'A', 'E', 'I', 'O', 'U', '\0' };`

8.6   a) *Error:* zPtr has not been initialized.
Correction: Initialize zPtr with zPtr = z;
b) *Error:* The pointer is not dereferenced.
Correction: Change the statement to number = *zPtr;
c) *Error:* zPtr[2] is not a pointer and should not be dereferenced.
Correction: Change *zPtr[2] to zPtr[2].
d) *Error:* Referring to an array element outside the array bounds with pointer subscripting.
Correction: To prevent this, change the relational operator in the for statement to < or change the 5 to a 4.
e) *Error:* Dereferencing a void pointer.
Correction: To dereference the void pointer, it must first be cast to an integer pointer. Change the statement to number = *static_cast< int * >(sPtr);
f) *Error:* Trying to modify an array name with pointer arithmetic.
Correction: Use a pointer variable instead of the array name to accomplish pointer arithmetic, or subscript the array name to refer to a specific element.

Exercises

8.7   State whether the following are *true* or *false*. If *false*, explain why.
a) Two pointers that point to different arrays cannot be compared meaningfully.
b) Because the name of an array is a pointer to the first element of the array, array names can be manipulated in precisely the same manner as pointers.

8.8   For each of the following, write C++ statements that perform the specified task. Assume that unsigned integers are stored in two bytes and that the starting address of the array is at location 1002500 in memory.
a) Declare an array of type unsigned int called values with five elements, and initialize the elements to the even integers from 2 to 10. Assume that the symbolic constant SIZE has been defined as 5.
b) Declare a pointer vPtr that points to an object of type unsigned int.
c) Use a for statement to print the elements of array values using array subscript notation.
d) Write two separate statements that assign the starting address of array values to pointer variable vPtr.
e) Use a for statement to print the elements of array values using pointer/offset notation.

    f) Use a `for` statement to print the elements of array `values` using pointer/offset notation with the array name as the pointer.

    g) Use a `for` statement to print the elements of array `values` by subscripting the pointer to the array.

    h) Refer to the fifth element of `values` using array subscript notation, pointer/offset notation with the array name as the pointer, pointer subscript notation and pointer/offset notation.

    i) What address is referenced by `vPtr + 3`? What value is stored at that location?

    j) Assuming that `vPtr` points to `values[ 4 ]`, what address is referenced by `vPtr -= 4`? What value is stored at that location?

8.9   For each of the following, write a single statement that performs the specified task. Assume that `long` variables `value1` and `value2` have been declared and `value1` has been initialized to 200000.

    a) Declare the variable `longPtr` to be a pointer to an object of type `long`.

    b) Assign the address of variable `value1` to pointer variable `longPtr`.

    c) Print the value of the object pointed to by `longPtr`.

    d) Assign the value of the object pointed to by `longPtr` to variable `value2`.

    e) Print the value of `value2`.

    f) Print the address of `value1`.

    g) Print the address stored in `longPtr`. Is the value printed the same as `value1`'s address?

8.10   Perform the task specified by each of the following statements:

    a) Write the function header for function `zero` that takes a long integer array parameter `bigIntegers` and does not return a value.

    b) Write the function prototype for the function in part (a).

    c) Write the function header for function `add1AndSum` that takes an integer array parameter `oneTooSmall` and returns an integer.

    d) Write the function prototype for the function described in part (c).

8.11   Find the error in each of the following segments. If the error can be corrected, explain how.

    a)
```
int *number;
cout << number << endl;
```

    b)
```
double *realPtr;
long *integerPtr;
integerPtr = realPtr;
```

    c)
```
int * x, y;
x = y;
```

    d)
```
char s[] = "this is a character array";
for ( ; *s != '\0'; s++)
   cout << *s << ' ';
```

    e)
```
short *numPtr, result;
void *genericPtr = numPtr;
result = *genericPtr + 7;
```

    f)
```
double x = 19.34;
double xPtr = &x;
cout << xPtr << endl;
```

8.12   (*Simulation: The Tortoise and the Hare*) In this exercise, you'll re-create the classic race of the tortoise and the hare. You'll use random number generation to develop a simulation of this memorable event.

    Our contenders begin the race at "square 1" of 70 squares. Each square represents a possible position along the race course. The finish line is at square 70. The first contender to reach or pass square 70 is rewarded with a pail of fresh carrots and lettuce. The course weaves its way up the side of a slippery mountain, so occasionally the contenders lose ground.

There is a clock that ticks once per second. With each tick of the clock, your program should use function `moveTortoise` and `moveHare` to adjust the position of the animals according to the rules in Fig. 8.21. These functions should use pointer-based pass-by-reference to modify the position of the tortoise and the hare.

Animal	Move type	Percentage of the time	Actual move
Tortoise	Fast plod	50%	3 squares to the right
	Slip	20%	6 squares to the left
	Slow plod	30%	1 square to the right
Hare	Sleep	20%	No move at all
	Big hop	20%	9 squares to the right
	Big slip	10%	12 squares to the left
	Small hop	30%	1 square to the right
	Small slip	20%	2 squares to the left

Fig. 8.21 | Rules for moving the tortoise and the hare.

Use variables to keep track of the positions of the animals (i.e., position numbers are 1–70). Start each animal at position 1 (i.e., the "starting gate"). If an animal slips left before square 1, move the animal back to square 1.

Generate the percentages in the preceding table by producing a random integer i in the range $1 \leq i \leq 10$. For the tortoise, perform a "fast plod" when $1 \leq i \leq 5$, a "slip" when $6 \leq i \leq 7$ or a "slow plod" when $8 \leq i \leq 10$. Use a similar technique to move the hare.

Begin the race by printing

```
BANG !!!!!
AND THEY'RE OFF !!!!!
```

For each tick of the clock (i.e., each repetition of a loop), print a 70-position line showing the letter T in the tortoise's position and the letter H in the hare's position. Occasionally, the contenders land on the same square. In this case, the tortoise bites the hare and your program should print OUCH!!! beginning at that position. All print positions other than the T, the H or the OUCH!!! (in case of a tie) should be blank.

After printing each line, test whether either animal has reached or passed square 70. If so, print the winner and terminate the simulation. If the tortoise wins, print TORTOISE WINS!!! YAY!!! If the hare wins, print Hare wins. Yuch. If both animals win on the same clock tick, you may want to favor the tortoise (the "underdog"), or you may want to print It's a tie. If neither animal wins, perform the loop again to simulate the next tick of the clock.

8.13   What does this program do?

```cpp
// Ex. 8.13: ex08_13.cpp
// What does this program do?
#include <iostream>
using namespace std;

void mystery1( char *, const char * ); // prototype

```

```
8    int main()
9    {
10      char string1[ 80 ];
11      char string2[ 80 ];
12
13      cout << "Enter two strings: ";
14      cin >> string1 >> string2;
15      mystery1( string1, string2 );
16      cout << string1 << endl;
17   } // end main
18
19   // What does this function do?
20   void mystery1( char *s1, const char *s2 )
21   {
22      while ( *s1 != '\0' )
23         s1++;
24
25      for ( ; *s1 = *s2; s1++, s2++ )
26         ; // empty statement
27   } // end function mystery1
```

8.14 What does this program do?

```
1    // Ex. 8.14: ex08_14.cpp
2    // What does this program do?
3    #include <iostream>
4    using namespace std;
5
6    int mystery2( const char * ); // prototype
7
8    int main()
9    {
10      char string1[ 80 ];
11
12      cout << "Enter a string: ";
13      cin >> string1;
14      cout << mystery2( string1 ) << endl;
15   } // end main
16
17   // What does this function do?
18   int mystery2( const char *s )
19   {
20      int x;
21
22      for ( x = 0; *s != '\0'; s++ )
23         x++;
24
25      return x;
26   } // end function mystery2
```

8.15 (*Quicksort*) You've previously seen the sorting techniques of the bucket sort and selection sort. We now present the recursive sorting technique called Quicksort. The basic algorithm for a single-subscripted array of values is as follows:

   a) *Partitioning Step:* Take the first element of the unsorted array and determine its final location in the sorted array (i.e., all values to the left of the element in the array are less than the element, and all values to the right of the element in the array are greater than the element). We now have one element in its proper location and two unsorted subarrays.

   b) *Recursive Step:* Perform *Step 1* on each unsorted subarray.

Each time *Step 1* is performed on a subarray, another element is placed in its final location of the sorted array, and two unsorted subarrays are created. When a subarray consists of one element, that subarray must be sorted; therefore, that element is in its final location.

The basic algorithm seems simple enough, but how do we determine the final position of the first element of each subarray? As an example, consider the following set of values (the element in bold is the partitioning element—it will be placed in its final location in the sorted array):

37 2 6 4 89 8 10 12 68 45

a) Starting from the rightmost element of the array, compare each element with **37** until an element less than **37** is found. Then swap **37** and that element. The first element less than **37** is 12, so **37** and 12 are swapped. The values now reside in the array as follows:

12 2 6 4 89 8 10 **37** 68 45

Element 12 is in italics to indicate that it was just swapped with **37**.

b) Starting from the left of the array, but beginning with the element after 12, compare each element with **37** until an element greater than **37** is found. Then swap **37** and that element. The first element greater than **37** is 89, so **37** and 89 are swapped. The values now reside in the array as follows:

12 2 6 4 **37** 8 10 *89* 68 45

c) Starting from the right, but beginning with the element before 89, compare each element with **37** until an element less than **37** is found. Then swap **37** and that element. The first element less than **37** is 10, so **37** and 10 are swapped. The values now reside in the array as follows:

12 2 6 4 *10* 8 **37** 89 68 45

d) Starting from the left, but beginning with the element after 10, compare each element with **37** until an element greater than **37** is found. Then swap **37** and that element. There are no more elements greater than **37**, so when we compare **37** with itself, we know that **37** has been placed in its final location of the sorted array.

Once the partition has been applied to the array, there are two unsorted subarrays. The subarray with values less than 37 contains 12, 2, 6, 4, 10 and 8. The subarray with values greater than 37 contains 89, 68 and 45. The sort continues with both subarrays being partitioned in the same manner as the original array.

Based on the preceding discussion, write recursive function `quickSort` to sort a single-subscripted integer array. The function should receive as arguments an integer array, a starting subscript and an ending subscript. Function `partition` should be called by `quickSort` to perform the partitioning step.

8.16 (*Maze Traversal*) The grid of hashes (#) and dots (.) in Fig. 8.22 is a two-dimensional array representation of a maze. In the two-dimensional array, the hashes represent the walls of the maze and the dots represent squares in the possible paths through the maze. Moves can be made only to a location in the array that contains a dot.

There is a simple algorithm for walking through a maze that guarantees finding the exit (assuming that there is an exit). If there is not an exit, you'll arrive at the starting location again. Place your right hand on the wall to your right and begin walking forward. Never remove your hand from the wall. If the maze turns to the right, you follow the wall to the right. As long as you do not remove your hand from the wall, eventually you'll arrive at the exit of the maze. There may be a shorter path than the one you've taken, but you are guaranteed to get out of the maze if you follow the algorithm.

```
# # # # # # # # # # #
# . . . # . . . . . #
. . # . # . # # # # . #
# # . # . . . . . # . #
# . . . # # # . # . .
# # # . # . # . # . #
# . . # . # . # . # . #
# # . # . # . # . # . #
# . . . . . . . . # . #
# # # # # . # # # . # #
# . . . . . # . . . #
# # # # # # # # # # #
```

Fig. 8.22 | Two-dimensional array representation of a maze.

Write recursive function `mazeTraverse` to walk through the maze. The function should receive arguments that include a 12-by-12 character array representing the maze and the starting location of the maze. As `mazeTraverse` attempts to locate the exit from the maze, it should place the character X in each square in the path. The function should display the maze after each move, so the user can watch as the maze is solved.

8.17 (*Generating Mazes Randomly*) Write a function `mazeGenerator` that randomly produces a maze. The function should take as arguments a two-dimensional 12-by-12 character array and pointers to the `int` variables that represent the row and column of the maze's entry point. Try your function `mazeTraverse` from Exercise 8.16, using several randomly generated mazes.

Special Section: Building Your Own Computer

In the next several problems, we take a temporary diversion away from the world of high-level-language programming. We "peel open" a computer and look at its internal structure. We introduce machine-language programming and write several machine-language programs. To make this an especially valuable experience, we then build a computer (using software-based *simulation*) on which you can execute your machine-language programs!

8.18 (*Machine-Language Programming*) Let's create a computer we'll call the Simpletron. As its name implies, it's a simple machine, but, as we'll soon see, it's a powerful one as well. The Simpletron runs programs written in the only language it directly understands, that is, Simpletron Machine Language, or SML for short.

The Simpletron contains an *accumulator*—a "special register" in which information is put before the Simpletron uses that information in calculations or examines it in various ways. All information in the Simpletron is handled in terms of *words*. A word is a signed four-digit decimal number, such as +3364, -1293, +0007, -0001, etc. The Simpletron is equipped with a 100-word memory, and these words are referenced by their location numbers 00, 01, ..., 99.

Before running an SML program, we must *load*, or place, the program into memory. The first instruction (or statement) of every SML program is always placed in location 00. The simulator will start executing at this location.

Each instruction written in SML occupies one word of the Simpletron's memory; thus, instructions are signed four-digit decimal numbers. Assume that the sign of an SML instruction is always plus, but the sign of a data word may be either plus or minus. Each location in the Simpletron's memory may contain an instruction, a data value used by a program or an unused (and hence undefined) area of memory. The first two digits of each SML instruction are the *operation code* that specifies the operation to be performed. SML operation codes are shown in Fig. 8.23.

The last two digits of an SML instruction are the *operand*—the address of the memory location containing the word to which the operation applies.

Operation code	Meaning
Input/output operations	
const int READ = 10;	Read a word from the keyboard into a specific location in memory.
const int WRITE = 11;	Write a word from a specific location in memory to the screen.
Load and store operations	
const int LOAD = 20;	Load a word from a specific location in memory into the accumulator.
const int STORE = 21;	Store a word from the accumulator into a specific location in memory.
Arithmetic operations	
const int ADD = 30;	Add a word from a specific location in memory to the word in the accumulator (leave result in accumulator).
const int SUBTRACT = 31;	Subtract a word from a specific location in memory from the word in the accumulator (leave result in accumulator).
const int DIVIDE = 32;	Divide a word from a specific location in memory into the word in the accumulator (leave result in accumulator).
const int MULTIPLY = 33;	Multiply a word from a specific location in memory by the word in the accumulator (leave result in accumulator).
Transfer-of-control operations	
const int BRANCH = 40;	Branch to a specific location in memory.
const int BRANCHNEG = 41;	Branch to a specific location in memory if the accumulator is negative.
const int BRANCHZERO = 42;	Branch to a specific location in memory if the accumulator is zero.
const int HALT = 43;	Halt—the program has completed its task.

Fig. 8.23 | Simpletron Machine Language (SML) operation codes.

Now let's consider two simple SML programs. The first (Fig. 8.24) reads two numbers from the keyboard and computes and prints their sum. The instruction +1007 reads the first number from the keyboard and places it into location 07 (which has been initialized to zero). Instruction +1008 reads the next number into location 08. The *load* instruction, +2007, places (copies) the first number into the accumulator, and the *add* instruction, +3008, adds the second number to the number in the accumulator. *All SML arithmetic instructions leave their results in the accumulator.* The *store* instruction, +2109, places (copies) the result back into memory location 09. Then the *write* instruction, +1109, takes the number and prints it (as a signed four-digit decimal number). The *halt* instruction, +4300, terminates execution.

The SML program in Fig. 8.25 reads two numbers from the keyboard, then determines and prints the larger value. Note the use of the instruction +4107 as a conditional transfer of control, much the same as C++'s if statement.

Location	Number	Instruction
00	+1007	(Read A)
01	+1008	(Read B)
02	+2007	(Load A)
03	+3008	(Add B)
04	+2109	(Store C)
05	+1109	(Write C)
06	+4300	(Halt)
07	+0000	(Variable A)
08	+0000	(Variable B)
09	+0000	(Result C)

Fig. 8.24 | SML Example 1.

Location	Number	Instruction
00	+1009	(Read A)
01	+1010	(Read B)
02	+2009	(Load A)
03	+3110	(Subtract B)
04	+4107	(Branch negative to 07)
05	+1109	(Write A)
06	+4300	(Halt)
07	+1110	(Write B)
08	+4300	(Halt)
09	+0000	(Variable A)
10	+0000	(Variable B)

Fig. 8.25 | SML Example 2.

Now write SML programs to accomplish each of the following tasks:
   a) Use a sentinel-controlled loop to read positive numbers and compute and print their sum. Terminate input when a negative number is entered.
   b) Use a counter-controlled loop to read seven numbers, some positive and some negative, and compute and print their average.
   c) Read a series of numbers, and determine and print the largest number. The first number read indicates how many numbers should be processed.

8.19   (*Computer Simulator*) It may at first seem outrageous, but in this problem you are going to build your own computer. No, you won't be soldering components together. Rather, you'll use the powerful technique of *software-based simulation* to create a *software model* of the Simpletron. Your Simpletron simulator will turn the computer you are using into a Simpletron, and you actually will be able to run, test and debug the SML programs you wrote in Exercise 8.18.

When you run your Simpletron simulator, it should begin by printing

```
*** Welcome to Simpletron! ***
```

```
*** Please enter your program one instruction ***
*** (or data word) at a time. I will type the ***
*** location number and a question mark (?).  ***
*** You then type the word for that location. ***
*** Type the sentinel -99999 to stop entering ***
*** your program. ***
```

Your program should simulate the Simpletron's memory with a single-subscripted, 100-element array memory. Now assume that the simulator is running, and let's examine the dialog as we enter the program of Example 2 of Exercise 8.18:

```
00 ? +1009
01 ? +1010
02 ? +2009
03 ? +3110
04 ? +4107
05 ? +1109
06 ? +4300
07 ? +1110
08 ? +4300
09 ? +0000
10 ? +0000
11 ? -99999

*** Program loading completed ***
*** Program execution begins  ***
```

The numbers to the right of each ? in the preceding dialog represent the SML program instructions input by the user.

The SML program has now been placed (or loaded) into array memory. Now the Simpletron executes your SML program. Execution begins with the instruction in location 00 and, like C++, continues sequentially, unless directed to some other part of the program by a transfer of control.

Use variable accumulator to represent the accumulator register. Use variable instructionCounter to keep track of the location in memory that contains the instruction being performed. Use variable operationCode to indicate the operation currently being performed (i.e., the left two digits of the instruction word). Use variable operand to indicate the memory location on which the current instruction operates. Thus, operand is the rightmost two digits of the instruction currently being performed. Do not execute instructions directly from memory. Rather, transfer the next instruction to be performed from memory to a variable called instructionRegister. Then "pick off" the left two digits and place them in operationCode, and "pick off" the right two digits and place them in operand. When Simpletron begins execution, the special registers are all initialized to zero.

Now let's "walk through" the execution of the first SML instruction, +1009 in memory location 00. This is called an *instruction execution cycle*.

The instructionCounter tells us the location of the next instruction to be performed. We *fetch* the contents of that location from memory by using the C++ statement

```
instructionRegister = memory[ instructionCounter ];
```

The operation code and operand are extracted from the instruction register by the statements

```
operationCode = instructionRegister / 100;
operand = instructionRegister % 100;
```

Now, the Simpletron must determine that the operation code is actually a *read* (versus a *write*, a *load*, etc.). A switch differentiates among the 12 operations of SML. In the switch statement, the behavior of various SML instructions is simulated as shown in Fig. 8.26 (we leave the others to you).

The *halt* instruction also causes the Simpletron to print the name and contents of each register, as well as the complete contents of memory. Such a printout is often called a *register and memory dump*. To help you program your dump function, a sample dump format is shown in Fig. 8.26. Note that a dump after executing a Simpletron program would show the actual values of instructions and data values at the moment execution terminated. To format numbers with their sign as shown in the dump, use stream manipulator **showpos**. To disable the display of the sign, use stream manipulator **noshowpos**. For numbers that have fewer than four digits, you can format numbers with leading zeros between the sign and the value by using the following statement before outputting the value:

```
cout << setfill( '0' ) << internal;
```

```
REGISTERS:
accumulator            +0000
instructionCounter        00
instructionRegister    +0000
operationCode             00
operand                   00

MEMORY:
        0     1     2     3     4     5     6     7     8     9
 0  +0000 +0000 +0000 +0000 +0000 +0000 +0000 +0000 +0000 +0000
10  +0000 +0000 +0000 +0000 +0000 +0000 +0000 +0000 +0000 +0000
20  +0000 +0000 +0000 +0000 +0000 +0000 +0000 +0000 +0000 +0000
30  +0000 +0000 +0000 +0000 +0000 +0000 +0000 +0000 +0000 +0000
40  +0000 +0000 +0000 +0000 +0000 +0000 +0000 +0000 +0000 +0000
50  +0000 +0000 +0000 +0000 +0000 +0000 +0000 +0000 +0000 +0000
60  +0000 +0000 +0000 +0000 +0000 +0000 +0000 +0000 +0000 +0000
70  +0000 +0000 +0000 +0000 +0000 +0000 +0000 +0000 +0000 +0000
80  +0000 +0000 +0000 +0000 +0000 +0000 +0000 +0000 +0000 +0000
90  +0000 +0000 +0000 +0000 +0000 +0000 +0000 +0000 +0000 +0000
```

Fig. 8.26 | A sample register and memory dump.

Parameterized stream manipulator **setfill** (from header <iomanip>) specifies the fill character that will appear between the sign and the value when a number is displayed with a field width of five characters but does not have four digits. (One position in the field width is reserved for the sign.) Stream manipulator **internal** indicates that the fill characters should appear between the sign and the numeric value .

Let's proceed with the execution of our program's first instruction—+1009 in location 00. As we've indicated, the switch statement simulates this by performing the C++ statement

```
cin >> memory[ operand ];
```

A question mark (?) should be displayed on the screen before the cin statement executes to prompt the user for input. The Simpletron waits for the user to type a value and press the *Enter* key. The value is then read into location 09.

At this point, simulation of the first instruction is complete. All that remains is to prepare the Simpletron to execute the next instruction. The instruction just performed was not a transfer of control, so we need merely increment the instruction counter register as follows:

```
++instructionCounter;
```

This completes the simulated execution of the first instruction. The entire process (i.e., the instruction execution cycle) begins anew with the fetch of the next instruction to execute.

Now let's consider how to simulate the branching instructions (i.e., the transfers of control). All we need to do is adjust the value in the instructionCounter appropriately. Therefore, the unconditional branch instruction (40) is simulated in the switch as

```
        instructionCounter = operand;
```

The conditional "branch if accumulator is zero" instruction is simulated as

```
        if ( accumulator == 0 )
            instructionCounter = operand;
```

At this point, you should implement your Simpletron simulator and run each of the SML programs you wrote in Exercise 8.18. The variables that represent the Simpletron simulator's memory and registers should be defined in main and passed to other functions by value or by reference as appropriate.

Your simulator should check for various types of errors. During the program loading phase, for example, each number the user types into the Simpletron's memory must be in the range -9999 to +9999. Your simulator should use a while loop to test that each number entered is in this range and, if not, keep prompting the user to reenter the number until the user enters a correct number.

During the execution phase, your simulator should check for various serious errors, such as attempts to divide by zero, attempts to execute invalid operation codes, accumulator overflows (i.e., arithmetic operations resulting in values larger than +9999 or smaller than -9999) and the like. Such serious errors are called **fatal errors**. When a fatal error is detected, your simulator should print an error message such as

```
        *** Attempt to divide by zero ***
        *** Simpletron execution abnormally terminated ***
```

and should print a full register and memory dump in the format we've discussed previously. This will help the user locate the error in the program.

8.20   (*Project: Modifications to the Simpletron Simulator*) In Exercise 8.19, you wrote a software simulation of a computer that executes programs written in Simpletron Machine Language (SML). In this exercise, we propose several modifications and enhancements to the Simpletron Simulator. In Exercises 20.31–20.35, we propose building a compiler that converts programs written in a high-level programming language (a variation of BASIC) to SML. Some of the following modifications and enhancements may be required to execute the programs produced by the compiler. [*Note:* Some modifications may conflict with others and therefore must be done separately.]

    a)   Extend the Simpletron Simulator's memory to contain 1000 memory locations to enable the Simpletron to handle larger programs.

    b)   Allow the simulator to perform modulus calculations. This requires an additional Simpletron Machine Language instruction.

    c)   Allow the simulator to perform exponentiation calculations. This requires an additional Simpletron Machine Language instruction.

    d)   Modify the simulator to use hexadecimal values rather than integer values to represent Simpletron Machine Language instructions.

    e)   Modify the simulator to allow output of a newline. This requires an additional Simpletron Machine Language instruction.

    f)   Modify the simulator to process floating-point values in addition to integer values.

    g)   Modify the simulator to handle string input. [*Hint:* Each Simpletron word can be divided into two groups, each holding a two-digit integer. Each two-digit integer represents the ASCII decimal equivalent of a character. Add a machine-language instruction that inputs a string and store the string beginning at a specific Simpletron memory location. The first half of the word at that location will be a count of the number of characters in the string (i.e., the length of the string). Each succeeding half-word contains one ASCII character expressed as two decimal digits. The machine-language instruction converts each character into its ASCII equivalent and assigns it to a half-word.]

h) Modify the simulator to handle output of strings stored in the format of part (g). [*Hint:* Add a machine-language instruction that will print a string beginning at a certain Simpletron memory location. The first half of the word at that location is a count of the number of characters in the string (i.e., the length of the string). Each succeeding half-word contains one ASCII character expressed as two decimal digits. The machine-language instruction checks the length and prints the string by translating each two-digit number into its equivalent character.]

i) Modify the simulator to include instruction SML_DEBUG that prints a memory dump after each instruction executes. Give SML_DEBUG an operation code of 44. The word +4401 turns on debug mode, and +4400 turns off debug mode.

Classes: A Deeper Look, Part I

9

*My object all sublime
I shall achieve in time.*
—W. S. Gilbert

Is it a world to hide virtues in?
—William Shakespeare

*Don't be "consistent," but be
simply true.*
—Oliver Wendell Holmes, Jr.

Objectives

In this chapter you'll learn:

- How to use a preprocessor wrapper to prevent multiple definition errors.

- To understand class scope and accessing class members via the name of an object, a reference to an object or a pointer to an object.

- To define constructors with default arguments.

- How destructors are used to perform "termination housekeeping" on an object before it's destroyed.

- When constructors and destructors are called and the order in which they're called.

- The logic errors that may occur when a **public** member function returns a reference to **private** data.

- To assign the data members of one object to those of another object by default memberwise assignment.

9.1 Introduction

In the preceding chapters, we introduced many basic terms and concepts of C++ object-oriented programming. We also discussed our program development methodology: We selected appropriate attributes and behaviors for each class and specified the manner in which objects of our classes collaborated with objects of C++ Standard Library classes to accomplish each program's overall goals.

In this chapter, we take a deeper look at classes. We use an integrated `Time` class case study in both this chapter and Chapter 10, Classes: A Deeper Look, Part 2 to demonstrate several class construction capabilities. We begin with a `Time` class that reviews several of the features presented in the preceding chapters. The example also demonstrates an important C++ software engineering concept—using a "preprocessor wrapper" in header files to prevent the code in the header from being included into the same source code file more than once. Since a class can be defined only once, using such preprocessor directives prevents multiple definition errors.

Next, we discuss class scope and the relationships among class members. We demonstrate how client code can access a class's `public` members via three types of "handles"—the name of an object, a reference to an object or a pointer to an object. As you'll see, object names and references can be used with the dot (`.`) member selection operator to access a `public` member, and pointers can be used with the arrow (`->`) member selection operator.

We discuss access functions that can read or display data in an object. A common use of access functions is to test the truth or falsity of conditions—such functions are known as predicate functions. We also demonstrate the notion of a utility function (also called a helper function)—a `private` member function that supports the operation of the class's `public` member functions, but is not intended for use by clients of the class.

In the second `Time` class case study example, we demonstrate how to pass arguments to constructors and show how default arguments can be used in a constructor to enable client code to initialize objects using a variety of arguments. Next, we discuss a special member function called a destructor that is part of every class and is used to perform "termination housekeeping" on an object before the object is destroyed. We then demonstrate the order in which constructors and destructors are called, because your programs' correctness depends on using properly initialized objects that have not yet been destroyed.

Our last example of the Time class case study in this chapter shows a dangerous programming practice in which a member function returns a reference to private data. We discuss how this breaks the encapsulation of a class and allows client code to directly access an object's data. This last example shows that objects of the same class can be assigned to one another using default memberwise assignment, which copies the data members in the object on the right side of the assignment into the corresponding data members of the object on the left side of the assignment. The chapter concludes with a discussion of software reusability.

9.2 Time Class Case Study

Our first example (Figs. 9.1–9.3) creates class Time and a driver program that tests the class. You've already created many classes in this book. In this section, we review many of the concepts covered in Chapter 3 and demonstrate an important C++ software engineering concept—using a "preprocessor wrapper" in header files to prevent the code in the header from being included into the same source code file more than once. Since a class can be defined only once, using such preprocessor directives prevents multiple-definition errors.

```
1   // Fig. 9.1: Time.h
2   // Declaration of class Time.
3   // Member functions are defined in Time.cpp
4
5   // prevent multiple inclusions of header file
6   #ifndef TIME_H
7   #define TIME_H
8
9   // Time class definition
10  class Time
11  {
12  public:
13     Time(); // constructor
14     void setTime( int, int, int ); // set hour, minute and second
15     void printUniversal(); // print time in universal-time format
16     void printStandard(); // print time in standard-time format
17  private:
18     int hour; // 0 - 23 (24-hour clock format)
19     int minute; // 0 - 59
20     int second; // 0 - 59
21  }; // end class Time
22
23  #endif
```

Fig. 9.1 | Time class definition.

Time Class Definition
The class definition (Fig. 9.1) contains prototypes (lines 13–16) for member functions Time, setTime, printUniversal and printStandard, and includes private integer members hour, minute and second (lines 18–20). Class Time's private data members can be accessed only by its four member functions. Chapter 12 introduces a third access specifier, protected, as we study inheritance and the part it plays in object-oriented programming.

Good Programming Practice 9.1

For clarity and readability, use each access specifier only once in a class definition. Place public *members first, where they're easy to locate.*

Software Engineering Observation 9.1

Each element of a class should have private *visibility unless it can be proven that the element needs* public *visibility. This is another example of the principle of least privilege.*

In Fig. 9.1, the class definition is enclosed in the following **preprocessor wrapper** (lines 6, 7 and 23):

```
// prevent multiple inclusions of header file
#ifndef TIME_H
#define TIME_H
   ...
#endif
```

When we build larger programs, other definitions and declarations will also be placed in header files. The preceding preprocessor wrapper prevents the code between **#ifndef** (which means "if not defined") and **#endif** from being included if the name TIME_H has been defined. If the header has not been included previously in a file, the name TIME_H is defined by the **#define** directive and the header file statements are included. If the header has been included previously, TIME_H is defined already and the header file is not included again. Attempts to include a header file multiple times (inadvertently) typically occur in large programs with many header files that may themselves include other header files. [*Note:* The commonly used convention for the symbolic constant name in the preprocessor directives is simply the header file name in upper case with the underscore character replacing the period.]

Error-Prevention Tip 9.1

Use #ifndef, #define *and* #endif *preprocessor directives to form a preprocessor wrapper that prevents header files from being included more than once in a program.*

Good Programming Practice 9.2

Use the name of the header file in upper case with the period replaced by an underscore in the #ifndef *and* #define *preprocessor directives of a header file.*

Time Class Member Functions

In Fig. 9.2, the Time constructor (lines 10–13) initializes the data members to 0—the universal-time equivalent of 12 AM. This ensures that the object begins in a consistent state. Invalid values cannot be stored in the data members of a Time object, because the constructor is called when the Time object is created, and all subsequent attempts by a client to modify the data members are scrutinized by function setTime (discussed shortly). Finally, it's important to note that you can define several overloaded constructors for a class.

The data members of a class cannot be initialized where they're declared in the class body. It's strongly recommended that these data members be initialized by the class's constructor (as there is no default initialization for fundamental-type data members). Data members can also be assigned values by Time's *set* functions. [*Note:* Chapter 10 demon-

```cpp
 1  // Fig. 9.2: Time.cpp
 2  // Member-function definitions for class Time.
 3  #include <iostream>
 4  #include <iomanip>
 5  #include "Time.h" // include definition of class Time from Time.h
 6  using namespace std;
 7
 8  // Time constructor initializes each data member to zero.
 9  // Ensures all Time objects start in a consistent state.
10  Time::Time()
11  {
12     hour = minute = second = 0;
13  } // end Time constructor
14
15  // set new Time value using universal time; ensure that
16  // the data remains consistent by setting invalid values to zero
17  void Time::setTime( int h, int m, int s )
18  {
19     hour = ( h >= 0 && h < 24 ) ? h : 0; // validate hour
20     minute = ( m >= 0 && m < 60 ) ? m : 0; // validate minute
21     second = ( s >= 0 && s < 60 ) ? s : 0; // validate second
22  } // end function setTime
23
24  // print Time in universal-time format (HH:MM:SS)
25  void Time::printUniversal()
26  {
27     cout << setfill( '0' ) << setw( 2 ) << hour << ":"
28        << setw( 2 ) << minute << ":" << setw( 2 ) << second;
29  } // end function printUniversal
30
31  // print Time in standard-time format (HH:MM:SS AM or PM)
32  void Time::printStandard()
33  {
34     cout << ( ( hour == 0 || hour == 12 ) ? 12 : hour % 12 ) << ":"
35        << setfill( '0' ) << setw( 2 ) << minute << ":" << setw( 2 )
36        << second << ( hour < 12 ? " AM" : " PM" );
37  } // end function printStandard
```

Fig. 9.2 | Time class member-function definitions.

strates that only a class's static const data members of integral or enum types can be initialized in the class's body.]

Common Programming Error 9.1

Attempting to initialize a non-static data member of a class explicitly in the class definition is a syntax error.

Function setTime (lines 17–22) is a public function that declares three int parameters and uses them to set the time. A conditional expression tests each argument to determine whether the value is in a specified range. For example, the hour value (line 19) must be greater than or equal to 0 and less than 24, because the universal-time format represents hours as integers from 0 to 23 (e.g., 1 PM is hour 13 and 11 PM is hour 23; midnight is hour 0 and noon is hour 12). Similarly, both minute and second values (lines 20 and 21) must be greater than or equal to 0 and less than 60. Any values outside these ranges are set to zero to ensure that a Time object always contains consistent data—that is, the object's data values are always kept in range, even if the values provided as arguments to function setTime were incorrect. In this example, zero is a consistent value for hour, minute and second.

A value passed to setTime is a correct value if it's in the allowed range for the member it's initializing. So, any number in the range 0–23 would be a correct value for the hour. A correct value is always a consistent value. However, a consistent value is not necessarily a correct value. If setTime sets hour to 0 because the argument received was out of range, then hour is correct only if the current time is coincidentally midnight.

Function printUniversal (lines 25–29 of Fig. 9.2) takes no arguments and outputs the time in universal-time format, consisting of three colon-separated pairs of digits for the hour, minute and second. For example, if the time were 1:30:07 PM, function printUniversal would return 13:30:07. Line 27 uses parameterized stream manipulator **setfill** to specify the **fill character** that is displayed when an integer is output in a field wider than the number of digits in the value. By default, the fill characters appear to the left of the digits in the number. In this example, if the minute value is 2, it will be displayed as 02, because the fill character is set to zero ('0'). If the number being output fills the specified field, the fill character will not be displayed. Once the fill character is specified with set-fill, it applies for all subsequent values that are displayed in fields wider than the value being displayed (i.e., setfill is a "sticky" setting). This is in contrast to setw, which applies only to the next value displayed (setw is a "nonsticky" setting).

> ### Error-Prevention Tip 9.2
> *Each sticky setting (such as a fill character or floating-point precision) should be restored to its previous setting when it's no longer needed. Failure to do so may result in incorrectly formatted output later in a program. Chapter 15, Stream Input/Output, discusses how to reset the fill character and precision.*

Function printStandard (lines 32–37) takes no arguments and outputs the date in standard-time format, consisting of the hour, minute and second values separated by colons and followed by an AM or PM indicator (e.g., 1:27:06 PM). Like function print-Universal, function printStandard uses setfill('0') to format the minute and second as two digit values with leading zeros if necessary. Line 34 uses the conditional operator (?:) to determine the value of hour to be displayed—if the hour is 0 or 12 (AM or PM), it appears as 12; otherwise, the hour appears as a value from 1 to 11. The conditional operator in line 36 determines whether AM or PM will be displayed.

Defining Member Functions Outside the Class Definition; Class Scope
Even though a member function declared in a class definition may be defined outside that class definition (and "tied" to the class via the binary scope resolution operator), that member function is still within that **class's scope**; i.e., its name is known only to other members of the class unless referred to via an object of the class, a reference to an object of the class, a pointer to an object of the class or the binary scope resolution operator. We'll say more about class scope shortly.

If a member function is defined in the body of a class definition, the compiler attempts to inline calls to the member function. Remember that the compiler reserves the right not to inline any function.

Performance Tip 9.1

Defining a member function inside the class definition inlines the member function (if the compiler chooses to do so). This can improve performance.

Software Engineering Observation 9.2

Defining a small member function inside the class definition does not promote the best software engineering, because clients of the class will be able to see the implementation of the function, and the client code must be recompiled if the function definition changes.

Software Engineering Observation 9.3

Only the simplest and most stable member functions (i.e., whose implementations are unlikely to change) should be defined in the class header.

Member Functions vs. Global Functions

The `printUniversal` and `printStandard` member functions take no arguments, because these member functions implicitly know that they're to print the data members of the particular `Time` object for which they're invoked. This can make member function calls more concise than conventional function calls in procedural programming.

Software Engineering Observation 9.4

Using an object-oriented programming approach often simplifies function calls by reducing the number of parameters. This benefit of object-oriented programming derives from the fact that encapsulating data members and member functions within an object gives the member functions the right to access the data members.

Software Engineering Observation 9.5

Member functions are usually shorter than functions in non object oriented programs, because the data stored in data members have ideally been validated by a constructor or by member functions that store new data. Because the data is already in the object, the member-function calls often have no arguments or fewer arguments than typical function calls in non-object-oriented languages. Thus, the calls are shorter, the function definitions are shorter and the function prototypes are shorter. This improves many aspects of program development.

Error-Prevention Tip 9.3

The fact that member function calls generally take either no arguments or substantially fewer arguments than conventional function calls in non-object-oriented languages reduces the likelihood of passing the wrong arguments, the wrong types of arguments or the wrong number of arguments.

Using Class Time

Once class `Time` has been defined, it can be used as a type in object, array, pointer and reference declarations as follows:

```
Time sunset; // object of type Time
Time arrayOfTimes[ 5 ]; // array of 5 Time objects
Time &dinnerTime = sunset; // reference to a Time object
Time *timePtr = &dinnerTime; // pointer to a Time object
```

Figure 9.3 uses class Time. Line 10 instantiates a single object of class Time called t. When the object is instantiated, the Time constructor is called to initialize each private data member to 0. Then, lines 14 and 16 print the time in universal and standard formats, respectively, to confirm that the members were initialized properly. Line 18 sets a new time by calling member function setTime, and lines 22 and 24 print the time again in

```cpp
1   // Fig. 9.3: fig09_03.cpp
2   // Program to test class Time.
3   // NOTE: This file must be compiled with Time.cpp.
4   #include <iostream>
5   #include "Time.h" // include definition of class Time from Time.h
6   using namespace std;
7
8   int main()
9   {
10      Time t; // instantiate object t of class Time
11
12      // output Time object t's initial values
13      cout << "The initial universal time is ";
14      t.printUniversal(); // 00:00:00
15      cout << "\nThe initial standard time is ";
16      t.printStandard(); // 12:00:00 AM
17
18      t.setTime( 13, 27, 6 ); // change time
19
20      // output Time object t's new values
21      cout << "\n\nUniversal time after setTime is ";
22      t.printUniversal(); // 13:27:06
23      cout << "\nStandard time after setTime is ";
24      t.printStandard(); // 1:27:06 PM
25
26      t.setTime( 99, 99, 99 ); // attempt invalid settings
27
28      // output t's values after specifying invalid values
29      cout << "\n\nAfter attempting invalid settings:"
30         << "\nUniversal time: ";
31      t.printUniversal(); // 00:00:00
32      cout << "\nStandard time: ";
33      t.printStandard(); // 12:00:00 AM
34      cout << endl;
35   } // end main
```

```
The initial universal time is 00:00:00
The initial standard time is 12:00:00 AM

Universal time after setTime is 13:27:06
Standard time after setTime is 1:27:06 PM

After attempting invalid settings:
Universal time: 00:00:00
Standard time: 12:00:00 AM
```

Fig. 9.3 | Program to test class Time.

both formats. Line 26 attempts to use `setTime` to set the data members to invalid values—function `setTime` recognizes this and sets the invalid values to 0 to maintain the object in a consistent state. Finally, lines 31 and 33 print the time again in both formats.

Looking Ahead to Composition and Inheritance

Often, classes do not have to be created "from scratch." Rather, they can include objects of other classes as members or they may be **derived** from other classes that provide attributes and behaviors the new classes can use. Such software reuse can greatly enhance productivity and simplify code maintenance. Including class objects as members of other classes is called **composition** (or **aggregation**) and is discussed in Chapter 10. Deriving new classes from existing classes is called **inheritance** and is discussed in Chapter 12.

Object Size

People new to object-oriented programming often suppose that objects must be quite large because they contain data members and member functions. Logically, this is true—you may think of objects as containing data and functions (and our discussion has certainly encouraged this view); physically, however, this is not true.

Performance Tip 9.2

Objects contain only data, so objects are much smaller than if they also contained member functions. Applying operator `sizeof` to a class name or to an object of that class will report only the size of the class's data members. The compiler creates one copy (only) of the member functions separate from all objects of the class. All objects of the class share this one copy. Each object, of course, needs its own copy of the class's data, because the data can vary among the objects. The function code is nonmodifiable and, hence, can be shared among all objects of one class.

9.3 **Class Scope and Accessing Class Members**

A class's data members (variables declared in the class definition) and member functions (functions declared in the class definition) belong to that class's scope. Nonmember functions are defined at global namespace scope.

Within a class's scope, class members are immediately accessible by all of that class's member functions and can be referenced by name. Outside a class's scope, `public` class members are referenced through one of the **handles** on an object—an object name, a reference to an object or a pointer to an object. The type of the object, reference or pointer specifies the interface (i.e., the member functions) accessible to the client. [We'll see in Chapter 10 that an implicit handle is inserted by the compiler on every reference to a data member or member function from within an object.]

Member functions of a class can be overloaded, but only by other member functions of that class. To overload a member function, simply provide in the class definition a prototype for each version of the overloaded function, and provide a separate function definition for each version of the function.

Variables declared in a member function have local scope and are known only to that function. If a member function defines a variable with the same name as a variable with class scope, the class-scope variable is hidden by the block-scope variable in the local scope. Such a hidden variable can be accessed by preceding the variable name with the class name followed by the scope resolution operator (::). Hidden global variables can be accessed with the unary scope resolution operator (see Chapter 6).

The dot member selection operator (.) is preceded by an object's name or with a reference to an object to access the object's members. The **arrow member selection operator** (->) is preceded by a pointer to an object to access the object's members.

Figure 9.4 uses a simple class called Count (lines 7–24) with private data member x of type int (line 23), public member function setX (lines 11–14) and public member function print (lines 17–20) to illustrate accessing class members with the member-selection operators. For simplicity, we've included this small class in the same file as main. Lines 28–30 create three variables related to type Count—counter (a Count object), counterPtr (a pointer to a Count object) and counterRef (a reference to a Count object). Variable counterRef refers to counter, and variable counterPtr points to counter. In lines 33–34 and 37–38, note that the program can invoke member functions setX and print by using the dot (.) member selection operator preceded by either the name of the object (counter) or a reference to the object (counterRef, which is an alias for counter). Similarly, lines 41–42 demonstrate that the program can invoke member functions setX and print by using a pointer (countPtr) and the arrow (->) member-selection operator.

```
1   // Fig. 9.4: fig09_04.cpp
2   // Demonstrating the class member access operators . and ->
3   #include <iostream>
4   using namespace std;
5
6   // class Count definition
7   class Count
8   {
9   public: // public data is dangerous
10      // sets the value of private data member x
11      void setX( int value )
12      {
13         x = value;
14      } // end function setX
15
16      // prints the value of private data member x
17      void print()
18      {
19         cout << x << endl;
20      } // end function print
21
22   private:
23      int x;
24   }; // end class Count
25
26   int main()
27   {
28      Count counter; // create counter object
29      Count *counterPtr = &counter; // create pointer to counter
30      Count &counterRef = counter; // create reference to counter
```

Fig. 9.4 | Accessing an object's member functions through each type of object handle—the object's name, a reference to the object and a pointer to the object. (Part 1 of 2.)

```
31
32       cout << "Set x to 1 and print using the object's name: ";
33       counter.setX( 1 ); // set data member x to 1
34       counter.print(); // call member function print
35
36       cout << "Set x to 2 and print using a reference to an object: ";
37       counterRef.setX( 2 ); // set data member x to 2
38       counterRef.print(); // call member function print
39
40       cout << "Set x to 3 and print using a pointer to an object: ";
41       counterPtr->setX( 3 ); // set data member x to 3
42       counterPtr->print(); // call member function print
43    } // end main
```

```
Set x to 1 and print using the object's name: 1
Set x to 2 and print using a reference to an object: 2
Set x to 3 and print using a pointer to an object: 3
```

Fig. 9.4 | Accessing an object's member functions through each type of object handle—the object's name, a reference to the object and a pointer to the object. (Part 2 of 2.)

9.4 Separating Interface from Implementation

In Chapter 3, we began by including a class's definition and member-function definitions in one file. We then demonstrated separating this code into two files—a header file for the class definition (i.e., the class's interface) and a source code file for the class's member-function definitions (i.e., the class's implementation). Recall that this makes it easier to modify programs—as far as clients of a class are concerned, changes in the class's implementation do not affect the client as long as the class's interface originally provided to the client remains unchanged.

Software Engineering Observation 9.6

Clients of a class do not need access to the class's source code in order to use the class. The clients do, however, need to be able to link to the class's object code (i.e., the compiled version of the class). This encourages independent software vendors (ISVs) to provide class libraries for sale or license. The ISVs provide in their products only the header files and the object modules. No proprietary information is revealed—as would be the case if source code were provided. The C++ user community benefits by having more ISV-produced class libraries available.

Actually, things are not quite this rosy. Header files do contain some portions of the implementation and hints about others. Inline member functions, for example, should be in a header file, so that when the compiler compiles a client, the client can include the `inline` function definition in place. A class's `private` members are listed in the class definition in the header file, so these members are visible to clients even though the clients may not access the `private` members. In Chapter 10, we show how to use a "proxy class" to hide even the `private` data of a class from clients of the class.

Software Engineering Observation 9.7

Information important to the interface of a class should be included in the header file. Information that will be used only internally in the class and will not be needed by clients of the class should be included in the unpublished source file. This is yet another example of the principle of least privilege.

9.5 Access Functions and Utility Functions

Access functions can read or display data. Another common use for access functions is to test the truth or falsity of conditions—such functions are often called **predicate functions**. An example of a predicate function would be an isEmpty function for any container class—a class capable of holding many objects, like a vector. A program might test isEmpty before attempting to read another item from the container object. An isFull predicate function might test a container-class object to determine whether it has no additional room. Useful predicate functions for our Time class might be isAM and isPM.

The program of Figs. 9.5–9.7 demonstrates the notion of a utility function (also called a **helper function**). A utility function is not part of a class's public interface; rather, it's a private member function that supports the operation of the class's public member functions. Utility functions are not intended to be used by clients of a class (but can be used by friends of a class, as we'll see in Chapter 10).

Class SalesPerson (Fig. 9.5) declares an array of 12 monthly sales figures (line 17) and the prototypes for the class's constructor and member functions that manipulate the array.

```
1   // Fig. 9.5: SalesPerson.h
2   // SalesPerson class definition.
3   // Member functions defined in SalesPerson.cpp.
4   #ifndef SALESP_H
5   #define SALESP_H
6
7   class SalesPerson
8   {
9   public:
10     static const int monthsPerYear = 12; // months in one year
11     SalesPerson(); // constructor
12     void getSalesFromUser(); // input sales from keyboard
13     void setSales( int, double ); // set sales for a specific month
14     void printAnnualSales(); // summarize and print sales
15   private:
16     double totalAnnualSales(); // prototype for utility function
17     double sales[ monthsPerYear ]; // 12 monthly sales figures
18   }; // end class SalesPerson
19
20   #endif
```

Fig. 9.5 | SalesPerson class definition.

In Fig. 9.6, the SalesPerson constructor (lines 9–13) initializes array sales to zero. The public member function setSales (lines 30–37) sets the sales figure for one month in array sales. The public member function printAnnualSales (lines 40–45) prints the total sales for the last 12 months. The private utility function totalAnnualSales (lines 48–56) totals the 12 monthly sales figures for the benefit of printAnnualSales. Member function printAnnualSales edits the sales figures into monetary format.

```cpp
1    // Fig. 9.6: SalesPerson.cpp
2    // SalesPerson class member-function definitions.
3    #include <iostream>
4    #include <iomanip>
5    #include "SalesPerson.h" // include SalesPerson class definition
6    using namespace std;
7
8    // initialize elements of array sales to 0.0
9    SalesPerson::SalesPerson()
10   {
11      for ( int i = 0; i < monthsPerYear; i++ )
12         sales[ i ] = 0.0;
13   } // end SalesPerson constructor
14
15   // get 12 sales figures from the user at the keyboard
16   void SalesPerson::getSalesFromUser()
17   {
18      double salesFigure;
19
20      for ( int i = 1; i <= monthsPerYear; i++ )
21      {
22         cout << "Enter sales amount for month " << i << ": ";
23         cin >> salesFigure;
24         setSales( i, salesFigure );
25      } // end for
26   } // end function getSalesFromUser
27
28   // set one of the 12 monthly sales figures; function subtracts
29   // one from month value for proper subscript in sales array
30   void SalesPerson::setSales( int month, double amount )
31   {
32      // test for valid month and amount values
33      if ( month >= 1 && month <= monthsPerYear && amount > 0 )
34         sales[ month - 1 ] = amount; // adjust for subscripts 0-11
35      else // invalid month or amount value
36         cout << "Invalid month or sales figure" << endl;
37   } // end function setSales
38
39   // print total annual sales (with the help of utility function)
40   void SalesPerson::printAnnualSales()
41   {
42      cout << setprecision( 2 ) << fixed
43         << "\nThe total annual sales are: $"
44         << totalAnnualSales() << endl; // call utility function
45   } // end function printAnnualSales
46
```

Fig. 9.6 | SalesPerson class member-function definitions. (Part 1 of 2.)

```
47    // private utility function to total annual sales
48    double SalesPerson::totalAnnualSales()
49    {
50       double total = 0.0; // initialize total
51
52       for ( int i = 0; i < monthsPerYear; i++ ) // summarize sales results
53          total += sales[ i ]; // add month i sales to total
54
55       return total;
56    } // end function totalAnnualSales
```

Fig. 9.6 | `SalesPerson` class member-function definitions. (Part 2 of 2.)

In Fig. 9.7, notice that the application's `main` function includes only a simple sequence of member-function calls—there are no control statements. The logic of manipulating the `sales` array is completely encapsulated in class `SalesPerson`'s member functions.

Software Engineering Observation 9.8

A phenomenon of object-oriented programming is that once a class is defined, creating and manipulating objects of that class often involve issuing only a simple sequence of member-function calls—few, if any, control statements are needed. By contrast, it's common to have control statements in the implementation of a class's member functions.

```
1    // Fig. 9.7: fig09_07.cpp
2    // Utility function demonstration.
3    // Compile this program with SalesPerson.cpp
4
5    // include SalesPerson class definition from SalesPerson.h
6    #include "SalesPerson.h"
7
8    int main()
9    {
10      SalesPerson s; // create SalesPerson object s
11
12      s.getSalesFromUser(); // note simple sequential code; there are
13      s.printAnnualSales(); // no control statements in main
14   } // end main
```

```
Enter sales amount for month 1: 5314.76
Enter sales amount for month 2: 4292.38
Enter sales amount for month 3: 4589.83
Enter sales amount for month 4: 5534.03
Enter sales amount for month 5: 4376.34
Enter sales amount for month 6: 5698.45
Enter sales amount for month 7: 4439.22
Enter sales amount for month 8: 5893.57
Enter sales amount for month 9: 4909.67
Enter sales amount for month 10: 5123.45
```

Fig. 9.7 | Utility function demonstration. (Part 1 of 2.)

```
Enter sales amount for month 11: 4024.97
Enter sales amount for month 12: 5923.92

The total annual sales are: $60120.59
```

Fig. 9.7 | Utility function demonstration. (Part 2 of 2.)

9.6 Time Class Case Study: Constructors with Default Arguments

The program of Figs. 9.8–9.10 enhances class Time to demonstrate how arguments are implicitly passed to a constructor. The constructor defined in Fig. 9.2 initialized hour, minute and second to 0 (i.e., midnight in universal time). Like other functions, constructors can specify default arguments. Line 13 of Fig. 9.8 declares the Time constructor to include default arguments, specifying a default value of zero for each argument passed to the constructor. In Fig. 9.9, lines 10–13 define the new version of the Time constructor that receives values for parameters hr, min and sec that will be used to initialize private data members hour, minute and second, respectively. Class Time provides *set* and *get* functions for each data member. The Time constructor now calls setTime, which calls the setHour, setMinute and setSecond functions to validate and assign values to the data members. The default arguments to the constructor ensure that, even if no values are provided in a constructor call, the constructor still initializes the data members to maintain the Time object in a consistent state. A constructor that defaults all its arguments is also a default constructor—i.e., a constructor that can be invoked with no arguments. There can be at most one default constructor per class.

```
1   // Fig. 9.8: Time.h
2   // Time class containing a constructor with default arguments.
3   // Member functions defined in Time.cpp.
4
5   // prevent multiple inclusions of header file
6   #ifndef TIME_H
7   #define TIME_H
8
9   // Time abstract data type definition
10  class Time
11  {
12  public:
13     Time( int = 0, int = 0, int = 0 ); // default constructor
14
15     // set functions
16     void setTime( int, int, int ); // set hour, minute, second
17     void setHour( int ); // set hour (after validation)
18     void setMinute( int ); // set minute (after validation)
19     void setSecond( int ); // set second (after validation)
20
21     // get functions
22     int getHour(); // return hour
```

Fig. 9.8 | Time class containing a constructor with default arguments. (Part 1 of 2.)

```
23        int getMinute(); // return minute
24        int getSecond(); // return second
25
26        void printUniversal(); // output time in universal-time format
27        void printStandard(); // output time in standard-time format
28     private:
29        int hour; // 0 - 23 (24-hour clock format)
30        int minute; // 0 - 59
31        int second; // 0 - 59
32     }; // end class Time
33
34     #endif
```

Fig. 9.8 | Time class containing a constructor with default arguments. (Part 2 of 2.)

In Fig. 9.9, line 12 of the constructor calls member function setTime with the values passed to the constructor (or the default values). Function setTime calls setHour to ensure that the value supplied for hour is in the range 0–23, then calls setMinute and setSecond to ensure that the values for minute and second are each in the range 0–59. If a value is out of range, that value is set to zero (to ensure that each data member remains in a consistent state). In Chapter 16, Exception Handling, we use exceptions to indicate when a value is out of range, rather than simply assigning a default consistent value.

```
 1     // Fig. 9.9: Time.cpp
 2     // Member-function definitions for class Time.
 3     #include <iostream>
 4     #include <iomanip>
 5     #include "Time.h" // include definition of class Time from Time.h
 6     using namespace std;
 7
 8     // Time constructor initializes each data member to zero;
 9     // ensures that Time objects start in a consistent state
10     Time::Time( int hr, int min, int sec )
11     {
12        setTime( hr, min, sec ); // validate and set time
13     } // end Time constructor
14
15     // set new Time value using universal time; ensure that
16     // the data remains consistent by setting invalid values to zero
17     void Time::setTime( int h, int m, int s )
18     {
19        setHour( h ); // set private field hour
20        setMinute( m ); // set private field minute
21        setSecond( s ); // set private field second
22     } // end function setTime
23
24     // set hour value
25     void Time::setHour( int h )
26     {
```

Fig. 9.9 | Time class member-function definitions including a constructor that takes arguments. (Part 1 of 2.)

```
27        hour = ( h >= 0 && h < 24 ) ? h : 0; // validate hour
28    } // end function setHour
29
30    // set minute value
31    void Time::setMinute( int m )
32    {
33        minute = ( m >= 0 && m < 60 ) ? m : 0; // validate minute
34    } // end function setMinute
35
36    // set second value
37    void Time::setSecond( int s )
38    {
39        second = ( s >= 0 && s < 60 ) ? s : 0; // validate second
40    } // end function setSecond
41
42    // return hour value
43    int Time::getHour()
44    {
45        return hour;
46    } // end function getHour
47
48    // return minute value
49    int Time::getMinute()
50    {
51        return minute;
52    } // end function getMinute
53
54    // return second value
55    int Time::getSecond()
56    {
57        return second;
58    } // end function getSecond
59
60    // print Time in universal-time format (HH:MM:SS)
61    void Time::printUniversal()
62    {
63        cout << setfill( '0' ) << setw( 2 ) << getHour() << ":"
64            << setw( 2 ) << getMinute() << ":" << setw( 2 ) << getSecond();
65    } // end function printUniversal
66
67    // print Time in standard-time format (HH:MM:SS AM or PM)
68    void Time::printStandard()
69    {
70        cout << ( ( getHour() == 0 || getHour() == 12 ) ? 12 : getHour() % 12 )
71            << ":" << setfill( '0' ) << setw( 2 ) << getMinute()
72            << ":" << setw( 2 ) << getSecond() << ( hour < 12 ? " AM" : " PM" );
73    } // end function printStandard
```

Fig. 9.9 | Time class member-function definitions including a constructor that takes arguments. (Part 2 of 2.)

The Time constructor could be written to include the same statements as member function setTime, or even the individual statements in the setHour, setMinute and set-Second functions. Calling setHour, setMinute and setSecond from the constructor may be slightly more efficient because the extra call to setTime would be eliminated. Similarly, copying the code from lines 27, 33 and 39 into constructor would eliminate the overhead of calling setTime, setHour, setMinute and setSecond. Coding the Time constructor or member function setTime as a copy of the code in lines 27, 33 and 39 would make maintenance of this class more difficult. If the implementations of setHour, setMinute and setSecond were to change, the implementation of any member function that duplicates lines 27, 33 and 39 would have to change accordingly. Having the Time constructor call setTime and having setTime call setHour, setMinute and setSecond enables us to limit the changes to code that validates the hour, minute or second to the corresponding *set* function. This reduces the likelihood of errors when altering the class's implementation. Also, the performance of the Time constructor and setTime can be enhanced by explicitly declaring them inline or by defining them in the class definition (which implicitly inlines the function definition).

Software Engineering Observation 9.9

If a member function of a class already provides all or part of the functionality required by a constructor (or other member function) of the class, call that member function from the constructor (or other member function). This simplifies the maintenance of the code and reduces the likelihood of an error if the implementation of the code is modified. As a general rule: Avoid repeating code.

Software Engineering Observation 9.10

Any change to the default argument values of a function requires the client code to be recompiled (to ensure that the program still functions correctly).

Function main in Fig. 9.10 initializes five Time objects—one with all three arguments defaulted in the implicit constructor call (line 9), one with one argument specified (line 10), one with two arguments specified (line 11), one with three arguments specified (line 12) and one with three invalid arguments specified (line 13). Then the program displays each object in universal-time and standard-time formats.

```
1   // Fig. 9.10: fig09_10.cpp
2   // Demonstrating a default constructor for class Time.
3   #include <iostream>
4   #include "Time.h" // include definition of class Time from Time.h
5   using namespace std;
6
7   int main()
8   {
9      Time t1; // all arguments defaulted
10     Time t2( 2 ); // hour specified; minute and second defaulted
11     Time t3( 21, 34 ); // hour and minute specified; second defaulted
12     Time t4( 12, 25, 42 ); // hour, minute and second specified
13     Time t5( 27, 74, 99 ); // all bad values specified
14
15     cout << "Constructed with:\n\nt1: all arguments defaulted\n   ";
16     t1.printUniversal(); // 00:00:00
17     cout << "\n   ";
```

Fig. 9.10 | Constructor with default arguments. (Part 1 of 2.)

```
18      t1.printStandard(); // 12:00:00 AM
19
20      cout << "\n\nt2: hour specified; minute and second defaulted\n   ";
21      t2.printUniversal(); // 02:00:00
22      cout << "\n   ";
23      t2.printStandard(); // 2:00:00 AM
24
25      cout << "\n\nt3: hour and minute specified; second defaulted\n   ";
26      t3.printUniversal(); // 21:34:00
27      cout << "\n   ";
28      t3.printStandard(); // 9:34:00 PM
29
30      cout << "\n\nt4: hour, minute and second specified\n   ";
31      t4.printUniversal(); // 12:25:42
32      cout << "\n   ";
33      t4.printStandard(); // 12:25:42 PM
34
35      cout << "\n\nt5: all invalid values specified\n   ";
36      t5.printUniversal(); // 00:00:00
37      cout << "\n   ";
38      t5.printStandard(); // 12:00:00 AM
39      cout << endl;
40   } // end main
```

```
Constructed with:

t1: all arguments defaulted
   00:00:00
   12:00:00 AM

t2: hour specified; minute and second defaulted
   02:00:00
   2:00:00 AM

t3: hour and minute specified; second defaulted
   21:34:00
   9:34:00 PM

t4: hour, minute and second specified
   12:25:42
   12:25:42 PM

t5: all invalid values specified
   00:00:00
   12:00:00 AM
```

Fig. 9.10 | Constructor with default arguments. (Part 2 of 2.)

*Notes Regarding Class **Time**'s* Set *and* Get *Functions and Constructor*

Time's *set* and *get* functions are called throughout the class's body. In particular, function setTime (lines 17–22 of Fig. 9.9) calls functions setHour, setMinute and setSecond, and functions printUniversal and printStandard call functions getHour, getMinute and getSecond in line 63–64 and lines 70–72, respectively. In each case, these functions could have accessed the class's private data directly. However, consider changing the representation of the time from three int values (requiring 12 bytes of memory) to a single int value representing the total number of seconds that have elapsed since midnight (requiring only four bytes of memory). If we made such a change, only the bodies of the functions that access the private data directly would need to change—in particular, the individual *set* and *get* functions for the hour, minute and second. There would be no need to modify the bodies of functions setTime, printUniversal or printStandard, because they do not access the data directly. Designing the class in this manner reduces the likelihood of programming errors when altering the class's implementation.

Similarly, the Time constructor could be written to include a copy of the appropriate statements from function setTime. Doing so may be slightly more efficient, because the extra constructor call and call to setTime are eliminated. However, duplicating statements in multiple functions or constructors makes changing the class's internal data representation more difficult. Having the Time constructor call function setTime directly requires any changes to the implementation of setTime to be made only once.

Common Programming Error 9.2

A constructor can call other member functions of the class, such as set or get functions, but because the constructor is initializing the object, the data members may not yet be in a consistent state. Using data members before they have been properly initialized can cause logic errors.

9.7 Destructors

A **destructor** is another type of special member function. The name of the destructor for a class is the **tilde character** (~) followed by the class name. This naming convention has intuitive appeal, because as we'll see in a later chapter, the tilde operator is the bitwise complement operator, and, in a sense, the destructor is the complement of the constructor. A destructor is often referred to with the abbreviation "dtor" in the literature. We prefer not to use this abbreviation.

A class's destructor is called implicitly when an object is destroyed. This occurs, for example, as an automatic object is destroyed when program execution leaves the scope in which that object was instantiated. *The destructor itself does not actually release the object's memory*—it performs **termination housekeeping** before the object's memory is reclaimed, so the memory may be reused to hold new objects.

A destructor receives no parameters and returns no value. A destructor may not specify a return type—not even void. A class may have only one destructor—destructor overloading is not allowed. A destructor must be public.

Common Programming Error 9.3

It's a syntax error to attempt to pass arguments to a destructor, to specify a return type for a destructor (even void cannot be specified), to return values from a destructor or to overload a destructor.

Even though destructors have not been provided for the classes presented so far, every class has a destructor. If you do not explicitly provide a destructor, the compiler creates an "empty" destructor. [*Note:* We'll see that such an implicitly created destructor does, in fact, perform important operations on objects that are created through composition

(Chapter 10) and inheritance (Chapter 12).] In Chapter 11, we'll build destructors appropriate for classes whose objects contain dynamically allocated memory (e.g., for arrays and strings) or use other system resources (e.g., files on disk, which we study in Chapter 17). We discuss how to dynamically allocate and deallocate memory in Chapter 10.

> **Software Engineering Observation 9.11**
>
> *As we'll see in the remainder of the book, constructors and destructors have much greater prominence in C++ and object-oriented programming than is possible to convey after only our brief introduction here.*

9.8 When Constructors and Destructors Are Called

Constructors and destructors are called implicitly by the compiler. The order in which these function calls occur depends on the order in which execution enters and leaves the scopes where the objects are instantiated. Generally, destructor calls are made in the reverse order of the corresponding constructor calls, but as we'll see in Figs. 9.11–9.13, the storage classes of objects can alter the order in which destructors are called.

Constructors are called for objects defined in global scope before any other function (including main) in that file begins execution (although the order of execution of global object constructors between files is not guaranteed). The corresponding destructors are called when main terminates. Function **exit** forces a program to terminate immediately and does not execute the destructors of automatic objects. The function often is used to terminate a program when an error is detected in the input or if a file to be processed by the program cannot be opened. Function **abort** performs similarly to function exit but forces the program to terminate immediately, without allowing the destructors of any objects to be called. Function abort is usually used to indicate an abnormal termination of the program. (See Appendix F, for more information on functions exit and abort.)

The constructor for an automatic local object is called when execution reaches the point where that object is defined—the corresponding destructor is called when execution leaves the object's scope (i.e., the block in which that object is defined has finished executing). Constructors and destructors for automatic objects are called each time execution enters and leaves the scope of the object. Destructors are not called for automatic objects if the program terminates with a call to function exit or function abort.

The constructor for a static local object is called only once, when execution first reaches the point where the object is defined—the corresponding destructor is called when main terminates or the program calls function exit. Global and static objects are destroyed in the reverse order of their creation. Destructors are not called for static objects if the program terminates with a call to function abort.

The program of Figs. 9.11–9.13 demonstrates the order in which constructors and destructors are called for objects of class CreateAndDestroy (Fig. 9.11 and Fig. 9.12) of various storage classes in several scopes. Each object of class CreateAndDestroy contains an integer (objectID) and a string (message) that are used in the program's output to identify the object (Fig. 9.11 lines 16–17). This mechanical example is purely for pedagogic purposes. For this reason, line 21 of the destructor in Fig. 9.12 determines whether the object being destroyed has an objectID value 1 or 6 and, if so, outputs a newline character. This line makes the program's output easier to follow.

```
1   // Fig. 9.11: CreateAndDestroy.h
2   // CreateAndDestroy class definition.
3   // Member functions defined in CreateAndDestroy.cpp.
4   #include <string>
5   using namespace std;
6
7   #ifndef CREATE_H
8   #define CREATE_H
9
10  class CreateAndDestroy
11  {
12  public:
13     CreateAndDestroy( int, string ); // constructor
14     ~CreateAndDestroy(); // destructor
15  private:
16     int objectID; // ID number for object
17     string message; // message describing object
18  }; // end class CreateAndDestroy
19
20  #endif
```

Fig. 9.11 | CreateAndDestroy class definition.

```
1   // Fig. 9.12: CreateAndDestroy.cpp
2   // CreateAndDestroy class member-function definitions.
3   #include <iostream>
4   #include "CreateAndDestroy.h"// include CreateAndDestroy class definition
5   using namespace std;
6
7   // constructor
8   CreateAndDestroy::CreateAndDestroy( int ID, string messageString )
9   {
10     objectID = ID; // set object's ID number
11     message = messageString; // set object's descriptive message
12
13     cout << "Object " << objectID << "   constructor runs   "
14        << message << endl;
15  } // end CreateAndDestroy constructor
16
17  // destructor
18  CreateAndDestroy::~CreateAndDestroy()
19  {
20     // output newline for certain objects; helps readability
21     cout << ( objectID == 1 || objectID == 6 ? "\n" : "" );
22
23     cout << "Object " << objectID << "   destructor runs   "
24        << message << endl;
25  } // end ~CreateAndDestroy destructor
```

Fig. 9.12 | CreateAndDestroy class member-function definitions.

Figure 9.13 defines object first (line 10) in global scope. Its constructor is actually called before any statements in main execute and its destructor is called at program termination after the destructors for all other objects have run.

Function main (lines 12–23) declares three objects. Objects second (line 15) and fourth (line 21) are local automatic objects, and object third (line 16) is a static local object. The constructor for each of these objects is called when execution reaches the point where that object is declared. The destructors for objects fourth then second are called (i.e., the reverse of the order in which their constructors were called) when execution reaches the end of main. Because object third is static, it exists until program termination. The destructor for object third is called before the destructor for global object first, but after all other objects are destroyed.

Function create (lines 26–33) declares three objects—fifth (line 29) and seventh (line 31) as local automatic objects, and sixth (line 30) as a static local object. The destructors for objects seventh thenfifth are called (i.e., the reverse of the order in which their constructors were called) when create terminates. Because sixth is static, it exists until program termination. The destructor for sixth is called before the destructors for third and first, but after all other objects are destroyed.

```cpp
1   // Fig. 9.13: fig09_13.cpp
2   // Demonstrating the order in which constructors and
3   // destructors are called.
4   #include <iostream>
5   #include "CreateAndDestroy.h" // include CreateAndDestroy class definition
6   using namespace std;
7
8   void create( void ); // prototype
9
10  CreateAndDestroy first( 1, "(global before main)" ); // global object
11
12  int main()
13  {
14     cout << "\nMAIN FUNCTION: EXECUTION BEGINS" << endl;
15     CreateAndDestroy second( 2, "(local automatic in main)" );
16     static CreateAndDestroy third( 3, "(local static in main)" );
17
18     create(); // call function to create objects
19
20     cout << "\nMAIN FUNCTION: EXECUTION RESUMES" << endl;
21     CreateAndDestroy fourth( 4, "(local automatic in main)" );
22     cout << "\nMAIN FUNCTION: EXECUTION ENDS" << endl;
23  } // end main
24
25  // function to create objects
26  void create( void )
27  {
28     cout << "\nCREATE FUNCTION: EXECUTION BEGINS" << endl;
29     CreateAndDestroy fifth( 5, "(local automatic in create)" );
30     static CreateAndDestroy sixth( 6, "(local static in create)" );
31     CreateAndDestroy seventh( 7, "(local automatic in create)" );
32     cout << "\nCREATE FUNCTION: EXECUTION ENDS" << endl;
33  } // end function create
```

Fig. 9.13 | Order in which constructors and destructors are called. (Part 1 of 2.)

```
Object 1    constructor runs   (global before main)

MAIN FUNCTION: EXECUTION BEGINS
Object 2    constructor runs   (local automatic in main)
Object 3    constructor runs   (local static in main)

CREATE FUNCTION: EXECUTION BEGINS
Object 5    constructor runs   (local automatic in create)
Object 6    constructor runs   (local static in create)
Object 7    constructor runs   (local automatic in create)

CREATE FUNCTION: EXECUTION ENDS
Object 7    destructor runs    (local automatic in create)
Object 5    destructor runs    (local automatic in create)

MAIN FUNCTION: EXECUTION RESUMES
Object 4    constructor runs   (local automatic in main)

MAIN FUNCTION: EXECUTION ENDS
Object 4    destructor runs    (local automatic in main)
Object 2    destructor runs    (local automatic in main)

Object 6    destructor runs    (local static in create)
Object 3    destructor runs    (local static in main)

Object 1    destructor runs    (global before main)
```

Fig. 9.13 | Order in which constructors and destructors are called. (Part 2 of 2.)

9.9 Time Class Case Study: A Subtle Trap—Returning a Reference to a private Data Member

A reference to an object is an alias for the name of the object and, hence, may be used on the left side of an assignment statement. In this context, the reference makes a perfectly acceptable *lvalue* that can receive a value. One way to use this capability (unfortunately!) is to have a public member function of a class return a reference to a private data member of that class. If a function returns a const reference, that reference cannot be used as a modifiable *lvalue*.

The program of Figs. 9.14–9.16 uses a simplified Time class (Fig. 9.14 and Fig. 9.15) to demonstrate returning a reference to a private data member with member function badSetHour (declared in Fig. 9.14 in line 15 and defined in Fig. 9.15 in lines 27–31). Such a reference return actually makes a call to member function badSetHour an alias for private data member hour! The function call can be used in any way that the private data member can be used, including as an *lvalue* in an assignment statement, thus *enabling clients of the class to clobber the class's private data at will!* The same problem would occur if a pointer to the private data were to be returned by the function.

```
1   // Fig. 9.14: Time.h
2   // Time class declaration.
3   // Member functions defined in Time.cpp
4
```

Fig. 9.14 | Time class declaration. (Part 1 of 2.)

```
 5   // prevent multiple inclusions of header file
 6   #ifndef TIME_H
 7   #define TIME_H
 8
 9   class Time
10   {
11   public:
12      Time( int = 0, int = 0, int = 0 );
13      void setTime( int, int, int );
14      int getHour();
15      int &badSetHour( int ); // DANGEROUS reference return
16   private:
17      int hour;
18      int minute;
19      int second;
20   }; // end class Time
21
22   #endif
```

Fig. 9.14 | Time class declaration. (Part 2 of 2.)

```
 1   // Fig. 9.15: Time.cpp
 2   // Time class member-function definitions.
 3   #include "Time.h" // include definition of class Time
 4
 5   // constructor function to initialize private data; calls member function
 6   // setTime to set variables; default values are 0 (see class definition)
 7   Time::Time( int hr, int min, int sec )
 8   {
 9      setTime( hr, min, sec );
10   } // end Time constructor
11
12   // set values of hour, minute and second
13   void Time::setTime( int h, int m, int s )
14   {
15      hour = ( h >= 0 && h < 24 ) ? h : 0; // validate hour
16      minute = ( m >= 0 && m < 60 ) ? m : 0; // validate minute
17      second = ( s >= 0 && s < 60 ) ? s : 0; // validate second
18   } // end function setTime
19
20   // return hour value
21   int Time::getHour()
22   {
23      return hour;
24   } // end function getHour
25
26   // POOR PRACTICE: Returning a reference to a private data member.
27   int &Time::badSetHour( int hh )
28   {
29      hour = ( hh >= 0 && hh < 24 ) ? hh : 0;
30      return hour; // DANGEROUS reference return
31   } // end function badSetHour
```

Fig. 9.15 | Time class member-function definitions.

Figure 9.16 declares Time object t (line 10) and reference hourRef (line 13), which is initialized with the reference returned by the call t.badSetHour(20). Line 15 displays the value of the alias hourRef. This shows how hourRef breaks the encapsulation of the class—statements in main should not have access to the private data of the class. Next, line 16 uses the alias to set the value of hour to 30 (an invalid value) and line 17 displays the value returned by function getHour to show that assigning a value to hourRef actually modifies the private data in the Time object t. Finally, line 21 uses the badSetHour function call itself as an *lvalue* and assigns 74 (another invalid value) to the reference returned by the function. Line 26 again displays the value returned by function getHour to show that assigning a value to the result of the function call in line 21 modifies the private data in the Time object t.

```cpp
1   // Fig. 9.16: fig09_16.cpp
2   // Demonstrating a public member function that
3   // returns a reference to a private data member.
4   #include <iostream>
5   #include "Time.h" // include definition of class Time
6   using namespace std;
7
8   int main()
9   {
10      Time t; // create Time object
11
12      // initialize hourRef with the reference returned by badSetHour
13      int &hourRef = t.badSetHour( 20 ); // 20 is a valid hour
14
15      cout << "Valid hour before modification: " << hourRef;
16      hourRef = 30; // use hourRef to set invalid value in Time object t
17      cout << "\nInvalid hour after modification: " << t.getHour();
18
19      // Dangerous: Function call that returns
20      // a reference can be used as an lvalue!
21      t.badSetHour( 12 ) = 74; // assign another invalid value to hour
22
23      cout << "\n\n*******************************************************\n"
24         << "POOR PROGRAMMING PRACTICE!!!!!!!!\n"
25         << "t.badSetHour( 12 ) as an lvalue, invalid hour: "
26         << t.getHour()
27         << "\n*******************************************************" << endl;
28   } // end main
```

```
Valid hour before modification: 20
Invalid hour after modification: 30

*******************************************************
POOR PROGRAMMING PRACTICE!!!!!!!!
t.badSetHour( 12 ) as an lvalue, invalid hour: 74
*******************************************************
```

Fig. 9.16 | Returning a reference to a private data member.

Error-Prevention Tip 9.4
*Returning a reference or a pointer to a private data member breaks the encapsulation of
the class and makes the client code dependent on the representation of the class's data; this
is a dangerous practice that should be avoided.*

9.10 Default Memberwise Assignment

The assignment operator (=) can be used to assign an object to another object of the
same type. By default, such assignment is performed by **memberwise assignment**—each
data member of the object on the right of the assignment operator is assigned individually to the same data member in the object on the left of the assignment operator.
Figures 9.17–9.18 define class Date for use in this example. Line 18 of Fig. 9.19 uses
default memberwise assignment to assign the data members of Date object date1 to the
corresponding data members of Date object date2. In this case, the month member of
date1 is assigned to the month member of date2, the day member of date1 is assigned
to the day member of date2 and the year member of date1 is assigned to the year member of date2. [*Caution:* Memberwise assignment can cause serious problems when used
with a class whose data members contain pointers to dynamically allocated memory; we
discuss these problems in Chapter 11 and show how to deal with them.] The Date constructor does not contain any error checking; we leave this to the exercises.

```
1   // Fig. 9.17: Date.h
2   // Date class declaration.  Member functions are defined in Date.cpp.
3
4   // prevent multiple inclusions of header file
5   #ifndef DATE_H
6   #define DATE_H
7
8   // class Date definition
9   class Date
10  {
11  public:
12     Date( int = 1, int = 1, int = 2000 ); // default constructor
13     void print();
14  private:
15     int month;
16     int day;
17     int year;
18  }; // end class Date
19
20  #endif
```

Fig. 9.17 | Date class declaration.

```
1   // Fig. 9.18: Date.cpp
2   // Date class member-function definitions.
3   #include <iostream>
4   #include "Date.h" // include definition of class Date from Date.h
```

Fig. 9.18 | Date class member-function definitions. (Part 1 of 2.)

```
5    using namespace std;
6
7    // Date constructor (should do range checking)
8    Date::Date( int m, int d, int y )
9    {
10       month = m;
11       day = d;
12       year = y;
13   } // end constructor Date
14
15   // print Date in the format mm/dd/yyyy
16   void Date::print()
17   {
18       cout << month << '/' << day << '/' << year;
19   } // end function print
```

Fig. 9.18 | Date class member-function definitions. (Part 2 of 2.)

```
1    // Fig. 9.19: fig09_19.cpp
2    // Demonstrating that class objects can be assigned
3    // to each other using default memberwise assignment.
4    #include <iostream>
5    #include "Date.h" // include definition of class Date from Date.h
6    using namespace std;
7
8    int main()
9    {
10       Date date1( 7, 4, 2004 );
11       Date date2; // date2 defaults to 1/1/2000
12
13       cout << "date1 = ";
14       date1.print();
15       cout << "\ndate2 = ";
16       date2.print();
17
18       date2 = date1; // default memberwise assignment
19
20       cout << "\n\nAfter default memberwise assignment, date2 = ";
21       date2.print();
22       cout << endl;
23   } // end main
```

```
date1 = 7/4/2004
date2 = 1/1/2000
After default memberwise assignment, date2 = 7/4/2004
```

Fig. 9.19 | Default memberwise assignment.

Objects may be passed as function arguments and may be returned from functions. Such passing and returning is performed using pass-by-value by default—a copy of the object is passed or returned. In such cases, C++ creates a new object and uses a **copy constructor** to copy the original object's values into the new object. For each class, the compiler provides a default copy constructor that copies each member of the original object into the corresponding member of the new object. Like memberwise assignment, copy constructors can cause serious problems when used with a class whose data members contain pointers to dynamically allocated memory. Chapter 11 discusses how to define customized copy constructors that properly copy objects containing pointers to dynamically allocated memory.

> **Performance Tip 9.3**
>
> *Passing an object by value is good from a security standpoint, because the called function has no access to the original object in the caller, but pass-by-value can degrade performance when making a copy of a large object. An object can be passed by reference by passing either a pointer or a reference to the object. Pass-by-reference offers good performance but is weaker from a security standpoint, because the called function is given access to the original object. Pass-by-const-reference is a safe, good-performing alternative (this can be implemented with a const reference parameter or with a pointer-to-const-data parameter).*

9.11 Wrap-Up

This chapter deepened our coverage of classes, using a rich Time class case study to introduce several new features. You saw that member functions are usually shorter than global functions because member functions can directly access an object's data members, so the member functions can receive fewer arguments than functions in procedural programming languages. You learned how to use the arrow operator to access an object's members via a pointer of the object's class type.

You learned that member functions have class scope—the member function's name is known only to the class's other members unless referred to via an object of the class, a reference to an object of the class, a pointer to an object of the class or the binary scope resolution operator. We also discussed access functions (commonly used to retrieve the values of data members or to test the truth or falsity of conditions) and utility functions (private member functions that support the operation of the class's public member functions).

You learned that a constructor can specify default arguments that enable it to be called in a variety of ways. You also learned that any constructor that can be called with no arguments is a default constructor and that there can be at most one default constructor per class. We discussed destructors and their purpose of performing termination housekeeping on an object of a class before that object is destroyed. We also demonstrated the order in which an object's constructors and destructors are called.

We demonstrated the problems that can occur when a member function returns a reference to a private data member, which breaks the encapsulation of the class. We also showed that objects of the same type can be assigned to one another using default memberwise assignment. We also discussed the benefits of using class libraries to enhance the speed with which code can be created and to increase the quality of software.

Chapter 10 presents additional class features. We'll demonstrate how const can be used to indicate that a member function does not modify an object of a class. You'll build classes with composition, which allows a class to contain objects of other classes as members. We'll show how a class can allow so-called "friend" functions to access the class's non-public members. We'll also show how a class's non-static member functions can use a special pointer named this to access an object's members.

Summary

Section 9.2 *Time Class Case Study*
- Preprocessor directives `#ifndef` (which means "if not defined") and `#endif` are used to prevent multiple inclusions of a header file. If the code between these directives has not previously been included in an application, `#define` defines a name that can be used to prevent future inclusions, and the code is included in the source code file.
- Data members cannot be initialized where they're declared in the class body (except for a class's `static const` data members of integral or `enum` types). Initialize these data members in the class's constructor (as there is no default initialization for data members of fundamental types).
- Stream manipulator `setfill` specifies the fill character that is displayed when an integer is output in a field that is wider than the number of digits in the value.
- By default, the fill characters appear before the digits in the number.
- Stream manipulator `setfill` is a "sticky" setting, meaning that once the fill character is set, it applies for all subsequent fields being printed.
- Even though a member function declared in a class definition may be defined outside that class definition (and "tied" to the class via the binary scope resolution operator), that member function is still within that class's scope.
- If a member function is defined in the body of a class definition, the C++ compiler attempts to inline calls to the member function.
- Classes can include objects of other classes as members or they may be derived from other classes that provide attributes and behaviors the new classes can use.

Section 9.3 *Class Scope and Accessing Class Members*
- A class's data members and member functions belong to that class's scope.
- Nonmember functions are defined at global namespace scope.
- Within a class's scope, class members are immediately accessible by all of that class's member functions and can be referenced by name.
- Outside a class's scope, class members are referenced through one of the handles on an object— an object name, a reference to an object or a pointer to an object.
- Member functions of a class can be overloaded, but only by other member functions of that class.
- To overload a member function, provide in the class definition a prototype for each version of the overloaded function, and provide a separate definition for each version of the function.
- Variables declared in a member function have local scope and are known only to that function.
- If a member function defines a variable with the same name as a variable with class scope, the class-scope variable is hidden by the block-scope variable in the local scope.
- The dot member selection operator (`.`) is preceded by an object's name or by a reference to an object to access the object's `public` members.
- The arrow member selection operator (`->`) is preceded by a pointer to an object to access that object's `public` members.

Section 9.4 *Separating Interface from Implementation*
- Header files contain some portions of a class's implementation and hints about others. Inline member functions, for example, should be in a header file, so that when the compiler compiles a client, the client can include the `inline` function definition in place.
- A class's `private` members that are listed in the class definition in the header file are visible to clients, even though the clients may not access the `private` members.

Section 9.5 Access Functions and Utility Functions

- A utility function is a `private` member function that supports the operation of the class's `public` member functions. Utility functions are not intended to be used by clients of a class.

Section 9.6 **Time** *Class Case Study: Constructors with Default Arguments*

- Like other functions, constructors can specify default arguments.

Section 9.7 Destructors

- A class's destructor is called implicitly when an object of the class is destroyed.

- The name of the destructor for a class is the tilde (~) character followed by the class name.

- A destructor does not release an object's storage—it performs termination housekeeping before the system reclaims an object's memory, so the memory may be reused to hold new objects.

- A destructor receives no parameters and returns no value. A class may have only one destructor.

- If you do not explicitly provide a destructor, the compiler creates an "empty" destructor, so every class has exactly one destructor.

Section 9.8 When Constructors and Destructors Are Called

- The order in which constructors and destructors are called depends on the order in which execution enters and leaves the scopes where the objects are instantiated.

- Generally, destructor calls are made in the reverse order of the corresponding constructor calls, but the storage classes of objects can alter the order in which destructors are called.

Section 9.9 **Time** *Class Case Study: A Subtle Trap—Returning a Reference to a* **private** *Data Member*

- A reference to an object is an alias for the name of the object and, hence, may be used on the left side of an assignment statement. In this context, the reference makes a perfectly acceptable *lvalue* that can receive a value.

- If the function returns a `const` reference, then the reference cannot be used as a modifiable *lvalue*.

Section 9.10 Default Memberwise Assignment

- The assignment operator (=) can be used to assign an object to another object of the same type. By default, such assignment is performed by memberwise assignment.

- Objects may be passed by value to or returned by value from functions. C++ creates a new object and uses a copy constructor to copy the original object's values into the new object.

- For each class, the compiler provides a default copy constructor that copies each member of the original object into the corresponding member of the new object.

Terminology

predicate function 406
preprocessor wrapper 398
setfill parameterized stream manipulator 400

termination housekeeping 414
tilde character (~) in a destructor name 414

Self-Review Exercises

9.1 Fill in the blanks in each of the following:

a) Class members are accessed via the _____ operator in conjunction with the name of an object (or reference to an object) of the class or via the _____ operator in conjunction with a pointer to an object of the class.

b) Class members specified as _____ are accessible only to member functions of the class and friends of the class.

c) Class members specified as _____ are accessible anywhere an object of the class is in scope.

d) _____ can be used to assign an object of a class to another object of the same class.

9.2 Find the error(s) in each of the following and explain how to correct it (them):

a) Assume the following prototype is declared in class Time:

```
void ~Time( int );
```

b) The following is a partial definition of class Time:

```
class Time
{
public:
    // function prototypes

private:
    int hour = 0;
    int minute = 0;
    int second = 0;
}; // end class Time
```

c) Assume the following prototype is declared in class Employee:

```
int Employee( string, string );
```

Answers to Self-Review Exercises

9.1 a) dot (.), arrow (->). b) private. c) public. d) Default memberwise assignment (performed by the assignment operator).

9.2 a) *Error:* Destructors are not allowed to return values (or even specify a return type) or take arguments.
Correction: Remove the return type void and the parameter int from the declaration.

b) *Error:* Members cannot be explicitly initialized in the class definition.
Correction: Remove the explicit initialization from the class definition and initialize the data members in a constructor.

c) *Error:* Constructors are not allowed to return values.
Correction: Remove the return type int from the declaration.

Exercises

9.3 What's the purpose of the scope resolution operator?

9.4 *(Enhancing Class Time)* Provide a constructor that is capable of using the current time from the time and localtime functions—declared in the C++ Standard Library header <ctime>—to initialize an object of the Time class.

9.5   *(Complex Class)* Create a class called Complex for performing arithmetic with complex numbers. Write a program to test your class. Complex numbers have the form

    realPart + imaginaryPart * i

where *i* is

$$\sqrt{-1}$$

Use double variables to represent the private data of the class. Provide a constructor that enables an object of this class to be initialized when it's declared. The constructor should contain default values in case no initializers are provided. Provide public member functions that perform the following tasks:

a) Adding two Complex numbers: The real parts are added together and the imaginary parts are added together.

b) Subtracting two Complex numbers: The real part of the right operand is subtracted from the real part of the left operand, and the imaginary part of the right operand is subtracted from the imaginary part of the left operand.

c) Printing Complex numbers in the form (a, b), where a is the real part and b is the imaginary part.

9.6   *(Rational Class)* Create a class called Rational for performing arithmetic with fractions. Write a program to test your class.

Use integer variables to represent the private data of the class—the numerator and the denominator. Provide a constructor that enables an object of this class to be initialized when it's declared. The constructor should contain default values in case no initializers are provided and should store the fraction in reduced form. For example, the fraction

$$\frac{2}{4}$$

would be stored in the object as 1 in the numerator and 2 in the denominator. Provide public member functions that perform each of the following tasks:

a) Adding two Rational numbers. The result should be stored in reduced form.

b) Subtracting two Rational numbers. The result should be stored in reduced form.

c) Multiplying two Rational numbers. The result should be stored in reduced form.

d) Dividing two Rational numbers. The result should be stored in reduced form.

e) Printing Rational numbers in the form a/b, where a is the numerator and b is the denominator.

f) Printing Rational numbers in floating-point format.

9.7   *(Enhancing Class Time)* Modify the Time class of Figs. 9.8–9.9 to include a tick member function that increments the time stored in a Time object by one second. The Time object should always remain in a consistent state. Write a program that tests the tick member function in a loop that prints the time in standard format during each iteration of the loop to illustrate that the tick member function works correctly. Be sure to test the following cases:

a) Incrementing into the next minute.

b) Incrementing into the next hour.

c) Incrementing into the next day (i.e., 11:59:59 PM to 12:00:00 AM).

9.8   *(Enhancing Class Date)* Modify the Date class of Figs. 9.17–9.18 to perform error checking on the initializer values for data members month, day and year. Also, provide a member function nextDay to increment the day by one. The Date object should always remain in a consistent state. Write a program that tests function nextDay in a loop that prints the date during each iteration to illustrate that nextDay works correctly. Be sure to test the following cases:

a) Incrementing into the next month.

b) Incrementing into the next year.

9.9 *(Combining Class* Time *and Class* Date*)* Combine the modified Time class of Exercise 9.7 and the modified Date class of Exercise 9.8 into one class called DateAndTime. (In Chapter 12, we'll discuss inheritance, which will enable us to accomplish this task quickly without modifying the existing class definitions.) Modify the tick function to call the nextDay function if the time increments into the next day. Modify functions printStandard and printUniversal to output the date and time. Write a program to test the new class DateAndTime. Specifically, test incrementing the time into the next day.

9.10 *(Returning Error Indicators from Class* Time*'s* set *Functions)* Modify the *set* functions in the Time class of Figs. 9.8–9.9 to return appropriate error values if an attempt is made to *set* a data member of an object of class Time to an invalid value. Write a program that tests your new version of class Time. Display error messages when *set* functions return error values.

9.11 *(*Rectangle *Class)* Create a class Rectangle with attributes length and width, each of which defaults to 1. Provide member functions that calculate the perimeter and the area of the rectangle. Also, provide *set* and *get* functions for the length and width attributes. The *set* functions should verify that length and width are each floating-point numbers larger than 0.0 and less than 20.0.

9.12 *(Enhancing Class* Rectangle*)* Create a more sophisticated Rectangle class than the one you created in Exercise 9.11. This class stores only the Cartesian coordinates of the four corners of the rectangle. The constructor calls a *set* function that accepts four sets of coordinates and verifies that each of these is in the first quadrant with no single *x*- or *y*-coordinate larger than 20.0. The *set* function also verifies that the supplied coordinates do, in fact, specify a rectangle. Provide member functions that calculate the length, width, perimeter and area. The length is the larger of the two dimensions. Include a predicate function square that determines whether the rectangle is a square.

9.13 *(Enhancing Class* Rectangle*)* Modify class Rectangle from Exercise 9.12 to include a draw function that displays the rectangle inside a 25-by-25 box enclosing the portion of the first quadrant in which the rectangle resides. Include a setFillCharacter function to specify the character out of which the body of the rectangle will be drawn. Include a setPerimeterCharacter function to specify the character that will be used to draw the border of the rectangle. If you feel ambitious, you might include functions to scale the size of the rectangle, rotate it, and move it around within the designated portion of the first quadrant.

9.14 *(*HugeInteger *Class)* Create a class HugeInteger that uses a 40-element array of digits to store integers as large as 40 digits each. Provide member functions input, output, add and subtract. For comparing HugeInteger objects, provide functions isEqualTo, isNotEqualTo, isGreaterThan, isLessThan, isGreaterThanOrEqualTo and isLessThanOrEqualTo—each of these is a "predicate" function that simply returns true if the relationship holds between the two HugeIntegers and returns false if the relationship does not hold. Also, provide a predicate function isZero. If you feel ambitious, provide member functions multiply, divide and modulus.

9.15 *(*TicTacToe *Class)* Create a class TicTacToe that will enable you to write a complete program to play the game of tic-tac-toe. The class contains as private data a 3-by-3 two-dimensional array of integers. The constructor should initialize the empty board to all zeros. Allow two human players. Wherever the first player moves, place a 1 in the specified square. Place a 2 wherever the second player moves. Each move must be to an empty square. After each move, determine whether the game has been won or is a draw. If you feel ambitious, modify your program so that the computer makes the moves for one of the players. Also, allow the player to specify whether he or she wants to go first or second. If you feel exceptionally ambitious, develop a program that will play three-dimensional tic-tac-toe on a 4-by-4-by-4 board. [*Caution:* This is an extremely challenging project that could take many weeks of effort!]

Classes: A Deeper Look, Part 2

10

But what, to serve our private ends,
Forbids the cheating of our friends?
—Charles Churchill

Instead of this absurd division into sexes they ought to class people as static and dynamic.
—Evelyn Waugh

Have no friends not equal to yourself.
—Confucius

Objectives

In this chapter you'll learn:

- To specify **const** (constant) objects and **const** member functions.

- To create objects composed of other objects.

- To use **friend** functions and **friend** classes.

- To use the **this** pointer.

- To use **static** data members and member functions.

- The concept of a container class.

- The notion of iterator classes that walk through the elements of container classes.

- To use proxy classes to hide implementation details from a class's clients.

10.1 Introduction

In this chapter, we continue our study of classes and data abstraction with several more advanced topics. We use const objects and const member functions to prevent modifications of objects and enforce the principle of least privilege. We discuss composition—a form of reuse in which a class can have objects of other classes as members. Next, we introduce friendship, which enables a class designer to specify nonmember functions that can access a class's non-public members—a technique that is often used in operator overloading (Chapter 11) for performance reasons. We discuss a special pointer (called this), which is an implicit argument to each of a class's non-static member functions. It allows those member functions to access the correct object's data members and other non-static member functions. Finally, we motivate the need for static class members and show how to use static data members and member functions in your own classes.

10.2 const (Constant) Objects and const Member Functions

Let's see how the principle of least privilege applies to objects. Some objects need to be modifiable and some do not. You may use keyword const to specify that an object is not modifiable and that any attempt to modify the object should result in a compilation error. The statement

```
const Time noon( 12, 0, 0 );
```

declares a const object noon of class Time and initializes it to 12 noon.

Software Engineering Observation 10.1
Attempts to modify a const object are caught at compile time rather than causing execution-time errors.

Performance Tip 10.1
Declaring variables and objects const when appropriate can improve performance—compilers can perform certain optimizations on constants that cannot be performed on variables.

C++ disallows member function calls for const objects unless the member functions themselves are also declared const. This is true even for *get* member functions that do not modify the object.

A member function is specified as const *both* in its prototype (Fig. 10.1; lines 19–24) and in its definition (Fig. 10.2; lines 43, 49, 55 and 61) by inserting the keyword const after the function's parameter list and, in the case of the function definition, before the left brace that begins the function body.

Common Programming Error 10.1
Defining as const a member function that modifies a data member of the object is a compilation error.

Common Programming Error 10.2
Defining as const a member function that calls a non-const member function of the class on the same object is a compilation error.

Common Programming Error 10.3
Invoking a non-const member function on a const object is a compilation error.

Software Engineering Observation 10.2
A const member function can be overloaded with a non-const version. The compiler chooses which overloaded member function to use based on the object on which the function is invoked. If the object is const, the compiler uses the const version. If the object is not const, the compiler uses the non-const version.

An interesting problem arises for constructors and destructors, each of which typically modifies objects. A constructor must be allowed to modify an object so that the object can be initialized properly. A destructor must be able to perform its termination housekeeping chores before an object's memory is reclaimed by the system.

Common Programming Error 10.4
Attempting to declare a constructor or destructor const is a compilation error.

Defining and Using const Member Functions

The program of Figs. 10.1–10.3 modifies class Time of Figs. 9.8–9.9 by making its *get* functions and printUniversal function const. In the header file Time.h (Fig. 10.1), lines 19–21 and 24 now include keyword const after each function's parameter list. The corresponding definition of each function in Fig. 10.2 (lines 43, 49, 55 and 61, respectively) also specifies keyword const after each function's parameter list.

```
1   // Fig. 10.1: Time.h
2   // Time class definition with const member functions.
3   // Member functions defined in Time.cpp.
4   #ifndef TIME_H
5   #define TIME_H
```

Fig. 10.1 | Time class definition with const member functions. (Part 1 of 2.)

```
6
7   class Time
8   {
9   public:
10     Time( int = 0, int = 0, int = 0 ); // default constructor
11
12     // set functions
13     void setTime( int, int, int ); // set time
14     void setHour( int ); // set hour
15     void setMinute( int ); // set minute
16     void setSecond( int ); // set second
17
18     // get functions (normally declared const)
19     int getHour() const; // return hour
20     int getMinute() const; // return minute
21     int getSecond() const; // return second
22
23     // print functions (normally declared const)
24     void printUniversal() const; // print universal time
25     void printStandard(); // print standard time (should be const)
26   private:
27     int hour; // 0 - 23 (24-hour clock format)
28     int minute; // 0 - 59
29     int second; // 0 - 59
30   }; // end class Time
31
32   #endif
```

Fig. 10.1 | Time class definition with **const** member functions. (Part 2 of 2.)

```
1   // Fig. 10.2: Time.cpp
2   // Time class member-function definitions.
3   #include <iostream>
4   #include <iomanip>
5   #include "Time.h" // include definition of class Time
6   using namespace std;
7
8   // constructor function to initialize private data;
9   // calls member function setTime to set variables;
10  // default values are 0 (see class definition)
11  Time::Time( int hour, int minute, int second )
12  {
13     setTime( hour, minute, second );
14  } // end Time constructor
15
16  // set hour, minute and second values
17  void Time::setTime( int hour, int minute, int second )
18  {
19     setHour( hour );
20     setMinute( minute );
21     setSecond( second );
22  } // end function setTime
```

Fig. 10.2 | Time class member-function definitions. (Part 1 of 2.)

```
23
24   // set hour value
25   void Time::setHour( int h )
26   {
27      hour = ( h >= 0 && h < 24 ) ? h : 0; // validate hour
28   } // end function setHour
29
30   // set minute value
31   void Time::setMinute( int m )
32   {
33      minute = ( m >= 0 && m < 60 ) ? m : 0; // validate minute
34   } // end function setMinute
35
36   // set second value
37   void Time::setSecond( int s )
38   {
39      second = ( s >= 0 && s < 60 ) ? s : 0; // validate second
40   } // end function setSecond
41
42   // return hour value
43   int Time::getHour() const // get functions should be const
44   {
45      return hour;
46   } // end function getHour
47
48   // return minute value
49   int Time::getMinute() const
50   {
51      return minute;
52   } // end function getMinute
53
54   // return second value
55   int Time::getSecond() const
56   {
57      return second;
58   } // end function getSecond
59
60   // print Time in universal-time format (HH:MM:SS)
61   void Time::printUniversal() const
62   {
63      cout << setfill( '0' ) << setw( 2 ) << hour << ":"
64         << setw( 2 ) << minute << ":" << setw( 2 ) << second;
65   } // end function printUniversal
66
67   // print Time in standard-time format (HH:MM:SS AM or PM)
68   void Time::printStandard() // note lack of const declaration
69   {
70      cout << ( ( hour == 0 || hour == 12 ) ? 12 : hour % 12 )
71         << ":" << setfill( '0' ) << setw( 2 ) << minute
72         << ":" << setw( 2 ) << second << ( hour < 12 ? " AM" : " PM" );
73   } // end function printStandard
```

Fig. 10.2 | Time class member-function definitions. (Part 2 of 2.)

Figure 10.3 instantiates two Time objects—non-const object wakeUp (line 7) and const object noon (line 8). The program attempts to invoke non-const member functions setHour (line 13) and printStandard (line 20) on the const object noon. In each case, the compiler generates an error message. The program also illustrates the three other member-function-call combinations on objects—a non-const member function on a non-const object (line 11), a const member function on a non-const object (line 15) and a const member function on a const object (lines 17–18). The error messages generated for non-const member functions called on a const object are shown in the output window.

```cpp
 1   // Fig. 10.3: fig10_03.cpp
 2   // Attempting to access a const object with non-const member functions.
 3   #include "Time.h" // include Time class definition
 4
 5   int main()
 6   {
 7      Time wakeUp( 6, 45, 0 ); // non-constant object
 8      const Time noon( 12, 0, 0 ); // constant object
 9
10                              // OBJECT      MEMBER FUNCTION
11      wakeUp.setHour( 18 );   // non-const   non-const
12
13      noon.setHour( 12 );     // const       non-const
14
15      wakeUp.getHour();       // non-const   const
16
17      noon.getMinute();       // const       const
18      noon.printUniversal();  // const       const
19
20      noon.printStandard();   // const       non-const
21   } // end main
```

Microsoft Visual C++ compiler error messages:

```
C:\cpphtp7_examples\ch10\Fig10_01_03\fig10_03.cpp(13) : error C2662:
   'Time::setHour' : cannot convert 'this' pointer from 'const Time' to
   'Time &'
        Conversion loses qualifiers
C:\cpphtp7_examples\ch10\Fig10_01_03\fig10_03.cpp(20) : error C2662:
   'Time::printStandard' : cannot convert 'this' pointer from 'const Time' to
   'Time &'
        Conversion loses qualifiers
```

GNU C++ compiler error messages:

```
fig10_03.cpp:13: error: passing 'const Time' as 'this' argument of
   'void Time::setHour(int)' discards qualifiers
fig10_03.cpp:20: error: passing 'const Time' as 'this' argument of
   'void Time::printStandard()' discards qualifiers
```

Fig. 10.3 | const objects and const member functions.

A constructor must be a non-const member function (Fig. 10.2, lines 11–14), but it can still be used to initialize a const object (Fig. 10.3, line 8). The Time constructor's definition (Fig. 10.2, lines 11–14) shows that it calls another non-const member function—setTime (lines 17–22)—to perform the initialization of a Time object. Invoking a non-const member function from the constructor call as part of the initialization of a const object is allowed. The "constness" of a const object is enforced from the time the constructor completes initialization of the object until that object's destructor is called.

Also, line 20 in Fig. 10.3 generates a compilation error even though member function printStandard of class Time does not modify the object on which it's invoked. The fact that a member function does not modify an object is not sufficient to indicate that the function is constant function—the function must *explicitly* be declared const.

Initializing a **const** Data Member with a Member Initializer

The program of Figs. 10.4–10.6 introduces using **member initializer syntax**. All data members *can* be initialized using member initializer syntax, but const data members and data members that are references *must* be initialized using member initializers. Later in this chapter, we'll see that member objects must be initialized this way as well.

```cpp
1   // Fig. 10.4: Increment.h
2   // Definition of class Increment.
3   #ifndef INCREMENT_H
4   #define INCREMENT_H
5
6   class Increment
7   {
8   public:
9      Increment( int c = 0, int i = 1 ); // default constructor
10
11     // function addIncrement definition
12     void addIncrement()
13     {
14        count += increment;
15     } // end function addIncrement
16
17     void print() const; // prints count and increment
18  private:
19     int count;
20     const int increment; // const data member
21  }; // end class Increment
22
23  #endif
```

Fig. 10.4 | Increment class definition containing non-const data member count and const data member increment.

```cpp
1   // Fig. 10.5: Increment.cpp
2   // Member-function definitions for class Increment demonstrate using a
3   // member initializer to initialize a constant of a built-in data type.
```

Fig. 10.5 | Member initializer used to initialize a constant of a built-in data type. (Part 1 of 2.)

```
 4  #include <iostream>
 5  #include "Increment.h" // include definition of class Increment
 6  using namespace std;
 7
 8  // constructor
 9  Increment::Increment( int c, int i )
10     : count( c ), // initializer for non-const member
11       increment( i ) // required initializer for const member
12  {
13     // empty body
14  } // end constructor Increment
15
16  // print count and increment values
17  void Increment::print() const
18  {
19     cout << "count = " << count << ", increment = " << increment << endl;
20  } // end function print
```

Fig. 10.5 | Member initializer used to initialize a constant of a built-in data type. (Part 2 of 2.)

```
 1  // Fig. 10.6: fig10_06.cpp
 2  // Program to test class Increment.
 3  #include <iostream>
 4  #include "Increment.h" // include definition of class Increment
 5  using namespace std;
 6
 7  int main()
 8  {
 9     Increment value( 10, 5 );
10
11     cout << "Before incrementing: ";
12     value.print();
13
14     for ( int j = 1; j <= 3; j++ )
15     {
16        value.addIncrement();
17        cout << "After increment " << j << ": ";
18        value.print();
19     } // end for
20  } // end main
```

```
Before incrementing: count = 10, increment = 5
After increment 1: count = 15, increment = 5
After increment 2: count = 20, increment = 5
After increment 3: count = 25, increment = 5
```

Fig. 10.6 | Invoking an Increment object's print and addIncrement member functions.

The constructor definition (Fig. 10.5, lines 9–14) uses a **member initializer list** to initialize class Increment's data members—non-const integer count and const integer increment (declared in lines 19–20 of Fig. 10.4). Member initializers appear between a constructor's parameter list and the left brace that begins the constructor's body. The member initializer list (Fig. 10.5, lines 10–11) is separated from the parameter list with a colon (:). Each member initializer consists of the data member name followed by parentheses containing the member's initial value. In this example, count is initialized with the value of constructor parameter c and increment is initialized with the value of constructor parameter i. Multiple member initializers are separated by commas. Also, the member initializer list executes before the body of the constructor executes.

Software Engineering Observation 10.3

A const object cannot be modified by assignment, so it must be initialized. When a data member of a class is declared const, a member initializer must be used to provide the constructor with the initial value of the data member for an object of the class. The same is true for references.

Erroneously Attempting to Initialize a const Data Member with an Assignment
The program of Figs. 10.7–10.9 illustrates the compilation errors caused by attempting to initialize const data member increment with an assignment statement (Fig. 10.8, line 12) in the Increment constructor's body rather than with a member initializer. Line 11 of Fig. 10.8 does not generate a compilation error, because count is not declared const.

Common Programming Error 10.5

Not providing a member initializer for a const data member is a compilation error.

Software Engineering Observation 10.4

Constant data members (const objects and const variables) and data members declared as references must be initialized with member initializer syntax; assignments for these types of data in the constructor body are not allowed.

```
I   // Fig. 10.7: Increment.h
2   // Definition of class Increment.
3   #ifndef INCREMENT_H
4   #define INCREMENT_H
5
6   class Increment
7   {
8   public:
9      Increment( int c = 0, int i = 1 ); // default constructor
10
11     // function addIncrement definition
12     void addIncrement()
13     {
14        count += increment;
15     } // end function addIncrement
16
17     void print() const; // prints count and increment
18  private:
19     int count;
```

Fig. 10.7 | Increment class definition containing non-const data member count and const data member increment. (Part 1 of 2.)

```
20      const int increment; // const data member
21    }; // end class Increment
22
23    #endif
```

Fig. 10.7 | Increment class definition containing non-const data member count and const data member increment. (Part 2 of 2.)

```
1    // Fig. 10.8: Increment.cpp
2    // Erroneous attempt to initialize a constant of a built-in data
3    // type by assignment.
4    #include <iostream>
5    #include "Increment.h" // include definition of class Increment
6    using namespace std;
7
8    // constructor; constant member 'increment' is not initialized
9    Increment::Increment( int c, int i )
10   {
11      count = c; // allowed because count is not constant
12      increment = i; // ERROR: Cannot modify a const object
13   } // end constructor Increment
14
15   // print count and increment values
16   void Increment::print() const
17   {
18      cout << "count = " << count << ", increment = " << increment << endl;
19   } // end function print
```

Fig. 10.8 | Erroneous attempt to initialize a constant of a built-in data type by assignment.

```
1    // Fig. 10.9: fig10_09.cpp
2    // Program to test class Increment.
3    #include <iostream>
4    #include "Increment.h" // include definition of class Increment
5    using namespace std;
6
7    int main()
8    {
9       Increment value( 10, 5 );
10
11      cout << "Before incrementing: ";
12      value.print();
13
14      for ( int j = 1; j <= 3; j++ )
15      {
16         value.addIncrement();
17         cout << "After increment " << j << ": ";
18         value.print();
19      } // end for
20   } // end main
```

Fig. 10.9 | Program to test class Increment generates compilation errors. (Part 1 of 2.)

Microsoft Visual C++ compiler error messages:

```
C:\cpphtp7_examples\ch10\Fig10_07_09\Increment.cpp(10) : error C2758:
    'Increment::increment' : must be initialized in constructor base/member
    initializer list
        C:\cpphtp7_examples\ch10\Fig10_07_09\increment.h(20) : see
            declaration of 'Increment::increment'
C:\cpphtp7_examples\ch10\Fig10_07_09\Increment.cpp(12) : error C2166:
    l-value specifies const object
```

GNU C++ compiler error messages:

```
Increment.cpp:9: error: uninitialized member 'Increment::increment' with
    'const' type 'const int'
Increment.cpp:12: error: assignment of read-only data-member
    'Increment::increment'
```

Fig. 10.9 | Program to test class `Increment` generates compilation errors. (Part 2 of 2.)

Function print (Fig. 10.8, lines 16–19) is declared const. It might seem strange to label this function const, because a program probably will never have a const Increment object. However, it's possible that a program will have a const reference to an Increment object or a pointer to const that points to an Increment object. Typically, this occurs when objects of class Increment are passed to functions or returned from functions. In these cases, only class Increment's const member functions can be called through the reference or pointer. Thus, it's reasonable to declare function print as const—doing so prevents errors in these situations where an Increment object is treated as a const object.

Error-Prevention Tip 10.1

Declare as const all of a class's member functions that do not modify the object in which they operate. Occasionally this may seem inappropriate, because you'll have no intention of creating const objects of that class or accessing objects of that class through const references or pointers to const. Declaring such member functions const does offer a benefit, though. If the member function is inadvertently written to modify the object, the compiler will issue an error message.

10.3 Composition: Objects as Members of Classes

An AlarmClock object needs to know when it's supposed to sound its alarm, so why not include a Time object as a member of the AlarmClock class? Such a capability is called **composition** and is sometimes referred to as a *has-a* **relationship**—a class can have objects of other classes as members.

Software Engineering Observation 10.5

A common form of software reusability is composition, in which a class has objects of other classes as members.

When an object is created, its constructor is called automatically. Previously, we saw how to pass arguments to the constructor of an object we created in main. This section shows how an object's constructor can pass arguments to member-object constructors via member initializers.

Software Engineering Observation 10.6

*Member objects are constructed in the order in which they're declared in the class definition (not in the order they're listed in the constructor's member initializer list) and before their enclosing class objects (sometimes called **host objects**) are constructed.*

The next program uses classes Date (Figs. 10.10–10.11) and Employee (Figs. 10.12–10.13) to demonstrate composition. Class Employee's definition (Fig. 10.12) contains private data members firstName, lastName, birthDate and hireDate. Members birthDate and hireDate are const objects of class Date, which contains private data members month, day and year. The Employee constructor's header (Fig. 10.13, lines 10–11) specifies that the constructor has four parameters (first, last, dateOfBirth and dateOfHire). The first two parameters are passed via member initializers to the string class constructor. The last two are passed via member initializers to the Date class constructor.

```
1   // Fig. 10.10: Date.h
2   // Date class definition; Member functions defined in Date.cpp
3   #ifndef DATE_H
4   #define DATE_H
5
6   class Date
7   {
8   public:
9      static const int monthsPerYear = 12; // number of months in a year
10     Date( int = 1, int = 1, int = 1900 ); // default constructor
11     void print() const; // print date in month/day/year format
12     ~Date(); // provided to confirm destruction order
13  private:
14     int month; // 1-12 (January-December)
15     int day; // 1-31 based on month
16     int year; // any year
17
18     // utility function to check if day is proper for month and year
19     int checkDay( int ) const;
20  }; // end class Date
21
22  #endif
```

Fig. 10.10 | Date class definition.

```
1   // Fig. 10.11: Date.cpp
2   // Date class member-function definitions.
3   #include <iostream>
4   #include "Date.h" // include Date class definition
5   using namespace std;
6
7   // constructor confirms proper value for month; calls
8   // utility function checkDay to confirm proper value for day
```

Fig. 10.11 | Date class member-function definitions. (Part 1 of 2.)

```
 9   Date::Date( int mn, int dy, int yr )
10   {
11      if ( mn > 0 && mn <= monthsPerYear ) // validate the month
12         month = mn;
13      else
14      {
15         month = 1; // invalid month set to 1
16         cout << "Invalid month (" << mn << ") set to 1.\n";
17      } // end else
18
19      year = yr; // could validate yr
20      day = checkDay( dy ); // validate the day
21
22      // output Date object to show when its constructor is called
23      cout << "Date object constructor for date ";
24      print();
25      cout << endl;
26   } // end Date constructor
27
28   // print Date object in form month/day/year
29   void Date::print() const
30   {
31      cout << month << '/' << day << '/' << year;
32   } // end function print
33
34   // output Date object to show when its destructor is called
35   Date::~Date()
36   {
37      cout << "Date object destructor for date ";
38      print();
39      cout << endl;
40   } // end ~Date destructor
41
42   // utility function to confirm proper day value based on
43   // month and year; handles leap years, too
44   int Date::checkDay( int testDay ) const
45   {
46      static const int daysPerMonth[ monthsPerYear + 1 ] =
47         { 0, 31, 28, 31, 30, 31, 30, 31, 31, 30, 31, 30, 31 };
48
49      // determine whether testDay is valid for specified month
50      if ( testDay > 0 && testDay <= daysPerMonth[ month ] )
51         return testDay;
52
53      // February 29 check for leap year
54      if ( month == 2 && testDay == 29 && ( year % 400 == 0 ||
55         ( year % 4 == 0 && year % 100 != 0 ) ) )
56         return testDay;
57
58      cout << "Invalid day (" << testDay << ") set to 1.\n";
59      return 1; // leave object in consistent state if bad value
60   } // end function checkDay
```

Fig. 10.11 | Date class member-function definitions. (Part 2 of 2.)

```
1    // Fig. 10.12: Employee.h
2    // Employee class definition showing composition.
3    // Member functions defined in Employee.cpp.
4    #ifndef EMPLOYEE_H
5    #define EMPLOYEE_H
6
7    #include <string>
8    #include "Date.h" // include Date class definition
9    using namespace std;
10
11   class Employee
12   {
13   public:
14      Employee( const string &, const string &,
15         const Date &, const Date & );
16      void print() const;
17      ~Employee(); // provided to confirm destruction order
18   private:
19      string firstName; // composition: member object
20      string lastName; // composition: member object
21      const Date birthDate; // composition: member object
22      const Date hireDate; // composition: member object
23   }; // end class Employee
24
25   #endif
```

Fig. 10.12 | Employee class definition showing composition.

```
1    // Fig. 10.13: Employee.cpp
2    // Employee class member-function definitions.
3    #include <iostream>
4    #include "Employee.h" // Employee class definition
5    #include "Date.h" // Date class definition
6    using namespace std;
7
8    // constructor uses member initializer list to pass initializer
9    // values to constructors of member objects
10   Employee::Employee( const string &first, const string &last,
11      const Date &dateOfBirth, const Date &dateOfHire )
12      : firstName( first ), // initialize firstName
13        lastName( last ), // initialize lastName
14        birthDate( dateOfBirth ), // initialize birthDate
15        hireDate( dateOfHire ) // initialize hireDate
16   {
17      // output Employee object to show when constructor is called
18      cout << "Employee object constructor: "
19         << firstName << ' ' << lastName << endl;
20   } // end Employee constructor
21
```

Fig. 10.13 | Employee class member-function definitions, including constructor with a member initializer list. (Part 1 of 2.)

```
22   // print Employee object
23   void Employee::print() const
24   {
25      cout << lastName << ", " << firstName << "  Hired: ";
26      hireDate.print();
27      cout << "  Birthday: ";
28      birthDate.print();
29      cout << endl;
30   } // end function print
31
32   // output Employee object to show when its destructor is called
33   Employee::~Employee()
34   {
35      cout << "Employee object destructor: "
36         << lastName << ", " << firstName << endl;
37   } // end ~Employee destructor
```

Fig. 10.13 | Employee class member-function definitions, including constructor with a member initializer list. (Part 2 of 2.)

Employee *Constructor's Member Initializer List*

The colon (:) following the constructor's header (Fig. 10.13, line 12) begins the member initializer list. The member initializers specify the Employee constructor parameters being passed to the constructors of the string and Date data members. Parameters first, last, dateOfBirth and dateOfHire are passed to the constructors for objects firstName's (Fig. 10.13, line 12), lastName (Fig. 10.13, line 13), birthDate (Fig. 10.13, line 14) and hireDate (Fig. 10.13, line 15), respectively. Again, member initializers are separated by commas.

Date *Class's Default Copy Constructor*

As you study class Date (Fig. 10.10), notice that the class does not provide a constructor that receives a parameter of type Date. So, why can the Employee constructor's member initializer list initialize the birthDate and hireDate objects by passing Date object's to their Date constructors? As we mentioned in Chapter 9, the compiler provides each class with a default copy constructor that copies each data member of the constructor's argument object into the corresponding member of the object being initialized. Chapter 11 discusses how you can define customized copy constructors.

Testing Classes Date *and* Employee

Figure 10.14 creates two Date objects (lines 9–10) and passes them as arguments to the constructor of the Employee object created in line 11. Line 14 outputs the Employee object's data. When each Date object is created in lines 9–10, the Date constructor defined in lines 9–26 of Fig. 10.11 displays a line of output to show that the constructor was called (see the first two lines of the sample output). [*Note:* Line 11 of Fig. 10.14 causes two additional Date constructor calls that do not appear in the program's output. When each of the Employee's Date member object's is initialized in the Employee constructor's member initializer list (Fig. 10.13, lines 14–15), the default copy constructor for class Date is called. Since this constructor is defined implicitly by the compiler, it does not contain any output statements to demonstrate when it's called.]

```
 1   // Fig. 10.14: fig10_14.cpp
 2   // Demonstrating composition--an object with member objects.
 3   #include <iostream>
 4   #include "Employee.h" // Employee class definition
 5   using namespace std;
 6
 7   int main()
 8   {
 9      Date birth( 7, 24, 1949 );
10      Date hire( 3, 12, 1988 );
11      Employee manager( "Bob", "Blue", birth, hire );
12
13      cout << endl;
14      manager.print();
15
16      cout << "\nTest Date constructor with invalid values:\n";
17      Date lastDayOff( 14, 35, 1994 ); // invalid month and day
18      cout << endl;
19   } // end main
```

```
Date object constructor for date 7/24/1949
Date object constructor for date 3/12/1988
Employee object constructor: Bob Blue ──────────

Blue, Bob  Hired: 3/12/1988  Birthday: 7/24/1949

Test Date constructor with invalid values:
Invalid month (14) set to 1.
Invalid day (35) set to 1.
Date object constructor for date 1/1/1994

Date object destructor for date 1/1/1994
Employee object destructor: Blue, Bob
Date object destructor for date 3/12/1988
Date object destructor for date 7/24/1949
Date object destructor for date 3/12/1988
Date object destructor for date 7/24/1949
```

There are actually five constructor calls when an **Employee** is constructed—two calls to the **string** class's constructor (lines 12–13 of Fig. 10.13), two calls to the **Date** class's default copy constructor (lines 14–15 of Fig. 10.13) and the call to the **Employee** class's constructor.

Fig. 10.14 | Demonstrating composition—an object with member objects.

Class Date and class Employee each include a destructor (lines 35–40 of Fig. 10.11 and lines 33–37 of Fig. 10.13, respectively) that prints a message when an object of its class is destructed. This enables us to confirm in the program output that objects are constructed from the *inside out* and destroyed in the reverse order, from the *outside in* (i.e., the Date member objects are destroyed after the Employee object that contains them). Notice the last four lines in the output of Fig. 10.14. The last two lines are the outputs of the Date destructor running on Date objects hire (line 10) and birth (line 9), respectively. These outputs confirm that the three objects created in main are destructed in the *reverse* of the order in which they were constructed. The Employee destructor output is five lines from the bottom. The fourth and third lines from the bottom of the output window show the destructors running for the Employee's member objects hireDate (Fig. 10.12, line 22) and birthDate (Fig. 10.12, line 21). These outputs confirm that the Employee object is destructed from the *outside in*—i.e., the Employee destructor runs first (output shown five lines from the bottom of the output window), then the member objects are destructed in the *reverse order* from which they were constructed. Class `string`'s destructor does not contain output statements, so we do not see the `firstName` and `lastName` objects being destructed. Again, Fig. 10.14's output did not show the constructors running for member objects `birthDate` and `hireDate`, because these objects were initialized with the default `Date` class copy constructors provided by the compiler.

What Happens When I Do Not Use the Member Initializer List?
If a member object is not initialized through a member initializer, the member object's default constructor will be called implicitly. Values, if any, established by the default constructor can be overridden by *set* functions. However, for complex initialization, this approach may require significant additional work and time.

Common Programming Error 10.6

A compilation error occurs if a member object is not initialized with a member initializer and the member object's class does not provide a default constructor (i.e., the member object's class defines one or more constructors, but none is a default constructor).

Performance Tip 10.2

Initialize member objects explicitly through member initializers. This eliminates the over-head of "doubly initializing" member objects—once when the member object's default constructor is called and again when set *functions are called in the constructor body (or later) to initialize the member object.*

Software Engineering Observation 10.7

If a class member is an object of another class, making that member object public *does not violate the encapsulation and hiding of that member object's* private *members. But, it does violate the encapsulation and hiding of the containing class's implementation, so member objects of class types should still be* private, *like all other data members.*

10.4 **friend** Functions and **friend** Classes

A **friend function** of a class is defined outside that class's scope, yet has the right to access the non-`public` (and `public`) members of the class. Standalone functions, entire classes or member functions of other classes may be declared to be friends of another class.

Using `friend` functions can enhance performance. This section presents a mechanical example of how a `friend` function works. Later in the book, `friend` functions are used to overload operators for use with class objects (Chapter 11) and to create iterator classes (Chapter 20, Data Structures). Objects of an iterator class can successively select items or perform an operation on items in a container class object. Objects of container classes can store items. Using friends is often appropriate when a member function cannot be used for certain operations, as we'll see in Chapter 11.

To declare a function as a friend of a class, precede the function prototype in the class definition with keyword `friend`. To declare all member functions of class `ClassTwo` as friends of class `ClassOne`, place a declaration of the form

```
friend class ClassTwo;
```

in the definition of class `ClassOne`.

Software Engineering Observation 10.8

Even though the prototypes for friend functions appear in the class definition, friends are not member functions.

Software Engineering Observation 10.9

Member access notions of private, protected and public are not relevant to friend declarations, so friend declarations can be placed anywhere in a class definition.

Good Programming Practice 10.1

Place all friendship declarations first inside the class definition's body and do not precede them with any access specifier.

Friendship is granted, not taken—i.e., for class B to be a friend of class A, class A must explicitly declare that class B is its friend. Also, the friendship relation is neither symmetric nor transitive; i.e., if class A is a friend of class B, and class B is a friend of class C, you cannot infer that class B is a friend of class A (again, friendship is not symmetric), that class C is a friend of class B (also because friendship is not symmetric), or that class A is a friend of class C (friendship is not transitive).

Software Engineering Observation 10.10

Some people in the OOP community feel that "friendship" corrupts information hiding and weakens the value of the object-oriented design approach. In this text, we identify several examples of the responsible use of friendship.

Modifying a Class's **private** Data with a Friend Function

Figure 10.15 is a mechanical example in which we define friend function setX to set the private data member x of class Count. The friend declaration (line 9) appears first (by convention) in the class definition, even before public member functions are declared. Again, this friend declaration can appear anywhere in the class.

```cpp
1   // Fig. 10.15: fig10_15.cpp
2   // Friends can access private members of a class.
3   #include <iostream>
4   using namespace std;
5
6   // Count class definition
7   class Count
8   {
9      friend void setX( Count &, int ); // friend declaration
10  public:
11     // constructor
12     Count()
13        : x( 0 ) // initialize x to 0
14     {
15        // empty body
16     } // end constructor Count
17
```

Fig. 10.15 | Friends can access private members of a class. (Part 1 of 2.)

```
18        // output x
19        void print() const
20        {
21           cout << x << endl;
22        } // end function print
23     private:
24        int x; // data member
25     }; // end class Count
26
27     // function setX can modify private data of Count
28     // because setX is declared as a friend of Count (line 9)
29     void setX( Count &c, int val )
30     {
31        c.x = val; // allowed because setX is a friend of Count
32     } // end function setX
33
34     int main()
35     {
36        Count counter; // create Count object
37
38        cout << "counter.x after instantiation: ";
39        counter.print();
40
41        setX( counter, 8 ); // set x using a friend function
42        cout << "counter.x after call to setX friend function: ";
43        counter.print();
44     } // end main
```

```
counter.x after instantiation: 0
counter.x after call to setX friend function: 8
```

Fig. 10.15 | Friends can access **private** members of a class. (Part 2 of 2.)

Function setX (lines 29–32) is a C-style, stand-alone function—it isn't a member function of class Count. For this reason, when setX is invoked for object counter, line 41 passes counter as an argument to setX rather than using a handle (such as the name of the object) to call the function, as in

```
counter.setX( 8 );
```

If you remove the friend declaration in line 9, you'll receive error messages indicating that function setX cannot modify class Count's private data member x.

As we mentioned, Fig. 10.15 is a mechanical example of using the friend construct. It would normally be appropriate to define function setX as a member function of class Count. It would also normally be appropriate to separate the program of Fig. 10.15 into three files:

1. A header file (e.g., Count.h) containing the Count class definition, which in turn contains the prototype of friend function setX

2. An implementation file (e.g., Count.cpp) containing the definitions of class Count's member functions and the definition of friend function setX

3. A test program (e.g., fig10_15.cpp) with main.

Overloaded friend Functions
It's possible to specify overloaded functions as friends of a class. Each function intended to be a friend must be explicitly declared in the class definition as a friend of the class.

10.5 Using the this Pointer

We've seen that an object's member functions can manipulate the object's data. How do member functions know *which* object's data members to manipulate? Every object has access to its own address through a pointer called **this** (a C++ keyword). The this pointer is *not* part of the object itself—i.e., the memory occupied by the this pointer is not reflected in the result of a sizeof operation on the object. Rather, the this pointer is passed (by the compiler) as an implicit argument to each of the object's non-static member functions. Section 10.6 introduces static class members and explains why the this pointer is *not* implicitly passed to static member functions.

Objects use the this pointer implicitly (as we've done to this point) or explicitly to reference their data members and member functions. The type of the this pointer depends on the type of the object and whether the member function in which this is used is declared const. For example, in a nonconstant member function of class Employee, the this pointer has type Employee * const (a constant pointer to a nonconstant Employee object). In a constant member function of the class Employee, the this pointer has the data type const Employee * const (a constant pointer to a constant Employee object).

The next example shows implicit and explicit use of the this pointer; later in this chapter and in Chapter 11, we show some substantial and subtle examples of using this.

*Implicitly and Explicitly Using the **this** Pointer to Access an Object's Data Members*
Figure 10.16 demonstrates the implicit and explicit use of the this pointer to enable a member function of class Test to print the private data x of a Test object.

```cpp
1   // Fig. 10.16: fig10_16.cpp
2   // Using the this pointer to refer to object members.
3   #include <iostream>
4   using namespace std;
5
6   class Test
7   {
8   public:
9      Test( int = 0 ); // default constructor
10     void print() const;
11  private:
12     int x;
13  }; // end class Test
14
15  // constructor
16  Test::Test( int value )
17     : x( value ) // initialize x to value
18  {
19     // empty body
20  } // end constructor Test
```

Fig. 10.16 | this pointer implicitly and explicitly accessing an object's members. (Part 1 of 2.)

```
21
22   // print x using implicit and explicit this pointers;
23   // the parentheses around *this are required
24   void Test::print() const
25   {
26      // implicitly use the this pointer to access the member x
27      cout << "        x = " << x;
28
29      // explicitly use the this pointer and the arrow operator
30      // to access the member x
31      cout << "\n  this->x = " << this->x;
32
33      // explicitly use the dereferenced this pointer and
34      // the dot operator to access the member x
35      cout << "\n(*this).x = " << ( *this ).x << endl;
36   } // end function print
37
38   int main()
39   {
40      Test testObject( 12 ); // instantiate and initialize testObject
41
42      testObject.print();
43   } // end main
```

```
        x = 12
  this->x = 12
(*this).x = 12
```

Fig. 10.16 | this pointer implicitly and explicitly accessing an object's members. (Part 2 of 2.)

For illustration purposes, member function print (lines 24–36) first prints x by using the this pointer implicitly (line 27)—only the name of the data member is specified. Then print uses two different notations to access x through the this pointer—the arrow operator (->) off the this pointer (line 31) and the dot operator (.) off the dereferenced this pointer (line 35). Note the parentheses around *this (line 35) when used with the dot member selection operator (.). The parentheses are required because the dot operator has higher precedence than the * operator. Without the parentheses, the expression *this.x would be evaluated as if it were parenthesized as *(this.x), which is a compilation error, because the dot operator cannot be used with a pointer.

Common Programming Error 10.7

Attempting to use the member selection operator (.) with a pointer to an object is a compilation error—the dot member selection operator may be used only with an lvalue such as an object's name, a reference to an object or a dereferenced pointer to an object.

One interesting use of the this pointer is to prevent an object from being assigned to itself. As we'll see in Chapter 11, self-assignment can cause serious errors when the object contains pointers to dynamically allocated storage.

Using the **this** Pointer to Enable Cascaded Function Calls

Another use of the this pointer is to enable **cascaded member-function calls**—that is, invoking multiple functions in the same statement (as in line 12 of Fig. 10.19). The program of Figs. 10.17–10.19 modifies class Time's *set* functions setTime, setHour, setMinute and setSecond such that each returns a reference to a Time object to enable cascaded member-function calls. Notice in Fig. 10.18 that the last statement in the body of each of these member functions returns *this (lines 22, 29, 36 and 43) into a return type of Time &.

```cpp
1   // Fig. 10.17: Time.h
2   // Cascading member function calls.
3
4   // Time class definition.
5   // Member functions defined in Time.cpp.
6   #ifndef TIME_H
7   #define TIME_H
8
9   class Time
10  {
11  public:
12     Time( int = 0, int = 0, int = 0 ); // default constructor
13
14     // set functions (the Time & return types enable cascading)
15     Time &setTime( int, int, int ); // set hour, minute, second
16     Time &setHour( int ); // set hour
17     Time &setMinute( int ); // set minute
18     Time &setSecond( int ); // set second
19
20     // get functions (normally declared const)
21     int getHour() const; // return hour
22     int getMinute() const; // return minute
23     int getSecond() const; // return second
24
25     // print functions (normally declared const)
26     void printUniversal() const; // print universal time
27     void printStandard() const; // print standard time
28  private:
29     int hour; // 0 - 23 (24-hour clock format)
30     int minute; // 0 - 59
31     int second; // 0 - 59
32  }; // end class Time
33
34  #endif
```

Fig. 10.17 | Time class definition modified to enable cascaded member-function calls.

```cpp
1   // Fig. 10.18: Time.cpp
2   // Time class member-function definitions.
3   #include <iostream>
4   #include <iomanip>
5   #include "Time.h" // Time class definition
6   using namespace std;
7
```

Fig. 10.18 | Time class member-function definitions modified to enable cascaded member-function calls. (Part 1 of 3.)

```
 8    // constructor function to initialize private data;
 9    // calls member function setTime to set variables;
10    // default values are 0 (see class definition)
11    Time::Time( int hr, int min, int sec )
12    {
13       setTime( hr, min, sec );
14    } // end Time constructor
15
16    // set values of hour, minute, and second
17    Time &Time::setTime( int h, int m, int s ) // note Time & return
18    {
19       setHour( h );
20       setMinute( m );
21       setSecond( s );
22       return *this; // enables cascading
23    } // end function setTime
24
25    // set hour value
26    Time &Time::setHour( int h ) // note Time & return
27    {
28       hour = ( h >= 0 && h < 24 ) ? h : 0; // validate hour
29       return *this; // enables cascading
30    } // end function setHour
31
32    // set minute value
33    Time &Time::setMinute( int m ) // note Time & return
34    {
35       minute = ( m >= 0 && m < 60 ) ? m : 0; // validate minute
36       return *this; // enables cascading
37    } // end function setMinute
38
39    // set second value
40    Time &Time::setSecond( int s ) // note Time & return
41    {
42       second = ( s >= 0 && s < 60 ) ? s : 0; // validate second
43       return *this; // enables cascading
44    } // end function setSecond
45
46    // get hour value
47    int Time::getHour() const
48    {
49       return hour;
50    } // end function getHour
51
52    // get minute value
53    int Time::getMinute() const
54    {
55       return minute;
56    } // end function getMinute
57
```

Fig. 10.18 | Time class member-function definitions modified to enable cascaded member-function calls. (Part 2 of 3.)

```
58   // get second value
59   int Time::getSecond() const
60   {
61      return second;
62   } // end function getSecond
63
64   // print Time in universal-time format (HH:MM:SS)
65   void Time::printUniversal() const
66   {
67      cout << setfill( '0' ) << setw( 2 ) << hour << ":"
68         << setw( 2 ) << minute << ":" << setw( 2 ) << second;
69   } // end function printUniversal
70
71   // print Time in standard-time format (HH:MM:SS AM or PM)
72   void Time::printStandard() const
73   {
74      cout << ( ( hour == 0 || hour == 12 ) ? 12 : hour % 12 )
75         << ":" << setfill( '0' ) << setw( 2 ) << minute
76         << ":" << setw( 2 ) << second << ( hour < 12 ? " AM" : " PM" );
77   } // end function printStandard
```

Fig. 10.18 | `Time` class member-function definitions modified to enable cascaded member-function calls. (Part 3 of 3.)

```
1    // Fig. 10.19: fig10_19.cpp
2    // Cascading member-function calls with the this pointer.
3    #include <iostream>
4    #include "Time.h" // Time class definition
5    using namespace std;
6
7    int main()
8    {
9       Time t; // create Time object
10
11      // cascaded function calls
12      t.setHour( 18 ).setMinute( 30 ).setSecond( 22 );
13
14      // output time in universal and standard formats
15      cout << "Universal time: ";
16      t.printUniversal();
17
18      cout << "\nStandard time: ";
19      t.printStandard();
20
21      cout << "\n\nNew standard time: ";
22
23      // cascaded function calls
24      t.setTime( 20, 20, 20 ).printStandard();
25      cout << endl;
26   } // end main
```

Fig. 10.19 | Cascading member-function calls with the `this` pointer. (Part 1 of 2.)

```
Universal time: 18:30:22
Standard time: 6:30:22 PM

New standard time: 8:20:20 PM
```

Fig. 10.19 | Cascading member-function calls with the this pointer. (Part 2 of 2.)

The program of Fig. 10.19 creates Time object t (line 9), then uses it in cascaded member-function calls (lines 12 and 24). Why does the technique of returning *this as a reference work? The dot operator (.) associates from left to right, so line 12 first evaluates t.setHour(18), then returns a reference to object t as the value of this function call. The remaining expression is then interpreted as

```
        t.setMinute( 30 ).setSecond( 22 );
```

The t.setMinute(30) call executes and returns a reference to the object t. The remaining expression is interpreted as

```
        t.setSecond( 22 );
```

Line 24 also uses cascading. The calls must appear in the order shown in line 24, because printStandard as defined in the class does not return a reference to t. Placing the call to printStandard before the call to setTime in line 24 results in a compilation error. Chapter 11 presents several practical examples of using cascaded function calls. One such example uses multiple << operators with cout to output multiple values in a single statement.

10.6 static Class Members

There is an important exception to the rule that each object of a class has its own copy of all the data members of the class. In certain cases, only one copy of a variable should be shared by all objects of a class. A **static data member** is used for these and other reasons. Such a variable represents "class-wide" information (i.e., a property that is shared by all instances and is not specific to any one object of the class). Recall that the versions of class GradeBook in Chapter 7 use static data members to store constants representing the number of grades that all GradeBook objects can hold.

Motivating Class-Wide Data
Let's further motivate the need for static class-wide data with an example. Suppose that we have a video game with Martians and other space creatures. Each Martian tends to be brave and willing to attack other space creatures when the Martian is aware that there are at least five Martians present. If fewer than five are present, each Martian becomes cowardly. So each Martian needs to know the martianCount. We could endow each instance of class Martian with martianCount as a data member. If we do, every Martian will have a separate copy of the data member. Every time we create a new Martian, we'll have to update the data member martianCount in all Martian objects. Doing this would require every Martian object to have, or have access to, handles to all other Martian objects in memory. This wastes space with the redundant copies and wastes time in updating the separate copies. Instead, we declare martianCount to be static. This makes martianCount class-wide data. Every Martian can access martianCount as if it were a data member of the

Martian, but only one copy of the static variable martianCount is maintained by C++. This saves space. We save time by having the Martian constructor increment static variable martianCount and having the Martian destructor decrement martianCount. Because there is only one copy, we do not have to increment or decrement separate copies of martianCount for each Martian object.

Performance Tip 10.3

Use static data members to save storage when a single copy of the data for all objects of a class will suffice.

Scope and Initialization of *static* Data Members

Although they may seem like global variables, a class's static data members have class scope. Also, static members can be declared public, private or protected. A fundamental-type static data member is initialized by default to 0. If you want a different initial value, a static data member can be initialized *once*. A static const data member of int or enum type can be initialized in its declaration in the class definition. However, all other static data members must be defined *at global namespace scope* (i.e., outside the body of the class definition) and can be initialized only in those definitions. If a static data member is an object of a class that provides a default constructor, the static data member need not be initialized because its default constructor will be called.

Accessing *static* Data Members

A class's private and protected static members are normally accessed through the class's public member functions or friends. A class's static members exist even when no objects of that class exist. To access a public static class member when no objects of the class exist, simply prefix the class name and the binary scope resolution operator (::) to the name of the data member. For example, if our preceding variable martianCount is public, it can be accessed with the expression Martian::martianCount when there are no Martian objects. (Of course, using public data is discouraged.)

To access a private or protected static class member when no objects of the class exist, provide a public **static member function** and call the function by prefixing its name with the class name and binary scope resolution operator. A static member function is a service of the *class*, not of a specific object of the class.

Software Engineering Observation 10.11

A class's static data members and static member functions exist and can be used even if no objects of that class have been instantiated.

Demonstrating *static* Data Members

The program of Figs. 10.20–10.22 demonstrates a private static data member called count (Fig. 10.20, line 25) and a public static member function called getCount (Fig. 10.20, line 19). In Fig. 10.21, line 8 defines and initializes the data member count to zero *at global namespace scope* and lines 12–15 define static member function getCount. Notice that neither line 8 nor line 12 includes keyword static, yet both lines refer to static class members. When static is applied to an item at global namespace scope, that item becomes known only in that file. The static class members need to be available to any client code that uses the class, so we declare them static only in the .h file. Data member count maintains a count of the number of objects of class Employee that have been instantiated. When objects of class Employee exist, member count can be referenced through any member function of an Employee object—in Fig. 10.21, count is referenced by both line 22 in the constructor and line 32 in the destructor.

Common Programming Error 10.8

It's a compilation error to include keyword static in the definition of a static data member at global namespace scope.

```
1   // Fig. 10.20: Employee.h
2   // Employee class definition with a static data member to
3   // track the number of Employee objects in memory
4   #ifndef EMPLOYEE_H
5   #define EMPLOYEE_H
6
7   #include <string>
8   using namespace std;
9
10  class Employee
11  {
12  public:
13     Employee( const string &, const string & ); // constructor
14     ~Employee(); // destructor
15     string getFirstName() const; // return first name
16     string getLastName() const; // return last name
17
18     // static member function
19     static int getCount(); // return number of objects instantiated
20  private:
21     string firstName;
22     string lastName;
23
24     // static data
25     static int count; // number of objects instantiated
26  }; // end class Employee
27
28  #endif
```

Fig. 10.20 | Employee class definition with a static data member to track the number of Employee objects in memory.

```
1   // Fig. 10.21: Employee.cpp
2   // Employee class member-function definitions.
3   #include <iostream>
4   #include "Employee.h" // Employee class definition
5   using namespace std;
6
```

Fig. 10.21 | Employee class member-function definitions. (Part 1 of 2.)

```
7   // define and initialize static data member at global namespace scope
8   int Employee::count = 0; // cannot include keyword static
9
10  // define static member function that returns number of
11  // Employee objects instantiated (declared static in Employee.h)
12  int Employee::getCount()
13  {
14     return count;
15  } // end static function getCount
16
17  // constructor initializes non-static data members and
18  // increments static data member count
19  Employee::Employee( const string &first, const string &last )
20     : firstName( first ), lastName( last )
21  {
22     ++count; // increment static count of employees
23     cout << "Employee constructor for " << firstName
24        << ' ' << lastName << " called." << endl;
25  } // end Employee constructor
26
27  // destructor deallocates dynamically allocated memory
28  Employee::~Employee()
29  {
30     cout << "~Employee() called for " << firstName
31        << ' ' << lastName << endl;
32     --count; // decrement static count of employees
33  } // end ~Employee destructor
34
35  // return first name of employee
36  string Employee::getFirstName() const
37  {
38     return firstName; // return copy of first name
39  } // end function getFirstName
40
41  // return last name of employee
42  string Employee::getLastName() const
43  {
44     return lastName; // return copy of last name
45  } // end function getLastName
```

Fig. 10.21 | Employee class member-function definitions. (Part 2 of 2.)

Figure 10.22 uses static member function getCount to determine the number of Employee objects in memory at various points in the program. The program calls Employee::getCount() before any Employee objects have been created (line 12), after two Employee objects have been created (line 23) and after those Employee objects have been destroyed (line 34). Lines 16–29 in main define a nested scope. Recall that local variables exist until the scope in which they are defined terminates. In this example, we create two Employee objects in lines 17–18 inside the nested scope. As each constructor executes, it increments class Employee's static data member count. These Employee objects are destroyed when the program reaches line 29. At that point, each object's destructor executes and decrements class Employee's static data member count.

```
 1   // Fig. 10.22: fig10_22.cpp
 2   // static data member tracking the number of objects of a class.
 3   #include <iostream>
 4   #include "Employee.h" // Employee class definition
 5   using namespace std;
 6
 7   int main()
 8   {
 9      // no objects exist; use class name and binary scope resolution
10      // operator to access static member function getCount
11      cout << "Number of employees before instantiation of any objects is "
12         << Employee::getCount() << endl; // use class name
13
14      // the following scope creates and destroys
15      // Employee objects before main terminates
16      {
17         Employee e1( "Susan", "Baker" );
18         Employee e2( "Robert", "Jones" );
19
20         // two objects exist; call static member function getCount again
21         // using the class name and the binary scope resolution operator
22         cout << "Number of employees after objects are instantiated is "
23            << Employee::getCount();
24
25         cout << "\n\nEmployee 1: "
26            << e1.getFirstName() << " " << e1.getLastName()
27            << "\nEmployee 2: "
28            << e2.getFirstName() << " " << e2.getLastName() << "\n\n";
29      } // end nested scope in main
30
31      // no objects exist, so call static member function getCount again
32      // using the class name and the binary scope resolution operator
33      cout << "\nNumber of employees after objects are deleted is "
34         << Employee::getCount() << endl;
35   } // end main
```

```
Number of employees before instantiation of any objects is 0
Employee constructor for Susan Baker called.
Employee constructor for Robert Jones called.
Number of employees after objects are instantiated is 2

Employee 1: Susan Baker
Employee 2: Robert Jones

~Employee() called for Robert Jones
~Employee() called for Susan Baker

Number of employees after objects are deleted is 0
```

Fig. 10.22 | static data member tracking the number of objects of a class.

A member function should be declared static if it does not access non-static data members or non-static member functions of the class. Unlike non-static member functions, a static member function does not have a this pointer, because static data members and `static` member functions exist independently of any objects of a class. The `this` pointer must refer to a specific object of the class, and when a `static` member function is called, there might not be any objects of its class in memory.

Common Programming Error 10.9
Using the `this` pointer in a `static` member function is a compilation error.

Common Programming Error 10.10
Declaring a `static` member function `const` is a compilation error. The `const` qualifier indicates that a function cannot modify the contents of the object in which it operates, but `static` member functions exist and operate independently of any objects of the class.

10.7 Data Abstraction and Information Hiding

Classes normally hide the details of their implementation from their clients. This is called **information hiding**. As an example, let's consider the stack data structure introduced in Section 6.11. Recall that the stack is a last-in-first-out (LIFO) data structure—the last item pushed (inserted) on the stack is the first item popped (removed) off the stack.

Stacks can be implemented with arrays and with other data structures, such as linked lists. (We discuss stacks in Chapter 14 and Chapter 20.) A client of a stack class need not be concerned with the stack's implementation. The client knows only that when data items are placed in the stack, they will be recalled in last-in, first-out order. The client cares about *what* functionality a stack offers, not about *how* that functionality is implemented. This concept is referred to as **data abstraction**. Although you might know the details of a class's implementation, you should not write code that depends on these details as the details may later change. This enables a particular class (such as one that implements a stack and its operations, *push* and *pop*) to be replaced with another version without affecting the rest of the system. As long as the `public` services of the class do not change (i.e., every original `public` member function still has the same prototype in the new class definition), the rest of the system is not affected.

Abstract Data Types

Many programming languages emphasize actions. In these languages, data exists to support the actions that programs must take. Data is "less interesting" than actions. Data is "crude." Only a few built-in data types exist, and it's difficult to create new types. C++ and the object-oriented style of programming elevate the importance of data. The primary activities of object-oriented programming in C++ are the creation of types (i.e., classes) and the expression of the interactions among objects of those types. To create languages that emphasize data, the programming-languages community needed to formalize some notions about data. The formalization we consider here is the notion of **abstract data types** (**ADTs**), which improve the application-development process.

What's an abstract data type? Consider the type `int`, which most people would associate with an integer in mathematics. Rather, an `int` is an abstract representation of an integer. Unlike mathematical integers, computer `int`s have a maximum size—on 32-bit machines is typically limited to the range –2,147,483,648 to +2,147,483,647. If the result of a calculation falls outside this range, an "overflow" error occurs and the computer responds in some machine-dependent manner. It might, for example, "quietly" produce an incorrect result, such as a value too large to fit in an int variable (commonly called **arithmetic overflow**). Mathematical integers do not have this problem. Therefore, the notion of a computer int is only an approximation of the notion of a real-world integer.

Types like int, double, char and others are all examples of abstract data types. They're essentially ways of representing real-world notions to some satisfactory level of precision within a computer system.

An abstract data type actually captures two notions—A **data representation** and the **operations** that can be performed on that data. For example, in C++, an int contains an integer value (data) and provides addition, subtraction, multiplication, division and modulus operations (among others)—division by zero is undefined. These allowed operations perform in a manner sensitive to machine parameters, such as the fixed word size of the underlying computer system. Another example is the notion of negative integers, whose operations and data representation are clear, but the operation of taking the square root of a negative integer is undefined. In C++, you can use classes to implement abstract data types and their services. For example, to implement a stack ADT, we create our own stack classes in Chapters 14 and 20, and we study the standard library stack class in Chapter 22, Standard Template Library (STL).

Software Engineering Observation 10.12

You can create new types through the class mechanism. These new types can be designed to be used as conveniently as the fundamental types. Thus, C++ is an extensible language. *Although the language is easy to extend with these new types, the base language itself cannot be changed.*

Queue Abstract Data Type

Each of us stands in line from time to time. A waiting line is also called a **queue**. Computer systems use waiting lines internally, so we need to write programs that implement queues. A queue is another example of an abstract data type.

Queues offer well-understood behavior to their clients. Clients put things in a queue one at a time—by invoking the queue's **enqueue** operation—and the clients get those things back one at a time on demand—by invoking the queue's **dequeue** operation. Conceptually, a queue can become infinitely long; a real queue, of course, is finite. Items are returned from a queue in **first-in, first-out** (**FIFO**) order—the first item inserted in the queue is the first item removed from the queue.

The queue hides an internal data representation that keeps track of the items currently waiting in line, and offers a set of operations to clients, namely, *enqueue* and *dequeue*. The clients are not concerned about the implementation of the queue. Clients merely want the queue to operate "as advertised." When a client enqueues a new item, the queue should accept that item and place it internally in some kind of first-in, first-out data structure. When the client wants the next item from the front of the queue, the queue should remove the item from its internal representation and deliver it to the client in FIFO order (i.e., the item that has been in the queue the longest should be the next one returned by the next *dequeue* operation).

The queue ADT guarantees the integrity of its internal data structure. Clients may not manipulate this data structure directly. Only the queue member functions have access to its internal data. Clients may cause only allowable operations to be performed on the data representation; operations not provided in the ADT's public interface are rejected in some appropriate manner. This could mean issuing an error message, throwing an exception (see Chapter 16), terminating execution or simply ignoring the operation request.

We create our own queue class in Chapter 20, and we study the Standard Library queue class in Chapter 22.

10.8 Wrap-Up

This chapter introduced several advanced topics related to classes and data abstraction. You learned how to specify `const` objects and `const` member functions to prevent modifications to objects, thus enforcing the principle of least privilege. You also learned that, through composition, a class can have objects of other classes as members. We introduced the topic of friendship and presented examples that demonstrate how to use `friend` functions.

You learned that the `this` pointer is passed as an implicit argument to each of a class's non-`static` member functions, allowing the functions to access the correct object's data members and other non-`static` member functions. You also saw explicit use of the `this` pointer to access the class's members and to enable cascaded member-function calls. We motivated the need for `static` data members and demonstrated how to declare and use `static` data members and `static` member functions in your own classes.

You learned about data abstraction and information hiding—two of the fundamental concepts of object-oriented programming. Finally, we discussed abstract data types—ways of representing real-world or conceptual notions to some satisfactory level of precision within a computer system.

In Chapter 11, we continue our study of classes and objects by showing how to enable C++'s operators to work with objects—a process called operator overloading. For example, you'll see how to "overload" the `<<` operator so it can be used to output a complete array without explicitly using a repetition statement.

Summary

Section 10.2 `const` (Constant) Objects and `const` Member Functions
- The keyword `const` can be used to specify that an object is not modifiable and that any attempt to modify the object should result in a compilation error.
- C++ compilers disallow non-`const` member function calls on `const` objects.
- An attempt by a `const` member function to modify an object of its class is a compilation error.
- A member function is specified as `const` both in its prototype and in its definition.
- A `const` object must be initialized.
- Constructors and destructors cannot be declared `const`.
- `const` data member and reference data members *must* be initialized using member initializers.

Section 10.3 Composition: Objects as Members of Classes
- A class can have objects of other classes as members—this concept is called composition.
- Member objects are constructed in the order in which they're declared in the class definition and before their enclosing class objects are constructed.
- If a member initializer is not provided for a member object, the member object's default constructor will be called implicitly.

Section 10.4 `friend` Functions and `friend` Classes
- A `friend` function of a class is defined outside that class's scope, yet has the right to access all of the class's members. Stand-alone functions or entire classes may be declared to be friends.
- A friend declaration can appear anywhere in the class.
- The friendship relation is neither symmetric nor transitive.

Section 10.5 Using the `this` Pointer
- Every object has access to its own address through the `this` pointer.
- An object's `this` pointer is not part of the object itself—i.e., the size of the memory occupied by the `this` pointer is not reflected in the result of a `sizeof` operation on the object.
- The `this` pointer is passed as an implicit argument to each non-`static` member function.
- Objects use the `this` pointer implicitly (as we've done to this point) or explicitly to reference their data members and member functions.
- The `this` pointer enables cascaded member-function calls in which multiple functions are invoked in the same statement.

Section 10.6 `static` Class Members
- A `static` data member represents "class-wide" information (i.e., a property of the class shared by all instances, not a property of a specific object of the class).
- `static` data members have class scope and can be declared `public`, `private` or `protected`.
- A class's `static` members exist even when no objects of that class exist.
- To access a `public` `static` class member when no objects of the class exist, simply prefix the class name and the binary scope resolution operator (`::`) to the name of the data member.
- A member function should be declared `static` if it does not access non `static` data members or non-static member functions of the class. Unlike non-static member functions, a `static` member function does not have a `this` pointer, because `static` data members and `static` member functions exist independently of any objects of a class.

Section 10.7 Data Abstraction and Information Hiding
- Abstract data types are ways of representing real-world and conceptual notions to some satisfactory level of precision within a computer system.
- An abstract data type captures two notions: a data representation and the operations that can be performed on that data.

Terminology

abstract data type (ADTs) 458
arithmetic overflow 459
cascaded member-function calls 449
composition 439
data abstraction 458
data representation 459
dequeue (queue operation) 459
enqueue (queue operation) 459
first-in, first-out (FIFO) 459
friend function 445
has-a relationship 439
host object 440

information hiding 458
member initializer 435
member initializer list 436
member initializer syntax 435
member object 439
member object constructor 439
operations in an ADT 460
queue 459
queue abstract data type 459
static data member 453
static member function 454
this pointer 448

Self-Review Exercises

10.1 Fill in the blanks in each of the following:
   a) _____ must be used to initialize constant members of a class.
   b) A nonmember function must be declared as a(n) _____ of a class to have access to that class's private data members.
   c) A constant object must be _____; it cannot be modified after it's created.
   d) A(n) _____ data member represents class-wide information.
   e) An object's non-static member functions have access to a "self pointer" to the object called the _____ pointer.
   f) Keyword _____ specifies that an object or variable is not modifiable.
   g) If a member initializer is not provided for a member object of a class, the object's _____ is called.
   h) A member function should be static if it does not access _____ class members.
   i) Member objects are constructed _____ their enclosing class object.

10.2 Find the errors in the following class and explain how to correct them:

```
class Example
{
public:
   Example( int y = 10 )
      : data( y )
   {
      // empty body
   } // end Example constructor

   int getIncrementedData() const
   {
      return data++;
   } // end function getIncrementedData

   static int getCount()
   {
      cout << "Data is " << data << endl;
      return count;
   } // end function getCount
private:
   int data;
   static int count;
}; // end class Example
```

Answers to Self-Review Exercises

10.1   a) member initializers. b) friend. c) initialized. d) static. e) this. f) const. g) default constructor. h) non-static. i) before.

10.2   *Error:* The class definition for Example has two errors. The first occurs in function get IncrementedData. The function is declared const, but it modifies the object.
   Correction: To correct the first error, remove the const keyword from the definition of get IncrementedData.
   Error: The second error occurs in function getCount. This function is declared static, so it isn't allowed to access any non-static member (i.e., data) of the class.
   Correction: To correct the second error, remove the output line from the getCount definition.

Exercises

10.3 Explain the notion of friendship. Explain the negative aspects of friendship as described in the text.

10.4 Can a correct Time class definition include both of the following constructors? If not, explain why not.

```
Time( int h = 0, int m = 0, int s = 0 );
Time();
```

10.5 What happens when a return type, even void, is specified for a constructor or destructor?

10.6 (*Date Class Modification*) Modify class Date in Fig. 10.10 to have the following capabilities:
a) Output the date in multiple formats such as

```
DDD YYYY
MM/DD/YY
June 14, 1992
```

b) Use overloaded constructors to create Date objects initialized with dates of the formats in part (a).
c) Create a Date constructor that reads the system date using the standard library functions of the <ctime> header and sets the Date members. (See your compiler's reference documentation or www.cplusplus.com/ref/ctime/index.html for information on the functions in header <ctime>.)

In Chapter 11, we'll be able to create operators for testing the equality of two dates and for comparing dates to determine whether one date is prior to, or after, another.

10.7 (*SavingsAccount Class*) Create a SavingsAccount class. Use a static data member annualInterestRate to store the annual interest rate for each of the savers. Each member of the class contains a private data member savingsBalance indicating the amount the saver currently has on deposit. Provide member function calculateMonthlyInterest that calculates the monthly interest by multiplying the balance by annualInterestRate divided by 12; this interest should be added to savingsBalance. Provide a static member function modifyInterestRate that sets the static annualInterestRate to a new value. Write a driver program to test class SavingsAccount. Instantiate two different objects of class SavingsAccount, saver1 and saver2, with balances of $2000.00 and $3000.00, respectively. Set the annualInterestRate to 3 percent. Then calculate the monthly interest and print the new balances for each of the savers. Then set the annualInterestRate to 4 percent, calculate the next month's interest and print the new balances for each of the savers.

10.8 (*IntegerSet Class*) Create class IntegerSet for which each object can hold integers in the range 0 through 100. Represent the set internally as a vector of bool values. Element a[i] is true if integer i is in the set. Element a[j] is false if integer j is not in the set. The default constructor initializes a set to the so-called "empty set," i.e., a set for which all elements contain false.

Provide member functions for the common set operations. For example, provide a unionOfSets member function that creates a third set that is the set-theoretic union of two existing sets (i.e., an element of the result is set to true if that element is true in either or both of the existing sets, and an element of the result is set to false if that element is false in each of the existing sets).

Provide an intersectionOfSets member function which creates a third set which is the set-theoretic intersection of two existing sets (i.e., an element of the result is set to false if that element is false in either or both of the existing sets, and an element of the result is set to true if that element is true in each of the existing sets).

Provide an insertElement member function that places a new integer k into a set by setting a[k] to true. Provide a deleteElement member function that deletes integer m by setting a[m] to false.

Provide a printSet member function that prints a set as a list of numbers separated by spaces. Print only those elements that are present in the set (i.e., their position in the vector has a value of true). Print --- for an empty set.

Provide an isEqualTo member function that determines whether two sets are equal.

Provide an additional constructor that receives an array of integers and the size of that array and uses the array to initialize a set object.

Now write a driver program to test your `IntegerSet` class. Instantiate several `IntegerSet` objects. Test that all your member functions work properly.

10.9 *(Time Class Modification)* It would be perfectly reasonable for the `Time` class of Figs. 10.17–10.18 to represent the time internally as the number of seconds since midnight rather than the three integer values `hour`, `minute` and `second`. Clients could use the same `public` methods and get the same results. Modify the `Time` class of Fig. 10.17 to implement the time as the number of seconds since midnight and show that there is no visible change in functionality to the clients of the class. [*Note:* This exercise nicely demonstrates the virtues of implementation hiding.]

10.10 *(Card Shuffling and Dealing)* Create a program to shuffle and deal a deck of cards. The program should consist of class `Card`, class `DeckOfCards` and a driver program. Class `Card` should provide:
    a) Data members `face` and `suit` of type `int`.
    b) A constructor that receives two `int`s representing the face and suit and uses them to initialize the data members.
    c) Two `static` arrays of `string`s representing the faces and suits.
    d) A `toString` function that returns the `Card` as a `string` in the form "*face* of *suit*." You can use the `+` operator to concatenate `string`s.
Class `DeckOfCards` should contain:
    a) A `vector` of `Card`s named `deck` to store the `Card`s.
    b) An integer `currentCard` representing the next card to deal.
    c) A default constructor that initializes the `Card`s in the deck. The constructor should use `vector` function `push_back` to add each `Card` to the end of the `vector` after the `Card` is created and initialized. This should be done for each of the 52 `Card`s in the deck.
    d) A `shuffle` function that shuffles the `Card`s in the deck. The shuffle algorithm should iterate through the `vector` of `Card`s. For each `Card`, randomly select another `Card` in the deck and swap the two `Card`s.
    e) A `dealCard` function that returns the next `Card` object from the deck.
    f) A `moreCards` function that returns a `bool` value indicating whether there are more `Card`s to deal.
The driver program should create a `DeckOfCards` object, shuffle the cards, then deal the 52 cards.

10.11 *(Card Shuffling and Dealing)* Modify the program you developed in Exercise 10.10 so that it deals a five-card poker hand. Then write functions to accomplish each of the following:
    a) Determine whether the hand contains a pair.
    b) Determine whether the hand contains two pairs.
    c) Determine whether the hand contains three of a kind (e.g., three jacks).
    d) Determine whether the hand contains four of a kind (e.g., four aces).
    e) Determine whether the hand contains a flush (i.e., all five cards of the same suit).
    f) Determine whether the hand contains a straight (i.e., five cards of consecutive face values).

Card Shuffling and Dealing Projects

10.12 *(Card Shuffling and Dealing)* Use the functions from Exercise 10.11 to write a program that deals two five-card poker hands, evaluates each hand and determines which is the better hand.

10.13 *(Card Shuffling and Dealing)* Modify the program you developed in Exercise 10.12 so that it can simulate the dealer. The dealer's five-card hand is dealt "face down" so the player cannot see it. The program should then evaluate the dealer's hand, and, based on the quality of the hand, the dealer should draw one, two or three more cards to replace the corresponding number of unneeded cards in the original hand. The program should then reevaluate the dealer's hand.

10.14 *(Card Shuffling and Dealing)* Modify the program you developed in Exercise 10.13 so that it handles the dealer's hand, but the player is allowed to decide which cards of the player's hand to replace. The program should then evaluate both hands and determine who wins. Now use this new program to play 20 games against the computer. Who wins more games, you or the computer? Have one of your friends play 20 games against the computer. Who wins more games? Based on the results of these games, make appropriate modifications to refine your poker-playing program. Play 20 more games. Does your modified program play a better game?

Making a Difference

10.15 *(Air Traffic Control Project)* Every day, according to the National Air Traffic Controllers Association (www.natca.org/mediacenter/bythenumbers.msp), there are more than 87,000 flights in the United States, including commercial flights, cargo flights, and so on, and the long-term trend is that air traffic activity will increase along with the population. As air traffic grows, so do the challenges to air traffic controllers, who monitor the flights and provide instructions to the pilots to ensure safety in the skies.

In this exercise, you'll create a Flight class that could be used in a simple air-traffic-control simulator. The application's main function will act as air traffic control. Visit sites such as

www.howstuffworks.com/air-traffic-control.htm

to research how the air-traffic-control system works. Then identify some key attributes of a Flight in an air-traffic-control system. Think about the different states a plane could be in from the time it's parked at an airport gate until it arrives at its destination—parked, taxiing, waiting to take off, taking off, climbing, and so on. Use a FlightStatus enumeration to represent these states. The attributes might include the plane's make and model, current air speed, current altitude, direction, carrier, departure time, estimated arrival time, origin and destination. The origin and destination should be specified using standard three-letter airport codes, such as BOS for Boston and LAX for Los Angeles (these codes are available at world-airport-codes.com). Provide *set* and *get* functions to manipulate these and any other attributes you identify. Next, identify the class's behaviors and implement them as functions of the class. Include behaviors such as changeAltitude, reduceSpeed and beginLandingApproach. The Flight constructor should initialize a Flight's attributes. You should also provide a toString function that returns a string representation of a Flight's current status (e.g., parked at the gate, taxiing, taking off, changing altitude). This string should include all of the object's instance-variable values.

When the application executes, main will display the message, "Air Traffic Control Simulator", then will create and interact with three Flight objects representing planes that are currently flying or preparing to fly. For simplicity, the Flight's confirmation of each action will be a message displayed on the screen when the appropriate function is called on the object. For example, if you call a flight's changeAltitude function, the method should:

    a) Display a message containing the airline, flight number, "changing altitude", the current altitude and the new altitude.

    b) Change the state of the status data member to CHANGING_ALTITUDE.

    c) Change the value of the newAltitude data member.

In main, create and initialize three Flight objects that are in different states—for example, one could be at the gate, one could be preparing for takeoff and one could be preparing for landing. The main function should send messages to (invoke functions on) the Flight objects. As a Flight object receives each message, it should display a confirmation message from the function being called—such as "[Airline name] [Flight number] changing altitude from 20000 to 25000 feet." The function should also update the appropriate state information in the Flight object. For example, if Air Traffic Control sends a message like "[Airline] [flight number] descend to 12000 feet," the program should execute a function call like flight1.changeAltitude(12000), which would display a confirmation message and would set data member newAltitude to 12000. [*Note:* Assume the Flight's currentAltitude data member is being set automatically by the plane's altimeter.]

11

Operator Overloading

The whole difference between construction and creation is exactly this: that a thing constructed can only be loved after it is constructed; but a thing created is loved before it exists.
—Gilbert Keith Chesterton

Our doctor would never really operate unless it was necessary. He was just that way. If he didn't need the money, he wouldn't lay a hand on you.
—Herb Shriner

Objectives

In this chapter you'll learn:

- What operator overloading is and how it simplifies programming.
- To overload operators for user-defined classes.
- To overload unary and binary operators.
- To convert objects from one class to another class.
- To create PhoneNumber, Array and Date classes that demonstrate operator overloading.
- To use overloaded operators and other features of C++'s string class.
- To use keyword explicit to prevent the compiler from using single-argument constructors to perform implicit conversions.

Outline

11.1 Introduction

Chapters 9–10 introduced the basics of C++ classes. Services were obtained from objects by sending messages (in the form of member-function calls) to the objects. This function call notation is cumbersome for certain kinds of classes (such as mathematical classes). Also, many common manipulations are performed with operators (e.g., input and output). We can use C++'s rich set of built-in operators to specify common object manipulations. This chapter shows how to enable C++'s operators to work with objects—a process called **operator overloading**.

One example of an overloaded operator built into C++ is <<, which is used both as the stream insertion operator and as the bitwise left-shift operator (which is discussed in Chapter 21, Bits, Characters, Strings and structs). Similarly, >> is also overloaded; it's used both as the stream extraction operator and as the bitwise right-shift operator. Both of these operators are overloaded in the C++ Standard Library.

Although operator overloading sounds like an exotic capability, most programmers implicitly use overloaded operators. For example, the C++ language overloads the addition operator (+) and the subtraction operator (-). These operators perform differently, depending on their context in integer, floating-point and pointer arithmetic.

C++ enables you to overload most operators to be sensitive to the context in which they're used—the compiler generates the appropriate code based on the context (in particular, the types of the operands). Some operators are overloaded frequently, especially the assignment, relational and various arithmetic operators such as + and -. The jobs performed by overloaded operators can also be performed by explicit function calls, but operator notation is often clearer and more familiar to programmers.

We discuss when to, and when not to, use operator overloading. We create classes `PhoneNumber`, `Array` and `Date` to demonstrate how to overload operators, including the stream insertion, stream extraction, assignment, equality, relational, subscript, logical negation and increment operators. We demonstrate C++'s Standard Library class `string`, which provides many overloaded operators. In the exercises, we ask you to implement several classes with overloaded operators. The exercises also use classes `Complex` (for complex numbers) and `HugeInt` (for integers larger than a computer can represent with type `long`) to demonstrate overloaded arithmetic operators + and -, and ask you to enhance those classes by overloading other arithmetic operators. Finally, we show how to create a proxy class to hide a class's implementation details (including its `private` data) from its clients.

11.2 Fundamentals of Operator Overloading

C++ programming is a type-sensitive and type-focused process. You can use fundamental types and can define new types. The fundamental types can be used with C++'s rich collection of operators. Operators provide you with a concise notation for expressing manipulations of data of fundamental types.

You can use operators with user-defined types as well. Although C++ does not allow new operators to be created, it does allow most existing operators to be overloaded so that, when they're used with objects, they have meaning appropriate to those objects.

Software Engineering Observation 11.1
Operator overloading contributes to C++'s extensibility—one of the language's most appealing attributes.

Good Programming Practice 11.1
Use operator overloading when it makes a program clearer than accomplishing the same operations with function calls.

Good Programming Practice 11.2
Overloaded operators should mimic the functionality of their built-in counterparts—for example, the + operator should be overloaded to perform addition, not subtraction. Avoid excessive or inconsistent use of operator overloading, as this can make a program cryptic and difficult to read.

An operator is overloaded by writing a non-`static` member function definition or global function definition as you normally would, except that the function name now becomes the keyword `operator` followed by the symbol for the operator being overloaded. For example, the function name `operator+` would be used to overload the addition operator (+). When operators are overloaded as member functions, they must be non-`static`, because they must be called on an object of the class and operate on that object.

To use an operator on class objects, that operator *must* be overloaded—with three exceptions. The assignment operator (=) may be used with every class to perform memberwise assignment of the class's data members—each data member is assigned from the assignment's "source" object to the "target" object. Memberwise assignment is dangerous for classes with pointer members; we'll explicitly overload the assignment operator for such classes. The address (&) and comma (,) operators may also be used with objects of any class without overloading. The address operator returns a pointer to the object. The comma operator evaluates the expression to its left then the expression to its right, and returns the value of the latter expression. Both of these operators can also be overloaded.

Overloading is especially appropriate for mathematical classes. These often require that a substantial set of operators be overloaded to ensure consistency with the way these mathematical classes are handled in the real world. For example, it would be unusual to overload only addition for a complex number class, because other arithmetic operators are also commonly used with complex numbers.

Operator overloading provides the same concise and familiar expressions for user-defined types that C++ provides with its rich collection of operators for fundamental types. Operator overloading is not automatic—you must write operator-overloading functions to perform the desired operations. Sometimes these functions are best made member functions; sometimes they're best as `friend` functions; occasionally they can be made global, non-`friend` functions. We present examples of each of these possibilities.

11.3 Restrictions on Operator Overloading

Most of C++'s operators can be overloaded. These are shown in Fig. 11.1. Figure 11.2 shows the operators that cannot be overloaded.

Operators that can be overloaded							
+	-	*	/	%	^	&	|
~	!	=	<	>	+=	-=	*=
/=	%=	^=	&=	|=	<<	>>	>>=
<<=	==	!=	<=	>=	&&	||	++
--	->*	,	->	[]	()	new	delete
new[]	delete[]						

Fig. 11.1 | Operators that can be overloaded.

Operators that cannot be overloaded			
.	.*	::	?:

Fig. 11.2 | Operators that cannot be overloaded.

Precedence, Associativity and Number of Operands
The precedence of an operator cannot be changed by overloading. This can lead to awkward situations in which an operator is overloaded in a manner for which its fixed precedence is inappropriate. However, parentheses can be used to force the order of evaluation of overloaded operators in an expression.

The associativity of an operator (i.e., whether the operator is applied right-to-left or left-to-right) cannot be changed by overloading.

It isn't possible to change the "arity" of an operator (i.e., the number of operands an operator takes): Overloaded unary operators remain unary operators; overloaded binary operators remain binary operators. C++'s only ternary operator (?:) cannot be overloaded. Operators &, *, + and - all have both unary and binary versions; these unary and binary versions can each be overloaded.

Common Programming Error 11.1
Attempting to change the "arity" of an operator via operator overloading is a compilation error.

Creating New Operators
It isn't possible to create new operators; only existing operators can be overloaded. Unfortunately, this prevents you from using popular notations like the ** operator used in some other programming languages for exponentiation. [*Note:* You could overload an existing operator to perform exponentiation.]

Common Programming Error 11.2
Attempting to create new operators via operator overloading is a syntax error.

Operators for Fundamental Types
The meaning of how an operator works on objects of fundamental types cannot be changed by operator overloading. You cannot, for example, change the meaning of how + adds two integers. Operator overloading works only with objects of user-defined types or with a mixture of an object of a user-defined type and an object of a fundamental type.

Software Engineering Observation 11.2
At least one argument of an operator function must be an object or reference of a user-defined type. This prevents you from changing how operators work on fundamental types.

Common Programming Error 11.3
Attempting to modify how an operator works with objects of fundamental types is a compilation error.

Related Operators
Overloading an assignment operator and an addition operator to allow statements like

```
object2 = object2 + object1;
```

does not imply that the += operator is also overloaded to allow statements such as

```
object2 += object1;
```

Such behavior can be achieved only by explicitly overloading operator += for that class.

Common Programming Error 11.4
Assuming that overloading an operator such as + overloads related operators such as += or that overloading == overloads a related operator like != can lead to errors. Operators can be overloaded only explicitly; there is no implicit overloading.

11.4 Operator Functions as Class Members vs. Global Functions

Operator functions can be member functions or global functions; global functions are often made friends for performance reasons. Member functions use the this pointer implicitly to obtain one of their class object arguments (the left operand for binary operators). Arguments for both operands of a binary operator must be explicitly listed in a global function call.

Operators That Must Be Overloaded as Member Functions

When overloading (), [], -> or any of the assignment operators, the operator overloading function must be declared as a class member. For the other operators, the operator overloading functions can be class members or standalone functions.

Operators as Member Functions and Global Functions

Whether an operator function is implemented as a member function or as a global function, the operator is still used the same way in expressions. So which is best?

When an operator function is implemented as a member function, the leftmost (or only) operand must be an object (or a reference to an object) of the operator's class. If the left operand must be an object of a different class or a fundamental type, this operator function must be implemented as a global function (as we'll do in Section 11.5 when overloading << and >> as the stream insertion and stream extraction operators, respectively). A global operator function can be made a friend of a class if that function must access private or protected members of that class directly.

Operator member functions of a specific class are called (implicitly by the compiler) only when the left operand of a binary operator is specifically an object of that class, or when the single operand of a unary operator is an object of that class.

Why Overloaded Stream Insertion and Stream Extraction Operators Are Overloaded as Global Functions

The overloaded stream insertion operator (<<) is used in an expression in which the left operand has type ostream &, as in cout << classObject. To use the operator in this manner where the *right* operand is an object of a user-defined class, it must be overloaded as a global function. To be a member function, operator << would have to be a member of the ostream class. This is not possible for user-defined classes, since we are not allowed to modify C++ Standard Library classes. Similarly, the overloaded stream extraction operator (>>) is used in an expression in which the left operand has type istream &, as in cin >> classObject, and the *right* operand is an object of a user-defined class, so it, too, must be a global function. Also, each of these overloaded operator functions may require access to the private data members of the class object being output or input, so these overloaded operator functions can be made friend functions of the class for performance reasons.

> **Performance Tip 11.1**
>
> *It's possible to overload an operator as a global, non-friend function, but such a function requiring access to a class's private or protected data would need to use set or get functions provided in that class's public interface. The overhead of calling these functions could cause poor performance, so these functions can be inlined to improve performance.*

Commutative Operators

Another reason why one might choose a global function to overload an operator is to enable the operator to be commutative. For example, suppose we have an object, number, of type long int, and an object bigInteger1, of class HugeInteger (a class in which integers may be arbitrarily large rather than being limited by the machine word size of the underlying hardware; class HugeInteger is developed in the chapter exercises). The addition operator (+) produces a temporary HugeInteger object as the sum of a HugeInteger and a long int (as in the expression bigInteger1 + number), or as the sum of a long int and a HugeInteger (as in the expression number + bigInteger1). Thus, we require the addition operator to be commutative (exactly as it is with two fundamental-type operands). The problem is that the class object must appear on the *left* of the addition operator if that operator is to be overloaded as a member function. So, we overload the operator as a global function to allow the HugeInteger to appear on the *right* of the addition. The operator+ function, which deals with the HugeInteger on the left, can still be a member function. The global function simply swaps its arguments and calls the member function.

11.5 Overloading Stream Insertion and Stream Extraction Operators

You can input and output fundamental-type data using the stream extraction operator >> and the stream insertion operator <<. The C++ class libraries overload these operators to process each fundamental type, including pointers and C-style char * strings. You can also overload these operators to perform input and output for your own types. The program of Figs. 11.3–11.5 overloads these operators to input and output PhoneNumber objects in the format "(000) 000-0000." The program assumes telephone numbers are input correctly.

```
1   // Fig. 11.3: PhoneNumber.h
2   // PhoneNumber class definition
3   #ifndef PHONENUMBER_H
4   #define PHONENUMBER_H
5
6   #include <iostream>
7   #include <string>
8   using namespace std;
9
10  class PhoneNumber
11  {
12     friend ostream &operator<<( ostream &, const PhoneNumber & );
13     friend istream &operator>>( istream &, PhoneNumber & );
14  private:
15     string areaCode; // 3-digit area code
16     string exchange; // 3-digit exchange
17     string line; // 4-digit line
18  }; // end class PhoneNumber
19
20  #endif
```

Fig. 11.3 | PhoneNumber class with overloaded stream insertion and stream extraction operators as friend functions.

```
1   // Fig. 11.4: PhoneNumber.cpp
2   // Overloaded stream insertion and stream extraction operators
3   // for class PhoneNumber.
4   #include <iomanip>
5   #include "PhoneNumber.h"
6   using namespace std;
```

Fig. 11.4 | Overloaded stream insertion and stream extraction operators for class PhoneNumber. (Part 1 of 2.)

```
7
8    // overloaded stream insertion operator; cannot be
9    // a member function if we would like to invoke it with
10   // cout << somePhoneNumber;
11   ostream &operator<<( ostream &output, const PhoneNumber &number )
12   {
13      output << "(" << number.areaCode << ") "
14         << number.exchange << "-" << number.line;
15      return output; // enables cout << a << b << c;
16   } // end function operator<<
17
18   // overloaded stream extraction operator; cannot be
19   // a member function if we would like to invoke it with
20   // cin >> somePhoneNumber;
21   istream &operator>>( istream &input, PhoneNumber &number )
22   {
23      input.ignore(); // skip (
24      input >> setw( 3 ) >> number.areaCode; // input area code
25      input.ignore( 2 ); // skip ) and space
26      input >> setw( 3 ) >> number.exchange; // input exchange
27      input.ignore(); // skip dash (-)
28      input >> setw( 4 ) >> number.line; // input line
29      return input; // enables cin >> a >> b >> c;
30   } // end function operator>>
```

Fig. 11.4 | Overloaded stream insertion and stream extraction operators for class `PhoneNumber`. (Part 2 of 2.)

```
1    // Fig. 11.5: fig11_05.cpp
2    // Demonstrating class PhoneNumber's overloaded stream insertion
3    // and stream extraction operators.
4    #include <iostream>
5    #include "PhoneNumber.h"
6    using namespace std;
7
8    int main()
9    {
10      PhoneNumber phone; // create object phone
11
12      cout << "Enter phone number in the form (123) 456-7890:" << endl;
13
14      // cin >> phone invokes operator>> by implicitly issuing
15      // the global function call operator>>( cin, phone )
16      cin >> phone;
17
18      cout << "The phone number entered was: ";
19
20      // cout << phone invokes operator<< by implicitly issuing
21      // the global function call operator<<( cout, phone )
22      cout << phone << endl;
23   } // end main
```

Fig. 11.5 | Overloaded stream insertion and stream extraction operators. (Part 1 of 2.)

```
Enter phone number in the form (123) 456-7890:
(800) 555-1212
The phone number entered was: (800) 555-1212
```

Fig. 11.5 | Overloaded stream insertion and stream extraction operators. (Part 2 of 2.)

The stream extraction operator function operator>> (Fig. 11.4, lines 21–30) takes istream reference input and PhoneNumber reference number as arguments and returns an istream reference. Operator function operator>> inputs phone numbers of the form

```
(800) 555-1212
```

into objects of class PhoneNumber. When the compiler sees the expression

```
cin >> phone
```

in line 16 of Fig. 11.5, the compiler generates the global function call

```
operator>>( cin, phone );
```

When this call executes, reference parameter input (Fig. 11.4, line 21) becomes an alias for cin and reference parameter number becomes an alias for phone. The operator function reads as strings the three parts of the telephone number into the areaCode (line 24), exchange (line 26) and line (line 28) members of the PhoneNumber object referenced by parameter number. Stream manipulator setw limits the number of characters read into each string. When used with cin and strings, setw restricts the number of characters read to the number of characters specified by its argument (i.e., setw(3) allows three characters to be read). The parentheses, space and dash characters are skipped by calling istream member function ignore (Fig. 11.4, lines 23, 25 and 27), which discards the specified number of characters in the input stream (one character by default). Function operator>> returns istream reference input (i.e., cin). This enables input operations on PhoneNumber objects to be cascaded with input operations on other PhoneNumber objects or on objects of other data types. For example, a program can input two PhoneNumber objects in one statement as follows:

```
cin >> phone1 >> phone2;
```

First, the expression cin >> phone1 executes by making the global function call

```
operator>>( cin, phone1 );
```

This call then returns a reference to cin as the value of cin >> phone1, so the remaining portion of the expression is interpreted simply as cin >> phone2. This executes by making the global function call

```
operator>>( cin, phone2 );
```

The stream insertion operator function (Fig. 11.4, lines 11–16) takes an ostream reference (output) and a const PhoneNumber reference (number) as arguments and returns an ostream reference. Function operator<< displays objects of type PhoneNumber. When the compiler sees the expression

```
cout << phone
```

in line 22 of Fig. 11.5, the compiler generates the global function call

```
operator<<( cout, phone );
```

Function `operator<<` displays the parts of the telephone number as `string`s, because they're stored as `string` objects.

Error-Prevention Tip 11.1

Returning a reference from an overloaded `<<` *or* `>>` *operator function is typically successful because* `cout`, `cin` *and most stream objects are global, or at least long-lived. Returning a reference to an automatic variable or other temporary object is dangerous—this can create "dangling references" to nonexisting objects.*

The functions `operator>>` and `operator<<` are declared in `PhoneNumber` as global, `friend` functions (Fig. 11.3, lines 12–13). They're global functions because the object of class `PhoneNumber` is the operator's right operand. Remember, overloaded operator functions for binary operators can be member functions only when the left operand is an object of the class in which the function is a member. Overloaded input and output operators are declared as `friend`s if they need to access non-`public` class members directly for performance reasons or because the class may not offer appropriate *get* functions. Also, the `PhoneNumber` reference in function `operator<<`'s parameter list (Fig. 11.4, line 11) is `const`, because the `PhoneNumber` will simply be output, and the `PhoneNumber` reference in function `operator>>`'s parameter list (line 21) is non-`const`, because the `PhoneNumber` object must be modified to store the input telephone number in the object.

Software Engineering Observation 11.3

New input/output capabilities for user-defined types are added to C++ without modifying standard input/output library classes. This is another example of C++'s extensibility.

11.6 Overloading Unary Operators

A unary operator for a class can be overloaded as a non-`static` member function with no arguments or as a global function with one argument that must be an object (or a reference to an object) of the class. Member functions that implement overloaded operators must be non-`static` so that they can access the non-`static` data in each object of the class. Remember that `static` member functions can access only `static` members of the class.

Later in this chapter, we'll overload unary operator `!` to test whether an object of the `String` class we create (Section 11.11) is empty and return a `bool` result. Consider the expression `!s`, in which `s` is an object of class `String`. When a unary operator such as `!` is overloaded as a member function with no arguments and the compiler sees the expression `!s`, the compiler generates the function call `s.operator!()`. The operand `s` is the class object for which the `String` class member function `operator!` is being invoked. The function is declared in the class definition as follows:

```
class String
{
public:
    bool operator!() const;
    ...
}; // end class String
```

A unary operator such as ! may be overloaded as a global function with one parameter in two different ways—either with a parameter that is an object (this requires a copy of the object, so the side effects of the function are not applied to the original object), or with a parameter that is a reference to an object (no copy of the original object is made, so all side effects of this function are applied to the original object). If s is a String class object (or a reference to a String class object), then !s is treated as if the call operator!(s) had been written, invoking the global operator! function that is declared as follows:

```
bool operator!( const String & );
```

11.7 Overloading Binary Operators

A binary operator can be overloaded as a non-static member function with one parameter or as a global function with two parameters (one of those parameters must be either a class object or a reference to a class object).

Later in this chapter, we'll overload < to compare two String objects. When overloading binary operator < as a non-static member function of a String class with one argument, if y and z are String-class objects, then y < z is treated as if y.operator<(z) had been written, invoking the operator< member function declared below

```
class String

public:
   bool operator<( const String & ) const;
   ...
}; // end class String
```

As a global function, binary operator < must take two arguments—one of which must be an object (or a reference to an object) of the class. If y and z are String-class objects or references to String-class objects, then y < z is treated as if the call operator<(y, z) had been written in the program, invoking global-function operator< declared as follows:

```
bool operator<( const String &, const String & );
```

11.8 Dynamic Memory Management

A standard C++ array data structure is fixed in size once it's created. The size is specified with a constant at compile time. Sometimes it's useful to determine the size of an array dynamically at execution time and then create the array. C++ enables you to control the allocation and deallocation of memory in a program for objects and for arrays of any built-in or user-defined type. This is known as **dynamic memory management** and is performed with the operators **new** and **delete**.

You can use the new operator to dynamically **allocate** (i.e., reserve) the exact amount of memory required to hold an object or array at execution time. The object or array is created in the **free store** (also called the **heap**)—a region of memory assigned to each program for storing dynamically allocated objects. Once memory is allocated in the free store, you can access it via the pointer that operator new returns. When you no longer need the memory, you can return it to the free store by using the delete operator to **deallocate** (i.e., release) the memory, which can then be reused by future new operations.

Obtaining Dynamic Memory with **new**

Let's discuss the details of using the new and delete operators to dynamically allocate memory to store objects, fundamental types and arrays. Consider the following statement:

```
Time *timePtr = new Time;
```

The new operator allocates storage of the proper size for an object of type Time, calls the default constructor to initialize the object and returns a pointer to the type specified to the right of the new operator (i.e., a Time *). If new is unable to find sufficient space in memory for the object, it indicates that an error occurred by "throwing an exception." Chapter 16, Exception Handling, discusses how to deal with new failures. In particular, we'll show how to "catch" the exception thrown by new and deal with it. When a program does not "catch" an exception, the program terminates immediately.

Releasing Dynamic Memory with **delete**

To destroy a dynamically allocated object and free the space for the object, use the delete operator as follows:

```
delete timePtr;
```

This statement first calls the destructor for the object to which timePtr points, then deallocates the memory associated with the object, returning the memory to the free store.

Common Programming Error 11.5

*Not releasing dynamically allocated memory when it's no longer needed can cause the system to run out of memory prematurely. This is sometimes called a "**memory leak**."*

Initializing Dynamic Memory

You can provide an **initializer** for a newly created fundamental-type variable, as in

```
double *ptr = new double( 3.14159 );
```

which initializes a newly created double to 3.14159 and assigns the resulting pointer to ptr. The same syntax can be used to specify a comma-separated list of arguments to the constructor of an object. For example,

```
Time *timePtr = new Time( 12, 45, 0 );
```

initializes a new Time object to 12:45 PM and assigns the resulting pointer to timePtr.

Dynamically Allocating Arrays with **new []**

You can also use the new operator to allocate arrays dynamically. For example, a 10-element integer array can be allocated and assigned to gradesArray as follows:

```
int *gradesArray = new int[ 10 ];
```

which declares int pointer gradesArray and assigns to it a pointer to the first element of a dynamically allocated 10-element array of ints. The size of an array created at compile time must be specified using a constant integral expression; however, a dynamically allocated array's size can be specified using *any* non-negative integral expression that can be evaluated at execution time. Also, when allocating an array of objects dynamically, you *cannot* pass arguments to each object's constructor—each object is initialized by its default constructor. For fundamental types, the elements are initialized to 0 or the equivalent of 0 (e.g., chars are initialized to the null character, '\0'). Although an array name is a pointer to the array's first element, the following is not allowed for dynamically allocated memory:

```
int gradesArray[] = new int[ 10 ];
```

Releasing Dynamically Allocated Arrays with **delete []**
To deallocate the memory to which gradesArray points, use the statement

```
delete [] gradesArray;
```

If the pointer points to an array of objects, the statement first calls the destructor for every object in the array, then deallocates the memory. If the preceding statement did not include the square brackets ([]) and gradesArray pointed to an array of objects, the result is undefined. Some compilers call the destructor only for the first object in the array. Using delete on a null pointer (i.e., a pointer with the value 0) has no effect.

Common Programming Error 11.6

Using delete instead of delete [] for arrays of objects can lead to runtime logic errors. To ensure that every object in the array receives a destructor call, always delete memory allocated as an array with operator delete []. Similarly, always delete memory allocated as an individual element with operator delete—the result of deleting a single object with operator delete [] is undefined.

11.9 Case Study: Array Class

We discussed arrays in Chapter 7. An array is not much more than a pointer to some space in memory. Pointer-based arrays have many problems, including:

- A program can easily "walk off" either end of an array, because C++ does not check whether subscripts fall outside the range of an array (though you can still do this explicitly).

- Arrays of size *n* must number their elements 0, …, *n* − 1; alternate subscript ranges are not allowed.

- An entire array cannot be input or output at once; each array element must be read or written individually (unless the array is a null-terminated C string).

- Two arrays cannot be meaningfully compared with equality or relational operators (because the array names are simply pointers to where the arrays begin in memory and two arrays will always be at different memory locations).

- When an array is passed to a general-purpose function designed to handle arrays of any size, the array's size must be passed as an additional argument.

- One array cannot be assigned to another with the assignment operator(s) (because array names are const pointers and a *constant* pointer cannot be used on the left side of an assignment operator).

C++ provides the means to implement more robust array capabilities via classes and operator overloading. You can develop an array class that is preferable to "raw" arrays. In this example, we create a powerful Array class that performs range checking to ensure that subscripts remain within the bounds of the Array. The class allows one array object to be assigned to another with the assignment operator. Array objects know their size, so the size does not need to be passed separately to functions that receive Array parameters. Entire Arrays can be input or output with the stream extraction and stream insertion operators, respectively. You can compare Arrays with the equality operators == and !=. Recall that C++ Standard Library class template vector (introduced in Chapter 7) provides many of these capabilities as well. Chapter 22 explains class template vector in detail.

This example will sharpen your appreciation of data abstraction. Class development is an interesting, creative and intellectually challenging activity—always with the goal of "crafting valuable classes." The program of Figs. 11.6–11.8 demonstrates class Array and its overloaded operators. First we walk through main (Fig. 11.8), then we consider the class definition (Fig. 11.6) and each of its member-function definitions (Fig. 11.7).

```cpp
1   // Fig. 11.6: Array.h
2   // Array class definition with overloaded operators.
3   #ifndef ARRAY_H
4   #define ARRAY_H
5
6   #include <iostream>
7   using namespace std;
8
9   class Array
10  {
11     friend ostream &operator<<( ostream &, const Array & );
12     friend istream &operator>>( istream &, Array & );
13  public:
14     Array( int = 10 ); // default constructor
15     Array( const Array & ); // copy constructor
16     ~Array(); // destructor
17     int getSize() const; // return size
18
19     const Array &operator=( const Array & ); // assignment operator
20     bool operator==( const Array & ) const; // equality operator
21
22     // inequality operator; returns opposite of == operator
23     bool operator!=( const Array &right ) const
24     {
25        return ! ( *this == right ); // invokes Array::operator==
26     } // end function operator!=
27
28     // subscript operator for non-const objects returns modifiable lvalue
29     int &operator[]( int );
30
31     // subscript operator for const objects returns rvalue
32     int operator[]( int ) const;
33  private:
34     int size; // pointer-based array size
35     int *ptr; // pointer to first element of pointer-based array
36  }; // end class Array
37
38  #endif
```

Fig. 11.6 | Array class definition with overloaded operators.

```cpp
1   // Fig 11.7: Array.cpp
2   // Array class member- and friend-function definitions.
3   #include <iostream>
4   #include <iomanip>
5   #include <cstdlib> // exit function prototype
6   #include "Array.h" // Array class definition
7   using namespace std;
8
9   // default constructor for class Array (default size 10)
10  Array::Array( int arraySize )
11  {
12     size = ( arraySize > 0 ? arraySize : 10 ); // validate arraySize
13     ptr = new int[ size ]; // create space for pointer-based array
14
15     for ( int i = 0; i < size; i++ )
16        ptr[ i ] = 0; // set pointer-based array element
17  } // end Array default constructor
18
19  // copy constructor for class Array;
20  // must receive a reference to prevent infinite recursion
21  Array::Array( const Array &arrayToCopy )
22     : size( arrayToCopy.size )
23  {
24     ptr = new int[ size ]; // create space for pointer-based array
25
26     for ( int i = 0; i < size; i++ )
27        ptr[ i ] = arrayToCopy.ptr[ i ]; // copy into object
28  } // end Array copy constructor
29
30  // destructor for class Array
31  Array::~Array()
32  {
33     delete [] ptr; // release pointer-based array space
34  } // end destructor
35
36  // return number of elements of Array
37  int Array::getSize() const
38  {
39     return size; // number of elements in Array
40  } // end function getSize
41
42  // overloaded assignment operator;
43  // const return avoids: ( a1 = a2 ) = a3
44  const Array &Array::operator=( const Array &right )
45  {
46     if ( &right != this ) // avoid self-assignment
47     {
48        // for Arrays of different sizes, deallocate original
49        // left-side array, then allocate new left-side array
50        if ( size != right.size )
51        {
52           delete [] ptr; // release space
53           size = right.size; // resize this object
```

Fig. 11.7 | Array class member- and `friend`-function definitions. (Part 1 of 3.)

```
54            ptr = new int[ size ]; // create space for array copy
55         } // end inner if
56
57         for ( int i = 0; i < size; i++ )
58            ptr[ i ] = right.ptr[ i ]; // copy array into object
59      } // end outer if
60
61      return *this; // enables x = y = z, for example
62   } // end function operator=
63
64   // determine if two Arrays are equal and
65   // return true, otherwise return false
66   bool Array::operator==( const Array &right ) const
67   {
68      if ( size != right.size )
69         return false; // arrays of different number of elements
70
71      for ( int i = 0; i < size; i++ )
72         if ( ptr[ i ] != right.ptr[ i ] )
73            return false; // Array contents are not equal
74
75      return true; // Arrays are equal
76   } // end function operator==
77
78   // overloaded subscript operator for non-const Arrays;
79   // reference return creates a modifiable lvalue
80   int &Array::operator[]( int subscript )
81   {
82      // check for subscript out-of-range error
83      if ( subscript < 0 || subscript >= size )
84      {
85         cerr << "\nError: Subscript " << subscript
86            << " out of range" << endl;
87         exit( 1 ); // terminate program; subscript out of range
88      } // end if
89
90      return ptr[ subscript ]; // reference return
91   } // end function operator[]
92
93   // overloaded subscript operator for const Arrays
94   // const reference return creates an rvalue
95   int Array::operator[]( int subscript ) const
96   {
97      // check for subscript out-of-range error
98      if ( subscript < 0 || subscript >= size )
99      {
100        cerr << "\nError: Subscript " << subscript
101           << " out of range" << endl;
102        exit( 1 ); // terminate program; subscript out of range
103     } // end if
104
105     return ptr[ subscript ]; // returns copy of this element
106  } // end function operator[]
```

Fig. 11.7 | Array class member- and friend-function definitions. (Part 2 of 3.)

```
107
108   // overloaded input operator for class Array;
109   // inputs values for entire Array
110   istream &operator>>( istream &input, Array &a )
111   {
112      for ( int i = 0; i < a.size; i++ )
113         input >> a.ptr[ i ];
114
115      return input; // enables cin >> x >> y;
116   } // end function
117
118   // overloaded output operator for class Array
119   ostream &operator<<( ostream &output, const Array &a )
120   {
121      int i;
122
123      // output private ptr-based array
124      for ( i = 0; i < a.size; i++ )
125      {
126         output << setw( 12 ) << a.ptr[ i ];
127
128         if ( ( i + 1 ) % 4 == 0 ) // 4 numbers per row of output
129            output << endl;
130      } // end for
131
132      if ( i % 4 != 0 ) // end last line of output
133         output << endl;
134
135      return output; // enables cout << x << y;
136   } // end function operator<<
```

Fig. 11.7 | Array class member- and `friend`-function definitions. (Part 3 of 3.)

```
1    // Fig. 11.8: fig11_08.cpp
2    // Array class test program.
3    #include <iostream>
4    #include "Array.h"
5    using namespace std;
6
7    int main()
8    {
9       Array integers1( 7 ); // seven-element Array
10      Array integers2; // 10-element Array by default
11
12      // print integers1 size and contents
13      cout << "Size of Array integers1 is "
14         << integers1.getSize()
15         << "\nArray after initialization:\n" << integers1;
16
```

Fig. 11.8 | Array class test program. (Part 1 of 3.)

```
17      // print integers2 size and contents
18      cout << "\nSize of Array integers2 is "
19         << integers2.getSize()
20         << "\nArray after initialization:\n" << integers2;
21
22      // input and print integers1 and integers2
23      cout << "\nEnter 17 integers:" << endl;
24      cin >> integers1 >> integers2;
25
26      cout << "\nAfter input, the Arrays contain:\n"
27         << "integers1:\n" << integers1
28         << "integers2:\n" << integers2;
29
30      // use overloaded inequality (!=) operator
31      cout << "\nEvaluating: integers1 != integers2" << endl;
32
33      if ( integers1 != integers2 )
34         cout << "integers1 and integers2 are not equal" << endl;
35
36      // create Array integers3 using integers1 as an
37      // initializer; print size and contents
38      Array integers3( integers1 ); // invokes copy constructor
39
40      cout << "\nSize of Array integers3 is "
41         << integers3.getSize()
42         << "\nArray after initialization:\n" << integers3;
43
44      // use overloaded assignment (=) operator
45      cout << "\nAssigning integers2 to integers1:" << endl;
46      integers1 = integers2; // note target Array is smaller
47
48      cout << "integers1:\n" << integers1
49         << "integers2:\n" << integers2;
50
51      // use overloaded equality (==) operator
52      cout << "\nEvaluating: integers1 == integers2" << endl;
53
54      if ( integers1 == integers2 )
55         cout << "integers1 and integers2 are equal" << endl;
56
57      // use overloaded subscript operator to create rvalue
58      cout << "\nintegers1[5] is " << integers1[ 5 ];
59
60      // use overloaded subscript operator to create lvalue
61      cout << "\n\nAssigning 1000 to integers1[5]" << endl;
62      integers1[ 5 ] = 1000;
63      cout << "integers1:\n" << integers1;
64
65      // attempt to use out-of-range subscript
66      cout << "\nAttempt to assign 1000 to integers1[15]" << endl;
67      integers1[ 15 ] = 1000; // ERROR: out of range
68   } // end main
```

Fig. 11.8 | Array class test program. (Part 2 of 3.)

```
Size of Array integers1 is 7
Array after initialization:
           0           0           0           0
           0           0           0

Size of Array integers2 is 10
Array after initialization:
           0           0           0           0
           0           0           0           0
           0           0

Enter 17 integers:
1 2 3 4 5 6 7 8 9 10 11 12 13 14 15 16 17

After input, the Arrays contain:
integers1:
           1           2           3           4
           5           6           7
integers2:
           8           9          10          11
          12          13          14          15
          16          17

Evaluating: integers1 != integers2
integers1 and integers2 are not equal

Size of Array integers3 is 7
Array after initialization:
           1           2           3           4
           5           6           7

Assigning integers2 to integers1:
integers1:
           8           9          10          11
          12          13          14          15
          16          17
integers2:
           8           9          10          11
          12          13          14          15
          16          17

Evaluating: integers1 == integers2
integers1 and integers2 are equal

integers1[5] is 13

Assigning 1000 to integers1[5]
integers1:
           8           9          10          11
          12        1000          14          15
          16          17

Attempt to assign 1000 to integers1[15]

Error: Subscript 15 out of range
```

Fig. 11.8 | Array class test program. (Part 3 of 3.)

*Creating **Arrays**, Outputting Their Size and Displaying Their Contents*
The program begins by instantiating two objects of class Array—integers1 (Fig. 11.8, line 9) with seven elements, and integers2 (Fig. 11.8, line 10) with the default Array size—10 elements (specified by the Array default constructor's prototype in Fig. 11.6, line 14). Lines 13–15 use member function getSize to determine the size of integers1 and output integers1, using the Array overloaded stream insertion operator. The sample output confirms that the Array elements were set correctly to zeros by the constructor. Next, lines 18–20 output the size of Array integers2 and output integers2, using the Array overloaded stream insertion operator.

*Using the Overloaded Stream Insertion Operator to Fill an **Array***
Line 23 prompts the user to input 17 integers. Line 24 uses the Array overloaded stream extraction operator to read these values into both arrays. The first seven values are stored in integers1 and the remaining 10 values are stored in integers2. Lines 26–28 output the two arrays with the overloaded Array stream insertion operator to confirm that the input was performed correctly.

Using the Overloaded Inequality Operator
Line 33 tests the overloaded inequality operator by evaluating the condition

```
integers1 != integers2
```

The program output shows that the Arrays are not equal.

*Initializing a New **Array** with a Copy of an Existing **Array**'s Contents*
Line 38 instantiates a third Array called integers3 and initializes it with a copy of Array integers1. This invokes the Array **copy constructor** to copy the elements of integers1 into integers3. We discuss the details of the copy constructor shortly. The copy constructor can also be invoked by writing line 38 as follows:

```
Array integers3 = integers1;
```

The equal sign in the preceding statement is *not* the assignment operator. When an equal sign appears in the declaration of an object, it invokes a constructor for that object. This form can be used to pass only a single argument to a constructor.

Lines 40–42 output the size of integers3 and output integers3, using the Array overloaded stream insertion operator to confirm that the Array elements were set correctly by the copy constructor.

Using the Overloaded Assignment Operator
Next, line 46 tests the overloaded assignment operator (=) by assigning integers2 to integers1. Lines 48–49 print both Array objects to confirm that the assignment was successful. Note that integers1 originally held 7 integers and was resized to hold a copy of the 10 elements in integers2. As we'll see, the overloaded assignment operator performs this resizing operation in a manner that is transparent to the client code.

Using the Overloaded Equality Operator
Next, line 54 uses the overloaded equality operator (==) to confirm that objects integers1 and integers2 are indeed identical after the assignment.

Using the Overloaded Subscript Operator

Line 58 uses the overloaded subscript operator to refer to integers1[5]—an in-range element of integers1. This subscripted name is used as an *rvalue* to print the value stored in integers1[5]. Line 62 uses integers1[5] as a modifiable *lvalue* on the left side of an assignment statement to assign a new value, 1000, to element 5 of integers1. We'll see that operator[] returns a reference to use as the modifiable *lvalue* after the operator confirms that 5 is a valid subscript for integers1.

Line 67 attempts to assign the value 1000 to integers1[15]—an out-of-range element. In this example, operator[] determines that the subscript is out of range, prints a message and terminates the program. We highlighted line 67 of the program in red to emphasize that it's an error to access an element that is out of range. This is a runtime logic error.

Interestingly, the array subscript operator [] is not restricted for use only with arrays; it also can be used, for example, to select elements from other kinds of container classes, such as linked lists, strings and dictionaries. Also, when operator[] functions are defined, subscripts no longer have to be integers—characters, strings, floats or even objects of user-defined classes also could be used. In Chapter 22, we discuss the STL map class that allows noninteger subscripts.

Array Class Definition

Now that we've seen how this program operates, let's walk through the class header (Fig. 11.6). As we refer to each member function in the header, we discuss that function's implementation in Fig. 11.7. In Fig. 11.6, lines 34–35 represent the private data members of class Array. Each Array object consists of a size member indicating the number of elements in the Array and an int pointer—ptr—that points to the dynamically allocated pointer-based array of integers managed by the Array object.

Overloading the Stream Insertion and Stream Extraction Operators as **friend***s*

Lines 11–12 of Fig. 11.6 declare the overloaded stream insertion operator and the overloaded stream extraction operator to be friends of class Array. When the compiler sees an expression like cout << arrayObject, it invokes global function operator<< with the call

```
operator<<( cout, arrayObject )
```

When the compiler sees an expression like cin >> arrayObject, it invokes global function operator>> with the call

```
operator>>( cin, arrayObject )
```

We note again that these stream insertion and stream extraction operator functions cannot be members of class Array, because the Array object is always mentioned on the right side of the stream insertion operator and the stream extraction operator. If these operator functions were to be members of class Array, the following awkward statements would have to be used to output and input an Array:

```
arrayObject << cout;
arrayObject >> cin;
```

Such statements would be confusing to most C++ programmers, who are familiar with cout and cin appearing as the left operands of << and >>, respectively.

Function operator<< (defined in Fig. 11.7, lines 119–136) prints the number of elements indicated by size from the integer array to which ptr points. Function operator>> (defined in Fig. 11.7, lines 110–116) inputs directly into the array to which ptr points. Each of these operator functions returns an appropriate reference to enable cascaded output or input statements, respectively. Each of these functions has access to an Array's private data because these functions are declared as friends of class Array. Also, class Array's getSize and operator[] functions could be used by operator<< and operator>>, in which case these operator functions would not need to be friends of class Array. However, the additional function calls might increase execution-time overhead.

Array Default Constructor

Line 14 of Fig. 11.6 declares the default constructor for the class and specifies a default size of 10 elements. When the compiler sees a declaration like line 10 in Fig. 11.8, it invokes class Array's default constructor (remember that the default constructor in this example actually receives a single int argument that has a default value of 10). The default constructor (defined in Fig. 11.7, lines 10–17) validates and assigns the argument to data member size, uses new to obtain the memory for the internal pointer-based representation of this array and assigns the pointer returned by new to data member ptr. Then the constructor uses a for statement to set all the elements of the array to zero. It's possible to have an Array class that does not initialize its members if, for example, these members are to be read at some later time; but this is considered to be a poor programming practice. Arrays, and objects in general, should be properly initialized and maintained in a consistent state.

Array Copy Constructor

Line 15 of Fig. 11.6 declares a copy constructor (defined in Fig. 11.7, lines 21–28) that initializes an Array by making a copy of an existing Array object. Such copying must be done carefully to avoid the pitfall of leaving both Array objects pointing to the same dynamically allocated memory. This is exactly the problem that would occur with default memberwise copying, if the compiler is allowed to define a default copy constructor for this class. Copy constructors are invoked whenever a copy of an object is needed, such as in passing an object by value to a function, returning an object by value from a function or initializing an object with a copy of another object of the same class. The copy constructor is called in a declaration when an object of class Array is instantiated and initialized with another object of class Array, as in the declaration in line 38 of Fig. 11.8.

Software Engineering Observation 11.4

The argument to a copy constructor should be a const reference to allow a const object to be copied.

Common Programming Error 11.7

A copy constructor must receive its argument by reference, not by value. Otherwise, the copy constructor call results in infinite recursion (a fatal logic error) because receiving an object by value requires the copy constructor to make a copy of the argument object. Recall that any time a copy of an object is required, the class's copy constructor is called. If the copy constructor received its argument by value, the copy constructor would call itself recursively to make a copy of its argument!

The copy constructor for `Array` uses a member initializer (Fig. 11.7, line 22) to copy the `size` of the initializer `Array` into data member `size`, uses `new` (line 24) to obtain the memory for the internal pointer-based representation of this `Array` and assigns the pointer returned by `new` to data member `ptr`.[1] Then the copy constructor uses a `for` statement to copy all the elements of the initializer `Array` into the new `Array` object. An object of a class can look at the `private` data of any other object of that class (using a handle that indicates which object to access).

Common Programming Error 11.8

If the copy constructor simply copied the pointer in the source object to the target object's pointer, then both objects would point to the same dynamically allocated memory. The first destructor to execute would then delete the dynamically allocated memory, and the other object's ptr *would be undefined, a situation called a **dangling pointer**—this would likely result in a serious run-time error (such as early program termination) when the pointer was used.*

Array Destructor
Line 16 of Fig. 11.6 declares the class's destructor (defined in Fig. 11.7, lines 31–34). The destructor is invoked when an object of class `Array` goes out of scope. The destructor uses `delete []` to release the memory allocated dynamically by `new` in the constructor.

Error-Prevention Tip 11.2

If after deleting dynamically allocated memory, the pointer will continue to exist in memory, set the pointer's value to 0 to indicate that the pointer no longer points to memory in the free store. By setting the pointer to 0, the program loses access to that free-store space, which could be reallocated for a different purpose. If you do not set the pointer to 0, your code could inadvertently access the reallocated memory, causing subtle, nonrepeatable logic errors.

getSize Member Function
Line 17 of Fig. 11.6 declares function `getSize` (defined in Fig. 11.7, lines 37–40) that returns the number of elements in the `Array`.

Overloaded Assignment Operator
Line 19 of Fig. 11.6 declares the overloaded assignment operator function for the class. When the compiler sees the expression `integers1 = integers2` in line 46 of Fig. 11.8, the compiler invokes member function `operator=` with the call

```
integers1.operator=( integers2 )
```

Member function `operator=`'s implementation (Fig. 11.7, lines 44–62) tests for **self-assignment** (line 46) in which an `Array` object is being assigned to itself. When `this` is equal to the `right` operand's address, a self-assignment is being attempted, so the assignment is skipped (i.e., the object already is itself; in a moment we'll see why self-assignment is dangerous). If it isn't a self-assignment, then the function determines whether the sizes of the

---

1. Operator `new` could fail to obtain the needed memory. We deal with `new` failures in Chapter 16.

two arrays are identical (line 50); in that case, the original array of integers in the left-side
Array object is not reallocated. Otherwise, operator= uses delete (line 52) to release the
memory originally allocated to the target array, copies the size of the source array to the
size of the target array (line 53), uses new to allocate memory for the target array and places the pointer returned by new into the array's ptr member. Then the for statement in
lines 57–58 copies the array elements from the source array to the target array. Regardless
of whether this is a self-assignment, the member function returns the current object (i.e.,
*this in line 61) as a constant reference; this enables cascaded Array assignments such as
x = y = z, but prevents ones like (x = y) = z because z cannot be assigned to the const
Array reference that is returned by (x = y). If self-assignment occurs, and function oper-
ator= did not test for this case, operator= would unnecessarily copy the elements of the
Array into itself.

Software Engineering Observation 11.5

*A copy constructor, a destructor and an overloaded assignment operator are usually
provided as a group for any class that uses dynamically allocated memory.*

Common Programming Error 11.9

*Not providing an overloaded assignment operator and a copy constructor for a class when
objects of that class contain pointers to dynamically allocated memory is a logic error.*

Software Engineering Observation 11.6

*It's possible to prevent one object of a class from being assigned to another. This is done by
declaring the assignment operator as a private member of the class.*

Software Engineering Observation 11.7

*It's possible to prevent class objects from being copied; to do this, simply make both the
overloaded assignment operator and the copy constructor of that class private.*

Overloaded Equality and Inequality Operators

Line 20 of Fig. 11.6 declares the overloaded equality operator (==) for the class. When the
compiler sees the expression integers1 == integers2 in line 54 of Fig. 11.8, the compiler
invokes member function operator== with the call

```
integers1.operator==( integers2 )
```

Member function operator== (defined in Fig. 11.7, lines 66–76) immediately returns
false if the size members of the arrays are not equal. Otherwise, operator== compares
each pair of elements. If they're all equal, the function returns true. The first pair of elements to differ causes the function to return false immediately.

Lines 23–26 of the header file define the overloaded inequality operator (!=) for the
class. Member function operator!= uses the overloaded operator== function to determine whether one Array is equal to another, then returns the opposite of that result.
Writing operator!= in this manner enables you to reuse operator==, which reduces the
amount of code that must be written in the class. Also, the full function definition for
operator!= is in the Array header file. This allows the compiler to inline the definition of
operator!= to eliminate the overhead of the extra function call.

Overloaded Subscript Operators

Lines 29 and 32 of Fig. 11.6 declare two overloaded subscript operators (defined in Fig. 11.7 in lines 80–91 and 95–106, respectively). When the compiler sees the expression integers1[5] (Fig. 11.8, line 58), it invokes the appropriate overloaded operator[] member function by generating the call

```
integers1.operator[]( 5 )
```

The compiler creates a call to the const version of operator[] (Fig. 11.7, lines 95–106) when the subscript operator is used on a const Array object. For example, if const object z is instantiated with the statement

```
const Array z( 5 );
```

then the const version of operator[] is required to execute a statement such as

```
cout << z[ 3 ] << endl;
```

Remember, a program can invoke only the const member functions of a const object.

Each definition of operator[] determines whether the subscript it receives as an argument is in range. If it isn't, each function prints an error message and terminates the program with a call to function exit (header <cstdlib>).[2] If the subscript is in range, the non-const version of operator[] returns the appropriate array element as a reference so that it may be used as a modifiable *lvalue* (e.g., on the left side of an assignment statement). If the subscript is in range, the const version of operator[] returns a copy of the appropriate element of the array. The returned character is an *rvalue*.

11.10 Converting between Types

Most programs process information of many types. Sometimes all the operations "stay within a type." For example, adding an int to an int produces an int. It's often necessary, however, to convert data of one type to data of another type. This can happen in assignments, in calculations, in passing values to functions and in returning values from functions. The compiler knows how to perform certain conversions among fundamental types. You can use cast operators to force conversions among fundamental types.

But what about user-defined types? The compiler cannot know in advance how to convert among user-defined types, and between user-defined types and fundamental types, so you must specify how to do this. Such conversions can be performed with **conversion constructors**—**single-argument constructors** that turn objects of other types (including fundamental types) into objects of a particular class.

A **conversion operator** (also called a **cast operator**) can be used to convert an object of one class into an object of another class or into an object of a fundamental type. Such a conversion operator must be a non-static member function. The function prototype

```
A::operator char *() const;
```

declares an overloaded cast operator function for converting an object of user-defined type A into a temporary char * object. The operator function is declared const because it does

---

2. It's more appropriate when a subscript is out of range to "throw an exception" indicating the out-of-range subscript. Then the program can "catch" that exception, process it and possibly continue execution. See Chapter 16 for more information on exceptions.

not modify the original object. An overloaded **cast operator function** does not specify a return type—the return type is the type to which the object is being converted. If s is a class object, when the compiler sees the expression static_cast< char * >(s), the compiler generates the call

```
s.operator char *()
```

The operand s is the class object s for which the member function operator char * is being invoked.

Overloaded cast operator functions can be defined to convert objects of user-defined types into fundamental types or into objects of other user-defined types. The prototypes

```
A::operator int() const;
A::operator OtherClass() const;
```

declare overloaded cast operator functions that can convert an object of user-defined type A into an integer or into an object of user-defined type OtherClass, respectively.

One of the nice features of cast operators and conversion constructors is that, when necessary, the compiler can call these functions implicitly to create temporary objects. For example, if an object s of a user-defined String class appears in a program at a location where an ordinary char * is expected, such as

```
cout << s;
```

the compiler can call the overloaded cast-operator function operator char * to convert the object into a char * and use the resulting char * in the expression. With this cast operator provided for a String class, the stream insertion operator does not have to be overloaded to output a String using cout.

11.11 Building a String Class

In Section 8.10, we introduced C-style, pointer-based string processing with character arrays. Our discussion of C strings continues in Section 21.10. As part of our coverage of crafting valuable classes, we implement our own String class that encapsulates a dynamically allocated C string and provides many capabilities that are similar to those we introduced in the Array class. To implement this class, we use several of the capabilities introduced in Sections 8.10 and 21.10. Because classes Array and String are so similar, we placed the String class code and discussion online at www.deitel.com/books/ cpphtp7/ under **Downloads and Resources for Registered Users**.

In this section, we discuss some of the features that are defined in the String class. The C++ standard library includes the similar, more robust class string, which we demonstrate in Section 11.14 and study in detail in Chapter 18.

String Conversion Constructor

Our String class provides a conversion constructor that takes a const char * argument and initializes a String object containing that same character string. Recall that any single-argument constructor can be thought of as a conversion constructor. Such constructors are helpful when we are doing any String operation using char * arguments. The conversion constructor can convert a char * string into a String object, which can then be assigned to the target String object. The availability of this conversion constructor means that it isn't necessary to supply an overloaded assignment operator for assigning character strings to String objects. When the compiler encounters the statement

```
myString = "hello";
```

where myString is a String object, the compiler invokes the conversion constructor to create a temporary String object containing the character string "hello"; then class String's overloaded assignment operator is invoked to assign the temporary String object to String object myString.

Software Engineering Observation 11.8

When a conversion constructor is used to perform an implicit conversion, C++ can apply only one implicit constructor call (i.e., a single user-defined conversion) to try to match the needs of another overloaded operator. The compiler will not satisfy an overloaded operator's needs by performing a series of implicit, user-defined conversions.

The String conversion constructor could be invoked in a declaration such as

```
String s1( "happy" );
```

It can also be invoked when you pass a C string to a function that expects a String argument or when you return a C string from a function with a String return type.

Overloaded Unary Negation Operator

The overloaded negation operator determines whether a String object is empty. For example, when the compiler sees the expression !string1, it generates the function call

```
string1.operator!()
```

This function returns true if the String's length is equal to zero, and false otherwise.

Overloaded Function Call Operator

Overloading the **function call operator ()** is powerful, because functions can take an arbitrary number of parameters. In class String, we overload this operator to select a substring from a String. The operator's two integer parameters specify the start location and the length of the substring to be selected. If the start location is out of range or the substring length is negative, the operator simply returns an empty String. If the substring length is 0, then the substring is selected to the end of the String object. Suppose string1 is a String object containing the string "AEIOU". When the compiler encounters the expression string1(2, 2), it generates the member-function call

```
string1.operator()( 2, 2 )
```

which returns a String containing "IO".

11.12 Overloading ++ and --

The prefix and postfix versions of the increment and decrement operators can all be overloaded. We'll see how the compiler distinguishes between the prefix version and the postfix version of an increment or decrement operator.

To overload the increment operator to allow both prefix and postfix increment usage, each overloaded operator function must have a distinct signature, so that the compiler will be able to determine which version of ++ is intended. The prefix versions are overloaded exactly as any other prefix unary operator would be.

Overloading the Prefix Increment Operator

Suppose, for example, that we want to add 1 to the day in Date object d1. When the compiler sees the preincrementing expression ++d1, the compiler generates the member-function call

```
d1.operator++()
```

The prototype for this operator function would be

```
Date &operator++();
```

If the prefix increment operator is implemented as a global function, then, when the compiler sees the expression ++d1, the compiler generates the function call

```
operator++( d1 )
```

The prototype for this operator function would be declared in the Date class as

```
Date &operator++( Date & );
```

Overloading the Postfix Increment Operator

Overloading the postfix increment operator presents a challenge, because the compiler must be able to distinguish between the signatures of the overloaded prefix and postfix increment operator functions. The *convention* that has been adopted in C++ is that, when the compiler sees the postincrementing expression d1++, it generates the member-function call

```
d1.operator++( 0 )
```

The prototype for this function is

```
Date operator++( int )
```

The argument 0 is strictly a "dummy value" that enables the compiler to distinguish between the prefix and postfix increment operator functions. The same syntax is used to differentiate between the prefix and postfix decrement operator functions.

If the postfix increment is implemented as a global function, then, when the compiler sees the expression d1++, the compiler generates the function call

```
operator++( d1, 0 )
```

The prototype for this function would be

```
Date operator++( Date &, int );
```

Once again, the 0 argument is used by the compiler to distinguish between the prefix and postfix increment operators implemented as global functions. Note that the postfix increment operator returns Date objects by value, whereas the prefix increment operator returns Date objects by reference, because the postfix increment operator typically returns a temporary object that contains the original value of the object before the increment occurred. C++ treats such objects as *rvalues*, which cannot be used on the left side of an assignment. The prefix increment operator returns the actual incremented object with its new value. Such an object can be used as an *lvalue* in a continuing expression.

Performance Tip 11.2

The extra object that is created by the postfix increment (or decrement) operator can result in a significant performance problem—especially when the operator is used in a loop. For this reason, you should use the postfix increment (or decrement) operator only when the logic of the program requires postincrementing (or postdecrementing).

Everything stated in this section for overloading prefix and postfix increment operators applies to overloading predecrement and postdecrement operators. Next, we examine a Date class with overloaded prefix and postfix increment operators.

11.13 Case Study: A Date Class

The program of Figs. 11.9–11.11 demonstrates a Date class, which uses overloaded prefix and postfix increment operators to add 1 to the day in a Date object, while causing appropriate increments to the month and year if necessary. The Date header file (Fig. 11.9) specifies that Date's public interface includes an overloaded stream insertion operator (line 11), a default constructor (line 13), a setDate function (line 14), an overloaded prefix increment operator (line 15), an overloaded postfix increment operator (line 16), an overloaded += addition assignment operator (line 17), a function to test for leap years (line 18) and a function to determine whether a day is the last day of the month (line 19).

```cpp
1   // Fig. 11.9: Date.h
2   // Date class definition with overloaded increment operators.
3   #ifndef DATE_H
4   #define DATE_H
5
6   #include <iostream>
7   using namespace std;
8
9   class Date
10  {
11     friend ostream &operator<<( ostream &, const Date & );
12  public:
13     Date( int m = 1, int d = 1, int y = 1900 ); // default constructor
14     void setDate( int, int, int ); // set month, day, year
15     Date &operator++(); // prefix increment operator
16     Date operator++( int ); // postfix increment operator
17     const Date &operator+=( int ); // add days, modify object
18     static bool leapYear( int ); // is date in a leap year?
19     bool endOfMonth( int ) const; // is date at the end of month?
20  private:
21     int month;
22     int day;
23     int year;
24
25     static const int days[]; // array of days per month
26     void helpIncrement(); // utility function for incrementing date
27  }; // end class Date
28
29  #endif
```

Fig. 11.9 | Date class definition with overloaded increment operators.

```cpp
1   // Fig. 11.10: Date.cpp
2   // Date class member- and friend-function definitions.
3   #include <iostream>
4   #include <string>
5   #include "Date.h"
6   using namespace std;
7
8   // initialize static member; one classwide copy
9   const int Date::days[] =
10     { 0, 31, 28, 31, 30, 31, 30, 31, 31, 30, 31, 30, 31 };
11
12  // Date constructor
13  Date::Date( int m, int d, int y )
14  {
15     setDate( m, d, y );
16  } // end Date constructor
17
18  // set month, day and year
19  void Date::setDate( int mm, int dd, int yy )
20  {
21     month = ( mm >= 1 && mm <= 12 ) ? mm : 1;
22     year = ( yy >= 1900 && yy <= 2100 ) ? yy : 1900;
23
24     // test for a leap year
25     if ( month == 2 && leapYear( year ) )
26        day = ( dd >= 1 && dd <= 29 ) ? dd : 1;
27     else
28        day = ( dd >= 1 && dd <= days[ month ] ) ? dd : 1;
29  } // end function setDate
30
31  // overloaded prefix increment operator
32  Date &Date::operator++()
33  {
34     helpIncrement(); // increment date
35     return *this; // reference return to create an lvalue
36  } // end function operator++
37
38  // overloaded postfix increment operator; note that the
39  // dummy integer parameter does not have a parameter name
40  Date Date::operator++( int )
41  {
42     Date temp = *this; // hold current state of object
43     helpIncrement();
44
45     // return unincremented, saved, temporary object
46     return temp; // value return; not a reference return
47  } // end function operator++
48
49  // add specified number of days to date
50  const Date &Date::operator+=( int additionalDays )
51  {
52     for ( int i = 0; i < additionalDays; i++ )
53        helpIncrement();
```

Fig. 11.10 | Date class member- and friend-function definitions. (Part 1 of 2.)

```
54
55      return *this; // enables cascading
56   } // end function operator+=
57
58   // if the year is a leap year, return true; otherwise, return false
59   bool Date::leapYear( int testYear )
60   {
61      if ( testYear % 400 == 0 ||
62         ( testYear % 100 != 0 && testYear % 4 == 0 ) )
63         return true; // a leap year
64      else
65         return false; // not a leap year
66   } // end function leapYear
67
68   // determine whether the day is the last day of the month
69   bool Date::endOfMonth( int testDay ) const
70   {
71      if ( month == 2 && leapYear( year ) )
72         return testDay == 29; // last day of Feb. in leap year
73      else
74         return testDay == days[ month ];
75   } // end function endOfMonth
76
77   // function to help increment the date
78   void Date::helpIncrement()
79   {
80      // day is not end of month
81      if ( !endOfMonth( day ) )
82         day++; // increment day
83      else
84         if ( month < 12 ) // day is end of month and month < 12
85         {
86            month++; // increment month
87            day = 1; // first day of new month
88         } // end if
89         else // last day of year
90         {
91            year++; // increment year
92            month = 1; // first month of new year
93            day = 1; // first day of new month
94         } // end else
95   } // end function helpIncrement
96
97   // overloaded output operator
98   ostream &operator<<( ostream &output, const Date &d )
99   {
100     static string monthName[ 13 ] = { "", "January", "February",
101        "March", "April", "May", "June", "July", "August",
102        "September", "October", "November", "December" };
103     output << monthName[ d.month ] << ' ' << d.day << ", " << d.year;
104     return output; // enables cascading
105  } // end function operator<<
```

Fig. 11.10 | Date class member- and friend-function definitions. (Part 2 of 2.)

```
 1    // Fig. 11.11: fig11_11.cpp
 2    // Date class test program.
 3    #include <iostream>
 4    #include "Date.h" // Date class definition
 5    using namespace std;
 6
 7    int main()
 8    {
 9       Date d1; // defaults to January 1, 1900
10       Date d2( 12, 27, 1992 ); // December 27, 1992
11       Date d3( 0, 99, 8045 ); // invalid date
12
13       cout << "d1 is " << d1 << "\nd2 is " << d2 << "\nd3 is " << d3;
14       cout << "\n\nd2 += 7 is " << ( d2 += 7 );
15
16       d3.setDate( 2, 28, 1992 );
17       cout << "\n\n  d3 is " << d3;
18       cout << "\n++d3 is " << ++d3 << " (leap year allows 29th)";
19
20       Date d4( 7, 13, 2002 );
21
22       cout << "\n\nTesting the prefix increment operator:\n"
23          << "  d4 is " << d4 << endl;
24       cout << "++d4 is " << ++d4 << endl;
25       cout << "  d4 is " << d4;
26
27       cout << "\n\nTesting the postfix increment operator:\n"
28          << "  d4 is " << d4 << endl;
29       cout << "d4++ is " << d4++ << endl;
30       cout << "  d4 is " << d4 << endl;
31    } // end main
```

```
d1 is January 1, 1900
d2 is December 27, 1992
d3 is January 1, 1900

d2 += 7 is January 3, 1993

  d3 is February 28, 1992
++d3 is February 29, 1992 (leap year allows 29th)

Testing the prefix increment operator:
  d4 is July 13, 2002
++d4 is July 14, 2002
  d4 is July 14, 2002

Testing the postfix increment operator:
  d4 is July 14, 2002
d4++ is July 14, 2002
  d4 is July 15, 2002
```

Fig. 11.11 | Date class test program.

Function main (Fig. 11.11) creates three Date objects (lines 9–11)—d1 is initialized by default to January 1, 1900; d2 is initialized to December 27, 1992; and d3 is initialized to an invalid date. The Date constructor (defined in Fig. 11.10, lines 13–16) calls setDate to validate the month, day and year specified. An invalid month is set to 1, an invalid year is set to 1900 and an invalid day is set to 1.

Line 13 of `main` output each of the constructed `Date` objects, using the overloaded stream insertion operator (defined in Fig. 11.10, lines 98–105). Line 14 of `main` uses the overloaded operator += to add seven days to d2. Line 16 uses function `setDate` to set d3 to February 28, 1992, which is a leap year. Then, line 18 preincrements d3 to show that the date increments properly to February 29. Next, line 20 creates a `Date` object, d4, which is initialized with the date July 13, 2002. Then line 24 increments d4 by 1 with the overloaded prefix increment operator. Lines 22–25 output d4 before and after the preincrement operation to confirm that it worked correctly. Finally, line 29 increments d4 with the overloaded postfix increment operator. Lines 27–30 output d4 before and after the postincrement operation to confirm that it worked correctly.

Overloading the prefix increment operator is straightforward. The prefix increment operator (defined in Fig. 11.10, lines 32–36) calls utility function `helpIncrement` (defined in Fig. 11.10, lines 78–95) to increment the date. This function deals with "wraparounds" or "carries" that occur when we increment the last day of the month. These carries require incrementing the month. If the month is already 12, then the year must also be incremented and the month must be set to 1. Function `helpIncrement` uses function `endOfMonth` to increment the day correctly.

The overloaded prefix increment operator returns a reference to the current `Date` object (i.e., the one that was just incremented). This occurs because the current object, `*this`, is returned as a `Date &`. This enables a preincremented `Date` object to be used as an *lvalue*, which is how the built-in prefix increment operator works for fundamental types.

Overloading the postfix increment operator (defined in Fig. 11.10, lines 40–47) is trickier. To emulate the effect of the postincrement, we must return an unincremented copy of the `Date` object. For example, if `int` variable x has the value 7, the statement

```
cout << x++ << endl;
```

outputs the original value of variable x. So we'd like our postfix increment operator to operate the same way on a `Date` object. On entry to `operator++`, we save the current object (`*this`) in `temp` (line 42). Next, we call `helpIncrement` to increment the current `Date` object. Then, line 46 returns the unincremented copy of the object previously stored in `temp`. This function cannot return a reference to the local `Date` object `temp`, because a local variable is destroyed when the function in which it's declared exits. Thus, declaring the return type to this function as `Date &` would return a reference to an object that no longer exists. Returning a reference (or a pointer) to a local variable is a common error for which most compilers will issue a warning.

11.14 Standard Library Class `string`

Building useful, reusable classes such as `Array` (Figs. 11.6–11.8) takes work. However, once such classes are tested and debugged, they can be reused by you, your colleagues, your company, many companies, an entire industry or even many industries (if they're placed in public or for-sale libraries). The designers of C++ did exactly that, building class `string` (which we've been using since Chapter 3) and class template `vector` (which we introduced in Chapter 7) into standard C++. These classes are available to anyone building applications with C++. As you'll see in Chapter 22, the C++ Standard Library provides several predefined class templates for use in your programs.

Figure 11.12 demonstrates many of class `string`'s overloaded operators, it's conversion constructor for C strings and several other useful member functions, including `empty`, `substr` and `at`. Function `empty` determines whether a `string` is empty, function `substr` returns a `string` that represents a portion of an existing `string` and function `at` returns the character at a specific index in a `string` (after checking that the index is in range). Chapter 18 presents class `string` in detail.

```cpp
1   // Fig. 11.12: fig11_12.cpp
2   // Standard Library string class test program.
3   #include <iostream>
4   #include <string>
5   using namespace std;
6
7   int main()
8   {
9      string s1( "happy" );
10     string s2( " birthday" );
11     string s3;
12
13     // test overloaded equality and relational operators
14     cout << "s1 is \"" << s1 << "\"; s2 is \"" << s2
15        << "\"; s3 is \"" << s3 << '\"'
16        << "\n\nThe results of comparing s2 and s1:"
17        << "\ns2 == s1 yields " << ( s2 == s1 ? "true" : "false" )
18        << "\ns2 != s1 yields " << ( s2 != s1 ? "true" : "false" )
19        << "\ns2 >  s1 yields " << ( s2 > s1 ? "true" : "false" )
20        << "\ns2 <  s1 yields " << ( s2 < s1 ? "true" : "false" )
21        << "\ns2 >= s1 yields " << ( s2 >= s1 ? "true" : "false" )
22        << "\ns2 <= s1 yields " << ( s2 <= s1 ? "true" : "false" );
23
24     // test string member-function empty
25     cout << "\n\nTesting s3.empty():" << endl;
26
27     if ( s3.empty() )
28     {
29        cout << "s3 is empty; assigning s1 to s3;" << endl;
30        s3 = s1; // assign s1 to s3
31        cout << "s3 is \"" << s3 << "\"";
32     } // end if
33
34     // test overloaded string concatenation operator
35     cout << "\n\ns1 += s2 yields s1 = ";
36     s1 += s2; // test overloaded concatenation
37     cout << s1;
38
39     // test overloaded string concatenation operator with C-style string
40     cout << "\n\ns1 += \" to you\" yields" << endl;
41     s1 += " to you";
42     cout << "s1 = " << s1 << "\n\n";
```

Fig. 11.12 | Standard Library class `string`. (Part 1 of 3.)

```
43
44      // test string member function substr
45      cout << "The substring of s1 starting at location 0 for\n"
46          << "14 characters, s1.substr(0, 14), is:\n"
47          << s1.substr( 0, 14 ) << "\n\n";
48
49      // test substr "to-end-of-string" option
50      cout << "The substring of s1 starting at\n"
51          << "location 15, s1.substr(15), is:\n"
52          << s1.substr( 15 ) << endl;
53
54      // test copy constructor
55      string s4( s1 );
56      cout << "\ns4 = " << s4 << "\n\n";
57
58      // test overloaded assignment (=) operator with self-assignment
59      cout << "assigning s4 to s4" << endl;
60      s4 = s4;
61      cout << "s4 = " << s4 << endl;
62
63      // test using overloaded subscript operator to create lvalue
64      s1[ 0 ] = 'H';
65      s1[ 6 ] = 'B';
66      cout << "\ns1 after s1[0] = 'H' and s1[6] = 'B' is: "
67          << s1 << "\n\n";
68
69      // test subscript out of range with string member function "at"
70      cout << "Attempt to assign 'd' to s1.at( 30 ) yields:" << endl;
71      s1.at( 30 ) = 'd'; // ERROR: subscript out of range
72   } // end main
```

```
s1 is "happy"; s2 is " birthday"; s3 is ""

The results of comparing s2 and s1:
s2 == s1 yields false
s2 != s1 yields true
s2 >  s1 yields false
s2 <  s1 yields true
s2 >= s1 yields false
s2 <= s1 yields true

Testing s3.empty():
s3 is empty; assigning s1 to s3;
s3 is "happy"

s1 += s2 yields s1 = happy birthday

s1 += " to you" yields
s1 = happy birthday to you

The substring of s1 starting at location 0 for
14 characters, s1.substr(0, 14), is:
happy birthday
```

Fig. 11.12 | Standard Library class `string`. (Part 2 of 3.)

```
The substring of s1 starting at
location 15, s1.substr(15), is:
to you

s4 = happy birthday to you

assigning s4 to s4
s4 = happy birthday to you

s1 after s1[0] = 'H' and s1[6] = 'B' is: Happy Birthday to you

Attempt to assign 'd' to s1.at( 30 ) yields:

This application has requested the Runtime to terminate it in an unusual way.
Please contact the application's support team for more information.
```

Fig. 11.12 | Standard Library class `string`. (Part 3 of 3.)

Lines 9–11 create three `string` objects—s1 is initialized with the literal "happy", s2 is initialized with the literal " birthday" and s3 uses the default string constructor to create an empty `string`. Lines 14–15 output these three objects, using `cout` and operator `<<`, which the `string` class designers overloaded to handle `string` objects. Then lines 16–22 show the results of comparing s2 to s1 by using class `string`'s overloaded equality and relational operators, which perform lexicographical comparisons using the numerical values of the characters (see Appendix B, ASCII Character Set) in each `string`.

Class `string` provides member function **empty** to determine whether a `string` is empty, which we demonstrate in line 27. Member function `empty` returns `true` if the `string` is empty; otherwise, it returns `false`.

Line 30 demonstrates class `string`'s overloaded assignment operator by assigning s1 to s3. Line 31 outputs s3 to demonstrate that the assignment worked correctly.

Line 36 demonstrates class `string`'s overloaded += operator for string concatenation. In this case, the contents of s2 are appended to s1. Then line 37 outputs the resulting string that is stored in s1. Line 41 demonstrates that a C-style string literal can be appended to a `string` object by using operator +=. Line 42 displays the result.

Class `string` provides member function **substr** (lines 47 and 52) to return a portion of a string as a `string` object. The call to `substr` in line 47 obtains a 14-character substring (specified by the second argument) of s1 starting at position 0 (specified by the first argument). The call to `substr` in line 52 obtains a substring starting from position 15 of s1. When the second argument is not specified, `substr` returns the remainder of the `string` on which it's called.

Line 55 creates `string` object s4 and initializes it with a copy of s1. This results in a call to class `string`'s copy constructor. Line 60 uses class `string`'s overloaded = operator to demonstrate that it handles self-assignment properly.

Lines 64–65 used class `string`'s overloaded [] operator to create *lvalues* that enable new characters to replace existing characters in s1. Line 67 outputs the new value of s1. *Class `string`'s overloaded [] operator does not perform any bounds checking.* Therefore, you must ensure that operations using standard class `string`'s overloaded [] operator do not accidentally manipulate elements outside the bounds of the `string`. Class `string` does provide bounds checking in its member function **at**, which "throws an exception" if its argument is an invalid subscript. By default, this causes a C++ program to terminate and display a system-specific error message.[3] If the subscript is valid, function `at` returns the character at the specified location as a modifiable *lvalue* or an unmodifiable *lvalue* (i.e., a const reference), depending on the context in which the call appears. Line 71 demonstrates a call to function at with an invalid subscript. The error message shown at the end of this program's output was produced when running the program on Windows Vista.

11.15 explicit Constructors

In Sections 11.9–11.10, we discussed that any single-argument constructor can be used by the compiler to perform an implicit conversion—the type received by the constructor is converted to an object of the class in which the constructor is defined. The conversion is automatic and you need not use a cast operator. In some situations, implicit conversions are undesirable or error-prone. For example, our Array class in Fig. 11.6 defines a constructor that takes a single int argument. The intent of this constructor is to create an Array object containing the number of elements specified by the int argument. However, this constructor can be misused by the compiler to perform an implicit conversion.

Common Programming Error 11.10

Unfortunately, the compiler might use implicit conversions in cases that you do not expect, resulting in ambiguous expressions that generate compilation errors or result in execution-time logic errors.

Accidentally Using a Single-Argument Constructor as a Conversion Constructor
The program (Fig. 11.13) uses the Array class of Figs. 11.6–11.7 to demonstrate an improper implicit conversion.

```
1   // Fig. 11.13: Fig11_13.cpp
2   // Driver for simple class Array.
3   #include <iostream>
4   #include "Array.h"
5   using namespace std;
6
7   void outputArray( const Array & ); // prototype
8
9   int main()
10  {
11     Array integers1( 7 ); // 7-element array
12     outputArray( integers1 ); // output Array integers1
13     outputArray( 3 ); // convert 3 to an Array and output Array's contents
14  } // end main
15
16  // print Array contents
17  void outputArray( const Array &arrayToOutput )
18  {
19     cout << "The Array received has " << arrayToOutput.getSize()
20        << " elements. The contents are:\n" << arrayToOutput << endl;
21  } // end outputArray
```

Fig. 11.13 | Single-argument constructors and implicit conversions. (Part 1 of 2.)

---

3. Again, Chapter 16 demonstrates how to "catch" and handle such exceptions.

```
The Array received has 7 elements. The contents are:
         0              0              0              0
         0              0              0
The Array received has 3 elements. The contents are:
         0              0              0
```

Fig. 11.13 | Single-argument constructors and implicit conversions. (Part 2 of 2.)

Line 11 in main instantiates Array object integers1 and calls the single argument constructor with the int value 7 to specify the number of elements in the Array. Recall from Fig. 11.7 that the Array constructor that receives an int argument initializes all the array elements to 0. Line 12 calls function outputArray (defined in lines 17–21), which receives as its argument a const Array & to an Array. The function outputs the number of elements in its Array argument and the contents of the Array. In this case, the size of the Array is 7, so seven 0s are output.

Line 13 calls function outputArray with the int value 3 as an argument. However, this program does not contain a function called outputArray that takes an int argument. So, the compiler determines whether class Array provides a conversion constructor that can convert an int into an Array. Since any constructor that receives a single argument is considered to be a conversion constructor, the compiler assumes the Array constructor that receives a single int is a conversion constructor and uses it to convert the argument 3 into a temporary Array object that contains three elements. Then, the compiler passes the temporary Array object to function outputArray to output the Array's contents. Thus, even though we do not explicitly provide an outputArray function that receives an int argument, the compiler is able to compile line 13. The output shows the contents of the three-element Array containing 0s.

Preventing Implicit Conversions with Single-Argument Constructors
C++ provides the keyword **explicit** to suppress implicit conversions via conversion constructors when such conversions should not be allowed. A constructor that is declared explicit cannot be used in an implicit conversion. Figure 11.14 declares an explicit constructor in class Array. The only modification to Array.h was the addition of the keyword explicit to the declaration of the single-argument constructor in line 14. No modifications are required to the source-code file containing class Array's member-function definitions.

```
1   // Fig. 11.14: Array.h
2   // Array class for storing arrays of integers.
3   #ifndef ARRAY_H
4   #define ARRAY_H
5
6   #include <iostream>
7   using namespace std;
8
```

Fig. 11.14 | Array class definition with explicit constructor. (Part 1 of 2.)

```
 9   class Array
10   {
11      friend ostream &operator<<( ostream &, const Array & );
12      friend istream &operator>>( istream &, Array & );
13   public:
14      explicit Array( int = 10 ); // default constructor
15      Array( const Array & ); // copy constructor
16      ~Array(); // destructor
17      int getSize() const; // return size
18
19      const Array &operator=( const Array & ); // assignment operator
20      bool operator==( const Array & ) const; // equality operator
21
22      // inequality operator; returns opposite of == operator
23      bool operator!=( const Array &right ) const
24      {
25         return ! ( *this == right ); // invokes Array::operator==
26      } // end function operator!=
27
28      // subscript operator for non-const objects returns lvalue
29      int &operator[]( int );
30
31      // subscript operator for const objects returns rvalue
32      const int &operator[]( int ) const;
33   private:
34      int size; // pointer-based array size
35      int *ptr; // pointer to first element of pointer-based array
36   }; // end class Array
37
38   #endif
```

Fig. 11.14 | Array class definition with `explicit` constructor. (Part 2 of 2.)

Figure 11.15 presents a slightly modified version of the program in Fig. 11.13. When this program is compiled, the compiler produces an error message indicating that the integer value passed to outputArray in line 13 cannot be converted to a const Array &. The compiler error message (from Visual C++) is shown in the output window. Line 14 demonstrates how the explicit constructor can be used to create a temporary Array of 3 elements and pass it to function outputArray.

```
 1   // Fig. 11.15: Fig11_15.cpp
 2   // Driver for simple class Array.
 3   #include <iostream>
 4   #include "Array.h"
 5   using namespace std;
 6
 7   void outputArray( const Array & ); // prototype
 8
```

Fig. 11.15 | Demonstrating an `explicit` constructor. (Part 1 of 2.)

```
 9   int main()
10   {
11      Array integers1( 7 ); // 7-element array
12      outputArray( integers1 ); // output Array integers1
13      outputArray( 3 ); // convert 3 to an Array and output Array's contents
14      outputArray( Array( 3 ) ); // explicit single-argument constructor call
15   } // end main
16
17   // print array contents
18   void outputArray( const Array &arrayToOutput )
19   {
20      cout << "The Array received has " << arrayToOutput.getSize()
21         << " elements. The contents are:\n" << arrayToOutput << endl;
22   } // end outputArray
```

```
c:\cpphtp7_examples\ch11\fig11_14_15\fig11_15.cpp(13) : error C2664:
'outputArray' : cannot convert parameter 1 from 'int' to 'const Array &'
        Reason: cannot convert from 'int' to 'const Array'
        Constructor for class 'Array' is declared 'explicit'
```

Fig. 11.15 | Demonstrating an `explicit` constructor. (Part 2 of 2.)

Common Programming Error 11.11
Attempting to invoke an explicit constructor for an implicit conversion is a compilation error.

Error-Prevention Tip 11.3
Use the explicit keyword on single-argument constructors that should not be used by the compiler to perform implicit conversions.

11.16 Proxy Classes

Recall that two of the fundamental principles of good software engineering are separating interface from implementation and hiding implementation details. We strive to achieve these goals by defining a class in a header file and implementing its member functions in a separate implementation file. As we pointed out in Chapter 9, however, header files *do* contain a portion of a class's implementation and hints about others. For example, a class's private members are listed in the class definition in a header file, so these members are visible to clients, even though the clients may not access the private members. Revealing a class's private data in this manner potentially exposes proprietary information to clients of the class. We now introduce the notion of a **proxy class** that allows you to hide even the private data of a class from clients of the class. Providing clients of your class with a proxy class that knows only the public interface to your class enables the clients to use your class's services without giving the clients access to your class's implementation details.

Implementing a proxy class requires several steps, which we demonstrate in Figs. 11.16–11.19. First, we create the class definition for the class that contains the proprietary implementation we would like to hide. Our example class, called Implementation, is shown in Fig. 11.16. The proxy class `Interface` is shown in Figs. 11.17–11.18. The test program and sample output are shown in Fig. 11.19.

Class `Implementation` (Fig. 11.16) provides a single `private` data member called `value` (the data we would like to hide from the client), a constructor to initialize `value` and functions `setValue` and `getValue`.

```
1   // Fig. 11.16: Implementation.h
2   // Implementation class definition.
3
4   class Implementation
5   {
6   public:
7      // constructor
8      Implementation( int v )
9         : value( v ) // initialize value with v
10     {
11        // empty body
12     } // end constructor Implementation
13
14     // set value to v
15     void setValue( int v )
16     {
17        value = v; // should validate v
18     } // end function setValue
19
20     // return value
21     int getValue() const
22     {
23        return value;
24     } // end function getValue
25  private:
26     int value; // data that we would like to hide from the client
27  }; // end class Implementation
```

Fig. 11.16 | `Implementation` class definition.

We define a proxy class called `Interface` (Fig. 11.17) with an identical `public` interface (except for the constructor and destructor names) to that of class `Implementation`. The proxy class's only `private` member is a pointer to an `Implementation` object. Using a pointer in this manner allows us to hide class `Implementation`'s implementation details from the client. Notice that the only mentions in class `Interface` of the proprietary `Implementation` class are in the pointer declaration (line 17) and in line 6, a **forward class declaration**. When a class definition uses only a pointer or reference to an object of another class (as in this case), the class header file for that other class (which would ordinarily reveal the `private` data of that class) is not required to be included with `#include`. This is because the compiler doesn't need to reserve space for an object of the class. The compiler does need to reserve space for the pointer or reference. The sizes of pointers and references are characteristics of the hardware platform on which the compiler runs, so the compiler already knows those sizes. You can simply declare that other class as a data type with a forward class declaration (line 6) before the type is used in the file.

```
1   // Fig. 11.17: Interface.h
2   // Proxy class Interface definition.
3   // Client sees this source code, but the source code does not reveal
4   // the data layout of class Implementation.
5
6   class Implementation; // forward class declaration required by line 17
7
8   class Interface
9   {
10  public:
11     Interface( int ); // constructor
12     void setValue( int ); // same public interface as
13     int getValue() const; // class Implementation has
14     ~Interface(); // destructor
15  private:
16     // requires previous forward declaration (line 6)
17     Implementation *ptr;
18  }; // end class Interface
```

Fig. 11.17 | Proxy class Interface definition.

The member-function implementation file for proxy class Interface (Fig. 11.18) is the only file that includes the header file Implementation.h (line 5) containing class Implementation. The file Interface.cpp (Fig. 11.18) is provided to the client as a precompiled object code file along with the header file Interface.h that includes the function prototypes of the services provided by the proxy class. Because file Interface.cpp is made available to the client only as object code, the client is not able to see the interactions between the proxy class and the proprietary class (lines 9, 17, 23 and 29). The proxy class imposes an extra "layer" of function calls as the "price to pay" for hiding the private data of class Implementation. Given the speed of today's computers and the fact that many compilers can inline simple function calls automatically, the effect of these extra function calls on performance is often negligible.

```
1   // Fig. 11.18: Interface.cpp
2   // Implementation of class Interface--client receives this file only
3   // as precompiled object code, keeping the implementation hidden.
4   #include "Interface.h" // Interface class definition
5   #include "Implementation.h" // Implementation class definition
6
7   // constructor
8   Interface::Interface( int v )
9      : ptr ( new Implementation( v ) ) // initialize ptr to point to
10  {                                     // a new Implementation object
11     // empty body
12  } // end Interface constructor
13
14  // call Implementation's setValue function
15  void Interface::setValue( int v )
16  {
```

Fig. 11.18 | Interface class member-function definitions. (Part 1 of 2.)

```
17        ptr->setValue( v );
18    } // end function setValue
19
20    // call Implementation's getValue function
21    int Interface::getValue() const
22    {
23        return ptr->getValue();
24    } // end function getValue
25
26    // destructor
27    Interface::~Interface()
28    {
29        delete ptr;
30    } // end ~Interface destructor
```

Fig. 11.18 | Interface class member-function definitions. (Part 2 of 2.)

Figure 11.19 tests class Interface. Notice that only the header file for Interface is included in the client code (line 4)—there is no mention of the existence of a separate class called Implementation. Thus, the client never sees the private data of class Implementation, nor can the client code become dependent on the Implementation code.

Software Engineering Observation 11.9
A proxy class insulates client code from implementation changes.

```
1     // Fig. 11.19: fig11_19.cpp
2     // Hiding a class's private data with a proxy class.
3     #include <iostream>
4     #include "Interface.h" // Interface class definition
5     using namespace std;
6
7     int main()
8     {
9        Interface i( 5 ); // create Interface object
10
11        cout << "Interface contains: " << i.getValue()
12           << " before setValue" << endl;
13
14        i.setValue( 10 );
15
16        cout << "Interface contains: " << i.getValue()
17           << " after setValue" << endl;
18    } // end main
```

```
Interface contains: 5 before setValue
Interface contains: 10 after setValue
```

Fig. 11.19 | Implementing a proxy class.

11.17 Wrap-Up

In this chapter, you learned how to build more robust classes by defining overloaded operators that enable you to use operators with objects of your classes. We presented basic operator overloading concepts, as well as several restrictions that the C++ standard places on overloaded operators. You learned reasons for implementing overloaded operators as member functions or as global functions. We discussed the differences between overloading unary and binary operators as member functions and global functions. With global functions, we showed how to input and output objects of our classes using the overloaded stream extraction and stream insertion operators, respectively. We introduced the concept of dynamic memory management. You learned that you can create and destroy objects dynamically with the new and delete operators, respectively. We showed a special syntax that is required to differentiate between the prefix and postfix versions of the increment (++) operator. We also demonstrated standard C++ class string, which makes extensive use of overloaded operators to create a robust, reusable class that can replace C-style, pointer-based strings. You learned how to use keyword explicit to prevent the compiler from using a single-argument constructor to perform implicit conversions. Finally, we showed how to create a proxy class to hide the implementation details of a class from the class's clients. In the next chapter, we continue our discussion of classes by introducing a form of software reuse called inheritance. We'll see that when classes share common attributes and behaviors, it's possible to define those attributes and behaviors in a common "base" class and "inherit" those capabilities into new class definitions, enabling you to create the new classes with a minimal amount of code.

Summary

Section 11.1 Introduction
- C++ enables you to overload most operators to be sensitive to the context in which they're used—the compiler generates the appropriate code based on the context (in particular, the types of the operands).
- Many of C++'s operators can be overloaded to work with user-defined types.
- One example of an overloaded operator built into C++ is operator <<, which is used both as the stream insertion operator and as the bitwise left-shift operator. Similarly, >> is also overloaded; it's used both as the stream extraction operator and as the bitwise right-shift operator. Both of these operators are overloaded in the C++ Standard Library.
- The C++ language itself overloads + and -. These operators perform differently, depending on their context in integer arithmetic, floating-point arithmetic and pointer arithmetic.
- The jobs performed by overloaded operators can also be performed by function calls, but operator notation is often clearer and more familiar to programmers.

Section 11.2 Fundamentals of Operator Overloading
- An operator is overloaded by writing a non-static member-function definition or global function definition in which the function name is the keyword operator followed by the symbol for the operator being overloaded.
- When operators are overloaded as member functions, they must be non-static, because they must be called on an object of the class and operate on that object.

- To use an operator on class objects, that operator *must* be overloaded, with three exceptions—the assignment operator (=), the address operator (&) and the comma operator (,).

Section 11.3 Restrictions on Operator Overloading
- You cannot change the precedence and associativity of an operator by overloading.
- You cannot change the "arity" of an operator (i.e., the number of operands an operator takes).
- You cannot create new operators—only existing operators can be overloaded.
- You cannot change the meaning of how an operator works on objects of fundamental types.
- Overloading an assignment operator and an addition operator for a class does not imply that the += operator is also overloaded. Such behavior can be achieved only by explicitly overloading operator += for that class.

Section 11.4 Operator Functions as Class Members vs. Global Functions
- Operator functions can be member functions or global functions—global functions are often made `friends` for performance reasons. Member functions use the `this` pointer implicitly to obtain one of their class object arguments (the left operand for binary operators). Arguments for both operands of a binary operator must be explicitly listed in a global function call.
- Overloaded (), [], -> and assignment operators must be declared as class members. For the other operators, the operator overloading functions can be class members or global functions.
- When an operator function is implemented as a member function, the leftmost (or only) operand must be an object (or a reference to an object) of the operator's class.
- If the left operand must be an object of a different class or a fundamental type, this operator function must be implemented as a global function.
- A global operator function can be made a `friend` of a class if that function must access `private` or `protected` members of that class directly.

Section 11.5 Overloading Stream Insertion and Stream Extraction Operators
- The overloaded stream insertion operator (<<) is used in an expression in which the left operand has type `ostream &`. For this reason, it must be overloaded as a global function. To be a member function, operator << would have to be a member of the `ostream` class, but this is not possible, since we are not allowed to modify C++ Standard Library classes. Similarly, the overloaded stream extraction operator (>>) must be a global function.
- Another reason to choose a global function to overload an operator is to enable the operator to be commutative.
- When used with `cin`, `setw` restricts the number of characters read to the number of characters specified by its argument.
- `istream` member function `ignore` discards the specified number of characters in the input stream (one character by default).
- Overloaded input and output operators are declared as `friends` if they need to access non-`public` class members directly for performance reasons.

Section 11.6 Overloading Unary Operators
- A unary operator for a class can be overloaded as a non-`static` member function with no arguments or as a global function with one argument; that argument must be either an object of the class or a reference to an object of the class.
- Member functions that implement overloaded operators must be non-`static` so that they can access the non-`static` data in each object of the class.

Section 11.7 Overloading Binary Operators

- A binary operator can be overloaded as a non-`static` member function with one argument or as a global function with two arguments (one of those arguments must be either a class object or a reference to a class object).

Section 11.8 Dynamic Memory Management

- Dynamic memory management enables you to control the allocation and deallocation of memory in a program for any built-in or user-defined type.

- The free store (sometimes called the heap) is a region of memory assigned to each program for storing objects dynamically allocated at execution time.

- The `new` operator allocates storage of the proper size for an object, runs the object's constructor and returns a pointer of the correct type. The `new` operator can be used to dynamically allocate any fundamental type (such as `int` or `double`) or class type. If `new` is unable to find space in memory for the object, it indicates that an error occurred by "throwing" an "exception." This usually causes the program to terminate immediately, unless the exception is handled.

- To destroy a dynamically allocated object and free its space, use the `delete` operator.

- An array of objects can be allocated dynamically with `new` as in

      int *ptr = new int[100];

  which allocates an array of 100 integers and assigns the starting location of the array to `ptr`. The preceding array of integers is deleted with the statement

      delete [] ptr;

Section 11.9 Case Study: **Array Class**

- A copy constructor initializes a new object of a class by copying the members of an existing one. Classes that contain dynamically allocated memory, typically provide a copy constructor, a destructor and an overloaded assignment operator.

- The implementation of member function `operator=` should test for self-assignment, in which an object is being assigned to itself.

- The compiler calls the `const` version of `operator[]` when the subscript operator is used on a `const` object and calls the non-`const` version of the operator when it's used on a non-`const` object.

- The array subscript operator (`[]`) can be used to select elements from other types of containers. Also, with overloading, the index values no longer need to be integers.

Section 11.10 Converting between Types

- The compiler cannot know in advance how to convert among user-defined types, and between user-defined types and fundamental types, so you must specify how to do this. Such conversions can be performed with conversion constructors—single-argument constructors that turn objects of other types (including fundamental types) into objects of a particular class.

- Any single-argument constructor can be thought of as a conversion constructor.

- A conversion operator can be used to convert an object of one class into an object of another class or into an object of a fundamental type. Such a conversion operator must be a non-`static` member function. Overloaded cast-operator functions can be defined for converting objects of user-defined types into fundamental types or into objects of other user-defined types.

- An overloaded cast operator function does not specify a return type—the return type is the type to which the object is being converted.

- When necessary, the compiler can call cast operators and conversion constructors implicitly to create temporary objects.

Section 11.11 Building a `String` Class

- Overloading the function call operator () is powerful, because functions can take an arbitrary number of parameters.

Section 11.12 Overloading ++ and --

- The prefix and postfix increment and decrement operator can all be overloaded.

- To overload the pre- and post-increment operators, each overloaded operator function must have a distinct signature. The prefix versions are overloaded like any other unary operator. The postfix increment operator's unique signature is accomplished by providing a second argument, which must be of type `int`. This argument is not supplied in the client code. It's used implicitly by the compiler to distinguish between the prefix and postfix versions of the increment operator. The same syntax is used to differentiate between the prefix and postfix decrement operator functions.

Section 11.14 Standard Library Class `string`

- Standard class `string` is defined in header `<string>` and belongs to namespace `std`.

- Class `string` provides many overloaded operators, including equality, relational, assignment, addition assignment (for concatenation) and subscript operators.

- Class `string` provides member function `empty`, which returns `true` if the `string` is empty; otherwise, it returns `false`.

- Standard class `string` member function `substr` obtains a substring of a length specified by the second argument, starting at the position specified by the first argument. When the second argument is not specified, `substr` returns the remainder of the `string` on which it's called.

- Class `string`'s overloaded `[]` operator does not perform any bounds checking. Therefore, you must ensure that operations using standard class `string`'s overloaded `[]` operator do not accidentally manipulate elements outside the bounds of the `string`.

- Standard class `string` provides bounds checking with member function `at`, which "throws an exception" if its argument is an invalid subscript. By default, this causes the program to terminate. If the subscript is valid, function `at` returns a reference or a `const` reference to the character at the specified location depending on the context.

Section 11.15 `explicit` Constructors

- C++ provides the keyword `explicit` to suppress implicit conversions via conversion constructors when such conversions should not be allowed. A constructor that is declared `explicit` cannot be used in an implicit conversion.

Section 11.16 Proxy Classes

- Providing clients of your class with a proxy class that knows only the `public` interface to your class enables the clients to use your class's services without giving the clients access to your class's implementation details, such as its `private` data.

- When a class definition uses only a pointer or reference to an object of another class, the class header file for that other class (which would ordinarily reveal the `private` data of that class) is not required to be included with `#include`. You can simply declare that other class as a data type with a forward class declaration before the type is used in the file.

- The implementation file containing the member functions for a proxy class is the only file that includes the header file for the class whose `private` data we would like to hide.

- The implementation file containing the member functions for the proxy class is provided to the client as a precompiled object code file along with the header file that includes the function prototypes of the services provided by the proxy class.

Terminology

at member function of class `string` 501	forward class declaration 506
allocate memory 476	free store 476
cast operator function 491	function call operator () 492
conversion constructor 490	heap 476
conversion operator 490	initializer 477
copy constructor 485, 487	memory leak 477
dangling pointer 488	`new` operator 476
deallocate memory 476	`new[]` operator 477
`delete` operator 476	operator overloading 467
`delete[]` operator 476	proxy class 505
dynamic memory management 476	self-assignment 488
empty member function of `string` 501	single-argument constructor 490
`explicit` constructor 503	substr member function of class `string` 501

Self-Review Exercises

11.1 Fill in the blanks in each of the following:

a) Suppose a and b are integer variables and we form the sum a + b. Now suppose c and d are floating-point variables and we form the sum c + d. The two + operators here are clearly being used for different purposes. This is an example of _____.

b) Keyword _____ introduces an overloaded-operator function definition.

c) To use operators on class objects, they must be overloaded, with the exception of operators _____, _____ and _____.

d) The _____, _____ and _____ of an operator cannot be changed by overloading the operator.

e) The operators that cannot be overloaded are _____, _____, _____ and _____.

f) The _____ operator reclaims memory previously allocated by new.

g) The _____ operator dynamically allocates memory for an object of a specified type and returns a(n) _____ to that type.

11.2 Explain the multiple meanings of the operators << and >>.

11.3 In what context might the name `operator/` be used?

11.4 (True/False) Only existing operators can be overloaded.

11.5 How does the precedence of an overloaded operator compare with the precedence of the original operator?

Answers to Self-Review Exercises

11.1 a) operator overloading. b) `operator`. c) assignment (=), address (&), comma (,). d) precedence, associativity, "arity." e) ., ?:, .*, and ::. f) `delete`. g) new, pointer.

11.2 Operator >> is both the right-shift operator and the stream extraction operator, depending on its context. Operator << is both the left-shift operator and the stream insertion operator, depending on its context.

11.3 For operator overloading: It would be the name of a function that would provide an overloaded version of the / operator for a specific class.

11.4 True.

11.5 The precedence is identical.

Exercises

11.6 Compare and contrast dynamic memory allocation and deallocation operators new, new [], delete and delete [].

11.7 *(Overloading the Parentheses Operator)* One nice example of overloading the function call operator () is to allow another form of double-array subscripting popular in some programming languages. Instead of saying

```
chessBoard[ row ][ column ]
```

for an array of objects, overload the function call operator to allow the alternate form

```
chessBoard( row, column )
```

Create a class DoubleSubscriptedArray that has similar features to class Array in Figs. 11.6–11.7. At construction time, the class should be able to create an array of any number of rows and any number of columns. The class should supply operator() to perform double-subscripting operations. For example, in a 3-by-5 DoubleSubscriptedArray called a, the user could write a(1, 3) to access the element at row 1 and column 3. Remember that operator() can receive any number of arguments. The underlying representation of the double-subscripted array should be a single-subscripted array of integers with *rows* * *columns* number of elements. Function operator() should perform the proper pointer arithmetic to access each element of the array. There should be two versions of operator()—one that returns int & (so that an element of a DoubleSubscriptedArray can be used as an *lvalue*) and one that returns const int & . The class should also provide the following operators: ==, !=, =, << (for outputting the array in row and column format) and >> (for inputting the entire array contents).

11.8 *(Complex Class)* Consider class Complex shown in Figs. 11.20–11.22. The class enables operations on so-called *complex numbers*. These are numbers of the form realPart + imaginaryPart * *i*, where *i* has the value

$$\sqrt{-1}$$

a) Modify the class to enable input and output of complex numbers via overloaded >> and << operators, respectively (you should remove the print function from the class).

b) Overload the multiplication operator to enable multiplication of two complex numbers as in algebra.

c) Overload the == and != operators to allow comparisons of complex numbers.

```cpp
1   // Fig. 11.20: Complex.h
2   // Complex class definition.
3   #ifndef COMPLEX_H
4   #define COMPLEX_H
5
6   class Complex
7   {
8   public:
9      Complex( double = 0.0, double = 0.0 ); // constructor
10     Complex operator+( const Complex & ) const; // addition
11     Complex operator-( const Complex & ) const; // subtraction
12     void print() const; // output
13  private:
14     double real; // real part
15     double imaginary; // imaginary part
16  }; // end class Complex
```

Fig. 11.20 | Complex class definition. (Part 1 of 2.)

```
17
18    #endif
```

Fig. 11.20 | Complex class definition. (Part 2 of 2.)

```
1     // Fig. 11.21: Complex.cpp
2     // Complex class member-function definitions.
3     #include <iostream>
4     #include "Complex.h" // Complex class definition
5     using namespace std;
6
7     // Constructor
8     Complex::Complex( double realPart, double imaginaryPart )
9        : real( realPart ),
10         imaginary( imaginaryPart )
11    {
12        // empty body
13    } // end Complex constructor
14
15    // addition operator
16    Complex Complex::operator+( const Complex &operand2 ) const
17    {
18        return Complex( real + operand2.real,
19            imaginary + operand2.imaginary );
20    } // end function operator+
21
22    // subtraction operator
23    Complex Complex::operator-( const Complex &operand2 ) const
24    {
25        return Complex( real - operand2.real,
26            imaginary - operand2.imaginary );
27    } // end function operator-
28
29    // display a Complex object in the form: (a, b)
30    void Complex::print() const
31    {
32        cout << '(' << real << ", " << imaginary << ')';
33    } // end function print
```

Fig. 11.21 | Complex class member-function definitions.

```
1     // Fig. 11.22: fig11_22.cpp
2     // Complex class test program.
3     #include <iostream>
4     #include "Complex.h"
5     using namespace std;
6
7     int main()
8     {
9        Complex x;
10       Complex y( 4.3, 8.2 );
11       Complex z( 3.3, 1.1 );
12
13       cout << "x: ";
14       x.print();
15       cout << "\ny: ";
```

Fig. 11.22 | Complex numbers. (Part 1 of 2.)

```
16      y.print();
17      cout << "\nz: ";
18      z.print();
19
20      x = y + z;
21      cout << "\n\nx = y + z:" << endl;
22      x.print();
23      cout << " = ";
24      y.print();
25      cout << " + ";
26      z.print();
27
28      x = y - z;
29      cout << "\n\nx = y - z:" << endl;
30      x.print();
31      cout << " = ";
32      y.print();
33      cout << " - ";
34      z.print();
35      cout << endl;
36   } // end main
```

```
x: (0, 0)
y: (4.3, 8.2)
z: (3.3, 1.1)

x = y + z:
(7.6, 9.3) = (4.3, 8.2) + (3.3, 1.1)

x = y - z:
(1, 7.1) = (4.3, 8.2) - (3.3, 1.1)
```

Fig. 11.22 | Complex numbers. (Part 2 of 2.)

11.9   *(HugeInt Class)* A machine with 32-bit integers can represent integers in the range of approximately –2 billion to +2 billion. This fixed-size restriction is rarely troublesome, but there are applications in which we would like to be able to use a much wider range of integers. This is what C++ was built to do, namely, create powerful new data types. Consider class HugeInt of Figs. 11.23–11.25. Study the class carefully, then answer the following:

a) Describe precisely how it operates.
b) What restrictions does the class have?
c) Overload the * multiplication operator.
d) Overload the / division operator.
e) Overload all the relational and equality operators.

[*Note:* We do not show an assignment operator or copy constructor for class HugeInteger, because the assignment operator and copy constructor provided by the compiler are capable of copying the entire array data member properly.]

```
1    // Fig. 11.23: Hugeint.h
2    // HugeInt class definition.
3    #ifndef HUGEINT_H
4    #define HUGEINT_H
5
6    #include <iostream>
7    #include <string>
```

Fig. 11.23 | HugeInt class definition. (Part 1 of 2.)

```
8   using namespace std;
9
10  class HugeInt
11  {
12     friend ostream &operator<<( ostream &, const HugeInt & );
13  public:
14     static const int digits = 30; // maximum digits in a HugeInt
15
16     HugeInt( long = 0 ); // conversion/default constructor
17     HugeInt( const string & ); // conversion constructor
18
19     // addition operator; HugeInt + HugeInt
20     HugeInt operator+( const HugeInt & ) const;
21
22     // addition operator; HugeInt + int
23     HugeInt operator+( int ) const;
24
25     // addition operator;
26     // HugeInt + string that represents large integer value
27     HugeInt operator+( const string & ) const;
28  private:
29     short integer[ digits ];
30  }; // end class HugetInt
31
32  #endif
```

Fig. 11.23 | HugeInt class definition. (Part 2 of 2.)

```
1   // Fig. 11.24: Hugeint.cpp
2   // HugeInt member-function and friend-function definitions.
3   #include <cctype> // isdigit function prototype
4   #include "Hugeint.h" // HugeInt class definition
5   using namespace std;
6
7   // default constructor; conversion constructor that converts
8   // a long integer into a HugeInt object
9   HugeInt::HugeInt( long value )
10  {
11     // initialize array to zero
12     for ( int i = 0; i < digits; i++ )
13        integer[ i ] = 0;
14
15     // place digits of argument into array
16     for ( int j = digits - 1; value != 0 && j >= 0; j-- )
17     {
18        integer[ j ] = value % 10;
19        value /= 10;
20     } // end for
21  } // end HugeInt default/conversion constructor
22
23  // conversion constructor that converts a character string
24  // representing a large integer into a HugeInt object
25  HugeInt::HugeInt( const string &number )
26  {
27     // initialize array to zero
28     for ( int i = 0; i < digits; i++ )
29        integer[ i ] = 0;
```

Fig. 11.24 | HugeInt class member-function and friend-function definitions. (Part 1 of 3.)

```
30
31      // place digits of argument into array
32      int length = number.size();
33
34      for ( int j = digits - length, k = 0; j < digits; j++, k++ )
35         if ( isdigit( number[ k ] ) ) // ensure that character is a digit
36            integer[ j ] = number[ k ] - '0';
37   } // end HugeInt conversion constructor
38
39   // addition operator; HugeInt + HugeInt
40   HugeInt HugeInt::operator+( const HugeInt &op2 ) const
41   {
42      HugeInt temp; // temporary result
43      int carry = 0;
44
45      for ( int i = digits - 1; i >= 0; i-- )
46      {
47         temp.integer[ i ] = integer[ i ] + op2.integer[ i ] + carry;
48
49         // determine whether to carry a 1
50         if ( temp.integer[ i ] > 9 )
51         {
52            temp.integer[ i ] %= 10;  // reduce to 0-9
53            carry = 1;
54         } // end if
55         else // no carry
56            carry = 0;
57      } // end for
58
59      return temp; // return copy of temporary object
60   } // end function operator+
61
62   // addition operator; HugeInt + int
63   HugeInt HugeInt::operator+( int op2 ) const
64   {
65      // convert op2 to a HugeInt, then invoke
66      // operator+ for two HugeInt objects
67      return *this + HugeInt( op2 );
68   } // end function operator+
69
70   // addition operator;
71   // HugeInt + string that represents large integer value
72   HugeInt HugeInt::operator+( const string &op2 ) const
73   {
74      // convert op2 to a HugeInt, then invoke
75      // operator+ for two HugeInt objects
76      return *this + HugeInt( op2 );
77   } // end operator+
78
79   // overloaded output operator
80   ostream& operator<<( ostream &output, const HugeInt &num )
81   {
82      int i;
83
84      for ( i = 0; ( num.integer[ i ] == 0 ) && ( i <= HugeInt::digits ); i++ )
85         ; // skip leading zeros
86
87      if ( i == HugeInt::digits )
88         output << 0;
```

Fig. 11.24 | HugeInt class member-function and friend-function definitions. (Part 2 of 3.)

```
89       else
90          for ( ; i < HugeInt::digits; i++ )
91             output << num.integer[ i ];
92
93       return output;
94   } // end function operator<<
```

Fig. 11.24 | HugeInt class member-function and **friend**-function definitions. (Part 3 of 3.)

```
 1   // Fig. 11.25: fig11_25.cpp
 2   // HugeInt test program.
 3   #include <iostream>
 4   #include "Hugeint.h"
 5   using namespace std;
 6
 7   int main()
 8   {
 9      HugeInt n1( 7654321 );
10      HugeInt n2( 7891234 );
11      HugeInt n3( "99999999999999999999999999999" );
12      HugeInt n4( "1" );
13      HugeInt n5;
14
15      cout << "n1 is " << n1 << "\nn2 is " << n2
16         << "\nn3 is " << n3 << "\nn4 is " << n4
17         << "\nn5 is " << n5 << "\n\n";
18
19      n5 = n1 + n2;
20      cout << n1 << " + " << n2 << " = " << n5 << "\n\n";
21
22      cout << n3 << " + " << n4 << "\n= " << ( n3 + n4 ) << "\n\n";
23
24      n5 = n1 + 9;
25      cout << n1 << " + " << 9 << " = " << n5 << "\n\n";
26
27      n5 = n2 + "10000";
28      cout << n2 << " + " << "10000" << " = " << n5 << endl;
29   } // end main
```

```
n1 is 7654321
n2 is 7891234
n3 is 99999999999999999999999999999
n4 is 1
n5 is 0

7654321 + 7891234 = 15545555

99999999999999999999999999999 + 1
= 100000000000000000000000000000

7654321 + 9 = 7654330

7891234 + 10000 = 7901234
```

Fig. 11.25 | Huge integers.

11.10 *(RationalNumber Class)* Create a class RationalNumber (fractions) with the following capabilities:

    a) Create a constructor that prevents a 0 denominator in a fraction, reduces or simplifies fractions that are not in reduced form and avoids negative denominators.

    b) Overload the addition, subtraction, multiplication and division operators for this class.

    c) Overload the relational and equality operators for this class.

11.11 *(Polynomial Class)* Develop class `Polynomial`. The internal representation of a `Polynomial` is an array of terms. Each term contains a coefficient and an exponent, e.g., the term

$$2x^4$$

has the coefficient 2 and the exponent 4. Develop a complete class containing proper constructor and destructor functions as well as *set* and *get* functions. The class should also provide the following overloaded operator capabilities:

    a) Overload the addition operator (+) to add two `Polynomial`s.

    b) Overload the subtraction operator (-) to subtract two `Polynomial`s.

    c) Overload the assignment operator to assign one `Polynomial` to another.

    d) Overload the multiplication operator (*) to multiply two `Polynomial`s.

    e) Overload the addition assignment operator (+=), subtraction assignment operator (-=), and multiplication assignment operator (*=).

Object-Oriented Programming: Inheritance

12

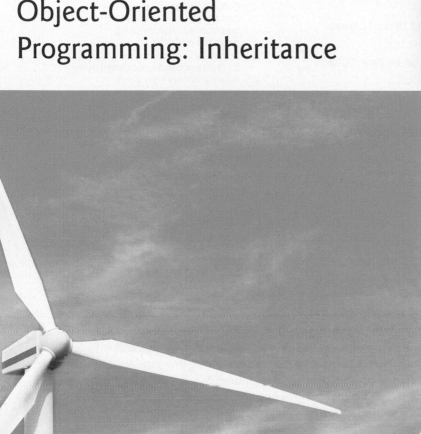

Say not you know another entirely, till you have divided an inheritance with him.
—Johann Kasper Lavater

This method is to define as the number of a class the class of all classes similar to the given class.
—Bertrand Russell

Good as it is to inherit a library, it is better to collect one.
—Augustine Birrell

Save base authority from others' books.
—William Shakespeare

Objectives

In this chapter you'll learn:

- To create classes by inheriting from existing classes.
- The notions of base classes and derived classes and the relationships between them.
- The **protected** member access specifier.
- The use of constructors and destructors in inheritance hierarchies.
- The order in which constructors and destructors are called in inheritance hierarchies.
- The differences between **public**, **protected** and **private** inheritance.
- To use inheritance to customize existing software.

12.1 Introduction

This chapter continues our discussion of object-oriented programming (OOP) by introducing another of its key features—**inheritance**. Inheritance is a form of software reuse in which you create a class that absorbs an existing class's data and behaviors and enhances them with new capabilities. Software reusability saves time during program development. It also encourages the reuse of proven, debugged, high-quality software, which increases the likelihood that a system will be implemented effectively.

When creating a class, instead of writing completely new data members and member functions, you can designate that the new class should **inherit** the members of an existing class. This existing class is called the **base class**, and the new class is referred to as the **derived class**. (Other programming languages, such as Java, refer to the base class as the **superclass** and the derived class as the **subclass**.) A derived class represents a more specialized group of objects. Typically, a derived class contains behaviors inherited from its base class plus additional behaviors. As we'll see, a derived class can also customize behaviors inherited from the base class. A **direct base class** is the base class from which a derived class explicitly inherits. An **indirect base class** is inherited from two or more levels up in the **class hierarchy**. In the case of **single inheritance**, a class is derived from one base class. C++ also supports **multiple inheritance**, in which a derived class inherits from multiple (possibly unrelated) base classes. Single inheritance is straightforward—we show several examples that should enable you to become proficient quickly. Multiple inheritance can be complex and error prone. We discuss multiple inheritance in Chapter 24, Other Topics.

C++ offers public, protected and private inheritance. In this chapter, we concentrate on public inheritance and briefly explain the other two. In Chapter 20, Data Structures, we show how private inheritance can be used as an alternative to composition. The third form, protected inheritance, is rarely used. With public inheritance, every object of a derived class is also an object of that derived class's base class. However, base-class objects are not objects of their derived classes. For example, if we have vehicle as a base class and car as a derived class, then all cars are vehicles, but not all vehicles are cars. As we continue our study of object-oriented programming in this chapter and Chapter 13, we take advantage of this relationship to perform some interesting manipulations.

Experience in building software systems indicates that significant amounts of code deal with closely related special cases. When you are preoccupied with special cases, the details can obscure the big picture. With object-oriented programming, you focus on the commonalities among objects in the system rather than on the special cases.

We distinguish between the **is-a relationship** and the *has-a* relationship. The *is-a* relationship represents inheritance. In an *is-a* relationship, an object of a derived class also can be treated as an object of its base class—for example, a car *is a* vehicle, so any attributes and behaviors of a vehicle are also attributes and behaviors of a car. By contrast, the *has-a* relationship represents composition. (Composition was discussed in Chapter 10.) In a *has-a* relationship, an object contains one or more objects of other classes as members. For example, a car includes many components—it *has a* steering wheel, *has a* brake pedal, *has a* transmission and *has* many other components.

Derived-class member functions might require access to base-class data members and member functions. A derived class can access the non-`private` members of its base class. Base-class members that should not be accessible to the member functions of derived classes should be declared `private` in the base class. A derived class *can* change the values of `private` base-class members, but only through non-`private` member functions provided in the base class and inherited into the derived class.

Software Engineering Observation 12.1

Member functions of a derived class cannot directly access `private` members of the base class.

Software Engineering Observation 12.2

If a derived class could access its base class's `private` members, classes that inherit from that derived class could access that data as well. This would propagate access to what should be `private` data, and the benefits of information hiding would be lost.

One problem with inheritance is that a derived class can inherit data members and member functions it does not need or should not have. It's the class designer's responsibility to ensure that the capabilities provided by a class are appropriate for future derived classes. Even when a base-class member function is appropriate for a derived class, the derived class often requires that the member function behave in a manner specific to the derived class. In such cases, the base-class member function can be redefined in the derived class with an appropriate implementation.

12.2 Base Classes and Derived Classes

Often, an object of one class *is an* object of another class, as well. For example, in geometry, a rectangle *is a* quadrilateral (as are squares, parallelograms and trapezoids). Thus, in C++, class `Rectangle` can be said to *inherit* from class `Quadrilateral`. In this context, class `Quadrilateral` is a base class, and class `Rectangle` is a derived class. A rectangle *is a* specific type of quadrilateral, but it's incorrect to claim that a quadrilateral *is a* rectangle—the quadrilateral could be a parallelogram or some other shape. Figure 12.1 lists several simple examples of base classes and derived classes.

Base class	Derived classes
Student	GraduateStudent, UndergraduateStudent
Shape	Circle, Triangle, Rectangle, Sphere, Cube
Loan	CarLoan, HomeImprovementLoan, MortgageLoan
Employee	Faculty, Staff
Account	CheckingAccount, SavingsAccount

Fig. 12.1 | Inheritance examples.

Because every derived-class object *is an* object of its base class, and one base class can have many derived classes, the set of objects represented by a base class typically is larger than the set of objects represented by any of its derived classes. For example, the base class Vehicle represents all vehicles, including cars, trucks, boats, airplanes, bicycles and so on. By contrast, derived class Car represents a smaller, more specific subset of all vehicles.

Inheritance relationships form treelike hierarchical structures. A base class exists in a hierarchical relationship with its derived classes. Although classes can exist independently, once they're employed in inheritance relationships, they become affiliated with other classes. A class becomes either a base class—supplying members to other classes, a derived class—inheriting its members from other classes, or both.

Let's develop a simple inheritance hierarchy with five levels (represented by the UML class diagram in Fig. 12.2). A university community has thousands of members.

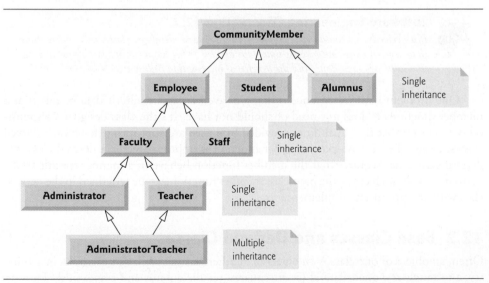

Fig. 12.2 | Inheritance hierarchy for university CommunityMembers.

These members consist of employees, students and alumni. Employees are either faculty members or staff members. Faculty members are either administrators (such as deans and department chairpersons) or teachers. Some administrators, however, also teach classes. Note that we've used multiple inheritance to form class AdministratorTeacher. Also, this inheritance hierarchy could contain many other classes. For example, students can be graduate or undergraduate students. Undergraduate students can be freshmen, sophomores, juniors and seniors.

Each arrow in the hierarchy (Fig. 12.2) represents an *is-a* relationship. For example, as we follow the arrows in this class hierarchy, we can state "an Employee *is a* Community-Member" and "a Teacher *is a* Faculty member." CommunityMember is the direct base class of Employee, Student and Alumnus. In addition, CommunityMember is an indirect base class of all the other classes in the diagram. Starting from the bottom of the diagram, you can follow the arrows and apply the *is-a* relationship to the topmost base class. For example, an AdministratorTeacher *is an* Administrator, *is a* Faculty member, *is an* Employee and *is a* CommunityMember.

Now consider the Shape inheritance hierarchy in Fig. 12.3. This hierarchy begins with base class Shape. Classes TwoDimensionalShape and ThreeDimensionalShape derive from base class Shape—Shapes are either TwoDimensionalShapes or ThreeDimensional-Shapes. The third level of this hierarchy contains some more specific types of TwoDimensionalShapes and ThreeDimensionalShapes. As in Fig. 12.2, we can follow the arrows from the bottom of the diagram to the topmost base class in this class hierarchy to identify several *is-a* relationships. For instance, a Triangle *is a* TwoDimensionalShape and *is a* Shape, while a Sphere *is a* ThreeDimensionalShape and *is a* Shape. This hierarchy could contain many other classes, such as Rectangles, Ellipses and Trapezoids, which are all TwoDimensionalShapes.

To specify that class TwoDimensionalShape (Fig. 12.3) is derived from (or inherits from) class Shape, class TwoDimensionalShape's definition could begin as follows:

```
class TwoDimensionalShape : public Shape
```

This is an example of **public inheritance**, the most commonly used form. We also will discuss **private inheritance** and **protected inheritance** (Section 12.6). With all forms of inheritance, private members of a base class are not accessible directly from that class's derived classes, but these private base-class members are still inherited (i.e., they're still considered parts of the derived classes). With public inheritance, all other base-class members retain their original member access when they become members of the derived class (e.g., public members of the base class become public members of the derived class, and, as we'll soon see, protected members of the base class become protected members of the

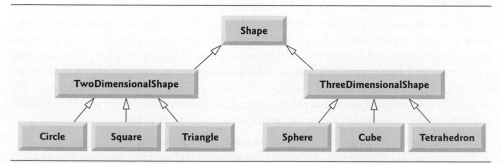

Fig. 12.3 | Inheritance hierarchy for Shapes.

derived class). Through these inherited base-class members, the derived class can manipulate private members of the base class (if these inherited members provide such functionality in the base class). Note that friend functions are not inherited.

Inheritance is not appropriate for every class relationship. In Chapter 10, we discussed the *has-a* relationship, in which classes have members that are objects of other classes. Such relationships create classes by composition of existing classes. For example, given the classes Employee, BirthDate and TelephoneNumber, it's improper to say that an Employee *is a* BirthDate or that an Employee *is a* TelephoneNumber. However, it's appropriate to say that an Employee *has a* BirthDate and that an Employee *has a* TelephoneNumber.

It's possible to treat base-class objects and derived-class objects similarly; their commonalities are expressed in the members of the base class. Objects of all classes derived from a common base class can be treated as objects of that base class (i.e., such objects have an *is-a* relationship with the base class). In Chapter 13, we consider many examples that take advantage of this relationship.

12.3 protected Members

Chapter 3 introduced access specifiers public and private. A base class's public members are accessible within its body and anywhere that the program has a handle (i.e., a name, reference or pointer) to an object of that class or one of its derived classes. A base class's private members are accessible only within its body and to the friends of that base class. In this section, we introduce the access specifier **protected**.

Using protected access offers an intermediate level of protection between public and private access. A base class's protected members can be accessed within the body of that base class, by members and friends of that base class, and by members and friends of any classes derived from that base class.

Derived-class member functions can refer to public and protected members of the base class simply by using the member names. When a derived-class member function redefines a base-class member function, the base-class member can be accessed from the derived class by preceding the base-class member name with the base-class name and the binary scope resolution operator (::). We discuss accessing redefined members of the base class in Section 12.4.5 and using protected data in Section 12.4.4.

12.4 Relationship between Base Classes and Derived Classes

In this section, we use an inheritance hierarchy containing types of employees in a company's payroll application to discuss the relationship between a base class and a derived class. Commission employees (who will be represented as objects of a base class) are paid a percentage of their sales, while base-salaried commission employees (who will be represented as objects of a derived class) receive a base salary plus a percentage of their sales. We divide our discussion of the relationship between commission employees and base-salaried commission employees into a carefully paced series of five examples:

1. In the first example, we create class CommissionEmployee, which contains as private data members a first name, last name, social security number, commission rate (percentage) and gross (i.e., total) sales amount.

2. The second example defines class BasePlusCommissionEmployee, which contains as private data members a first name, last name, social security number, commission rate, gross sales amount and base salary. We create the latter class by writing every line of code the class requires—we'll soon see that it's much more efficient to create this class simply by inheriting from class CommissionEmployee.

3. The third example defines a new version of class BasePlusCommissionEmployee class that inherits directly from class CommissionEmployee (i.e., a BasePlus-CommissionEmployee *is a* CommissionEmployee who also has a base salary) and attempts to access class CommissionEmployee's private members—this results in compilation errors, because the derived class does not have access to the base class's private data.

4. The fourth example shows that if CommissionEmployee's data is declared as protected, a new version of class BasePlusCommissionEmployee that inherits from class CommissionEmployee *can* access that data directly. For this purpose, we define a new version of class CommissionEmployee with protected data. Both the inherited and noninherited BasePlusCommissionEmployee classes contain identical functionality, but we show how the version of BasePlusCommissionEmployee that inherits from class CommissionEmployee is easier to create and manage.

5. After we discuss the convenience of using protected data, we create the fifth example, which sets the CommissionEmployee data members back to private to enforce good software engineering. This example demonstrates that derived class BasePlusCommissionEmployee can use base class CommissionEmployee's public member functions to manipulate CommissionEmployee's private data.

12.4.1 Creating and Using a CommissionEmployee Class

Let's examine CommissionEmployee's class definition (Figs. 12.4–12.5). The CommissionEmployee header file (Fig. 12.4) specifies class CommissionEmployee's public services, which include a constructor (lines 12–13) and member functions earnings (line 30) and print (line 31). Lines 15–28 declare public *get* and *set* functions that manipulate the class's data members (declared in lines 33–37) firstName, lastName, socialSecurityNumber, grossSales and commissionRate. The CommissionEmployee header file specifies that these data members are private, so objects of other classes cannot directly access this data. Declaring data members as private and providing non-private *get* and *set* functions to manipulate and validate the data members helps enforce good software engineering. Member functions setGrossSales (defined in lines 56–59 of Fig. 12.5) and setCommissionRate (defined in lines 68–71 of Fig. 12.5), for example, validate their arguments before assigning the values to data members grossSales and commissionRate, respectively.

```
1   // Fig. 12.4: CommissionEmployee.h
2   // CommissionEmployee class definition represents a commission employee.
3   #ifndef COMMISSION_H
4   #define COMMISSION_H
5
```

Fig. 12.4 | CommissionEmployee class header file. (Part 1 of 2.)

```
 6    #include <string> // C++ standard string class
 7    using namespace std;
 8
 9    class CommissionEmployee
10    {
11    public:
12       CommissionEmployee( const string &, const string &, const string &,
13          double = 0.0, double = 0.0 );
14
15       void setFirstName( const string & ); // set first name
16       string getFirstName() const; // return first name
17
18       void setLastName( const string & ); // set last name
19       string getLastName() const; // return last name
20
21       void setSocialSecurityNumber( const string & ); // set SSN
22       string getSocialSecurityNumber() const; // return SSN
23
24       void setGrossSales( double ); // set gross sales amount
25       double getGrossSales() const; // return gross sales amount
26
27       void setCommissionRate( double ); // set commission rate (percentage)
28       double getCommissionRate() const; // return commission rate
29
30       double earnings() const; // calculate earnings
31       void print() const; // print CommissionEmployee object
32    private:
33       string firstName;
34       string lastName;
35       string socialSecurityNumber;
36       double grossSales; // gross weekly sales
37       double commissionRate; // commission percentage
38    }; // end class CommissionEmployee
39
40    #endif
```

Fig. 12.4 | CommissionEmployee class header file. (Part 2 of 2.)

```
 1    // Fig. 12.5: CommissionEmployee.cpp
 2    // Class CommissionEmployee member-function definitions.
 3    #include <iostream>
 4    #include "CommissionEmployee.h" // CommissionEmployee class definition
 5    using namespace std;
 6
 7    // constructor
 8    CommissionEmployee::CommissionEmployee(
 9       const string &first, const string &last, const string &ssn,
10       double sales, double rate )
11    {
12       firstName = first; // should validate
```

Fig. 12.5 | Implementation file for CommissionEmployee class that represents an employee who is paid a percentage of gross sales. (Part 1 of 3.)

```
13        lastName = last; // should validate
14        socialSecurityNumber = ssn; // should validate
15        setGrossSales( sales ); // validate and store gross sales
16        setCommissionRate( rate ); // validate and store commission rate
17     } // end CommissionEmployee constructor
18
19     // set first name
20     void CommissionEmployee::setFirstName( const string &first )
21     {
22        firstName = first; // should validate
23     } // end function setFirstName
24
25     // return first name
26     string CommissionEmployee::getFirstName() const
27     {
28        return firstName;
29     } // end function getFirstName
30
31     // set last name
32     void CommissionEmployee::setLastName( const string &last )
33     {
34        lastName = last; // should validate
35     } // end function setLastName
36
37     // return last name
38     string CommissionEmployee::getLastName() const
39     {
40        return lastName;
41     ] // end function getLastName
42
43     // set social security number
44     void CommissionEmployee::setSocialSecurityNumber( const string &ssn )
45     [
46        socialSecurityNumber = ssn; // should validate
47     } // end function setSocialSecurityNumber
48
49     // return social security number
50     string CommissionEmployee::getSocialSecurityNumber() const
51     {
52        return socialSecurityNumber;
53     } // end function getSocialSecurityNumber
54
55     // set gross sales amount
56     void CommissionEmployee::setGrossSales( double sales )
57     {
58        grossSales = ( sales < 0.0 ) ? 0.0 : sales;
59     } // end function setGrossSales
60
61     // return gross sales amount
62     double CommissionEmployee::getGrossSales() const
63     {
```

Fig. 12.5 | Implementation file for CommissionEmployee class that represents an employee who is paid a percentage of gross sales. (Part 2 of 3.)

```
64        return grossSales;
65    } // end function getGrossSales
66
67    // set commission rate
68    void CommissionEmployee::setCommissionRate( double rate )
69    {
70        commissionRate = ( rate > 0.0 && rate < 1.0 ) ? rate : 0.0;
71    } // end function setCommissionRate
72
73    // return commission rate
74    double CommissionEmployee::getCommissionRate() const
75    {
76        return commissionRate;
77    } // end function getCommissionRate
78
79    // calculate earnings
80    double CommissionEmployee::earnings() const
81    {
82        return commissionRate * grossSales;
83    } // end function earnings
84
85    // print CommissionEmployee object
86    void CommissionEmployee::print() const
87    {
88        cout << "commission employee: " << firstName << ' ' << lastName
89            << "\nsocial security number: " << socialSecurityNumber
90            << "\ngross sales: " << grossSales
91            << "\ncommission rate: " << commissionRate;
92    } // end function print
```

Fig. 12.5 | Implementation file for `CommissionEmployee` class that represents an employee who is paid a percentage of gross sales. (Part 3 of 3.)

The `CommissionEmployee` constructor definition purposely does not use member-initializer syntax in the first several examples of this section, so that we can demonstrate how `private` and `protected` specifiers affect member access in derived classes. As shown in Fig. 12.5, lines 12–14, we assign values to data members `firstName`, `lastName` and `socialSecurityNumber` in the constructor body. Later in this section, we'll return to using member-initializer lists in the constructors.

We do not validate the values of the constructor's arguments `first`, `last` and `ssn` before assigning them to the corresponding data members. We certainly could validate the first and last names—perhaps by ensuring that they're of a reasonable length. Similarly, a social security number could be validated to ensure that it contains nine digits, with or without dashes (e.g., 123-45-6789 or 123456789).

Member function `earnings` (lines 80–83) calculates a `CommissionEmployee`'s earnings. Line 82 multiplies the `commissionRate` by the `grossSales` and returns the result. Member function `print` (lines 86–92) displays the values of a `CommissionEmployee` object's data members.

Figure 12.6 tests class `CommissionEmployee`. Lines 11–12 instantiate object `employee` of class `CommissionEmployee` and invoke `CommissionEmployee`'s constructor to initialize the object with "Sue" as the first name, "Jones" as the last name, "222-22-2222" as the

```cpp
1   // Fig. 12.6: fig12_06.cpp
2   // Testing class CommissionEmployee.
3   #include <iostream>
4   #include <iomanip>
5   #include "CommissionEmployee.h" // CommissionEmployee class definition
6   using namespace std;
7
8   int main()
9   {
10      // instantiate a CommissionEmployee object
11      CommissionEmployee employee(
12         "Sue", "Jones", "222-22-2222", 10000, .06 );
13
14      // set floating-point output formatting
15      cout << fixed << setprecision( 2 );
16
17      // get commission employee data
18      cout << "Employee information obtained by get functions: \n"
19         << "\nFirst name is " << employee.getFirstName()
20         << "\nLast name is " << employee.getLastName()
21         << "\nSocial security number is "
22         << employee.getSocialSecurityNumber()
23         << "\nGross sales is " << employee.getGrossSales()
24         << "\nCommission rate is " << employee.getCommissionRate() << endl;
25
26      employee.setGrossSales( 8000 ); // set gross sales
27      employee.setCommissionRate( .1 ); // set commission rate
28
29      cout << "\nUpdated employee information output by print function: \n"
30         << endl;
31      employee.print(); // display the new employee information
32
33      // display the employee's earnings
34      cout << "\n\nEmployee's earnings: $" << employee.earnings() << endl;
35   } // end main
```

```
Employee information obtained by get functions:

First name is Sue
Last name is Jones
Social security number is 222-22-2222
Gross sales is 10000.00
Commission rate is 0.06

Updated employee information output by print function:

commission employee: Sue Jones
social security number: 222-22-2222
gross sales: 8000.00
commission rate: 0.10

Employee's earnings: $800.00
```

Fig. 12.6 | CommissionEmployee class test program.

social security number, 10000 as the gross sales amount and .06 as the commission rate. Lines 19–24 use employee's *get* functions to display the values of its data members. Lines 26–27 invoke the object's member functions setGrossSales and setCommissionRate to change the values of data members grossSales and commissionRate, respectively. Line 31 then calls employee's print member function to output the updated CommissionEmployee information. Finally, line 34 displays the CommissionEmployee's earnings, calculated by the object's earnings member function using the updated values of data members gross-Sales and commissionRate.

12.4.2 Creating a BasePlusCommissionEmployee Class Without Using Inheritance

We now discuss the second part of our introduction to inheritance by creating and testing (a completely new and independent) class BasePlusCommissionEmployee (Figs. 12.7–12.8), which contains a first name, last name, social security number, gross sales amount, commission rate *and* base salary.

```cpp
1   // Fig. 12.7: BasePlusCommissionEmployee.h
2   // BasePlusCommissionEmployee class definition represents an employee
3   // that receives a base salary in addition to commission.
4   #ifndef BASEPLUS_H
5   #define BASEPLUS_H
6
7   #include <string> // C++ standard string class
8   using namespace std;
9
10  class BasePlusCommissionEmployee
11  {
12  public:
13     BasePlusCommissionEmployee( const string &, const string &,
14        const string &, double = 0.0, double = 0.0, double = 0.0 );
15
16     void setFirstName( const string & ); // set first name
17     string getFirstName() const; // return first name
18
19     void setLastName( const string & ); // set last name
20     string getLastName() const; // return last name
21
22     void setSocialSecurityNumber( const string & ); // set SSN
23     string getSocialSecurityNumber() const; // return SSN
24
25     void setGrossSales( double ); // set gross sales amount
26     double getGrossSales() const; // return gross sales amount
27
28     void setCommissionRate( double ); // set commission rate
29     double getCommissionRate() const; // return commission rate
30
31     void setBaseSalary( double ); // set base salary
32     double getBaseSalary() const; // return base salary
33
```

Fig. 12.7 | BasePlusCommissionEmployee class header file. (Part 1 of 2.)

```
34      double earnings() const; // calculate earnings
35      void print() const; // print BasePlusCommissionEmployee object
36   private:
37      string firstName;
38      string lastName;
39      string socialSecurityNumber;
40      double grossSales; // gross weekly sales
41      double commissionRate; // commission percentage
42      double baseSalary; // base salary
43   }; // end class BasePlusCommissionEmployee
44
45   #endif
```

Fig. 12.7 | BasePlusCommissionEmployee class header file. (Part 2 of 2.)

```
1    // Fig. 12.8: BasePlusCommissionEmployee.cpp
2    // Class BasePlusCommissionEmployee member-function definitions.
3    #include <iostream>
4    #include "BasePlusCommissionEmployee.h"
5    using namespace std;
6
7    // constructor
8    BasePlusCommissionEmployee::BasePlusCommissionEmployee(
9       const string &first, const string &last, const string &ssn,
10      double sales, double rate, double salary )
11   {
12      firstName = first; // should validate
13      lastName = last; // should validate
14      socialSecurityNumber = ssn; // should validate
15      setGrossSales( sales ); // validate and store gross sales
16      setCommissionRate( rate ); // validate and store commission rate
17      setBaseSalary( salary ); // validate and store base salary
18   } // end BasePlusCommissionEmployee constructor
19
20   // set first name
21   void BasePlusCommissionEmployee::setFirstName( const string &first )
22   {
23      firstName = first; // should validate
24   } // end function setFirstName
25
26   // return first name
27   string BasePlusCommissionEmployee::getFirstName() const
28   {
29      return firstName;
30   } // end function getFirstName
31
32   // set last name
33   void BasePlusCommissionEmployee::setLastName( const string &last )
34   {
35      lastName = last; // should validate
36   } // end function setLastName
```

Fig. 12.8 | BasePlusCommissionEmployee class represents an employee who receives a base salary in addition to a commission. (Part I of 3.)

```
37
38    // return last name
39    string BasePlusCommissionEmployee::getLastName() const
40    {
41       return lastName;
42    } // end function getLastName
43
44    // set social security number
45    void BasePlusCommissionEmployee::setSocialSecurityNumber(
46       const string &ssn )
47    {
48       socialSecurityNumber = ssn; // should validate
49    } // end function setSocialSecurityNumber
50
51    // return social security number
52    string BasePlusCommissionEmployee::getSocialSecurityNumber() const
53    {
54       return socialSecurityNumber;
55    } // end function getSocialSecurityNumber
56
57    // set gross sales amount
58    void BasePlusCommissionEmployee::setGrossSales( double sales )
59    {
60       grossSales = ( sales < 0.0 ) ? 0.0 : sales;
61    } // end function setGrossSales
62
63    // return gross sales amount
64    double BasePlusCommissionEmployee::getGrossSales() const
65    {
66       return grossSales;
67    } // end function getGrossSales
68
69    // set commission rate
70    void BasePlusCommissionEmployee::setCommissionRate( double rate )
71    {
72       commissionRate = ( rate > 0.0 && rate < 1.0 ) ? rate : 0.0;
73    } // end function setCommissionRate
74
75    // return commission rate
76    double BasePlusCommissionEmployee::getCommissionRate() const
77    {
78       return commissionRate;
79    } // end function getCommissionRate
80
81    // set base salary
82    void BasePlusCommissionEmployee::setBaseSalary( double salary )
83    {
84       baseSalary = ( salary < 0.0 ) ? 0.0 : salary;
85    } // end function setBaseSalary
86
```

Fig. 12.8 | BasePlusCommissionEmployee class represents an employee who receives a base salary in addition to a commission. (Part 2 of 3.)

```
87    // return base salary
88    double BasePlusCommissionEmployee::getBaseSalary() const
89    {
90       return baseSalary;
91    } // end function getBaseSalary
92
93    // calculate earnings
94    double BasePlusCommissionEmployee::earnings() const
95    {
96       return baseSalary + ( commissionRate * grossSales );
97    } // end function earnings
98
99    // print BasePlusCommissionEmployee object
100   void BasePlusCommissionEmployee::print() const
101   {
102      cout << "base-salaried commission employee: " << firstName << ' '
103         << lastName << "\nsocial security number: " << socialSecurityNumber
104         << "\ngross sales: " << grossSales
105         << "\ncommission rate: " << commissionRate
106         << "\nbase salary: " << baseSalary;
107   } // end function print
```

Fig. 12.8 | BasePlusCommissionEmployee class represents an employee who receives a base salary in addition to a commission. (Part 3 of 3.)

Defining Class *BasePlusCommissionEmployee*

The BasePlusCommissionEmployee header file (Fig. 12.7) specifies class BasePlusCommissionEmployee's public services, which include the BasePlusCommissionEmployee constructor (lines 13–14) and member functions earnings (line 34) and print (line 35). Lines 16–32 declare public *get* and *set* functions for the class's private data members (declared in lines 37–42) firstName, lastName, socialSecurityNumber, grossSales, commissionRate and baseSalary. These variables and member functions encapsulate all the necessary features of a base-salaried commission employee. Note the similarity between this class and class CommissionEmployee (Figs. 12.4–12.5)—in this example, we won't yet exploit that similarity.

Class BasePlusCommissionEmployee's earnings member function (defined in lines 94–97 of Fig. 12.8) computes the earnings of a base-salaried commission employee. Line 96 returns the result of adding the employee's base salary to the product of the commission rate and the employee's gross sales.

Testing Class *BasePlusCommissionEmployee*

Figure 12.9 tests class BasePlusCommissionEmployee. Lines 11–12 instantiate object employee of class BasePlusCommissionEmployee, passing "Bob", "Lewis", "333-33-3333", 5000, .04 and 300 to the constructor as the first name, last name, social security number, gross sales, commission rate and base salary, respectively. Lines 19–25 use BasePlusCommissionEmployee's *get* functions to retrieve the values of the object's data members for output. Line 27 invokes the object's setBaseSalary member function to change the base salary. Member function setBaseSalary (Fig. 12.8, lines 82–85) ensures that data member baseSalary is not assigned a negative value, because an employee's base salary cannot

```cpp
 1   // Fig. 12.9: fig12_09.cpp
 2   // Testing class BasePlusCommissionEmployee.
 3   #include <iostream>
 4   #include <iomanip>
 5   #include "BasePlusCommissionEmployee.h"
 6   using namespace std;
 7
 8   int main()
 9   {
10      // instantiate BasePlusCommissionEmployee object
11      BasePlusCommissionEmployee
12         employee( "Bob", "Lewis", "333-33-3333", 5000, .04, 300 );
13
14      // set floating-point output formatting
15      cout << fixed << setprecision( 2 );
16
17      // get commission employee data
18      cout << "Employee information obtained by get functions: \n"
19         << "\nFirst name is " << employee.getFirstName()
20         << "\nLast name is " << employee.getLastName()
21         << "\nSocial security number is "
22         << employee.getSocialSecurityNumber()
23         << "\nGross sales is " << employee.getGrossSales()
24         << "\nCommission rate is " << employee.getCommissionRate()
25         << "\nBase salary is " << employee.getBaseSalary() << endl;
26
27      employee.setBaseSalary( 1000 ); // set base salary
28
29      cout << "\nUpdated employee information output by print function: \n"
30         << endl;
31      employee.print(); // display the new employee information
32
33      // display the employee's earnings
34      cout << "\n\nEmployee's earnings: $" << employee.earnings() << endl;
35   } // end main
```

```
Employee information obtained by get functions:

First name is Bob
Last name is Lewis
Social security number is 333-33-3333
Gross sales is 5000.00
Commission rate is 0.04
Base salary is 300.00

Updated employee information output by print function:

base-salaried commission employee: Bob Lewis
social security number: 333-33-3333
gross sales: 5000.00
commission rate: 0.04
base salary: 1000.00

Employee's earnings: $1200.00
```

Fig. 12.9 | BasePlusCommissionEmployee class test program.

be negative. Line 31 of Fig. 12.9 invokes the object's print member function to output the updated BasePlusCommissionEmployee's information, and line 34 calls member function earnings to display the BasePlusCommissionEmployee's earnings.

Exploring the Similarities Between Class BasePlusCommissionEmployee and Class CommissionEmployee

Most of the code for class BasePlusCommissionEmployee (Figs. 12.7–12.8) is similar, if not identical, to the code for class CommissionEmployee (Figs. 12.4–12.5). For example, in class BasePlusCommissionEmployee, private data members firstName and lastName and member functions setFirstName, getFirstName, setLastName and getLastName are identical to those of class CommissionEmployee. Classes CommissionEmployee and BasePlusCommissionEmployee also both contain private data members socialSecurityNumber, commissionRate and grossSales, as well as *get* and *set* functions to manipulate these members. In addition, the BasePlusCommissionEmployee constructor is almost identical to that of class CommissionEmployee, except that BasePlusCommissionEmployee's constructor also sets the baseSalary. The other additions to class BasePlusCommissionEmployee are private data member baseSalary and member functions setBaseSalary and getBaseSalary. Class BasePlusCommissionEmployee's print member function is nearly identical to that of class CommissionEmployee, except that BasePlusCommissionEmployee's print also outputs the value of data member baseSalary.

We literally copied code from class CommissionEmployee and pasted it into class BasePlusCommissionEmployee, then modified class BasePlusCommissionEmployee to include a base salary and member functions that manipulate the base salary. This "copy-and-paste" approach is error prone and time consuming. Worse yet, it can spread many physical copies of the same code throughout a system, creating a code-maintenance nightmare. Is there a way to "absorb" the data members and member functions of a class in a way that makes them part of another class without duplicating code? In the next several examples, we do exactly this, using inheritance.

Software Engineering Observation 12.3

Copying and pasting code from one class to another can spread errors across multiple source code files. To avoid duplicating code (and possibly errors), use inheritance, rather than the "copy-and-paste" approach, in situations where you want one class to "absorb" the data members and member functions of another class.

Software Engineering Observation 12.4

With inheritance, the common data members and member functions of all the classes in the hierarchy are declared in a base class. When changes are required for these common features, you need to make the changes only in the base class—derived classes then inherit the changes. Without inheritance, changes would need to be made to all the source code files that contain a copy of the code in question.

12.4.3 Creating a CommissionEmployee– BasePlusCommissionEmployee Inheritance Hierarchy

Now we create and test a new BasePlusCommissionEmployee class (Figs. 12.10–12.11) that derives from class CommissionEmployee (Figs. 12.4–12.5). In this example, a BasePlusCommissionEmployee object *is a* CommissionEmployee (because inheritance passes on the capabilities of class CommissionEmployee), but class BasePlusCommission-Employee also has data member baseSalary (Fig. 12.10, line 23). The colon (:) in line 11 of the class definition indicates inheritance. Keyword public indicates the type of inheritance. As a derived class (formed with public inheritance), BasePlusCommissionEmployee inherits all the members of class CommissionEmployee, except for the constructor—each class provides its own constructors that are specific to the class. (Destructors, too, are not inherited.) Thus, the public services of BasePlusCommissionEmployee include its constructor (lines 14–15) and the public member functions inherited from class CommissionEmployee—although we cannot see these inherited member functions in BasePlusCommissionEmployee's source code, they're nevertheless a part of derived class BasePlusCommissionEmployee. The derived class's public services also include member functions setBaseSalary, getBaseSalary, earnings and print (lines 17–21).

```cpp
 1   // Fig. 12.10: BasePlusCommissionEmployee.h
 2   // BasePlusCommissionEmployee class derived from class
 3   // CommissionEmployee.
 4   #ifndef BASEPLUS_H
 5   #define BASEPLUS_H
 6
 7   #include <string> // C++ standard string class
 8   #include "CommissionEmployee.h" // CommissionEmployee class declaration
 9   using namespace std;
10
11   class BasePlusCommissionEmployee : public CommissionEmployee
12   {
13   public:
14      BasePlusCommissionEmployee( const string &, const string &,
15         const string &, double = 0.0, double = 0.0, double = 0.0 );
16
17      void setBaseSalary( double ); // set base salary
18      double getBaseSalary() const; // return base salary
19
20      double earnings() const; // calculate earnings
21      void print() const; // print BasePlusCommissionEmployee object
22   private:
23      double baseSalary; // base salary
24   }; // end class BasePlusCommissionEmployee
25
26   #endif
```

Fig. 12.10 | BasePlusCommissionEmployee class definition indicating inheritance relationship with class CommissionEmployee.

```cpp
 1   // Fig. 12.11: BasePlusCommissionEmployee.cpp
 2   // Class BasePlusCommissionEmployee member-function definitions.
 3   #include <iostream>
 4   #include "BasePlusCommissionEmployee.h"
 5   using namespace std;
```

Fig. 12.11 | BasePlusCommissionEmployee implementation file: private base-class data cannot be accessed from derived class. (Part 1 of 3.)

```
 6
 7   // constructor
 8   BasePlusCommissionEmployee::BasePlusCommissionEmployee(
 9      const string &first, const string &last, const string &ssn,
10      double sales, double rate, double salary )
11      // explicitly call base-class constructor
12      : CommissionEmployee( first, last, ssn, sales, rate )
13   {
14      setBaseSalary( salary ); // validate and store base salary
15   } // end BasePlusCommissionEmployee constructor
16
17   // set base salary
18   void BasePlusCommissionEmployee::setBaseSalary( double salary )
19   {
20      baseSalary = ( salary < 0.0 ) ? 0.0 : salary;
21   } // end function setBaseSalary
22
23   // return base salary
24   double BasePlusCommissionEmployee::getBaseSalary() const
25   {
26      return baseSalary;
27   } // end function getBaseSalary
28
29   // calculate earnings
30   double BasePlusCommissionEmployee::earnings() const
31   {
32      // derived class cannot access the base class's private data
33      return baseSalary + ( commissionRate * grossSales );
34   } // end function earnings
35
36   // print BasePlusCommissionEmployee object
37   void BasePlusCommissionEmployee::print() const
38   {
39      // derived class cannot access the base class's private data
40      cout << "base-salaried commission employee: " << firstName << ' '
41         << lastName << "\nsocial security number: " << socialSecurityNumber
42         << "\ngross sales: " << grossSales
43         << "\ncommission rate: " << commissionRate
44         << "\nbase salary: " << baseSalary;
45   } // end function print
```

```
C:\cpphtp7_examples\ch12\Fig12_10_11\BasePlusCommissionEmployee.cpp(33) :
   error C2248: 'CommissionEmployee::commissionRate' :
   cannot access private member declared in class 'CommissionEmployee'

C:\cpphtp7_examples\ch12\Fig12_10_11\BasePlusCommissionEmployee.cpp(33) :
   error C2248: 'CommissionEmployee::grossSales' :
   cannot access private member declared in class 'CommissionEmployee'

C:\cpphtp7_examples\ch12\Fig12_10_11\BasePlusCommissionEmployee.cpp(40) :
   error C2248: 'CommissionEmployee::firstName' :
   cannot access private member declared in class 'CommissionEmployee'
```

Fig. 12.11 | BasePlusCommissionEmployee implementation file: private base-class data cannot be accessed from derived class. (Part 2 of 3.)

```
C:\cpphtp7_examples\ch12\Fig12_10_11\BasePlusCommissionEmployee.cpp(41) :
   error C2248: 'CommissionEmployee::lastName' :
   cannot access private member declared in class 'CommissionEmployee'

C:\cpphtp7_examples\ch12\Fig12_10_11\BasePlusCommissionEmployee.cpp(41) :
   error C2248: 'CommissionEmployee::socialSecurityNumber' :
   cannot access private member declared in class 'CommissionEmployee'

C:\cpphtp7_examples\ch12\Fig12_10_11\BasePlusCommissionEmployee.cpp(42) :
   error C2248: 'CommissionEmployee::grossSales' :
   cannot access private member declared in class 'CommissionEmployee'

C:\cpphtp7_examples\ch12\Fig12_10_11\BasePlusCommissionEmployee.cpp(43) :
   error C2248: 'CommissionEmployee::commissionRate' :
   cannot access private member declared in class 'CommissionEmployee'
```

Fig. 12.11 | `BasePlusCommissionEmployee` implementation file: `private` base-class data cannot be accessed from derived class. (Part 3 of 3.)

Figure 12.11 shows `BasePlusCommissionEmployee`'s member-function implementations. The constructor (lines 8–15) introduces **base-class initializer syntax** (line 12), which uses a member initializer to pass arguments to the base-class (`CommissionEmployee`) constructor. C++ requires that a derived-class constructor call its base-class constructor to initialize the base-class data members that are inherited into the derived class. Line 12 accomplishes this task by invoking the `CommissionEmployee` constructor by name, passing the constructor's parameters `first`, `last`, `ssn`, `sales` and `rate` as arguments to initialize base-class data members `firstName`, `lastName`, `socialSecurityNumber`, `grossSales` and `commissionRate`. If `BasePlusCommissionEmployee`'s constructor did not invoke class `CommissionEmployee`'s constructor explicitly, C++ would attempt to invoke class `CommissionEmployee`'s default constructor—but the class does not have such a constructor, so the compiler would issue an error. Recall from Chapter 3 that the compiler provides a default constructor with no parameters in any class that does not explicitly include a constructor. However, `CommissionEmployee` *does* explicitly include a constructor, so a default constructor is not provided, and any attempts to implicitly call `CommissionEmployee`'s default constructor would result in compilation errors.

Common Programming Error 12.1

When a derived-class constructor calls a base-class constructor, the arguments passed to the base-class constructor must be consistent with the number and types of parameters specified in one of the base-class constructors; otherwise, a compilation error occurs.

Performance Tip 12.1

In a derived-class constructor, initializing member objects and invoking base-class constructors explicitly in the member initializer list prevents duplicate initialization in which a default constructor is called, then data members are modified again in the derived-class constructor's body.

The compiler generates errors for line 33 of Fig. 12.11 because base class `CommissionEmployee`'s data members `commissionRate` and `grossSales` are `private`—derived class `BasePlusCommissionEmployee`'s member functions are not allowed to access base class

CommissionEmployee's private data. We used red text in Fig. 12.11 to indicate erroneous code. The compiler issues additional errors in lines 40–43 of BasePlusCommission-Employee's print member function for the same reason. As you can see, C++ rigidly enforces restrictions on accessing private data members, so that even a derived class (which is intimately related to its base class) cannot access the base class's private data. [*Note:* To save space, we show only the error messages from Visual C++ in this example and we removed some of the error messages. The error messages produced by your compiler may differ from those shown here.]

We purposely included the erroneous code in Fig. 12.11 to emphasize that a derived class's member functions cannot access its base class's private data. The errors in Base-PlusCommissionEmployee could have been prevented by using the *get* member functions inherited from class CommissionEmployee. For example, line 33 could have invoked get-CommissionRate and getGrossSales to access CommissionEmployee's private data members commissionRate and grossSales, respectively. Similarly, lines 40–43 could have used appropriate *get* member functions to retrieve the values of the base class's data members. In the next example, we show how using protected data also allows us to avoid the errors encountered in this example.

Including the Base-Class Header File in the Derived-Class Header File with #include
Notice that we #include the base class's header file in the derived class's header file (line 8 of Fig. 12.10). This is necessary for three reasons. First, for the derived class to use the base class's name in line 10, we must tell the compiler that the base class exists—the class definition in CommissionEmployee.h does exactly that.

The second reason is that the compiler uses a class definition to determine the size of an object of that class (as we discussed in Section 3.7). A client program that creates an object of a class must #include the class definition to enable the compiler to reserve the proper amount of memory for the object. When using inheritance, a derived-class object's size depends on the data members declared explicitly in its class definition *and* the data members inherited from its direct and indirect base classes. Including the base class's definition in line 8 allows the compiler to determine the memory requirements for the base class's data members that become part of a derived-class object and thus contribute to the total size of the derived-class object.

The last reason for line 8 is to allow the compiler to determine whether the derived class uses the base class's inherited members properly. For example, in the program of Figs. 12.10–12.11, the compiler uses the base-class header file to determine that the data members being accessed by the derived class are private in the base class. Since these are inaccessible to the derived class, the compiler generates errors. The compiler also uses the base class's function prototypes to validate function calls made by the derived class to the inherited base-class functions—you'll see an example of such a function call in Fig. 12.15.

Linking Process in an Inheritance Hierarchy
In Section 3.8, we discussed the linking process for creating an executable GradeBook application. In that example, you saw that the client's object code was linked with the object code for class GradeBook, as well as the object code for any C++ Standard Library classes used in either the client code or in class GradeBook.

The linking process is similar for a program that uses classes in an inheritance hierarchy. The process requires the object code for all classes used in the program and the object code for the direct and indirect base classes of any derived classes used by the program. Suppose a client wants to create an application that uses class BasePlusCommission-Employee, which is a derived class of CommissionEmployee (we'll see an example of this in Section 12.4.4). When compiling the client application, the client's object code must be linked with the object code for classes BasePlusCommissionEmployee and Commission-Employee, because BasePlusCommissionEmployee inherits member functions from its base class CommissionEmployee. The code is also linked with the object code for any C++ Standard Library classes used in class CommissionEmployee, class BasePlusCommission-Employee or the client code. This provides the program with access to the implementations of all of the functionality that the program may use.

12.4.4 CommissionEmployee–BasePlusCommissionEmployee Inheritance Hierarchy Using protected Data

To enable class BasePlusCommissionEmployee to directly access CommissionEmployee data members firstName, lastName, socialSecurityNumber, grossSales and commissionRate, we can declare those members as protected in the base class. As we discussed in Section 12.3, a base class's protected members can be accessed by members and friends of the base class and by members and friends of any classes derived from that base class.

Good Programming Practice 12.1

Declare public members first, protected members second and private members last.

Defining Base Class CommissionEmployee with protected Data
Class CommissionEmployee (Figs. 12.12–12.13) now declares data members firstName, lastName, socialSecurityNumber, grossSales and commissionRate as protected (Fig. 12.12, lines 32–37) rather than private. The member-function implementations in Fig. 12.13 are identical to those in Fig. 12.5.

```
1   // Fig. 12.12: CommissionEmployee.h
2   // CommissionEmployee class definition with protected data.
3   #ifndef COMMISSION_H
4   #define COMMISSION_H
5
6   #include <string> // C++ standard string class
7   using namespace std;
8
9   class CommissionEmployee
10  {
11  public:
12     CommissionEmployee( const string &, const string &, const string &,
13        double = 0.0, double = 0.0 );
14
15     void setFirstName( const string & ); // set first name
16     string getFirstName() const; // return first name
```

Fig. 12.12 | CommissionEmployee class definition that declares protected data to allow access by derived classes. (Part 1 of 2.)

```
17
18      void setLastName( const string & ); // set last name
19      string getLastName() const; // return last name
20
21      void setSocialSecurityNumber( const string & ); // set SSN
22      string getSocialSecurityNumber() const; // return SSN
23
24      void setGrossSales( double ); // set gross sales amount
25      double getGrossSales() const; // return gross sales amount
26
27      void setCommissionRate( double ); // set commission rate
28      double getCommissionRate() const; // return commission rate
29
30      double earnings() const; // calculate earnings
31      void print() const; // print CommissionEmployee object
32   protected:
33      string firstName;
34      string lastName;
35      string socialSecurityNumber;
36      double grossSales; // gross weekly sales
37      double commissionRate; // commission percentage
38   }; // end class CommissionEmployee
39
40   #endif
```

Fig. 12.12 | CommissionEmployee class definition that declares protected data to allow access by derived classes. (Part 2 of 2.)

```
1    // Fig. 12.13: CommissionEmployee.cpp
2    // Class CommissionEmployee member-function definitions.
3    #include <iostream>
4    #include "CommissionEmployee.h" // CommissionEmployee class definition
5    using namespace std;
6
7    // constructor
8    CommissionEmployee::CommissionEmployee(
9       const string &first, const string &last, const string &ssn,
10      double sales, double rate )
11   {
12      firstName = first; // should validate
13      lastName = last; // should validate
14      socialSecurityNumber = ssn; // should validate
15      setGrossSales( sales ); // validate and store gross sales
16      setCommissionRate( rate ); // validate and store commission rate
17   } // end CommissionEmployee constructor
18
19   // set first name
20   void CommissionEmployee::setFirstName( const string &first )
21   {
22      firstName = first; // should validate
23   } // end function setFirstName
```

Fig. 12.13 | CommissionEmployee class with protected data. (Part 1 of 3.)

```
24
25   // return first name
26   string CommissionEmployee::getFirstName() const
27   {
28      return firstName;
29   } // end function getFirstName
30
31   // set last name
32   void CommissionEmployee::setLastName( const string &last )
33   {
34      lastName = last; // should validate
35   } // end function setLastName
36
37   // return last name
38   string CommissionEmployee::getLastName() const
39   {
40      return lastName;
41   } // end function getLastName
42
43   // set social security number
44   void CommissionEmployee::setSocialSecurityNumber( const string &ssn )
45   {
46      socialSecurityNumber = ssn; // should validate
47   } // end function setSocialSecurityNumber
48
49   // return social security number
50   string CommissionEmployee::getSocialSecurityNumber() const
51   {
52      return socialSecurityNumber;
53   } // end function getSocialSecurityNumber
54
55   // set gross sales amount
56   void CommissionEmployee::setGrossSales( double sales )
57   {
58      grossSales = ( sales < 0.0 ) ? 0.0 : sales;
59   } // end function setGrossSales
60
61   // return gross sales amount
62   double CommissionEmployee::getGrossSales() const
63   {
64      return grossSales;
65   } // end function getGrossSales
66
67   // set commission rate
68   void CommissionEmployee::setCommissionRate( double rate )
69   {
70      commissionRate = ( rate > 0.0 && rate < 1.0 ) ? rate : 0.0;
71   } // end function setCommissionRate
72
73   // return commission rate
74   double CommissionEmployee::getCommissionRate() const
75   {
```

Fig. 12.13 | CommissionEmployee class with protected data. (Part 2 of 3.)

```
76        return commissionRate;
77    } // end function getCommissionRate
78
79    // calculate earnings
80    double CommissionEmployee::earnings() const
81    {
82        return commissionRate * grossSales;
83    } // end function earnings
84
85    // print CommissionEmployee object
86    void CommissionEmployee::print() const
87    {
88        cout << "commission employee: " << firstName << ' ' << lastName
89            << "\nsocial security number: " << socialSecurityNumber
90            << "\ngross sales: " << grossSales
91            << "\ncommission rate: " << commissionRate;
92    } // end function print
```

Fig. 12.13 | CommissionEmployee class with protected data. (Part 3 of 3.)

Modifying Derived Class BasePlusCommissionEmployee

The version of class BasePlusCommissionEmployee in Figs. 12.14–12.15 inherits from class CommissionEmployee in Figs. 12.12–12.13. Objects of class BasePlusCommission-Employee can access inherited data members that are declared protected in class Commission-sionEmployee (i.e., data members firstName, lastName, socialSecurityNumber, grossSales and commissionRate). As a result, the compiler does not generate errors when compiling the BasePlusCommissionEmployee earnings and print member-function definitions in Fig. 12.15 (lines 30–34 and 37–45, respectively). This shows the special privileges that a derived class is granted to access protected base-class data members. Objects of a derived class also can access protected members in any of that derived class's indirect base classes.

```
 1    // Fig. 12.14: BasePlusCommissionEmployee.h
 2    // BasePlusCommissionEmployee class derived from class
 3    // CommissionEmployee.
 4    #ifndef BASEPLUS_H
 5    #define BASEPLUS_H
 6
 7    #include <string> // C++ standard string class
 8    #include "CommissionEmployee.h" // CommissionEmployee class declaration
 9    using namespace std;
10
11    class BasePlusCommissionEmployee : public CommissionEmployee
12    {
13    public:
14        BasePlusCommissionEmployee( const string &, const string &,
15            const string &, double = 0.0, double = 0.0, double = 0.0 );
16
```

Fig. 12.14 | BasePlusCommissionEmployee class header file. (Part 1 of 2.)

```
17     void setBaseSalary( double ); // set base salary
18     double getBaseSalary() const; // return base salary
19
20     double earnings() const; // calculate earnings
21     void print() const; // print BasePlusCommissionEmployee object
22  private:
23     double baseSalary; // base salary
24  }; // end class BasePlusCommissionEmployee
25
26  #endif
```

Fig. 12.14 | BasePlusCommissionEmployee class header file. (Part 2 of 2.)

```
1   // Fig. 12.15: BasePlusCommissionEmployee.cpp
2   // Class BasePlusCommissionEmployee member-function definitions.
3   #include <iostream>
4   #include "BasePlusCommissionEmployee.h"
5   using namespace std;
6
7   // constructor
8   BasePlusCommissionEmployee::BasePlusCommissionEmployee(
9      const string &first, const string &last, const string &ssn,
10     double sales, double rate, double salary )
11     // explicitly call base-class constructor
12     : CommissionEmployee( first, last, ssn, sales, rate )
13  {
14     setBaseSalary( salary ); // validate and store base salary
15  } // end BasePlusCommissionEmployee constructor
16
17  // set base salary
18  void BasePlusCommissionEmployee::setBaseSalary( double salary )
19  {
20     baseSalary = ( salary < 0.0 ) ? 0.0 : salary;
21  } // end function setBaseSalary
22
23  // return base salary
24  double BasePlusCommissionEmployee::getBaseSalary() const
25  {
26     return baseSalary;
27  } // end function getBaseSalary
28
29  // calculate earnings
30  double BasePlusCommissionEmployee::earnings() const
31  {
32     // can access protected data of base class
33     return baseSalary + ( commissionRate * grossSales );
34  } // end function earnings
35
```

Fig. 12.15 | BasePlusCommissionEmployee implementation file for
BasePlusCommissionEmployee class that inherits protected data from CommissionEmployee.
(Part 1 of 2.)

```
36    // print BasePlusCommissionEmployee object
37    void BasePlusCommissionEmployee::print() const
38    {
39       // can access protected data of base class
40       cout << "base-salaried commission employee: " << firstName << ' '
41          << lastName << "\nsocial security number: " << socialSecurityNumber
42          << "\ngross sales: " << grossSales
43          << "\ncommission rate: " << commissionRate
44          << "\nbase salary: " << baseSalary;
45    } // end function print
```

Fig. 12.15 | BasePlusCommissionEmployee implementation file for
BasePlusCommissionEmployee class that inherits protected data from CommissionEmployee.
(Part 2 of 2.)

Class BasePlusCommissionEmployee does not inherit class CommissionEmployee's constructor. However, class BasePlusCommissionEmployee's constructor (Fig. 12.15, lines 8–15) calls class CommissionEmployee's constructor explicitly with member initializer syntax (line 12). Recall that BasePlusCommissionEmployee's constructor must explicitly call the constructor of class CommissionEmployee, because CommissionEmployee does not contain a default constructor that could be invoked implicitly.

*Testing the Modified **BasePlusCommissionEmployee** Class*
Figure 12.16 uses a BasePlusCommissionEmployee object to perform the same tasks that Fig. 12.9 performed on an object of the first version of class BasePlusCommissionEmployee (Figs. 12.7–12.8). The code and outputs of the two programs are identical. We created the first class BasePlusCommissionEmployee without using inheritance and created this version of BasePlusCommissionEmployee using inheritance; however, both classes provide the same functionality. The code for class BasePlusCommissionEmployee (i.e., the header and implementation files), which is 71 lines, is considerably shorter than the code for the noninherited version of the class, which is 152 lines, because the inherited version absorbs part of its functionality from CommissionEmployee, whereas the noninherited version does not absorb any functionality. Also, there is now only one copy of the CommissionEmployee functionality declared and defined in class CommissionEmployee. This makes the source code easier to maintain, modify and debug, because the source code related to a CommissionEmployee exists only in the files of Figs. 12.12–12.13.

```
1    // Fig. 12.16: fig12_16.cpp
2    // Testing class BasePlusCommissionEmployee.
3    #include <iostream>
4    #include <iomanip>
5    #include "BasePlusCommissionEmployee.h"
6    using namespace std;
7
8    int main()
9    {
```

Fig. 12.16 | protected base-class data can be accessed from derived class. (Part 1 of 2.)

```
10      // instantiate BasePlusCommissionEmployee object
11      BasePlusCommissionEmployee
12         employee( "Bob", "Lewis", "333-33-3333", 5000, .04, 300 );
13
14      // set floating-point output formatting
15      cout << fixed << setprecision( 2 );
16
17      // get commission employee data
18      cout << "Employee information obtained by get functions: \n"
19         << "\nFirst name is " << employee.getFirstName()
20         << "\nLast name is " << employee.getLastName()
21         << "\nSocial security number is "
22         << employee.getSocialSecurityNumber()
23         << "\nGross sales is " << employee.getGrossSales()
24         << "\nCommission rate is " << employee.getCommissionRate()
25         << "\nBase salary is " << employee.getBaseSalary() << endl;
26
27      employee.setBaseSalary( 1000 ); // set base salary
28
29      cout << "\nUpdated employee information output by print function: \n"
30         << endl;
31      employee.print(); // display the new employee information
32
33      // display the employee's earnings
34      cout << "\n\nEmployee's earnings: $" << employee.earnings() << endl;
35   } // end main
```

```
Employee information obtained by get functions:

First name is Bob
Last name is Lewis
Social security number is 333-33-3333
Gross sales is 5000.00
Commission rate is 0.04
Base salary is 300.00

Updated employee information output by print function:

base-salaried commission employee: Bob Lewis
social security number: 333-33-3333
gross sales: 5000.00
commission rate: 0.04
base salary: 1000.00

Employee's earnings: $1200.00
```

Fig. 12.16 | protected base-class data can be accessed from derived class. (Part 2 of 2.)

Notes on Using protected Data

In this example, we declared base-class data members as protected, so derived classes can modify the data directly. Inheriting protected data members slightly increases performance, because we can directly access the members without incurring the overhead of calls to *set* or *get* member functions. In most cases, however, it's better to use private data members to encourage proper software engineering, and leave code optimization issues to the compiler. Your code will be easier to maintain, modify and debug.

Using `protected` data members creates two serious problems. First, the derived-class object does not have to use a member function to set the value of the base class's `protected` data member. An invalid value can easily be assigned to the `protected` data member, thus leaving the object in an inconsistent state—e.g., with `CommissionEmployee`'s data member `grossSales` declared as `protected`, a derived-class object can assign a negative value to `grossSales`. The second problem with using `protected` data members is that derived-class member functions are more likely to be written so that they depend on the base-class implementation. Derived classes should depend only on the base-class services (i.e., non-private member functions) and not on the base-class implementation. With `protected` data members in the base class, if the base-class implementation changes, we may need to modify all derived classes of that base class. For example, if for some reason we were to change the names of data members `firstName` and `lastName` to `first` and `last`, then we'd have to do so for all occurrences in which a derived class references these base-class data members directly. Such software is said to be **fragile** or **brittle**, because a small change in the base class can "break" derived-class implementation. You should be able to change the base-class implementation while still providing the same services to derived classes. (Of course, if the base-class services change, we must reimplement our derived classes—good object-oriented design attempts to prevent this.)

Software Engineering Observation 12.5

It's appropriate to use the `protected` access specifier when a base class should provide a service (i.e., a member function) only to its derived classes and `friends`.

Software Engineering Observation 12.6

Declaring base-class data members `private` (as opposed to declaring them `protected`) enables you to change the base-class implementation without having to change derived-class implementations.

Error-Prevention Tip 12.1

When possible, avoid including `protected` data members in a base class. Rather, include non-private member functions that access `private` data members, ensuring that the object maintains a consistent state.

12.4.5 CommissionEmployee-BasePlusCommissionEmployee Inheritance Hierarchy Using private Data

We now reexamine our hierarchy once more, this time using the best software engineering practices. Class `CommissionEmployee` (Figs. 12.17–12.18) now declares data members `firstName`, `lastName`, `socialSecurityNumber`, `grossSales` and `commissionRate` as private (Fig. 12.17, lines 32–37) and provides public member functions `setFirstName`, `getFirstName`, `setLastName`, `getLastName`, `setSocialSecurityNumber`, `getSocialSecurityNumber`, `setGrossSales`, `getGrossSales`, `setCommissionRate`, `getCommissionRate`, `earnings` and `print` for manipulating these values. If we decide to change the data member names, the `earnings` and `print` definitions will not require modification—only the definitions of the *get* and *set* member functions that directly manipulate the data members will need to change. These changes occur solely within the base class—no changes to the derived class are needed. Localizing the effects of changes like this is a good

software engineering practice. Derived class `BasePlusCommissionEmployee`
(Figs. 12.19–12.20) inherits `CommissionEmployee`'s member functions and can access the
`private` base-class members via the inherited non-private member functions.

```cpp
1   // Fig. 12.17: CommissionEmployee.h
2   // CommissionEmployee class definition with good software engineering.
3   #ifndef COMMISSION_H
4   #define COMMISSION_H
5
6   #include <string> // C++ standard string class
7   using namespace std;
8
9   class CommissionEmployee
10  {
11  public:
12     CommissionEmployee( const string &, const string &, const string &,
13        double = 0.0, double = 0.0 );
14
15     void setFirstName( const string & ); // set first name
16     string getFirstName() const; // return first name
17
18     void setLastName( const string & ); // set last name
19     string getLastName() const; // return last name
20
21     void setSocialSecurityNumber( const string & ); // set SSN
22     string getSocialSecurityNumber() const; // return SSN
23
24     void setGrossSales( double ); // set gross sales amount
25     double getGrossSales() const; // return gross sales amount
26
27     void setCommissionRate( double ); // set commission rate
28     double getCommissionRate() const; // return commission rate
29
30     double earnings() const; // calculate earnings
31     void print() const; // print CommissionEmployee object
32  private:
33     string firstName;
34     string lastName;
35     string socialSecurityNumber;
36     double grossSales; // gross weekly sales
37     double commissionRate; // commission percentage
38  }; // end class CommissionEmployee
39
40  #endif
```

Fig. 12.17 | `CommissionEmployee` class defined using good software engineering practices.

In the `CommissionEmployee` constructor implementation (Fig. 12.18, lines 8–15), we
use member initializers (line 11) to set the values of members `firstName`, `lastName` and
`socialSecurityNumber`. We show how derived-class `BasePlusCommissionEmployee`
(Figs. 12.19–12.20) can invoke non-private base-class member functions (`setFirst-
Name`, `getFirstName`, `setLastName`, `getLastName`, `setSocialSecurityNumber` and `getSo-
cialSecurityNumber`) to manipulate these data members.

Performance Tip 12.2

Using a member function to access a data member's value can be slightly slower than accessing the data directly. However, today's optimizing compilers are carefully designed to perform many optimizations implicitly (such as inlining set *and* get *member-function calls). You should write code that adheres to proper software engineering principles, and leave optimization to the compiler. A good rule is, "Do not second-guess the compiler."*

```cpp
1   // Fig. 12.18: CommissionEmployee.cpp
2   // Class CommissionEmployee member-function definitions.
3   #include <iostream>
4   #include "CommissionEmployee.h" // CommissionEmployee class definition
5   using namespace std;
6
7   // constructor
8   CommissionEmployee::CommissionEmployee(
9      const string &first, const string &last, const string &ssn,
10     double sales, double rate )
11     : firstName( first ), lastName( last ), socialSecurityNumber( ssn )
12  {
13     setGrossSales( sales ); // validate and store gross sales
14     setCommissionRate( rate ); // validate and store commission rate
15  } // end CommissionEmployee constructor
16
17  // set first name
18  void CommissionEmployee::setFirstName( const string &first )
19  {
20     firstName = first; // should validate
21  } // end function setFirstName
22
23  // return first name
24  string CommissionEmployee::getFirstName() const
25  {
26     return firstName;
27  } // end function getFirstName
28
29  // set last name
30  void CommissionEmployee::setLastName( const string &last )
31  {
32     lastName = last; // should validate
33  } // end function setLastName
34
35  // return last name
36  string CommissionEmployee::getLastName() const
37  {
38     return lastName;
39  } // end function getLastName
40
41  // set social security number
42  void CommissionEmployee::setSocialSecurityNumber( const string &ssn )
43  {
```

Fig. 12.18 | CommissionEmployee class implementation file: CommissionEmployee class uses member functions to manipulate its private data. (Part 1 of 2.)

```
44        socialSecurityNumber = ssn; // should validate
45   } // end function setSocialSecurityNumber
46
47   // return social security number
48   string CommissionEmployee::getSocialSecurityNumber() const
49   {
50        return socialSecurityNumber;
51   } // end function getSocialSecurityNumber
52
53   // set gross sales amount
54   void CommissionEmployee::setGrossSales( double sales )
55   {
56        grossSales = ( sales < 0.0 ) ? 0.0 : sales;
57   } // end function setGrossSales
58
59   // return gross sales amount
60   double CommissionEmployee::getGrossSales() const
61   {
62        return grossSales;
63   } // end function getGrossSales
64
65   // set commission rate
66   void CommissionEmployee::setCommissionRate( double rate )
67   {
68        commissionRate = ( rate > 0.0 && rate < 1.0 ) ? rate : 0.0;
69   } // end function setCommissionRate
70
71   // return commission rate
72   double CommissionEmployee::getCommissionRate() const
73   {
74        return commissionRate;
75   } // end function getCommissionRate
76
77   // calculate earnings
78   double CommissionEmployee::earnings() const
79   {
80        return getCommissionRate() * getGrossSales();
81   } // end function earnings
82
83   // print CommissionEmployee object
84   void CommissionEmployee::print() const
85   {
86        cout << "commission employee: "
87           << getFirstName() << ' ' << getLastName()
88           << "\nsocial security number: " << getSocialSecurityNumber()
89           << "\ngross sales: " << getGrossSales()
90           << "\ncommission rate: " << getCommissionRate();
91   } // end function print
```

Fig. 12.18 | CommissionEmployee class implementation file: CommissionEmployee class uses member functions to manipulate its private data. (Part 2 of 2.)

Class BasePlusCommissionEmployee (Figs. 12.19–12.20) has several changes to its member-function implementations (Fig. 12.20) that distinguish it from the previous version of the class (Figs. 12.14–12.15). Member functions earnings (Fig. 12.20, lines 30–33) and print (lines 36–44) each invoke member function getBaseSalary to obtain the base salary value, rather than accessing baseSalary directly. This insulates earnings and print from potential changes to the implementation of data member baseSalary. For example, if we decide to rename data member baseSalary or change its type, only member functions set-BaseSalary and getBaseSalary will need to change.

```cpp
1   // Fig. 12.19: BasePlusCommissionEmployee.h
2   // BasePlusCommissionEmployee class derived from class
3   // CommissionEmployee.
4   #ifndef BASEPLUS_H
5   #define BASEPLUS_H
6
7   #include <string> // C++ standard string class
8   #include "CommissionEmployee.h" // CommissionEmployee class declaration
9   using namespace std;
10
11  class BasePlusCommissionEmployee : public CommissionEmployee
12  {
13  public:
14     BasePlusCommissionEmployee( const string &, const string &,
15        const string &, double = 0.0, double = 0.0, double = 0.0 );
16
17     void setBaseSalary( double ); // set base salary
18     double getBaseSalary() const; // return base salary
19
20     double earnings() const; // calculate earnings
21     void print() const; // print BasePlusCommissionEmployee object
22  private:
23     double baseSalary; // base salary
24  }; // end class BasePlusCommissionEmployee
25
26  #endif
```

Fig. 12.19 | BasePlusCommissionEmployee class header file.

```cpp
1   // Fig. 12.20: BasePlusCommissionEmployee.cpp
2   // Class BasePlusCommissionEmployee member-function definitions.
3   #include <iostream>
4   #include "BasePlusCommissionEmployee.h"
5   using namespace std;
6
7   // constructor
8   BasePlusCommissionEmployee::BasePlusCommissionEmployee(
9      const string &first, const string &last, const string &ssn,
10     double sales, double rate, double salary )
11     // explicitly call base-class constructor
12     : CommissionEmployee( first, last, ssn, sales, rate )
13  {
```

Fig. 12.20 | BasePlusCommissionEmployee class that inherits from class CommissionEmployee but cannot directly access the class's private data. (Part 1 of 2.)

```
14     setBaseSalary( salary ); // validate and store base salary
15  } // end BasePlusCommissionEmployee constructor
16
17  // set base salary
18  void BasePlusCommissionEmployee::setBaseSalary( double salary )
19  {
20     baseSalary = ( salary < 0.0 ) ? 0.0 : salary;
21  } // end function setBaseSalary
22
23  // return base salary
24  double BasePlusCommissionEmployee::getBaseSalary() const
25  {
26     return baseSalary;
27  } // end function getBaseSalary
28
29  // calculate earnings
30  double BasePlusCommissionEmployee::earnings() const
31  {
32     return getBaseSalary() + CommissionEmployee::earnings();
33  } // end function earnings
34
35  // print BasePlusCommissionEmployee object
36  void BasePlusCommissionEmployee::print() const
37  {
38     cout << "base-salaried ";
39
40     // invoke CommissionEmployee's print function
41     CommissionEmployee::print();
42
43     cout << "\nbase salary: " << getBaseSalary();
44  } // end function print
```

Fig. 12.20 | BasePlusCommissionEmployee class that inherits from class
CommissionEmployee but cannot directly access the class's private data. (Part 2 of 2.)

Class BasePlusCommissionEmployee's earnings function (Fig. 12.20, lines 30–33)
redefines class CommissionEmployee's earnings member function (Fig. 12.18, lines 78–
81) to calculate the earnings of a base-salaried commission employee. Class BasePlusCommissionEmployee's version of earnings obtains the portion of the employee's earnings
based on commission alone by calling base-class CommissionEmployee's earnings function with the expression CommissionEmployee::earnings() (Fig. 12.20, line 32).
BasePlusCommissionEmployee's earnings function then adds the base salary to this value
to calculate the total earnings of the employee. Note the syntax used to invoke a redefined
base-class member function from a derived class—place the base-class name and the binary
scope resolution operator (::) before the base-class member-function name. This member-
function invocation is a good software engineering practice: Recall from *Software Engineering Observation 9.9* that, if an object's member function performs the actions needed
by another object, we should call that member function rather than duplicating its code
body. By having BasePlusCommissionEmployee's earnings function invoke Commission-
Employee's earnings function to calculate part of a BasePlusCommissionEmployee
object's earnings, we avoid duplicating the code and reduce code-maintenance problems.

Common Programming Error 12.2

When a base-class member function is redefined in a derived class, the derived-class version often calls the base-class version to do additional work. Failure to use the :: operator prefixed with the name of the base class when referencing the base class's member function causes infinite recursion, because the derived-class member function would then call itself.

Similarly, BasePlusCommissionEmployee's print function (Fig. 12.20, lines 36–44) redefines class CommissionEmployee's print function (Fig. 12.18, lines 84–91) to output the appropriate base-salaried commission employee information. The new version displays part of a BasePlusCommissionEmployee object's information (i.e., the string "commission employee" and the values of class CommissionEmployee's private data members) by calling CommissionEmployee's print member function with the qualified name CommissionEmployee::print() (Fig. 12.20, line 41). BasePlusCommissionEmployee's print function then outputs the remainder of a BasePlusCommissionEmployee object's information (i.e., the value of class BasePlusCommissionEmployee's base salary).

Figure 12.21 performs the same manipulations on a BasePlusCommissionEmployee object as did Fig. 12.9 and Fig. 12.16 on objects of classes CommissionEmployee and BasePlusCommissionEmployee, respectively. Although each "base-salaried commission employee" class behaves identically, class BasePlusCommissionEmployee is the best engineered. By using inheritance and by calling member functions that hide the data and ensure consistency, we've efficiently and effectively constructed a well-engineered class.

```cpp
1   // Fig. 12.21: fig12_21.cpp
2   // Testing class BasePlusCommissionEmployee.
3   #include <iostream>
4   #include <iomanip>
5   #include "BasePlusCommissionEmployee.h"
6   using namespace std;
7
8   int main()
9   {
10     // instantiate BasePlusCommissionEmployee object
11     BasePlusCommissionEmployee
12        employee( "Bob", "Lewis", "333-33-3333", 5000, .04, 300 );
13
14     // set floating-point output formatting
15     cout << fixed << setprecision( 2 );
16
17     // get commission employee data
18     cout << "Employee information obtained by get functions: \n"
19        << "\nFirst name is " << employee.getFirstName()
20        << "\nLast name is " << employee.getLastName()
21        << "\nSocial security number is "
22        << employee.getSocialSecurityNumber()
23        << "\nGross sales is " << employee.getGrossSales()
24        << "\nCommission rate is " << employee.getCommissionRate()
25        << "\nBase salary is " << employee.getBaseSalary() << endl;
```

Fig. 12.21 | Base-class private data is accessible to a derived class via public or protected member function inherited by the derived class. (Part 1 of 2.)

```
26
27      employee.setBaseSalary( 1000 ); // set base salary
28
29      cout << "\nUpdated employee information output by print function: \n"
30         << endl;
31      employee.print(); // display the new employee information
32
33      // display the employee's earnings
34      cout << "\n\nEmployee's earnings: $" << employee.earnings() << endl;
35   } // end main
```

```
Employee information obtained by get functions:

First name is Bob
Last name is Lewis
Social security number is 333-33-3333
Gross sales is 5000.00
Commission rate is 0.04
Base salary is 300.00

Updated employee information output by print function:

base-salaried commission employee: Bob Lewis
social security number: 333-33-3333
gross sales: 5000.00
commission rate: 0.04
base salary: 1000.00

Employee's earnings: $1200.00
```

Fig. 12.21 | Base-class `private` data is accessible to a derived class via `public` or `protected` member function inherited by the derived class. (Part 2 of 2.)

In this section, you saw an evolutionary set of examples that was carefully designed to teach key capabilities for good software engineering with inheritance. You learned how to create a derived class using inheritance, how to use `protected` base-class members to enable a derived class to access inherited base-class data members and how to redefine base-class functions to provide versions that are more appropriate for derived-class objects. In addition, you learned how to apply software engineering techniques from Chapters 9–10 and this chapter to create classes that are easy to maintain, modify and debug.

12.5 Constructors and Destructors in Derived Classes

As we explained in the preceding section, instantiating a derived-class object begins a chain of constructor calls in which the derived-class constructor, before performing its own tasks, invokes its direct base class's constructor either explicitly (via a base-class member initializer) or implicitly (calling the base class's default constructor). Similarly, if the base class is derived from another class, the base-class constructor is required to invoke the constructor of the next class up in the hierarchy, and so on. The last constructor called in this chain is the constructor of the class at the base of the hierarchy, whose body actually finishes executing first. The original derived-class constructor's body finishes executing last. Each base-class constructor initializes the base-class data members that the derived-class object inherits. For example, consider the CommissionEmployee/BasePlusCommissionEmployee hierarchy from Figs. 12.17–12.20. When a program creates an object of class BasePlusCommissionEmployee, the CommissionEmployee constructor is called. Since class CommissionEmployee is at the base of the hierarchy, its constructor executes, initializing the private data members of CommissionEmployee that are part of the BasePlusCommissionEmployee object. When CommissionEmployee's constructor completes execution, it returns control to BasePlusCommissionEmployee's constructor, which initializes the BasePlusCommissionEmployee object's baseSalary.

Software Engineering Observation 12.7

When a program creates a derived-class object, the derived-class constructor immediately calls the base-class constructor, the base-class constructor's body executes, then the derived class's member initializers execute and finally the derived-class constructor's body executes. This process cascades up the hierarchy if it contains more than two levels.

When a derived-class object is destroyed, the program calls that object's destructor. This begins a chain (or cascade) of destructor calls in which the derived-class destructor and the destructors of the direct and indirect base classes and the classes' members execute in reverse of the order in which the constructors executed. When a derived-class object's destructor is called, the destructor performs its task, then invokes the destructor of the next base class up the hierarchy. This process repeats until the destructor of the final base class at the top of the hierarchy is called. Then the object is removed from memory.

Software Engineering Observation 12.8

Suppose that we create an object of a derived class where both the base class and the derived class contain (via composition) objects of other classes. When an object of that derived class is created, first the constructors for the base class's member objects execute, then the base-class constructor executes, then the constructors for the derived class's member objects execute, then the derived class's constructor executes. Destructors for derived-class objects are called in the reverse of the order in which their corresponding constructors are called.

Base-class constructors, destructors and overloaded assignment operators (see Chapter 11, Operator Overloading) are not inherited by derived classes. Derived-class constructors, destructors and overloaded assignment operators, however, can call base-class constructors, destructors and overloaded assignment operators.

Our next example defines class CommissionEmployee (Figs. 12.22–12.23) and class BasePlusCommissionEmployee (Figs. 12.24–12.25) with constructors and destructors that each print a message when invoked. As you'll see in the output in Fig. 12.26, these messages demonstrate the order in which the constructors and destructors are called for objects in an inheritance hierarchy.

```
1   // Fig. 12.22: CommissionEmployee.h
2   // CommissionEmployee class definition represents a commission employee.
3   #ifndef COMMISSION_H
4   #define COMMISSION_H
5
```

Fig. 12.22 | CommissionEmployee class header file. (Part 1 of 2.)

```
6    #include <string> // C++ standard string class
7    using namespace std;
8
9    class CommissionEmployee
10   {
11   public:
12      CommissionEmployee( const string &, const string &, const string &,
13         double = 0.0, double = 0.0 );
14      ~CommissionEmployee(); // destructor
15
16      void setFirstName( const string & ); // set first name
17      string getFirstName() const; // return first name
18
19      void setLastName( const string & ); // set last name
20      string getLastName() const; // return last name
21
22      void setSocialSecurityNumber( const string & ); // set SSN
23      string getSocialSecurityNumber() const; // return SSN
24
25      void setGrossSales( double ); // set gross sales amount
26      double getGrossSales() const; // return gross sales amount
27
28      void setCommissionRate( double ); // set commission rate
29      double getCommissionRate() const; // return commission rate
30
31      double earnings() const; // calculate earnings
32      void print() const; // print CommissionEmployee object
33   private:
34      string firstName;
35      string lastName;
36      string socialSecurityNumber;
37      double grossSales; // gross weekly sales
38      double commissionRate; // commission percentage
39   }; // end class CommissionEmployee
40
41   #endif
```

Fig. 12.22 | CommissionEmployee class header file. (Part 2 of 2.)

```
1    // Fig. 12.23: CommissionEmployee.cpp
2    // Class CommissionEmployee member-function definitions.
3    #include <iostream>
4    #include "CommissionEmployee.h" // CommissionEmployee class definition
5    using namespace std;
6
7    // constructor
8    CommissionEmployee::CommissionEmployee(
9       const string &first, const string &last, const string &ssn,
10      double sales, double rate )
11      : firstName( first ), lastName( last ), socialSecurityNumber( ssn )
12   {
```

Fig. 12.23 | CommissionEmployee's constructor and destructor output text. (Part 1 of 3.)

```
13        setGrossSales( sales ); // validate and store gross sales
14        setCommissionRate( rate ); // validate and store commission rate
15
16        cout << "CommissionEmployee constructor: " << endl;
17        print();
18        cout << "\n\n";
19    } // end CommissionEmployee constructor
20
21    // destructor
22    CommissionEmployee::~CommissionEmployee()
23    {
24        cout << "CommissionEmployee destructor: " << endl;
25        print();
26        cout << "\n\n";
27    } // end CommissionEmployee destructor
28
29    // set first name
30    void CommissionEmployee::setFirstName( const string &first )
31    {
32        firstName = first; // should validate
33    } // end function setFirstName
34
35    // return first name
36    string CommissionEmployee::getFirstName() const
37    {
38        return firstName;
39    } // end function getFirstName
40
41    // set last name
42    void CommissionEmployee::setLastName( const string &last )
43    {
44        lastName = last; // should validate
45    } // end function setLastName
46
47    // return last name
48    string CommissionEmployee::getLastName() const
49    {
50        return lastName;
51    } // end function getLastName
52
53    // set social security number
54    void CommissionEmployee::setSocialSecurityNumber( const string &ssn )
55    {
56        socialSecurityNumber = ssn; // should validate
57    } // end function setSocialSecurityNumber
58
59    // return social security number
60    string CommissionEmployee::getSocialSecurityNumber() const
61    {
62        return socialSecurityNumber;
63    } // end function getSocialSecurityNumber
64
```

Fig. 12.23 | CommissionEmployee's constructor and destructor output text. (Part 2 of 3.)

```cpp
65    // set gross sales amount
66    void CommissionEmployee::setGrossSales( double sales )
67    {
68       grossSales = ( sales < 0.0 ) ? 0.0 : sales;
69    } // end function setGrossSales
70
71    // return gross sales amount
72    double CommissionEmployee::getGrossSales() const
73    {
74       return grossSales;
75    } // end function getGrossSales
76
77    // set commission rate
78    void CommissionEmployee::setCommissionRate( double rate )
79    {
80       commissionRate = ( rate > 0.0 && rate < 1.0 ) ? rate : 0.0;
81    } // end function setCommissionRate
82
83    // return commission rate
84    double CommissionEmployee::getCommissionRate() const
85    {
86       return commissionRate;
87    } // end function getCommissionRate
88
89    // calculate earnings
90    double CommissionEmployee::earnings() const
91    {
92       return getCommissionRate() * getGrossSales();
93    } // end function earnings
94
95    // print CommissionEmployee object
96    void CommissionEmployee::print() const
97    {
98       cout << "commission employee: "
99          << getFirstName() << ' ' << getLastName()
100          << "\nsocial security number: " << getSocialSecurityNumber()
101          << "\ngross sales: " << getGrossSales()
102          << "\ncommission rate: " << getCommissionRate();
103    } // end function print
```

Fig. 12.23 | CommissionEmployee's constructor and destructor output text. (Part 3 of 3.)

```cpp
1    // Fig. 12.24: BasePlusCommissionEmployee.h
2    // BasePlusCommissionEmployee class derived from class
3    // CommissionEmployee.
4    #ifndef BASEPLUS_H
5    #define BASEPLUS_H
6
7    #include <string> // C++ standard string class
8    #include "CommissionEmployee.h" // CommissionEmployee class declaration
9    using namespace std;
10
```

Fig. 12.24 | BasePlusCommissionEmployee class header file. (Part 1 of 2.)

```
11   class BasePlusCommissionEmployee : public CommissionEmployee
12   {
13   public:
14      BasePlusCommissionEmployee( const string &, const string &,
15         const string &, double = 0.0, double = 0.0, double = 0.0 );
16      ~BasePlusCommissionEmployee(); // destructor
17
18      void setBaseSalary( double ); // set base salary
19      double getBaseSalary() const; // return base salary
20
21      double earnings() const; // calculate earnings
22      void print() const; // print BasePlusCommissionEmployee object
23   private:
24      double baseSalary; // base salary
25   }; // end class BasePlusCommissionEmployee
26
27   #endif
```

Fig. 12.24 | BasePlusCommissionEmployee class header file. (Part 2 of 2.)

```
1    // Fig. 12.25: BasePlusCommissionEmployee.cpp
2    // Class BasePlusCommissionEmployee member-function definitions.
3    #include <iostream>
4    #include "BasePlusCommissionEmployee.h"
5    using namespace std;
6
7    // constructor
8    BasePlusCommissionEmployee::BasePlusCommissionEmployee(
9       const string &first, const string &last, const string &ssn,
10      double sales, double rate, double salary )
11      // explicitly call base-class constructor
12      : CommissionEmployee( first, last, ssn, sales, rate )
13   {
14      setBaseSalary( salary ); // validate and store base salary
15
16      cout << "BasePlusCommissionEmployee constructor: " << endl;
17      print();
18      cout << "\n\n";
19   } // end BasePlusCommissionEmployee constructor
20
21   // destructor
22   BasePlusCommissionEmployee::~BasePlusCommissionEmployee()
23   {
24      cout << "BasePlusCommissionEmployee destructor: " << endl;
25      print();
26      cout << "\n\n";
27   } // end BasePlusCommissionEmployee destructor
28
29   // set base salary
30   void BasePlusCommissionEmployee::setBaseSalary( double salary )
31   {
```

Fig. 12.25 | BasePlusCommissionEmployee's constructor and destructor output text. (Part 1 of 2.)

```
32        baseSalary = ( salary < 0.0 ) ? 0.0 : salary;
33    } // end function setBaseSalary
34
35    // return base salary
36    double BasePlusCommissionEmployee::getBaseSalary() const
37    {
38        return baseSalary;
39    } // end function getBaseSalary
40
41    // calculate earnings
42    double BasePlusCommissionEmployee::earnings() const
43    {
44        return getBaseSalary() + CommissionEmployee::earnings();
45    } // end function earnings
46
47    // print BasePlusCommissionEmployee object
48    void BasePlusCommissionEmployee::print() const
49    {
50        cout << "base-salaried ";
51
52        // invoke CommissionEmployee's print function
53        CommissionEmployee::print();
54
55        cout << "\nbase salary: " << getBaseSalary();
56    } // end function print
```

Fig. 12.25 | BasePlusCommissionEmployee's constructor and destructor output text. (Part 2 of 2.)

In this example, we modified the CommissionEmployee constructor (lines 8–19 of Fig. 12.23) and included a CommissionEmployee destructor (lines 22–27), each of which outputs a line of text upon its invocation. We also modified the BasePlusCommissionEmployee constructor (lines 8–19 of Fig. 12.25) and included a BasePlusCommissionEmployee destructor (lines 22–27), each of which outputs a line of text upon its invocation.

Figure 12.26 demonstrates the order in which constructors and destructors are called for objects of classes that are part of an inheritance hierarchy. Function main instantiates CommissionEmployee object employee1 (lines 15–16) in a separate block inside main (lines 14–17). The object goes in and out of scope—the end of the block is reached immediately after the object is created—so both the CommissionEmployee constructor and destructor are called. Next, lines 20–21 instantiate BasePlusCommissionEmployee object employee2. This invokes the CommissionEmployee constructor to display outputs with values passed from the BasePlusCommissionEmployee constructor, then the output specified in the BasePlusCommissionEmployee constructor is performed. Lines 24–25 then instantiate BasePlusCommissionEmployee object employee3. Again, the CommissionEmployee and BasePlusCommissionEmployee constructors are both called. In each case, the body of the CommissionEmployee constructor executes before the body of the BasePlusCommission-Employee constructor executes. When the end of main is reached, the destructors are called for objects employee2 and employee3. But, because destructors are called in the reverse order of their corresponding constructors, the BasePlusCommissionEmployee destructor and CommissionEmployee destructor are called (in that order) for object employee3, then the BasePlusCommissionEmployee and CommissionEmployee destructors are called (in that order) for object employee2.

```cpp
1   // Fig. 12.26: fig12_26.cpp
2   // Display order in which base-class and derived-class constructors
3   // and destructors are called.
4   #include <iostream>
5   #include <iomanip>
6   #include "BasePlusCommissionEmployee.h"
7   using namespace std;
8
9   int main()
10  {
11     // set floating-point output formatting
12     cout << fixed << setprecision( 2 );
13
14     { // begin new scope
15        CommissionEmployee employee1(
16           "Bob", "Lewis", "333-33-3333", 5000, .04 );
17     } // end scope
18
19     cout << endl;
20     BasePlusCommissionEmployee
21        employee2( "Lisa", "Jones", "555-55-5555", 2000, .06, 800 );
22
23     cout << endl;
24     BasePlusCommissionEmployee
25        employee3( "Mark", "Sands", "888-88-8888", 8000, .15, 2000 );
26     cout << endl;
27  } // end main
```

```
CommissionEmployee constructor:
commission employee: Bob Lewis
social security number: 333-33-3333
gross sales: 5000.00
commission rate: 0.04

CommissionEmployee destructor:
commission employee: Bob Lewis
social security number: 333-33-3333
gross sales: 5000.00
commission rate: 0.04


CommissionEmployee constructor:
commission employee: Lisa Jones
social security number: 555-55-5555
gross sales: 2000.00
commission rate: 0.06

BasePlusCommissionEmployee constructor:
base-salaried commission employee: Lisa Jones
social security number: 555-55-5555
```

Fig. 12.26 | Constructor and destructor call order. (Part 1 of 2.)

```
gross sales: 2000.00
commission rate: 0.06
base salary: 800.00


CommissionEmployee constructor:
commission employee: Mark Sands
social security number: 888-88-8888
gross sales: 8000.00
commission rate: 0.15

BasePlusCommissionEmployee constructor:
base-salaried commission employee: Mark Sands
social security number: 888-88-8888
gross sales: 8000.00
commission rate: 0.15
base salary: 2000.00


BasePlusCommissionEmployee destructor:
base-salaried commission employee: Mark Sands
social security number: 888-88-8888
gross sales: 8000.00
commission rate: 0.15
base salary: 2000.00

CommissionEmployee destructor:
commission employee: Mark Sands
social security number: 888-88-8888
gross sales: 8000.00
commission rate: 0.15

BasePlusCommissionEmployee destructor:
base-salaried commission employee: Lisa Jones
social security number: 555-55-5555
gross sales: 2000.00
commission rate: 0.06
base salary: 800.00

CommissionEmployee destructor:
commission employee: Lisa Jones
social security number: 555-55-5555
gross sales: 2000.00
commission rate: 0.06
```

Fig. 12.26 | Constructor and destructor call order. (Part 2 of 2.)

12.6 public, protected and private Inheritance

When deriving a class from a base class, the base class may be inherited through public, protected or private inheritance. Use of protected and private inheritance is rare, and each should be used only with great care; we normally use public inheritance in this book. (Chapter 20 demonstrates private inheritance as an alternative to composition.) Figure 12.27 summarizes for each type of inheritance the accessibility of base-class members in a derived class. The first column contains the base-class access specifiers.

Base-class member-access specifier	Type of inheritance		
	public inheritance	**protected** inheritance	**private** inheritance
public	**public** in derived class. Can be accessed directly by member functions, **friend** functions and nonmember functions.	**protected** in derived class. Can be accessed directly by member functions and **friend** functions.	**private** in derived class. Can be accessed directly by member functions and **friend** functions.
protected	**protected** in derived class. Can be accessed directly by member functions and **friend** functions.	**protected** in derived class. Can be accessed directly by member functions and **friend** functions.	**private** in derived class. Can be accessed directly by member functions and **friend** functions.
private	Hidden in derived class. Can be accessed by member functions and **friend** functions through **public** or **protected** member functions of the base class.	Hidden in derived class. Can be accessed by member functions and **friend** functions through **public** or **protected** member functions of the base class.	Hidden in derived class. Can be accessed by member functions and **friend** functions through **public** or **protected** member functions of the base class.

Fig. 12.27 | Summary of base-class member accessibility in a derived class.

When deriving a class from a `public` base class, `public` members of the base class become `public` members of the derived class, and `protected` members of the base class become `protected` members of the derived class. A base class's `private` members are never accessible directly from a derived class, but can be accessed through calls to the `public` and `protected` members of the base class.

When deriving from a `protected` base class, `public` and `protected` members of the base class become `protected` members of the derived class. When deriving from a `private` base class, `public` and `protected` members of the base class become `private` members (e.g., the functions become utility functions) of the derived class. `Private` and `protected` inheritance are not *is-a* relationships.

12.7 Software Engineering with Inheritance

In this section, we discuss the use of inheritance to customize existing software. When we use inheritance to create a new class from an existing one, the new class inherits the data members and member functions of the existing class, as described in Fig. 12.27. We can customize the new class to meet our needs by including additional members and by redefining base-class members. The derived-class programmer does this in C++ without accessing the base class's source code. The derived class must be able to link to the base class's object code. This powerful capability is attractive to independent software vendors (ISVs).

ISVs can develop proprietary classes for sale or license and make these classes available to users in object-code format. Users then can derive new classes from these library classes rapidly and without accessing the ISVs' proprietary source code. All the ISVs need to supply with the object code are the header files.

Sometimes it's difficult for students to appreciate the scope of problems faced by designers who work on large-scale software projects in industry. People experienced with such projects say that effective software reuse improves the software development process. Object-oriented programming facilitates software reuse, thus shortening development times and enhancing software quality.

The availability of substantial and useful class libraries delivers the maximum benefits of software reuse through inheritance. Just as shrink-wrapped software produced by independent software vendors became an explosive-growth industry with the arrival of the personal computer, interest in the creation and sale of class libraries is growing exponentially. Application designers build their applications with these libraries, and library designers are rewarded by having their libraries included with the applications. The standard C++ libraries that are shipped with C++ compilers tend to be rather general purpose and limited in scope. However, there is massive worldwide commitment to the development of class libraries for a huge variety of applications arenas.

Software Engineering Observation 12.9

At the design stage in an object-oriented system, the designer often determines that certain classes are closely related. The designer should "factor out" common attributes and behaviors and place these in a base class, then use inheritance to form derived classes, endowing them with capabilities beyond those inherited from the base class.

Software Engineering Observation 12.10

The creation of a derived class does not affect its base class's source code. Inheritance preserves the integrity of a base class.

Performance Tip 12.3

If classes produced through inheritance are larger than they need to be (i.e., contain too much functionality), memory and processing resources might be wasted. Inherit from the class whose functionality is "closest" to what's needed.

Reading derived-class definitions can be confusing, because inherited members are not shown physically in the derived classes, but nevertheless are present. A similar problem exists when documenting derived-class members.

12.8 Wrap-Up

This chapter introduced inheritance—the ability to create a class by absorbing an existing class's data members and member functions and embellishing them with new capabilities. Through a series of examples using an employee inheritance hierarchy, you learned the notions of base classes and derived classes and used `public` inheritance to create a derived class that inherits members from a base class. The chapter introduced the access specifier `protected`—derived-class member functions can access `protected` base-class members. You learned how to access redefined base-class members by qualifying their names with the base-class name and binary scope resolution operator (`::`). You also saw the order in which constructors and destructors are called for objects of classes that are part of an inheritance hierarchy. Finally, we explained the three types of inheritance—public, protected and private—and the accessibility of base-class members in a derived class when using each type.

In Chapter 13, Object-Oriented Programming: Polymorphism, we build on our discussion of inheritance by introducing polymorphism—an object-oriented concept that enables us to write programs that handle, in a more general manner, objects of a wide variety of classes related by inheritance. After studying Chapter 13, you'll be familiar with classes, objects, encapsulation, inheritance and polymorphism—the essential concepts of object-oriented programming.

Summary

Section 12.1 Introduction
- Software reuse reduces program development time and cost.

Section 12.2 Base Classes and Derived Classes
- Inheritance is a form of software reuse in which you create a class that absorbs an existing class's data and behaviors and enhances them with new capabilities. The existing class is called the base class, and the new class is referred to as the derived class.
- A direct base class is the one from which a derived class explicitly inherits. An indirect base class is inherited from two or more levels up the class hierarchy.
- With single inheritance, a class is derived from one base class. With multiple inheritance, a class inherits from multiple (possibly unrelated) base classes.
- A derived class represents a more specialized group of objects. Typically, a derived class contains behaviors inherited from its base class plus additional behaviors. A derived class can also customize behaviors inherited from the base class.
- Every object of a derived class is also an object of that class's base class. However, a base-class object is not an object of that class's derived classes.
- The *is-a* relationship represents inheritance. In an *is-a* relationship, an object of a derived class also can be treated as an object of its base class.
- The *has-a* relationship represents composition—an object contains one or more objects of other classes as members, but does not disclose their behavior directly in its interface.
- A derived class cannot access the private members of its base class directly. A derived class can access the public and protected members of its base class directly.
- A derived class can effect state changes in private base-class members, but only through non-private member functions provided in the base class and inherited into the derived class.
- A base-class member function can be redefined in a derived class.
- Single-inheritance relationships form treelike hierarchical structures.
- It's possible to treat base-class objects and derived-class objects similarly; the commonality shared between the object types is expressed in the base class's data members and member functions.

Section 12.3 protected Members
- A base class's public members are accessible anywhere that the program has a handle to an object of that base class or to an object of one of that base class's derived classes—or, when using the binary scope resolution operator, whenever the class's name is in scope.

- A base class's `private` members are accessible only within the base class or from its friends.
- A base class's `protected` members can be accessed by members and `friends` of that base class and by members and `friends` of any classes derived from that base class.
- When a derived-class member function redefines a base-class member function, the base-class member function can be accessed from the derived class by qualifying the base-class member function name with the base-class name and the binary scope resolution operator (`::`).

Section 12.5 Constructors and Destructors in Derived Classes
- When an object of a derived class is instantiated, the base class's constructor is called immediately to initialize the base-class data members in the derived-class object, then the derived-class constructor initializes the additional derived-class data members.
- When a derived-class object is destroyed, the destructors are called in the reverse order of the constructors—first the derived-class destructor is called, then the base-class destructor is called.

Section 12.6 *public, protected and private Inheritance*
- Declaring data members `private`, while providing non-`private` member functions to manipulate and perform validity checking on this data, enforces good software engineering.
- When deriving a class, the base class may be declared as either `public`, `protected` or `private`.
- When deriving a class from a `public` base class, `public` members of the base class become `public` members of the derived class, and `protected` members of the base class become `protected` members of the derived class.
- When deriving a class from a `protected` base class, `public` and `protected` members of the base class become `protected` members of the derived class.
- When deriving a class from a `private` base class, `public` and `protected` members of the base class become `private` members of the derived class.

Terminology

base class 522
base-class initializer syntax 540
brittle software 549
class hierarchy 522
derived class 522
direct base class 522
fragile software 549
has-a relationship 523
indirect base class 522
inheritance 522

is-a relationship 523
multiple inheritance 522
`private` inheritance 525
`protected` inheritance 525
`protected` keyword 526
`public` inheritance 525
single inheritance 522
subclass 522
superclass 522

Self-Review Exercises

12.1   Fill in the blanks in each of the following statements:

    a) _____ is a form of software reuse in which new classes absorb the data and behaviors of existing classes and embellish these classes with new capabilities.

    b) A base class's _____ members can be accessed in the base-class definition, in derived-class definitions and in `friends` of the base class its derived classes.

    c) In a(n) _____ relationship, an object of a derived class also can be treated as an object of its base class.

    d) In a(n) _____ relationship, a class object has one or more objects of other classes as members.

    e) In single inheritance, a class exists in a(n) _____ relationship with its derived classes.

    f) A base class's _____ members are accessible within that base class and anywhere that the program has a handle to an object of that class or one of its derived classes.

    g) A base class's `protected` access members have a level of protection between those of `public` and _____ access.

    h) C++ provides for _____, which allows a derived class to inherit from many base classes, even if the base classes are unrelated.

    i) When an object of a derived class is instantiated, the base class's _____ is called implicitly or explicitly to do any necessary initialization of the base-class data members in the derived-class object.

    j) When deriving a class from a base class with `public` inheritance, `public` members of the base class become _____ members of the derived class, and `protected` members of the base class become _____ members of the derived class.

    k) When deriving a class from a base class with `protected` inheritance, `public` members of the base class become _____ members of the derived class, and `protected` members of the base class become _____ members of the derived class.

12.2   State whether each of the following is *true* or *false*. If *false*, explain why.

    a) Base-class constructors are not inherited by derived classes.

    b) A *has-a* relationship is implemented via inheritance.

    c) A `Car` class has an *is-a* relationship with the `SteeringWheel` and `Brakes` classes.

    d) Inheritance encourages the reuse of proven high-quality software.

    e) When a derived-class object is destroyed, the destructors are called in the reverse order of the constructors.

Answers to Self-Review Exercises

12.1   a) Inheritance. b) `protected`. c) *is-a* or inheritance. d) *has-a* or composition or aggregation. e) hierarchical. f) `public`. g) `private`. h) multiple inheritance. i) constructor. j) `public`, `protected`. k) `protected`, `protected`.

12.2   a) True. b) False. A *has-a* relationship is implemented via composition. An *is-a* relationship is implemented via inheritance. c) False. This is an example of a *has-a* relationship. Class `Car` has an *is-a* relationship with class `Vehicle`. d) True. e) True.

Exercises

12.3   *(Composition as an Alternative to Inheritance)* Many programs written with inheritance could be written with composition instead, and vice versa. Rewrite class `BasePlusCommissionEmployee` of the `CommissionEmployee`–`BasePlusCommissionEmployee` hierarchy to use composition rather than inheritance. After you do this, assess the relative merits of the two approaches for designing classes `CommissionEmployee` and `BasePlusCommissionEmployee`, as well as for object-oriented programs in general. Which approach is more natural? Why?

12.4   *(Inheritance Advantage)* Discuss the ways in which inheritance promotes software reuse, saves time during program development and helps prevent errors.

12.5   *(Protected vs. Private Base Classes)* Some programmers prefer not to use `protected` access because they believe it breaks the encapsulation of the base class. Discuss the relative merits of using `protected` access vs. using `private` access in base classes.

12.6   *(Student Inheritance Hierarchy)* Draw an inheritance hierarchy for students at a university similar to the hierarchy shown in Fig. 12.2. Use `Student` as the base class of the hierarchy, then include classes UndergraduateStudent and GraduateStudent that derive from Student. Continue to extend the hierarchy as deep (i.e., as many levels) as possible. For example, Freshman, Sophomore, Junior and Senior might derive from UndergraduateStudent, and DoctoralStudent and MastersStudent might derive from GraduateStudent. After drawing the hierarchy, discuss the relationships that exist between the classes. [*Note:* You do not need to write any code for this exercise.]

12.7 *(Richer Shape Hierarchy)* The world of shapes is much richer than the shapes included in the inheritance hierarchy of Fig. 12.3. Write down all the shapes you can think of—both two-dimensional and three-dimensional—and form them into a more complete Shape hierarchy with as many levels as possible. Your hierarchy should have the base class Shape from which class TwoDimensionalShape and class ThreeDimensionalShape are derived. [*Note:* You do not need to write any code for this exercise.] We'll use this hierarchy in the exercises of Chapter 13 to process a set of distinct shapes as objects of base-class Shape. (This technique, called polymorphism, is the subject of Chapter 13.)

12.8 *(Quadrilateral Inheritance Hierarchy)* Draw an inheritance hierarchy for classes Quadrilateral, Trapezoid, Parallelogram, Rectangle and Square. Use Quadrilateral as the base class of the hierarchy. Make the hierarchy as deep as possible.

12.9 *(Package Inheritance Hierarchy)* Package-delivery services, such as FedEx®, DHL® and UPS®, offer a number of different shipping options, each with specific costs associated. Create an inheritance hierarchy to represent various types of packages. Use Package as the base class of the hierarchy, then include classes TwoDayPackage and OvernightPackage that derive from Package. Base class Package should include data members representing the name, address, city, state and ZIP code for both the sender and the recipient of the package, in addition to data members that store the weight (in ounces) and cost per ounce to ship the package. Package's constructor should initialize these data members. Ensure that the weight and cost per ounce contain positive values. Package should provide a public member function calculateCost that returns a double indicating the cost associated with shipping the package. Package's calculateCost function should determine the cost by multiplying the weight by the cost per ounce. Derived class TwoDayPackage should inherit the functionality of base class Package, but also include a data member that represents a flat fee that the shipping company charges for two-day-delivery service. TwoDayPackage's constructor should receive a value to initialize this data member. TwoDayPackage should redefine member function calculateCost so that it computes the shipping cost by adding the flat fee to the weight-based cost calculated by base class Package's calculateCost function. Class OvernightPackage should inherit directly from class Package and contain an additional data member representing an additional fee per ounce charged for overnight-delivery service. OvernightPackage should redefine member function calculateCost so that it adds the additional fee per ounce to the standard cost per ounce before calculating the shipping cost. Write a test program that creates objects of each type of Package and tests member function calculateCost.

12.10 *(Account Inheritance Hierarchy)* Create an inheritance hierarchy that a bank might use to represent customers' bank accounts. All customers at this bank can deposit (i.e., credit) money into their accounts and withdraw (i.e., debit) money from their accounts. More specific types of accounts also exist. Savings accounts, for instance, earn interest on the money they hold. Checking accounts, on the other hand, charge a fee per transaction (i.e., credit or debit).

Create an inheritance hierarchy containing base class Account and derived classes SavingsAccount and CheckingAccount that inherit from class Account. Base class Account should include one data member of type double to represent the account balance. The class should provide a constructor that receives an initial balance and uses it to initialize the data member. The constructor should validate the initial balance to ensure that it's greater than or equal to 0.0. If not, the balance should be set to 0.0 and the constructor should display an error message, indicating that the initial balance was invalid. The class should provide three member functions. Member function credit should add an amount to the current balance. Member function debit should withdraw money from the Account and ensure that the debit amount does not exceed the Account's balance. If it does, the balance should be left unchanged and the function should print the message "Debit amount exceeded account balance." Member function getBalance should return the current balance.

Derived class SavingsAccount should inherit the functionality of an Account, but also include a data member of type double indicating the interest rate (percentage) assigned to the Account. SavingsAccount's constructor should receive the initial balance, as well as an initial value for the SavingsAccount's interest rate. SavingsAccount should provide a public member function calculateInterest that returns a double indicating the amount of interest earned by an account. Member function calculateInterest should determine this amount by multiplying the interest rate by the account balance. [*Note:* SavingsAccount should inherit member functions credit and debit as is without redefining them.]

Derived class CheckingAccount should inherit from base class Account and include an additional data member of type double that represents the fee charged per transaction. CheckingAccount's constructor should receive the initial balance, as well as a parameter indicating a fee amount. Class CheckingAccount should redefine member functions credit and debit so that they subtract the fee from the account balance whenever either transaction is performed successfully. CheckingAccount's versions of these functions should invoke the base-class Account version to perform the updates to an account balance. CheckingAccount's debit function should charge a fee only if money is actually withdrawn (i.e., the debit amount does not exceed the account balance). [*Hint:* Define Account's debit function so that it returns a bool indicating whether money was withdrawn. Then use the return value to determine whether a fee should be charged.]

After defining the classes in this hierarchy, write a program that creates objects of each class and tests their member functions. Add interest to the SavingsAccount object by first invoking its calculateInterest function, then passing the returned interest amount to the object's credit function.

13

Object-Oriented Programming: Polymorphism

*One Ring to rule them all,
One Ring to find them,
One Ring to bring them all
and in the darkness bind them.*
—John Ronald Reuel Tolkien

*The silence often of pure
innocence
Persuades when speaking fails.*
—William Shakespeare

*General propositions do not
decide concrete cases.*
—Oliver Wendell Holmes

*A philosopher of imposing
stature doesn't think in a
vacuum. Even his most abstract
ideas are, to some extent,
conditioned by what is or is not
known in the time when he lives.*
—Alfred North Whitehead

Objectives

In this chapter you'll learn:

- How polymorphism makes programming more convenient and systems more extensible.

- The distinction between abstract and concrete classes and how to create abstract classes.

- To use runtime type information (RTTI).

- How C++ implements **virtual** functions and dynamic binding.

- How **virtual** destructors ensure that all appropriate destructors run on an object.

13.1 Introduction

In Chapters 9–12, we discussed key object-oriented programming technologies including classes, objects, encapsulation, operator overloading and inheritance. We now continue our study of OOP by explaining and demonstrating **polymorphism** with inheritance hierarchies. Polymorphism enables us to "program in the general" rather than "program in the specific." In particular, polymorphism enables us to write programs that process objects of classes that are part of the same class hierarchy as if they were all objects of the hierarchy's base class. As we'll soon see, polymorphism works off base-class pointer handles and base-class reference handles, but not off name handles.

Suppose we create a polymorphic program that simulates the movement of several types of animals for a biological study. Classes `Fish`, `Frog` and `Bird` represent the three types of animals under investigation. Imagine that each of these classes inherits from base class `Animal`, which contains a function move and maintains an animal's current location. Each derived class implements move. Our program maintains a vector of `Animal` pointers to objects of the derived classes. To simulate the animals' movements, the program sends each object the same message once per second—namely, move. However, each specific type of `Animal` responds to a move message in its own way—a `Fish` might swim two feet, a `Frog` might jump three feet and a `Bird` might fly ten feet. The program issues the same message (i.e., move) to each animal object, but each object knows how to modify its location for its specific type of movement. Relying on each object to know how to "do the right thing" in response to the same function call is the key concept of polymorphism. The same message sent to a variety of objects has "many forms" of results—hence the term polymorphism.

With polymorphism, we can design and implement systems that are easily extensible—new classes can be added with little or no modification to the general portions of the program, as long as the new classes are part of the inheritance hierarchy that the program processes generically. The only parts of a program that must be altered to accommodate new classes are those that require direct knowledge of the new classes that you add to the hierarchy. For example, if we create class `Tortoise` that inherits from class `Animal` (which might respond to a move message by crawling one inch), we need to write only the `Tortoise` class and the part of the simulation that instantiates a `Tortoise` object. The portions of the simulation that process each `Animal` generically can remain the same.

We begin with a sequence of small, focused examples that lead up to an understanding of `virtual` functions and dynamic binding—polymorphism's two underlying technologies. We then present a case study that revisits Chapter 12's `Employee` hierarchy. In the case study, we define a common "interface" (i.e., set of functionality) for all the classes in the hierarchy. This common functionality among employees is defined in a so-called abstract base class, `Employee`, from which classes `SalariedEmployee`, `HourlyEmployee` and `CommissionEmployee` inherit directly and class `BaseCommissionEmployee` inherits indirectly. We'll soon see what makes a class "abstract" or its opposite—"concrete."

In this hierarchy, every employee has an `earnings` function to calculate the employee's weekly pay. These `earnings` functions vary by employee type—for instance, `SalariedEmployees` are paid a fixed weekly salary regardless of the number of hours worked, while `HourlyEmployees` are paid by the hour and receive overtime pay. We show how to process each employee "in the general"—that is, using base-class pointers to call the `earnings` function of several derived-class objects. This way, you need to be concerned with only one type of function call, which can be used to execute several different functions based on the objects referred to by the base-class pointers.

A key feature of this chapter is its (optional) detailed discussion of polymorphism, `virtual` functions and dynamic binding "under the hood," which uses a detailed diagram to explain how polymorphism can be implemented in C++.

Occasionally, when performing polymorphic processing, we need to program "in the specific," meaning that operations need to be performed on a specific type of object in a hierarchy—the operation cannot be generally applied to several types of objects. We reuse our `Employee` hierarchy to demonstrate the powerful capabilities of **runtime type information (RTTI)** and **dynamic casting**, which enable a program to determine the type of an object at execution time and act on that object accordingly. We use these capabilities to determine whether a particular employee object is a `BasePlusCommissionEmployee`, then give that employee a 10 percent bonus on his or her base salary.

13.2 Polymorphism Examples

In this section, we discuss several polymorphism examples. With polymorphism, one function can cause different actions to occur, depending on the type of the object on which the function is invoked. This gives you tremendous expressive capability. If class `Rectangle` is derived from class `Quadrilateral`, then a `Rectangle` object is a more specific version of a `Quadrilateral` object. Therefore, any operation (such as calculating the perimeter or the area) that can be performed on an object of class `Quadrilateral` also can be performed on an object of class `Rectangle`. Such operations also can be performed on other kinds of `Quadrilaterals`, such as `Squares`, `Parallelograms` and `Trapezoids`. The polymorphism occurs when a program invokes a virtual function through a base-class (i.e., Quadrilateral) pointer or reference—C++ dynamically (i.e., at execution time) chooses the correct function for the class from which the object was instantiated. You'll see a code example that illustrates this process in Section 13.3.

As another example, suppose that we design a video game that manipulates objects of many different types, including objects of classes Martian, Venutian, Plutonian, SpaceShip and LaserBeam. Imagine that each of these classes inherits from the common base class SpaceObject, which contains member function draw. Each derived class implements this function in a manner appropriate for that class. A screen-manager program maintains a container (e.g., a vector) that holds SpaceObject pointers to objects of the various classes. To refresh the screen, the screen manager periodically sends each object the same message—namely, draw. Each type of object responds in a unique way. For example, a Martian object might draw itself in red with the appropriate number of antennae. A SpaceShip object might draw itself as a silver flying saucer. A LaserBeam object might draw itself as a bright red beam across the screen. Again, the same message (in this case, draw) sent to a variety of objects has "many forms" of results.

A polymorphic screen manager facilitates adding new classes to a system with minimal modifications to its code. Suppose that we want to add objects of class Mercurian to our video game. To do so, we must build a class Mercurian that inherits from SpaceObject, but provides its own definition of member function draw. Then, when pointers to objects of class Mercurian appear in the container, you do not need to modify the code for the screen manager. The screen manager invokes member function draw on every object in the container, regardless of the object's type, so the new Mercurian objects simply "plug right in." Thus, without modifying the system (other than to build and include the classes themselves), you can use polymorphism to accommodate additional classes, including ones that were not even envisioned when the system was created.

Software Engineering Observation 13.1

With virtual functions and polymorphism, you can deal in generalities and let the execution-time environment concern itself with the specifics. You can direct a variety of objects to behave in manners appropriate to those objects without even knowing their types—as long as those objects belong to the same inheritance hierarchy and are being accessed off a common base-class pointer or a common base-class reference.

Software Engineering Observation 13.2

Polymorphism promotes extensibility: Software written to invoke polymorphic behavior is written independently of the types of the objects to which messages are sent. Thus, new types of objects that can respond to existing messages can be incorporated into such a system without modifying the base system. Only client code that instantiates new objects must be modified to accommodate new types.

13.3 Relationships Among Objects in an Inheritance Hierarchy

Section 12.4 created an employee class hierarchy, in which class BasePlusCommissionEmployee inherited from class CommissionEmployee. The Chapter 12 examples manipulated CommissionEmployee and BasePlusCommissionEmployee objects by using the objects' names to invoke their member functions. We now examine the relationships among classes in a hierarchy more closely. The next several sections present a series of examples that demonstrate how base-class and derived-class pointers can be aimed at base-class and derived-class objects, and how those pointers can be used to invoke member functions that manipulate those objects. In Section 13.3.4, we demonstrate how to get polymorphic behavior from base-class pointers aimed at derived-class objects.

In Section 13.3.1, we assign the address of a derived-class object to a base-class pointer, then show that invoking a function via the base-class pointer invokes the base-class functionality—i.e., the type of the handle determines which function is called. In Section 13.3.2, we assign the address of a base-class object to a derived-class pointer, which results in a compilation error. We discuss the error message and investigate why the compiler does not allow such an assignment. In Section 13.3.3, we assign the address of a derived-class object to a base-class pointer, then examine how the base-class pointer can be used to invoke only the base-class functionality—when we attempt to invoke derived-class member functions through the base-class pointer, compilation errors occur. Finally, in Section 13.3.4, we introduce virtual functions and polymorphism by declaring a base-class function as virtual. We then assign the address of a derived-class object to the base-class pointer and use that pointer to invoke derived-class functionality—precisely the capability we need to achieve polymorphic behavior.

A key concept in these examples is to demonstrate that an object of a derived class can be treated as an object of its base class. This enables various interesting manipulations. For example, a program can create an array of base-class pointers that point to objects of many derived-class types. Despite the fact that the derived-class objects are of different types, the compiler allows this because each derived-class object *is an* object of its base class. However, we cannot treat a base-class object as an object of any of its derived classes. For example, a CommissionEmployee is not a BasePlusCommissionEmployee in the hierarchy defined in Chapter 12—a CommissionEmployee does not have a baseSalary data member and does not have member functions setBaseSalary and getBaseSalary. The *is-a* relationship applies only from a derived class to its direct and indirect base classes.

13.3.1 Invoking Base-Class Functions from Derived-Class Objects

The example in Figs. 13.1–13.5 demonstrates three ways to aim base and derived-class pointers at base and derived-class objects. The first two are straightforward—we aim a base-class pointer at a base-class object (and invoke base-class functionality), and we aim a derived-class pointer at a derived-class object (and invoke derived-class functionality). Then, we demonstrate the relationship between derived classes and base classes (i.e., the *is-a* relationship of inheritance) by aiming a base-class pointer at a derived-class object (and showing that the base-class functionality is indeed available in the derived-class object).

Class CommissionEmployee (Figs. 13.1–13.2), which we discussed in Chapter 12, is used to represent employees who are paid a percentage of their sales. Class BasePlusCommissionEmployee (Figs. 13.3–13.4), which we also discussed in Chapter 12, is used to represent employees who receive a base salary plus a percentage of their sales. Each BasePlusCommissionEmployee object *is a* CommissionEmployee that also has a base salary. Class BasePlusCommissionEmployee's earnings member function (lines 30–33 of Fig. 13.4) redefines class CommissionEmployee's earnings member function (lines 78–81 of Fig. 13.2) to include the object's base salary. Class BasePlusCommissionEmployee's print member function (lines 36–44 of Fig. 13.4) redefines class CommissionEmployee's version (lines 84–91 of Fig. 13.2) to display the same information plus the employee's base salary.

```
1   // Fig. 13.1: CommissionEmployee.h
2   // CommissionEmployee class definition represents a commission employee.
3   #ifndef COMMISSION_H
4   #define COMMISSION_H
5
6   #include <string> // C++ standard string class
7   using namespace std;
8
9   class CommissionEmployee
10  {
11  public:
12     CommissionEmployee( const string &, const string &, const string &,
13        double = 0.0, double = 0.0 );
14
15     void setFirstName( const string & ); // set first name
16     string getFirstName() const; // return first name
17
18     void setLastName( const string & ); // set last name
19     string getLastName() const; // return last name
20
21     void setSocialSecurityNumber( const string & ); // set SSN
22     string getSocialSecurityNumber() const; // return SSN
23
24     void setGrossSales( double ); // set gross sales amount
25     double getGrossSales() const; // return gross sales amount
26
27     void setCommissionRate( double ); // set commission rate
28     double getCommissionRate() const; // return commission rate
29
30     double earnings() const; // calculate earnings
31     void print() const; // print CommissionEmployee object
32  private:
33     string firstName;
34     string lastName;
35     string socialSecurityNumber;
36     double grossSales; // gross weekly sales
37     double commissionRate; // commission percentage
38  }; // end class CommissionEmployee
39
40  #endif
```

Fig. 13.1 | CommissionEmployee class header file.

```
1   // Fig. 13.2: CommissionEmployee.cpp
2   // Class CommissionEmployee member-function definitions.
3   #include <iostream>
4   #include "CommissionEmployee.h" // CommissionEmployee class definition
```

Fig. 13.2 | CommissionEmployee class implementation file. (Part 1 of 3.)

```cpp
 5   using namespace std;
 6
 7   // constructor
 8   CommissionEmployee::CommissionEmployee(
 9      const string &first, const string &last, const string &ssn,
10      double sales, double rate )
11      : firstName( first ), lastName( last ), socialSecurityNumber( ssn )
12   {
13      setGrossSales( sales ); // validate and store gross sales
14      setCommissionRate( rate ); // validate and store commission rate
15   } // end CommissionEmployee constructor
16
17   // set first name
18   void CommissionEmployee::setFirstName( const string &first )
19   {
20      firstName = first; // should validate
21   } // end function setFirstName
22
23   // return first name
24   string CommissionEmployee::getFirstName() const
25   {
26      return firstName;
27   } // end function getFirstName
28
29   // set last name
30   void CommissionEmployee::setLastName( const string &last )
31   {
32      lastName = last;  // should validate
33   } // end function setLastName
34
35   // return last name
36   string CommissionEmployee::getLastName() const
37   {
38      return lastName;
39   } // end function getLastName
40
41   // set social security number
42   void CommissionEmployee::setSocialSecurityNumber( const string &ssn )
43   {
44      socialSecurityNumber = ssn; // should validate
45   } // end function setSocialSecurityNumber
46
47   // return social security number
48   string CommissionEmployee::getSocialSecurityNumber() const
49   {
50      return socialSecurityNumber;
51   } // end function getSocialSecurityNumber
52
53   // set gross sales amount
54   void CommissionEmployee::setGrossSales( double sales )
55   {
56      grossSales = ( sales < 0.0 ) ? 0.0 : sales;
57   } // end function setGrossSales
```

Fig. 13.2 | CommissionEmployee class implementation file. (Part 2 of 3.)

```
58
59   // return gross sales amount
60   double CommissionEmployee::getGrossSales() const
61   {
62      return grossSales;
63   } // end function getGrossSales
64
65   // set commission rate
66   void CommissionEmployee::setCommissionRate( double rate )
67   {
68      commissionRate = ( rate > 0.0 && rate < 1.0 ) ? rate : 0.0;
69   } // end function setCommissionRate
70
71   // return commission rate
72   double CommissionEmployee::getCommissionRate() const
73   {
74      return commissionRate;
75   } // end function getCommissionRate
76
77   // calculate earnings
78   double CommissionEmployee::earnings() const
79   {
80      return getCommissionRate() * getGrossSales();
81   } // end function earnings
82
83   // print CommissionEmployee object
84   void CommissionEmployee::print() const
85   {
86      cout << "commission employee: "
87         << getFirstName() << ' ' << getLastName()
88         << "\nsocial security number: " << getSocialSecurityNumber()
89         << "\ngross sales: " << getGrossSales()
90         << "\ncommission rate: " << getCommissionRate();
91   } // end function print
```

Fig. 13.2 | CommissionEmployee class implementation file. (Part 3 of 3.)

```
1    // Fig. 13.3: BasePlusCommissionEmployee.h
2    // BasePlusCommissionEmployee class derived from class
3    // CommissionEmployee.
4    #ifndef BASEPLUS_H
5    #define BASEPLUS_H
6
7    #include <string> // C++ standard string class
8    #include "CommissionEmployee.h" // CommissionEmployee class declaration
9    using namespace std;
10
11   class BasePlusCommissionEmployee : public CommissionEmployee
12   {
13   public:
14      BasePlusCommissionEmployee( const string &, const string &,
15         const string &, double = 0.0, double = 0.0, double = 0.0 );
```

Fig. 13.3 | BasePlusCommissionEmployee class header file. (Part 1 of 2.)

```
16
17     void setBaseSalary( double ); // set base salary
18     double getBaseSalary() const; // return base salary
19
20     double earnings() const; // calculate earnings
21     void print() const; // print BasePlusCommissionEmployee object
22  private:
23     double baseSalary; // base salary
24  }; // end class BasePlusCommissionEmployee
25
26  #endif
```

Fig. 13.3 | BasePlusCommissionEmployee class header file. (Part 2 of 2.)

```
1   // Fig. 13.4: BasePlusCommissionEmployee.cpp
2   // Class BasePlusCommissionEmployee member-function definitions.
3   #include <iostream>
4   #include "BasePlusCommissionEmployee.h"
5   using namespace std;
6
7   // constructor
8   BasePlusCommissionEmployee::BasePlusCommissionEmployee(
9      const string &first, const string &last, const string &ssn,
10     double sales, double rate, double salary )
11     // explicitly call base-class constructor
12     : CommissionEmployee( first, last, ssn, sales, rate )
13  {
14     setBaseSalary( salary ); // validate and store base salary
15  } // end BasePlusCommissionEmployee constructor
16
17  // set base salary
18  void BasePlusCommissionEmployee::setBaseSalary( double salary )
19  {
20     baseSalary = ( salary < 0.0 ) ? 0.0 : salary;
21  } // end function setBaseSalary
22
23  // return base salary
24  double BasePlusCommissionEmployee::getBaseSalary() const
25  {
26     return baseSalary;
27  } // end function getBaseSalary
28
29  // calculate earnings
30  double BasePlusCommissionEmployee::earnings() const
31  {
32     return getBaseSalary() + CommissionEmployee::earnings();
33  } // end function earnings
34
35  // print BasePlusCommissionEmployee object
36  void BasePlusCommissionEmployee::print() const
37  {
38     cout << "base-salaried ";
```

Fig. 13.4 | BasePlusCommissionEmployee class implementation file. (Part 1 of 2.)

```
39
40     // invoke CommissionEmployee's print function
41     CommissionEmployee::print();
42
43     cout << "\nbase salary: " << getBaseSalary();
44 } // end function print
```

Fig. 13.4 | BasePlusCommissionEmployee class implementation file. (Part 2 of 2.)

In Fig. 13.5, lines 13–14 create a CommissionEmployee object and line 17 creates a pointer to a CommissionEmployee object; lines 20–21 create a BasePlusCommission-Employee object and line 24 creates a pointer to a BasePlusCommissionEmployee object. Lines 31 and 33 use each object's name to invoke its print member function. Line 36 assigns the address of base-class object commissionEmployee to base-class pointer commissionEmployeePtr, which line 39 uses to invoke member function print on that CommissionEmployee object. This invokes the version of print defined in base class CommissionEmployee. Similarly, line 42 assigns the address of derived-class object basePlusCommissionEmployee to derived-class pointer basePlusCommissionEmployeePtr, which line 46 uses to invoke member function print on that BasePlusCommissionEmployee object. This invokes the version of print defined in derived class BasePlusCommissionEmployee. Line 49 then assigns the address of derived-class object basePlusCommissionEmployee to base-class pointer commissionEmployeePtr, which line 53 uses to invoke member function print. This "crossover" is allowed because an object of a derived class *is an* object of its base class. Note that despite the fact that the base class CommissionEmployee pointer points to a derived class BasePlusCommissionEmployee object, the base class CommissionEmployee's print member function is invoked (rather than BasePlusCommissionEmployee's print function). The output of each print member-function invocation in this program reveals that *the invoked functionality depends on the type of the handle (i.e., the pointer or reference type) used to invoke the function, not the type of the object to which the handle points.* In Section 13.3.4, when we introduce virtual functions, we demonstrate that it's possible to invoke the object type's functionality, rather than invoke the handle type's functionality. We'll see that this is crucial to implementing polymorphic behavior—the key topic of this chapter.

```
1  // Fig. 13.5: fig13_05.cpp
2  // Aiming base-class and derived-class pointers at base-class
3  // and derived-class objects, respectively.
4  #include <iostream>
5  #include <iomanip>
6  #include "CommissionEmployee.h"
7  #include "BasePlusCommissionEmployee.h"
8  using namespace std;
9
10 int main()
11 {
```

Fig. 13.5 | Assigning addresses of base-class and derived-class objects to base-class and derived-class pointers. (Part 1 of 3.)

```
12      // create base-class object
13      CommissionEmployee commissionEmployee(
14         "Sue", "Jones", "222-22-2222", 10000, .06 );
15
16      // create base-class pointer
17      CommissionEmployee *commissionEmployeePtr = 0;
18
19      // create derived-class object
20      BasePlusCommissionEmployee basePlusCommissionEmployee(
21         "Bob", "Lewis", "333-33-3333", 5000, .04, 300 );
22
23      // create derived-class pointer
24      BasePlusCommissionEmployee *basePlusCommissionEmployeePtr = 0;
25
26      // set floating-point output formatting
27      cout << fixed << setprecision( 2 );
28
29      // output objects commissionEmployee and basePlusCommissionEmployee
30      cout << "Print base-class and derived-class objects:\n\n";
31      commissionEmployee.print(); // invokes base-class print
32      cout << "\n\n";
33      basePlusCommissionEmployee.print(); // invokes derived-class print
34
35      // aim base-class pointer at base-class object and print
36      commissionEmployeePtr = &commissionEmployee; // perfectly natural
37      cout << "\n\n\nCalling print with base-class pointer to "
38         << "\nbase-class object invokes base-class print function:\n\n";
39      commissionEmployeePtr->print(); // invokes base-class print
40
41      // aim derived-class pointer at derived-class object and print
42      basePlusCommissionEmployeePtr = &basePlusCommissionEmployee; // natural
43      cout << "\n\n\nCalling print with derived-class pointer to "
44         << "\nderived-class object invokes derived-class "
45         << "print function:\n\n";
46      basePlusCommissionEmployeePtr->print(); // invokes derived-class print
47
48      // aim base-class pointer at derived-class object and print
49      commissionEmployeePtr = &basePlusCommissionEmployee;
50      cout << "\n\n\nCalling print with base-class pointer to "
51         << "derived-class object\ninvokes base-class print "
52         << "function on that derived-class object:\n\n";
53      commissionEmployeePtr->print(); // invokes base-class print
54      cout << endl;
55   } // end main
```

```
Print base-class and derived-class objects:

commission employee: Sue Jones
social security number: 222-22-2222
gross sales: 10000.00
commission rate: 0.06
```

Fig. 13.5 | Assigning addresses of base-class and derived-class objects to base-class and derived-class pointers. (Part 2 of 3.)

```
base-salaried commission employee: Bob Lewis
social security number: 333-33-3333
gross sales: 5000.00
commission rate: 0.04
base salary: 300.00


Calling print with base-class pointer to
base-class object invokes base-class print function:

commission employee: Sue Jones
social security number: 222-22-2222
gross sales: 10000.00
commission rate: 0.06


Calling print with derived-class pointer to
derived-class object invokes derived-class print function:

base-salaried commission employee: Bob Lewis
social security number: 333-33-3333
gross sales: 5000.00
commission rate: 0.04
base salary: 300.00


Calling print with base-class pointer to derived-class object
invokes base-class print function on that derived-class object:

commission employee: Bob Lewis
social security number: 333-33-3333
gross sales: 5000.00
commission rate: 0.04
```

Fig. 13.5 | Assigning addresses of base-class and derived-class objects to base-class and derived-class pointers. (Part 3 of 3.)

13.3.2 Aiming Derived-Class Pointers at Base-Class Objects

In Section 13.3.1, we assigned the address of a derived-class object to a base-class pointer and explained that the C++ compiler allows this assignment, because a derived-class object *is a* base-class object. We take the opposite approach in Fig. 13.6, as we aim a derived-class pointer at a base-class object. [*Note:* This program uses classes CommissionEmployee and BasePlusCommissionEmployee of Figs. 13.1–13.4.] Lines 8–9 of Fig. 13.6 create a CommissionEmployee object, and line 10 creates a BasePlusCommissionEmployee pointer. Line 14 attempts to assign the address of base-class object commissionEmployee to derived-class pointer basePlusCommissionEmployeePtr, but the C++ compiler generates an error. The compiler prevents this assignment, because a CommissionEmployee is not a BasePlusCommissionEmployee. Consider the consequences if the compiler were to allow this assignment. Through a BasePlusCommissionEmployee pointer, we can invoke every BasePlusCommissionEmployee member function, including setBaseSalary, for the object to which the pointer points (i.e., the base-class object commissionEmployee). However, the CommissionEmployee object does not provide a setBaseSalary member function, nor does it provide a baseSalary data member to set. This could lead to problems, because member function setBaseSalary would assume that there is a baseSalary data member to set at its "usual location" in a BasePlusCommissionEmployee object. This memory does not belong to the CommissionEmployee object, so member function setBaseSalary might overwrite other important data in memory, possibly data that belongs to a different object.

```
 1   // Fig. 13.6: fig13_06.cpp
 2   // Aiming a derived-class pointer at a base-class object.
 3   #include "CommissionEmployee.h"
 4   #include "BasePlusCommissionEmployee.h"
 5
 6   int main()
 7   {
 8      CommissionEmployee commissionEmployee(
 9         "Sue", "Jones", "222-22-2222", 10000, .06 );
10      BasePlusCommissionEmployee *basePlusCommissionEmployeePtr = 0;
11
12      // aim derived-class pointer at base-class object
13      // Error: a CommissionEmployee is not a BasePlusCommissionEmployee
14      basePlusCommissionEmployeePtr = &commissionEmployee;
15   } // end main
```

Microsoft Visual C++ compiler error messages:

```
C:\cpphtp7_examples\ch13\Fig13_06\fig13_06.cpp(14) : error C2440: '=' :
cannot convert from 'CommissionEmployee *' to 'BasePlusCommissionEmployee *'
       Cast from base to derived requires dynamic_cast or static_cast
```

GNU C++ compiler error messages:

```
fig13_06.cpp:14: error: invalid conversion from `CommissionEmployee*' to
   `BasePlusCommissionEmployee*'
```

Fig. 13.6 | Aiming a derived-class pointer at a base-class object.

13.3.3 Derived-Class Member-Function Calls via Base-Class Pointers

Off a base-class pointer, the compiler allows us to invoke only base-class member functions. Thus, if a base-class pointer is aimed at a derived-class object, and an attempt is made to access a *derived-class-only member function*, a compilation error will occur.

Figure 13.7 shows the consequences of attempting to invoke a derived-class member function off a base-class pointer. [*Note:* We are again using classes CommissionEmployee and BasePlusCommissionEmployee of Figs. 13.1–13.4.] Line 9 creates commissionEmployeePtr—a pointer to a CommissionEmployee object—and lines 10–11 create a BasePlusCommissionEmployee object. Line 14 aims commissionEmployeePtr at derived-class object basePlusCommissionEmployee. Recall from Section 13.3.1 that this is allowed, because a BasePlusCommissionEmployee *is a* CommissionEmployee (in the sense that a BasePlusCommissionEmployee object contains all the functionality of a CommissionEmployee object). Lines 18–22 invoke base-class member functions getFirstName, getLastName, getSocialSecurityNumber, getGrossSales and getCommissionRate off the base-class pointer. All of these calls are legitimate, because `BasePlusCommissionEmployee` inherits these member functions from `CommissionEmployee`. We know that `commission-EmployeePtr` is aimed at a `BasePlusCommissionEmployee` object, so in lines 26–27 we attempt to invoke `BasePlusCommissionEmployee` member functions `getBaseSalary` and `setBaseSalary`. The compiler generates errors on both of these calls, because they're not made to member functions of base-class `CommissionEmployee`. The handle can be used to invoke only those functions that are members of that handle's associated class type. (In this case, off a `CommissionEmployee *`, we can invoke only `CommissionEmployee` member functions `setFirstName`, `getFirstName`, `setLastName`, `getLastName`, `setSocialSecurityNumber`, `getSocialSecurityNumber`, `setGrossSales`, `getGrossSales`, `setCommissionRate`, `getCommissionRate`, `earnings` and `print`.)

```
1   // Fig. 13.7: fig13_07.cpp
2   // Attempting to invoke derived-class-only member functions
3   // through a base-class pointer.
4   #include "CommissionEmployee.h"
5   #include "BasePlusCommissionEmployee.h"
6
7   int main()
8   {
9       CommissionEmployee *commissionEmployeePtr = 0; // base class
10      BasePlusCommissionEmployee basePlusCommissionEmployee(
11          "Bob", "Lewis", "333-33-3333", 5000, .04, 300 ); // derived class
12
13      // aim base-class pointer at derived-class object
14      commissionEmployeePtr = &basePlusCommissionEmployee;
15
16      // invoke base-class member functions on derived-class
17      // object through base-class pointer (allowed)
18      string firstName = commissionEmployeePtr->getFirstName();
19      string lastName = commissionEmployeePtr->getLastName();
20      string ssn = commissionEmployeePtr->getSocialSecurityNumber();
21      double grossSales = commissionEmployeePtr->getGrossSales();
22      double commissionRate = commissionEmployeePtr->getCommissionRate();
23
24      // attempt to invoke derived-class-only member functions
25      // on derived-class object through base-class pointer (disallowed)
26      double baseSalary = commissionEmployeePtr->getBaseSalary();
27      commissionEmployeePtr->setBaseSalary( 500 );
28  } // end main
```

Microsoft Visual C++ compiler error messages:

```
C:\cpphtp7_examples\ch13\Fig13_07\fig13_07.cpp(26) : error C2039:
   'getBaseSalary' : is not a member of 'CommissionEmployee'
      C:\cpphtp7_examples\ch13\Fig13_07\CommissionEmployee.h(10) :
         see declaration of 'CommissionEmployee'
C:\cpphtp7_examples\ch13\Fig13_07\fig13_07.cpp(27) : error C2039:
   'setBaseSalary' : is not a member of 'CommissionEmployee'
      C:\cpphtp7_examples\ch13\Fig13_07\CommissionEmployee.h(10) :
         see declaration of 'CommissionEmployee'
```

Fig. 13.7 | Attempting to invoke derived-class-only functions via a base-class pointer. (Part 1 of 2.)

GNU C++ compiler error messages:

```
fig13_07.cpp:26: error: `getBaseSalary' undeclared (first use this function)
fig13_07.cpp:26: error: (Each undeclared identifier is reported only once for
  each function it appears in.)
fig13_07.cpp:27: error: `setBaseSalary' undeclared (first use this function)
```

Fig. 13.7 | Attempting to invoke derived-class-only functions via a base-class pointer. (Part 2 of 2.)

The compiler allows access to derived-class-only members from a base-class pointer that is aimed at a derived-class object *if* we explicitly cast the base-class pointer to a derived-class pointer—known as **downcasting**. As you know, it's possible to aim a base-class pointer at a derived-class object. However, as we demonstrated in Fig. 13.7, a base-class pointer can be used to invoke only the functions declared in the base class. Downcasting allows a derived-class-specific operation on a derived-class object pointed to by a base-class pointer. After a downcast, the program can invoke derived-class functions that are not in the base class. Section 13.8 shows a concrete example of downcasting.

Software Engineering Observation 13.3

If the address of a derived-class object has been assigned to a pointer of one of its direct or indirect base classes, it's acceptable to cast that base-class pointer back to a pointer of the derived-class type. In fact, this must be done to send that derived-class object messages that do not appear in the base class.

13.3.4 Virtual Functions

In Section 13.3.1, we aimed a base-class `CommissionEmployee` pointer at a derived-class `BasePlusCommissionEmployee` object, then invoked member function `print` through that pointer. Recall that the type of the handle determines which class's functionality to invoke. In that case, the `CommissionEmployee` pointer invoked the `CommissionEmployee` member function `print` on the `BasePlusCommissionEmployee` object, even though the pointer was aimed at a `BasePlusCommissionEmployee` object that has its own customized `print` function. *With* `virtual` *functions, the type of the object being pointed to, not the type of the handle, determines which version of a* `virtual` *function to invoke.*

First, we consider why `virtual` functions are useful. Suppose that shape classes such as `Circle`, `Triangle`, `Rectangle` and `Square` are all derived from base class `Shape`. Each of these classes might be endowed with the ability to draw itself via a member function `draw`. Although each class has its own `draw` function, the function for each shape is quite different. In a program that draws a set of shapes, it would be useful to be able to treat all the shapes generically as objects of the base class `Shape`. Then, to draw any shape, we could simply use a base-class `Shape` pointer to invoke function `draw` and let the program determine *dynamically* (i.e., at runtime) which derived-class `draw` function to use, based on the type of the object to which the base-class `Shape` pointer points at any given time.

To enable this behavior, we declare `draw` in the base class as a **virtual function**, and we **override** `draw` in each of the derived classes to draw the appropriate shape. From an implementation perspective, overriding a function is no different than redefining one (which is the approach we've been using until now). An overridden function in a derived class has the same signature and return type (i.e., prototype) as the function it overrides in its base class. If we do not declare the base-class function as `virtual`, we can redefine that function. By contrast, if we declare the base-class function as `virtual`, we can override that function to enable polymorphic behavior. We declare a `virtual` function by preceding the function's prototype with the keyword `virtual` in the base class. For example,

```
virtual void draw() const;
```

would appear in base class `Shape`. The preceding prototype declares that function `draw` is a `virtual` function that takes no arguments and returns nothing. This function is declared `const` because a `draw` function typically would not make changes to the `Shape` object on which it's invoked—virtual functions do not have to be `const` functions.

Software Engineering Observation 13.4

Once a function is declared `virtual`, it remains `virtual` all the way down the inheritance hierarchy from that point, even if that function is not explicitly declared `virtual` when a derived class overrides it.

Good Programming Practice 13.1

Even though certain functions are implicitly `virtual` because of a declaration made higher in the class hierarchy, explicitly declare these functions `virtual` at every level of the hierarchy to promote program clarity.

Error-Prevention Tip 13.1

When you browse a class hierarchy to locate a class to reuse, it's possible that a function in that class will exhibit `virtual` function behavior even though it isn't explicitly declared `virtual`. This happens when the class inherits a `virtual` function from its base class, and it can lead to subtle logic errors. Such errors can be avoided by explicitly declaring all `virtual` functions `virtual` throughout the inheritance hierarchy.

Software Engineering Observation 13.5

When a derived class chooses not to override a `virtual` function from its base class, the derived class simply inherits its base class's `virtual` function implementation.

If a program invokes a `virtual` function through a base-class pointer to a derived-class object (e.g., `shapePtr->draw()`) or a base-class reference to a derived-class object (e.g., `shapeRef.draw()`), the program will choose the correct derived-class `draw` function dynamically (i.e., at execution time) based on the object type—not the pointer or reference type. Choosing the appropriate function to call at execution time (rather than at compile time) is known as **dynamic binding** or **late binding**.

When a `virtual` function is called by referencing a specific object by name and using the dot member-selection operator (e.g., `squareObject.draw()`), the function invocation is resolved at compile time (this is called **static binding**) and the `virtual` function that is called is the one defined for (or inherited by) the class of that particular object—this is not polymorphic behavior. Thus, dynamic binding with `virtual` functions occurs only off pointer (and, as we'll soon see, reference) handles.

Now let's see how `virtual` functions can enable polymorphic behavior in our employee hierarchy. Figures 13.8–13.9 are the header files for classes `CommissionEmployee` and `BasePlusCommissionEmployee`, respectively. The only difference between these files and those of Fig. 13.1 and Fig. 13.3 is that we specify each class's `earnings` and print member functions as virtual (lines 30–31 of Fig. 13.8 and lines 20–21 of Fig. 13.9). Because functions earnings and print are virtual in class CommissionEmployee, class BasePlusCommissionEmployee's earnings and print functions override class CommissionEmployee's. Now, if we aim a base-class CommissionEmployee pointer at a derived-class BasePlusCommissionEmployee object, and the program uses that pointer to call either function earnings or print, the BasePlusCommissionEmployee object's corresponding function will be invoked. There were no changes to the member-function implementations of classes CommissionEmployee and BasePlusCommissionEmployee, so we reuse the versions of Fig. 13.2 and Fig. 13.4.

```cpp
1   // Fig. 13.8: CommissionEmployee.h
2   // CommissionEmployee class definition represents a commission employee.
3   #ifndef COMMISSION_H
4   #define COMMISSION_H
5
6   #include <string> // C++ standard string class
7   using namespace std;
8
9   class CommissionEmployee
10  {
11  public:
12     CommissionEmployee( const string &, const string &, const string &,
13        double = 0.0, double = 0.0 );
14
15     void setFirstName( const string & ); // set first name
16     string getFirstName() const; // return first name
17
18     void setLastName( const string & ); // set last name
19     string getLastName() const; // return last name
20
21     void setSocialSecurityNumber( const string & ); // set SSN
22     string getSocialSecurityNumber() const; // return SSN
23
24     void setGrossSales( double ); // set gross sales amount
25     double getGrossSales() const; // return gross sales amount
26
27     void setCommissionRate( double ); // set commission rate
28     double getCommissionRate() const; // return commission rate
29
30     virtual double earnings() const; // calculate earnings
31     virtual void print() const; // print CommissionEmployee object
32  private:
33     string firstName;
34     string lastName;
35     string socialSecurityNumber;
36     double grossSales; // gross weekly sales
37     double commissionRate; // commission percentage
38  }; // end class CommissionEmployee
39
40  #endif
```

Fig. 13.8 | CommissionEmployee class header file declares earnings and print functions as virtual.

```
1    // Fig. 13.9: BasePlusCommissionEmployee.h
2    // BasePlusCommissionEmployee class derived from class
3    // CommissionEmployee.
4    #ifndef BASEPLUS_H
5    #define BASEPLUS_H
6
7    #include <string> // C++ standard string class
8    #include "CommissionEmployee.h" // CommissionEmployee class declaration
9    using namespace std;
10
11   class BasePlusCommissionEmployee : public CommissionEmployee
12   {
13   public:
14      BasePlusCommissionEmployee( const string &, const string &,
15         const string &, double = 0.0, double = 0.0, double = 0.0 );
16
17      void setBaseSalary( double ); // set base salary
18      double getBaseSalary() const; // return base salary
19
20      virtual double earnings() const; // calculate earnings
21      virtual void print() const; // print BasePlusCommissionEmployee object
22   private:
23      double baseSalary; // base salary
24   }; // end class BasePlusCommissionEmployee
25
26   #endif
```

Fig. 13.9 | BasePlusCommissionEmployee class header file declares earnings and print functions as virtual.

We modified Fig. 13.5 to create the program of Fig. 13.10. Lines 40–51 demonstrate again that a CommissionEmployee pointer aimed at a CommissionEmployee object can be used to invoke CommissionEmployee functionality, and a BasePlusCommissionEmployee pointer aimed at a BasePlusCommissionEmployee object can be used to invoke BasePlusCommissionEmployee functionality. Line 54 aims base-class pointer commissionEmployeePtr at derived-class object basePlusCommissionEmployee. Note that when line 61 invokes member function print off the base-class pointer, the derived-class BasePlusCommissionEmployee's print member function is invoked, so line 61 outputs different text than line 53 does in Fig. 13.5 (when member function print was not declared virtual). We see that declaring a member function virtual causes the program to dynamically determine which function to invoke based on the type of object to which the handle points, rather than on the type of the handle. Note again that when commissionEmployeePtr points to a CommissionEmployee object (line 40), class CommissionEmployee's print function is invoked, and when CommissionEmployeePtr points to a BasePlusCommissionEmployee object, class BasePlusCommissionEmployee's print function is invoked. Thus, the same message—print, in this case—sent (off a base-class pointer) to a variety of objects related by inheritance to that base class, takes on many forms—this is polymorphic behavior.

```cpp
 1   // Fig. 13.10: fig13_10.cpp
 2   // Introducing polymorphism, virtual functions and dynamic binding.
 3   #include <iostream>
 4   #include <iomanip>
 5   #include "CommissionEmployee.h"
 6   #include "BasePlusCommissionEmployee.h"
 7   using namespace std;
 8
 9   int main()
10   {
11      // create base-class object
12      CommissionEmployee commissionEmployee(
13         "Sue", "Jones", "222-22-2222", 10000, .06 );
14
15      // create base-class pointer
16      CommissionEmployee *commissionEmployeePtr = 0;
17
18      // create derived-class object
19      BasePlusCommissionEmployee basePlusCommissionEmployee(
20         "Bob", "Lewis", "333-33-3333", 5000, .04, 300 );
21
22      // create derived-class pointer
23      BasePlusCommissionEmployee *basePlusCommissionEmployeePtr = 0;
24
25      // set floating-point output formatting
26      cout << fixed << setprecision( 2 );
27
28      // output objects using static binding
29      cout << "Invoking print function on base-class and derived-class "
30         << "\nobjects with static binding\n\n";
31      commissionEmployee.print(); // static binding
32      cout << "\n\n";
33      basePlusCommissionEmployee.print(); // static binding
34
35      // output objects using dynamic binding
36      cout << "\n\n\nInvoking print function on base-class and "
37         << "derived-class \nobjects with dynamic binding";
38
39      // aim base-class pointer at base-class object and print
40      commissionEmployeePtr = &commissionEmployee;
41      cout << "\n\nCalling virtual function print with base-class pointer"
42         << "\nto base-class object invokes base-class "
43         << "print function:\n\n";
44      commissionEmployeePtr->print(); // invokes base-class print
45
46      // aim derived-class pointer at derived-class object and print
47      basePlusCommissionEmployeePtr = &basePlusCommissionEmployee;
48      cout << "\n\nCalling virtual function print with derived-class "
49         << "pointer\nto derived-class object invokes derived-class "
50         << "print function:\n\n";
51      basePlusCommissionEmployeePtr->print(); // invokes derived-class print
```

Fig. 13.10 | Demonstrating polymorphism by invoking a derived-class virtual function via a base-class pointer to a derived-class object. (Part 1 of 2.)

```
52
53       // aim base-class pointer at derived-class object and print
54       commissionEmployeePtr = &basePlusCommissionEmployee;
55       cout << "\n\nCalling virtual function print with base-class pointer"
56          << "\nto derived-class object invokes derived-class "
57          << "print function:\n\n";
58
59       // polymorphism; invokes BasePlusCommissionEmployee's print;
60       // base-class pointer to derived-class object
61       commissionEmployeePtr->print();
62       cout << endl;
63    } // end main
```

```
Invoking print function on base-class and derived-class
objects with static binding

commission employee: Sue Jones
social security number: 222-22-2222
gross sales: 10000.00
commission rate: 0.06

base-salaried commission employee: Bob Lewis
social security number: 333-33-3333
gross sales: 5000.00
commission rate: 0.04
base salary: 300.00


Invoking print function on base-class and derived-class
objects with dynamic binding

Calling virtual function print with base-class pointer
to base-class object invokes base-class print function:

commission employee: Sue Jones
social security number: 222-22-2222
gross sales: 10000.00
commission rate: 0.06

Calling virtual function print with derived-class pointer
to derived-class object invokes derived-class print function:

base-salaried commission employee: Bob Lewis
social security number: 333-33-3333
gross sales: 5000.00
commission rate: 0.04
base salary: 300.00

Calling virtual function print with base-class pointer
to derived-class object invokes derived-class print function:

base-salaried commission employee: Bob Lewis
social security number: 333-33-3333
gross sales: 5000.00
commission rate: 0.04
base salary: 300.00
```

Fig. 13.10 | Demonstrating polymorphism by invoking a derived-class `virtual` function via a base-class pointer to a derived-class object. (Part 2 of 2.)

13.3.5 Summary of the Allowed Assignments Between Base-Class and Derived-Class Objects and Pointers

Now that you've seen a complete application that processes diverse objects polymorphically, we summarize what you can and cannot do with base-class and derived-class objects and pointers. Although a derived-class object also *is a* base-class object, the two objects are nevertheless different. As discussed previously, derived-class objects can be treated as if they were base-class objects. This is a logical relationship, because the derived class contains all the members of the base class. However, base-class objects cannot be treated as if they were derived-class objects—the derived class can have additional derived-class-only members. For this reason, aiming a derived-class pointer at a base-class object is not allowed without an explicit cast—such an assignment would leave the derived-class-only members undefined on the base-class object. The cast relieves the compiler of the responsibility of issuing an error message. In a sense, by using the cast you are saying, "I know that what I'm doing is dangerous and I take full responsibility for my actions."

We've discussed four ways to aim base-class pointers and derived-class pointers at base-class objects and derived-class objects:

1. Aiming a base-class pointer at a base-class object is straightforward—calls made off the base-class pointer simply invoke base-class functionality.

2. Aiming a derived-class pointer at a derived-class object is straightforward—calls made off the derived-class pointer simply invoke derived-class functionality.

3. Aiming a base-class pointer at a derived-class object is safe, because the derived-class object *is an* object of its base class. However, this pointer can be used to invoke only base-class member functions. If you attempt to refer to a derived-class-only member through the base-class pointer, the compiler reports an error. To avoid this error, you must cast the base-class pointer to a derived-class pointer. The derived-class pointer can then be used to invoke the derived-class object's complete functionality. This technique, called downcasting, is a potentially dangerous operation—Section 13.8 demonstrates how to safely use downcasting. If a virtual function is defined in the base and derived classes (either by inheritance or overriding), and if that function is invoked on a derived-class object via a base-class pointer, then the derived-class version of that function is called. This is an example of the polymorphic behavior that occurs only with virtual functions.

4. Aiming a derived-class pointer at a base-class object generates a compilation error. The *is-a* relationship applies only from a derived class to its direct and indirect base classes, and not vice versa. A base-class object does not contain the derived-class-only members that can be invoked off a derived-class pointer.

Common Programming Error 13.1

After aiming a base-class pointer at a derived-class object, attempting to reference derived-class-only members with the base-class pointer is a compilation error.

Common Programming Error 13.2

Treating a base-class object as a derived-class object can cause errors.

13.4 **Type Fields and `switch` Statements**

One way to determine the type of an object is to use a `switch` statement to check the value of a field in the object. This allows us to distinguish among object types, then invoke an appropriate action for a particular object. For example, in a hierarchy of shapes in which each shape object has a `shapeType` attribute, a `switch` statement could check the object's `shapeType` to determine which `print` function to call.

Using `switch` logic exposes programs to a variety of potential problems. For example, you might forget to include a type test when one is warranted, or might forget to test all possible cases in a `switch` statement. When modifying a `switch`-based system by adding new types, you might forget to insert the new cases in all relevant `switch` statements. Every addition or deletion of a class requires the modification of every `switch` statement in the system; tracking these statements down can be time consuming and error prone.

Software Engineering Observation 13.6

Polymorphic programming can eliminate the need for `switch` logic. By using the polymorphism mechanism to perform the equivalent logic, you can avoid the kinds of errors typically associated with `switch` logic.

Software Engineering Observation 13.7

An interesting consequence of using polymorphism is that programs take on a simplified appearance. They contain less branching logic and simpler sequential code. This simplification facilitates testing, debugging and program maintenance.

13.5 **Abstract Classes and Pure `virtual` Functions**

When we think of a class as a type, we assume that programs will create objects of that type. However, there are cases in which it's useful to define classes from which you never intend to instantiate any objects. Such classes are called **abstract classes**. Because these classes normally are used as base classes in inheritance hierarchies, we refer to them as **abstract base classes**. These classes cannot be used to instantiate objects, because, as we'll soon see, abstract classes are incomplete—derived classes must define the "missing pieces." We build programs with abstract classes in Section 13.6.

An abstract class provides a base class from which other classes can inherit. Classes that can be used to instantiate objects are called **concrete classes**. Such classes define every member function they declare. We could have an abstract base class `TwoDimensionalShape` and derive such concrete classes as `Square`, `Circle` and `Triangle`. We could also have an abstract base class `ThreeDimensionalShape` and derive such concrete classes as `Cube`, `Sphere` and `Cylinder`. Abstract base classes are too generic to define real objects; we need to be more specific before we can think of instantiating objects. For example, if someone tells you to "draw the two-dimensional shape," what shape would you draw? Concrete classes provide the specifics that make it reasonable to instantiate objects.

An inheritance hierarchy does not need to contain any abstract classes, but many object-oriented systems have class hierarchies headed by abstract base classes. In some cases, abstract classes constitute the top few levels of the hierarchy. A good example of this is the shape hierarchy in Fig. 12.3, which begins with abstract base class `Shape`. On the next level of the hierarchy we have two more abstract base classes, namely, `TwoDimension-`

alShape and ThreeDimensionalShape. The next level of the hierarchy defines concrete classes for two-dimensional shapes (namely, Circle, Square and Triangle) and for three-dimensional shapes (namely, Sphere, Cube and Tetrahedron).

A class is made abstract by declaring one or more of its virtual functions to be "pure." A **pure virtual function** is specified by placing "= 0" in its declaration, as in

```
virtual void draw() const = 0; // pure virtual function
```

The "= 0" is a **pure specifier**. Pure virtual functions do not provide implementations. Every concrete derived class *must* override all base-class pure virtual functions with concrete implementations of those functions. The difference between a virtual function and a pure virtual function is that a virtual function has an implementation and gives the derived class the *option* of overriding the function; by contrast, a pure virtual function does not provide an implementation and *requires* the derived class to override the function for that derived class to be concrete; otherwise the derived class remains abstract.

Pure virtual functions are used when it does not make sense for the base class to have an implementation of a function, but you want all concrete derived classes to implement the function. Returning to our earlier example of space objects, it does not make sense for the base class SpaceObject to have an implementation for function draw (as there is no way to draw a generic space object without having more information about what type of space object is being drawn). An example of a function that would be defined as virtual (and not pure virtual) would be one that returns a name for the object. We can name a generic SpaceObject (for instance, as "space object"), so a default implementation for this function can be provided, and the function does not need to be pure virtual. The function is still declared virtual, however, because it's expected that derived classes will override this function to provide more specific names for the derived-class objects.

Software Engineering Observation 13.8

An abstract class defines a common public interface for the various classes in a class hierarchy. An abstract class contains one or more pure virtual functions that concrete derived classes must override.

Common Programming Error 13.3

Attempting to instantiate an object of an abstract class causes a compilation error.

Common Programming Error 13.4

Failure to override a pure virtual function in a derived class, then attempting to instantiate objects of that class, is a compilation error.

Software Engineering Observation 13.9

An abstract class has at least one pure virtual function. An abstract class also can have data members and concrete functions (including constructors and destructors), which are subject to the normal rules of inheritance by derived classes.

Although we cannot instantiate objects of an abstract base class, we *can* use the abstract base class to declare pointers and references that can refer to objects of any concrete classes derived from the abstract class. Programs typically use such pointers and references to manipulate derived-class objects polymorphically.

Consider another application of polymorphism. A screen manager needs to display a variety of objects, including new types of objects that you'll add to the system after writing the screen manager. The system might need to display various shapes, such as Circles, Triangles or Rectangles, which are derived from abstract base class Shape. The screen manager uses Shape pointers to manage the objects that are displayed. To draw any object (regardless of the level at which that object's class appears in the inheritance hierarchy), the screen manager uses a base-class pointer to the object to invoke the object's draw function, which is a pure virtual function in base class Shape; therefore, each concrete derived class must implement function draw. Each Shape object in the inheritance hierarchy knows how to draw itself. The screen manager does not have to worry about the type of each object or whether the screen manager has ever encountered objects of that type.

Polymorphism is particularly effective for implementing layered software systems. In operating systems, for example, each type of physical device could operate quite differently from the others. Even so, commands to *read* or *write* data from and to devices may have a certain uniformity. The *write* message sent to a device-driver object needs to be interpreted specifically in the context of that device driver and how that device driver manipulates devices of a specific type. However, the *write* call itself really is no different from the *write* to any other device in the system—place some number of bytes from memory onto that device. An object-oriented operating system might use an abstract base class to provide an interface appropriate for all device drivers. Then, through inheritance from that abstract base class, derived classes are formed that all operate similarly. The capabilities (i.e., the public functions) offered by the device drivers are provided as pure virtual functions in the abstract base class. The implementations of these pure virtual functions are provided in the derived classes that correspond to the specific types of device drivers. This architecture also allows new devices to be added to a system easily, even after the operating system has been defined. The user can just plug in the device and install its new device driver. The operating system "talks" to this new device through its device driver, which has the same public member functions as all other device drivers—those defined in the device driver abstract base class.

It's common in object-oriented programming to define an **iterator class** that can traverse all the objects in a container (such as an array). For example, a program can print a list of objects in a vector by creating an iterator object, then using the iterator to obtain the next element of the list each time the iterator is called. Iterators often are used in polymorphic programming to traverse an array or a linked list of pointers to objects from various levels of a hierarchy. The pointers in such a list are all base-class pointers. (Chapter 22, Standard Template Library (STL), presents a thorough treatment of iterators.) A list of pointers to objects of base class TwoDimensionalShape could contain pointers to objects of classes Square, Circle, Triangle and so on. Using polymorphism to send a draw message, off a TwoDimensionalShape * pointer, to each object in the list would draw each object correctly on the screen.

13.6 Case Study: Payroll System Using Polymorphism

This section reexamines the CommissionEmployee-BasePlusCommissionEmployee hierarchy that we explored throughout Section 12.4. In this example, we use an abstract class and polymorphism to perform payroll calculations based on the type of employee. We create an enhanced employee hierarchy to solve the following problem:

> *A company pays its employees weekly. The employees are of four types: Salaried employees are paid a fixed weekly salary regardless of the number of hours worked, hourly employees are paid by the hour and receive overtime pay for all hours worked in excess of 40 hours, commission employees are paid a percentage of their sales and base-salary-plus-commission employees receive a base salary plus a percentage of their sales. For the current pay period, the company has decided to reward base-salary-plus-commission employees by adding 10 percent to their base salaries. The company wants to implement a C++ program that performs its payroll calculations polymorphically.*

We use abstract class `Employee` to represent the general concept of an employee. The classes that derive directly from `Employee` are `SalariedEmployee`, `CommissionEmployee` and `HourlyEmployee`. Class `BasePlusCommissionEmployee`—derived from `Commission-Employee`—represents the last employee type. The UML class diagram in Fig. 13.11 shows the inheritance hierarchy for our polymorphic employee payroll application. The abstract class name `Employee` is italicized, as per the convention of the UML.

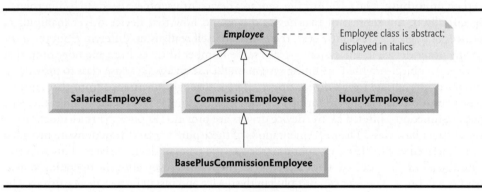

Fig. 13.11 | `Employee` hierarchy UML class diagram.

Abstract base class `Employee` declares the "interface" to the hierarchy—that is, the set of member functions that a program can invoke on all `Employee` objects. Each employee, regardless of the way his or her earnings are calculated, has a first name, a last name and a social security number, so `private` data members `firstName`, `lastName` and `socialSecurityNumber` appear in abstract base class `Employee`.

Software Engineering Observation 13.10

*A derived class can inherit interface or implementation from a base class. Hierarchies designed for **implementation inheritance** tend to have their functionality high in the hierarchy—each new derived class inherits one or more member functions that were defined in a base class, and the derived class uses the base-class definitions. Hierarchies designed for **interface inheritance** tend to have their functionality lower in the hierarchy—a base class specifies one or more functions that should be defined for each class in the hierarchy (i.e., they have the same prototype), but the individual derived classes provide their own implementations of the function(s).*

The following sections implement the `Employee` class hierarchy. The first five each implement one of the abstract or concrete classes. The last section implements a test program that builds objects of all these classes and processes the objects polymorphically.

13.6.1 Creating Abstract Base Class Employee

Class Employee (Figs. 13.13–13.14, discussed in further detail shortly) provides functions earnings and print, in addition to various *get* and *set* functions that manipulate Employee's data members. An earnings function certainly applies generically to all employees, but each earnings calculation depends on the employee's class. So we declare earnings as pure virtual in base class Employee because a default implementation does not make sense for that function—there is not enough information to determine what amount earnings should return. Each derived class overrides earnings with an appropriate implementation. To calculate an employee's earnings, the program assigns the address of an employee's object to a base class Employee pointer, then invokes the earnings function on that object. We maintain a vector of Employee pointers, each of which points to an Employee object (of course, there cannot be Employee objects, because Employee is an abstract class—because of inheritance, however, all objects of all derived classes of Employee may nevertheless be thought of as Employee objects). The program iterates through the vector and calls function earnings for each Employee object. C++ processes these function calls polymorphically. Including earnings as a pure virtual function in Employee forces every direct derived class of Employee that wishes to be a concrete class to override earnings. This enables the designer of the class hierarchy to demand that each derived class provide an appropriate pay calculation, if indeed that derived class is to be concrete.

Function print in class Employee displays the first name, last name and social security number of the employee. As we'll see, each derived class of Employee overrides function print to output the employee's type (e.g., "salaried employee:") followed by the rest of the employee's information. Function print could also call earnings, even though print is a pure-virtual function in class Employee.

The diagram in Fig. 13.12 shows each of the five classes in the hierarchy down the left side and functions earnings and print across the top. For each class, the diagram shows the desired results of each function. Class Employee specifies "= 0" for function earnings to indicate that this is a pure virtual function. Each derived class overrides this function to provide an appropriate implementation. We do not list base class Employee's *get* and *set* functions because they're not overridden in any of the derived classes—each of these functions is inherited and used "as is" by each of the derived classes.

Let's consider class Employee's header file (Fig. 13.13). The public member functions include a constructor that takes the first name, last name and social security number as arguments (line 12); *set* functions that set the first name, last name and social security number (lines 14, 17 and 20, respectively); *get* functions that return the first name, last name and social security number (lines 15, 18 and 21, respectively); pure virtual function earnings (line 24) and virtual function print (line 25).

Recall that we declared earnings as a pure virtual function because first we must know the specific Employee type to determine the appropriate earnings calculations. Declaring this function as pure virtual indicates that each concrete derived class *must* provide an earnings implementation and that a program can use base-class Employee pointers to invoke function earnings polymorphically for any type of Employee.

Figure 13.14 contains the member-function implementations for class Employee. No implementation is provided for virtual function earnings. The Employee constructor (lines 9–14) does not validate the social security number. Normally, such validation should be provided.

	earnings	print
Employee	= 0	*firstName lastName* social security number: *SSN*
Salaried-Employee	weeklySalary	salaried employee: *firstName lastName* social security number: *SSN* weekly salary: *weeklysalary*
Hourly-Employee	*If hours <= 40* wage * hours *If hours > 40* (40 * wage) + ((hours - 40) * wage * 1.5)	hourly employee: *firstName lastName* social security number: *SSN* hourly wage: *wage*; hours worked: *hours*
Commission-Employee	commissionRate * grossSales	commission employee: *firstName lastName* social security number: *SSN* gross sales: *grossSales*; commission rate: *commissionRate*
BasePlus-Commission-Employee	baseSalary + (commissionRate * grossSales)	base salaried commission employee: *firstName lastName* social security number: *SSN* gross sales: *grossSales*; commission rate: *commissionRate*; base salary: *baseSalary*

Fig. 13.12 | Polymorphic interface for the Employee hierarchy classes.

```cpp
1   // Fig. 13.13: Employee.h
2   // Employee abstract base class.
3   #ifndef EMPLOYEE_H
4   #define EMPLOYEE_H
5
6   #include <string> // C++ standard string class
7   using namespace std;
8
9   class Employee
10  {
11  public:
12     Employee( const string &, const string &, const string & );
13
14     void setFirstName( const string & ); // set first name
15     string getFirstName() const; // return first name
16
17     void setLastName( const string & ); // set last name
18     string getLastName() const; // return last name
19
20     void setSocialSecurityNumber( const string & ); // set SSN
21     string getSocialSecurityNumber() const; // return SSN
```

Fig. 13.13 | Employee class header file. (Part 1 of 2.)

```
22
23      // pure virtual function makes Employee abstract base class
24      virtual double earnings() const = 0; // pure virtual
25      virtual void print() const; // virtual
26   private:
27      string firstName;
28      string lastName;
29      string socialSecurityNumber;
30   }; // end class Employee
31
32   #endif // EMPLOYEE_H
```

Fig. 13.13 | Employee class header file. (Part 2 of 2.)

```
1   // Fig. 13.14: Employee.cpp
2   // Abstract-base-class Employee member-function definitions.
3   // Note: No definitions are given for pure virtual functions.
4   #include <iostream>
5   #include "Employee.h" // Employee class definition
6   using namespace std;
7
8   // constructor
9   Employee::Employee( const string &first, const string &last,
10     const string &ssn )
11     : firstName( first ), lastName( last ), socialSecurityNumber( ssn )
12   {
13      // empty body
14   } // end Employee constructor
15
16   // set first name
17   void Employee::setFirstName( const string &first )
18   {
19      firstName = first;
20   } // end function setFirstName
21
22   // return first name
23   string Employee::getFirstName() const
24   {
25      return firstName;
26   } // end function getFirstName
27
28   // set last name
29   void Employee::setLastName( const string &last )
30   {
31      lastName = last;
32   } // end function setLastName
33
34   // return last name
35   string Employee::getLastName() const
36   {
37      return lastName;
38   } // end function getLastName
```

Fig. 13.14 | Employee class implementation file. (Part 1 of 2.)

```
39
40   // set social security number
41   void Employee::setSocialSecurityNumber( const string &ssn )
42   {
43      socialSecurityNumber = ssn; // should validate
44   } // end function setSocialSecurityNumber
45
46   // return social security number
47   string Employee::getSocialSecurityNumber() const
48   {
49      return socialSecurityNumber;
50   } // end function getSocialSecurityNumber
51
52   // print Employee's information (virtual, but not pure virtual)
53   void Employee::print() const
54   {
55      cout << getFirstName() << ' ' << getLastName()
56         << "\nsocial security number: " << getSocialSecurityNumber();
57   } // end function print
```

Fig. 13.14 | Employee class implementation file. (Part 2 of 2.)

Note that virtual function print (Fig. 13.14, lines 53–57) provides an implementation that will be overridden in each of the derived classes. Each of these functions will, however, use the abstract class's version of print to print information common to all classes in the Employee hierarchy.

13.6.2 Creating Concrete Derived Class SalariedEmployee

Class SalariedEmployee (Figs. 13.15–13.16) derives from class Employee (line 8 of Fig. 13.15). The public member functions include a constructor that takes a first name, a last name, a social security number and a weekly salary as arguments (lines 11–12); a *set* function to assign a new nonnegative value to data member weeklySalary (line 14); a *get* function to return weeklySalary's value (line 15); a virtual function earnings that calculates a SalariedEmployee's earnings (line 18) and a virtual function print (line 19) that outputs the employee's type, namely, "salaried employee: " followed by employee-specific information produced by base class Employee's print function and SalariedEmployee's getWeeklySalary function.

```
1   // Fig. 13.15: SalariedEmployee.h
2   // SalariedEmployee class derived from Employee.
3   #ifndef SALARIED_H
4   #define SALARIED_H
5
6   #include "Employee.h" // Employee class definition
7
8   class SalariedEmployee : public Employee
9   {
```

Fig. 13.15 | SalariedEmployee class header file. (Part 1 of 2.)

```
10    public:
11       SalariedEmployee( const string &, const string &,
12          const string &, double = 0.0 );
13
14       void setWeeklySalary( double ); // set weekly salary
15       double getWeeklySalary() const; // return weekly salary
16
17       // keyword virtual signals intent to override
18       virtual double earnings() const; // calculate earnings
19       virtual void print() const; // print SalariedEmployee object
20    private:
21       double weeklySalary; // salary per week
22    }; // end class SalariedEmployee
23
24    #endif // SALARIED_H
```

Fig. 13.15 | SalariedEmployee class header file. (Part 2 of 2.)

Figure 13.16 contains the member-function implementations for SalariedEmployee. The class's constructor passes the first name, last name and social security number to the Employee constructor (line 10) to initialize the private data members that are inherited from the base class, but not accessible in the derived class. Function earnings (line 29–32) overrides pure virtual function earnings in Employee to provide a concrete implementation that returns the SalariedEmployee's weekly salary. If we did not implement earnings, class SalariedEmployee would be an abstract class, and any attempt to instantiate an object of the class would result in a compilation error (and, of course, we want SalariedEmployee here to be a concrete class). In class SalariedEmployee's header file, we declared member functions earnings and print as virtual (lines 18–19 of Fig. 13.15)—actually, placing the virtual keyword before these member functions is redundant. We defined them as virtual in base class Employee, so they remain virtual functions throughout the class hierarchy. Recall from *Good Programming Practice 13.1* that explicitly declaring such functions virtual at every level of the hierarchy can promote program clarity.

```
1    // Fig. 13.16: SalariedEmployee.cpp
2    // SalariedEmployee class member-function definitions.
3    #include <iostream>
4    #include "SalariedEmployee.h" // SalariedEmployee class definition
5    using namespace std;
6
7    // constructor
8    SalariedEmployee::SalariedEmployee( const string &first,
9       const string &last, const string &ssn, double salary )
10      : Employee( first, last, ssn )
11   {
12      setWeeklySalary( salary );
13   } // end SalariedEmployee constructor
```

Fig. 13.16 | SalariedEmployee class implementation file. (Part 1 of 2.)

```
14
15   // set salary
16   void SalariedEmployee::setWeeklySalary( double salary )
17   {
18      weeklySalary = ( salary < 0.0 ) ? 0.0 : salary;
19   } // end function setWeeklySalary
20
21   // return salary
22   double SalariedEmployee::getWeeklySalary() const
23   {
24      return weeklySalary;
25   } // end function getWeeklySalary
26
27   // calculate earnings;
28   // override pure virtual function earnings in Employee
29   double SalariedEmployee::earnings() const
30   {
31      return getWeeklySalary();
32   } // end function earnings
33
34   // print SalariedEmployee's information
35   void SalariedEmployee::print() const
36   {
37      cout << "salaried employee: ";
38      Employee::print(); // reuse abstract base-class print function
39      cout << "\nweekly salary: " << getWeeklySalary();
40   } // end function print
```

Fig. 13.16 | SalariedEmployee class implementation file. (Part 2 of 2.)

Function print of class SalariedEmployee (lines 35–40 of Fig. 13.16) overrides Employee function print. If class SalariedEmployee did not override print, Salaried-Employee would inherit the Employee version of print. In that case, SalariedEmployee's print function would simply return the employee's full name and social security number, which does not adequately represent a SalariedEmployee. To print a SalariedEmployee's complete information, the derived class's print function outputs "salaried employee: " followed by the base-class Employee-specific information (i.e., first name, last name and social security number) printed by invoking the base class's print function using the scope resolution operator (line 38)—this is a nice example of code reuse. The output produced by SalariedEmployee's print function contains the employee's weekly salary obtained by invoking the class's getWeeklySalary function.

13.6.3 Creating Concrete Derived Class HourlyEmployee

Class HourlyEmployee (Figs. 13.17–13.18) also derives from class Employee (line 8 of Fig. 13.17). The public member functions include a constructor (lines 13–14) that takes as arguments a first name, a last name, a social security number, an hourly wage and the number of hours worked; *set* functions that assign new values to data members wage and hours, respectively (lines 16 and 19); *get* functions to return the values of wage and hours, respectively (lines 17 and 20); a virtual function earnings that calculates an HourlyEmployee's earnings (line 23) and a virtual function print that outputs the employee's type, namely, "hourly employee: " and employee-specific information (line 24).

```
1   // Fig. 13.17: HourlyEmployee.h
2   // HourlyEmployee class definition.
3   #ifndef HOURLY_H
4   #define HOURLY_H
5
6   #include "Employee.h" // Employee class definition
7
8   class HourlyEmployee : public Employee
9   {
10  public:
11     static const int hoursPerWeek = 168; // hours in one week
12
13     HourlyEmployee( const string &, const string &,
14        const string &, double = 0.0, double = 0.0 );
15
16     void setWage( double ); // set hourly wage
17     double getWage() const; // return hourly wage
18
19     void setHours( double ); // set hours worked
20     double getHours() const; // return hours worked
21
22     // keyword virtual signals intent to override
23     virtual double earnings() const; // calculate earnings
24     virtual void print() const; // print HourlyEmployee object
25  private:
26     double wage; // wage per hour
27     double hours; // hours worked for week
28  }; // end class HourlyEmployee
29
30  #endif // HOURLY_H
```

Fig. 13.17 | HourlyEmployee class header file.

Figure 13.18 contains the member-function implementations for class HourlyEmployee. Lines 17–20 and 29–33 define *set* functions that assign new values to data members wage and hours, respectively. Function setWage (lines 17–20) ensures that wage is non-negative, and function setHours (lines 29–33) ensures that data member hours is between 0 and hoursPerWeek (i.e., 168). Class HourlyEmployee's *get* functions are implemented in lines 23–26 and 36–39. We do not declare these functions virtual, so classes derived from class HourlyEmployee cannot override them (although derived classes certainly can redefine them). The HourlyEmployee constructor, like the SalariedEmployee constructor, passes the first name, last name and social security number to the base class Employee constructor (line 10) to initialize the inherited private data members declared in the base class. In addition, HourlyEmployee's print function calls base-class function print (line 55) to output the Employee-specific information (i.e., first name, last name and social security number)—this is another nice example of code reuse.

```cpp
1   // Fig. 13.18: HourlyEmployee.cpp
2   // HourlyEmployee class member-function definitions.
3   #include <iostream>
4   #include "HourlyEmployee.h" // HourlyEmployee class definition
5   using namespace std;
6
7   // constructor
8   HourlyEmployee::HourlyEmployee( const string &first, const string &last,
9      const string &ssn, double hourlyWage, double hoursWorked )
10     : Employee( first, last, ssn )
11  {
12     setWage( hourlyWage ); // validate hourly wage
13     setHours( hoursWorked ); // validate hours worked
14  } // end HourlyEmployee constructor
15
16  // set wage
17  void HourlyEmployee::setWage( double hourlyWage )
18  {
19     wage = ( hourlyWage < 0.0 ? 0.0 : hourlyWage );
20  } // end function setWage
21
22  // return wage
23  double HourlyEmployee::getWage() const
24  {
25     return wage;
26  } // end function getWage
27
28  // set hours worked
29  void HourlyEmployee::setHours( double hoursWorked )
30  {
31     hours = ( ( ( hoursWorked >= 0.0 ) &&
32        ( hoursWorked <= hoursPerWeek ) ) ? hoursWorked : 0.0 );
33  } // end function setHours
34
35  // return hours worked
36  double HourlyEmployee::getHours() const
37  {
38     return hours;
39  } // end function getHours
40
41  // calculate earnings;
42  // override pure virtual function earnings in Employee
43  double HourlyEmployee::earnings() const
44  {
45     if ( getHours() <= 40 ) // no overtime
46        return getWage() * getHours();
47     else
48        return 40 * getWage() + ( ( getHours() - 40 ) * getWage() * 1.5 );
49  } // end function earnings
50
51  // print HourlyEmployee's information
52  void HourlyEmployee::print() const
53  {
```

Fig. 13.18 | HourlyEmployee class implementation file. (Part 1 of 2.)

```
54      cout << "hourly employee: ";
55      Employee::print(); // code reuse
56      cout << "\nhourly wage: " << getWage() <<
57         "; hours worked: " << getHours();
58   } // end function print
```

Fig. 13.18 | HourlyEmployee class implementation file. (Part 2 of 2.)

13.6.4 Creating Concrete Derived Class CommissionEmployee

Class CommissionEmployee (Figs. 13.19–13.20) derives from Employee (Fig. 13.19, line 8). The member-function implementations (Fig. 13.20) include a constructor (lines 8–14) that takes a first name, last name, social security number, sales amount and commission rate; *set* functions (lines 17–20 and 29–32) to assign new values to data members commissionRate and grossSales, respectively; *get* functions (lines 23–26 and 35–38) that retrieve their values; function earnings (lines 41–44) to calculate a CommissionEmployee's earnings; and function print (lines 47–53) to output the employee's type, namely, "commission employee: " and employee-specific information. The constructor passes the first name, last name and social security number to the Employee constructor (line 10) to initialize Employee's private data members. Function print calls base-class function print (line 50) to display the Employee-specific information.

```
1   // Fig. 13.19: CommissionEmployee.h
2   // CommissionEmployee class derived from Employee.
3   #ifndef COMMISSION_H
4   #define COMMISSION_H
5
6   #include "Employee.h" // Employee class definition
7
8   class CommissionEmployee : public Employee
9   {
10  public:
11     CommissionEmployee( const string &, const string &,
12        const string &, double = 0.0, double = 0.0 );
13
14     void setCommissionRate( double ); // set commission rate
15     double getCommissionRate() const; // return commission rate
16
17     void setGrossSales( double ); // set gross sales amount
18     double getGrossSales() const; // return gross sales amount
19
20     // keyword virtual signals intent to override
21     virtual double earnings() const; // calculate earnings
22     virtual void print() const; // print CommissionEmployee object
23  private:
24     double grossSales; // gross weekly sales
25     double commissionRate; // commission percentage
26  }; // end class CommissionEmployee
27
28  #endif // COMMISSION_H
```

Fig. 13.19 | CommissionEmployee class header file.

```cpp
1   // Fig. 13.20: CommissionEmployee.cpp
2   // CommissionEmployee class member-function definitions.
3   #include <iostream>
4   #include "CommissionEmployee.h" // CommissionEmployee class definition
5   using namespace std;
6
7   // constructor
8   CommissionEmployee::CommissionEmployee( const string &first,
9      const string &last, const string &ssn, double sales, double rate )
10     : Employee( first, last, ssn )
11  {
12     setGrossSales( sales );
13     setCommissionRate( rate );
14  } // end CommissionEmployee constructor
15
16  // set commission rate
17  void CommissionEmployee::setCommissionRate( double rate )
18  {
19     commissionRate = ( ( rate > 0.0 && rate < 1.0 ) ? rate : 0.0 );
20  } // end function setCommissionRate
21
22  // return commission rate
23  double CommissionEmployee::getCommissionRate() const
24  {
25      return commissionRate;
26  } // end function getCommissionRate
27
28  // set gross sales amount
29  void CommissionEmployee::setGrossSales( double sales )
30  {
31     grossSales = ( ( sales < 0.0 ) ? 0.0 : sales );
32  } // end function setGrossSales
33
34  // return gross sales amount
35  double CommissionEmployee::getGrossSales() const
36  {
37      return grossSales;
38  } // end function getGrossSales
39
40  // calculate earnings; override pure virtual function earnings in Employee
41  double CommissionEmployee::earnings() const
42  {
43     return getCommissionRate() * getGrossSales();
44  } // end function earnings
45
46  // print CommissionEmployee's information
47  void CommissionEmployee::print() const
48  {
49     cout << "commission employee: ";
50     Employee::print(); // code reuse
51     cout << "\ngross sales: " << getGrossSales()
52        << "; commission rate: " << getCommissionRate();
53  } // end function print
```

Fig. 13.20 | CommissionEmployee class implementation file.

13.6.5 Creating Indirect Concrete Derived Class BasePlusCommissionEmployee

Class BasePlusCommissionEmployee (Figs. 13.21–13.22) directly inherits from class CommissionEmployee (line 8 of Fig. 13.21) and therefore is an *indirect* derived class of class Employee. Class BasePlusCommissionEmployee's member-function implementations include a constructor (lines 8–14 of Fig. 13.22) that takes as arguments a first name, a last name, a social security number, a sales amount, a commission rate and a base salary. It then passes the first name, last name, social security number, sales amount and commission rate to the CommissionEmployee constructor (line 11) to initialize the inherited members. BasePlusCommissionEmployee also contains a *set* function (lines 17–20) to assign a new value to data member baseSalary and a *get* function (lines 23–26) to return baseSalary's value. Function earnings (lines 30–33) calculates a BasePlusCommissionEmployee's earnings. Line 32 in function earnings calls base-class CommissionEmployee's earnings function to calculate the commission-based portion of the employee's earnings. This is a nice example of code reuse. BasePlusCommissionEmployee's print function (lines 36–41) outputs "base-salaried", followed by the output of base-class CommissionEmployee's print function (another example of code reuse), then the base salary. The resulting output begins with "base-salaried commission employee: " followed by the rest of the BasePlusCommissionEmployee's information. Recall that CommissionEmployee's print displays the employee's first name, last name and social security number by invoking the print function of its base class (i.e., Employee)—yet another example of code reuse. BasePlusCommissionEmployee's print initiates a chain of functions calls that spans all three levels of the Employee hierarchy.

```
1   // Fig. 13.21: BasePlusCommissionEmployee.h
2   // BasePlusCommissionEmployee class derived from CommissionEmployee.
3   #ifndef BASEPLUS_H
4   #define BASEPLUS_H
5
6   #include "CommissionEmployee.h" // CommissionEmployee class definition
7
8   class BasePlusCommissionEmployee : public CommissionEmployee
9   {
10  public:
11     BasePlusCommissionEmployee( const string &, const string &,
12        const string &, double = 0.0, double = 0.0, double = 0.0 );
13
14     void setBaseSalary( double ); // set base salary
15     double getBaseSalary() const; // return base salary
16
17     // keyword virtual signals intent to override
18     virtual double earnings() const; // calculate earnings
19     virtual void print() const; // print BasePlusCommissionEmployee object
20  private:
21     double baseSalary; // base salary per week
22  }; // end class BasePlusCommissionEmployee
23
24  #endif // BASEPLUS_H
```

Fig. 13.21 | BasePlusCommissionEmployee class header file.

```cpp
1   // Fig. 13.22: BasePlusCommissionEmployee.cpp
2   // BasePlusCommissionEmployee member-function definitions.
3   #include <iostream>
4   #include "BasePlusCommissionEmployee.h"
5   using namespace std;
6
7   // constructor
8   BasePlusCommissionEmployee::BasePlusCommissionEmployee(
9      const string &first, const string &last, const string &ssn,
10     double sales, double rate, double salary )
11     : CommissionEmployee( first, last, ssn, sales, rate )
12  {
13     setBaseSalary( salary ); // validate and store base salary
14  } // end BasePlusCommissionEmployee constructor
15
16  // set base salary
17  void BasePlusCommissionEmployee::setBaseSalary( double salary )
18  {
19     baseSalary = ( ( salary < 0.0 ) ? 0.0 : salary );
20  } // end function setBaseSalary
21
22  // return base salary
23  double BasePlusCommissionEmployee::getBaseSalary() const
24  {
25     return baseSalary;
26  } // end function getBaseSalary
27
28  // calculate earnings;
29  // override virtual function earnings in CommissionEmployee
30  double BasePlusCommissionEmployee::earnings() const
31  {
32     return getBaseSalary() + CommissionEmployee::earnings();
33  } // end function earnings
34
35  // print BasePlusCommissionEmployee's information
36  void BasePlusCommissionEmployee::print() const
37  {
38     cout << "base-salaried ";
39     CommissionEmployee::print(); // code reuse
40     cout << "; base salary: " << getBaseSalary();
41  } // end function print
```

Fig. 13.22 | BasePlusCommissionEmployee class implementation file.

13.6.6 Demonstrating Polymorphic Processing

To test our Employee hierarchy, the program in Fig. 13.23 creates an object of each of the four concrete classes SalariedEmployee, HourlyEmployee, CommissionEmployee and BasePlusCommissionEmployee. The program manipulates these objects, first with static binding, then polymorphically, using a vector of Employee pointers. Lines 23–30 create objects of each of the four concrete Employee derived classes. Lines 35–43 output each Employee's information and earnings. Each member-function invocation in lines 35–43 is an example of static binding—at compile time, because we are using name handles (not pointers or references that could be set at execution time), the compiler can identify each object's type to determine which print and earnings functions are called.

```cpp
1   // Fig. 13.23: fig13_23.cpp
2   // Processing Employee derived-class objects individually
3   // and polymorphically using dynamic binding.
4   #include <iostream>
5   #include <iomanip>
6   #include <vector>
7   #include "Employee.h"
8   #include "SalariedEmployee.h"
9   #include "HourlyEmployee.h"
10  #include "CommissionEmployee.h"
11  #include "BasePlusCommissionEmployee.h"
12  using namespace std;
13
14  void virtualViaPointer( const Employee * const ); // prototype
15  void virtualViaReference( const Employee & ); // prototype
16
17  int main()
18  {
19     // set floating-point output formatting
20     cout << fixed << setprecision( 2 );
21
22     // create derived-class objects
23     SalariedEmployee salariedEmployee(
24        "John", "Smith", "111-11-1111", 800 );
25     HourlyEmployee hourlyEmployee(
26        "Karen", "Price", "222-22-2222", 16.75, 40 );
27     CommissionEmployee commissionEmployee(
28        "Sue", "Jones", "333-33-3333", 10000, .06 );
29     BasePlusCommissionEmployee basePlusCommissionEmployee(
30        "Bob", "Lewis", "444-44-4444", 5000, .04, 300 );
31
32     cout << "Employees processed individually using static binding:\n\n";
33
34     // output each Employee's information and earnings using static binding
35     salariedEmployee.print();
36     cout << "\nearned $" << salariedEmployee.earnings() << "\n\n";
37     hourlyEmployee.print();
38     cout << "\nearned $" << hourlyEmployee.earnings() << "\n\n";
39     commissionEmployee.print();
40     cout << "\nearned $" << commissionEmployee.earnings() << "\n\n";
41     basePlusCommissionEmployee.print();
42     cout << "\nearned $" << basePlusCommissionEmployee.earnings()
43        << "\n\n";
44
45     // create vector of four base-class pointers
46     vector < Employee * > employees( 4 );
47
48     // initialize vector with Employees
49     employees[ 0 ] = &salariedEmployee;
```

Fig. 13.23 | Employee class hierarchy driver program. (Part 1 of 3.)

```
50      employees[ 1 ] = &hourlyEmployee;
51      employees[ 2 ] = &commissionEmployee;
52      employees[ 3 ] = &basePlusCommissionEmployee;
53
54      cout << "Employees processed polymorphically via dynamic binding:\n\n";
55
56      // call virtualViaPointer to print each Employee's information
57      // and earnings using dynamic binding
58      cout << "Virtual function calls made off base-class pointers:\n\n";
59
60      for ( size_t i = 0; i < employees.size(); i++ )
61         virtualViaPointer( employees[ i ] );
62
63      // call virtualViaReference to print each Employee's information
64      // and earnings using dynamic binding
65      cout << "Virtual function calls made off base-class references:\n\n";
66
67      for ( size_t i = 0; i < employees.size(); i++ )
68         virtualViaReference( *employees[ i ] ); // note dereferencing
69   } // end main
70
71   // call Employee virtual functions print and earnings off a
72   // base-class pointer using dynamic binding
73   void virtualViaPointer( const Employee * const baseClassPtr )
74   {
75      baseClassPtr->print();
76      cout << "\nearned $" << baseClassPtr->earnings() << "\n\n";
77   } // end function virtualViaPointer
78
79   // call Employee virtual functions print and earnings off a
80   // base-class reference using dynamic binding
81   void virtualViaReference( const Employee &baseClassRef )
82   {
83      baseClassRef.print();
84      cout << "\nearned $" << baseClassRef.earnings() << "\n\n";
85   } // end function virtualViaReference
```

```
Employees processed individually using static binding:

salaried employee: John Smith
social security number: 111-11-1111
weekly salary: 800.00
earned $800.00

hourly employee: Karen Price
social security number: 222-22-2222
hourly wage: 16.75; hours worked: 40.00
earned $670.00

commission employee: Sue Jones
social security number: 333-33-3333
gross sales: 10000.00; commission rate: 0.06
earned $600.00
```

Fig. 13.23 | Employee class hierarchy driver program. (Part 2 of 3.)

```
base-salaried commission employee: Bob Lewis
social security number: 444-44-4444
gross sales: 5000.00; commission rate: 0.04; base salary: 300.00
earned $500.00

Employees processed polymorphically using dynamic binding:

Virtual function calls made off base-class pointers:

salaried employee: John Smith
social security number: 111-11-1111
weekly salary: 800.00
earned $800.00

hourly employee: Karen Price
social security number: 222-22-2222
hourly wage: 16.75; hours worked: 40.00
earned $670.00

commission employee: Sue Jones
social security number: 333-33-3333
gross sales: 10000.00; commission rate: 0.06
earned $600.00

base-salaried commission employee: Bob Lewis
social security number: 444-44-4444
gross sales: 5000.00; commission rate: 0.04; base salary: 300.00
earned $500.00

Virtual function calls made off base-class references:

salaried employee: John Smith
social security number: 111-11-1111
weekly salary: 800.00
earned $800.00

hourly employee: Karen Price
social security number: 222-22-2222
hourly wage: 16.75; hours worked: 40.00
earned $670.00

commission employee: Sue Jones
social security number: 333-33-3333
gross sales: 10000.00; commission rate: 0.06
earned $600.00

base-salaried commission employee: Bob Lewis
social security number: 444-44-4444
gross sales: 5000.00; commission rate: 0.04; base salary: 300.00
earned $500.00
```

Fig. 13.23 | Employee class hierarchy driver program. (Part 3 of 3.)

Line 46 allocates vector employees, which contains four Employee pointers. Line 49 aims employees[0] at object salariedEmployee. Line 50 aims employees[1] at object hourlyEmployee. Line 51 aims employees[2] at object commissionEmployee. Line 52 aims employee[3] at object basePlusCommissionEmployee. The compiler allows these assignments, because a SalariedEmployee *is an* Employee, an HourlyEmployee *is an*

Employee, a CommissionEmployee *is an* Employee and a BasePlusCommissionEmployee *is an* Employee. Therefore, we can assign the addresses of SalariedEmployee, HourlyEmployee, CommissionEmployee and BasePlusCommissionEmployee objects to base-class Employee pointers (even though Employee is an abstract class).

The loop in lines 60–61 traverses vector employees and invokes function virtualViaPointer (lines 73–77) for each element in employees. Function virtualViaPointer receives in parameter baseClassPtr (of type const Employee * const) the address stored in an employees element. Each call to virtualViaPointer uses baseClassPtr to invoke virtual functions print (line 75) and earnings (line 76). Note that function virtualViaPointer does not contain any SalariedEmployee, HourlyEmployee, CommissionEmployee or BasePlusCommissionEmployee type information. The function knows only about base-class type Employee. Therefore, the compiler cannot know which concrete class's functions to call through baseClassPtr. Yet at execution time, each virtual-function invocation calls the function on the object to which baseClassPtr points at that moment. The output illustrates that the appropriate functions for each class are indeed invoked and that each object's proper information is displayed. For instance, the weekly salary is displayed for the SalariedEmployee, and the gross sales are displayed for the CommissionEmployee and BasePlusCommissionEmployee. Also, obtaining the earnings of each Employee polymorphically in line 76 produces the same results as obtaining these employees' earnings via static binding in lines 36, 38, 40 and 42. All virtual function calls to print and earnings are resolved at runtime with dynamic binding.

Finally, another for statement (lines 67–68) traverses employees and invokes function virtualViaReference (lines 81–85) for each element in the vector. Function virtualViaReference receives in its parameter baseClassRef (of type const Employee &) a reference to the object obtained by dereferencing the pointer stored in each employees element (line 68). Each call to virtualViaReference invokes virtual functions print (line 83) and earnings (line 84) via reference baseClassRef to demonstrate that polymorphic processing occurs with base-class references as well. Each virtual-function invocation calls the function on the object to which baseClassRef refers at runtime. This is another example of dynamic binding. The output produced using base-class references is identical to the output produced using base-class pointers.

13.7 (Optional) Polymorphism, Virtual Functions and Dynamic Binding "Under the Hood"

C++ makes polymorphism easy to program. It's certainly possible to program for polymorphism in non-object-oriented languages such as C, but doing so requires complex and potentially dangerous pointer manipulations. This section discusses how C++ can implement polymorphism, virtual functions and dynamic binding internally. This will give you a solid understanding of how these capabilities really work. More importantly, it will help you appreciate the overhead of polymorphism—in terms of additional memory consumption and processor time. This will help you determine when to use polymorphism and when to avoid it. As you'll see in Chapter 22, the STL components were implemented without polymorphism and virtual functions—this was done to avoid the associated execution-time overhead and achieve optimal performance to meet the unique requirements of the STL.

First, we'll explain the data structures that the C++ compiler builds at compile time to support polymorphism at execution time. You'll see that polymorphism is accomplished through three levels of pointers (i.e., "triple indirection"). Then we'll show how an executing program uses these data structures to execute virtual functions and achieve the dynamic binding associated with polymorphism. Our discussion explains one possible implementation; this is not a language requirement.

When C++ compiles a class that has one or more virtual functions, it builds a **virtual function table (*vtable*)** for that class. An executing program uses the *vtable* to select the proper function implementation each time a virtual function of that class is called. The leftmost column of Fig. 13.24 illustrates the *vtables* for classes Employee, SalariedEmployee, HourlyEmployee, CommissionEmployee and BasePlusCommissionEmployee.

In the *vtable* for class Employee, the first function pointer is set to 0 (i.e., the null pointer). This is done because function earnings is a pure virtual function and therefore lacks an implementation. The second function pointer points to function print, which displays the employee's full name and social security number. [*Note:* We've abbreviated the output of each print function in this figure to conserve space.] Any class that has one or more null pointers in its *vtable* is an abstract class. Classes without any null *vtable* pointers (such as SalariedEmployee, HourlyEmployee, CommissionEmployee and BasePlusCommissionEmployee) are concrete classes.

Class SalariedEmployee overrides function earnings to return the employee's weekly salary, so the function pointer points to the earnings function of class SalariedEmployee. SalariedEmployee also overrides print, so the corresponding function pointer points to the SalariedEmployee member function that prints "salaried employee: " followed by the employee's name, social security number and weekly salary.

The earnings function pointer in the *vtable* for class HourlyEmployee points to HourlyEmployee's earnings function that returns the employee's wage multiplied by the number of hours worked. To conserve space, we've omitted the fact that hourly employees receive time-and-a-half pay for overtime hours worked. The print function pointer points to the HourlyEmployee version of the function, which prints "hourly employee: ", the employee's name, social security number, hourly wage and hours worked. Both functions override the functions in class Employee.

The earnings function pointer in the *vtable* for class CommissionEmployee points to CommissionEmployee's earnings function that returns the employee's gross sales multiplied by the commission rate. The print function pointer points to the CommissionEmployee version of the function, which prints the employee's type, name, social security number, commission rate and gross sales. As in class HourlyEmployee, both functions override the functions in class Employee.

The earnings function pointer in the *vtable* for class BasePlusCommissionEmployee points to the BasePlusCommissionEmployee's earnings function, which returns the employee's base salary plus gross sales multiplied by commission rate. The print function pointer points to the BasePlusCommissionEmployee version of the function, which prints the employee's base salary plus the type, name, social security number, commission rate and gross sales. Both functions override the functions in class CommissionEmployee.

Notice that in our Employee case study, each concrete class provides its own implementation for virtual functions earnings and print. You've learned that each class which inherits directly from abstract base class Employee must implement earnings in

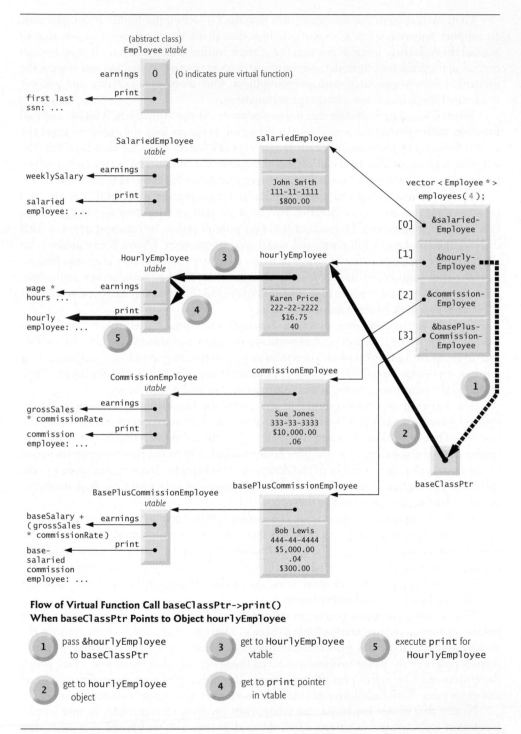

Flow of Virtual Function Call baseClassPtr->print()
When baseClassPtr Points to Object hourlyEmployee

1. pass &hourlyEmployee to baseClassPtr
2. get to hourlyEmployee object
3. get to HourlyEmployee vtable
4. get to print pointer in vtable
5. execute print for HourlyEmployee

Fig. 13.24 | How virtual function calls work.

order to be a concrete class, because earnings is a pure virtual function. These classes do not need to implement function print, however, to be considered concrete—print is not a pure virtual function and derived classes can inherit class Employee's implementation of print. Furthermore, class BasePlusCommissionEmployee does not have to implement either function print or earnings—both function implementations can be inherited from class CommissionEmployee. If a class in our hierarchy were to inherit function implementations in this manner, the *vtable* pointers for these functions would simply point to the function implementation that was being inherited. For example, if BasePlusCommissionEmployee did not override earnings, the earnings function pointer in the *vtable* for class BasePlusCommissionEmployee would point to the same earnings function as the *vtable* for class CommissionEmployee points to.

Polymorphism is accomplished through an elegant data structure involving three levels of pointers. We've discussed one level—the function pointers in the *vtable*. These point to the actual functions that execute when a virtual function is invoked.

Now we consider the second level of pointers. Whenever an object of a class with one or more virtual functions is instantiated, the compiler attaches to the object a pointer to the *vtable* for that class. This pointer is normally at the front of the object, but it isn't required to be implemented that way. In Fig. 13.24, these pointers are associated with the objects created in Fig. 13.23 (one object for each of the types SalariedEmployee, HourlyEmployee, CommissionEmployee and BasePlusCommissionEmployee). Notice that the diagram displays each of the object's data member values. For example, the salariedEmployee object contains a pointer to the SalariedEmployee *vtable*; the object also contains the values John Smith, 111-11-1111 and $800.00.

The third level of pointers simply contains the handles to the objects that receive the virtual function calls. The handles in this level may also be references. Fig. 13.24 depicts the vector employees that contains Employee pointers.

Now let's see how a typical virtual function call executes. Consider the call baseClassPtr->print() in function virtualViaPointer (line 75 of Fig. 13.23). Assume that baseClassPtr contains employees[1] (i.e., the address of object hourlyEmployee in employees). When the compiler compiles this statement, it determines that the call is indeed being made via a base-class pointer and that print is a virtual function.

The compiler determines that print is the *second* entry in each of the *vtables*. To locate this entry, the compiler notes that it will need to skip the first entry. Thus, the compiler compiles an **offset** or **displacement** of four bytes (four bytes for each pointer on today's popular 32-bit machines, and only one pointer needs to be skipped) into the table of machine-language object-code pointers to find the code that will execute the virtual function call.

The compiler generates code that performs the following operations [*Note:* The numbers in the list correspond to the circled numbers in Fig. 13.24]:

1. Select the ith entry of employees (in this case, the address of object hourlyEmployee), and pass it as an argument to function virtualViaPointer. This sets parameter baseClassPtr to point to hourlyEmployee.

2. Dereference that pointer to get to the hourlyEmployee object—which, as you recall, begins with a pointer to the HourlyEmployee *vtable*.

3. Dereference hourlyEmployee's *vtable* pointer to get to the HourlyEmployee *vtable*.

4. Skip the offset of four bytes to select the print function pointer.

5. Dereference the print function pointer to form the "name" of the actual function to execute, and use the function call operator () to execute the appropriate print function, which in this case prints the employee's type, name, social security number, hourly wage and hours worked.

Fig. 13.24's data structures may appear to be complex, but this complexity is managed by the compiler and hidden from you, making polymorphic programming straightforward. The pointer dereferencing operations and memory accesses that occur on every virtual function call require some additional execution time. The *vtables* and the *vtable* pointers added to the objects require some additional memory. You now have enough information to determine whether virtual functions are appropriate for your programs.

Performance Tip 13.1
Polymorphism, as typically implemented with virtual functions and dynamic binding in C++, is efficient. You can use these capabilities with nominal impact on performance.

Performance Tip 13.2
Virtual functions and dynamic binding enable polymorphic programming as an alternative to switch logic programming. Optimizing compilers normally generate polymorphic code that runs as efficiently as hand-coded switch-based logic. Polymorphism's overhead is acceptable for most applications. But in some situations—such as real-time applications with stringent performance requirements—polymorphism's overhead may be too high.

Software Engineering Observation 13.11
Dynamic binding enables independent software vendors (ISVs) to distribute software without revealing proprietary secrets. Software distributions can consist of only header files and object files—no source code needs to be revealed. Software developers can then use inheritance to derive new classes from those provided by the ISVs. Other software that worked with the classes the ISVs provided will still work with the derived classes and will use the overridden virtual functions provided in these classes (via dynamic binding).

13.8 Case Study: Payroll System Using Polymorphism and Runtime Type Information with Downcasting, dynamic_cast, typeid and type_info

Recall from the problem statement at the beginning of Section 13.6 that, for the current pay period, our fictitious company has decided to reward BasePlusCommissionEmployees by adding 10 percent to their base salaries. When processing Employee objects polymorphically in Section 13.6.6, we did not need to worry about the "specifics." Now, however, to adjust the base salaries of BasePlusCommissionEmployees, we have to determine the specific type of each Employee object at execution time, then act appropriately. This section demonstrates the powerful capabilities of runtime type information (RTTI) and dynamic casting, which enable a program to determine the type of an object at execution time and act on that object accordingly.

[*Note:* Some compilers require that RTTI be enabled before it can be used in a program. In Visual C++ 2008, this option is enabled by default.]

Figure 13.25 uses the `Employee` hierarchy developed in Section 13.6 and increases by 10 percent the base salary of each `BasePlusCommissionEmployee`. Line 22 declares four-element `vector` `employees` that stores pointers to `Employee` objects. Lines 25–32 populate the `vector` with the addresses of dynamically allocated objects of classes `SalariedEmployee` (Figs. 13.15–13.16), `HourlyEmployee` (Figs. 13.17–13.18), `CommissionEmployee` (Figs. 13.19–13.20) and `BasePlusCommissionEmployee` (Figs. 13.21–13.22).

```cpp
1   // Fig. 13.25: fig13_25.cpp
2   // Demonstrating downcasting and runtime type information.
3   // NOTE: You may need to enable RTTI on your compiler
4   // before you can execute this application.
5   #include <iostream>
6   #include <iomanip>
7   #include <vector>
8   #include <typeinfo>
9   #include "Employee.h"
10  #include "SalariedEmployee.h"
11  #include "HourlyEmployee.h"
12  #include "CommissionEmployee.h"
13  #include "BasePlusCommissionEmployee.h"
14  using namespace std;
15
16  int main()
17  {
18     // set floating-point output formatting
19     cout << fixed << setprecision( 2 );
20
21     // create vector of four base-class pointers
22     vector < Employee * > employees( 4 );
23
24     // initialize vector with various kinds of Employees
25     employees[ 0 ] = new SalariedEmployee(
26        "John", "Smith", "111-11-1111", 800 );
27     employees[ 1 ] = new HourlyEmployee(
28        "Karen", "Price", "222-22-2222", 16.75, 40 );
29     employees[ 2 ] = new CommissionEmployee(
30        "Sue", "Jones", "333-33-3333", 10000, .06 );
31     employees[ 3 ] = new BasePlusCommissionEmployee(
32        "Bob", "Lewis", "444-44-4444", 5000, .04, 300 );
33
34     // polymorphically process each element in vector employees
35     for ( size_t i = 0; i < employees.size(); i++ )
36     {
37        employees[ i ]->print(); // output employee information
38        cout << endl;
39
40        // downcast pointer
41        BasePlusCommissionEmployee *derivedPtr =
42           dynamic_cast < BasePlusCommissionEmployee * >
43              ( employees[ i ] );
44
```

Fig. 13.25 | Demonstrating downcasting and runtime type information. (Part 1 of 2.)

```
45          // determine whether element points to base-salaried
46          // commission employee
47          if ( derivedPtr != 0 ) // 0 if not a BasePlusCommissionEmployee
48          {
49              double oldBaseSalary = derivedPtr->getBaseSalary();
50              cout << "old base salary: $" << oldBaseSalary << endl;
51              derivedPtr->setBaseSalary( 1.10 * oldBaseSalary );
52              cout << "new base salary with 10% increase is: $"
53                  << derivedPtr->getBaseSalary() << endl;
54          } // end if
55
56          cout << "earned $" << employees[ i ]->earnings() << "\n\n";
57      } // end for
58
59      // release objects pointed to by vector's elements
60      for ( size_t j = 0; j < employees.size(); j++ )
61      {
62          // output class name
63          cout << "deleting object of "
64              << typeid( *employees[ j ] ).name() << endl;
65
66          delete employees[ j ];
67      } // end for
68  } // end main
```

```
salaried employee: John Smith
social security number: 111-11-1111
weekly salary: 800.00
earned $800.00

hourly employee: Karen Price
social security number: 222-22-2222
hourly wage: 16.75; hours worked: 40.00
earned $670.00

commission employee: Sue Jones
social security number: 333-33-3333
gross sales: 10000.00; commission rate: 0.06
earned $600.00

base-salaried commission employee: Bob Lewis
social security number: 444-44-4444
gross sales: 5000.00; commission rate: 0.04; base salary: 300.00
old base salary: $300.00
new base salary with 10% increase is: $330.00
earned $530.00

deleting object of class SalariedEmployee
deleting object of class HourlyEmployee
deleting object of class CommissionEmployee
deleting object of class BasePlusCommissionEmployee
```

Fig. 13.25 | Demonstrating downcasting and runtime type information. (Part 2 of 2.)

The for statement in lines 35–57 iterates through the employees vector and displays each Employee's information by invoking member function print (line 37). Recall that because print is declared virtual in base class Employee, the system invokes the appropriate derived-class object's print function.

In this example, as we encounter BasePlusCommissionEmployee objects, we wish to increase their base salary by 10 percent. Since we process the employees generically (i.e., polymorphically), we cannot (with the techniques we've learned) be certain as to which type of Employee is being manipulated at any given time. This creates a problem, because BasePlusCommissionEmployee employees must be identified when we encounter them so they can receive the 10 percent salary increase. To accomplish this, we use operator **dynamic_cast** (line 42) to determine whether the type of each object is BasePlusCommissionEmployee. This is the downcast operation we referred to in Section 13.3.3. Lines 41–43 dynamically downcast employees[i] from type Employee * to type BasePlusCommissionEmployee *. If the vector element points to an object that *is a* BasePlusCommissionEmployee object, then that object's address is assigned to commissionPtr; otherwise, 0 is assigned to derived-class pointer derivedPtr.

If the value returned by the dynamic_cast operator in lines 41–43 is not 0, the object is the correct type, and the if statement (lines 47–54) performs the special processing required for the BasePlusCommissionEmployee object. Lines 49, 51 and 53 invoke BasePlusCommissionEmployee functions getBaseSalary and setBaseSalary to retrieve and update the employee's salary.

Line 56 invokes member function earnings on the object to which employees[i] points. Recall that earnings is declared virtual in the base class, so the program invokes the derived-class object's earnings function—another example of dynamic binding.

Lines 60–67 display each employee's object type and uses the delete operator to deallocate the dynamic memory to which each vector element points. Operator **typeid** (line 64) returns a reference to an object of class **type_info** that contains the information about the type of its operand, including the name of that type. When invoked, type_info member function **name** (line 64) returns a pointer-based string that contains the type name (e.g., "class BasePlusCommissionEmployee") of the argument passed to typeid. To use typeid, the program must include header file **<typeinfo>** (line 8).

Portability Tip 13.1

The string returned by type_info member function name may vary by compiler.

We avoid several compilation errors in this example by downcasting an Employee pointer to a BasePlusCommissionEmployee pointer (lines 41–43). If we remove the dynamic_cast from line 42 and attempt to assign the current Employee pointer directly to BasePlusCommissionEmployee pointer derivedPtr, we'll receive a compilation error. C++ does not allow a program to assign a base-class pointer to a derived-class pointer because the *is-a* relationship does not apply—a CommissionEmployee is *not* a BasePlusCommissionEmployee. The *is-a* relationship applies only between the derived class and its base classes, not vice versa.

Similarly, if lines 49, 51 and 53 used the current base-class pointer from employees, rather than derived-class pointer derivedPtr, to invoke derived-class-only functions getBaseSalary and setBaseSalary, we would receive a compilation error at each of these lines. As you learned in Section 13.3.3, attempting to invoke derived-class-only functions through a base-class pointer is not allowed. Although lines 49, 51 and 53 execute only if commissionPtr is not 0 (i.e., if the cast can be performed), we cannot attempt to invoke derived-class BasePlusCommissionEmployee functions getBaseSalary and setBaseSalary on the base-class Employee pointer. Recall that, using a base class Employee pointer, we can invoke only functions found in base class Employee—earnings, print and Employee's *get* and *set* functions.

13.9 Virtual Destructors

A problem can occur when using polymorphism to process dynamically allocated objects of a class hierarchy. So far you've seen **nonvirtual destructors**—destructors that are not declared with keyword virtual. If a derived-class object with a nonvirtual destructor is destroyed explicitly by applying the delete operator to a base-class pointer to the object, the C++ standard specifies that the behavior is undefined.

The simple solution to this problem is to create a **virtual destructor** (i.e., a destructor that is declared with keyword virtual) in the base class. This makes all derived-class destructors virtual *even though they do not have the same name as the base-class destructor.* Now, if an object in the hierarchy is destroyed explicitly by applying the delete operator to a base-class pointer, the destructor for the appropriate class is called based on the object to which the base-class pointer points. Remember, when a derived-class object is destroyed, the base-class part of the derived-class object is also destroyed, so it's important for the destructors of both the derived class and base class to execute. The base-class destructor automatically executes after the derived-class destructor.

Error-Prevention Tip 13.2

If a class has virtual functions, provide a virtual destructor, even if one is not required for the class. This ensures that a custom derived-class destructor (if there is one) will be invoked when a derived-class object is deleted via a base class pointer.

Common Programming Error 13.5

Constructors cannot be virtual. Declaring a constructor virtual is a compilation error.

13.10 Wrap-Up

In this chapter we discussed polymorphism, which enables us to "program in the general" rather than "program in the specific," and we showed how this makes programs more extensible. We began with an example of how polymorphism would allow a screen manager to display several "space" objects. We then demonstrated how base-class and derived-class pointers can be aimed at base-class and derived-class objects. We said that aiming base-class pointers at base-class objects is natural, as is aiming derived-class pointers at derived-class objects. Aiming base-class pointers at derived-class objects is also natural because a derived-class object *is an* object of its base class. You learned why aiming derived-class pointers at base-class objects is dangerous and why the compiler disallows such assignments. We introduced virtual functions, which enable the proper functions to be called when objects at various levels of an inheritance hierarchy are referenced (at execution time) via base-class pointers. This is known as dynamic or late binding. We then discussed pure virtual functions (virtual functions that do not provide an implementation) and abstract classes

(classes with one or more pure virtual functions). You learned that abstract classes cannot be used to instantiate objects, while concrete classes can. We then demonstrated using abstract classes in an inheritance hierarchy. You learned how polymorphism works "under the hood" with *vtables* that are created by the compiler. We used runtime type information (RTTI) and dynamic casting to determine the type of an object at execution time and act on that object accordingly. The chapter concluded with a discussion of virtual destructors, and how they ensure that all appropriate destructors in an inheritance hierarchy run on a derived-class object when that object is deleted via a base-class pointer.

In the next chapter, we discuss templates, a sophisticated feature of C++ that enables you to define a family of related classes or functions with a single code segment.

Summary

Section 13.1 Introduction
- Polymorphism enables us to "program in the general" rather than "program in the specific."
- Polymorphism enables us to write programs that process objects of classes that are part of the same class hierarchy as if they were all objects of the hierarchy's base class.
- With polymorphism, we can design and implement systems that are easily extensible—new classes can be added with little or no modification to the general portions of the program. The only parts of a program that must be altered to accommodate new classes are those that require direct knowledge of the new classes that you add to the hierarchy.
- Runtime type information (RTTI) and dynamic casting enable a program to determine the type of an object at execution time and act on that object accordingly.

Section 13.2 Polymorphism Examples
- With polymorphism, one function can cause different actions to occur, depending on the type of the object on which the function is invoked.
- This makes it possible to design and implement more extensible systems. Programs can be written to process objects of types that may not exist when the program is under development.

Section 13.3 Relationships Among Objects in an Inheritance Hierarchy
- C++ enables polymorphism—the ability for objects of different classes related by inheritance to respond differently to the same member-function call.
- Polymorphism is implemented via virtual functions and dynamic binding.
- When a base-class pointer or reference is used to call a virtual function, C++ chooses the correct overridden function in the appropriate derived class associated with the object.
- If a virtual function is called by referencing a specific object by name and using the dot member-selection operator, the reference is resolved at compile time (this is called static binding); the virtual function that is called is the one defined for the class of that particular object.
- Derived classes can provide their own implementations of a base-class virtual function if necessary, but if they do not, the base class's implementation is used.

Section 13.4 Type Fields and switch Statements
- Polymorphic programming with virtual functions can eliminate the need for switch logic. You can use the virtual function mechanism to perform the equivalent logic automatically, thus avoiding the kinds of errors typically associated with switch logic.

Section 13.5 Abstract Classes and Pure `virtual` Functions

- Abstract classes are typically used as base classes, so we refer to them as abstract base classes. No objects of an abstract class may be instantiated.

- Classes from which objects can be instantiated are concrete classes.

- You create an abstract class by declaring one or more pure `virtual` functions with pure specifiers (= 0) in their declarations.

- If a class is derived from a class with a pure `virtual` function and that derived class does not supply a definition for that pure `virtual` function, then that `virtual` function remains pure in the derived class. Consequently, the derived class is also an abstract class.

- Although we cannot instantiate objects of abstract base classes, we can declare pointers and references to objects of abstract base classes. Such pointers and references can be used to enable polymorphic manipulations of derived-class objects instantiated from concrete derived classes.

Section 13.7 (Optional) Polymorphism, Virtual Functions and Dynamic Binding "Under the Hood"

- Dynamic binding requires that at runtime, the call to a virtual member function be routed to the `virtual` function version appropriate for the class. A `virtual` function table called the *vtable* is implemented as an array containing function pointers. Each class with `virtual` functions has a *vtable*. For each `virtual` function in the class, the *vtable* has an entry containing a function pointer to the version of the `virtual` function to use for an object of that class. The `virtual` function to use for a particular class could be the function defined in that class, or it could be a function inherited either directly or indirectly from a base class higher in the hierarchy.

- When a base class provides a `virtual` member function, derived classes can override the `virtual` function, but they do not have to override it.

- Each object of a class with `virtual` functions contains a pointer to the *vtable* for that class. When a function call is made from a base-class pointer to a derived-class object, the appropriate function pointer in the *vtable* is obtained and dereferenced to complete the call at execution time.

- Any class that has one or more 0 pointers in its *vtable* is an abstract class. Classes without any 0 *vtable* pointers are concrete classes.

- New kinds of classes are regularly added to systems and accommodated by dynamic binding.

Section 13.8 Case Study: Payroll System Using Polymorphism and Runtime Type Information with Downcasting, `dynamic_cast`, `typeid` and `type_info`

- Operator `dynamic_cast` checks the type of the object to which a pointer points, then determines whether the type has an *is-a* relationship with the type to which the pointer is being converted. If so, `dynamic_cast` returns the object's address. If not, `dynamic_cast` returns 0.

- Operator `typeid` returns a reference to a `type_info` object that contains information about the operand's type, including the type name. To use `typeid`, the program must include header file `<typeinfo>`.

- When invoked, `type_info` member function `name` returns a pointer-based string that contains the name of the type that the `type_info` object represents.

- Operators `dynamic_cast` and `typeid` are part of C++'s runtime type information (RTTI) feature, which allows a program to determine an object's type at runtime.

Section 13.9 Virtual Destructors

- Declare the base-class destructor `virtual` if the class contains `virtual` functions. This makes all derived-class destructors virtual, even though they do not have the same name as the base-class destructor. If an object in the hierarchy is destroyed explicitly by applying the `delete` operator to a base-class pointer to a derived-class object, the destructor for the appropriate class is called. After a derived-class destructor runs, the destructors for all of that class's base classes run all the way up the hierarchy.

Terminology

abstract base classes 593	offset into a *vtable* 615
abstract classes 593	override 586
concrete classes 593	polymorphism 573
displacement into a *vtable* 615	pure specifier (with virtual functions) 594
downcasting 586	pure virtual function 594
dynamic binding 587	runtime type information (RTTI) 574
dynamic casting 574	static binding 587
dynamic_cast 619	typeid operator 619
implementation inheritance 596	type_info class 619
interface inheritance 596	<typeinfo> header file 619
iterator class 595	virtual destructor 620
late binding 587	virtual function 586
name function of class type_info 619	virtual function table (*vtable*) 613
nonvirtual destructor 620	

Self-Review Exercises

13.1 Fill in the blanks in each of the following statements:

a) Treating a base-class object as a(n) _____ can cause errors.
b) Polymorphism helps eliminate _____ logic.
c) If a class contains at least one pure virtual function, it's a(n) _____ class.
d) Classes from which objects can be instantiated are called _____ classes.
e) Operator _____ can be used to downcast base-class pointers safely.
f) Operator typeid returns a reference to a(n) _____ object.
g) _____ involves using a base-class pointer or reference to invoke virtual functions on base-class and derived-class objects.
h) Overridable functions are declared using keyword _____.
i) Casting a base-class pointer to a derived-class pointer is called _____.

13.2 State whether each of the following is *true* or *false*. If *false*, explain why.

a) All virtual functions in an abstract base class must be declared as pure virtual functions.
b) Referring to a derived-class object with a base-class handle is dangerous.
c) A class is made abstract by declaring that class virtual.
d) If a base class declares a pure virtual function, a derived class must implement that function to become a concrete class.
e) Polymorphic programming can eliminate the need for switch logic.

Answers to Self-Review Exercises

13.1 a) derived-class object. b) switch. c) abstract. d) concrete. e) dynamic_cast. f) type_info. g) Polymorphism. h) virtual. i) downcasting.

13.2 a) False. An abstract base class can include virtual functions with implementations. b) False. Referring to a base-class object with a derived-class handle is dangerous. c) False. Classes are never declared virtual. Rather, a class is made abstract by including at least one pure virtual function in the class. d) True. e) True.

Exercises

13.3 How is it that polymorphism enables you to program "in the general" rather than "in the specific"? Discuss the key advantages of programming "in the general."

13.4 Discuss the problems of programming with switch logic. Explain why polymorphism can be an effective alternative to using switch logic.

13.5 Distinguish between inheriting interface and inheriting implementation. How do inheritance hierarchies designed for inheriting interface differ from those designed for inheriting implementation?

13.6 What are virtual functions? Describe a circumstance in which virtual functions would be appropriate.

13.7 Distinguish between static binding and dynamic binding. Explain the use of virtual functions and the *vtable* in dynamic binding.

13.8 Distinguish between virtual functions and pure virtual functions.

13.9 *(Abstract Base Classes)* Suggest one or more levels of abstract base classes for the Shape hierarchy discussed in this chapter and shown in Fig. 12.3. (The first level is Shape, and the second level consists of the classes TwoDimensionalShape and ThreeDimensionalShape.)

13.10 How does polymorphism promote extensibility?

13.11 You've been asked to develop a flight simulator that will have elaborate graphical outputs. Explain why polymorphic programming could be especially effective for a problem of this nature.

13.12 *(Payroll System Modification)* Modify the payroll system of Figs. 13.13–13.23 to include private data member birthDate in class Employee. Use class Date from Figs. 11.9–11.10 to represent an employee's birthday. Assume that payroll is processed once per month. Create a vector of Employee references to store the various employee objects. In a loop, calculate the payroll for each Employee (polymorphically), and add a $100.00 bonus to the person's payroll amount if the current month is the month in which the Employee's birthday occurs.

13.13 *(Shape Hierarchy)* Implement the Shape hierarchy designed in Exercise 12.7 (which is based on the hierarchy in Fig. 12.3). Each TwoDimensionalShape should contain function getArea to calculate the area of the two-dimensional shape. Each ThreeDimensionalShape should have member functions getArea and getVolume to calculate the surface area and volume, respectively, of the three-dimensional shape. Create a program that uses a vector of Shape pointers to objects of each concrete class in the hierarchy. The program should print the object to which each vector element points. Also, in the loop that processes all the shapes in the vector, determine whether each shape is a TwoDimensionalShape or a ThreeDimensionalShape. If a shape is a TwoDimensionalShape, display its area. If a shape is a ThreeDimensionalShape, display its area and volume.

13.14 *(Project: Polymorphic Screen Manager Using Shape Hierarchy)* Develop a basic graphics package. Use the Shape hierarchy implemented in Exercise 13.13. Limit yourself to two-dimensional shapes such as squares, rectangles, triangles and circles. Interact with the user. Let the user specify the position, size, shape and fill characters to be used in drawing each shape. The user can specify more than one of the same shape. As you create each shape, place a Shape * pointer to each new Shape object into an array. Each Shape class should now have its own draw member function. Write a polymorphic screen manager that walks through the array, sending draw messages to each object in the array to form a screen image. Redraw the screen image each time the user specifies an additional shape.

13.15 *(Package Inheritance Hierarchy)* Use the Package inheritance hierarchy created in Exercise 12.9 to create a program that displays the address information and calculates the shipping costs for several Packages. The program should contain a vector of Package pointers to objects of classes TwoDayPackage and OvernightPackage. Loop through the vector to process the Packages polymorphically. For each Package, invoke *get* functions to obtain the address information of the sender and the recipient, then print the two addresses as they would appear on mailing labels. Also, call each Package's calculateCost member function and print the result. Keep track of the total shipping cost for all Packages in the vector, and display this total when the loop terminates.

13.16 *(Polymorphic Banking Program Using* Account *Hierarchy)* Develop a polymorphic banking program using the Account hierarchy created in Exercise 12.10. Create a vector of Account pointers to SavingsAccount and CheckingAccount objects. For each Account in the vector, allow the user to specify an amount of money to withdraw from the Account using member function debit and an amount of money to deposit into the Account using member function credit. As you process each Account, determine its type. If an Account is a SavingsAccount, calculate the amount of interest owed to the Account using member function calculateInterest, then add the interest to the account balance using member function credit. After processing an Account, print the updated account balance obtained by invoking base-class member function getBalance.

Making a Difference

13.17 *(CarbonFootprint Abstract Class: Polymorphism)* Using an abstract class with only pure virtual functions, you can specify similar behaviors for possibly disparate classes. Governments and companies worldwide are becoming increasingly concerned with carbon footprints (annual releases of carbon dioxide into the atmosphere) from buildings burning various types of fuels for heat, vehicles burning fuels for power, and the like. Many scientists blame these greenhouse gases for the phenomenon called global warming. Create three small classes unrelated by inheritance—classes Building, Car and Bicycle. Give each class some unique appropriate attributes and behaviors that it does not have in common with other classes. Write an abstract class CarbonFootprint with only a pure virtual getCarbonFootprint method. Have each of your classes inherit from that abstract class and implement the getCarbonFootprint method to calculate an appropriate carbon footprint for that class (check out a few websites that explain how to calculate carbon footprints). Write an application that creates objects of each of the three classes, places pointers to those objects in a vector of CarbonFootprint pointers, then iterates through the vector, polymorphically invoking each object's getCarbonFootprint method. For each object, print some identifying information and the object's carbon footprint.

14

Templates

Behind that outside pattern the dim shapes get clearer every day.
It is always the same shape, only very numerous.
—Charlotte Perkins Gilman

Every man of genius sees the world at a different angle from his fellows.
—Havelock Ellis

...our special individuality, as distinguished from our generic humanity.
—Oliver Wendell Holmes, Sr

Objectives

In this chapter you'll learn:

- To use function templates to conveniently create a group of related (overloaded) functions.

- To distinguish between function templates and function-template specializations.

- To use class templates to create groups of related types.

- To distinguish between class templates and class-template specializations.

- To overload function templates.

- To understand the relationships among templates, friends, inheritance and static members.

14.1 Introduction

In this chapter, we discuss one of C++'s more powerful software reuse features, namely **templates**. **Function templates** and **class templates** enable you to specify, with a single code segment, an entire range of related (overloaded) functions—called **function-template specializations**—or an entire range of related classes—called **class-template specializations**. This technique is called **generic programming**.

We might write a single function template for an array-sort function, then have C++ generate separate function-template specializations that will sort `int` arrays, `float` arrays, `string` arrays and so on. We introduced function templates in Chapter 6. We present an additional discussion and example in this chapter.

We might write a single class template for a stack class, then have C++ generate separate class-template specializations, such as a stack-of-`int` class, a stack-of-`float` class, a stack-of-`string` class and so on.

Note the distinction between templates and template specializations: Function templates and class templates are like stencils out of which we trace shapes; function-template specializations and class-template specializations are like the separate tracings that all have the same shape, but could, for example, be drawn in different colors.

In this chapter, we present a function template and a class template. We also consider the relationships between templates and other C++ features, such as overloading, inheritance, friends and `static` members. The design and details of the template mechanisms discussed here are based on the work of Bjarne Stroustrup as presented in his paper, "Parameterized Types for C++"—published in the *Proceedings of the USENIX C++ Conference* held in Denver, Colorado, in October 1988.

This chapter is only an introduction to templates. Chapter 22, Standard Template Library (STL), presents an in-depth treatment of the template container classes, iterators and algorithms of the STL. Chapter 22 contains dozens of live-code template-based examples illustrating more sophisticated template-programming techniques than those used here.

Software Engineering Observation 14.1

Most C++ compilers require the complete definition of a template to appear in the client source-code file that uses the template. For this reason and for reusability, templates are often defined in header files, which are then #included into the appropriate client source-code files. For class templates, this means that the member functions are also defined in the header file.

14.2 Function Templates

Overloaded functions normally perform *similar* or *identical* operations on different types of data. If the operations are *identical* for each type, they can be expressed more compactly and conveniently using function templates. Initially, you write a single function-template definition. Based on the argument types provided explicitly or inferred from calls to this function, the compiler generates separate source-code functions (i.e., function-template specializations) to handle each function call appropriately. In C, this task can be performed using **macros** created with the preprocessor directive #define (see Appendix E, Preprocessor). However, macros can have serious side effects and do not enable the compiler to perform type checking. Function templates provide a compact solution, like macros, but enable full type checking.

Error-Prevention Tip 14.1

Function templates, like macros, enable software reuse. Unlike macros, function templates help eliminate many types of errors through the scrutiny of full C++ type checking.

All **function-template definitions** begin with keyword **template** followed by a list of **template parameters** to the function template enclosed in **angle brackets** (< and >); each template parameter that represents a type must be preceded by either of the interchangeable keywords class or **typename**, as in

```
template< typename T >
```

or

```
template< class ElementType >
```

or

```
template< typename BorderType, typename FillType >
```

The type template parameters of a function-template definition are used to specify the types of the arguments to the function, to specify the return type of the function and to declare variables within the function. The function definition follows and appears like any other function definition. Keywords typename and class used to specify function-template parameters actually mean "any fundamental type or user-defined type."

Common Programming Error 14.1

Not placing keyword class or keyword typename before each type template parameter of a function template is a syntax error.

Example: Function Template *printArray*
Let's examine function template printArray in Fig. 14.1, lines 7–14. Function template printArray declares (line 7) a single template parameter T (T can be any valid identifier) for the type of the array to be printed by function printArray; T is referred to as a **type template parameter**, or type parameter. You'll see nontype template parameters in Section 14.5.

```
1    // Fig. 14.1: fig14_01.cpp
2    // Using template functions.
3    #include <iostream>
4    using namespace std;
5
6    // function template printArray definition
7    template< typename T >
8    void printArray( const T * const array, int count )
9    {
10      for ( int i = 0; i < count; i++ )
11         cout << array[ i ] << " ";
12
13      cout << endl;
14   } // end function template printArray
15
16   int main()
17   {
18      const int aCount = 5; // size of array a
19      const int bCount = 7; // size of array b
20      const int cCount = 6; // size of array c
21
22      int a[ aCount ] = { 1, 2, 3, 4, 5 };
23      double b[ bCount ] = { 1.1, 2.2, 3.3, 4.4, 5.5, 6.6, 7.7 };
24      char c[ cCount ] = "HELLO"; // 6th position for null
25
26      cout << "Array a contains:" << endl;
27
28      // call integer function-template specialization
29      printArray( a, aCount );
30
31      cout << "Array b contains:" << endl;
32
33      // call double function-template specialization
34      printArray( b, bCount );
35
36      cout << "Array c contains:" << endl;
37
38      // call character function-template specialization
39      printArray( c, cCount );
40   } // end main
```

```
Array a contains:
1 2 3 4 5
Array b contains:
1.1 2.2 3.3 4.4 5.5 6.6 7.7
Array c contains:
H E L L O
```

Fig. 14.1 | Function-template specializations of function template printArray.

When the compiler detects a printArray function invocation in the client program (e.g., lines 29, 34 and 39), the compiler uses its overload resolution capabilities to find a definition of function printArray that best matches the function call. In this case, the only `printArray` function with the appropriate number of parameters is the `printArray` function template (lines 7–14). Consider the function call at line 29. The compiler compares the type of `printArray`'s first argument (`int *` at line 29) to the `printArray` function template's first parameter (`const T * const` at line 8) and deduces that replacing the type parameter `T` with `int` would make the argument consistent with the parameter. Then, the compiler substitutes `int` for `T` throughout the template definition and compiles a `printArray` specialization that can display an array of `int` values. In Fig. 14.1, the compiler creates three `printArray` specializations—one that expects an `int` array, one that expects a `double` array and one that expects a `char` array. For example, the function-template specialization for type `int` is

```
void printArray( const int * const array, int count )
{
   for ( int i = 0; i < count; i++ )
      cout << array[ i ] << " ";

   cout << endl;
} // end function printArray
```

As with function parameters, the names of template parameters must be unique inside a template definition. Template parameter names need not be unique across different function templates.

Figure 14.1 demonstrates function template `printArray` (lines 7–14). The program begins by declaring five-element `int` array a, seven-element `double` array b and six-element `char` array c (lines 22–24, respectively). Then, the program outputs each array by calling `printArray`—once with a first argument a of type `int *` (line 29), once with a first argument b of type `double *` (line 34) and once with a first argument c of type `char *` (line 39). The call in line 29, for example, causes the compiler to infer that `T` is `int` and to instantiate a `printArray` function-template specialization, for which type parameter `T` is `int`. The call in line 34 causes the compiler to infer that `T` is `double` and to instantiate a second `printArray` function-template specialization, for which type parameter `T` is `double`. The call in line 39 causes the compiler to infer that `T` is `char` and to instantiate a third `printArray` function-template specialization, for which type parameter `T` is `char`. It's important to note that if `T` (line 7) represents a user-defined type (which it does not in Fig. 14.1), there must be an overloaded stream insertion operator for that type; otherwise, the first stream insertion operator in line 11 will not compile.

Common Programming Error 14.2

If a template is invoked with a user-defined type, and if that template uses functions or operators (e.g., ==, +, <=) with objects of that class type, then those functions and operators must be overloaded for the user-defined type. Forgetting to overload such operators causes compilation errors.

In this example, the template mechanism saves you from having to write three separate overloaded functions with prototypes

```
void printArray( const int * const, int );
void printArray( const double * const, int );
void printArray( const char * const, int );
```

that all use the same code, except for type `T` (as used in line 8).

Performance Tip 14.1

Although templates offer software-reusability benefits, remember that multiple function-template specializations and class-template specializations are instantiated in a program (at compile time), despite the fact that the templates are written only once. These copies can consume considerable memory. This is not normally an issue, though, because the code generated by the template is the same size as the code you'd have written to produce the separate overloaded functions.

14.3 Overloading Function Templates

Function templates and overloading are intimately related. The function-template specializations generated from a function template all have the same name, so the compiler uses overloading resolution to invoke the proper function.

A function template may be overloaded in several ways. We can provide other function templates that specify the same function name but different function parameters. For example, function template printArray of Fig. 14.1 could be overloaded with another printArray function template with additional parameters lowSubscript and highSubscript to specify the portion of the array to output (see Exercise 14.4).

A function template also can be overloaded by providing nontemplate functions with the same function name but different function arguments. For example, function template printArray of Fig. 14.1 could be overloaded with a nontemplate version that specifically prints an array of character strings in neat, tabular format (see Exercise 14.5).

The compiler performs a matching process to determine what function to call when a function is invoked. First, the compiler tries to find and use a precise match in which the function names and argument types are consistent with those of the function call. If this fails, the compiler determines whether a function template is available that can be used to generate a function-template specialization with a precise match of function name and argument types. If such a function template is found, the compiler generates and uses the appropriate function-template specialization. If not, the compiler generates an error message. Also, if there are multiple matches for the function call, the compiler considers the call to be ambiguous and the compiler generates an error message.

Common Programming Error 14.3

A compilation error occurs if no matching function definition can be found for a particular function call or if there are multiple matches that the compiler considers ambiguous.

14.4 Class Templates

It's possible to understand the concept of a "stack" (a data structure into which we insert items at the top and retrieve those items in last-in, first-out order) independent of the type of the items being placed in the stack. However, to instantiate a stack, a data type must be specified. This creates a wonderful opportunity for software reusability. We need the means for describing the notion of a stack generically and instantiating classes that are type-specific versions of this generic stack class. C++ provides this capability through class templates.

Software Engineering Observation 14.2

Class templates encourage software reusability by enabling type-specific versions of generic classes to be instantiated.

Class templates are called **parameterized types**, because they require one or more type parameters to specify how to customize a "generic class" template to form a class-template specialization.

To produce a variety of class-template specializations you write only one class-template definition. Each time an additional class-template specialization is needed, you use a concise, simple notation, and the compiler writes the source code for the specialization you require. One Stack class template, for example, could thus become the basis for creating many Stack classes (such as "Stack of double," "Stack of int," "Stack of char," "Stack of Employee," etc.) used in a program.

Creating Class Template Stack< T >

Note the Stack class-template definition in Fig. 14.2. It looks like a conventional class definition, except that it's preceded by the header (line 6)

```
template< typename T >
```

to specify a class-template definition with type parameter T which acts as a placeholder for the type of the Stack class to be created. You need not specifically use identifier T—any valid identifier can be used. The type of element to be stored on this Stack is mentioned generically as T throughout the Stack class header and member-function definitions. In a moment, we show how T becomes associated with a specific type, such as double or int. Due to the way this class template is designed, there are two constraints for nonfundamental data types used with this Stack—they must have a default constructor (for use in line 44 to create the array that stores the stack elements), and their assignment operators must properly copy objects into the Stack (lines 56 and 70).

```
 1   // Fig. 14.2: Stack.h
 2   // Stack class template.
 3   #ifndef STACK_H
 4   #define STACK_H
 5
 6   template< typename T >
 7   class Stack
 8   {
 9   public:
10      Stack( int = 10 ); // default constructor (Stack size 10)
11
12      // destructor
13      ~Stack()
14      {
15         delete [] stackPtr; // deallocate internal space for Stack
16      } // end ~Stack destructor
17
18      bool push( const T & ); // push an element onto the Stack
19      bool pop( T & ); // pop an element off the Stack
```

Fig. 14.2 | Class template Stack. (Part 1 of 3.)

```
20
21     // determine whether Stack is empty
22     bool isEmpty() const
23     {
24        return top == -1;
25     } // end function isEmpty
26
27     // determine whether Stack is full
28     bool isFull() const
29     {
30        return top == size - 1;
31     } // end function isFull
32
33  private:
34     int size; // # of elements in the Stack
35     int top; // location of the top element (-1 means empty)
36     T *stackPtr; // pointer to internal representation of the Stack
37  }; // end class template Stack
38
39  // constructor template
40  template< typename T >
41  Stack< T >::Stack( int s )
42     : size( s > 0 ? s : 10 ), // validate size
43       top( -1 ), // Stack initially empty
44       stackPtr( new T[ size ] ) // allocate memory for elements
45  {
46     // empty body
47  } // end Stack constructor template
48
49  // push element onto Stack;
50  // if successful, return true; otherwise, return false
51  template< typename T >
52  bool Stack< T >::push( const T &pushValue )
53  {
54     if ( !isFull() )
55     {
56        stackPtr[ ++top ] = pushValue; // place item on Stack
57        return true; // push successful
58     } // end if
59
60     return false; // push unsuccessful
61  } // end function template push
62
63  // pop element off Stack;
64  // if successful, return true; otherwise, return false
65  template< typename T >
66  bool Stack< T >::pop( T &popValue )
67  {
68     if ( !isEmpty() )
69     {
70        popValue = stackPtr[ top-- ]; // remove item from Stack
71        return true; // pop successful
72     } // end if
```

Fig. 14.2 | Class template Stack. (Part 2 of 3.)

```
73
74      return false; // pop unsuccessful
75   } // end function template pop
76
77   #endif
```

Fig. 14.2 | Class template Stack. (Part 3 of 3.)

The member-function definitions of a class template are function templates. The member-function definitions that appear outside the class template definition each begin with the header

```
    template< typename T >
```

(lines 40, 51 and 65). Thus, each definition resembles a conventional function definition, except that the Stack element type always is listed generically as type parameter T. The binary scope resolution operator is used with the class-template name Stack< T > (lines 41, 52 and 66) to tie each member-function definition to the class template's scope. In this case, the generic class name is Stack< T >. When doubleStack is instantiated as type Stack<double>, the Stack constructor function-template specialization uses new to create an array of elements of type double to represent the stack (line 44). The statement

```
    stackPtr( new T[ size ] );
```

in the Stack class-template definition is generated by the compiler in the class-template specialization Stack<double> as

```
    stackPtr( new double[ size ] );
```

Creating a Driver to Test Class Template **Stack< T >**
Now, let's consider the driver (Fig. 14.3) that exercises the Stack class template. The driver begins by instantiating object doubleStack of size 5 (line 9). This object is declared to be of class Stack< double > (pronounced "Stack of double"). The compiler associates type double with type parameter T in the class template to produce the source code for a Stack class of type double. Although templates offer software-reusability benefits, remember that multiple class-template specializations are instantiated in a program (at compile time), even though the template is written only once.

```
1   // Fig. 14.3: fig14_03.cpp
2   // Stack class template test program.
3   #include <iostream>
4   #include "Stack.h" // Stack class template definition
5   using namespace std;
6
7   int main()
8   {
9      Stack< double > doubleStack( 5 ); // size 5
10     double doubleValue = 1.1;
11
```

Fig. 14.3 | Class template Stack test program. (Part 1 of 2.)

```
12      cout << "Pushing elements onto doubleStack\n";
13
14      // push 5 doubles onto doubleStack
15      while ( doubleStack.push( doubleValue ) )
16      {
17         cout << doubleValue << ' ';
18         doubleValue += 1.1;
19      } // end while
20
21      cout << "\nStack is full. Cannot push " << doubleValue
22         << "\n\nPopping elements from doubleStack\n";
23
24      // pop elements from doubleStack
25      while ( doubleStack.pop( doubleValue ) )
26         cout << doubleValue << ' ';
27
28      cout << "\nStack is empty. Cannot pop\n";
29
30      Stack< int > intStack; // default size 10
31      int intValue = 1;
32      cout << "\nPushing elements onto intStack\n";
33
34      // push 10 integers onto intStack
35      while ( intStack.push( intValue ) )
36      {
37         cout << intValue++ << ' ';
38      } // end while
39
40      cout << "\nStack is full. Cannot push " << intValue
41         << "\n\nPopping elements from intStack\n";
42
43      // pop elements from intStack
44      while ( intStack.pop( intValue ) )
45         cout << intValue << ' ';
46
47      cout << "\nStack is empty. Cannot pop" << endl;
48   } // end main
```

```
Pushing elements onto doubleStack
1.1 2.2 3.3 4.4 5.5
Stack is full. Cannot push 6.6

Popping elements from doubleStack
5.5 4.4 3.3 2.2 1.1
Stack is empty. Cannot pop

Pushing elements onto intStack
1 2 3 4 5 6 7 8 9 10
Stack is full. Cannot push 11

Popping elements from intStack
10 9 8 7 6 5 4 3 2 1
Stack is empty. Cannot pop
```

Fig. 14.3 | Class template Stack test program. (Part 2 of 2.)

Lines 15–19 invoke push to place the double values 1.1, 2.2, 3.3, 4.4 and 5.5 onto doubleStack. The while loop terminates when the driver attempts to push a sixth value onto doubleStack (which is full, because it holds a maximum of five elements). Function push returns false when it's unable to push a value onto the stack.[1]

Lines 25–26 invoke pop in a while loop to remove the five values from the stack (note, in the output of Fig. 14.3, that the values do pop off in last-in, first-out order). When the driver attempts to pop a sixth value, the doubleStack is empty, so the pop loop terminates.

Line 30 instantiates integer stack intStack with the declaration

```
Stack< int > intStack;
```

(pronounced "intStack is a Stack of int"). Because no size is specified, the size defaults to 10 as specified in the default constructor (Fig. 14.2, line 10). Lines 35–38 loop and invoke push to place values onto intStack until it's full, then lines 44–45 loop and invoke pop to remove values from intStack until it's empty. Once again, notice in the output that the values pop off in last-in, first-out order.

*Creating Function Templates to Test Class Template **Stack< T >***
Notice that the code in function main of Fig. 14.3 is almost identical for both the double-Stack manipulations in lines 9–28 and the intStack manipulations in lines 30–47. This presents another opportunity to use a function template. Figure 14.4 defines function template testStack (lines 10–34) to perform the same tasks as main in Fig. 14.3—push a series of values onto a Stack< T > and pop the values off a Stack< T >. Function template testStack uses template parameter T (specified at line 10) to represent the data type stored in the Stack< T >. The function template takes four arguments (lines 12–15)—a reference to an object of type Stack< T >, a value of type T that will be the first value pushed onto the Stack< T >, a value of type T used to increment the values pushed onto the Stack< T > and a string that represents the name of the Stack< T > object for output purposes. Function main (lines 36–43) instantiates an object of type Stack< double > called doubleStack (line 38) and an object of type Stack< int > called intStack (line 39) and uses these objects in lines 41 and 42. The compiler infers the type of T for testStack from the type used to instantiate the function's first argument (i.e., the type used to instantiate double-Stack or intStack). The output of Fig. 14.4 precisely matches the output of Fig. 14.3.

```
1   // Fig. 14.4: fig14_04.cpp
2   // Stack class template test program. Function main uses a
3   // function template to manipulate objects of type Stack< T >.
4   #include <iostream>
5   #include <string>
6   #include "Stack.h" // Stack class template definition
```

Fig. 14.4 | Passing a Stack template object to a function template. (Part 1 of 2.)

---

1. Class Stack (Fig. 14.2) provides the function isFull, which you can use to determine whether the stack is full before attempting a push operation. This would avoid the potential error of pushing onto a full stack. As we discuss in Chapter 16, Exception Handling, if the operation cannot be completed, function push would "throw an exception." You can write code to "catch" that exception, then decide how to handle it appropriately for the application. The same technique can be used with function pop when an attempt is made to pop an element from an empty stack.

```
 7   using namespace std;
 8
 9   // function template to manipulate Stack< T >
10   template< typename T >
11   void testStack(
12      Stack< T > &theStack, // reference to Stack< T >
13      T value, // initial value to push
14      T increment, // increment for subsequent values
15      const string stackName ) // name of the Stack< T > object
16   {
17      cout << "\nPushing elements onto " << stackName << '\n';
18
19      // push element onto Stack
20      while ( theStack.push( value ) )
21      {
22         cout << value << ' ';
23         value += increment;
24      } // end while
25
26      cout << "\nStack is full. Cannot push " << value
27         << "\n\nPopping elements from " << stackName << '\n';
28
29      // pop elements from Stack
30      while ( theStack.pop( value ) )
31         cout << value << ' ';
32
33      cout << "\nStack is empty. Cannot pop" << endl;
34   } // end function template testStack
35
36   int main()
37   {
38      Stack< double > doubleStack( 5 ); // size 5
39      Stack< int > intStack; // default size 10
40
41      testStack( doubleStack, 1.1, 1.1, "doubleStack" );
42      testStack( intStack, 1, 1, "intStack" );
43   } // end main
```

```
Pushing elements onto doubleStack
1.1 2.2 3.3 4.4 5.5
Stack is full. Cannot push 6.6

Popping elements from doubleStack
5.5 4.4 3.3 2.2 1.1
Stack is empty. Cannot pop

Pushing elements onto intStack
1 2 3 4 5 6 7 8 9 10
Stack is full. Cannot push 11

Popping elements from intStack
10 9 8 7 6 5 4 3 2 1
Stack is empty. Cannot pop
```

Fig. 14.4 | Passing a Stack template object to a function template. (Part 2 of 2.)

14.5 Nontype Parameters and Default Types for Class Templates

Class template `Stack` of Section 14.4 used only a type parameter in the template header (Fig. 14.2, line 6). It's also possible to use **non-type template parameters**, which can have default arguments and are treated as `const`s. For example, the template header could be modified to take an `int elements` parameter as follows:

```
template< typename T, int elements > // nontype parameter elements
```

Then, a declaration such as

```
Stack< double, 100 > mostRecentSalesFigures;
```

could be used to instantiate (at compile time) a 100-element `Stack` class-template specialization of `double` values named `mostRecentSalesFigures`; this class-template specialization would be of type `Stack< double, 100 >`. The class definition then might contain a `private` data member with an array declaration such as

```
T stackHolder[ elements ]; // array to hold Stack contents
```

In addition, a type parameter can specify a **default type**. For example,

```
template< typename T = string > // defaults to type string
```

might specify that a `Stack` contains `string` objects by default. Then, a declaration such as

```
Stack<> jobDescriptions;
```

could be used to instantiate a `Stack` class-template specialization of `string`s named `jobDescriptions`; this class-template specialization would be of type `Stack< string >`. Default type parameters must be the rightmost (trailing) parameters in a template's type-parameter list. When one is instantiating a class with two or more default types, if an omitted type is not the rightmost type parameter in the type-parameter list, then all type parameters to the right of that type also must be omitted.

Performance Tip 14.2
When appropriate, specify the size of a container class (such as an array class or a stack class) at compile time (possibly through a nontype template parameter). This eliminates the execution-time overhead of using new to create the space dynamically.

Software Engineering Observation 14.3
Specifying the size of a container at compile time avoids the potentially fatal execution-time error if new is unable to obtain the needed memory.

In the exercises, you'll be asked to use a nontype parameter to create a template for our class `Array` from Chapter 11. This template will enable `Array` objects to be instantiated with a specified number of elements of a specified type at compile time, rather than creating space for the `Array` objects at execution time.

In some cases, it may not be possible to use a particular type with a class template. For example, the `Stack` template of Fig. 14.2 requires that user-defined types that will be stored in a `Stack` must provide a default constructor and an assignment operator that properly copies objects. If a particular user-defined type will not work with our `Stack` template or requires customized processing, you can define an **explicit specialization** of the class template for a particular type. Let's assume we want to create an explicit specialization `Stack` for `Employee` objects. To do this, form a new class with the name `Stack< Employee >` as follows:

```
template<>
class Stack< Employee >
{
   // body of class definition
};
```

The `Stack<Employee>` explicit specialization is a complete replacement for the `Stack` class template that is specific to type `Employee`—it does not use anything from the original class template and can even have different members.

14.6 Notes on Templates and Inheritance

Templates and inheritance relate in several ways:

- A class template can be derived from a class-template specialization.
- A class template can be derived from a nontemplate class.
- A class-template specialization can be derived from a class-template specialization.
- A nontemplate class can be derived from a class-template specialization.

14.7 Notes on Templates and Friends

We've seen that functions and entire classes can be declared as `friends` of nontemplate classes. With class templates, friendship can be established between a class template and a global function, a member function of another class (possibly a class-template specialization), or even an entire class (possibly a class-template specialization).

Throughout this section, we assume that we've defined a class template for a class named X with a single type parameter T, as in:

```
template< typename T > class X
```

Under this assumption, it's possible to make a function f1 a friend of every class-template specialization instantiated from the class template for class X. To do so, use a friendship declaration of the form

```
friend void f1();
```

For example, function f1 is a friend of X< double >, X< string > and X< Employee >, etc.

It's also possible to make a function f2 a friend of only a class-template specialization with the same type argument. To do so, use a friendship declaration of the form

```
friend void f2( X< T > & );
```

For example, if T is a `float`, function f2(X< float > &) is a friend of class-template specialization X< float > but not a friend of class-template specification X< string >.

You can declare that a member function of another class is a friend of any class-template specialization generated from the class template. To do so, the `friend` declaration must qualify the name of the other class's member function using the class name and the binary scope resolution operator, as in:

```
friend void A::f3();
```

The declaration makes member function f3 of class A a friend of every class-template specialization instantiated from the preceding class template. For example, function f3 of class A is a friend of X< double >, X< string > and X< Employee >, etc.

As with a global function, another class's member function can be a friend of only a class-template specialization with the same type argument. A friendship declaration of the form

```
friend void C< T >::f4( X< T > & );
```

for a particular type T such as float makes class C's member function

```
C< float >::f4( X< float > & )
```

a friend function of *only* class-template specialization X< float >.

In some cases, it's desirable to make an entire class's set of member functions friends of a class template. In this case, a friend declaration of the form

```
friend class Y;
```

makes every member function of class Y a friend of every class-template specialization produced from the class template X.

Finally, it's possible to make all member functions of one class-template specialization friends of another class-template specialization with the same type argument. For example, a friend declaration of the form:

```
friend class Z< T >;
```

indicates that when a class-template specialization is instantiated with a particular type for T (such as float), all members of class Z< float > become friends of class-template specialization X< float >. We use this particular relationship in Chapter 20, Data Structures.

14.8 Notes on Templates and static Members

What about static data members? Recall that, with a nontemplate class, one copy of each static data member is shared among all objects of the class, and the static data member must be initialized at global namespace scope.

Each class-template specialization instantiated from a class template has its own copy of each static data member of the class template; all objects of that specialization share that one static data member. In addition, as with static data members of nontemplate classes, static data members of class-template specializations must be defined and, if necessary, initialized at global namespace scope. Each class-template specialization gets its own copy of the class template's static member functions.

14.9 Wrap-Up

This chapter introduced one of C++'s most powerful features—templates. You learned how to use function templates to enable the compiler to produce a set of function-template specializations that represent a group of related overloaded functions. We also discussed how to overload a function template to create a specialized version of a function that handles a particular data type's processing in a manner that differs from the other function-template specializations. Next, you learned about class templates and class-template specializations. You saw examples of how to use a class template to create a group of related types that each perform identical processing on different data types. Finally, you learned about some of the relationships among templates, friends, inheritance and static members. In the next chapter, we discuss many of C++'s I/O capabilities and demonstrate several stream manipulators that perform various formatting tasks.

Summary

Section 14.1 Introduction
- Templates enable us to specify a range of related (overloaded) functions—called function-template specializations—or a range of related classes—called class-template specializations.

Section 14.2 Function Templates
- To use function-template specializations, you write a single function-template definition. Based on the argument types provided in calls to this function, C++ generates separate specializations to handle each type of call appropriately.
- All function-template definitions begin with the keyword template followed by template parameters enclosed in angle brackets (< and >); each template parameter that represents a type must be preceded by keyword class or typename. Keywords typename and class used to specify function-template parameters mean "any fundamental type or user-defined type."
- Template-definition template parameters are used to specify the kinds of arguments to the function, the return type of the function and to declare variables in the function.
- As with function parameters, the names of template parameters must be unique inside a template definition. Template parameter names need not be unique across different function templates.

Section 14.3 Overloading Function Templates
- A function template may be overloaded in several ways. We can provide other function templates that specify the same function name but different function parameters. A function template can also be overloaded by providing other nontemplate functions with the same function name, but different function parameters. If both the template and non-template versions match a call, the non-template version will be used.

Section 14.4 Class Templates
- Class templates provide the means for describing a class generically and for instantiating classes that are type-specific versions of this generic class.
- Class templates are called parameterized types; they require type parameters to specify how to customize a generic class template to form a specific class-template specialization.
- To use class-template specializations you write one class template. When you need a new type-specific class, the compiler writes the source code for the class-template specialization.
- A class-template definition looks like a conventional class definition, except that it's preceded by template< typename T > (or template< class T >) to indicate this is a class-template definition. Type parameter T acts as a placeholder for the type of the class to create. The type T is mentioned throughout the class definition and member-function definitions as a generic type name.

- Member-function definitions outside a class template each begin with `template<typename T>` (or `template<class T>`). Then, each function definition resembles a conventional function definition, except that the generic data in the class always is listed generically as type parameter `T`. The binary scope-resolution operator is used with the class-template name to tie each member-function definition to the class template's scope.

Section 14.5 Nontype Parameters and Default Types for Class Templates
- It's possible to use nontype parameters in the header of a class or function template.
- You can specify a default type for a type parameter in the type-parameter list.
- An explicit specialization of a class template overrides a class template for a specific type.

Section 14.6 Notes on Templates and Inheritance
- A class template can be derived from a class-template specialization. A class template can be derived from a nontemplate class. A class-template specialization can be derived from a class-template specialization. A nontemplate class can be derived from a class-template specialization.

Section 14.7 Notes on Templates and Friends
- Functions and entire classes can be declared as friends of nontemplate classes. With class templates, friendship arrangements can be declared. Friendship can be established between a class template and a global function, a member function of another class (possibly a class-template specialization) or even an entire class (possibly a class-template specialization).

Section 14.8 Notes on Templates and `static` Members
- Each class-template specialization has its own copy of each `static` data member; all objects of that specialization share that `static` data member. Such data members must be defined and, if necessary, initialized at global namespace scope.
- Each class-template specialization gets a copy of the class template's `static` member functions.

Terminology

angle brackets (< and >) 628
`class` keyword in a template type parameter 628
class template 627
class-template definition 632
class-template specialization 627
default type for a type parameter 638
explicit specialization 639
`friend` of a template 639
function template 627
function-template definition 628
function-template specialization 627
generic programming 627
macro 628
member function of a class-template specialization 639

non-type template parameter 638
overloading a function template 631
parameterized type 632
`static` data member of a class template 640
`static` data member of a class-template specialization 640
`static` member function of a class template 640
`static` member function of a class-template specialization 640
template 627
`template` keyword 628
template parameter 628
type parameter 628
type template parameter 628
`typename` keyword 628

Self-Review Exercises

14.1 State which of the following are *true* and which are *false*. If *false*, explain why.
 a) The template parameters of a function-template definition are used to specify the types of the arguments to the function, to specify the return type of the function and to declare variables within the function.

    b) Keywords typename and class as used with a template type parameter specifically mean "any user-defined class type."

    c) A function template can be overloaded by another function template with the same function name.

    d) Template parameter names among template definitions must be unique.

    e) Each member-function definition outside a class template must begin with a template header.

    f) A friend function of a class template must be a function-template specialization.

    g) If several class-template specializations are generated from a single class template with a single static data member, each of the class-template specializations shares a single copy of the class template's static data member.

14.2   Fill in the blanks in each of the following:

    a) Templates enable us to specify, with a single code segment, an entire range of related functions called _____, or an entire range of related classes called _____.

    b) All function-template definitions begin with the keyword _____, followed by a list of template parameters to the function template enclosed in _____.

    c) The related functions generated from a function template all have the same name, so the compiler uses _____ resolution to invoke the proper function.

    d) Class templates also are called _____ types.

    e) The _____ operator is used with a class-template name to tie each member-function definition to the class template's scope.

    f) As with static data members of nontemplate classes, static data members of class-template specializations must also be defined and, if necessary, initialized at _____ scope.

Answers to Self-Review Exercises

14.1   a) True. b) False. Keywords typename and class in this context also allow for a type parameter of a fundamental type. c) True. d) False. Template parameter names among function templates need not be unique. e) True. f) False. It could be a nontemplate function. g) False. Each class-template specialization will have its own copy of the static data member.

14.2   a) function-template specializations, class-template specializations. b) template, angle brackets (< and >). c) overloading. d) parameterized. e) binary scope resolution. f) global namespace.

Exercises

14.3   *(Selection Sort Function Template)* Write a function template selectionSort based on Fig. 8.13. Write a driver program that inputs, sorts and outputs an int array and a float array.

14.4   *(Print Array Range)* Overload function template printArray of Fig. 14.1 so that it takes two additional integer arguments, namely int lowSubscript and int highSubscript. A call to this function will print only the designated portion of the array. Validate lowSubscript and highSubscript; if either is out of range or if highSubscript is less than or equal to lowSubscript, the overloaded printArray function should return 0; otherwise, printArray should return the number of elements printed. Then modify main to exercise both versions of printArray on arrays a, b and c (lines 22–24 of Fig. 14.1). Be sure to test all capabilities of both versions of printArray.

14.5   *(Function Template Overloading)* Overload function template printArray of Fig. 14.1 with a nontemplate version that prints an array of character strings in neat, tabular, column format.

14.6   *(Operator Overloads in Templates)* Write a simple function template for predicate function isEqualTo that compares its two arguments of the same type with the equality operator (==) and returns true if they are equal and false otherwise. Use this function template in a program that calls isEqualTo only with a variety of fundamental types. Now write a separate version of the program that calls isEqualTo with a user-defined class type, but does not overload the equality operator. What happens when you attempt to run this program? Now overload the equality operator (with the operator function) operator==. Now what happens when you attempt to run this program?

14.7 *(Array Class Template)* Use an int template nontype parameter numberOfElements and a type parameter elementType to help create a template for the Array class (Figs. 11.6–11.7) we developed in Chapter 11. This template will enable Array objects to be instantiated with a specified number of elements of a specified element type at compile time.

Write a program with class template Array. The template can instantiate an Array of any element type. Override the template with a specific definition for an Array of float elements (class Array<float>). The driver should demonstrate the instantiation of an Array of int through the template and should show that an attempt to instantiate an Array of float uses the definition provided in class Array<float>.

14.8 Distinguish between the terms "function template" and "function-template specialization."

14.9 Explain which is more like a stencil—a class template or a class-template specialization?

14.10 What's the relationship between function templates and overloading?

14.11 Why might you choose to use a function template instead of a macro?

14.12 What performance problem can result from using function templates and class templates?

14.13 The compiler performs a matching process to determine which function-template specialization to call when a function is invoked. Under what circumstances does an attempt to make a match result in a compile error?

14.14 Why is it appropriate to refer to a class template as a parameterized type?

14.15 Explain why a C++ program would use the statement

```
Array< Employee > workerList( 100 );
```

14.16 Review your answer to Exercise 14.15. Explain why a C++ program might use the statement

```
Array< Employee > workerList;
```

14.17 Explain the use of the following notation in a C++ program:

```
template< typename T > Array< T >::Array( int s )
```

14.18 Why might you use a nontype parameter with a class template for a container such as an array or stack?

14.19 Suppose that a class template has the header

```
template< typename T > class Ct1
```

Describe the friendship relationships established by placing each of the following friend declarations inside this class template. Identifiers beginning with "f" are functions, identifiers beginning with "C" are classes, identifiers beginning with "Ct" are class templates and T is a template type parameter (i.e., T can represent any fundamental or class type).
  a) friend void f1();
  b) friend void f2(Ct1< T > &);
  c) friend void C2::f3();
  d) friend void Ct3< T >::f4(Ct1< T > &);
  e) friend class C4;
  f) friend class Ct5< T >;

14.20 Suppose that class template Employee has a static data member count. Suppose that three class-template specializations are instantiated from the class template. How many copies of the static data member will exist? How will the use of each be constrained (if at all)?

Stream Input/Output

15

Consciousness ... does not appear to itself chopped up in bits ... A "river" or a "stream" are the metaphors by which it is most naturally described.
—William James

Objectives

In this chapter you'll learn:

- To use C++ object-oriented stream input/output.

- To format input and output.

- The stream-I/O class hierarchy.

- To use stream manipulators.

- To control justification and padding.

- To determine the success or failure of input/output operations.

- To tie output streams to input streams.

15.1 Introduction

The C++ standard libraries provide an extensive set of input/output capabilities. This chapter discusses a range of capabilities sufficient for performing most common I/O operations and overviews the remaining capabilities. We discussed some of these features earlier in the text; now we provide a more complete treatment. Many of the I/O features that we'll discuss are object oriented. This style of I/O makes use of other C++ features, such as references, function overloading and operator overloading.

C++ uses **type-safe I/O**. Each I/O operation is executed in a manner sensitive to the data type. If an I/O member function has been defined to handle a particular data type, then that member function is called to handle that data type. If there is no match between the type of the actual data and a function for handling that data type, the compiler generates an error. Thus, improper data cannot "sneak" through the system (as can occur in C, allowing for some subtle and bizarre errors).

Users can specify how to perform I/O for objects of user-defined types by overloading the stream insertion operator (<<) and the stream extraction operator (>>). This **extensibility** is one of C++'s most valuable features.

Software Engineering Observation 15.1
Use the C++-style I/O exclusively in C++ programs, even though C-style I/O is available to C++ programmers.

Error-Prevention Tip 15.1

C++ I/O is type safe.

Software Engineering Observation 15.2

C++ enables a common treatment of I/O for predefined types and user-defined types. This commonality facilitates software development and reuse.

15.2 Streams

C++ I/O occurs in **streams**, which are sequences of bytes. In input operations, the bytes flow from a device (e.g., a keyboard, a disk drive, a network connection, etc.) to main memory. In output operations, bytes flow from main memory to a device (e.g., a display screen, a printer, a disk drive, a network connection, etc.).

An application associates meaning with bytes. The bytes could represent characters, raw data, graphics images, digital speech, digital video or any other information an application may require.

The system I/O mechanisms should transfer bytes from devices to memory (and vice versa) consistently and reliably. Such transfers often involve some mechanical motion, such as the rotation of a disk or a tape, or the typing of keystrokes at a keyboard. The time these transfers take is typically much greater than the time the processor requires to manipulate data internally. Thus, I/O operations require careful planning and tuning to ensure optimal performance.

C++ provides both "low-level" and "high-level" I/O capabilities. Low-level I/O capabilities (i.e., **unformatted I/O**) specify that some number of bytes should be transferred device-to-memory or memory-to-device. In such transfers, the individual byte is the item of interest. Such low-level capabilities provide high-speed, high-volume transfers but are not particularly convenient.

Programmers generally prefer a higher-level view of I/O (i.e., **formatted I/O**), in which bytes are grouped into meaningful units, such as integers, floating-point numbers, characters, strings and user-defined types. These type-oriented capabilities are satisfactory for most I/O other than high-volume file processing.

Performance Tip 15.1

Use unformatted I/O for the best performance in high-volume file processing.

Portability Tip 15.1

Using unformatted I/O can lead to portability problems, because unformatted data is not portable across all platforms.

15.2.1 Classic Streams vs. Standard Streams

In the past, the C++ **classic stream libraries** enabled input and output of chars. Because a char normally occupies one byte, it can represent only a limited set of characters (such as those in the ASCII character set). However, many languages use alphabets that contain more characters than a single-byte char can represent. The ASCII character set does not provide these characters; the **Unicode® character set** does. Unicode is an extensive international character set that represents the majority of the world's "commercially viable" languages, mathematical symbols and much more. For more information on Unicode, visit www.unicode.org.

C++ includes the **standard stream libraries**, which enable developers to build systems capable of performing I/O operations with Unicode characters. For this purpose, C++ includes an additional character type called **wchar_t**, which can store 2-byte Unicode characters. The C++ standard also redesigned the classic C++ stream classes, which processed only chars, as class templates with separate specializations for processing characters of types char and wchar_t, respectively. We use the char type of class templates throughout this book.

15.2.2 iostream Library Header Files

The C++ iostream library provides hundreds of I/O capabilities. Several header files contain portions of the library interface.

Most C++ programs include the <iostream> header file, which declares basic services required for all stream-I/O operations. The <iostream> header file defines the cin, cout, cerr and clog objects, which correspond to the standard input stream, the standard output stream, the unbuffered standard error stream and the buffered standard error stream, respectively. (cerr and clog are discussed in Section 15.2.3.) Both unformatted- and formatted-I/O services are provided.

The <iomanip> header declares services useful for performing formatted I/O with so-called **parameterized stream manipulators**, such as setw and setprecision.

The <fstream> header declares services for user-controlled file processing. We use this header in the file-processing programs of Chapter 17.

C++ implementations generally contain other I/O-related libraries that provide system-specific capabilities, such as the controlling of special-purpose devices for audio and video I/O.

15.2.3 Stream Input/Output Classes and Objects

The iostream library provides many templates for handling common I/O operations. For example, class template **basic_istream** supports stream-input operations, class template **basic_ostream** supports stream-output operations, and class template basic_iostream supports both stream-input and stream-output operations. Each template has a predefined template specialization that enables char I/O. In addition, the iostream library provides a set of typedefs that provide aliases for these template specializations. The **typedef** specifier declares synonyms (aliases) for previously defined data types. Programmers sometimes use typedef to create shorter or more readable type names. For example, the statement

```
typedef Card *CardPtr;
```

defines an additional type name, CardPtr, as a synonym for type Card *. Creating a name using typedef does not create a data type; typedef creates only a type name that may be used in the program. Section 21.5 discusses typedef in detail. The typedef **istream** represents a specialization of basic_istream that enables char input. Similarly, the typedef **ostream** represents a specialization of basic_ostream that enables char output. Also, the typedef **iostream** represents a specialization of basic_iostream that enables both char input and output. We use these typedefs throughout this chapter.

Stream-I/O Template Hierarchy and Operator Overloading

Templates `basic_istream` and `basic_ostream` both derive through single inheritance from base template `basic_ios`.[1] Template `basic_iostream` derives through multiple inheritance[2] from templates `basic_istream` and `basic_ostream`. The UML class diagram of Fig. 15.1 summarizes these inheritance relationships.

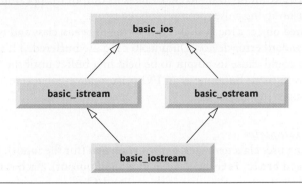

Fig. 15.1 | Stream-I/O template hierarchy portion.

Operator overloading provides a convenient notation for performing input/output. The left-shift operator (`<<`) is overloaded to designate stream output and is referred to as the stream insertion operator. The right-shift operator (`>>`) is overloaded to designate stream input and is referred to as the stream extraction operator. These operators are used with the standard stream objects `cin`, `cout`, `cerr` and `clog` and, commonly, with user-defined stream objects.

Standard Stream Objects `cin`, `cout`, `cerr` and `clog`

Predefined object `cin` is an `istream` instance and is said to be "connected to" (or attached to) the standard input device, which usually is the keyboard. The stream extraction operator (`>>`) as used in the following statement causes a value for integer variable `grade` (assuming that `grade` has been declared as an `int` variable) to be input from `cin` to memory:

```
cin >> grade; // data "flows" in the direction of the arrows
```

The compiler determines the data type of `grade` and selects the appropriate overloaded stream extraction operator. Assuming that `grade` has been declared properly, the stream extraction operator does not require additional type information (as is the case, for example, in C-style I/O). The `>>` operator is overloaded to input data items of fundamental types, strings and pointer values.

The predefined object `cout` is an `ostream` instance and is said to be "connected to" the standard output device, which usually is the display screen. The stream insertion operator (`<<`), as used in the following statement, causes the value of variable `grade` to be output from memory to the standard output device:

```
cout << grade; // data "flows" in the direction of the arrows
```

---

1. This chapter discusses templates only in the context of the template specializations for char I/O.
2. Multiple inheritance is discussed in Chapter 24, Other Topics.

The compiler determines the data type of grade (assuming grade has been declared properly) and selects the appropriate stream insertion operator. The << operator is overloaded to output data items of fundamental types, strings and pointer values.

The predefined object cerr is an ostream instance and is said to be "connected to" the standard error device, normally the screen. Outputs to object cerr are **unbuffered**, implying that each stream insertion to cerr causes its output to appear immediately—this is appropriate for notifying a user promptly about errors.

The predefined object clog is an instance of the ostream class and is said to be "connected to" the standard error device. Outputs to clog are **buffered**. This means that each insertion to clog could cause its output to be held in a buffer until the buffer is filled or until the buffer is flushed. Buffering is an I/O performance-enhancement technique discussed in operating-systems courses.

File-Processing Templates

C++ file processing uses class templates **basic_ifstream** (for file input), **basic_ofstream** (for file output) and **basic_fstream** (for file input and output). Each class template has a predefined template specialization that enables char I/O. C++ provides a set of typedefs that provide aliases for these template specializations. For example, the typedef **ifstream** represents a specialization of basic_ifstream that enables char input from a file. Similarly, typedef **ofstream** represents a specialization of basic_ofstream that enables char output to a file. Also, typedef **fstream** represents a specialization of basic_fstream that enables char input from, and output to, a file. Template basic_ifstream inherits from basic_istream, basic_ofstream inherits from basic_ostream and basic_fstream inherits from basic_iostream. The UML class diagram of Fig. 15.2 summarizes the various inheritance relationships of the I/O-related classes. The full stream-I/O class hierarchy provides most of the capabilities that you need. Consult the class-library reference for your C++ system for additional file-processing information.

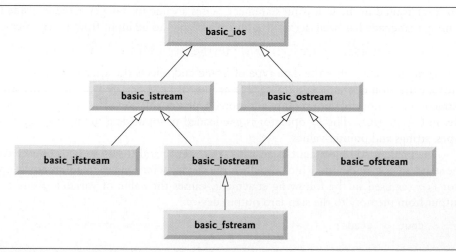

Fig. 15.2 | Stream-I/O template hierarchy portion showing the main file-processing templates.

15.3 **Stream Output**

Formatted and unformatted output capabilities are provided by ostream. Capabilities include output of standard data types with the stream insertion operator (<<); output of characters via the put member function; unformatted output via the write member function (Section 15.5); output of integers in decimal, octal and hexadecimal formats (Section 15.6.1); output of floating-point values with various precision (Section 15.6.2), with forced decimal points (Section 15.7.1), in scientific notation and in fixed notation (Section 15.7.5); output of data justified in fields of designated widths (Section 15.7.2); output of data in fields padded with specified characters (Section 15.7.3); and output of uppercase letters in scientific notation and hexadecimal notation (Section 15.7.6).

15.3.1 Output of char * Variables

C++ determines data types automatically—an improvement over C. This feature sometimes "gets in the way." For example, suppose we want to print the address stored in a char * pointer. The << operator has been overloaded to output a char * as a null-terminated string. To output the address, you can cast the char * to a void * (this can be done to any pointer variable). Figure 15.3 demonstrates printing a char * variable in both string and address formats. The address prints as a hexadecimal (base-16) number, which might differ among computers. To learn more about hexadecimal numbers, read Appendix D. We say more about controlling the bases of numbers in Section 15.6.1 and Section 15.7.4.

```
1   // Fig. 15.3: Fig15_03.cpp
2   // Printing the address stored in a char * variable.
3   #include <iostream>
4   using namespace std;
5
6   int main()
7   {
8      const char *const word = "again";
9
10     // display value of char *, then display value of char *
11     // static_cast to void *
12     cout << "Value of word is: " << word << endl
13        << "Value of static_cast< void * >( word ) is: "
14        << static_cast< void * >( word ) << endl;
15  } // end main
```

```
Value of word is: again
Value of static_cast< void * >( word ) is: 00428300
```

Fig. 15.3 | Printing the address stored in a char * variable.

15.3.2 Character Output Using Member Function put

We can use the put member function to output characters. For example, the statement

```
cout.put( 'A' );
```

displays a single character A. Calls to put may be cascaded, as in the statement

```
cout.put( 'A' ).put( '\n' );
```

which outputs the letter A followed by a newline character. As with <<, the preceding statement executes in this manner, because the dot operator (.) associates from left to right, and the put member function returns a reference to the ostream object (cout) that received the put call. The put function also may be called with a numeric expression that represents an ASCII value, as in the following statement

```
cout.put( 65 );
```

which also outputs A.

15.4 Stream Input

Now let's consider stream input. Formatted and unformatted input capabilities are provided by istream. The stream extraction operator (>>) normally skips **white-space characters** (such as blanks, tabs and newlines) in the input stream; later we'll see how to change this behavior. After each input, the stream extraction operator returns a reference to the stream object that received the extraction message (e.g., cin in the expression cin >> grade). If that reference is used as a condition (e.g., in a while statement's loop-continuation condition), the stream's overloaded void * cast operator function is implicitly invoked to convert the reference into a non-null pointer value or the null pointer based on the success or failure of the last input operation. A non-null pointer converts to the bool value true to indicate success and the null pointer converts to the bool value false to indicate failure. When an attempt is made to read past the end of a stream, the stream's overloaded void * cast operator returns the null pointer to indicate end-of-file.

Each stream object contains a set of **state bits** used to control the stream's state (i.e., formatting, setting error states, etc.). These bits are used by the stream's overloaded void * cast operator to determine whether to return a non-null pointer or the null pointer. Stream extraction causes the stream's **failbit** to be set if data of the wrong type is input and causes the stream's **badbit** to be set if the operation fails. Section 15.7 and Section 15.8 discuss stream state bits in detail, then show how to test these bits after an I/O operation.

15.4.1 get and getline Member Functions

The **get** member function with no arguments inputs one character from the designated stream (including white-space characters and other nongraphic characters, such as the key sequence that represents end-of-file) and returns it as the value of the function call. This version of get returns EOF when end-of-file is encountered on the stream.

*Using Member Functions **eof**, **get** and **put***

Figure 15.4 demonstrates the use of member functions eof and get on input stream cin and member function put on output stream cout. The program first prints the value of cin.eof()—i.e., false (0 on the output)—to show that end-of-file has not occurred on cin. The user enters a line of text and presses *Enter* followed by end-of-file (*<Ctrl>-z* on Microsoft Windows systems, *<Ctrl>-d* on UNIX and Macintosh systems). Line 15 reads each character, which line 16 outputs to cout using member function put. When end-of-file is encountered, the while statement ends, and line 20 displays the value of cin.eof(), which is now true (1 on the output), to show that end-of-file has been set on cin. This program uses the version of istream member function get that takes no arguments and returns the character being input (line 15). Function eof returns true only after the program attempts to read past the last character in the stream.

```
1    // Fig. 15.4: Fig15_04.cpp
2    // Using member functions get, put and eof.
3    #include <iostream>
4    using namespace std;
5
6    int main()
7    {
8       int character; // use int, because char cannot represent EOF
9
10      // prompt user to enter line of text
11      cout << "Before input, cin.eof() is " << cin.eof() << endl
12         << "Enter a sentence followed by end-of-file:" << endl;
13
14      // use get to read each character; use put to display it
15      while ( ( character = cin.get() ) != EOF )
16         cout.put( character );
17
18      // display end-of-file character
19      cout << "\nEOF in this system is: " << character << endl;
20      cout << "After input of EOF, cin.eof() is " << cin.eof() << endl;
21   } // end main
```

```
Before input, cin.eof() is 0
Enter a sentence followed by end-of-file:
Testing the get and put member functions
Testing the get and put member functions
^Z

EOF in this system is: -1
After input of EOF, cin.eof() is 1
```

Fig. 15.4 | get, put and eof member functions.

The get member function with a character-reference argument inputs the next character from the input stream (even if this is a white-space character) and stores it in the character argument. This version of get returns a reference to the istream object for which the get member function is being invoked.

A third version of get takes three arguments—a character array, a size limit and a delimiter (with default value '\n'). This version reads characters from the input stream. It either reads one fewer than the specified maximum number of characters and terminates or terminates as soon as the delimiter is read. A null character is inserted to terminate the input string in the character array used as a buffer by the program. The delimiter is not placed in the character array but does remain in the input stream (the delimiter will be the next character read). Thus, the result of a second consecutive get is an empty line, unless the delimiter character is removed from the input stream (possibly with cin.ignore()).

Comparing `cin` *and* `cin.get`

Figure 15.5 compares input using stream extraction with `cin` (which reads characters until a white-space character is encountered) and input using `cin.get`. The call to `cin.get` (line 22) does not specify a delimiter, so the default `'\n'` character is used.

```cpp
1   // Fig. 15.5: Fig15_05.cpp
2   // Contrasting input of a string via cin and cin.get.
3   #include <iostream>
4   using namespace std;
5
6   int main()
7   {
8      // create two char arrays, each with 80 elements
9      const int SIZE = 80;
10     char buffer1[ SIZE ];
11     char buffer2[ SIZE ];
12
13     // use cin to input characters into buffer1
14     cout << "Enter a sentence:" << endl;
15     cin >> buffer1;
16
17     // display buffer1 contents
18     cout << "\nThe string read with cin was:" << endl
19        << buffer1 << endl << endl;
20
21     // use cin.get to input characters into buffer2
22     cin.get( buffer2, SIZE );
23
24     // display buffer2 contents
25     cout << "The string read with cin.get was:" << endl
26        << buffer2 << endl;
27  } // end main
```

```
Enter a sentence:
Contrasting string input with cin and cin.get

The string read with cin was:
Contrasting

The string read with cin.get was:
 string input with cin and cin.get
```

Fig. 15.5 | Input of a string using `cin` with stream extraction contrasted with input using `cin.get`.

Using Member Function `getline`

Member function **`getline`** operates similarly to the third version of the `get` member function and inserts a null character after the line in the character array. The `getline` function removes the delimiter from the stream (i.e., reads the character and discards it), but does not store it in the character array. The program of Fig. 15.6 demonstrates the use of the `getline` member function to input a line of text (line 13).

```
 1   // Fig. 15.6: Fig15_06.cpp
 2   // Inputting characters using cin member function getline.
 3   #include <iostream>
 4   using namespace std;
 5
 6   int main()
 7   {
 8      const int SIZE = 80;
 9      char buffer[ SIZE ]; // create array of 80 characters
10
11      // input characters in buffer via cin function getline
12      cout << "Enter a sentence:" << endl;
13      cin.getline( buffer, SIZE );
14
15      // display buffer contents
16      cout << "\nThe sentence entered is:" << endl << buffer << endl;
17   } // end main
```

```
Enter a sentence:
Using the getline member function

The sentence entered is:
Using the getline member function
```

Fig. 15.6 | Inputting character data with cin member function getline.

15.4.2 istream Member Functions peek, putback and ignore

The **ignore** member function of istream reads and discards a designated number of characters (the default is one) or terminates upon encountering a designated delimiter (the default is EOF, which causes ignore to skip to the end of the file when reading from a file).

The **putback** member function places the previous character obtained by a get from an input stream back into that stream. This function is useful for applications that scan an input stream looking for a field beginning with a specific character. When that character is input, the application returns the character to the stream, so the character can be included in the input data.

The **peek** member function returns the next character from an input stream but does not remove the character from the stream.

15.4.3 Type-Safe I/O

C++ offers type-safe I/O. The << and >> operators are overloaded to accept data items of specific types. If unexpected data is processed, various error bits are set, which the user may test to determine whether an I/O operation succeeded or failed. If operator << has not been overloaded for a user-defined type and you attempt to input into or output the contents of an object of that user-defined type, the compiler reports an error. This enables the program to "stay in control." We discuss these error states in Section 15.8.

15.5 Unformatted I/O Using read, write and gcount

Unformatted input/output is performed using the **read** and **write** member functions of istream and ostream, respectively. Member function read inputs bytes to a character array in memory; member function write outputs bytes from a character array. These bytes are not formatted in any way. They're input or output as raw bytes. For example, the call

```
char buffer[] = "HAPPY BIRTHDAY";
cout.write( buffer, 10 );
```

outputs the first 10 bytes of buffer (including null characters, if any, that would cause output with cout and << to terminate). The call

```
cout.write( "ABCDEFGHIJKLMNOPQRSTUVWXYZ", 10 );
```

displays the first 10 characters of the alphabet.

The read member function inputs a designated number of characters into a character array. If fewer than the designated number of characters are read, failbit is set. Section 15.8 shows how to determine whether failbit has been set. Member function **gcount** reports the number of characters read by the last input operation.

Figure 15.7 demonstrates istream member functions read and gcount, and ostream member function write. The program inputs 20 characters (from a longer input sequence) into the array buffer with read (line 13), determines the number of characters input with gcount (line 17) and outputs the characters in buffer with write (line 17).

```
1   // Fig. 15.7: Fig15_07.cpp
2   // Unformatted I/O using read, gcount and write.
3   #include <iostream>
4   using namespace std;
5
6   int main()
7   {
8      const int SIZE = 80;
9      char buffer[ SIZE ]; // create array of 80 characters
10
11     // use function read to input characters into buffer
12     cout << "Enter a sentence:" << endl;
13     cin.read( buffer, 20 );
14
15     // use functions write and gcount to display buffer characters
16     cout << endl << "The sentence entered was:" << endl;
17     cout.write( buffer, cin.gcount() );
18     cout << endl;
19  } // end main
```

```
Enter a sentence:
Using the read, write, and gcount member functions
The sentence entered was:
Using the read, writ
```

Fig. 15.7 | Unformatted I/O using the read, gcount and write member functions.

15.6 Introduction to Stream Manipulators

C++ provides various **stream manipulators** that perform formatting tasks. The stream manipulators provide capabilities such as setting field widths, setting precision, setting and unsetting format state, setting the fill character in fields, flushing streams, inserting a new-line into the output stream (and flushing the stream), inserting a null character into the output stream and skipping white space in the input stream. These features are described in the following sections.

15.6.1 Integral Stream Base: dec, oct, hex and setbase

Integers are interpreted normally as decimal (base-10) values. To change the base in which integers are interpreted on a stream, insert the **hex** manipulator to set the base to hexadecimal (base 16) or insert the **oct** manipulator to set the base to octal (base 8). Insert the **dec** manipulator to reset the stream base to decimal. These are all sticky manipulators.

The base of a stream also may be changed by the **setbase** stream manipulator, which takes one integer argument of 10, 8, or 16 to set the base to decimal, octal or hexadecimal, respectively. Because setbase takes an argument, it's called a parameterized stream manipulator. Using setbase (or any other parameterized manipulator) requires the inclusion of the <iomanip> header file. The stream base value remains the same until changed explicitly; setbase settings are "sticky." Figure 15.8 demonstrates stream manipulators hex, oct, dec and setbase.

```cpp
 1   // Fig. 15.8: Fig15_08.cpp
 2   // Using stream manipulators hex, oct, dec and setbase.
 3   #include <iostream>
 4   #include <iomanip>
 5   using namespace std;
 6
 7   int main()
 8   {
 9      int number;
10
11      cout << "Enter a decimal number: ";
12      cin >> number; // input number
13
14      // use hex stream manipulator to show hexadecimal number
15      cout << number << " in hexadecimal is: " << hex
16         << number << endl;
17
18      // use oct stream manipulator to show octal number
19      cout << dec << number << " in octal is: "
20         << oct << number << endl;
21
22      // use setbase stream manipulator to show decimal number
23      cout << setbase( 10 ) << number << " in decimal is: "
24         << number << endl;
25   } // end main
```

```
Enter a decimal number: 20
20 in hexadecimal is: 14
20 in octal is: 24
20 in decimal is: 20
```

Fig. 15.8 | Stream manipulators hex, oct, dec and setbase.

15.6.2 Floating-Point Precision (precision, setprecision)

We can control the **precision** of floating-point numbers (i.e., the number of digits to the right of the decimal point) by using either the setprecision stream manipulator or the **precision** member function of ios_base. A call to either of these sets the precision for all subsequent output operations until the next precision-setting call. A call to member function precision with no argument returns the current precision setting (this is what you need to use so that you can restore the original precision eventually after a "sticky" setting is no longer needed). The program of Fig. 15.9 uses both member function precision (line 22) and the setprecision manipulator (line 31) to print a table that shows the square root of 2, with precision varying from 0 to 9.

```cpp
1   // Fig. 15.9: Fig15_09.cpp
2   // Controlling precision of floating-point values.
3   #include <iostream>
4   #include <iomanip>
5   #include <cmath>
6   using namespace std;
7
8   int main()
9   {
10     double root2 = sqrt( 2.0 ); // calculate square root of 2
11     int places; // precision, vary from 0-9
12
13     cout << "Square root of 2 with precisions 0-9." << endl
14        << "Precision set by ios_base member function "
15        << "precision:" << endl;
16
17     cout << fixed; // use fixed-point notation
18
19     // display square root using ios_base function precision
20     for ( places = 0; places <= 9; places++ )
21     {
22        cout.precision( places );
23        cout << root2 << endl;
24     } // end for
25
26     cout << "\nPrecision set by stream manipulator "
27        << "setprecision:" << endl;
28
29     // set precision for each digit, then display square root
30     for ( places = 0; places <= 9; places++ )
31        cout << setprecision( places ) << root2 << endl;
32   } // end main
```

```
Square root of 2 with precisions 0-9.
Precision set by ios_base member function precision:
1
1.4
1.41
1.414
```

Fig. 15.9 | Precision of floating-point values. (Part 1 of 2.)

```
1.4142
1.41421
1.414214
1.4142136
1.41421356
1.414213562

Precision set by stream manipulator setprecision:
1
1.4
1.41
1.414
1.4142
1.41421
1.414214
1.4142136
1.41421356
1.414213562
```

Fig. 15.9 | Precision of floating-point values. (Part 2 of 2.)

15.6.3 Field Width (width, setw)

The **width** member function (of base class ios_base) sets the field width (i.e., the number of character positions in which a value should be output or the maximum number of characters that should be input) and returns the previous width. If values output are narrower than the field width, **fill characters** are inserted as **padding.** A value wider than the designated width will not be truncated—the full number will be printed. The width function with no argument returns the current setting.

> **Common Programming Error 15.1**
> *The width setting applies only for the next insertion or extraction (i.e., the width setting is not "sticky"); afterward, the width is set implicitly to 0 (i.e., input and output will be performed with default settings). Assuming that the width setting applies to all subsequent outputs is a logic error.*

> **Common Programming Error 15.2**
> *When a field is not sufficiently wide to handle outputs, the outputs print as wide as necessary, which can yield confusing outputs.*

Figure 15.10 demonstrates the use of the width member function on both input and output. On input into a char array, a maximum of one fewer characters than the width will be read, because provision is made for the null character to be placed in the input string. Remember that stream extraction terminates when nonleading white space is encountered. The setw stream manipulator also may be used to set the field width.

```
1   // Fig. 15.10: Fig15_10.cpp
2   // Demonstrating member function width.
3   #include <iostream>
4   using namespace std;
```

Fig. 15.10 | width member function of class ios_base. (Part 1 of 2.)

```
5
6    int main()
7    {
8       int widthValue = 4;
9       char sentence[ 10 ];
10
11      cout << "Enter a sentence:" << endl;
12      cin.width( 5 ); // input only 5 characters from sentence
13
14      // set field width, then display characters based on that width
15      while ( cin >> sentence )
16      {
17         cout.width( widthValue++ );
18         cout << sentence << endl;
19         cin.width( 5 ); // input 5 more characters from sentence
20      } // end while
21   } // end main
```

```
Enter a sentence:
This is a test of the width member function
This
   is
    a
 test
   of
   the
   widt
      h
    memb
      er
     func
      tion
```

Fig. 15.10 | width member function of class `ios_base`. (Part 2 of 2.)

[*Note:* When prompted for input in Fig. 15.10, the user should enter a line of text and press *Enter* followed by end-of-file (*<Ctrl>-z* on Microsoft Windows systems, *<Ctrl>-d* on UNIX and Macintosh systems).]

15.6.4 User-Defined Output Stream Manipulators

You can create your own stream manipulators.[3] Figure 15.11 shows the creation and use of new nonparameterized stream manipulators bell (lines 8–11), carriageReturn (lines 14–17), tab (lines 20–23) and endLine (lines 27–30). For output stream manipulators, the return type and parameter must be of type ostream &. When line 35 inserts the endLine manipulator in the output stream, function endLine is called and line 29 outputs the escape sequence \n and the flush manipulator to the standard output stream cout. Similarly, when lines 35–44 insert the manipulators tab, bell and carriageReturn in the output stream, their corresponding functions—tab (line 20), bell (line 8) and carriageReturn (line 14) are called, which in turn output various escape sequences.

---

3. You also may create your own parameterized stream manipulators. This concept is beyond the scope of this book.

```
1   // Fig. 15.11: Fig15_11.cpp
2   // Creating and testing user-defined, nonparameterized
3   // stream manipulators.
4   #include <iostream>
5   using namespace std;
6
7   // bell manipulator (using escape sequence \a)
8   ostream& bell( ostream& output )
9   {
10     return output << '\a'; // issue system beep
11  } // end bell manipulator
12
13  // carriageReturn manipulator (using escape sequence \r)
14  ostream& carriageReturn( ostream& output )
15  {
16     return output << '\r'; // issue carriage return
17  } // end carriageReturn manipulator
18
19  // tab manipulator (using escape sequence \t)
20  ostream& tab( ostream& output )
21  {
22     return output << '\t'; // issue tab
23  } // end tab manipulator
24
25  // endLine manipulator (using escape sequence \n and member
26  // function flush)
27  ostream& endLine( ostream& output )
28  {
29     return output << '\n' << flush; // issue endl-like end of line
30  } // end endLine manipulator
31
32  int main()
33  {
34     // use tab and endLine manipulators
35     cout << "Testing the tab manipulator:" << endLine
36        << 'a' << tab << 'b' << tab << 'c' << endLine;
37
38     cout << "Testing the carriageReturn and bell manipulators:"
39        << endLine << "..........";
40
41     cout << bell; // use bell manipulator
42
43     // use carriageReturn and endLine manipulators
44     cout << carriageReturn << "-----" << endLine;
45  } // end main
```

```
Testing the tab manipulator:
a       b       c
Testing the carriageReturn and bell manipulators:
-----.....
```

Fig. 15.11 | User-defined, nonparameterized stream manipulators.

15.7 **Stream Format States and Stream Manipulators**

Various stream manipulators can be used to specify the kinds of formatting to be performed during stream-I/O operations. Stream manipulators control the output's format settings. Figure 15.12 lists each stream manipulator that controls a given stream's format state. All these manipulators belong to class ios_base. We show examples of most of these stream manipulators in the next several sections.

Stream manipulator	Description
skipws	Skip white-space characters on an input stream. This setting is reset with stream manipulator noskipws.
left	Left justify output in a field. Padding characters appear to the right if necessary.
right	Right justify output in a field. Padding characters appear to the left if necessary.
internal	Indicate that a number's sign should be left justified in a field and a number's magnitude should be right justified in that same field (i.e., padding characters appear between the sign and the number).
dec	Specify that integers should be treated as decimal (base 10) values.
oct	Specify that integers should be treated as octal (base 8) values.
hex	Specify that integers should be treated as hexadecimal (base 16) values.
showbase	Specify that the base of a number is to be output ahead of the number (a leading 0 for octals; a leading 0x or 0X for hexadecimals). This setting is reset with stream manipulator noshowbase.
showpoint	Specify that floating-point numbers should be output with a decimal point. This is used normally with fixed to guarantee a certain number of digits to the right of the decimal point, even if they're zeros. This setting is reset with stream manipulator noshowpoint.
uppercase	Specify that uppercase letters (i.e., X and A through F) should be used in a hexadecimal integer and that uppercase E should be used when representing a floating-point value in scientific notation. This setting is reset with stream manipulator nouppercase.
showpos	Specify that positive numbers should be preceded by a plus sign (+). This setting is reset with stream manipulator noshowpos.
scientific	Specify output of a floating-point value in scientific notation.
fixed	Specify output of a floating-point value in fixed-point notation with a specific number of digits to the right of the decimal point.

Fig. 15.12 | Format state stream manipulators from <iostream>.

15.7.1 Trailing Zeros and Decimal Points (showpoint)

Stream manipulator **showpoint** forces a floating-point number to be output with its decimal point and trailing zeros. For example, the floating-point value 79.0 prints as 79 without using showpoint and prints as 79.000000 (or as many trailing zeros as are specified by the current precision) using showpoint. To reset the showpoint setting, output the stream manipulator **noshowpoint**. The program in Fig. 15.13 shows how to use stream manipulator showpoint to control the printing of trailing zeros and decimal points for floating-point values. Recall that the default precision of a floating-point number is 6. When neither the fixed nor the scientific stream manipulator is used, the precision represents the number of significant digits to display (i.e., the total number of digits to display), not the number of digits to display after decimal point.

```cpp
 1   // Fig. 15.13: Fig15_13.cpp
 2   // Controlling the printing of trailing zeros and
 3   // decimal points in floating-point values.
 4   #include <iostream>
 5   using namespace std;
 6
 7   int main()
 8   {
 9      // display double values with default stream format
10      cout << "Before using showpoint" << endl
11         << "9.9900 prints as: " << 9.9900 << endl
12         << "9.9000 prints as: " << 9.9000 << endl
13         << "9.0000 prints as: " << 9.0000 << endl << endl;
14
15      // display double value after showpoint
16      cout << showpoint
17         << "After using showpoint" << endl
18         << "9.9900 prints as: " << 9.9900 << endl
19         << "9.9000 prints as: " << 9.9000 << endl
20         << "9.0000 prints as: " << 9.0000 << endl;
21   } // end main
```

```
Before using showpoint
9.9900 prints as: 9.99
9.9000 prints as: 9.9
9.0000 prints as: 9

After using showpoint
9.9900 prints as: 9.99000
9.9000 prints as: 9.90000
9.0000 prints as: 9.00000
```

Fig. 15.13 | Controlling the printing of trailing zeros and decimal points in floating-point values.

15.7.2 Justification (left, right and internal)

Stream manipulators **left** and **right** enable fields to be left justified with padding characters to the right or right justified with padding characters to the left, respectively. The padding character is specified by the fill member function or the setfill parameterized stream manipulator (which we discuss in Section 15.7.3). Figure 15.14 uses the setw, left and right manipulators to left justify and right justify integer data in a field.

```
1    // Fig. 15.14: Fig15_14.cpp
2    // Left and right justification with stream manipulators left and right.
3    #include <iostream>
4    #include <iomanip>
5    using namespace std;
6
7    int main()
8    {
9       int x = 12345;
10
11      // display x right justified (default)
12      cout << "Default is right justified:" << endl
13         << setw( 10 ) << x;
14
15      // use left manipulator to display x left justified
16      cout << "\n\nUse std::left to left justify x:\n"
17         << left << setw( 10 ) << x;
18
19      // use right manipulator to display x right justified
20      cout << "\n\nUse std::right to right justify x:\n"
21         << right << setw( 10 ) << x << endl;
22   } // end main
```

```
Default is right justified:
     12345

Use std::left to left justify x:
12345

Use std::right to right justify x:
     12345
```

Fig. 15.14 | Left justification and right justification with stream manipulators `left` and `right`.

Stream manipulator **internal** indicates that a number's sign (or base when using stream manipulator `showbase`) should be left justified within a field, that the number's magnitude should be right justified and that intervening spaces should be padded with the fill character. Figure 15.15 shows the `internal` stream manipulator specifying internal spacing (line 10). Note that **showpos** forces the plus sign to print (line 10). To reset the showpos setting, output the stream manipulator **noshowpos**.

```
1    // Fig. 15.15: Fig15_15.cpp
2    // Printing an integer with internal spacing and plus sign.
3    #include <iostream>
4    #include <iomanip>
5    using namespace std;
6
7    int main()
8    {
```

Fig. 15.15 | Printing an integer with internal spacing and plus sign. (Part 1 of 2.)

```
 9        // display value with internal spacing and plus sign
10        cout << internal << showpos << setw( 10 ) << 123 << endl;
11     } // end main
```

```
+         123
```

Fig. 15.15 | Printing an integer with internal spacing and plus sign. (Part 2 of 2.)

15.7.3 Padding (fill, setfill)

The **fill member function** specifies the fill character to be used with justified fields; if no value is specified, spaces are used for padding. The fill function returns the prior padding character. The **setfill manipulator** also sets the padding character. Figure 15.16 demonstrates using member function fill (line 30) and stream manipulator setfill (lines 34 and 37) to set the fill character.

```
 1    // Fig. 15.16: Fig15_16.cpp
 2    // Using member function fill and stream manipulator setfill to change
 3    // the padding character for fields larger than the printed value.
 4    #include <iostream>
 5    #include <iomanip>
 6    using namespace std;
 7
 8    int main()
 9    {
10       int x = 10000;
11
12       // display x
13       cout << x << " printed as int right and left justified\n"
14          << "and as hex with internal justification.\n"
15          << "Using the default pad character (space):" << endl;
16
17       // display x with base
18       cout << showbase << setw( 10 ) << x << endl;
19
20       // display x with left justification
21       cout << left << setw( 10 ) << x << endl;
22
23       // display x as hex with internal justification
24       cout << internal << setw( 10 ) << hex << x << endl << endl;
25
26       cout << "Using various padding characters:" << endl;
27
28       // display x using padded characters (right justification)
29       cout << right;
30       cout.fill( '*' );
31       cout << setw( 10 ) << dec << x << endl;
32
33       // display x using padded characters (left justification)
34       cout << left << setw( 10 ) << setfill( '%' ) << x << endl;
```

Fig. 15.16 | Using member function fill and stream manipulator setfill to change the padding character for fields larger than the values being printed. (Part 1 of 2.)

```
35
36      // display x using padded characters (internal justification)
37      cout << internal << setw( 10 ) << setfill( '^' ) << hex
38         << x << endl;
39  } // end main
```

```
10000 printed as int right and left justified
and as hex with internal justification.
Using the default pad character (space):
     10000
10000
0x    2710

Using various padding characters:
*****10000
10000%%%%%
0x^^^^2710
```

Fig. 15.16 | Using member function `fill` and stream manipulator `setfill` to change the padding character for fields larger than the values being printed. (Part 2 of 2.)

15.7.4 Integral Stream Base (dec, oct, hex, showbase)

C++ provides stream manipulators **dec**, **hex** and **oct** to specify that integers are to be displayed as decimal, hexadecimal and octal values, respectively. Stream insertions default to decimal if none of these manipulators is used. With stream extraction, integers prefixed with 0 (zero) are treated as octal values, integers prefixed with 0x or 0X are treated as hexadecimal values, and all other integers are treated as decimal values. Once a particular base is specified for a stream, all integers on that stream are processed using that base until a different base is specified or until the program terminates.

Stream manipulator **showbase** forces the base of an integral value to be output. Decimal numbers are output by default, octal numbers are output with a leading 0, and hexadecimal numbers are output with either a leading 0x or a leading 0X (as we discuss in Section 15.7.6, stream manipulator **uppercase** determines which option is chosen). Figure 15.17 demonstrates the use of stream manipulator **showbase** to force an integer to print in decimal, octal and hexadecimal formats. To reset the showbase setting, output the stream manipulator **noshowbase**.

```
1   // Fig. 15.17: Fig15_17.cpp
2   // Using stream manipulator showbase.
3   #include <iostream>
4   using namespace std;
5
6   int main()
7   {
8      int x = 100;
9
10     // use showbase to show number base
11     cout << "Printing integers preceded by their base:" << endl
12        << showbase;
```

Fig. 15.17 | Stream manipulator `showbase`. (Part 1 of 2.)

```
13
14     cout << x << endl; // print decimal value
15     cout << oct << x << endl; // print octal value
16     cout << hex << x << endl; // print hexadecimal value
17  } // end main
```

```
Printing integers preceded by their base:
100
0144
0x64
```

Fig. 15.17 | Stream manipulator `showbase`. (Part 2 of 2.)

15.7.5 Floating-Point Numbers; Scientific and Fixed Notation (`scientific`, `fixed`)

Stream manipulators `scientific` and `fixed` control the output format of floating-point numbers. Stream manipulator **scientific** forces the output of a floating-point number to display in scientific format. Stream manipulator **fixed** forces a floating-point number to display a specific number of digits (as specified by member function `precision` or stream manipulator `setprecision`) to the right of the decimal point. Without using another manipulator, the floating-point-number value determines the output format.

Figure 15.18 demonstrates displaying floating-point numbers in fixed and scientific formats using stream manipulators `scientific` (line 18) and `fixed` (line 22). The exponent format in scientific notation might differ across different compilers.

```
 1  // Fig. 15.18: Fig15_18.cpp
 2  // Displaying floating-point values in system default,
 3  // scientific and fixed formats.
 4  #include <iostream>
 5  using namespace std;
 6
 7  int main()
 8  {
 9     double x = 0.001234567;
10     double y = 1.946e9;
11
12     // display x and y in default format
13     cout << "Displayed in default format:" << endl
14        << x << '\t' << y << endl;
15
16     // display x and y in scientific format
17     cout << "\nDisplayed in scientific format:" << endl
18        << scientific << x << '\t' << y << endl;
19
20     // display x and y in fixed format
21     cout << "\nDisplayed in fixed format:" << endl
22        << fixed << x << '\t' << y << endl;
23  } // end main
```

Fig. 15.18 | Floating-point values displayed in default, scientific and fixed formats. (Part 1 of 2.)

```
Displayed in default format:
0.00123457      1.946e+009

Displayed in scientific format:
1.234567e-003   1.946000e+009

Displayed in fixed format:
0.001235        1946000000.000000
```

Fig. 15.18 | Floating-point values displayed in default, scientific and fixed formats. (Part 2 of 2.)

15.7.6 Uppercase/Lowercase Control (uppercase)

Stream manipulator **uppercase** outputs an uppercase X or E with hexadecimal-integer values or with scientific notation floating-point values, respectively (Fig. 15.19). Using stream manipulator uppercase also causes all letters in a hexadecimal value to be uppercase. By default, the letters for hexadecimal values and the exponents in scientific notation floating-point values appear in lowercase. To reset the uppercase setting, output the stream manipulator **nouppercase**.

```
 1    // Fig. 15.19: Fig15_19.cpp
 2    // Stream manipulator uppercase.
 3    #include <iostream>
 4    using namespace std;
 5
 6    int main()
 7    {
 8       cout << "Printing uppercase letters in scientific" << endl
 9          << "notation exponents and hexadecimal values:" << endl;
10
11       // use std:uppercase to display uppercase letters; use std::hex and
12       // std::showbase to display hexadecimal value and its base
13       cout << uppercase << 4.345e10 << endl
14          << hex << showbase << 123456789 << endl;
15    } // end main
```

```
Printing uppercase letters in scientific
notation exponents and hexadecimal values:
4.345E+010
0X75BCD15
```

Fig. 15.19 | Stream manipulator uppercase.

15.7.7 Specifying Boolean Format (boolalpha)

C++ provides data type bool, whose values may be false or true, as a preferred alternative to the old style of using 0 to indicate false and nonzero to indicate true. A bool variable outputs as 0 or 1 by default. However, we can use stream manipulator **boolalpha** to set the output stream to display bool values as the strings "true" and "false". Use stream manipulator **noboolalpha** to set the output stream to display bool values as integers (i.e., the default setting). The program of Fig. 15.20 demonstrates these stream manipulators.

Line 11 displays the bool value, which line 8 sets to true, as an integer. Line 15 uses manipulator boolalpha to display the bool value as a string. Lines 18–19 then change the bool's value and use manipulator noboolalpha, so line 22 can display the bool value as an integer. Line 26 uses manipulator boolalpha to display the bool value as a string. Both boolalpha and noboolalpha are "sticky" settings.

Good Programming Practice 15.1

Displaying bool values as true or false, rather than nonzero or 0, respectively, makes program outputs clearer.

```cpp
1   // Fig. 15.20: Fig15_20.cpp
2   // Demonstrating stream manipulators boolalpha and noboolalpha.
3   #include <iostream>
4   using namespace std;
5
6   int main()
7   {
8      bool booleanValue = true;
9
10     // display default true booleanValue
11     cout << "booleanValue is " << booleanValue << endl;
12
13     // display booleanValue after using boolalpha
14     cout << "booleanValue (after using boolalpha) is "
15        << boolalpha << booleanValue << endl << endl;
16
17     cout << "switch booleanValue and use noboolalpha" << endl;
18     booleanValue = false; // change booleanValue
19     cout << noboolalpha << endl; // use noboolalpha
20
21     // display default false booleanValue after using noboolalpha
22     cout << "booleanValue is " << booleanValue << endl;
23
24     // display booleanValue after using boolalpha again
25     cout << "booleanValue (after using boolalpha) is "
26        << boolalpha << booleanValue << endl;
27   } // end main
```

```
booleanValue is 1
booleanValue (after using boolalpha) is true

switch booleanValue and use noboolalpha

booleanValue is 0
booleanValue (after using boolalpha) is false
```

Fig. 15.20 | Stream manipulators boolalpha and noboolalpha.

15.7.8 Setting and Resetting the Format State via Member Function flags

Throughout Section 15.7, we've been using stream manipulators to change output format characteristics. We now discuss how to return an output stream's format to its default state after having applied several manipulations. Member function **flags** without an argument returns the current format settings as a **fmtflags** data type (of class ios_base), which represents the **format state**. Member function flags with a fmtflags argument sets the format state as specified by the argument and returns the prior state settings. The initial settings of the value that flags returns might differ across several systems. The program of Fig. 15.21 uses member function flags to save the stream's original format state (line 17), then restore the original format settings (line 25).

```cpp
1   // Fig. 15.21: Fig15_21.cpp
2   // Demonstrating the flags member function.
3   #include <iostream>
4   using namespace std;
5
6   int main()
7   {
8      int integerValue = 1000;
9      double doubleValue = 0.0947628;
10
11     // display flags value, int and double values (original format)
12     cout << "The value of the flags variable is: " << cout.flags()
13        << "\nPrint int and double in original format:\n"
14        << integerValue << '\t' << doubleValue << endl << endl;
15
16     // use cout flags function to save original format
17     ios_base::fmtflags originalFormat = cout.flags();
18     cout << showbase << oct << scientific; // change format
19
20     // display flags value, int and double values (new format)
21     cout << "The value of the flags variable is: " << cout.flags()
22        << "\nPrint int and double in a new format:\n"
23        << integerValue << '\t' << doubleValue << endl << endl;
24
25     cout.flags( originalFormat ); // restore format
26
27     // display flags value, int and double values (original format)
28     cout << "The restored value of the flags variable is: "
29        << cout.flags()
30        << "\nPrint values in original format again:\n"
31        << integerValue << '\t' << doubleValue << endl;
32  } // end main
```

```
The value of the flags variable is: 513
Print int and double in original format:
1000    0.0947628

The value of the flags variable is: 012011
Print int and double in a new format:
01750   9.476280e-002

The restored value of the flags variable is: 513
Print values in original format again:
1000    0.0947628
```

Fig. 15.21 | flags member function.

15.8 **Stream Error States**

The state of a stream may be tested through bits in class `ios_base`. In a moment, we show how to test these bits, in the example of Fig. 15.22.

The **eofbit** is set for an input stream after end-of-file is encountered. A program can use member function `eof` to determine whether end-of-file has been encountered on a stream after an attempt to extract data beyond the end of the stream. The call

```
cin.eof()
```

returns `true` if end-of-file has been encountered on `cin` and `false` otherwise.

The `failbit` is set for a stream when a format error occurs on the stream and no characters are input (e.g., when you attempt to read a number and the user enters a string). When such an error occurs, the characters are not lost. The **fail** member function reports whether a stream operation has failed. Usually, recovering from such errors is possible.

```cpp
1   // Fig. 15.22: Fig15_22.cpp
2   // Testing error states.
3   #include <iostream>
4   using namespace std;
5
6   int main()
7   {
8      int integerValue;
9
10     // display results of cin functions
11     cout << "Before a bad input operation:"
12        << "\ncin.rdstate(): " << cin.rdstate()
13        << "\n    cin.eof(): " << cin.eof()
14        << "\n    cin.fail(): " << cin.fail()
15        << "\n    cin.bad(): " << cin.bad()
16        << "\n    cin.good(): " << cin.good()
17        << "\n\nExpects an integer, but enter a character: ";
18
19     cin >> integerValue; // enter character value
20     cout << endl;
21
22     // display results of cin functions after bad input
23     cout << "After a bad input operation:"
24        << "\ncin.rdstate(): " << cin.rdstate()
25        << "\n    cin.eof(): " << cin.eof()
26        << "\n    cin.fail(): " << cin.fail()
27        << "\n    cin.bad(): " << cin.bad()
28        << "\n    cin.good(): " << cin.good() << endl << endl;
29
30     cin.clear(); // clear stream
31
32     // display results of cin functions after clearing cin
33     cout << "After cin.clear()" << "\ncin.fail(): " << cin.fail()
34        << "\ncin.good(): " << cin.good() << endl;
35   } // end main
```

Fig. 15.22 | Testing error states. (Part 1 of 2.)

```
Before a bad input operation:
cin.rdstate(): 0
    cin.eof(): 0
   cin.fail(): 0
    cin.bad(): 0
   cin.good(): 1

Expects an integer, but enter a character: A

After a bad input operation:
cin.rdstate(): 2
    cin.eof(): 0
   cin.fail(): 1
    cin.bad(): 0
   cin.good(): 0

After cin.clear()
cin.fail(): 0
cin.good(): 1
```

Fig. 15.22 | Testing error states. (Part 2 of 2.)

The badbit is set for a stream when an error occurs that results in the loss of data. The **bad** member function reports whether a stream operation failed. Generally, such serious failures are nonrecoverable.

The **goodbit** is set for a stream if none of the bits eofbit, failbit or badbit is set for the stream.

The **good** member function returns true if the bad, fail and eof functions would all return false. I/O operations should be performed only on "good" streams.

The **rdstate** member function returns the stream's error state. Calling cout.rdstate, for example, would return the stream's state, which then could be tested by a switch statement that examines eofbit, badbit, failbit and goodbit. The preferred means of testing the state of a stream is to use member functions eof, bad, fail and good—using these functions does not require you to be familiar with particular status bits.

The **clear** member function is used to restore a stream's state to "good," so that I/O may proceed on that stream. The default argument for clear is goodbit, so the statement

```
    cin.clear();
```

clears cin and sets goodbit for the stream. The statement

```
    cin.clear( ios::failbit )
```

sets the failbit. You might want to do this when performing input on cin with a user-defined type and encountering a problem. The name clear might seem inappropriate in this context, but it's correct.

The program of Fig. 15.22 demonstrates member functions rdstate, eof, fail, bad, good and clear. [*Note:* The actual values output may differ across different compilers.]

The operator! member function of basic_ios returns true if the badbit is set, the failbit is set or both are set. The operator void * member function returns false (0) if the badbit is set, the failbit is set or both are set. These functions are useful in file processing when a true/false condition is being tested under the control of a selection statement or repetition statement.

15.9 **Tying an Output Stream to an Input Stream**

Interactive applications generally involve an istream for input and an ostream for output. When a prompting message appears on the screen, the user responds by entering the appropriate data. Obviously, the prompt needs to appear before the input operation proceeds. With output buffering, outputs appear only when the buffer fills, when outputs are flushed explicitly by the program or automatically at the end of the program. C++ provides member function **tie** to synchronize (i.e., "tie together") the operation of an istream and an ostream to ensure that outputs appear before their subsequent inputs. The call

```
cin.tie( &cout );
```

ties cout (an ostream) to cin (an istream). Actually, this particular call is redundant, because C++ performs this operation automatically to create a user's standard input/output environment. However, the user would tie other istream/ostream pairs explicitly. To untie an input stream, inputStream, from an output stream, use the call

```
inputStream.tie( 0 );
```

15.10 **Wrap-Up**

This chapter summarized how C++ performs input/output using streams. You learned about the stream-I/O classes and objects, as well as the stream I/O template class hierarchy. We discussed ostream's formatted and unformatted output capabilities performed by the put and write functions. You saw examples using istream's formatted and unformatted input capabilities performed by the eof, get, getline, peek, putback, ignore and read functions. Next, we discussed stream manipulators and member functions that perform formatting tasks—dec, oct, hex and setbase for displaying integers; precision and setprecision for controlling floating-point precision; and width and setw for setting field width. You also learned additional formatting iostream manipulators and member functions—showpoint for displaying decimal point and trailing zeros; left, right and internal for justification; fill and setfill for padding; scientific and fixed for displaying floating-point numbers in scientific and fixed notation; uppercase for uppercase/lowercase control; boolalpha for specifying boolean format; and flags and fmtflags for resetting the format state.

In the next chapter, we introduce exception handling, which allows you to deal with certain problems that may occur during a program's execution. We demonstrate basic exception-handling techniques that often permit a program to continue executing as if no problem had been encountered. We also present several classes that the C++ Standard Library provides for handling exceptions.

Summary

Section 15.1 Introduction
- I/O operations are performed in a manner sensitive to the type of the data.

Section 15.2 Streams
- C++ I/O occurs in streams. A stream is a sequence of bytes.

- I/O mechanisms move bytes from devices to memory and vice versa efficiently and reliably.
- C++ provides "low-level" and "high-level" I/O capabilities. Low-level I/O-capabilities specify that bytes should be transferred device-to-memory or memory-to-device. High-level I/O is performed with bytes grouped into meaningful units such as integers, strings and user-defined types.
- C++ provides both unformatted-I/O and formatted-I/O operations. Unformatted-I/O transfers are fast, but process raw data that is difficult for people to use. Formatted I/O processes data in meaningful units, but requires extra processing time that can degrade the performance.
- The <iostream> header file declares all stream-I/O operations.
- The <iomanip> header declares the parameterized stream manipulators.
- The <fstream> header declares file-processing operations.
- The basic_istream template supports stream-input operations.
- The basic_ostream template supports stream-output operations.
- The basic_iostream template supports both stream-input and stream-output operations.
- Templates basic_istream and the basic_ostream each derive from the basic_ios template.
- Template basic_iostream derives from both the basic_istream and basic_ostream templates.
- The istream object cin is tied to the standard input device, normally the keyboard.
- The ostream object cout is tied to the standard output device, normally the screen.
- The ostream object cerr is tied to the standard error device, normally the screen. Outputs to cerr are unbuffered; each insertion to cerr appears immediately.
- The ostream object clog is tied to the standard error device, normally the screen. Outputs to clog are buffered.
- The C++ compiler determines data types automatically for input and output.

Section 15.3 Stream Output
- Addresses are displayed in hexadecimal format by default.
- To print the address in a pointer variable, cast the pointer to void *.
- Member function put outputs one character. Calls to put may be cascaded.

Section 15.4 Stream Input
- Stream input is performed with the stream extraction operator >>, which automatically skips white-space characters in the input stream and returns false after end-of-file is encountered.
- Stream extraction causes failbit to be set for improper input and badbit to be set if the operation fails.
- A series of values can be input using the stream extraction operation in a while loop header. The extraction returns 0 when end-of-file is encountered or an error occurs.
- The get member function with no arguments inputs one character and returns the character; EOF is returned if end-of-file is encountered on the stream.
- Member function get with a character-reference argument inputs the next character from the input stream and stores it in the character argument. This version of get returns a reference to the istream object for which the get member function is being invoked.
- Member function get with three arguments—a character array, a size limit and a delimiter (with default value newline)—reads characters from the input stream up to a maximum of limit – 1 characters, or until the delimiter is read. The input string is terminated with a null character. The delimiter is not placed in the character array but remains in the input stream.
- The getline member function operates like the three-argument get member function. The getline function removes the delimiter from the input stream but does not store it in the string.

- Member function ignore skips the specified number of characters (the default is 1) in the input stream; it terminates if the specified delimiter is encountered (the default delimiter is EOF).
- The putback member function places the previous character obtained by a get on a stream back into that stream.
- The peek member function returns the next character from an input stream but does not extract (remove) the character from the stream.
- C++ offers type-safe I/O. If unexpected data is processed by the << and >> operators, various error bits are set, which can be tested to determine whether an I/O operation succeeded or failed. If operator << has not been overloaded for a user-defined type, a compiler error is reported.

Section 15.5 Unformatted I/O Using **read, write** and **gcount**
- Unformatted I/O is performed with member functions read and write. These input or output bytes to or from memory, beginning at a designated memory address.
- The gcount member function returns the number of characters input by the previous read operation on that stream.
- Member function read inputs a specified number of characters into a character array. failbit is set if fewer than the specified number of characters are read.

Section 15.6 Introduction to Stream Manipulators
- To change the base in which integers output, use the manipulator hex to set the base to hexadecimal (base 16) or oct to set the base to octal (base 8). Use manipulator dec to reset the base to decimal. The base remains the same until changed explicitly.
- The parameterized stream manipulator setbase also sets the base for integer output. setbase takes one integer argument of 10, 8 or 16 to set the base.
- Floating-point precision can be controlled with the setprecision stream manipulator or the precision member function. Both set the precision for all subsequent output operations until the next precision-setting call. The precision member function with no argument returns the current precision value.
- Parameterized manipulators require the inclusion of the <iomanip> header file.
- Member function width sets the field width and returns the previous width. Values narrower than the field are padded with fill characters. The field-width setting applies only for the next insertion or extraction; the field width is set to 0 implicitly (subsequent values will be output as large as necessary). Values wider than a field are printed in their entirety. Function width with no argument returns the current width setting. Manipulator setw also sets the width.
- For input, the setw stream manipulator establishes a maximum string size; if a larger string is entered, the larger line is broken into pieces no larger than the designated size.
- You can create your own stream manipulators.

Section 15.7 Stream Format States and Stream Manipulators
- Stream manipulator showpoint forces a floating-point number to be output with a decimal point and with the number of significant digits specified by the precision.
- Stream manipulators left and right cause fields to be left justified with padding characters to the right or right justified with padding characters to the left.
- Stream manipulator internal indicates that a number's sign (or base when using stream manipulator showbase) should be left justified within a field, its magnitude should be right justified and intervening spaces should be padded with the fill character.

- Member function `fill` specifies the fill character to be used with stream manipulators `left`, `right` and `internal` (space is the default); the prior padding character is returned. Stream manipulator `setfill` also sets the fill character.

- Stream manipulators `oct`, `hex` and `dec` specify that integers are to be treated as octal, hexadecimal or decimal values, respectively. Integer output defaults to decimal if none of these bits is set; stream extractions process the data in the form the data is supplied.

- Stream manipulator `showbase` forces the base of an integral value to be output.

- Stream manipulator `scientific` is used to output a floating-point number in scientific format. Stream manipulator `fixed` is used to output a floating-point number with the precision specified by the `precision` member function.

- Stream manipulator `uppercase` outputs an uppercase `X` or `E` for hexadecimal integers and scientific notation floating-point values, respectively. Hexadecimal values appear in all uppercase.

- Member function `flags` with no argument returns the `long` value of the current format state settings. Function `flags` with a `long` argument sets the format state specified by the argument.

Section 15.8 Stream Error States

- The state of a stream may be tested through bits in class `ios_base`.

- The `eofbit` is set for an input stream after end-of-file is encountered during an input operation. The `eof` member function reports whether the `eofbit` has been set.

- A stream's `failbit` is set when a format error occurs. The `fail` member function reports whether a stream operation has failed; it's normally possible to recover from such errors.

- A stream's `badbit` is set when an error occurs that results in data loss. Member function `bad` reports whether such a stream operation failed. Such serious failures are normally nonrecoverable.

- The `good` member function returns true if the `bad`, `fail` and `eof` functions would all return `false`. I/O operations should be performed only on "good" streams.

- The `rdstate` member function returns the error state of the stream.

- Member function `clear` restores a stream's state to "good," so that I/O may proceed.

Section 15.9 Tying an Output Stream to an Input Stream

- C++ provides the `tie` member function to synchronize `istream` and `ostream` operations to ensure that outputs appear before subsequent inputs.

Terminology

Self-Review Exercises

15.1 Answer each of the following:

    a) Input/output in C++ occurs as _____ of bytes.

    b) The stream manipulators that format justification are _____, _____ and _____.

    c) Member function _____ can be used to set and reset format state.

    d) Most C++ programs that do I/O should include the _____ header file that contains the declarations required for all stream-I/O operations.

    e) When using parameterized manipulators, the header file _____ must be included.

    f) Header file _____ contains the declarations required for file processing.

    g) The ostream member function _____ is used to perform unformatted output.

    h) Input operations are supported by class _____.

    i) Standard error stream outputs are directed to the stream objects _____ or _____.

    j) Output operations are supported by class _____.

    k) The symbol for the stream insertion operator is _____.

    l) The four objects that correspond to the standard devices on the system include _____, _____, _____ and _____.

    m) The symbol for the stream extraction operator is _____.

    n) The stream manipulators _____, _____ and _____ specify that integers should be displayed in octal, hexadecimal and decimal formats, respectively.

    o) The _____ stream manipulator causes positive numbers to display with a plus sign.

15.2 State whether the following are *true* or *false*. If the answer is *false*, explain why.

    a) The stream member function flags with a long argument sets the flags state variable to its argument and returns its previous value.

b) The stream insertion operator << and the stream extraction operator >> are overloaded to handle all standard data types—including strings and memory addresses (stream insertion only)—and all user-defined data types.

c) The stream member function flags with no arguments resets the stream's format state.

d) The stream extraction operator >> can be overloaded with an operator function that takes an istream reference and a reference to a user-defined type as arguments and returns an istream reference.

e) The stream insertion operator << can be overloaded with an operator function that takes an istream reference and a reference to a user-defined type as arguments and returns an istream reference.

f) Input with the stream extraction operator >> always skips leading white-space characters in the input stream, by default.

g) The stream member function rdstate returns the current state of the stream.

h) The cout stream normally is connected to the display screen.

i) The stream member function good returns true if the bad, fail and eof member functions all return false.

j) The cin stream normally is connected to the display screen.

k) If a nonrecoverable error occurs during a stream operation, the bad member function will return true.

l) Output to cerr is unbuffered and output to clog is buffered.

m) Stream manipulator showpoint forces floating-point values to print with the default six digits of precision unless the precision value has been changed, in which case floating-point values print with the specified precision.

n) The ostream member function put outputs the specified number of characters.

o) The stream manipulators dec, oct and hex affect only the next integer output operation.

p) By default, memory addresses are displayed as long integers.

15.3 For each of the following, write a single statement that performs the indicated task.

a) Output the string "Enter your name: ".

b) Use a stream manipulator that causes the exponent in scientific notation and the letters in hexadecimal values to print in capital letters.

c) Output the address of the variable myString of type char *.

d) Use a stream manipulator to ensure that floating-point values print in scientific notation.

e) Output the address in variable integerPtr of type int *.

f) Use a stream manipulator such that, when integer values are output, the integer base for octal and hexadecimal values is displayed.

g) Output the value pointed to by floatPtr of type float *.

h) Use a stream member function to set the fill character to '*' for printing in field widths larger than the values being output. Repeat this statement with a stream manipulator.

i) Output the characters 'O' and 'K' in one statement with ostream function put.

j) Get the value of the next character to input without extracting it from the stream.

k) Input a single character into variable charValue of type char, using the istream member function get in two different ways.

l) Input and discard the next six characters in the input stream.

m) Use istream member function read to input 50 characters into char array line.

n) Read 10 characters into character array name. Stop reading characters if the '.' delimiter is encountered. Do not remove the delimiter from the input stream. Write another statement that performs this task and removes the delimiter from the input.

o) Use the istream member function gcount to determine the number of characters input into character array line by the last call to istream member function read, and output that number of characters, using ostream member function write.

p) Output 124, 18.376, 'Z', 1000000 and "String", separated by spaces.

q) Print the current precision setting, using a member function of object cout.

r) Input an integer value into int variable months and a floating-point value into float variable percentageRate.

s) Print 1.92, 1.925 and 1.9258 separated by tabs and with 3 digits of precision, using a stream manipulator.

t) Print integer 100 in octal, hexadecimal and decimal, using stream manipulators and separated by tabs.

u) Print integer 100 in decimal, octal and hexadecimal separated by tabs, using a stream manipulator to change the base.

v) Print 1234 right justified in a 10-digit field.

w) Read characters into character array line until the character 'z' is encountered, up to a limit of 20 characters (including a terminating null character). Do not extract the delimiter character from the stream.

x) Use integer variables x and y to specify the field width and precision used to display the double value 87.4573, and display the value.

15.4 Identify the error in each of the following statements and explain how to correct it.

a) cout << "Value of x <= y is: " << x <= y;

b) The following statement should print the integer value of 'c'.

cout << 'c';

c) cout << ""A string in quotes"";

15.5 For each of the following, show the output.

a) cout << "12345" << endl;
cout.width(5);
cout.fill('*');
cout << 123 << endl << 123;

b) cout << setw(10) << setfill('$') << 10000;

c) cout << setw(8) << setprecision(3) << 1024.987654;

d) cout << showbase << oct << 99 << endl << hex << 99;

e) cout << 100000 << endl << showpos << 100000;

f) cout << setw(10) << setprecision(2) << scientific << 444.93738;

Answers to Self-Review Exercises

15.1   a) streams. b) left, right and internal. c) flags. d) <iostream>. e) <iomanip>. f) <fstream>. g) write. h) istream. i) cerr or clog. j) ostream. k) <<. l) cin, cout, cerr and clog. m) >>. n) oct, hex and dec. o) showpos.

15.2   a) False. The stream member function flags with a fmtflags argument sets the flags state variable to its argument and returns the prior state settings. b) False. The stream insertion and stream extraction operators are not overloaded for all user-defined types. You must specifically provide the overloaded operator functions to overload the stream operators for use with each user-defined type you create. c) False. The stream member function flags with no arguments returns the current format settings as a fmtflags data type, which represents the format state. d) True. e) False. To overload the stream insertion operator <<, the overloaded operator function must take an ostream reference and a reference to a user-defined type as arguments and return an ostream reference. f) True. g) True. h) True. i) True. j) False. The cin stream is connected to the standard input of the computer, which normally is the keyboard. k) True. l) True. m) True. n) False. The ostream member function put outputs its single-character argument. o) False. The stream manipulators dec, oct and hex set the output format state for integers to the specified base until the base is changed again or the program terminates. p) False. Memory addresses are displayed in hexadecimal format by default. To display addresses as long integers, the address must be cast to a long value.

15.3   a)   `cout << "Enter your name: ";`

        b)   `cout << uppercase;`

        c)   `cout << static_cast< void * >( myString );`

        d)   `cout << scientific;`

        e)   `cout << integerPtr;`

        f)   `cout << showbase;`

        g)   `cout << *floatPtr;`

        h)   `cout.fill( '*' );`

           `cout << setfill( '*' );`

        i)   `cout.put( 'O' ).put( 'K' );`

        j)   `cin.peek();`

        k)   `charValue = cin.get();`

           `cin.get( charValue );`

        l)   `cin.ignore( 6 );`

       m)   `cin.read( line, 50 );`

        n)   `cin.get( name, 10, '.' );`

           `cin.getline( name, 10, '.' );`

        o)   `cout.write( line, cin.gcount() );`

        p)   `cout << 124 << ' ' << 18.376 << ' ' << "Z " << 1000000 << " String";`

        q)   `cout << cout.precision();`

        r)   `cin >> months >> percentageRate;`

        s)   `cout << setprecision( 3 ) << 1.92 << '\t' << 1.925 << '\t' << 1.9258;`

        t)   `cout << oct << 100 << '\t' << hex << 100 << '\t' << dec << 100;`

        u)   `cout << 100 << '\t' << setbase( 8 ) << 100 << '\t' << setbase( 16 ) << 100;`

        v)   `cout << setw( 10 ) << 1234;`

       w)   `cin.get( line, 20, 'z' );`

        x)   `cout << setw( x ) << setprecision( y ) << 87.4573;`

15.4   a)   *Error:* The precedence of the << operator is higher than that of <=, which causes the statement to be evaluated improperly and also causes a compiler error.

           Correction: Place parentheses around the expression x <= y.

        b)   *Error:* In C++, characters are not treated as small integers, as they are in C.

           Correction: To print the numerical value for a character in the computer's character set, the character must be cast to an integer value, as in the following:

               `cout << static_cast< int >( 'c' );`

        c)   *Error:* Quote characters cannot be printed in a string unless an escape sequence is used.

           Correction: Print the string in one of the following ways:

               `cout << "\"A string in quotes\"";`

15.5   a)   `12345`

           `**123`

           `123`

        b)   `$$$$$10000`

        c)   `1024.988`

        d)   `0143`

           `0x63`

        e)   `100000`

           `+100000`

        f)   `4.45e+002`

Exercises

15.6   Write a statement for each of the following:

   a) Print integer 40000 left justified in a 15-digit field.

   b) Read a string into character array variable state.

   c) Print 200 with and without a sign.

   d) Print the decimal value 100 in hexadecimal form preceded by 0x.

   e) Read characters into array charArray until the character 'p' is encountered, up to a limit of 10 characters (including the terminating null character). Extract the delimiter from the input stream, and discard it.

   f) Print 1.234 in a 9-digit field with preceding zeros.

15.7   *(Inputting Decimal, Octal and Hexadecimal Values)* Write a program to test the inputting of integer values in decimal, octal and hexadecimal formats. Output each integer read by the program in all three formats. Test the program with the following input data: 10, 010, 0x10.

15.8   *(Printing Pointer Values as Integers)* Write a program that prints pointer values, using casts to all the integer data types. Which ones print strange values? Which ones cause errors?

15.9   *(Printing with Field Widths)* Write a program to test the results of printing the integer value 12345 and the floating-point value 1.2345 in various-sized fields. What happens when the values are printed in fields containing fewer digits than the values?

15.10   *(Rounding)* Write a program that prints the value 100.453627 rounded to the nearest digit, tenth, hundredth, thousandth and ten-thousandth.

15.11   Write a program that inputs a string from the keyboard and determines the length of the string. Print the string in a field width that is twice the length of the string.

15.12   *(Converting Fahrenheit to Celsius)* Write a program that converts integer Fahrenheit temperatures from 0 to 212 degrees to floating-point Celsius temperatures with 3 digits of precision. Use the formula

```
celsius = 5.0 / 9.0 * ( fahrenheit - 32 );
```

to perform the calculation. The output should be printed in two right-justified columns and the Celsius temperatures should be preceded by a sign for both positive and negative values.

15.13   In some programming languages, strings are entered surrounded by either single or double quotation marks. Write a program that reads the three strings suzy, "suzy" and 'suzy'. Are the single and double quotes ignored or read as part of the string?

15.14   *(Reading Phone Numbers with and Overloaded Stream Extraction Operator)* In Fig. 11.5, the stream extraction and stream insertion operators were overloaded for input and output of objects of the PhoneNumber class. Rewrite the stream extraction operator to perform the following error checking on input. The operator>> function will need to be reimplemented.

   a) Input the entire phone number into an array. Test that the proper number of characters has been entered. There should be a total of 14 characters read for a phone number of the form (800) 555-1212. Use ios_base-member-function clear to set failbit for improper input.

   b) The area code and exchange do not begin with 0 or 1. Test the first digit of the areacode and exchange portions of the phone number to be sure that neither begins with 0 or 1. Use ios_base-member-function clear to set failbit for improper input.

   c) The middle digit of an area code used to be limited to 0 or 1 (although this has changed recently). Test the middle digit for a value of 0 or 1. Use the ios_base-member-function clear to set failbit for improper input. If none of the above operations results in fail bit being set for improper input, copy the three parts of the telephone number into the areaCode, exchange and line members of the PhoneNumber object. If failbit has been set on the input, have the program print an error message and end, rather than print the phone number.

15.15 *(Point Class)* Write a program that accomplishes each of the following:

    a) Create a user-defined class Point that contains the private integer data members xCoordinate and yCoordinate and declares stream insertion and stream extraction overloaded operator functions as friends of the class.

    b) Define the stream insertion and stream extraction operator functions. The stream extraction operator function should determine whether the data entered is valid, and, if not, it should set the failbit to indicate improper input. The stream insertion operator should not be able to display the point after an input error occurred.

    c) Write a main function that tests input and output of user-defined class Point, using the overloaded stream extraction and stream insertion operators.

15.16 *(Complex Class)* Write a program that accomplishes each of the following:

    a) Create a user-defined class Complex that contains the private integer data members real and imaginary and declares stream insertion and stream extraction overloaded operator functions as friends of the class.

    b) Define the stream insertion and stream extraction operator functions. The stream extraction operator function should determine whether the data entered is valid, and, if not, it should set failbit to indicate improper input. The input should be of the form

       3 + 8i

    c) The values can be negative or positive, and it's possible that one of the two values is not provided, in which case the appropriate data member should be set to 0. The stream insertion operator should not be able to display the point if an input error occurred. For negative imaginary values, a minus sign should be printed rather than a plus sign.

    d) Write a main function that tests input and output of user-defined class Complex, using the overloaded stream extraction and stream insertion operators.

15.17 *(Printing a Table of ASCII Values)* Write a program that uses a for statement to print a table of ASCII values for the characters in the ASCII character set from 33 to 126. The program should print the decimal value, octal value, hexadecimal value and character value for each character. Use the stream manipulators dec, oct and hex to print the integer values.

15.18 Write a program to show that the getline and three-argument get istream member functions both end the input string with a string-terminating null character. Also, show that get leaves the delimiter character on the input stream, whereas getline extracts the delimiter character and discards it. What happens to the unread characters in the stream?

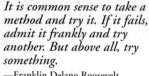

Exception Handling

It is common sense to take a method and try it. If it fails, admit it frankly and try another. But above all, try something.
—Franklin Delano Roosevelt

If they're running and they don't look where they're going I have to come out from somewhere and catch them.
—Jerome David Salinger

I never forget a face, but in your case I'll make an exception.
—Groucho Marx

Objectives

In this chapter you'll learn:

- What exceptions are and when to use them.

- To use **try**, **catch** and **throw** to detect, handle and indicate exceptions, respectively.

- To process uncaught and unexpected exceptions.

- To declare new exception classes.

- How stack unwinding enables exceptions not caught in one scope to be caught in another scope.

- To handle **new** failures.

- To use **auto_ptr** to prevent memory leaks.

- To understand the standard exception hierarchy.

16.1 Introduction

In this chapter, we introduce **exception handling**. An **exception** is an indication of a problem that occurs during a program's execution. The name "exception" implies that the problem occurs infrequently—if the "rule" is that a statement normally executes correctly, then the "exception to the rule" is that a problem occurs. Exception handling enables you to create applications that can resolve (or handle) exceptions. In many cases, handling an exception allows a program to continue executing as if no problem had been encountered. A more severe problem could prevent a program from continuing normal execution, instead requiring the program to notify the user of the problem before terminating in a controlled manner. The features presented in this chapter enable you to write **robust** and **fault-tolerant programs** that can deal with problems that may arise and continue executing or terminate gracefully. The style and details of C++ exception handling are based in part on the work of Andrew Koenig and Bjarne Stroustrup, as presented in their paper, "Exception Handling for C++ (revised)."[1]

Error-Prevention Tip 16.1
Exception handling helps improve a program's fault tolerance.

Software Engineering Observation 16.1
Exception handling provides a standard mechanism for processing errors. This is especially important when working on a project with a large team of programmers.

We begin with an overview of exception-handling concepts, then demonstrates basic exception-handling techniques. We show these techniques via an example that demonstrates handling an exception that occurs when a function attempts to divide by zero. We then discuss additional exception-handling issues, such as how to handle exceptions that occur in a constructor or destructor and how to handle exceptions that occur if operator **new** fails to allocate memory for an object. We conclude the chapter by introducing several classes that the C++ Standard Library provides for handling exceptions.

---

1. Koenig, A., and B. Stroustrup, "Exception Handling for C++ (revised)," *Proceedings of the Usenix C++ Conference*, pp. 149–176, San Francisco, April 1990.

16.2 Exception-Handling Overview

Program logic frequently tests conditions that determine how program execution proceeds. Consider the following pseudocode:

> *Perform a task*
>
> *If the preceding task did not execute correctly*
> > *Perform error processing*
>
> *Perform next task*
>
> *If the preceding task did not execute correctly*
> > *Perform error processing*
>
> ...

In this pseudocode, we begin by performing a task. We then test whether that task executed correctly. If not, we perform error processing. Otherwise, we continue with the next task. Although this form of error handling works, intermixing program logic with error-handling logic can make the program difficult to read, modify, maintain and debug—especially in large applications.

Performance Tip 16.1

If the potential problems occur infrequently, intermixing program logic and error-handling logic can degrade a program's performance, because the program must (potentially frequently) perform tests to determine whether the task executed correctly and the next task can be performed.

Exception handling enables you to remove error-handling code from the "main line" of the program's execution, which improves program clarity and enhances modifiability. You can decide to handle any exceptions you choose—all exceptions, all exceptions of a certain type or all exceptions of a group of related types (e.g., exception types that belong to an inheritance hierarchy). Such flexibility reduces the likelihood that errors will be overlooked and thereby makes a program more robust.

With programming languages that do not support exception handling, programmers often delay writing error-processing code or sometimes forget to include it. This results in less robust software products. C++ enables you to deal with exception handling easily from the inception of a project.

16.3 Example: Handling an Attempt to Divide by Zero

Let's consider a simple example of exception handling (Figs. 16.1–16.2). The purpose of this example is to show how to prevent a common arithmetic problem—division by zero. In C++, division by zero using integer arithmetic typically causes a program to terminate prematurely. In floating-point arithmetic, some C++ implementations allow division by zero, in which case positive or negative infinity is displayed as INF or -INF, respectively.

In this example, we define a function named quotient that receives two integers input by the user and divides its first int parameter by its second int parameter. Before performing the division, the function casts the first int parameter's value to type double.

Then, the second int parameter's value is promoted to type double for the calculation. So function quotient actually performs the division using two double values and returns a double result.

Although division by zero is allowed in floating-point arithmetic, for the purpose of this example we treat any attempt to divide by zero as an error. Thus, function quotient tests its second parameter to ensure that it isn't zero before allowing the division to proceed. If the second parameter is zero, the function uses an exception to indicate to the caller that a problem occurred. The caller (main in this example) can then process the exception and allow the user to type two new values before calling function quotient again. In this way, the program can continue to execute even after an improper value is entered, thus making the program more robust.

The example consists of two files. DivideByZeroException.h (Fig. 16.1) defines an exception class that represents the type of the problem that might occur in the example, and fig16_02.cpp (Fig. 16.2) defines the quotient function and the main function that calls it. Function main contains the code that demonstrates exception handling.

Defining an Exception Class to Represent the Type of Problem That Might Occur

Figure 16.1 defines class DivideByZeroException as a derived class of Standard Library class **runtime_error** (defined in header file **<stdexcept>**). Class runtime_error—a derived class of Standard Library class **exception** (defined in header file **<exception>**)—is the C++ standard base class for representing runtime errors. Class exception is the standard C++ base class for all exceptions. (Section 16.13 discusses class exception and its derived classes in detail.) A typical exception class that derives from the runtime_error class defines only a constructor (e.g., lines 12–13) that passes an error-message string to the base-class runtime_error constructor. Every exception class that derives directly or indirectly from exception contains the virtual function **what**, which returns an exception object's error message. You are not required to derive a custom exception class, such as DivideByZeroException, from the standard exception classes provided by C++. However, doing so allows you to use the virtual function what to obtain an appropriate error message. We use an object of this DivideByZeroException class in Fig. 16.2 to indicate when an attempt is made to divide by zero.

```
 1  // Fig. 16.1: DivideByZeroException.h
 2  // Class DivideByZeroException definition.
 3  #include <stdexcept> // stdexcept header file contains runtime_error
 4  using namespace std;
 5
 6  // DivideByZeroException objects should be thrown by functions
 7  // upon detecting division-by-zero exceptions
 8  class DivideByZeroException : public runtime_error
 9  {
10  public:
11     // constructor specifies default error message
12     DivideByZeroException()
13        : runtime_error( "attempted to divide by zero" ) {}
14  }; // end class DivideByZeroException
```

Fig. 16.1 | Class DivideByZeroException definition.

Demonstrating Exception Handling

The program in Fig. 16.2 uses exception handling to wrap code that might throw a "divide-by-zero" exception and to handle that exception, should one occur. The application enables the user to enter two integers, which are passed as arguments to function `quotient` (lines 10–18). This function divides its first parameter (`numerator`) by its second parameter (`denominator`). Assuming that the user does not specify 0 as the denominator for the division, function `quotient` returns the division result. However, if the user inputs 0 for the denominator, function `quotient` throws an exception. In the sample output, the first two lines show a successful calculation, and the next two lines show a failed calculation due to an attempt to divide by zero. When the exception occurs, the program informs the user of the mistake and prompts the user to input two new integers. After we discuss the code, we'll consider the user inputs and flow of program control that yield these outputs.

```cpp
1   // Fig. 16.2: Fig16_02.cpp
2   // A simple exception-handling example that checks for
3   // divide-by-zero exceptions.
4   #include <iostream>
5   #include "DivideByZeroException.h" // DivideByZeroException class
6   using namespace std;
7
8   // perform division and throw DivideByZeroException object if
9   // divide-by-zero exception occurs
10  double quotient( int numerator, int denominator )
11  {
12     // throw DivideByZeroException if trying to divide by zero
13     if ( denominator == 0 )
14        throw DivideByZeroException(); // terminate function
15
16     // return division result
17     return static_cast< double >( numerator ) / denominator;
18  } // end function quotient
19
20  int main()
21  {
22     int number1; // user-specified numerator
23     int number2; // user-specified denominator
24     double result; // result of division
25
26     cout << "Enter two integers (end-of-file to end): ";
27
28     // enable user to enter two integers to divide
29     while ( cin >> number1 >> number2 )
30     {
31        // try block contains code that might throw exception
32        // and code that should not execute if an exception occurs
33        try
34        {
35           result = quotient( number1, number2 );
```

Fig. 16.2 | Exception-handling example that throws exceptions on attempts to divide by zero. (Part 1 of 2.)

```
36              cout << "The quotient is: " << result << endl;
37         } // end try
38         catch ( DivideByZeroException &divideByZeroException )
39         {
40              cout << "Exception occurred: "
41                   << divideByZeroException.what() << endl;
42         } // end catch
43
44         cout << "\nEnter two integers (end-of-file to end): ";
45     } // end while
46
47     cout << endl;
48  } // end main
```

```
Enter two integers (end-of-file to end): 100 7
The quotient is: 14.2857

Enter two integers (end-of-file to end): 100 0
Exception occurred: attempted to divide by zero

Enter two integers (end-of-file to end): ^Z
```

Fig. 16.2 | Exception-handling example that throws exceptions on attempts to divide by zero. (Part 2 of 2.)

Enclosing Code in a try Block

The program begins by prompting the user to enter two integers. The integers are input in the condition of the while loop (line 29). Line 35 passes the values to function quotient (lines 10–18), which either divides the integers and returns a result, or **throws an exception** (i.e., indicates that an error occurred) on an attempt to divide by zero. Exception handling is geared to situations in which the function that detects an error is unable to handle it.

C++ provides **try blocks** to enable exception handling. A try block consists of keyword **try** followed by braces ({}) that define a block of code in which exceptions might occur. The try block encloses statements that might cause exceptions and statements that should be skipped if an exception occurs.

A try block (lines 33–37) encloses the invocation of function quotient and the statement that displays the division result. In this example, because the invocation of function quotient (line 35) can throw an exception, we enclose this function invocation in a try block. Enclosing the output statement (line 36) in the try block ensures that the output will occur only if function quotient returns a result.

Software Engineering Observation 16.2

Exceptions may surface through explicitly mentioned code in a try block, through calls to other functions and through deeply nested function calls initiated by code in a try block.

Defining a catch Handler to Process a DivideByZeroException

Exceptions are processed by **catch handlers** (also called **exception handlers**), which catch and handle exceptions. At least one catch handler (lines 38–42) must immediately follow each `try` block. Each `catch` handler begins with the keyword **catch** and specifies in parentheses an **exception parameter** that represents the type of exception the `catch` handler can process (`DivideByZeroException` in this case). When an exception occurs in a `try` block, the `catch` handler that executes is the one whose type matches the type of the exception that occurred (i.e., the type in the `catch` block matches the thrown exception type exactly or is a base class of it). If an exception parameter includes an optional parameter name, the `catch` handler can use that parameter name to interact with the caught exception in the body of the `catch` handler, which is delimited by braces ({ and }). A `catch` handler typically reports the error to the user, logs it to a file, terminates the program gracefully or tries an alternate strategy to accomplish the failed task. In this example, the `catch` handler simply reports that the user attempted to divide by zero. Then the program prompts the user to enter two new integer values.

Common Programming Error 16.1

It's a syntax error to place code between a `try` block and its corresponding `catch` handlers or between its `catch` handlers.

Common Programming Error 16.2

Each `catch` handler can have only a single parameter—specifying a comma-separated list of exception parameters is a syntax error.

Common Programming Error 16.3

It's a logic error to catch the same type in two different `catch` handlers following a single `try` block.

Termination Model of Exception Handling

If an exception occurs as the result of a statement in a `try` block, the `try` block expires (i.e., terminates immediately). Next, the program searches for the first `catch` handler that can process the type of exception that occurred. The program locates the matching `catch` by comparing the thrown exception's type to each `catch`'s exception-parameter type until the program finds a match. A match occurs if the types are identical or if the thrown exception's type is a derived class of the exception-parameter type. When a match occurs, the code contained in the matching `catch` handler executes. When a `catch` handler finishes processing by reaching its closing right brace (}), the exception is considered handled and the local variables defined within the `catch` handler (including the `catch` parameter) go out of scope. Program control does not return to the point at which the exception occurred (known as the **throw point**), because the `try` block has expired. Rather, control resumes with the first statement (line 44) after the last `catch` handler following the `try` block. This is known as the **termination model of exception handling**. [*Note:* Some languages use the **resumption model of exception handling**, in which, after an exception is handled, control resumes just after the throw point.] As with any other block of code, when a `try` block terminates, local variables defined in the block go out of scope.

Common Programming Error 16.4

Logic errors can occur if you assume that after an exception is handled, control will return to the first statement after the throw point.

Error-Prevention Tip 16.2

With exception handling, a program can continue executing (rather than terminating) after dealing with a problem. This helps ensure the kind of robust applications that contribute to what's called mission-critical computing or business-critical computing.

If the try block completes its execution successfully (i.e., no exceptions occur in the try block), then the program ignores the catch handlers and program control continues with the first statement after the last catch following that try block.

If an exception that occurs in a try block has no matching catch handler, or if an exception occurs in a statement that is not in a try block, the function that contains the statement terminates immediately, and the program attempts to locate an enclosing try block in the calling function. This process is called **stack unwinding** and is discussed in Section 16.8.

Flow of Program Control When the User Enters a Nonzero Denominator

Consider the flow of control when the user inputs the numerator 100 and the denominator 7 (i.e., the first two lines of output in Fig. 16.2). In line 13, function quotient determines that the denominator does not equal zero, so line 17 performs the division and returns the result (14.2857) to line 35 as a double. Program control then continues sequentially from line 35, so line 36 displays the division result—line 37 ends the try block. Because the try block completed successfully and did not throw an exception, the program does not execute the statements contained in the catch handler (lines 38–42), and control continues to line 44 (the first line of code after the catch handler), which prompts the user to enter two more integers.

Flow of Program Control When the User Enters a Denominator of Zero

Now let's consider a more interesting case in which the user inputs the numerator 100 and the denominator 0 (i.e., the third and fourth lines of output in Fig. 16.2). In line 13, quotient determines that the denominator equals zero, which indicates an attempt to divide by zero. Line 14 throws an exception, which we represent as an object of class DivideByZeroException (Fig. 16.1).

To throw an exception, line 14 uses keyword **throw** followed by an operand that represents the type of exception to throw. Normally, a throw statement specifies one operand. (In Section 16.5, we discuss how to use a throw statement with no operand.) The operand of a throw can be of any type. If the operand is an object, we call it an **exception object**—in this example, the exception object is an object of type DivideByZeroException. However, a throw operand also can assume other values, such as the value of an expression that does not result in an object (e.g., throw x > 5) or the value of an int (e.g., throw 5). The examples in this chapter focus exclusively on throwing exception objects.

Common Programming Error 16.5

Use caution when throwing the result of a conditional expression (?:)—promotion rules could cause the value to be of a type different from the one expected. For example, when throwing an int or a double from the same conditional expression, the int is promoted to a double. So, a catch handler that catches an int would never execute based on such a conditional expression.

As part of throwing an exception, the `throw` operand is created and used to initialize the parameter in the `catch` handler, which we discuss momentarily. In this example, the `throw` statement in line 14 creates an object of class `DivideByZeroException`. When line 14 throws the exception, function `quotient` exits immediately. Therefore, line 14 throws the exception before function `quotient` can perform the division in line 17. This is a central characteristic of exception handling: A function should throw an exception *before* the error has an opportunity to occur.

Because we enclosed the call to `quotient` (line 35) in a `try` block, program control enters the `catch` handler (lines 38–42) that immediately follows the `try` block. This `catch` handler serves as the exception handler for the divide-by-zero exception. In general, when an exception is thrown within a `try` block, the exception is caught by a `catch` handler that specifies the type matching the thrown exception. In this program, the `catch` handler specifies that it catches `DivideByZeroException` objects—this type matches the object type thrown in function `quotient`. Actually, the `catch` handler catches a reference to the `DivideByZeroException` object created by function `quotient`'s `throw` statement (line 14). The exception object is maintained by the exception-handling mechanism.

Performance Tip 16.2
Catching an exception object by reference eliminates the overhead of copying the object that represents the thrown exception.

Good Programming Practice 16.1
Associating each type of runtime error with an appropriately named exception object improves program clarity.

The `catch` handler's body (lines 40–41) prints the associated error message returned by calling function `what` of base-class `runtime_error`. This function returns the string that the `DivideByZeroException` constructor (lines 12–13 in Fig. 16.1) passed to the `runtime_error` base-class constructor.

16.4 When to Use Exception Handling

Exception handling is designed to process **synchronous errors**, which occur when a statement executes. Common examples of these errors are out-of-range array subscripts, arithmetic overflow (i.e., a value outside the representable range of values), division by zero, invalid function parameters and unsuccessful memory allocation (due to lack of memory). Exception handling is not designed to process errors associated with **asynchronous events** (e.g., disk I/O completions, network message arrivals, mouse clicks and keystrokes), which occur in parallel with, and independent of, the program's flow of control.

Software Engineering Observation 16.3
Incorporate your exception-handling strategy into your system from inception. Including effective exception handling after a system has been implemented can be difficult.

Software Engineering Observation 16.4
Exception handling provides a single, uniform technique for processing problems. This helps programmers on large projects understand each other's error-processing code.

Software Engineering Observation 16.5
Avoid using exception handling as an alternate form of flow of control. These "additional" exceptions can "get in the way" of genuine error-type exceptions.

Software Engineering Observation 16.6
Exception handling enables predefined software components to communicate problems to application-specific components, which can then process the problems in an application-specific manner.

The exception-handling mechanism also is useful for processing problems that occur when a program interacts with software elements, such as member functions, constructors, destructors and classes. Rather than handling problems internally, such software elements often use exceptions to notify programs when problems occur. This enables you to implement customized error handling for each application.

Performance Tip 16.3
When no exceptions occur, exception-handling code incurs little or no performance penalty. Thus, programs that implement exception handling operate more efficiently than do programs that intermix error-handling code with program logic.

Software Engineering Observation 16.7
Functions with common error conditions should return 0 or NULL (or other appropriate values) rather than throw exceptions. A program calling such a function can check the return value to determine success or failure of the function call.

Complex applications normally consist of predefined software components and application-specific components that use the predefined components. When a predefined component encounters a problem, that component needs a mechanism to communicate the problem to the application-specific component—the predefined component cannot know in advance how each application processes a problem that occurs.

16.5 Rethrowing an Exception

It's possible that an exception handler, upon receiving an exception, might decide either that it cannot process that exception or that it can process the exception only partially. In such cases, the exception handler can defer the exception handling (or perhaps a portion of it) to another exception handler. In either case, you achieve this by **rethrowing the exception** via the statement

```
throw;
```

Regardless of whether a handler can process (even partially) an exception, the handler can rethrow the exception for further processing outside the handler. The next enclosing try block detects the rethrown exception, which a catch handler listed after that enclosing try block attempts to handle.

Common Programming Error 16.6
*Executing an empty throw statement outside a catch handler calls function **terminate**, which abandons exception processing and terminates the program immediately.*

The program of Fig. 16.3 demonstrates rethrowing an exception. In main's try block (lines 29–34), line 32 calls function throwException (lines 8–24). The throwException function also contains a try block (lines 11–15), from which the throw statement in line 14 throws an instance of standard-library-class exception. Function throwException's catch handler (lines 16–21) catches this exception, prints an error message (lines 18–19) and rethrows the exception (line 20). This terminates function throwException and returns control to line 32 in the try...catch block in main. The try block terminates (so line 33 does not execute), and the catch handler in main (lines 35–38) catches this exception and prints an error message (line 37). [*Note:* Since we do not use the exception parameters in the catch handlers of this example, we omit the exception parameter names and specify only the type of exception to catch (lines 16 and 35).]

```cpp
1   // Fig. 16.3: Fig16_03.cpp
2   // Demonstrating exception rethrowing.
3   #include <iostream>
4   #include <exception>
5   using namespace std;
6
7   // throw, catch and rethrow exception
8   void throwException()
9   {
10     // throw exception and catch it immediately
11     try
12     {
13        cout << "  Function throwException throws an exception\n";
14        throw exception(); // generate exception
15     } // end try
16     catch ( exception & ) // handle exception
17     {
18        cout << "  Exception handled in function throwException"
19           << "\n  Function throwException rethrows exception";
20        throw; // rethrow exception for further processing
21     } // end catch
22
23     cout << "This also should not print\n";
24   } // end function throwException
25
26   int main()
27   {
28     // throw exception
29     try
30     {
31        cout << "\nmain invokes function throwException\n";
32        throwException();
33        cout << "This should not print\n";
34     } // end try
35     catch ( exception & ) // handle exception
36     {
37        cout << "\n\nException handled in main\n";
38     } // end catch
```

Fig. 16.3 | Rethrowing an exception. (Part 1 of 2.)

```
39
40      cout << "Program control continues after catch in main\n";
41   } // end main
```

```
main invokes function throwException
  Function throwException throws an exception
  Exception handled in function throwException
  Function throwException rethrows exception

Exception handled in main
Program control continues after catch in main
```

Fig. 16.3 | Rethrowing an exception. (Part 2 of 2.)

16.6 Exception Specifications

An optional **exception specification** (also called a **throw list**) enumerates a list of exceptions that a function can throw. For example, consider the function declaration

```
int someFunction( double value )
    throw ( ExceptionA, ExceptionB, ExceptionC )
{
    // function body
}
```

In this definition, the exception specification, which begins with keyword throw immediately following the closing parenthesis of the function's parameter list, indicates that function someFunction can throw exceptions of types ExceptionA, ExceptionB and ExceptionC. A function can throw only exceptions of the types indicated by the specification or exceptions of any type derived from these types. If the function throws an exception that does not belong to a specified type, the exception-handling mechanism calls function **unexpected**, which terminates the program.

A function that does not provide an exception specification can throw any exception. Placing throw()—an **empty exception specification**—after a function's parameter list states that the function does not throw exceptions. If the function attempts to throw an exception, function unexpected is invoked. Section 16.7 shows how function unexpected can be customized by calling function **set_unexpected**. [*Note:* Some compilers ignore exception specifications.]

Common Programming Error 16.7

Throwing an exception that has not been declared in a function's exception specification causes a call to function unexpected.

Error-Prevention Tip 16.3

The compiler will not generate a compilation error if a function contains a throw expression for an exception not listed in the function's exception specification. An error occurs only when that function attempts to throw that exception at execution time. To avoid surprises at execution time, carefully check your code to ensure that functions do not throw exceptions not listed in their exception specifications.

Software Engineering Observation 16.8

It's generally recommended that you do not use exception specifications unless you're overriding a base-class member function that already has an exception specification. In this case, the exception specification is required for the derived-class member function.

16.7 Processing Unexpected Exceptions

Function unexpected calls the function registered with function set_unexpected (defined in header file <exception>). If no function has been registered in this manner, function terminate is called by default. Cases in which function terminate is called include:

1. the exception mechanism cannot find a matching catch for a thrown exception

2. a destructor attempts to throw an exception during stack unwinding

3. an attempt is made to rethrow an exception when there is no exception currently being handled

4. a call to function unexpected defaults to calling function terminate

(Section 15.5.1 of the C++ Standard Document discusses several additional cases.) Function **set_terminate** can specify the function to invoke when terminate is called. Otherwise, terminate calls **abort**, which terminates the program without calling the destructors of any remaining objects of automatic or static storage class. This could lead to resource leaks when a program terminates prematurely.

Common Programming Error 16.8

*Aborting a program component due to an uncaught exception could leave a resource— such as a file stream or an I/O device—in a state in which other programs are unable to acquire the resource. This is known as a **resource leak**.*

Function set_terminate and function set_unexpected each return a pointer to the last function called by terminate and unexpected, respectively (0, the first time each is called). This enables you to save the function pointer so it can be restored later. Functions set_terminate and set_unexpected take as arguments pointers to functions with void return types and no arguments.

If the last action of a programmer-defined termination function is not to exit a program, function abort will be called to end program execution after the other statements of the programmer-defined termination function are executed.

16.8 Stack Unwinding

When an exception is thrown but not caught in a particular scope, the function call stack is "unwound," and an attempt is made to catch the exception in the next outer try...catch block. Unwinding the function call stack means that the function in which the exception was not caught terminates, all local variables in that function are destroyed and control returns to the statement that originally invoked that function. If a try block encloses that statement, an attempt is made to catch the exception. If a try block does not enclose that statement, stack unwinding occurs again. If no catch handler ever catches this exception, function terminate is called to terminate the program. The program of Fig. 16.4 demonstrates stack unwinding.

```
 1   // Fig. 16.4: Fig16_04.cpp
 2   // Demonstrating stack unwinding.
 3   #include <iostream>
 4   #include <stdexcept>
 5   using namespace std;
 6
 7   // function3 throws runtime error
 8   void function3() throw ( runtime_error )
 9   {
10      cout << "In function 3" << endl;
11
12      // no try block, stack unwinding occurs, return control to function2
13      throw runtime_error( "runtime_error in function3" ); // no print
14   } // end function3
15
16   // function2 invokes function3
17   void function2() throw ( runtime_error )
18   {
19      cout << "function3 is called inside function2" << endl;
20      function3(); // stack unwinding occurs, return control to function1
21   } // end function2
22
23   // function1 invokes function2
24   void function1() throw ( runtime_error )
25   {
26      cout << "function2 is called inside function1" << endl;
27      function2(); // stack unwinding occurs, return control to main
28   } // end function1
29
30   // demonstrate stack unwinding
31   int main()
32   {
33      // invoke function1
34      try
35      {
36         cout << "function1 is called inside main" << endl;
37         function1(); // call function1 which throws runtime_error
38      } // end try
39      catch ( runtime_error &error ) // handle runtime error
40      {
41         cout << "Exception occurred: " << error.what() << endl;
42         cout << "Exception handled in main" << endl;
43      } // end catch
44   } // end main
```

```
function1 is called inside main
function2 is called inside function1
function3 is called inside function2
In function 3
Exception occurred: runtime_error in function3
Exception handled in main
```

Fig. 16.4 | Stack unwinding.

In main, the try block (lines 34–38) calls function1 (lines 24–28). Next, function1 calls function2 (lines 17–21), which in turn calls function3 (lines 8–14). Line 13 of function3 throws a runtime_error object. However, because no try block encloses the throw statement in line 13, stack unwinding occurs—function3 terminates at line 13, then returns control to the statement in function2 that invoked function3 (i.e., line 20). Because no try block encloses line 20, stack unwinding occurs again—function2 terminates at line 20 and returns control to the statement in function1 that invoked function2 (i.e., line 27). Because no try block encloses line 27, stack unwinding occurs one more time—function1 terminates at line 27 and returns control to the statement in main that invoked function1 (i.e., line 37). The try block of lines 34–38 encloses this statement, so the first matching catch handler located after this try block (line 39–43) catches and processes the exception. Line 41 uses function what to display the exception message. Recall that function what is a virtual function of class exception that can be overridden by a derived class to return an appropriate error message.

16.9 Constructors, Destructors and Exception Handling

First, let's discuss an issue that we've mentioned but not yet resolved satisfactorily: What happens when an error is detected in a constructor? For example, how should an object's constructor respond when new fails because it was unable to allocate required memory for storing that object's internal representation? Because the constructor cannot return a value to indicate an error, we must choose an alternative means of indicating that the object has not been constructed properly. One scheme is to return the improperly constructed object and hope that anyone using it would make appropriate tests to determine that it's in an inconsistent state. Another scheme is to set some variable outside the constructor. The preferred alternative is to require the constructor to throw an exception that contains the error information, thus offering an opportunity for the program to handle the failure.

Before an exception is thrown by a constructor, destructors are called for any member objects built as part of the object being constructed. Destructors are called for every automatic object constructed in a try block before an exception is thrown. Stack unwinding is guaranteed to have been completed at the point that an exception handler begins executing. If a destructor invoked as a result of stack unwinding throws an exception, terminate is called.

If an object has member objects, and if an exception is thrown before the outer object is fully constructed, then destructors will be executed for the member objects that have been constructed prior to the occurrence of the exception. If an array of objects has been partially constructed when an exception occurs, only the destructors for the constructed objects in the array will be called.

An exception could preclude the operation of code that would normally release a resource (such as memory or a file), thus causing a resource leak. One technique to resolve this problem is to initialize a local object to acquire the resource. When an exception occurs, the destructor for that object will be invoked and can free the resource.

Error-Prevention Tip 16.4

When an exception is thrown from the constructor for an object that is created in a new expression, the dynamically allocated memory for that object is released.

16.10 Exceptions and Inheritance

Various exception classes can be derived from a common base class, as we discussed in Section 16.3, when we created class DivideByZeroException as a derived class of class exception. If a catch handler catches a pointer or reference to an exception object of a base-class type, it also can catch a pointer or reference to all objects of classes publicly derived from that base class—this allows for polymorphic processing of related errors.

Error-Prevention Tip 16.5

Using inheritance with exceptions enables an exception handler to catch related errors with concise notation. One approach is to catch each type of pointer or reference to a derived-class exception object individually, but a more concise approach is to catch pointers or references to base-class exception objects instead. Also, catching pointers or references to derived-class exception objects individually is error prone, especially if you forget to test explicitly for one or more of the derived-class pointer or reference types.

16.11 Processing new Failures

The C++ standard specifies that, when operator new fails, it throws a **bad_alloc** exception (defined in header file <new>).In this section, we present two examples of new failing. The first uses the version of new that throws a bad_alloc exception when new fails. The second uses function **set_new_handler** to handle new failures. [*Note:* The examples in Figs. 16.5–16.6 allocate large amounts of dynamic memory, which could cause your computer to become sluggish.]

*new Throwing **bad_alloc** on Failure*
Figure 16.5 demonstrates new throwing bad_alloc on failure to allocate the requested memory. The for statement (lines 16–20) inside the try block should loop 50 times and, on each pass, allocate an array of 50,000,000 double values. If new fails and throws a bad_alloc exception, the loop terminates, and the program continues in line 22, where the catch handler catches and processes the exception. Lines 24–25 print the message "Exception occurred:" followed by the message returned from the base-class-exception version of function what (i.e., an implementation-defined exception-specific message, such as "Allocation Failure" in Microsoft Visual C++). The output shows that the program performed only four iterations of the loop before new failed and threw the bad_alloc exception. Your output might differ based on the physical memory, disk space available for virtual memory on your system and the compiler you are using.

```
1   // Fig. 16.5: Fig16_05.cpp
2   // Demonstrating standard new throwing bad_alloc when memory
3   // cannot be allocated.
4   #include <iostream>
5   #include <new> // bad_alloc class is defined here
6   using namespace std;
7
```

Fig. 16.5 | new throwing bad_alloc on failure. (Part 1 of 2.)

```
 8   int main()
 9   {
10      double *ptr[ 50 ];
11
12      // aim each ptr[i] at a big block of memory
13      try
14      {
15         // allocate memory for ptr[ i ]; new throws bad_alloc on failure
16         for ( int i = 0; i < 50; i++ )
17         {
18            ptr[ i ] = new double[ 50000000 ]; // may throw exception
19            cout << "ptr[" << i << "] points to 50,000,000 new doubles\n";
20         } // end for
21      } // end try
22      catch ( bad_alloc &memoryAllocationException )
23      {
24         cerr << "Exception occurred: "
25            << memoryAllocationException.what() << endl;
26      } // end catch
27   } // end main
```

```
ptr[0] points to 50,000,000 new doubles
ptr[1] points to 50,000,000 new doubles
ptr[2] points to 50,000,000 new doubles
ptr[3] points to 50,000,000 new doubles
Exception occurred: bad allocation
```

Fig. 16.5 | new throwing bad_alloc on failure. (Part 2 of 2.)

new *Returning 0 on Failure*

In old versions of C++, operator new returned 0 when it failed to allocate memory. The C++ standard specifies that standard-compliant compilers can continue to use a version of new that returns 0 upon failure. For this purpose, header file <new> defines object **nothrow** (of type nothrow_t), which is used as follows:

```
double *ptr = new( nothrow ) double[ 50000000 ];
```

The preceding statement uses the version of new that does not throw bad_alloc exceptions (i.e., nothrow) to allocate an array of 50,000,000 doubles.

> **Software Engineering Observation 16.9**
>
> *To make programs more robust, use the version of new that throws bad_alloc exceptions on failure.*

Handling new *Failures Using Function* set_new_handler

An additional feature for handling new failures is function set_new_handler (prototyped in standard header file <new>). This function takes as its argument a pointer to a function that takes no arguments and returns void. This pointer points to the function that will be called if new fails. This provides you with a uniform approach to handling all new failures, regardless of where a failure occurs in the program. Once set_new_handler registers a **new handler** in the program, operator new does not throw bad_alloc on failure; rather, it defers the error handling to the new-handler function.

If new allocates memory successfully, it returns a pointer to that memory. If new fails to allocate memory and set_new_handler did not register a new-handler function, new throws a bad_alloc exception. If new fails to allocate memory and a new-handler function has been registered, the new-handler function is called. The C++ standard specifies that the new-handler function should perform one of the following tasks:

1. Make more memory available by deleting other dynamically allocated memory (or telling the user to close other applications) and return to operator new to attempt to allocate memory again.

2. Throw an exception of type bad_alloc.

3. Call function abort or exit (both found in header file <cstdlib>) to terminate the program.

Figure 16.6 demonstrates set_new_handler. Function customNewHandler (lines 9–13) prints an error message (line 11), then calls abort (line 12) to terminate the program. The output shows that the loop iterated four times before new failed and invoked function customNewHandler. Your output might differ based on the physical memory, disk space available for virtual memory on your system and your compiler.

```cpp
 1   // Fig. 16.6: Fig16_06.cpp
 2   // Demonstrating set_new_handler.
 3   #include <iostream>
 4   #include <new> // set_new_handler function prototype
 5   #include <cstdlib> // abort function prototype
 6   using namespace std;
 7
 8   // handle memory allocation failure
 9   void customNewHandler()
10   {
11      cerr << "customNewHandler was called";
12      abort();
13   } // end function customNewHandler
14
15   // using set_new_handler to handle failed memory allocation
16   int main()
17   {
18      double *ptr[ 50 ];
19
20      // specify that customNewHandler should be called on
21      // memory allocation failure
22      set_new_handler( customNewHandler );
23
24      // aim each ptr[i] at a big block of memory; customNewHandler will be
25      // called on failed memory allocation
26      for ( int i = 0; i < 50; i++ )
27      {
28         ptr[ i ] = new double[ 50000000 ]; // may throw exception
29         cout << "ptr[" << i << "] points to 50,000,000 new doubles\n";
30      } // end for
31   } // end main
```

Fig. 16.6 | set_new_handler specifying the function to call when new fails. (Part 1 of 2.)

```
ptr[0] points to 50,000,000 new doubles
ptr[1] points to 50,000,000 new doubles
ptr[2] points to 50,000,000 new doubles
ptr[3] points to 50,000,000 new doubles
customNewHandler was called
This application has requested the Runtime to terminate it in an unusual way.
Please contact the application's support team for more information.
```

Fig. 16.6 | set_new_handler specifying the function to call when new fails. (Part 2 of 2.)

16.12 Class auto_ptr and Dynamic Memory Allocation

A common programming practice is to allocate dynamic memory, assign the address of that memory to a pointer, use the pointer to manipulate the memory and deallocate the memory with delete when the memory is no longer needed. If an exception occurs after successful memory allocation but before the delete statement executes, a memory leak could occur. The C++ standard provides class template **auto_ptr** in header file **<memory>** to deal with this situation.

An object of class auto_ptr maintains a pointer to dynamically allocated memory. When an auto_ptr object destructor is called (for example, when an auto_ptr object goes out of scope), it performs a delete operation on its pointer data member. Class template auto_ptr provides overloaded operators * and -> so that an auto_ptr object can be used just as a regular pointer variable is. Figure 16.9 demonstrates an auto_ptr object that points to a dynamically allocated object of class Integer (Figs. 16.7–16.8).

```
1   // Fig. 16.7: Integer.h
2   // Integer class definition.
3
4   class Integer
5   {
6   public:
7      Integer( int i = 0 ); // Integer default constructor
8      ~Integer(); // Integer destructor
9      void setInteger( int i ); // functions to set Integer
10     int getInteger() const; // function to return Integer
11  private:
12     int value;
13  }; // end class Integer
```

Fig. 16.7 | Integer class definition.

```
1   // Fig. 16.8: Integer.cpp
2   // Integer member function definitions.
3   #include <iostream>
4   #include "Integer.h"
5   using namespace std;
6
```

Fig. 16.8 | Member function definitions of class Integer. (Part 1 of 2.)

```
 7   // Integer default constructor
 8   Integer::Integer( int i )
 9      : value( i )
10   {
11      cout << "Constructor for Integer " << value << endl;
12   } // end Integer constructor
13
14   // Integer destructor
15   Integer::~Integer()
16   {
17      cout << "Destructor for Integer " << value << endl;
18   } // end Integer destructor
19
20   // set Integer value
21   void Integer::setInteger( int i )
22   {
23      value = i;
24   } // end function setInteger
25
26   // return Integer value
27   int Integer::getInteger() const
28   {
29      return value;
30   } // end function getInteger
```

Fig. 16.8 | Member function definitions of class `Integer`. (Part 2 of 2.)

Line 15 of Fig. 16.9 creates `auto_ptr` object `ptrToInteger` and initializes it with a pointer to a dynamically allocated `Integer` object that contains the value 7. Line 18 uses the `auto_ptr` overloaded `->` operator to invoke function `setInteger` on the `Integer` object that `ptrToInteger` manages. Line 21 uses the `auto_ptr` overloaded `*` operator to dereference `ptrToInteger`, then uses the dot (`.`) operator to invoke function `getInteger` on the `Integer` object. Like a regular pointer, an `auto_ptr`'s `->` and `*` overloaded operators can be used to access the object to which the `auto_ptr` points.

```
 1   // Fig. 16.9: Fig16_09.cpp
 2   // Demonstrating auto_ptr.
 3   #include <iostream>
 4   #include <memory>
 5   using namespace std;
 6
 7   #include "Integer.h"
 8
 9   // use auto_ptr to manipulate Integer object
10   int main()
11   {
12      cout << "Creating an auto_ptr object that points to an Integer\n";
13
14      // "aim" auto_ptr at Integer object
15      auto_ptr< Integer > ptrToInteger( new Integer( 7 ) );
```

Fig. 16.9 | `auto_ptr` object manages dynamically allocated memory. (Part 1 of 2.)

```
16
17        cout << "\nUsing the auto_ptr to manipulate the Integer\n";
18        ptrToInteger->setInteger( 99 ); // use auto_ptr to set Integer value
19
20        // use auto_ptr to get Integer value
21        cout << "Integer after setInteger: " << ( *ptrToInteger ).getInteger()
22    } // end main
```

```
Creating an auto_ptr object that points to an Integer
Constructor for Integer 7

Using the auto_ptr to manipulate the Integer
Integer after setInteger: 99

Destructor for Integer 99
```

Fig. 16.9 | `auto_ptr` object manages dynamically allocated memory. (Part 2 of 2.)

Because `ptrToInteger` is a local automatic variable in `main`, `ptrToInteger` is destroyed when `main` terminates. The `auto_ptr` destructor forces a `delete` of the `Integer` object pointed to by `ptrToInteger`, which in turn calls the `Integer` class destructor. The memory that `Integer` occupies is released, regardless of how control leaves the block (e.g., by a `return` statement or by an exception). Most importantly, using this technique can prevent memory leaks. For example, suppose a function returns a pointer aimed at some object. Unfortunately, the function caller that receives this pointer might not `delete` the object, thus resulting in a memory leak. However, if the function returns an `auto_ptr` to the object, the object will be deleted automatically when the `auto_ptr` object's destructor gets called.

Only one `auto_ptr` at a time can own a dynamically allocated object and the object cannot be an array. By using its overloaded assignment operator or copy constructor, an `auto_ptr` can transfer ownership of the dynamic memory it manages. The last `auto_ptr` object that maintains the pointer to the dynamic memory will delete the memory. This makes `auto_ptr` an ideal mechanism for returning dynamically allocated memory to client code. When the `auto_ptr` goes out of scope in the client code, the `auto_ptr`'s destructor deletes the dynamic memory.

Common Programming Error 16.9

Because auto_ptr objects transfer ownership of memory when they are copied, they cannot be used with Standard Library container classes like vector*. Container classes often make copies of objects. This causes ownership of a container element to be transferred to another object, which might then be accidentally deleted when the copy goes out of scope. The* Boost.Smart_ptr *library (Section 23.6) provides memory management features similar* auto_ptr *that can be used with containers.*

16.13 Standard Library Exception Hierarchy

Experience has shown that exceptions fall nicely into a number of categories. The C++ Standard Library includes a hierarchy of exception classes, some of which are shown in Fig. 16.10. As we first discussed in Section 16.3, this hierarchy is headed by base-class exception (defined in header file <exception>), which contains virtual function what, which derived classes can override to issue appropriate error messages.

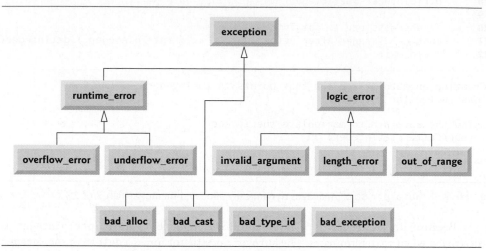

Fig. 16.10 | Some of the Standard Library exception classes.

Immediate derived classes of base-class exception include runtime_error and **logic_error** (both defined in header <stdexcept>), each of which has several derived classes. Also derived from exception are the exceptions thrown by C++ operators—for example, bad_alloc is thrown by new (Section 16.11), **bad_cast** is thrown by dynamic_cast (Chapter 13) and **bad_typeid** is thrown by typeid (Chapter 13). Including **bad_exception** in the throw list of a function means that, if an unexpected exception occurs, function unexpected can throw bad_exception rather than terminating the program's execution (by default) or calling another function specified by set_unexpected.

Common Programming Error 16.10

Placing a catch *handler that catches a base-class object before a* catch *that catches an object of a class derived from that base class is a logic error. The base-class* catch *catches all objects of classes derived from that base class, so the derived-class* catch *will never execute.*

Class logic_error is the base class of several standard exception classes that indicate errors in program logic. For example, class **invalid_argument** indicates that an invalid argument was passed to a function. (Proper coding can, of course, prevent invalid arguments from reaching a function.) Class **length_error** indicates that a length larger than the maximum size allowed for the object being manipulated was used for that object. Class **out_of_range** indicates that a value, such as a subscript into an array, exceeded its allowed range of values.

Class runtime_error, which we used briefly in Section 16.8, is the base class of several other standard exception classes that indicate execution-time errors. For example, class **overflow_error** describes an **arithmetic overflow error** (i.e., the result of an arithmetic operation is larger than the largest number that can be stored in the computer) and class

underflow_error describes an **arithmetic underflow error** (i.e., the result of an arithmetic operation is smaller than the smallest number that can be stored in the computer).

> **Common Programming Error 16.11**
> *Exception classes need not be derived from class* exception, *so catching type* exception *is not guaranteed to* catch *all exceptions a program could encounter.*

> **Error-Prevention Tip 16.6**
> *To catch all exceptions potentially thrown in a try block, use* catch(...). *One weakness with catching exceptions in this way is that the type of the caught exception is unknown at compile time. Another weakness is that, without a named parameter, there is no way to refer to the exception object inside the exception handler.*

> **Software Engineering Observation 16.10**
> *The standard* exception *hierarchy is a good starting point for creating exceptions. You can build programs that can* throw *standard exceptions,* throw *exceptions derived from the standard exceptions or* throw *your own exceptions not derived from the standard exceptions.*

> **Software Engineering Observation 16.11**
> *Use* catch(...) *to perform recovery that does not depend on the exception type (e.g., releasing common resources). The exception can be rethrown to alert more specific enclosing* catch *handlers.*

16.14 Other Error-Handling Techniques

We've discussed several ways to deal with exceptional situations prior to this chapter. The following summarizes these and other error-handling techniques:

- Ignore the exception. If an exception occurs, the program might fail as a result of the uncaught exception. This is devastating for commercial software products and special-purpose mission-critical software, but, for software developed for your own purposes, ignoring many kinds of errors is common.

- Abort the program. This, of course, prevents a program from running to completion and producing incorrect results. For many types of errors, this is appropriate, especially for nonfatal errors that enable a program to run to completion (potentially misleading you to think that the program functioned correctly). This strategy is inappropriate for mission-critical applications. Resource issues also are important here—if a program obtains a resource, the program should release that resource before program termination.

- Set error indicators. The problem with this approach is that programs might not check these error indicators at all points at which the errors could be troublesome. Another problem is that the program, after processing the problem, might not clear the error indicators.

- Test for the error condition, issue an error message and call exit (in <cstdlib>) to pass an appropriate error code to the program's environment.

- Certain kinds of errors have dedicated capabilities for handling them. For example, when operator new fails to allocate memory, a new_handler function can be called to handle the error. This function can be customized by supplying a function name as the argument to set_new_handler, as we discussed in Section 16.11.

16.15 Wrap-Up

In this chapter, you learned how to use exception handling to deal with errors in a program. You learned that exception handling enables you to remove error-handling code from the "main line" of the program's execution. We demonstrated exception handling in the context of a divide-by-zero example. We also showed how to use try blocks to enclose code that may throw an exception, and how to use catch handlers to deal with exceptions that may arise. You learned how to throw and rethrow exceptions, and how to handle the exceptions that occur in constructors. The chapter continued with discussions of processing new failures, dynamic memory allocation with class auto_ptr and the standard library exception hierarchy. In the next chapter, you'll learn about file processing, including how persistent data is stored and how to manipulate it.

Summary

Section 16.1 Introduction

- An exception is an indication of a problem that occurs during a program's execution.
- Exception handling enables you to create programs that can resolve problems that occur at execution time—often allowing programs to continue executing as if no problems had been encountered. More severe problems may require a program to notify the user of the problem before terminating in a controlled manner.

Section 16.2 Exception-Handling Overview

- Exception handling enables you to remove error-handling code from the "main line" of the program's execution, which improves program clarity and enhances modifiability.

Section 16.3 Example: Handling an Attempt to Divide by Zero

- Class exception is the standard C++ base class for exceptions. Class exception provides virtual function what that returns an appropriate error message and can be overridden in derived classes.
- Class runtime_error (defined in header <stdexcept>) is the C++ standard base class for representing runtime errors.
- C++ uses the termination model of exception handling.
- A try block consists of keyword try followed by braces ({}) that define a block of code in which exceptions might occur. The try block encloses statements that might cause exceptions and statements that should not execute if exceptions occur.
- At least one catch handler must immediately follow a try block. Each catch handler specifies an exception parameter that represents the type of exception the catch handler can process.
- If an exception parameter includes an optional parameter name, the catch handler can use that parameter name to interact with a caught exception object.
- The point in the program at which an exception occurs is called the throw point.

- If an exception occurs in a try block, the try block expires and program control transfers to the first catch in which the exception parameter's type matches that of the thrown exception.

- When a try block terminates, local variables defined in the block go out of scope.

- When a try block terminates due to an exception, the program searches for the first catch handler that matches the type of exception that occurred. A match occurs if the types are identical or if the thrown exception's type is a derived class of the exception-parameter type. When a match occurs, the code contained within the matching catch handler executes.

- When a catch handler finishes processing, the catch parameter and local variables defined within the catch handler go out of scope. Any remaining catch handlers that correspond to the try block are ignored, and execution resumes at the first line of code after the try...catch sequence.

- If no exceptions occur in a try block, the program ignores the catch handler(s) for that block. Program execution resumes with the next statement after the try...catch sequence.

- If an exception that occurs in a try block has no matching catch handler, or if an exception occurs in a statement that is not in a try block, the function that contains the statement terminates immediately, and the program attempts to locate an enclosing try block in the calling function. This process is called stack unwinding.

- To throw an exception, use keyword throw followed by an operand that represents the type of exception to throw. The operand of a throw can be of any type.

Section 16.4 When to Use Exception Handling
- Exception handling is for synchronous errors, which occur when a statement executes.

- Exception handling is not designed to process errors associated with asynchronous events, which occur in parallel with, and independent of, the program's flow of control.

Section 16.5 Rethrowing an Exception
- The exception handler can defer the exception handling (or perhaps a portion of it) to another exception handler. In either case, the handler achieves this by rethrowing the exception.

- Common examples of exceptions are out-of-range array subscripts, arithmetic overflow, division by zero, invalid function parameters and unsuccessful memory allocations.

Section 16.6 Exception Specifications
- An optional exception specification enumerates a list of exceptions that a function can throw. A function can throw only exceptions of the types indicated by the exception specification or exceptions of any type derived from these types. If the function throws an exception that does not belong to a specified type, function unexpected is called and the program terminates.

- A function with no exception specification can throw any exception. The empty exception specification throw() indicates that a function does not throw exceptions. If a function with an empty exception specification attempts to throw an exception, function unexpected is invoked.

Section 16.7 Processing Unexpected Exceptions
- Function unexpected calls the function registered with function set_unexpected. If no function has been registered in this manner, function terminate is called by default.

- Function set_terminate can specify the function to invoke when terminate is called. Otherwise, terminate calls abort, which terminates the program without calling the destructors of objects that are declared static and auto.

- Functions set_terminate and set_unexpected each return a pointer to the last function called by terminate and unexpected, respectively (0, the first time each is called). This enables you to save the function pointer so it can be restored later.

- Functions `set_terminate` and `set_unexpected` take as arguments pointers to functions with `void` return types and no arguments.
- If a programmer-defined termination function does not exit a program, function `abort` will be called after the programmer-defined termination function completes execution.

Section 16.8 Stack Unwinding

- Unwinding the function call stack means that the function in which the exception was not caught terminates, all local variables in that function are destroyed and control returns to the statement that originally invoked that function.

Section 16.9 Constructors, Destructors and Exception Handling

- Exceptions thrown by a constructor cause destructors to be called for any objects built as part of the object being constructed before the exception is thrown.
- Each automatic object constructed in a `try` block is destructed before an exception is thrown.
- Stack unwinding completes before an exception handler begins executing.
- If a destructor invoked as a result of stack unwinding throws an exception, `terminate` is called.
- If an object has member objects, and if an exception is thrown before the outer object is fully constructed, then destructors will be executed for the member objects that have been constructed before the exception occurs.
- If an array of objects has been partially constructed when an exception occurs, only the destructors for the constructed array element objects will be called.
- When an exception is thrown from the constructor for an object that is created in a `new` expression, the dynamically allocated memory for that object is released.

Section 16.10 Exceptions and Inheritance

- If a `catch` handler catches a pointer or reference to an exception object of a base-class type, it also can catch a pointer or reference to all objects of classes derived publicly from that base class—this allows for polymorphic processing of related errors.

Section 16.11 Processing **new** Failures

- The C++ standard document specifies that, when operator `new` fails, it throws a `bad_alloc` exception (defined in header file `<new>`).
- Function `set_new_handler` takes as its argument a pointer to a function that takes no arguments and returns `void`. This pointer points to the function that will be called if `new` fails.
- Once `set_new_handler` registers a `new` handler in the program, operator `new` does not throw `bad_alloc` on failure; rather, it defers the error handling to the new-handler function.
- If `new` allocates memory successfully, it returns a pointer to that memory.
- If an exception occurs after successful memory allocation but before the `delete` statement executes, a memory leak could occur.

Section 16.12 Class **auto_ptr** and Dynamic Memory Allocation

- The C++ Standard Library provides class template `auto_ptr` to deal with memory leaks.
- An object of class `auto_ptr` maintains a pointer to dynamically allocated memory. An `auto_ptr` object's destructor performs a `delete` operation on the `auto_ptr`'s pointer data member.
- Class template `auto_ptr` provides overloaded operators `*` and `->` so that an `auto_ptr` object can be used just as a regular pointer variable is. An `auto_ptr` also transfers ownership of the dynamic memory it manages via its copy constructor and overloaded assignment operator.

Section 16.13 Standard Library Exception Hierarchy

- The C++ Standard Library includes a hierarchy of exception classes. This hierarchy is headed by base-class exception.

- Immediate derived classes of base class exception include runtime_error and logic_error (both defined in header <stdexcept>), each of which has several derived classes.

- Several operators throw standard exceptions—operator new throws bad_alloc, operator dynamic_cast throws bad_cast and operator typeid throws bad_typeid.

- Including bad_exception in the throw list of a function means that, if an unexpected exception occurs, function unexpected can throw bad_exception rather than terminating the program's execution or calling another function specified by set_unexpected.

Terminology

abort function 695
arithmetic overflow error 704
arithmetic underflow error 705
asynchronous event 691
auto_ptr class template 701
bad_alloc exception 698
bad_cast exception 704
bad_exception exception 704
bad_typeid exception 704
catch handler 688
catch keyword 689
empty exception specification 694
exception 684
exception class 686
exception handler 688
exception handling 684
<exception> header file 686
exception object 690
exception parameter 689
exception specification 694
fault-tolerant program 684
invalid_argument exception 704
length_error exception 704
logic_error exception 704
<memory> header file 701
new handler 699

nothrow object 699
out_of_range exception 704
overflow_error exception 704
resource leak 695
resumption model of exception handling 689
rethrowing the exception 692
robust program 684
runtime_error exception 686
set_new_handler function 698
set_terminate function 695
set_unexpected function 694
stack unwinding 690
<stdexcept> header file 686
synchronous error 691
terminate function 692
termination model of exception handling 689
throw 690
throws an exception 688
throw keyword 690
throw list 694
throw point 689
try block 688
try keyword 688
underflow_error exception 705
unexpected function 694
what virtual function of class exception 686

Self-Review Exercises

16.1 List five common examples of exceptions.

16.2 Give several reasons why exception-handling techniques should not be used for conventional program control.

16.3 Why are exceptions appropriate for dealing with errors produced by library functions?

16.4 What's a "resource leak"?

16.5 If no exceptions are thrown in a try block, where does control proceed to after the try block completes execution?

16.6   What happens if an exception is thrown outside a try block?

16.7   Give a key advantage and a key disadvantage of using catch(...).

16.8   What happens if no catch handler matches the type of a thrown object?

16.9   What happens if several handlers match the type of the thrown object?

16.10   Why would you specify a base-class type as the type of a catch handler, then throw objects of derived-class types?

16.11   Suppose a catch handler with a precise match to an exception object type is available. Under what circumstances might a different handler be executed for exception objects of that type?

16.12   Must throwing an exception cause program termination?

16.13   What happens when a catch handler throws an exception?

16.14   What does the statement throw; do?

16.15   How do you restrict the exception types that a function can throw?

16.16   What happens if a function throws an exception of a type not allowed by the exception specification for the function?

16.17   What happens to the automatic objects that have been constructed in a try block when that block throws an exception?

Answers to Self-Review Exercises

16.1   Insufficient memory to satisfy a new request, array subscript out of bounds, arithmetic overflow, division by zero, invalid function parameters.

16.2   (a) Exception handling is designed to handle infrequently occurring situations that often result in program termination, so compiler writers are not required to implement exception handling to perform optimally. (b) Flow of control with conventional control structures generally is clearer and more efficient than with exceptions. (c) Problems can occur because the stack is unwound when an exception occurs and resources allocated prior to the exception might not be freed. (d) The "additional" exceptions make it more difficult for you to handle the larger number of exception cases.

16.3   It's unlikely that a library function will perform error processing that will meet the unique needs of all users.

16.4   A program that terminates abruptly could leave a resource in a state in which other programs would not be able to acquire the resource, or the program itself might not be able to reacquire a "leaked" resource.

16.5   The exception handlers (in the catch handlers) for that try block are skipped, and the program resumes execution after the last catch handler.

16.6   An exception thrown outside a try block causes a call to terminate.

16.7   The form catch(...) catches any type of exception thrown in a try block. An advantage is that all possible exceptions will be caught. A disadvantage is that the catch has no parameter, so it cannot reference information in the thrown object and cannot know the cause of the exception.

16.8   This causes the search for a match to continue in the next enclosing try block if there is one. As this process continues, it might eventually be determined that there is no handler in the program that matches the type of the thrown object; in this case, terminate is called, which by default calls abort. An alternative terminate function can be provided as an argument to set_terminate.

16.9   The first matching exception handler after the try block is executed.

16.10 This is a nice way to `catch` related types of exceptions.

16.11 A base-class handler would catch objects of all derived-class types.

16.12 No, but it does terminate the block in which the exception is thrown.

16.13 The exception will be processed by a `catch` handler (if one exists) associated with the `try` block (if one exists) enclosing the `catch` handler that caused the exception.

16.14 It rethrows the exception if it appears in a `catch` handler; otherwise, function `unexpected` is called.

16.15 Provide an exception specification listing the exception types that the function can throw.

16.16 Function `unexpected` is called.

16.17 The `try` block expires, causing destructors to be called for each of these objects.

Exercises

16.18 List various exceptional conditions that have occurred throughout this text. List as many additional exceptional conditions as you can. For each of these exceptions, describe briefly how a program typically would handle the exception, using the exception-handling techniques discussed in this chapter. Some typical exceptions are division by zero, arithmetic overflow, array subscript out of bounds, exhaustion of the free store, etc.

16.19 Under what circumstances would you not provide a parameter name when defining the type of the object that will be caught by a handler?

16.20 A program contains the statement

```
throw;
```

Where would you normally expect to find such a statement? What if that statement appeared in a different part of the program?

16.21 Compare and contrast exception handling with the various other error-processing schemes discussed in the text.

16.22 Why should exceptions not be used as an alternate form of program control?

16.23 Describe a technique for handling related exceptions.

16.24 *(Throwing Exceptions from a **catch**)* Suppose a program `throws` an exception and the appropriate exception handler begins executing. Now suppose that the exception handler itself `throws` the same exception. Does this create infinite recursion? Write a program to check your observation.

16.25 *(Catching Derived-Class Exceptions)* Use inheritance to create various derived classes of `runtime_error`. Then show that a `catch` handler specifying the base class can `catch` derived-class exceptions.

16.26 *(Throwing the Result of a Conditional Expression)* Throw the result of a conditional expression that returns either a `double` or an `int`. Provide an `int` catch handler and a `double` catch handler. Show that only the `double` catch handler executes, regardless of whether the `int` or the `double` is returned.

16.27 *(Local Variable Destructors)* Write a program illustrating that all destructors for objects constructed in a block are called before an exception is thrown from that block.

16.28 *(Member Object Destructors)* Write a program illustrating that member object destructors are called for only those member objects that were constructed before an exception occurred.

16.29 *(Cathing All Exceptions)* Write a program that demonstrates several exception types being caught with the `catch(...)` exception handler.

16.30 *(Order of Exception Handlers)* Write a program illustrating that the order of exception handlers is important. The first matching handler is the one that executes. Attempt to compile and run your program two different ways to show that two different handlers execute with two different effects.

16.31 *(Constructors Throwing Exceptions)* Write a program that shows a constructor passing information about constructor failure to an exception handler after a `try` block.

16.32 *(Rethrowing Exceptions)* Write a program that illustrates rethrowing an exception.

16.33 *(Uncaught Exceptions)* Write a program that illustrates that a function with its own `try` block does not have to catch every possible error generated within the `try`. Some exceptions can slip through to, and be handled in, outer scopes.

16.34 *(Stack Unwinding)* Write a program that `throws` an exception from a deeply nested function and still has the `catch` handler following the `try` block enclosing the call chain catch the exception.

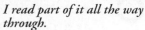

File Processing

17

I read part of it all the way through.
—Samuel Goldwyn

A great memory does not make a philosopher,
any more than a dictionary can be called grammar.
—John Henry, Cardinal Newman

I can only assume that a "Do Not File" document is filed in a "Do Not File" file.
—Senator Frank Church
Senate Intelligence Subcommittee
Hearing, 1975

Objectives

In this chapter you'll learn:

- To create, read, write and update files.

- Sequential file processing.

- Random-access file processing.

- To use high-performance unformatted I/O operations.

- The differences between formatted-data and raw-data file processing.

- To build a transaction-processing program using random-access file processing.

17.1 Introduction

Storage of data in memory is temporary. **Files** are used for **data persistence**—permanent retention of data. Computers store files on **secondary storage devices,** such as hard disks, CDs, DVDs, flash drives and tapes. In this chapter, we explain how to build C++ programs that create, update and process data files. We consider both sequential files and random-access files. We compare formatted-data file processing and raw-data file processing. We examine techniques for input of data from, and output of data to, string streams rather than files in Chapter 18, Class string and String Stream Processing.

17.2 Data Hierarchy

Ultimately, all data items that digital computers process are reduced to combinations of zeros and ones. This occurs because it's simple and economical to build electronic devices that can assume two stable states—one state represents 0 and the other represents 1. It's remarkable that the impressive functions performed by computers ultimately involve only the most fundamental manipulations of 0s and 1s.

The smallest data item that computers support is called a **bit** (short for "**binary digit**"—a digit that can assume one of two values). Each data item, or bit, can assume either the value 0 or the value 1. Computer circuitry performs various simple bit manipulations, such as examining the value of a bit, setting the value of a bit and reversing a bit (from 1 to 0 or from 0 to 1).

Programming with data in the low-level form of bits is cumbersome. It's preferable to program with data in forms such as **decimal digits** (0–9), **letters** (A–Z and a–z) and **special symbols** (e.g., $, @, %, &, * and many others). Digits, letters and special symbols are referred to as **characters**. The set of all characters used to write programs and represent data items on a particular computer is called that computer's **character set**. Because computers can process only 1s and 0s, every character in a computer's character set is represented as a pattern of 1s and 0s. **Bytes** are composed of eight bits. You create programs and data items with characters; computers manipulate and process these characters as patterns of bits. For example, C++ provides data type char. Each char typically occupies one byte. C++ also provides data type wchar_t, which can occupy more than one byte (to support larger character sets, such as the **Unicode® character set**; for more information on Unicode®, visit www.unicode.org).

Just as characters are composed of bits, **fields** are composed of characters. A field is a group of characters that conveys some meaning. For example, a field consisting of uppercase and lowercase letters can represent a person's name.

Data items processed by computers form a **data hierarchy** (Fig. 17.1), in which data items become larger and more complex in structure as we progress from bits, to characters, to fields and to larger data aggregates.

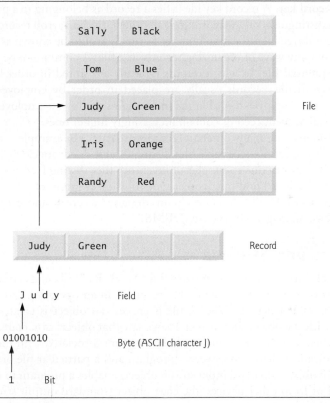

Fig. 17.1 | Data hierarchy.

Typically, a **record** (which can be represented as a class in C++) is composed of several fields (called data members in C++). In a payroll system, for example, a record for a particular employee might include the following fields:

1. Employee identification number
2. Name
3. Address
4. Hourly pay rate
5. Number of exemptions claimed
6. Year-to-date earnings
7. Amount of taxes withheld

Thus, a record is a group of related fields. In the preceding example, each field is associated with the same employee. A file is a group of related records.[1] A company's payroll file normally contains one record for each employee. Thus, a payroll file for a small company might contain only 22 records, whereas one for a large company might contain 100,000 records. It isn't unusual for a company to have many files, some containing millions, billions, trillions or more characters of information.

To facilitate retrieving specific records from a file, at least one field in each record is chosen as a **record key**. A record key identifies a record as belonging to a particular person or entity and distinguishes that record from all others. In the payroll record described previously, the employee identification number normally would be chosen as the record key.

There are many ways of organizing records in a file. A common type of organization is called a **sequential file,** in which records typically are stored in order by a record-key field. In a payroll file, records usually are placed in order by employee identification number. The first employee record in the file contains the lowest employee identification number, and subsequent records contain increasingly higher ones.

Most businesses use many different files to store data. For example, a company might have payroll files, accounts-receivable files (listing money due from clients), accounts-payable files (listing money due to suppliers), inventory files (listing facts about all the items handled by the business) and many other types of files. A group of related files often are stored in a **database.** A collection of programs designed to create and manage databases is called a **database management system (DBMS).**

17.3 Files and Streams

C++ views each file as a sequence of bytes (Fig. 17.2). Each file ends either with an **end-of-file marker** or at a specific byte number recorded in an operating-system-maintained, administrative data structure. When a file is *opened*, an object is created, and a stream is associated with the object. In Chapter 15, we saw that objects cin, cout, cerr and clog are created when <iostream> is included. The streams associated with these objects provide communication channels between a program and a particular file or device. For example, the cin object (standard input stream object) enables a program to input data from the keyboard or from other devices, the cout object (standard output stream object) enables a program to output data to the screen or other devices, and the cerr and clog objects (standard error stream objects) enable a program to output error messages to the screen or other devices.

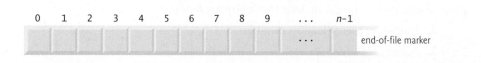

Fig. 17.2 | C++'s view of a file of n bytes.

---

1. Generally, a file can contain arbitrary data in arbitrary formats. In some operating systems, a file is viewed as nothing more than a collection of bytes. In such an operating system, any organization of the bytes in a file (such as organizing the data into records) is a view created by the application programmer.

To perform file processing in C++, header files <iostream> and <fstream> must be included. Header <fstream> includes the definitions for the stream class templates basic_ifstream (for file input), basic_ofstream (for file output) and basic_fstream (for file input and output). Each class template has a predefined template specialization that enables char I/O. In addition, the <fstream> library provides typedef aliases for these template specializations. For example, the typedef ifstream represents a specialization of basic_ifstream that enables char input from a file. Similarly, typedef ofstream represents a specialization of basic_ofstream that enables char output to files. Also, typedef fstream represents a specialization of basic_fstream that enables char input from, and output to, files.

Files are opened by creating objects of these stream template specializations. These templates "derive" from class templates basic_istream, basic_ostream and basic_iostream, respectively. Thus, all member functions, operators and manipulators that belong to these templates (which we described in Chapter 15) also can be applied to file streams. Figure 17.3 summarizes the inheritance relationships of the I/O classes that we've discussed to this point.

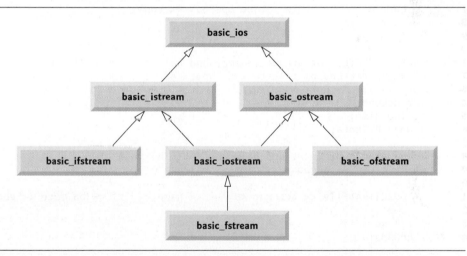

Fig. 17.3 | Portion of stream I/O template hierarchy.

17.4 Creating a Sequential File

C++ imposes no structure on a file. Thus, a concept like that of a "record" does not exist in a C++ file. Therefore, you must structure files to meet the application's requirements. In the following example, we see how you can impose a simple record structure on a file.

Figure 17.4 creates a sequential file that might be used in an accounts-receivable system to help manage the money owed by a company's credit clients. For each client, the program obtains the client's account number, name and balance (i.e., the amount the client owes the company for goods and services received in the past). The data obtained for each client constitutes a record for that client. The account number serves as the record key; that is, the program creates and maintains the file in account number order. This program assumes the user enters the records in account number order. In a comprehensive accounts receivable system, a sorting capability would be provided for the user to enter records in any order—the records then would be sorted and written to the file.

```cpp
 1   // Fig. 17.4: Fig17_04.cpp
 2   // Create a sequential file.
 3   #include <iostream>
 4   #include <string>
 5   #include <fstream> // file stream
 6   #include <cstdlib>
 7   using namespace std;
 8
 9   int main()
10   {
11      // ofstream constructor opens file
12      ofstream outClientFile( "clients.dat", ios::out );
13
14      // exit program if unable to create file
15      if ( !outClientFile ) // overloaded ! operator
16      {
17         cerr << "File could not be opened" << endl;
18         exit( 1 );
19      } // end if
20
21      cout << "Enter the account, name, and balance." << endl
22         << "Enter end-of-file to end input.\n? ";
23
24      int account;
25      string name;
26      double balance;
27
28      // read account, name and balance from cin, then place in file
29      while ( cin >> account >> name >> balance )
30      {
31         outClientFile << account << ' ' << name << ' ' << balance << endl;
32         cout << "? ";
33      } // end while
34   } // end main
```

```
Enter the account, name, and balance.
Enter end-of-file to end input.
? 100 Jones 24.98
? 200 Doe 345.67
? 300 White 0.00
? 400 Stone -42.16
? 500 Rich 224.62
? ^Z
```

Fig. 17.4 | Creating a sequential file.

Let's examine this program. As stated previously, files are opened by creating ifstream, ofstream or fstream objects. In Fig. 17.4, the file is to be opened for output, so an ofstream object is created. Two arguments are passed to the object's constructor— the **filename** and the **file-open mode** (line 12). For an ofstream object, the file-open mode can be either **ios::out** to output data to a file or **ios::app** to append data to the end of a file (without modifying any data already in the file). Existing files opened with mode ios::out are **truncated**—all data in the file is discarded. If the specified file does not yet exist, then the ofstream object creates the file, using that filename.

Line 12 creates an ofstream object named outClientFile associated with the file clients.dat that is opened for output. The arguments "clients.dat" and ios::out are passed to the ofstream constructor, which opens the file—this establishes a "line of communication" with the file. By default, ofstream objects are opened for output, so line 12 could have used the alternate statement

```
ofstream outClientFile( "clients.dat" );
```

to open clients.dat for output. Figure 17.5 lists the file-open modes.

Common Programming Error 17.1

Use caution when opening an existing file for output (ios::out), especially when you want to preserve the file's contents, which will be discarded without warning.

Mode	Description
ios::app	Append all output to the end of the file.
ios::ate	Open a file for output and move to the end of the file (normally used to append data to a file). Data can be written anywhere in the file.
ios::in	Open a file for input.
ios::out	Open a file for output.
ios::trunc	Discard the file's contents (this also is the default action for ios::out).
ios::binary	Open a file for binary (i.e., nontext) input or output.

Fig. 17.5 | File open modes.

An ofstream object can be created without opening a specific file—a file can be attached to the object later. For example, the statement

```
ofstream outClientFile;
```

creates an ofstream object named outClientFile. The ofstream member function **open** opens a file and attaches it to an existing ofstream object as follows:

```
outClientFile.open( "clients.dat", ios::out );
```

Common Programming Error 17.2

Not opening a file before attempting to reference it in a program will result in an error.

After creating an ofstream object and attempting to open it, the program tests whether the open operation was successful. The if statement in lines 15–19 uses the overloaded ios member function operator! to determine whether the open operation succeeded. The condition returns a true value if either the failbit or the badbit is set for the stream on the open operation. Some possible errors are attempting to open a nonexistent file for reading, attempting to open a file for reading or writing without permission, and opening a file for writing when no disk space is available.

If the condition indicates an unsuccessful attempt to open the file, line 17 outputs the error message "File could not be opened", and line 18 invokes function exit to terminate the program. The argument to exit is returned to the environment from which the program was invoked. Argument 0 indicates that the program terminated normally; any other value indicates that the program terminated due to an error. The calling environment (most likely the operating system) uses the value returned by exit to respond appropriately to the error.

Another overloaded ios member function—operator void *—converts the stream to a pointer, so it can be tested as 0 (i.e., the null pointer) or nonzero (i.e., any other pointer value). When a pointer value is used as a condition, C++ interprets a null pointer in a condition as the bool value false and interprets a non-null pointer as the bool value true. If the failbit or badbit (see Chapter 15) has been set for the stream, 0 (false) is returned. The condition in the while statement of lines 29–33 invokes the operator void * member function on cin implicitly. The condition remains true as long as neither the failbit nor the badbit has been set for cin. Entering the end-of-file indicator sets the failbit for cin. The operator void * function can be used to test an input object for end-of-file instead of calling the eof member function explicitly on the input object.

If line 12 opened the file successfully, the program begins processing data. Lines 21–22 prompt the user to enter either the various fields for each record or the end-of-file indicator when data entry is complete. Figure 17.6 lists the keyboard combinations for entering end-of-file for various computer systems.

Computer system	Keyboard combination
UNIX/Linux/Mac OS X	*<Ctrl-d>* (on a line by itself)
Microsoft Windows	*<Ctrl-z>* (sometimes followed by pressing *Enter*)
VAX (VMS)	*<Ctrl-z>*

Fig. 17.6 | End-of-file key combinations for various popular computer systems.

Line 29 extracts each set of data and determines whether end-of-file has been entered. When end-of-file is encountered or bad data is entered, operator void * returns the null pointer (which converts to the bool value false) and the while statement terminates. The user enters end-of-file to inform the program to process no additional data. The end-of-file indicator is set when the user enters the end-of-file key combination. The while statement loops until the end-of-file indicator is set.

Line 31 writes a set of data to the file clients.dat, using the stream insertion operator << and the outClientFile object associated with the file at the beginning of the program. The data may be retrieved by a program designed to read the file (see Section 17.5). The file created in Fig. 17.4 is simply a text file, so it can be viewed by any text editor.

Once the user enters the end-of-file indicator, main terminates. This implicitly invokes outClientFile's destructor, which closes the clients.dat file. You also can close the ofstream object explicitly, using member function **close** in the statement

```
outClientFile.close();
```

Performance Tip 17.1

Closing files explicitly when the program no longer needs to reference them can reduce re-source usage (especially if the program continues execution after closing the files).

In the sample execution for the program of Fig. 17.4, the user enters information for five accounts, then signals that data entry is complete by entering end-of-file (^Z is displayed for Microsoft Windows). This dialog window does not show how the data records appear in the file. To verify that the program created the file successfully, the next section shows how to create a program that reads this file and prints its contents.

17.5 Reading Data from a Sequential File

Files store data so it may be retrieved for processing when needed. The previous section demonstrated how to create a file for sequential access. In this section, we discuss how to read data sequentially from a file.

Figure 17.7 reads records from the `clients.dat` file that we created using the program of Fig. 17.4 and displays the contents of these records. Creating an `ifstream` object opens a file for input. The `ifstream` constructor can receive the filename and the file open mode as arguments. Line 15 creates an `ifstream` object called `inClientFile` and associates it with the `clients.dat` file. The arguments in parentheses are passed to the `ifstream` constructor function, which opens the file and establishes a "line of communication" with the file.

Good Programming Practice 17.1

Open a file for input only (using `ios::in`) if the file's contents should not be modified. This prevents unintentional modification of the file's contents and is an example of the principle of least privilege.

```
1   // Fig. 17.7: Fig17_07.cpp
2   // Reading and printing a sequential file.
3   #include <iostream>
4   #include <fstream> // file stream
5   #include <iomanip>
6   #include <string>
7   #include <cstdlib>
8   using namespace std;
9
10  void outputLine( int, const string, double ); // prototype
11
12  int main()
13  {
14     // ifstream constructor opens the file
15     ifstream inClientFile( "clients.dat", ios::in );
16
17     // exit program if ifstream could not open file
18     if ( !inClientFile )
19     {
20        cerr << "File could not be opened" << endl;
```

Fig. 17.7 | Reading and printing a sequential file. (Part 1 of 2.)

```
21          exit( 1 );
22       } // end if
23
24       int account;
25       string name;
26       double balance;
27
28       cout << left << setw( 10 ) << "Account" << setw( 13 )
29          << "Name" << "Balance" << endl << fixed << showpoint;
30
31       // display each record in file
32       while ( inClientFile >> account >> name >> balance )
33          outputLine( account, name, balance );
34    } // end main
35
36    // display single record from file
37    void outputLine( int account, const string name, double balance )
38    {
39       cout << left << setw( 10 ) << account << setw( 13 ) << name
40          << setw( 7 ) << setprecision( 2 ) << right << balance << endl;
41    } // end function outputLine
```

```
Account    Name       Balance
100        Jones        24.98
200        Doe         345.67
300        White         0.00
400        Stone       -42.16
500        Rich        224.62
```

Fig. 17.7 | Reading and printing a sequential file. (Part 2 of 2.)

Objects of class ifstream are opened for input by default. We could have used the statement

```
ifstream inClientFile( "clients.dat" );
```

to open clients.dat for input. Just as with an ofstream object, an ifstream object can be created without opening a specific file, because a file can be attached to it later.

The program uses the condition !inClientFile to determine whether the file was opened successfully before attempting to retrieve data from the file. Line 32 reads a set of data (i.e., a record) from the file. After the preceding line is executed the first time, account has the value 100, name has the value "Jones" and balance has the value 24.98. Each time line 32 executes, it reads another record from the file into the variables account, name and balance. Line 33 displays the records, using function outputLine (lines 37–41), which uses parameterized stream manipulators to format the data for display. When the end of file has been reached, the implicit call to operator void * in the while condition returns the null pointer (which converts to the bool value false), the ifstream destructor function closes the file and the program terminates.

To retrieve data sequentially from a file, programs normally start reading from the beginning of the file and read all the data consecutively until the desired data is found. It might be necessary to process the file sequentially several times (from the beginning of the file) during the execution of a program. Both istream and ostream provide member functions for repositioning the **file-position pointer** (the byte number of the next byte in the file to be read or written). These member functions are **seekg** ("seek get") for istream and **seekp** ("seek put") for ostream. Each istream object has a "get pointer," which indicates the byte number in the file from which the next input is to occur, and each ostream object has a "put pointer," which indicates the byte number in the file at which the next output should be placed. The statement

```
inClientFile.seekg( 0 );
```

repositions the file-position pointer to the beginning of the file (location 0) attached to in-ClientFile. The argument to seekg normally is a long integer. A second argument can be specified to indicate the **seek direction**, which can be **ios::beg** (the default) for positioning relative to the beginning of a stream, **ios::cur** for positioning relative to the current position in a stream or **ios::end** for positioning relative to the end of a stream. The file-position pointer is an integer value that specifies the location in the file as a number of bytes from the file's starting location (this is also referred to as the **offset** from the beginning of the file). Some examples of positioning the "get" file-position pointer are

```
// position to the nth byte of fileObject (assumes ios::beg)
fileObject.seekg( n );
// position n bytes forward in fileObject
fileObject.seekg( n, ios::cur );
// position n bytes back from end of fileObject
fileObject.seekg( n, ios::end );
// position at end of fileObject
fileObject.seekg( 0, ios::end );
```

The same operations can be performed using ostream member function seekp. Member functions **tellg** and **tellp** are provided to return the current locations of the "get" and "put" pointers, respectively. The following statement assigns the "get" file-position pointer value to variable location of type long:

```
location = fileObject.tellg();
```

Figure 17.8 enables a credit manager to display the account information for those customers with zero balances (i.e., customers who do not owe the company any money), credit (negative) balances (i.e., customers to whom the company owes money), and debit (positive) balances (i.e., customers who owe the company money for goods and services received in the past). The program displays a menu and allows the credit manager to enter one of three options to obtain credit information. Option 1 produces a list of accounts with zero balances. Option 2 produces a list of accounts with credit balances. Option 3 produces a list of accounts with debit balances. Option 4 terminates program execution. Entering an invalid option displays the prompt to enter another choice. Lines 65–66 enable the program to read from the beginning of the file after the EOF marker has been read.

```
1   // Fig. 17.8: Fig17_08.cpp
2   // Credit inquiry program.
3   #include <iostream>
4   #include <fstream>
```

Fig. 17.8 | Credit inquiry program. (Part 1 of 4.)

```
5    #include <iomanip>
6    #include <string>
7    #include <cstdlib>
8    using namespace std;
9
10   enum RequestType { ZERO_BALANCE = 1, CREDIT_BALANCE, DEBIT_BALANCE, END };
11   int getRequest();
12   bool shouldDisplay( int, double );
13   void outputLine( int, const string, double );
14
15   int main()
16   {
17      // ifstream constructor opens the file
18      ifstream inClientFile( "clients.dat", ios::in );
19
20      // exit program if ifstream could not open file
21      if ( !inClientFile )
22      {
23         cerr << "File could not be opened" << endl;
24         exit( 1 );
25      } // end if
26
27      int request;
28      int account;
29      string name;
30      double balance;
31
32      // get user's request (e.g., zero, credit or debit balance)
33      request = getRequest();
34
35      // process user's request
36      while ( request != END )
37      {
38         switch ( request )
39         {
40            case ZERO_BALANCE:
41               cout << "\nAccounts with zero balances:\n";
42               break;
43            case CREDIT_BALANCE:
44               cout << "\nAccounts with credit balances:\n";
45               break;
46            case DEBIT_BALANCE:
47               cout << "\nAccounts with debit balances:\n";
48               break;
49         } // end switch
50
51         // read account, name and balance from file
52         inClientFile >> account >> name >> balance;
53
54         // display file contents (until eof)
55         while ( !inClientFile.eof() )
56         {
```

Fig. 17.8 | Credit inquiry program. (Part 2 of 4.)

```
57           // display record
58           if ( shouldDisplay( request, balance ) )
59              outputLine( account, name, balance );
60
61           // read account, name and balance from file
62           inClientFile >> account >> name >> balance;
63        } // end inner while
64
65        inClientFile.clear(); // reset eof for next input
66        inClientFile.seekg( 0 ); // reposition to beginning of file
67        request = getRequest(); // get additional request from user
68     } // end outer while
69
70     cout << "End of run." << endl;
71  } // end main
72
73  // obtain request from user
74  int getRequest()
75  {
76     int request; // request from user
77
78     // display request options
79     cout << "\nEnter request" << endl
80        << " 1 - List accounts with zero balances" << endl
81        << " 2 - List accounts with credit balances" << endl
82        << " 3 - List accounts with debit balances" << endl
83        << " 4 - End of run" << fixed << showpoint;
84
85     do // input user request
86     {
87        cout << "\n? ";
88        cin >> request;
89     } while ( request < ZERO_BALANCE && request > END );
90
91     return request;
92  } // end function getRequest
93
94  // determine whether to display given record
95  bool shouldDisplay( int type, double balance )
96  {
97     // determine whether to display zero balances
98     if ( type == ZERO_BALANCE && balance == 0 )
99        return true;
100
101     // determine whether to display credit balances
102     if ( type == CREDIT_BALANCE && balance < 0 )
103        return true;
104
105     // determine whether to display debit balances
106     if ( type == DEBIT_BALANCE && balance > 0 )
107        return true;
108
```

Fig. 17.8 | Credit inquiry program. (Part 3 of 4.)

```
109      return false;
110  } // end function shouldDisplay
111
112  // display single record from file
113  void outputLine( int account, const string name, double balance )
114  {
115     cout << left << setw( 10 ) << account << setw( 13 ) << name
116        << setw( 7 ) << setprecision( 2 ) << right << balance << endl;
117  } // end function outputLine
```

```
Enter request
 1 - List accounts with zero balances
 2 - List accounts with credit balances
 3 - List accounts with debit balances
 4 - End of run
? 1

Accounts with zero balances:
300       White           0.00

Enter request
 1 - List accounts with zero balances
 2 - List accounts with credit balances
 3 - List accounts with debit balances
 4 - End of run
? 2

Accounts with credit balances:
400       Stone          -42.16

Enter request
 1 - List accounts with zero balances
 2 - List accounts with credit balances
 3 - List accounts with debit balances
 4 - End of run
? 3

Accounts with debit balances:
100       Jones          24.98
200       Doe           345.67
500       Rich          224.62

Enter request
 1 - List accounts with zero balances
 2 - List accounts with credit balances
 3 - List accounts with debit balances
 4 - End of run
? 4
End of run.
```

Fig. 17.8 | Credit inquiry program. (Part 4 of 4.)

17.6 Updating Sequential Files

Data that is formatted and written to a sequential file as shown in Section 17.4 cannot be modified without the risk of destroying other data in the file. For example, if the name

"White" needs to be changed to "Worthington," the old name cannot be overwritten without corrupting the file. The record for White was written to the file as

```
300 White 0.00
```

If this record were rewritten beginning at the same location in the file using the longer name, the record would be

```
300 Worthington 0.00
```

The new record contains six more characters than the original record. Therefore, the characters beyond the second "o" in "Worthington" would overwrite the beginning of the next sequential record in the file. The problem is that, in the formatted input/output model using the stream insertion operator << and the stream extraction operator >>, fields—and hence records—can vary in size. For example, values 7, 14, –117, 2074, and 27383 are all ints, which store the same number of "raw data" bytes internally (typically four bytes on today's popular 32-bit machines). However, these integers become different-sized fields when output as formatted text (character sequences). Therefore, the formatted input/output model usually is not used to update records in place.

Such updating can be done awkwardly. For example, to make the preceding name change, the records before 300 White 0.00 in a sequential file could be copied to a new file, the updated record then written to the new file, and the records after 300 White 0.00 copied to the new file. This requires processing every record in the file to update one record. If many records are being updated in one pass of the file, though, this technique can be acceptable.

17.7 Random-Access Files

So far, we've seen how to create sequential files and search them to locate information. Sequential files are inappropriate for **instant-access applications**, in which a particular record must be located immediately. Common instant-access applications are airline reservation systems, banking systems, point-of-sale systems, automated teller machines and other kinds of **transaction-processing systems** that require rapid access to specific data. A bank might have hundreds of thousands (or even millions) of other customers, yet, when a customer uses an automated teller machine, the program checks that customer's account in a few seconds or less for sufficient funds. This kind of instant access is made possible with **random-access files.** Individual records of a random-access file can be accessed directly (and quickly) without having to search other records.

As we've said, C++ does not impose structure on a file. So the application that wants to use random-access files must create them. A variety of techniques can be used. Perhaps the easiest method is to require that all records in a file be of the same fixed length. Using same-size, fixed-length records makes it easy for a program to calculate (as a function of the record size and the record key) the exact location of any record relative to the beginning of the file. We soon will see how this facilitates immediate access to specific records, even in large files.

Figure 17.9 illustrates C++'s view of a random-access file composed of fixed-length records (each record, in this case, is 100 bytes long). A random-access file is like a railroad train with many same-size cars—some empty and some with contents.

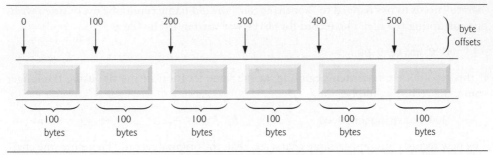

Fig. 17.9 | C++ view of a random-access file.

Data can be inserted into a random-access file without destroying other data in the file. Data stored previously also can be updated or deleted without rewriting the entire file. In the following sections, we explain how to create a random-access file, enter data into the file, read the data both sequentially and randomly, update the data and delete data that is no longer needed.

17.8 Creating a Random-Access File

The `ostream` member function `write` outputs a fixed number of bytes, beginning at a specific location in memory, to the specified stream. When the stream is associated with a file, function `write` writes the data at the location in the file specified by the "put" file-position pointer. The `istream` member function `read` inputs a fixed number of bytes from the specified stream to an area in memory beginning at a specified address. If the stream is associated with a file, function `read` inputs bytes at the location in the file specified by the "get" file-position pointer.

Writing Bytes with ***ostream*** *Member Function* ***write***
When writing the integer `number` to a file, instead of using the statement

```
outFile << number;
```

which for a four-byte integer could print as few digits as one or as many as 11 (10 digits plus a sign, each requiring a single byte of storage), we can use the statement

```
outFile.write( reinterpret_cast< const char * >( &number ),
   sizeof( number ) );
```

which always writes the binary version of the integer's four bytes (on a machine with four-byte integers). Function `write` treats its first argument as a group of bytes by viewing the object in memory as a `const char *`, which is a pointer to a byte. Starting from that location, function `write` outputs the number of bytes specified by its second argument—an integer of type `size_t`. As we'll see, `istream` function `read` can subsequently be used to read the four bytes back into integer variable `number`.

Converting Between Pointer Types with the ***reinterpret_cast*** *Operator*
Unfortunately, most pointers that we pass to function `write` as the first argument are not of type `const char *`. To output objects of other types, we must convert the pointers to those objects to type `const char *`; otherwise, the compiler will not compile calls to func-

tion `write`. C++ provides the **`reinterpret_cast`** operator for cases like this in which a pointer of one type must be cast to an unrelated pointer type. Without a `reinterpret_cast`, the `write` statement that outputs the integer `number` will not compile because the compiler does not allow a pointer of type `int *` (the type returned by the expression `&number`) to be passed to a function that expects an argument of type `const char *`—as far as the compiler is concerned, these types are incompatible.

A `reinterpret_cast` is performed at compile time and does not change the value of the object to which its operand points. Instead, it requests that the compiler reinterpret the operand as the target type (specified in the angle brackets following the keyword `reinterpret_cast`). In Fig. 17.12, we use `reinterpret_cast` to convert a `ClientData` pointer to a `const char *`, which reinterprets a `ClientData` object as bytes to be output to a file. Random-access file-processing programs rarely write a single field to a file. Typically, they write one object of a class at a time, as we show in the following examples.

Error-Prevention Tip 17.1

It's easy to use `reinterpret_cast` to perform dangerous manipulations that could lead to serious execution-time errors.

Portability Tip 17.1

Using `reinterpret_cast` is compiler dependent and can cause programs to behave differently on different platforms. The `reinterpret_cast` operator should not be used unless absolutely necessary.

Portability Tip 17.2

A program that reads unformatted data (written by `write`) must be compiled and executed on a system compatible with the program that wrote the data, because different systems may represent internal data differently.

Credit Processing Program

Consider the following problem statement:

> *Create a credit-processing program capable of storing at most 100 fixed-length records for a company that can have up to 100 customers. Each record should consist of an account number that acts as the record key, a last name, a first name and a balance. The program should be able to update an account, insert a new account, delete an account and insert all the account records into a formatted text file for printing.*

The next several sections introduce the techniques for creating this credit-processing program. Figure 17.12 illustrates opening a random-access file, defining the record format using an object of class `ClientData` (Figs. 17.10–17.11) and writing data to the disk in binary format. This program initializes all 100 records of the file `credit.dat` with empty objects, using function `write`. Each empty object contains 0 for the account number, the null string (represented by empty quotation marks) for the last and first name and 0.0 for the balance. Each record is initialized with the amount of empty space in which the account data will be stored.

Objects of class `string` do not have uniform size, rather they use dynamically allocated memory to accommodate strings of various lengths. We must maintain fixed-length records, so class `ClientData` stores the client's first and last name in fixed-length char arrays (declared in Fig. 17.10, lines 32–33). Member functions `setLastName` (Fig. 17.11, lines 36–43) and setFirstName (Fig. 17.11, lines 52–59) each copy the characters of a string object into the corresponding char array. Consider function setLastName. Line 39 invokes string member function **size** to get the length of lastNameString. Line 40 ensures that length is fewer than 15 characters, then line 41 copies length characters from lastNameString into the char array lastName using string member function copy. Member function setFirstName performs the same steps for the first name.

```
1    // Fig. 17.10: ClientData.h
2    // Class ClientData definition used in Fig. 17.12-Fig. 17.15.
3    #ifndef CLIENTDATA_H
4    #define CLIENTDATA_H
5
6    #include <string>
7    using namespace std;
8
9    class ClientData
10   {
11   public:
12      // default ClientData constructor
13      ClientData( int = 0, string = "", string = "", double = 0.0 );
14
15      // accessor functions for accountNumber
16      void setAccountNumber( int );
17      int getAccountNumber() const;
18
19      // accessor functions for lastName
20      void setLastName( string );
21      string getLastName() const;
22
23      // accessor functions for firstName
24      void setFirstName( string );
25      string getFirstName() const;
26
27      // accessor functions for balance
28      void setBalance( double );
29      double getBalance() const;
30   private:
31      int accountNumber;
32      char lastName[ 15 ];
33      char firstName[ 10 ];
34      double balance;
35   }; // end class ClientData
36
37   #endif
```

Fig. 17.10 | ClientData class header file.

```
1    // Fig. 17.11: ClientData.cpp
2    // Class ClientData stores customer's credit information.
3    #include <string>
```

Fig. 17.11 | ClientData class represents a customer's credit information. (Part 1 of 3.)

```
 4   #include "ClientData.h"
 5   using namespace std;
 6
 7   // default ClientData constructor
 8   ClientData::ClientData( int accountNumberValue,
 9      string lastNameValue, string firstNameValue, double balanceValue )
10   {
11      setAccountNumber( accountNumberValue );
12      setLastName( lastNameValue );
13      setFirstName( firstNameValue );
14      setBalance( balanceValue );
15   } // end ClientData constructor
16
17   // get account-number value
18   int ClientData::getAccountNumber() const
19   {
20      return accountNumber;
21   } // end function getAccountNumber
22
23   // set account-number value
24   void ClientData::setAccountNumber( int accountNumberValue )
25   {
26      accountNumber = accountNumberValue; // should validate
27   } // end function setAccountNumber
28
29   // get last-name value
30   string ClientData::getLastName() const
31   {
32      return lastName;
33   } // end function getLastName
34
35   // set last-name value
36   void ClientData::setLastName( string lastNameString )
37   {
38      // copy at most 15 characters from string to lastName
39      int length = lastNameString.size();
40      length = ( length < 15 ? length : 14 );
41      lastNameString.copy( lastName, length );
42      lastName[ length ] = '\0'; // append null character to lastName
43   } // end function setLastName
44
45   // get first-name value
46   string ClientData::getFirstName() const
47   {
48      return firstName;
49   } // end function getFirstName
50
51   // set first-name value
52   void ClientData::setFirstName( string firstNameString )
53   {
54      // copy at most 10 characters from string to firstName
55      int length = firstNameString.size();
56      length = ( length < 10 ? length : 9 );
```

Fig. 17.11 | ClientData class represents a customer's credit information. (Part 2 of 3.)

```
57        firstNameString.copy( firstName, length );
58        firstName[ length ] = '\0'; // append null character to firstName
59    } // end function setFirstName
60
61    // get balance value
62    double ClientData::getBalance() const
63    {
64        return balance;
65    } // end function getBalance
66
67    // set balance value
68    void ClientData::setBalance( double balanceValue )
69    {
70        balance = balanceValue;
71    } // end function setBalance
```

Fig. 17.11 | `ClientData` class represents a customer's credit information. (Part 3 of 3.)

In Fig. 17.12, line 11 creates an `ofstream` object for the file `credit.dat`. The second argument to the constructor—`ios::out | ios::binary`—indicates that we are opening the file for output in binary mode, which is required if we are to write fixed-length records. Lines 24–25 cause the `blankClient` to be written to the `credit.dat` file associated with `ofstream` object `outCredit`. Remember that operator `sizeof` returns the size in bytes of the object contained in parentheses (see Chapter 8). The first argument to function `write` at line 24 must be of type `const char *`. However, the data type of `&blankClient` is `ClientData *`. To convert `&blankClient` to `const char *`, line 24 uses the cast operator `reinterpret_cast`, so the call to `write` compiles without issuing a compilation error.

```
1    // Fig. 17.12: Fig17_12.cpp
2    // Creating a randomly accessed file.
3    #include <iostream>
4    #include <fstream>
5    #include <cstdlib>
6    #include "ClientData.h" // ClientData class definition
7    using namespace std;
8
9    int main()
10   {
11       ofstream outCredit( "credit.dat", ios::out | ios::binary );
12
13       // exit program if ofstream could not open file
14       if ( !outCredit )
15       {
16          cerr << "File could not be opened." << endl;
17          exit( 1 );
18       } // end if
19
20       ClientData blankClient; // constructor zeros out each data member
21
```

Fig. 17.12 | Creating a random-access file with 100 blank records sequentially. (Part 1 of 2.)

```
22      // output 100 blank records to file
23      for ( int i = 0; i < 100; i++ )
24         outCredit.write( reinterpret_cast< const char * >( &blankClient ),
25            sizeof( ClientData ) );
26   } // end main
```

Fig. 17.12 | Creating a random-access file with 100 blank records sequentially. (Part 2 of 2.)

17.9 Writing Data Randomly to a Random-Access File

Figure 17.13 writes data to the file credit.dat and uses the combination of fstream functions seekp and write to store data at exact locations in the file. Function seekp sets the "put" file-position pointer to a specific position in the file, then write outputs the data. Line 6 includes the header file ClientData.h defined in Fig. 17.10, so the program can use ClientData objects.

```
1   // Fig. 17.13: Fig17_13.cpp
2   // Writing to a random-access file.
3   #include <iostream>
4   #include <fstream>
5   #include <cstdlib>
6   #include "ClientData.h" // ClientData class definition
7   using namespace std;
8
9   int main()
10  {
11     int accountNumber;
12     string lastName;
13     string firstName;
14     double balance;
15
16     fstream outCredit( "credit.dat", ios::in | ios::out | ios::binary );
17
18     // exit program if fstream cannot open file
19     if ( !outCredit )
20     {
21        cerr << "File could not be opened." << endl;
22        exit( 1 );
23     } // end if
24
25     cout << "Enter account number (1 to 100, 0 to end input)\n? ";
26
27     // require user to specify account number
28     ClientData client;
29     cin >> accountNumber;
30
31     // user enters information, which is copied into file
32     while ( accountNumber > 0 && accountNumber <= 100 )
33     {
```

Fig. 17.13 | Writing to a random-access file. (Part 1 of 2.)

```
34          // user enters last name, first name and balance
35          cout << "Enter lastname, firstname, balance\n? ";
36          cin >> lastName;
37          cin >> firstName;
38          cin >> balance;
39
40          // set record accountNumber, lastName, firstName and balance values
41          client.setAccountNumber( accountNumber );
42          client.setLastName( lastName );
43          client.setFirstName( firstName );
44          client.setBalance( balance );
45
46          // seek position in file of user-specified record
47          outCredit.seekp( ( client.getAccountNumber() - 1 ) *
48             sizeof( ClientData ) );
49
50          // write user-specified information in file
51          outCredit.write( reinterpret_cast< const char * >( &client ),
52             sizeof( ClientData ) );
53
54          // enable user to enter another account
55          cout << "Enter account number\n? ";
56          cin >> accountNumber;
57       } // end while
58    } // end main
```

```
Enter account number (1 to 100, 0 to end input)
? 37
Enter lastname, firstname, balance
? Barker Doug 0.00
Enter account number
? 29
Enter lastname, firstname, balance
? Brown Nancy -24.54
Enter account number
? 96
Enter lastname, firstname, balance
? Stone Sam 34.98
Enter account number
? 88
Enter lastname, firstname, balance
? Smith Dave 258.34
Enter account number
? 33
Enter lastname, firstname, balance
? Dunn Stacey 314.33
Enter account number
? 0
```

Fig. 17.13 | Writing to a random-access file. (Part 2 of 2.)

Lines 47–48 position the "put" file-position pointer for object outCredit to the byte location calculated by

```
( client.getAccountNumber() - 1 ) * sizeof( ClientData )
```

Because the account number is between 1 and 100, 1 is subtracted from the account number when calculating the byte location of the record. Thus, for record 1, the file-position pointer is set to byte 0 of the file. Line 16 uses the `fstream` object `outCredit` to open the existing `credit.dat` file. The file is opened for input and output in binary mode by combining the file-open modes `ios::in`, `ios::out` and `ios::binary`. Multiple file-open modes are combined by separating each open mode from the next with the bitwise inclusive OR operator (|). Opening the existing `credit.dat` file in this manner ensures that this program can manipulate the records written to the file by the program of Fig. 17.12, rather than creating the file from scratch. Chapter 21, Bits, Characters, C Strings and structs, discusses the bitwise inclusive OR operator in detail.

17.10 Reading from a Random-Access File Sequentially

In the previous sections, we created a random-access file and wrote data to that file. In this section, we develop a program that reads the file sequentially and prints only those records that contain data. These programs produce an additional benefit. See if you can determine what it is; we'll reveal it at the end of this section.

The `istream` function `read` inputs a specified number of bytes from the current position in the specified stream into an object. For example, lines 30–31 from Fig. 17.14 read the number of bytes specified by `sizeof(ClientData)` from the file associated with `ifstream` object `inCredit` and store the data in the `client` record. Function `read` requires a first argument of type `char *`. Since `&client` is of type `ClientData *`, `&client` must be cast to `char *` using the cast operator `reinterpret_cast`.

```cpp
1   // Fig. 17.14: Fig17_14.cpp
2   // Reading a random-access file sequentially.
3   #include <iostream>
4   #include <iomanip>
5   #include <fstream>
6   #include <cstdlib>
7   #include "ClientData.h" // ClientData class definition
8   using namespace std;
9
10  void outputLine( ostream&, const ClientData & ); // prototype
11
12  int main()
13  {
14     ifstream inCredit( "credit.dat", ios::in | ios::binary );
15
16     // exit program if ifstream cannot open file
17     if ( !inCredit )
18     {
19        cerr << "File could not be opened." << endl;
20        exit( 1 );
21     } // end if
22
```

Fig. 17.14 | Reading a random-access file sequentially. (Part 1 of 2.)

```
23        cout << left << setw( 10 ) << "Account" << setw( 16 )
24            << "Last Name" << setw( 11 ) << "First Name" << left
25            << setw( 10 ) << right << "Balance" << endl;
26
27        ClientData client; // create record
28
29        // read first record from file
30        inCredit.read( reinterpret_cast< char * >( &client ),
31            sizeof( ClientData ) );
32
33        // read all records from file
34        while ( inCredit && !inCredit.eof() )
35        {
36            // display record
37            if ( client.getAccountNumber() != 0 )
38                outputLine( cout, client );
39
40            // read next from file
41            inCredit.read( reinterpret_cast< char * >( &client ),
42                sizeof( ClientData ) );
43        } // end while
44    } // end main
45
46    // display single record
47    void outputLine( ostream &output, const ClientData &record )
48    {
49        output << left << setw( 10 ) << record.getAccountNumber()
50            << setw( 16 ) << record.getLastName()
51            << setw( 11 ) << record.getFirstName()
52            << setw( 10 ) << setprecision( 2 ) << right << fixed
53            << showpoint << record.getBalance() << endl;
54    } // end function outputLine
```

Account	Last Name	First Name	Balance
29	Brown	Nancy	-24.54
33	Dunn	Stacey	314.33
37	Barker	Doug	0.00
88	Smith	Dave	258.34
96	Stone	Sam	34.98

Fig. 17.14 | Reading a random-access file sequentially. (Part 2 of 2.)

Figure 17.14 reads every record in the credit.dat file sequentially, checks each record to determine whether it contains data, and displays formatted outputs for records containing data. The condition in line 34 uses the ios member function eof to determine when the end of file is reached and causes execution of the while statement to terminate. Also, if an error occurs when reading from the file, the loop terminates, because inCredit evaluates to false. The data input from the file is output by function outputLine (lines 47–54), which takes two arguments—an ostream object and a clientData structure to be output. The ostream parameter type is interesting, because any ostream object (such as cout) or any object of a derived class of ostream (such as an object of type ofstream) can be supplied as the argument. This means that the same function can be used, for example, to perform output to the standard-output stream and to a file stream without writing separate functions.

What about that additional benefit we promised? If you examine the output window, you'll notice that the records are listed in sorted order (by account number). This is a consequence of how we stored these records in the file, using direct-access techniques. Compared to the insertion sort we used in Chapter 7, sorting using direct-access techniques is relatively fast. The speed is achieved by making the file large enough to hold every possible record that might be created. This, of course, means that the file could be occupied sparsely most of the time, resulting in a waste of storage. This is another example of the space-time trade-off: By using large amounts of space, we can develop a much faster sorting algorithm. Fortunately, the continuous reduction in price of storage units has made this less of an issue.

17.11 Case Study: A Transaction-Processing Program

We now present a substantial transaction-processing program (Fig. 17.15) using a random-access file to achieve "instant-access" processing. The program maintains a bank's account information. The program updates existing accounts, adds new accounts, deletes accounts and stores a formatted listing of all current accounts in a text file. We assume that the program of Fig. 17.12 has been executed to create the file `credit.dat` and that the program of Fig. 17.13 has been executed to insert the initial data.

```cpp
 1   // Fig. 17.15: Fig17_15.cpp
 2   // This program reads a random-access file sequentially, updates
 3   // data previously written to the file, creates data to be placed
 4   // in the file, and deletes data previously stored in the file.
 5   #include <iostream>
 6   #include <fstream>
 7   #include <iomanip>
 8   #include <cstdlib>
 9   #include "ClientData.h" // ClientData class definition
10   using namespace std;
11
12   int enterChoice();
13   void createTextFile( fstream& );
14   void updateRecord( fstream& );
15   void newRecord( fstream& );
16   void deleteRecord( fstream& );
17   void outputLine( ostream&, const ClientData & );
18   int getAccount( const char * const );
19
20   enum Choices { PRINT = 1, UPDATE, NEW, DELETE, END };
21
22   int main()
23   {
24      // open file for reading and writing
25      fstream inOutCredit( "credit.dat", ios::in | ios::out | ios::binary );
26
```

Fig. 17.15 | Bank account program. (Part 1 of 6.)

```
27      // exit program if fstream cannot open file
28      if ( !inOutCredit )
29      {
30         cerr << "File could not be opened." << endl;
31         exit ( 1 );
32      } // end if
33
34      int choice; // store user choice
35
36      // enable user to specify action
37      while ( ( choice = enterChoice() ) != END )
38      {
39         switch ( choice )
40         {
41            case PRINT: // create text file from record file
42               createTextFile( inOutCredit );
43               break;
44            case UPDATE: // update record
45               updateRecord( inOutCredit );
46               break;
47            case NEW: // create record
48               newRecord( inOutCredit );
49               break;
50            case DELETE: // delete existing record
51               deleteRecord( inOutCredit );
52               break;
53            default: // display error if user does not select valid choice
54               cerr << "Incorrect choice" << endl;
55               break;
56         } // end switch
57
58         inOutCredit.clear(); // reset end-of-file indicator
59      } // end while
60   } // end main
61
62   // enable user to input menu choice
63   int enterChoice()
64   {
65      // display available options
66      cout << "\nEnter your choice" << endl
67         << "1 - store a formatted text file of accounts" << endl
68         << "    called \"print.txt\" for printing" << endl
69         << "2 - update an account" << endl
70         << "3 - add a new account" << endl
71         << "4 - delete an account" << endl
72         << "5 - end program\n? ";
73
74      int menuChoice;
75      cin >> menuChoice; // input menu selection from user
76      return menuChoice;
77   } // end function enterChoice
78
```

Fig. 17.15 | Bank account program. (Part 2 of 6.)

```
79   // create formatted text file for printing
80   void createTextFile( fstream &readFromFile )
81   {
82      // create text file
83      ofstream outPrintFile( "print.txt", ios::out );
84
85      // exit program if ofstream cannot create file
86      if ( !outPrintFile )
87      {
88         cerr << "File could not be created." << endl;
89         exit( 1 );
90      } // end if
91
92      outPrintFile << left << setw( 10 ) << "Account" << setw( 16 )
93         << "Last Name" << setw( 11 ) << "First Name" << right
94         << setw( 10 ) << "Balance" << endl;
95
96      // set file-position pointer to beginning of readFromFile
97      readFromFile.seekg( 0 );
98
99      // read first record from record file
100     ClientData client;
101     readFromFile.read( reinterpret_cast< char * >( &client ),
102        sizeof( ClientData ) );
103
104     // copy all records from record file into text file
105     while ( !readFromFile.eof() )
106     {
107        // write single record to text file
108        if ( client.getAccountNumber() != 0 ) // skip empty records
109           outputLine( outPrintFile, client );
110
111        // read next record from record file
112        readFromFile.read( reinterpret_cast< char * >( &client ),
113           sizeof( ClientData ) );
114     } // end while
115  } // end function createTextFile
116
117  // update balance in record
118  void updateRecord( fstream &updateFile )
119  {
120     // obtain number of account to update
121     int accountNumber = getAccount( "Enter account to update" );
122
123     // move file-position pointer to correct record in file
124     updateFile.seekg( ( accountNumber - 1 ) * sizeof( ClientData ) );
125
126     // read first record from file
127     ClientData client;
128     updateFile.read( reinterpret_cast< char * >( &client ),
129        sizeof( ClientData ) );
130
```

Fig. 17.15 | Bank account program. (Part 3 of 6.)

```
131      // update record
132      if ( client.getAccountNumber() != 0 )
133      {
134         outputLine( cout, client ); // display the record
135
136         // request user to specify transaction
137         cout << "\nEnter charge (+) or payment (-): ";
138         double transaction; // charge or payment
139         cin >> transaction;
140
141         // update record balance
142         double oldBalance = client.getBalance();
143         client.setBalance( oldBalance + transaction );
144         outputLine( cout, client ); // display the record
145
146         // move file-position pointer to correct record in file
147         updateFile.seekp( ( accountNumber - 1 ) * sizeof( ClientData ) );
148
149         // write updated record over old record in file
150         updateFile.write( reinterpret_cast< const char * >( &client ),
151            sizeof( ClientData ) );
152      } // end if
153      else // display error if account does not exist
154         cerr << "Account #" << accountNumber
155            << " has no information." << endl;
156   } // end function updateRecord
157
158   // create and insert record
159   void newRecord( fstream &insertInFile )
160   {
161      // obtain number of account to create
162      int accountNumber = getAccount( "Enter new account number" );
163
164      // move file-position pointer to correct record in file
165      insertInFile.seekg( ( accountNumber - 1 ) * sizeof( ClientData ) );
166
167      // read record from file
168      ClientData client;
169      insertInFile.read( reinterpret_cast< char * >( &client ),
170         sizeof( ClientData ) );
171
172      // create record, if record does not previously exist
173      if ( client.getAccountNumber() == 0 )
174      {
175         string lastName;
176         string firstName;
177         double balance;
178
179         // user enters last name, first name and balance
180         cout << "Enter lastname, firstname, balance\n? ";
181         cin >> setw( 15 ) >> lastName;
182         cin >> setw( 10 ) >> firstName;
183         cin >> balance;
```

Fig. 17.15 | Bank account program. (Part 4 of 6.)

```
184
185        // use values to populate account values
186        client.setLastName( lastName );
187        client.setFirstName( firstName );
188        client.setBalance( balance );
189        client.setAccountNumber( accountNumber );
190
191        // move file-position pointer to correct record in file
192        insertInFile.seekp( ( accountNumber - 1 ) * sizeof( ClientData ) );
193
194        // insert record in file
195        insertInFile.write( reinterpret_cast< const char * >( &client ),
196           sizeof( ClientData ) );
197     } // end if
198     else // display error if account already exists
199        cerr << "Account #" << accountNumber
200           << " already contains information." << endl;
201  } // end function newRecord
202
203  // delete an existing record
204  void deleteRecord( fstream &deleteFromFile )
205  {
206     // obtain number of account to delete
207     int accountNumber = getAccount( "Enter account to delete" );
208
209     // move file-position pointer to correct record in file
210     deleteFromFile.seekg( ( accountNumber - 1 ) * sizeof( ClientData ) );
211
212     // read record from file
213     ClientData client;
214     deleteFromFile.read( reinterpret_cast< char * >( &client ),
215        sizeof( ClientData ) );
216
217     // delete record, if record exists in file
218     if ( client.getAccountNumber() != 0 )
219     {
220        ClientData blankClient; // create blank record
221
222        // move file-position pointer to correct record in file
223        deleteFromFile.seekp( ( accountNumber - 1 ) *
224           sizeof( ClientData ) );
225
226        // replace existing record with blank record
227        deleteFromFile.write(
228           reinterpret_cast< const char * >( &blankClient ),
229           sizeof( ClientData ) );
230
231        cout << "Account #" << accountNumber << " deleted.\n";
232     } // end if
233     else // display error if record does not exist
234        cerr << "Account #" << accountNumber << " is empty.\n";
235  } // end deleteRecord
236
```

Fig. 17.15 | Bank account program. (Part 5 of 6.)

```
237    // display single record
238    void outputLine( ostream &output, const ClientData &record )
239    {
240       output << left << setw( 10 ) << record.getAccountNumber()
241          << setw( 16 ) << record.getLastName()
242          << setw( 11 ) << record.getFirstName()
243          << setw( 10 ) << setprecision( 2 ) << right << fixed
244          << showpoint << record.getBalance() << endl;
245    } // end function outputLine
246
247    // obtain account-number value from user
248    int getAccount( const char * const prompt )
249    {
250       int accountNumber;
251
252       // obtain account-number value
253       do
254       {
255          cout << prompt << " (1 - 100): ";
256          cin >> accountNumber;
257       } while ( accountNumber < 1 || accountNumber > 100 );
258
259       return accountNumber;
260    } // end function getAccount
```

Fig. 17.15 | Bank account program. (Part 6 of 6.)

The program has five options (Option 5 is for terminating the program). Option 1 calls function createTextFile to store a formatted list of all the account information in a text file called print.txt that may be printed. Function createTextFile (lines 80–115) takes an fstream object as an argument to be used to input data from the credit.dat file. Function createTextFile invokes istream member function read (lines 101–102) and uses the sequential-file-access techniques of Fig. 17.14 to input data from credit.dat. Function outputLine, discussed in Section 17.10, is used to output the data to file print.txt. Note that createTextFile uses istream member function seekg (line 97) to ensure that the file-position pointer is at the beginning of the file. After choosing Option 1, the print.txt file contains

Account	Last Name	First Name	Balance
29	Brown	Nancy	-24.54
33	Dunn	Stacey	314.33
37	Barker	Doug	0.00
88	Smith	Dave	258.34
96	Stone	Sam	34.98

Option 2 calls updateRecord (lines 118–156) to update an account. This function updates only an existing record, so the function first determines whether the specified record is empty. Lines 128–129 read data into object client, using istream member function read. Then line 132 compares the value returned by getAccountNumber of the client object to zero to determine whether the record contains information. If this value is zero, lines 154–155 print an error message indicating that the record is empty. If the record contains information, line 134 displays the record, using function outputLine, line 139 inputs the transaction amount and lines 142–151 calculate the new balance and rewrite the record to the file. A typical output for Option 2 is

```
Enter account to update (1 - 100): 37
37          Barker          Doug              0.00

Enter charge (+) or payment (-): +87.99
37          Barker          Doug             87.99
```

Option 3 calls function newRecord (lines 159–201) to add a new account to the file. If the user enters an account number for an existing account, newRecord displays an error message indicating that the account exists (lines 199–200). This function adds a new account in the same manner as the program of Fig. 17.12. A typical output for Option 3 is

```
Enter new account number (1 - 100): 22
Enter lastname, firstname, balance
? Johnston Sarah 247.45
```

Option 4 calls function deleteRecord (lines 204–235) to delete a record from the file. Line 207 prompts the user to enter the account number. Only an existing record may be deleted, so, if the specified account is empty, line 234 displays an error message. If the account exists, lines 227–229 reinitialize that account by copying an empty record (blank-Client) to the file. Line 231 displays a message to inform the user that the record has been deleted. A typical output for Option 4 is

```
Enter account to delete (1 - 100): 29
Account #29 deleted.
```

Line 25 opens the credit.dat file by creating an fstream object for both reading and writing, using modes ios::in and ios::out "or-ed" together.

17.12 Overview of Object Serialization

This chapter and Chapter 15 introduced the object-oriented style of input/output. However, our examples concentrated on I/O of fundamental types rather than objects of user-defined types. In Chapter 11, we showed how to input and output objects using operator overloading. We accomplished object input by overloading the stream extraction operator, >>, for the appropriate istream. We accomplished object output by overloading the stream insertion operator, <<, for the appropriate ostream. In both cases, only an object's data members were input or output, and, in each case, they were in a format meaningful only for objects of that particular type. An object's member functions are not input or output with the object's data; rather, one copy of the class's member functions remains available internally and is shared by all objects of the class.

When object data members are output to a disk file, we lose the object's type information. We store only the values of the object's attributes, not type information, on the disk. If the program that reads this data knows the object type to which the data corresponds, the program can read the data into an object of that type as we did in our random-access file examples.

An interesting problem occurs when we store objects of different types in the same file. How can we distinguish them (or their collections of data members) as we read them into a program? The problem is that objects typically do not have type fields (we discussed this issue in Chapter 13).

One approach used by several programming languages is called **object serialization**. A so-called **serialized object** is an object represented as a sequence of bytes that includes the object's data as well as information about the object's type and the types of data stored in the object. After a serialized object has been written to a file, it can be read from the file and **deserialized**—that is, the type information and bytes that represent the object and its data can be used to recreate the object in memory. C++ does not provide a built-in serialization mechanism; however, there are third party and open source C++ libraries that support object serialization. The open source Boost C++ Libraries (www.boost.org) provide support for serializing objects in text, binary and extensible markup language (XML) formats (www.boost.org/libs/serialization/doc/index.html). We overview the Boost C++ Libraries in Chapter 23.

17.13 Wrap-Up

In this chapter, we presented various file-processing techniques to manipulate persistent data. You learned that data is stored in computers in the form of 0s and 1s, and that combinations of these values form bytes, fields, records and eventually files. You were introduced to the differences between character-based and byte-based streams, and to several file-processing class templates in header file <fstream>. Then, you learned how to use sequential file processing to manipulate records stored in order, by the record-key field. You also learned how to use random-access files to instantly retrieve and manipulate fixed-length records. We presented a substantial transaction-processing case study using a random-access file to achieve "instant-access" processing. Finally, we discussed the basic concepts of object serialization. In the next chapter, we discuss typical string-manipulation operations provided by class template basic_string. We also introduce string stream-processing capabilities that allow strings to be input from and output to memory.

Summary

Section 17.1 Introduction
- Files are used for data persistence—permanent retention of data.
- Computers store files on secondary storage devices, such as hard disks, CDs, DVDs, flash memory and tapes.

Section 17.2 Data Hierarchy
- The smallest data item that computers support is called a bit (short for "binary digit"—a digit that can assume one of two values, 0 or 1).
- Digits, letters and special symbols are referred to as characters.

- The set of all characters used to write programs and represent data items on a particular computer is called that computer's character set.

- Bytes are composed of eight bits.

- Just as characters are composed of bits, fields are composed of characters. A field is a group of characters that conveys some meaning.

- Typically, a record (i.e., a class in C++) is composed of several fields (i.e., data members in C++).

- At least one field in a record is chosen as a record key to identify a record as belonging to a particular person or entity that is distinct from all other records in the file.

- In a sequential file, records typically are stored in order by a record-key field.

Section 17.3 Files and Streams

- C++ views each file as a sequence of bytes.

- Each file ends either with an end-of-file marker or at a specific byte number recorded in a system-maintained, administrative data structure.

- When a file is opened, an object is created, and a stream is associated with the object.

- To perform file processing in C++, header files `<iostream>` and `<fstream>` must be included.

- Header `<fstream>` includes the definitions for the stream class templates `basic_ifstream` (for file input), `basic_ofstream` (for file output) and `basic_fstream` (for file input and output).

- Each class template has a predefined template specialization that enables char I/O. The `<fstream>` library provides `typedef` aliases for these template specializations. The `typedef` `ifstream` represents a specialization of `basic_ifstream` that enables char input from a file. The `typedef` `ofstream` represents a specialization of `basic_ofstream` that enables char output to files. The `typedef` `fstream` represents a specialization of `basic_fstream` that enables char input from, and output to, files.

- The file-processing templates derive from class templates `basic_istream`, `basic_ostream` and `basic_iostream`, respectively. Thus, all member functions, operators and manipulators that belong to these templates also can be applied to file streams.

Section 17.4 Creating a Sequential File

- C++ imposes no structure on a file; you must structure files to meet the application's requirements.

- A file can be opened for output when an `ofstream` object is created. Two arguments are passed to the object's constructor—the filename and the file-open mode.

- For an `ofstream` object, the file-open mode can be either `ios::out` to output data to a file or `ios::app` to append data to the end of a file. Existing files opened with mode `ios::out` are truncated. If the specified file does not exist, the `ofstream` object creates the file using that filename.

- By default, `ofstream` objects are opened for output.

- An `ofstream` object can be created without opening a specific file—a file can be attached to the object later with member function `open`.

- The `ios` member function `operator!` determines whether a stream was opened correctly. This operator can be used in a condition that returns a true value if either the `failbit` or the `badbit` is set for the stream on the open operation.

- The `ios` member function `operator void *` converts a stream to a pointer, so it can be compared to 0. When a pointer value is used as a condition, a null pointer represents `false` and a non-null pointer represents `true`. If the `failbit` or `badbit` has been set for a stream, 0 (`false`) is returned.

- Entering the end-of-file indicator sets the `failbit` for `cin`.

- The `operator void *` function can be used to test an input object for end-of-file instead of calling the `eof` member function explicitly on the input object.

- When a stream object's destructor is called, the corresponding stream is closed. You also can close the stream object explicitly, using the stream's `close` member function.
- Closing files explicitly when they're no longer needed can reduce a program's resource usage.

Section 17.5 Reading Data from a Sequential File
- Files store data so it may be retrieved for processing when needed.
- Creating an `ifstream` object opens a file for input. The `ifstream` constructor can receive the filename and the file open mode as arguments.
- Open a file for input only if the file's contents should not be modified.
- Objects of class `ifstream` are opened for input by default.
- An `ifstream` object can be created without opening a specific file; a file can be attached to it later.
- To retrieve data sequentially from a file, programs normally start reading from the beginning of the file and read all the data consecutively until the desired data is found.
- Both `istream` and `ostream` provide member functions for repositioning the file-position pointer. These member functions are `seekg` ("seek get") for `istream` and `seekp` ("seek put") for `ostream`. Each `istream` object has a "get pointer," which indicates the byte number in the file from which the next input is to occur, and each `ostream` object has a "put pointer," which indicates the byte number in the file at which the next output should be placed.
- The argument to `seekg` normally is a long integer. A second argument can be specified to indicate the seek direction, which can be `ios::beg` (the default) for positioning relative to the beginning of a stream, `ios::cur` for positioning relative to the current position in a stream or `ios::end` for positioning relative to the end of a stream.
- The file-position pointer is an integer value that specifies the location in the file as a number of bytes from the file's starting location (i.e., the offset from the beginning of the file).
- Member functions `tellg` and `tellp` are provided to return the current locations of the "get" and "put" pointers, respectively.

Section 17.6 Updating Sequential Files
- Data that is formatted and written to a sequential file cannot be modified without the risk of destroying other data in the file. The problem is that records can vary in size.

Section 17.7 Random-Access Files
- Sequential files are inappropriate for instant-access applications, in which a particular record must be located immediately.
- Instant access is made possible with random-access files. Individual records of a random-access file can be accessed directly (and quickly) without having to search other records.
- The easiest method to format files for random access is to require that all records in a file be of the same fixed length. Using same-size, fixed-length records makes it easy for a program to calculate (as a function of the record size and the record key) the exact location of any record relative to the beginning of the file.
- Data can be inserted into a random-access file without destroying other data in the file.
- Data stored previously can be updated or deleted without rewriting the entire file.

Section 17.8 Creating a Random-Access File
- The `ostream` member function `write` outputs a fixed number of bytes, beginning at a specific location in memory, to the specified stream. Function `write` writes the data at the location in the file specified by the "put" file-position pointer.

- The `istream` member function `read` inputs a fixed number of bytes from the specified stream to an area in memory beginning at a specified address. If the stream is associated with a file, function read inputs bytes at the location in the file specified by the "get" file-position pointer.

- Function `write` treats its first argument as a group of bytes by viewing the object in memory as a `const char *`, which is a pointer to a byte (remember that a char is one byte). Starting from that location, function `write` outputs the number of bytes specified by its second argument. The `istream` function read can subsequently be used to read the bytes back into memory.

- The `reinterpret_cast` operator converts a pointer of one type to an unrelated pointer type.

- A `reinterpret_cast` is performed at compile time and does not change the value of the object to which its operand points.

- A program that reads unformatted data must be compiled and executed on a system compatible with the program that wrote the data—different systems may represent internal data differently.

- Objects of class `string` do not have uniform size, rather they use dynamically allocated memory to accommodate strings of various lengths.

- The `string` member function `data` returns an array containing the characters of the `string`. This array is not guaranteed to be null terminated.

- The string member function `size` gets the length of a `string`.

- The file open mode `ios::binary` indicates that a file should be opened in binary mode.

Section 17.9 Writing Data Randomly to a Random-Access File
- Multiple file-open modes are combined by separating each open mode from the next with the bitwise inclusive OR operator (|).

Section 17.10 Reading from a Random-Access File Sequentially
- The `istream` function `read` inputs a specified number of bytes from the current position in the specified stream into an object.

- A function that receives an `ostream` parameter can receive any `ostream` object (such as `cout`) or any object of a derived class of `ostream` (such as an object of type `ofstream`) as an argument. This means that the same function can be used, for example, to perform output to the standard-output stream and to a file stream without writing separate functions.

Section 17.12 Overview of Object Serialization
- When object data members are output to a disk file, we lose the object's type information. We store only the values of the object's attributes, not type information, on the disk. If the program that reads this data knows the object type to which the data corresponds, the program can read the data into an object of that type.

- Several programming languages support object serialization. A so-called serialized object is an object represented as a sequence of bytes that includes the object's data as well as information about the object's type and the types of data stored in the object. A serialized object can be read from the file and deserialized.

- The open source Boost Libraries provide support for serializing objects in text, binary and extensible markup language (XML) formats (`www.boost.org/libs/serialization/doc/index.html`).

Terminology

Self-Review Exercises

17.1   Fill in the blanks in each of the following:

a) Ultimately, all data items processed by a computer are reduced to combinations of _____ and _____.

b) The smallest data item a computer can process is called a(n) _____.

c) A(n) _____ is a group of related records.

d) Digits, letters and special symbols are referred to as _____.

e) A group of related files is called a(n) _____.

f) Member function _____ of the file streams fstream, ifstream and ofstream closes a file.

g) The istream member function _____ reads a character from the specified stream.

h) Member function _____ of the file streams fstream, ifstream and ofstream opens a file.

i) The istream member function _____ is normally used when reading data from a file in random-access applications.

j) Member functions _____ and _____ of istream and ostream set the file-position pointer to a specific location in an input or output stream, respectively.

17.2   State which of the following are *true* and which are *false*. If *false*, explain why.

a) Member function read cannot be used to read data from the input object cin.

b) You must create the cin, cout, cerr and clog objects explicitly.

c) A program must call function close explicitly to close a file associated with an ifstream, ofstream or fstream object.

d) If the file-position pointer points to a location in a sequential file other than the beginning of the file, the file must be closed and reopened to read from the beginning of the file.

e) The ostream member function write can write to standard-output stream cout.

f) Data in sequential files always is updated without overwriting nearby data.

g) Searching all records in a random-access file to find a specific record is unnecessary.

h) Records in random-access files must be of uniform length.

i) Member functions seekp and seekg must seek relative to the beginning of a file.

17.3 Assume that each of the following statements applies to the same program.

a) Write a statement that opens file oldmast.dat for input; use an ifstream object called inOldMaster.

b) Write a statement that opens file trans.dat for input; use an ifstream object called inTransaction.

c) Write a statement that opens file newmast.dat for output (and creation); use ofstream objcct outNewMaster.

d) Write a statement that reads a record from the file oldmast.dat. The record consists of integer accountNumber, string name and floating-point currentBalance; use ifstream object inOldMaster.

e) Write a statement that reads a record from the file trans.dat. The record consists of integer accountNum and floating-point dollarAmount; use ifstream object inTransaction.

f) Write a statement that writes a record to the file newmast.dat. The record consists of integer accountNum, string name, and floating-point currentBalance; use ofstream object outNewMaster.

17.4 Find the error(s) and show how to correct it (them) in each of the following.

a) File payables.dat referred to by ofstream object outPayable has not been opened.

```
outPayable << account << company << amount << endl;
```

b) The following statement should read a record from the file payables.dat. The ifstream object inPayable refers to this file, and istream object inReceivable refers to the file receivables.dat.

```
inReceivable >> account >> company >> amount;
```

c) The file tools.dat should be opened to add data to the file without discarding the current data.

```
ofstream outTools( "tools.dat", ios::out );
```

Answers to Self-Review Exercises

17.1 a) 1s, 0s. b) bit. c) file. d) characters. e) database. f) close. g) get. h) open. i) read. j) seekg, seekp.

17.2 a) False. Function read can read from any input stream object derived from istream.

b) False. These four streams are created automatically for you. The <iostream> header must be included in a file to use them. This header includes declarations for each stream object.

c) False. The files will be closed when destructors for ifstream, ofstream or fstream objects execute when the stream objects go out of scope or before program execution terminates, but it's a good programming practice to close all files explicitly with close once they're no longer needed.

d) False. Member function seekp or seekg can be used to reposition the "put" or "get" file-position pointer to the beginning of the file.

e) True.

f) False. In most cases, sequential file records are not of uniform length. Therefore, it's possible that updating a record will cause other data to be overwritten.

g) True.

h) False. Records in a random-access file normally are of uniform length.

i) False. It's possible to seek from the beginning of the file, from the end of the file and from the current position in the file.

17.3   a) `ifstream inOldMaster( "oldmast.dat", ios::in );`
       b) `ifstream inTransaction( "trans.dat", ios::in );`
       c) `ofstream outNewMaster( "newmast.dat", ios::out );`
       d) `inOldMaster >> accountNumber >> name >> currentBalance;`
       e) `inTransaction >> accountNum >> dollarAmount;`
       f) `outNewMaster << accountNum << name << currentBalance;`

17.4   a) *Error:* The file `payables.dat` has not been opened before the attempt is made to output data to the stream.
       Correction: Use `ostream` function `open` to open `payables.dat` for output.
      b) *Error:* The incorrect `istream` object is being used to read a record from the file named `payables.dat`.
       Correction: Use `istream` object `inPayable` to refer to `payables.dat`.
      c) *Error:* The file's contents are discarded because the file is opened for output (`ios::out`).
       Correction: To add data to the file, open the file either for updating (`ios::ate`) or for appending (`ios::app`).

Exercises

17.5   Fill in the blanks in each of the following:
    a) Computers store large amounts of data on secondary storage devices as _____.
    b) A(n) _____ is composed of several fields.
    c) To facilitate the retrieval of specific records from a file, one field in each record is chosen as a(n) _____.
    d) The vast majority of information stored in computer systems is stored in _____ files.
    e) A group of related characters that conveys meaning is called a(n) _____.
    f) The standard stream objects declared by header `<iostream>` are _____, _____, _____ and _____.
    g) `ostream` member function _____ outputs a character to the specified stream.
    h) `ostream` member function _____ is generally used to write data to a randomly accessed file.
    i) `istream` member function _____ repositions the file-position pointer in a file.

17.6   State which of the following are *true* and which are *false*. If *false*, explain why.
    a) The impressive functions performed by computers essentially involve the manipulation of zeros and ones.
    b) People prefer to manipulate bits instead of characters and fields because bits are more compact.
    c) People specify programs and data items as characters; computers then manipulate and process these characters as groups of zeros and ones.
    d) A person's 5-digit zip code is an example of a numeric field.
    e) A person's street address is generally considered to be an alphabetic field in computer applications.
    f) Data items represented in computers form a data hierarchy in which data items become larger and more complex as we progress from fields to characters to bits, etc.
    g) A record key identifies a record as belonging to a particular field.
    h) Most organizations store all information in a single file to facilitate computer processing.
    i) When a program creates a file, the file is automatically retained by the computer for future reference; i.e., files are said to be persistent.

17.7   *(File Matching)* Exercise 17.3 asked you to write a series of single statements. Actually, these statements form the core of an important type of file-processing program, namely, a file-matching program. In commercial data processing, it's common to have several files in each application system. In an accounts receivable system, for example, there is generally a master file containing detailed information about each customer, such as the customer's name, address, telephone number, outstanding balance, credit limit, discount terms, contract arrangements and, possibly, a condensed history of recent purchases and cash payments.

As transactions occur (e.g., sales are made and cash payments arrive), they're entered into a file. At the end of each business period (a month for some companies, a week for others and a day in some cases), the file of transactions (called `trans.dat` in Exercise 17.3) is applied to the master file (called `oldmast.dat` in Exercise 17.3), thus updating each account's record of purchases and payments. During an updating run, the master file is rewritten as a new file (`newmast.dat`), which is then used at the end of the next business period to begin the updating process again.

File-matching programs must deal with certain problems that do not exist in single-file programs. For example, a match does not always occur. A customer on the master file might not have made any purchases or cash payments in the current business period, and therefore no record for this customer will appear on the transaction file. Similarly, a customer who did make some purchases or cash payments may have just moved to this community, and the company may not have had a chance to create a master record for this customer.

Use the statements from Exercise 17.3 as a basis for writing a complete file-matching accounts receivable program. Use the account number on each file as the record key for matching purposes. Assume that each file is a sequential file with records stored in increasing order by account number.

When a match occurs (i.e., records with the same account number appear on both the master and transaction files), add the dollar amount on the transaction file to the current balance on the master file, and write the `newmast.dat` record. (Assume purchases are indicated by positive amounts on the transaction file and payments are indicated by negative amounts.) When there is a master record for a particular account but no corresponding transaction record, merely write the master record to `newmast.dat`. When there is a transaction record but no corresponding master record, print the error message "`Unmatched transaction record for account number ...`" (fill in the account number from the transaction record).

17.8 *(File Matching Test Data)* After writing the program of Exercise 17.7, write a simple program to create some test data for checking out the program. Use the following sample account data:

Master file Account number	Name	Balance
100	Alan Jones	348.17
300	Mary Smith	27.19
500	Sam Sharp	0.00
700	Suzy Green	−14.22

Transaction file Account number	Transaction amount
100	27.14
300	62.11
400	100.56
900	82.17

17.9 *(File Matching Test)* Run the program of Exercise 17.7, using the files of test data created in Exercise 17.8. Print the new master file. Check that the accounts have been updated correctly.

17.10 *(File Matching Enhancement)* It's common to have several transaction records with the same record key, because a particular customer might make several purchases and cash payments during a business period. Rewrite your accounts receivable file-matching program of Exercise 17.7 to provide for the possibility of handling several transaction records with the same record key. Modify the test data of Exercise 17.8 to include the following additional transaction records:

Account number	Dollar amount
300	83.89
700	80.78
700	1.53

17.11 Write a series of statements that accomplish each of the following. Assume that we've defined class `Person` that contains the `private` data members

```
string lastName;
string firstName;
string age;
int id;
```

and `public` member functions

```
// accessor functions for id
void setId( int );
int getId() const;

// accessor functions for lastName
void setLastName( string );
string getLastName() const;

// accessor functions for firstName
void setFirstName( string );
string getFirstName() const;

// accessor functions for age
void setAge( string );
string getAge() const;
```

Also assume that any random-access files have been opened properly.

a) Initialize the file `nameage.dat` with 100 records that store values `lastName` = "unassigned", `firstName` = "" and `age` = "0".

b) Input 10 last names, first names and ages, and write them to the file.

c) Update a record that already contains information. If the record does not contain information, inform the user "No info".

d) Delete a record that contains information by reinitializing that particular record.

17.12 *(Hardware Inventory)* You are the owner of a hardware store and need to keep an inventory that can tell you what different tools you have, how many of each you have on hand and the cost of each one. Write a program that initializes the random-access file `hardware.dat` to 100 empty records, lets you input the data concerning each tool, enables you to list all your tools, lets you delete a record for a tool that you no longer have and lets you update *any* information in the file. The tool identification number should be the record number. Use the following information to start your file:

Record #	Tool name	Quantity	Cost
3	Electric sander	7	57.98
17	Hammer	76	11.99

Record #	Tool name	Quantity	Cost
24	Jig saw	21	11.00
39	Lawn mower	3	79.50
56	Power saw	18	99.99
68	Screwdriver	106	6.99
77	Sledge hammer	11	21.50
83	Wrench	34	7.50

17.13 (*Telephone Number Word Generator*) Standard telephone keypads contain the digits 0 through 9. The numbers 2 through 9 each have three letters associated with them, as is indicated by the following table:

Digit	Letter
2	A B C
3	D E F
4	G H I
5	J K L
6	M N O
7	P R S
8	T U V
9	W X Y

Many people find it difficult to memorize phone numbers, so they use the correspondence between digits and letters to develop seven-letter words that correspond to their phone numbers. For example, a person whose telephone number is 686-2377 might use the correspondence indicated in the above table to develop the seven-letter word "NUMBERS."

Businesses frequently attempt to get telephone numbers that are easy for their clients to remember. If a business can advertise a simple word for its customers to dial, then no doubt the business will receive a few more calls.

Each seven-letter word corresponds to exactly one seven-digit telephone number. The restaurant wishing to increase its take-home business could surely do so with the number 825-3688 (i.e., "TAKEOUT").

Each seven-digit phone number corresponds to many separate seven-letter words. Unfortunately, most of these represent unrecognizable juxtapositions of letters. It's possible, however, that the owner of a barber shop would be pleased to know that the shop's telephone number, 424-7288, corresponds to "HAIRCUT." A veterinarian with the phone number 738-2273 would be pleased to know that the number corresponds to "PETCARE."

Write a program that, given a seven-digit number, writes to a file every possible seven-letter word corresponding to that number. There are 2187 (3 to the seventh power) such words. Avoid phone numbers with the digits 0 and 1.

17.14 Write a program that uses the `sizeof` operator to determine the sizes in bytes of the various data types on your computer system. Write the results to the file `datasize.dat`, so that you may print the results later. The results should be displayed in two-column format with the type name in the left column and the size of the type in right column, as in:

```
char                    1
unsigned char           1
short int               2
unsigned short int      2
int                     4
unsigned int            4
long int                4
unsigned long int       4
float                   4
double                  8
long double            10
```

[*Note:* The sizes of the built-in data types on your computer might differ from those listed above.]

Making a Difference

17.15 *(Phishing Scanner)* Phishing is a form of identity theft in which, in an e-mail, a sender posing as a trustworthy source attempts to acquire private information, such as your user names, passwords, credit-card numbers and social security number. Phishing e-mails claiming to be from popular banks, credit-card companies, auction sites, social networks and online payment services may look quite legitimate. These fraudulent messages often provide links to spoofed (fake) websites where you're asked to enter sensitive information.

Visit McAfee® (www.mcafee.com/us/threat_center/anti_phishing/phishing_top10.html), Security Extra (www.securityextra.com/), www.snopes.com and other websites to find lists of the top phishing scams. Also check out the Anti-Phishing Working Group (www.antiphishing.org/), and the FBI's Cyber Investigations website (www.fbi.gov/cyberinvest/cyberhome.htm), where you'll find information about the latest scams and how to protect yourself.

Create a list of 30 words, phrases and company names commonly found in phishing messages. Assign a point value to each based on your estimate of its likeliness to be in a phishing message (e.g., one point if it's somewhat likely, two points if moderately likely, or three points if highly likely). Write a program that scans a file of text for these terms and phrases. For each occurrence of a keyword or phrase within the text file, add the assigned point value to the total points for that word or phrase. For each keyword or phrase found, output one line with the word or phrase, the number of occurrences and the point total. Then show the point total for the entire message. Does your program assign a high point total to some actual phishing e-mails you've received? Does it assign a high point total to some legitimate e-mails you've received?

Class string and String Stream Processing

18

Suit the action to the word, the word to the action; with this special observance, that you o'erstep not the modesty of nature.
—William Shakespeare

The difference between the almost-right word and the right word is really a large matter — it's the difference between the lightning bug and the lightning.
—Mark Twain

Mum's the word.
—Miguel de Cervantes

I have made this letter longer than usual, because I lack the time to make it short.
—Blaise Pascal

Objectives

In this chapter you'll learn:

- To assign, concatenate, compare, search and swap **string**s.

- To determine **string** characteristics.

- To find, replace and insert characters in **string**s.

- To convert **string**s to C-style strings and vice versa.

- To use **string** iterators.

- To perform input from and output to **string**s in memory.

18.1 Introduction

The class template **basic_string** provides typical string-manipulation operations such as copying, searching, etc. The template definition and all support facilities are defined in namespace std; these include the typedef statement

```
typedef basic_string< char > string;
```

that creates the alias type string for **basic_string<char>**. A typedef is also provided for the **wchar_t** type (wstring). Type wchar_t[1] stores characters (e.g., two-byte characters, four-byte characters, etc.) for supporting other character sets. We use string exclusively throughout this chapter. To use strings, include header file <string>.

A string object can be initialized with a constructor argument such as

```
string text( "Hello" ); // creates a string from a const char *
```

which creates a string containing the characters in "Hello", or with two constructor arguments as in

```
string name( 8, 'x' ); // string of 8 'x' characters
```

which creates a string containing eight 'x' characters. Class string also provides a default constructor (which creates an empty string) and a copy constructor. An **empty string** is a string that does not contain any characters.

A string also can be initialized via the alternate constructor syntax in the definition of a string as in

```
string month = "March"; // same as: string month( "March" );
```

Remember that operator = in the preceding declaration is not an assignment; rather it's an implicit call to the string class constructor, which does the conversion.

---

1. Type wchar_t commonly is used to represent Unicode®, which does have 16-bit characters, but the size of wchar_t is not fixed by the standard. The Unicode Standard outlines a specification to produce consistent encoding of the world's characters and *symbols*. To learn more about the Unicode Standard, visit www.unicode.org.

Class `string` provides no conversions from `int` or `char` to `string` in a `string` definition. For example, the definitions

```
string error1 = 'c';
string error2( 'u' );
string error3 = 22;
string error4( 8 );
```

result in syntax errors. Assigning a single character to a `string` object is permitted in an assignment statement as in

```
string1 = 'n';
```

Common Programming Error 18.1

Attempting to convert an `int` or `char` to a `string` via an initialization in a declaration or via a constructor argument is a compilation error.

Unlike C-style `char *` strings, `strings` are not necessarily null terminated. [*Note:* The C++ standard document provides only a description of the interface for class `string`—implementation is platform dependent.] The length of a `string` can be retrieved with member function **length** and with member function **size**. The subscript operator, [], can be used with `strings` to access and modify individual characters. Like C-style strings, `strings` have a first subscript of 0 and a last subscript of `length() - 1`.

Most `string` member functions take as arguments a starting subscript location and the number of characters on which to operate.

The stream extraction operator (>>) is overloaded to support `strings`. The statements

```
string stringObject;
cin >> stringObject;
```

declare a `string` object and read a `string` from `cin`. Input is delimited by white-space characters. When a delimiter is encountered, the input operation is terminated. Function **getline** also is overloaded for `strings`. Assuming `string1` is a `string`, the statement

```
getline( cin, string1 );
```

reads a `string` from the keyboard into `string1`. Input is delimited by a newline ('\n'), so `getLine` can read a line of text into a `string` object.

18.2 **string** Assignment and Concatenation

Figure 18.1 demonstrates `string` assignment and concatenation. Line 4 includes header `<string>` for class `string`. The `strings` `string1`, `string2` and `string3` are created in lines 9–11. Line 13 assigns the value of `string1` to `string2`. After the assignment takes place, `string2` is a copy of `string1`. Line 14 uses member function **assign** to copy `string1` into `string3`. A separate copy is made (i.e., `string1` and `string3` are independent objects). Class `string` also provides an overloaded version of member function `assign` that copies a specified number of characters, as in

```
targetString.assign( sourceString, start, numberOfCharacters );
```

where `sourceString` is the `string` to be copied, `start` is the starting subscript and `numberOfCharacters` is the number of characters to copy.

```cpp
1   // Fig. 18.1: Fig18_01.cpp
2   // Demonstrating string assignment and concatenation.
3   #include <iostream>
4   #include <string>
5   using namespace std;
6
7   int main()
8   {
9      string string1( "cat" );
10     string string2; // initialized to the empty string
11     string string3; // initialized to the empty string
12
13     string2 = string1; // assign string1 to string2
14     string3.assign( string1 ); // assign string1 to string3
15     cout << "string1: " << string1 << "\nstring2: " << string2
16        << "\nstring3: " << string3 << "\n\n";
17
18     // modify string2 and string3
19     string2[ 0 ] = string3[ 2 ] = 'r';
20
21     cout << "After modification of string2 and string3:\n" << "string1: "
22        << string1 << "\nstring2: " << string2 << "\nstring3: ";
23
24     // demonstrating member function at
25     for ( int i = 0; i < string3.length(); i++ )
26        cout << string3.at( i );
27
28     // declare string4 and string5
29     string string4( string1 + "apult" ); // concatenation
30     string string5;
31
32     // overloaded +=
33     string3 += "pet"; // create "carpet"
34     string1.append( "acomb" ); // create "catacomb"
35
36     // append subscript locations 4 through end of string1 to
37     // create string "comb" (string5 was initially empty)
38     string5.append( string1, 4, string1.length() - 4 );
39
40     cout << "\n\nAfter concatenation:\nstring1: " << string1
41        << "\nstring2: " << string2 << "\nstring3: " << string3
42        << "\nstring4: " << string4 << "\nstring5: " << string5 << endl;
43  } // end main
```

```
string1: cat
string2: cat
string3: cat

After modification of string2 and string3:
string1: cat
string2: rat
string3: car
```

Fig. 18.1 | Demonstrating `string` assignment and concatenation. (Part 1 of 2.)

```
After concatenation:
string1: catacomb
string2: rat
string3: carpet
string4: catapult
string5: comb
```

Fig. 18.1 | Demonstrating string assignment and concatenation. (Part 2 of 2.)

Line 19 uses the subscript operator to assign 'r' to string3[2] (forming "car") and to assign 'r' to string2[0] (forming "rat"). The strings are then output.

Lines 25–26 output the contents of string3 one character at a time using member function **at**. Member function at provides **checked access** (or **range checking**); i.e., going past the end of the string throws an out_of_range exception. (See Chapter 16 for a detailed discussion of exception handling.) The subscript operator, [], does not provide checked access. This is consistent with its use on arrays.

Common Programming Error 18.2

Accessing a string subscript outside the bounds of the string using function at is a logic error that causes an out_of_range exception.

Common Programming Error 18.3

Accessing an element beyond the size of the string using the subscript operator is an unreported logic error.

String string4 is declared (line 29) and initialized to the result of concatenating string1 and "apult" using the overloaded + operator, which for class string denotes concatenation. Line 33 uses the addition assignment operator, +=, to concatenate string3 and "pet". Line 34 uses member function **append** to concatenate string1 and "acomb".

Line 38 appends the string "comb" to empty string string5. This member function is passed the string (string1) to retrieve characters from, the starting subscript in the string (4) and the number of characters to append (the value returned by string1.length() - 4).

18.3 **Comparing strings**

Class string provides member functions for comparing strings. Figure 18.2 demonstrates class string's comparison capabilities.

```
1  // Fig. 18.2: Fig18_02.cpp
2  // Demonstrating string comparison capabilities.
3  #include <iostream>
4  #include <string>
5  using namespace std;
6
7  int main()
8  {
```

Fig. 18.2 | Comparing strings. (Part 1 of 3.)

```
 9      string string1( "Testing the comparison functions." );
10      string string2( "Hello" );
11      string string3( "stinger" );
12      string string4( string2 );
13
14      cout << "string1: " << string1 << "\nstring2: " << string2
15         << "\nstring3: " << string3 << "\nstring4: " << string4 << "\n\n";
16
17      // comparing string1 and string4
18      if ( string1 == string4 )
19         cout << "string1 == string4\n";
20      else // string1 != string4
21      {
22         if ( string1 > string4 )
23            cout << "string1 > string4\n";
24         else // string1 < string4
25            cout << "string1 < string4\n";
26      } // end else
27
28      // comparing string1 and string2
29      int result = string1.compare( string2 );
30
31      if ( result == 0 )
32         cout << "string1.compare( string2 ) == 0\n";
33      else // result != 0
34      {
35         if ( result > 0 )
36            cout << "string1.compare( string2 ) > 0\n";
37         else // result < 0
38            cout << "string1.compare( string2 ) < 0\n";
39      } // end else
40
41      // comparing string1 (elements 2-5) and string3 (elements 0-5)
42      result = string1.compare( 2, 5, string3, 0, 5 );
43
44      if ( result == 0 )
45         cout << "string1.compare( 2, 5, string3, 0, 5 ) == 0\n";
46      else // result != 0
47      {
48         if ( result > 0 )
49            cout << "string1.compare( 2, 5, string3, 0, 5 ) > 0\n";
50         else // result < 0
51            cout << "string1.compare( 2, 5, string3, 0, 5 ) < 0\n";
52      } // end else
53
54      // comparing string2 and string4
55      result = string4.compare( 0, string2.length(), string2 );
56
57      if ( result == 0 )
58         cout << "string4.compare( 0, string2.length(), "
59            << "string2 ) == 0" << endl;
60      else // result != 0
61      {
```

Fig. 18.2 | Comparing `string`s. (Part 2 of 3.)

```
62        if ( result > 0 )
63           cout << "string4.compare( 0, string2.length(), "
64              << "string2 ) > 0" << endl;
65        else // result < 0
66           cout << "string4.compare( 0, string2.length(), "
67              << "string2 ) < 0" << endl;
68     } // end else
69
70     // comparing string2 and string4
71     result = string2.compare( 0, 3, string4 );
72
73     if ( result == 0 )
74        cout << "string2.compare( 0, 3, string4 ) == 0" << endl;
75     else // result != 0
76     {
77        if ( result > 0 )
78           cout << "string2.compare( 0, 3, string4 ) > 0" << endl;
79        else // result < 0
80           cout << "string2.compare( 0, 3, string4 ) < 0" << endl;
81     } // end else
82  } // end main
```

```
string1: Testing the comparison functions.
string2: Hello
string3: stinger
string4: Hello

string1 > string4
string1.compare( string2 ) > 0
string1.compare( 2, 5, string3, 0, 5 ) == 0
string4.compare( 0, string2.length(), string2 ) == 0
string2.compare( 0, 3, string4 ) < 0
```

Fig. 18.2 | Comparing strings. (Part 3 of 3.)

The program declares four strings (lines 9–12) and outputs each (lines 14–15). Line 18 tests string1 against string4 for equality using the overloaded equality operator. If the condition is true, "string1 == string4" is output. If the condition is false, the condition in line 22 is tested. All the string class overloaded relational and equality operator functions return bool values.

Line 29 uses string member function **compare** to compare string1 to string2. Variable result is assigned 0 if the strings are equivalent, a positive number if string1 is **lexicographically** greater than string2 or a negative number if string1 is lexicographically less than string2. Because a string starting with 'T' is considered lexicographically greater than a string starting with 'H', result is assigned a value greater than 0, as confirmed by the output. A lexicon is a dictionary. When we say that a string is lexicographically less than another, we mean that the compare method uses the numerical values of the characters (see Appendix B, ASCII Character Set) in each string to determine that the first string is less than the second.

Line 42 compares portions of string1 and string3 using an overloaded version of member function compare. The first two arguments (2 and 5) specify the starting subscript and length of the portion of string1 ("sting") to compare with string3. The third argument is the comparison `string`. The last two arguments (0 and 5) are the starting subscript and length of the portion of the comparison `string` being compared (also `"sting"`). The value assigned to `result` is 0 for equality, a positive number if `string1` is lexicographically greater than `string3` or a negative number if `string1` is lexicographically less than `string3`. The two pieces being compared here are identical, so `result` is assigned 0.

Line 55 uses another overloaded version of function `compare` to compare `string4` and `string2`. The first two arguments are the same—the starting subscript and length. The last argument is the comparison `string`. The value returned is also the same—0 for equality, a positive number if `string4` is lexicographically greater than `string2` or a negative number if `string4` is lexicographically less than `string2`. Because the two pieces of strings being compared here are identical, `result` is assigned 0.

Line 71 calls member function `compare` to compare the first 3 characters in `string2` to `string4`. Because `"Hel"` is less than `"Hello"`, a value less than zero is returned.

18.4 Substrings

Class `string` provides member function **`substr`** for retrieving a substring from a `string`. The result is a new `string` object that is copied from the source `string`. Figure 18.3 demonstrates `substr`. The program declares and initializes a `string` at line 9. Line 13 uses member function `substr` to retrieve a substring from `string1`. The first argument specifies the beginning subscript of the desired substring; the second argument specifies the substring's length.

```
1   // Fig. 18.3: Fig18_03.cpp
2   // Demonstrating string member function substr.
3   #include <iostream>
4   #include <string>
5   using namespace std;
6
7   int main()
8   {
9      string string1( "The airplane landed on time." );
10
11     // retrieve substring "plane" which
12     // begins at subscript 7 and consists of 5 characters
13     cout << string1.substr( 7, 5 ) << endl;
14  } // end main
```

```
plane
```

Fig. 18.3 | Demonstrating `string` member function `substr`.

18.5 Swapping strings

Class `string` provides member function **`swap`** for swapping strings. Figure 18.4 swaps two strings. Lines 9–10 declare and initialize strings `first` and `second`. Each `string` is then output. Line 15 uses `string` member function `swap` to swap the values of `first` and `second`. The two strings are printed again to confirm that they were indeed swapped. The `string` member function `swap` is useful for implementing programs that sort strings.

```
 1   // Fig. 18.4: Fig18_04.cpp
 2   // Using the swap function to swap two strings.
 3   #include <iostream>
 4   #include <string>
 5   using namespace std;
 6
 7   int main()
 8   {
 9      string first( "one" );
10      string second( "two" );
11
12      // output strings
13      cout << "Before swap:\n first: " << first << "\nsecond: " << second;
14
15      first.swap( second ); // swap strings
16
17      cout << "\n\nAfter swap:\n first: " << first
18         << "\nsecond: " << second << endl;
19   } // end main
```

```
Before swap:
 first: one
second: two

After swap:
 first: two
second: one
```

Fig. 18.4 | Using function swap to swap two strings.

18.6 string Characteristics

Class string provides member functions for gathering information about a string's size, length, capacity, maximum length and other characteristics. A string's size or length is the number of characters currently stored in the string. A string's **capacity** is the number of characters that can be stored in the string without allocating more memory. The capacity of a string must be at least equal to the current size of the string, though it can be greater. The exact capacity of a string depends on the implementation. The **maximum size** is the largest possible size a string can have. If this value is exceeded, a length_error exception is thrown. Figure 18.5 demonstrates string class member functions for determining various characteristics of strings.

```
 1   // Fig. 18.5: Fig18_05.cpp
 2   // Demonstrating member functions related to size and capacity.
 3   #include <iostream>
 4   #include <string>
 5   using namespace std;
 6
 7   void printStatistics( const string & );
```

Fig. 18.5 | Printing string characteristics. (Part 1 of 3.)

```
 8
 9   int main()
10   {
11      string string1; // empty string
12
13      cout << "Statistics before input:\n" << boolalpha;
14      printStatistics( string1 );
15
16      // read in only "tomato" from "tomato soup"
17      cout << "\n\nEnter a string: ";
18      cin >> string1; // delimited by whitespace
19      cout << "The string entered was: " << string1;
20
21      cout << "\nStatistics after input:\n";
22      printStatistics( string1 );
23
24      // read in "soup"
25      cin >> string1; // delimited by whitespace
26      cout << "\n\nThe remaining string is: " << string1 << endl;
27      printStatistics( string1 );
28
29      // append 46 characters to string1
30      string1 += "1234567890abcdefghijklmnopqrstuvwxyz1234567890";
31      cout << "\n\nstring1 is now: " << string1 << endl;
32      printStatistics( string1 );
33
34      // add 10 elements to string1
35      string1.resize( string1.length() + 10 );
36      cout << "\n\nStats after resizing by (length + 10):\n";
37      printStatistics( string1 );
38      cout << endl;
39   } // end main
40
41   // display string statistics
42   void printStatistics( const string &stringRef )
43   {
44      cout << "capacity: " << stringRef.capacity() << "\nmax size: "
45         << stringRef.max_size() << "\nsize: " << stringRef.size()
46         << "\nlength: " << stringRef.length()
47         << "\nempty: " << stringRef.empty();
48   } // end printStatistics
```

```
Statistics before input:
capacity: 0
max size: 4294967293
size: 0
length: 0
empty: true

Enter a string: tomato soup
The string entered was: tomato
Statistics after input:
capacity: 15
```

Fig. 18.5 | Printing `string` characteristics. (Part 2 of 3.)

```
max size: 4294967293
size: 6
length: 6
empty: false

The remaining string is: soup
capacity: 15
max size: 4294967293
size: 4
length: 4
empty: false

string1 is now: soup1234567890abcdefghijklmnopqrstuvwxyz1234567890
capacity: 63
max size: 4294967293
size: 50
length: 50
empty: false

Stats after resizing by (length + 10):
capacity: 63
max size: 4294967293
size: 60
length: 60
empty: false
```

Fig. 18.5 | Printing string characteristics. (Part 3 of 3.)

The program declares empty string string1 (line 11) and passes it to function printStatistics (line 14). Function printStatistics (lines 42–48) takes a reference to a const string as an argument and outputs the capacity (using member function **capacity**), maximum size (using member function **max_size**), size (using member function size), length (using member function length) and whether the string is empty (using member function empty). The initial call to printStatistics indicates that the initial values for the capacity, size and length of string1 are 0.

The size and length of 0 indicate that there are no characters stored in string. Because the initial capacity is 0, when characters are placed in string1, memory is allocated to accommodate the new characters. Recall that the size and length are always identical. In this implementation, the maximum size is 4294967293. Object string1 is an empty string, so function empty returns true.

Line 18 inputs a string. In this example, "tomato soup" is input. Because a space character is a delimiter, only "tomato" is stored in string1; however, "soup" remains in the input buffer. Line 22 calls function printStatistics to output statistics for string1. Notice in the output that the length is 6 and the capacity is 15.

> **Performance Tip 18.1**
> *To minimize the number of times memory is allocated and deallocated, some string class implementations provide a default capacity that is larger than the length of the string.*

Line 25 reads "soup" from the input buffer and stores it in string1, thereby replacing "tomato". Line 27 passes string1 to printStatistics.

Line 30 uses the overloaded += operator to concatenate a 46-character-long string to string1. Line 32 passes string1 to printStatistics. The capacity has increased to 63 elements and the length is now 50.

Line 35 uses member function **resize** to increase the length of string1 by 10 characters. The additional elements are set to null characters. The output shows that the capacity has not changed and the length is now 60.

18.7 Finding Substrings and Characters in a `string`

Class `string` provides `const` member functions for finding substrings and characters in a `string`. Figure 18.6 demonstrates the find functions.

```cpp
 1   // Fig. 18.6: Fig18_06.cpp
 2   // Demonstrating the string find member functions.
 3   #include <iostream>
 4   #include <string>
 5   using namespace std;
 6
 7   int main()
 8   {
 9      string string1( "noon is 12 pm; midnight is not." );
10      int location;
11
12      // find "is" at location 5 and 24
13      cout << "Original string:\n" << string1
14         << "\n\n(find) \"is\" was found at: " << string1.find( "is" )
15         << "\n(rfind) \"is\" was found at: " << string1.rfind( "is" );
16
17      // find 'o' at location 1
18      location = string1.find_first_of( "misop" );
19      cout << "\n\n(find_first_of) found '" << string1[ location ]
20         << "' from the group \"misop\" at: " << location;
21
22      // find 'o' at location 29
23      location = string1.find_last_of( "misop" );
24      cout << "\n\n(find_last_of) found '" << string1[ location ]
25         << "' from the group \"misop\" at: " << location;
26
27      // find '1' at location 8
28      location = string1.find_first_not_of( "noi spm" );
29      cout << "\n\n(find_first_not_of) '" << string1[ location ]
30         << "' is not contained in \"noi spm\" and was found at: "
31         << location;
32
33      // find '.' at location 12
34      location = string1.find_first_not_of( "12noi spm" );
35      cout << "\n\n(find_first_not_of) '" << string1[ location ]
36         << "' is not contained in \"12noi spm\" and was "
37         << "found at: " << location << endl;
38
```

Fig. 18.6 | Demonstrating the `string` `find` functions. (Part 1 of 2.)

```
39      // search for characters not in string1
40      location = string1.find_first_not_of(
41         "noon is 12 pm; midnight is not." );
42      cout << "\nfind_first_not_of(\"noon is 12 pm; midnight is not.\")"
43         << " returned: " << location << endl;
44   } // end main
```

```
Original string:
noon is 12 pm; midnight is not.

(find) "is" was found at: 5
(rfind) "is" was found at: 24

(find_first_of) found 'o' from the group "misop" at: 1

(find_last_of) found 'o' from the group "misop" at: 29

(find_first_not_of) '1' is not contained in "noi spm" and was found at: 8

(find_first_not_of) '.' is not contained in "12noi spm" and was found at: 12

find_first_not_of("noon is 12 pm; midnight is not.") returned: -1
```

Fig. 18.6 | Demonstrating the `string` find functions. (Part 2 of 2.)

String `string1` is declared and initialized in line 9. Line 14 attempts to find `"is"` in `string1` using function **find**. If `"is"` is found, the subscript of the starting location of that string is returned. If the `string` is not found, the value **string::npos** (a public static constant defined in class `string`) is returned. This value is returned by the `string` find-related functions to indicate that a substring or character was not found in the `string`.

Line 15 uses member function **rfind** to search `string1` backward (i.e., right-to-left). If `"is"` is found, the subscript location is returned. If the string is not found, `string::npos` is returned. [*Note:* The rest of the find functions presented in this section return the same type unless otherwise noted.]

Line 18 uses member function **find_first_of** to locate the first occurrence in `string1` of any character in `"misop"`. The searching is done from the beginning of `string1`. The character `'o'` is found in element 1.

Line 23 uses member function **find_last_of** to find the last occurrence in `string1` of any character in `"misop"`. The searching is done from the end of `string1`. The character `'o'` is found in element 29.

Line 28 uses member function **find_first_not_of** to find the first character in `string1` not contained in `"noi spm"`. The character `'1'` is found in element 8. Searching is done from the beginning of `string1`.

Line 34 uses member function `find_first_not_of` to find the first character not contained in `"12noi spm"`. The character `'.'` is found in element 12. Searching is done from the end of `string1`.

Lines 40–41 use member function `find_first_not_of` to find the first character not contained in `"noon is 12 pm; midnight is not."`. In this case, the `string` being searched contains every character specified in the string argument. Because a character was not found, `string::npos` (which has the value –1 in this case) is returned.

18.8 **Replacing Characters in a** `string`

Figure 18.7 demonstrates `string` member functions for replacing and erasing characters. Lines 10–14 declare and initialize `string string1`. Line 20 uses `string` member function **erase** to erase everything from (and including) the character in position 62 to the end of `string1`. [*Note:* Each newline character occupies one element in the `string`.]

```cpp
1   // Fig. 18.7: Fig18_07.cpp
2   // Demonstrating string member functions erase and replace.
3   #include <iostream>
4   #include <string>
5   using namespace std;
6
7   int main()
8   {
9      // compiler concatenates all parts into one string
10     string string1( "The values in any left subtree"
11        "\nare less than the value in the"
12        "\nparent node and the values in"
13        "\nany right subtree are greater"
14        "\nthan the value in the parent node" );
15
16     cout << "Original string:\n" << string1 << endl << endl;
17
18     // remove all characters from (and including) location 62
19     // through the end of string1
20     string1.erase( 62 );
21
22     // output new string
23     cout << "Original string after erase:\n" << string1
24        << "\n\nAfter first replacement:\n";
25
26     int position = string1.find( " " ); // find first space
27
28     // replace all spaces with period
29     while ( position != string::npos )
30     {
31        string1.replace( position, 1, "." );
32        position = string1.find( " ", position + 1 );
33     } // end while
34
35     cout << string1 << "\n\nAfter second replacement:\n";
36
37     position = string1.find( "." ); // find first period
38
39     // replace all periods with two semicolons
40     // NOTE: this will overwrite characters
41     while ( position != string::npos )
42     {
43        string1.replace( position, 2, "xxxxx;;yyy", 5, 2 );
44        position = string1.find( ".", position + 1 );
45     } // end while
```

Fig. 18.7 | Demonstrating functions **erase** and **replace**. (Part I of 2.)

```
46
47      cout << string1 << endl;
48   } // end main
```

```
Original string:
The values in any left subtree
are less than the value in the
parent node and the values in
any right subtree are greater
than the value in the parent node

Original string after erase:
The values in any left subtree
are less than the value in the


After first replacement:
The.values.in.any.left.subtree
are.less.than.the.value.in.the


After second replacement:
The;;alues;;n;;ny;;eft;;ubtree
are;;ess;;han;;he;;alue;;n;;he
```

Fig. 18.7 | Demonstrating functions `erase` and `replace`. (Part 2 of 2.)

Lines 26–33 use `find` to locate each occurrence of the space character. Each space is then replaced with a period by a call to `string` member function **replace**. Function `replace` takes three arguments: the subscript of the character in the `string` at which replacement should begin, the number of characters to replace and the replacement string. Member function `find` returns `string::npos` when the search character is not found. In line 32, 1 is added to `position` to continue searching at the location of the next character.

Lines 37–45 use function `find` to find every period and another overloaded function `replace` to replace every period and its following character with two semicolons. The arguments passed to this version of `replace` are the subscript of the element where the replace operation begins, the number of characters to replace, a replacement character string from which a substring is selected to use as replacement characters, the element in the character string where the replacement substring begins and the number of characters in the replacement character string to use.

18.9 Inserting Characters into a `string`

Class `string` provides member functions for inserting characters into a `string`. Figure 18.8 demonstrates the `string insert` capabilities.

The program declares, initializes then outputs `strings string1`, `string2`, `string3` and `string4`. Line 19 uses `string` member function **insert** to insert `string2`'s content before element 10 of `string1`.

Line 22 uses `insert` to insert `string4` before `string3`'s element 3. The last two arguments specify the starting and last element of `string4` that should be inserted. Using `string::npos` causes the entire `string` to be inserted.

```cpp
 1  // Fig. 18.8: Fig18_08.cpp
 2  // Demonstrating class string insert member functions.
 3  #include <iostream>
 4  #include <string>
 5  using namespace std;
 6
 7  int main()
 8  {
 9     string string1( "beginning end" );
10     string string2( "middle " );
11     string string3( "12345678" );
12     string string4( "xx" );
13
14     cout << "Initial strings:\nstring1: " << string1
15        << "\nstring2: " << string2 << "\nstring3: " << string3
16        << "\nstring4: " << string4 << "\n\n";
17
18     // insert "middle" at location 10 in string1
19     string1.insert( 10, string2 );
20
21     // insert "xx" at location 3 in string3
22     string3.insert( 3, string4, 0, string::npos );
23
24     cout << "Strings after insert:\nstring1: " << string1
25        << "\nstring2: " << string2 << "\nstring3: " << string3
26        << "\nstring4: " << string4 << endl;
27  } // end main
```

```
Initial strings:
string1: beginning end
string2: middle
string3: 12345678
string4: xx

Strings after insert:
string1: beginning middle end
string2: middle
string3: 123xx45678
string4: xx
```

Fig. 18.8 | Demonstrating the `string insert` member functions.

18.10 Conversion to C-Style Pointer-Based char * Strings

Class `string` provides member functions for converting `string` class objects to C-style pointer-based strings. As mentioned earlier, unlike pointer-based strings, `string`s are not necessarily null terminated. These conversion functions are useful when a given function takes a pointer-based string as an argument. Figure 18.9 demonstrates conversion of `string`s to pointer-based strings.

The program declares a `string`, an `int` and two `char` pointers (lines 9–12). The `string string1` is initialized to `"STRINGS"`, `ptr1` is initialized to 0 and `length` is initialized to the length of `string1`. Memory of sufficient size to hold a pointer-based string equivalent of `string string1` is allocated dynamically and attached to `char` pointer `ptr2`.

```cpp
 1   // Fig. 18.9: Fig18_09.cpp
 2   // Converting to C-style strings.
 3   #include <iostream>
 4   #include <string>
 5   using namespace std;
 6
 7   int main()
 8   {
 9      string string1( "STRINGS" ); // string constructor with char* arg
10      const char *ptr1 = 0; // initialize *ptr1
11      int length = string1.length();
12      char *ptr2 = new char[ length + 1 ]; // including null
13
14      // copy characters from string1 into allocated memory
15      string1.copy( ptr2, length, 0 ); // copy string1 to ptr2 char*
16      ptr2[ length ] = '\0'; // add null terminator
17
18      cout << "string string1 is " << string1
19         << "\nstring1 converted to a C-Style string is "
20         << string1.c_str()   << "\nptr1 is ";
21
22      // Assign to pointer ptr1 the const char * returned by
23      // function data(). NOTE: this is a potentially dangerous
24      // assignment. If string1 is modified, pointer ptr1 can
25      // become invalid.
26      ptr1 = string1.data();
27
28      // output each character using pointer
29      for ( int i = 0; i < length; i++ )
30         cout << *( ptr1 + i ); // use pointer arithmetic
31
32      cout << "\nptr2 is " << ptr2 << endl;
33      delete [] ptr2; // reclaim dynamically allocated memory
34   } // end main
```

```
string string1 is STRINGS
string1 converted to a C-Style string is STRINGS
ptr1 is STRINGS
ptr2 is STRINGS
```

Fig. 18.9 | Converting strings to C-style strings and character arrays.

Line 15 uses string member function **copy** to copy object string1 into the char array pointed to by ptr2. Line 16 manually places a terminating null character in the array pointed to by ptr2.

Line 20 uses function **c_str** to obtain a const char * that points to a null terminated C-style string with the same content as string1. The pointer is passed to the stream insertion operator for output.

Line 26 assigns the const char * ptr1 a pointer returned by class string member function **data**. This member function returns a non-null-terminated C-style character array. We do not modify string string1 in this example. If string1 were to be modified (e.g., the string's dynamic memory changes its address due to a member function call such as `string1.insert( 0, "abcd" );`), `ptr1` could become invalid—which could lead to unpredictable results.

Lines 29–30 use pointer arithmetic to output the character array pointed to by `ptr1`. In lines 32–33, the C-style string pointed to by `ptr2` is output and the memory allocated for `ptr2` is `delete`d to avoid a memory leak.

Common Programming Error 18.4

Not terminating the character array returned by `data` *with a null character can lead to execution-time errors.*

Good Programming Practice 18.1

Whenever possible, use the more robust `string` *class objects rather than C-style pointer-based strings.*

18.11 Iterators

Class `string` provides iterators for forward and backward traversal of `strings`. Iterators provide access to individual characters with syntax that is similar to pointer operations. Iterators are not range checked. In this section we provide "mechanical examples" to demonstrate the use of iterators. We discuss more robust uses of iterators in Chapter 22, Standard Template Library (STL). Figure 18.10 demonstrates iterators.

```cpp
1   // Fig. 18.10: Fig18_10.cpp
2   // Using an iterator to output a string.
3   #include <iostream>
4   #include <string>
5   using namespace std;
6
7   int main()
8   {
9      string string1( "Testing iterators" );
10     string::const_iterator iterator1 = string1.begin();
11
12     cout << "string1 = " << string1
13        << "\n(Using iterator iterator1) string1 is: ";
14
15     // iterate through string
16     while ( iterator1 != string1.end() )
17     {
18        cout << *iterator1; // dereference iterator to get char
19        iterator1++; // advance iterator to next char
20     } // end while
21
22     cout << endl;
23  } // end main
```

```
string1 = Testing iterators
(Using iterator iterator1) string1 is: Testing iterators
```

Fig. 18.10 | Using an iterator to output a `string`.

Lines 9–10 declare `string string1` and **`string::const_iterator`** `iterator1`. A `const_iterator` is an iterator that cannot modify the `string`—in this case the `string` through which it's iterating. Iterator `iterator1` is initialized to the beginning of `string1` with the `string` class member function **begin**. Two versions of begin exist—one that returns an `iterator` for iterating through a non-const `string` and a const version that returns a `const_iterator` for iterating through a const `string`. Line 12 outputs `string1`.

Lines 16–20 use iterator `iterator1` to "walk through" `string1`. Class string member function **end** returns an `iterator` (or a `const_iterator`) for the position past the last element of `string1`. Each element is printed by dereferencing the iterator much as you'd dereference a pointer, and the iterator is advanced one position using operator ++.

Class `string` provides member functions **rend** and **rbegin** for accessing individual `string` characters in reverse from the end of a `string` toward the beginning. Member functions rend and rbegin return **reverse_iterators** or **const_reverse_iterators** (based on whether the `string` is non-const or const). In the exercises, we ask you to write a program that demonstrates these capabilities. We'll use iterators and reverse iterators more in Chapter 22.

Error-Prevention Tip 18.1

Use `string` member function at (rather than iterators) when you want the benefit of range checking.

Good Programming Practice 18.2

When the operations involving the iterator should not modify the data being processed, use a `const_iterator`. This is another example of employing the principle of least privilege.

18.12 String Stream Processing

In addition to standard stream I/O and file stream I/O, C++ stream I/O includes capabilities for inputting from, and outputting to, `string`s in memory. These capabilities often are referred to as **in-memory I/O** or **string stream processing**.

Input from a `string` is supported by class **`istringstream`**. Output to a `string` is supported by class **`ostringstream`**. The class names `istringstream` and `ostringstream` are actually aliases defined by the `typedef`s

```
typedef basic_istringstream< char > istringstream;
typedef basic_ostringstream< char > ostringstream;
```

Class templates `basic_istringstream` and `basic_ostringstream` provide the same functionality as classes `istream` and `ostream` plus other member functions specific to in-memory formatting. Programs that use in-memory formatting must include the **`<sstream>`** and `<iostream>` header files.

One application of these techniques is data validation. A program can read an entire line at a time from the input stream into a `string`. Next, a validation routine can scrutinize the contents of the `string` and correct (or repair) the data, if necessary. Then the program can proceed to input from the `string`, knowing that the input data is in the proper format.

Outputting to a `string` is a nice way to take advantage of the powerful output formatting capabilities of C++ streams. Data can be prepared in a `string` to mimic the edited screen format. That `string` could be written to a disk file to preserve the screen image.

An ostringstream object uses a `string` object to store the output data. The **str** member function of class `ostringstream` returns a copy of that `string`.

Figure 18.11 demonstrates an `ostringstream` object. The program creates ostring-stream object `outputString` (line 10) and uses the stream insertion operator to output a series of `string`s and numerical values to the object.

```cpp
1   // Fig. 18.11: Fig18_11.cpp
2   // Using an ostringstream object.
3   #include <iostream>
4   #include <string>
5   #include <sstream> // header file for string stream processing
6   using namespace std;
7
8   int main()
9   {
10      ostringstream outputString; // create ostringstream instance
11
12      string string1( "Output of several data types " );
13      string string2( "to an ostringstream object:" );
14      string string3( "\n         double: " );
15      string string4( "\n            int: " );
16      string string5( "\naddress of int: " );
17
18      double double1 = 123.4567;
19      int integer = 22;
20
21      // output strings, double and int to ostringstream outputString
22      outputString << string1 << string2 << string3 << double1
23         << string4 << integer << string5 << &integer;
24
25      // call str to obtain string contents of the ostringstream
26      cout << "outputString contains:\n" << outputString.str();
27
28      // add additional characters and call str to output string
29      outputString << "\nmore characters added";
30      cout << "\n\nafter additional stream insertions,\n"
31         << "outputString contains:\n" << outputString.str() << endl;
32   } // end main
```

```
outputString contains:
Output of several data types to an ostringstream object:
        double: 123.457
           int: 22
address of int: 0012F540

after additional stream insertions,
outputString contains:
Output of several data types to an ostringstream object:
        double: 123.457
           int: 22
address of int: 0012F540
more characters added
```

Fig. 18.11 | Using an `ostringstream` object.

Lines 22–23 output string string1, string string2, string string3, double double1, string string4, int integer, string string5 and the address of int integer—all to outputString in memory. Line 26 uses the stream insertion operator and the call outputString.str() to display a copy of the string created in lines 22–23. Line 29 demonstrates that more data can be appended to the string in memory by simply issuing another stream insertion operation to outputString. Lines 30–31 display string outputString after appending additional characters.

An istringstream object inputs data from a string in memory to program variables. Data is stored in an istringstream object as characters. Input from the istringstream object works identically to input from any file. The end of the string is interpreted by the istringstream object as end-of-file.

Figure 18.12 demonstrates input from an istringstream object. Lines 10–11 create string input containing the data and istringstream object inputString constructed to contain the data in string input. The string input contains the data

```
Input test 123 4.7 A
```

which, when read as input to the program, consist of two strings ("Input" and "test"), an int (123), a double (4.7) and a char ('A'). These characters are extracted to variables string1, string2, integer, double1 and character in line 18.

```cpp
1   // Fig. 18.12: Fig18_12.cpp
2   // Demonstrating input from an istringstream object.
3   #include <iostream>
4   #include <string>
5   #include <sstream>
6   using namespace std;
7
8   int main()
9   {
10     string input( "Input test 123 4.7 A" );
11     istringstream inputString( input );
12     string string1;
13     string string2;
14     int integer;
15     double double1;
16     char character;
17
18     inputString >> string1 >> string2 >> integer >> double1 >> character;
19
20     cout << "The following items were extracted\n"
21       << "from the istringstream object:" << "\nstring: " << string1
22       << "\nstring: " << string2 << "\n   int: " << integer
23       << "\ndouble: " << double1 << "\n  char: " << character;
24
25     // attempt to read from empty stream
26     long value;
27     inputString >> value;
28
```

Fig. 18.12 | Demonstrating input from an istringstream object. (Part 1 of 2.)

```
29      // test stream results
30      if ( inputString.good() )
31          cout << "\n\nlong value is: " << value << endl;
32      else
33          cout << "\n\ninputString is empty" << endl;
34   } // end main
```

```
The following items were extracted
from the istringstream object:
string: Input
string: test
   int: 123
double: 4.7
  char: A

inputString is empty
```

Fig. 18.12 | Demonstrating input from an `istringstream` object. (Part 2 of 2.)

The data is then output in lines 20–23. The program attempts to read from input-String again in line 27. The `if` condition in line 30 uses function good (Section 15.8) to test if any data remains. Because no data remains, the function returns `false` and the `else` part of the `if...else` statement is executed.

18.13 Wrap-Up

This chapter discussed the details of C++ Standard Library class `string`. We discussed assigning, concatenating, comparing, searching and swapping strings. We also introduced a number of methods to determine string characteristics, to find, replace and insert characters in a string, and to convert strings to C-style strings and vice versa. You also learned about string iterators and performing input from and output to strings in memory. In Chapter 19, Searching and Sorting, we discuss the binary search algorithm and the merge sort algorithm. We also use Big O notation to analyze and compare the efficiency of various searching and sorting algorithms.

Summary

Section 18.1 Introduction

- Class template `basic_string` provides typical string-manipulation operations.
- The `typedef` statement

      typedef basic_string< char > string;

  creates the alias type `string` for `basic_string<char>`. A `typedef` also is provided for the `wchar_t` type (`wstring`). Type `wchar_t` normally stores two-byte (16-bit) characters for supporting other character sets. The size of `wchar_t` is not fixed by the standard.

- To use strings, include C++ Standard Library header file `<string>`.
- Assigning a single character to a `string` object is permitted in an assignment statement.
- `strings` are not necessarily null terminated.

- Most string member functions take as arguments a starting subscript location and the number of characters on which to operate.

Section 18.2 string *Assignment and Concatenation*
- Class string provides overloaded operator= and member function assign for assignments.
- The subscript operator, [], provides read/write access to any element of a string.
- string member function at provides checked access—going past either end of the string throws an out_of_range exception. The subscript operator, [], does not provide checked access.
- The overloaded + and += operators and member function append perform string concatenation.

Section 18.3 *Comparing* strings
- Class string provides overloaded ==, !=, <, >, <= and >= operators for string comparisons.
- string member function compare compares two strings (or substrings) and returns 0 if the strings are equal, a positive number if the first string is lexicographically greater than the second or a negative number if the first string is lexicographically less than the second.

Section 18.4 *Substrings*
- string member function substr retrieves a substring from a string.

Section 18.5 *Swapping* strings
- string member function swap swaps the contents of two strings.

Section 18.6 string *Characteristics*
- string member functions size and length return the number of characters currently stored in a string.
- string member function capacity returns the total number of characters that can be stored in a string without increasing the amount of memory allocated to the string.
- string member function max_size returns the maximum size a string can have.
- string member function resize changes the length of a string.

Section 18.7 *Finding Substrings and Characters in a* string
- Class string find functions find, rfind, find_first_of, find_last_of and find_first_not_of locate substrings or characters in a string.

Section 18.8 *Replacing Characters in a* string
- string member function erase deletes elements of a string.x
- string member function replace replaces characters in a string.

Section 18.9 *Inserting Characters into a* string
- string member function insert inserts characters in a string.

Section 18.10 *Conversion to C-Style Pointer-Based* char * *Strings*
- string member function c_str returns a const char * pointing to a null-terminated C-style character string that contains all the characters in a string.
- string member function data returns a const char * pointing to a non-null-terminated C-style character array that contains all the characters in a string.

Section 18.11 *Iterators*
- Class string provides member functions end and begin to iterate through individual elements.

- Class `string` provides member functions `rend` and `rbegin` for accessing individual `string` characters in reverse from the end of a `string` toward the beginning.

Section 18.12 String Stream Processing
- Input from a `string` is supported by type `istringstream`. Output to a `string` is supported by type `ostringstream`.
- `ostringstream` member function `str` returns the `string` from the stream.

Terminology

append member function of class string 759
assign member function of class string 757
at member function of class string 759
basic_string<char> 756
basic_string class template 756
begin member function of class string 773
c_str member function of class string 771
capacity of a string 763
capacity member function of class string 765
checked access 759
compare member function of class string 761
const_iterator 773
const_reverse_iterator 773
copy member function of class string 771
data member function of class string 771
empty string 756
end member function of class string 773
erase member function of class string 768
find member function of class string 767
find_first_not_of member function of class string 767
find_first_of member function of class string 767
find_last_of member function of class string 767
getline member function of class string 757

in-memory I/O 773
insert member function of class string 769
istringstream class 773
length member function of class string 757
lexicographical comparison 761
max_size member function of class string 765
maximum size of a string 763
ostringstream class 773
range checking 759
rbegin member function of class string 773
rend member function of class string 773
replace member function of class string 769
resize member function of class string 766
reverse_iterator 773
rfind member function of class string 767
size member function of class string 757
<sstream> header file 773
str member function of class ostringstream 774
string::const_iterator 773
string::npos constant 767
string stream processing 773
substr member function of class string 762
swap member function of class string 762
wchar_t type 756

Self-Review Exercises

18.1 Fill in the blanks in each of the following:
  a) Header _____ must be included for class string.
  b) Class string belongs to the _____ namespace.
  c) Function _____ deletes characters from a string.
  d) Function _____ finds the first occurrence of any character from a string.

18.2 State which of the following statements are *true* and which are *false*. If a statement is *false*, explain why.
  a) Concatenation of string objects can be performed with the addition assignment operator, +=.
  b) Characters within a string begin at index 0.
  c) The assignment operator, =, copies a string.
  d) A C-style string is a string object.

18.3 Find the error(s) in each of the following, and explain how to correct it (them):
a) `string string1( 28 ); // construct string1`
   `string string2( 'z' ); // construct string2`
b) `// assume std namespace is known`
   `const char *ptr = name.data(); // name is "joe bob"`
   `ptr[ 3 ] = '-';`
   `cout << ptr << endl;`

Answers to Self-Review Exercises

18.1 a) `<string>`. b) `std`. c) `erase`. d) `find_first_of`.

18.2 a) True.
b) True.
c) True.
d) False. A `string` is an object that provides many different services. A C-style string does not provide any services. C-style strings are null terminated; `string`s are not necessarily null terminated. C-style strings are pointers and `string`s are objects.

18.3 a) Constructors for class `string` do not exist for integer and character arguments. Other valid constructors should be used—converting the arguments to `string`s if need be.
b) Function `data` does not add a null terminator. Also, the code attempts to modify a `const char`. Replace all of the lines with the code:
   `cout << name.substr( 0, 3 ) + "-" + name.substr( 4 ) << endl;`

Exercises

18.4 Fill in the blanks in each of the following:
a) Class `string` member functions _____ and _____ convert `string`s to C-style strings.
b) Class `string` member function _____ is used for assignment.
c) _____ is the return type of function `rbegin`.
d) Class `string` member function _____ is used to retrieve a substring.

18.5 State which of the following statements are *true* and which are *false*. If a statement is *false*, explain why.
a) `string`s are always null terminated.
b) Class `string` member function `max_size` returns the maximum size for a `string`.
c) Class `string` member function `at` can throw an `out_of_range` exception.
d) Class `string` member function `begin` returns an `iterator`.

18.6 Find any errors in the following and explain how to correct them:
a) `std::cout << s.data() << std::endl; // s is "hello"`
b) `erase( s.rfind( "x" ), 1 ); // s is "xenon"`
c) `string& foo()`
   `{`
      `string s( "Hello" );`
      `...    // other statements`
      `return;`
   `} // end function foo`

18.7 (*Simple Encryption*) Some information on the Internet may be encrypted with a simple algorithm known as "rot13," which rotates each character by 13 positions in the alphabet. Thus, `'a'` corresponds to `'n'`, and `'x'` corresponds to `'k'`. rot13 is an example of **symmetric key encryption**. With symmetric key encryption, both the encrypter and decrypter use the same key.

   a) Write a program that encrypts a message using rot13.
   b) Write a program that decrypts the scrambled message using 13 as the key.
   c) After writing the programs of part (a) and part (b), briefly answer the following question: If you did not know the key for part (b), how difficult do you think it would be to break the code? What if you had access to substantial computing power (e.g., supercomputers)? In Exercise 18.25 we ask you to write a program to accomplish this.

18.8   *(Using string Iterators)* Write a program using iterators that demonstrates the use of functions `rbegin` and `rend`.

18.9   *(Words Ending in "r" or "ay")* Write a program that reads in several `strings` and prints only those ending in "r" or "ay". Only lowercase letters should be considered.

18.10   *(string Concatenation)* Write a program that separately inputs a first name and a last name and concatenates the two into a new `string`. Show two techniques for accomplishing this task.

18.11   *(Hangman Game)* Write a program that plays the game of Hangman. The program should pick a word (which is either coded directly into the program or read from a text file) and display the following:

```
Guess the word:    XXXXXX
```

Each X represents a letter. The user tries to guess the letters in the word. The appropriate response yes or no should be displayed after each guess. After each incorrect guess, display the diagram with another body part filled. After seven incorrect guesses, the user should be hanged. The display should look as follows:

After each guess, display all user guesses. If the user guesses the word correctly, the program should display

```
Congratulations!!! You guessed my word. Play again? yes/no
```

18.12   *(Printing a string Backward)* Write a program that inputs a `string` and prints the `string` backward. Convert all uppercase characters to lowercase and all lowercase characters to uppercase.

18.13   *(Alphabetizing Animal Names)* Write a program that uses the comparison capabilities introduced in this chapter to alphabetize a series of animal names. Only uppercase letters should be used for the comparisons.

18.14   *(Cryptograms)* Write a program that creates a cryptogram out of a `string`. A cryptogram is a message or word in which each letter is replaced with another letter. For example the `string`

```
The bird was named squawk
```

might be scrambled to form

```
cin vrjs otz ethns zxqtop
```

Spaces are not scrambled. In this particular case, 'T' was replaced with 'x', each 'a' was replaced with 'h', etc. Uppercase letters become lowercase letters in the cryptogram. Use techniques similar to those in Exercise 18.7.

18.15   *(Solving Cryptograms)* Modify Exercise 18.14 to allow the user to solve the cryptogram. The user should input two characters at a time: The first character specifies a letter in the cryptogram, and the second letter specifies the replacement letter. If the replacement letter is correct, replace the letter in the cryptogram with the replacement letter in uppercase.

18.16 *(Counting Palindromes)* Write a program that inputs a sentence and counts the number of palindromes in it. A palindrome is a word that reads the same backward and forward. For example, "tree" is not a palindrome, but "noon" is.

18.17 *(Counting Vowels)* Write a program that counts the total number of vowels in a sentence. Output the frequency of each vowel.

18.18 Write a program that inserts the characters "******" in the exact middle of a `string`.

18.19 *(Erasing Characters from a `string`)* Write a program that erases the sequences "by" and "BY" from a `string`.

18.20 *(Replacing Punctuation and Tokenizing `strings`)* Write a program that inputs a line of text, replaces all punctuation marks with spaces and uses the C-string library function `strtok` to tokenize the `string` into individual words.

18.21 *(Reversing a `string` with Iterators)* Write a program that inputs a line of text and prints the text backward. Use iterators in your solution.

18.22 *(Reversing a `string` with Iterators using Recursion)* Write a recursive version of Exercise 18.21.

18.23 *(Using the `erase` Functions with Iterator Arguments)* Write a program that demonstrates the use of the erase functions that take `iterator` arguments.

18.24 *(Letter Pyramid)* Write a program that generates the following from the `string` "abcdefghijklmnopqrstuvwxyz{":

```
            a
           bcb
          cdedc
         defgfed
        efghihgfe
       fghijkjihgf
      ghijklmlkjihg
     hijklmnonmlkjih
    ijklmnopqponmlkji
   jklmnopqrsrqponmlkj
  klmnopqrstutsrqponmlk
 lmnopqrstuvwvutsrqponml
mnopqrstuvwxyxwvutsrqponm
nopqrstuvwxyz{zyxwvutsrqpon
```

18.25 *(Simple Decryption)* In Exercise 18.7, we asked you to write a simple encryption algorithm. Write a program that will attempt to decrypt a "rot13" message using simple frequency substitution. (Assume that you do not know the key.) The most frequent letters in the encrypted phrase should be replaced with the most commonly used English letters (a, e, i, o, u, s, t, r, etc.). Write the possibilities to a file. What made the code breaking easy? How can the encryption mechanism be improved?

18.26 *(Sorting `strings`)* Write a version of the selection sort routine (Fig. 8.20) that sorts `strings`. Use function `swap` in your solution.

18.27 *(Enhanced `Employee` Class)* Modify class `Employee` in Figs. 13.6–13.7 by adding a `private` utility function called `isValidSocialSecurityNumber`. This member function should validate the format of a social security number (e.g., ###-##-####, where # is a digit). If the format is valid, return `true`; otherwise return `false`.

Making a Difference

18.28 *(Cooking with Healthier Ingredients)* Obesity in the United States is increasing at an alarming rate. Check the map from the Centers for Disease Control and Prevention (CDC) at `www.cdc.gov/nccdphp/dnpa/Obesity/trend/maps/index.htm`, which shows obesity trends in the United States over the last 20 years. As obesity increases, so do occurrences of related problems (e.g., heart disease, high blood pressure, high cholesterol, type 2 diabetes). Write a program that helps users choose healthier ingredients when cooking, and helps those allergic to certain foods (e.g., nuts, gluten) find substitutes. The program should read a recipe from the user and suggest healthier replacements for some of the ingredients. For simplicity, your program should assume the recipe has no abbreviations for measures such as teaspoons, cups, and tablespoons, and uses numerical digits for quantities (e.g., 1 egg, 2 cups) rather than spelling them out (one egg, two cups). Some common substitutions are shown in Fig. 18.13. Your program should display a warning such as, "Always consult your physician before making significant changes to your diet."

Ingredient	Substitution
1 cup sour cream	1 cup yogurt
1 cup milk	1/2 cup evaporated milk and 1/2 cup water
1 teaspoon lemon juice	1/2 teaspoon vinegar
1 cup sugar	1/2 cup honey, 1 cup molasses or 1/4 cup agave nectar
1 cup butter	1 cup margarine or yogurt
1 cup flour	1 cup rye or rice flour
1 cup mayonnaise	1 cup cottage cheese or 1/8 cup mayonnaise and 7/8 cup yogurt
1 egg	2 tablespoons cornstarch, arrowroot flour or potato starch or 2 egg whites or 1/2 of a large banana (mashed)
1 cup milk	1 cup soy milk
1/4 cup oil	1/4 cup applesauce
white bread	whole-grain bread

Fig. 18.13 | Typical ingredient substitutes.

Your program should take into consideration that replacements are not always one-for-one. For example, if a cake recipe calls for three eggs, it might reasonably use six egg whites instead. Conversion data for measurements and substitutes can be obtained at websites such as:

```
chinesefood.about.com/od/recipeconversionfaqs/f/usmetricrecipes.htm
www.pioneerthinking.com/eggsub.html
www.gourmetsleuth.com/conversions.htm
```

Your program should consider the user's health concerns, such as high cholesterol, high blood pressure, weight loss, gluten allergy, and so on. For high cholesterol, the program should suggest substitutes for eggs and dairy products; if the user wishes to lose weight, low-calorie substitutes for ingredients such as sugar should be suggested.

18.29 *(Spam Scanner)* Spam (or junk e-mail) costs U.S. organizations billions of dollars a year in spam-prevention software, equipment, network resources, bandwidth, and lost productivity. Research online some of the most common spam e-mail messages and words, and check your own junk e-mail folder. Create a list of 30 words and phrases commonly found in spam messages. Write an application in which the user enters an e-mail message. Then, scan the message for each of the

30 keywords or phrases. For each occurrence of one of these within the message, add a point to the message's "spam score." Next, rate the likelihood that the message is spam, based on the number of points it received.

18.30 *(SMS Language)* Short Message Service (SMS) is a communications service that allows sending text messages of 160 or fewer characters between mobile phones. With the proliferation of mobile phone use worldwide, SMS is being used in many developing nations for political purposes (e.g., voicing opinions and opposition), reporting news about natural disasters, and so on. For example, check out comunica.org/radio2.0/archives/87. Since the length of SMS messages is limited, SMS Language—abbreviations of common words and phrases in mobile text messages, e-mails, instant messages, etc.—is often used. For example, "in my opinion" is "IMO" in SMS Language. Research SMS Language online. Write a program in which the user can enter a message using SMS Language, then the program should translate it into English (or your own language). Also provide a mechanism to translate text written in English (or your own language) into SMS Language. One potential problem is that one SMS abbreviation could expand into a variety of phrases. For example, IMO (as used above) could also stand for "International Maritime Organization," "in memory of," "in my opinion," etc.

19

Searching and Sorting

*With sobs and tears
he sorted out
Those of the largest size ...*
—Lewis Carroll

*Attempt the end, and never
stand to doubt;
Nothing's so hard, but search
will find it out.*
—Robert Herrick

*'Tis in my memory lock'd,
And you yourself shall keep the
key of it.*
—William Shakespeare

*It is an immutable law in
business that words are words,
explanations are explanations,
promises are promises — but
only performance is reality.*
—Harold S. Green

Objectives

In this chapter you'll learn:

- To search for a given value in a vector using binary search.

- To use Big O notation to express the efficiency of searching and sorting algorithms and to compare their performance.

- To sort a vector using the recursive merge sort algorithm.

- To understand the nature of algorithms of constant, linear and quadratic runtime.

19.1 Introduction

Searching data involves determining whether a value (referred to as the **search key**) is present in the data and, if so, finding the value's location. Two popular search algorithms are the simple linear search (introduced in Section 7.7) and the faster but more complex binary search, which is introduced in this chapter.

Sorting places data in order, typically ascending or descending, based on one or more **sort keys**. A list of names could be sorted alphabetically, bank accounts could be sorted by account number, employee payroll records could be sorted by social security number, and so on. Previously, you learned about insertion sort (Section 7.8) and selection sort (Section 8.6). This chapter introduces the more efficient, but more complex merge sort. Figure 19.1 summarizes the searching and sorting algorithms discussed in the examples and exercises of this book. This chapter also introduces **Big O notation**, which is used to estimate the worst-case runtime for an algorithm—that is, how hard an algorithm may have to work to solve a problem.

Algorithm	Location
Searching Algorithms	
Linear search	Section 7.7
Binary search	Section 19.2.2
Recursive linear search	Exercise 19.8
Recursive binary search	Exercise 19.9
Binary tree search	Section 20.7
Linear search of a linked list	Exercise 20.21
binary_search standard library function	Section 22.5.6
Sorting Algorithms	
Insertion sort	Section 7.8
Selection sort	Section 8.6
Recursive merge sort	Section 19.3.3
Bubble sort	Exercises 19.5 and 19.6
Bucket sort	Exercise 19.7
Recursive quicksort	Exercise 19.10

Fig. 19.1 | Searching and sorting algorithms in this text. (Part 1 of 2.)

Algorithm	Location
Binary tree sort	Section 20.7
sort standard library function	Section 22.5.6
Heap sort	Section 22.5.12

Fig. 19.1 | Searching and sorting algorithms in this text. (Part 2 of 2.)

19.2 Searching Algorithms

Looking up a phone number, accessing a website and checking the definition of a word in a dictionary all involve searching large amounts of data. Searching algorithms all accomplish the same goal—finding an element that matches a given search key, if such an element does, in fact, exist. There are, however, a number of things that differentiate search algorithms from one another. The major difference is the amount of effort they require to complete the search. One way to describe this effort is with Big O notation. For searching and sorting algorithms, this is particularly dependent on the number of data elements.

In Chapter 7, we discussed the linear search algorithm, which is a simple and easy-to-implement searching algorithm. We'll now discuss the efficiency of the linear search algorithm as measured by Big O notation. Then, we'll introduce a searching algorithm that is relatively efficient but more complex and difficult to implement.

19.2.1 Efficiency of Linear Search

Suppose an algorithm simply tests whether the first element of a vector is equal to the second element of the vector. If the vector has 10 elements, this algorithm requires only one comparison. If the vector has 1000 elements, the algorithm still requires only one comparison. In fact, the algorithm is independent of the number of vector elements. This algorithm is said to have a **constant runtime**, which is represented in Big O notation as $O(1)$. An algorithm that is $O(1)$ does not necessarily require only one comparison. $O(1)$ just means that the number of comparisons is *constant*—it does not grow as the size of the vector increases. An algorithm that tests whether the first element of a vector is equal to any of the next three elements will always require three comparisons, but in Big O notation it's still considered $O(1)$. $O(1)$ is often pronounced "on the order of 1" or more simply "**order 1**."

An algorithm that tests whether the first element of a vector is equal to *any* of the other elements of the vector requires at most $n - 1$ comparisons, where n is the number of elements in the vector. If the vector has 10 elements, the algorithm requires up to nine comparisons. If the vector has 1000 elements, the algorithm requires up to 999 comparisons. As n grows larger, the n part of the expression "dominates," and subtracting one becomes inconsequential. Big O is designed to highlight these dominant terms and ignore terms that become unimportant as n grows. For this reason, an algorithm that requires a total of $n - 1$ comparisons (such as the one we described in this paragraph) is said to be $O(n)$. An $O(n)$ algorithm is referred to as having a **linear runtime**. $O(n)$ is often pronounced "on the order of n" or more simply "**order n**."

Now suppose you have an algorithm that tests whether *any* element of a vector is duplicated elsewhere in the vector. The first element must be compared with every other element in the vector. The second element must be compared with every other element except the first (it was already compared to the first). The third element must be compared with every other element except the first two. In the end, this algorithm will end up making $(n - 1) + (n - 2) + \ldots + 2 + 1$ or $n^2/2 - n/2$ comparisons. As n increases, the n^2 term dominates and the n term becomes inconsequential. Again, Big O notation highlights the n^2 term, leaving $n^2/2$. As we'll soon see, however, constant factors are omitted in Big O notation.

Big O is concerned with how an algorithm's runtime grows in relation to the number of items processed. Suppose an algorithm requires n^2 comparisons. With four elements, the algorithm will require 16 comparisons; with eight elements, 64 comparisons. With this algorithm, doubling the number of elements quadruples the number of comparisons. Consider a similar algorithm requiring $n^2/2$ comparisons. With four elements, the algorithm will require eight comparisons; with eight elements, 32 comparisons. Again, doubling the number of elements quadruples the number of comparisons. Both of these algorithms grow as the square of n, so Big O ignores the constant, and both algorithms are considered to be $O(n^2)$, which is referred to as **quadratic runtime** and pronounced "on the order of n-squared" or more simply "**order n-squared**."

When n is small, $O(n^2)$ algorithms (running on today's billion-operation-per-second personal computers) will not noticeably affect performance. But as n grows, you'll start to notice the performance degradation. An $O(n^2)$ algorithm running on a million-element vector would require a trillion "operations" (where each could actually require several machine instructions to execute). This could require a few hours to execute. A billion-element vector would require a quintillion operations, a number so large that the algorithm could take decades! Unfortunately, $O(n^2)$ algorithms tend to be easy to write. In this chapter, you'll see algorithms with more favorable Big O measures. These efficient algorithms often take a bit more cleverness and effort to create, but their superior performance can be worth the extra effort, especially as n gets large and as algorithms are compounded into larger programs.

The linear search algorithm runs in $O(n)$ time. The worst case in this algorithm is that every element must be checked to determine whether the search key exists in the vector. If the size of the vector is doubled, the number of comparisons that the algorithm must perform is also doubled. Linear search can provide outstanding performance if the element matching the search key happens to be at or near the front of the vector. But we seek algorithms that perform well, on average, across all searches, including those where the element matching the search key is near the end of the vector.

Linear search is the easiest search algorithm to implement, but it can be slow compared to other search algorithms. If a program needs to perform many searches on large vectors, it may be better to implement a different, more efficient algorithm, such as the binary search which we present in the next section.

Performance Tip 19.1

Sometimes the simplest algorithms perform poorly. Their virtue is that they're easy to program, test and debug. Sometimes more complex algorithms are required to realize maximum performance.

19.2.2 Binary Search

The **binary search algorithm** is more efficient than the linear search algorithm, but it requires that the vector first be sorted. This is only worthwhile when the vector, once sorted, will be searched a great many times—or when the searching application has stringent performance requirements. The first iteration of this algorithm tests the middle element in the vector. If this matches the search key, the algorithm ends. Assuming the vector is sorted in ascending order, then if the search key is less than the middle element, the search key cannot match any element in the second half of the vector and the algorithm continues with only the first half of the vector (i.e., the first element up to, but not including, the middle element). If the search key is greater than the middle element, the search key cannot match any element in the first half of the vector and the algorithm continues with only the second half of the vector (i.e., the element after the middle element through the last element). Each iteration tests the middle value of the remaining portion of the vector. If the element does not match the search key, the algorithm eliminates half of the remaining elements. The algorithm ends either by finding an element that matches the search key or by reducing the subvector to zero size.

As an example, consider the sorted 15-element vector

2	3	5	10	27	30	34	51	56	65	77	81	82	93	99

and the search key 65. A binary search would first check whether 51 is the search key (because 51 is the middle element of the vector). The search key (65) is larger than 51, so 51 is eliminated from consideration along with the first half of the vector (all elements smaller than 51.) Next, the algorithm checks whether 81 (the middle element of the remainder of the vector) matches the search key. The search key (65) is smaller than 81, so 81 is eliminated from consideration along with the elements larger than 81. After just two tests, the algorithm has narrowed the number of elements to check to three (56, 65 and 77). The algorithm then checks 65 (which matches the search key), and returns the index (9) of the vector element containing 65. In this case, the algorithm required just three comparisons to determine whether a vector element matched the search key. Using a linear search algorithm would have required 10 comparisons. [*Note:* In this example, we've chosen to use a vector with 15 elements, so that there will always be an obvious middle element in the vector. With an even number of elements, the middle of the vector lies between two elements. We implement the algorithm to choose the larger of those two elements.]

Figures 19.2–19.3 define class `BinarySearch` and its member functions, respectively. Class `BinarySearch` is similar to `LinearSearch` (Section 7.7)—it has a constructor, a search function (`binarySearch`), a `displayElements` function, two `private` data members and a `private` utility function (`displaySubElements`). Lines 11–21 of Fig. 19.3 define the constructor. After initializing the vector with random `int`s from 10–99 (lines 17–18), line 20 calls the Standard Library function `sort` on the vector `data`. Recall that the binary search algorithm will work only on a sorted vector. Function **sort** requires two arguments that specify the range of elements to sort. These arguments are specified with iterators (discussed in detail in Chapter 22, Standard Template Library (STL)). The vector member functions `begin` and `end` return iterators that can be used with function `sort` to indicate that all the elements from the beginning to the end should be sorted.

Lines 24–54 define function `binarySearch`. The search key is passed into parameter `searchElement` (line 24). Lines 26–28 calculate the `low` end index, `high` end index and

```
 1   // Fig 19.2: BinarySearch.h
 2   // Class that contains a vector of random integers and a function
 3   // that uses binary search to find an integer.
 4   #include <vector>
 5   using namespace std;
 6
 7   class BinarySearch
 8   {
 9   public:
10      BinarySearch( int ); // constructor initializes vector
11      int binarySearch( int ) const; // perform a binary search on vector
12      void displayElements() const; // display vector elements
13   private:
14      int size; // vector size
15      vector< int > data; // vector of ints
16      void displaySubElements( int, int ) const; // display range of values
17   }; // end class BinarySearch
```

Fig. 19.2 | BinarySearch class definition.

```
 1   // Fig 19.3: BinarySearch.cpp
 2   // BinarySearch class member-function definition.
 3   #include <iostream>
 4   #include <cstdlib> // prototypes for functions srand and rand
 5   #include <ctime> // prototype for function time
 6   #include <algorithm> // prototype for sort function
 7   #include "BinarySearch.h" // class BinarySearch definition
 8   using namespace std;
 9
10   // constructor initializes vector with random ints and sorts the vector
11   BinarySearch::BinarySearch( int vectorSize )
12   {
13      size = ( vectorSize > 0 ? vectorSize : 10 ); // validate vectorSize
14      srand( time( 0 ) ); // seed using current time
15
16      // fill vector with random ints in range 10-99
17      for ( int i = 0; i < size; i++ )
18         data.push_back( 10 + rand() % 90 ); // 10-99
19
20      std::sort( data.begin(), data.end() ); // sort the data
21   } // end BinarySearch constructor
22
23   // perform a binary search on the data
24   int BinarySearch::binarySearch( int searchElement ) const
25   {
26      int low = 0; // low end of the search area
27      int high = size - 1; // high end of the search area
28      int middle = ( low + high + 1 ) / 2; // middle element
29      int location = -1; // return value; -1 if not found
30
31      do // loop to search for element
32      {
```

Fig. 19.3 | BinarySearch class member-function definition. (Part 1 of 2.)

```
33        // print remaining elements of vector to be searched
34        displaySubElements( low, high );
35
36        // output spaces for alignment
37        for ( int i = 0; i < middle; i++ )
38           cout << "   ";
39
40        cout << " * " << endl; // indicate current middle
41
42        // if the element is found at the middle
43        if ( searchElement == data[ middle ] )
44           location = middle; // location is the current middle
45        else if ( searchElement < data[ middle ] ) // middle is too high
46           high = middle - 1; // eliminate the higher half
47        else // middle element is too low
48           low = middle + 1; // eliminate the lower half
49
50        middle = ( low + high + 1 ) / 2; // recalculate the middle
51     } while ( ( low <= high ) && ( location == -1 ) );
52
53     return location; // return location of search key
54  } // end function binarySearch
55
56  // display values in vector
57  void BinarySearch::displayElements() const
58  {
59     displaySubElements( 0, size - 1 );
60  } // end function displayElements
61
62  // display certain values in vector
63  void BinarySearch::displaySubElements( int low, int high ) const
64  {
65     for ( int i = 0; i < low; i++ ) // output spaces for alignment
66        cout << "   ";
67
68     for ( int i = low; i <= high; i++ ) // output elements left in vector
69        cout << data[ i ] << " ";
70
71     cout << endl;
72  } // end function displaySubElements
```

Fig. 19.3 | BinarySearch class member-function definition. (Part 2 of 2.)

middle index of the portion of the vector that the program is currently searching. At the beginning of the function, the low end is 0, the high end is the size of the vector minus 1 and the middle is the average of these two values. Line 29 initializes the location of the found element to -1—the value that will be returned if the search key is not found. Lines 31–51 loop until low is greater than high (this occurs when the element is not found) or location does not equal -1 (indicating that the search key was found). Line 43 tests whether the value in the middle element is equal to searchElement. If this is true, line 44 assigns middle to location. Then the loop terminates and location is returned to the caller. Each iteration of the loop tests a single value (line 43) and eliminates half of the remaining values in the vector (line 46 or 48).

Lines 22–38 of Fig. 19.4 loop until the user enters the value -1. For each other number the user enters, the program performs a binary search on the data to determine whether it matches an element in the vector. The first line of output from this program is the vector of ints, in increasing order. When the user instructs the program to search for 38, the program first tests the middle element, which is 67 (as indicated by *). The search key is less than 67, so the program eliminates the second half of the vector and tests the middle element from the first half of the vector. The search key equals 38, so the program returns the index 3.

```cpp
 1   // Fig 19.4: Fig19_04.cpp
 2   // BinarySearch test program.
 3   #include <iostream>
 4   #include "BinarySearch.h" // class BinarySearch definition
 5   using namespace std;
 6
 7   int main()
 8   {
 9      int searchInt; // search key
10      int position; // location of search key in vector
11
12      // create vector and output it
13      BinarySearch searchVector ( 15 );
14      searchVector.displayElements();
15
16      // get input from user
17      cout << "\nPlease enter an integer value (-1 to quit): ";
18      cin >> searchInt; // read an int from user
19      cout << endl;
20
21      // repeatedly input an integer; -1 terminates the program
22      while ( searchInt != -1 )
23      {
24         // use binary search to try to find integer
25         position = searchVector.binarySearch( searchInt );
26
27         // return value of -1 indicates integer was not found
28         if ( position == -1 )
29            cout << "The integer " << searchInt << " was not found.\n";
30         else
31            cout << "The integer " << searchInt
32               << " was found in position " << position << ".\n";
33
34         // get input from user
35         cout << "\n\nPlease enter an integer value (-1 to quit): ";
36         cin >> searchInt; // read an int from user
37         cout << endl;
38      } // end while
39   } // end main
```

Fig. 19.4 | BinarySearch test program. (Part 1 of 2.)

```
26 31 33 38 47 49 49 67 73 74 82 89 90 91 95

Please enter an integer value (-1 to quit): 38

26 31 33 38 47 49 49 67 73 74 82 89 90 91 95
            *
26 31 33 38 47 49 49
         *
The integer 38 was found in position 3.


Please enter an integer value (-1 to quit): 91

26 31 33 38 47 49 49 67 73 74 82 89 90 91 95
            *
                     73 74 82 89 90 91 95
                              *
                              90 91 95
                                 *
The integer 91 was found in position 13.


Please enter an integer value (-1 to quit): 25

26 31 33 38 47 49 49 67 73 74 82 89 90 91 95
            *
26 31 33 38 47 49 49
         *
26 31 33
     *
26
*
The integer 25 was not found.


Please enter an integer value (-1 to quit): -1
```

Fig. 19.4 | BinarySearch test program. (Part 2 of 2.)

Efficiency of Binary Search

In the worst-case scenario, searching a sorted vector of 1023 elements will take only 10 comparisons when using a binary search. Repeatedly dividing 1023 by 2 (because, after each comparison, we can eliminate from consideration half of the remaining vector) and rounding down (because we also remove the middle element) yields the values 511, 255, 127, 63, 31, 15, 7, 3, 1 and 0. The number 1023 ($2^{10} - 1$) is divided by 2 only 10 times to get the value 0, which indicates that there are no more elements to test. Dividing by 2 is equivalent to one comparison in the binary search algorithm. Thus, a vector of 1,048,575 ($2^{20} - 1$) elements takes a maximum of 20 comparisons to find the key, and a vector of about one billion elements takes a maximum of 30 comparisons to find the key. This is a tremendous improvement in performance over the linear search. For a one-billion-element vector, this is a difference between an average of 500 million comparisons for the linear search and a maximum of only 30 comparisons for the binary search! The maximum number of comparisons needed for the binary search of any sorted vector is the exponent of the first power of 2 greater than the number of elements in the vector, which is represented as $\log_2 n$. All logarithms grow at roughly the same rate, so in Big O notation the base can be omitted. This results in a Big O of $O(\log n)$ for a binary search, which is also known as **logarithmic runtime** and pronounced "on the order of log n" or more simply "**order log n**."

19.3 Sorting Algorithms

Sorting data (i.e., placing the data into some particular order, such as ascending or descending) is one of the most important computing applications. A bank sorts all of its checks by account number so that it can prepare individual bank statements at the end of each month. Telephone companies sort their lists of accounts by last name and, further, by first name to make it easy to find phone numbers. Virtually every organization must sort some data, and often, massive amounts of it. Sorting data is an intriguing, computer-intensive problem that has attracted intense research efforts.

An important point to understand about sorting is that the end result—the sorted vector—will be the same no matter which algorithm you use to sort the vector. The choice of algorithm affects only the runtime and memory use of the program. In previous chapters, we introduced the selection sort and insertion sort—simple algorithms to implement, but inefficient. The next section examines the efficiency of these two algorithms using Big O notation. The last algorithm—merge sort, which we introduce in this chapter—is much faster but is more difficult to implement.

19.3.1 Efficiency of Selection Sort

Selection sort is an easy-to-implement, but inefficient, sorting algorithm. The first iteration of the algorithm selects the smallest element in the vector and swaps it with the first element. The second iteration selects the second-smallest element (which is the smallest element of the remaining elements) and swaps it with the second element. The algorithm continues until the last iteration selects the second-largest element and swaps it with the second-to-last element, leaving the largest element in the last index. After the ith iteration, the smallest i elements of the vector will be sorted into increasing order in the first i elements of the vector.

The selection sort algorithm iterates $n-1$ times, each time swapping the smallest remaining element into its sorted position. Locating the smallest remaining element requires $n-1$ comparisons during the first iteration, $n-2$ during the second iteration, then $n-3, \ldots, 3, 2, 1$. This results in a total of $n(n-1)/2$ or $(n^2-n)/2$ comparisons. In Big O notation, smaller terms drop out and constants are ignored, leaving a final Big O of $O(n^2)$.

19.3.2 Efficiency of Insertion Sort

Insertion sort is another simple, but inefficient, sorting algorithm. The algorithm's first iteration takes the second element in the vector and, if it's less than the first element, swaps it with the first element. The second iteration looks at the third element and inserts it into the correct position with respect to the first two elements, so all three elements are in order. At the ith iteration of this algorithm, the first i elements in the original vector will be sorted.

Insertion sort iterates $n-1$ times, inserting an element into the appropriate position in the elements sorted so far. For each iteration, determining where to insert the element can require comparing the element to each of the preceding elements—$n-1$ comparisons in the worst case. Each individual repetition statement runs in $O(n)$ time. For determining Big O notation, nested statements mean that you must multiply the number of comparisons. For each iteration of an outer loop, there will be a certain number of iterations of the inner loop. In this algorithm, for each $O(n)$ iteration of the outer loop, there will be $O(n)$ iterations of the inner loop, resulting in a Big O of $O(n * n)$ or $O(n^2)$.

19.3.3 Merge Sort (A Recursive Implementation)

Merge sort is an efficient sorting algorithm but is conceptually more complex than selection sort and insertion sort. The merge sort algorithm sorts a vector by splitting it into two equal-sized subvectors, sorting each subvector then merging them into one larger vector. With an odd number of elements, the algorithm creates the two subvectors such that one has one more element than the other.

Merge sort performs the merge by looking at the first element in each vector, which is also the smallest element in the vector. Merge sort takes the smallest of these and places it in the first element of the larger, sorted vector. If there are still elements in the subvector, merge sort looks at the second element in that subvector (which is now the smallest element remaining) and compares it to the first element in the other subvector. Merge sort continues this process until the larger vector is filled.

The implementation of merge sort in this example is recursive. The base case is a vector with one element. A one-element vector is, of course, sorted, so merge sort immediately returns when it's called with a one-element vector. The recursion step splits a vector of two or more elements into two equal-sized subvectors, recursively sorts each subvector, then merges them into one larger, sorted vector. [Again, if there is an odd number of elements, one subvector is one element larger than the other.]

Suppose the algorithm has already merged smaller vectors to create sorted vectors A:

4	10	34	56	77

and B:

5	30	51	52	93

Merge sort combines these two vectors into one larger, sorted vector. The smallest value in A is 4 (located in the zeroth element of A). The smallest value in B is 5 (located in the zeroth element of B). In order to determine the smallest element in the larger vector, the algorithm compares 4 and 5. The value from A is smaller, so 4 becomes the value of the first element in the merged vector. The algorithm continues by comparing 10 (the value of the second element in A) to 5 (the value of the first element in B). The value from B is smaller, so 5 becomes the value of the second element in the larger vector. The algorithm continues by comparing 10 to 30, with 10 becoming the value of the third element in the vector, and so on.

Figure 19.5 defines class `MergeSort`, and lines 22–25 of Fig. 19.6 define the `sort` function. Line 24 calls function `sortSubVector` with 0 and `size - 1` as the arguments. These arguments correspond to the beginning and ending indices of the vector to be sorted, causing `sortSubVector` to operate on the entire vector. Function `sortSubVector` is defined in lines 28–52. Line 31 tests the base case. If the size of the vector is 0, the vector is already sorted, so the function simply returns immediately. If the size of the vector is greater than or equal to 1, the function splits the vector in two, recursively calls function `sortSubVector` to sort the two subvectors, then merges them. Line 46 recursively calls function `sortSub-`

Vector on the first half of the vector, and line 47 recursively calls function `sortSubVector` on the second half of the vector. When these two function calls return, each half of the vector has been sorted. Line 50 calls function `merge` (lines 55–99) on the two halves of the vector to combine the two sorted vectors into one larger sorted vector.

```
 1   // Fig 19.5: MergeSort.h
 2   // Class that creates a vector filled with random integers.
 3   // Provides a function to sort the vector with merge sort.
 4   #include <vector>
 5   using namespace std;
 6
 7   // MergeSort class definition
 8   class MergeSort
 9   {
10   public:
11      MergeSort( int ); // constructor initializes vector
12      void sort(); // sort vector using merge sort
13      void displayElements() const; // display vector elements
14   private:
15      int size; // vector size
16      vector< int > data; // vector of ints
17      void sortSubVector( int, int ); // sort subvector
18      void merge( int, int, int, int ); // merge two sorted vectors
19      void displaySubVector( int, int ) const; // display subvector
20   }; // end class SelectionSort
```

Fig. 19.5 | `MergeSort` class definition.

```
 1   // Fig 19.6: MergeSort.cpp
 2   // Class MergeSort member-function definition.
 3   #include <iostream>
 4   #include <vector>
 5   #include <cstdlib> // prototypes for functions srand and rand
 6   #include <ctime> // prototype for function time
 7   #include "MergeSort.h" // class MergeSort definition
 8   using namespace std;
 9
10   // constructor fill vector with random integers
11   MergeSort::MergeSort( int vectorSize )
12   {
13      size = ( vectorSize > 0 ? vectorSize : 10 ); // validate vectorSize
14      srand( time( 0 ) ); // seed random number generator using current time
15
16      // fill vector with random ints in range 10-99
17      for ( int i = 0; i < size; i++ )
18         data.push_back( 10 + rand() % 90 );
19   } // end MergeSort constructor
20
21   // split vector, sort subvectors and merge subvectors into sorted vector
22   void MergeSort::sort()
23   {
```

Fig. 19.6 | `MergeSort` class member-function definition. (Part 1 of 3.)

```
24          sortSubVector( 0, size - 1 ); // recursively sort entire vector
25      } // end function sort
26
27      // recursive function to sort subvectors
28      void MergeSort::sortSubVector( int low, int high )
29      {
30          // test base case; size of vector equals 1
31          if ( ( high - low ) >= 1 ) // if not base case
32          {
33              int middle1 = ( low + high ) / 2; // calculate middle of vector
34              int middle2 = middle1 + 1; // calculate next element over
35
36              // output split step
37              cout << "split:   ";
38              displaySubVector( low, high );
39              cout << endl << "         ";
40              displaySubVector( low, middle1 );
41              cout << endl << "         ";
42              displaySubVector( middle2, high );
43              cout << endl << endl;
44
45              // split vector in half; sort each half (recursive calls)
46              sortSubVector( low, middle1 ); // first half of vector
47              sortSubVector( middle2, high ); // second half of vector
48
49              // merge two sorted vectors after split calls return
50              merge( low, middle1, middle2, high );
51          } // end if
52      } // end function sortSubVector
53
54      // merge two sorted subvectors into one sorted subvector
55      void MergeSort::merge( int left, int middle1, int middle2, int right )
56      {
57          int leftIndex = left; // index into left subvector
58          int rightIndex = middle2; // index into right subvector
59          int combinedIndex = left; // index into temporary working vector
60          vector< int > combined( size ); // working vector
61
62          // output two subvectors before merging
63          cout << "merge:   ";
64          displaySubVector( left, middle1 );
65          cout << endl << "         ";
66          displaySubVector( middle2, right );
67          cout << endl;
68
69          // merge vectors until reaching end of either
70          while ( leftIndex <= middle1 && rightIndex <= right )
71          {
72              // place smaller of two current elements into result
73              // and move to next space in vector
74              if ( data[ leftIndex ] <= data[ rightIndex ] )
75                  combined[ combinedIndex++ ] = data[ leftIndex++ ];
```

Fig. 19.6 | MergeSort class member-function definition. (Part 2 of 3.)

```
76          else
77              combined[ combinedIndex++ ] = data[ rightIndex++ ];
78      } // end while
79
80      if ( leftIndex == middle2 ) // if at end of left vector
81      {
82          while ( rightIndex <= right ) // copy in rest of right vector
83              combined[ combinedIndex++ ] = data[ rightIndex++ ];
84      } // end if
85      else // at end of right vector
86      {
87          while ( leftIndex <= middle1 ) // copy in rest of left vector
88              combined[ combinedIndex++ ] = data[ leftIndex++ ];
89      } // end else
90
91      // copy values back into original vector
92      for ( int i = left; i <= right; i++ )
93          data[ i ] = combined[ i ];
94
95      // output merged vector
96      cout << "            ";
97      displaySubVector( left, right );
98      cout << endl << endl;
99  } // end function merge
100
101 // display elements in vector
102 void MergeSort::displayElements() const
103 {
104     displaySubVector( 0, size - 1 );
105 } // end function displayElements
106
107 // display certain values in vector
108 void MergeSort::displaySubVector( int low, int high ) const
109 {
110     // output spaces for alignment
111     for ( int i = 0; i < low; i++ )
112         cout << "   ";
113
114     // output elements left in vector
115     for ( int i = low; i <= high; i++ )
116         cout << " " << data[ i ];
117 } // end function displaySubVector
```

Fig. 19.6 | MergeSort class member-function definition. (Part 3 of 3.)

Lines 70–78 in function merge loop until the program reaches the end of either subvector. Line 74 tests which element at the beginning of the vectors is smaller. If the element in the left vector is smaller, line 75 places it in position in the combined vector. If the element in the right vector is smaller, line 77 places it in position in the combined vector. When the while loop has completed (line 78), one entire subvector is placed in the combined vector, but the other subvector still contains data. Line 80 tests whether the left vector has reached the end. If so, lines 82–83 fill the combined vector with the elements of the right vector. If the left vector has not reached the end, then the right vector must have reached the end, and lines 87–88 fill the combined vector with the elements of the left vector. Finally, lines 92–93 copy the combined vector into the original vector. Figure 19.7 creates and uses a MergeSort object. The output from this program displays the splits and merges performed by merge sort, showing the progress of the sort at each step of the algorithm.

Efficiency of Merge Sort

Merge sort is a far more efficient algorithm than either insertion sort or selection sort (although that may be difficult to believe when looking at the rather busy output in Fig. 19.7). Consider the first (nonrecursive) call to function sortSubVector (line 24). This results in two recursive calls to function sortSubVector with subvectors each approximately half the size of the original vector, and a single call to function merge. This call to function merge requires, at worst, $n - 1$ comparisons to fill the original vector, which is $O(n)$. (Recall that each vector element is chosen by comparing one element from each of the subvectors.) The two calls to function sortSubVector result in four more recursive calls to function sortSubVector—each with a subvector approximately one-quarter the size of the original vector—and two calls to function merge. These two calls to function merge each require, at worst, $n/2 - 1$ comparisons, for a total number of comparisons of $O(n)$. This process continues, each call to sortSubVector generating two additional calls to sortSubVector and a call to merge, until the algorithm has split the vector into one-element subvectors. At each level, $O(n)$ comparisons are required to merge the subvectors. Each level splits the size of the vectors in half, so doubling the size of the vector requires one more level. Quadrupling the size of the vector requires two more levels. This pattern is logarithmic and results in $\log_2 n$ levels. This results in a total efficiency of $O(n \log n)$.

```
1   // Fig 19.7: Fig19_07.cpp
2   // MergeSort test program.
3   #include <iostream>
4   #include "MergeSort.h" // class MergeSort definition
5   using namespace std;
6
7   int main()
8   {
9      // create object to perform merge sort
10     MergeSort sortVector( 10 );
11
12     cout << "Unsorted vector:" << endl;
13     sortVector.displayElements(); // print unsorted vector
14     cout << endl << endl;
15
16     sortVector.sort(); // sort vector
17
18     cout << "Sorted vector:" << endl;
19     sortVector.displayElements(); // print sorted vector
20     cout << endl;
21  } // end main
```

Fig. 19.7 | MergeSort test program. (Part 1 of 3.)

```
Unsorted vector:
 30 47 22 67 79 18 60 78 26 54

split:     30 47 22 67 79 18 60 78 26 54
           30 47 22 67 79
                         18 60 78 26 54

split:     30 47 22 67 79
           30 47 22
                   67 79

split:     30 47 22
           30 47
                 22

split:     30 47
           30
              47

merge:     30
              47
           30 47

merge:     30 47
                 22
           22 30 47

split:              67 79
                    67
                       79

merge:              67
                       79
                    67 79

merge:     22 30 47
                    67 79
           22 30 47 67 79

split:                   18 60 78 26 54
                         18 60 78
                                  26 54

split:                   18 60 78
                         18 60
                               78

split:                   18 60
                         18
                            60

merge:                   18
                            60
                         18 60

merge:                   18 60
                               78
                         18 60 78
```

Fig. 19.7 | MergeSort test program. (Part 2 of 3.)

```
split:                        26 54
                              26
                                 54

merge:                        26
                                 54
                              26 54

merge:              18 60 78
                              26 54
                    18 26 54 60 78

merge:    22 30 47 67 79
                    18 26 54 60 78
          18 22 26 30 47 54 60 67 78 79

Sorted vector:
 18 22 26 30 47 54 60 67 78 79
```

Fig. 19.7 | MergeSort test program. (Part 3 of 3.)

Figure 19.8 summarizes the searching and sorting algorithms we cover in this book and lists the Big O for each. Figure 19.9 lists the Big O categories we've covered in this chapter along with a number of values for *n* to highlight the differences in the growth rates.

Algorithm	Location	Big O
Searching Algorithms		
Linear search	Section 7.7	$O(n)$
Binary search	Section 19.2.2	$O(\log n)$
Recursive linear search	Exercise 19.8	$O(n)$
Recursive binary search	Exercise 19.9	$O(\log n)$
Sorting Algorithms		
Insertion sort	Section 7.8	$O(n^2)$
Selection sort	Section 8.6	$O(n^2)$
Merge sort	Section 19.3.3	$O(n \log n)$
Bubble sort	Exercises 19.5 and 19.6	$O(n^2)$
Quicksort	Exercise 19.10	Worst case: $O(n^2)$
		Average case: $O(n \log n)$

Fig. 19.8 | Searching and sorting algorithms with Big O values.

n	Approximate decimal value	$O(\log n)$	$O(n)$	$O(n \log n)$	$O(n^2)$
2^{10}	1000	10	2^{10}	$10 \cdot 2^{10}$	2^{20}
2^{20}	1,000,000	20	2^{20}	$20 \cdot 2^{20}$	2^{40}
2^{30}	1,000,000,000	30	2^{30}	$30 \cdot 2^{30}$	2^{60}

Fig. 19.9 | Approximate number of comparisons for common Big O notations.

19.4 Wrap-Up

This chapter discussed searching and sorting data. We discussed the binary search algorithm, which is faster but more complex than linear search (Section 7.7). The binary search algorithm will work only on a sorted array, but each iteration of binary search eliminates from consideration half of the elements in the array. You also learned the merge sort algorithm, which is more efficient than either insertion sort (Section 7.8) or selection sort (Section 8.6). We also introduced Big O notation, which helps you express the efficiency of an algorithm. Big O notation measures the worst-case runtime for an algorithm. The Big O value is useful for comparing algorithms to choose the most efficient one. In the next chapter, you'll learn about dynamic data structures that can grow or shrink at execution time.

Summary

Section 19.1 Introduction

- Searching data involves determining whether a search key is present in the data and, if so, finding its location.
- Sorting involves arranging data into order.
- One way to describe the efficiency of an algorithm is with Big O notation, which indicates how hard an algorithm may have to work to solve a problem.

Section 19.2 Searching Algorithms

- A key difference among searching algorithms is the amount of effort they require to return a result.

Section 19.2.1 Efficiency of Linear Search

- For searching and sorting algorithms, Big O describes how the amount of effort of a particular algorithm varies depending on how many elements are in the data.
- An algorithm that is $O(1)$ is said to have a constant runtime. This does not mean that the algorithm requires only one comparison—it just means that the number of comparisons does not grow as the size of the vector increases.
- An $O(n)$ algorithm is referred to as having a linear runtime.
- Big O highlights dominant factors and ignores terms that are unimportant with high values of n.
- Big O notation represents the growth rate of algorithm runtimes, so constants are ignored.
- The linear search algorithm runs in $O(n)$ time.
- In the worst case for linear search every element must be checked to determine whether the search element exists. This occurs if the search key is the last element in the vector or is not present.

Section 19.2.2 Binary Search

- Binary search is more efficient than linear search, but it requires that the vector first be sorted. This is worthwhile only when the vector, once sorted, will be searched many times.
- The first iteration of binary search tests the middle element. If this is the search key, the algorithm returns its location. If the search key is less than the middle element, binary search continues with the first half of the vector. If the search key is greater than the middle element, binary search continues with the second half. Each iteration tests the middle value of the remaining vector and, if the element is not found, eliminates from consideration half of the remaining elements.

- Binary search is more efficient than linear search, because with each comparison it eliminates from consideration half of the elements in the vector.
- Binary search runs in $O(\log n)$ time.
- If the size of the vector is doubled, binary search requires only one extra comparison to complete.

Section 19.3.1 Efficiency of Selection Sort
- Selection sort is a simple, but inefficient, sorting algorithm.
- The first iteration of selection sort selects the smallest element and swaps it with the first element. The second iteration selects the second-smallest element (which is the smallest remaining element) and swaps it with the second element. This continues until the last iteration selects the second-largest element and swaps it with the second-to-last index, leaving the largest element in the last index. At the ith iteration, the smallest i elements are sorted into the first i elements.

Section 19.3.2 Efficiency of Insertion Sort
- The selection sort algorithm runs in $O(n^2)$ time.
- The first iteration of insertion sort takes the second element value and, if it's less than the first, swaps it with the first. The second iteration looks at the third element value and inserts it in the correct position with respect to the first two element values. After the ith iteration of insertion sort, the first i element values in the original vector are sorted. Only $n - 1$ iterations are required.
- The insertion sort algorithm runs in $O(n^2)$ time.

Section 19.3.3 Merge Sort (A Recursive Implementation)
- Merge sort is faster, but more complex to implement, than selection sort and insertion sort.
- The merge sort algorithm sorts a vector by splitting the vector into two equal-sized subvectors, sorting each subvector and merging the subvectors into one larger vector.
- Merge sort's base case is a vector with one element. A one-element vector is already sorted, so merge sort immediately returns when it's called with a one-element vector. The merge part of merge sort takes two sorted vectors (these could be one-element vectors) and combines them into one larger sorted vector.
- Merge sort performs the merge by looking at the first element in each vector, which is also the smallest element in the vector. Merge sort takes the smallest of these and places it in the first element of the larger, sorted vector. If there are still elements in the subvector, merge sort looks at the second element in that subvector (which is now the smallest element remaining) and compares it to the first element in the other subvector. Merge sort continues this process until the larger vector is filled.
- In the worst case, the first call to merge sort has to make $O(n)$ comparisons to fill the n slots in the final vector.
- The merging portion of the merge sort algorithm is performed on two subvectors, each of approximately size $n/2$. Creating each of these subvectors requires $n/2 - 1$ comparisons for each subvector, or $O(n)$ comparisons total. This pattern continues, as each level works on twice as many vectors, but each is half the size of the previous vector.
- Similar to binary search, this halving results in $\log n$ levels, each level requiring $O(n)$ comparisons, for a total efficiency of $O(n \log n)$.

Terminology

Big O notation 785
binary search algorithm 788

constant runtime 786
linear runtime 786

Self-Review Exercises

19.1   Fill in the blanks in each of the following statements:
   a) A selection sort application would take approximately _____ times as long to run on a 128-element vector as on a 32-element vector.
   b) The efficiency of merge sort is _____.

19.2   What key aspect of both the binary search and the merge sort accounts for the logarithmic portion of their respective Big Os?

19.3   In what sense is the insertion sort superior to the merge sort? In what sense is the merge sort superior to the insertion sort?

19.4   In the text, we say that after the merge sort splits the vector into two subvectors, it then sorts these two subvectors and merges them. Why might someone be puzzled by our statement that "it then sorts these two subvectors"?

Answers to Self-Review Exercises

19.1   a) 16, because an $O(n^2)$ algorithm takes 16 times as long to sort four times as much information. b) $O(n \log n)$.

19.2   Both of these algorithms incorporate "halving"—somehow reducing something by half. The binary search eliminates from consideration half of the vector after each comparison. The merge sort splits the vector in half each time it's called.

19.3   The insertion sort is easier to understand and to implement than the merge sort. The merge sort is far more efficient ($O(n \log n)$) than the insertion sort ($O(n^2)$).

19.4   In a sense, it does not really sort these two subvectors. It simply keeps splitting the original vector in half until it provides a one-element subvector, which is, of course, sorted. It then builds up the original two subvectors by merging these one-element vectors to form larger subvectors, which are then merged, and so on.

Exercises

[*Note:* Most of the exercises shown here are duplicates of exercises from Chapters 7–8. We include the exercises again here as a convenience for readers studying searching and sorting in this chapter.]

19.5   (*Bubble Sort*) Implement bubble sort—another simple yet inefficient sorting technique. It's called bubble sort or sinking sort because smaller values gradually "bubble" their way to the top of the vector (i.e., toward the first element) like air bubbles rising in water, while the larger values sink to the bottom (end) of the vector. The technique uses nested loops to make several passes through the vector. Each pass compares successive pairs of elements. If a pair is in increasing order (or the values are equal), the bubble sort leaves the values as they are. If a pair is in decreasing order, the bubble sort swaps their values in the vector.

The first pass compares the first two element values of the vector and swaps them if necessary. It then compares the second and third element values in the vector. The end of this pass compares the last two element values in the vector and swaps them if necessary. After one pass, the largest value will be in the last element. After two passes, the largest two values will be in the last two elements. Explain why bubble sort is an $O(n^2)$ algorithm.

19.6   (*Enhanced Bubble Sort*) Make the following simple modifications to improve the performance of the bubble sort you developed in Exercise 19.5:

a) After the first pass, the largest value is guaranteed to be in the highest-numbered element of the vector; after the second pass, the two highest values are "in place"; and so on. Instead of making nine comparisons (for a 10-element vector) on every pass, modify the bubble sort to make only the eight necessary comparisons on the second pass, seven on the third pass, and so on.

b) The data in the vector may already be in the proper order or near-proper order, so why make nine passes (of a 10-element vector) if fewer will suffice? Modify the sort to check at the end of each pass whether any swaps have been made. If none have been made, the data must already be in the proper order, so the program should terminate. If swaps have been made, at least one more pass is needed.

19.7   (*Bucket Sort*) A bucket sort begins with a one-dimensional vector of positive integers to be sorted and a two-dimensional vector of integers with rows indexed from 0 to 9 and columns indexed from 0 to $n - 1$, where n is the number of values to be sorted. Each row of the two-dimensional vector is referred to as a *bucket*. Write a class named BucketSort containing a function called sort that operates as follows:

a) Place each value of the one-dimensional vector into a row of the bucket vector, based on the value's "ones" (rightmost) digit. For example, 97 is placed in row 7, 3 is placed in row 3 and 100 is placed in row 0. This procedure is called a *distribution pass*.

b) Loop through the bucket vector row by row, and copy the values back to the original vector. This procedure is called a *gathering pass*. The new order of the preceding values in the one-dimensional vector is 100, 3 and 97.

c) Repeat this process for each subsequent digit position (tens, hundreds, thousands, etc.).

   On the second (tens digit) pass, 100 is placed in row 0, 3 is placed in row 0 (because 3 has no tens digit) and 97 is placed in row 9. After the gathering pass, the order of the values in the one-dimensional vector is 100, 3 and 97. On the third (hundreds digit) pass, 100 is placed in row 1, 3 is placed in row 0 and 97 is placed in row 0 (after the 3). After this last gathering pass, the original vector is in sorted order.

   Note that the two-dimensional vector of buckets is 10 times the length of the integer vector being sorted. This sorting technique provides better performance than a bubble sort, but requires much more memory—the bubble sort requires space for only one additional element of data. This comparison is an example of the space–time trade-off: The bucket sort uses more memory than the bubble sort, but performs better. This version of the bucket sort requires copying all the data back to the original vector on each pass. Another possibility is to create a second two-dimensional bucket vector and repeatedly swap the data between the two bucket vectors.

19.8   (*Recursive Linear Search*) Modify Exercise 7.33 to use recursive function recursiveLinearSearch to perform a linear search of the vector. The function should receive the search key and starting index as arguments. If the search key is found, return its index in the vector; otherwise, return –1. Each call to the recursive function should check one element value in the vector.

19.9   (*Recursive Binary Search*) Modify Fig. 19.3 to use recursive function recursiveBinarySearch to perform a binary search of the vector. The function should receive the search key, starting index and ending index as arguments. If the search key is found, return its index in the vector. If the search key is not found, return -1.

19.10 *(Quicksort)* The recursive sorting technique called quicksort uses the following basic algorithm for a one-dimensional vector of values:

    a) *Partitioning Step*: Take the first element of the unsorted vector and determine its final location in the sorted vector (i.e., all values to the left of the element in the vector are less than the element's value, and all values to the right of the element in the vector are greater than the element's value—we show how to do this below). We now have one value in its proper location and two unsorted subvectors.

    b) *Recursion Step*: Perform the *Partitioning Step* on each unsorted subvector. Each time the *Partitioning Step* is performed on a subvector, another value is placed in its final location of the sorted vector, and two unsorted subvectors are created. When a subvector consists of one element, that element's value is in its final location (because a one-element vector is already sorted).

        The basic algorithm seems simple enough, but how do we determine the final position of the first element value of each subvector? As an example, consider the following set of values (the value in bold is for the partitioning element—it will be placed in its final location in the sorted vector):

        37 2 6 4 89 8 10 12 68 45

Starting from the rightmost element of the vector, compare each element value with 37 until an element value less than 37 is found; then swap 37 and that element's value. The first element value less than 37 is 12, so 37 and 12 are swapped. The new vector is

        12 2 6 4 89 8 10 **37** 68 45

Element value 12 is in italics to indicate that it was just swapped with 37.

        Starting from the left of the vector, but beginning with the element value after 12, compare each element value with 37 until an element value greater than 37 is found—then swap 37 and that element value. The first element value greater than 37 is 89, so 37 and 89 are swapped. The new vector is

        12 2 6 4 **37** 8 10 *89* 68 45

Starting from the right, but beginning with the element value before 89, compare each element value with 37 until an element value less than 37 is found—then swap 37 and that element value. The first element value less than 37 is 10, so 37 and 10 are swapped. The new vector is

        12 2 6 4 *10* 8 **37** 89 68 45

Starting from the left, but beginning with the element value after 10, compare each element value with 37 until an element value greater than 37 is found—then swap 37 and that element value. There are no more element values greater than 37, so when we compare 37 with itself, we know that 37 has been placed in its final location of the sorted vector. Every value to the left of 37 is smaller than it, and every value to the right of 37 is larger than it.

        Once the partition has been applied on the previous vector, there are two unsorted subvectors. The subvector with values less than 37 contains 12, 2, 6, 4, 10 and 8. The subvector with values greater than 37 contains 89, 68 and 45. The sort continues recursively, with both subvectors being partitioned in the same manner as the original vector.

        Based on the preceding discussion, write recursive function `quickSortHelper` to sort a one-dimensional integer vector. The function should receive as arguments a starting index and an ending index on the original vector being sorted.

20

Data Structures

Much that I bound,
I could not free;
Much that I freed
returned to me.
—Lee Wilson Dodd

'Will you walk a little faster?'
said a whiting to a snail,
'There's a porpoise close behind
us, and he's treading on my tail.'
—Lewis Carroll

There is always room at the top.
—Daniel Webster

Push on—keep moving.
—Thomas Morton

I'll turn over a new leaf.
—Miguel de Cervantes

Objectives

In this chapter you'll learn:

- To form linked data structures using pointers, self-referential classes and recursion.

- To create and manipulate dynamic data structures such as linked lists, queues, stacks and binary trees.

- To use binary search trees for high-speed searching and sorting.

- To understand various important applications of linked data structures.

- To understand how to create reusable data structures with class templates, inheritance and composition.

20.1 Introduction

We've studied fixed-size **data structures** such as one-dimensional arrays and two-dimensional arrays. This chapter introduces **dynamic data structures** that grow and shrink during execution. **Linked lists** are collections of data items logically "lined up in a row"—insertions and removals are made anywhere in a linked list. **Stacks** are important in compilers and operating systems: Insertions and removals are made only at one end of a stack—its **top**. **Queues** represent waiting lines; insertions are made at the back (also referred to as the **tail**) of a queue and removals are made from the front (also referred to as the **head**) of a queue. **Binary trees** facilitate high-speed searching and sorting of data, efficient elimination of duplicate data items, representation of file-system directories and compilation of expressions into machine language. These data structures have many other interesting applications.

We discuss several popular and important data structures and implement programs that create and manipulate them. We use classes, class templates, inheritance and composition to create and package these data structures for reusability and maintainability.

This chapter is solid preparation for Chapter 22, Standard Template Library (STL). The STL is a major portion of the C++ Standard Library. The STL provides containers, iterators for traversing those containers and algorithms for processing the containers' elements. You'll see that the STL has taken each of the data structures we discuss in this chapter and packaged them into templatized classes. The STL code is carefully written to be portable, efficient and extensible. Once you understand the principles and construction of data structures, you'll be able to make the best use of the prepackaged data structures, iterators and algorithms in the STL, a world-class set of reusable components.

The chapter examples are practical programs that you'll be able to use in more advanced courses and in industry applications. The programs employ extensive pointer manipulation. The exercises include a rich collection of useful applications.

We encourage you to attempt the major project described in the special section Building Your Own Compiler. You've been using a C++ compiler to translate your programs to machine language so that you could execute these programs on your computer. In this project, you'll actually build your own compiler. It will read a file of statements written in a simple, yet powerful, high-level language similar to early versions of the popular language BASIC. Your compiler will translate these statements into a file of Simpletron Machine Language (SML) instructions—SML is the language you learned in the Chapter 8 special section, Building Your Own Computer. Your Simpletron Simulator program will then execute the SML program produced by your compiler! The special section carefully walks you through the specifications of the high-level language and describes the algorithms you'll need to convert each type of high-level language statement into machine-language instructions. This chapter's exercises also suggest many enhancements to both the compiler and the Simpletron Simulator.

20.2 Self-Referential Classes

A **self-referential class** contains a pointer member that points to a class object of the same class type. For example, the definition

```
class Node
{
public:
   Node( int ); // constructor
   void setData( int ); // set data member
   int getData() const; // get data member
   void setNextPtr( Node * ); // set pointer to next Node
   Node *getNextPtr() const; // get pointer to next Node
private:
   int data; // data stored in this Node
   Node *nextPtr; // pointer to another object of same type
}; // end class Node
```

defines a type, Node. Type Node has two private data members—integer member data and pointer member nextPtr. Member nextPtr points to an object of type Node—another object of the same type as the one being declared here, hence the term "self-referential class." Member nextPtr is referred to as a **link**—i.e., nextPtr can "tie" an object of type Node to another object of the same type. Type Node also has five member functions—a constructor that receives an integer to initialize member data, a setData function to set the value of member data, a getData function to return the value of member data, a setNextPtr function to set the value of member nextPtr and a getNextPtr function to return the value of member nextPtr.

Self-referential class objects can be linked together to form useful data structures such as lists, queues, stacks and trees. Figure 20.1 illustrates two self-referential class objects linked together to form a list. Note that a slash—representing a null (0) pointer—is placed in the link member of the second self-referential class object to indicate that the link does not point to another object. The slash is only for illustration purposes; it does not correspond to the backslash character in C++. A null pointer normally indicates the end of a data structure just as the null character ('\0') indicates the end of a string.

Fig. 20.1 | Two self-referential class objects linked together.

Common Programming Error 20.1
Not setting the link in the last node of a linked data structure to null (0) is a (possibly fatal) logic error.

20.3 **Dynamic Memory Allocation and Data Structures**

Creating and maintaining dynamic data structures requires dynamic memory allocation, which enables a program to obtain more memory at execution time to hold new nodes. When that memory is no longer needed by the program, the memory can be released so that it can be reused to allocate other objects in the future. The limit for dynamic memory allocation can be as large as the amount of available physical memory in the computer or the amount of available virtual memory in a virtual memory system. Often, the limits are much smaller, because available memory must be shared among many programs.

The new operator takes as an argument the type of the object being dynamically allocated and returns a pointer to an object of that type. For example, the statement

```
Node *newPtr = new Node( 10 ); // create Node with data 10
```

allocates sizeof(Node) bytes, runs the Node constructor and assigns the new Node's address to newPtr. If no memory is available, new throws a bad_alloc exception. The value 10 is passed to the Node constructor which initializes the Node's data member to 10.

The delete operator runs the Node destructor and deallocates memory allocated with new—the memory is returned to the system so that the memory can be reallocated in the future. To free memory dynamically allocated by the preceding new, use the statement

```
delete newPtr;
```

Note that newPtr itself is not deleted; rather the space newPtr points to is deleted. If pointer newPtr has the null pointer value 0, the preceding statement has no effect. It isn't an error to delete a null pointer.

The following sections discuss lists, stacks, queues and trees. The data structures presented in this chapter are created and maintained with dynamic memory allocation, self-referential classes, class templates and function templates.

20.4 **Linked Lists**

A linked list is a linear collection of self-referential class objects, called **nodes**, connected by **pointer links**—hence, the term "linked" list. A linked list is accessed via a pointer to the list's first node. Each subsequent node is accessed via the link-pointer member stored in the previous node. By convention, the link pointer in the last node of a list is set to null (0) to mark the end of the list. Data is stored in a linked list dynamically—each node is created as necessary. A node can contain data of any type, including objects of other classes. If nodes contain base-class pointers to base-class and derived-class objects related by inheritance, we can have a linked list of such nodes and process them polymorphically using virtual function calls. Stacks and queues are also **linear data structures** and, as we'll see, can be viewed as constrained versions of linked lists. Trees are **nonlinear data structures**.

Lists of data can be stored in arrays, but linked lists provide several advantages. A linked list is appropriate when the number of data elements to be represented at one time is unpredictable. Linked lists are dynamic, so the length of a list can increase or decrease as necessary. The size of a "conventional" C++ array, however, cannot be altered, because the array size is fixed at compile time. "Conventional" arrays can become full. Linked lists become full only when the system has insufficient memory to satisfy dynamic storage allocation requests.

Performance Tip 20.1

An array can be declared to contain more elements than the number of items expected, but this can waste memory. Linked lists can provide better memory utilization in these situations. Linked lists allow the program to adapt at runtime. Class template vector *(Section 7.11) implements a dynamically resizable array-based data structure.*

Linked lists can be maintained in sorted order by inserting each new element at the proper point in the list. Existing list elements do not need to be moved. Pointers merely need to be updated to point to the correct node.

Performance Tip 20.2

Insertion and deletion in a sorted array can be time consuming—all the elements following the inserted or deleted element must be shifted appropriately. A linked list allows efficient insertion operations anywhere in the list.

Performance Tip 20.3

The elements of an array are stored contiguously in memory. This allows immediate access to any element, because an element's address can be calculated directly based on its position relative to the beginning of the array. Linked lists do not afford such immediate "direct access" to their elements. So accessing individual elements in a linked list can be considerably more expensive than accessing individual elements in an array. The selection of a data structure is typically based on the performance of specific operations used by a program and the order in which the data items are maintained in the data structure. For example, it's typically more efficient to insert an item in a sorted linked list than a sorted array.

Linked-list nodes are not stored contiguously in memory, but logically they appear to be contiguous. Figure 20.2 illustrates a linked list with several nodes.

Performance Tip 20.4

Using dynamic memory allocation (instead of fixed-size arrays) for data structures that grow and shrink at execution time can save memory. Keep in mind, however, that pointers occupy space and that dynamic memory allocation incurs the overhead of function calls.

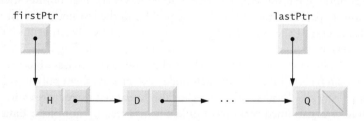

Fig. 20.2 | A graphical representation of a list.

Linked List Implementation

The program of Figs. 20.3–20.5 uses a List class template (see Chapter 14 for information on class templates) to manipulate a list of integer values and a list of floating-point values. The driver program (Fig. 20.5) provides five options: 1) Insert a value at the beginning of the list, 2) insert a value at the end of the list, 3) delete a value from the beginning of the list, 4) delete a value from the end of the list and 5) end the list processing. A detailed discussion of the program follows. Exercise 20.20 asks you to implement a recursive function that prints a linked list backward, and Exercise 20.21 asks you to implement a recursive function that searches a linked list for a particular data item.

The program uses class templates ListNode (Fig. 20.3) and List (Fig. 20.4). Encapsulated in each List object is a linked list of ListNode objects. Class template ListNode (Fig. 20.3) contains private members data and nextPtr (lines 19–20), a constructor to initialize these members and function getData to return the data in a node. Member data stores a value of type NODETYPE, the type parameter passed to the class template. Member nextPtr stores a pointer to the next ListNode object in the linked list. Line 13 of the List-Node class template definition declares class List< NODETYPE > as a friend. This makes all member functions of a given specialization of class template List friends of the corresponding specialization of class template ListNode, so they can access the private members of ListNode objects of that type. Because the ListNode template parameter NODETYPE is used as the template argument for List in the friend declaration, ListNodes specialized with a particular type can be processed only by a List specialized with the same type (e.g., a List of int values manages ListNode objects that store int values).

```
1   // Fig. 20.3: ListNode.h
2   // Template ListNode class definition.
3   #ifndef LISTNODE_H
4   #define LISTNODE_H
5
6   // forward declaration of class List required to announce that class
7   // List exists so it can be used in the friend declaration at line 13
8   template< typename NODETYPE > class List;
9
10  template< typename NODETYPE >
11  class ListNode
12  {
13     friend class List< NODETYPE >; // make List a friend
14
15  public:
16     ListNode( const NODETYPE & ); // constructor
17     NODETYPE getData() const; // return data in node
18  private:
19     NODETYPE data; // data
20     ListNode< NODETYPE > *nextPtr; // next node in list
21  }; // end class ListNode
22
23  // constructor
24  template< typename NODETYPE>
25  ListNode< NODETYPE >::ListNode( const NODETYPE &info )
26     : data( info ), nextPtr( 0 )
27  {
28     // empty body
29  } // end ListNode constructor
30
```

Fig. 20.3 | ListNode class-template definition. (Part 1 of 2.)

```
31    // return copy of data in node
32    template< typename NODETYPE >
33    NODETYPE ListNode< NODETYPE >::getData() const
34    {
35       return data;
36    } // end function getData
37
38    #endif
```

Fig. 20.3 | `ListNode` class-template definition. (Part 2 of 2.)

Lines 23–24 of the `List` class template (Fig. 20.4) declare `private` data members `firstPtr` (a pointer to the first `ListNode` in a `List`) and `lastPtr` (a pointer to the last `ListNode` in a `List`). The default constructor (lines 31–36) initializes both pointers to 0 (null). The destructor (lines 39–59) ensures that all `ListNode` objects in a `List` object are destroyed when that `List` object is destroyed. The primary `List` functions are `insertAtFront` (lines 62–74), `insertAtBack` (lines 77–89), `removeFromFront` (lines 92–110) and `removeFromBack` (lines 113–140).

Function `isEmpty` (lines 143–147) is called a predicate function—it does not alter the `List`; rather, it determines whether the `List` is empty (i.e., the pointer to the first node of the `List` is null). If the `List` is empty, `true` is returned; otherwise, `false` is returned. Function `print` (lines 158–178) displays the `List`'s contents. Utility function `getNewNode` (lines 150–155) returns a dynamically allocated `ListNode` object. This function is called from functions `insertAtFront` and `insertAtBack`.

Error-Prevention Tip 20.1

Assign null (0) to the link member of a new node. Pointers must be initialized before they're used.

```
1     // Fig. 20.4: List.h
2     // Template List class definition.
3     #ifndef LIST_H
4     #define LIST_H
5
6     #include <iostream>
7     #include "ListNode.h" // ListNode class definition
8     using namespace std;
9
10    template< typename NODETYPE >
11    class List
12    {
13    public:
14       List(); // constructor
15       ~List(); // destructor
16       void insertAtFront( const NODETYPE & );
17       void insertAtBack( const NODETYPE & );
18       bool removeFromFront( NODETYPE & );
19       bool removeFromBack( NODETYPE & );
```

Fig. 20.4 | `List` class-template definition. (Part 1 of 5.)

```
20      bool isEmpty() const;
21      void print() const;
22   private:
23      ListNode< NODETYPE > *firstPtr; // pointer to first node
24      ListNode< NODETYPE > *lastPtr; // pointer to last node
25
26      // utility function to allocate new node
27      ListNode< NODETYPE > *getNewNode( const NODETYPE & );
28   }; // end class List
29
30   // default constructor
31   template< typename NODETYPE >
32   List< NODETYPE >::List()
33      : firstPtr( 0 ), lastPtr( 0 )
34   {
35      // empty body
36   } // end List constructor
37
38   // destructor
39   template< typename NODETYPE >
40   List< NODETYPE >::~List()
41   {
42      if ( !isEmpty() ) // List is not empty
43      {
44         cout << "Destroying nodes ...\n";
45
46         ListNode< NODETYPE > *currentPtr = firstPtr;
47         ListNode< NODETYPE > *tempPtr;
48
49         while ( currentPtr != 0 ) // delete remaining nodes
50         {
51            tempPtr = currentPtr;
52            cout << tempPtr->data << '\n';
53            currentPtr = currentPtr->nextPtr;
54            delete tempPtr;
55         } // end while
56      } // end if
57
58      cout << "All nodes destroyed\n\n";
59   } // end List destructor
60
61   // insert node at front of list
62   template< typename NODETYPE >
63   void List< NODETYPE >::insertAtFront( const NODETYPE &value )
64   {
65      ListNode< NODETYPE > *newPtr = getNewNode( value ); // new node
66
67      if ( isEmpty() ) // List is empty
68         firstPtr = lastPtr = newPtr; // new list has only one node
69      else // List is not empty
70      {
71         newPtr->nextPtr = firstPtr; // point new node to previous 1st node
```

Fig. 20.4 | List class-template definition. (Part 2 of 5.)

```
72            firstPtr = newPtr; // aim firstPtr at new node
73         } // end else
74      } // end function insertAtFront
75
76      // insert node at back of list
77      template< typename NODETYPE >
78      void List< NODETYPE >::insertAtBack( const NODETYPE &value )
79      {
80         ListNode< NODETYPE > *newPtr = getNewNode( value ); // new node
81
82         if ( isEmpty() ) // List is empty
83            firstPtr = lastPtr = newPtr; // new list has only one node
84         else // List is not empty
85         {
86            lastPtr->nextPtr = newPtr; // update previous last node
87            lastPtr = newPtr; // new last node
88         } // end else
89      } // end function insertAtBack
90
91      // delete node from front of list
92      template< typename NODETYPE >
93      bool List< NODETYPE >::removeFromFront( NODETYPE &value )
94      {
95         if ( isEmpty() ) // List is empty
96            return false; // delete unsuccessful
97         else
98         {
99            ListNode< NODETYPE > *tempPtr = firstPtr; // hold tempPtr to delete
100
101            if ( firstPtr == lastPtr )
102               firstPtr = lastPtr = 0; // no nodes remain after removal
103            else
104               firstPtr = firstPtr->nextPtr; // point to previous 2nd node
105
106            value = tempPtr->data; // return data being removed
107            delete tempPtr; // reclaim previous front node
108            return true; // delete successful
109         } // end else
110      } // end function removeFromFront
111
112      // delete node from back of list
113      template< typename NODETYPE >
114      bool List< NODETYPE >::removeFromBack( NODETYPE &value )
115      {
116         if ( isEmpty() ) // List is empty
117            return false; // delete unsuccessful
118         else
119         {
120            ListNode< NODETYPE > *tempPtr = lastPtr; // hold tempPtr to delete
121
122            if ( firstPtr == lastPtr ) // List has one element
123               firstPtr = lastPtr = 0; // no nodes remain after removal
```

Fig. 20.4 | List class-template definition. (Part 3 of 5.)

```
124            else
125            {
126                ListNode< NODETYPE > *currentPtr = firstPtr;
127
128                // locate second-to-last element
129                while ( currentPtr->nextPtr != lastPtr )
130                    currentPtr = currentPtr->nextPtr; // move to next node
131
132                lastPtr = currentPtr; // remove last node
133                currentPtr->nextPtr = 0; // this is now the last node
134            } // end else
135
136            value = tempPtr->data; // return value from old last node
137            delete tempPtr; // reclaim former last node
138            return true; // delete successful
139        } // end else
140    } // end function removeFromBack
141
142    // is List empty?
143    template< typename NODETYPE >
144    bool List< NODETYPE >::isEmpty() const
145    {
146        return firstPtr == 0;
147    } // end function isEmpty
148
149    // return pointer to newly allocated node
150    template< typename NODETYPE >
151    ListNode< NODETYPE > *List< NODETYPE >::getNewNode(
152        const NODETYPE &value )
153    {
154        return new ListNode< NODETYPE >( value );
155    } // end function getNewNode
156
157    // display contents of List
158    template< typename NODETYPE >
159    void List< NODETYPE >::print() const
160    {
161        if ( isEmpty() ) // List is empty
162        {
163            cout << "The list is empty\n\n";
164            return;
165        } // end if
166
167        ListNode< NODETYPE > *currentPtr = firstPtr;
168
169        cout << "The list is: ";
170
171        while ( currentPtr != 0 ) // get element data
172        {
173            cout << currentPtr->data << ' ';
174            currentPtr = currentPtr->nextPtr;
175        } // end while
176
```

Fig. 20.4 | List class-template definition. (Part 4 of 5.)

```
177      cout << "\n\n";
178   } // end function print
179
180   #endif
```

Fig. 20.4 | List class-template definition. (Part 5 of 5.)

In Fig. 20.5, Lines 69 and 73 create List objects for types int and double, respectively. Lines 70 and 74 invoke the testList function template to manipulate objects.

```
1    // Fig. 20.5: Fig21_05.cpp
2    // List class test program.
3    #include <iostream>
4    #include <string>
5    #include "List.h" // List class definition
6    using namespace std;
7
8    // display program instructions to user
9    void instructions()
10   {
11      cout << "Enter one of the following:\n"
12         << "  1 to insert at beginning of list\n"
13         << "  2 to insert at end of list\n"
14         << "  3 to delete from beginning of list\n"
15         << "  4 to delete from end of list\n"
16         << "  5 to end list processing\n";
17   } // end function instructions
18
19   // function to test a List
20   template< typename T >
21   void testList( List< T > &listObject, const string &typeName )
22   {
23      cout << "Testing a List of " << typeName << " values\n";
24      instructions(); // display instructions
25
26      int choice; // store user choice
27      T value; // store input value
28
29      do // perform user-selected actions
30      {
31         cout << "? ";
32         cin >> choice;
33
34         switch ( choice )
35         {
36            case 1: // insert at beginning
37               cout << "Enter " << typeName << ": ";
38               cin >> value;
39               listObject.insertAtFront( value );
40               listObject.print();
41               break;
```

Fig. 20.5 | Manipulating a linked list. (Part 1 of 4.)

```
42              case 2: // insert at end
43                  cout << "Enter " << typeName << ": ";
44                  cin >> value;
45                  listObject.insertAtBack( value );
46                  listObject.print();
47                  break;
48              case 3: // remove from beginning
49                  if ( listObject.removeFromFront( value ) )
50                      cout << value << " removed from list\n";
51
52                  listObject.print();
53                  break;
54              case 4: // remove from end
55                  if ( listObject.removeFromBack( value ) )
56                      cout << value << " removed from list\n";
57
58                  listObject.print();
59                  break;
60          } // end switch
61      } while ( choice < 5 ); // end do...while
62
63      cout << "End list test\n\n";
64  } // end function testList
65
66  int main()
67  {
68      // test List of int values
69      List< int > integerList;
70      testList( integerList, "integer" );
71
72      // test List of double values
73      List< double > doubleList;
74      testList( doubleList, "double" );
75  } // end main
```

```
Testing a List of integer values
Enter one of the following:
  1 to insert at beginning of list
  2 to insert at end of list
  3 to delete from beginning of list
  4 to delete from end of list
  5 to end list processing
? 1
Enter integer: 1
The list is: 1

? 1
Enter integer: 2
The list is: 2 1

? 2
Enter integer: 3
The list is: 2 1 3
```

Fig. 20.5 | Manipulating a linked list. (Part 2 of 4.)

```
? 2
Enter integer: 4
The list is: 2 1 3 4

? 3
2 removed from list
The list is: 1 3 4

? 3
1 removed from list
The list is: 3 4

? 4
4 removed from list
The list is: 3

? 4
3 removed from list
The list is empty

? 5
End list test

Testing a List of double values
Enter one of the following:
   1 to insert at beginning of list
   2 to insert at end of list
   3 to delete from beginning of list
   4 to delete from end of list
   5 to end list processing
? 1
Enter double: 1.1
The list is: 1.1

? 1
Enter double: 2.2
The list is: 2.2 1.1

? 2
Enter double: 3.3
The list is: 2.2 1.1 3.3

? 2
Enter double: 4.4
The list is: 2.2 1.1 3.3 4.4

? 3
2.2 removed from list
The list is: 1.1 3.3 4.4

? 3
1.1 removed from list
The list is: 3.3 4.4

? 4
4.4 removed from list
The list is: 3.3
```

Fig. 20.5 | Manipulating a linked list. (Part 3 of 4.)

```
? 4
3.3 removed from list
The list is empty

? 5
End list test

All nodes destroyed

All nodes destroyed
```

Fig. 20.5 | Manipulating a linked list. (Part 4 of 4.)

Member Function `insertAtFront`

Over the next several pages, we discuss each of the member functions of class `List` in detail. Function `insertAtFront` (Fig. 20.4, lines 62–74) places a new node at the front of the list. The function consists of several steps:

1. Call function `getNewNode` (line 65), passing it `value`, which is a constant reference to the node value to be inserted.

2. Function `getNewNode` (lines 150–155) uses operator `new` to create a new list node and return a pointer to this newly allocated node, which is assigned to `newPtr` in `insertAtFront` (line 65).

3. If the list is empty (line 67), `firstPtr` and `lastPtr` are set to `newPtr` (line 68)—i.e., the first and last node are the same node.

4. If the list is not empty (line 69), then the node pointed to by `newPtr` is threaded into the list by copying `firstPtr` to `newPtr->nextPtr` (line 71), so that the new node points to what used to be the first node of the list, and copying `newPtr` to `firstPtr` (line 72), so that `firstPtr` now points to the new first node of the list.

Figure 20.6 illustrates function `insertAtFront`. Part (a) shows the list and the new node before calling `insertAtFront`. The dashed arrows in part (b) illustrate *Step 4* of the `insertAtFront` operation that enables the node containing 12 to become the new list front.

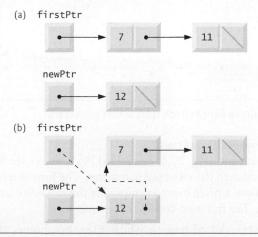

Fig. 20.6 | Operation `insertAtFront` represented graphically.

Member Function `insertAtBack`

Function `insertAtBack` (Fig. 20.4, lines 77–89) places a new node at the back of the list. The function consists of several steps:

1. Call function `getNewNode` (line 80), passing it `value`, which is a constant reference to the node value to be inserted.

2. Function `getNewNode` (lines 150–155) uses operator `new` to create a new list node and return a pointer to this newly allocated node, which is assigned to `newPtr` in `insertAtBack` (line 80).

3. If the list is empty (line 82), then both `firstPtr` and `lastPtr` are set to `newPtr` (line 83).

4. If the list is not empty (line 84), then the node pointed to by `newPtr` is threaded into the list by copying `newPtr` into `lastPtr->nextPtr` (line 86), so that the new node is pointed to by what used to be the last node of the list, and copying `newPtr` to `lastPtr` (line 87), so that `lastPtr` now points to the new last node of the list.

Figure 20.7 illustrates an `insertAtBack` operation. Part (a) of the figure shows the list and the new node before the operation. The dashed arrows in part (b) illustrate *Step 4* of function `insertAtBack` that enables a new node to be added to the end of a list that is not empty.

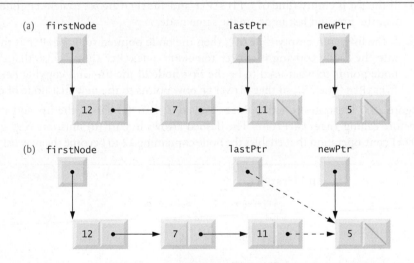

Fig. 20.7 | Operation `insertAtBack` represented graphically.

Member Function `removeFromFront`

Function `removeFromFront` (Fig. 20.4, lines 92–110) removes the front node of the list and copies the node value to the reference parameter. The function returns `false` if an attempt is made to remove a node from an empty list (lines 95–96) and returns `true` if the removal is successful. The function consists of several steps:

1. Assign `tempPtr` the address to which `firstPtr` points (line 99). Eventually, `tempPtr` will be used to delete the node being removed.

2. If firstPtr is equal to lastPtr (line 101), i.e., if the list has only one element prior to the removal attempt, then set firstPtr and lastPtr to zero (line 102) to dethread that node from the list (leaving the list empty).

3. If the list has more than one node prior to removal, then leave lastPtr as is and set firstPtr to firstPtr->nextPtr (line 104); i.e., modify firstPtr to point to what was the second node prior to removal (and is now the new first node).

4. After all these pointer manipulations are complete, copy to reference parameter value the data member of the node being removed (line 106).

5. Now delete the node pointed to by tempPtr (line 107).

6. Return true, indicating successful removal (line 108).

Figure 20.8 illustrates function removeFromFront. Part (a) illustrates the list before the removal operation. Part (b) shows the actual pointer manipulations for removing the front node from a nonempty list.

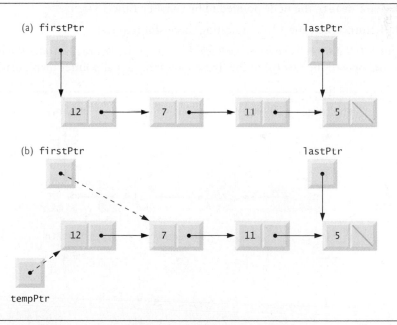

Fig. 20.8 | Operation removeFromFront represented graphically.

Member Function *removeFromBack*

Function removeFromBack (Fig. 20.4, lines 113–140) removes the back node of the list and copies the node value to the reference parameter. The function returns false if an attempt is made to remove a node from an empty list (lines 116–117) and returns true if the removal is successful. The function consists of several steps:

1. Assign to tempPtr the address to which lastPtr points (line 120). Eventually, tempPtr will be used to delete the node being removed.

2. If firstPtr is equal to lastPtr (line 122), i.e., if the list has only one element prior to the removal attempt, then set firstPtr and lastPtr to zero (line 123) to dethread that node from the list (leaving the list empty).

3. If the list has more than one node prior to removal, then assign currentPtr the address to which firstPtr points (line 126) to prepare to "walk the list."

4. Now "walk the list" with currentPtr until it points to the node before the last node. This node will become the last node after the remove operation completes. This is done with a while loop (lines 129–130) that keeps replacing currentPtr by currentPtr->nextPtr, while currentPtr->nextPtr is not lastPtr.

5. Assign lastPtr to the address to which currentPtr points (line 132) to dethread the back node from the list.

6. Set currentPtr->nextPtr to zero (line 133) in the new last node of the list.

7. After all the pointer manipulations are complete, copy to reference parameter value the data member of the node being removed (line 136).

8. Now delete the node pointed to by tempPtr (line 137).

9. Return true (line 138), indicating successful removal.

Figure 20.9 illustrates removeFromBack. Part (a) of the figure illustrates the list before the removal operation. Part (b) of the figure shows the actual pointer manipulations.

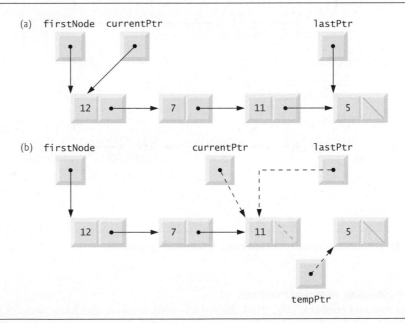

Fig. 20.9 | Operation removeFromBack represented graphically.

Member Function print
Function print (lines 158–178) first determines whether the list is empty (line 161). If so, it prints "The list is empty" and returns (lines 163–164). Otherwise, it iterates through

the list and outputs the value in each node. The function initializes `currentPtr` as a copy of `firstPtr` (line 167), then prints the string `"The list is: "` (line 169). While `currentPtr` is not null (line 171), `currentPtr->data` is printed (line 173) and `currentPtr` is assigned the value of `currentPtr->nextPtr` (line 174). Note that if the link in the last node of the list is not null, the printing algorithm will erroneously attempt to print past the end of the list. The printing algorithm is identical for linked lists, stacks and queues (because we base each of these data structures on the same linked list infrastructure).

Circular Linked Lists and Double Linked Lists

The kind of linked list we've been discussing is a **singly linked list**—the list begins with a pointer to the first node, and each node contains a pointer to the next node "in sequence." This list terminates with a node whose pointer member has the value 0. A singly linked list may be traversed in only one direction.

A **circular, singly linked list** (Fig. 20.10) begins with a pointer to the first node, and each node contains a pointer to the next node. The "last node" does not contain a 0 pointer; rather, the pointer in the last node points back to the first node, thus closing the "circle."

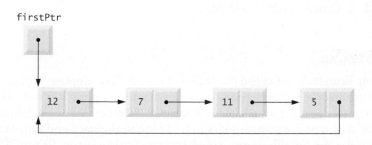

Fig. 20.10 | Circular, singly linked list.

A **doubly linked list** (Fig. 20.11) allows traversals both forward and backward. Such a list is often implemented with two "start pointers"—one that points to the first element of the list to allow front-to-back traversal of the list and one that points to the last element to allow back-to-front traversal. Each node has both a forward pointer to the next node in the list in the forward direction and a backward pointer to the next node in the list in the backward direction. If your list contains an alphabetized telephone directory, for example, a search for someone whose name begins with a letter near the front of the alphabet might

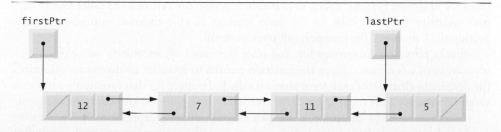

Fig. 20.11 | Doubly linked list.

begin from the front of the list. Searching for someone whose name begins with a letter near the end of the alphabet might begin from the back of the list.

In a **circular, doubly linked list** (Fig. 20.12), the forward pointer of the last node points to the first node, and the backward pointer of the first node points to the last node, thus closing the "circle."

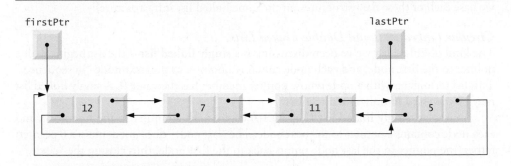

Fig. 20.12 | Circular, doubly linked list.

20.5 Stacks

Chapter 14, Templates, explained the notion of a stack class template with an underlying array implementation. In this section, we use an underlying pointer-based linked-list implementation. We also discuss stacks in Chapter 22, Standard Template Library (STL).

A stack data structure allows nodes to be added to the stack and removed from the stack only at the top. For this reason, a stack is referred to as a last-in, first-out (LIFO) data structure. One way to implement a stack is as a constrained version of a linked list. In such an implementation, the link member in the last node of the stack is set to null (zero) to indicate the bottom of the stack.

The primary member functions used to manipulate a stack are push and pop. Function push inserts a new node at the top of the stack. Function pop removes a node from the top of the stack, stores the popped value in a reference variable that is passed to the calling function and returns true if the pop operation was successful (false otherwise).

Stacks have many interesting applications. For example, when a function call is made, the called function must know how to return to its caller, so the return address is pushed onto a stack. If a series of function calls occurs, the successive return values are pushed onto the stack in last-in, first-out order, so that each function can return to its caller. Stacks support recursive function calls in the same manner as conventional nonrecursive calls. Section 6.11 discusses the function call stack in detail.

Stacks provide the memory for, and store the values of, automatic variables on each invocation of a function. When the function returns to its caller or throws an exception, the destructor (if any) for each local object is called, the space for that function's automatic variables is popped off the stack and those variables are no longer known to the program.

Stacks are used by compilers in the process of evaluating expressions and generating machine-language code. The exercises explore several applications of stacks, including using them to develop your own complete working compiler.

We'll take advantage of the close relationship between lists and stacks to implement a stack class primarily by reusing a list class. First, we implement the stack class through private inheritance of the list class. Then we implement an identically performing stack class through composition by including a list object as a private member of a stack class. Of course, all of the data structures in this chapter, including these two stack classes, are implemented as templates to encourage further reusability.

The program of Figs. 20.13–20.14 creates a Stack class template (Fig. 20.13) primarily through private inheritance (line 9) of the List class template of Fig. 20.4. We want the Stack to have member functions push (lines 13–16), pop (lines 19–22), isStackEmpty (lines 25–28) and printStack (lines 31–34). Note that these are essentially the insertAtFront, removeFromFront, isEmpty and print functions of the List class template. Of course, the List class template contains other member functions (i.e., insertAtBack and removeFromBack) that we would not want to make accessible through the public interface to the Stack class. So when we indicate that the Stack class template is to inherit from the List class template, we specify private inheritance. This makes all the List class template's member functions private in the Stack class template. When we implement the Stack's member functions, we then have each of these call the appropriate member function of the List class—push calls insertAtFront (line 15), pop calls removeFromFront (line 21), isStackEmpty calls isEmpty (line 27) and printStack calls print (line 33)—this is referred to as **delegation**.

```
1   // Fig. 20.13: Stack.h
2   // Template Stack class definition derived from class List.
3   #ifndef STACK_H
4   #define STACK_H
5
6   #include "List.h" // List class definition
7
8   template< typename STACKTYPE >
9   class Stack : private List< STACKTYPE >
10  {
11  public:
12     // push calls the List function insertAtFront
13     void push( const STACKTYPE &data )
14     {
15        insertAtFront( data );
16     } // end function push
17
18     // pop calls the List function removeFromFront
19     bool pop( STACKTYPE &data )
20     {
21        return removeFromFront( data );
22     } // end function pop
23
24     // isStackEmpty calls the List function isEmpty
25     bool isStackEmpty() const
26     {
27        return this->isEmpty();
28     } // end function isStackEmpty
```

Fig. 20.13 | Stack class-template definition. (Part I of 2.)

```
29
30      // printStack calls the List function print
31      void printStack() const
32      {
33         this->print();
34      } // end function print
35   }; // end class Stack
36
37   #endif
```

Fig. 20.13 | Stack class-template definition. (Part 2 of 2.)

The explicit use of the this pointer on lines 27 and 33 is required so the compiler can resolve identifiers in template definitions properly. A **dependent name** is an identifier that depends on a template parameter. For example, the call to removeFromFront (line 21) depends on the argument data which has a type that is dependent on the template parameter STACKTYPE. Resolution of dependent names occurs when the template is instantiated. In contrast, the identifier for a function that takes no arguments like isEmpty or print in the List superclass is a **non-dependent name**. Such identifiers are normally resolved at the point where the template is defined. If the template has not yet been instantiated, then the code for the function with the non-dependent name does not yet exist and some compilers will generate compilation errors. Adding the explicit use of this-> in lines 27 and 33 makes the calls to the base class's member functions dependent on the template parameter and ensures that the code will compile properly.

The stack class template is used in main (Fig. 20.14) to instantiate integer stack intStack of type Stack< int > (line 9). Integers 0 through 2 are pushed onto intStack (lines 14–18), then popped off intStack (lines 23–28). The program uses the Stack class template to create doubleStack of type Stack< double > (line 30). Values 1.1, 2.2 and 3.3 are pushed onto doubleStack (lines 36–41), then popped off doubleStack (lines 46–51).

```
1    // Fig. 20.14: Fig21_14.cpp
2    // Template Stack class test program.
3    #include <iostream>
4    #include "Stack.h" // Stack class definition
5    using namespace std;
6
7    int main()
8    {
9       Stack< int > intStack; // create Stack of ints
10
11      cout << "processing an integer Stack" << endl;
12
13      // push integers onto intStack
14      for ( int i = 0; i < 3; i++ )
15      {
16         intStack.push( i );
17         intStack.printStack();
18      } // end for
```

Fig. 20.14 | A simple stack program. (Part 1 of 3.)

```
19
20      int popInteger; // store int popped from stack
21
22      // pop integers from intStack
23      while ( !intStack.isStackEmpty() )
24      {
25         intStack.pop( popInteger );
26         cout << popInteger << " popped from stack" << endl;
27         intStack.printStack();
28      } // end while
29
30      Stack< double > doubleStack; // create Stack of doubles
31      double value = 1.1;
32
33      cout << "processing a double Stack" << endl;
34
35      // push floating-point values onto doubleStack
36      for ( int j = 0; j < 3; j++ )
37      {
38         doubleStack.push( value );
39         doubleStack.printStack();
40         value += 1.1;
41      } // end for
42
43      double popDouble; // store double popped from stack
44
45      // pop floating-point values from doubleStack
46      while ( !doubleStack.isStackEmpty() )
47      {
48         doubleStack.pop( popDouble );
49         cout << popDouble << " popped from stack" << endl;
50         doubleStack.printStack();
51      } // end while
52   } // end main
```

```
processing an integer Stack
The list is: 0

The list is: 1 0

The list is: 2 1 0

2 popped from stack
The list is: 1 0

1 popped from stack
The list is: 0

0 popped from stack
The list is empty

processing a double Stack
The list is: 1.1

The list is: 2.2 1.1
```

Fig. 20.14 | A simple stack program. (Part 2 of 3.)

```
The list is: 3.3 2.2 1.1

3.3 popped from stack
The list is: 2.2 1.1

2.2 popped from stack
The list is: 1.1

1.1 popped from stack
The list is empty

All nodes destroyed

All nodes destroyed
```

Fig. 20.14 | A simple stack program. (Part 3 of 3.)

Another way to implement a Stack class template is by reusing the List class template through composition. Figure 20.15 is a new implementation of the Stack class template that contains a List< STACKTYPE > object called stackList (line 38). This version of the Stack class template uses class List from Fig. 20.4. To test this class, use the driver program in Fig. 20.14, but include the new header file—Stackcomposition.h in line 6 of that file. The output of the program is identical for both versions of class Stack.

```
 1   // Fig. 20.15: Stackcomposition.h
 2   // Template Stack class definition with composed List object.
 3   #ifndef STACKCOMPOSITION_H
 4   #define STACKCOMPOSITION_H
 5
 6   #include "List.h" // List class definition
 7
 8   template< typename STACKTYPE >
 9   class Stack
10   {
11   public:
12      // no constructor; List constructor does initialization
13
14      // push calls stackList object's insertAtFront member function
15      void push( const STACKTYPE &data )
16      {
17         stackList.insertAtFront( data );
18      } // end function push
19
20      // pop calls stackList object's removeFromFront member function
21      bool pop( STACKTYPE &data )
22      {
23         return stackList.removeFromFront( data );
24      } // end function pop
25
26      // isStackEmpty calls stackList object's isEmpty member function
27      bool isStackEmpty() const
28      {
```

Fig. 20.15 | Stack class template with a composed List object. (Part 1 of 2.)

```
29          return stackList.isEmpty();
30       } // end function isStackEmpty
31
32       // printStack calls stackList object's print member function
33       void printStack() const
34       {
35          stackList.print();
36       } // end function printStack
37    private:
38       List< STACKTYPE > stackList; // composed List object
39    }; // end class Stack
40
41    #endif
```

Fig. 20.15 | Stack class template with a composed List object. (Part 2 of 2.)

20.6 Queues

A **queue** is similar to a supermarket checkout line—the first person in line is serviced first, and other customers enter the line at the end and wait to be serviced. Queue nodes are removed only from the head of the queue and are inserted only at the tail of the queue. For this reason, a queue is referred to as a first-in, first-out (FIFO) data structure. The insert and remove operations are known as **enqueue** and **dequeue**.

Queues have many applications in computer systems. Computers that have a single processor can service only one user at a time. Entries for the other users are placed in a queue. Each entry gradually advances to the front of the queue as users receive service. The entry at the front of the queue is the next to receive service.

Queues are also used to support **print spooling**. For example, a single printer might be shared by all users of a network. Many users can send print jobs to the printer, even when the printer is already busy. These print jobs are placed in a queue until the printer becomes available. A program called a **spooler** manages the queue to ensure that, as each print job completes, the next print job is sent to the printer.

Information packets also wait in queues in computer networks. Each time a packet arrives at a network node, it must be routed to the next node on the network along the path to the packet's final destination. The routing node routes one packet at a time, so additional packets are enqueued until the router can route them.

A file server in a computer network handles file access requests from many clients throughout the network. Servers have a limited capacity to service requests from clients. When that capacity is exceeded, client requests wait in queues.

The program of Figs. 20.16–20.17 creates a Queue class template (Fig. 20.16) through private inheritance (line 9) of the List class template (Fig. 20.4). The Queue has member functions enqueue (lines 13–16), dequeue (lines 19–22), isQueueEmpty (lines 25–28) and printQueue (lines 31–34). These are essentially the insertAtBack, removeFromFront, isEmpty and print functions of the List class template. Of course, the List class template contains other member functions that we do not want to make accessible through the public interface to the Queue class. So when we indicate that the Queue class template is to inherit the List class template, we specify private inheritance. This makes all the List class template's member functions private in the Queue class template. When we implement the Queue's member functions, we have each of these call the appropriate member function of the list class—enqueue calls insertAtBack (line 15), dequeue calls removeFromFront (line 21), isQueueEmpty calls isEmpty (line 27) and printQueue calls print (line 33). As with the Stack example in Fig. 20.13, this delegation requires explicit use of the this pointer in isQueueEmpty and printQueue to avoid compilation errors.

```cpp
 1   // Fig. 20.16: Queue.h
 2   // Template Queue class definition derived from class List.
 3   #ifndef QUEUE_H
 4   #define QUEUE_H
 5
 6   #include "List.h" // List class definition
 7
 8   template< typename QUEUETYPE >
 9   class Queue : private List< QUEUETYPE >
10   {
11   public:
12      // enqueue calls List member function insertAtBack
13      void enqueue( const QUEUETYPE &data )
14      {
15         insertAtBack( data );
16      } // end function enqueue
17
18      // dequeue calls List member function removeFromFront
19      bool dequeue( QUEUETYPE &data )
20      {
21         return removeFromFront( data );
22      } // end function dequeue
23
24      // isQueueEmpty calls List member function isEmpty
25      bool isQueueEmpty() const
26      {
27         return this->isEmpty();
28      } // end function isQueueEmpty
29
30      // printQueue calls List member function print
31      void printQueue() const
32      {
33         this->print();
34      } // end function printQueue
35   }; // end class Queue
36
37   #endif
```

Fig. 20.16 | Queue class-template definition.

Figure 20.17 uses the Queue class template to instantiate integer queue intQueue of type Queue< int > (line 9). Integers 0 through 2 are enqueued to intQueue (lines 14–18), then dequeued from intQueue in first-in, first-out order (lines 23–28). Next, the program instantiates queue doubleQueue of type Queue< double > (line 30). Values 1.1, 2.2 and 3.3 are enqueued to doubleQueue (lines 36–41), then dequeued from doubleQueue in first-in, first-out order (lines 46–51).

```cpp
 1   // Fig. 20.17: Fig21_17.cpp
 2   // Template Queue class test program.
 3   #include <iostream>
 4   #include "Queue.h" // Queue class definition
 5   using namespace std;
 6
 7   int main()
 8   {
 9      Queue< int > intQueue; // create Queue of integers
10
11      cout << "processing an integer Queue" << endl;
12
13      // enqueue integers onto intQueue
14      for ( int i = 0; i < 3; i++ )
15      {
16         intQueue.enqueue( i );
17         intQueue.printQueue();
18      } // end for
19
20      int dequeueInteger; // store dequeued integer
21
22      // dequeue integers from intQueue
23      while ( !intQueue.isQueueEmpty() )
24      {
25         intQueue.dequeue( dequeueInteger );
26         cout << dequeueInteger << " dequeued" << endl;
27         intQueue.printQueue();
28      } // end while
29
30      Queue< double > doubleQueue; // create Queue of doubles
31      double value = 1.1;
32
33      cout << "processing a double Queue" << endl;
34
35      // enqueue floating-point values onto doubleQueue
36      for ( int j = 0; j < 3; j++ )
37      {
38         doubleQueue.enqueue( value );
39         doubleQueue.printQueue();
40         value += 1.1;
41      } // end for
42
43      double dequeueDouble; // store dequeued double
44
45      // dequeue floating-point values from doubleQueue
46      while ( !doubleQueue.isQueueEmpty() )
47      {
48         doubleQueue.dequeue( dequeueDouble );
49         cout << dequeueDouble << " dequeued" << endl;
50         doubleQueue.printQueue();
51      } // end while
52   } // end main
```

Fig. 20.17 | Queue-processing program. (Part 1 of 2.)

```
processing an integer Queue
The list is: 0

The list is: 0 1

The list is: 0 1 2

0 dequeued
The list is: 1 2

1 dequeued
The list is: 2

2 dequeued
The list is empty

processing a double Queue
The list is: 1.1

The list is: 1.1 2.2

The list is: 1.1 2.2 3.3

1.1 dequeued
The list is: 2.2 3.3

2.2 dequeued
The list is: 3.3

3.3 dequeued
The list is empty

All nodes destroyed

All nodes destroyed
```

Fig. 20.17 | Queue-processing program. (Part 2 of 2.)

20.7 Trees

Linked lists, stacks and queues are linear data structures. A tree is a nonlinear, two-dimensional data structure. Tree nodes contain two or more links. This section discusses **binary trees** (Fig. 20.18)—trees whose nodes all contain two links (none, one or both of which may be null).

Basic Terminology

For this discussion, refer to nodes A, B, C and D in Fig. 20.18. The **root node** (node B) is the first node in a tree. Each link in the root node refers to a **child** (nodes A and D). The **left child** (node A) is the root node of the **left subtree** (which contains only node A), and the **right child** (node D) is the root node of the **right subtree** (which contains nodes D and C). The children of a given node are called **siblings** (e.g., nodes A and D are siblings). A node with no children is a **leaf node** (e.g., nodes A and C are leaf nodes). Computer scientists normally draw trees from the root node down—the opposite of how trees grow in nature.

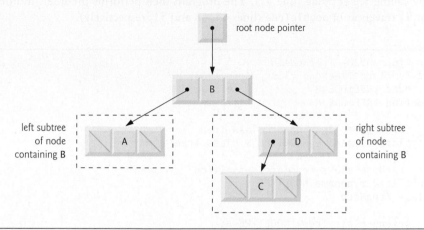

Fig. 20.18 | A graphical representation of a binary tree.

Binary Search Trees

A **binary search tree** (with no duplicate node values) has the characteristic that the values in any left subtree are less than the value in its **parent node**, and the values in any right subtree are greater than the value in its parent node. Figure 20.19 illustrates a binary search tree with 9 values. Note that the shape of the binary search tree that corresponds to a set of data can vary, depending on the order in which the values are inserted into the tree.

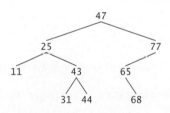

Fig. 20.19 | A binary search tree.

Implementing the Binary Search Tree Program

The program of Figs. 20.20–20.22 creates a binary search tree and traverses it (i.e., walks through all its nodes) three ways—using recursive **inorder**, **preorder** and **postorder traversals**. We explain these traversal algorithms shortly.

We begin our discussion with the driver program (Fig. 20.22), then continue with the implementations of classes TreeNode (Fig. 20.20) and Tree (Fig. 20.21). Function main (Fig. 20.22) begins by instantiating integer tree intTree of type Tree< int > (line 10). The program prompts for 10 integers, each of which is inserted in the binary tree by calling insertNode (line 19). The program then performs preorder, inorder and postorder traversals (these are explained shortly) of intTree (lines 23, 26 and 29, respectively). The program then instantiates floating-point tree doubleTree of type Tree< double > (line 31). The program prompts for 10 double values, each of which is inserted in the binary tree by calling `insertNode` (line 41). The program then performs preorder, inorder and postorder traversals of `doubleTree` (lines 45, 48 and 51, respectively).

```cpp
 1   // Fig. 20.20: TreeNode.h
 2   // Template TreeNode class definition.
 3   #ifndef TREENODE_H
 4   #define TREENODE_H
 5
 6   // forward declaration of class Tree
 7   template< typename NODETYPE > class Tree;
 8
 9   // TreeNode class-template definition
10   template< typename NODETYPE >
11   class TreeNode
12   {
13      friend class Tree< NODETYPE >;
14   public:
15      // constructor
16      TreeNode( const NODETYPE &d )
17         : leftPtr( 0 ), // pointer to left subtree
18           data( d ), // tree node data
19           rightPtr( 0 ) // pointer to right substree
20      {
21         // empty body
22      } // end TreeNode constructor
23
24      // return copy of node's data
25      NODETYPE getData() const
26      {
27         return data;
28      } // end getData function
29   private:
30      TreeNode< NODETYPE > *leftPtr; // pointer to left subtree
31      NODETYPE data;
32      TreeNode< NODETYPE > *rightPtr; // pointer to right subtree
33   }; // end class TreeNode
34
35   #endif
```

Fig. 20.20 | `TreeNode` class-template definition.

```cpp
 1   // Fig. 20.21: Tree.h
 2   // Template Tree class definition.
 3   #ifndef TREE_H
 4   #define TREE_H
 5
 6   #include <iostream>
 7   #include "TreeNode.h"
 8   using namespace std;
 9
```

Fig. 20.21 | `Tree` class-template definition. (Part 1 of 4.)

```
10    // Tree class-template definition
11    template< typename NODETYPE > class Tree
12    {
13    public:
14       Tree(); // constructor
15       void insertNode( const NODETYPE & );
16       void preOrderTraversal() const;
17       void inOrderTraversal() const;
18       void postOrderTraversal() const;
19    private:
20       TreeNode< NODETYPE > *rootPtr;
21
22       // utility functions
23       void insertNodeHelper( TreeNode< NODETYPE > **, const NODETYPE & );
24       void preOrderHelper( TreeNode< NODETYPE > * ) const;
25       void inOrderHelper( TreeNode< NODETYPE > * ) const;
26       void postOrderHelper( TreeNode< NODETYPE > * ) const;
27    }; // end class Tree
28
29    // constructor
30    template< typename NODETYPE >
31    Tree< NODETYPE >::Tree()
32    {
33       rootPtr = 0; // indicate tree is initially empty
34    } // end Tree constructor
35
36    // insert node in Tree
37    template< typename NODETYPE >
38    void Tree< NODETYPE >::insertNode( const NODETYPE &value )
39    {
40       insertNodeHelper( &rootPtr, value );
41    } // end function insertNode
42
43    // utility function called by insertNode; receives a pointer
44    // to a pointer so that the function can modify pointer's value
45    template< typename NODETYPE >
46    void Tree< NODETYPE >::insertNodeHelper(
47       TreeNode< NODETYPE > **ptr, const NODETYPE &value )
48    {
49       // subtree is empty; create new TreeNode containing value
50       if ( *ptr == 0 )
51          *ptr = new TreeNode< NODETYPE >( value );
52       else // subtree is not empty
53       {
54          // data to insert is less than data in current node
55          if ( value < ( *ptr )->data )
56             insertNodeHelper( &( ( *ptr )->leftPtr ), value );
57          else
58          {
59             // data to insert is greater than data in current node
60             if ( value > ( *ptr )->data )
61                insertNodeHelper( &( ( *ptr )->rightPtr ), value );
```

Fig. 20.21 | Tree class-template definition. (Part 2 of 4.)

```
62            else // duplicate data value ignored
63               cout << value << " dup" << endl;
64         } // end else
65      } // end else
66   } // end function insertNodeHelper
67
68   // begin preorder traversal of Tree
69   template< typename NODETYPE >
70   void Tree< NODETYPE >::preOrderTraversal() const
71   {
72      preOrderHelper( rootPtr );
73   } // end function preOrderTraversal
74
75   // utility function to perform preorder traversal of Tree
76   template< typename NODETYPE >
77   void Tree< NODETYPE >::preOrderHelper( TreeNode< NODETYPE > *ptr ) const
78   {
79      if ( ptr != 0 )
80      {
81         cout << ptr->data << ' '; // process node
82         preOrderHelper( ptr->leftPtr ); // traverse left subtree
83         preOrderHelper( ptr->rightPtr ); // traverse right subtree
84      } // end if
85   } // end function preOrderHelper
86
87   // begin inorder traversal of Tree
88   template< typename NODETYPE >
89   void Tree< NODETYPE >::inOrderTraversal() const
90   {
91      inOrderHelper( rootPtr );
92   } // end function inOrderTraversal
93
94   // utility function to perform inorder traversal of Tree
95   template< typename NODETYPE >
96   void Tree< NODETYPE >::inOrderHelper( TreeNode< NODETYPE > *ptr ) const
97   {
98      if ( ptr != 0 )
99      {
100        inOrderHelper( ptr->leftPtr ); // traverse left subtree
101        cout << ptr->data << ' '; // process node
102        inOrderHelper( ptr->rightPtr ); // traverse right subtree
103     } // end if
104  } // end function inOrderHelper
105
106  // begin postorder traversal of Tree
107  template< typename NODETYPE >
108  void Tree< NODETYPE >::postOrderTraversal() const
109  {
110     postOrderHelper( rootPtr );
111  } // end function postOrderTraversal
112
```

Fig. 20.21 | Tree class-template definition. (Part 3 of 4.)

```
113  // utility function to perform postorder traversal of Tree
114  template< typename NODETYPE >
115  void Tree< NODETYPE >::postOrderHelper(
116     TreeNode< NODETYPE > *ptr ) const
117  {
118     if ( ptr != 0 )
119     {
120        postOrderHelper( ptr->leftPtr ); // traverse left subtree
121        postOrderHelper( ptr->rightPtr ); // traverse right subtree
122        cout << ptr->data << ' '; // process node
123     } // end if
124  } // end function postOrderHelper
125
126  #endif
```

Fig. 20.21 | Tree class-template definition. (Part 4 of 4.)

```
1   // Fig. 20.22: Fig21_22.cpp
2   // Tree class test program.
3   #include <iostream>
4   #include <iomanip>
5   #include "Tree.h" // Tree class definition
6   using namespace std;
7
8   int main()
9   {
10     Tree< int > intTree; // create Tree of int values
11     int intValue;
12
13     cout << "Enter 10 integer values:\n";
14
15     // insert 10 integers to intTree
16     for ( int i = 0; i < 10; i++ )
17     {
18        cin >> intValue;
19        intTree.insertNode( intValue );
20     } // end for
21
22     cout << "\nPreorder traversal\n";
23     intTree.preOrderTraversal();
24
25     cout << "\nInorder traversal\n";
26     intTree.inOrderTraversal();
27
28     cout << "\nPostorder traversal\n";
29     intTree.postOrderTraversal();
30
31     Tree< double > doubleTree; // create Tree of double values
32     double doubleValue;
33
34     cout << fixed << setprecision( 1 )
35        << "\n\n\nEnter 10 double values:\n";
```

Fig. 20.22 | Creating and traversing a binary tree. (Part 1 of 2.)

```
36
37      // insert 10 doubles to doubleTree
38      for ( int j = 0; j < 10; j++ )
39      {
40         cin >> doubleValue;
41         doubleTree.insertNode( doubleValue );
42      } // end for
43
44      cout << "\nPreorder traversal\n";
45      doubleTree.preOrderTraversal();
46
47      cout << "\nInorder traversal\n";
48      doubleTree.inOrderTraversal();
49
50      cout << "\nPostorder traversal\n";
51      doubleTree.postOrderTraversal();
52      cout << endl;
53   } // end main
```

```
Enter 10 integer values:
50 25 75 12 33 67 88 6 13 68

Preorder traversal
50 25 12 6 13 33 75 67 68 88
Inorder traversal
6 12 13 25 33 50 67 68 75 88
Postorder traversal
6 13 12 33 25 68 67 88 75 50


Enter 10 double values:
39.2 16.5 82.7 3.3 65.2 90.8 1.1 4.4 89.5 92.5

Preorder traversal
39.2 16.5 3.3 1.1 4.4 82.7 65.2 90.8 89.5 92.5
Inorder traversal
1.1 3.3 4.4 16.5 39.2 65.2 82.7 89.5 90.8 92.5
Postorder traversal
1.1 4.4 3.3 16.5 65.2 89.5 92.5 90.8 82.7 39.2
```

Fig. 20.22 | Creating and traversing a binary tree. (Part 2 of 2.)

The TreeNode class template (Fig. 20.20) definition declares Tree<NODETYPE> as its friend (line 13). This makes all member functions of a given specialization of class template Tree (Fig. 20.21) friends of the corresponding specialization of class template TreeNode, so they can access the private members of TreeNode objects of that type. Because the TreeNode template parameter NODETYPE is used as the template argument for Tree in the friend declaration, TreeNodes specialized with a particular type can be processed only by a Tree specialized with the same type (e.g., a Tree of int values manages TreeNode objects that store int values).

Lines 30–32 declare a TreeNode's private data—the node's data value, and pointers leftPtr (to the node's left subtree) and rightPtr (to the node's right subtree). The constructor (lines 16–22) sets data to the value supplied as a constructor argument and sets pointers `leftPtr` and `rightPtr` to zero (thus initializing this node to be a leaf node). Member function `getData` (lines 25–28) returns the `data` value.

Class template `Tree` (Fig. 20.21) has as `private` data `rootPtr` (line 20), a pointer to the tree's root node. Lines 15–18 declare the `public` member functions `insertNode` (that inserts a new node in the tree) and `preOrderTraversal`, `inOrderTraversal` and `postOrderTraversal`, each of which walks the tree in the designated manner. Each of these member functions calls its own recursive utility function to perform the appropriate operations on the internal representation of the tree, so the program is not required to access the underlying `private` data to perform these functions. Remember that the recursion requires us to pass in a pointer that represents the next subtree to process. The `Tree` constructor initializes `rootPtr` to zero to indicate that the tree is initially empty.

The `Tree` class's utility function `insertNodeHelper` (lines 45–66) is called by `insertNode` (lines 37–41) to recursively insert a node into the tree. *A node can only be inserted as a leaf node in a binary search tree.* If the tree is empty, a new `TreeNode` is created, initialized and inserted in the tree (lines 51–52).

If the tree is not empty, the program compares the value to be inserted with the `data` value in the root node. If the insert value is smaller (line 55), the program recursively calls `insertNodeHelper` (line 56) to insert the value in the left subtree. If the insert value is larger (line 60), the program recursively calls `insertNodeHelper` (line 61) to insert the value in the right subtree. If the value to be inserted is identical to the data value in the root node, the program prints the message " dup" (line 63) and returns without inserting the duplicate value into the tree. Note that `insertNode` passes the address of `rootPtr` to `insertNodeHelper` (line 40) so it can modify the value stored in `rootPtr` (i.e., the address of the root node). To receive a pointer to `rootPtr` (which is also a pointer), `insertNodeHelper`'s first argument is declared as a pointer to a pointer to a `TreeNode`.

Member functions `inOrderTraversal` (lines 88–92), `preOrderTraversal` (lines 69–73) and `postOrderTraversal` (lines 107–111) traverse the tree and print the node values. For the purpose of the following discussion, we use the binary search tree in Fig. 20.23.

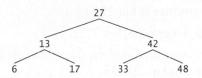

Fig. 20.23 | A binary search tree.

Inorder Traversal Algorithm

Function `inOrderTraversal` invokes utility function `inOrderHelper` to perform the inorder traversal of the binary tree. The steps for an inorder traversal are:

1. Traverse the left subtree with an inorder traversal. (This is performed by the call to `inOrderHelper` at line 100.)

2. Process the value in the node—i.e., print the node value (line 101).

3. Traverse the right subtree with an inorder traversal. (This is performed by the call to `inOrderHelper` at line 102.)

The value in a node is not processed until the values in its left subtree are processed, because each call to inOrderHelper immediately calls inOrderHelper again with the pointer to the left subtree. The inorder traversal of the tree in Fig. 20.23 is

```
6 13 17 27 33 42 48
```

Note that the inorder traversal of a binary search tree prints the node values in ascending order. The process of creating a binary search tree actually sorts the data—thus, this process is called the **binary tree sort**.

Preorder Traversal Algorithm

Function preOrderTraversal invokes utility function preOrderHelper to perform the preorder traversal of the binary tree. The steps for an preorder traversal are:

1. Process the value in the node (line 81).
2. Traverse the left subtree with a preorder traversal. (This is performed by the call to preOrderHelper at line 82.)
3. Traverse the right subtree with a preorder traversal. (This is performed by the call to preOrderHelper at line 83.)

The value in each node is processed as the node is visited. After the value in a given node is processed, the values in the left subtree are processed. Then the values in the right subtree are processed. The preorder traversal of the tree in Fig. 20.23 is

```
27 13 6 17 42 33 48
```

Postorder Traversal Algorithm

Function postOrderTraversal invokes utility function postOrderHelper to perform the postorder traversal of the binary tree. The steps for a postorder traversal are:

1. Traverse the left subtree with a postorder traversal. (This is performed by the call to postOrderHelper at line 120.)
2. Traverse the right subtree with a postorder traversal. (This is performed by the call to postOrderHelper at line 121.)
3. Process the value in the node (line 122).

The value in each node is not printed until the values of its children are printed. The postOrderTraversal of the tree in Fig. 20.23 is

```
6 17 13 33 48 42 27
```

Duplicate Elimination

The binary search tree facilitates **duplicate elimination**. As the tree is being created, an attempt to insert a duplicate value will be recognized, because a duplicate will follow the same "go left" or "go right" decisions on each comparison as the original value did when it was inserted in the tree. Thus, the duplicate will eventually be compared with a node containing the same value. The duplicate value may be discarded at this point.

Searching a binary tree for a value that matches a key value is also fast. If the tree is balanced, then each branch contains about half the number of nodes in the tree. Each comparison of a node to the search key eliminates half the nodes. This is called an $O(\log n)$ algorithm (Big O notation is discussed in Chapter 19). So a binary search tree with n elements would require a maximum of $\log_2 n$ comparisons either to find a match or to determine that no match exists. This means, for example, that when searching a (balanced) 1000-element binary search tree, no more than 10 comparisons need to be made, because $2^{10} > 1000$. When searching a (balanced) 1,000,000-element binary search tree, no more than 20 comparisons need to be made, because $2^{20} > 1,000,000$.

Overview of the Binary Tree Exercises

In the exercises, algorithms are presented for several other binary tree operations such as deleting an item from a binary tree, printing a binary tree in a two-dimensional tree format and performing a **level-order traversal** of a binary tree. The level-order traversal of a binary tree visits the nodes of the tree row by row, starting at the root node level. On each level of the tree, the nodes are visited from left to right. Other binary tree exercises include allowing a binary search tree to contain duplicate values, inserting string values in a binary tree and determining how many levels are contained in a binary tree.

20.8 Wrap-Up

In this chapter, you learned that linked lists are collections of data items that are "linked up in a chain." You also learned that a program can perform insertions and deletions anywhere in a linked list (though our implementation only performed insertions and deletions at the ends of the list). We demonstrated that the stack and queue data structures are constrained versions of lists. For stacks, you saw that insertions and deletions are made only at the top. For queues, you saw that insertions are made at the tail and deletions are made from the head. We also presented the binary tree data structure. You saw a binary search tree that facilitated high-speed searching and sorting of data and efficient duplicate elimination. You learned how to create these data structures for reusability (as templates) and maintainability. In the next chapter, we introduce structs, which are similar to classes, and discuss the manipulation of bits, characters and C-style strings.

Summary

Section 20.1 Introduction

- Dynamic data structures grow and shrink during execution.
- Linked lists are collections of data items "lined up in a row"—insertions and removals are made anywhere in a linked list.
- Stacks are important in compilers and operating systems: Insertions and removals are made only at one end of a stack—its top.
- Queues represent waiting lines; insertions are made at the back (also referred to as the tail) of a queue and removals are made from the front (also referred to as the head).
- Binary trees facilitate high-speed searching and sorting of data, efficient duplicate elimination, representation of file-system directories and compilation of expressions into machine language.

Section 20.2 Self-Referential Classes

- A self-referential class contains a pointer member that points to an object of the same class type.
- Self-referential class objects can be linked together to form useful data structures such as lists, queues, stacks and trees.

Section 20.3 Dynamic Memory Allocation and Data Structures

- The limit for dynamic memory allocation can be as large as the amount of available physical memory in the computer or the amount of available virtual memory in a virtual memory system.

Section 20.4 Linked Lists

- A linked list is a linear collection of self-referential class objects, called nodes, connected by pointer links—hence, the term "linked" list.
- A linked list is accessed via a pointer to the first node of the list. Each subsequent node is accessed via the link-pointer member stored in the previous node.
- Linked lists, stacks and queues are linear data structures. Trees are nonlinear data structures.
- A linked list is appropriate when the number of data elements to be represented is unpredictable.
- Linked lists are dynamic, so the length of a list can increase or decrease as necessary.
- A singly linked list begins with a pointer to the first node, and each node contains a pointer to the next node "in sequence."
- A circular, singly linked list begins with a pointer to the first node, and each node contains a pointer to the next node. The "last node" does not contain a null pointer; rather, the pointer in the last node points back to the first node, thus closing the "circle."
- A doubly linked list allows traversals both forward and backward.
- A doubly linked list is often implemented with two "start pointers"—one that points to the first element to allow front-to-back traversal of the list and one that points to the last element to allow back-to-front traversal. Each node has a pointer to both the next and previous nodes.
- In a circular, doubly linked list, the forward pointer of the last node points to the first node, and the backward pointer of the first node points to the last node, thus closing the "circle."

Section 20.5 Stacks

- A stack data structure allows nodes to be added to and removed from the stack only at the top.
- A stack is referred to as a last-in, first-out (LIFO) data structure.
- The primary member functions used to manipulate a stack are push and pop. Function push inserts a new node at the top of the stack. Function pop removes a node from the top of the stack.
- A dependent name is an identifier that depends on the value of a template parameter. Resolution of dependent names occurs when the template is instantiated.
- Non-dependent names are resolved at the point where the template is defined.

Section 20.6 Queues

- A queue is similar to a supermarket checkout line—the first person in line is serviced first, and other customers enter the line at the end and wait to be serviced.
- Queue nodes are removed only from a queue's head and are inserted only at its tail.
- A queue is referred to as a first-in, first-out (FIFO) data structure. The insert and remove operations are known as enqueue and dequeue.

Section 20.7 Trees

- Binary trees are trees whose nodes all contain two links (none, one or both of which may be null).
- The root node is the first node in a tree.
- Each link in the root node refers to a child. The left child is the root node of the left subtree, and the right child is the root node of the right subtree.
- The children of a single node are called siblings. A node with no children is called a leaf node.

- A binary search tree (with no duplicate node values) has the characteristic that the values in any left subtree are less than the value in its parent node, and the values in any right subtree are greater than the value in its parent node.

- A node can only be inserted as a leaf node in a binary search tree.

- An inorder traversal of a binary tree traverses the left subtree, processes the value in the root node then traverses the right subtree. The value in a node is not processed until the values in its left subtree are processed.

- A preorder traversal processes the value in the root node, traverses the left subtree, then traverses the right subtree. The value in each node is processed as the node is encountered.

- A postorder traversal traverses the left subtree, traverses the right subtree, then processes the root node's value. The value in each node is not processed until the values in both subtrees are processed.

- The binary search tree helps eliminate duplicate data. As the tree is being created, an attempt to insert a duplicate value will be recognized and the duplicate value may be discarded.

- The level-order traversal of a binary tree visits the nodes of the tree row by row, starting at the root node level. On each level of the tree, the nodes are visited from left to right.

Terminology

binary search tree 833
binary tree sort 840
binary tree 807
child node 832
circular, doubly linked list 824
circular, singly linked list 823
data structure 807
delegation 825
dependent name 826
dequeue 829
doubly linked list 823
duplicate elimination 840
dynamic data structure 807
enqueue 829
first-in, first-out (FIFO) 829
head of a queue 807
infix notation 846
inorder traversal of a binary tree 839
inserting a node
last-in, first-out (LIFO) 824
leaf node 832
left child 832
left subtree 832
level-order traversal 841
linear data structure 809

link 808
linked list 807
node 809
non-dependent name 826
nonlinear data structure 809
parent node 833
pointer link 809
pop 824
postfix notation 846
postorder traversal of a binary tree 833
preorder traversal of a binary tree 833
print spooling 829
push 824
queue 829
right child 832
right subtree 832
root node 832
self-referential class 808
sibling node 832
singly linked list 823
spooler 829
stack 807
tail of a queue 807
top of a stack 807

Self-Review Exercises

20.1 Fill in the blanks in each of the following:
    a) A self-_____ class is used to form dynamic data structures that can grow and shrink at execution time

b) The _____ operator is used to dynamically allocate memory and construct an object; this operator returns a pointer to the object.

c) A(n) _____ is a constrained version of a linked list in which nodes can be inserted and deleted only from the start of the list and node values are returned in last-in, first-out order.

d) A function that does not alter a linked list, but looks at the list to determine whether it's empty, is an example of a(n) _____ function.

e) A queue is referred to as a(n) _____ data structure, because the first nodes inserted are the first nodes removed.

f) The pointer to the next node in a linked list is referred to as a(n) _____.

g) The _____ operator is used to destroy an object and release dynamically allocated memory.

h) A(n) _____ is a constrained version of a linked list in which nodes can be inserted only at the end of the list and deleted only from the start of the list.

i) A(n) _____ is a nonlinear, two-dimensional data structure that contains nodes with two or more links.

j) A stack is referred to as a(n) _____ data structure, because the last node inserted is the first node removed.

k) The nodes of a(n) _____ tree contain two link members.

l) The first node of a tree is the _____ node.

m) Each link in a tree node points to a(n) _____ or _____ of that node.

n) A tree node that has no children is called a(n) _____ node.

o) The four traversal algorithms we mentioned in the text for binary search trees are _____, _____, _____ and _____.

20.2 What are the differences between a linked list and a stack?

20.3 What are the differences between a stack and a queue?

20.4 Perhaps a more appropriate title for this chapter would have been "Reusable Data Structures." Comment on how each of the following entities or concepts contributes to the reusability of data structures:

a) classes
b) class templates
c) inheritance
d) `private` inheritance
e) composition

20.5 Manually provide the inorder, preorder and postorder traversals of the binary search tree of Fig. 20.24.

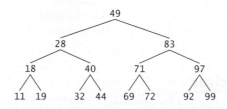

Fig. 20.24 | A 15-node binary search tree.

Answers to Self-Review Exercises

20.1 a) referential. b) new. c) stack. d) predicate. e) first-in, first-out (FIFO). f) link.
g) delete. h) queue. i) tree. j) last-in, first-out (LIFO). k) binary. l) root. m) child or subtree.
n) leaf. o) inorder, preorder, postorder and level order.

20.2 It's possible to insert a node anywhere in a linked list and remove a node from anywhere in
a linked list. Nodes in a stack may only be inserted at the top of the stack and removed from the top
of a stack.

20.3 A queue data structure allows nodes to be removed only from the head of the queue and
inserted only at the tail of the queue. A queue is referred to as a first-in, first-out (FIFO) data structure. A stack data structure allows nodes to be added to the stack and removed from the stack only
at the top. A stack is referred to as a last-in, first-out (LIFO) data structure.

20.4 a) Classes allow us to instantiate as many data structure objects of a certain type (i.e., class)
as we wish.
b) Class templates enable us to instantiate related classes, each based on different type parameters—we can then generate as many objects of each template class as we like.
c) Inheritance enables us to reuse code from a base class in a derived class, so that the derived-class data structure is also a base-class data structure (with public inheritance, that
is).
d) Private inheritance enables us to reuse portions of the code from a base class to form a
derived-class data structure; because the inheritance is private, all public base-class
member functions become private in the derived class. This enables us to prevent clients of the derived-class data structure from accessing base-class member functions that
do not apply to the derived class.
e) Composition enables us to reuse code by making a class object data structure a member
of a composed class; if we make the class object a private member of the composed
class, then the class object's public member functions are not available through the
composed object's interface.

20.5 The inorder traversal is

        11 18 19 28 32 40 44 49 69 71 72 83 92 97 99

The preorder traversal is

        49 28 18 11 19 40 32 44 83 71 69 72 97 92 99

The postorder traversal is

        11 19 18 32 44 40 28 69 72 71 92 99 97 83 49

Exercises

20.6 *(Concatenating Lists)* Write a program that concatenates two linked list objects of characters. The program should include function concatenate, which takes references to both list objects
as arguments and concatenates the second list to the first list.

20.7 *(Merging Ordered Lists)* Write a program that merges two ordered list objects of integers
into a single ordered list object of integers. Function merge should receive references to each of the
list objects to be merged and reference to a list object into which the merged elements will be placed.

20.8 *(Summing and Averaging Elements in a List)* Write a program that inserts 25 random integers from 0 to 100 in order in a linked list object. The program should calculate the sum of the
elements and the floating-point average of the elements.

20.9 *(Copying a List in Reverse Order)* Write a program that creates a linked list object of 10 characters and creates a second list object containing a copy of the first list, but in reverse order.

20.10 *(Printing a Sentence in Reverse Order with a Stack)* Write a program that inputs a line of text and uses a stack object to print the line reversed.

20.11 *(Palindrome Testing with Stacks)* Write a program that uses a stack object to determine if a string is a palindrome (i.e., the string is spelled identically backward and forward). The program should ignore spaces and punctuation.

20.12 *(Infix-to-Postfix Conversion)* Stacks are used by compilers to help in the process of evaluating expressions and generating machine language code. In this and the next exercise, we investigate how compilers evaluate arithmetic expressions consisting only of constants, operators and parentheses.

Humans generally write expressions like 3 + 4 and 7 / 9 in which the operator (+ or / here) is written between its operands—this is called **infix notation**. Computers "prefer" **postfix notation** in which the operator is written to the right of its two operands. The preceding infix expressions would appear in postfix notation as 3 4 + and 7 9 /, respectively.

To evaluate a complex infix expression, a compiler would first convert the expression to postfix notation and evaluate the postfix version of the expression. Each of these algorithms requires only a single left-to-right pass of the expression. Each algorithm uses a stack object in support of its operation, and in each algorithm the stack is used for a different purpose.

In this exercise, you'll write a C++ version of the infix-to-postfix conversion algorithm. In the next exercise, you'll write a C++ version of the postfix expression evaluation algorithm. Later in the chapter, you'll discover that code you write in this exercise can help you implement a complete working compiler.

Write a program that converts an ordinary infix arithmetic expression (assume a valid expression is entered) with single-digit integers such as

    (6 + 2) * 5 - 8 / 4

to a postfix expression. The postfix version of the preceding infix expression is

    6 2 + 5 * 8 4 / -

The program should read the expression into string infix and use modified versions of the stack functions implemented in this chapter to help create the postfix expression in string postfix. The algorithm for creating a postfix expression is as follows:

1) Push a left parenthesis '(' onto the stack.
2) Append a right parenthesis ')' to the end of infix.
3) While the stack is not empty, read infix from left to right and do the following:
   If the current character in infix is a digit, copy it to the next element of postfix.
   If the current character in infix is a left parenthesis, push it onto the stack.
   If the current character in infix is an operator,
      Pop operators (if there are any) at the top of the stack while they have equal or higher precedence than the current operator, and insert the popped operators in postfix.
      Push the current character in infix onto the stack.
   If the current character in infix is a right parenthesis
      Pop operators from the top of the stack and insert them in postfix until a left parenthesis is at the top of the stack.
      Pop (and discard) the left parenthesis from the stack.

The following arithmetic operations are allowed in an expression:

+   addition
-   subtraction
*   multiplication

/   division
∧   exponentiation
%   modulus

[*Note:* We assume left-to-right associativity for all operators for the purpose of this exercise.] The stack should be maintained with stack nodes, each containing a data member and a pointer to the next stack node.

Some of the functional capabilities you may want to provide are:

a) function `convertToPostfix` that converts the infix expression to postfix notation
b) function `isOperator` that determines whether c is an operator
c) function `precedence` that determines whether the precedence of `operator1` is greater than or equalt to the precedence of `operator2`, and, if so, returns `true`.
d) function `push` that pushes a value onto the stack
e) function `pop` that pops a value off the stack
f) function `stackTop` that returns the top value of the stack without popping the stack
g) function `isEmpty` that determines if the stack is empty
h) function `printStack` that prints the stack

20.13   *(Postfix Evaluation)* Write a program that evaluates a postfix expression (assume it's valid) such as

6 2 + 5 * 8 4 / -

The program should read a postfix expression consisting of digits and operators into a `string`. Using modified versions of the stack functions implemented earlier in this chapter, the program should scan the expression and evaluate it. The algorithm is as follows:

1) While you have not reached the end of the `string`, read the expression from left to right.
      If the current character is a digit,
            Push its integer value onto the stack (the integer value of a digit character is its value in the computer's character set minus the value of `'0'` in the computer's character set).
      Otherwise, if the current character is an *operator*,
            Pop the two top elements of the stack into variables x and y.
            Calculate y *operator* x.
            Push the result of the calculation onto the stack.
2) When you reach the end of the `string`, pop the top value of the stack. This is the result of the postfix expression.

[*Note:* In *Step 2* above, if the operator is `'/'`, the top of the stack is 2 and the next element in the stack is 8, then pop 2 into x, pop 8 into y, evaluate 8 / 2 and push the result, 4, back onto the stack. This note also applies to operator `'-'`.] The arithmetic operations allowed in an expression are

+   addition
–   subtraction
*   multiplication
/   division
∧   exponentiation
%   modulus

[*Note:* We assume left-to-right associativity for all operators for the purpose of this exercise.] The stack should be maintained with stack nodes that contain an `int` data member and a pointer to the next stack node. You may want to provide the following functional capabilities:

a) function `evaluatePostfixExpression` that evaluates the postfix expression
b) function `calculate` that evaluates the expression op1 operator op2
c) function `push` that pushes a value onto the stack

    d) function `pop` that pops a value off the stack
    e) function `isEmpty` that determines if the stack is empty
    f) function `printStack` that prints the stack

20.14 *(Postfix Evaluation Enhanced)* Modify the postfix evaluator program of Exercise 20.13 so that it can process integer operands larger than 9.

20.15 *(Supermarket Simulation)* Write a program that simulates a checkout line at a supermarket. The line is a queue object. Customers (i.e., customer objects) arrive in random integer intervals of 1–4 minutes. Also, each customer is served in random integer intervals of 1–4 minutes. Obviously, the rates need to be balanced. If the average arrival rate is larger than the average service rate, the queue will grow infinitely. Even with "balanced" rates, randomness can still cause long lines. Run the supermarket simulation for a 12-hour day (720 minutes) using the following algorithm:

    1) Choose a random integer between 1 and 4 to determine the minute at which the first customer arrives.
    2) At the first customer's arrival time:
        Determine customer's service time (random integer from 1 to 4);
        Begin servicing the customer;
        Schedule arrival time of next customer (random integer 1 to 4 added to the current time).
    3) For each minute of the day:
        If the next customer arrives,
            Say so,
            Enqueue the customer;
            Schedule the arrival time of the next customer;
        If service was completed for the last customer;
            Say so
            Dequeue next customer to be serviced
            Determine customer's service completion time
                (random integer from 1 to 4 added to the current time).

Now run your simulation for 720 minutes, and answer each of the following:
    a) What's the maximum number of customers in the queue at any time?
    b) What's the longest wait any one customer experiences?
    c) What happens if the arrival interval is changed from 1–4 minutes to 1–3 minutes?

20.16 *(Allowing Duplicates in Binary Trees)* Modify the program of Figs. 20.20–20.22 to allow the binary tree object to contain duplicates.

20.17 *(Binary Tree of Strings)* Write a program based on Figs. 20.20–20.22 that inputs a line of text, tokenizes the sentence into separate words (you may want to use the `istringstream` library class), inserts the words in a binary search tree and prints the inorder, preorder and postorder traversals of the tree. Use an OOP approach.

20.18 *(Duplicate Elimination)* In this chapter, we saw that duplicate elimination is straightforward when creating a binary search tree. Describe how you'd perform duplicate elimination using only a one-dimensional array. Compare the performance of array-based duplicate elimination with the performance of binary-search-tree-based duplicate elimination.

20.19 *(Depth of a Binary Tree)* Write a function `depth` that receives a binary tree and determines how many levels it has.

20.20 *(Recursively Print a List Backward)* Write a member function `printListBackward` that recursively outputs the items in a linked list object in reverse order. Write a test program that creates a sorted list of integers and prints the list in reverse order.

20.21 (*Recursively Search a List*) Write a member function searchList that recursively searches a linked list object for a specified value. The function should return a pointer to the value if it's found; otherwise, null should be returned. Use your function in a test program that creates a list of integers. The program should prompt the user for a value to locate in the list.

20.22 (*Binary Tree Delete*) Deleting items from binary search trees is not as straightforward as the insertion algorithm. There are three cases that are encountered when deleting an item—the item is contained in a leaf node (i.e., it has no children), the item is contained in a node that has one child or the item is contained in a node that has two children.

If the item to be deleted is contained in a leaf node, the node is deleted and the pointer in the parent node is set to null.

If the item to be deleted is contained in a node with one child, the pointer in the parent node is set to point to the child node and the node containing the data item is deleted. This causes the child node to take the place of the deleted node in the tree.

The last case is the most difficult. When a node with two children is deleted, another node in the tree must take its place. However, the pointer in the parent node cannot be assigned to point to one of the children of the node to be deleted. In most cases, the resulting binary search tree would not adhere to the following characteristic of binary search trees (with no duplicate values): *The values in any left subtree are less than the value in the parent node, and the values in any right subtree are greater than the value in the parent node.*

Which node is used as a *replacement node* to maintain this characteristic? Either the node containing the largest value in the tree less than the value in the node being deleted, or the node containing the smallest value in the tree greater than the value in the node being deleted. Let's consider the node with the smaller value. In a binary search tree, the largest value less than a parent's value is located in the left subtree of the parent node and is guaranteed to be contained in the rightmost node of the subtree. This node is located by walking down the left subtree to the right until the pointer to the right child of the current node is null. We are now pointing to the replacement node, which is either a leaf node or a node with one child to its left. If the replacement node is a leaf node, the steps to perform the deletion are as follows:

1) Store the pointer to the node to be deleted in a temporary pointer variable (this pointer is used to delete the dynamically allocated memory).
2) Set the pointer in the parent of the node being deleted to point to the replacement node.
3) Set the pointer in the parent of the replacement node to null.
4) Set the pointer to the right subtree in the replacement node to point to the right subtree of the node to be deleted.
5) Delete the node to which the temporary pointer variable points.

The deletion steps for a replacement node with a left child are similar to those for a replacement node with no children, but the algorithm also must move the child into the replacement node's position in the tree. If the replacement node is a node with a left child, the steps to perform the deletion are as follows:

1) Store the pointer to the node to be deleted in a temporary pointer variable.
2) Set the pointer in the parent of the node being deleted to point to the replacement node.
3) Set the pointer in the parent of the replacement node to point to the left child of the replacement node.
4) Set the pointer to the right subtree in the replacement node to point to the right subtree of the node to be deleted.
5) Delete the node to which the temporary pointer variable points.

Write member function deleteNode, which takes as its arguments a pointer to the root node of the tree object and the value to be deleted. The function should locate in the tree the node containing the value to be deleted and use the algorithms discussed here to delete the node. The function should print a message that indicates whether the value is deleted. Modify the program of

Figs. 20.20–20.22 to use this function. After deleting an item, call the inOrder, preOrder and postOrder traversal functions to confirm that the delete operation was performed correctly.

20.23 (*Binary Tree Search*) Write member function binaryTreeSearch, which attempts to locate a specified value in a binary search tree object. The function should take as arguments a pointer to the root node of the binary tree and a search key to be located. If the node containing the search key is found, the function should return a pointer to that node; otherwise, the function should return a null pointer.

20.24 (*Level-Order Binary Tree Traversal*) The program of Figs. 20.20–20.22 illustrated three recursive methods of traversing a binary tree—inorder, preorder and postorder traversals. This exercise presents the *level-order traversal* of a binary tree, in which the node values are printed level by level, starting at the root node level. The nodes on each level are printed from left to right. The level-order traversal is not a recursive algorithm. It uses a queue object to control the output of the nodes. The algorithm is as follows:

1) Insert the root node in the queue
2) While there are nodes left in the queue,
    Get the next node in the queue
    Print the node's value
    If the pointer to the left child of the node is not null
        Insert the left child node in the queue
    If the pointer to the right child of the node is not null
        Insert the right child node in the queue.

Write member function levelOrder to perform a level-order traversal of a binary tree object. Modify the program of Figs. 20.20–20.22 to use this function. [*Note:* You'll also need to modify and incorporate the queue-processing functions of Fig. 20.16 in this program.]

20.25 (*Printing Trees*) Write a recursive member function outputTree to display a binary tree object on the screen. The function should output the tree row by row, with the top of the tree at the left of the screen and the bottom of the tree toward the right of the screen. Each row is output vertically. For example, the binary tree illustrated in Fig. 20.24 is output as shown in Fig. 20.25. Note that the rightmost leaf node appears at the top of the output in the rightmost column and the root node appears at the left of the output. Each column of output starts five spaces to the right of the previous column. Function outputTree should receive an argument totalSpaces representing the number of spaces preceding the value to be output (this variable should start at zero, so the root node is output at the left of the screen). The function uses a modified inorder traversal to output the tree—it starts at the rightmost node in the tree and works back to the left. The algorithm is as follows:

Fig. 20.25 | Output from displaying a binary tree.

> While the pointer to the current node is not null
>> Recursively call `outputTree` with the current node's right subtree and `totalSpaces + 5`
>> Use a for structure to count from 1 to `totalSpaces` and output spaces
>> Output the value in the current node
>> Set the pointer to the current node to point to the left subtree of the current node
>> Increment `totalSpaces` by 5.

20.26   *(Insert/Delete Anywhere in a Linked List)* Our linked list class template allowed insertions and deletions at only the front and the back of the linked list. These capabilities were convenient for us when we used `private` inheritance and composition to produce a stack class template and a queue class template with a minimal amount of code by reusing the list class template. Actually, linked lists are more general than those we provided. Modify the linked list class template we developed in this chapter to handle insertions and deletions anywhere in the list.

20.27   *(List and Queues without Tail Pointers)* Our implementation of a linked list (Figs. 20.3–20.5) used both a `firstPtr` and a `lastPtr`. The `lastPtr` was useful for the `insertAtBack` and `removeFromBack` member functions of the `List` class. The `insertAtBack` function corresponds to the `enqueue` member function of the `Queue` class. Rewrite the `List` class so that it does not use a `lastPtr`. Thus, any operations on the tail of a list must begin searching the list from the front. Does this affect our implementation of the `Queue` class (Fig. 20.16)?

20.28   Use the composition version of the stack program (Fig. 20.15) to form a complete working stack program. Modify this program to `inline` the member functions. Compare the two approaches. Summarize the advantages and disadvantages of inlining member functions.

20.29   *(Performance of Binary Tree Sorting and Searching)* One problem with the binary tree sort is that the order in which the data is inserted affects the shape of the tree—for the same collection of data, different orderings can yield binary trees of dramatically different shapes. The performance of the binary tree sorting and searching algorithms is sensitive to the shape of the binary tree. What shape would a binary tree have if its data were inserted in increasing order? in decreasing order? What shape should the tree have to achieve maximal searching performance?

20.30   *(Indexed Lists)* As presented in the text, linked lists must be searched sequentially. For large lists, this can result in poor performance. A common technique for improving list searching performance is to create and maintain an index to the list. An index is a set of pointers to various key places in the list. For example, an application that searches a large list of names could improve performance by creating an index with 26 entries—one for each letter of the alphabet. A search operation for a last name beginning with 'Y' would first search the index to determine where the 'Y' entries begin and "jump into" the list at that point and search linearly until the desired name was found. This would be much faster than searching the linked list from the beginning. Use the `List` class of Figs. 20.3–20.5 as the basis of an `IndexedList` class. Write a program that demonstrates the operation of indexed lists. Be sure to include member functions `insertInIndexedList`, `searchInIndexedList` and `deleteFromIndexedList`.

Special Section: Building Your Own Compiler

In Exercises 8.18–8.19 and 8.20, we introduced Simpletron Machine Language (SML), and you implemented a Simpletron computer simulator to execute SML programs. In Exercises 20.31—20.35, we build a compiler that converts programs written in a high-level programming language to SML. This section "ties" together the entire programming process. You'll write programs in this new high-level language, compile them on the compiler you build and run them on the simulator you built in Exercise 8.19. You should make every effort to implement your compiler in an object-oriented manner. [*Note:* Due to the size of the descriptions for Exercises 20.31—20.35, we've posted them in a PDF document located at www.deitel.com/books/cpphtp7/.]

21

Bits, Characters, C Strings and structs

*The same old charitable lie
Repeated as the years scoot by
Perpetually makes a hit—
"You really haven't changed a
bit!"*
—Margaret Fishback

*The chief defect of Henry King
Was chewing little bits of string.*
—Hilaire Belloc

*Vigorous writing is concise. A
sentence should contain no
unnecessary words, a paragraph
no unnecessary sentences.*
—William Strunk, Jr.

Objectives

In this chapter you'll learn:

- To create and use structs.

- To pass structs by value
  and by reference.

- To use typedef to create
  aliases for previously defined
  data types and structs.

- To manipulate data with the
  bitwise operators and to
  create bit fields for storing
  data compactly.

- To use the functions of the
  character-handling library
  <cctype>.

- To use the string-conversion
  functions of the general-
  utilities library <cstdlib>.

- To use the string-processing
  functions of the string-
  handling library <cstring>.

21.1 **Introduction**

We now discuss structures and the manipulation of bits, characters and C-style strings. Many of the techniques we present here are included for the benefit of those who will work with legacy C and C++ code.

C++'s designers evolved structures into the notion of a class. Like a class, C++ structures may contain access specifiers, member functions, constructors and destructors. In fact, the only differences between structures and classes in C++ is that structure members default to public access and class members default to private access when no access specifiers are used, and that structures default to public inheritance, whereas classes default to private inheritance. Classes have been covered thoroughly in the book, so there is really no need for us to discuss structures in detail. Our presentation of structures in this chapter focuses on their use in C, where structures contain only public data members. This use of structures is typical of the legacy C code and early C++ code you'll see in industry.

We discuss how to declare, initialize and pass structures to functions. Then, we present a high-performance card shuffling and dealing simulation in which we use structure objects and C-style strings to represent the cards. We discuss the bitwise operators that allow you to access and manipulate the individual bits in bytes of data. We also present bitfields—special structures that can be used to specify the exact number of bits a variable occupies in memory. These bit manipulation techniques are common in C and C++ programs that interact directly with hardware devices that have limited memory. The chapter finishes with examples of many character and C string manipulation functions—some of which are designed to process blocks of memory as arrays of bytes. The detailed C string treatment in this chapter is mostly for reasons of legacy code support and because there are still remnants of C string use in C++, such as command-line arguments (Appendix F). New development should use C++ string objects rather than C strings.

21.2 **Structure Definitions**

Structures are **aggregate data types**—that is, they can be built using elements of several types including other structs. Consider the following structure definition:

```
struct Card
{
   string face;
   string suit;
}; // end struct Card
```

Keyword **struct** introduces the definition for structure Card. The identifier Card is the **structure name** and is used in C++ to declare variables of the **structure type** (in C, the type name of the preceding structure is `struct Card`). In this example, the structure type is Card. Data (and possibly functions—just as with classes) declared within the braces of the structure definition are the structure's **members**. Members of the same structure must have unique names, but two different structures may contain members of the same name without conflict. Each structure definition must end with a semicolon.

Common Programming Error 21.1

Forgetting the semicolon that terminates a structure definition is a syntax error.

Card's definition contains two `string` members—face and suit. Structure members can be variables of the fundamental data types (e.g., `int`, `double`, etc.) or aggregates, such as arrays, other structures and classes. Data members in a single structure definition can be of many data types. For example, an Employee structure might contain character-string members for the first and last names, an `int` member for the employee's age, a `char` member containing `'M'` or `'F'` for the employee's gender, a `double` member for the employee's hourly salary and so on.

A structure cannot contain an instance of itself. For example, a structure variable Card cannot be declared in the definition for structure Card. A pointer to a Card structure, however, can be included. A structure containing a member that is a pointer to the same structure type is referred to as a **self-referential structure.** We used a similar construct—self-referential classes—in Chapter 20, Data Structures, to build various kinds of linked data structures.

The Card structure definition does not reserve any space in memory; rather, it creates a new data type that is used to declare structure variables. Structure variables are declared like variables of other types. The following declarations

```
Card oneCard;
Card deck[ 52 ];
Card *cardPtr;
```

declare oneCard to be a structure variable of type Card, deck to be an array with 52 elements of type Card and cardPtr to be a pointer to a Card structure. Variables of a given structure type can also be declared by placing a comma-separated list of the variable names between the closing brace of the structure definition and the semicolon that ends the structure definition. For example, the preceding declarations could have been incorporated into the Card structure definition as follows:

```
struct Card
{
   string face;
   string suit;
} oneCard, deck[ 52 ], *cardPtr;
```

The structure name is optional. If a structure definition does not contain a structure name, variables of the structure type may be declared only between the closing right brace of the structure definition and the semicolon that terminates the structure definition.

Software Engineering Observation 21.1

Provide a structure name when creating a structure type. The structure name is required for declaring new variables of the structure type later in the program, declaring parameters of the structure type and, if the structure is being used like a C++ class, specifying the name of the constructor and destructor.

The only valid built-in operations that may be performed on structure objects are assigning one structure object to another of the same type, taking the address (&) of a structure object, accessing the members of a structure object (in the same manner as members of a class are accessed) and using the `sizeof` operator to determine the size of a structure. As with classes, most operators can be overloaded to work with objects of a structure type.

Structure members are not necessarily stored in consecutive bytes of memory. Sometimes there are "holes" in a structure, because some computers store specific data types only on certain memory boundaries for performance reasons, such as half-word, word or double-word boundaries. A word is a standard memory unit used to store data in a computer—usually two bytes or four bytes and typically four bytes on today's popular 32-bit systems. Consider the following structure definition in which structure objects `sample1` and `sample2` of type `Example` are declared:

```
struct Example
{
    char c;
    int i;
} sample1, sample2;
```

A computer with two-byte words might require that each of the members of `Example` be aligned on a word boundary (i.e., at the beginning of a word— this is machine dependent). Figure 21.1 shows a sample storage alignment for an object of type `Example` that has been assigned the character `'a'` and the integer 97 (the bit representations of the values are shown). If the members are stored beginning at word boundaries, there is a one-byte hole (byte 1 in the figure) in the storage for objects of type `Example`. The value in the one-byte hole is undefined. If the member values of `sample1` and `sample2` are in fact equal, the structure objects are not necessarily equal, because the undefined one-byte holes are not likely to contain identical values.

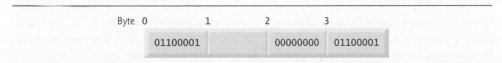

Fig. 21.1 | Possible storage alignment for a variable of type `Example`, showing an undefined area in memory.

Common Programming Error 21.2

Comparing variables of structure types is a compilation error.

Portability Tip 21.1

Because the size of data items of a particular type is machine dependent, and because storage alignment considerations are machine dependent, so too is the representation of a structure.

21.3 Initializing Structures

Structures can be initialized using initializer lists, like arrays. For example, the declaration

```
Card oneCard = { "Three", "Hearts" };
```

creates `Card` variable `oneCard` and initializes member `face` to `"Three"` and member `suit` to `"Hearts"`. If there are fewer initializers in the list than members in the structure, the remaining members are initialized to their default values. Structure variables declared outside a function definition (i.e., externally) are initialized to their default values if they're not explicitly initialized in the external declaration. Structure variables may also be set in assignment expressions by assigning a structure variable of the same type or by assigning values to the individual data members of the structure.

21.4 Using Structures with Functions

There are two ways to pass the information in structures to functions. You can either pass the entire structure or pass the individual members of a structure. By default, structures are passed by value. Structures and their members can also be passed by reference by passing either references or pointers. To pass a structure by reference, pass the address of the structure object or a reference to the structure object.

In Chapter 7, we stated that an array could be passed by value by using a structure. To pass an array by value, create a structure (or a class) with the array as a member, then pass an object of that structure (or class) type to a function by value. Because structure objects are passed by value, the array member, too, is passed by value.

Performance Tip 21.1

Passing structures (and especially large structures) by reference is more efficient than passing them by value (which requires the entire structure to be copied).

21.5 typedef

Keyword **typedef** provides a mechanism for creating synonyms (or aliases) for previously defined data types. Names for structure types are often defined with `typedef` to create shorter, simpler or more readable type names. For example, the statement

```
typedef Card *CardPtr;
```

defines the new type name `CardPtr` as a synonym for type `Card *`.

Good Programming Practice 21.1

Capitalize `typedef` names to emphasize that they are synonyms for other type names.

Creating a new name with `typedef` does not create a new type; `typedef` simply creates a new type name that can then be used in the program as an alias for an existing type name.

> **Portability Tip 21.2**
> *Synonyms for built-in data types can be created with* `typedef` *to make programs more portable. For example, a program can use* `typedef` *to create alias* `Integer` *for four-byte integers.* `Integer` *can then be aliased to* `int` *on systems with four-byte integers and can be aliased to* `long int` *on systems with two-byte integers where* `long int` *values occupy four bytes. Then, you simply declare all four-byte integer variables to be of type* `Integer`*.*

21.6 Example: Card Shuffling and Dealing Simulation

The card shuffling and dealing program in Figs. 21.2–21.4 is similar to the one described in Exercise 10.10. This program represents the deck of cards as a `vector` of structures and uses high-performance shuffling and dealing algorithms.

The constructor (lines 12–32 of Fig. 21.3) initializes the `Card` vector in order with character strings representing Ace through King of each suit. Function `shuffle` implements the high-performance shuffling algorithm. The function loops through all 52 cards (subscripts 0 to 51). For each card, a number between 0 and 51 is picked randomly. Next, the current `Card` structure and the randomly selected `Card` structure are swapped in the vector. A total of 52 swaps are made in a single pass of the entire vector, and the vector of `Card` structures is shuffled. Because the `Card` structures were swapped in place in the vector, the dealing algorithm implemented in function `deal` requires only one pass of the vector to deal the shuffled cards.

```
 1   // Fig. 21.2: DeckOfCards.h
 2   // Definition of class DeckOfCards that
 3   // represents a deck of playing cards.
 4   #include <string>
 5   #include <vector>
 6   using namespace std;
 7
 8   // Card structure definition
 9   struct Card
10   {
11      string face;
12      string suit;
13   }; // end structure Card
14
15   // DeckOfCards class definition
16   class DeckOfCards
17   {
18   public:
19      static const int numberOfCards = 52;
20      static const int faces = 13;
21      static const int suits = 4;
22
```

Fig. 21.2 | Header file for `DeckOfCards` class. (Part 1 of 2.)

```
23       DeckOfCards(); // constructor initializes deck
24       void shuffle(); // shuffles cards in deck
25       void deal() const; // deals cards in deck
26
27    private:
28       vector< Card > deck; // represents deck of cards
29    }; // end class DeckOfCards
```

Fig. 21.2 | Header file for `DeckOfCards` class. (Part 2 of 2.)

```
 1    // Fig. 21.3: DeckOfCards.cpp
 2    // Member-function definitions for class DeckOfCards that simulates
 3    // the shuffling and dealing of a deck of playing cards.
 4    #include <iostream>
 5    #include <iomanip>
 6    #include <cstdlib> // prototypes for rand and srand
 7    #include <ctime> // prototype for time
 8    #include "DeckOfCards.h" // DeckOfCards class definition
 9    using namespace std;
10
11    // no-argument DeckOfCards constructor intializes deck
12    DeckOfCards::DeckOfCards()
13       : deck( numberOfCards )
14    {
15       // initialize suit array
16       static string suit[ suits ] =
17          { "Hearts", "Diamonds", "Clubs", "Spades" };
18
19       // initialize face array
20       static string face[ faces ] =
21          { "Ace", "Deuce", "Three", "Four", "Five", "Six", "Seven",
22            "Eight", "Nine", "Ten", "Jack", "Queen", "King" };
23
24       // set values for deck of 52 Cards
25       for ( int i = 0; i < numberOfCards; i++ )
26       {
27          deck[ i ].face = face[ i % faces ];
28          deck[ i ].suit = suit[ i / faces ];
29       } // end for
30
31       srand( time( 0 ) ); // seed random number generator
32    } // end no-argument DeckOfCards constructor
33
34    // shuffle cards in deck
35    void DeckOfCards::shuffle()
36    {
37       // shuffle cards randomly
38       for ( int i = 0; i < numberOfCards; i++ )
39       {
40          int j = rand() % numberOfCards;
41          Card temp = deck[ i ];
42          deck[ i ] = deck[ j ];
```

Fig. 21.3 | Class file for `DeckOfCards`. (Part 1 of 2.)

```
43          deck[ j ] = temp;
44      } // end for
45  } // end function shuffle
46
47  // deal cards in deck
48  void DeckOfCards::deal() const
49  {
50      // display each card's face and suit
51      for ( int i = 0; i < numberOfCards; i++ )
52          cout << right << setw( 5 ) << deck[ i ].face << " of "
53              << left << setw( 8 ) << deck[ i ].suit
54              << ( ( i + 1 ) % 2 ? '\t' : '\n' );
55  } // end function deal
```

Fig. 21.3 | Class file for `DeckOfCards`. (Part 2 of 2.)

```
 1  // Fig. 21.4: fig21_04.cpp
 2  // Card shuffling and dealing program.
 3  #include "DeckOfCards.h" // DeckOfCards class definition
 4
 5  int main()
 6  {
 7      DeckOfCards deckOfCards; // create DeckOfCards object
 8      deckOfCards.shuffle(); // shuffle the cards in the deck
 9      deckOfCards.deal(); // deal the cards in the deck
10  } // end main
```

```
  King of Clubs         Ten of Diamonds
 Five of Diamonds      Jack of Clubs
Seven of Spades       Five of Clubs
Three of Spades       King of Hearts
  Ten of Clubs        Eight of Spades
Eight of Hearts        Six of Hearts
 Nine of Diamonds     Nine of Clubs
Three of Diamonds    Queen of Hearts
  Six of Clubs        Seven of Hearts
Seven of Diamonds     Jack of Diamonds
 Jack of Spades       King of Diamonds
Deuce of Diamonds     Four of Clubs
Three of Clubs        Five of Hearts
Eight of Clubs         Ace of Hearts
Deuce of Spades        Ace of Clubs
  Ten of Spades      Eight of Diamonds
  Ten of Hearts        Six of Spades
Queen of Diamonds     Nine of Hearts
Seven of Clubs       Queen of Clubs
Deuce of Clubs       Queen of Spades
Three of Hearts       Five of Spades
Deuce of Hearts       Jack of Hearts
 Four of Hearts        Ace of Diamonds
 Nine of Spades       Four of Diamonds
  Ace of Spades        Six of Diamonds
 Four of Spades       King of Spades
```

Fig. 21.4 | High-performance card shuffling and dealing simulation.

21.7 Bitwise Operators

C++ provides extensive bit-manipulation capabilities for getting down to the so-called "bits-and-bytes" level. Operating systems, test-equipment software, networking software and many other kinds of software require that you communicate "directly with the hardware." This and the next several sections discuss bit manipulation. We introduce each of C++'s many bitwise operators, and we discuss how to save memory by using bit fields.

All data is represented internally by computers as sequences of bits. Each bit can assume the value 0 or the value 1. On most systems, a sequence of 8 bits forms a **byte**— the standard storage unit for a variable of type char. Other data types are stored in larger numbers of bytes. Bitwise operators are used to manipulate the bits of integral operands (char, short, int and long; both signed and unsigned). Unsigned integers are normally used with the bitwise operators.

Portability Tip 21.3

Bitwise data manipulations are machine dependent.

The bitwise operator discussions in this section show the binary representations of the integer operands. For a detailed explanation of the binary (also called base-2) number system, see Appendix D, Number Systems. Because of the machine-dependent nature of bitwise manipulations, some of these programs might not work on your system without modification.

The bitwise operators are: **bitwise AND (&)**, **bitwise inclusive OR (|)**, **bitwise exclusive OR (∧)**, **left shift (<<)**, **right shift (>>)** and **bitwise complement (~)**—also known as the **one's complement**. (Note that we've been using &, << and >> for other purposes. This is a classic example of operator overloading.) The bitwise AND, bitwise inclusive OR and bitwise exclusive OR operators compare their two operands bit by bit. The bitwise AND operator sets each bit in the result to 1 if the corresponding bit in both operands is 1. The bitwise inclusive-OR operator sets each bit in the result to 1 if the corresponding bit in either (or both) operand(s) is 1. The bitwise exclusive-OR operator sets each bit in the result to 1 if the corresponding bit in either operand—but not both—is 1. The left-shift operator shifts the bits of its left operand to the left by the number of bits specified in its right operand. The right-shift operator shifts the bits in its left operand to the right by the number of bits specified in its right operand. The bitwise complement operator sets all 0 bits in its operand to 1 in the result and sets all 1 bits in its operand to 0 in the result. Detailed discussions of each bitwise operator appear in the following examples. The bitwise operators are summarized in Fig. 21.5.

Operator	Name	Description
&	bitwise AND	The bits in the result are set to 1 if the corresponding bits in the two operands are both 1.
|	bitwise inclusive OR	The bits in the result are set to 1 if one or both of the corresponding bits in the two operands is 1.

Fig. 21.5 | Bitwise operators. (Part 1 of 2.)

Operator	Name	Description
^	bitwise exclusive OR	The bits in the result are set to 1 if exactly one of the corresponding bits in the two operands is 1.
<<	left shift	Shifts the bits of the first operand left by the number of bits specified by the second operand; fill from right with 0 bits.
>>	right shift with sign extension	Shifts the bits of the first operand right by the number of bits specified by the second operand; the method of filling from the left is machine dependent.
~	bitwise complement	All 0 bits are set to 1 and all 1 bits are set to 0.

Fig. 21.5 | Bitwise operators. (Part 2 of 2.)

Printing a Binary Representation of an Integral Value

When using the bitwise operators, it's useful to illustrate their precise effects by printing values in their binary representation. The program of Fig. 21.6 prints an unsigned integer in its binary representation in groups of eight bits each.

```cpp
1   // Fig. 21.6: fig21_06.cpp
2   // Printing an unsigned integer in bits.
3   #include <iostream>
4   #include <iomanip>
5   using namespace std;
6
7   void displayBits( unsigned ); // prototype
8
9   int main()
10  {
11     unsigned inputValue; // integral value to print in binary
12
13     cout << "Enter an unsigned integer: ";
14     cin >> inputValue;
15     displayBits( inputValue );
16  } // end main
17
18  // display bits of an unsigned integer value
19  void displayBits( unsigned value )
20  {
21     const int SHIFT = 8 * sizeof( unsigned ) - 1;
22     const unsigned MASK = 1 << SHIFT;
23
24     cout << setw( 10 ) << value << " = ";
25
26     // display bits
27     for ( unsigned i = 1; i <= SHIFT + 1; i++ )
28     {
29        cout << ( value & MASK ? '1' : '0' );
30        value <<= 1; // shift value left by 1
```

Fig. 21.6 | Printing an unsigned integer in bits. (Part 1 of 2.)

```
31
32          if ( i % 8 == 0 ) // output a space after 8 bits
33             cout << ' ';
34       } // end for
35
36       cout << endl;
37  } // end function displayBits
```

```
Enter an unsigned integer: 65000
    65000 = 00000000 00000000 11111101 11101000
```

```
Enter an unsigned integer: 29
    29 = 00000000 00000000 00000000 00011101
```

Fig. 21.6 | Printing an unsigned integer in bits. (Part 2 of 2.)

Function `displayBits` (lines 19–37) uses the bitwise AND operator to combine variable `value` with constant `MASK`. Often, the bitwise AND operator is used with an operand called a **mask**—an integer value with specific bits set to 1. Masks are used to hide some bits in a value while selecting other bits. In `displayBits`, line 22 assigns constant `MASK` the value `1 << SHIFT`. The value of constant `SHIFT` was calculated in line 21 with the expression

```
8 * sizeof( unsigned ) - 1
```

which multiplies the number of bytes an `unsigned` object requires in memory by 8 (the number of bits in a byte) to get the total number of bits required to store an `unsigned` object, then subtracts 1. The bit representation of `1 << SHIFT` on a computer that represents `unsigned` objects in four bytes of memory is

```
10000000 00000000 00000000 00000000
```

The left-shift operator shifts the value 1 from the low-order (rightmost) bit to the high-order (leftmost) bit in `MASK`, and fills in 0 bits from the right. Line 29 prints a 1 or a 0 for the current leftmost bit of variable `value`. Assume that variable `value` contains 65000 (00000000 00000000 11111101 11101000). When `value` and `MASK` are combined using &, all the bits except the high-order bit in variable `value` are "masked off" (hidden), because any bit "ANDed" with 0 yields 0. If the leftmost bit is 1, `value & MASK` evaluates to

```
00000000 00000000 11111101 11101000    (value)
10000000 00000000 00000000 00000000    (MASK)
------------------------------------
00000000 00000000 00000000 00000000    (value & MASK)
```

which is interpreted as `false`, and 0 is printed. Then line 30 shifts variable `value` left by one bit with the expression `value <<= 1` (i.e., `value = value << 1`). These steps are repeated for each bit variable `value`. Eventually, a bit with a value of 1 is shifted into the leftmost bit position, and the bit manipulation is as follows:

```
11111101 11101000 00000000 00000000    (value)
10000000 00000000 00000000 00000000    (MASK)
------------------------------------
10000000 00000000 00000000 00000000    (value & MASK)
```

Because both left bits are 1s, the expression's result is nonzero (true) and 1 is printed. Figure 21.7 summarizes the results of combining two bits with the bitwise AND operator.

Common Programming Error 21.3

Using the logical AND operator (&&) for the bitwise AND operator (&) and vice versa is a logic error.

Bit 1	Bit 2	Bit 1 & Bit 2
0	0	0
1	0	0
0	1	0
1	1	1

Fig. 21.7 | Results of combining two bits with the bitwise AND operator (&).

The program of Fig. 21.8 demonstrates the bitwise AND operator, the bitwise inclusive OR operator, the bitwise exclusive OR operator and the bitwise complement operator. Function displayBits (lines 53–71) prints the unsigned integer values.

```cpp
1   // Fig. 21.8: fig21_08.cpp
2   // Bitwise AND, inclusive OR,
3   // exclusive OR and complement operators.
4   #include <iostream>
5   #include <iomanip>
6   using namespace std;
7
8   void displayBits( unsigned ); // prototype
9
10  int main()
11  {
12     unsigned number1;
13     unsigned number2;
14     unsigned mask;
15     unsigned setBits;
16
17     // demonstrate bitwise &
18     number1 = 2179876355;
19     mask = 1;
20     cout << "The result of combining the following\n";
21     displayBits( number1 );
22     displayBits( mask );
23     cout << "using the bitwise AND operator & is\n";
24     displayBits( number1 & mask );
25
```

Fig. 21.8 | Bitwise AND, inclusive-OR, exclusive-OR and complement operators. (Part 1 of 3.)

```
26        // demonstrate bitwise |
27        number1 = 15;
28        setBits = 241;
29        cout << "\nThe result of combining the following\n";
30        displayBits( number1 );
31        displayBits( setBits );
32        cout << "using the bitwise inclusive OR operator | is\n";
33        displayBits( number1 | setBits );
34
35        // demonstrate bitwise exclusive OR
36        number1 = 139;
37        number2 = 199;
38        cout << "\nThe result of combining the following\n";
39        displayBits( number1 );
40        displayBits( number2 );
41        cout << "using the bitwise exclusive OR operator ^ is\n";
42        displayBits( number1 ^ number2 );
43
44        // demonstrate bitwise complement
45        number1 = 21845;
46        cout << "\nThe one's complement of\n";
47        displayBits( number1 );
48        cout << "is" << endl;
49        displayBits( ~number1 );
50  } // end main
51
52  // display bits of an unsigned integer value
53  void displayBits( unsigned value )
54  {
55        const int SHIFT = 8 * sizeof( unsigned ) - 1;
56        const unsigned MASK = 1 << SHIFT;
57
58        cout << setw( 10 ) << value << " = ";
59
60        // display bits
61        for ( unsigned i = 1; i <= SHIFT + 1; i++ )
62        {
63           cout << ( value & MASK ? '1' : '0' );
64           value <<= 1; // shift value left by 1
65
66           if ( i % 8 == 0 ) // output a space after 8 bits
67              cout << ' ';
68        } // end for
69
70        cout << endl;
71  } // end function displayBits
```

```
The result of combining the following
2179876355 = 10000001 11101110 01000110 00000011
         1 = 00000000 00000000 00000000 00000001
using the bitwise AND operator & is
         1 = 00000000 00000000 00000000 00000001
```

Fig. 21.8 | Bitwise AND, inclusive-OR, exclusive-OR and complement operators. (Part 2 of 3.)

```
The result of combining the following
2179876355 = 10000001 11101110 01000110 00000011
         1 = 00000000 00000000 00000000 00000001
using the bitwise AND operator & is
         1 = 00000000 00000000 00000000 00000001

The result of combining the following
        15 = 00000000 00000000 00000000 00001111
       241 = 00000000 00000000 00000000 11110001
using the bitwise inclusive OR operator | is
       255 = 00000000 00000000 00000000 11111111

The result of combining the following
       139 = 00000000 00000000 00000000 10001011
       199 = 00000000 00000000 00000000 11000111
using the bitwise exclusive OR operator ^ is
        76 = 00000000 00000000 00000000 01001100

The one's complement of
     21845 = 00000000 00000000 01010101 01010101
is
4294945450 = 11111111 11111111 10101010 10101010
```

Fig. 21.8 | Bitwise AND, inclusive-OR, exclusive-OR and complement operators. (Part 3 of 3.)

Bitwise AND Operator (&)

In Fig. 21.8, line 18 assigns 2179876355 (10000001 11101110 01000110 00000011) to variable number1, and line 19 assigns 1 (00000000 00000000 00000000 00000001) to variable mask. When mask and number1 are combined using the bitwise AND operator (&) in the expression number1 & mask (line 24), the result is 00000000 00000000 00000000 00000001. All the bits except the low-order bit in variable number1 are "masked off" (hidden) by "ANDing" with constant MASK.

Bitwise Inclusive OR Operator (|)

The bitwise inclusive-OR operator is used to set specific bits to 1 in an operand. In Fig. 21.8, line 27 assigns 15 (00000000 00000000 00000000 00001111) to variable number1, and line 28 assigns 241 (00000000 00000000 00000000 11110001) to variable setBits. When number1 and setBits are combined using the bitwise OR operator in the expression number1 | setBits (line 33), the result is 255 (00000000 00000000 00000000 11111111). Figure 21.9 summarizes the results of combining two bits with the bitwise inclusive-OR operator.

Bit 1	Bit 2	Bit 1 | Bit 2
0	0	0
1	0	1
0	1	1
1	1	1

Fig. 21.9 | Combining two bits with the bitwise inclusive-OR operator (|).

Common Programming Error 21.4

Using the logical OR operator (||) for the bitwise OR operator (|) and vice versa is a logic error.

Bitwise Exclusive OR (∧)

The bitwise exclusive OR operator (∧) sets each bit in the result to 1 if *exactly* one of the corresponding bits in its two operands is 1. In Fig. 21.8, lines 36–37 assign variables number1 and number2 the values 139 (00000000 00000000 00000000 10001011) and 199 (00000000 00000000 00000000 11000111), respectively. When these variables are combined with the exclusive-OR operator in the expression number1 ∧ number2 (line 42), the result is 00000000 00000000 00000000 01001100. Figure 21.10 summarizes the results of combining two bits with the bitwise exclusive-OR operator.

Bit 1	Bit 2	Bit 1 ∧ Bit 2
0	0	0
1	0	1
0	1	1
1	1	0

Fig. 21.10 | Combining two bits with the bitwise exclusive-OR operator (∧).

Bitwise Complement (~)

The bitwise complement operator (~) sets all 1 bits in its operand to 0 in the result and sets all 0 bits to 1 in the result—otherwise referred to as "taking the one's complement of the value." In Fig. 21.8, line 45 assigns variable number1 the value 21845 (00000000 00000000 01010101 01010101). When the expression ~number1 evaluates, the result is (11111111 11111111 10101010 10101010).

Figure 21.11 demonstrates the left-shift operator (<<) and the right-shift operator (>>). Function displayBits (lines 27–45) prints the unsigned integer values.

```
 1   // Fig. 21.11: fig21_11.cpp
 2   // Using the bitwise shift operators.
 3   #include <iostream>
 4   #include <iomanip>
 5   using namespace std;
 6
 7   void displayBits( unsigned ); // prototype
 8
 9   int main()
10   {
11      unsigned number1 = 960;
12
```

Fig. 21.11 | Bitwise shift operators. (Part 1 of 2.)

```
13        // demonstrate bitwise left shift
14        cout << "The result of left shifting\n";
15        displayBits( number1 );
16        cout << "8 bit positions using the left-shift operator is\n";
17        displayBits( number1 << 8 );
18
19        // demonstrate bitwise right shift
20        cout << "\nThe result of right shifting\n";
21        displayBits( number1 );
22        cout << "8 bit positions using the right-shift operator is\n";
23        displayBits( number1 >> 8 );
24    } // end main
25
26    // display bits of an unsigned integer value
27    void displayBits( unsigned value )
28    {
29        const int SHIFT = 8 * sizeof( unsigned ) - 1;
30        const unsigned MASK = 1 << SHIFT;
31
32        cout << setw( 10 ) << value << " = ";
33
34        // display bits
35        for ( unsigned i = 1; i <= SHIFT + 1; i++ )
36        {
37            cout << ( value & MASK ? '1' : '0' );
38            value <<= 1; // shift value left by 1
39
40            if ( i % 8 == 0 ) // output a space after 8 bits
41                cout << ' ';
42        } // end for
43
44        cout << endl;
45    } // end function displayBits
```

```
The result of left shifting
       960 = 00000000 00000000 00000011 11000000
8 bit positions using the left-shift operator is
    245760 = 00000000 00000011 11000000 00000000

The result of right shifting
       960 = 00000000 00000000 00000011 11000000
8 bit positions using the right-shift operator is
         3 = 00000000 00000000 00000000 00000011
```

Fig. 21.11 | Bitwise shift operators. (Part 2 of 2.)

Left-Shift Operator

The left-shift operator (<<) shifts the bits of its left operand to the left by the number of bits specified in its right operand. Bits vacated to the right are replaced with 0s; bits shifted off the left are lost. In the program of Fig. 21.11, line 11 assigns variable number1 the value 960 (00000000 00000000 00000011 11000000). The result of left-shifting variable number1 8 bits in the expression number1 << 8 (line 17) is 245760 (00000000 00000011 11000000 00000000).

Right-Shift Operator
The right-shift operator (>>) shifts the bits of its left operand to the right by the number of bits specified in its right operand. Performing a right shift on an `unsigned` integer causes the vacated bits at the left to be replaced by 0s; bits shifted off the right are lost. In the program of Fig. 21.11, the result of right-shifting `number1` in the expression `number1 >> 8` (line 23) is 3 (00000000 00000000 00000000 00000011).

Common Programming Error 21.5
The result of shifting a value is undefined if the right operand is negative or if the right operand is greater than or equal to the number of bits in which the left operand is stored.

Portability Tip 21.4
The result of right-shifting a signed value is machine dependent. Some machines fill with zeros and others use the sign bit.

Bitwise Assignment Operators
Each bitwise operator (except the bitwise complement operator) has a corresponding assignment operator. These **bitwise assignment operators** are shown in Fig. 21.12; they're used in a similar manner to the arithmetic assignment operators introduced in Chapter 2.

Bitwise assignment operators	
&=	Bitwise AND assignment operator.
|=	Bitwise inclusive-OR assignment operator.
^=	Bitwise exclusive-OR assignment operator.
<<=	Left-shift assignment operator.
>>=	Right-shift with sign extension assignment operator.

Fig. 21.12 | Bitwise assignment operators.

Figure 21.13 shows the precedence and associativity of the operators introduced up to this point in the text. They're shown top to bottom in decreasing order of precedence.

Operators	Associativity	Type
:: (unary; right to left) :: (binary; left to right)	left to right	highest
() [] . -> ++ -- static_cast< *type* >()	left to right	unary
++ -- + - ! delete sizeof * ~ & new	right to left	unary
* / %	left to right	multiplicative
+ -	left to right	additive
<< >>	left to right	shifting

Fig. 21.13 | Operator precedence and associativity. (Part 1 of 2.)

Operators	Associativity	Type
< <= > >=	left to right	relational
== !=	left to right	equality
&	left to right	bitwise AND
^	left to right	bitwise XOR
|	left to right	bitwise OR
&&	left to right	logical AND
||	left to right	logical OR
?:	right to left	conditional
= += -= *= /= %= &= |= ^= <<= >>=	right to left	assignment
,	left to right	comma

Fig. 21.13 | Operator precedence and associativity. (Part 2 of 2.)

21.8 Bit Fields

C++ provides the ability to specify the number of bits in which an integral type or enum type member of a class or a structure is stored. Such a member is referred to as a **bit field.** Bit fields enable better memory utilization by storing data in the minimum number of bits required. Bit field members *must* be declared as an integral or enum type.

Performance Tip 21.2
Bit fields help conserve storage.

Consider the following structure definition:

```
struct BitCard
{
   unsigned face : 4;
   unsigned suit : 2;
   unsigned color : 1;
}; // end struct BitCard
```

The definition contains three unsigned bit fields—face, suit and color—used to represent a card from a deck of 52 cards. A bit field is declared by following an integral type or enum type member with a colon (:) and an integer constant representing the **width of the bit field** (i.e., the number of bits in which the member is stored). The width must be an integer constant.

The preceding structure definition indicates that member face is stored in 4 bits, member suit in 2 bits and member color in 1 bit. The number of bits is based on the desired range of values for each structure member. Member face stores values between 0 (Ace) and 12 (King)—4 bits can store a value between 0 and 15. Member suit stores values between 0 and 3 (0 = Diamonds, 1 = Hearts, 2 = Clubs, 3 = Spades)—2 bits can store a value between 0 and 3. Finally, member color stores either 0 (Red) or 1 (Black)— 1 bit can store either 0 or 1.

The program in Figs. 21.14–21.16 creates `vector` `deck` containing `BitCard` structures (line 27 of Fig. 21.14). The constructor inserts the 52 cards in the `deck` `vector`, and function `deal` prints the 52 cards. Notice that bit fields are accessed exactly as any other structure member is (lines 15–17 and 26–31 of Fig. 21.15). The member `color` is included as a means of indicating the card color.

```
1   // Fig. 21.14: DeckOfCards.h
2   // Definition of class DeckOfCards that
3   // represents a deck of playing cards.
4   #include <vector>
5   using namespace std;
6
7   // BitCard structure definition with bit fields
8   struct BitCard
9   {
10     unsigned face : 4; // 4 bits; 0-15
11     unsigned suit : 2; // 2 bits; 0-3
12     unsigned color : 1; // 1 bit; 0-1
13  }; // end struct BitCard
14
15  // DeckOfCards class definition
16  class DeckOfCards
17  {
18  public:
19     static const int faces = 13;
20     static const int colors = 2; // black and red
21     static const int numberOfCards = 52;
22
23     DeckOfCards(); // constructor initializes deck
24     void deal(); // deals cards in deck
25
26  private:
27     vector< BitCard > deck; // represents deck of cards
28  }; // end class DeckOfCards
```

Fig. 21.14 | Header file for class `DeckOfCards`.

```
1   // Fig. 21.15: DeckOfCards.cpp
2   // Member-function definitions for class DeckOfCards that simulates
3   // the shuffling and dealing of a deck of playing cards.
4   #include <iostream>
5   #include <iomanip>
6   #include "DeckOfCards.h" // DeckOfCards class definition
7   using namespace std;
8
9   // no-argument DeckOfCards constructor intializes deck
10  DeckOfCards::DeckOfCards()
11
12  {
13     for ( int i = 0; i < numberOfCards; i++ )
14     {
```

Fig. 21.15 | Class file for `DeckOfCards`. (Part 1 of 2.)

```
15            deck[ i ].face = i % faces; // faces in order
16             deck[ i ].suit = i / faces; // suits in order
17             deck[ i ].color = i / ( faces * colors ); // colors in order
18         } // end for
19    } // end no-argument DeckOfCards constructor
20
21    // deal cards in deck
22    void DeckOfCards::deal()
23    {
24        for ( int k1 = 0, k2 = k1 + numberOfCards / 2;
25            k1 < numberOfCards / 2 - 1; k1++, k2++ )
26            cout << "Card:" << setw( 3 ) << deck[ k1 ].face
27                 << " Suit:" << setw( 2 ) << deck[ k1 ].suit
28                 << " Color:" << setw( 2 ) << deck[ k1 ].color
29                 << "  " << "Card:" << setw( 3 ) << deck[ k2 ].face
30                 << " Suit:" << setw( 2 ) << deck[ k2 ].suit
31                 << " Color:" << setw( 2 ) << deck[ k2 ].color << endl;
32    } // end function deal
```

Fig. 21.15 | Class file for `DeckOfCards`. (Part 2 of 2.)

```
1    // Fig. 21.16: fig21_16.cpp
2    // Card shuffling and dealing program.
3    #include "DeckOfCards.h" // DeckOfCards class definition
4
5    int main()
6    {
7        DeckOfCards deckOfCards; // create DeckOfCards object
8        deckOfCards.deal(); // deal the cards in the deck
9    } // end main
```

```
Card:  0  Suit: 0  Color: 0    Card:  0  Suit: 2  Color: 1
Card:  1  Suit: 0  Color: 0    Card:  1  Suit: 2  Color: 1
Card:  2  Suit: 0  Color: 0    Card:  2  Suit: 2  Color: 1
Card:  3  Suit: 0  Color: 0    Card:  3  Suit: 2  Color: 1
Card:  4  Suit: 0  Color: 0    Card:  4  Suit: 2  Color: 1
Card:  5  Suit: 0  Color: 0    Card:  5  Suit: 2  Color: 1
Card:  6  Suit: 0  Color: 0    Card:  6  Suit: 2  Color: 1
Card:  7  Suit: 0  Color: 0    Card:  7  Suit: 2  Color: 1
Card:  8  Suit: 0  Color: 0    Card:  8  Suit: 2  Color: 1
Card:  9  Suit: 0  Color: 0    Card:  9  Suit: 2  Color: 1
Card: 10  Suit: 0  Color: 0    Card: 10  Suit: 2  Color: 1
Card: 11  Suit: 0  Color: 0    Card: 11  Suit: 2  Color: 1
Card: 12  Suit: 0  Color: 0    Card: 12  Suit: 2  Color: 1
Card:  0  Suit: 1  Color: 0    Card:  0  Suit: 3  Color: 1
Card:  1  Suit: 1  Color: 0    Card:  1  Suit: 3  Color: 1
Card:  2  Suit: 1  Color: 0    Card:  2  Suit: 3  Color: 1
Card:  3  Suit: 1  Color: 0    Card:  3  Suit: 3  Color: 1
Card:  4  Suit: 1  Color: 0    Card:  4  Suit: 3  Color: 1
Card:  5  Suit: 1  Color: 0    Card:  5  Suit: 3  Color: 1
Card:  6  Suit: 1  Color: 0    Card:  6  Suit: 3  Color: 1
Card:  7  Suit: 1  Color: 0    Card:  7  Suit: 3  Color: 1
```

Fig. 21.16 | Bit fields used to store a deck of cards. (Part 1 of 2.)

```
Card:  8   Suit: 1   Color: 0      Card:  8   Suit: 3   Color: 1
Card:  9   Suit: 1   Color: 0      Card:  9   Suit: 3   Color: 1
Card: 10   Suit: 1   Color: 0      Card: 10   Suit: 3   Color: 1
Card: 11   Suit: 1   Color: 0      Card: 11   Suit: 3   Color: 1
Card: 12   Suit: 1   Color: 0      Card: 12   Suit: 3   Color: 1
```

Fig. 21.16 | Bit fields used to store a deck of cards. (Part 2 of 2.)

It's possible to specify an **unnamed bit field**, in which case the field is used as **padding** in the structure. For example, the structure definition uses an unnamed 3-bit field as padding—nothing can be stored in those 3 bits. Member b is stored in another storage unit.

```
struct Example
{
    unsigned a : 13;
    unsigned   : 3; // align to next storage-unit boundary
    unsigned b : 4;
}; // end struct Example
```

An **unnamed bit field with a zero width** is used to align the next bit field on a new storage-unit boundary. For example, the structure definition

```
struct Example
{
    unsigned a : 13;
    unsigned   : 0; // align to next storage-unit boundary
    unsigned b : 4;
}; // end struct Example
```

uses an unnamed 0-bit field to skip the remaining bits (as many as there are) of the storage unit in which a is stored and align b on the next storage-unit boundary.

Portability Tip 21.5

Bit-field manipulations are machine dependent. For example, some computers allow bit fields to cross word boundaries, whereas others do not.

Common Programming Error 21.6

Attempting to access individual bits of a bit field with subscripting as if they were elements of an array is a compilation error. Bit fields are not "arrays of bits."

Common Programming Error 21.7

Attempting to take the address of a bit field (the & operator may not be used with bit fields because a pointer can designate only a particular byte in memory and bit fields can start in the middle of a byte) is a compilation error.

Performance Tip 21.3

Although bit fields save space, using them can cause the compiler to generate slower-executing machine-language code. This occurs because it takes extra machine-language operations to access only portions of an addressable storage unit. This is one of many examples of the space–time trade-offs that occur in computer science.

21.9 Character-Handling Library

Most data is entered into computers as characters—including letters, digits and various special symbols. In this section, we discuss C++'s capabilities for examining and manipulating individual characters. In the remainder of the chapter, we continue the discussion of character-string manipulation that we began in Chapter 8.

The character-handling library includes several functions that perform useful tests and manipulations of character data. Each function receives a character—represented as an int—or EOF as an argument. Characters are often manipulated as integers. Remember that EOF normally has the value –1 and that some hardware architectures do not allow negative values to be stored in char variables. Therefore, the character-handling functions manipulate characters as integers. Figure 21.17 summarizes the functions of the character-handling library. When using functions from the character-handling library, include the <cctype> header file.

Prototype	Description
int isdigit(int c)	Returns 1 if c is a digit and 0 otherwise.
int isalpha(int c)	Returns 1 if c is a letter and 0 otherwise.
int isalnum(int c)	Returns 1 if c is a digit or a letter and 0 otherwise.
int isxdigit(int c)	Returns 1 if c is a hexadecimal digit character and 0 otherwise. (See Appendix D, Number Systems, for a detailed explanation of binary, octal, decimal and hexadecimal numbers.)
int islower(int c)	Returns 1 if c is a lowercase letter and 0 otherwise.
int isupper(int c)	Returns 1 if c is an uppercase letter; 0 otherwise.
int tolower(int c)	If c is an uppercase letter, tolower returns c as a lowercase letter. Otherwise, tolower returns the argument unchanged.
int toupper(int c)	If c is a lowercase letter, toupper returns c as an uppercase letter. Otherwise, toupper returns the argument unchanged.
int isspace(int c)	Returns 1 if c is a white-space character—newline ('\n'), space (' '), form feed ('\f'), carriage return ('\r'), horizontal tab ('\t'), or vertical tab ('\v')—and 0 otherwise.
int iscntrl(int c)	Returns 1 if c is a control character, such as newline ('\n'), form feed ('\f'), carriage return ('\r'), horizontal tab ('\t'), vertical tab ('\v'), alert ('\a'), or backspace ('\b')—and 0 otherwise.
int ispunct(int c)	Returns 1 if c is a printing character other than a space, a digit, or a letter and 0 otherwise.
int isprint(int c)	Returns 1 if c is a printing character including space (' ') and 0 otherwise.
int isgraph(int c)	Returns 1 if c is a printing character other than space (' ') and 0 otherwise.

Fig. 21.17 | Character-handling library functions.

Figure 21.18 demonstrates functions **isdigit**, **isalpha**, **isalnum** and **isxdigit**. Function isdigit determines whether its argument is a digit (0–9). Function isalpha determines whether its argument is an uppercase letter (A–Z) or a lowercase letter (a–z). Function isalnum determines whether its argument is an uppercase letter, a lowercase letter or a digit. Function isxdigit determines whether its argument is a hexadecimal digit (A–F, a–f, 0–9).

```cpp
 1  // Fig. 21.18: fig21_18.cpp
 2  // Character-handling functions isdigit, isalpha, isalnum and isxdigit.
 3  #include <iostream>
 4  #include <cctype> // character-handling function prototypes
 5  using namespace std;
 6
 7  int main()
 8  {
 9     cout << "According to isdigit:\n"
10        << ( isdigit( '8' ) ? "8 is a" : "8 is not a" ) << " digit\n"
11        << ( isdigit( '#' ) ? "# is a" : "# is not a" ) << " digit\n";
12
13     cout << "\nAccording to isalpha:\n"
14        << ( isalpha( 'A' ) ? "A is a" : "A is not a" ) << " letter\n"
15        << ( isalpha( 'b' ) ? "b is a" : "b is not a" ) << " letter\n"
16        << ( isalpha( '&' ) ? "& is a" : "& is not a" ) << " letter\n"
17        << ( isalpha( '4' ) ? "4 is a" : "4 is not a" ) << " letter\n";
18
19     cout << "\nAccording to isalnum:\n"
20        << ( isalnum( 'A' ) ? "A is a" : "A is not a" )
21        << " digit or a letter\n"
22        << ( isalnum( '8' ) ? "8 is a" : "8 is not a" )
23        << " digit or a letter\n"
24        << ( isalnum( '#' ) ? "# is a" : "# is not a" )
25        << " digit or a letter\n";
26
27     cout << "\nAccording to isxdigit:\n"
28        << ( isxdigit( 'F' ) ? "F is a" : "F is not a" )
29        << " hexadecimal digit\n"
30        << ( isxdigit( 'J' ) ? "J is a" : "J is not a" )
31        << " hexadecimal digit\n"
32        << ( isxdigit( '7' ) ? "7 is a" : "7 is not a" )
33        << " hexadecimal digit\n"
34        << ( isxdigit( '$' ) ? "$ is a" : "$ is not a" )
35        << " hexadecimal digit\n"
36        << ( isxdigit( 'f' ) ? "f is a" : "f is not a" )
37        << " hexadecimal digit" << endl;
38  } // end main
```

```
According to isdigit:
8 is a digit
# is not a digit
```

Fig. 21.18 | Character-handling functions isdigit, isalpha, isalnum and isxdigit. (Part I of 2.)

```
According to isalpha:
A is a letter
b is a letter
& is not a letter
4 is not a letter

According to isalnum:
A is a digit or a letter
8 is a digit or a letter
# is not a digit or a letter

According to isxdigit:
F is a hexadecimal digit
J is not a hexadecimal digit
7 is a hexadecimal digit
$ is not a hexadecimal digit
f is a hexadecimal digit
```

Fig. 21.18 | Character-handling functions `isdigit`, `isalpha`, `isalnum` and `isxdigit`. (Part 2 of 2.)

Figure 21.18 uses the conditional operator (?:) with each function to determine whether the string " is a " or the string " is not a " should be printed in the output for each character tested. For example, line 10 indicates that if '8' is a digit—i.e., if `isdigit` returns a true (nonzero) value—the string "8 is a " is printed. If '8' is not a digit (i.e., if `isdigit` returns 0), the string "8 is not a " is printed.

Figure 21.19 demonstrates functions **islower**, **isupper**, **tolower** and **toupper**. Function `islower` determines whether its argument is a lowercase letter (a–z). Function `isupper` determines whether its argument is an uppercase letter (A–Z). Function `tolower` converts an uppercase letter to lowercase and returns the lowercase letter—if the argument is not an uppercase letter, `tolower` returns the argument value unchanged. Function `toupper` converts a lowercase letter to uppercase and returns the uppercase letter—if the argument is not a lowercase letter, `toupper` returns the argument value unchanged.

```
1   // Fig. 21.19: fig21_19.cpp
2   // Character-handling functions islower, isupper, tolower and toupper.
3   #include <iostream>
4   #include <cctype> // character-handling function prototypes
5   using namespace std;
6
7   int main()
8   {
9      cout << "According to islower:\n"
10        << ( islower( 'p' ) ? "p is a" : "p is not a" )
11        << " lowercase letter\n"
12        << ( islower( 'P' ) ? "P is a" : "P is not a" )
13        << " lowercase letter\n"
14        << ( islower( '5' ) ? "5 is a" : "5 is not a" )
```

Fig. 21.19 | Character-handling functions `islower`, `isupper`, `tolower` and `toupper`. (Part 1 of 2.)

```
15              << " lowercase letter\n"
16              << ( islower( '!' ) ? "! is a" : "! is not a" )
17              << " lowercase letter\n";
18
19      cout << "\nAccording to isupper:\n"
20              << ( isupper( 'D' ) ? "D is an" : "D is not an" )
21              << " uppercase letter\n"
22              << ( isupper( 'd' ) ? "d is an" : "d is not an" )
23              << " uppercase letter\n"
24              << ( isupper( '8' ) ? "8 is an" : "8 is not an" )
25              << " uppercase letter\n"
26              << ( isupper( '$' ) ? "$ is an" : "$ is not an" )
27              << " uppercase letter\n";
28
29      cout << "\nu converted to uppercase is "
30              << static_cast< char >( toupper( 'u' ) )
31              << "\n7 converted to uppercase is "
32              << static_cast< char >( toupper( '7' ) )
33              << "\n$ converted to uppercase is "
34              << static_cast< char >( toupper( '$' ) )
35              << "\nL converted to lowercase is "
36              << static_cast< char >( tolower( 'L' ) ) << endl;
37   } // end main
```

```
According to islower:
p is a lowercase letter
P is not a lowercase letter
5 is not a lowercase letter
! is not a lowercase letter

According to isupper:
D is an uppercase letter
d is not an uppercase letter
8 is not an uppercase letter
$ is not an uppercase letter

u converted to uppercase is U
7 converted to uppercase is 7
$ converted to uppercase is $
L converted to lowercase is l
```

Fig. 21.19 | Character-handling functions `islower`, `isupper`, `tolower` and `toupper`. (Part 2 of 2.)

Figure 21.20 demonstrates functions **isspace**, **iscntrl**, **ispunct**, **isprint** and **isgraph**. Function `isspace` determines whether its argument is a white-space character, such as space (' '), form feed ('\f'), newline ('\n'), carriage return ('\r'), horizontal tab ('\t') or vertical tab ('\v'). Function `iscntrl` determines whether its argument is a control character such as horizontal tab ('\t'), vertical tab ('\v'), form feed ('\f'), alert ('\a'), backspace ('\b'), carriage return ('\r') or newline ('\n'). Function `ispunct` determines whether its argument is a printing character other than a space, digit or letter, such as $, #, (,), [,], {, }, ;, : or %. Function `isprint` determines whether its argument is a character that can be displayed on the screen (including the space character). Function `isgraph` tests for the same characters as `isprint`, but the space character is not included.

```
1   // Fig. 21.20: fig21_20.cpp
2   // Using functions isspace, iscntrl, ispunct, isprint, isgraph.
3   #include <iostream>
4   #include <cctype> // character-handling function prototypes
5   using namespace std;
6
7   int main()
8   {
9      cout << "According to isspace:\nNewline "
10        << ( isspace( '\n' ) ? "is a" : "is not a" )
11        << " whitespace character\nHorizontal tab "
12        << ( isspace( '\t' ) ? "is a" : "is not a" )
13        << " whitespace character\n"
14        << ( isspace( '%' ) ? "% is a" : "% is not a" )
15        << " whitespace character\n";
16
17     cout << "\nAccording to iscntrl:\nNewline "
18        << ( iscntrl( '\n' ) ? "is a" : "is not a" )
19        << " control character\n"
20        << ( iscntrl( '$' ) ? "$ is a" : "$ is not a" )
21        << " control character\n";
22
23     cout << "\nAccording to ispunct:\n"
24        << ( ispunct( ';' ) ? "; is a" : "; is not a" )
25        << " punctuation character\n"
26        << ( ispunct( 'Y' ) ? "Y is a" : "Y is not a" )
27        << " punctuation character\n"
28        << ( ispunct( '#' ) ? "# is a" : "# is not a" )
29        << " punctuation character\n";
30
31     cout << "\nAccording to isprint:\n"
32        << ( isprint( '$' ) ? "$ is a" : "$ is not a" )
33        << " printing character\nAlert "
34        << ( isprint( '\a' ) ? "is a" : "is not a" )
35        << " printing character\nSpace "
36        << ( isprint( ' ' ) ? "is a" : "is not a" )
37        << " printing character\n";
38
39     cout << "\nAccording to isgraph:\n"
40        << ( isgraph( 'Q' ) ? "Q is a" : "Q is not a" )
41        << " printing character other than a space\nSpace "
42        << ( isgraph( ' ' ) ? "is a" : "is not a" )
43        << " printing character other than a space" << endl;
44  } // end main
```

```
According to isspace:
Newline is a whitespace character
Horizontal tab is a whitespace character
% is not a whitespace character
```

Fig. 21.20 | Character-handling functions isspace, iscntrl, ispunct, isprint and isgraph. (Part 1 of 2.)

```
According to iscntrl:
Newline is a control character
$ is not a control character

According to ispunct:
; is a punctuation character
Y is not a punctuation character
# is a punctuation character

According to isprint:
$ is a printing character
Alert is not a printing character
Space is a printing character

According to isgraph:
Q is a printing character other than a space
Space is not a printing character other than a space
```

Fig. 21.20 | Character-handling functions `isspace`, `iscntrl`, `ispunct`, `isprint` and `isgraph`. (Part 2 of 2.)

21.10 Pointer-Based String Manipulation Functions

The string-handling library provides many useful functions for manipulating string data, comparing strings, searching strings for characters and other strings, tokenizing strings (separating strings into logical pieces such as the separate words in a sentence) and determining the length of strings. This section presents some common string-manipulation functions of the string-handling library (from the C++ standard library). The functions are summarized in Fig. 21.21; then each is used in a live-code example. The prototypes for these functions are located in header file `<cstring>`.

Function prototype	Function description
`char *strcpy( char *s1, const char *s2 );`	
	Copies the string s2 into the character array s1. The value of s1 is returned.
`char *strncpy( char *s1, const char *s2, size_t n );`	
	Copies at most n characters of the string s2 into the character array s1. The value of s1 is returned.
`char *strcat( char *s1, const char *s2 );`	
	Appends the string s2 to s1. The first character of s2 overwrites the terminating null character of s1. The value of s1 is returned.
`char *strncat( char *s1, const char *s2, size_t n );`	
	Appends at most n characters of string s2 to string s1. The first character of s2 overwrites the terminating null character of s1. The value of s1 is returned.

Fig. 21.21 | String-manipulation functions of the string-handling library. (Part 1 of 2.)

Function prototype	Function description
`int strcmp( const char *s1, const char *s2 );`	
	Compares the string s1 with the string s2. The function returns a value of zero, less than zero or greater than zero if s1 is equal to, less than or greater than s2, respectively.
`int strncmp( const char *s1, const char *s2, size_t n );`	
	Compares up to n characters of the string s1 with the string s2. The function returns zero, less than zero or greater than zero if the n-character portion of s1 is equal to, less than or greater than the corresponding n-character portion of s2, respectively.
`char *strtok( char *s1, const char *s2 );`	
	A sequence of calls to strtok breaks string s1 into "tokens"—logical pieces such as words in a line of text. The string is broken up based on the characters contained in string s2. For instance, if we were to break the string "this:is:a:string" into tokens based on the character ':', the resulting tokens would be "this", "is", "a" and "string". Function strtok returns only one token at a time—the first call contains s1 as the first argument, and subsequent calls to continue tokenizing the same string contain NULL as the first argument. A pointer to the current token is returned by each call. If there are no more tokens when the function is called, NULL is returned.
`size_t strlen( const char *s );`	
	Determines the length of string s. The number of characters preceding the terminating null character is returned.

Fig. 21.21 | String-manipulation functions of the string-handling library. (Part 2 of 2.)

Several functions in Fig. 21.21 contain parameters with data type `size_t`. This type is defined in the header file `<cstring>` to be an unsigned integral type such as `unsigned int` or `unsigned long`.

Common Programming Error 21.8
Forgetting to include the <cstring> header file when using functions from the string-handling library causes compilation errors.

Copying Strings with *strcpy and strncpy*

Function **strcpy** copies its second argument—a string—into its first argument—a character array that must be large enough to store the string and its terminating null character, (which is also copied). Function **strncpy** is much like strcpy, except that strncpy specifies the number of characters to be copied from the string into the array. Function strncpy does not necessarily copy the terminating null character of its second argument—a terminating null character is written only if the number of characters to be copied is at least one more than the length of the string. For example, if "test" is the second argument, a terminating null character is written only if the third argument to strncpy is at least 5 (four characters in "test" plus one terminating null character). If the third argument is larger than 5, null characters are appended to the array until the total number of characters specified by the third argument is written.

> **Common Programming Error 21.9**
> *When using `strncpy`, the terminating null character of the second argument (a char * string) will not be copied if the number of characters specified by `strncpy`'s third argument is not greater than the second argument's length. In that case, a fatal error may occur if you do not manually terminate the resulting char * string with a null character.*

Figure 21.22 uses `strcpy` (line 13) to copy the entire string in array x into array y and uses `strncpy` (line 19) to copy the first 14 characters of array x into array z. Line 20 appends a null character (`'\0'`) to array z, because the call to `strncpy` in the program does not write a terminating null character. (The third argument is less than the string length of the second argument plus one.)

```cpp
1   // Fig. 21.22: fig21_22.cpp
2   // Using strcpy and strncpy.
3   #include <iostream>
4   #include <cstring> // prototypes for strcpy and strncpy
5   using namespace std;
6
7   int main()
8   {
9      char x[] = "Happy Birthday to You"; // string length 21
10     char y[ 25 ];
11     char z[ 15 ];
12
13     strcpy( y, x ); // copy contents of x into y
14
15     cout << "The string in array x is: " << x
16        << "\nThe string in array y is: " << y << '\n';
17
18     // copy first 14 characters of x into z
19     strncpy( z, x, 14 ); // does not copy null character
20     z[ 14 ] = '\0'; // append '\0' to z's contents
21
22     cout << "The string in array z is: " << z << endl;
23  } // end main
```

```
The string in array x is: Happy Birthday to You
The string in array y is: Happy Birthday to You
The string in array z is: Happy Birthday
```

Fig. 21.22 | `strcpy` and `strncpy`.

Concatenating Strings with `strcat` and `strncat`

Function **strcat** appends its second argument (a string) to its first argument (a character array containing a string). The first character of the second argument replaces the null character (`'\0'`) that terminates the string in the first argument. You must ensure that the array used to store the first string is large enough to store the combination of the first string, the second string and the terminating null character (copied from the second string). Function

strncat appends a specified number of characters from the second string to the first string and appends a terminating null character to the result. The program of Fig. 21.23 demonstrates function strcat (lines 15 and 25) and function strncat (line 20).

```
1    // Fig. 21.23: fig23_23.cpp
2    // Using strcat and strncat.
3    #include <iostream>
4    #include <cstring> // prototypes for strcat and strncat
5    using namespace std;
6
7    int main()
8    {
9       char s1[ 20 ] = "Happy "; // length 6
10      char s2[] = "New Year "; // length 9
11      char s3[ 40 ] = "";
12
13      cout << "s1 = " << s1 << "\ns2 = " << s2;
14
15      strcat( s1, s2 ); // concatenate s2 to s1 (length 15)
16
17      cout << "\n\nAfter strcat(s1, s2):\ns1 = " << s1 << "\ns2 = " << s2;
18
19      // concatenate first 6 characters of s1 to s3
20      strncat( s3, s1, 6 ); // places '\0' after last character
21
22      cout << "\n\nAfter strncat(s3, s1, 6):\ns1 = " << s1
23         << "\ns3 = " << s3;
24
25      strcat( s3, s1 ); // concatenate s1 to s3
26      cout << "\n\nAfter strcat(s3, s1):\ns1 = " << s1
27         << "\ns3 = " << s3 << endl;
28   } // end main
```

```
s1 = Happy
s2 = New Year

After strcat(s1, s2):
s1 = Happy New Year
s2 = New Year

After strncat(s3, s1, 6):
s1 = Happy New Year
s3 = Happy

After strcat(s3, s1):
s1 = Happy New Year
s3 = Happy Happy New Year
```

Fig. 21.23 | strcat and strncat.

*Comparing Strings with **strcmp** and **strncmp***

Figure 21.24 compares three strings using strcmp (lines 15–17) and strncmp (lines 20–22). Function strcmp compares its first string argument with its second string argument character by character. The function returns zero if the strings are equal, a negative value if the first string is less than the second string and a positive value if the first string is greater than the second string. Function `strncmp` is equivalent to `strcmp`, except that `strncmp` compares up to a specified number of characters. Function `strncmp` stops comparing characters if it reaches the null character in one of its string arguments. The program prints the integer value returned by each function call.

Common Programming Error 21.10

Assuming that `strcmp` and `strncmp` return one (a true value) when their arguments are equal is a logic error. Both functions return zero (C++'s false value) for equality. Therefore, when testing two strings for equality, the result of the `strcmp` or `strncmp` function should be compared with zero to determine whether the strings are equal.

```cpp
1   // Fig. 21.24: fig21_24.cpp
2   // Using strcmp and strncmp.
3   #include <iostream>
4   #include <iomanip>
5   #include <cstring> // prototypes for strcmp and strncmp
6   using namespace std;
7
8   int main()
9   {
10     char *s1 = "Happy New Year";
11     char *s2 = "Happy New Year";
12     char *s3 = "Happy Holidays";
13
14     cout << "s1 = " << s1 << "\ns2 = " << s2 << "\ns3 = " << s3
15        << "\n\nstrcmp(s1, s2) = " << setw( 2 ) << strcmp( s1, s2 )
16        << "\nstrcmp(s1, s3) = " << setw( 2 ) << strcmp( s1, s3 )
17        << "\nstrcmp(s3, s1) = " << setw( 2 ) << strcmp( s3, s1 );
18
19     cout << "\n\nstrncmp(s1, s3, 6) = " << setw( 2 )
20        << strncmp( s1, s3, 6 ) << "\nstrncmp(s1, s3, 7) = " << setw( 2 )
21        << strncmp( s1, s3, 7 ) << "\nstrncmp(s3, s1, 7) = " << setw( 2 )
22        << strncmp( s3, s1, 7 ) << endl;
23   } // end main
```

```
s1 = Happy New Year
s2 = Happy New Year
s3 = Happy Holidays

strcmp(s1, s2) =  0
strcmp(s1, s3) =  1
strcmp(s3, s1) = -1

strncmp(s1, s3, 6) =  0
strncmp(s1, s3, 7) =  1
strncmp(s3, s1, 7) = -1
```

Fig. 21.24 | `strcmp` and `strncmp`.

To understand what it means for one string to be "greater than" or "less than" another, consider the process of alphabetizing last names. You'd, no doubt, place "Jones" before "Smith," because the first letter of "Jones" comes before the first letter of "Smith" in the alphabet. But the alphabet is more than just a list of 26 letters—it's an *ordered* list of characters. Each letter occurs in a specific position within the list. "Z" is more than just a letter of the alphabet; "Z" is specifically the 26th letter of the alphabet.

How does the computer know that one letter comes before another? All characters are represented inside the computer as numeric codes; when the computer compares two strings, it actually compares the numeric codes of the characters in the strings.

In an effort to standardize character representations, most computer manufacturers have designed their machines to utilize one of two popular coding schemes—ASCII or EBCDIC. Recall that ASCII stands for "American Standard Code for Information Interchange." EBCDIC stands for "Extended Binary Coded Decimal Interchange Code." There are other coding schemes as well.

ASCII and EBCDIC are called character codes, or character sets. Most readers of this book will be using desktop or notebook computers that use the ASCII character set. IBM mainframe computers use the EBCDIC character set. As Internet and World Wide Web usage becomes pervasive, the newer Unicode character set is growing in popularity (www.unicode.org). String and character manipulations actually involve the manipulation of the appropriate numeric codes and not the characters themselves. This explains the interchangeability of characters and small integers in C++. Since it's meaningful to say that one numeric code is greater than, less than or equal to another numeric code, it becomes possible to relate various characters or strings to one another by referring to the character codes. Appendix B contains the ASCII character codes.

Portability Tip 21.6
The internal numeric codes used to represent characters may be different on different computers that use different character sets.

Portability Tip 21.7
Do not explicitly test for ASCII codes, as in if (rating == 65); rather, use the corresponding character constant, as in if (rating == 'A').

[*Note:* With some compilers, functions strcmp and strncmp always return -1, 0 or 1, as in the sample output of Fig. 21.24. With other compilers, these functions return 0 or the difference between the numeric codes of the first characters that differ in the strings being compared. For example, when s1 and s3 are compared, the first characters that differ between them are the first character of the second word in each string—N (numeric code 78) in s1 and H (numeric code 72) in s3, respectively. In this case, the return value will be 6 (or -6 if s3 is compared to s1).]

Tokenizing a String with strtok

Function **strtok** breaks a string into a series of **tokens**. A token is a sequence of characters separated by **delimiting characters** (usually spaces or punctuation marks). For example, in a line of text, each word can be considered a token, and the spaces separating the words can be considered delimiters.

Multiple calls to strtok are required to break a string into tokens (assuming that the string contains more than one token). The first call to strtok contains two arguments, a string to be tokenized and a string containing characters that separate the tokens (i.e., delimiters). Line 16 in Fig. 21.25 assigns to `tokenPtr` a pointer to the first token in `sentence`. The second argument, `" "`, indicates that tokens in `sentence` are separated by spaces. Function `strtok` searches for the first character in `sentence` that is not a delimiting character (space). This begins the first token. The function then finds the next delimiting character in the string and replaces it with a null (`'\0'`) character. This terminates the current token. Function `strtok` saves (in a `static` variable) a pointer to the next character following the token in `sentence` and returns a pointer to the current token.

```cpp
1   // Fig. 21.25: fig21_25.cpp
2   // Using strtok to tokenize a string.
3   #include <iostream>
4   #include <cstring> // prototype for strtok
5   using namespace std;
6
7   int main()
8   {
9      char sentence[] = "This is a sentence with 7 tokens";
10     char *tokenPtr;
11
12     cout << "The string to be tokenized is:\n" << sentence
13        << "\n\nThe tokens are:\n\n";
14
15     // begin tokenization of sentence
16     tokenPtr = strtok( sentence, " " );
17
18     // continue tokenizing sentence until tokenPtr becomes NULL
19     while ( tokenPtr != NULL )
20     {
21        cout << tokenPtr << '\n';
22        tokenPtr = strtok( NULL, " " ); // get next token
23     } // end while
24
25     cout << "\nAfter strtok, sentence = " << sentence << endl;
26  } // end main
```

```
The string to be tokenized is:
This is a sentence with 7 tokens

The tokens are:

This
is
a
sentence
with
7
tokens

After strtok, sentence = This
```

Fig. 21.25 | Using `strtok` to tokenize a string.

Subsequent calls to `strtok` to continue tokenizing `sentence` contain NULL as the first argument (line 22). The NULL argument indicates that the call to `strtok` should continue tokenizing from the location in sentence saved by the last call to strtok. Function strtok maintains this saved information in a manner that is not visible to you. If no tokens remain when strtok is called, strtok returns NULL. The program of Fig. 21.25 uses strtok to tokenize the string "This is a sentence with 7 tokens". The program prints each token on a separate line. Line 25 outputs sentence after tokenization. Note that *strtok modifies the input string*; therefore, a copy of the string should be made if the program requires the original after the calls to strtok. When sentence is output after tokenization, only the word "This" prints, because strtok replaced each blank in sentence with a null character ('\0') during the tokenization process.

Common Programming Error 21.11

Not realizing that strtok *modifies the string being tokenized, then attempting to use that string as if it were the original unmodified string is a logic error.*

Determining String Lengths

Function **strlen** takes a string as an argument and returns the number of characters in the string—the terminating null character is not included in the length. The length is also the index of the null character. The program of Fig. 21.26 demonstrates function strlen.

```cpp
 1  // Fig. 21.26: fig21_26.cpp
 2  // Using strlen.
 3  #include <iostream>
 4  #include <cstring> // prototype for strlen
 5  using namespace std;
 6
 7  int main()
 8  {
 9     char *string1 = "abcdefghijklmnopqrstuvwxyz";
10     char *string2 = "four";
11     char *string3 = "Boston";
12
13     cout << "The length of \"" << string1 << "\" is " << strlen( string1 )
14        << "\nThe length of \"" << string2 << "\" is " << strlen( string2 )
15        << "\nThe length of \"" << string3 << "\" is " << strlen( string3 )
16        << endl;
17  } // end main
```

```
The length of "abcdefghijklmnopqrstuvwxyz" is 26
The length of "four" is 4
The length of "Boston" is 6
```

Fig. 21.26 | strlen returns the length of a char * string.

21.11 Pointer-Based String-Conversion Functions

In Section 21.10, we discussed several of C++'s most popular pointer-based string-manipulation functions. In the next several sections, we cover the remaining functions, including functions for converting strings to numeric values, functions for searching strings and functions for manipulating, comparing and searching blocks of memory.

This section presents the pointer-based **string-conversion functions** from the **general-utilities library `<cstdlib>`**. These functions convert pointer-based strings of characters to integer and floating-point values. In new code development, C++ programmers typically use the string stream processing capabilities introduced in Chapter 18 to perform such conversions. Figure 21.27 summarizes the pointer-based string-conversion functions. Note the use of const to declare variable nPtr in the function headers (read from right to left as "nPtr is a pointer to a character constant"). When using functions from the general-utilities library, include the `<cstdlib>` header file.

Prototype	Description
`double atof( const char *nPtr )`	Converts the string nPtr to double. If the string cannot be converted, 0 is returned.
`int atoi( const char *nPtr )`	Converts the string nPtr to int. If the string cannot be converted, 0 is returned.
`long atol( const char *nPtr )`	Converts the string nPtr to long int. If the string cannot be converted, 0 is returned.
`double strtod( const char *nPtr, char **endPtr )`	Converts the string nPtr to double. endPtr is the address of a pointer to the rest of the string after the double. If the string cannot be converted, 0 is returned.
`long strtol( const char *nPtr, char **endPtr, int base )`	Converts the string nPtr to long. endPtr is the address of a pointer to the rest of the string after the long. If the string cannot be converted, 0 is returned. The base parameter indicates the base of the number to convert (e.g., 8 for octal, 10 for decimal or 16 for hexadecimal). The default is decimal.
`unsigned long strtoul( const char *nPtr, char **endPtr, int base )`	Converts the string nPtr to unsigned long. endPtr is the address of a pointer to the rest of the string after the unsigned long. If the string cannot be converted, 0 is returned. The base parameter indicates the base of the number to convert (e.g., 8 for octal, 10 for decimal or 16 for hexadecimal). The default is decimal.

Fig. 21.27 | Pointer-based string-conversion functions of the general-utilities library.

Function **atof** (Fig. 21.28, line 9) converts its argument—a string that represents a floating-point number—to a double value. The function returns the double value. If the string cannot be converted—for example, if the first character of the string is not a digit—function atof returns zero.

Function **atoi** (Fig. 21.29, line 9) converts its argument—a string of digits that represents an integer—to an int value. The function returns the int value. If the string cannot be converted, function atoi returns zero.

```
 I   // Fig. 21.28: fig21_28.cpp
 2   // Using atof.
 3   #include <iostream>
 4   #include <cstdlib> // atof prototype
 5   using namespace std;
 6
 7   int main()
 8   {
 9      double d = atof( "99.0" ); // convert string to double
10
11      cout << "The string \"99.0\" converted to double is " << d
12         << "\nThe converted value divided by 2 is " << d / 2.0 << endl;
13   } // end main
```

```
The string "99.0" converted to double is 99
The converted value divided by 2 is 49.5
```

Fig. 21.28 | String-conversion function atof.

```
 I   // Fig. 21.29: Fig21_29.cpp
 2   // Using atoi.
 3   #include <iostream>
 4   #include <cstdlib> // atoi prototype
 5   using namespace std;
 6
 7   int main()
 8   {
 9      int i = atoi( "2593" ); // convert string to int
10
11      cout << "The string \"2593\" converted to int is " << i
12         << "\nThe converted value minus 593 is " << i - 593 << endl;
13   } // end main
```

```
The string "2593" converted to int is 2593
The converted value minus 593 is 2000
```

Fig. 21.29 | String-conversion function atoi.

Function **atol** (Fig. 21.30, line 9) converts its argument—a string of digits representing a long integer—to a long value. The function returns the long value. If the string cannot be converted, function atol returns zero. If int and long are both stored in four bytes, function atoi and function atol work identically.

```
 I   // Fig. 21.30: fig21_30.cpp
 2   // Using atol.
 3   #include <iostream>
 4   #include <cstdlib> // atol prototype
 5   using namespace std;
```

Fig. 21.30 | String-conversion function atol. (Part 1 of 2.)

```
6
7   int main()
8   {
9      long x = atol( "1000000" ); // convert string to long
10
11     cout << "The string \"1000000\" converted to long is " << x
12        << "\nThe converted value divided by 2 is " << x / 2 << endl;
13  } // end main
```

```
The string "1000000" converted to long int is 1000000
The converted value divided by 2 is 500000
```

Fig. 21.30 | String-conversion function `atol`. (Part 2 of 2.)

Function **strtod** (Fig. 21.31) converts a sequence of characters representing a floating-point value to `double`. Function `strtod` receives two arguments—a string (`char *`) and the address of a `char *` pointer (i.e., a `char **`). The string contains the character sequence to be converted to `double`. The second argument enables `strtod` to modify a `char *` pointer in the calling function, such that the pointer points to the location of the first character after the converted portion of the string. Line 13 indicates that d is assigned the `double` value converted from `string` and that `stringPtr` is assigned the location of the first character after the converted value (51.2) in `string`.

```
1   // Fig. 21.31: fig21_31.cpp
2   // Using strtod.
3   #include <iostream>
4   #include <cstdlib> // strtod prototype
5   using namespace std;
6
7   int main()
8   {
9      double d;
10     const char *string1 = "51.2% are admitted";
11     char *stringPtr;
12
13     d = strtod( string1, &stringPtr ); // convert characters to double
14
15     cout << "The string \"" << string1
16        << "\" is converted to the\ndouble value " << d
17        << " and the string \"" << stringPtr << "\"" << endl;
18  } // end main
```

```
The string "51.2% are admitted" is converted to the
double value 51.2 and the string "% are admitted"
```

Fig. 21.31 | String-conversion function `strtod`.

Function **strtol** (Fig. 21.32) converts to `long` a sequence of characters representing an integer. The function receives a string (`char *`), the address of a `char *` pointer and an integer. The string contains the character sequence to convert. The second argument is assigned the location of the first character after the converted portion of the string. The integer specifies the *base* of the value being converted. Line 13 indicates that x is assigned the long value converted from string and that remainderPtr is assigned the location of the first character after the converted value (-1234567) in string1. Using a null pointer for the second argument causes the remainder of the string to be ignored. The third argument, 0, indicates that the value to be converted can be in octal (base 8), decimal (base 10) or hexadecimal (base 16). This is determined by the initial characters in the string—0 indicates an octal number, 0x indicates hexadecimal and a number from 1–9 indicates decimal.

```cpp
1   // Fig. 21.32: fig21_32.cpp
2   // Using strtol.
3   #include <iostream>
4   #include <cstdlib> // strtol prototype
5   using namespace std;
6
7   int main()
8   {
9      long x;
10     const char *string1 = "-1234567abc";
11     char *remainderPtr;
12
13     x = strtol( string1, &remainderPtr, 0 ); // convert characters to long
14
15     cout << "The original string is \"" << string1
16        << "\"\nThe converted value is " << x
17        << "\"\nThe remainder of the original string is \"" << remainderPtr
18        << "\"\nThe converted value plus 567 is " << x + 567 << endl;
19  } // end main
```

```
The original string is "-1234567abc"
The converted value is -1234567
The remainder of the original string is "abc"
The converted value plus 567 is -1234000
```

Fig. 21.32 | String-conversion function strtol.

In a call to function strtol, the base can be specified as zero or as any value between 2 and 36. (See Appendix D for a detailed explanation of the octal, decimal, hexadecimal and binary number systems.) Numeric representations of integers from base 11 to base 36 use the characters A–Z to represent the values 10 to 35. For example, hexadecimal values can consist of the digits 0–9 and the characters A–F. A base-11 integer can consist of the digits 0–9 and the character A. A base-24 integer can consist of the digits 0–9 and the characters A–N. A base-36 integer can consist of the digits 0–9 and the characters A–Z. [*Note:* The case of the letter used is ignored.]

Function **strtoul** (Fig. 21.33) converts to unsigned long a sequence of characters representing an unsigned long integer. The function works identically to strtol. Line 14 indicates that x is assigned the unsigned long value converted from string and that remainderPtr is assigned the location of the first character after the converted value (1234567) in string1. The third argument, 0, indicates that the value to be converted can be in octal, decimal or hexadecimal format, depending on the initial characters.

```
1   // Fig. 21.33: fig21_33.cpp
2   // Using strtoul.
3   #include <iostream>
4   #include <cstdlib> // strtoul prototype
5   using namespace std;
6
7   int main()
8   {
9      unsigned long x;
10     const char *string1 = "1234567abc";
11     char *remainderPtr;
12
13     // convert a sequence of characters to unsigned long
14     x = strtoul( string1, &remainderPtr, 0 );
15
16     cout << "The original string is \"" << string1
17        << "\"\nThe converted value is " << x
18        << "\"\nThe remainder of the original string is \"" << remainderPtr
19        << "\"\nThe converted value minus 567 is " << x - 567 << endl;
20  } // end main
```

```
The original string is "1234567abc"
The converted value is 1234567
The remainder of the original string is "abc"
The converted value minus 567 is 1234000
```

Fig. 21.33 | String-conversion function `strtoul`.

21.12 Search Functions of the Pointer-Based String-Handling Library

This section presents the functions of the string-handling library used to search strings for characters and other strings. The functions are summarized in Fig. 21.34. Functions `strcspn` and `strspn` specify return type `size_t`. Type `size_t` is a type defined by the standard as the integral type of the value returned by operator `sizeof`.

Prototype	Description
`char *strchr( const char *s, int c )`	
	Locates the first occurrence of character c in string s. If c is found, a pointer to c in s is returned. Otherwise, a null pointer is returned.
`char *strrchr( const char *s, int c )`	
	Searches from the end of string s and locates the last occurrence of character c in string s. If c is found, a pointer to c in string s is returned. Otherwise, a null pointer is returned.

Fig. 21.34 | Search functions of the pointer-based string-handling library. (Part 1 of 2.)

Prototype	Description

`size_t strspn( const char *s1, const char *s2 )`

> Determines and returns the length of the initial segment of string s1 consisting only of characters contained in string s2.

`char *strpbrk( const char *s1, const char *s2 )`

> Locates the first occurrence in string s1 of any character in string s2. If a character from string s2 is found, a pointer to the character in string s1 is returned. Otherwise, a null pointer is returned.

`size_t strcspn( const char *s1, const char *s2 )`

> Determines and returns the length of the initial segment of string s1 consisting of characters not contained in string s2.

`char *strstr( const char *s1, const char *s2 )`

> Locates the first occurrence in string s1 of string s2. If the string is found, a pointer to the string in s1 is returned. Otherwise, a null pointer is returned.

Fig. 21.34 | Search functions of the pointer-based string-handling library. (Part 2 of 2.)

Function **strchr** searches for the first occurrence of a character in a string. If the character is found, strchr returns a pointer to the character in the string; otherwise, strchr returns a null pointer. The program of Fig. 21.35 uses strchr (lines 14 and 22) to search for the first occurrences of 'a' and 'z' in the string "This is a test".

```cpp
1   // Fig. 21.35: fig21_35.cpp
2   // Using strchr.
3   #include <iostream>
4   #include <cstring> // strchr prototype
5   using namespace std;
6
7   int main()
8   {
9      const char *string1 = "This is a test";
10     char character1 = 'a';
11     char character2 = 'z';
12
13     // search for character1 in string1
14     if ( strchr( string1, character1 ) != NULL )
15        cout << '\'' << character1 << "' was found in \""
16           << string1 << "\".\n";
17     else
18        cout << '\'' << character1 << "' was not found in \""
19           << string1 << "\".\n";
20
21     // search for character2 in string1
22     if ( strchr( string1, character2 ) != NULL )
23        cout << '\'' << character2 << "' was found in \""
24           << string1 << "\".\n";
```

Fig. 21.35 | String-search function strchr. (Part 1 of 2.)

```
25      else
26          cout << '\'' << character2 << "' was not found in \""
27              << string1 << "\"." << endl;
28  } // end main
```

```
'a' was found in "This is a test".
'z' was not found in "This is a test".
```

Fig. 21.35 | String-search function strchr. (Part 2 of 2.)

Function **strcspn** (Fig. 21.36, line 15) determines the length of the initial part of the string in its first argument that does not contain any characters from the string in its second argument. The function returns the length of the segment.

```
1   // Fig. 21.36: fig21_36.cpp
2   // Using strcspn.
3   #include <iostream>
4   #include <cstring> // strcspn prototype
5   using namespace std;
6
7   int main()
8   {
9      const char *string1 = "The value is 3.14159";
10     const char *string2 = "1234567890";
11
12     cout << "string1 = " << string1 << "\nstring2 = " << string2
13         << "\n\nThe length of the initial segment of string1"
14         << "\ncontaining no characters from string2 = "
15         << strcspn( string1, string2 ) << endl;
16  } // end main
```

```
string1 = The value is 3.14159
string2 = 1234567890

The length of the initial segment of string1
containing no characters from string2 = 13
```

Fig. 21.36 | String-search function strcspn.

Function **strpbrk** searches for the first occurrence in its first string argument of any character in its second string argument. If a character from the second argument is found, strpbrk returns a pointer to the character in the first argument; otherwise, strpbrk returns a null pointer. Line 13 of Fig. 21.37 locates the first occurrence in string1 of any character from string2.

```
1   // Fig. 21.37: fig21_37.cpp
2   // Using strpbrk.
3   #include <iostream>
```

Fig. 21.37 | String-search function strpbrk. (Part 1 of 2.)

```
 4   #include <cstring> // strpbrk prototype
 5   using namespace std;
 6
 7   int main()
 8   {
 9      const char *string1 = "This is a test";
10      const char *string2 = "beware";
11
12      cout << "Of the characters in \"" << string2 << "\"\n'"
13         << *strpbrk( string1, string2 ) << "\' is the first character "
14         << "to appear in\n\"" << string1 << '\"' << endl;
15   } // end main
```

```
Of the characters in "beware"
'a' is the first character to appear in
"This is a test"
```

Fig. 21.37 | String-search function `strpbrk`. (Part 2 of 2.)

Function **strrchr** searches for the last occurrence of the specified character in a string. If the character is found, strrchr returns a pointer to the character in the string; otherwise, strrchr returns 0. Line 15 of Fig. 21.38 searches for the last occurrence of the character 'z' in the string "A zoo has many animals including zebras".

```
 1   // Fig. 21.38: fig21_38.cpp
 2   // Using strrchr.
 3   #include <iostream>
 4   #include <cstring> // strrchr prototype
 5   using namespace std;
 6
 7   int main()
 8   {
 9      const char *string1 = "A zoo has many animals including zebras";
10      char c = 'z';
11
12      cout << "string1 = " << string1 << "\n" << endl;
13      cout << "The remainder of string1 beginning with the\n"
14         << "last occurrence of character '"
15         << c << "' is: \"" << strrchr( string1, c ) << '\"' << endl;
16   } // end main
```

```
string1 = A zoo has many animals including zebras

The remainder of string1 beginning with the
last occurrence of character 'z' is: "zebras"
```

Fig. 21.38 | String-search function `strrchr`.

Function **strspn** (Fig. 21.39, line 15) determines the length of the initial part of the string in its first argument that contains only characters from the string in its second argument. The function returns the length of the segment.

```
 1   // Fig. 21.39: fig21_39.cpp
 2   // Using strspn.
 3   #include <iostream>
 4   #include <cstring> // strspn prototype
 5   using namespace std;
 6
 7   int main()
 8   {
 9      const char *string1 = "The value is 3.14159";
10      const char *string2 = "aehils Tuv";
11
12      cout << "string1 = " << string1 << "\nstring2 = " << string2
13         << "\n\nThe length of the initial segment of string1\n"
14         << "containing only characters from string2 = "
15         << strspn( string1, string2 ) << endl;
16   } // end main
```

```
string1 = The value is 3.14159
string2 = aehils Tuv

The length of the initial segment of string1
containing only characters from string2 = 13
```

Fig. 21.39 | String-search function `strspn`.

Function **strstr** searches for the first occurrence of its second string argument in its first string argument. If the second string is found in the first string, a pointer to the location of the string in the first argument is returned; otherwise, it returns 0. Line 15 of Fig. 21.40 uses `strstr` to find the string "def" in the string "abcdefabcdef".

```
 1   // Fig. 21.40: fig21_40.cpp
 2   // Using strstr.
 3   #include <iostream>
 4   #include <cstring> // strstr prototype
 5   using namespace std;
 6
 7   int main()
 8   {
 9      const char *string1 = "abcdefabcdef";
10      const char *string2 = "def";
11
12      cout << "string1 = " << string1 << "\nstring2 = " << string2
13         << "\n\nThe remainder of string1 beginning with the\n"
14         << "first occurrence of string2 is: "
15         << strstr( string1, string2 ) << endl;
16   } // end main
```

```
string1 = abcdefabcdef
string2 = def

The remainder of string1 beginning with the
first occurrence of string2 is: defabcdef
```

Fig. 21.40 | String-search function `strstr`.

21.13 Memory Functions of the Pointer-Based String-Handling Library

The string-handling library functions presented in this section facilitate manipulating, comparing and searching blocks of memory. The functions treat blocks of memory as arrays of bytes. These functions can manipulate any block of data. Figure 21.41 summarizes the memory functions of the string-handling library. In the function discussions, "object" refers to a block of data. [*Note:* The string-processing functions in prior sections operate on null-terminated strings. The ones in this section operate on arrays of bytes. The null-character value (i.e., a byte containing 0) has no significance with the functions in this section.]

Prototype	Description
`void *memcpy( void *s1, const void *s2, size_t n )`	
	Copies n characters from the object pointed to by s2 into the object pointed to by s1. A pointer to the resulting object is returned. The area from which characters are copied is not allowed to overlap the area to which characters are copied.
`void *memmove( void *s1, const void *s2, size_t n )`	
	Copies n characters from the object pointed to by s2 into the object pointed to by s1. The copy is performed as if the characters were first copied from the object pointed to by s2 into a temporary array, then copied from the temporary array into the object pointed to by s1. A pointer to the resulting object is returned. The area from which characters are copied is allowed to overlap the area to which characters are copied.
`int memcmp( const void *s1, const void *s2, size_t n )`	
	Compares the first n characters of the objects pointed to by s1 and s2. The function returns 0, less than 0, or greater than 0 if s1 is equal to, less than or greater than s2, respectively.
`void *memchr( const void *s, int c, size_t n )`	
	Locates the first occurrence of c (converted to unsigned char) in the first n characters of the object pointed to by s. If c is found, a pointer to c in the object is returned. Otherwise, 0 is returned.
`void *memset( void *s, int c, size_t n )`	
	Copies c (converted to unsigned char) into the first n characters of the object pointed to by s. A pointer to the result is returned.

Fig. 21.41 | Memory functions of the string-handling library.

The pointer parameters to these functions are declared void *. In Chapter 8, we saw that a pointer to any data type can be assigned directly to a pointer of type void *. For this reason, these functions can receive pointers to any data type. Remember that a pointer of type void * cannot be assigned directly to a pointer of any other data type. Because a void * pointer cannot be dereferenced, each function receives a size argument that specifies the number of characters (bytes) the function will process. For simplicity, the examples in this section manipulate character arrays (blocks of characters).

Function **memcpy** copies a specified number of characters (bytes) from the object pointed to by its second argument into the object pointed to by its first argument. The function can receive a pointer to any type of object. The result of this function is undefined if the two objects overlap in memory (i.e., are parts of the same object). The program of Fig. 21.42 uses memcpy (line 14) to copy the string in array s2 to array s1.

```cpp
1   // Fig. 21.42: fig21_36.cpp
2   // Using memcpy.
3   #include <iostream>
4   #include <cstring> // memcpy prototype
5   using namespace std;
6
7   int main()
8   {
9      char s1[ 17 ];
10
11     // 17 total characters (includes terminating null)
12     char s2[] = "Copy this string";
13
14     memcpy( s1, s2, 17 ); // copy 17 characters from s2 to s1
15
16     cout << "After s2 is copied into s1 with memcpy,\n"
17        << "s1 contains \"" << s1 << '\"' << endl;
18  } // end main
```

```
After s2 is copied into s1 with memcpy,
s1 contains "Copy this string"
```

Fig. 21.42 | Memory-handling function `memcpy`.

Function **memmove**, like memcpy, copies a specified number of bytes from the object pointed to by its second argument into the object pointed to by its first argument. Copying is performed as if the bytes were copied from the second argument to a temporary array of characters, then copied from the temporary array to the first argument. This allows characters from one part of a string to be copied into another part of the same string.

 Common Programming Error 21.12
String-manipulation functions other than memmove that copy characters have undefined results when copying takes place between parts of the same string.

The program in Fig. 21.43 uses memmove (line 13) to copy the last 10 bytes of array x into the first 10 bytes of array x.

```cpp
1   // Fig. 21.43: fig21_37.cpp
2   // Using memmove.
3   #include <iostream>
4   #include <cstring> // memmove prototype
5   using namespace std;
```

Fig. 21.43 | Memory-handling function `memmove`. (Part 1 of 2.)

```
 6
 7    int main()
 8    {
 9       char x[] = "Home Sweet Home";
10
11       cout << "The string in array x before memmove is: " << x;
12       cout << "\nThe string in array x after memmove is:  "
13          << static_cast< char * >( memmove( x, &x[ 5 ], 10 ) ) << endl;
14    } // end main
```

```
The string in array x before memmove is: Home Sweet Home
The string in array x after memmove is:  Sweet Home Home
```

Fig. 21.43 | Memory-handling function memmove. (Part 2 of 2.)

Function **memcmp** (Fig. 21.44, lines 14–16) compares the specified number of characters of its first argument with the corresponding characters of its second argument. The function returns a value greater than zero if the first argument is greater than the second argument, zero if the arguments are equal, and a value less than zero if the first argument is less than the second argument. [*Note:* With some compilers, function memcmp returns –1, 0 or 1, as in the sample output of Fig. 21.44. With other compilers, this function returns 0 or the difference between the numeric codes of the first characters that differ in the strings being compared. For example, when s1 and s2 are compared, the first character that differs between them is the fifth character of each string—E (numeric code 69) for s1 and X (numeric code 72) for s2. In this case, the return value will be 19 (or –19 when s2 is compared to s1).]

```
 1    // Fig. 21.44: fig21_38.cpp
 2    // Using memcmp.
 3    #include <iostream>
 4    #include <iomanip>
 5    #include <cstring> // memcmp prototype
 6    using namespace std;
 7
 8    int main()
 9    {
10       char s1[] = "ABCDEFG";
11       char s2[] = "ABCDXYZ";
12
13       cout << "s1 = " << s1 << "\ns2 = " << s2 << endl
14          << "\nmemcmp(s1, s2, 4) = " << setw( 3 ) << memcmp( s1, s2, 4 )
15          << "\nmemcmp(s1, s2, 7) = " << setw( 3 ) << memcmp( s1, s2, 7 )
16          << "\nmemcmp(s2, s1, 7) = " << setw( 3 ) << memcmp( s2, s1, 7 )
17          << endl;
18    } // end main
```

```
s1 = ABCDEFG
s2 = ABCDXYZ
```

Fig. 21.44 | Memory-handling function memcmp. (Part 1 of 2.)

```
memcmp(s1, s2, 4) =   0
memcmp(s1, s2, 7) =  -1
memcmp(s2, s1, 7) =   1
```

Fig. 21.44 | Memory-handling function `memcmp`. (Part 2 of 2.)

Function **memchr** searches for the first occurrence of a byte, represented as `unsigned char`, in the specified number of bytes of an object. If the byte is found in the object, a pointer to it is returned; otherwise, the function returns a null pointer. Line 13 of Fig. 21.45 searches for the character (byte) `'r'` in the string `"This is a string"`.

```
1    // Fig. 21.45: fig21_39.cpp
2    // Using memchr.
3    #include <iostream>
4    #include <cstring> // memchr prototype
5    using namespace std;
6
7    int main()
8    {
9       char s[] = "This is a string";
10
11      cout << "s = " << s << "\n" << endl;
12      cout << "The remainder of s after character 'r' is found is \""
13         << static_cast< char * >( memchr( s, 'r', 16 ) ) << '\"' << endl;
14   } // end main
```

```
s = This is a string

The remainder of s after character 'r' is found is "ring"
```

Fig. 21.45 | Memory-handling function `memchr`.

Function **memset** copies the value of the byte in its second argument into a specified number of bytes of the object pointed to by its first argument. Line 13 in Fig. 21.46 uses memset to copy `'b'` into the first 7 bytes of string1.

```
1    // Fig. 21.46: fig21_40.cpp
2    // Using memset.
3    #include <iostream>
4    #include <cstring> // memset prototype
5    using namespace std;
6
7    int main()
8    {
9       char string1[ 15 ] = "BBBBBBBBBBBBBB";
10
11      cout << "string1 = " << string1 << endl;
12      cout << "string1 after memset = "
13         << static_cast< char * >( memset( string1, 'b', 7 ) ) << endl;
14   } // end main
```

Fig. 21.46 | Memory-handling function `memset`. (Part 1 of 2.)

```
string1 = BBBBBBBBBBBBBB
string1 after memset = bbbbbbbBBBBBBB
```

Fig. 21.46 | Memory-handling function `memset`. (Part 2 of 2.)

21.14 Wrap-Up

This chapter introduced `struct` definitions, initializing `struct`s and using them with functions. We discussed `typedef`, using it to create aliases to help promote portability. We also introduced bitwise operators to manipulate data and bit fields for storing data compactly. You also learned about the string-conversion functions in `<cstlib>` and the string-processing functions in `<cstring>`. In the next chapter, we continue our discussion of data structures by discussing containers—data structures defined in the C++ Standard Template Library. We also present the many algorithms defined in the STL as well.

Summary

Section 21.2 Structure Definitions
- Structures are collections of related variables (or aggregates) under one name.
- Structures can contain variables of different data types.
- Keyword `struct` begins every structure definition. Between the braces of the structure definition are the structure member declarations.
- Members of the same structure must have unique names.
- A structure definition creates a new data type that can be used to declare variables.

Section 21.3 Initializing Structures
- A structure can be initialized with an initializer list by following the variable in the declaration with an equal sign and a comma-separated list of initializers enclosed in braces. If there are fewer initializers in the list than members in the structure, the remaining members are initialized to zero (or a null pointer for pointer members).
- Entire structure variables may be assigned to structure variables of the same type.
- A structure variable may be initialized with a structure variable of the same type.

Section 21.4 Using Structures with Functions
- Structure variables and individual structure members are passed to functions by value.
- To pass a structure by reference, pass the address of the structure variable or a reference to the structure variable. An array of structures is passed by reference. To pass an array by value, create a structure with the array as a member.

Section 21.5 `typedef`
- Creating a new type name with `typedef` does not create a new type; it creates a name that is synonymous with a type defined previously.

Section 21.7 Bitwise Operators
- The bitwise AND operator (`&`) takes two integral operands. A bit in the result is set to one if the corresponding bits in each of the operands are one.

- Masks are used with bitwise AND to hide some bits while preserving others.
- The bitwise inclusive-OR operator (|) takes two operands. A bit in the result is set to one if the corresponding bit in either operand is set to one.
- Each of the bitwise operators (except complement) has a corresponding assignment operator.
- The bitwise exclusive-OR operator (∧) takes two operands. A bit in the result is set to one if exactly one of the corresponding bits in the two operands is set to one.
- The left-shift operator (<<) shifts the bits of its left operand left by the number of bits specified by its right operand. Bits vacated to the right are replaced with zeros.
- The right-shift operator (>>) shifts the bits of its left operand right by the number of bits specified in its right operand. Right shifting an unsigned integer causes bits vacated at the left to be replaced by zeros. Vacated bits in signed integers can be replaced with zeros or ones.
- The bitwise complement operator (~) takes one operand and inverts its bits—this produces the one's complement of the operand.

Section 21.8 Bit Fields
- Bit fields reduce storage use by storing data in the minimum number of bits required. Bit-field members must be declared as `int` or `unsigned`.
- A bit field is declared by following an `unsigned` or `int` member name with a colon and the width of the bit field.
- The bit-field width must be an integer constant.
- If a bit field is specified without a name, the field is used as padding in the structure.
- An unnamed bit field with width 0 aligns the next bit field on a new machine-word boundary.

Section 21.9 Character-Handling Library
- Function `islower` determines whether its argument is a lowercase letter (a–z). Function `isupper` determines whether its argument is an uppercase letter (A–Z).
- Function `isdigit` determines whether its argument is a digit (0–9).
- Function `isalpha` determines whether its argument is an uppercase (A–Z) or lowercase letter (a–z).
- Function `isalnum` determines whether its argument is an uppercase letter (A–Z), a lowercase letter (a–z), or a digit (0–9).
- Function `isxdigit` determines whether its argument is a hexadecimal digit (A–F, a–f, 0–9).
- Function `toupper` converts a lowercase letter to an uppercase letter. Function `tolower` converts an uppercase letter to a lowercase letter.
- Function `isspace` determines whether its argument is one of the following white-space characters: ' ' (space), '\f', '\n', '\r', '\t' or '\v'.
- Function `iscntrl` determines whether its argument is a control character, such as '\t', '\v', '\f', '\a', '\b', '\r' or '\n'.
- Function `ispunct` determines whether its argument is a printing character other than a space, a digit or a letter.
- Function `isprint` determines whether its argument is any printing character, including space.
- Function `isgraph` determines whether its argument is a printing character other than space.

Section 21.10 Pointer-Based String Manipulation Functions
- Function `strcpy` copies its second argument into its first argument. You must ensure that the target array is large enough to store the string and its terminating null character.

- Function strncpy is equivalent to strcpy, but it specifies the number of characters to be copied from the string into the array. The terminating null character will be copied only if the number of characters to be copied is at least one more than the length of the string.

- Function strcat appends its second string argument—including the terminating null character—to its first string argument. The first character of the second string replaces the null ('\0') character of the first string. You must ensure that the target array used to store the first string is large enough to store both the first string and the second string.

- Function strncat is equivalent to strcat, but it appends a specified number of characters from the second string to the first string. A terminating null character is appended to the result.

- Function strcmp compares its first string argument with its second string argument character by character. The function returns zero if the strings are equal, a negative value if the first string is less than the second string and a positive value if the first string is greater than the second string.

- Function strncmp is equivalent to strcmp, but it compares a specified number of characters. If the number of characters in one of the strings is less than the number of characters specified, strncmp compares characters until the null character in the shorter string is encountered.

- A sequence of calls to strtok breaks a string into tokens that are separated by characters contained in a second string argument. The first call specifies the string to be tokenized as the first argument, and subsequent calls to continue tokenizing the same string specify NULL as the first argument. The function returns a pointer to the current token from each call. If there are no more tokens when strtok is called, NULL is returned.

- Function strlen takes a string as an argument and returns the number of characters in the string—the terminating null character is not included in the length of the string.

Section 21.11 Pointer-Based String-Conversion Functions

- Function atof converts its argument—a string beginning with a series of digits that represents a floating-point number—to a double value.

- Function atoi converts its argument—a string beginning with a series of digits that represents an integer—to an int value.

- Function atol converts its argument—a string beginning with a series of digits that represents a long integer—to a long value.

- Function strtod converts a sequence of characters representing a floating-point value to double. The function receives two arguments—a string (char *) and the address of a char * pointer. The string contains the character sequence to be converted, and the pointer to char * is assigned the remainder of the string after the conversion.

- Function strtol converts a sequence of characters representing an integer to long. The function receives a string (char *), the address of a char * pointer and an integer. The string contains the character sequence to be converted, the pointer to char * is assigned the location of the first character after the converted value and the integer specifies the base of the value being converted.

- Function strtoul converts a sequence of characters representing an integer to unsigned long. The function receives a string (char *), the address of a char * pointer and an integer. The string contains the character sequence to be converted, the pointer to char * is assigned the location of the first character after the converted value and the integer specifies the base of the value being converted.

Section 21.12 Search Functions of the Pointer-Based String-Handling Library

- Function strchr searches for the first occurrence of a character in a string. If found, strchr returns a pointer to the character in the string; otherwise, strchr returns a null pointer.

- Function `strcspn` determines the length of the initial part of the string in its first argument that does not contain any characters from the string in its second argument. The function returns the length of the segment.

- Function `strpbrk` searches for the first occurrence in its first argument of any character that appears in its second argument. If a character from the second argument is found, `strpbrk` returns a pointer to the character; otherwise, `strpbrk` returns a null pointer.

- Function `strrchr` searches for the last occurrence of a character in a string. If the character is found, `strrchr` returns a pointer to the character in the string; otherwise, it returns a null pointer.

- Function `strspn` determines the length of the initial part of its first argument that contains only characters from the string in its second argument and returns the length of the segment.

- Function `strstr` searches for the first occurrence of its second string argument in its first string argument. If the second string is found in the first string, a pointer to the location of the string in the first argument is returned; otherwise it returns 0.

Section 21.13 Memory Functions of the Pointer-Based String-Handling Library

- Function `memcpy` copies a specified number of characters from the object to which its second argument points into the object to which its first argument points. The function can receive a pointer to any object. The pointers are received as `void` pointers and converted to `char` pointers for use in the function. Function `memcpy` manipulates the bytes of its argument as characters.

- Function `memmove` copies a specified number of bytes from the object pointed to by its second argument to the object pointed to by its first argument. Copying is accomplished as if the bytes were copied from the second argument to a temporary character array, then copied from the temporary array to the first argument.

- Function `memcmp` compares the specified number of characters of its first and second arguments.

- Function `memchr` searches for the first occurrence of a byte, represented as `unsigned char`, in the specified number of bytes of an object. If the byte is found, a pointer to it is returned; otherwise, a null pointer is returned.

- Function `memset` copies its second argument, treated as an `unsigned char`, to a specified number of bytes of the object pointed to by the first argument.

Terminology

Self-Review Exercises

21.1   Fill in the blanks in each of the following:

    a) A(n) _____ is a collection of related variables under one name.

    b) The bits in the result of an expression using the _____ operator are set to one if the corresponding bits in each operand are set to one. Otherwise, the bits are set to zero.

    c) The variables declared in a structure definition are called its _____.

    d) The bits in the result of an expression using the _____ operator are set to one if at least one of the corresponding bits in either operand is set to one. Otherwise, the bits are set to zero.

    e) Keyword _____ introduces a structure declaration.

    f) Keyword _____ is used to create a synonym for a previously defined data type.

    g) Each bit in the result of an expression using the _____ operator is set to one if exactly one of the corresponding bits in either operand is set to one.

    h) The bitwise AND operator & is often used to _____ bits (i.e., to select certain bits from a bit string while zeroing others).

    i) A structure member is accessed with either operator _____ or _____.

    j) The _____ and _____ operators are used to shift the bits of a value to the left or to the right, respectively.

21.2   State whether each of the following is *true* or *false*. If *false*, explain why.

    a) Structures may contain only one data type.

    b) Members of different structures must have unique names.

    c) Keyword typedef is used to define new data types.

    d) Structures are always passed to functions by reference.

21.3   Write a single statement or a set of statements to accomplish each of the following:

    a) Define a structure called Part containing int variable partNumber and char array part-Name, whose values may be as long as 25 characters.

    b) Define PartPtr to be a synonym for the type Part *.

    c) Use separate statements to declare variable a to be of type Part, array b[10] to be of type Part and variable ptr to be of type pointer to Part.

    d) Read a part number and a part name from the keyboard into the members of variable a.

    e) Assign the member values of variable a to element three of array b.

    f) Assign the address of array b to the pointer variable ptr.

    g) Print the member values of element three of array b, using the variable ptr and the structure pointer operator to refer to the members.

21.4   Find the error in each of the following:

    a) Assume that `struct Card` has been defined as containing two pointers to type `char`— namely, `face` and `suit`. Also, the variable c has been declared to be of type `Card`, and the variable `cPtr` has been declared to be of type pointer to `Card`. Variable `cPtr` has been assigned the address of c.

```
cout << *cPtr.face << endl;
```

    b) Assume that `struct Card` has been defined as containing two pointers to type `char`— namely, `face` and `suit`. Also, the array `hearts[13]` has been declared to be of type `Card`. The following statement should print the member `face` of element 10 of the array.

```
cout << hearts.face << endl;
```

    c)
```
struct Person
{
    char lastName[ 15 ];
    char firstName[ 15 ];
    int age;
}
```

    d) Assume that variable p has been declared as type `Person` and that variable c has been declared as type `Card`.

```
p = c;
```

21.5   Write a single statement to accomplish each of the following. Assume that variables c (which stores a character), x, y and z are of type `int`; variables d, e and f are of type `double`; variable ptr is of type `char *` and arrays `s1[ 100 ]` and `s2[ 100 ]` are of type `char`.

    a) Convert the character stored in variable c to an uppercase letter. Assign the result to variable c.

    b) Determine if the value of variable c is a digit. Use the conditional operator as shown in Figs. 21.18–21.20 to print " is a " or " is not a " when the result is displayed.

    c) Convert the string `"1234567"` to `long`, and print the value.

    d) Determine whether the value of variable c is a control character. Use the conditional operator to print " is a " or " is not a " when the result is displayed.

    e) Assign to ptr the location of the last occurrence of c in s1.

    f) Convert the string `"8.63582"` to `double`, and print the value.

    g) Determine whether the value of c is a letter. Use the conditional operator to print " is a " or " is not a " when the result is displayed.

    h) Assign to ptr the location of the first occurrence of s2 in s1.

    i) Determine whether the value of variable c is a printing character. Use the conditional operator to print " is a " or " is not a " when the result is displayed.

    j) Assign to ptr the location of the first occurrence in s1 of any character from s2.

    k) Assign to ptr the location of the first occurrence of c in s1.

    l) Convert the string `"-21"` to `int`, and print the value.

Answers to Self-Review Exercises

21.1   a) structure. b) bitwise AND (&). c) members. d) bitwise inclusive-OR (|). e) `struct`. f) `typedef`. g) bitwise exclusive-OR (^). h) mask. i) structure member (.), structure pointer (->). j) left-shift operator (<<), right-shift operator (>>).

21.2   a) False. A structure can contain many data types.

    b) False. The members of separate structures can have the same names, but the members of the same structure must have unique names.

c) False. `typedef` is used to define aliases for previously defined data types.

d) False. Structures are passed to functions by value by default and may be passed by reference.

21.3 a)
```
struct Part
{
    int partNumber;
    char partName[ 26 ];
};
```

b) `typedef Part * PartPtr;`

c)
```
Part a;
Part b[ 10 ];
Part *ptr;
```

d) `cin >> a.partNumber >> a.partName;`

e) `b[ 3 ] = a;`

f) `ptr = b;`

g)
```
cout << ( ptr + 3 )->partNumber << ' '
     << ( ptr + 3 )->partName << endl;
```

21.4 a) *Error:* The parentheses that should enclose *cPtr have been omitted, causing the order of evaluation of the expression to be incorrect.

b) *Error:* The array subscript has been omitted. The expression should be
`hearts[ 10 ].face`.

c) *Error:* A semicolon is required to end a structure definition.

d) *Error:* Variables of different structure types cannot be assigned to one another.

21.5 a) `c = toupper( c );`

b)
```
cout << '\'' << c << "\' "
     << ( isdigit( c ) ? "is a" : "is not a" )
     << " digit" << endl;
```

c) `cout << atol( "1234567" ) << endl;`

d)
```
cout << '\'' << c << "\' "
     << ( iscntrl( c ) ? "is a" : "is not a" )
     << " control character" << endl;
```

e) `ptr = strrchr( s1, c );`

f) `out << atof( "8.63582" ) << endl;`

g)
```
cout << '\'' << c << "\' "
     << ( isalpha( c ) ? "is a" : "is not a" )
     << " letter" << endl;
```

h) `ptr = strstr( s1, s2 );`

i)
```
cout << '\'' << c << "\' "
     << ( isprint( c ) ? "is a" : "is not a" )
     << " printing character" << endl;
```

j) `ptr = strpbrk( s1, s2 );`

k) `ptr = strchr( s1, c );`

l) `cout << atoi( "-21" ) << endl;`

Exercises

21.6 Provide the definition for each of the following structures:

a) Structure `Inventory`, containing character array `partName[ 30 ]`, integer `partNumber`, floating-point `price`, integer `stock` and integer `reorder`.

b) A structure called `Address` that contains character arrays `streetAddress[25]`, `city[20]`, `state[3]` and `zipCode[6]`.

c) Structure `Student`, containing arrays `firstName[ 15 ]` and `lastName[ 15 ]` and variable `homeAddress` of type `struct Address` from part (b).

d) Structure `Test`, containing 16 bit fields with widths of 1 bit. The names of the bit fields are the letters a to p.

21.7 Consider the following structure definitions and variable declarations:

```
struct Customer {
    char lastName[ 15 ];
    char firstName[ 15 ];
    int customerNumber;

    struct {
        char phoneNumber[ 11 ];
        char address[ 50 ];
        char city[ 15 ];
        char state[ 3 ];
        char zipCode[ 6 ];
    } personal;

} customerRecord, *customerPtr;

customerPtr = &customerRecord;
```

Write a separate expression that accesses the structure members in each of the following parts:

a) Member `lastName` of structure `customerRecord`.

b) Member `lastName` of the structure pointed to by `customerPtr`.

c) Member `firstName` of structure `customerRecord`.

d) Member `firstName` of the structure pointed to by `customerPtr`.

e) Member `customerNumber` of structure `customerRecord`.

f) Member `customerNumber` of the structure pointed to by `customerPtr`.

g) Member `phoneNumber` of member `personal` of structure `customerRecord`.

h) Member `phoneNumber` of member `personal` of the structure pointed to by `customerPtr`.

i) Member `address` of member `personal` of structure `customerRecord`.

j) Member `address` of member `personal` of the structure pointed to by `customerPtr`.

k) Member `city` of member `personal` of structure `customerRecord`.

l) Member `city` of member `personal` of the structure pointed to by `customerPtr`.

m) Member `state` of member `personal` of structure `customerRecord`.

n) Member `state` of member `personal` of the structure pointed to by `customerPtr`.

o) Member `zipCode` of member `personal` of structure `customerRecord`.

p) Member `zipCode` of member `personal` of the structure pointed to by `customerPtr`.

21.8 *(Card Shufflling and Dealing)* Modify Fig. 21.14 to shuffle the cards using a high-performance shuffle, as shown in Fig. 21.3. Print the resulting deck in two-column format. Precede each card with its color.

21.9 *(Shifting and Printing an Integer)* Write a program that right-shifts an integer variable 4 bits. The program should print the integer in bits before and after the shift operation. Does your system place zeros or ones in the vacated bits?

21.10 *(Multiplication Via Bit Shifting)* Left-shifting an `unsigned` integer by 1 bit is equivalent to multiplying the value by 2. Write function `power2` that takes two integer arguments, `number` and `pow`, and calculates

$$number * 2^{pow}$$

Use a shift operator to calculate the result. The program should print the values as integers and as bits.

21.11 *(Packing Characters into Unsigned Integers)* The left-shift operator can be used to pack two character values into a two-byte unsigned integer variable. Write a program that inputs two characters from the keyboard and passes them to function packCharacters. To pack two characters into an unsigned integer variable, assign the first character to the unsigned variable, shift the unsigned variable left by 8 bit positions and combine the unsigned variable with the second character using the bitwise inclusive-OR operator. The program should output the characters in their bit format before and after they're packed into the unsigned integer to prove that they're in fact packed correctly in the unsigned variable.

21.12 *(Unpacking Characters from Unsigned Integers)* Using the right-shift operator, the bitwise AND operator and a mask, write function unpackCharacters that takes the unsigned integer from Exercise 21.11 and unpacks it into two characters. To unpack two characters from an unsigned two-byte integer, combine the unsigned integer with the mask 65280 (11111111 00000000) and right-shift the result 8 bits. Assign the resulting value to a char variable. Then, combine the unsigned integer with the mask 255 (00000000 11111111). Assign the result to another char variable. The program should print the unsigned integer in bits before it's unpacked, then print the characters in bits to confirm that they were unpacked correctly.

21.13 *(Packing Characters into Unsigned Integers)* If your system uses four-byte integers, rewrite the program of Exercise 21.11 to pack four characters.

21.14 *(Unpacking Characters from Unsigned Integers)* If your system uses four-byte integers, rewrite the function unpackCharacters of Exercise 21.12 to unpack four characters. Create the masks you need to unpack the four characters by left-shifting the value 255 in the mask variable by 8 bits 0, 1, 2 or 3 times (depending on the byte you are unpacking).

21.15 *(Reversing Bits)* Write a program that reverses the order of the bits in an unsigned integer value. The program should input the value from the user and call function reverseBits to print the bits in reverse order. Print the value in bits both before and after the bits are reversed to confirm that the bits are reversed properly.

21.16 *(Passing an Array by Value)* Write a program that demonstrates passing an array by value. [*Hint:* Use a struct.] Prove that a copy was passed by modifying the array copy in the called function.

21.17 *(Testing Characters with the **<cctype>** Functions)* Write a program that inputs a character from the keyboard and tests the character with each function in the character-handling library. Print the value returned by each function.

21.18 The following program uses function multiple to determine whether the integer entered from the keyboard is a multiple of some integer X. Examine function multiple, then determine the value of X.

```
 1    // Exercise 21.18: ex21_18.cpp
 2    // This program determines if a value is a multiple of X.
 3    #include <iostream>
 4    using namespace std;
 5
 6    bool multiple( int );
 7
 8    int main()
 9    {
10       int y;
11
12       cout << "Enter an integer between 1 and 32000: ";
13       cin >> y;
14
```

```
15      if ( multiple( y ) )
16         cout << y << " is a multiple of X" << endl;
17      else
18         cout << y << " is not a multiple of X" << endl;
19   } // end main
20
21   // determine if num is a multiple of X
22   bool multiple( int num )
23   {
24      bool mult = true;
25
26      for ( int i = 0, mask = 1; i < 10; i++, mask <<= 1 )
27         if ( ( num & mask ) != 0 )
28         {
29            mult = false;
30            break;
31         } // end if
32
33      return mult;
34   } // end function multiple
```

21.19 What does the following program do?

```
1    // Exercise 21.19: ex21_19.cpp
2    #include <iostream>
3    using namespace std;
4
5    bool mystery( unsigned );
6
7    int main()
8    {
9       unsigned x;
10
11      cout << "Enter an integer: ";
12      cin >> x;
13      cout << boolalpha
14           << "The result is " << mystery( x ) << endl;
15   } // end main
16
17   // What does this function do?
18   bool mystery( unsigned bits )
19   {
20      const int SHIFT = 8 * sizeof( unsigned ) - 1;
21      const unsigned MASK = 1 << SHIFT;
22      unsigned total = 0;
23
24      for ( int i = 0; i < SHIFT + 1; i++, bits <<= 1 )
25         if ( ( bits & MASK ) == MASK )
26            ++total;
27
28      return !( total % 2 );
29   } // end function mystery
```

21.20 Write a program that inputs a line of text with `istream` member function `getline` (as in Chapter 15) into character array `s[100]`. Output the line in uppercase letters and lowercase letters.

21.21 *(Converting Strings to Integers)* Write a program that inputs four strings that represent integers, converts the strings to integers, sums the values and prints the total of the four values. Use only the C-style string-processing techniques shown in this chapter.

21.22 *(Converting Strings to Floating-Point Numbers)* Write a program that inputs four strings that represent floating-point values, converts the strings to double values, sums the values and prints the total of the four values. Use only the C-style string-processing techniques shown in this chapter.

21.23 *(Searching for Substrings)* Write a program that inputs a line of text and a search string from the keyboard. Using function strstr, locate the first occurrence of the search string in the line of text, and assign the location to variable searchPtr of type char *. If the search string is found, print the remainder of the line of text beginning with the search string. Then use strstr again to locate the next occurrence of the search string in the line of text. If a second occurrence is found, print the remainder of the line of text beginning with the second occurrence. [*Hint:* The second call to strstr should contain the expression searchPtr + 1 as its first argument.]

21.24 *(Searching for Substrings)* Write a program based on the program of Exercise 21.23 that inputs several lines of text and a search string, then uses function strstr to determine the total number of occurrences of the string in the lines of text. Print the result.

21.25 *(Searching for Characters)* Write a program that inputs several lines of text and a search character and uses function strchr to determine the total number of occurrences of the character in the lines of text.

21.26 *(Searching for Characters)* Write a program based on the program of Exercise 21.25 that inputs several lines of text and uses function strchr to determine the total number of occurrences of each letter of the alphabet in the text. Uppercase and lowercase letters should be counted together. Store the totals for each letter in an array, and print the values in tabular format after the totals have been determined.

21.27 The chart in Appendix B shows the numeric code representations for the characters in the ASCII character set. Study this chart, then state whether each of the following is *true* or *false*:
- a) The letter "A" comes before the letter "B."
- b) The digit "9" comes before the digit "0."
- c) The commonly used symbols for addition, subtraction, multiplication and division all come before any of the digits.
- d) The digits come before the letters.
- e) If a sort program sorts strings into ascending sequence, then the program will place the symbol for a right parenthesis before the symbol for a left parenthesis.

21.28 *(Strings Beginning with b)* Write a program that reads a series of strings and prints only those strings beginning with the letter "b."

21.29 *(Strings Ending with ED)* Write a program that reads a series of strings and prints only those strings that end with the letters "ED."

21.30 *(Displaying Characters for Given ASCII Codes)* Write a program that inputs an ASCII code and prints the corresponding character. Modify this program so that it generates all possible three-digit codes in the range 000–255 and attempts to print the corresponding characters. What happens when this program is run?

21.31 *(Write Your Own Character Handling Functions)* Using the ASCII character chart in Appendix B as a guide, write your own versions of the character-handling functions in Fig. 21.17.

21.32 *(Write Your Own String Conversion Functions)* Write your own versions of the functions in Fig. 21.27 for converting strings to numbers.

21.33 *(Write Your Own String Searching Functions)* Write your own versions of the functions in Fig. 21.34 for searching strings.

21.34 *(Write Your Own Memory Handling Functions)* Write your own versions of the functions in Fig. 21.41 for manipulating blocks of memory.

21.35   What does this program do?

```cpp
// Ex. 21.35: ex21_35.cpp
// What does this program do?
#include <iostream>
using namespace std;

bool mystery3( const char *, const char * ); // prototype

int main()
{
   char string1[ 80 ], string2[ 80 ];

   cout << "Enter two strings: ";
   cin >> string1 >> string2;
   cout << "The result is " << mystery3( string1, string2 ) << endl;
} // end main

// What does this function do?
bool mystery3( const char *s1, const char *s2 )
{
   for ( ; *s1 != '\0' && *s2 != '\0'; s1++, s2++ )

      if ( *s1 != *s2 )
         return false;

   return true;
} // end function mystery3
```

21.36   *(Comparing Strings)* Write a program that uses function `strcmp` to compare two strings input by the user. The program should state whether the first string is less than, equal to or greater than the second string.

21.37   *(Comparing Strings)* Write a program that uses function `strncmp` to compare two strings input by the user. The program should input the number of characters to compare. The program should state whether the first string is less than, equal to or greater than the second string.

21.38   *(Randomly Creating Sentences)* Write a program that uses random number generation to create sentences. The program should use four arrays of pointers to char called `article`, `noun`, `verb` and `preposition`. The program should create a sentence by selecting a word at random from each array in the following order: `article`, `noun`, `verb`, `preposition`, `article` and `noun`. As each word is picked, it should be concatenated to the previous words in a character array that is large enough to hold the entire sentence. The words should be separated by spaces. When the final sentence is output, it should start with a capital letter and end with a period. The program should generate 20 such sentences.

The arrays should be filled as follows: The `article` array should contain the articles `"the"`, `"a"`, `"one"`, `"some"` and `"any"`; the `noun` array should contain the nouns `"boy"`, `"girl"`, `"dog"`, `"town"` and `"car"`; the `verb` array should contain the verbs `"drove"`, `"jumped"`, `"ran"`, `"walked"` and `"skipped"`; the `preposition` array should contain the prepositions `"to"`, `"from"`, `"over"`, `"under"` and `"on"`.

After completing the program, modify it to produce a short story consisting of several of these sentences. (How about a random term-paper writer!)

21.39   *(Limericks)* A limerick is a humorous five-line verse in which the first and second lines rhyme with the fifth, and the third line rhymes with the fourth. Using techniques similar to those developed in Exercise 21.38, write a C++ program that produces random limericks. Polishing this program to produce good limericks is a challenging problem, but the result will be worth the effort!

21.40 *(Pig Latin)* Write a program that encodes English language phrases into pig Latin. Pig Latin is a form of coded language often used for amusement. Many variations exist in the methods used to form pig Latin phrases. For simplicity, use the following algorithm: To form a pig-Latin phrase from an English-language phrase, tokenize the phrase into words with function strtok. To translate each English word into a pig-Latin word, place the first letter of the English word at the end of the English word and add the letters "ay." Thus, the word "jump" becomes "umpjay," the word "the" becomes "hetay" and the word "computer" becomes "omputercay." Blanks between words remain as blanks. Assume that the English phrase consists of words separated by blanks, there are no punctuation marks and all words have two or more letters. Function printLatinWord should display each word. [*Hint:* Each time a token is found in a call to strtok, pass the token pointer to function printLatinWord and print the pig-Latin word.]

21.41 *(Tokenizing Phone Numbers)* Write a program that inputs a telephone number as a string in the form (555) 555-5555. The program should use function strtok to extract the area code as a token, the first three digits of the phone number as a token, and the last four digits of the phone number as a token. The seven digits of the phone number should be concatenated into one string. Both the area code and the phone number should be printed.

21.42 *(Tokenizing and Reversing a Sentence)* Write a program that inputs a line of text, tokenizes the line with function strtok and outputs the tokens in reverse order.

21.43 *(Alphabetizing Strings)* Use the string-comparison functions discussed in Section 21.10 and the techniques for sorting arrays developed in Chapter 7 to write a program that alphabetizes a list of strings. Use the names of 10 towns in your area as data for your program.

21.44 *(Write Your Own String Copy and Concatenation Functions)* Write two versions of each string copy and string-concatenation function in Fig. 21.21. The first version should use array subscripting, and the second should use pointers and pointer arithmetic.

21.45 *(Write Your Own String Comparison Functions)* Write two versions of each string-comparison function in Fig. 21.21. The first version should use array subscripting, and the second should use pointers and pointer arithmetic.

21.46 *(Write Your Own String Length Function)* Write two versions of function strlen in Fig. 21.21. The first version should use array subscripting, and the second should use pointers and pointer arithmetic.

Special Section: Advanced String-Manipulation Exercises

The preceding exercises are keyed to the text and designed to test your understanding of fundamental string-manipulation concepts. This section includes a collection of intermediate and advanced string-manipulation exercises. You should find these problems challenging, yet enjoyable. The problems vary considerably in difficulty. Some require an hour or two of program writing and implementation. Others are useful for lab assignments that might require two or three weeks of study and implementation. Some are challenging term projects.

21.47 *(Text Analysis)* The availability of computers with string-manipulation capabilities has resulted in some rather interesting approaches to analyzing the writings of great authors. Much attention has been focused on whether William Shakespeare ever lived. Some scholars believe there is substantial evidence that Francis Bacon, Christopher Marlowe or other authors actually penned the masterpieces attributed to Shakespeare. Researchers have used computers to find similarities in the writings of these authors. This exercise examines three methods for analyzing texts with a computer. Thousands of texts, including Shakespeare, are available online at www.gutenberg.org.

    a)   Write a program that reads several lines of text from the keyboard and prints a table indicating the number of occurrences of each letter of the alphabet in the text. For example, the phrase

```
To be, or not to be: that is the question:
```

contains one "a," two "b's," no "c's," etc.

b) Write a program that reads several lines of text and prints a table indicating the number of one-letter words, two-letter words, three-letter words, etc., appearing in the text. For example, the phrase

```
Whether 'tis nobler in the mind to suffer
```

contains the following word lengths and occurrences:

Word length	Occurrences
1	0
2	2
3	1
4	2 (including 'tis)
5	0
6	2
7	1

c) Write a program that reads several lines of text and prints a table indicating the number of occurrences of each different word in the text. The first version of your program should include the words in the table in the same order in which they appear in the text. For example, the lines

```
To be, or not to be: that is the question:
Whether 'tis nobler in the mind to suffer
```

contain the word "to" three times, the word "be" two times, the word "or" once, etc. A more interesting (and useful) printout should then be attempted in which the words are sorted alphabetically.

21.48 *(Word Processing)* One important function in word-processing systems is *type justification*—the alignment of words to both the left and right margins of a page. This generates a professional-looking document that gives the appearance of being set in type rather than prepared on a typewriter. Type justification can be accomplished on computer systems by inserting blank characters between the words in a line so that the rightmost word aligns with the right margin.

Write a program that reads several lines of text and prints this text in type-justified format. Assume that the text is to be printed on paper 8-1/2 inches wide and that one-inch margins are to be allowed on both the left and right sides. Assume that the computer prints 10 characters to the horizontal inch. Therefore, your program should print 6-1/2 inches of text, or 65 characters per line.

21.49 *(Printing Dates in Various Formats)* Dates are commonly printed in several different formats in business correspondence. Two of the more common formats are

```
07/21/1955
July 21, 1955
```

Write a program that reads a date in the first format and prints that date in the second format.

21.50 *(Check Protection)* Computers are frequently employed in check-writing systems such as payroll and accounts-payable applications. Many strange stories circulate regarding weekly paychecks being printed (by mistake) for amounts in excess of $1 million. Weird amounts are printed by computerized check-writing systems, because of human error or machine failure. Systems designers build controls into their systems to prevent such erroneous checks from being issued.

Another serious problem is the intentional alteration of a check amount by someone who intends to cash a check fraudulently. To prevent a dollar amount from being altered, most computerized check-writing systems employ a technique called *check protection.*

Checks designed for imprinting by computer contain a fixed number of spaces in which the computer may print an amount. Suppose that a paycheck contains eight blank spaces in which the computer is supposed to print the amount of a weekly paycheck. If the amount is large, then all eight of those spaces will be filled, for example,

```
1,230.60    (check amount)
--------
12345678    (position numbers)
```

On the other hand, if the amount is less than $1000, then several of the spaces would ordinarily be left blank. For example,

```
   99.87
--------
12345678
```

contains three blank spaces. If a check is printed with blank spaces, it's easier for someone to alter the amount of the check. To prevent a check from being altered, many check-writing systems insert *leading asterisks* to protect the amount as follows:

```
***99.87
--------
12345678
```

Write a program that inputs a dollar amount to be printed on a check then prints the amount in check-protected format with leading asterisks if necessary. Assume that nine spaces are available for printing an amount.

21.51 *(Writing the Word Equivalent of a Check Amount)* Continuing the discussion of the previous example, we reiterate the importance of designing check-writing systems to prevent alteration of check amounts. One common security method requires that the check amount be both written in numbers and "spelled out" in words. Even if someone is able to alter the numerical amount of the check, it's extremely difficult to change the amount in words.

Write a program that inputs a numeric check amount and writes the word equivalent of the amount. Your program should be able to handle check amounts as large as $99.99. For example, the amount 112.43 should be written as

```
ONE HUNDRED TWELVE and 43/100
```

21.52 *(Morse Code)* Perhaps the most famous of all coding schemes is the Morse code, developed by Samuel Morse in 1832 for use with the telegraph system. The Morse code assigns a series of dots and dashes to each letter of the alphabet, each digit and a few special characters (such as period, comma, colon and semicolon). In sound-oriented systems, the dot represents a short sound, and the dash represents a long sound. Other representations of dots and dashes are used with light-oriented systems and signal-flag systems.

Separation between words is indicated by a space, or, quite simply, the absence of a dot or dash. In a sound-oriented system, a space is indicated by a short period of time during which no sound is transmitted. The international version of the Morse code appears in Fig. 21.47.

Write a program that reads an English-language phrase and encodes it into Morse code. Also write a program that reads a phrase in Morse code and converts it into the English-language equivalent. Use one blank between each Morse-coded letter and three blanks between each Morse-coded word.

Character	Code	Character	Code
A	.-	N	-.
B	-...	O	---
C	-.-.	P	.--.
D	-..	Q	--.-
E	.	R	.-.
F	..-.	S	...
G	--.	T	-
H	....	U	..-
I	..	V	...-
J	.---	W	.--
K	-.-	X	-..-
L	.-..	Y	-.--
M	--	Z	--..
Digits			
1	.----	6	-....
2	..---	7	--...
3	...--	8	---..
4	....-	9	----.
5	.....	0	-----

Fig. 21.47 | Morse code alphabet and numbers.

21.53 *(Metric Conversion Program)* Write a program that will assist the user with metric conversions. Your program should allow the user to specify the names of the units as strings (i.e., centimeters, liters, grams, etc., for the metric system and inches, quarts, pounds, etc., for the English system) and should respond to simple questions such as

```
"How many inches are in 2 meters?"
"How many liters are in 10 quarts?"
```

Your program should recognize invalid conversions. For example, the question

```
"How many feet are in 5 kilograms?"
```

is not meaningful, because "feet" are units of length, while "kilograms" are units of weight.

Challenging String-Manipulation Projects

21.54 *(Crossword Puzzle Generator)* Most people have worked a crossword puzzle, but few have ever attempted to generate one. Generating a crossword puzzle is a difficult problem. It's suggested here as a string-manipulation project requiring substantial sophistication and effort. There are many issues that you must resolve to get even the simplest crossword puzzle generator program working. For example, how does one represent the grid of a crossword puzzle inside the computer? Should one use a series of strings, or should two-dimensional arrays be used? You need a source of words (i.e., a computerized dictionary) that can be directly referenced by the program. In what form should these words be stored to facilitate the complex manipulations required by the program? The really ambitious reader will want to generate the "clues" portion of the puzzle, in which the brief hints for each "across" word and each "down" word are printed for the puzzle worker. Merely printing a version of the blank puzzle itself is not a simple problem.

21.55 *(Spelling Checker)* Many popular word-processing software packages have built-in spell checkers. We used spell-checking capabilities in preparing this book and discovered that, no matter how careful we thought we were in writing a chapter, the software was always able to find a few more spelling errors than we were able to catch manually.

In this project, you are asked to develop your own spell-checker utility. We make suggestions to help get you started. You should then consider adding more capabilities. You might find it helpful to use a computerized dictionary as a source of words.

Why do we type so many words with incorrect spellings? In some cases, it's because we simply do not know the correct spelling, so we make a "best guess." In some cases, it's because we transpose two letters (e.g., "defualt" instead of "default"). Sometimes we double-type a letter accidentally (e.g., "hanndy" instead of "handy"). Sometimes we type a nearby key instead of the one we intended (e.g., "biryhday" instead of "birthday"). And so on.

Design and implement a spell-checker program. Your program maintains an array wordList of character strings. You can either enter these strings or obtain them from a computerized dictionary.

Your program asks a user to enter a word. The program then looks up that word in the wordList array. If the word is present in the array, your program should print "Word is spelled correctly."

If the word is not present in the array, your program should print "Word is not spelled correctly." Then your program should try to locate other words in wordList that might be the word the user intended to type. For example, you can try all possible single transpositions of adjacent letters to discover that the word "default" is a direct match to a word in wordList. Of course, this implies that your program will check all other single transpositions, such as "edfault," "dfeault," "deafult," "defalut" and "defautl." When you find a new word that matches one in wordList, print that word in a message such as "Did you mean "default?"."

Implement other tests, such as the replacing of each double letter with a single letter and any other tests you can develop to improve the value of your spell checker.

22

Standard Template Library (STL)

The shapes a bright container can contain!
—Theodore Roethke

Journey over all the universe in a map.
—Miguel de Cervantes

O! thou hast damnable iteration, and art indeed able to corrupt a saint.
—William Shakespeare

That great dust heap called "history."
—Augustine Birrell

The historian is a prophet in reverse.
—Friedrich von Schlegel

Attempt the end, and never stand to doubt; Nothing's so hard but search will find it out.
—Robert Herrick

Objectives

In this chapter you'll learn:

- To use the STL containers, container adapters and "near containers."

- To program with the dozens of STL algorithms.

- To use iterators to access the elements of STL containers.

22.1 Introduction to the Standard Template Library (STL)

We've repeatedly emphasized the importance of software reuse. Recognizing that many data structures and algorithms are commonly used, the C++ standard committee added the **Standard Template Library (STL)** to the C++ Standard Library. The STL defines powerful, template-based, reusable components that implement many common data structures and algorithms used to process those data structures. The STL offers proof of concept for generic programming with templates—introduced in Chapter 14, Templates, and used extensively in Chapter 20, Data Structures. [*Note:* In industry, the features presented in this chapter are often referred to as the Standard Template Library or STL. However, these terms are not used in the C++ standard document, because these features are simply considered to be part of the C++ Standard Library.]

The STL was developed by Alexander Stepanov and Meng Lee at Hewlett-Packard and is based on their research in the field of generic programming, with significant contributions from David Musser. As you'll see, the STL was conceived and designed for performance and flexibility.

This chapter introduces the STL and discusses its three key components—**containers** (popular templatized data structures), **iterators** and **algorithms**. The STL containers are data structures capable of storing objects of almost any data type (there are some restrictions). We'll see that there are three styles of container classes—**first-class containers**, **adapters** and **near containers**.

Performance Tip 22.1

For any particular application, several different STL containers might be appropriate. Select the most appropriate container that achieves the best performance (i.e., balance of speed and size) for that application. Efficiency was a crucial consideration in the STL's design.

Performance Tip 22.2

Standard Library capabilities are implemented to operate efficiently across many applications. For some applications with unique performance requirements, it might be necessary to write your own customized implementations.

Each STL container has associated member functions. A subset of these member functions is defined in all STL containers. We illustrate most of this common functionality in our examples of STL containers `vector` (a dynamically resizable array which we introduced in Chapter 7), `list` (a doubly linked list) and **deque** (a double-ended queue, pronounced "deck"). We introduce container-specific functionality in examples for each of the other STL containers.

STL iterators, which have properties similar to those of pointers, are used by programs to manipulate the STL-container elements. In fact, standard arrays can be manipulated by STL algorithms, using standard pointers as iterators. We'll see that manipulating containers with iterators is convenient and provides tremendous expressive power when combined with STL algorithms—in some cases, reducing many lines of code to a single statement. There are five categories of iterators, each of which we discuss in Section 22.1.2 and use throughout this chapter.

STL algorithms are functions that perform such common data manipulations as searching, sorting and comparing elements (or entire containers). The STL provides approximately 70 algorithms. Most of them use iterators to access container elements. Each algorithm has minimum requirements for the types of iterators that can be used with it. We'll see that each first-class container supports specific iterator types, some more powerful than others. A container's supported iterator type determines whether the container can be used with a specific algorithm. Iterators encapsulate the mechanism used to access container elements. This encapsulation enables many of the STL algorithms to be applied to several containers without regard for the underlying container implementation. As long as a container's iterators support the minimum requirements of the algorithm, then the algorithm can process that container's elements. This also enables you to create new algorithms that can process the elements of multiple container types.

Software Engineering Observation 22.1

The STL approach allows general programs to be written so that the code does not depend on the underlying container. Such a programming style is called generic programming.

In Chapter 20, we studied data structures. We built linked lists, queues, stacks and trees. We carefully wove link objects together with pointers. Pointer-based code is complex, and the slightest omission or oversight can lead to serious memory-access violations and memory-leak errors with no compiler complaints. Implementing additional data structures, such as deques, priority queues, sets and maps, requires substantial extra work. In addition, if many programmers on a large project implement similar containers and algorithms for different tasks, the code becomes difficult to modify, maintain and debug. An advantage of the STL is that you can reuse the STL containers, iterators and algorithms to implement common data representations and manipulations. This reuse can save substantial development time, money and effort.

Software Engineering Observation 22.2

Avoid reinventing the wheel; program with the reusable components of the C++ Standard Library. STL includes many of the most popular data structures as containers and provides various popular algorithms to process data in these containers.

Error-Prevention Tip 22.1

When programming pointer-based data structures and algorithms, we must do our own debugging and testing to be sure our data structures, classes and algorithms function properly. It's easy to make errors when manipulating pointers at this low level. Memory leaks and memory-access violations are common in such custom code. The prepackaged, templatized containers of the STL are sufficient for most programmers. Using the STL helps you reduce testing and debugging time. One caution is that, for large projects, template compile time can be significant.

This chapter introduces the STL. It's by no means complete or comprehensive. However, it's a friendly, accessible chapter that should convince you of the value of the STL in software reuse and encourage further study.

22.1.1 Introduction to Containers

The STL container types are shown in Fig. 22.1. The containers are divided into three major categories—**sequence containers**, **associative containers** and **container adapters**.

Standard Library container class	Description
Sequence containers	
vector	Rapid insertions and deletions at back. Direct access to any element.
deque	Rapid insertions and deletions at front or back. Direct access to any element.
list	Doubly linked list, rapid insertion and deletion anywhere.
Associative containers	
set	Rapid lookup, no duplicates allowed.
multiset	Rapid lookup, duplicates allowed.
map	One-to-one mapping, no duplicates allowed, rapid key-based lookup.
multimap	One-to-many mapping, duplicates allowed, rapid key-based lookup.

Fig. 22.1 | Standard Library container classes. (Part 1 of 2.)

Standard Library container class	Description
Container adapters	
stack	Last-in, first-out (LIFO).
queue	First-in, first-out (FIFO).
priority_queue	Highest-priority element is always the first element out.

Fig. 22.1 | Standard Library container classes. (Part 2 of 2.)

STL Containers Overview

The sequence containers represent linear data structures, such as vectors and linked lists. Associative containers are nonlinear containers that typically can locate elements stored in the containers quickly. Such containers can store sets of values or **key/value pairs**. The sequence containers and associative containers are collectively referred to as the first-class containers. As we saw in Chapter 20, stacks and queues actually are constrained versions of sequential containers. For this reason, STL implements stacks and queues as container adapters that enable a program to view a sequential container in a constrained manner. There are other container types that are considered "near containers"—C-like pointer-based arrays (discussed in Chapter 7), bitsets for maintaining sets of flag values and valarrays for performing high-speed mathematical vector operations (this last class is optimized for computation performance and is not as flexible as the first-class containers). These types are considered "near containers" because they exhibit capabilities similar to those of the first-class containers, but do not support all the first-class-container capabilities. Type string (discussed in Chapter 18) supports the same functionality as a sequence container, but stores only character data.

STL Container Common Functions

Most STL containers provide similar functionality. Many generic operations, such as member function size, apply to all containers, and other operations apply to subsets of similar containers. This encourages extensibility of the STL with new classes. Figure 22.2 describes the functions common to all Standard Library containers. [*Note:* Overloaded operators operator<, operator<=, operator>, operator>=, operator== and operator!= are not provided for priority_queues.]

Member function	Description
default constructor	A constructor to create an empty container. Normally, each container has several constructors that provide different initialization methods for the container.
copy constructor	A constructor that initializes the container to be a copy of an existing container of the same type.
destructor	Destructor function for cleanup after a container is no longer needed.

Fig. 22.2 | Common member functions for most STL containers. (Part 1 of 2.)

Member function	Description
empty	Returns true if there are no elements in the container; otherwise, returns false.
insert	Inserts an item in the container.
size	Returns the number of elements currently in the container.
operator=	Assigns one container to another.
operator<	Returns true if the first container is less than the second container; otherwise, returns false.
operator<=	Returns true if the first container is less than or equal to the second container; otherwise, returns false.
operator>	Returns true if the first container is greater than the second container; otherwise, returns false.
operator>=	Returns true if the first container is greater than or equal to the second container; otherwise, returns false.
operator==	Returns true if the first container is equal to the second container; otherwise, returns false.
operator!=	Returns true if the first container is not equal to the second container; otherwise, returns false.
swap	Swaps the elements of two containers.
Functions found only in first-class containers	
max_size	Returns the maximum number of elements for a container.
begin	The two versions of this function return either an iterator or a const_iterator that refers to the first element of the container.
end	The two versions of this function return either an iterator or a const_iterator that refers to the next position after the end of the container.
rbegin	The two versions of this function return either a reverse_iterator or a const_reverse_iterator that refers to the last element of the container.
rend	The two versions of this function return either a reverse_iterator or a const_reverse_iterator that refers to the next position after the last element of the reversed container.
erase	Erases one or more elements from the container.
clear	Erases all elements from the container.

Fig. 22.2 | Common member functions for most STL containers. (Part 2 of 2.)

STL Container Header Files

The header files for each of the Standard Library containers are shown in Fig. 22.3. The contents of these header files are all in namespace std.

First-Class Container Common typedefs

Figure 22.4 shows the common typedefs (to create synonyms or aliases for lengthy type names) found in first-class containers. These typedefs are used in generic declarations of variables, parameters to functions and return values from functions. For example, value_type in each container is always a `typedef` that represents the type of value stored in the container.

Standard Library container header files
<vector>
<list>
<deque>
<queue>   Contains both queue and priority_queue.
<stack>
<map>   Contains both map and multimap.
<set>   Contains both set and multiset.
<valarray>
<bitset>

Fig. 22.3 | Standard Library container header files.

typedef	Description
allocator_type	The type of the object used to allocate the container's memory.
value_type	The type of element stored in the container.
reference	A reference to the type of element stored in the container.
const_reference	A constant reference to the type of element stored in the container. Such a reference can be used only for *reading* elements in the container and for performing const operations.
pointer	A pointer to the type of element stored in the container.
const_pointer	A pointer to a constant of the container's element type.
iterator	An iterator that points to an element of the container's element type.
const_iterator	A constant iterator that points to the type of element stored in the container and can be used only to *read* elements.
reverse_iterator	A reverse iterator that points to the type of element stored in the container. This type of iterator is for iterating through a container in reverse.
const_reverse_iterator	A constant reverse iterator that points to the type of element stored in the container and can be used only to *read* elements. This type of iterator is for iterating through a container in reverse.
difference_type	The type of the result of subtracting two iterators that refer to the same container (operator − is not defined for iterators of lists and associative containers).
size_type	The type used to count items in a container and index through a sequence container (cannot index through a list).

Fig. 22.4 | typedefs found in first-class containers.

Performance Tip 22.3

STL generally avoids inheritance and virtual *functions in favor of using generic programming with templates to achieve better execution-time performance.*

Portability Tip 22.1

Programming with STL will enhance the portability of your code.

When preparing to use an STL container, it's important to ensure that the type of element being stored in the container supports a minimum set of functionality. When an element is inserted into a container, a copy of that element is made. For this reason, the element type should provide its own copy constructor and assignment operator. [*Note:* This is required only if default memberwise copy and default memberwise assignment do not perform proper copy and assignment operations for the element type.] Also, the associative containers and many algorithms require elements to be compared. For this reason, the element type should provide an equality operator (==) and a less-than operator (<).

Software Engineering Observation 22.3

The STL containers do not require their elements to be comparable with the equality and less-than operators unless a program uses a container member function that must compare the container elements (e.g., the sort *function in class* list*). Some pre-standard C++ compilers are not capable of ignoring parts of a template that are not used in a particular program. On compilers with this problem, you may not be able to use the STL containers with objects of classes that do not define overloaded less-than and equality operators.*

22.1.2 Introduction to Iterators

Iterators have many features in common with pointers and are used to point to the elements of first-class containers (and for a few other purposes, as we'll see). Iterators hold state information sensitive to the particular containers on which they operate; thus, iterators are implemented appropriately for each type of container. Certain iterator operations are uniform across containers. For example, the dereferencing operator (*) dereferences an iterator so that you can use the element to which it points. The ++ operation on an iterator moves it to the next element of the container (much as incrementing a pointer into an array aims the pointer at the next element of the array).

STL first-class containers provide member functions begin and end. Function **begin** returns an iterator pointing to the first element of the container. Function **end** returns an iterator pointing to the first element past the end of the container (an element that doesn't exist). If iterator i points to a particular element, then ++i points to the "next" element and *i refers to the element pointed to by i. The iterator resulting from end is typically used in an equality or inequality comparison to determine whether the "moving iterator" (i in this case) has reached the end of the container.

An object of type iterator refers to a container element that can be modified. An object of type const_iterator refers to a container element that cannot be modified.

Using *istream_iterator for Input and Using *ostream_iterator *for Output*

We use iterators with **sequences** (also called **ranges**). These sequences can be in containers, or they can be **input sequences** or **output sequences**. The program of Fig. 22.5 demonstrates input from the standard input (a sequence of data for input into a program), using an **istream_iterator**, and output to the standard output (a sequence of data for output from a program), using an **ostream_iterator**. The program inputs two integers from the user at the keyboard and displays the sum of the integers.

```cpp
1   // Fig. 22.5: Fig22_05.cpp
2   // Demonstrating input and output with iterators.
3   #include <iostream>
4   #include <iterator> // ostream_iterator and istream_iterator
5   using namespace std;
6
7   int main()
8   {
9      cout << "Enter two integers: ";
10
11     // create istream_iterator for reading int values from cin
12     istream_iterator< int > inputInt( cin );
13
14     int number1 = *inputInt; // read int from standard input
15     ++inputInt; // move iterator to next input value
16     int number2 = *inputInt; // read int from standard input
17
18     // create ostream_iterator for writing int values to cout
19     ostream_iterator< int > outputInt( cout );
20
21     cout << "The sum is: ";
22     *outputInt = number1 + number2; // output result to cout
23     cout << endl;
24  } // end main
```

```
Enter two integers: 12 25
The sum is: 37
```

Fig. 22.5 | Input and output stream iterators.

Line 12 creates an `istream_iterator` that is capable of extracting (inputting) `int` values in a type-safe manner from the standard input object `cin`. Line 14 dereferences iterator `inputInt` to read the first integer from `cin` and assigns that integer to `number1`. The dereferencing operator `*` applied to `inputInt` gets the value from the stream associated with `inputInt`; this is similar to dereferencing a pointer. Line 15 positions iterator `inputInt` to the next value in the input stream. Line 16 inputs the next integer from `inputInt` and assigns it to `number2`.

Line 19 creates an `ostream_iterator` that is capable of inserting (outputting) `int` values in the standard output object cout. Line 22 outputs an integer to `cout` by assigning to `*outputInt` the sum of `number1` and `number2`. Notice the use of the dereferencing operator `*` to use `*outputInt` as an *lvalue* in the assignment statement. If you want to output another value using `outputInt`, the iterator must be incremented with `++` (both the prefix and postfix increment can be used, but the prefix form should be preferred for performance reasons).

Error-Prevention Tip 22.2

The * (dereferencing) operator of any const *iterator returns a* const *reference to the container element, disallowing the use of non-*const *member functions.*

Common Programming Error 22.1

Attempting to dereference an iterator positioned outside its container is a runtime logic error. In particular, the iterator returned by end *cannot be dereferenced or incremented.*

Common Programming Error 22.2

*Attempting to create a non-*const *iterator for a* const *container results in a compilation error.*

Iterator Categories and Iterator Category Hierarchy

Figure 22.6 shows the categories of STL iterators. Each category provides a specific set of functionality. Figure 22.7 illustrates the hierarchy of iterator categories. As you follow the hierarchy from top to bottom, each iterator category supports all the functionality of the categories above it in the figure. Thus the "weakest" iterator types are at the top and the most powerful one is at the bottom. Note that this is not an inheritance hierarchy.

Category	Description
input	Used to read an element from a container. An input iterator can move only in the forward direction (i.e., from the beginning of the container to the end) one element at a time. Input iterators support only one-pass algorithms—the same input iterator cannot be used to pass through a sequence twice.
output	Used to write an element to a container. An output iterator can move only in the forward direction one element at a time. Output iterators support only one-pass algorithms—the same output iterator cannot be used to pass through a sequence twice.
forward	Combines the capabilities of input and output iterators and retains their position in the container (as state information).
bidirectional	Combines the capabilities of a forward iterator with the ability to move in the backward direction (i.e., from the end of the container toward the beginning). Bidirectional iterators support multipass algorithms.
random access	Combines the capabilities of a bidirectional iterator with the ability to directly access any element of the container, i.e., to jump forward or backward by an arbitrary number of elements.

Fig. 22.6 | Iterator categories.

The iterator category that each container supports determines whether that container can be used with specific algorithms in the STL. Containers that support random-access iterators can be used with all algorithms in the STL. As we'll see, pointers into arrays can be used in place of iterators in most STL algorithms, including those that require random-access iterators. Figure 22.8 shows the iterator category of each of the STL containers. The first-class containers (vectors, deques, lists, sets, multisets, maps and multimaps), strings and arrays are all traversable with iterators.

Software Engineering Observation 22.4

Using the "weakest iterator" that yields acceptable performance helps produce maximally reusable components. For example, if an algorithm requires only forward iterators, it can be used with any container that supports forward iterators, bidirectional iterators or random-access iterators. However, an algorithm that requires random-access iterators can be used only with containers that have random-access iterators.

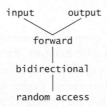

Fig. 22.7 | Iterator category hierarchy.

Container	Type of iterator supported
Sequence containers (first class)	
vector	random access
deque	random access
list	bidirectional
Associative containers (first class)	
set	bidirectional
multiset	bidirectional
map	bidirectional
multimap	bidirectional
Container adapters	
stack	no iterators supported
queue	no iterators supported
priority_queue	no iterators supported

Fig. 22.8 | Iterator types supported by each container.

Predefined Iterator **typedefs**

Figure 22.9 shows the predefined iterator typedefs that are found in the class definitions of the STL containers. Not every typedef is defined for every container. We use const versions of the iterators for traversing read-only containers. We use reverse iterators to traverse containers in the reverse direction.

Predefined `typedefs` for iterator types	Direction of ++	Capability
`iterator`	forward	read/write
`const_iterator`	forward	read
`reverse_iterator`	backward	read/write
`const_reverse_iterator`	backward	read

Fig. 22.9 | Iterator `typedefs`.

Error-Prevention Tip 22.3

Operations performed on a `const_iterator` return const references to prevent modification to elements of the container being manipulated. Using `const_iterators` where appropriate is another example of the principle of least privilege.

Iterator Operations

Figure 22.10 shows some operations that can be performed on each iterator type. The operations for each iterator type include all operations preceding that type in the figure. For input iterators and output iterators, it's not possible to save the iterator then use the saved value later.

Iterator operation	Description
All iterators	
`++p`	Preincrement an iterator.
`p++`	Postincrement an iterator.
Input iterators	
`*p`	Dereference an iterator.
`p = p1`	Assign one iterator to another.
`p == p1`	Compare iterators for equality.
`p != p1`	Compare iterators for inequality.
Output iterators	
`*p`	Dereference an iterator.
`p = p1`	Assign one iterator to another.
Forward iterators	Forward iterators provide all the functionality of both input iterators and output iterators.
Bidirectional iterators	
`--p`	Predecrement an iterator.
`p--`	Postdecrement an iterator.
Random-access iterators	
`p += i`	Increment the iterator p by i positions.

Fig. 22.10 | Iterator operations for each type of iterator. (Part 1 of 2.)

Iterator operation	Description
p -= i	Decrement the iterator p by i positions.
p + i *or* i + p	Expression value is an iterator positioned at p incremented by i positions.
p - i	Expression value is an iterator positioned at p decremented by i positions.
p - p1	Expression value is an integer representing the distance between two elements in the same container.
p[i]	Return a reference to the element offset from p by i positions
p < p1	Return true if iterator p is less than iterator p1 (i.e., iterator p is before iterator p1 in the container); otherwise, return false.
p <= p1	Return true if iterator p is less than or equal to iterator p1 (i.e., iterator p is before iterator p1 or at the same location as iterator p1 in the container); otherwise, return false.
p > p1	Return true if iterator p is greater than iterator p1 (i.e., iterator p is after iterator p1 in the container); otherwise, return false.
p >= p1	Return true if iterator p is greater than or equal to iterator p1 (i.e., iterator p is after iterator p1 or at the same location as iterator p1 in the container); otherwise, return false.

Fig. 22.10 | Iterator operations for each type of iterator. (Part 2 of 2.)

22.1.3 Introduction to Algorithms

STL algorithms can be used generically across a variety of containers. STL provides many algorithms you'll use frequently to manipulate containers. Inserting, deleting, searching, sorting and others are appropriate for some or all of the STL containers.

The STL includes approximately 70 standard algorithms. We show most of these and summarize the others. The algorithms operate on container elements only indirectly through iterators. Many algorithms operate on sequences of elements defined by pairs of iterators—one pointing to the first element of the sequence and one pointing to one element past the last element. Also, it's possible to create your own new algorithms that operate in a similar fashion so they can be used with the STL containers and iterators.

Algorithms often return iterators that indicate the results of the algorithms. Algorithm find, for example, locates an element and returns an iterator to that element. If the element is not found, find returns the "one past the end" iterator that was passed in to define the end of the range to be searched, which can be tested to determine whether an element was not found. The find algorithm can be used with any first-class STL container. STL algorithms create yet another opportunity for reuse—using the rich collection of popular algorithms can save you much time and effort.

If an algorithm uses less powerful iterators, the algorithm can also be used with containers that support more powerful iterators. Some algorithms demand powerful iterators; e.g., sort demands random-access iterators.

Software Engineering Observation 22.5

The STL is extensible. It's straightforward to add new algorithms and to do so without changes to STL containers.

Software Engineering Observation 22.6
The STL is implemented concisely. The algorithms are separated from the containers and operate on elements of the containers only indirectly through iterators. This separation makes it easier to write generic algorithms applicable to many container classes.

Software Engineering Observation 22.7
STL algorithms can operate on STL containers and on pointer-based, C-like arrays.

Portability Tip 22.2
Because STL algorithms process containers only indirectly through iterators, one algorithm can often be used with many different containers.

Figure 22.11 shows many of the **mutating-sequence algorithms**—i.e., the algorithms that result in modifications of the containers to which the algorithms are applied.

Mutating-sequence algorithms			
copy	partition	replace_copy	stable_partition
copy_backward	random_shuffle	replace_copy_if	swap
fill	remove	replace_if	swap_ranges
fill_n	remove_copy	reverse	transform
generate	remove_copy_if	reverse_copy	unique
generate_n	remove_if	rotate	unique_copy
iter_swap	replace	rotate_copy	

Fig. 22.11 | Mutating-sequence algorithms.

Figure 22.12 shows many of the nonmodifying sequence algorithms—i.e., the algorithms that do not result in modifications of the containers to which they're applied. Figure 22.13 shows the numerical algorithms of the header file **<numeric>**.

Nonmodifying sequence algorithms			
adjacent_find	equal	find_end	mismatch
count	find	find_first_of	search
count_if	find_each	find_if	search_n

Fig. 22.12 | Nonmodifying sequence algorithms.

Numerical algorithms from header file **<numeric>**	
accumulate	partial_sum
inner_product	adjacent_difference

Fig. 22.13 | Numerical algorithms from header file <numeric>.

22.2 Sequence Containers

The C++ Standard Template Library provides three sequence containers—vector, list and deque. Class template vector and class template deque both are based on arrays. Class template list implements a linked-list data structure similar to our List class presented in Chapter 20, but more robust.

One of the most popular containers in the STL is vector. Recall that we introduced class template vector in Chapter 7 as a more robust type of array. A vector changes size dynamically. Unlike C and C++ "raw" arrays (see Chapter 7), vectors can be assigned to one another. This is not possible with pointer-based, C-like arrays, because those array names are constant pointers and cannot be the targets of assignments. Just as with C arrays, vector subscripting does not perform automatic range checking, but class template vector does provide this capability via member function at (also discussed in Chapter 7).

Performance Tip 22.4

Insertion at the back of a vector is efficient. The vector simply grows, if necessary, to accommodate the new item. It's expensive to insert (or delete) an element in the middle of a vector—the entire portion of the vector after the insertion (or deletion) point must be moved, because vector elements occupy contiguous cells in memory just as C or C++ "raw" arrays do.

Figure 22.2 presented the operations common to all the STL containers. Beyond these operations, each container typically provides a variety of other capabilities. Many of these capabilities are common to several containers, but they're not always equally efficient for each container. You must choose the container most appropriate for the application.

Performance Tip 22.5

Applications that require frequent insertions and deletions at both ends of a container normally use a deque rather than a vector. Although we can insert and delete elements at the front and back of both a vector and a deque, class deque is more efficient than vector for doing insertions and deletions at the front.

Performance Tip 22.6

Applications with frequent insertions and deletions in the middle and/or at the extremes of a container normally use a list, due to its efficient implementation of insertion and deletion anywhere in the data structure.

In addition to the common operations described in Fig. 22.2, the sequence containers have several other common operations—**front** to return a reference to the first element in a non-empty container, **back** to return a reference to the last element in a non-empty container, push_back to insert a new element at the end of the container and pop_back to remove the last element of the container.

22.2.1 vector Sequence Container

Class template vector provides a data structure with contiguous memory locations. This enables efficient, direct access to any element of a vector via the subscript operator [], exactly as with a C or C++ "raw" array. Class template vector is most commonly used when the data in the container must be easily accessible via a subscript or will be sorted. When a vector's memory is exhausted, the vector allocates a larger contiguous area of memory, copies the original elements into the new memory and deallocates the old memory.

Performance Tip 22.7

Choose the vector container for the best random-access performance.

Performance Tip 22.8

Objects of class template vector provide rapid indexed access with the overloaded subscript operator [] because they're stored in contiguous memory like a C or C++ raw array.

Performance Tip 22.9

It's faster to insert many elements at once than one at a time.

An important part of every container is the type of iterator it supports. This determines which algorithms can be applied to the container. A vector supports random-access iterators—i.e., all iterator operations shown in Fig. 22.10 can be applied to a vector iterator. All STL algorithms can operate on a vector. The iterators for a vector are sometimes implemented as pointers to elements of the vector. Each STL algorithm that takes iterator arguments requires those iterators to provide a minimum level of functionality. If an algorithm requires a forward iterator, for example, that algorithm can operate on any container that provides forward iterators, bidirectional iterators or random-access iterators. As long as the container supports the algorithm's minimum iterator functionality, the algorithm can operate on the container.

Using Vector and Iterators

Figure 22.14 illustrates several functions of the vector class template. Many of these functions are available in every first-class container. You must include header file <vector> to use class template vector.

```
 1  // Fig. 22.14: Fig22_14.cpp
 2  // Demonstrating Standard Library vector class template.
 3  #include <iostream>
 4  #include <vector> // vector class-template definition
 5  using namespace std;
 6
 7  // prototype for function template printVector
 8  template < typename T > void printVector( const vector< T > &integers2 );
 9
10  int main()
11  {
12     const int SIZE = 6; // define array size
13     int array[ SIZE ] = { 1, 2, 3, 4, 5, 6 }; // initialize array
14     vector< int > integers; // create vector of ints
```

Fig. 22.14 | Standard Library vector class template. (Part 1 of 2.)

```
15
16      cout << "The initial size of integers is: " << integers.size()
17         << "\nThe initial capacity of integers is: " << integers.capacity();
18
19      // function push_back is in every sequence collection
20      integers.push_back( 2 );
21      integers.push_back( 3 );
22      integers.push_back( 4 );
23
24      cout << "\nThe size of integers is: " << integers.size()
25         << "\nThe capacity of integers is: " << integers.capacity();
26      cout << "\n\nOutput array using pointer notation: ";
27
28      // display array using pointer notation
29      for ( int *ptr = array; ptr != array + SIZE; ptr++ )
30         cout << *ptr << ' ';
31
32      cout << "\nOutput vector using iterator notation: ";
33      printVector( integers );
34      cout << "\nReversed contents of vector integers: ";
35
36      // two const reverse iterators
37      vector< int >::const_reverse_iterator reverseIterator;
38      vector< int >::const_reverse_iterator tempIterator = integers.rend();
39
40      // display vector in reverse order using reverse_iterator
41      for ( reverseIterator = integers.rbegin();
42         reverseIterator!= tempIterator; ++reverseIterator )
43         cout << *reverseIterator << ' ';
44
45      cout << endl;
46   } // end main
47
48   // function template for outputting vector elements
49   template < typename T > void printVector( const vector< T > &integers2 )
50   {
51      typename vector< T >::const_iterator constIterator; // const_iterator
52
53      // display vector elements using const_iterator
54      for ( constIterator = integers2.begin();
55         constIterator != integers2.end(); ++constIterator )
56         cout << *constIterator << ' ';
57   } // end function printVector
```

```
The initial size of integers is: 0
The initial capacity of integers is: 0
The size of integers is: 3
The capacity of integers is: 4

Output array using pointer notation: 1 2 3 4 5 6
Output vector using iterator notation: 2 3 4
Reversed contents of vector integers: 4 3 2
```

Fig. 22.14 | Standard Library vector class template. (Part 2 of 2.)

Line 14 defines an instance called integers of class template vector that stores int values. When this object is instantiated, an empty vector is created with size 0 (i.e., the number of elements stored in the vector) and capacity 0 (i.e., the number of elements that can be stored without allocating more memory to the vector).

Lines 16 and 17 demonstrate the size and capacity functions; each initially returns 0 for vector v in this example. Function size—available in every container—returns the number of elements currently stored in the container. Function **capacity** returns the number of elements that can be stored in the vector before the vector needs to dynamically resize itself to accommodate more elements.

Lines 20–22 use function **push_back**—available in all sequence containers—to add an element to the end of the vector. If an element is added to a full vector, the vector increases its size—some STL implementations have the vector double its capacity.

Performance Tip 22.10

It can be wasteful to double a vector's size when more space is needed. For example, a full vector of 1,000,000 elements resizes to accommodate 2,000,000 elements when a new element is added. This leaves 999,999 unused elements. You can use resize *and* reserve *to control space usage better.*

Lines 24 and 25 use size and capacity to illustrate the new size and capacity of the vector after the three push_back operations. Function size returns 3—the number of elements added to the vector. Function capacity returns 4, indicating that we can add one more element before the vector needs to add more memory. When we added the first element, the vector allocated space for one element, and the size became 1 to indicate that the vector contained only one element. When we added the second element, the capacity doubled to 2 and the size became 2 as well. When we added the third element, the capacity doubled again to 4. So we can actually add another element before the vector needs to allocate more space. When the vector eventually fills its allocated capacity and the program attempts to add one more element to the vector, the vector will double its capacity to 8 elements.

The manner in which a vector grows to accommodate more elements—a time consuming operation—is not specified by the C++ Standard Document. C++ library implementors use various clever schemes to minimize the overhead of resizing a vector. Hence, the output of this program may vary, depending on the version of vector that comes with your compiler. Some library implementors allocate a large initial capacity. If a vector stores a small number of elements, such capacity may be a waste of space. However, it can greatly improve performance if a program adds many elements to a vector and does not have to reallocate memory to accommodate those elements. This is a classic space–time trade-off. Library implementors must balance the amount of memory used against the amount of time required to perform various vector operations.

Lines 29–30 demonstrate how to output the contents of an array using pointers and pointer arithmetic. Line 33 calls function printVector (defined in lines 49–57) to output the contents of a vector using iterators. Function template printVector receives a const reference to a vector (integers2) as its argument. Line 51 defines a const_iterator called constIterator that iterates through the vector and outputs its contents. Notice that the declaration in line 51 is prefixed with the keyword typename. Because printVector is a function template and vector< T > will be specialized differently for each function-template specialization, the compiler cannot tell at compile time whether or not vector< T >::const_iterator is a type. In a particular specialization, const_iterator could be a static variable. The compiler needs this information to compile the program correctly. Therefore, you must tell the compiler that a qualified name, when the qualifier is a dependent type, is expected to be a type in every specialization.

A const_iterator enables the program to read the elements of the vector, but does not allow the program to modify the elements. The for statement in lines 54–56 initializes constIterator using vector member function begin, which returns a const_iterator to the first element in the vector—there is another version of begin that returns an iterator that can be used for non-const containers. A const_iterator is returned because the identifier integers2 was declared const in the parameter list of function printVector. The loop continues as long as constIterator has not reached the end of the vector. This is determined by comparing constIterator to the result of integers2.end(), which returns an iterator indicating the location past the last element of the vector. If constIterator is equal to this value, the end of the vector has been reached. Functions begin and end are available for all first-class containers. The body of the loop dereferences iterator constIterator to get the value in the current element of the vector. Remember that the iterator acts like a pointer to the element and that operator * is overloaded to return a reference to the element. The expression ++constIterator (line 55) positions the iterator to the next element of the vector.

Performance Tip 22.11
Use prefix increment when applied to STL iterators because the prefix increment operator does not return a value that must be stored in a temporary object.

Error-Prevention Tip 22.4
Only random-access iterators support <. It's better to use != and end to test for the end of a container.

Line 37 declares a const_reverse_iterator that can be used to iterate through a vector backward. Line 38 declares a const_reverse_iterator variable tempIterator and initializes it to the iterator returned by function **rend** (i.e., the iterator for the ending point when iterating through the container in reverse). All first-class containers support this type of iterator. Lines 41–43 use a for statement similar to that in function printVector to iterate through the vector. In this loop, function **rbegin** (i.e., the iterator for the starting point when iterating through the container in reverse) and tempIterator delineate the range of elements to output. As with functions begin and end, rbegin and rend can return a const_reverse_iterator or a reverse_iterator, based on whether or not the container is constant.

Performance Tip 22.12
For performance reasons, capture the loop ending value before the loop and compare against that, rather than having a (potentially expensive) function call for each iteration.

Vector Element-Manipulation Functions
Figure 22.15 illustrates functions that enable retrieval and manipulation of the elements of a vector. Line 15 uses an overloaded vector constructor that takes two iterators as ar-

guments to initialize `integers`. Remember that pointers into an array can be used as iterators. Line 15 initializes `integers` with the contents of `array` from location `array` up to—but not including—location `array + SIZE`.

```cpp
1   // Fig. 22.15: Fig22_15.cpp
2   // Testing Standard Library vector class template
3   // element-manipulation functions.
4   #include <iostream>
5   #include <vector> // vector class-template definition
6   #include <algorithm> // copy algorithm
7   #include <iterator> // ostream_iterator iterator
8   #include <stdexcept> // out_of_range exception
9   using namespace std;
10
11  int main()
12  {
13     const int SIZE = 6;
14     int array[ SIZE ] = { 1, 2, 3, 4, 5, 6 };
15     vector< int > integers( array, array + SIZE );
16     ostream_iterator< int > output( cout, " " );
17
18     cout << "Vector integers contains: ";
19     copy( integers.begin(), integers.end(), output );
20
21     cout << "\nFirst element of integers: " << integers.front()
22        << "\nLast element of integers: " << integers.back();
23
24     integers[ 0 ] = 7; // set first element to 7
25     integers.at( 2 ) = 10; // set element at position 2 to 10
26
27     // insert 22 as 2nd element
28     integers.insert( integers.begin() + 1, 22 );
29
30     cout << "\n\nContents of vector integers after changes: ";
31     copy( integers.begin(), integers.end(), output );
32
33     // access out-of-range element
34     try
35     {
36        integers.at( 100 ) = 777;
37     } // end try
38     catch ( out_of_range &outOfRange ) // out_of_range exception
39     {
40        cout << "\n\nException: " << outOfRange.what();
41     } // end catch
42
43     // erase first element
44     integers.erase( integers.begin() );
45     cout << "\n\nVector integers after erasing first element: ";
46     copy( integers.begin(), integers.end(), output );
47
```

Fig. 22.15 | `vector` class template element-manipulation functions. (Part 1 of 2.)

```
48      // erase remaining elements
49      integers.erase( integers.begin(), integers.end() );
50      cout << "\nAfter erasing all elements, vector integers "
51         << ( integers.empty() ? "is" : "is not" ) << " empty";
52
53      // insert elements from array
54      integers.insert( integers.begin(), array, array + SIZE );
55      cout << "\n\nContents of vector integers before clear: ";
56      copy( integers.begin(), integers.end(), output );
57
58      // empty integers; clear calls erase to empty a collection
59      integers.clear();
60      cout << "\nAfter clear, vector integers "
61         << ( integers.empty() ? "is" : "is not" ) << " empty" << endl;
62   } // end main
```

```
Vector integers contains: 1 2 3 4 5 6
First element of integers: 1
Last element of integers: 6

Contents of vector integers after changes: 7 22 2 10 4 5 6

Exception: invalid vector<T> subscript

Vector integers after erasing first element: 22 2 10 4 5 6
After erasing all elements, vector integers is empty

Contents of vector integers before clear: 1 2 3 4 5 6
After clear, vector integers is empty
```

Fig. 22.15 | vector class template element-manipulation functions. (Part 2 of 2.)

Line 16 defines an ostream_iterator called output that can be used to output integers separated by single spaces via cout. An ostream_iterator< int > is a type-safe output mechanism that outputs only values of type int or a compatible type. The first argument to the constructor specifies the output stream, and the second argument is a string specifying the separator for the values output—in this case, the string contains a space character. We use the ostream_iterator (defined in header <iterator>) to output the contents of the vector in this example.

Line 19 uses algorithm **copy** from the Standard Library to output the entire contents of vector integers to the standard output. Algorithm copy copies each element in the container starting with the location specified by the iterator in its first argument and continuing up to—but not including—the location specified by the iterator in its second argument. The first and second arguments must satisfy input iterator requirements—they must be iterators through which values can be read from a container. Also, applying ++ to the first iterator must eventually cause it to reach the second iterator argument in the container. The elements are copied to the location specified by the output iterator (i.e., an iterator through which a value can be stored or output) specified as the last argument. In this case, the output iterator is an ostream_iterator (output) that is attached to cout, so the elements are copied to the standard output. To use the algorithms of the Standard Library, you must include the header file **<algorithm>**.

Lines 21–22 use functions front and back (available for all sequence containers) to determine the vector's first and last elements, respectively. Notice the difference between functions front and begin. Function front returns a reference to the first element in the vector, while function begin returns a random access iterator pointing to the first element in the vector. Also notice the difference between functions back and end. Function back returns a reference to the last element in the vector, while function end returns a random access iterator pointing to the end of the vector (the location after the last element).

> **Common Programming Error 22.3**
>
> *The vector must not be empty; otherwise, results of the front and back functions are undefined.*

Lines 24–25 illustrate two ways to subscript through a vector (which also can be used with the deque containers). Line 26 uses the subscript operator that is overloaded to return either a reference to the value at the specified location or a constant reference to that value, depending on whether the container is constant. Function at (line 25) performs the same operation, but with bounds checking. Function at first checks the value supplied as an argument and determines whether it's in the bounds of the vector. If not, function at throws an out_of_range exception defined in header <stdexcept> (as demonstrated in lines 34–41). Figure 22.16 shows some of the STL exception types. (The Standard Library exception types are discussed in Chapter 16, Exception Handling.)

STL exception types	Description
out_of_range	Indicates when subscript is out of range—e.g., when an invalid subscript is specified to vector member function at.
invalid_argument	Indicates an invalid argument was passed to a function.
length_error	Indicates an attempt to create too long a container, string, etc.
bad_alloc	Indicates that an attempt to allocate memory with new (or with an allocator) failed because not enough memory was available.

Fig. 22.16 | Some STL exception types.

Line 28 uses one of the three overloaded **insert** functions provided by each sequence container. Line 28 inserts the value 22 before the element at the location specified by the iterator in the first argument. In this example, the iterator is pointing to the second element of the vector, so 22 is inserted as the second element and the original second element becomes the third element of the vector. Other versions of insert allow inserting multiple copies of the same value starting at a particular position in the container, or inserting a range of values from another container (or array), starting at a particular position in the original container.

Lines 44 and 49 use the two **erase** functions that are available in all first-class containers. Line 44 indicates that the element at the location specified by the iterator argument should be removed from the container (in this example, the element at the beginning of the vector). Line 49 specifies that all elements in the range starting with the location of the first argument up to—but not including—the location of the second argument should be erased from the container. In this example, all the elements are erased from the vector. Line 51 uses function **empty** (available for all containers and adapters) to confirm that the vector is empty.

Common Programming Error 22.4

Erasing an element that contains a pointer to a dynamically allocated object does not de-lete that object; this can lead to a memory leak.

Line 54 demonstrates the version of function insert that uses the second and third arguments to specify the starting location and ending location in a sequence of values (possibly from another container; in this case, from array of integers array) that should be inserted into the vector. Remember that the ending location specifies the position in the sequence after the last element to be inserted; copying is performed up to—but not including—this location.

Finally, line 59 uses function **clear** (found in all first-class containers) to empty the vector. This function calls the version of erase used in line 51 to empty the vector.

[*Note:* Other functions that are common to all containers and common to all sequence containers have not yet been covered. We'll cover most of these in the next few sections. We'll also cover many functions that are specific to each container.]

22.2.2 list Sequence Container

The list sequence container provides an efficient implementation for insertion and deletion operations at any location in the container. If most of the insertions and deletions occur at the ends of the container, the deque data structure (Section 22.2.3) provides a more efficient implementation. Class template list is implemented as a doubly linked list—every node in the list contains a pointer to the previous node in the list and to the next node in the list. This enables class template list to support bidirectional iterators that allow the container to be traversed both forward and backward. Any algorithm that requires input, output, forward or bidirectional iterators can operate on a list. Many list member functions manipulate the elements of the container as an ordered set of elements.

In addition to the member functions of all STL containers in Fig. 22.2 and the common member functions of all sequence containers discussed in Section 22.2, class template list provides nine other member functions—splice, push_front, pop_front, remove, remove_if, unique, merge, reverse and sort. Several of these member functions are list-optimized implementations of STL algorithms presented in Section 22.5. Figure 22.17 demonstrates several features of class list. Remember that many of the functions presented in Figs. 22.14–22.15 can be used with class list. Header file **<list>** must be included to use class list.

```
1   // Fig. 22.17: Fig22_17.cpp
2   // Standard library list class template test program.
3   #include <iostream>
4   #include <list> // list class-template definition
5   #include <algorithm> // copy algorithm
6   #include <iterator> // ostream_iterator
7   using namespace std;
```

Fig. 22.17 | Standard Library list class template. (Part 1 of 4.)

```
 8
 9    // prototype for function template printList
10    template < typename T > void printList( const list< T > &listRef );
11
12    int main()
13    {
14       const int SIZE = 4;
15       int array[ SIZE ] = { 2, 6, 4, 8 };
16       list< int > values; // create list of ints
17       list< int > otherValues; // create list of ints
18
19       // insert items in values
20       values.push_front( 1 );
21       values.push_front( 2 );
22       values.push_back( 4 );
23       values.push_back( 3 );
24
25       cout << "values contains: ";
26       printList( values );
27
28       values.sort(); // sort values
29       cout << "\nvalues after sorting contains: ";
30       printList( values );
31
32       // insert elements of array into otherValues
33       otherValues.insert( otherValues.begin(), array, array + SIZE );
34       cout << "\nAfter insert, otherValues contains: ";
35       printList( otherValues );
36
37       // remove otherValues elements and insert at end of values
38       values.splice( values.end(), otherValues );
39       cout << "\nAfter splice, values contains: ";
40       printList( values );
41
42       values.sort(); // sort values
43       cout << "\nAfter sort, values contains: ";
44       printList( values );
45
46       // insert elements of array into otherValues
47       otherValues.insert( otherValues.begin(), array, array + SIZE );
48       otherValues.sort();
49       cout << "\nAfter insert and sort, otherValues contains: ";
50       printList( otherValues );
51
52       // remove otherValues elements and insert into values in sorted order
53       values.merge( otherValues );
54       cout << "\nAfter merge:\n   values contains: ";
55       printList( values );
56       cout << "\n   otherValues contains: ";
57       printList( otherValues );
58
59       values.pop_front(); // remove element from front
60       values.pop_back(); // remove element from back
```

Fig. 22.17 | Standard Library list class template. (Part 2 of 4.)

```
61      cout << "\nAfter pop_front and pop_back:\n   values contains: "
62      printList( values );
63
64      values.unique(); // remove duplicate elements
65      cout << "\nAfter unique, values contains: ";
66      printList( values );
67
68      // swap elements of values and otherValues
69      values.swap( otherValues );
70      cout << "\nAfter swap:\n   values contains: ";
71      printList( values );
72      cout << "\n   otherValues contains: ";
73      printList( otherValues );
74
75      // replace contents of values with elements of otherValues
76      values.assign( otherValues.begin(), otherValues.end() );
77      cout << "\nAfter assign, values contains: ";
78      printList( values );
79
80      // remove otherValues elements and insert into values in sorted order
81      values.merge( otherValues );
82      cout << "\nAfter merge, values contains: ";
83      printList( values );
84
85      values.remove( 4 ); // remove all 4s
86      cout << "\nAfter remove( 4 ), values contains: ";
87      printList( values );
88      cout << endl;
89   } // end main
90
91   // printList function template definition; uses
92   // ostream_iterator and copy algorithm to output list elements
93   template < typename T > void printList( const list< T > &listRef )
94   {
95      if ( listRef.empty() ) // list is empty
96         cout << "List is empty";
97      else
98      {
99         ostream_iterator< T > output( cout, " " );
100        copy( listRef.begin(), listRef.end(), output );
101     } // end else
102   } // end function printList
```

```
values contains: 2 1 4 3
values after sorting contains: 1 2 3 4
After insert, otherValues contains: 2 6 4 8
After splice, values contains: 1 2 3 4 2 6 4 8
After sort, values contains: 1 2 2 3 4 4 6 8
After insert and sort, otherValues contains: 2 4 6 8
After merge:
   values contains: 1 2 2 2 3 4 4 4 6 6 8 8
   otherValues contains: List is empty
```

Fig. 22.17 | Standard Library `list` class template. (Part 3 of 4.)

```
After pop_front and pop_back:
   values contains: 2 2 2 3 4 4 4 6 6 8
After unique, values contains: 2 3 4 6 8
After swap:
   values contains: List is empty
   otherValues contains: 2 3 4 6 8
After assign, values contains: 2 3 4 6 8
After merge, values contains: 2 2 3 3 4 4 6 6 8 8
After remove( 4 ), values contains: 2 2 3 3 6 6 8 8
```

Fig. 22.17 | Standard Library `list` class template. (Part 4 of 4.)

Lines 16–17 instantiate two `list` objects capable of storing integers. Lines 20–21 use function **push_front** to insert integers at the beginning of `values`. Function push_front is specific to classes `list` and `deque` (not to `vector`). Lines 22–23 use function push_back to insert integers at the end of `values`. Remember that function push_back is common to all sequence containers.

Line 28 uses `list` member function **sort** to arrange the elements in the `list` in ascending order. [*Note:* This is different from the `sort` in the STL algorithms.] A second version of function `sort` allows you to supply a binary predicate function that takes two arguments (values in the list), performs a comparison and returns a `bool` value indicating the result. This function determines the order in which the elements of the `list` are sorted. This version could be particularly useful for a `list` that stores pointers rather than values. [*Note:* We demonstrate a unary predicate function in Fig. 22.28. A unary predicate function takes a single argument, performs a comparison using that argument and returns a `bool` value indicating the result.]

Line 38 uses `list` function **splice** to remove the elements in `otherValues` and insert them into `values` before the iterator position specified as the first argument. There are two other versions of this function. Function `splice` with three arguments allows one element to be removed from the container specified as the second argument from the location specified by the iterator in the third argument. Function `splice` with four arguments uses the last two arguments to specify a range of locations that should be removed from the container in the second argument and placed at the location specified in the first argument.

After inserting more elements in `otherValues` and sorting both `values` and `otherValues`, line 53 uses `list` member function **merge** to remove all elements of `otherValues` and insert them in sorted order into `values`. Both `list`s must be sorted in the same order before this operation is performed. A second version of `merge` enables you to supply a predicate function that takes two arguments (values in the list) and returns a `bool` value. The predicate function specifies the sorting order used by `merge`.

Line 59 uses `list` function **pop_front** to remove the first element in the `list`. Line 60 uses function **pop_back** (available for all sequence containers) to remove the last element in the `list`.

Line 64 uses `list` function **unique** to remove duplicate elements in the `list`. The `list` should be in sorted order (so that all duplicates are side by side) before this operation is performed, to guarantee that all duplicates are eliminated. A second version of `unique` enables you to supply a predicate function that takes two arguments (values in the list) and returns a `bool` value specifying whether two elements are equal.

Line 69 uses function **swap** (available to all first-class containers) to exchange the contents of values with the contents of otherValues.

Line 76 uses list function **assign** (available to all sequence containers) to replace the contents of values with the contents of otherValues in the range specified by the two iterator arguments. A second version of assign replaces the original contents with copies of the value specified in the second argument. The first argument of the function specifies the number of copies. Line 85 uses list function **remove** to delete all copies of the value 4 from the list.

22.2.3 deque Sequence Container

Class deque provides many of the benefits of a vector and a list in one container. The term deque is short for "double-ended queue." Class deque is implemented to provide efficient indexed access (using subscripting) for reading and modifying its elements, much like a vector. Class deque is also implemented for efficient insertion and deletion operations at its front and back, much like a list (although a list is also capable of efficient insertions and deletions in the middle of the list). Class deque provides support for random-access iterators, so deques can be used with all STL algorithms. One of the most common uses of a deque is to maintain a first-in, first-out queue of elements. In fact, a deque is the default underlying implementation for the queue adaptor (Section 22.4.2).

Additional storage for a deque can be allocated at either end of the deque in blocks of memory that are typically maintained as an array of pointers to those blocks.[1] Due to the noncontiguous memory layout of a deque, a deque iterator must be more intelligent than the pointers that are used to iterate through vectors or pointer-based arrays.

Performance Tip 22.13
In general, deque has higher overhead than vector.

Performance Tip 22.14
Insertions and deletions in the middle of a deque are optimized to minimize the number of elements copied, so it's more efficient than a vector but less efficient than a list for this kind of modification.

Class deque provides the same basic operations as class vector, but like list adds member functions push_front and pop_front to allow insertion and deletion at the beginning of the deque, respectively.

Figure 22.18 demonstrates features of class deque. Remember that many of the functions presented in Fig. 22.14, Fig. 22.15 and Fig. 22.17 also can be used with class deque. Header file **<deque>** must be included to use class deque.

Line 11 instantiates a deque that can store double values. Lines 15–17 use functions push_front and push_back to insert elements at the beginning and end of the deque.

---

1. This is an implementation-specific detail, not a requirement of the C++ standard.

Remember that push_back is available for all sequence containers, but push_front is available only for class list and class deque.

```cpp
1   // Fig. 22.18: Fig22_18.cpp
2   // Standard Library class deque test program.
3   #include <iostream>
4   #include <deque> // deque class-template definition
5   #include <algorithm> // copy algorithm
6   #include <iterator> // ostream_iterator
7   using namespace std;
8
9   int main()
10  {
11     deque< double > values; // create deque of doubles
12     ostream_iterator< double > output( cout, " " );
13
14     // insert elements in values
15     values.push_front( 2.2 );
16     values.push_front( 3.5 );
17     values.push_back( 1.1 );
18
19     cout << "values contains: ";
20
21     // use subscript operator to obtain elements of values
22     for ( unsigned int i = 0; i < values.size(); i++ )
23        cout << values[ i ] << ' ';
24
25     values.pop_front(); // remove first element
26     cout << "\nAfter pop_front, values contains: ";
27     copy( values.begin(), values.end(), output );
28
29     // use subscript operator to modify element at location 1
30     values[ 1 ] = 5.4;
31     cout << "\nAfter values[ 1 ] = 5.4, values contains: ";
32     copy( values.begin(), values.end(), output );
33     cout << endl;
34  } // end main
```

```
values contains: 3.5 2.2 1.1
After pop_front, values contains: 2.2 1.1
After values[ 1 ] = 5.4, values contains: 2.2 5.4
```

Fig. 22.18 | Standard Library deque class template.

The for statement in lines 22–23 uses the subscript operator to retrieve the value in each element of the deque for output. The condition uses function size to ensure that we do not attempt to access an element outside the bounds of the deque.

Line 25 uses function pop_front to demonstrate removing the first element of the deque. Remember that pop_front is available only for class list and class deque (not for class vector).

Line 30 uses the subscript operator to create an *lvalue*. This enables values to be assigned directly to any element of the deque.

22.3 Associative Containers

The STL's associative containers provide direct access to store and retrieve elements via **keys** (often called **search keys**). The four associative containers are `multiset`, `set`, `multimap` and `map`. Each associative container maintains its keys in sorted order. Iterating through an associative container traverses it in the sort order for that container. Classes **multiset** and **set** provide operations for manipulating sets of values where the values are the keys—there is not a separate value associated with each key. The primary difference between a `multiset` and a `set` is that a `multiset` allows duplicate keys and a `set` does not. Classes **multimap** and **map** provide operations for manipulating values associated with keys (these values are sometimes referred to as **mapped values**). The primary difference between a `multimap` and a `map` is that a `multimap` allows duplicate keys with associated values to be stored and a `map` allows only unique keys with associated values. In addition to the common member functions of all containers presented in Fig. 22.2, all associative containers also support several other member functions, including `find`, `lower_bound`, `upper_bound` and `count`. Examples of each of the associative containers and the common associative container member functions are presented in the next several subsections.

22.3.1 `multiset` Associative Container

The `multiset` associative container provides fast storage and retrieval of keys and allows duplicate keys. The ordering of the elements is determined by a **comparator function object**. For example, in an integer `multiset`, elements can be sorted in ascending order by ordering the keys with **comparator function object `less<int>`**. We discuss function objects in detail in Section 22.7. The data type of the keys in all associative containers must support comparison properly based on the comparator function object specified—keys sorted with `less< T >` must support comparison with `operator<`. If the keys used in the associative containers are of user-defined data types, those types must supply the appropriate comparison operators. A `multiset` supports bidirectional iterators (but not random-access iterators).

Figure 22.19 demonstrates the `multiset` associative container for a `multiset` of integers sorted in ascending order. Header file **<set>** must be included to use class `multiset`. Containers `multiset` and `set` provide the same basic functionality.

```
1   // Fig. 22.19: Fig22_19.cpp
2   // Testing Standard Library class multiset
3   #include <iostream>
4   #include <set> // multiset class-template definition
5   #include <algorithm> // copy algorithm
6   #include <iterator> // ostream_iterator
7   using namespace std;
8
9   // define short name for multiset type used in this program
10  typedef multiset< int, less< int > > Ims;
11
12  int main()
13  {
```

Fig. 22.19 | Standard Library `multiset` class template. (Part 1 of 3.)

```
14       const int SIZE = 10;
15       int a[ SIZE ] = { 7, 22, 9, 1, 18, 30, 100, 22, 85, 13 };
16       Ims intMultiset; // Ims is typedef for "integer multiset"
17       ostream_iterator< int > output( cout, " " );
18
19       cout << "There are currently " << intMultiset.count( 15 )
20          << " values of 15 in the multiset\n";
21
22       intMultiset.insert( 15 ); // insert 15 in intMultiset
23       intMultiset.insert( 15 ); // insert 15 in intMultiset
24       cout << "After inserts, there are " << intMultiset.count( 15 )
25          << " values of 15 in the multiset\n\n";
26
27       // iterator that cannot be used to change element values
28       Ims::const_iterator result;
29
30       // find 15 in intMultiset; find returns iterator
31       result = intMultiset.find( 15 );
32
33       if ( result != intMultiset.end() ) // if iterator not at end
34          cout << "Found value 15\n"; // found search value 15
35
36       // find 20 in intMultiset; find returns iterator
37       result = intMultiset.find( 20 );
38
39       if ( result == intMultiset.end() ) // will be true hence
40          cout << "Did not find value 20\n"; // did not find 20
41
42       // insert elements of array a into intMultiset
43       intMultiset.insert( a, a + SIZE );
44       cout << "\nAfter insert, intMultiset contains:\n";
45       copy( intMultiset.begin(), intMultiset.end(), output );
46
47       // determine lower and upper bound of 22 in intMultiset
48       cout << "\n\nLower bound of 22: "
49          << *( intMultiset.lower_bound( 22 ) );
50       cout << "\nUpper bound of 22: " << *( intMultiset.upper_bound( 22 ) );
51
52       // p represents pair of const_iterators
53       pair< Ims::const_iterator, Ims::const_iterator > p;
54
55       // use equal_range to determine lower and upper bound
56       // of 22 in intMultiset
57       p = intMultiset.equal_range( 22 );
58
59       cout << "\n\nequal_range of 22:" << "\n   Lower bound: "
60          << *( p.first ) << "\n   Upper bound: " << *( p.second );
61       cout << endl;
62   } // end main
```

```
There are currently 0 values of 15 in the multiset
After inserts, there are 2 values of 15 in the multiset
```

Fig. 22.19 | Standard Library multiset class template. (Part 2 of 3.)

```
Found value 15
Did not find value 20

After insert, intMultiset contains:
1 7 9 13 15 15 18 22 22 30 85 100

Lower bound of 22: 22
Upper bound of 22: 30

equal_range of 22:
   Lower bound: 22
   Upper bound: 30
```

Fig. 22.19 | Standard Library `multiset` class template. (Part 3 of 3.)

Line 10 uses a `typedef` to create a new type name (alias) for a `multiset` of integers ordered in ascending order, using the function object `less< int >`. Ascending order is the default for a `multiset`, so `less< int >` can be omitted in line 10. This new type (`Ims`) is then used to instantiate an integer `multiset` object, `intMultiset` (line 16).

Good Programming Practice 22.1

Use typedefs to make code with long type names (such as multisets) easier to read.

The output statement in line 19 uses function **count** (available to all associative containers) to count the number of occurrences of the value 15 currently in the `multiset`.

Lines 22–23 use one of the three versions of function `insert` to add the value 15 to the `multiset` twice. A second version of `insert` takes an iterator and a value as arguments and begins the search for the insertion point from the iterator position specified. A third version of `insert` takes two iterators as arguments that specify a range of values to add to the `multiset` from another container.

Line 31 uses function **find** (available to all associative containers) to locate the value 15 in the `multiset`. Function `find` returns an `iterator` or a `const_iterator` pointing to the earliest location at which the value is found. If the value is not found, `find` returns an `iterator` or a `const_iterator` equal to the value returned by a call to `end`. Line 40 demonstrates this case.

Line 43 uses function **insert** to insert the elements of array `a` into the `multiset`. In line 45, the `copy` algorithm copies the elements of the `multiset` to the standard output in ascending order.

Lines 49 and 50 use functions **lower_bound** and **upper_bound** (available in all associative containers) to locate the earliest occurrence of the value 22 in the `multiset` and the element *after* the last occurrence of the value 22 in the `multiset`. Both functions return `iterators` or `const_iterators` pointing to the appropriate location or the iterator returned by `end` if the value is not in the `multiset`.

Line 53 instantiates an instance of class `pair` called `p`. Objects of class `pair` are used to associate pairs of values. In this example, the contents of a `pair` are two `const_iterators` for our integer-based `multiset`. The purpose of `p` is to store the return value of `multiset` function **equal_range** that returns a `pair` containing the results of both a `lower_bound` and an `upper_bound` operation. Type `pair` contains two `public` data members called **first** and **second**.

Line 57 uses function equal_range to determine the lower_bound and upper_bound of 22 in the multiset. Line 60 uses p.first and p.second, respectively, to access the lower_bound and upper_bound. We dereferenced the iterators to output the values at the locations returned from equal_range.

22.3.2 set Associative Container

The set associative container is used for fast storage and retrieval of unique keys. The implementation of a set is identical to that of a multiset, except that a set must have unique keys. Therefore, if an attempt is made to insert a duplicate key into a set, the duplicate is ignored; because this is the intended mathematical behavior of a set, we do not identify it as a common programming error. A set supports bidirectional iterators (but not random-access iterators). Figure 22.20 demonstrates a set of doubles. Header file <set> must be included to use class set.

```cpp
1   // Fig. 22.20: Fig22_20.cpp
2   // Standard Library class set test program.
3   #include <iostream>
4   #include <set>
5   #include <algorithm>
6   #include <iterator> // ostream_iterator
7   using namespace std;
8
9   // define short name for set type used in this program
10  typedef set< double, less< double > > DoubleSet;
11
12  int main()
13  {
14     const int SIZE = 5;
15     double a[ SIZE ] = { 2.1, 4.2, 9.5, 2.1, 3.7 };
16     DoubleSet doubleSet( a, a + SIZE );
17     ostream_iterator< double > output( cout, " " );
18
19     cout << "doubleSet contains: ";
20     copy( doubleSet.begin(), doubleSet.end(), output );
21
22     // p represents pair containing const_iterator and bool
23     pair< DoubleSet::const_iterator, bool > p;
24
25     // insert 13.8 in doubleSet; insert returns pair in which
26     // p.first represents location of 13.8 in doubleSet and
27     // p.second represents whether 13.8 was inserted
28     p = doubleSet.insert( 13.8 ); // value not in set
29     cout << "\n\n" << *( p.first )
30        << ( p.second ? " was" : " was not" ) << " inserted";
31     cout << "\ndoubleSet contains: ";
32     copy( doubleSet.begin(), doubleSet.end(), output );
33
34     // insert 9.5 in doubleSet
35     p = doubleSet.insert( 9.5 ); // value already in set
```

Fig. 22.20 | Standard Library set class template. (Part 1 of 2.)

```
36        cout << "\n\n" << *( p.first )
37           << ( p.second ? " was" : " was not" ) << " inserted";
38        cout << "\ndoubleSet contains: ";
39        copy( doubleSet.begin(), doubleSet.end(), output );
40        cout << endl;
41    } // end main
```

```
doubleSet contains: 2.1 3.7 4.2 9.5

13.8 was inserted
doubleSet contains: 2.1 3.7 4.2 9.5 13.8

9.5 was not inserted
doubleSet contains: 2.1 3.7 4.2 9.5 13.8
```

Fig. 22.20 | Standard Library set class template. (Part 2 of 2.)

Line 10 uses typedef to create a new type name (DoubleSet) for a set of double values ordered in ascending order, using the function object less< double >.

Line 16 uses the new type DoubleSet to instantiate object doubleSet. The constructor call takes the elements in array a between a and a + SIZE (i.e., the entire array) and inserts them into the set. Line 20 uses algorithm copy to output the contents of the set. Notice that the value 2.1—which appeared twice in array a—appears only once in doubleSet. This is because container set does not allow duplicates.

Line 23 defines a pair consisting of a const_iterator for a DoubleSet and a bool value. This object stores the result of a call to set function insert.

Line 28 uses function insert to place the value 13.8 in the set. The returned pair, p, contains an iterator p.first pointing to the value 13.8 in the set and a bool value that is true if the value was inserted and false if the value was not inserted (because it was already in the set). In this case, 13.8 was not in the set, so it was inserted. Line 35 attempts to insert 9.5, which is already in the set. The output of lines 36–37 shows that 9.5 was not inserted.

22.3.3 multimap Associative Container

The multimap associative container is used for fast storage and retrieval of keys and associated values (often called key/value pairs). Many of the functions used with multisets and sets are also used with multimaps and maps. The elements of multimaps and maps are pairs of keys and values instead of individual values. When inserting into a multimap or map, a pair object that contains the key and the value is used. The ordering of the keys is determined by a comparator function object. For example, in a multimap that uses integers as the key type, keys can be sorted in ascending order by ordering them with comparator function object less< int >. Duplicate keys are allowed in a multimap, so multiple values can be associated with a single key. This is often called a one-to-many relationship. For example, in a credit-card transaction-processing system, one credit-card account can have many associated transactions; in a university, one student can take many courses, and one professor can teach many students; in the military, one rank (like "private") has many people. A multimap supports bidirectional iterators, but not random-access iterators.

Figure 22.21 demonstrates the `multimap` associative container. Header file **<map>** must be included to use class `multimap`.

Performance Tip 22.15

A `multimap` is implemented to efficiently locate all values paired with a given key.

Line 8 uses `typedef` to define alias `Mmid` for a `multimap` type in which the key type is `int`, the type of a key's associated value is `double` and the elements are ordered in ascending order. Line 12 uses the new type to instantiate a `multimap` called `pairs`. Line 14 uses function `count` to determine the number of key/value pairs with a key of 15.

```cpp
1   // Fig. 22.21: Fig22_21.cpp
2   // Standard Library class multimap test program.
3   #include <iostream>
4   #include <map> // multimap class-template definition
5   using namespace std;
6
7   // define short name for multimap type used in this program
8   typedef multimap< int, double, less< int > > Mmid;
9
10  int main()
11  {
12     Mmid pairs; // declare the multimap pairs
13
14     cout << "There are currently " << pairs.count( 15 )
15        << " pairs with key 15 in the multimap\n";
16
17     // insert two value_type objects in pairs
18     pairs.insert( Mmid::value_type( 15, 2.7 ) );
19     pairs.insert( Mmid::value_type( 15, 99.3 ) );
20
21     cout << "After inserts, there are " << pairs.count( 15 )
22        << " pairs with key 15\n\n";
23
24     // insert five value_type objects in pairs
25     pairs.insert( Mmid::value_type( 30, 111.11 ) );
26     pairs.insert( Mmid::value_type( 10, 22.22 ) );
27     pairs.insert( Mmid::value_type( 25, 33.333 ) );
28     pairs.insert( Mmid::value_type( 20, 9.345 ) );
29     pairs.insert( Mmid::value_type( 5, 77.54 ) );
30
31     cout << "Multimap pairs contains:\nKey\tValue\n";
32
33     // use const_iterator to walk through elements of pairs
34     for ( Mmid::const_iterator iter = pairs.begin();
35        iter != pairs.end(); ++iter )
36        cout << iter->first << '\t' << iter->second << '\n';
37
38     cout << endl;
39  } // end main
```

Fig. 22.21 | Standard Library `multimap` class template. (Part 1 of 2.)

```
There are currently 0 pairs with key 15 in the multimap
After inserts, there are 2 pairs with key 15

Multimap pairs contains:
Key     Value
5       77.54
10      22.22
15      2.7
15      99.3
20      9.345
25      33.333
30      111.11
```

Fig. 22.21 | Standard Library `multimap` class template. (Part 2 of 2.)

Line 18 uses function `insert` to add a new key/value pair to the `multimap`. The expression `Mmid::value_type( 15, 2.7 )` creates a `pair` object in which `first` is the key (`15`) of type `int` and `second` is the value (`2.7`) of type `double`. The type `Mmid::value_type` is defined as part of the `typedef` for the `multimap`. Line 19 inserts another `pair` object with the key `15` and the value `99.3`. Then lines 21–22 output the number of pairs with key `15`.

Lines 25–29 insert five additional `pairs` into the `multimap`. The `for` statement in lines 34–36 outputs the contents of the `multimap`, including both keys and values. Line 36 uses the `const_iterator` called `iter` to access the members of the `pair` in each element of the `multimap`. Notice in the output that the keys appear in ascending order.

22.3.4 map Associative Container

The `map` associative container performs fast storage and retrieval of unique keys and associated values. Duplicate keys are not allowed—a single value can be associated with each key. This is called a **one-to-one mapping**. For example, a company that uses unique employee numbers, such as 100, 200 and 300, might have a `map` that associates employee numbers with their telephone extensions—4321, 4115 and 5217, respectively. With a `map` you specify the key and get back the associated data quickly. A `map` is also known as an **associative array**. Providing the key in a `map`'s subscript operator `[]` locates the value associated with that key in the `map`. Insertions and deletions can be made anywhere in a `map`.

Figure 22.22 demonstrates a `map` and uses the same features as Fig. 22.21 to demonstrate the subscript operator. Header file `<map>` must be included to use class `map`. Lines 31–32 use the subscript operator of class `map`. When the subscript is a key that is already in the `map` (line 31), the operator returns a reference to the associated value. When the subscript is a key that is not in the `map` (line 32), the operator inserts the key in the `map` and returns a reference that can be used to associate a value with that key. Line 31 replaces the value for the key `25` (previously `33.333` as specified in line 19) with a new value, `9999.99`. Line 32 inserts a new key/value `pair` in the `map` (called **creating an association**).

```
1  // Fig. 22.22: Fig22_22.cpp
2  // Standard Library class map test program.
3  #include <iostream>
4  #include <map> // map class-template definition
```

Fig. 22.22 | Standard Library `map` class template. (Part 1 of 3.)

```
5   using namespace std;
6
7   // define short name for map type used in this program
8   typedef map< int, double, less< int > > Mid;
9
10  int main()
11  {
12     Mid pairs;
13
14     // insert eight value_type objects in pairs
15     pairs.insert( Mid::value_type( 15, 2.7 ) );
16     pairs.insert( Mid::value_type( 30, 111.11 ) );
17     pairs.insert( Mid::value_type( 5, 1010.1 ) );
18     pairs.insert( Mid::value_type( 10, 22.22 ) );
19     pairs.insert( Mid::value_type( 25, 33.333 ) );
20     pairs.insert( Mid::value_type( 5, 77.54 ) ); // dup ignored
21     pairs.insert( Mid::value_type( 20, 9.345 ) );
22     pairs.insert( Mid::value_type( 15, 99.3 ) ); // dup ignored
23
24     cout << "pairs contains:\nKey\tValue\n";
25
26     // use const_iterator to walk through elements of pairs
27     for ( Mid::const_iterator iter = pairs.begin();
28        iter != pairs.end(); ++iter )
29        cout << iter->first << '\t' << iter->second << '\n';
30
31     pairs[ 25 ] = 9999.99; // use subscripting to change value for key 25
32     pairs[ 40 ] = 8765.43; // use subscripting to insert value for key 40
33
34     cout << "\nAfter subscript operations, pairs contains:\nKey\tValue\n";
35
36     // use const_iterator to walk through elements of pairs
37     for ( Mid::const_iterator iter2 = pairs.begin();
38        iter2 != pairs.end(); ++iter2 )
39        cout << iter2->first << '\t' << iter2->second << '\n';
40
41     cout << endl;
42  } // end main
```

```
pairs contains:
Key     Value
5       1010.1
10      22.22
15      2.7
20      9.345
25      33.333
30      111.11

After subscript operations, pairs contains:
Key     Value
5       1010.1
10      22.22
```

Fig. 22.22 | Standard Library map class template. (Part 2 of 3.)

15	2.7
20	9.345
25	9999.99
30	111.11
40	8765.43

Fig. 22.22 | Standard Library map class template. (Part 3 of 3.)

22.4 Container Adapters

The STL provides three **container adapters**—stack, queue and priority_queue. Adapters are not first-class containers, because they do not provide the actual data-structure implementation in which elements can be stored and because adapters do not support iterators. The benefit of an adapter class is that you can choose an appropriate underlying data structure. All three adapter classes provide member functions **push** and **pop** that properly insert an element into each adapter data structure and properly remove an element from each adapter data structure. The next several subsections provide examples of the adapter classes.

22.4.1 stack Adapter

Class **stack** enables insertions into and deletions from the underlying data structure at one end (commonly referred to as a last-in, first-out data structure). A stack can be implemented with any of the sequence containers: vector, list and deque. This example creates three integer stacks, using each of the sequence containers of the Standard Library as the underlying data structure to represent the stack. By default, a stack is implemented with a deque. The stack operations are push to insert an element at the top of the stack (implemented by calling function push_back of the underlying container), pop to remove the top element of the stack (implemented by calling function pop_back of the underlying container), **top** to get a reference to the top element of the stack (implemented by calling function back of the underlying container), empty to determine whether the stack is empty (implemented by calling function empty of the underlying container) and size to get the number of elements in the stack (implemented by calling function size of the underlying container).

Performance Tip 22.16

Each of the common operations of a stack is implemented as an inline function that calls the appropriate function of the underlying container. This avoids the overhead of a second function call.

Performance Tip 22.17

For the best performance, use class vector as the underlying container for a stack.

Figure 22.23 demonstrates the stack adapter class. Header file **<stack>** must be included to use class stack.

Lines 18, 21 and 24 instantiate three integer stacks. Line 18 specifies a stack of integers that uses the default deque container as its underlying data structure. Line 21 specifies

```cpp
 1   // Fig. 22.23: Fig22_23.cpp
 2   // Standard Library adapter stack test program.
 3   #include <iostream>
 4   #include <stack> // stack adapter definition
 5   #include <vector> // vector class-template definition
 6   #include <list> // list class-template definition
 7   using namespace std;
 8
 9   // pushElements function-template prototype
10   template< typename T > void pushElements( T &stackRef );
11
12   // popElements function-template prototype
13   template< typename T > void popElements( T &stackRef );
14
15   int main()
16   {
17      // stack with default underlying deque
18      stack< int > intDequeStack;
19
20      // stack with underlying vector
21      stack< int, vector< int > > intVectorStack;
22
23      // stack with underlying list
24      stack< int, list< int > > intListStack;
25
26      // push the values 0-9 onto each stack
27      cout << "Pushing onto intDequeStack: ";
28      pushElements( intDequeStack );
29      cout << "\nPushing onto intVectorStack: ";
30      pushElements( intVectorStack );
31      cout << "\nPushing onto intListStack: ";
32      pushElements( intListStack );
33      cout << endl << endl;
34
35      // display and remove elements from each stack
36      cout << "Popping from intDequeStack: ";
37      popElements( intDequeStack );
38      cout << "\nPopping from intVectorStack: ";
39      popElements( intVectorStack );
40      cout << "\nPopping from intListStack: ";
41      popElements( intListStack );
42      cout << endl;
43   } // end main
44
45   // push elements onto stack object to which stackRef refers
46   template< typename T > void pushElements( T &stackRef )
47   {
48      for ( int i = 0; i < 10; i++ )
49      {
50         stackRef.push( i ); // push element onto stack
51         cout << stackRef.top() << ' '; // view (and display) top element
52      } // end for
53   } // end function pushElements
```

Fig. 22.23 | Standard Library stack adapter class. (Part 1 of 2.)

```
54
55   // pop elements from stack object to which stackRef refers
56   template< typename T > void popElements( T &stackRef )
57   {
58      while ( !stackRef.empty() )
59      {
60         cout << stackRef.top() << ' '; // view (and display) top element
61         stackRef.pop(); // remove top element
62      } // end while
63   } // end function popElements
```

```
Pushing onto intDequeStack: 0 1 2 3 4 5 6 7 8 9
Pushing onto intVectorStack: 0 1 2 3 4 5 6 7 8 9
Pushing onto intListStack: 0 1 2 3 4 5 6 7 8 9

Popping from intDequeStack: 9 8 7 6 5 4 3 2 1 0
Popping from intVectorStack: 9 8 7 6 5 4 3 2 1 0
Popping from intListStack: 9 8 7 6 5 4 3 2 1 0
```

Fig. 22.23 | Standard Library stack adapter class. (Part 2 of 2.)

a stack of integers that uses a vector of integers as its underlying data structure. Line 24 specifies a stack of integers that uses a list of integers as its underlying data structure.

Function pushElements (lines 46–53) pushes the elements onto each stack. Line 50 uses function push (available in each adapter class) to place an integer on top of the stack. Line 51 uses stack function top to retrieve the top element of the stack for output. Function top does not remove the top element.

Function popElements (lines 56–63) pops the elements off each stack. Line 60 uses stack function top to retrieve the top element of the stack for output. Line 61 uses function pop (available in each adapter class) to remove the top element of the stack. Function pop does not return a value.

22.4.2 queue Adapter

Class **queue** enables insertions at the back of the underlying data structure and deletions from the front (commonly referred to as a first-in, first-out data structure). A queue can be implemented with STL data structure list or deque. By default, a queue is implemented with a deque. The common queue operations are push to insert an element at the back of the queue (implemented by calling function push_back of the underlying container), pop to remove the element at the front of the queue (implemented by calling function pop_front of the underlying container), **front** to get a reference to the first element in the queue (implemented by calling function front of the underlying container), **back** to get a reference to the last element in the queue (implemented by calling function back of the underlying container), empty to determine whether the queue is empty (implemented by calling function empty of the underlying container) and size to get the number of elements in the queue (implemented by calling function size of the underlying container).

Performance Tip 22.18

For the best performance, use class deque as the underlying container for a queue.

Performance Tip 22.19

Each of the common operations of a queue is implemented as an inline *function that calls the appropriate function of the underlying container. This avoids the overhead of a second function call.*

Figure 22.24 demonstrates the queue adapter class. Header file **<queue>** must be included to use a queue.

```cpp
 1  // Fig. 22.24: Fig22_24.cpp
 2  // Standard Library adapter queue test program.
 3  #include <iostream>
 4  #include <queue> // queue adapter definition
 5  using namespace std;
 6
 7  int main()
 8  {
 9     queue< double > values; // queue with doubles
10
11     // push elements onto queue values
12     values.push( 3.2 );
13     values.push( 9.8 );
14     values.push( 5.4 );
15
16     cout << "Popping from values: ";
17
18     // pop elements from queue
19     while ( !values.empty() )
20     {
21        cout << values.front() << ' '; // view front element
22        values.pop(); // remove element
23     } // end while
24
25     cout << endl;
26  } // end main
```

```
Popping from values: 3.2 9.8 5.4
```

Fig. 22.24 | Standard Library queue adapter class templates.

Line 9 instantiates a queue that stores double values. Lines 12–14 use function push to add elements to the queue. The while statement in lines 19–23 uses function empty (available in all containers) to determine whether the queue is empty (line 19). While there are more elements in the queue, line 21 uses queue function front to read (but not remove) the first element in the queue for output. Line 22 removes the first element in the queue with function pop (available in all adapter classes).

22.4.3 priority_queue Adapter

Class **priority_queue** provides functionality that enables insertions in sorted order into the underlying data structure and deletions from the front of the underlying data structure. A priority_queue can be implemented with STL sequence containers vector or deque. By default, a priority_queue is implemented with a vector as the underlying container. When elements are added to a priority_queue, they're inserted in priority order, such that the highest-priority element (i.e., the largest value) will be the first element removed from the priority_queue. This is usually accomplished by arranging the elements in a binary tree structure called a **heap** that always maintains the largest value (i.e., highest-priority element) at the front of the data structure. We discuss the STL's heap algorithms in Section 22.5.12. The comparison of elements is performed with comparator function object less< T > by default, but you can supply a different comparator.

There are several common priority_queue operations. push inserts an element at the appropriate location based on priority order of the priority_queue (implemented by calling function push_back of the underlying container, then reordering the elements using heapsort). pop removes the highest-priority element of the priority_queue (implemented by calling function pop_back of the underlying container after removing the top element of the heap). **top** gets a reference to the top element of the priority_queue (implemented by calling function front of the underlying container). empty determines whether the priority_queue is empty (implemented by calling function empty of the underlying container). size gets the number of elements in the priority_queue (implemented by calling function size of the underlying container).

Performance Tip 22.20

Each of the common operations of a priority_queue is implemented as an inline function that calls the appropriate function of the underlying container. This avoids the overhead of a second function call.

Performance Tip 22.21

For the best performance, use class vector as the underlying container for a priority_queue.

Figure 22.25 demonstrates the priority_queue adapter class. Header file <queue> must be included to use class priority_queue.

```cpp
1   // Fig. 22.25: Fig22_25.cpp
2   // Standard Library adapter priority_queue test program.
3   #include <iostream>
4   #include <queue> // priority_queue adapter definition
5   using namespace std;
6
7   int main()
8   {
9      priority_queue< double > priorities; // create priority_queue
10
11     // push elements onto priorities
12     priorities.push( 3.2 );
13     priorities.push( 9.8 );
14     priorities.push( 5.4 );
15
16     cout << "Popping from priorities: ";
```

Fig. 22.25 | Standard Library priority_queue adapter class.   (Part 1 of 2.)

```
17
18      // pop element from priority_queue
19      while ( !priorities.empty() )
20      {
21         cout << priorities.top() << ' '; // view top element
22         priorities.pop(); // remove top element
23      } // end while
24
25      cout << endl;
26   } // end main
```

```
Popping from priorities: 9.8 5.4 3.2
```

Fig. 22.25 | Standard Library `priority_queue` adapter class.   (Part 2 of 2.)

Line 9 instantiates a `priority_queue` that stores `double` values and uses a `vector` as the underlying data structure. Lines 12–14 use function `push` to add elements to the `priority_queue`. The `while` statement in lines 19–23 uses function `empty` (available in all containers) to determine whether the `priority_queue` is empty (line 19). While there are more elements, line 21 uses `priority_queue` function `top` to retrieve the highest-priority element in the `priority_queue` for output. Line 22 removes the highest-priority element in the `priority_queue` with function `pop` (available in all adapter classes).

22.5 **Algorithms**

Until the STL, class libraries of containers and algorithms were essentially incompatible among vendors. Early container libraries generally used inheritance and polymorphism, with the associated overhead of `virtual` function calls. Early libraries built the algorithms into the container classes as class behaviors. The STL separates the algorithms from the containers. This makes it much easier to add new algorithms. With the STL, the elements of containers are accessed through iterators. The next several subsections demonstrate many of the STL algorithms.

Performance Tip 22.22
The STL is implemented for efficiency. It avoids the overhead of `virtual` function calls.

Software Engineering Observation 22.8
STL algorithms do not depend on the implementation details of the containers on which they operate. As long as the container's (or array's) iterators satisfy the requirements of the algorithm, STL algorithms can work on C-style, pointer-based arrays, on STL containers and on user-defined data structures.

Software Engineering Observation 22.9
Algorithms can be added easily to the STL without modifying the container classes.

22.5.1 fill, fill_n, generate and generate_n

Figure 22.26 demonstrates algorithms fill, fill_n, generate and generate_n. Functions **fill** and **fill_n** set every element in a range of container elements to a specific value. Functions **generate** and **generate_n** use a **generator function** to create values for every element in a range of container elements. The generator function takes no arguments and returns a value that can be placed in an element of the container.

```cpp
1   // Fig. 22.26: Fig22_26.cpp
2   // Standard Library algorithms fill, fill_n, generate and generate_n.
3   #include <iostream>
4   #include <algorithm> // algorithm definitions
5   #include <vector> // vector class-template definition
6   #include <iterator> // ostream_iterator
7   using namespace std;
8
9   char nextLetter(); // prototype of generator function
10
11  int main()
12  {
13     vector< char > chars( 10 );
14     ostream_iterator< char > output( cout, " " );
15     fill( chars.begin(), chars.end(), '5' ); // fill chars with 5s
16
17     cout << "Vector chars after filling with 5s:\n";
18     copy( chars.begin(), chars.end(), output );
19
20     // fill first five elements of chars with As
21     fill_n( chars.begin(), 5, 'A' );
22
23     cout << "\n\nVector chars after filling five elements with As:\n";
24     copy( chars.begin(), chars.end(), output );
25
26     // generate values for all elements of chars with nextLetter
27     generate( chars.begin(), chars.end(), nextLetter );
28
29     cout << "\n\nVector chars after generating letters A-J:\n";
30     copy( chars.begin(), chars.end(), output );
31
32     // generate values for first five elements of chars with nextLetter
33     generate_n( chars.begin(), 5, nextLetter );
34
35     cout << "\n\nVector chars after generating K-O for the"
36        << " first five elements:\n";
37     copy( chars.begin(), chars.end(), output );
38     cout << endl;
39  } // end main
40
41  // generator function returns next letter (starts with A)
42  char nextLetter()
43  {
44     static char letter = 'A';
```

Fig. 22.26 | Algorithms fill, fill_n, generate and generate_n. (Part 1 of 2.)

```
45        return letter++;
46    } // end function nextLetter
```

```
Vector chars after filling with 5s:
5 5 5 5 5 5 5 5 5 5

Vector chars after filling five elements with As:
A A A A A 5 5 5 5 5

Vector chars after generating letters A-J:
A B C D E F G H I J

Vector chars after generating K-O for the first five elements:
K L M N O F G H I J
```

Fig. 22.26 | Algorithms fill, fill_n, generate and generate_n. (Part 2 of 2.)

Line 13 defines a 10-element vector that stores char values. Line 15 uses function fill to place the character '5' in every element of vector chars from chars.begin() up to, but not including, chars.end(). The iterators supplied as the first and second argument must be at least forward iterators (i.e., they can be used for both input from a container and output to a container in the forward direction).

Line 21 uses function fill_n to place the character 'A' in the first five elements of vector chars. The iterator supplied as the first argument must be at least an output iterator (i.e., it can be used for output to a container in the forward direction). The second argument specifies the number of elements to fill. The third argument specifies the value to place in each element.

Line 27 uses function generate to place the result of a call to generator function nextLetter in every element of vector chars from chars.begin() up to, but not including, chars.end(). The iterators supplied as the first and second arguments must be at least forward iterators. Function nextLetter (lines 42–46) begins with the character 'A' maintained in a static local variable. The statement in line 45 postincrements the value of letter and returns the old value of letter each time nextLetter is called.

Line 33 uses function generate_n to place the result of a call to generator function nextLetter in five elements of vector chars, starting from chars.begin(). The iterator supplied as the first argument must be at least an output iterator.

22.5.2 equal, mismatch and lexicographical_compare

Figure 22.27 demonstrates comparing sequences of values for equality using algorithms equal, mismatch and lexicographical_compare.

```
1   // Fig. 22.27: Fig22_27.cpp
2   // Standard Library functions equal, mismatch and lexicographical_compare.
3   #include <iostream>
4   #include <algorithm> // algorithm definitions
5   #include <vector> // vector class-template definition
6   #include <iterator> // ostream_iterator
7   using namespace std;
```

Fig. 22.27 | Algorithms equal, mismatch and lexicographical_compare. (Part 1 of 3.)

```
8
9   int main()
10  {
11     const int SIZE = 10;
12     int a1[ SIZE ] = { 1, 2, 3, 4, 5, 6, 7, 8, 9, 10 };
13     int a2[ SIZE ] = { 1, 2, 3, 4, 1000, 6, 7, 8, 9, 10 };
14     vector< int > v1( a1, a1 + SIZE ); // copy of a1
15     vector< int > v2( a1, a1 + SIZE ); // copy of a1
16     vector< int > v3( a2, a2 + SIZE ); // copy of a2
17     ostream_iterator< int > output( cout, " " );
18
19     cout << "Vector v1 contains: ";
20     copy( v1.begin(), v1.end(), output );
21     cout << "\nVector v2 contains: ";
22     copy( v2.begin(), v2.end(), output );
23     cout << "\nVector v3 contains: ";
24     copy( v3.begin(), v3.end(), output );
25
26     // compare vectors v1 and v2 for equality
27     bool result = equal( v1.begin(), v1.end(), v2.begin() );
28     cout << "\n\nVector v1 " << ( result ? "is" : "is not" )
29        << " equal to vector v2.\n";
30
31     // compare vectors v1 and v3 for equality
32     result = equal( v1.begin(), v1.end(), v3.begin() );
33     cout << "Vector v1 " << ( result ? "is" : "is not" )
34        << " equal to vector v3.\n";
35
36     // location represents pair of vector iterators
37     pair< vector< int >::iterator, vector< int >::iterator > location;
38
39     // check for mismatch between v1 and v3
40     location = mismatch( v1.begin(), v1.end(), v3.begin() );
41     cout << "\nThere is a mismatch between v1 and v3 at location "
42        << ( location.first - v1.begin() ) << "\nwhere v1 contains "
43        << *location.first << " and v3 contains " << *location.second
44        << "\n\n";
45
46     char c1[ SIZE ] = "HELLO";
47     char c2[ SIZE ] = "BYE BYE";
48
49     // perform lexicographical comparison of c1 and c2
50     result = lexicographical_compare( c1, c1 + SIZE, c2, c2 + SIZE );
51     cout << c1 << ( result ? " is less than " :
52        " is greater than or equal to " )  << c2 << endl;
53  } // end main
```

```
Vector v1 contains: 1 2 3 4 5 6 7 8 9 10
Vector v2 contains: 1 2 3 4 5 6 7 8 9 10
Vector v3 contains: 1 2 3 4 1000 6 7 8 9 10

Vector v1 is equal to vector v2.
Vector v1 is not equal to vector v3.
```

Fig. 22.27 | Algorithms equal, mismatch and lexicographical_compare. (Part 2 of 3.)

```
There is a mismatch between v1 and v3 at location 4
where v1 contains 5 and v3 contains 1000

HELLO is greater than or equal to BYE BYE
```

Fig. 22.27 | Algorithms `equal`, `mismatch` and `lexicographical_compare`. (Part 3 of 3.)

Line 27 uses function **equal** to compare two sequences of values for equality. Each sequence need not necessarily contain the same number of elements—equal returns `false` if the sequences are not of the same length. The `==` operator (whether built-in or overloaded) performs the comparison of the elements. In this example, the elements in vector v1 from v1.begin() up to, but not including, v1.end() are compared to the elements in vector v2 starting from v2.begin(). In this example, v1 and v2 are equal. The three iterator arguments must be at least input iterators (i.e., they can be used for input from a sequence in the forward direction). Line 32 uses function equal to compare vectors v1 and v3, which are not equal.

There is another version of function equal that takes a binary predicate function as a fourth parameter. The binary predicate function receives the two elements being compared and returns a bool value indicating whether the elements are equal. This can be useful in sequences that store objects or pointers to values rather than actual values, because you can define one or more comparisons. For example, you can compare Employee objects for age, social security number, or location rather than comparing entire objects. You can compare what pointers refer to rather than comparing the pointer values (i.e., the addresses stored in the pointers).

Lines 37–40 begin by instantiating a pair of iterators called location for a vector of integers. This object stores the result of the call to mismatch (line 40). Function **mismatch** compares two sequences of values and returns a pair of iterators indicating the location in each sequence of the mismatched elements. If all the elements match, the two iterators in the pair are equal to the last iterator for each sequence. The three iterator arguments must be at least input iterators. Line 42 determines the actual location of the mismatch in the vectors with the expression location.first - v1.begin(). The result of this calculation is the number of elements between the iterators (this is analogous to pointer arithmetic, which we studied in Chapter 8). This corresponds to the element number in this example, because the comparison is performed from the beginning of each vector. As with function equal, there is another version of function mismatch that takes a binary predicate function as a fourth parameter.

Line 50 uses function **lexicographical_compare** to compare the contents of two character arrays. This function's four iterator arguments must be at least input iterators. As you know, pointers into arrays are random-access iterators. The first two iterator arguments specify the range of locations in the first sequence. The last two specify the range of locations in the second sequence. While iterating through the sequences, the lexicographical_compare checks if the element in the first sequence is less than the corresponding element in the second sequence. If so, the function returns true. If the element in the first sequence is greater than or equal to the element in the second sequence, the function returns false. This function can be used to arrange sequences lexicographically. Typically, such sequences contain strings.

22.5.3 remove, remove_if, remove_copy and remove_copy_if

Figure 22.28 demonstrates removing values from a sequence with algorithms remove, remove_if, remove_copy and remove_copy_if.

```cpp
1   // Fig. 22.28: Fig22_28.cpp
2   // Standard Library functions remove, remove_if,
3   // remove_copy and remove_copy_if.
4   #include <iostream>
5   #include <algorithm> // algorithm definitions
6   #include <vector> // vector class-template definition
7   #include <iterator> // ostream_iterator
8   using namespace std;
9
10  bool greater9( int ); // prototype
11
12  int main()
13  {
14     const int SIZE = 10;
15     int a[ SIZE ] = { 10, 2, 10, 4, 16, 6, 14, 8, 12, 10 };
16     ostream_iterator< int > output( cout, " " );
17     vector< int > v( a, a + SIZE ); // copy of a
18     vector< int >::iterator newLastElement;
19
20     cout << "Vector v before removing all 10s:\n   ";
21     copy( v.begin(), v.end(), output );
22
23     // remove all 10s from v
24     newLastElement = remove( v.begin(), v.end(), 10 );
25     cout << "\nVector v after removing all 10s:\n   ";
26     copy( v.begin(), newLastElement, output );
27
28     vector< int > v2( a, a + SIZE ); // copy of a
29     vector< int > c( SIZE, 0 ); // instantiate vector c
30     cout << "\n\nVector v2 before removing all 10s and copying:\n   ";
31     copy( v2.begin(), v2.end(), output );
32
33     // copy from v2 to c, removing 10s in the process
34     remove_copy( v2.begin(), v2.end(), c.begin(), 10 );
35     cout << "\nVector c after removing all 10s from v2:\n   ";
36     copy( c.begin(), c.end(), output );
37
38     vector< int > v3( a, a + SIZE ); // copy of a
39     cout << "\n\nVector v3 before removing all elements"
40        << "\ngreater than 9:\n   ";
41     copy( v3.begin(), v3.end(), output );
42
43     // remove elements greater than 9 from v3
44     newLastElement = remove_if( v3.begin(), v3.end(), greater9 );
45     cout << "\nVector v3 after removing all elements"
46        << "\ngreater than 9:\n   ";
47     copy( v3.begin(), newLastElement, output );
48
```

Fig. 22.28 | Algorithms remove, remove_if, remove_copy and remove_copy_if. (Part 1 of 2.)

```
49      vector< int > v4( a, a + SIZE ); // copy of a
50      vector< int > c2( SIZE, 0 ); // instantiate vector c2
51      cout << "\n\nVector v4 before removing all elements"
52         << "\ngreater than 9 and copying:\n   ";
53      copy( v4.begin(), v4.end(), output );
54
55      // copy elements from v4 to c2, removing elements greater
56      // than 9 in the process
57      remove_copy_if( v4.begin(), v4.end(), c2.begin(), greater9 );
58      cout << "\nVector c2 after removing all elements"
59         << "\ngreater than 9 from v4:\n   ";
60      copy( c2.begin(), c2.end(), output );
61      cout << endl;
62   } // end main
63
64   // determine whether argument is greater than 9
65   bool greater9( int x )
66   {
67      return x > 9;
68   } // end function greater9
```

```
Vector v before removing all 10s:
   10 2 10 4 16 6 14 8 12 10
Vector v after removing all 10s:
   2 4 16 6 14 8 12

Vector v2 before removing all 10s and copying:
   10 2 10 4 16 6 14 8 12 10
Vector c after removing all 10s from v2:
   2 4 16 6 14 8 12 0 0 0

Vector v3 before removing all elements
greater than 9:
   10 2 10 4 16 6 14 8 12 10
Vector v3 after removing all elements
greater than 9:
   2 4 6 8

Vector v4 before removing all elements
greater than 9 and copying:
   10 2 10 4 16 6 14 8 12 10
Vector c2 after removing all elements
greater than 9 from v4:
   2 4 6 8 0 0 0 0 0 0
```

Fig. 22.28 | Algorithms remove, remove_if, remove_copy and remove_copy_if. (Part 2 of 2.)

Line 24 uses function **remove** to eliminate all elements with the value 10 in the range from v.begin() up to, but not including, v.end() from v. The first two iterator arguments must be forward iterators so that the algorithm can modify the elements in the sequence. This function does not modify the number of elements in the vector or destroy the eliminated elements, but it does move all elements that are not eliminated toward the beginning of the vector. The function returns an iterator positioned after the last vector element that was not deleted. Elements from the iterator position to the end of the vector have undefined values (in this example, each "undefined" position has value 0).

Line 34 uses function **remove_copy** to copy all elements that do not have the value 10 in the range from v2.begin() up to, but not including, v2.end() from v2. The elements are placed in c, starting at position c.begin(). The iterators supplied as the first two arguments must be input iterators. The iterator supplied as the third argument must be an output iterator so that the element being copied can be inserted into the copy location. This function returns an iterator positioned after the last element copied into vector c. Note, in line 29, the use of the vector constructor that receives the number of elements in the vector and the initial values of those elements.

Line 44 uses function **remove_if** to delete all those elements in the range from v3.begin() up to, but not including, v3.end() from v3 for which our user-defined unary predicate function greater9 returns true. Function greater9 (defined in lines 65–68) returns true if the value passed to it's greater than 9; otherwise, it returns false. The iterators supplied as the first two arguments must be forward iterators so that the algorithm can modify the elements in the sequence. This function does not modify the number of elements in the vector, but it does move to the beginning of the vector all elements that are not eliminated. This function returns an iterator positioned after the last element in the vector that was not deleted. All elements from the iterator position to the end of the vector have undefined values.

Line 57 uses function **remove_copy_if** to copy all those elements in the range from v4.begin() up to, but not including, v4.end() from v4 for which the unary predicate function greater9 returns true. The elements are placed in c2, starting at position c2.begin(). The iterators supplied as the first two arguments must be input iterators. The iterator supplied as the third argument must be an output iterator so that the element being copied can be inserted into the copy location. This function returns an iterator positioned after the last element copied into c2.

22.5.4 replace, replace_if, replace_copy and replace_copy_if

Figure 22.29 demonstrates replacing values from a sequence using algorithms replace, replace_if, replace_copy and replace_copy_if.

```
1   // Fig. 22.29: Fig22_29.cpp
2   // Standard Library functions replace, replace_if,
3   // replace_copy and replace_copy_if.
4   #include <iostream>
5   #include <algorithm>
6   #include <vector>
7   #include <iterator> // ostream_iterator
8   using namespace std;
9
10  bool greater9( int ); // predicate function prototype
11
12  int main()
13  {
14      const int SIZE = 10;
```

Fig. 22.29 | Algorithms replace, replace_if, replace_copy and replace_copy_if. (Part 1 of 3.)

```
15       int a[ SIZE ] = { 10, 2, 10, 4, 16, 6, 14, 8, 12, 10 };
16       ostream_iterator< int > output( cout, " " );
17
18       vector< int > v1( a, a + SIZE ); // copy of a
19       cout << "Vector v1 before replacing all 10s:\n   ";
20       copy( v1.begin(), v1.end(), output );
21
22       // replace all 10s in v1 with 100
23       replace( v1.begin(), v1.end(), 10, 100 );
24       cout << "\nVector v1 after replacing 10s with 100s:\n   ";
25       copy( v1.begin(), v1.end(), output );
26
27       vector< int > v2( a, a + SIZE ); // copy of a
28       vector< int > c1( SIZE ); // instantiate vector c1
29       cout << "\n\nVector v2 before replacing all 10s and copying:\n   ";
30       copy( v2.begin(), v2.end(), output );
31
32       // copy from v2 to c1, replacing 10s with 100s
33       replace_copy( v2.begin(), v2.end(), c1.begin(), 10, 100 );
34       cout << "\nVector c1 after replacing all 10s in v2:\n   ";
35       copy( c1.begin(), c1.end(), output );
36
37       vector< int > v3( a, a + SIZE ); // copy of a
38       cout << "\n\nVector v3 before replacing values greater than 9:\n   ";
39       copy( v3.begin(), v3.end(), output );
40
41       // replace values greater than 9 in v3 with 100
42       replace_if( v3.begin(), v3.end(), greater9, 100 );
43       cout << "\nVector v3 after replacing all values greater"
44          << "\nthan 9 with 100s:\n   ";
45       copy( v3.begin(), v3.end(), output );
46
47       vector< int > v4( a, a + SIZE ); // copy of a
48       vector< int > c2( SIZE ); // instantiate vector c2
49       cout << "\n\nVector v4 before replacing all values greater "
50          << "than 9 and copying:\n   ";
51       copy( v4.begin(), v4.end(), output );
52
53       // copy v4 to c2, replacing elements greater than 9 with 100
54       replace_copy_if( v4.begin(), v4.end(), c2.begin(), greater9, 100 );
55       cout << "\nVector c2 after replacing all values greater "
56          << "than 9 in v4:\n   ";
57       copy( c2.begin(), c2.end(), output );
58       cout << endl;
59    } // end main
60
61    // determine whether argument is greater than 9
62    bool greater9( int x )
63    {
64       return x > 9;
65    } // end function greater9
```

Fig. 22.29 | Algorithms replace, replace_if, replace_copy and replace_copy_if. (Part 2 of 3.)

```
Vector v1 before replacing all 10s:
   10 2 10 4 16 6 14 8 12 10
Vector v1 after replacing 10s with 100s:
   100 2 100 4 16 6 14 8 12 100

Vector v2 before replacing all 10s and copying:
   10 2 10 4 16 6 14 8 12 10
Vector c1 after replacing all 10s in v2:
   100 2 100 4 16 6 14 8 12 100

Vector v3 before replacing values greater than 9:
   10 2 10 4 16 6 14 8 12 10
Vector v3 after replacing all values greater
than 9 with 100s:
   100 2 100 4 100 6 100 8 100 100

Vector v4 before replacing all values greater than 9 and copying:
   10 2 10 4 16 6 14 8 12 10
Vector c2 after replacing all values greater than 9 in v4:
   100 2 100 4 100 6 100 8 100 100
```

Fig. 22.29 | Algorithms `replace`, `replace_if`, `replace_copy` and `replace_copy_if`. (Part 3 of 3.)

Line 23 uses function **replace** to replace all elements with the value 10 in the range from v1.begin() up to, but not including, v1.end() in v1 with the new value 100. The iterators supplied as the first two arguments must be forward iterators so that the algorithm can modify the elements in the sequence.

Line 33 uses function **replace_copy** to copy all elements in the range from v2.begin() up to, but not including, v2.end() from v2, replacing all elements with the value 10 with the new value 100. The elements are copied into c1, starting at position c1.begin(). The iterators supplied as the first two arguments must be input iterators. The iterator supplied as the third argument must be an output iterator so that the element being copied can be inserted into the copy location. This function returns an iterator positioned after the last element copied into c1.

Line 42 uses function **replace_if** to replace all those elements in the range from v3.begin() up to, but not including, v3.end() in v3 for which the unary predicate function greater9 returns true. Function greater9 (defined in lines 62–65) returns true if the value passed to it's greater than 9; otherwise, it returns false. The value 100 replaces each value greater than 9. The iterators supplied as the first two arguments must be forward iterators so that the algorithm can modify the elements in the sequence.

Line 54 uses function **replace_copy_if** to copy all elements in the range from v4.begin() up to, but not including, v4.end() from v4. Elements for which the unary predicate function greater9 returns true are replaced with the value 100. The elements are placed in c2, starting at position c2.begin(). The iterators supplied as the first two arguments must be input iterators. The iterator supplied as the third argument must be an output iterator so that the element being copied can be inserted into the copy location. This function returns an iterator positioned after the last element copied into c2.

22.5.5 Mathematical Algorithms

Figure 22.30 demonstrates several common mathematical algorithms from the STL, including `random_shuffle`, `count`, `count_if`, `min_element`, `max_element`, `accumulate`, `for_each` and `transform`.

```cpp
1   // Fig. 22.30: Fig22_30.cpp
2   // Mathematical algorithms of the Standard Library.
3   #include <iostream>
4   #include <algorithm> // algorithm definitions
5   #include <numeric> // accumulate is defined here
6   #include <vector>
7   #include <iterator>
8   using namespace std;
9
10  bool greater9( int ); // predicate function prototype
11  void outputSquare( int ); // output square of a value
12  int calculateCube( int ); // calculate cube of a value
13
14  int main()
15  {
16     const int SIZE = 10;
17     int a1[ SIZE ] = { 1, 2, 3, 4, 5, 6, 7, 8, 9, 10 };
18     vector< int > v( a1, a1 + SIZE ); // copy of a1
19     ostream_iterator< int > output( cout, " " );
20
21     cout << "Vector v before random_shuffle: ";
22     copy( v.begin(), v.end(), output );
23
24     random_shuffle( v.begin(), v.end() ); // shuffle elements of v
25     cout << "\nVector v after random_shuffle: ";
26     copy( v.begin(), v.end(), output );
27
28     int a2[ SIZE ] = { 100, 2, 8, 1, 50, 3, 8, 8, 9, 10 };
29     vector< int > v2( a2, a2 + SIZE ); // copy of a2
30     cout << "\n\nVector v2 contains: ";
31     copy( v2.begin(), v2.end(), output );
32
33     // count number of elements in v2 with value 8
34     int result = count( v2.begin(), v2.end(), 8 );
35     cout << "\nNumber of elements matching 8: " << result;
36
37     // count number of elements in v2 that are greater than 9
38     result = count_if( v2.begin(), v2.end(), greater9 );
39     cout << "\nNumber of elements greater than 9: " << result;
40
41     // locate minimum element in v2
42     cout << "\n\nMinimum element in Vector v2 is: "
43        << *( min_element( v2.begin(), v2.end() ) );
44
45     // locate maximum element in v2
46     cout << "\nMaximum element in Vector v2 is: "
47        << *( max_element( v2.begin(), v2.end() ) );
```

Fig. 22.30 | Mathematical algorithms of the Standard Library. (Part 1 of 2.)

```
48
49      // calculate sum of elements in v
50      cout << "\n\nThe total of the elements in Vector v is: "
51         << accumulate( v.begin(), v.end(), 0 );
52
53      // output square of every element in v
54      cout << "\n\nThe square of every integer in Vector v is:\n";
55      for_each( v.begin(), v.end(), outputSquare );
56
57      vector< int > cubes( SIZE ); // instantiate vector cubes
58
59      // calculate cube of each element in v; place results in cubes
60      transform( v.begin(), v.end(), cubes.begin(), calculateCube );
61      cout << "\n\nThe cube of every integer in Vector v is:\n";
62      copy( cubes.begin(), cubes.end(), output );
63      cout << endl;
64   } // end main
65
66   // determine whether argument is greater than 9
67   bool greater9( int value )
68   {
69      return value > 9;
70   } // end function greater9
71
72   // output square of argument
73   void outputSquare( int value )
74   {
75      cout << value * value << ' ';
76   } // end function outputSquare
77
78   // return cube of argument
79   int calculateCube( int value )
80   {
81      return value * value * value;
82   } // end function calculateCube
```

```
Vector v before random_shuffle: 1 2 3 4 5 6 7 8 9 10
Vector v after random_shuffle: 5 4 1 3 7 8 9 10 6 2

Vector v2 contains: 100 2 8 1 50 3 8 8 9 10
Number of elements matching 8: 3
Number of elements greater than 9: 3

Minimum element in Vector v2 is: 1
Maximum element in Vector v2 is: 100

The total of the elements in Vector v is: 55

The square of every integer in Vector v is:
25 16 1 9 49 64 81 100 36 4

The cube of every integer in Vector v is:
125 64 1 27 343 512 729 1000 216 8
```

Fig. 22.30 | Mathematical algorithms of the Standard Library. (Part 2 of 2.)

Line 24 uses function **random_shuffle** to reorder randomly the elements in the range from v.begin() up to, but not including, v.end() in v. This function takes two random-access iterator arguments.

Line 34 uses function **count** to count the elements with the value 8 in the range from v2.begin() up to, but not including, v2.end() in v2. This function requires its two iterator arguments to be at least input iterators.

Line 38 uses function **count_if** to count elements in the range from v2.begin() up to, but not including, v2.end() in v2 for which the predicate function greater9 returns true. Function count_if requires its two iterator arguments to be at least input iterators.

Line 43 uses function **min_element** to locate the smallest element in the range from v2.begin() up to, but not including, v2.end(). The function returns a forward iterator located at the smallest element, or v2.end() if the range is empty. The function's two iterator arguments must be at least input iterators. A second version of this function takes as its third argument a binary function that compares two elements in the sequence. This function returns the bool value true if the first argument is less than the second.

Good Programming Practice 22.2

It's a good practice to check that the range specified in a call to min_element is not empty and that the return value is not the "past the end" iterator.

Line 47 uses function **max_element** to locate the largest element in the range from v2.begin() up to, but not including, v2.end() in v2. The function returns an input iterator located at the largest element. The function's two iterator arguments must be at least input iterators. A second version of this function takes as its third argument a binary predicate function that compares the elements in the sequence. The binary function takes two arguments and returns the bool value true if the first argument is less than the second.

Line 51 uses function **accumulate** (the template of which is in header file <numeric>) to sum the values in the range from v.begin() up to, but not including, v.end() in v. The function's two iterator arguments must be at least input iterators and its third argument represents the initial value of the total. A second version of this function takes as its fourth argument a general function that determines how elements are accumulated. The general function must take two arguments and return a result. The first argument to this function is the current value of the accumulation. The second argument is the value of the current element in the sequence being accumulated.

Line 55 uses function **for_each** to apply a general function to every element in the range from v.begin() up to, but not including, v.end(). The general function takes the current element as an argument and may modify that element (if it's received by reference). Function for_each requires its two iterator arguments to be at least input iterators.

Line 60 uses function **transform** to apply a general function to every element in the range from v.begin() up to, but not including, v.end() in v. The general function (the fourth argument) should take the current element as an argument, should not modify the element and should return the transformed value. Function transform requires its first two iterator arguments to be at least input iterators and its third argument to be at least an output iterator. The third argument specifies where the transformed values should be placed. Note that the third argument can equal the first. Another version of transform accepts five arguments—the first two arguments are input iterators that specify a range of elements from one source container, the third argument is an input iterator that specifies the first element in another source container, the fourth argument is an output iterator that specifies where the transformed values should be placed and the last argument is a general function that takes two arguments. This version of transform takes one element from each of the two input sources and applies the general function to that pair of elements, then places the transformed value at the location specified by the fourth argument.

22.5.6 Basic Searching and Sorting Algorithms

Figure 22.31 demonstrates some basic searching and sorting capabilities of the Standard Library, including find, find_if, sort and binary_search.

```cpp
1   // Fig. 22.31: Fig22_31.cpp
2   // Standard Library search and sort algorithms.
3   #include <iostream>
4   #include <algorithm> // algorithm definitions
5   #include <vector> // vector class-template definition
6   #include <iterator>
7   using namespace std;
8
9   bool greater10( int value ); // predicate function prototype
10
11  int main()
12  {
13     const int SIZE = 10;
14     int a[ SIZE ] = { 10, 2, 17, 5, 16, 8, 13, 11, 20, 7 };
15     vector< int > v( a, a + SIZE ); // copy of a
16     ostream_iterator< int > output( cout, " " );
17
18     cout << "Vector v contains: ";
19     copy( v.begin(), v.end(), output ); // display output vector
20
21     // locate first occurrence of 16 in v
22     vector< int >::iterator location;
23     location = find( v.begin(), v.end(), 16 );
24
25     if ( location != v.end() ) // found 16
26        cout << "\n\nFound 16 at location " << ( location - v.begin() );
27     else // 16 not found
28        cout << "\n\n16 not found";
29
30     // locate first occurrence of 100 in v
31     location = find( v.begin(), v.end(), 100 );
32
33     if ( location != v.end() ) // found 100
34        cout << "\nFound 100 at location " << ( location - v.begin() );
35     else // 100 not found
36        cout << "\n100 not found";
37
38     // locate first occurrence of value greater than 10 in v
39     location = find_if( v.begin(), v.end(), greater10 );
40
```

Fig. 22.31 | Basic searching and sorting algorithms of the Standard Library. (Part 1 of 2.)

```
41        if ( location != v.end() ) // found value greater than 10
42            cout << "\n\nThe first value greater than 10 is " << *location
43                << "\nfound at location " << ( location - v.begin() );
44        else // value greater than 10 not found
45            cout << "\n\nNo values greater than 10 were found";
46
47        // sort elements of v
48        sort( v.begin(), v.end() );
49        cout << "\n\nVector v after sort: ";
50        copy( v.begin(), v.end(), output );
51
52        // use binary_search to locate 13 in v
53        if ( binary_search( v.begin(), v.end(), 13 ) )
54            cout << "\n\n13 was found in v";
55        else
56            cout << "\n\n13 was not found in v";
57
58        // use binary_search to locate 100 in v
59        if ( binary_search( v.begin(), v.end(), 100 ) )
60            cout << "\n100 was found in v";
61        else
62            cout << "\n100 was not found in v";
63
64        cout << endl;
65    } // end main
66
67    // determine whether argument is greater than 10
68    bool greater10( int value )
69    {
70        return value > 10;
71    } // end function greater10
```

```
Vector v contains: 10 2 17 5 16 8 13 11 20 7

Found 16 at location 4
100 not found

The first value greater than 10 is 17
found at location 2

Vector v after sort: 2 5 7 8 10 11 13 16 17 20

13 was found in v
100 was not found in v
```

Fig. 22.31 | Basic searching and sorting algorithms of the Standard Library. (Part 2 of 2.)

Line 23 uses function **find** to locate the value 16 in the range from v.begin() up to, but not including, v.end() in v. The function requires its two iterator arguments to be at least input iterators and returns an input iterator that either is positioned at the first element containing the value or indicates the end of the sequence (as is the case in line 31).

Line 39 uses function **find_if** to locate the first value in the range from v.begin() up to, but not including, v.end() in v for which the unary predicate function greater10 returns true. Function greater10 (defined in lines 71–74) takes an integer and returns a bool value indicating whether the integer argument is greater than 10. Function find_if requires its two iterator arguments to be at least input iterators. The function returns an input iterator that either is positioned at the first element containing a value for which the predicate function returns true or indicates the end of the sequence.

Line 48 uses function **sort** to arrange the elements in the range from v.begin() up to, but not including, v.end() in v in ascending order. The function requires its two iterator arguments to be random-access iterators. A second version of this function takes a third argument that is a binary predicate function taking two arguments that are values in the sequence and returning a bool indicating the sorting order—if the return value is true, the two elements being compared are in sorted order.

Common Programming Error 22.5

Attempting to sort a container by using an iterator other than a random-access iterator is a compilation error. Function sort requires a random-access iterator.

Line 53 uses function **binary_search** to determine whether the value 13 is in the range from v.begin() up to, but not including, v.end() in v. The sequence of values must be sorted in ascending order first. Function binary_search requires its two iterator arguments to be at least forward iterators. The function returns a bool indicating whether the value was found in the sequence. Line 59 demonstrates a call to function binary_search in which the value is not found. A second version of this function takes a fourth argument that is a binary predicate function taking two arguments that are values in the sequence and returning a bool. The predicate function returns true if the two elements being compared are in sorted order. To obtain the location of the search key in the container, use the lower_bound or find algorithms.

22.5.7 swap, iter_swap and swap_ranges

Figure 22.32 demonstrates algorithms swap, iter_swap and swap_ranges for swapping elements. Line 18 uses function **swap** to exchange two values. In this example, the first and second elements of array a are exchanged. The function takes as arguments references to the two values being exchanged.

```
1   // Fig. 22.32: Fig22_32.cpp
2   // Standard Library algorithms iter_swap, swap and swap_ranges.
3   #include <iostream>
4   #include <algorithm> // algorithm definitions
5   #include <iterator>
6   using namespace std;
7
8   int main()
9   {
10      const int SIZE = 10;
11      int a[ SIZE ] = { 1, 2, 3, 4, 5, 6, 7, 8, 9, 10 };
12      ostream_iterator< int > output( cout, " " );
13
14      cout << "Array a contains:\n   ";
15      copy( a, a + SIZE, output ); // display array a
```

Fig. 22.32 | Demonstrating swap, iter_swap and swap_ranges. (Part 1 of 2.)

```
16
17        // swap elements at locations 0 and 1 of array a
18        swap( a[ 0 ], a[ 1 ] );
19
20        cout << "\nArray a after swapping a[0] and a[1] using swap:\n    ";
21        copy( a, a + SIZE, output ); // display array a
22
23        // use iterators to swap elements at locations 0 and 1 of array a
24        iter_swap( &a[ 0 ], &a[ 1 ] ); // swap with iterators
25        cout << "\nArray a after swapping a[0] and a[1] using iter_swap:\n    ";
26        copy( a, a + SIZE, output );
27
28        // swap elements in first five elements of array a with
29        // elements in last five elements of array a
30        swap_ranges( a, a + 5, a + 5 );
31
32        cout << "\nArray a after swapping the first five elements\n"
33            << "with the last five elements:\n    ";
34        copy( a, a + SIZE, output );
35        cout << endl;
36    } // end main
```

```
Array a contains:
   1 2 3 4 5 6 7 8 9 10
Array a after swapping a[0] and a[1] using swap:
   2 1 3 4 5 6 7 8 9 10
Array a after swapping a[0] and a[1] using iter_swap:
   1 2 3 4 5 6 7 8 9 10
Array a after swapping the first five elements
with the last five elements:
   6 7 8 9 10 1 2 3 4 5
```

Fig. 22.32 | Demonstrating swap, iter_swap and swap_ranges. (Part 2 of 2.)

Line 24 uses function **iter_swap** to exchange the two elements. The function takes two forward iterator arguments (in this case, pointers to elements of an array) and exchanges the values in the elements to which the iterators refer.

Line 30 uses function **swap_ranges** to exchange the elements from a up to, but not including, a + 5 with the elements beginning at position a + 5. The function requires three forward iterator arguments. The first two arguments specify the range of elements in the first sequence that will be exchanged with the elements in the second sequence starting from the iterator in the third argument. In this example, the two sequences of values are in the same array, but the sequences can be from different arrays or containers.

22.5.8 copy_backward, merge, unique and reverse

Figure 22.33 demonstrates STL algorithms copy_backward, merge, unique and reverse. Line 26 uses function **copy_backward** to copy elements in the range from v1.begin() up to, but not including, v1.end(), placing the elements in results by starting from the element before results.end() and working toward the beginning of the vector. The function returns an iterator positioned at the last element copied into the results (i.e., the beginning of results, because of the backward copy). The elements are placed in results in the same order as v1. This function requires three bidirectional iterator arguments (iterators that can be incremented and decremented to iterate forward and backward through a sequence, respectively). One difference between copy_backward and copy is that the iterator returned from copy is positioned *after* the last element copied and the one returned from copy_backward is positioned *at* the last element copied (i.e., the first element in the sequence). Also, copy_backward can manipulate overlapping ranges of elements in a container as long as the first element to copy is not in the destination range of elements.

```cpp
1   // Fig. 22.33: Fig22_33.cpp
2   // Standard Library functions copy_backward, merge, unique and reverse.
3   #include <iostream>
4   #include <algorithm> // algorithm definitions
5   #include <vector> // vector class-template definition
6   #include <iterator> // ostream_iterator
7   using namespace std;
8
9   int main()
10  {
11     const int SIZE = 5;
12     int a1[ SIZE ] = { 1, 3, 5, 7, 9 };
13     int a2[ SIZE ] = { 2, 4, 5, 7, 9 };
14     vector< int > v1( a1, a1 + SIZE ); // copy of a1
15     vector< int > v2( a2, a2 + SIZE ); // copy of a2
16     ostream_iterator< int > output( cout, " " );
17
18     cout << "Vector v1 contains: ";
19     copy( v1.begin(), v1.end(), output ); // display vector output
20     cout << "\nVector v2 contains: ";
21     copy( v2.begin(), v2.end(), output ); // display vector output
22
23     vector< int > results( v1.size() );
24
25     // place elements of v1 into results in reverse order
26     copy_backward( v1.begin(), v1.end(), results.end() );
27     cout << "\n\nAfter copy_backward, results contains: ";
28     copy( results.begin(), results.end(), output );
29
30     vector< int > results2( v1.size() + v2.size() );
31
32     // merge elements of v1 and v2 into results2 in sorted order
33     merge( v1.begin(), v1.end(), v2.begin(), v2.end(), results2.begin() );
34
35     cout << "\n\nAfter merge of v1 and v2 results2 contains:\n";
36     copy( results2.begin(), results2.end(), output );
37
38     // eliminate duplicate values from results2
39     vector< int >::iterator endLocation;
40     endLocation = unique( results2.begin(), results2.end() );
41
42     cout << "\n\nAfter unique results2 contains:\n";
43     copy( results2.begin(), endLocation, output );
```

Fig. 22.33 | Demonstrating copy_backward, merge, unique and reverse. (Part 1 of 2.)

```
44
45        cout << "\n\nVector v1 after reverse: ";
46        reverse( v1.begin(), v1.end() ); // reverse elements of v1
47        copy( v1.begin(), v1.end(), output );
48        cout << endl;
49   } // end main
```

```
Vector v1 contains: 1 3 5 7 9
Vector v2 contains: 2 4 5 7 9

After copy_backward, results contains: 1 3 5 7 9

After merge of v1 and v2 results2 contains:
1 2 3 4 5 5 7 7 9 9

After unique results2 contains:
1 2 3 4 5 7 9

Vector v1 after reverse: 9 7 5 3 1
```

Fig. 22.33 | Demonstrating copy_backward, merge, unique and reverse. (Part 2 of 2.)

Line 33 uses function **merge** to combine two sorted ascending sequences of values into a third sorted ascending sequence. The function requires five iterator arguments. The first four must be at least input iterators and the last must be at least an output iterator. The first two arguments specify the range of elements in the first sorted sequence (v1), the second two arguments specify the range of elements in the second sorted sequence (v2) and the last argument specifies the starting location in the third sequence (results2) where the elements will be merged. A second version of this function takes as its sixth argument a binary predicate function that specifies the sorting order.

Line 30 creates vector results2 with the number of elements v1.size() + v2.size(). Using the merge function as shown here requires that the sequence where the results are stored be at least the size of the two sequences being merged. If you do not want to allocate the number of elements for the resulting sequence before the merge operation, you can use the following statements:

```
vector< int > results2;
merge( v1.begin(), v1.end(), v2.begin(), v2.end(),
    back_inserter( results2 ) );
```

The argument back_inserter(results2) uses function template **back_inserter** (header file <iterator>) for the container results2. A back_inserter calls the container's default push_back function to insert an element at the end of the container. If an element is inserted into a container that has no more space available, *the container grows in size*. Thus, the number of elements in the container does not have to be known in advance. There are two other inserters—**front_inserter** (to insert an element at the beginning of a container specified as its argument) and **inserter** (to insert an element before the iterator supplied as its second argument in the container supplied as its first argument).

Line 40 uses function **unique** on the sorted sequence of elements in the range from results2.begin() up to, but not including, results2.end() in results2. After this function is applied to a sorted sequence with duplicate values, only a single copy of each value remains in the sequence. The function takes two arguments that must be at least forward iterators. The function returns an iterator positioned after the last element in the sequence of unique values. The values of all elements in the container after the last unique value are undefined. A second version of this function takes as a third argument a binary predicate function specifying how to compare two elements for equality.

Line 46 uses function **reverse** to reverse all the elements in the range from `v1.begin()` up to, but not including, `v1.end()` in `v1`. The function takes two arguments that must be at least bidirectional iterators.

22.5.9 `inplace_merge`, `unique_copy` and `reverse_copy`

Figure 22.34 demonstrates algorithms `inplace_merge`, `unique_copy` and `reverse_copy`. Line 22 uses function **inplace_merge** to merge two sorted sequences of elements in the same container. In this example, the elements from `v1.begin()` up to, but not including, `v1.begin() + 5` are merged with the elements from `v1.begin() + 5` up to, but not including, `v1.end()`. This function requires its three iterator arguments to be at least bidirectional iterators. A second version of this function takes as a fourth argument a binary predicate function for comparing elements in the two sequences.

```cpp
1   // Fig. 22.34: Fig22_34.cpp
2   // Standard Library algorithms inplace_merge,
3   // reverse_copy and unique_copy.
4   #include <iostream>
5   #include <algorithm> // algorithm definitions
6   #include <vector> // vector class-template definition
7   #include <iterator> // back_inserter definition
8   using namespace std;
9
10  int main()
11  {
12     const int SIZE = 10;
13     int a1[ SIZE ] = { 1, 3, 5, 7, 9, 1, 3, 5, 7, 9 };
14     vector< int > v1( a1, a1 + SIZE ); // copy of a
15     ostream_iterator< int > output( cout, " " );
16
17     cout << "Vector v1 contains: ";
18     copy( v1.begin(), v1.end(), output );
19
20     // merge first half of v1 with second half of v1 such that
21     // v1 contains sorted set of elements after merge
22     inplace_merge( v1.begin(), v1.begin() + 5, v1.end() );
23
24     cout << "\nAfter inplace_merge, v1 contains: ";
25     copy( v1.begin(), v1.end(), output );
26
27     vector< int > results1;
28
29     // copy only unique elements of v1 into results1
30     unique_copy( v1.begin(), v1.end(), back_inserter( results1 ) );
31     cout << "\nAfter unique_copy results1 contains: ";
```

Fig. 22.34 | Algorithms `inplace_merge`, `unique_copy` and `reverse_copy`. (Part 1 of 2.)

```
32        copy( results1.begin(), results1.end(), output );
33
34        vector< int > results2;
35
36        // copy elements of v1 into results2 in reverse order
37        reverse_copy( v1.begin(), v1.end(), back_inserter( results2 ) );
38        cout << "\nAfter reverse_copy, results2 contains: ";
39        copy( results2.begin(), results2.end(), output );
40        cout << endl;
41     } // end main
```

```
Vector v1 contains: 1 3 5 7 9 1 3 5 7 9
After inplace_merge, v1 contains: 1 1 3 3 5 5 7 7 9 9
After unique_copy results1 contains: 1 3 5 7 9
After reverse_copy, results2 contains: 9 9 7 7 5 5 3 3 1 1
```

Fig. 22.34 | Algorithms `inplace_merge`, `unique_copy` and `reverse_copy`. (Part 2 of 2.)

Line 30 uses function **unique_copy** to make a copy of all the unique elements in the sorted sequence of values from `v1.begin()` up to, but not including, `v1.end()`. The copied elements are placed into `vector` `results1`. The first two arguments must be at least input iterators and the last must be at least an output iterator. In this example, we did not preallocate enough elements in `results1` to store all the elements copied from `v1`. Instead, we use function `back_inserter` (defined in header file `<iterator>`) to add elements to the end of `v1`. The `back_inserter` uses class `vector`'s capability to insert elements at the end of the `vector`. Because the `back_inserter` inserts an element rather than replacing an existing element's value, the `vector` is able to grow to accommodate additional elements. A second version of the `unique_copy` function takes as a fourth argument a binary predicate function for comparing elements for equality.

Line 37 uses function **reverse_copy** to make a reversed copy of the elements in the range from `v1.begin()` up to, but not including, `v1.end()`. The copied elements are inserted into `results2` using a `back_inserter` object to ensure that the `vector` can grow to accommodate the appropriate number of elements copied. Function `reverse_copy` requires its first two iterator arguments to be at least bidirectional iterators and its third to be at least an output iterator.

22.5.10 Set Operations

Figure 22.35 demonstrates functions `includes`, `set_difference`, `set_intersection`, `set_symmetric_difference` and `set_union` for manipulating sets of sorted values. To demonstrate that STL functions can be applied to arrays and containers, this example uses only arrays (remember, a pointer into an array is a random-access iterator).

Lines 25 and 31 call function **includes**. Function `includes` compares two sets of sorted values to determine whether every element of the second set is in the first set. If so, `includes` returns `true`; otherwise, it returns `false`. The first two iterator arguments must be at least input iterators and must describe the first set of values. In line 25, the first set consists of the elements from `a1` up to, but not including, `a1 + SIZE1`. The last two iterator arguments must be at least input iterators and must describe the second set of values. In this example, the second set consists of the elements from `a2` up to, but not including, `a2`

+ SIZE2. A second version of function `includes` takes a fifth argument that is a binary predicate function indicating the order in which the elements were originally sorted. The two sequences must be sorted using the same comparison function.

```cpp
1   // Fig. 22.35: Fig22_35.cpp
2   // Standard Library algorithms includes, set_difference,
3   // set_intersection, set_symmetric_difference and set_union.
4   #include <iostream>
5   #include <algorithm> // algorithm definitions
6   #include <iterator> // ostream_iterator
7   using namespace std;
8
9   int main()
10  {
11     const int SIZE1 = 10, SIZE2 = 5, SIZE3 = 20;
12     int a1[ SIZE1 ] = { 1, 2, 3, 4, 5, 6, 7, 8, 9, 10 };
13     int a2[ SIZE2 ] = { 4, 5, 6, 7, 8 };
14     int a3[ SIZE2 ] = { 4, 5, 6, 11, 15 };
15     ostream_iterator< int > output( cout, " " );
16
17     cout << "a1 contains: ";
18     copy( a1, a1 + SIZE1, output ); // display array a1
19     cout << "\na2 contains: ";
20     copy( a2, a2 + SIZE2, output ); // display array a2
21     cout << "\na3 contains: ";
22     copy( a3, a3 + SIZE2, output ); // display array a3
23
24     // determine whether set a2 is completely contained in a1
25     if ( includes( a1, a1 + SIZE1, a2, a2 + SIZE2 ) )
26        cout << "\n\na1 includes a2";
27     else
28        cout << "\n\na1 does not include a2";
29
30     // determine whether set a3 is completely contained in a1
31     if ( includes( a1, a1 + SIZE1, a3, a3 + SIZE2 ) )
32        cout << "\na1 includes a3";
33     else
34        cout << "\na1 does not include a3";
35
36     int difference[ SIZE1 ];
37
38     // determine elements of a1 not in a2
39     int *ptr = set_difference( a1, a1 + SIZE1,
40        a2, a2 + SIZE2, difference );
41     cout << "\n\nset_difference of a1 and a2 is: ";
42     copy( difference, ptr, output );
43
44     int intersection[ SIZE1 ];
45
46     // determine elements in both a1 and a2
47     ptr = set_intersection( a1, a1 + SIZE1,
48        a2, a2 + SIZE2, intersection );
```

Fig. 22.35 | set operations of the Standard Library. (Part 1 of 2.)

```
49        cout << "\n\nset_intersection of a1 and a2 is: ";
50        copy( intersection, ptr, output );
51
52        int symmetric_difference[ SIZE1 + SIZE2 ];
53
54        // determine elements of a1 that are not in a2 and
55        // elements of a2 that are not in a1
56        ptr = set_symmetric_difference( a1, a1 + SIZE1,
57           a3, a3 + SIZE2, symmetric_difference );
58        cout << "\n\nset_symmetric_difference of a1 and a3 is: ";
59        copy( symmetric_difference, ptr, output );
60
61        int unionSet[ SIZE3 ];
62
63        // determine elements that are in either or both sets
64        ptr = set_union( a1, a1 + SIZE1, a3, a3 + SIZE2, unionSet );
65        cout << "\n\nset_union of a1 and a3 is: ";
66        copy( unionSet, ptr, output );
67        cout << endl;
68     } // end main
```

```
a1 contains: 1 2 3 4 5 6 7 8 9 10
a2 contains: 4 5 6 7 8
a3 contains: 4 5 6 11 15

a1 includes a2
a1 does not include a3

set_difference of a1 and a2 is: 1 2 3 9 10

set_intersection of a1 and a2 is: 4 5 6 7 8

set_symmetric_difference of a1 and a3 is: 1 2 3 7 8 9 10 11 15

set_union of a1 and a3 is: 1 2 3 4 5 6 7 8 9 10 11 15
```

Fig. 22.35 | set operations of the Standard Library. (Part 2 of 2.)

Lines 39–40 use function **set_difference** to find the elements from the first set of sorted values that are not in the second set of sorted values (both sets of values must be in ascending order). The elements that are different are copied into the fifth argument (in this case, the array difference). The first two iterator arguments must be at least input iterators for the first set of values. The next two iterator arguments must be at least input iterators for the second set of values. The fifth argument must be at least an output iterator indicating where to store a copy of the values that are different. The function returns an output iterator positioned immediately after the last value copied into the set to which the fifth argument points. A second version of function set_difference takes a sixth argument that is a binary predicate function indicating the order in which the elements were originally sorted. The two sequences must be sorted using the same comparison function.

Lines 47–48 use function **set_intersection** to determine the elements from the first set of sorted values that are in the second set of sorted values (both sets of values must be in ascending order). The elements common to both sets are copied into the fifth argument (in this case, array `intersection`). The first two iterator arguments must be at least input iterators for the first set of values. The next two iterator arguments must be at least input iterators for the second set of values. The fifth argument must be at least an output iterator indicating where to store a copy of the values that are the same. The function returns an output iterator positioned immediately after the last value copied into the set to which the fifth argument points. A second version of function `set_intersection` takes a sixth argument that is a binary predicate function indicating the order in which the elements were originally sorted. The two sequences must be sorted using the same comparison function.

Lines 56–57 use function **`set_symmetric_difference`** to determine the elements in the first set that are not in the second set and the elements in the second set that are not in the first set (both sets must be in ascending order). The elements that are different are copied from both sets into the fifth argument (the array `symmetric_difference`). The first two iterator arguments must be at least input iterators for the first set of values. The next two iterator arguments must be at least input iterators for the second set of values. The fifth argument must be at least an output iterator indicating where to store a copy of the values that are different. The function returns an output iterator positioned immediately after the last value copied into the set to which the fifth argument points. A second version of function `set_symmetric_difference` takes a sixth argument that is a binary predicate function indicating the order in which the elements were originally sorted. The two sequences must be sorted using the same comparison function.

Line 64 uses function **`set_union`** to create a set of all the elements that are in either or both of the two sorted sets (both sets of values must be in ascending order). The elements are copied from both sets into the fifth argument (in this case the array `unionSet`). Elements that appear in both sets are only copied from the first set. The first two iterator arguments must be at least input iterators for the first set of values. The next two iterator arguments must be at least input iterators for the second set of values. The fifth argument must be at least an output iterator indicating where to store the copied elements. The function returns an output iterator positioned immediately after the last value copied into the set to which the fifth argument points. A second version of `set_union` takes a sixth argument that is a binary predicate function indicating the order in which the elements were originally sorted. The two sequences must be sorted using the same comparison function.

22.5.11 `lower_bound`, `upper_bound` and `equal_range`

Figure 22.36 demonstrates functions `lower_bound`, `upper_bound` and `equal_range`. Line 22 uses function **`lower_bound`** to find the first location in a sorted sequence of values at which the third argument could be inserted in the sequence such that the sequence would still be sorted in ascending order. The first two iterator arguments must be at least forward iterators. The third argument is the value for which to determine the lower bound. The function returns a forward iterator pointing to the position at which the insert can occur. A second version of function `lower_bound` takes as a fourth argument a binary predicate function indicating the order in which the elements were originally sorted.

Line 28 uses function **`upper_bound`** to find the last location in a sorted sequence of values at which the third argument could be inserted in the sequence such that the sequence would still be sorted in ascending order. The first two iterator arguments must be at least forward iterators. The third argument is the value for which to determine the upper bound. The function returns a forward iterator pointing to the position at which the insert can occur. A second version of upper_bound takes as a fourth argument a binary predicate function indicating the order in which the elements were originally sorted.

```cpp
1   // Fig. 22.36: Fig22_36.cpp
2   // Standard Library functions lower_bound, upper_bound and
3   // equal_range for a sorted sequence of values.
4   #include <iostream>
5   #include <algorithm> // algorithm definitions
6   #include <vector> // vector class-template definition
7   #include <iterator> // ostream_iterator
8   using namespace std;
9
10  int main()
11  {
12     const int SIZE = 10;
13     int a1[ SIZE ] = { 2, 2, 4, 4, 4, 6, 6, 6, 6, 8 };
14     vector< int > v( a1, a1 + SIZE ); // copy of a1
15     ostream_iterator< int > output( cout, " " );
16
17     cout << "Vector v contains:\n";
18     copy( v.begin(), v.end(), output );
19
20     // determine lower-bound insertion point for 6 in v
21     vector< int >::iterator lower;
22     lower = lower_bound( v.begin(), v.end(), 6 );
23     cout << "\n\nLower bound of 6 is element "
24        << ( lower - v.begin() ) << " of vector v";
25
26     // determine upper-bound insertion point for 6 in v
27     vector< int >::iterator upper;
28     upper = upper_bound( v.begin(), v.end(), 6 );
29     cout << "\nUpper bound of 6 is element "
30        << ( upper - v.begin() ) << " of vector v";
31
32     // use equal_range to determine both the lower- and
33     // upper-bound insertion points for 6
34     pair< vector< int >::iterator, vector< int >::iterator > eq;
35     eq = equal_range( v.begin(), v.end(), 6 );
36     cout << "\nUsing equal_range:\n   Lower bound of 6 is element "
37        << ( eq.first - v.begin() ) << " of vector v";
38     cout << "\n   Upper bound of 6 is element "
39        << ( eq.second - v.begin() ) << " of vector v";
40     cout << "\n\nUse lower_bound to locate the first point\n"
41        << "at which 5 can be inserted in order";
42
43     // determine lower-bound insertion point for 5 in v
44     lower = lower_bound( v.begin(), v.end(), 5 );
45     cout << "\n   Lower bound of 5 is element "
46        << ( lower - v.begin() ) << " of vector v";
47     cout << "\n\nUse upper_bound to locate the last point\n"
48        << "at which 7 can be inserted in order";
49
```

Fig. 22.36 | Algorithms lower_bound, upper_bound and equal_range. (Part 1 of 2.)

```
50        // determine upper-bound insertion point for 7 in v
51        upper = upper_bound( v.begin(), v.end(), 7 );
52        cout << "\n   Upper bound of 7 is element "
53           << ( upper - v.begin() ) << " of vector v";
54        cout << "\n\nUse equal_range to locate the first and\n"
55           << "last point at which 5 can be inserted in order";
56
57        // use equal_range to determine both the lower- and
58        // upper-bound insertion points for 5
59        eq = equal_range( v.begin(), v.end(), 5 );
60        cout << "\n   Lower bound of 5 is element "
61           << ( eq.first - v.begin() ) << " of vector v";
62        cout << "\n   Upper bound of 5 is element "
63           << ( eq.second - v.begin() ) << " of vector v" << endl;
64     } // end main
```

```
Vector v contains:
2 2 4 4 4 6 6 6 6 8

Lower bound of 6 is element 5 of vector v
Upper bound of 6 is element 9 of vector v
Using equal_range:
   Lower bound of 6 is element 5 of vector v
   Upper bound of 6 is element 9 of vector v

Use lower_bound to locate the first point
at which 5 can be inserted in order
   Lower bound of 5 is element 5 of vector v

Use upper_bound to locate the last point
at which 7 can be inserted in order
   Upper bound of 7 is element 9 of vector v

Use equal_range to locate the first and
last point at which 5 can be inserted in order
   Lower bound of 5 is element 5 of vector v
   Upper bound of 5 is element 5 of vector v
```

Fig. 22.36 | Algorithms `lower_bound`, `upper_bound` and `equal_range`. (Part 2 of 2.)

Line 35 uses function **equal_range** to return a pair of forward iterators containing the results of performing both a lower_bound and an upper_bound operation. The first two arguments must be at least forward iterators. The third is the value for which to locate the equal range. The function returns a pair of forward iterators for the lower bound (eq.first) and upper bound (eq.second), respectively.

Functions lower_bound, upper_bound and equal_range are often used to locate insertion points in sorted sequences. Line 44 uses lower_bound to locate the first point at which 5 can be inserted in order in v. Line 51 uses upper_bound to locate the last point at which 7 can be inserted in order in v. Line 59 uses equal_range to locate the first and last points at which 5 can be inserted in order in v.

22.5.12 Heapsort

Figure 22.37 demonstrates the Standard Library functions for performing the **heapsort sorting algorithm**. Heapsort is a sorting algorithm in which an array of elements is arranged into a special binary tree called a heap. The key features of a heap are that the largest element is always at the top of the heap and the values of the children of any node in the binary tree are always less than or equal to that node's value. A heap arranged in this manner is often called a **maxheap**. Heapsort is discussed in detail in computer science courses called "Data Structures" and "Algorithms."

```cpp
1   // Fig. 22.37: Fig22_37.cpp
2   // Standard Library algorithms push_heap, pop_heap,
3   // make_heap and sort_heap.
4   #include <iostream>
5   #include <algorithm>
6   #include <vector>
7   #include <iterator>
8   using namespace std;
9
10  int main()
11  {
12     const int SIZE = 10;
13     int a[ SIZE ] = { 3, 100, 52, 77, 22, 31, 1, 98, 13, 40 };
14     vector< int > v( a, a + SIZE ); // copy of a
15     vector< int > v2;
16     ostream_iterator< int > output( cout, " " );
17
18     cout << "Vector v before make_heap:\n";
19     copy( v.begin(), v.end(), output );
20
21     make_heap( v.begin(), v.end() ); // create heap from vector v
22     cout << "\nVector v after make_heap:\n";
23     copy( v.begin(), v.end(), output );
24
25     sort_heap( v.begin(), v.end() ); // sort elements with sort_heap
26     cout << "\nVector v after sort_heap:\n";
27     copy( v.begin(), v.end(), output );
28
29     // perform the heapsort with push_heap and pop_heap
30     cout << "\n\nArray a contains: ";
31     copy( a, a + SIZE, output ); // display array a
32     cout << endl;
33
34     // place elements of array a into v2 and
35     // maintain elements of v2 in heap
36     for ( int i = 0; i < SIZE; i++ )
37     {
38        v2.push_back( a[ i ] );
39        push_heap( v2.begin(), v2.end() );
40        cout << "\nv2 after push_heap(a[" << i << "]): ";
41        copy( v2.begin(), v2.end(), output );
42     } // end for
43
44     cout << endl;
45
```

Fig. 22.37 | Using Standard Library functions to perform a heapsort. (Part 1 of 2.)

```
46      // remove elements from heap in sorted order
47      for ( unsigned int j = 0; j < v2.size(); j++ )
48      {
49         cout << "\nv2 after " << v2[ 0 ] << " popped from heap\n";
50         pop_heap( v2.begin(), v2.end() - j );
51         copy( v2.begin(), v2.end(), output );
52      } // end for
53
54      cout << endl;
55   } // end main
```

```
Vector v before make_heap:
3 100 52 77 22 31 1 98 13 40
Vector v after make_heap:
100 98 52 77 40 31 1 3 13 22
Vector v after sort_heap:
1 3 13 22 31 40 52 77 98 100

Array a contains: 3 100 52 77 22 31 1 98 13 40

v2 after push_heap(a[0]): 3
v2 after push_heap(a[1]): 100 3
v2 after push_heap(a[2]): 100 3 52
v2 after push_heap(a[3]): 100 77 52 3
v2 after push_heap(a[4]): 100 77 52 3 22
v2 after push_heap(a[5]): 100 77 52 3 22 31
v2 after push_heap(a[6]): 100 77 52 3 22 31 1
v2 after push_heap(a[7]): 100 98 52 77 22 31 1 3
v2 after push_heap(a[8]): 100 98 52 77 22 31 1 3 13
v2 after push_heap(a[9]): 100 98 52 77 40 31 1 3 13 22

v2 after 100 popped from heap
98 77 52 22 40 31 1 3 13 100
v2 after 98 popped from heap
77 40 52 22 13 31 1 3 98 100
v2 after 77 popped from heap
52 40 31 22 13 3 1 77 98 100
v2 after 52 popped from heap
40 22 31 1 13 3 52 77 98 100
v2 after 40 popped from heap
31 22 3 1 13 40 52 77 98 100
v2 after 31 popped from heap
22 13 3 1 31 40 52 77 98 100
v2 after 22 popped from heap
13 1 3 22 31 40 52 77 98 100
v2 after 13 popped from heap
3 1 13 22 31 40 52 77 98 100
v2 after 3 popped from heap
1 3 13 22 31 40 52 77 98 100
v2 after 1 popped from heap
1 3 13 22 31 40 52 77 98 100
```

Fig. 22.37 | Using Standard Library functions to perform a heapsort. (Part 2 of 2.)

Line 21 uses function **make_heap** to take a sequence of values in the range from v.begin() up to, but not including, v.end() and create a heap that can be used to produce a sorted sequence. The two iterator arguments must be random-access iterators, so this function will work only with arrays, vectors and deques. A second version of this function takes as a third argument a binary predicate function for comparing values.

Line 25 uses function **sort_heap** to sort a sequence of values in the range from v.begin() up to, but not including, v.end() that are already arranged in a heap. The two iterator arguments must be random-access iterators. A second version of this function takes as a third argument a binary predicate function for comparing values.

Line 39 uses function **push_heap** to add a new value into a heap. We take one element of array a at a time, append it to the end of vector v2 and perform the push_heap operation. If the appended element is the only element in the vector, the vector is already a heap. Otherwise, function push_heap rearranges the vector elements into a heap. Each time push_heap is called, it assumes that the last element currently in the vector (i.e., the one that is appended before the push_heap function call) is the element being added to the heap and that all other elements in the vector are already arranged as a heap. The two iterator arguments to push_heap must be random-access iterators. A second version of this function takes as a third argument a binary predicate function for comparing values.

Line 50 uses **pop_heap** to remove the top heap element. This function assumes that the elements in the range specified by its two random-access iterator arguments are already a heap. Repeatedly removing the top heap element results in a sorted sequence of values. Function pop_heap swaps the first heap element (v2.begin()) with the last heap element (the element before v2.end() - i), then ensures that the elements up to, but not including, the last element still form a heap. Notice in the output that, after the pop_heap operations, the vector is sorted in ascending order. A second version of this function takes as a third argument a binary predicate function for comparing values.

22.5.13 min and max

Algorithms **min** and **max** determine the minimum and the maximum of two elements, respectively. Figure 22.38 demonstrates min and max for int and char values.

```cpp
1   // Fig. 22.38: Fig22_38.cpp
2   // Standard Library algorithms min and max.
3   #include <iostream>
4   #include <algorithm>
5   using namespace std;
6
7   int main()
8   {
9      cout << "The minimum of 12 and 7 is: " << min( 12, 7 );
10     cout << "\nThe maximum of 12 and 7 is: " << max( 12, 7 );
11     cout << "\nThe minimum of 'G' and 'Z' is: " << min( 'G', 'Z' );
12     cout << "\nThe maximum of 'G' and 'Z' is: " << max( 'G', 'Z' );
13     cout << endl;
14  } // end main
```

```
The minimum of 12 and 7 is: 7
The maximum of 12 and 7 is: 12
The minimum of 'G' and 'Z' is: G
The maximum of 'G' and 'Z' is: Z
```

Fig. 22.38 | Algorithms min and max.

22.5.14 STL Algorithms Not Covered in This Chapter

Figure 22.39 summarizes the STL algorithms that are not covered in this chapter.

Algorithm	Description
inner_product	Calculate the sum of the products of two sequences by taking corresponding elements in each sequence, multiplying those elements and adding the result to a total.
adjacent_difference	Beginning with the second element in a sequence, calculate the difference (using operator –) between the current and previous elements, and store the result. The first two input iterator arguments indicate the range of elements in the container and the third indicates where the results should be stored. A second version of this algorithm takes as a fourth argument a binary function to perform a calculation between the current element and the previous element.
partial_sum	Calculate a running total (using operator +) of the values in a sequence. The first two input iterator arguments indicate the range of elements in the container and the third indicates where the results should be stored. A second version of this algorithm takes as a fourth argument a binary function that performs a calculation between the current value in the sequence and the running total.
nth_element	Use three random-access iterators to partition a range of elements. The first and last arguments represent the range of elements. The second argument is the partitioning element's location. After this algorithm executes, all elements before the partitioning element are less than that element and all elements after the partitioning element are greater than or equal to that element. A second version of this algorithm takes as a fourth argument a binary comparison function.
partition	This algorithm is similar to nth_element, but requires less powerful bidirectional iterators, making it more flexible. It requires two bidirectional iterators indicating the range of elements to partition. The third argument is a unary predicate function that helps partition the elements so that all elements for which the predicate is true are to the left (toward the beginning of the sequence) of those for which the predicate is false. A bidirectional iterator is returned indicating the first element in the sequence for which the predicate returns false.
stable_partition	Similar to partition except that this algorithm guarantees that equivalent elements will be maintained in their original order.
next_permutation	Next lexicographical permutation of a sequence.
prev_permutation	Previous lexicographical permutation of a sequence.
rotate	Use three forward iterator arguments to rotate the sequence indicated by the first and last argument by the number of positions indicated by subtracting the first argument from the second argument. For example, the sequence 1, 2, 3, 4, 5 rotated by two positions would be 4, 5, 1, 2, 3.

Fig. 22.39 | Algorithms not covered in this chapter. (Part 1 of 2.)

Algorithm	Description
rotate_copy	This algorithm is identical to rotate except that the results are stored in a separate sequence indicated by the fourth argument—an output iterator. The two sequences must have the same number of elements.
adjacent_find	This algorithm returns an input iterator indicating the first of two identical adjacent elements in a sequence. If there are no identical adjacent elements, the iterator is positioned at the end of the sequence.
search	This algorithm searches for a subsequence of elements within a sequence of elements and, if such a subsequence is found, returns a forward iterator that indicates the first element of that subsequence. If there are no matches, the iterator is positioned at the end of the sequence to be searched.
search_n	This algorithm searches a sequence of elements looking for a subsequence in which the values of a specified number of elements have a particular value and, if such a subsequence is found, returns a forward iterator that indicates the first element of that subsequence. If there are no matches, the iterator is positioned at the end of the sequence to be searched.
partial_sort	Use three random-access iterators to sort part of a sequence. The first and last arguments indicate the sequence of elements. The second argument indicates the ending location for the sorted part of the sequence. By default, elements are ordered using operator < (a binary predicate function can also be supplied). The elements from the second argument iterator to the end of the sequence are in an undefined order.
partial_sort_copy	Use two input iterators and two random-access iterators to sort part of the sequence indicated by the two input iterator arguments. The results are stored in the sequence indicated by the two random-access iterator arguments. By default, elements are ordered using operator < (a binary predicate function can also be supplied). The number of elements sorted is the smaller of the number of elements in the result and the number of elements in the original sequence.
stable_sort	The algorithm is similar to sort except that all equivalent elements are maintained in their original order. This sort is $O(n \log n)$ if enough memory is available; otherwise, it's $O(n(\log n)^2)$.

Fig. 22.39 | Algorithms not covered in this chapter. (Part 2 of 2.)

22.6 Class bitset

Class **bitset** makes it easy to create and manipulate **bit sets**, which are useful for representing a set of bit flags. bitsets are fixed in size at compile time. Class bitset is an alternate tool for bit manipulation, discussed in Chapter 21. The declaration

```
bitset< size > b;
```

creates `bitset b`, in which every bit is initially 0. The statement

```
b.set( bitNumber );
```

sets bit `bitNumber` of `bitset b` "on." The expression `b.set()` sets all bits in b "on."
The statement

```
b.reset( bitNumber );
```

sets bit `bitNumber` of `bitset b` "off." The expression `b.reset()` sets all bits in b "off." The
statement

```
b.flip( bitNumber );
```

"flips" bit `bitNumber` of `bitset b` (e.g., if the bit is on, `flip` sets it off). The expression
`b.flip()` flips all bits in b. The statement

```
b[ bitNumber ];
```

returns a reference to the bit `bitNumber` of `bitset b`. Similarly,

```
b.at( bitNumber );
```

performs range checking on `bitNumber` first. Then, if `bitNumber` is in range, at returns a
reference to the bit. Otherwise, at throws an `out_of_range` exception. The statement

```
b.test( bitNumber );
```

performs range checking on `bitNumber` first. If `bitNumber` is in range, `test` returns `true`
if the bit is on, `false` it's off. Otherwise, `test` throws an `out_of_range` exception. The
expression

```
b.size()
```

returns the number of bits in `bitset b`. The expression

```
b.count()
```

returns the number of bits that are set in `bitset b`. The expression

```
b.any()
```

returns `true` if any bit is set in `bitset b`. The expression

```
b.none()
```

returns `true` if none of the bits is set in `bitset b`. The expressions

```
b == b1
b != b1
```

compare the two `bitsets` for equality and inequality, respectively.

Each of the bitwise assignment operators &=, |= and ^= can be used to combine `bit-sets`. For example,

```
b &= b1;
```

performs a bit-by-bit logical AND between `bitset`s b and b1. The result is stored in b. Bitwise logical OR and bitwise logical XOR are performed by

```
b |= b1;
b ^= b2;
```

The expression

```
b >>= n;
```

shifts the bits in `bitset` b right by n positions. The expression

```
b <<= n;
```

shifts the bits in `bitset` b left by n positions. The expressions

```
b.to_string()
b.to_ulong()
```

convert `bitset` b to a `string` and an `unsigned long`, respectively.

Sieve of Eratosthenes with *bitset*
Figure 22.40 revisits the Sieve of Eratosthenes for finding prime numbers that we discussed in Exercise 7.29. A `bitset` is used instead of an array to implement the algorithm. The program displays all the prime numbers from 2 to 1023, then allows the user to enter a number to determine whether that number is prime.

```cpp
1   // Fig. 22.40: Fig22_40.cpp
2   // Using a bitset to demonstrate the Sieve of Eratosthenes.
3   #include <iostream>
4   #include <iomanip>
5   #include <cmath>
6   #include <bitset> // bitset class definition
7   using namespace std;
8
9   int main()
10  {
11     const int SIZE = 1024;
12     int value;
13     bitset< SIZE > sieve; // create bitset of 1024 bits
14     sieve.flip(); // flip all bits in bitset sieve
15     sieve.reset( 0 ); // reset first bit (number 0)
16     sieve.reset( 1 ); // reset second bit (number 1)
17
18     // perform Sieve of Eratosthenes
19     int finalBit = sqrt( static_cast< double >( sieve.size() ) ) + 1;
20
21     // determine all prime numbers from 2 to 1024
22     for ( int i = 2; i < finalBit; i++ )
23     {
24        if ( sieve.test( i ) ) // bit i is on
25        {
```

Fig. 22.40 | Class `bitset` and the Sieve of Eratosthenes. (Part 1 of 3.)

```
26              for ( int j = 2 * i; j < SIZE; j += i )
27                  sieve.reset( j ); // set bit j off
28          } // end if
29      } // end for
30
31      cout << "The prime numbers in the range 2 to 1023 are:\n";
32
33      // display prime numbers in range 2-1023
34      for ( int k = 2, counter = 1; k < SIZE; k++ )
35      {
36          if ( sieve.test( k ) ) // bit k is on
37          {
38              cout << setw( 5 ) << k;
39
40              if ( counter++ % 12 == 0 ) // counter is a multiple of 12
41                  cout << '\n';
42          } // end if
43      } // end for
44
45      cout << endl;
46
47      // get value from user to determine whether value is prime
48      cout << "\nEnter a value from 2 to 1023 (-1 to end): ";
49      cin >> value;
50
51      // determine whether user input is prime
52      while ( value != -1 )
53      {
54          if ( sieve[ value ] ) // prime number
55              cout << value << " is a prime number\n";
56          else // not a prime number
57              cout << value << " is not a prime number\n";
58
59          cout << "\nEnter a value from 2 to 1023 (-1 to end): ";
60          cin >> value;
61      } // end while
62  } // end main
```

```
The prime numbers in the range 2 to 1023 are:
    2    3    5    7   11   13   17   19   23   29   31   37
   41   43   47   53   59   61   67   71   73   79   83   89
   97  101  103  107  109  113  127  131  137  139  149  151
  157  163  167  173  179  181  191  193  197  199  211  223
  227  229  233  239  241  251  257  263  269  271  277  281
  283  293  307  311  313  317  331  337  347  349  353  359
  367  373  379  383  389  397  401  409  419  421  431  433
  439  443  449  457  461  463  467  479  487  491  499  503
  509  521  523  541  547  557  563  569  571  577  587  593
  599  601  607  613  617  619  631  641  643  647  653  659
  661  673  677  683  691  701  709  719  727  733  739  743
  751  757  761  769  773  787  797  809  811  821  823  827
  829  839  853  857  859  863  877  881  883  887  907  911
  919  929  937  941  947  953  967  971  977  983  991  997
 1009 1013 1019 1021
```

Fig. 22.40 | Class bitset and the Sieve of Eratosthenes. (Part 2 of 3.)

```
Enter a value from 2 to 1023 (-1 to end): 389
389 is a prime number

Enter a value from 2 to 1023 (-1 to end): 88
88 is not a prime number

Enter a value from 2 to 1023 (-1 to end): -1
```

Fig. 22.40 | Class bitset and the Sieve of Eratosthenes. (Part 3 of 3.)

Line 13 creates a bitset of size bits (size is 1024 in this example). By default, all the bits in the bitset are set "off." Line 14 calls function **flip** to set all bits "on." Numbers 0 and 1 are not prime numbers, so lines 15–16 call function **reset** to set bits 0 and 1 "off." Lines 22–29 determine all the prime numbers from 2 to 1023. The integer finalBit (line 19) is used to determine when the algorithm is complete. The basic algorithm is that a number is prime if it has no divisors other than 1 and itself. Starting with the number 2, we can eliminate all multiples of that number. The number 2 is divisible only by 1 and itself, so it's prime. Therefore, we can eliminate 4, 6, 8 and so on. The number 3 is divisible only by 1 and itself. Therefore, we can eliminate all multiples of 3 (keep in mind that all even numbers have already been eliminated).

22.7 Function Objects

Many STL algorithms allow you to pass a function pointer into the algorithm to help the algorithm perform its task. For example, the binary_search algorithm that we discussed in Section 22.5.6 is overloaded with a version that requires as its fourth parameter a pointer to a function that takes two arguments and returns a bool value. The binary_search algorithm uses this function to compare the search key to an element in the collection. The function returns true if the search key and element being compared are equal; otherwise, the function returns false. This enables binary_search to search a collection of elements for which the element type does not provide an overloaded equality == operator.

STL's designers made the algorithms more flexible by allowing any algorithm that can receive a function pointer to receive an object of a class that overloads the parentheses operator with a function named operator(), provided that the overloaded operator meets the requirements of the algorithm—in the case of binary_search, it must receive two arguments and return a bool. An object of such a class is known as a **function object** and can be used syntactically and semantically like a function or function pointer—the overloaded parentheses operator is invoked by using a function object's name followed by parentheses containing the arguments to the function. Together, function objects and functions used are know as **functors**. Most algorithms can use function objects and functions interchangeably.

Function objects provide several advantages over function pointers. Since function objects are commonly implemented as class templates that are included into each source code file that uses them, the compiler can inline an overloaded operator() to improve performance. Also, since they're objects of classes, function objects can have data members that operator() can use to perform its task.

Predefined Function Objects of the Standard Template Library
Many predefined function objects can be found in the header **<functional>**. Figure 22.41 lists several of the STL function objects, which are all implemented as class templates. We used the function object less< T > in the set, multiset and priority_queue examples, to specify the sorting order for elements in a container.

STL function objects	Type	STL function objects	Type
divides< T >	arithmetic	logical_or< T >	logical
equal_to< T >	relational	minus< T >	arithmetic
greater< T >	relational	modulus< T >	arithmetic
greater_equal< T >	relational	negate< T >	arithmetic
less< T >	relational	not_equal_to< T >	relational
less_equal< T >	relational	plus< T >	arithmetic
logical_and< T >	logical	multiplies< T >	arithmetic
logical_not< T >	logical		

Fig. 22.41 | Function objects in the Standard Library.

*Using the STL **Accumulate** Algorithm*
Figure 22.42 demonstrates the accumulate numeric algorithm (discussed in Fig. 22.30) to calculate the sum of the squares of the elements in a vector. The fourth argument to accumulate is a **binary function object** (that is, a function object for which operator() takes two arguments) or a function pointer to a **binary function** (that is, a function that takes two arguments). Function accumulate is demonstrated twice—once with a function pointer and once with a function object.

```
1   // Fig. 22.42: Fig22_42.cpp
2   // Demonstrating function objects.
3   #include <iostream>
4   #include <vector> // vector class-template definition
5   #include <algorithm> // copy algorithm
6   #include <numeric> // accumulate algorithm
7   #include <functional> // binary_function definition
8   #include <iterator> // ostream_iterator
9   using namespace std;
10
11  // binary function adds square of its second argument and the
12  // running total in its first argument, then returns the sum
13  int sumSquares( int total, int value )
14  {
15     return total + value * value;
16  } // end function sumSquares
17
```

Fig. 22.42 | Binary function object. (Part 1 of 2.)

```
18   // binary function class template defines overloaded operator()
19   // that adds the square of its second argument and running
20   // total in its first argument, then returns sum
21   template< typename T >
22   class SumSquaresClass : public binary_function< T, T, T >
23   {
24   public:
25      // add square of value to total and return result
26      T operator()( const T &total, const T &value )
27      {
28         return total + value * value;
29      } // end function operator()
30   }; // end class SumSquaresClass
31
32   int main()
33   {
34      const int SIZE = 10;
35      int array[ SIZE ] = { 1, 2, 3, 4, 5, 6, 7, 8, 9, 10 };
36      vector< int > integers( array, array + SIZE ); // copy of array
37      ostream_iterator< int > output( cout, " " );
38      int result;
39
40      cout << "vector integers contains:\n";
41      copy( integers.begin(), integers.end(), output );
42
43      // calculate sum of squares of elements of vector integers
44      // using binary function sumSquares
45      result = accumulate( integers.begin(), integers.end(),
46         0, sumSquares );
47
48      cout << "\n\nSum of squares of elements in integers using "
49         << "binary\nfunction sumSquares: " << result;
50
51      // calculate sum of squares of elements of vector integers
52      // using binary function object
53      result = accumulate( integers.begin(), integers.end(),
54         0, SumSquaresClass< int >() );
55
56      cout << "\n\nSum of squares of elements in integers using "
57         << "binary\nfunction object of type "
58         << "SumSquaresClass< int >: " << result << endl;
59   } // end main
```

```
vector integers contains:
1 2 3 4 5 6 7 8 9 10

Sum of squares of elements in integers using binary
function sumSquares: 385

Sum of squares of elements in integers using binary
function object of type SumSquaresClass< int >: 385
```

Fig. 22.42 | Binary function object. (Part 2 of 2.)

Lines 13–16 define a function sumSquares that squares its second argument value, adds that square and its first argument total and returns the sum. Function accumulate will pass each of the elements of the sequence over which it iterates as the second argument to sumSquares in the example. On the first call to sumSquares, the first argument will be the initial value of the total (which is supplied as the third argument to accumulate; 0 in this program). All subsequent calls to sumSquares receive as the first argument the running sum returned by the previous call to sumSquares. When accumulate completes, it returns the sum of the squares of all the elements in the sequence.

Lines 21–30 define a class SumSquaresClass that inherits from the class template **binary_function** (in header file <functional>)—an empty base class for creating function objects in which operator receives two parameters and returns a value. Class binary_function accepts three type parameters that represent the types of the first argument, second argument and return value of operator, respectively. In this example, the type of these parameters is T (line 22). On the first call to the function object, the first argument will be the initial value of the total (which is supplied as the third argument to accumulate: 0 in this program) and the second argument will be the first element in vector integers. All subsequent calls to operator receive as the first argument the result returned by the previous call to the function object, and the second argument will be the next element in the vector. When accumulate completes, it returns the sum of the squares of all the elements in the vector.

Lines 45–46 call function accumulate with a pointer to function sumSquares as its last argument. The statement in lines 53–54 calls function accumulate with an object of class SumSquaresClass as the last argument. The expression SumSquaresClass< int >() creates an instance of class SumSquaresClass (a function object) that is passed to accumulate, which sends the object the message (invokes the function) operator. The statement could be written as two separate statements, as follows:

```
SumSquaresClass< int > sumSquaresObject;
result = accumulate( integers.begin(), integers.end(),
   0, sumSquaresObject );
```

The first line defines an object of class SumSquaresClass. That object is then passed to function accumulate.

22.8 Wrap-Up

In this chapter, we introduced the Standard Template Library and discussed its three key components—containers, iterators and algorithms. You learned the STL sequence containers, vector, deque and list, which represent linear data structures. We discussed associative containers, set, multiset, map and multimap, which represent nonlinear data structures. You also saw that the container adapters stack, queue and priority_queue can be used to restrict the operations of the sequence containers for the purpose of implementing the specialized data structures represented by the container adapters. We then demonstrated many of the STL algorithms, including mathematical algorithms, basic searching and sorting algorithms and set operations. You learned the types of iterators each algorithm requires and that each algorithm can be used with any container that supports the minimum iterator functionality the algorithm requires. You also learned class bitset, which makes it easy to create and manipulate bit sets as a container. Finally, we introduced function objects that work syntactically and semantically like ordinary functions, but offer advantages such as performance and the ability to store data.

The next chapter discusses the future of C++. A new standard, known as C++0x, will be released in 2010 or 2011. You'll learn about the new libraries and core language features being added to C++. You'll also learn about the Boost Libraries, which many of the libraries being added to C++0x are based on. We'll demonstrate how to use two of the new libraries to work with regular expressions and smart pointers.

22.9 STL Web Resources

Our C++ Resource Center (www.deitel.com/cplusplus/) focuses on the enormous amount of free C++ content available online. Start your search here for resources, downloads, tutorials, documentation, books, e-books, journals, articles, blogs, RSS feeds and more that will help you develop C++ applications. The C++ Resource Center includes links to many STL resources and tutorials.

Summary

Section 22.1 Introduction to the Standard Template Library (STL)
- The Standard Template Library defines powerful, template-based, reusable components that implement many common data structures, and algorithms used to process those data structures.
- The STL has three key components—containers, iterators and algorithms.
- The STL containers are data structures capable of storing objects of any data type. There are three styles of container classes—first-class containers, container adapters and near containers.
- STL algorithms are functions that perform such common data manipulations as searching, sorting and comparing elements or entire containers.

Section 22.1.1 Introduction to Containers
- The containers are divided into sequence containers, associative containers and container adapters.
- The sequence containers represent linear data structures, such as vectors and linked lists.
- Associative containers are nonlinear containers that quickly locate elements stored in them, such as sets of values or key/value pairs.
- Sequence containers and associative containers are collectively referred to as first-class containers.

Section 22.1.2 Introduction to Iterators
- First-class container function `begin` returns an iterator pointing to the first element of a container. Function `end` returns an iterator pointing to the first element past the end of the container (an element that doesn't exist and is typically used in a loop to indicate when to terminate processing of the container's elements).
- An `istream_iterator` is capable of extracting values in a type-safe manner from an input stream. An `ostream_iterator` is capable of inserting values in an output stream.
- Input and output iterators can move only in the forward direction (i.e., from the beginning of the container to the end) one element at a time.
- A forward iterator combines the capabilities of input and output iterators.
- A bidirectional iterator has the capabilities of a forward iterator and the ability to move in the backward direction (i.e., from the end of the container toward the beginning).

- A random-access iterator has the capabilities of a bidirectional iterator and the ability to directly access any element of the container.

Section 22.1.3 Introduction to Algorithms
- Containers that support random-access iterators can be used with all algorithms in the STL.

Section 22.2 Sequence Containers
- The STL provides sequence containers vector, list and deque. Class templates vector and deque both are based on arrays. Class template list implements a linked-list data structure.

Section 22.2.1 **vector** Sequence Container
- Function capacity returns the number of elements that can be stored in a vector before the vector dynamically resizes itself to accommodate more elements.
- Sequence container function push_back adds an element to the end of a container.
- To use the algorithms of the STL, you must include the header file <algorithm>.
- Algorithm copy copies each element in a container starting with the location specified by the iterator in its first argument and up to—but not including—the location specified by the iterator in its second argument.
- Function front returns a reference to the first element in a sequence container. Function begin returns an iterator pointing to the beginning of a sequence container.
- Function back returns a reference to the last element in a sequence container. Function end returns an iterator pointing to the element one past the end of a sequence container.
- Sequence container function insert inserts value(s) before the element at a specific location.
- Function erase (in all first-class containers) removes specific element(s) from the container.
- Function empty (in all containers and adapters) returns true if the container is empty.
- Function clear (in all first-class containers) empties the container.

Section 22.2.2 **list** Sequence Container
- The list sequence container provides an efficient implementation for insertion and deletion operations at any location in the container. Header file <list> must be included to use class template list.
- The list member function push_front inserts values at the beginning of a list.
- The list member function sort arranges the elements in the list in ascending order.
- The list member function splice removes elements in one list and inserts them into another list at a specific position.
- The list member function unique removes duplicate elements in a list.
- The list member function assign replaces the contents of one list with the contents of another.
- The list member function remove deletes all copies of a specified value from a list.

Section 22.2.3 **deque** Sequence Container
- Class template deque provides the same operations as vector, but adds member functions push_front and pop_front to allow insertion and deletion at the beginning of a deque, respectively. Header file <deque> must be included to use class template deque.

Section 22.3 Associative Containers
- The STL's associative containers provide direct access to store and retrieve elements via keys.
- The four associative containers are multiset, set, multimap and map.

- Class templates `multiset` and `set` provide operations for manipulating sets of values where the values are the keys—there is not a separate value associated with each key. Header file `<set>` must be included to use class templates `set` and `multiset`.

- A `multiset` allows duplicate keys and a `set` does not.

Section 22.3.1 `multiset` Associative Container
- The `multiset` associative container provides fast storage and retrieval of keys and allows duplicate keys. The ordering of the elements is determined by a comparator function object.

- A `multiset`'s keys can be sorted in ascending order by ordering the keys with comparator function object `less<T>`.

- The type of the keys in all associative containers must support comparison properly based on the comparator function object specified.

- A `multiset` supports bidirectional iterators.

- Header file `<set>` must be included to use class `multiset`.

Section 22.3.2 `set` Associative Container
- The `set` associative container is used for fast storage and retrieval of unique keys.

- If an attempt is made to insert a duplicate key into a `set`, the duplicate is ignored.

- A `set` supports bidirectional iterators.

- Header file `<set>` must be included to use class `set`.

Section 22.3.3 `multimap` Associative Container
- Containers `multimap` and `map` provide operations for manipulating values associated with keys.

- The primary difference between a `multimap` and a `map` is that a `multimap` allows duplicate keys with associated values to be stored and a `map` allows only unique keys with associated values.

- Function `count` (available to all associative containers) counts the number of occurrences of the specified value currently in a container.

- Function `find` (available to all associative containers) locates a specified value in a container.

- Functions `lower_bound` and `upper_bound` (available in all associative containers) locate the earliest occurrence of the specified value in a container and the element after the last occurrence of the specified value in a container, respectively.

- Function `equal_range` (available in all associative containers) returns a `pair` containing the results of both a `lower_bound` and an `upper_bound` operation.

- The `multimap` associative container is used for fast storage and retrieval of keys and associated values (often called key/value pairs).

- Duplicate keys are allowed in a `multimap`, so multiple values can be associated with a single key. This is called a one-to-many relationship.

- Header file `<map>` must be included to use class templates `map` and `multimap`.

Section 22.3.4 `map` Associative Container
- Duplicate keys are not allowed in a `map`, so only a single value can be associated with each key. This is called a one-to-one mapping.

- A `map` is commonly called an associative array.

Section 22.4 Container Adapters
- The STL provides three container adapters—`stack`, `queue` and `priority_queue`.

- Adapters are not first-class containers, because they do not provide the actual data structure implementation in which elements can be stored and they do not support iterators.
- All three adapter class templates provide member functions push and pop that properly insert an element into and remove an element from each adapter data structure, respectively.

Section 22.4.1 stack *Adapter*

- Class template stack is a last-in, first-out data structure. Header file <stack> must be included to use class template stack.
- The stack member function top returns a reference to the top element of the stack (implemented by calling function back of the underlying container).
- The stack member function empty determines whether the stack is empty (implemented by calling function empty of the underlying container).
- The stack member function size returns the number of elements in the stack (implemented by calling function size of the underlying container).

Section 22.4.2 queue *Adapter*

- Class template queue enables insertions at the back of the underlying data structure and deletions from the front of the underlying data structure (commonly referred to as a first-in, first-out data structure). Header file <queue> must be included to use a queue or a priority_queue.
- The queue member function front returns a reference to the first element in the queue (implemented by calling function front of the underlying container).
- The queue member function back returns a reference to the last element in the queue (implemented by calling function back of the underlying container).
- The queue member function empty determines whether the queue is empty (implemented by calling function empty of the underlying container).
- The queue member function size returns the number of elements in the queue (implemented by calling function size of the underlying container).

Section 22.4.3 priority_queue *Adapter*

- Class template priority_queue provides functionality that enables insertions in sorted order into the underlying data structure and deletions from the front of the underlying data structure.
- The common priority_queue operations are push, pop, top, empty and size.

Section 22.5.1 fill, fill_n, generate *and* generate_n

- Algorithms fill and fill_n set every element in a range of container elements to a specific value.
- Algorithms generate and generate_n use a generator function or function object to create values for every element in a range of container elements.

Section 22.5.2 equal, mismatch *and* lexicographical_compare

- Algorithm equal compares two sequences of values for equality.
- Algorithm mismatch compares two sequences of values and returns a pair of iterators indicating the location in each sequence of the mismatched elements.
- Algorithm lexicographical_compare compares the contents of two sequences.

Section 22.5.3 remove, remove_if, remove_copy *and* remove_copy_if

- Algorithm remove eliminates all elements with a specific value in a certain range.
- Algorithm remove_copy copies all elements that do not have a specific value in a certain range.

- Algorithm `remove_if` deletes all elements that satisfy the `if` condition in a certain range.
- Algorithm `remove_copy_if` copies all elements that satisfy the `if` condition in a certain range.

Section 22.5.4 `replace`, `replace_if`, `replace_copy` and `replace_copy_if`
- Algorithm `replace` replaces all elements with a specific value in certain range.
- Algorithm `replace_copy` copies all elements with a specific value in a certain range.
- Algorithm `replace_if` replaces all elements that satisfy the `if` condition in a certain range.
- Algorithm `replace_copy_if` copies all elements that satisfy the `if` condition in a certain range.

Section 22.5.5 Mathematical Algorithms
- Algorithm `random_shuffle` reorders randomly the elements in a certain range.
- Algorithm `count` counts the elements with a specific value in a certain range.
- Algorithm `count_if` counts the elements that satisfy the `if` condition in a certain range.
- Algorithm `min_element` locates the smallest element in a certain range.
- Algorithm `max_element` locates the largest element in a certain range.
- Algorithm `accumulate` sums the values in a certain range.
- Algorithm `for_each` applies a general function or function object to every element in a range.
- Algorithm `transform` applies a general function or function object to every element in a range and replaces each element with the result of the function.

Section 22.5.6 Basic Searching and Sorting Algorithms
- Algorithm `find` locates a specific value in a certain range.
- Algorithm `find_if` locates the first value in a certain range that satisfies the `if` condition.
- Algorithm `sort` arranges the elements in a certain range in ascending order or an order specified by a predicate.
- Algorithm `binary_search` determines whether a specific value is in a sorted range of elements.

Section 22.5.7 `swap`, `iter_swap` and `swap_ranges`
- Algorithm `swap` exchanges two values.
- Algorithm `iter_swap` exchanges the two elements.
- Algorithm `swap_ranges` exchanges the elements in a certain range.

Section 22.5.8 `copy_backward`, `merge`, `unique` and `reverse`
- Algorithm `copy_backward` copies elements in a range and places the elements into a container starting from the end and working toward the front.
- Algorithm `merge` combines two sorted ascending sequences of values into a third sorted ascending sequence.
- Algorithm `unique` removes duplicated elements in a certain range of a sorted sequence.
- Algorithm `reverse` reverses all the elements in a certain range.

Section 22.5.9 `inplace_merge`, `unique_copy` and `reverse_copy`
- Algorithm `inplace_merge` merges two sorted sequences of elements in the same container.
- Algorithm `unique_copy` makes a copy of all the unique elements in the sorted sequence of values in a certain range.
- Algorithm `reverse_copy` makes a reversed copy of the elements in a certain range.

Section 22.5.10 Set Operations

- The set function includes compares two sets of sorted values to determine whether every element of the second set is in the first set.

- The set function set_difference finds the elements from the first set of sorted values that are not in the second set of sorted values (both sets of values must be in ascending order).

- The set function set_intersection determines the elements from the first set of sorted values that are in the second set of sorted values (both sets of values must be in ascending order).

- The set function set_symmetric_difference determines the elements in the first set that are not in the second set and the elements in the second set that are not in the first set (both sets of values must be in ascending order).

- The set function set_union creates a set of all the elements that are in either or both of the two sorted sets (both sets of values must be in ascending order).

Section 22.5.11 lower_bound, upper_bound and equal_range

- Algorithm lower_bound finds the first location in a sorted sequence of values at which the third argument could be inserted in the sequence such that the sequence would still be sorted in ascending order.

- Algorithm upper_bound finds the last location in a sorted sequence of values at which the third argument could be inserted in the sequence such that the sequence would still be sorted in ascending order.

- Algorithm equal_range performs returns the lower bound and upper bound as a pair.

Section 22.5.12 Heapsort

- Algorithm make_heap takes a sequence of values in a certain range and creates a heap that can be used to produce a sorted sequence.

- Algorithm sort_heap sorts a sequence of values in a certain range of a heap.

- Algorithm pop_heap removes the top heap element.

Section 22.5.13 min and max

- Algorithms min and max determine the minimum of two elements and the maximum of two elements, respectively.

Section 22.6 Class bitset

- Class template bitset makes it easy to create and manipulate bit sets, which are useful for representing a set of bit flags.

Section 22.7 Function Objects

- A function object is an instance of a class that overloads operator().

- STL provides many predefined function objects, which can be found in header <functional>.

- Binary function objects are function objects that take two arguments and return a value. Class template binary_function is an empty base class for creating binary function objects that provides standard type names for the function's parameters and result.

Terminology

Self-Review Exercises

State whether the following are *true* or *false* or fill in the blanks. If the answer is *false*, explain why,.

22.1   (T/F) The STL makes abundant use of inheritance and virtual functions.

22.2   The two types of first-class STL containers are sequence containers and _____ containers.

22.3   The five main iterator types are _____, _____, _____, _____ and _____.

22.4   (T/F) An iterator acts like a pointer to an element.

22.5   (T/F) STL algorithms can operate on C-like pointer-based arrays.

22.6   (T/F) STL algorithms are encapsulated as member functions within each container class.

22.7   (T/F) When using the remove algorithm on a vector, the algorithm does not decrease the size of the vector from which elements are being removed.

22.8   The three STL container adapters are _____, _____ and _____.

22.9 (T/F) Container member function end yields the position of the container's last element.

22.10 STL algorithms operate on container elements indirectly, using _____.

22.11 The sort algorithm requires a(n) _____ iterator.

Answers to Self-Review Exercises

22.1 False. These were avoided for performance reasons.

22.2 Associative.

22.3 Input, output, forward, bidirectional, random access.

22.4 True.

22.5 True.

22.6 False. STL algorithms are not member functions. They operate indirectly on containers, through iterators.

22.7 True.

22.8 `stack`, `queue`, `priority_queue`.

22.9 False. It actually yields the position just after the end of the container.

22.10 Iterators.

22.11 Random-access.

Exercises

22.12 *(Palindromes)* Write a function template `palindrome` that takes a `vector` parameter and returns `true` or `false` according to whether the `vector` does or does not read the same forward as backward (e.g., a `vector` containing 1, 2, 3, 2, 1 is a palindrome, but a `vector` containing 1, 2, 3, 4 is not).

22.13 *(Sieve of Eratosthenes)* Modify Fig. 22.40, the Sieve of Eratosthenes, so that, if the number the user inputs into the program is not prime, the program displays the prime factors of the number. Remember that a prime number's factors are only 1 and the prime number itself. Every nonprime number has a unique prime factorization. For example, the factors of 54 are 2, 3, 3 and 3. When these values are multiplied together, the result is 54. For the number 54, the prime factors output should be 2 and 3.

22.14 *(Prime Numbers)* Modify Exercise 22.13 so that, if the number the user inputs into the program is not prime, the program displays the prime factors of the number and the number of times each prime factor appears in the unique prime factorization. For example, the output for the number 54 should be

```
The unique prime factorization of 54 is: 2 * 3 * 3 * 3
```

Recommended Reading

Ammeraal, L. *STL for C++ Programmers.* New York: John Wiley & Sons, 1997.

Austern, M. H. *Generic Programming and the STL: Using and Extending the C++ Standard Template Library.* Boston, MA: Addison-Wesley, 1998.

Glass, G., and B. Schuchert. *The STL <Primer>.* Upper Saddle River, NJ: Prentice Hall PTR, 1995.

Henricson, M., and E. Nyquist. *Industrial Strength C++: Rules and Recommendations.* Upper Saddle River, NJ: Prentice Hall, 1997.

Josuttis, N. *The C++ Standard Library: A Tutorial and Handbook.* Boston, MA: Addison-Wesley, 1999.

Koenig, A., and B. Moo. *Ruminations on C++.* Boston, MA: Addison-Wesley, 1997.

Meyers, S. *Effective STL: 50 Specific Ways to Improve Your Use of the Standard Template Library.* Boston, MA: Addison-Wesley, 2001.

Musser, D. R., G. Derge and A. Saini. *STL Tutorial and Reference Guide: C++ Programming with the Standard Template Library, Second Edition.* Boston, MA: Addison-Wesley, 2002.

Musser, D. R., and A. A. Stepanov. "Algorithm-Oriented Generic Libraries," *Software Practice and Experience,* Vol. 24, No. 7, July 1994.

Nelson, M. *C++ Programmer's Guide to the Standard Template Library.* Foster City, CA: Programmer's Press, 1995.

Pohl, I. *C++ Distilled: A Concise ANSI/ISO Reference and Style Guide.* Boston, MA: Addison-Wesley, 1997.

Pohl, I. *Object-Oriented Programming Using C++, Second Edition.* Boston, MA: Addison-Wesley, 1997.

Reese, G. *C++ Standard Library Practical Tips.* Hingham, MA: Charles River Media, 2005.

Robson, R. *Using the STL: The C++ Standard Template Library, Second Edition.* New York: Springer, 2010.

Schildt, H. *STL Programming from the Ground Up,* New York: Osborne McGraw-Hill, 1999.

Stepanov, A., and M. Lee. "The Standard Template Library," *Internet Distribution* 31 October 1995 <www.cs.rpi.edu/~musser/doc.ps>.

Stroustrup, B. "Making a vector Fit for a Standard," *The C++ Report,* October 1994.

Stroustrup, B. *The Design and Evolution of C++.* Boston, MA: Addison-Wesley, 1994.

Stroustrup, B. *The C++ Programming Language, Third Edition.* Boston, MA: Addison-Wesley, 1997.

Vandevoorde, D., and N. Josuttis. *C++ Templates: The Complete Guide.* Boston, MA: Addison-Wesley, 2002.

Vilot, M. J. "An Introduction to the Standard Template Library," *The C++ Report,* Vol. 6, No. 8, October 1994.

Wilson, M. *Extended STL, Volume 1: Collections and Iterators.* Boston, MA: Addison-Wesley, 2007

Chapters on the Web

The following chapters are available as PDF documents from this book's Companion Website (www.pearsonhighered.com/deitel/):

- Chapter 23, Boost Libraries, Technical Report 1 and C++0x
- Chapter 24, Other Topics
- Chapter 25, ATM Case Study, Part 1: Object-Oriented Design with the UML
- Chapter 26, ATM Case Study, Part 2: Implementing an Object-Oriented Design
- Chapter 27, Game Programming with Ogre

These files can be viewed in Adobe® Reader® (get.adobe.com/reader). The index entries for these chapters have uppercase Roman numeral page numbers.

New copies of this book come with a Companion Website access code that is located on the card inside the book's front cover. If the access code is already visible or there is no card, you purchased a used book or an edition that does not come with an access code. In this case, you can purchase access directly from the Companion Website.

A

Operator Precedence and Associativity

Operators are shown in decreasing order of precedence from top to bottom (Fig. A.1).

Operator	Type	Associativity
::	binary scope resolution	left to right
::	unary scope resolution	
()	parentheses	left to right
[]	array subscript	
.	member selection via object	
->	member selection via pointer	
++	unary postfix increment	
--	unary postfix decrement	
typeid	runtime type information	
dynamic_cast < *type* >	runtime type-checked cast	
static_cast< *type* >	compile-time type-checked cast	
reinterpret_cast< *type* >	cast for nonstandard conversions	
const_cast< *type* >	cast away const-ness	
++	unary prefix increment	right to left
--	unary prefix decrement	
+	unary plus	
-	unary minus	
!	unary logical negation	
~	unary bitwise complement	
sizeof	determine size in bytes	
&	address	
*	dereference	
new	dynamic memory allocation	
new[]	dynamic array allocation	
delete	dynamic memory deallocation	
delete[]	dynamic array deallocation	
(*type*)	C-style unary cast	right to left
.*	pointer to member via object	left to right
->*	pointer to member via pointer	

Fig. A.1 | Operator precedence and associativity chart. (Part 1 of 2.)

Operator	Type	Associativity
* / %	multiplication division modulus	left to right
+ −	addition subtraction	left to right
<< >>	bitwise left shift bitwise right shift	left to right
< <= > >=	relational less than relational less than or equal to relational greater than relational greater than or equal to	left to right
== !=	relational is equal to relational is not equal to	left to right
&	bitwise AND	left to right
^	bitwise exclusive OR	left to right
|	bitwise inclusive OR	left to right
&&	logical AND	left to right
||	logical OR	left to right
?:	ternary conditional	right to left
= += −= *= /= %= &= ^= |= <<= >>=	assignment addition assignment subtraction assignment multiplication assignment division assignment modulus assignment bitwise AND assignment bitwise exclusive OR assignment bitwise inclusive OR assignment bitwise left-shift assignment bitwise right-shift assignment	right to left
,	comma	left to right

Fig. A.1 | Operator precedence and associativity chart. (Part 2 of 2.)

ASCII Character Set

	0	1	2	3	4	5	6	7	8	9
0	nul	soh	stx	etx	eot	enq	ack	bel	bs	ht
1	nl	vt	ff	cr	so	si	dle	dc1	dc2	dc3
2	dc4	nak	syn	etb	can	em	sub	esc	fs	gs
3	rs	us	sp	!	"	#	$	%	&	'
4	(	)	*	+	,	-	.	/	0	1
5	2	3	4	5	6	7	8	9	:	;
6	<	=	>	?	@	A	B	C	D	E
7	F	G	H	I	J	K	L	M	N	O
8	P	Q	R	S	T	U	V	W	X	Y
9	Z	[	\	]	^	_	'	a	b	c
10	d	e	f	g	h	i	j	k	l	m
11	n	o	p	q	r	s	t	u	v	w
12	x	y	z	{			}	~	del		

Fig. B.1 | ASCII character set.

The digits at the left of the table are the left digits of the decimal equivalents (0–127) of the character codes, and the digits at the top of the table are the right digits of the character codes. For example, the character code for "F" is 70, and the character code for "&" is 38.

Most users of this book are interested in the ASCII character set used to represent English characters on many computers. The ASCII character set is a subset of the Unicode character set that represents characters from most of the world's languages.

C

Fundamental Types

Figure C.1 lists C++'s fundamental types. The C++ Standard Document does not provide the exact number of bytes required to store variables of these types in memory. However, the C++ Standard Document does indicate how the memory requirements for fundamental types relate to one another. By order of increasing memory requirements, the signed integer types are signed char, short int, int and long int. This means that a short int must provide at least as much storage as a signed char; an int must provide at least as much storage as a short int; and a long int must provide at least as much storage as an int. Each signed integer type has a corresponding unsigned integer type that has the same memory requirements. Unsigned types cannot represent negative values, but can represent twice as many positive values as their associated signed types. By order of increasing memory requirements, the floating-point types are float, double and long double. Like integer types, a double must provide at least as much storage as a float and a long double must provide at least as much storage as a double.

Integral types	Floating-point types
bool	float
char	double
signed char	long double
unsigned char	
short int	
unsigned short int	
int	
unsigned int	
long int	
unsigned long int	
wchar_t	

Fig. C.1 | C++ fundamental types.

The exact sizes and ranges of values for the fundamental types are implementation dependent. The header files <climits> (for the integral types) and <cfloat> (for the floating-point types) specify the ranges of values supported on your system.

The range of values a type supports depends on the number of bytes that are used to represent that type. For example, consider a system with 4 byte (32 bit) ints. For the signed int type, the nonnegative values are in the range 0 to 2,147,483,647 ($2^{31} - 1$). The negative values are in the range -1 to $-2,147,483,648$ (-2^{31}). This is a total of 2^{32} possible values. An unsigned int on the same system would use the same number of bits to represent data, but would not represent any negative values. This results in values in the range 0 to 4,294,967,295 ($2^{32} - 1$). On the same system, a short int could not use more than 32 bits to represent its data and a long int must use at least 32 bits.

C++ provides the data type bool for variables that can hold only the values true and false.

Number Systems

D

Here are only numbers ratified.
—William Shakespeare

Objectives

In this appendix you'll learn:

- To understand basic number systems concepts, such as base, positional value and symbol value.

- To understand how to work with numbers in the binary, octal and hexadecimal number systems.

- To abbreviate binary numbers as octal numbers or hexadecimal numbers.

- To convert octal numbers and hexadecimal numbers to binary numbers.

- To convert back and forth between decimal numbers and their binary, octal and hexadecimal equivalents.

- To understand binary arithmetic and how negative binary numbers are represented using two's complement notation.

D.1 Introduction

In this appendix, we introduce the key number systems that C++ programmers use, especially when they are working on software projects that require close interaction with machine-level hardware. Projects like this include operating systems, computer networking software, compilers, database systems and applications requiring high performance.

When we write an integer such as 227 or –63 in a C++ program, the number is assumed to be in the **decimal (base 10) number system**. The **digits** in the decimal number system are 0, 1, 2, 3, 4, 5, 6, 7, 8 and 9. The lowest digit is 0 and the highest is 9—one less than the base of 10. Internally, computers use the **binary (base 2) number system**. The binary number system has only two digits, namely 0 and 1. Its lowest digit is 0 and its highest is 1—one less than the base of 2.

As we'll see, binary numbers tend to be much longer than their decimal equivalents. Programmers who work in assembly languages, and in high-level languages like C++ that enable them to reach down to the machine level, find it cumbersome to work with binary numbers. So two other number systems—the **octal number system (base 8)** and the **hexadecimal number system (base 16)**—are popular, primarily because they make it convenient to abbreviate binary numbers.

In the octal number system, the digits range from 0 to 7. Because both the binary and the octal number systems have fewer digits than the decimal number system, their digits are the same as the corresponding digits in decimal.

The hexadecimal number system poses a problem because it requires 16 digits—a lowest digit of 0 and a highest digit with a value equivalent to decimal 15 (one less than the base of 16). By convention, we use the letters A through F to represent the hexadecimal digits corresponding to decimal values 10 through 15. Thus in hexadecimal we can have numbers like 876 consisting solely of decimal-like digits, numbers like 8A55F consisting of digits and letters and numbers like FFE consisting solely of letters. Occasionally, a hexadecimal number spells a common word such as FACE or FEED—this can appear strange to programmers accustomed to working with numbers. The digits of the binary, octal, decimal and hexadecimal number systems are summarized in Figs. D.1–D.2.

Each of these number systems uses **positional notation**—each position in which a digit is written has a different **positional value**. For example, in the decimal number 937 (the 9, the 3 and the 7 are referred to as **symbol values**), we say that the 7 is written in the ones position, the 3 is written in the tens position and the 9 is written in the hundreds position. Note that each of these positions is a power of the base (base 10) and that these powers begin at 0 and increase by 1 as we move left in the number (Fig. D.3).

Binary digit	Octal digit	Decimal digit	Hexadecimal digit
0	0	0	0
1	1	1	1
	2	2	2
	3	3	3
	4	4	4
	5	5	5
	6	6	6
	7	7	7
		8	8
		9	9
			A (decimal value of 10)
			B (decimal value of 11)
			C (decimal value of 12)
			D (decimal value of 13)
			E (decimal value of 14)
			F (decimal value of 15)

Fig. D.I | Digits of the binary, octal, decimal and hexadecimal number systems.

Attribute	Binary	Octal	Decimal	Hexadecimal
Base	2	8	10	16
Lowest digit	0	0	0	0
Highest digit	1	7	9	F

Fig. D.2 | Comparing the binary, octal, decimal and hexadecimal number systems.

Positional values in the decimal number system			
Decimal digit	9	3	7
Position name	Hundreds	Tens	Ones
Positional value	100	10	1
Positional value as a power of the base (10)	10^2	10^1	10^0

Fig. D.3 | Positional values in the decimal number system.

For longer decimal numbers, the next positions to the left would be the thousands position (10 to the 3rd power), the ten-thousands position (10 to the 4th power), the hundred-thousands position (10 to the 5th power), the millions position (10 to the 6th power), the ten-millions position (10 to the 7th power) and so on.

In the binary number 101, the rightmost 1 is written in the ones position, the 0 is written in the twos position and the leftmost 1 is written in the fours position. Note that each position is a power of the base (base 2) and that these powers begin at 0 and increase by 1 as we move left in the number (Fig. D.4). So, $101 = 2^2 + 2^0 = 4 + 1 = 5$.

Positional values in the binary number system			
Binary digit	1	0	1
Position name	Fours	Twos	Ones
Positional value	4	2	1
Positional value as a power of the base (2)	2^2	2^1	2^0

Fig. D.4 | Positional values in the binary number system.

For longer binary numbers, the next positions to the left would be the eights position (2 to the 3rd power), the sixteens position (2 to the 4th power), the thirty-twos position (2 to the 5th power), the sixty-fours position (2 to the 6th power) and so on.

In the octal number 425, we say that the 5 is written in the ones position, the 2 is written in the eights position and the 4 is written in the sixty-fours position. Note that each of these positions is a power of the base (base 8) and that these powers begin at 0 and increase by 1 as we move left in the number (Fig. D.5).

Positional values in the octal number system			
Decimal digit	4	2	5
Position name	Sixty-fours	Eights	Ones
Positional value	64	8	1
Positional value as a power of the base (8)	8^2	8^1	8^0

Fig. D.5 | Positional values in the octal number system.

For longer octal numbers, the next positions to the left would be the five-hundred-and-twelves position (8 to the 3rd power), the four-thousand-and-ninety-sixes position (8 to the 4th power), the thirty-two-thousand-seven-hundred-and-sixty-eights position (8 to the 5th power) and so on.

In the hexadecimal number 3DA, we say that the A is written in the ones position, the D is written in the sixteens position and the 3 is written in the two-hundred-and-fifty-sixes position. Note that each of these positions is a power of the base (base 16) and that these powers begin at 0 and increase by 1 as we move left in the number (Fig. D.6).

For longer hexadecimal numbers, the next positions to the left would be the four-thousand-and-ninety-sixes position (16 to the 3rd power), the sixty-five-thousand-five-hundred-and-thirty-sixes position (16 to the 4th power) and so on.

Positional values in the hexadecimal number system			
Decimal digit	3	D	A
Position name	Two-hundred-and-fifty-sixes	Sixteens	Ones
Positional value	256	16	1
Positional value as a power of the base (16)	16^2	16^1	16^0

Fig. D.6 | Positional values in the hexadecimal number system.

D.2 Abbreviating Binary Numbers as Octal and Hexadecimal Numbers

The main use for octal and hexadecimal numbers in computing is for abbreviating lengthy binary representations. Figure D.7 highlights the fact that lengthy binary numbers can be expressed concisely in number systems with higher bases than the binary number system.

Decimal number	Binary representation	Octal representation	Hexadecimal representation
0	0	0	0
1	1	1	1
2	10	2	2
3	11	3	3
4	100	4	4
5	101	5	5
6	110	6	6
7	111	7	7
8	1000	10	8
9	1001	11	9
10	1010	12	A
11	1011	13	B
12	1100	14	C
13	1101	15	D
14	1110	16	E
15	1111	17	F
16	10000	20	10

Fig. D.7 | Decimal, binary, octal and hexadecimal equivalents.

A particularly important relationship that both the octal number system and the hexadecimal number system have to the binary system is that the bases of octal and hexadecimal (8 and 16 respectively) are powers of the base of the binary number system (base 2).

Consider the following 12-digit binary number and its octal and hexadecimal equivalents. See if you can determine how this relationship makes it convenient to abbreviate binary numbers in octal or hexadecimal. The answers follow the numbers.

Binary number	Octal equivalent	Hexadecimal equivalent
100011010001	4321	8D1

To see how the binary number converts easily to octal, simply break the 12-digit binary number into groups of three consecutive bits each, starting from the right, and write those groups over the corresponding digits of the octal number as follows:

100	011	010	001
4	3	2	1

Note that the octal digit you've written under each group of three bits corresponds precisely to the octal equivalent of that 3-digit binary number, as shown in Fig. D.7.

The same kind of relationship can be observed in converting from binary to hexadecimal. Break the 12-digit binary number into groups of four consecutive bits each, starting from the right, and write those groups over the corresponding digits of the hexadecimal number as follows:

1000	1101	0001
8	D	1

Notice that the hexadecimal digit you wrote under each group of four bits corresponds precisely to the hexadecimal equivalent of that 4-digit binary number as shown in Fig. D.7.

D.3 Converting Octal and Hexadecimal Numbers to Binary Numbers

In the previous section, we saw how to convert binary numbers to their octal and hexadecimal equivalents by forming groups of binary digits and simply rewriting them as their equivalent octal digit values or hexadecimal digit values. This process may be used in reverse to produce the binary equivalent of a given octal or hexadecimal number.

For example, the octal number 653 is converted to binary simply by writing the 6 as its 3-digit binary equivalent 110, the 5 as its 3-digit binary equivalent 101 and the 3 as its 3-digit binary equivalent 011 to form the 9-digit binary number 110101011.

The hexadecimal number FAD5 is converted to binary simply by writing the F as its 4-digit binary equivalent 1111, the A as its 4-digit binary equivalent 1010, the D as its 4-digit binary equivalent 1101 and the 5 as its 4-digit binary equivalent 0101 to form the 16-digit 1111101011010101.

D.4 Converting from Binary, Octal or Hexadecimal to Decimal

We are accustomed to working in decimal, and therefore it is often convenient to convert a binary, octal, or hexadecimal number to decimal to get a sense of what the number is "really" worth. Our diagrams in Section D.1 express the positional values in decimal. To convert a number to decimal from another base, multiply the decimal equivalent of each digit by its positional value and sum these products. For example, the binary number 110101 is converted to decimal 53 as shown in Fig. D.8.

Converting a binary number to decimal					
Positional values:	32	16	8	4	2	1
Symbol values:	1	1	0	1	0	1
Products:	1*32=32	1*16=16	0*8=0	1*4=4	0*2=0	1*1=1
Sum:	= 32 + 16 + 0 + 4 + 0s + 1 = 53					

Fig. D.8 | Converting a binary number to decimal.

To convert octal 7614 to decimal 3980, we use the same technique, this time using appropriate octal positional values, as shown in Fig. D.9.

Converting an octal number to decimal			
Positional values:	512	64	8	1
Symbol values:	7	6	1	4
Products	7*512=3584	6*64=384	1*8=8	4*1=4
Sum:	= 3584 + 384 + 8 + 4 = 3980			

Fig. D.9 | Converting an octal number to decimal.

To convert hexadecimal AD3B to decimal 44347, we use the same technique, this time using appropriate hexadecimal positional values, as shown in Fig. D.10.

Converting a hexadecimal number to decimal			
Positional values:	4096	256	16	1
Symbol values:	A	D	3	B
Products	A*4096=40960	D*256=3328	3*16=48	B*1=11
Sum:	= 40960 + 3328 + 48 + 11 = 44347			

Fig. D.10 | Converting a hexadecimal number to decimal.

D.5 Converting from Decimal to Binary, Octal or Hexadecimal

The conversions in Section D.4 follow naturally from the positional notation conventions. Converting from decimal to binary, octal, or hexadecimal also follows these conventions.

Suppose we wish to convert decimal 57 to binary. We begin by writing the positional values of the columns right to left until we reach a column whose positional value is greater than the decimal number. We do not need that column, so we discard it. Thus, we first write:

Positional values:	64	32	16	8	4	2	1

Then we discard the column with positional value 64, leaving:

Positional values:	32	16	8	4	2	1

Next we work from the leftmost column to the right. We divide 32 into 57 and observe that there is one 32 in 57 with a remainder of 25, so we write 1 in the 32 column. We divide 16 into 25 and observe that there is one 16 in 25 with a remainder of 9 and write 1 in the 16 column. We divide 8 into 9 and observe that there is one 8 in 9 with a remainder of 1. The next two columns each produce quotients of 0 when their positional values are divided into 1, so we write 0s in the 4 and 2 columns. Finally, 1 into 1 is 1, so we write 1 in the 1 column. This yields:

Positional values:	32	16	8	4	2	1
Symbol values:	1	1	1	0	0	1

and thus decimal 57 is equivalent to binary 111001.

To convert decimal 103 to octal, we begin by writing the positional values of the columns until we reach a column whose positional value is greater than the decimal number. We do not need that column, so we discard it. Thus, we first write:

Positional values:	512	64	8	1

Then we discard the column with positional value 512, yielding:

Positional values:	64	8	1

Next we work from the leftmost column to the right. We divide 64 into 103 and observe that there is one 64 in 103 with a remainder of 39, so we write 1 in the 64 column. We divide 8 into 39 and observe that there are four 8s in 39 with a remainder of 7 and write 4 in the 8 column. Finally, we divide 1 into 7 and observe that there are seven 1s in 7 with no remainder, so we write 7 in the 1 column. This yields:

Positional values:	64	8	1
Symbol values:	1	4	7

and thus decimal 103 is equivalent to octal 147.

To convert decimal 375 to hexadecimal, we begin by writing the positional values of the columns until we reach a column whose positional value is greater than the decimal number. We do not need that column, so we discard it. Thus, we first write:

Positional values:	4096	256	16	1

Then we discard the column with positional value 4096, yielding:

Positional values:	256	16	1

Next we work from the leftmost column to the right. We divide 256 into 375 and observe that there is one 256 in 375 with a remainder of 119, so we write 1 in the 256 column. We divide 16 into 119 and observe that there are seven 16s in 119 with a remainder of 7 and write 7 in the 16 column. Finally, we divide 1 into 7 and observe that there are seven 1s in 7 with no remainder, so we write 7 in the 1 column. This yields:

Positional values:	256	16	1
Symbol values:	1	7	7

and thus decimal 375 is equivalent to hexadecimal 177.

D.6 Negative Binary Numbers: Two's Complement Notation

The discussion so far in this appendix has focused on positive numbers. In this section, we explain how computers represent negative numbers using **two's complement notation**. First we explain how the two's complement of a binary number is formed, then we show why it represents the negative value of the given binary number.

Consider a machine with 32-bit integers. Suppose

```
int value = 13;
```

The 32-bit representation of value is

```
00000000 00000000 00000000 00001101
```

To form the negative of value we first form its **one's complement** by applying C++'s **bitwise complement operator** (~):

```
onesComplementOfValue = ~value;
```

Internally, ~value is now value with each of its bits reversed—ones become zeros and zeros become ones, as follows:

```
value:
00000000 00000000 00000000 00001101

~value (i.e., value's one's complement):
11111111 11111111 11111111 11110010
```

To form the two's complement of value, we simply add 1 to value's one's complement. Thus

```
Two's complement of value:
11111111 11111111 11111111 11110011
```

Now if this is in fact equal to −13, we should be able to add it to binary 13 and obtain a result of 0. Let's try this:

```
 00000000 00000000 00000000 00001101
+11111111 11111111 11111111 11110011
-------------------------------------
 00000000 00000000 00000000 00000000
```

The carry bit coming out of the leftmost column is discarded and we indeed get 0 as a result. If we add the one's complement of a number to the number, the result will be all 1s. The key to getting a result of all zeros is that the two's complement is one more than the one's complement. The addition of 1 causes each column to add to 0 with a carry of 1. The carry keeps moving leftward until it is discarded from the leftmost bit, and thus the resulting number is all zeros.

Computers actually perform a subtraction, such as

```
x = a - value;
```

by adding the two's complement of value to a, as follows:

```
x = a + (~value + 1);
```

Suppose a is 27 and value is 13 as before. If the two's complement of value is actually the negative of value, then adding the two's complement of value to a should produce the result 14. Let's try this:

```
a (i.e., 27)        00000000 00000000 00000000 00011011
+(~value + 1)      +11111111 11111111 11111111 11110011
                   -------------------------------------
                    00000000 00000000 00000000 00001110
```

which is indeed equal to 14.

Summary

- An integer such as 19 or 227 or –63 in a C++ program is assumed to be in the decimal (base 10) number system. The digits in the decimal number system are 0, 1, 2, 3, 4, 5, 6, 7, 8 and 9. The lowest digit is 0 and the highest is 9—one less than the base of 10.

- Computers use the binary (base 2) number system. The binary number system has only two digits, namely 0 and 1. Its lowest digit is 0 and its highest is 1—one less than the base of 2.

- The octal number system (base 8) and the hexadecimal number system (base 16) are popular primarily because they make it convenient to abbreviate binary numbers.

- The digits of the octal number system range from 0 to 7.

- The hexadecimal number system poses a problem because it requires 16 digits—a lowest digit of 0 and a highest digit with a value equivalent to decimal 15 (one less than the base of 16). By convention, we use the letters A through F to represent the hexadecimal digits corresponding to decimal values 10 through 15.

- Each number system uses positional notation—each position in which a digit is written has a different positional value.

- A particularly important relationship of both the octal and the hexadecimal number systems to the binary system is that their bases (8 and 16 respectively) are powers of the base of the binary number system (base 2).

- To convert from octal to binary, replace each octal digit with its three-digit binary equivalent.

- To convert a hexadecimal to a binary number, simply replace each hexadecimal digit with its four-digit binary equivalent.

- Because we are accustomed to working in decimal, it is convenient to convert a binary, octal or hexadecimal number to decimal to get a sense of the number's "real" worth.

- To convert a number to decimal from another base, multiply the decimal equivalent of each digit by its positional value and sum the products.

- Computers represent negative numbers using two's complement notation.

- To form the negative of a value in binary, first form its one's complement by applying C++'s bitwise complement operator (~). This reverses the bits of the value. To form the two's complement of a value, simply add one to the value's one's complement.

Terminology

bitwise complement operator (~) 1019
decimal number system 1012
digit 1012
hexadecimal number system 1012
negative value 1019
octal number system 1012

one's complement notation 1019
positional notation 1012
positional value 1012
symbol value 1012
two's complement notation 1019

Self-Review Exercises

D.1   The bases of the decimal, binary, octal and hexadecimal number systems are _____, _____, _____ and _____ respectively.

D.2   In general, the decimal, octal and hexadecimal representations of a given binary number contain (more/fewer) digits than the binary number contains.

D.3   (*True/False*) A popular reason for using the decimal number system is that it forms a convenient notation for abbreviating binary numbers simply by substituting one decimal digit per group of four binary bits.

D.4   The [octal/hexadecimal/decimal] representation of a large binary value is the most concise (of the given alternatives).

D.5   (*True/False*) The highest digit in any base is one more than the base.

D.6   (*True/False*) The lowest digit in any base is one less than the base.

D.7   The positional value of the rightmost digit of any number in either binary, octal, decimal or hexadecimal is always _____.

D.8   The positional value of the digit to the left of the rightmost digit of any number in binary, octal, decimal or hexadecimal is always equal to _____.

D.9   Fill in the missing values in this chart of positional values for the rightmost four positions in each of the indicated number systems:

	1000	100	10	1
decimal	1000	100	10	1
hexadecimal	...	256	...	...
binary	...	...	...	...
octal	512	...	8	...

D.10   Convert binary 110101011000 to octal and to hexadecimal.

D.11   Convert hexadecimal FACE to binary.

D.12   Convert octal 7316 to binary.

D.13   Convert hexadecimal 4FEC to octal. [*Hint:* First convert 4FEC to binary, then convert that binary number to octal.]

D.14   Convert binary 1101110 to decimal.

D.15   Convert octal 317 to decimal.

D.16   Convert hexadecimal EFD4 to decimal.

D.17   Convert decimal 177 to binary, to octal and to hexadecimal.

D.18   Show the binary representation of decimal 417. Then show the one's complement of 417 and the two's complement of 417.

D.19   What's the result when a number and its two's complement are added to each other?

Answers to Self-Review Exercises

D.1   10, 2, 8, 16.

D.2   Fewer.

D.3   False. Hexadecimal does this.

D.4   Hexadecimal.

D.5   False. The highest digit in any base is one less than the base.

D.6   False. The lowest digit in any base is zero.

D.7   1 (the base raised to the zero power).

D.8   The base of the number system.

D.9   Filled in chart shown below:

decimal	1000	100	10	1
hexadecimal	4096	256	16	1
binary	8	4	2	1
octal	512	64	8	1

D.10   Octal 6530; Hexadecimal D58.

D.11   Binary 1111 1010 1100 1110.

D.12   Binary 111 011 001 110.

D.13   Binary 0 100 111 111 101 100; Octal 47754.

D.14   Decimal 2 + 4 + 8 + 32 + 64 = 110.

D.15   Decimal 7 + 1 * 8 + 3 * 64 = 7 + 8 + 192 = 207.

D.16   Decimal 4 + 13 * 16 + 15 * 256 + 14 * 4096 = 61396.

D.17   Decimal 177
to binary:

```
256 128 64 32 16 8 4 2 1
128 64 32 16 8 4 2 1
(1*128)+(0*64)+(1*32)+(1*16)+(0*8)+(0*4)+(0*2)+(1*1)
10110001
```

to octal:

```
512 64 8 1
64 8 1
(2*64)+(6*8)+(1*1)
261
```

to hexadecimal:

```
256 16 1
16 1
(11*16)+(1*1)
(B*16)+(1*1)
B1
```

D.18   Binary:

```
512 256 128 64 32 16 8 4 2 1
256 128 64 32 16 8 4 2 1
(1*256)+(1*128)+(0*64)+(1*32)+(0*16)+(0*8)+(0*4)+(0*2)+(1*1)
110100001
```

One's complement: 001011110
Two's complement: 001011111
Check: Original binary number + its two's complement

```
110100001
001011111
---------
000000000
```

D.19   Zero.

Exercises

D.20   Some people argue that many of our calculations would be easier in the base 12 than in the base 10 (decimal) number system because 12 is divisible by so many more numbers than 10. What's the lowest digit in base 12? What would be the highest symbol for the digit in base 12? What are the positional values of the rightmost four positions of any number in the base 12 number system?

D.21   Complete the following chart of positional values for the rightmost four positions in each of the indicated number systems:

decimal	1000	100	10	1
base 6	...	...	6	...
base 13	...	169	...	...
base 3	27	...	...	...

D.22   Convert binary 100101111010 to octal and to hexadecimal.

D.23   Convert hexadecimal 3A7D to binary.

D.24   Convert hexadecimal 765F to octal. [*Hint:* First convert 765F to binary, then convert that binary number to octal.]

D.25   Convert binary 1011110 to decimal.

D.26   Convert octal 426 to decimal.

D.27   Convert hexadecimal FFFF to decimal.

D.28   Convert decimal 299 to binary, to octal and to hexadecimal.

D.29   Show the binary representation of decimal 779. Then show the one's complement of 779 and the two's complement of 779.

D.30   Show the two's complement of integer value −1 on a machine with 32-bit integers.

E

Preprocessor

Objectives

In this appendix you'll learn:

- To use `#include` for developing large programs.
- To use `#define` to create macros and macros with arguments.
- To understand conditional compilation.
- To display error messages during conditional compilation.
- To use assertions to test if the values of expressions are correct.

E.1 Introduction

This chapter introduces the **preprocessor**. Preprocessing occurs before a program is compiled. Some possible actions are inclusion of other files in the file being compiled, definition of **symbolic constants** and **macros**, **conditional compilation** of program code and **conditional execution of preprocessor directives.** All preprocessor directives begin with #, and only white-space characters may appear before a preprocessor directive on a line. Preprocessor directives are not C++ statements, so they do not end in a semicolon (;). Preprocessor directives are processed fully before compilation begins.

Common Programming Error E.1
Placing a semicolon at the end of a preprocessor directive can lead to a variety of errors, depending on the type of preprocessor directive.

Software Engineering Observation E.1
Many preprocessor features (especially macros) are more appropriate for C programmers than for C++ programmers. C++ programmers should familiarize themselves with the preprocessor, because they might need to work with C legacy code.

E.2 #include Preprocessor Directive

The **#include preprocessor directive** has been used throughout this text. The #include directive causes a copy of a specified file to be included in place of the directive. The two forms of the #include directive are

```
#include <filename>
#include "filename"
```

The difference between these is the location the preprocessor searches for the file to be included. If the filename is enclosed in angle brackets (< and >)—used for standard library header files—the preprocessor searches for the specified file in an implementation-dependent manner, normally through predesignated directories. If the file name is enclosed in quotes, the preprocessor searches first in the same directory as the file being compiled, then in the same implementation-dependent manner as for a file name enclosed in angle brackets. This method is normally used to include programmer-defined header files.

The #include directive is used to include standard header files such as <iostream> and <iomanip>. The #include directive is also used with programs consisting of several source files that are to be compiled together. A header file containing declarations and definitions common to the separate program files is often created and included in the file. Examples of such declarations and definitions are classes, structures, unions, enumerations, function prototypes, constants and stream objects (e.g., cin).

E.3 #define Preprocessor Directive: Symbolic Constants

The **#define preprocessor directive** creates **symbolic constants**—constants represented as symbols—and macros—operations defined as symbols. The #define preprocessor directive format is

    #define   identifier   replacement-text

When this line appears in a file, all subsequent occurrences (except those inside a string) of *identifier* in that file will be replaced by *replacement-text* before the program is compiled. For example,

    #define PI 3.14159

replaces all subsequent occurrences of the symbolic constant PI with the numeric constant 3.14159. Symbolic constants enable you to create a name for a constant and use the name throughout the program. Later, if the constant needs to be modified throughout the program, it can be modified once in the #define preprocessor directive—and when the program is recompiled, all occurrences of the constant in the program will be modified. [*Note:* Everything to the right of the symbolic constant name replaces the symbolic constant. For example, #define PI = 3.14159 causes the preprocessor to replace every occurrence of PI with = 3.14159. Such replacement is the cause of many subtle logic and syntax errors.] Redefining a symbolic constant with a new value without first undefining it is also an error. Note that const variables in C++ are preferred over symbolic constants. Constant variables have a specific data type and are visible by name to a debugger. Once a symbolic constant is replaced with its replacement text, only the replacement text is visible to a debugger. A disadvantage of const variables is that they might require a memory location of their data type size—symbolic constants do not require any additional memory.

Common Programming Error E.2
Using symbolic constants in a file other than the file in which the symbolic constants are defined is a compilation error (unless they are #included from a header file).

Good Programming Practice E.1
Using meaningful names for symbolic constants makes programs more self-documenting.

E.4 #define Preprocessor Directive: Macros

[*Note:* This section is included for the benefit of C++ programmers who will need to work with C legacy code. In C++, macros can often be replaced by templates and inline functions.] A macro is an operation defined in a #define preprocessor directive. As with symbolic constants, the *macro-identifier* is replaced with the *replacement-text* before the program is compiled. Macros may be defined with or without *arguments*. A macro without arguments is processed like a symbolic constant. In a macro with arguments, the arguments are substituted in the *replacement-text*, then the macro is expanded—i.e., the *replacement-text* replaces the macro-identifier and argument list in the program. There is no data type checking for macro arguments. A macro is used simply for text substitution.

Consider the following macro definition with one argument for the area of a circle:

```
#define CIRCLE_AREA( x ) ( PI * ( x ) * ( x ) )
```

Wherever CIRCLE_AREA(y) appears in the file, the value of y is substituted for x in the replacement text, the symbolic constant PI is replaced by its value (defined previously) and the macro is expanded in the program. For example, the statement

```
area = CIRCLE_AREA( 4 );
```

is expanded to

```
area = ( 3.14159 * ( 4 ) * ( 4 ) );
```

Because the expression consists only of constants, at compile time the value of the expression can be evaluated, and the result is assigned to area at runtime. The parentheses around each x in the replacement text and around the entire expression force the proper order of evaluation when the macro argument is an expression. For example, the statement

```
area = CIRCLE_AREA( c + 2 );
```

is expanded to

```
area = ( 3.14159 * ( c + 2 ) * ( c + 2 ) );
```

which evaluates correctly, because the parentheses force the proper order of evaluation. If the parentheses are omitted, the macro expansion is

```
area = 3.14159 * c + 2 * c + 2;
```

which evaluates incorrectly as

```
area = ( 3.14159 * c ) + ( 2 * c ) + 2;
```

because of the rules of operator precedence.

Common Programming Error E.3

Forgetting to enclose macro arguments in parentheses in the replacement text is an error.

Macro CIRCLE_AREA could be defined as a function. Function circleArea, as in

```
double circleArea( double x ) { return 3.14159 * x * x; }
```

performs the same calculation as CIRCLE_AREA, but the overhead of a function call is associated with function circleArea. The advantages of CIRCLE_AREA are that macros insert code directly in the program—avoiding function overhead—and the program remains readable because CIRCLE_AREA is defined separately and named meaningfully. A disadvantage is that its argument is evaluated twice. Also, every time a macro appears in a program, the macro is expanded. If the macro is large, this produces an increase in program size. Thus, there is a trade-off between execution speed and program size (if disk space is low).

Note that `inline` functions (see Chapter 6) are preferred to obtain the performance of macros and the software engineering benefits of functions.

Performance Tip E.1

Macros can sometimes be used to replace a function call with `inline` code prior to execution time. This eliminates the overhead of a function call. Inline functions are preferable to macros because they offer the type-checking services of functions.

The following is a macro definition with two arguments for the area of a rectangle:

```
#define RECTANGLE_AREA( x, y ) ( ( x ) * ( y ) )
```

Wherever RECTANGLE_AREA(a, b) appears in the program, the values of a and b are substituted in the macro replacement text, and the macro is expanded in place of the macro name. For example, the statement

```
rectArea = RECTANGLE_AREA( a + 4, b + 7 );
```

is expanded to

```
rectArea = ( ( a + 4 ) * ( b + 7 ) );
```

The value of the expression is evaluated and assigned to variable rectArea.

The replacement text for a macro or symbolic constant is normally any text on the line after the identifier in the #define directive. If the replacement text for a macro or symbolic constant is longer than the remainder of the line, a backslash (\) must be placed at the end of each line of the macro (except the last line), indicating that the replacement text continues on the next line.

Symbolic constants and macros can be discarded using the **#undef preprocessor directive**. Directive #undef "undefines" a symbolic constant or macro name. The scope of a symbolic constant or macro is from its definition until it is either undefined with #undef or the end of the file is reached. Once undefined, a name can be redefined with #define.

Note that expressions with side effects (e.g., variable values are modified) should not be passed to a macro, because macro arguments may be evaluated more than once.

Common Programming Error E.4

Macros often replace a name that wasn't intended to be a use of the macro but just happened to be spelled the same. This can lead to exceptionally mysterious compilation and syntax errors.

E.5 Conditional Compilation

Conditional compilation enables you to control the execution of preprocessor directives and the compilation of program code. Each of the conditional preprocessor directives evaluates a constant integer expression that will determine whether the code will be compiled. Cast expressions, `sizeof` expressions and enumeration constants cannot be evaluated in preprocessor directives because these are all determined by the compiler and preprocessing happens before compilation.

The conditional preprocessor construct is much like the `if` selection structure. Consider the following preprocessor code:

```
#ifndef NULL
    #define NULL 0
#endif
```

which determines whether the symbolic constant NULL is already defined. The expression #ifndef NULL includes the code up to #endif if NULL is not defined, and skips the code if NULL is defined. Every **#if** construct ends with **#endif**. Directives **#ifdef** and **#ifndef** are shorthand for #if defined(*name*) and #if !defined(*name*). A multiple-part conditional preprocessor construct may be tested using the #elif (the equivalent of else if in an if structure) and the #else (the equivalent of else in an if structure) directives.

During program development, programmers often find it helpful to "comment out" large portions of code to prevent it from being compiled. If the code contains C-style comments, /* and */ cannot be used to accomplish this task, because the first */ encountered would terminate the comment. Instead, you can use the following preprocessor construct:

```
#if 0
    code prevented from compiling
#endif
```

To enable the code to be compiled, simply replace the value 0 in the preceding construct with the value 1.

Conditional compilation is commonly used as a debugging aid. Output statements are often used to print variable values and to confirm the flow of control. These output statements can be enclosed in conditional preprocessor directives so that the statements are compiled only until the debugging process is completed. For example,

```
#ifdef DEBUG
    cerr << "Variable x = " << x << endl;
#endif
```

causes the cerr statement to be compiled in the program if the symbolic constant DEBUG has been defined before directive #ifdef DEBUG. This symbolic constant is normally set by a command-line compiler or by settings in the IDE (e.g., Visual Studio) and not by an explicit #define definition. When debugging is completed, the #define directive is removed from the source file, and the output statements inserted for debugging purposes are ignored during compilation. In larger programs, it might be desirable to define several different symbolic constants that control the conditional compilation in separate sections of the source file.

Common Programming Error E.5

Inserting conditionally compiled output statements for debugging purposes in locations where C++ currently expects a single statement can lead to syntax errors and logic errors. In this case, the conditionally compiled statement should be enclosed in a compound statement. Thus, when the program is compiled with debugging statements, the flow of control of the program is not altered.

E.6 #error and #pragma Preprocessor Directives

The **#error directive**

```
#error tokens
```

prints an implementation-dependent message including the *tokens* specified in the directive. The tokens are sequences of characters separated by spaces. For example,

```
#error 1 - Out of range error
```

contains six tokens. In one popular C++ compiler, for example, when a #error directive is processed, the tokens in the directive are displayed as an error message, preprocessing stops and the program does not compile.

The **#pragma directive**

```
#pragma tokens
```

causes an implementation-defined action. A pragma not recognized by the implementation is ignored. A particular C++ compiler, for example, might recognize pragmas that enable you to take advantage of that compiler's specific capabilities. For more information on #error and #pragma, see the documentation for your C++ implementation.

E.7 Operators # and

The # and ## preprocessor operators are available in C++ and ANSI/ISO C. The # operator causes a replacement-text token to be converted to a string surrounded by quotes. Consider the following macro definition:

```
#define HELLO( x ) cout << "Hello, " #x << endl;
```

When HELLO(John) appears in a program file, it is expanded to

```
cout << "Hello, " "John" << endl;
```

The string "John" replaces #x in the replacement text. Strings separated by whitespace are concatenated during preprocessing, so the above statement is equivalent to

```
cout << "Hello, John" << endl;
```

Note that the # operator must be used in a macro with arguments, because the operand of # refers to an argument of the macro.

The ## operator concatenates two tokens. Consider the following macro definition:

```
cout << "Hello, John" << endl;
#define TOKENCONCAT( x, y )  x ## y
```

When TOKENCONCAT appears in the program, its arguments are concatenated and used to replace the macro. For example, TOKENCONCAT(O, K) is replaced by OK in the program. The ## operator must have two operands.

E.8 Predefined Symbolic Constants

There are six **predefined symbolic constants** (Fig. E.1). The identifiers for each of these begin and (except for __cplusplus) end with *two* underscores. These identifiers and preprocessor operator defined (Section E.5) cannot be used in #define or #undef directives.

Symbolic constant	Description
__LINE__	The line number of the current source-code line (an integer constant).
__FILE__	The presumed name of the source file (a string).
__DATE__	The date the source file is compiled (a string of the form "Mmm dd yyyy" such as "Aug 19 2002").
__STDC__	Indicates whether the program conforms to the ANSI/ISO C standard. Contains value 1 if there is full conformance and is undefined otherwise.
__TIME__	The time the source file is compiled (a string literal of the form "hh:mm:ss").
__cplusplus	Contains the value 199711L (the date the ISO C++ standard was approved) if the file is being compiled by a C++ compiler, undefined otherwise. Allows a file to be set up to be compiled as either C or C++.

Fig. E.1 | The predefined symbolic constants.

E.9 Assertions

The **assert macro**—defined in the **<cassert>** header file—tests the value of an expression. If the value of the expression is 0 (false), then assert prints an error message and calls function **abort** (of the general utilities library—<cstdlib>) to terminate program execution. This is a useful debugging tool for testing whether a variable has a correct value. For example, suppose variable x should never be larger than 10 in a program. An assertion may be used to test the value of x and print an error message if the value of x is incorrect. The statement would be

```
assert( x <= 10 );
```

If x is greater than 10 when the preceding statement is encountered in a program, an error message containing the line number and file name is printed, and the program terminates. You may then concentrate on this area of the code to find the error. If the symbolic constant NDEBUG is defined, subsequent assertions will be ignored. Thus, when assertions are no longer needed (i.e., when debugging is complete), we insert the line

```
#define NDEBUG
```

in the program file rather than deleting each assertion manually. As with the DEBUG symbolic constant, NDEBUG is often set by compiler command-line options or through a setting in the IDE.

Most C++ compilers now include exception handling. C++ programmers prefer using exceptions rather than assertions. But assertions are still valuable for C++ programmers who work with C legacy code.

E.10 Wrap-Up

This appendix discussed the #include directive, which is used to develop larger programs. You also learned about the #define directive, which is used to create macros. We introduced conditional compilation, displaying error messages and using assertions.

Summary

Section E.2 #include *Preprocessor Directive*

- All preprocessor directives begin with # and are processed before the program is compiled.

- Only white-space characters may appear before a preprocessor directive on a line.

- The #include directive includes a copy of the specified file. If the filename is enclosed in quotes, the preprocessor begins searching in the same directory as the file being compiled for the file to be included. If the filename is enclosed in angle brackets (< and >), the search is performed in an implementation-defined manner.

Section E.3 #define *Preprocessor Directive: Symbolic Constants*

- The #define preprocessor directive is used to create symbolic constants and macros.

- A symbolic constant is a name for a constant.

Section E.4 #define *Preprocessor Directive: Macros*

- A macro is an operation defined in a #define preprocessor directive. Macros may be defined with or without arguments.

- The replacement text for a macro or symbolic constant is any text remaining on the line after the identifier (and, if any, the macro argument list) in the #define directive. If the replacement text for a macro or symbolic constant is too long to fit on one line, a backslash (\) is placed at the end of the line, indicating that the replacement text continues on the next line.

- Symbolic constants and macros can be discarded using the #undef preprocessor directive. Directive #undef "undefines" the symbolic constant or macro name.

- The scope of a symbolic constant or macro is from its definition until it is either undefined with #undef or the end of the file is reached.

Section E.5 *Conditional Compilation*

- Conditional compilation enables you to control the execution of preprocessor directives and the compilation of program code.

- The conditional preprocessor directives evaluate constant integer expressions. Cast expressions, sizeof expressions and enumeration constants cannot be evaluated in preprocessor directives.

- Every #if construct ends with #endif.

- Directives #ifdef and #ifndef are provided as shorthand for #if defined(*name*) and #if !defined(*name*).

- A multiple-part conditional preprocessor construct is tested with directives #elif and #else.

Section E.6 #error *and* #pragma *Preprocessor Directives*

- The #error directive prints an implementation-dependent message that includes the tokens specified in the directive and terminates preprocessing and compiling.

- The #pragma directive causes an implementation-defined action. If the pragma is not recognized by the implementation, the pragma is ignored.

Section E.7 *Operators* # *and*

- The # operator causes the following replacement text token to be converted to a string surrounded by quotes. The # operator must be used in a macro with arguments, because the operand of # must be an argument of the macro.

- The ## operator concatenates two tokens. The ## operator must have two operands.

Section E.8 Predefined Symbolic Constants

- There are six predefined symbolic constants. Constant `__LINE__` is the line number of the current source-code line (an integer). Constant `__FILE__` is the presumed name of the file (a string). Constant `__DATE__` is the date the source file is compiled (a string). Constant `__TIME__` is the time the source file is compiled (a string). Note that each of the predefined symbolic constants begins (and, with the exception of `__cplusplus`, ends) with two underscores.

Section E.9 Assertions

- The `assert` macro—defined in the `<cassert>` header file—tests the value of an expression. If the value of the expression is 0 (false), then `assert` prints an error message and calls function `abort` to terminate program execution.

Terminology

1030
1030
\ (backslash) continuation character 1028
abort 1031
argument 1027
assert macro 1031
`<cassert>` 1031
conditional compilation 1025
conditional execution of preprocessor
    directives 1025
convert-to-string preprocessor directive
`__cplusplus` 1030
`<cstdio>`
`<cstdlib>` 1031
`__DATE__` 1031
debugger 1026
`#define` preprocessor directive 1026
directives 1025
`#elif` 1029
`#else` 1029
`#endif` 1029
`#error` directive 1029

expand a macro 1027
`__FILE__` 1031
header file 1025
`#if` 1029
`#ifdef` 1029
`#ifndef` 1029
`#include` preprocessor directive 1025
`__LINE__` 1031
macro 1025
macro identifier 1026
macro with arguments 1027
`#pragma` directive 1030
predefined symbolic constants 1030
preprocessing directive 1025
preprocessor 1025
replacement-text 1026
scope of a symbolic constant or macro 1028
standard library header files 1025
symbolic constant 1025, 1026
`__TIME__` 1031
`#undef` preprocessor directive 1028

Self-Review Exercises

E.1 Fill in the blanks in each of the following:
 a) Every preprocessor directive must begin with _____.
 b) The conditional compilation construct may be extended to test for multiple cases by using the _____ and the _____ directives.
 c) The _____ directive creates macros and symbolic constants.
 d) Only _____ characters may appear before a preprocessor directive on a line.
 e) The _____ directive discards symbolic constant and macro names.
 f) The _____ and _____ directives are provided as shorthand notation for `#if defined(`*name*`)` and `#if !defined(`*name*`)`.
 g) _____ enables you to control the execution of preprocessor directives and the compilation of program code.

h) The _____ macro prints a message and terminates program execution if the value of the expression the macro evaluates is 0.

i) The _____ directive inserts a file in another file.

j) The _____ operator concatenates its two arguments.

k) The _____ operator converts its operand to a string.

l) The character _____ indicates that the replacement text for a symbolic constant or macro continues on the next line.

E.2 Write a program to print the values of the predefined symbolic constants __LINE__, __FILE__, __DATE__ and __TIME__ listed in Fig. E.1.

E.3 Write a preprocessor directive to accomplish each of the following:

a) Define symbolic constant YES to have the value 1.

b) Define symbolic constant NO to have the value 0.

c) Include the header file common.h. The header is found in the same directory as the file being compiled.

d) If symbolic constant TRUE is defined, undefine it, and redefine it as 1. Do not use #ifdef.

e) If symbolic constant TRUE is defined, undefine it, and redefine it as 1. Use the #ifdef preprocessor directive.

f) If symbolic constant ACTIVE is not equal to 0, define symbolic constant INACTIVE as 0. Otherwise, define INACTIVE as 1.

g) Define macro CUBE_VOLUME that computes the volume of a cube (takes one argument).

Answers to Self-Review Exercises

E.1 a) #. b) #elif, #else. c) #define. d) white-space. e) #undef. f) #ifdef, #ifndef. g) Conditional compilation. h) assert. i) #include. j) ##. k) #. l) \.

E.2 (See below.)

```
1   // exF_02.cpp
2   // Self-Review Exercise E.2 solution.
3   #include <iostream>
4   using namespace std;
5
6   int main()
7   {
8      cout << "__LINE__   = " << __LINE__   << endl
9           << "__FILE__   = " << __FILE__   << endl
10          << "__DATE__   = " << __DATE__   << endl
11          << "__TIME__   = " << __TIME__   << endl
12          << "__cplusplus = " << __cplusplus << endl;
13  } // end main
```

```
__LINE__   = 9
__FILE__   = c:\cpp4e\ch19\ex19_02.CPP
__DATE__   = Jul 17 2002
__TIME__   = 09:55:58
__cplusplus = 199711L
```

E.3 a) #define YES 1

b) #define NO 0

c) #include "common.h"

```
d)  #if defined(TRUE)
        #undef TRUE
        #define TRUE 1
    #endif
e)  #ifdef TRUE
        #undef TRUE
        #define TRUE 1
    #endif
f)  #if ACTIVE
        #define INACTIVE 0
    #else
        #define INACTIVE 1
    #endif
g)  #define CUBE_VOLUME( x )  ( ( x ) * ( x ) * ( x ) )
```

Exercises

E.4   Write a program that defines a macro with one argument to compute the volume of a sphere. The program should compute the volume for spheres of radii from 1 to 10 and print the results in tabular format. The formula for the volume of a sphere is

$$(4.0 / 3) * \pi * r^3$$

where π is 3.14159.

E.5   Write a program that produces the following output:

```
The sum of x and y is 13
```

The program should define macro SUM with two arguments, x and y, and use SUM to produce the output.

E.6   Write a program that uses macro MINIMUM2 to determine the smaller of two numeric values. Input the values from the keyboard.

E.7   Write a program that uses macro MINIMUM3 to determine the smallest of three numeric values. Macro MINIMUM3 should use macro MINIMUM2 defined in Exercise E.6 to determine the smallest number. Input the values from the keyboard.

E.8   Write a program that uses macro PRINT to print a string value.

E.9   Write a program that uses macro PRINTARRAY to print an array of integers. The macro should receive the array and the number of elements in the array as arguments.

E.10   Write a program that uses macro SUMARRAY to sum the values in a numeric array. The macro should receive the array and the number of elements in the array as arguments.

E.11   Rewrite the solutions to Exercises E.4–E.10 as inline functions.

E.12   For each of the following macros, identify the possible problems (if any) when the preprocessor expands the macros:

```
a)  #define SQR( x ) x * x
b)  #define SQR( x ) ( x * x )
c)  #define SQR( x ) ( x ) * ( x )
d)  #define SQR( x ) ( ( x ) * ( x ) )
```

Appendices on the Web

The following appendices are available as PDF documents from this book's Companion Website (www.pearsonhighered.com/deitel/):

- Appendix F, C Legacy Code Topics
- Appendix G, UML 2: Additional Diagram Types
- Appendix H, Using the Visual Studio Debugger
- Appendix I, Using the GNU C++ Debugger

These files can be viewed in Adobe® Reader® (get.adobe.com/reader). The index entries for these appendices have uppercase Roman numeral page numbers.

New copies of this book come with a Companion Website access code that is located on the card inside the book's front cover. If the access code is already visible or there is no card, you purchased a used book or an edition that does not come with an access code. In this case, you can purchase access directly from the Companion Website.

Index